Tax Formula for Individuals

Income (broadly conceived)	$xx,xxx
Less: Exclusions.	(x,xxx)
Gross income	$xx,xxx
Less: Deductions *for* adjusted gross income	(x,xxx)
Adjusted gross income....................................	$xx,xxx
Less: The greater of— Total itemized deductions *or* standard deduction	(x,xxx)
Less: Personal and dependency exemptions	(x,xxx)
Taxable income	$xx,xxx
Tax on taxable income....................................	$ x,xxx
Less: Tax credits (including Federal income tax withheld and other prepayments of Federal income taxes)	(xxx)
Tax due (or refund)......................................	$ xxx

Basic Standard Deduction Amounts

	Standard Deduction Amount	
Filing Status	**2010**	**2011**
Single	$ 5,700	$ 5,800
Married, filing jointly	11,400	11,600
Surviving spouse	11,400	11,600
Head of household	8,400	8,500
Married, filing separately	5,700	5,800

2012

5,9

Amount of Each Additional Standard Deduction

Filing Status	**2010**	**2011**
Single	$1,400	$1,450
Married, filing jointly	1,100	1,150
Surviving spouse	1,100	1,150
Head of household	1,400	1,450
Married, filing separately	1,100	1,150

Personal and Dependency Exemption

2010	**2011**
$3,650	$3,700

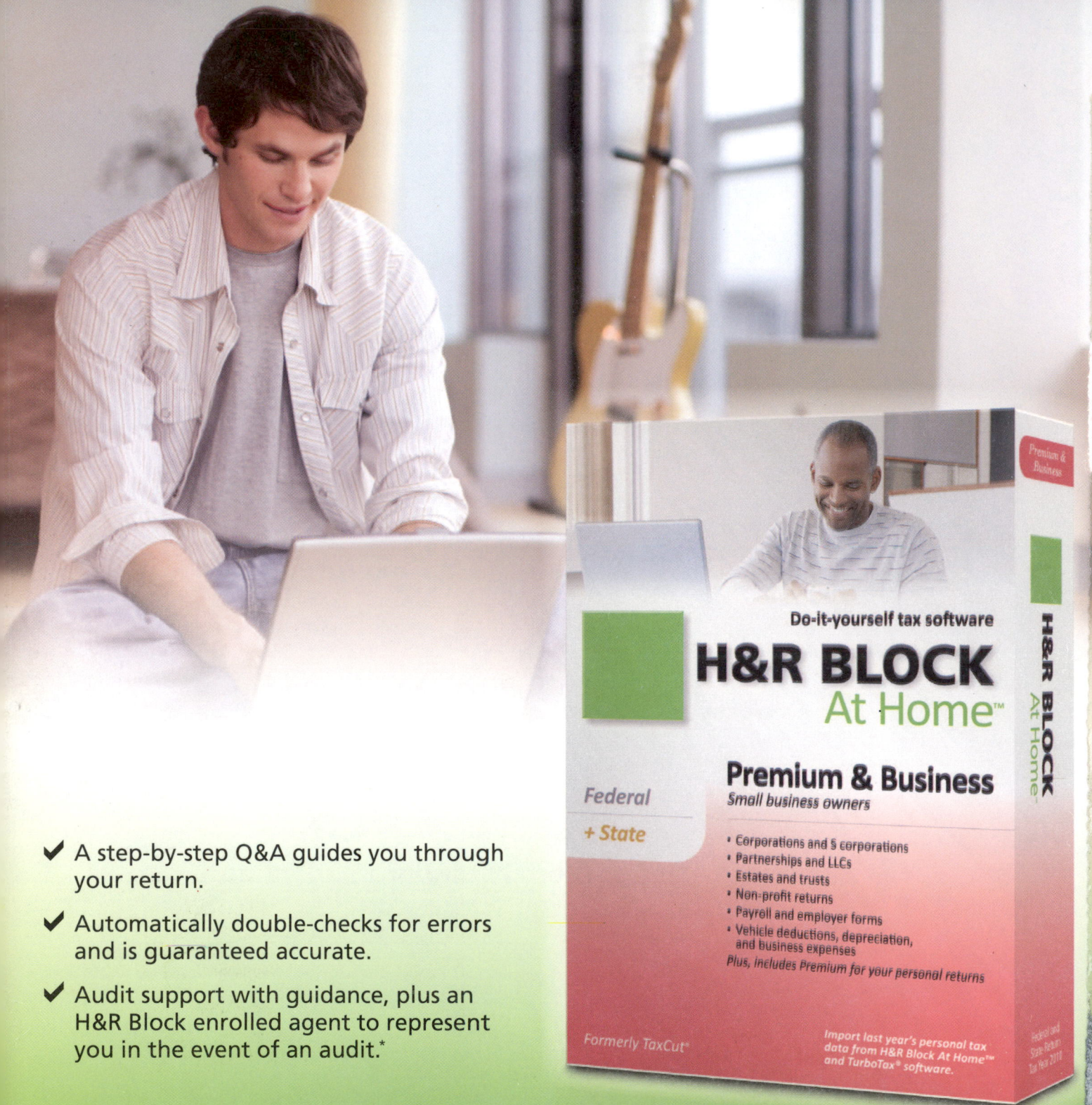

Do-it-yourself tax software

H&R BLOCK
At Home™

Premium & Business
Small business owners

- Corporations and S corporations
- Partnerships and LLCs
- Estates and trusts
- Non-profit returns
- Payroll and employer forms
- Vehicle deductions, depreciation, and business expenses

Plus, includes Premium for your personal returns

Federal
+ State

Formerly TaxCut®

Import last year's personal tax data from H&R Block At Home™ and TurboTax® software.

Premium & Business

Federal and State Returns Tax Year 2010

✔ A step-by-step Q&A guides you through your return.

✔ Automatically double-checks for errors and is guaranteed accurate.

✔ Audit support with guidance, plus an H&R Block enrolled agent to represent you in the event of an audit.*

Trust the **tax experts at H&R Block**® to make it easy.

Two powerful programs in one for your personal and business taxes.†

SOUTH-WESTERN
FEDERAL TAXATION

INDIVIDUAL INCOME TAXES

2012 EDITION

GENERAL EDITORS

William H. Hoffman, Jr.
J.D., Ph.D., CPA

James E. Smith
Ph.D., CPA

CONTRIBUTING AUTHORS

James H. Boyd
Ph.D., CPA
Arizona State University

D. Larry Crumbley
Ph.D., CPA
Louisiana State University

Steven C. Dilley
J.D., Ph.D., CPA
Michigan State University

William H. Hoffman, Jr.
J.D., Ph.D., CPA
University of Houston

David M. Maloney
Ph.D., CPA
University of Virginia

Gary A. McGill
Ph.D., CPA
University of Florida

William A. Raabe
Ph.D., CPA
The Ohio State University

Boyd C. Randall
J.D., Ph.D.
Brigham Young University

W. Eugene Seago
J.D., Ph.D., CPA
Virginia Polytechnic Institute and State University

James E. Smith
Ph.D., CPA
College of William and Mary

James C. Young
Ph.D., CPA
Northern Illinois University

SOUTH-WESTERN
CENGAGE Learning

Australia • Brazil • Japan • Korea • Mexico • Singapore • Spain • United Kingdom • United States

SOUTH-WESTERN
CENGAGE Learning™

South-Western Federal Taxation:
Individual Income Taxes, 2012 Edition

William H. Hoffman, Jr., James E. Smith

Vice President of Editorial, Business: Jack W. Calhoun

Editor-in-Chief: Rob Dewey

Senior Acquisitions Editor: Mike Schenk

Senior Developmental Editor: Craig Avery

Editorial Assistant: Ann Mazzaro

Marketing Manager: Natalie Livingston

Senior Content Project Manager: Colleen A. Farmer

Media Editor: Chris Valentine

Senior Frontlist Buyer, Manufacturing: Doug Wilke

Marketing Communications Manager: Libby Shipp

Production Service: Cadmus Communications

Senior Art Director: Michelle Kunkler

Internal and Cover Designer: Chris Miller

Cover Image: ©iolo72/Shutterstock

Rights Acquisitions Specialist – Text: John Hill

For product information and technology assistance, contact us at
Cengage Learning Customer & Sales Support,
1-800-354-9706

For permission to use material from this text or product, submit all requests online at **www.cengage.com/permissions**
Further permissions questions can be emailed to
permissionrequest@cengage.com

Student Edition ISBN 13: 978-1-111-22168-3
Student Edition ISBN 10: 1-111-22168-5
Student Edition with CD ISBN 13: 978-1-111-22167-6
Student Edition with CD ISBN 10: 1-111-22167-7

ISSN: 0272-0329
2012 Annual Edition

South-Western
5191 Natorp Boulevard
Mason, OH 45040
USA

Cengage Learning products are represented in Canada by Nelson Education, Ltd.

For your course and learning solutions, visit **www.cengage.com**
Purchase any of our products at your local college store or at our preferred online store **www.cengagebrain.com**

Printed in the United States of America
1 2 3 4 5 6 7 15 14 13 12 11

Preface

To The Student

THE LEADERSHIP YOU TRUST.
THE INNOVATION YOU EXPECT.
THE SERVICE YOU DESERVE.

South-Western Federal Taxation is the most trusted and best-selling series in college taxation. We are focused exclusively on providing the most useful, comprehensive, and up-to-date tax texts, online study aids, tax preparation tools, and printed study guides to help you succeed in your tax courses and beyond.

Studying Is Easier with the Right Tools. *Individual Income Taxes, 2012 Edition* provides a dynamic learning experience inside and outside of the classroom. Built with resources and tools that students have identified as the most important, our complete study system provides options for the way you learn.

Here's how *Individual Income Taxes, 2012 Edition* is designed to help you learn!

PRACTICAL TAX SCENARIOS AT THE START OF EVERY CHAPTER...

The Big Picture: Tax Solutions for the Real World. Taxation comes alive at the start of each chapter. **The Big Picture** is a glimpse into the lives, families, careers, and tax situations of typical individual filers. Each **Big Picture** case asks you to apply what you will learn in the upcoming chapter to develop the best tax solution to these real-life dilemmas.

THE BIG PICTURE	Tax Solutions for the Real World
EDUCATION TAX CREDITS	Tom and Jennifer Snyder have two children in college. Lora is a freshman, and her tuition and required fees in 2011 total $14,000. Lora has a partial scholarship amounting to $6,500, and the Snyders paid the balance of her tuition ($7,500), plus room and board of $8,500. Sam is a junior, and the Snyders paid $8,100 for his tuition plus $7,200 for his room and board. Both students qualify as Tom and Jennifer's dependents.
	The Snyders have AGI of $158,000. They would like to know what tax options are available to them related to these educational expenses. They have heard about education tax credits, but they believe that their income is too high for them to get any benefit. Are they correct? **Read the chapter and formulate your response.**

... BIG PICTURE EXAMPLES TO HELP YOU FOLLOW CLIENTS THROUGH THE CHAPTER...

Among the many examples in every chapter are an average of almost four examples per chapter based on the Big Picture tax situation that opens the text. That means less confusion understanding new topics, a more consistent application of data for you to learn, and practical tax stories that span the whole chapter.

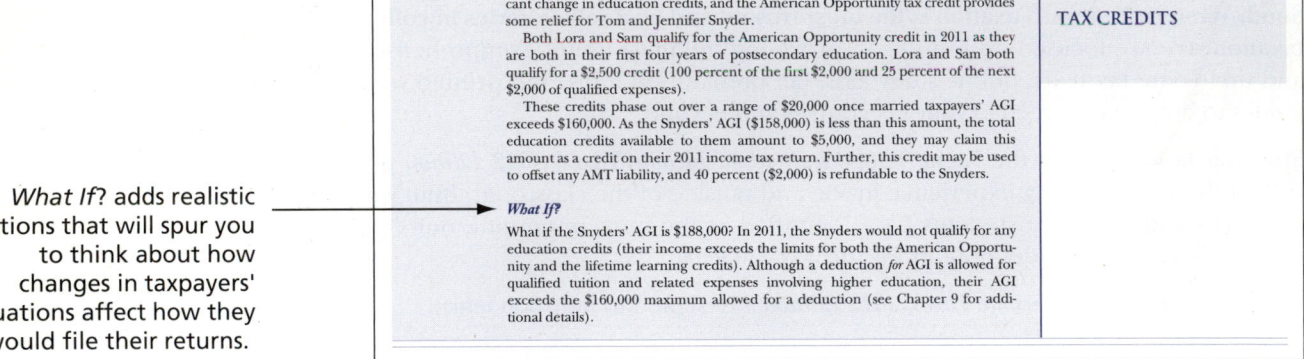

Return to the facts of *The Big Picture* on p. 13-2. Now assume that Tom and Jennifer's modified AGI for 2011 is $172,000 instead of $158,000. Tom and Jennifer are eligible to claim a $2,000 American Opportunity credit for 2011. Their $5,000 available American Opportunity credit must be reduced because their AGI exceeds the $160,000 limit for married taxpayers. The percentage reduction is computed as the amount by which modified AGI exceeds the limit, expressed as a percentage of the phaseout range, or [($172,000 − $160,000)/$20,000)], resulting in a 60% reduction. Therefore, the maximum available credit for 2011 is $2,000 ($5,000 × 40% allowable portion). ■

. . .AND PRACTICAL CONCLUSIONS TO THOSE TAX SCENARIOS

Refocus on the Big Picture. Returning to the client situations introduced in the chapter-opening **Big Picture**, these end-of-chapter summaries and tax planning scenarios apply concepts and topics from the chapter in a reasonable and professional solution. A **What If?** section then demonstrates how tax treatments might change as a result of potential changes in the filer's situation—making **What If?** a valuable consideration in tax planning.

What If? adds realistic options that will spur you to think about how changes in taxpayers' situations affect how they would file their returns.

REFOCUS ON THE BIG PICTURE

EDUCATION TAX CREDITS

The American Recovery and Reinvestment Tax Act (ARRTA) of 2009 made a significant change in education credits, and the American Opportunity tax credit provides some relief for Tom and Jennifer Snyder.

Both Lora and Sam qualify for the American Opportunity credit in 2011 as they are both in their first four years of postsecondary education. Lora and Sam both qualify for a $2,500 credit (100 percent of the first $2,000 and 25 percent of the next $2,000 of qualified expenses).

These credits phase out over a range of $20,000 once married taxpayers' AGI exceeds $160,000. As the Snyders' AGI ($158,000) is less than this amount, the total education credits available to them amount to $5,000, and they may claim this amount as a credit on their 2011 income tax return. Further, this credit may be used to offset any AMT liability, and 40 percent ($2,000) is refundable to the Snyders.

What If?

What if the Snyders' AGI is $188,000? In 2011, the Snyders would not qualify for any education credits (their income exceeds the limits for both the American Opportunity and the lifetime learning credits). Although a deduction *for* AGI is allowed for qualified tuition and related expenses involving higher education, their AGI exceeds the $160,000 maximum allowed for a deduction (see Chapter 9 for additional details).

NEW FINANCIAL DISCLOSURE INSIGHTS

Increasingly, tax professionals need to understand how taxes affect the income statement and balance sheet. These features, appearing throughout the text, use current data about existing taxpayers to highlight book-tax reporting differences, effective tax rates, and trends in reporting conventions. **Financial Disclosure Insights** help you integrate financial knowledge with the results of state and Federal tax law. **SWFT's coverage of the role of tax data on the financial statements far exceeds that of any other tax text.**

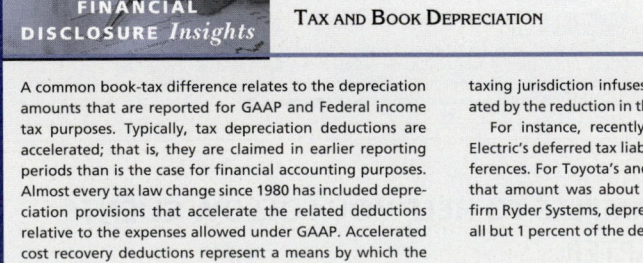

FINANCIAL DISCLOSURE *Insights* — **TAX AND BOOK DEPRECIATION**

A common book-tax difference relates to the depreciation amounts that are reported for GAAP and Federal income tax purposes. Typically, tax depreciation deductions are accelerated; that is, they are claimed in earlier reporting periods than is the case for financial accounting purposes. Almost every tax law change since 1980 has included depreciation provisions that accelerate the related deductions relative to the expenses allowed under GAAP. Accelerated cost recovery deductions represent a means by which the taxing jurisdiction infuses the business with cash flow created by the reduction in the year's tax liabilities.

For instance, recently about one-quarter of General Electric's deferred tax liabilities related to depreciation differences. For Toyota's and Ford's depreciation differences, that amount was about one-third. And for the trucking firm Ryder Systems, depreciation differences accounted for all but 1 percent of the deferred tax liabilities.

ORGANIZED AROUND KEY TAX CONCEPTS, LEARNING OBJECTIVES, AND EXAMPLES

Fitting It All Together: The Income Tax Formula for Individuals. This study feature introduced in Chapter 3 demonstrates how topics within the text are aligned, using the Income Tax Formula for Individuals as the framework.

Chapter-Opening Tax Formula Framework Using Form 1040. Framework 1040, the Tax Formula Framework for Individuals, helps you organize your understanding of key topics within each chapter in terms of the basic tax formula and then identifies where these items are reported on the individual tax Form 1040. **Framework 1040** is a **handy navigation tool** that helps explain how tax concepts are organized.

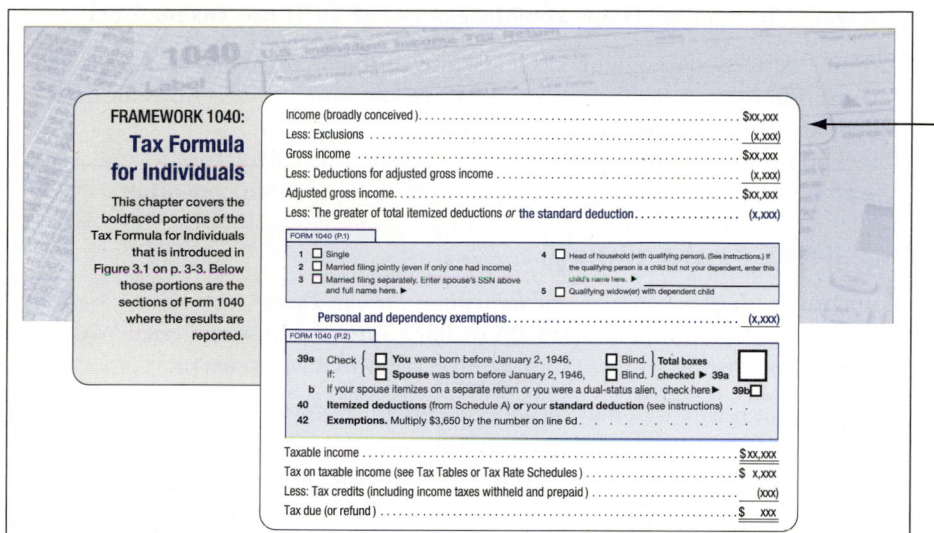

Use this chapter-opening **Framework 1040**, which shows the topics as they appear in the individual tax formula, to understand where on Form 1040 these chapter topics would appear.

Examples You'll Use in Every Chapter. An **average of over 40 examples in each chapter** use realistic situations to illustrate the complexities of the tax law and demonstrate concepts.

EXAMPLE 17	Jennifer, age 17, lives in the same household with her parents during the entire year. If her parents file separate returns, the one with the higher AGI has priority as to the dependency exemption. ∎

Homework Linked to Chapter Learning Objectives. Students tell us that for maximum learning value, homework assignments should refer back to specific chapter topics and sections. Each end-of-chapter Question and Problem is labeled with the Learning Objective(s) that appear beside key topics in the text margins. **Now it is easier to go back to the section of the text where the concept in the homework item is covered—saving you time, better organizing your study, and increasing your confidence in earning a better grade.**

> 43. **LO.1, 3, 7** Ava, age 18, is claimed as a dependent on her parents' 2011 return, on which they report taxable income of $100,000 (no qualified dividends or capital gains). Ava earned $2,900 pet sitting and $3,000 in interest on a savings account. What are Ava's taxable income and tax liability for 2011?

ONLINE RESOURCES AND STUDY TOOLS

Aplia™ is an online interactive homework solution that improves learning by increasing student effort and engagement. Aplia for tax ensures that you stay on top of your coursework with regularly scheduled homework assignments. The Aplia assignments are derived from select end-of-chapter problems from the textbook, allowing you to apply what you learn. To explore the benefits Aplia offers, ask your instructor or visit **www.aplia.com/tax**.

CHECKPOINT® STUDENT EDITION

Checkpoint® Student Edition from Thomson Reuters comes with every new copy of this textbook to help you succeed in the tax research portion of your studies.*

3 Simple Ways Checkpoint® Helps You Make Sense of All Those Taxes:

- Intuitive web-based design makes it fast and simple to find what you need.
- A comprehensive collection of primary tax law, cases, and rulings along with analytical insight you simply can't find anywhere else.
- Checkpoint® has built-in productivity tools such as calculators to make research more efficient—a resource more tax pros use than any other.

CPAexcel CPA EXAM REVIEW

With your purchase of a new copy of *Individual Income Taxes**, you have a 6-month access to CPAexcel content, the best CPA review course for busy students! With CPA exam content matched to your taxation course, you will have access to:

- Online exam review that may be accessed anytime, anywhere.
- Over 800 past exam and proficiency questions.
- Exam-identical simulations and comprehensive diagnostics.

H&R BLOCK AT HOME™

More than software: Put the experience of H&R Block tax professionals on your side.

- A step-by-step interview guides you through a customized process.
- Accurate calculations and 100% satisfaction—guaranteed.
- Worry-free Audit Support™ and tax advice from an H&R Block tax professional.

H&R Block At Home™ is offered with each new copy of **South-Western Federal Taxation**—at no additional cost to students!

ONLINE STUDENT RESOURCES

Go to **www.cengagebrain.com** for free resources to help you study as well as the opportunity to purchase additional study aids. These valuable free study resources will help you earn a better grade:

- **Interactive quizzes** are short and auto-graded to help you brush up on important chapter topics.
- **Flashcards** use chapter terms and definitions to aid you in learning tax terminology for each chapter.
- **Online glossary** for each chapter provides terms and definitions from the text in alphabetical order for easy reference.
- **Learning objectives** can be downloaded for each chapter to help keep you on track.

---

*Not available with the Professional Editions of *South-Western Federal Taxation*.

- **Tax Tips for the Recent Graduate** introduce the college graduate to some common tax considerations that could be beneficial in reducing the dreaded "tax bite."
- **Tax Updates** provide the most recent tax information and major changes to the tax law.
- **Tax tables** used in the textbook are downloadable for reference.

ADDITIONAL STUDENT RESOURCES

Study Guide, ISBN 1-111-82451-7
Do you need more help studying for your taxation class? Order the study guide to receive:

- **Study Highlights**—an outline of key topics for each chapter.
- **Key Terms** used in the chapter.
- **Self-Quizzing** with helpful, annotated answers that are keyed to pages in the 2012 Edition.

Check with your bookstore or order on **CengageBrain.com**.

Individual Practice Sets, ISBN 1-111-82452-5
Ask your instructor about assigning these practice sets.

Written specifically for *Individual Income Taxes, 2012 Edition*, these practice sets are comprehensive and designed to be completed near the end of the course using tax preparation software such as H&R Block at Home™.

Check with your instructor before ordering practice sets. Solutions are available to instructors only.

For over 35 years, the **South-Western Federal Taxation** Series has guided more than 1.5 million students through the ever-changing field of Federal taxation.

With our promise of leadership, innovation, and service, we are committed to your success both now and in the future.

About the Editors

WILLIAM H. HOFFMAN JR. earned B.A. and J.D. degrees from the University of Michigan and M.B.A. and Ph.D. degrees from The University of Texas. He is a licensed CPA and attorney in Texas. His teaching experience includes The University of Texas (1957–1961), Louisiana State University (1961–1967), and the University of Houston (1967–1999). Professor Hoffman has addressed many tax institutes and conferences and has published extensively in academic and professional journals. His articles appear in *The Journal of Taxation, The Tax Adviser, Taxes—The Tax Magazine, The Journal of Accountancy, The Accounting Review,* and *Taxation for Accountants.*

JAMES E. SMITH is the John S. Quinn Professor of Accounting at the College of William and Mary. He has been a member of the Accounting Faculty for over 30 years. He received his Ph.D. degree from the University of Arizona. Professor Smith has served as a discussion leader for Continuing Professional Education programs for the AICPA, Federal Tax Workshops, and various state CPA societies. He has conducted programs in more than 40 states for approximately 25,000 CPAs. He has been the recipient of the AICPA's Outstanding Discussion Leader Award and the American Taxation Association/Arthur Andersen Teaching Innovation Award. Among his other awards are the Virginia Society of CPAs' Outstanding Accounting Educator Award and the James Madison University's Outstanding Accounting Educator Award. He was the President of the Administrators of Accounting Programs Group (AAPG) in 1991–1992. He was the faculty adviser for the William and Mary teams that received first place in the Andersen Tax Challenge in 1994, 1995, 1997, 2000, and 2001 and in the Deloitte Tax Case Study Competition in 2002, 2004, 2005, 2006, and 2008.

Brief Contents

Contents

PART 5: Property Transactions

PART 7: Corporations and Partnerships

APPENDIXES

Introduction and Basic Tax Model

Part 1 provides an introduction to taxation in the United States. Although the primary orientation of this text is income taxation, other types of taxes are also discussed briefly. The purposes of the Federal tax law are examined, and the legislative, administrative, and judicial sources of Federal tax law, including their application to the tax research process, are analyzed. Part 1 concludes with the introduction of the basic tax model for the individual taxpayer.

An Introduction to Taxation and Understanding the Federal Tax Law

CHAPTER

1

LEARNING OBJECTIVES

After completing Chapter 1, you should be able to:

LO.1

Appreciate why taxation is important.

LO.2

Describe some of the history and trends of the Federal income tax.

LO.3

Assess some of the criteria for selecting a tax structure; understand the components of a tax structure.

LO.4

Identify the different taxes imposed in the United States at the Federal, state, and local levels.

LO.5

Explain the administration of the tax law, including the audit process utilized by the IRS.

LO.6

Evaluate some of the ethical guidelines involved in tax practice.

LO.7

Recognize the economic, social, equity, and political considerations that justify various aspects of the tax law.

LO.8

Describe the role played by the IRS and the courts in the evolution of the Federal tax system.

OUTLINE

Tax Solutions for the Real World

**FAMILY AND
TAXES—A
TYPICAL YEAR**

Travis and Betty Carter are married and live in a state that imposes both a sales tax and an income tax. They have two children, April (age 17) and Martin (age 18). Travis is a mining engineer who specializes in land reclamation. After several years with a mining corporation, Travis established a consulting practice that involves a considerable amount of travel. Betty is a registered nurse who, until recently, was a homemaker. In November of this year, she decided to reenter the job market and accepted a position with a medical clinic. The Carters live only a few blocks from Ernest and Mary Walker, Betty Carter's parents. The Walkers are retired and live on interest, dividends, and Social Security benefits.

Various developments occurring during the year with possible tax ramifications are summarized below.

- The ad valorem property taxes on the Carters' residence are increased, while those on the Walkers' residence are lowered.
- When Travis registers an automobile purchased last year in another state, he is forced to pay a sales tax to his home state.
- As an anniversary present, the Carters gave the Walkers a recreational vehicle (RV).
- When Travis made a consulting trip to Chicago, the client withheld Illinois state income tax from the payment made to Travis for his services.
- Travis employs his children to draft blueprints and prepare scale models for use in his work. Both April and Martin have had training in drafting and topography.
- Early in the year the Carters are audited by the state on an income tax return filed several years ago. Later in the year, they are audited by the IRS on a Form 1040 they filed for the same year. In each case, a tax deficiency and interest were assessed.
- The Walkers are audited by the IRS. Unlike the Carters, they did not have to deal with an agent but settled the matter by mail.

Explain these developments and resolve the issues raised. **Read the chapter and formulate your response.**

T he primary objective of this chapter is to provide an overview of the Federal tax system. Among the topics discussed are the following:

- The importance and relevance of taxation.
- The history of the Federal income tax in brief.
- The types of taxes imposed at the Federal, state, and local levels.
- Some highlights of tax law administration.
- Tax concepts that help explain the reasons for various tax provisions.
- The influence that the Internal Revenue Service (IRS) and the courts have had in the evolution of current tax law.

1.1 LEARNING AND COPING WITH TAXATION

LO.1

Appreciate why taxation is important.

The study of taxation is important because taxes permeate our society. Even the simplest of decisions can carry tax implications. Does it matter, for example, which son or daughter pays the medical bills when all of four adult children contribute to the support of their widowed mother? Or if you use your automobile in a business, is it worth your time and effort to use the actual cost method of calculating the expenses rather than the simpler automatic mileage method?

Effectively coping with taxes often involves making decisions based on timing considerations. Does the employee who is trying to decide between a traditional Individual Retirement Account (IRA) and a Roth IRA want the tax benefit up front (i.e., traditional) or at retirement (i.e., Roth)? Timing considerations are paramount when it is deemed desirable to accelerate (or defer) income or accelerate (or defer) deductions for any one year.

The study of taxation teaches us not to overlook the less obvious taxes that can block our intended objective. A grandson inherits his grandmother's personal residence. He has heard that rental property can generate significant income tax benefits. But does he realize that a change of ownership may unlock an appraised-value freeze on the property? Or that conversion from residential to income-producing use will cause an increase in ad valorem taxes on realty? Thus, an attractive income tax result could be materially diminished by adverse property tax consequences.

It is essential in working with taxation to maintain a balanced perspective. A corporation that is deciding where to locate a new factory does not automatically select the city or state that offers the most generous tax benefits. Nor does the person who is retiring to a warmer climate pick Belize over Arizona because the former has no income tax while the latter does. Tax considerations should not control, but they remain one of many factors to be considered.

The study of taxation involves reviewing a multitude of rules and exceptions and, when possible, trying to understand the justification for them. But the desired goal of this learning process is the ability to recognize issues that carry tax implications. Suppose, for example, that you come upon a situation that involves a discharge of indebtedness. If you know that forgiveness of debt results in income but there are exceptions to this rule, the battle is won! The issue has been identified, and the outcome (i.e., when an exception applies) can easily be resolved by additional research.

1.2 HISTORY OF U.S. TAXATION

EARLY PERIODS

The concept of an income tax can hardly be regarded as a newcomer to the Western Hemisphere. An income tax was first enacted in 1634 by the English colonists in the Massachusetts Bay Colony, but the Federal government did not adopt this form of taxation until 1861. In fact, both the Federal Union and the Confederate States of America used the income tax to raise funds to finance the Civil War. Although modest in its reach and characterized by broad exemptions and low rates, the income tax generated $376 million of revenue for the Federal government during the Civil War.

When the Civil War ended, the need for additional revenue disappeared, and the income tax was repealed. Once again the Federal government was able to finance its operations almost exclusively from customs duties (tariffs). It is interesting to note that the courts held that the Civil War income tax was not contrary to the Constitution.

When a new Federal income tax on individuals was enacted in 1894, its opponents were prepared and were able to successfully challenge its constitutionality. The U.S. Constitution provided that "No Capitation, or other direct, Tax shall be laid, unless in Proportion to the Census or Enumeration herein before directed to be taken." In *Pollock v. Farmers' Loan and Trust Co.*, the U.S. Supreme Court found that taxes on the income of real and personal property were the legal equivalent of a tax on the property involved and, therefore, required apportionment.[1]

A Federal corporate income tax, enacted by Congress in 1909, fared better in the judicial system. The U.S. Supreme Court found this tax to be constitutional because it was treated as an excise tax.[2] In essence, it was a tax on the right to do business in the

---

[1] 3 AFTR 2602, 15 S.Ct. 912 (USSC, 1895). See Chapter 2 for an explanation of the citations of judicial decisions.

[2] *Flint v. Stone Tracy Co.*, 3 AFTR 2834, 31 S.Ct. 342 (USSC, 1911).

FIGURE 1.1	Federal Budget Receipts—2011	
Individual income taxes		44%
Corporation income taxes		12
Social insurance taxes and contributions		36
Excise taxes		3
Other		5
		100%

corporate form. As such, it was likened to a form of the franchise tax.[3] The corporate form of doing business had been developed in the late nineteenth century and was an unfamiliar concept to the framers of the U.S. Constitution. Since a corporation is an entity created under law, jurisdictions possess the right to tax its creation and operation. Using this rationale, many states still impose franchise taxes on corporations.

The ratification of the Sixteenth Amendment to the U.S. Constitution in 1913 sanctioned both the Federal individual and corporate income taxes and, as a consequence, neutralized the continuing effect of the *Pollock* decision.

REVENUE ACTS

Following ratification of the Sixteenth Amendment, Congress enacted the Revenue Act of 1913. Under this Act, the first Form 1040 was due on March 1, 1914. The law allowed various deductions and personal exemptions of $3,000 for a single individual and $4,000 for married taxpayers. Rates ranged from a low of 2 percent to a high of 6 percent. The 6 percent rate applied only to taxable income in excess of $500,000![4]

Various revenue acts were passed between 1913 and 1939. In 1939, all of these revenue laws were codified into the Internal Revenue Code of 1939. In 1954, a similar codification of the revenue law took place. The current law is entitled the Internal Revenue Code of 1986, which largely carries over the provisions of the 1954 Code. To date, the Code has been amended numerous times since 1986. This matter is discussed further in Chapter 2 under Origin of the Internal Revenue Code.

HISTORICAL TRENDS

The income tax has proved to be a major source of revenue for the Federal government. Figure 1.1, which contains a breakdown of the major revenue sources,[5] demonstrates the importance of the income tax. *Estimated* income tax collections from individuals and corporations amount to 56 percent of the total receipts.

The need for revenues to finance the war effort during World War II converted the income tax into a *mass tax*. For example, in 1939, less than 6 percent of the U.S. population was subject to the Federal income tax. In 1945, more than 74 percent of the population was subject to the Federal income tax.[6]

Certain changes in the income tax law are of particular significance in understanding the Federal income tax. In 1943, Congress passed the Current Tax Payment Act, which provided for the first pay-as-you-go tax system. A pay-as-you-go income tax system requires employers to withhold for taxes a specified portion of an employee's wages. Persons with income from other than wages may have to make quarterly payments to the IRS for estimated taxes due for the year.

One trend that has caused considerable concern is the increasing complexity of the Federal income tax laws. In the name of tax reform, Congress has added to this complexity by frequently changing the tax laws. Most recent legislation continues this trend. Increasingly, this complexity forces many taxpayers to seek assistance. According to

[3]See the discussion of state franchise taxes later in the chapter.
[4]This should be contrasted with the highest 2011 tax rate of 35%, which applies once taxable income exceeds $379,150.

[5]The Budget of the United States Government for Fiscal Year 2011, Office of Management and Budget (Washington, D.C.: U.S. Government Printing Office, 2010).
[6]Richard Goode, *The Individual Income Tax* (Washington, D.C.: The Brookings Institution, 1964), pp. 2–4.

TAX in the NEWS   **ADAM SMITH STOPPED TOO SOON**

The American Institute of Certified Public Accountants (AICPA) has issued suggestions for Federal tax policy. Titled *Guiding Principles of Good Tax Policy: A Framework for Evaluating Tax Proposals,* the monograph sets forth 10 tax principles that are commonly used as indicators of desirable tax policy.

The first four principles are adapted from Adam Smith's *The Wealth of Nations.* The other six are summarized below:

- The tax system should be simple.
- The tax should be neutral in terms of its effect on business decisions.

- The tax system should not reduce economic growth and efficiency.
- The tax should be clear and readily understood so that taxpayers know about it and when it applies.
- The tax should be structured so as to minimize noncompliance.
- The tax system should enable the IRS to predict the amount and timing of revenue production.

Source: Adapted from a Tax Policy Concept Statement issued by the Tax Division of the AICPA.

recent estimates, about 64 percent of all taxpayers who file a return pay a preparer, and slightly more than 20 percent purchase tax software. At this time, therefore, substantial support exists for tax law simplification.

1.3 CRITERIA USED IN THE SELECTION OF A TAX STRUCTURE

In the eighteenth century, Adam Smith identified the following *canons of taxation,* which are still considered when evaluating a particular tax structure:[7]

- *Equality.* Each taxpayer enjoys fair or equitable treatment by paying taxes in proportion to his or her income level. Ability to pay a tax is the measure of how equitably a tax is distributed among taxpayers.
- *Convenience.* Administrative simplicity has long been valued in formulating tax policy. If a tax is easily assessed and collected and its administrative costs are low, it should be favored. An advantage of the withholding (pay-as-you-go) system is its convenience for taxpayers.
- *Certainty.* A tax structure is *good* if the taxpayer can readily predict when, where, and how a tax will be levied. Individuals and businesses need to know the likely tax consequences of a particular type of transaction.
- *Economy.* A *good* tax system involves only nominal collection costs by the government and minimal compliance costs on the part of the taxpayer. Although the government's cost of collecting Federal taxes amounts to less than one-half of 1 percent of the revenue collected, the complexity of our current tax structure imposes substantial taxpayer compliance costs.

By these canons, the Federal income tax is a contentious product. *Equality* is present as long as one accepts ability to pay as an ingredient of this component. *Convenience* exists due to a heavy reliance on pay-as-you-go procedures. *Certainty* probably generates the greatest controversy. In one sense, certainty is present since a mass of administrative and judicial guidelines exists to aid in interpreting the tax law. In another sense, however, certainty does not exist since many questions remain unanswered and frequent changes in the tax law by Congress lessen stability. Particularly troublesome in this regard are tax provisions that are given a limited life (e.g., 2010). If not extended by Congress, the provisions expire. All too often, Congress does not give the necessary approval in time, and the extension has to be applied retroactively. *Economy*

LO.3

Assess some of the criteria for selecting a tax structure; understand the components of a tax structure.

---
[7] *The Wealth of Nations* (New York: Dutton, 1910), Book V, Chapter II, Part II.

is present if only the collection procedure of the IRS is considered. Economy is not present, however, if one focuses instead on taxpayer compliance efforts and costs.

1.4 THE TAX STRUCTURE

TAX BASE

A tax base is the amount to which the tax rate is applied. In the case of the Federal income tax, the tax base is *taxable income*. As noted later in the chapter (Figure 1.2), taxable income is gross income reduced by certain deductions (both business and personal).

TAX RATES

Tax rates are applied to the tax base to determine a taxpayer's liability. The tax rates may be proportional or progressive. A tax is *proportional* if the rate of tax remains constant for any given income level. Examples of proportional taxes include most excise taxes, general sales taxes, and employment taxes (FICA, FUTA).

EXAMPLE 1

Bill has $10,000 of taxable income and pays a tax of $3,000, or 30%. Bob's taxable income is $50,000, and the tax on this amount is $15,000, or 30%. If this constant rate is applied throughout the rate structure, the tax is proportional. ∎

A tax is *progressive* if a higher rate of tax applies as the tax base increases. The Federal income tax, Federal gift and estate taxes, and most state income tax rate structures are progressive.

EXAMPLE 2

If Cora, a married individual filing jointly, has taxable income of $10,000, her tax for 2011 is $1,000 for an average tax rate of 10%. If, however, Cora's taxable income is $50,000, her tax will be $6,650 for an average tax rate of 13.3%. The tax is progressive since higher rates are applied to greater amounts of taxable income. ∎

INCIDENCE OF TAXATION

The degree to which various segments of society share the total tax burden is difficult to assess. Assumptions must be made concerning who absorbs the burden of paying the tax. For example, since dividend payments to shareholders are not deductible by a corporation and are generally taxable to shareholders, the same income is subject to a form of double taxation. Concern over double taxation is valid to the extent that corporations are *not* able to shift the corporate tax to the consumer through higher commodity prices. Many research studies have shown a high degree of shifting of the corporate income tax, converting it into a consumption tax that is borne by the ultimate purchasers of goods.

The progressiveness of the Federal income tax rate structure for individuals has varied over the years. As late as 1986, for example, there were 15 rates, ranging from 0 to 50 percent. These later were reduced to two rates of 15 and 28 percent. Currently, there are six rates ranging from 10 to 35 percent.

LO.4

Identify the different taxes imposed in the United States at the Federal, state, and local levels.

1.5 MAJOR TYPES OF TAXES

Why does a text devoted primarily to the Federal individual income tax discuss state and local taxes? A simple illustration shows the importance of non-Federal taxes.

EXAMPLE 3

Rick is employed by Flamingo Corporation in San Antonio, Texas, at a salary of $74,000. Rick's employer offers him a chance to transfer to its New York City office at a salary of $94,000. A quick computation indicates that the additional taxes (Federal, state, and local) involve approximately $12,000. ∎

Although Rick must consider many nontax factors before he decides on a job change, he should also evaluate the tax climate. How do state and local taxes compare? For example, neither Texas nor San Antonio imposes an income tax, but New York State and New York City both do. Consequently, what appears to be a $20,000 pay increase is only $8,000 when the additional taxes of $12,000 are taken into account.

PROPERTY TAXES

Correctly referred to as **ad valorem taxes** because they are based on value, property taxes are a tax on wealth, or capital. In this regard, they have much in common with estate taxes and gift taxes discussed later in the chapter. Although property taxes do not tax income, the income actually derived (or the potential for any income) may be relevant insofar as it affects the value of the property being taxed.

Property taxes fall into *two* categories: those imposed on realty and those imposed on personalty, or assets other than land and buildings. Both have added importance since they usually generate a deduction for Federal income tax purposes (see Chapter 10).

Ad Valorem Taxes on Realty

Property taxes on realty are used exclusively by states and their local political subdivisions, such as cities, counties, and school districts. They represent a major source of revenue for *local* governments, but their importance at the *state* level has waned over the past few years. Some states, for example, have imposed freezes on upward revaluations of residential housing.

How realty is defined can have an important bearing on which assets are subject to tax. This is especially true in jurisdictions that do not impose ad valorem taxes on personalty. Primarily a question of state property law, **realty** generally includes real estate and any capital improvements that are classified as fixtures. Simply stated, a *fixture* is something so permanently attached to the real estate that its removal will cause irreparable damage. A built-in bookcase might well be a fixture, whereas a movable bookcase would not be a fixture. Certain items such as electrical wiring and plumbing cease to be personalty when installed in a building and become realty.

The following are some of the characteristics of ad valorem taxes on realty:

- Property owned by the Federal government is exempt from tax. Similar immunity usually is extended to property owned by state and local governments and by certain charitable organizations.
- Some states provide for lower valuations on property dedicated to agricultural use or other special uses (e.g., wildlife sanctuaries). Reductions in appraised valuations may also be available when the property is subject to a conservation easement (e.g., a limitation on further development).
- Some states partially exempt the homestead, or personal residence, portion of property from taxation. Additionally, modern homestead laws normally protect some or all of a personal residence (including a farm or ranch) from the actions of creditors pursuing claims against the owner.
- Lower taxes may apply to a residence owned by a taxpayer age 65 or older.
- When non-income-producing property (e.g., a personal residence) is converted to income-producing property (e.g., a rental house), typically the appraised value increases.
- Some jurisdictions extend immunity from tax for a specified period of time (a *tax holiday*) to new or relocated businesses. A tax holiday can backfire, however, and cause more harm than good. If it is too generous, it can damage the local infrastructure (e.g., less funding for public works and education).

EXAMPLE 4
THE BIG PICTURE

Return to the facts of *The Big Picture* on p. 1-2. Why did the Walkers' taxes decrease while those of the Carters increased? A likely explanation is that one (or both) of the Walkers achieved senior citizen status. In the case of the Carters, the assessed value of their property was probably increased (see below). Perhaps they made significant home improvements (e.g., kitchen/bathroom renovation, addition of a sundeck). ∎

TAX in the NEWS

THE BACKDOOR TAX INCREASE

Can a landowner's property taxes increase even though the tax rate has not changed? Yes, if the assessed value of the property is increased! Known as a "backdoor tax increase," this procedure allows the taxing authority to generate additional revenue without having to secure voter approval for an increase in the tax rate. Even more aggravating for the property owner is an increase in assessed value that is based on past market values and does not reflect the true current value. This kind of increase often occurs during periods of economic downturn, when real estate prices decline. Under these conditions, increases in assessed value are likely to cause considerable taxpayer dissatisfaction and lead to proposals for legislative relief, such as a freeze on upward property assessments.

Source: Adapted from Jennifer Levitz, "Calls Grow to Cap Property Taxes," *Wall Street Journal,* January 5, 2009, p. A3.

Unlike the ad valorem tax on personalty (see below), the tax on realty is difficult to avoid. Since real estate is impossible to hide, a high degree of taxpayer compliance is not surprising. The only avoidance possibility that is generally available is associated with the assessed value of the property. For this reason, the assessed value of the property—particularly, a value that is reassessed upward—may be subject to controversy and litigation.

The history of the ad valorem tax on realty has been marked by inconsistent application due to a lack of competent tax administration and definitive guidelines for assessment procedures. In recent years, however, some significant improvements have occurred. Some jurisdictions, for example, have computerized their reassessment procedures so that they will immediately affect all property located within the jurisdiction.

Several jurisdictions provide homeowners with a measure of protection from increased property taxes by "freezing" existing assessments and limiting future upward adjustments. Such restrictions on reassessments, however, do not carry over to the new owner when the property is sold. Thus, such measures tend to lock in ownership and restrict the mobility of those who might otherwise change residences.

Ad Valorem Taxes on Personalty

Personalty can be defined as all assets that are not realty. It may be helpful to distinguish between the *classification* of an asset (realty or personalty) and the *use* to which it is put. Both realty and personalty can be either business use or personal use property. Examples include a residence (realty that is personal use), an office building (realty that is business use), surgical instruments (personalty that is business use), and regular wearing apparel (personalty that is personal use).[8]

Personalty can also be classified as tangible property or intangible property. For ad valorem tax purposes, intangible personalty includes stocks, bonds, and various other securities (e.g., bank shares).

The following generalizations may be made concerning the ad valorem taxes on personalty:

- Particularly with personalty devoted to personal use (e.g., jewelry, household furnishings), taxpayer compliance ranges from poor to zero. Some jurisdictions do not even attempt to enforce the tax on these items. For automobiles devoted to personal use, many jurisdictions have converted from value as the tax base to arbitrary license fees based on the weight of the vehicle. Some jurisdictions also consider the vehicle's age (e.g., automobiles six years or older are not subject to the ad valorem tax because they are presumed to have little, if any, value).

---

[8]The distinction, important for ad valorem and for Federal income tax purposes, often becomes confused when personalty is referred to as "personal" property to distinguish it from "real" property. This designation does not give a complete picture of what is involved. The description "personal" residence, however, is clearer, since a residence can be identified as being realty. What is meant, in this case, is realty that is personal use property.

TAX in the NEWS

MORE EXCISE TAXES FROM THE FEDERAL GOVERNMENT—GOOD OR BAD?

The recent increase in the Federal excise tax on tobacco (from $0.39 to $1.01 per package of cigarettes) has met with a mixed reaction. On the positive side, the increase will fund a good cause—SCHIP (State Children's Health Insurance Program). Likewise, no one can take issue with a sin tax that purports to reduce smoking.

As for the negative aspects, most heavy smokers are lower-income taxpayers. Thus, this tax increase will largely fall on the poor. Furthermore, various states have increased their tobacco taxes as well. Faced with a substantially higher cost for cigarettes, smokers who cannot kick the habit may see the cheaper price provided by an illegal market (i.e., smuggling) as an attractive alternative. Tax increases that foster criminal activity are not a good way to raise revenue.

More importantly, does this foray into tobacco taxes portend a new trend on the part of Congress to find new sources of revenue? Note that the cigarette tax increase has recently been followed by a new excise tax on tanning salons. Will other new excise taxes be imposed (e.g., a tax on soft drinks) or existing excise taxes increased (e.g., more taxes on alcoholic beverages)?

- For personalty devoted to business use (e.g., inventories, trucks, machinery, equipment), taxpayer compliance and enforcement procedures are measurably better.
- Which jurisdiction possesses the authority to tax movable personalty (e.g., railroad rolling stock) always has been and continues to be a troublesome issue.
- A few states levy an ad valorem tax on intangibles such as stocks and bonds. Taxpayer compliance may be negligible if the state lacks a means of verifying security transactions and ownership.

TRANSACTION TAXES

Transaction taxes, which characteristically are imposed at the manufacturer's, wholesaler's, or retailer's level, cover a wide range of transfers. Like many other types of taxes (e.g., income taxes, estate taxes, and gift taxes), transaction taxes usually are not within the exclusive province of any level of taxing authority (Federal, state, local government). As the description implies, these levies place a tax on transfers of property and normally are determined by multiplying the value involved by a percentage rate.

Federal Excise Taxes

Long one of the mainstays of the Federal tax system, Federal **excise taxes** had declined in relative importance until recently. In recent years, Congress substantially increased the Federal excise taxes on such items as tobacco products, fuel and gasoline sales, and air travel. Other Federal excise taxes include the following:

- Manufacturers' excise taxes on trucks, trailers, tires, firearms, sporting equipment, and coal and the gas guzzler tax on automobiles.[9]
- Alcohol taxes.
- Miscellaneous taxes (e.g., the tax on wagering).

The list of transactions covered, although seemingly impressive, has diminished over the years. At one time, for example, there was a Federal excise tax on admission to amusement facilities (e.g., theaters) and on the sale of such items as leather goods, jewelry, furs, and cosmetics.

When reviewing the list of both Federal and state excise taxes, one should recognize the possibility that the tax laws may be trying to influence social behavior. For example, the gas guzzler tax is intended as an incentive for the automobile companies to build fuel-efficient cars.

---

[9]The gas guzzler tax is imposed on the manufacturers of automobiles (both domestic and foreign) and increases in amount as the mileage ratings per gallon of gas decrease. For example, a Maserati Gran Turismo manages 19 miles per gallon in combined city/highway driving and starts at $121,100, which includes a $2,100 gas guzzler tax.

TEXAS'S "POLE TAX"—"SIN TAX" OR TAX ON FREE SPEECH?

A 2007 Texas law imposes a $5-per-visit excise tax on patrons who visit one of the state's roughly 170 strip clubs. The tax is being challenged in the courts as a discriminatory way to raise revenue and a measure that squelches freedom of speech. Arguably, "pole dancing" involves a form of emotional expression that is protected by the First Amendment to the U.S. Constitution. Supporters of the pole tax disagree and maintain that its purpose is to combat sexual assault by discouraging the "combustible combination" of drinking and nude dancing. The state of Utah has imposed a similar tax that has been sustained by the state supreme court but probably will be appealed to the U.S. Supreme Court.

Depending on what happens to these taxes in the courts, other states seeking new sources of revenue are likely to respond accordingly.

Source: Adapted from Leslie Eaton, "'Sin Tax' Called Naked Money Grab," *Wall Street Journal*, March 26, 2010, p. A3.

State and Local Excise Taxes

Many state and local excise taxes parallel the Federal version. Thus, all states tax the sale of gasoline, liquor, and tobacco products; however, unlike the Federal version, the rates vary significantly. For gasoline products, for example, compare the 37.5 cents per gallon imposed by the state of Washington with the 7.5 cents per gallon levied by the state of Georgia. For tobacco sales, contrast the 17 cents per pack of 20 cigarettes in effect in Missouri with the $4.35 per pack applicable in the state of New York. Given the latter situation, is it surprising that the smuggling of cigarettes for resale elsewhere is so widespread?

Other excise taxes found at some state and local levels include those on admission to amusement facilities, on the sale of playing cards, and on prepared foods. Most states impose a transaction tax on the transfer of property that requires the recording of documents (e.g., real estate sales).[10] Some extend the tax to the transfer of stocks and other securities.

Over the last few years, two types of excise taxes imposed at the local level have become increasingly popular: the hotel occupancy tax and the rental car "surcharge." Since they tax the visitor who cannot vote, they are a political windfall and are often used to finance special projects that generate civic pride (e.g., convention centers, state-of-the-art sports arenas). These levies can be significant, as demonstrated by Houston's hotel tax of 17 percent and the car rental tax and fees of 35 percent at the Kansas City, Missouri airport.

General Sales Taxes

The distinction between an excise tax and a general **sales tax** is easy to make. One is restricted to a particular transaction (e.g., the 18.4 cents per gallon Federal excise tax on the sale of gasoline), while the other covers a multitude of transactions (e.g., a 5 percent tax on *all* retail sales). In actual practice, however, the distinction is not always that clear. Some state statutes exempt certain transactions from the application of the general sales taxes (e.g., sales of food to be consumed off the premises, sales of certain medicines and drugs). Also, it is not uncommon to find that rates vary depending on the commodity involved. Many states, for example, allow preferential rates for the sale of agricultural equipment or apply different rates (either higher or lower than the general rate) to the sale of automobiles. With many of these special exceptions and classifications of rates, a general sales tax can take on the appearance of a collection of individual excise taxes.

A **use tax** is an ad valorem tax, usually at the same rate as the sales tax, on the use, consumption, or storage of tangible property purchased outside the state but used within the state. The purpose of a use tax is to prevent the avoidance of a sales tax.

---

[10]This type of tax has much in common with the stamp tax levied by Great Britain on the American colonies during the pre-Revolutionary War period in U.S. history.

Every state that imposes a general sales tax levied on the consumer also has a use tax. Alaska, Delaware, Montana, New Hampshire, and Oregon have neither tax. There is no Federal general sales or use tax.

EXAMPLE 5
THE BIG PICTURE

Return to the facts of *The Big Picture* on p. 1-2. The payment Travis made when he registered the car is probably a use tax. When the car was purchased in another state, likely no (or a lesser) sales tax was levied. The current payment makes up for the amount of sales tax he would have paid had the car been purchased in his home state. ∎

The use tax is difficult to enforce for many purchases and therefore the purchaser often does not pay it. In some cases, for example, it may be worthwhile to make purchases through an out-of-state mail-order business or the websites of local vendors. In spite of shipping costs, the avoidance of the local sales tax that otherwise might be incurred can lower the cost of such products as computer components. Some states are taking steps to curtail this loss of revenue. For items such as automobiles (refer to Example 5), the use tax probably will be collected when the purchaser registers the item in his or her home state.

ETHICS & Equity

MAKING GOOD USE OF OUT-OF-STATE RELATIVES

Marcus, a resident of Texas, has found the ideal gift for his wife in celebration of their upcoming wedding anniversary— a $22,000 diamond tennis bracelet. However, Marcus is appalled at the prospect of paying the state and local sales tax of $1,815 (combined rate of 8.25 percent). He, therefore, asks his aunt, a resident of Montana, to purchase the bracelet. The jewelry store lists the aunt as the buyer and ships the bracelet to her. Prior to the anniversary, Marcus receives the bracelet from his aunt. Is Marcus able to save $1,815 on the present for his wife? What can go wrong?

Local general sales taxes, over and above those levied by the state, are common. It is not unusual to find taxpayers living in the same state but paying different general sales taxes due to the location of their residence.

EXAMPLE 6

Pete and Sam both live in a state that has a general sales tax of 3%. Sam, however, resides in a city that imposes an additional general sales tax of 2%. Even though Pete and Sam live in the same state, one is subject to a rate of 3%, while the other pays a tax of 5%. ∎

For various reasons, some jurisdictions will suspend the application of a general sales tax. New York City does so to stimulate shopping. Illinois has permanently suspended the tax on construction materials used to build power-generating plants. Texas and numerous other states do so annually on clothing right before the beginning of the school year. Such suspensions are similar to the tax holidays granted for ad valorem tax purposes. As state revenues have declined in recent years, many states have had misgivings about the advisability of scheduling further sales tax holidays. Turning off the spigot could have political consequences, however. These holidays are extremely popular with both merchants and shoppers, so their termination could cause voter backlash at the polls.

Severance Taxes

Severance taxes are transaction taxes that are based on the notion that the state has an interest in its natural resources (e.g., oil, gas, iron ore, coal). Therefore, a tax is imposed when the natural resources are extracted.

For some states, severance taxes can be a significant source of revenue. Due to the severance tax on oil production, Alaska has been able to avoid both a state income tax and a state general sales tax.

TAXES ON TRANSFERS AT DEATH

The right to transfer property or to receive property upon the death of the owner may be subject to estate and/or inheritance taxes. Consequently, such taxes fall into the category of excise taxes. If the tax is imposed on the right to pass property at death, it is classified as an **estate tax**. If it taxes the right to receive property from a decedent, it is termed an **inheritance tax**. As is typical of other types of excise taxes, the value of the property transferred provides the base for determining the amount of the tax.

The Federal government imposes only an estate tax. Many state governments, however, levy inheritance taxes, estate taxes, or both. Some states (e.g., Florida, Texas) levy neither tax.

EXAMPLE 7	At the time of her death, Wilma lived in a state that imposes an inheritance tax but not an estate tax. Mary, one of Wilma's heirs, lives in the same state. Wilma's estate is subject to the Federal estate tax, and Mary is subject to the state inheritance tax. ∎

The Federal Estate Tax

The Revenue Act of 1916 incorporated the estate tax into the tax law. The tax was originally intended to prevent large concentrations of wealth from being kept within a family for many generations. Whether this objective has been accomplished is debatable. Like the income tax, estate taxes can be reduced through various planning procedures.

The gross estate includes property the decedent owned at the time of death. It also includes property interests, such as life insurance proceeds paid to the estate or to a beneficiary other than the estate if the deceased-insured had any ownership rights in the policy. Quite simply, the gross estate represents property interests subject to Federal estate taxation.[11] All property included in the gross estate is valued as of the date of death or, if the alternate valuation date is elected, six months later.[12]

Deductions from the gross estate in arriving at the taxable estate include funeral and administration expenses, certain taxes, debts of the decedent, casualty losses[13] incurred during the administration of the estate, transfers to charitable organizations, and, in some cases, the marital deduction. The *marital deduction* is available for amounts actually passing to a surviving spouse (a widow or widower).

Once the taxable estate has been determined and certain taxable gifts made by the decedent during life have been added to it, the estate tax can be computed. From the amount derived from the appropriate tax rate schedules, various credits should be subtracted to arrive at the tax, if any, that is due.[14] Although many other credits are also available, probably the most significant is the *unified transfer tax credit*. The main reason for this credit is to eliminate or reduce the estate tax liability for modest estates. For 2011, the amount of the credit is $1,730,800. Based on the estate tax rates, the credit exempts a tax base of up to $5 million.

EXAMPLE 8	Ned made no taxable gifts before his death in 2011. If Ned's taxable estate amounts to $5 million or less, no Federal estate tax is due because of the application of the unified transfer tax credit. Under the tax law, the estate tax on a taxable estate of $5 million is $1,730,800. ∎

---

[11]For further information on these matters, see *South-Western Federal Taxation: Corporations, Partnerships, Estates, and Trusts.*

[12]See the discussion of the alternate valuation date in Chapter 14.

[13]For a definition of "casualty losses," see the Glossary in Appendix C.

[14]For tax purposes, it is always crucial to appreciate the difference between a deduction and a credit. A *credit* is a dollar-for-dollar reduction of tax liability.

A *deduction*, however, benefits the taxpayer only to the extent of his or her tax bracket. An estate in a 50% tax bracket, for example, would need $2 of deductions to prevent $1 of tax liability. In contrast, $1 of credit neutralizes $1 of tax liability.

State Taxes on Transfers at Death

As noted earlier, most states levy an inheritance tax, an estate tax, or both. The two forms of taxes on transfers at death differ according to whether the tax is imposed on the heirs or on the estate.

Characteristically, an inheritance tax divides the heirs into classes based on their relationship to the decedent. The more closely related the heir, the lower the rates imposed and the greater the exemption allowed. Some states completely exempt from taxation amounts passing to a surviving spouse.

GIFT TAXES

Like taxes on transfers at death, a **gift tax** is an excise tax levied on the right to transfer property. In this case, however, the tax is imposed on transfers made during the owner's life and not at death. A gift tax applies only to transfers that are not offset by full and adequate consideration.

	EXAMPLE 9

Carl sells property worth $50,000 to his daughter for $1,000. Although property worth $50,000 has been transferred, only $49,000 represents a gift, since this is the portion not supported by full and adequate consideration. ∎

The Federal Gift Tax

First enacted in 1932, the Federal gift tax was intended to complement the estate tax. If lifetime transfers by gift were not taxed, it would be possible to avoid the estate tax and escape taxation entirely.

Only taxable gifts are subject to the gift tax. For this purpose, a taxable gift is measured by the fair market value of the property on the date of transfer less the *annual exclusion per donee* and, in some cases, less the *marital deduction*, which allows tax-free transfers between spouses. Each donor is allowed an annual exclusion of $13,000 in 2011 for each donee.[15]

	EXAMPLE 10

On December 31, 2010, Louise (a widow) gives $13,000 to each of her four married children, their spouses, and her eight grandchildren. On January 2, 2011, she repeats the procedure, giving $13,000 to each recipient. Due to the annual exclusion, Louise has not made a taxable gift, although she transferred $208,000 [$13,000(annual exclusion) × 16 (donees)] in 2010 and $208,000 [$13,000 (annual exclusion) × 16 (donees)] in 2011, for a total of $416,000 ($208,000 + $208,000). ∎

A special election applicable to married persons allows one-half of the gift made by the donor-spouse to be treated as being made by the nondonor-spouse (*gift splitting*). This election to split the gifts of property made to third persons has the effect of increasing the number of annual exclusions available. Also, it allows the use of the nondonor-spouse's unified transfer tax credit and may lower the tax rates that will apply.

	EXAMPLE 11 THE BIG PICTURE

Return to the facts of *The Big Picture* on p. 1-2. Although the value of the RV is not stated, it is highly likely to exceed the annual exclusion allowed—$52,000 for two donees (the Walkers) from two donors (the Carters). Thus, a taxable gift results, and a Form 709 (Gift Tax Return) must be filed. Whether any gift tax is due depends on the past taxable gifts the Carters have made and how much of their unified transfer tax credit (see below) is still available. ∎

---

[15]The purpose of the annual exclusion is to avoid the need to report and pay a tax on *modest* gifts. Without the exclusion, the IRS could face a real problem of taxpayer noncompliance. The annual exclusion is indexed as the level of inflation warrants. The exclusion was $12,000 from 2006 through 2008.

The gift tax rate schedule is the same as that applicable to the estate tax. The schedule is commonly referred to as the *unified transfer tax schedule.*

The Federal gift tax is *cumulative* in effect. What this means is that the tax base for current taxable gifts includes past taxable gifts. Although a credit is allowed for prior gift taxes, the result of adding past taxable gifts to current taxable gifts could be to force the donor into a higher tax bracket.[16] Like the Federal estate tax rates, the Federal gift tax rates are progressive (see Example 2 earlier in this chapter).

The unified transfer tax credit is available for all taxable gifts; the amount of this credit for 2011 is $1,730,800. There is, however, only one unified transfer tax credit, and it applies both to taxable gifts and to the Federal estate tax. In a manner of speaking, therefore, once the unified transfer tax credit has been exhausted for Federal gift tax purposes, it is no longer available to insulate a decedent's transfers from the Federal estate tax, except to the extent of the excess of the credit amount for estate tax purposes over that for gift tax purposes.

Even though a unified transfer tax credit of $1,730,800 in 2011 is available for transfers by death, lifetime gifts continue to be attractive. If income-producing property is involved (e.g., marketable securities, rental real estate), a gift may reduce income taxes for the family unit by shifting subsequent income to lower-bracket donees. If the gift involves property that is expected to appreciate in value (e.g., life insurance policies, real estate, artworks), future increases in value will be assigned to the donee and will not be included in the donor's estate. Also important is that due to the annual exclusion ($13,000 per donee in 2011), some of the gift is not subject to any gift tax. Recall that the gift-splitting election enables married donors to double up on the annual exclusion.

INCOME TAXES

Income taxes are levied by the Federal government, most states, and some local governments. The trend in recent years has been to place greater reliance on this method of taxation. This trend is not consistent with what is happening in other countries, and in this sense, our system of taxation is somewhat different.

Income taxes generally are imposed on individuals, corporations, and certain fiduciaries (estates and trusts). Most jurisdictions attempt to assure the collection of income taxes by requiring pay-as-you-go procedures, including withholding requirements for employees and estimated tax prepayments for all taxpayers.

Federal Income Taxes

The Federal income tax that is imposed on individuals follows the formula set forth in Figure 1.2. The formula for the individual income tax establishes the framework followed in the text. Beginning with Chapter 3, each component of the formula is illustrated and explained. In large part, the text coverage of individual taxpayers follows the same order as the components in the formula.

Like its individual counterpart, the Federal corporate income tax is progressive in nature. But its application does not require the computation of adjusted gross income (AGI) and does not provide for the standard deduction and personal and dependency exemptions. All allowable deductions of a corporation fall into the business-expense category. In effect, therefore, the taxable income of a corporation is the difference between gross income (net of exclusions) and deductions.

While Chapters 3 through 19 cover the Federal income tax applicable to individuals, Chapter 20 summarizes the rules relating to corporations. For an in-depth treatment of the Federal income tax as it affects corporations, partnerships, estates, and trusts, see *South-Western Federal Taxation: Corporations, Partnerships, Estates, and Trusts,* 2012 Edition, Chapters 2 through 9, 12, and 20.

---

[16]For further information on the Federal gift tax, see *South-Western Federal Taxation: Corporations, Partnerships, Estates, and Trusts.*

FIGURE 1.2	Formula for Federal Income Tax on Individuals	
Income (broadly conceived)		$xx,xxx
Less: Exclusions (income that is not subject to tax)		(x,xxx)
Gross income (income that is subject to tax)		$xx,xxx
Less: Certain deductions (usually referred to as deductions *for* adjusted gross income)		(x,xxx)
Adjusted gross income		$xx,xxx
Less: The greater of certain personal and employee deductions (usually referred to as *itemized deductions*)		
or		
The standard deduction (including any additional standard deduction)		(x,xxx)
and		
Less: Personal and dependency exemptions		(x,xxx)
Taxable income		$xx,xxx
Tax on taxable income (see the Tax Tables and Tax Rate Schedules in Appendix A)		$ x,xxx
Less: Tax credits (including Federal income tax withheld and other prepayments of Federal income taxes)		(xxx)
Tax due (or refund)		$ xxx

State Income Taxes

All but the following states impose an income tax on individuals: Alaska, Florida, Nevada, South Dakota, Texas, Washington, and Wyoming. New Hampshire and Tennessee impose an individual income tax only on interest and dividends.

Some of the characteristics of state income taxes are summarized as follows:

- With few exceptions, all states require some form of withholding procedures.
- Most states use as the tax base the income determination made for Federal income tax purposes.
- A minority of states go even further and impose a flat rate upon AGI as computed for Federal income tax purposes. Several apply a rate to the Federal income tax liability. This is often referred to as the piggyback approach to state income taxation. Although the term *piggyback* does not lend itself to precise definition, in this context, it means making use, for state income tax purposes, of what was done for Federal income tax purposes.
- Some states are somewhat eroding the piggyback approach by "decoupling" from selected recent tax reductions passed by Congress. The purpose of the decoupling is to retain state revenue that would otherwise be lost. In other words, the state cannot afford to allow its taxpayers the same deductions for state purposes that are allowed for Federal purposes.
- Because of the tie-ins to the Federal return, a state may be notified of any changes made by the IRS upon audit of a Federal return. In recent years, the exchange of information between the IRS and state taxing authorities has increased. Lately, some states (e.g., California) are playing a major role in revealing tax shelter abuses to the IRS.
- Most states allow a deduction for personal and dependency exemptions. Some states substitute a tax credit for a deduction.
- A diminishing minority of states allow a deduction for Federal income taxes.
- Virtually all state income tax returns provide checkoff boxes for donations to various causes. Many are dedicated to medical research and wildlife programs, but special projects are not uncommon. For example, Oklahoma has one to retire the debt incurred for its new capitol dome, while Wisconsin tries to finance part of the renovation of Lambeau Field (home of the Green

---

FINANCIAL DISCLOSURE *Insights*

WHAT DO YOU MEAN BY "INCOME" ANYWAY?

Most business taxpayers keep at least "two sets of books," in that they report one amount of "income" for financial accounting purposes and another amount of "taxable income" as required by various taxing jurisdictions—the definition that will be used throughout this book. In fact, "income" might be defined in many different ways, as required by the recipients of the income reports of the enterprise. For instance, a business entity might prepare markedly different income reports for lenders, employee unions, managers in operating divisions, and international agencies.

Financial accounting income guidance is provided for U.S. businesses by the **Financial Accounting Standards Board (FASB)**, using the accumulated **Generally Accepted Accounting Principles (GAAP)** for the reporting period. When an entity conducts business outside the United States, the **International Financial Reporting Standards (IFRS)** of the **International Accounting Standards Board (IASB)** also may apply.

Throughout this book, we will point out some of the effects that Federal income tax provisions can have on the taxpayer's financial accounting results for the tax year. The vast majority of an entity's business transactions receive identical treatment under GAAP, IFRS, and the Federal tax law. But when the applicable provisions differ, "income" can be reported as different amounts—accounting professionals often refer to these as "book-tax differences." A tax professional must be able to identify and explain the various constructs of "income" so that the business entity's operating results will be accurately reflected in its stock price, loan covenants, and cash-flow demands.

Bay Packers). These checkoff boxes have been criticized as adding complexity to the returns (e.g., one state has 24 boxes) and misleading taxpayers.[17]

- Most states allow their residents some form of tax credit for income taxes paid to other states.

EXAMPLE 12
THE BIG PICTURE

Return to the facts of *The Big Picture* on p. 1-2. Because the income earned by Travis on his Chicago trip will be subject to tax by his home state, he probably will be able to claim an offsetting credit. Whether this negates the double taxation of the same income depends on the amount of credit allowed. ■

- The objective of most states is to tax the income of residents and those who regularly conduct business within the state (e.g., nonresidents who commute to work). These states also purport to tax the income of nonresidents who earn income within the state on an itinerant basis. Usually, however, the only visitors actually taxed are highly paid athletes and entertainers. This so-called *jock tax* has been much criticized as being discriminatory due to its selective imposition.
- The due date for filing generally is the same as for the Federal income tax (the fifteenth day of the fourth month following the close of the tax year).
- Some states have occasionally instituted amnesty programs that allow taxpayers to pay back taxes (and interest) on unreported income with no (or reduced) penalty. In many cases, the tax amnesty has generated enough revenue to warrant the authorization of follow-up programs covering future years—one state has had four amnesty periods, and seven states have had at least three.[18] Amnesties usually include other taxes as well (e.g., sales, franchise, severance). One major advantage of amnesty programs is

---

[17]Many taxpayers do not realize that they are paying for the checkoff donation (usually with some of their income tax refund). Unlike the presidential election campaign fund available for Federal income tax purposes ($3 in this case), the contribution is *not made* by the government.

[18]Although the suggestion has been made, no comparable amnesty program has been offered for the Federal income tax.

TAX in the NEWS

WAS LEBRON JAMES AWARE OF THE TAX SAVINGS INVOLVED WHEN HE CHOSE THE MIAMI HEAT?

As a free agent, basketball star LeBron James had narrowed his choices to the Cavaliers (Ohio), the Knicks (New York), the Nets (New Jersey), and the Heat (Florida). In terms of state (and local) income taxes, was he aware that the maximum rates involved were quite varied—7+ percent, 12.85 percent, 9 percent, and 0 percent, respectively? Projecting a salary of $100 million over five years, what is the saving between a tax of 12.85 percent (Knicks) and 0 percent (Heat)? Although some of the salary will be subject to the jock tax (when an away game is played in a state that imposes an income tax), what about the considerable income from endorsements? This will be assigned to LeBron's place of residence, Florida, which imposes no income tax.

Undoubtedly, LeBron chose to sign with the Heat for basketball reasons. For tax purposes, though, the choice has probably saved him millions of dollars currently and over the next few years.

Source: Adapted from "LeBron's Tax Holiday," *Wall Street Journal*, July 10–11, 2010, p. A12.

that they uncover taxpayers that were previously unknown to the taxing authority.

- Because many consumers do not pay state and local sales taxes on out-of-state purchases, state income tax returns often contain a separate line for the reporting of the use tax that is due. The instructions to the form may provide tables of suggested amounts based on income levels for those who lack records on the purchases not previously taxed. Thus, the income tax return serves as a means of collecting delinquent sales taxes.

Nearly all states have an income tax applicable to corporations. It is difficult to determine those that do not because a state franchise tax (discussed later in the chapter) sometimes is based in part on the income earned by the corporation.

Local Income Taxes

Cities imposing an income tax include, but are not limited to, Baltimore, Cincinnati, Cleveland, Detroit, Kansas City (Missouri), New York, Philadelphia, and St. Louis. The application of a city income tax is not limited to local residents.

EMPLOYMENT TAXES

Classification as an employee usually leads to the imposition of **employment taxes** and to the requirement that the employer withhold specified amounts for income taxes. The rules governing the withholding for income taxes are discussed in Chapter 13. The material that follows concentrates on the two major employment taxes: FICA (Federal Insurance Contributions Act—commonly referred to as the Social Security tax) and FUTA (Federal Unemployment Tax Act). Both taxes can be justified by social and public welfare considerations: FICA offers some measure of retirement security, and FUTA provides a modest source of income in the event of loss of employment.

Employment taxes come into play only if two conditions are satisfied. First, is the individual involved an *employee* (as opposed to *self-employed*)? The differences between an employee and a self-employed person are discussed in Chapter 9. Second, if the individual involved is an employee, is he or she covered under FICA or

FUTA or both? The coverage of both of these taxes is summarized in Exhibit 13.4 in Chapter 13.[19]

FICA Taxes

The **FICA tax** rates and wage base have increased steadily over the years. It is difficult to imagine that the initial rate in 1937 was only 1 percent of the first $3,000 of covered wages. Thus, the maximum tax due was only $30!

Currently, the FICA tax has two components: Social Security tax (old age, survivors, and disability insurance) *and* Medicare tax (hospital insurance). The Social Security tax rate is 6.2 percent for 2010 and 4.2 percent for 2011, and the Medicare tax rate is 1.45 percent for these years. The base amount for Social Security is $106,800 for 2010 and 2011. There is no limit on the base amount for the Medicare tax. The employer must match the employee's portion for both the Social Security tax and the Medicare tax. Note that for 2011, the Social Security tax matching for the employer is at the 6.2 percent rate.

A spouse employed by another spouse is subject to FICA. However, children under the age of 18 who are employed in a parent's unincorporated trade or business are exempted.

EXAMPLE 13
THE BIG PICTURE

Return to the facts of *The Big Picture* on p. 1-2. Presuming April and Martin perform meaningful services for Travis (which the facts seem to imply), they are legitimate employees. April is not subject to Social Security tax because she is under age 18. However, Martin is age 18 and needs to be covered. Furthermore, recall that Betty Carter is now working and will likewise be subject to Social Security tax. Travis, as an independent contractor, is subject to self-employment tax. ■

Taxpayers who are not employees (e.g., sole proprietors, independent contractors) may also be subject to Social Security taxes. Known as the self-employment tax, the rates are 12.4 percent (10.4 percent for 2011) for Social Security and 2.9 percent for Medicare, or twice that applicable to an employee. The tax is imposed on net self-employment income up to a base amount of $106,800 for 2010 and 2011.

FUTA Taxes

The purpose of the **FUTA tax** is to provide funds that the states can use to administer unemployment benefits. This leads to the somewhat unusual situation of one tax being handled by both Federal and state governments. The end result of such joint administration is to compel the employer to observe two sets of rules. Thus, state and Federal returns must be filed and payments made to both governmental units.

In 2011, FUTA is 6.2 percent (6.0 percent plus a 0.2 percent surtax) on the first $7,000 of covered wages paid during the year to each employee. The Federal government allows a credit for FUTA paid (or allowed under a merit rating system) to the state. The credit cannot exceed 5.4 percent of the covered wages. Thus, the amount required to be paid to the IRS could be as low as 0.8 percent (6.2% − 5.4%).

States follow a policy of reducing the unemployment tax on employers who experience stable employment. Thus, an employer with little or no employee turnover might find that the state rate drops to as low as 0.1 percent or, in some states, even to zero. The reason for the merit rating credit is that the state has to pay fewer unemployment benefits when employment is steady.

---

[19]Chapter 13 includes coverage of the self-employment tax (the Social Security and Medicare taxes for self-employed persons). See also Circular E, *Employer's Tax Guide*, issued by the IRS as Publication 15.

FUTA differs from FICA in the sense that the incidence of taxation falls entirely upon the employer. A few states, however, levy a special tax on employees to provide either disability benefits or supplemental unemployment compensation, or both.

OTHER U.S. TAXES

To complete the overview of the U.S. tax system, some missing links need to be covered that do not fit into the classifications discussed elsewhere in this chapter.

Federal Customs Duties

One tax that has not yet been mentioned is the tariff on certain imported goods.[20] Generally referred to as customs duties or levies, this tax, together with selective excise taxes, provided most of the revenues needed by the Federal government during the nineteenth century. In view of present times, it is remarkable to note that tariffs and excise taxes alone paid off the national debt in 1835 and enabled the U.S. Treasury to pay a surplus of $28 million to the states.

In recent years, tariffs have served the nation more as an instrument for carrying out protectionist policies than as a means of generating revenue. Thus, a particular U.S. industry might be saved from economic disaster, so the argument goes, by imposing customs duties on the importation of foreign goods that can be sold at lower prices. Protectionists contend that the tariff thereby neutralizes the competitive edge held by the producer of the foreign goods.[21]

Protectionist policies seem more appropriate for less-developed countries whose industrial capacity has not yet matured. In a world where a developed country should have everything to gain by encouraging international free trade, such policies may be of dubious value. History shows that tariffs often lead to retaliatory action on the part of the nation or nations affected.

Miscellaneous State and Local Taxes

Most states impose a franchise tax on corporations. Basically, a **franchise tax** is levied on the right to do business in the state. The base used for the determination of the tax varies from state to state. Although corporate income considerations may come into play, this tax most often is based on the capitalization of the corporation (either with or without certain long-term indebtedness).

Closely akin to the franchise tax are **occupational fees** applicable to various trades or businesses, such as a liquor store license, a taxicab permit, or a fee to practice a profession such as law, medicine, or accounting. Most of these are not significant revenue producers and fall more into the category of licenses than taxes. The revenue derived is used to defray the cost incurred by the jurisdiction in regulating the business or profession in the interest of the public good.

EXAMPLE 14
THE BIG PICTURE

Return to the facts of *The Big Picture* on p. 1-2. Although the facts do not mention the matter, both Travis and Betty will almost certainly pay occupational fees—Travis for engineering and Betty for nursing. ∎

PROPOSED U.S. TAXES

Considerable dissatisfaction with the U.S. Federal income tax has led to several recent proposals that, to say the least, are rather drastic in nature. One proposal

---

[20]Less-developed countries that rely principally on one or more major commodities (e.g., oil, coffee) are prone to favor *export* duties as well.

[21]The North American Free Trade Agreement (NAFTA), enacted in 1993, substantially reduced the tariffs on trade between Canada, Mexico, and the United States. The General Agreement on Tariffs and Trade (GATT) legislation enacted in 1994 also reduced tariffs on selected commodities among 124 signatory nations.

would retain the income tax but with substantial change. Two other proposals would replace the Federal income tax with an entirely different system of taxation.

The Flat Tax

One proposal is for a **flat tax** that would replace the current graduated income tax with a single rate of 17 percent. Large personal exemptions (e.g., approximately $30,000 for a family of four) would allow many low- and middle-income taxpayers to pay no tax. All other deductions would be eliminated, and no tax would be imposed on income from investments.

Various other versions of the flat tax have been suggested that would retain selected deductions (e.g., interest on home mortgages and charitable contributions) and not exclude all investment income from taxation.

The major advantage of the flat tax is its simplicity. Everyone agrees that the current Federal income tax is inappropriately complex. Consequently, compliance costs are disproportionately high. Proponents of the flat tax further believe that simplifying the income tax will significantly reduce the current "tax gap" (i.e., the difference between the amount of taxes that *should be paid* and what is *actually paid*).

Political considerations are a major obstacle to the enactment of a flat tax in its pure form. Special interest groups, such as charitable organizations and mortgage companies, are not apt to be complacent over the elimination of a tax deduction that benefits their industry. In addition, there is uncertainty as to the economic effects of the tax.

It is interesting to note that Russia's attempt at a progressive income tax was quite disastrous. Not only did high rates drive capital out of the country but also failure to report income was rampant. In early 2000, the income tax was repealed and replaced with a 13 percent flat tax. To date, the flat tax has worked quite well. Several Baltic states (Estonia, Latvia, and Lithuania) have followed Russia's example. Albania, Romania, Slovakia, Georgia, Ukraine, and Serbia have also adopted a flat tax.

Value Added Tax

The **value added tax (VAT)** is one of two proposals that would replace the Federal income tax. Under the VAT, a business would pay the tax (approximately 17 percent) on all of the materials and services required to manufacture its product. In effect, the VAT taxes the increment in value as goods move through production and manufacturing stages to the marketplace. Moreover, the VAT paid by the producer will be reflected in the selling price of the goods. Thus, the VAT is a tax on consumption.

The United States is the only country in the OECD (Organization for Economic Cooperation and Development) that does not have a VAT. Approximately 136 countries around the world use a VAT, ranging from 5 percent in Japan to 25 percent in Denmark. Instead, the United States relies heavily on income taxes.

The VAT is an effective generator of revenue. Many view this trait as a major disadvantage. With additional revenue available, the government may be tempted to expand the entitlements available to the general public in the future.

Sales Tax

A **national sales tax** differs from a VAT in that it would be collected on the final sale of goods and services. Consequently, it is collected from the consumer and not from businesses that add value to the product. Like the VAT, the national sales tax is intended to replace the Federal income tax.

A current proposal for a national sales tax, called the "Fair Tax," would tax all purchases, including food and medicine, at approximately 23 percent. Exempt items include business expenses, used goods, and the costs of education. The "Fair Tax" would replace not only the income tax (both individual and corporate) but also payroll taxes (including the self-employment tax) and the gift and estate taxes.

Current sponsors of this proposal, which is reintroduced in each new Congress, include Saxby Chambliss (R–Ga.) in the Senate and John Linder (R–Ga.) in the House.

Critics contend that both forms of consumption taxes, a VAT and a national sales tax, are regressive. They impose more of a burden on low-income taxpayers who must spend larger proportions of their incomes on essential purchases. The proposals attempt to remedy this inequity by granting some sort of credit, rebate, or exemption to low-income taxpayers.

In terms of taxpayer compliance, a VAT is preferable to a national sales tax. Without significant collection efforts, a national sales tax could easily be circumvented by resorting to a barter system of doing business. Its high rate would also encourage smuggling and black market activities.

1.6 Tax Administration

INTERNAL REVENUE SERVICE

> **LO.5**
>
> Explain the administration of the tax law, including the audit process utilized by the IRS.

The responsibility for administering the Federal tax laws rests with the Treasury Department. Administratively, the IRS is part of the Department of the Treasury and is responsible for enforcing the tax laws. The Commissioner of Internal Revenue is appointed by the President and is responsible for establishing policy and supervising the activities of the IRS.

THE AUDIT PROCESS

Selection of Returns for Audit

Due to budgetary limitations, only a small minority of tax returns are audited. For the fiscal year ended September 30, 2009, the IRS audited only 1 percent of all individual income tax returns filed.

The IRS utilizes mathematical formulas and statistical sampling techniques to select tax returns that are most likely to contain errors and to yield substantial amounts of additional tax revenues upon audit. The mathematical formula yields what is called a Discriminant Information Function (DIF) score. It is the DIF score given to a particular return that may lead to its selection for audit.

To update the DIF components, the IRS selects a cross section of returns, which are subject to various degrees of inspection (i.e., information return verification, correspondence, and face-to-face audits with filers). The results of these audits highlight areas of taxpayer noncompliance and enable the IRS to use its auditors more productively. In recent years, IRS audits have resulted in an increasing number of "no change" results. This indicates that the IRS is not always choosing the right returns to audit (i.e., the ones with errors).

Though the IRS does not openly disclose all of its audit selection techniques, the following observations may be made concerning the probability of selection for audit:

- Certain groups of taxpayers are subject to audit much more frequently than others. These groups include individuals with large amounts of gross income, self-employed individuals with substantial business income and deductions, and taxpayers with prior tax deficiencies. Also vulnerable are businesses that receive a large proportion of their receipts in cash (e.g., cafés and small service businesses) and thus have a high potential for tax avoidance.

EXAMPLE 15

Jack owns and operates a liquor store on a cash-and-carry basis. Since all of Jack's sales are for cash, he might well be a prime candidate for an audit by the IRS. Cash transactions are easier to conceal than those made on credit. ∎

- If information returns (e.g., Form 1099, Form W–2) are not in substantial agreement with reported income, an audit can be anticipated.
- If an individual's itemized deductions are in excess of norms established for various income levels, the probability of an audit is increased.
- Filing of a refund claim by the taxpayer may prompt an audit of the return.
- Information obtained from other sources (e.g., informants, news items) may lead to an audit. Recently, for example, the IRS advised its agents to be on the alert for newspaper accounts of large civil court judgments. The advice was based on the assumption that many successful plaintiffs were not reporting as income the taxable punitive damages portion of awards.

The tax law permits the IRS to pay rewards to persons who provide information that leads to the detection and punishment of those who violate the tax laws. The rewards may not exceed 30 percent of the taxes, fines, and penalties recovered as a result of such information.

EXAMPLE 16

After 15 years of service, Rita is discharged by her employer, Dr. Smith. Shortly thereafter, the IRS receives an anonymous letter stating that Dr. Smith keeps two separate sets of books and that the one used for tax reporting substantially understates his cash receipts. ■

EXAMPLE 17

During a divorce proceeding, it is revealed that Leo, a public official, kept large amounts of cash in a shoe box at home. This information is widely disseminated by the news media and comes to the attention of the IRS. Needless to say, the IRS is interested in knowing whether these funds originated from a taxable source and, if so, whether they were reported on Leo's income tax returns. ■

Types of Audits

Once a return is selected for audit, the taxpayer is notified. If the issue involved is minor, the matter often can be resolved simply by correspondence (a **correspondence audit**) between the IRS and the taxpayer.

EXAMPLE 18

During 2009, Janet received dividend income from Green Corporation. In early 2010, Green Corporation reported the payment on Form 1099–DIV (an information return for reporting dividend payments), the original being sent to the IRS and a copy to Janet. When preparing her income tax return for 2009, Janet apparently overlooked this particular Form 1099–DIV and failed to include the dividend on Schedule B, Interest and Dividend Income, of Form 1040. In 2011, the IRS sends a notice to Janet calling her attention to the omission and requesting a remittance for additional tax, interest, and penalty. Janet promptly mails a check to the IRS for the requested amount, and the matter is closed. ■

Other examinations are generally classified as either office audits or field audits. An **office audit** usually is restricted in scope and is conducted in the facilities of the IRS. In contrast, a **field audit** involves an examination of numerous items reported on the return and is conducted on the premises of the taxpayer or the taxpayer's representative.

EXAMPLE 19
THE BIG PICTURE

Return to the facts of *The Big Picture* on p. 1-2. The audit of the Walkers by the IRS obviously was a correspondence type. The reason for the audit was probably a minor oversight, such as the omission of some interest or dividend income (see Example 18). The audit of the Carters, however, was more serious—probably a field or office type. Since the Federal audit followed a state audit that was productive (i.e., led to the assessment of a deficiency), there may have been an exchange of information between the two taxing authorities—see p. 16 in this chapter. ■

TAX in the NEWS　　　　**PAY OR SHAME!**

An increasing number of states and local jurisdictions are learning that the threat of public humiliation can be rewarding. When someone owes taxes but does not pay, the prospect of having one's name listed on a public website may make a difference. Often payment is made in order to avoid the cybershame that comes from being exposed as a tax deadbeat. Some taxing jurisdictions have found the shaming procedure so productive that they maintain sepa-

rate lists for different types of taxes (e.g., sales taxes, income taxes) or different types of delinquents (e.g., personal, business). As of yet, the IRS has not considered this approach for Federal tax scofflaws. Perhaps the length of the list would be too overwhelming!

Source: Adapted from Amy Merrick, "Cash-Starved States Put Tax Scofflaws in Crosshairs," *Wall Street Journal*, March 12, 2010, p. A3.

Upon the conclusion of the audit, the examining agent issues a Revenue Agent's Report (RAR) that summarizes the findings. The RAR will result in a refund (the tax was overpaid), a deficiency (the tax was underpaid), or a *no change* (the tax was correct) finding. If, during the course of an audit, a special agent accompanies (or takes over from) the regular auditor, this means the IRS suspects fraud. If the matter has progressed to an investigation for fraud, the taxpayer should retain competent counsel.

Settlement Procedures

If an audit results in an assessment of additional tax and no settlement is reached with the IRS agent, the taxpayer may attempt to negotiate a settlement with a higher level of the IRS. If an appeal is desired, an appropriate request must be made to the Appeals Division of the IRS. The Appeals Division is authorized to settle all disputes based on the *hazard of litigation* (the probability of favorable resolution of the disputed issue or issues if litigated). In some cases, a taxpayer may be able to obtain a percentage settlement or a favorable settlement of one or more disputed issues.

If a satisfactory settlement is not reached within the administrative appeal process, the taxpayer can litigate the case in the Tax Court, a Federal District Court, or the Court of Federal Claims. However, litigation is recommended only as a last resort because of the legal costs involved and the uncertainty of the final outcome. Tax litigation considerations are discussed more fully in Chapter 2.

STATUTE OF LIMITATIONS

A **statute of limitations** is a provision in the law that offers a party a defense against a suit brought by another party after the expiration of a specified period of time. The purpose of a statute of limitations is to preclude parties from prosecuting stale claims. The passage of time makes the defense of such claims difficult since witnesses may no longer be available or evidence may have been lost or destroyed. Found at the state and Federal levels, such statutes cover a multitude of suits, both civil and criminal.

For our purposes, the relevant statutes deal with the Federal income tax. The two categories involved cover both the period of limitations applicable to the assessment of additional tax deficiencies by the IRS and the period applicable to claims for refunds by taxpayers.

Assessment by the IRS

Under the general rule, the IRS may assess an additional tax liability against a taxpayer within *three years* of the filing of the income tax return. If the return is filed early, the three-year period begins to run from the due date of the return (usually April 15 for a calendar year individual taxpayer). If the taxpayer files the return late (i.e., beyond the due date), the three-year period begins to run on the date filed.

If a taxpayer omits an amount of gross income in excess of 25 percent of the gross income reported on the return, the statute of limitations is increased to six years.

| EXAMPLE 20 | For 2011, Mark, a calendar year taxpayer, reported gross income of $400,000 on a timely filed income tax return. If Mark omitted more than $100,000 (25% × $400,000), the six-year statute of limitations would apply to the 2011 tax year. ■ |

The six-year provision on assessments by the IRS applies only to the omission of income and does not cover other factors that might lead to an understatement of tax liability, such as overstatement of deductions and credits.

There is *no* statute of limitations on assessments of tax if *no return* is filed or if a *fraudulent* return is filed.

Limitations on Refunds

If a taxpayer believes that an overpayment of Federal income tax was made, a claim for refund should be filed with the IRS. A *claim for refund,* therefore, is a request to the IRS that it return to the taxpayer excessive income taxes paid.[22]

A claim for refund generally must be filed within *three years* from the date the return was filed *or* within *two years* from the date the tax was paid, whichever is later. Income tax returns that are filed early are deemed to have been filed on the date the return was due.

INTEREST AND PENALTIES

Interest rates are determined quarterly by the IRS based on the existing Federal short-term rate. Currently, the rates for tax refunds (overpayments) for individual taxpayers are the same as those applicable to assessments (underpayments). For the first quarter (January 1–March 31) of 2011, the rates are 3 percent for refunds and assessments.[23]

For assessments of additional taxes, the interest begins running on the unextended due date of the return. With refunds, however, no interest is allowed if the overpayment is refunded to the taxpayer within 45 days of the date the return is filed. For this purpose, returns filed early are deemed to have been filed on the due date.

In addition to interest, the tax law provides various penalties for lack of compliance by taxpayers. Some of these penalties are summarized as follows:

- For a *failure to file* a tax return by the due date (including extension—see Chapter 3), a penalty of 5 percent per month up to a maximum of 25 percent is imposed on the amount of tax shown as due on the return. Any fraction of a month counts as a full month.
- A penalty for a *failure to pay* the tax due as shown on the return is imposed in the amount of 0.5 percent per month up to a maximum of 25 percent. Again, any fraction of a month counts as full month. During any month in which both the failure to file penalty and the failure to pay penalty apply, the failure to file penalty is reduced by the amount of the failure to pay penalty.

---

[22]Generally, an individual filing a claim for refund should use Form 1040X.

[23]The rates applicable after March 31, 2011, were not available when this text went to press.

EXAMPLE 21

Adam files his tax return 18 days after the due date of the return. Along with the return, he remits a check for $1,000, which is the balance of the tax he owed. Disregarding the interest element, Adam's total penalties are as follows:

Failure to pay penalty (0.5% × $1,000)		$ 5
Plus:		
Failure to file penalty (5% × $1,000)	$50	
Less failure to pay penalty for the same period	(5)	
Failure to file penalty		45
Total penalties		$50

Note that the penalties for one full month are imposed even though Adam was delinquent by only 18 days. Unlike the method used to compute interest, any part of a month is treated as a whole month. ■

- A *negligence* penalty of 20 percent is imposed if any of the underpayment was for intentional disregard of rules and regulations without intent to defraud. The penalty applies to just that portion attributable to the negligence.

EXAMPLE 22

Cindy underpaid her taxes for 2010 in the amount of $20,000, of which $15,000 is attributable to negligence. Cindy's negligence penalty is $3,000 (20% × $15,000). ■

- Various penalties may be imposed in the case of *fraud*. Fraud involves specific intent on the part of the taxpayer to evade a tax. In the case of *civil* fraud, the penalty is 75 percent of the underpayment attributable to fraud. In the case of *criminal* fraud, the penalties can include large fines as well as prison sentences. The difference between civil and criminal fraud is one of degree. Criminal fraud involves the presence of willfulness on the part of the taxpayer. Also, the burden of proof, which is on the IRS in both situations, is more stringent for criminal fraud than for civil fraud. The negligence penalty is not imposed when the fraud penalty applies. For possible fraud situations, refer to Examples 16 and 17.

TAX PRACTICE

If a practitioner is a member of a profession, such as law or public accounting, he or she must abide by certain ethical standards. Furthermore, the Internal Revenue Code imposes penalties upon the preparers of Federal tax returns who violate proscribed acts and procedures.

Ethical Guidelines

The American Institute of CPAs has issued numerous pronouncements dealing with CPAs engaged in tax practice. Originally called "Statements on Responsibilities in Tax Practice," these pronouncements were intended to be only *guides* to action. In 2000, however, the AICPA redesignated the pronouncements as "Statements on Standards for Tax Services" and made them *enforceable* as part of its Code of Professional Conduct. They include the provisions summarized below.

> **LO.6**
>
> Evaluate some of the ethical guidelines involved in tax practice.

- Do not take questionable positions on a client's tax return in the hope that the return will not be selected for audit by the IRS. Any positions taken should be supported by a good-faith belief that they have a realistic possibility of being sustained if challenged. The client should be fully advised of the risks involved and of the penalties that will result if the position taken is not successful.
- A practitioner can use a client's estimates if they are reasonable under the circumstances. If the tax law requires receipts or other verification, the client should be so advised. In no event should an estimate be given the

appearance of greater accuracy than is the case. For example, an estimate of $1,000 should not be deducted on a return as $999.

- Every effort should be made to answer questions appearing on tax returns. A question need not be answered if the information requested is not readily available, the answer is voluminous, or the question's meaning is uncertain. The failure to answer a question on a return cannot be justified on the grounds that the answer could prove disadvantageous to the taxpayer.
- Upon learning of an error on a past tax return, advise the client to correct it. Do not, however, inform the IRS of the error. If the error is material and the client refuses to correct it, consider withdrawing from the engagement. This will be necessary if the error has a carryover effect and prevents the current year's tax liability from being determined correctly.

ETHICS & Equity   LET BYGONES BE BYGONES

Arturo is a new client who wants you to prepare his Federal income tax return for 2011. In the past, he has prepared his own returns but has become overwhelmed by the time and effort involved. In your first meeting with Arturo, you learn that he inherited some foreign rental property several years ago. As of yet, however, he has not reported any transactions regarding the property on his tax returns. He is not averse to including the rent income on his 2011 return but wishes to avoid the hassle of filing amended returns. He prefers to "let bygones be bygones."

Under these circumstances, do you accept the engagement? Why or why not?

Statutory Penalties Imposed on Tax Return Preparers

In addition to ethical constraints, a tax return preparer may be subject to certain statutorily sanctioned penalties, including the following:

- Various penalties involving procedural matters. Examples include failing to furnish the taxpayer with a copy of the return; endorsing a taxpayer's refund check; failing to sign the return as a preparer; failing to furnish one's identification number; and failing to keep copies of returns or maintain a client list.
- Penalty for understatement of a tax liability based on a position that lacks any realistic possibility of being sustained. If the position is not frivolous, the penalty can be avoided by disclosing it on the return.
- Penalty for any willful attempt to understate taxes. This usually results when a preparer disregards or makes no effort to obtain pertinent information from a client.
- Penalty for failure to exercise due diligence in determining eligibility for, or the amount of, an earned income tax credit.

1.7 UNDERSTANDING THE FEDERAL TAX LAW

L0.7

Recognize the economic, social, equity, and political considerations that justify various aspects of the tax law.

The Federal tax law is a mosaic of statutory provisions, administrative pronouncements, and court decisions. Anyone who has attempted to work with this body of knowledge would have to admit to its complexity. For the person who has to trudge through a mass of rules to find the solution to a tax problem, it may be of some consolation to know that the law's complexity can generally be explained. Whether sound or not, there is a reason for the formulation of every rule. Knowing these reasons, therefore, is a considerable step toward understanding the Federal tax law.

The Federal tax law has as its *major objective* the raising of revenue. But although the fiscal needs of the government are important, other considerations explain certain portions of the law. Economic, social, equity, and political factors also play a

GLOBAL *Tax Issues*

OUTSOURCING OF TAX RETURN PREPARATION

The use of foreign nationals to carry out certain job assignments for U.S. businesses is an increasingly popular practice. Outsourcing such activities as telemarketing to India, for example, usually produces the same satisfactory result as having the work done in the United States but at a much lower cost.

Outsourcing is also being applied to the preparation of tax returns. Not only can this practice be expected to continue, but it probably will increase in volume. Outsourcing tax return preparation does not violate Federal law and is compatible with accounting ethical guidelines as long as three safeguards are followed: First, the practitioner must make sure that client confidentiality is maintained. Second, the practitioner must verify the accuracy of the work that has been outsourced. Third, the practitioner must inform clients, preferably in writing, when any third-party contractor is used to provide professional services.

Practitioners justify outsourcing as a means of conserving time and effort that can be applied toward more meaningful tax planning on behalf of their clients.

Source: AICPA Ethics Ruling No. 1 (under Rule 301), see **www.aicpa.org/Research/standards/CodeofConduct/Pages/et_391.aspx**.

---

significant role. Added to these factors is the marked impact the IRS and the courts have had and will continue to have on the evolution of Federal tax law. These matters are treated in the remainder of the chapter, and, wherever appropriate, the discussion is referenced to subjects covered later in the text.

REVENUE NEEDS

The foundation of any tax system has to be the raising of revenue to cover the cost of government operations. Ideally, annual outlays should not exceed anticipated revenues, thereby leading to a balanced budget with no resulting deficit.

When enacting tax legislation, a deficit-conscious Congress often has been guided by the concept of **revenue neutrality**. Also referred to as "pay-as-you-go" ("paygo"), the concept means that every new tax law that lowers taxes must include a revenue offset that makes up for the loss. Revenue neutrality does not mean that any one taxpayer's tax liability will remain the same. Since the circumstances involved will differ, one taxpayer's increased tax liability could be another's tax savings. Although revenue-neutral tax reform does not reduce deficits, at least it does not aggravate the problem.

In addition to making changes in the tax law revenue neutral, several other procedures can be taken to mitigate any revenue loss. When tax reductions are involved, the full impact of the legislation can be phased in over a period of years.[24] Or, as an alternative, the tax reduction can be limited to a period of years. When the period expires, the prior law is reinstated through a **sunset provision**. Most of the major tax bills recently passed by Congress have contained numerous sunset provisions. They provide some semblance of revenue neutrality as some of the bills include tax cuts that were not offset by new sources of revenue. It remains to be seen, however, whether Congress will allow the sunset provisions to take effect and, thereby, kill the tax cuts that were enacted.

Does the recent passage of the American Recovery and Reinvestment Tax Act of 2009 (ARRTA), which contains almost $300 billion in tax relief and negligible revenue offsets, foretell the abandonment of the pay-go approach? Probably not. ARRTA represents a drastic attempt to use the tax system as a means of coping with the current economic downturn. As an emergency measure, it should be regarded as an exception to the norm.

---

[24]The same approach can be taken with tax increases. The phaseout and phase-in of limitations on the deductibility of personal exemptions and itemized deductions for certain high-bracket taxpayers (see Chapters 3 and 10) are examples of both of these approaches.

ECONOMIC CONSIDERATIONS

Using the tax system in an effort to accomplish economic objectives has become increasingly popular in recent years. Generally, proponents of this goal use tax legislation to amend the Internal Revenue Code in ways designed to help control the economy or encourage certain activities and businesses.

Control of the Economy

Congress has used depreciation write-offs as a means of controlling the economy. Theoretically, shorter asset lives and accelerated methods should encourage additional investment in depreciable property acquired for business use. Conversely, longer asset lives and the required use of the straight-line method of depreciation dampen the tax incentive for capital outlays.

Another approach that utilizes depreciation as a means of controlling capital investment is the amount of write-off allowed upon the acquisition of assets. This is the approach followed by the § 179 election to expense assets.

A change in the tax rate structure has a more immediate impact on the economy. With lower tax rates, taxpayers are able to retain additional spendable funds. If lower tax rates are accompanied by the elimination of certain deductions, exclusions, and credits, however, the overall result may not be lower tax liabilities.

Encouragement of Certain Activities

Without passing judgment on the wisdom of any such choices, it is quite clear that the tax law encourages certain types of economic activity or segments of the economy. For example, the favorable treatment allowed research and development expenditures can be explained by the desire to foster technological progress. Under the tax law, such expenditures can be either deducted in the year incurred or capitalized and amortized over a period of 60 months or more. In terms of the timing of the tax savings, these options usually are preferable to capitalizing the cost with a write-off over the estimated useful life of the asset created. If the asset developed has an indefinite useful life, no write-off would be available without the two options allowed by the tax law.

Part of the tax law addresses the energy crisis—in terms of both our reliance on foreign oil and the need to ease the problem of global warming. For example, a tax credit is allowed for electricity produced from renewable sources, such as biomass, solar, and wind. In addition, tax credits are available to those who purchase motor vehicles that operate on alternative (i.e., nonfossil) fuels. Residential energy credits are allowed for home improvements that conserve energy or make its use more efficient (e.g., solar hot water, geothermal heat pumps). Ecological considerations justify a tax provision that permits a more rapid expensing of the costs of installing pollution control facilities. Measures such as these that aid in maintaining a clean air environment and conserving energy resources can also be justified under social considerations.

Is it wise to stimulate U.S. exports of services? Along this line, Congress has deemed it advisable to establish incentives for U.S. citizens who accept employment overseas. Such persons receive generous tax breaks through special treatment of their foreign-source income.

Is saving desirable for the economy? Saving leads to capital formation and thereby makes funds available to finance home construction and industrial expansion. The tax law encourages saving by according preferential treatment to private retirement plans. Not only are contributions to Keogh (H.R. 10) plans and certain IRAs deductible, but income from the contributions accumulates free of tax. As noted below, the encouragement of private-sector pension plans can also be justified under social considerations.

Encouragement of Certain Industries

No one can question the proposition that a sound agricultural base is necessary for a well-balanced national economy. Undoubtedly, this can explain why farmers are accorded special treatment under the Federal tax system. Among the benefits are the election to expense rather than capitalize certain soil and water conservation expenditures and fertilizers and the election to defer the recognition of gain on the receipt of crop insurance proceeds.

To stimulate the manufacturing industry, Congress enacted a domestic production activities deduction. The provision provides a tax benefit in the form of a deduction for profits derived from manufacturing activities conducted within the United States. By restricting the deduction to manufacturing income attributable to wages reportable to the IRS, new U.S. jobs will result, and the outsourcing of labor is discouraged. Thus, the tax system is used to encourage both domestic manufacturing and job growth.

Encouragement of Small Business

At least in the United States, a consensus exists that what is good for small business is good for the economy as a whole. Whether valid or not, this assumption has led to a definite bias in the tax law favoring small business.

In the corporate tax area, several provisions can be explained by the desire to benefit small business. One provision permits the shareholders of a small business corporation to make a special election that generally will avoid the imposition of the corporate income tax.[25] Furthermore, such an election enables the corporation to pass through its operating losses to its shareholders.

SOCIAL CONSIDERATIONS

Some provisions of the Federal tax law, particularly those dealing with the income tax of individuals, can be explained by social considerations. Some notable examples and their rationales include the following:

- Certain benefits provided to employees through accident and health plans financed by employers are nontaxable to employees. Encouraging such plans is considered socially desirable since they provide medical benefits in the event of an employee's illness or injury.

- Most premiums paid by an employer for group term insurance covering the life of the employee are nontaxable to the employee. These arrangements can be justified on social grounds in that they provide funds for the family unit to help it adjust to the loss of wages caused by the employee's death.

- A contribution made by an employer to a qualified pension or profit sharing plan for an employee may receive special treatment. The contribution and any income it generates are not taxed to the employee until the funds are distributed. Such an arrangement also benefits the employer by allowing a tax deduction when the contribution is made to the qualified plan. Private retirement plans are encouraged to supplement the subsistence income level the employee otherwise would have under the Social Security system.[26]

- A deduction is allowed for contributions to qualified charitable organizations. The deduction attempts to shift some of the financial and administrative burden of socially desirable programs from the public (the government) to the private (the citizens) sector.

- A tax credit is allowed for amounts spent to furnish care for certain minor or disabled dependents to enable the taxpayer to seek or maintain gainful employment. Who could deny the social desirability of encouraging taxpayers to provide care for their children while they work?

- Various tax credits, deductions, and exclusions are designed to encourage taxpayers to obtain additional education.[27]

- A tax deduction is not allowed for certain expenditures deemed to be contrary to public policy. This disallowance extends to such items as fines, penalties, illegal kickbacks, bribes to government officials, and gambling losses

---

[25]Known as the S election, it is discussed in Chapter 20.

[26]The same rationale explains the availability of similar arrangements for self-employed persons (the H.R. 10, or Keogh, plan). See Chapter 19.

[27]These provisions can also be justified under the category of economic considerations. No one can take issue with the conclusion that a better educated workforce carries a positive economic impact.

in excess of gains. Social considerations dictate that the tax law should not encourage these activities by permitting a deduction.

Many other examples could be cited, but the conclusion would be unchanged. Social considerations do explain a significant part of the Federal tax law.

EQUITY CONSIDERATIONS

The concept of equity is relative. Reasonable persons can, and often do, disagree about what is fair or unfair. In the tax area, moreover, equity is most often tied to a particular taxpayer's personal situation. To illustrate, compare the tax positions of those who rent their personal residences with those who own their homes. Renters receive no Federal income tax benefit from the rent they pay. For homeowners, however, a large portion of the house payments they make may qualify for the Federal interest and property tax deductions. Although renters may have difficulty understanding this difference in tax treatment, the encouragement of home ownership can be justified on both economic and social grounds.

In the same vein, compare the tax treatment of a corporation with that of a partnership. Although the two businesses may be of equal size, similarly situated, and competitors in the production of goods or services, they are not treated comparably under the tax law. The corporation is subject to a separate Federal income tax; the partnership is not. Whether the differences in tax treatment can be justified logically in terms of equity is beside the point. The point is that the tax law can and does make a distinction between these business forms.

Equity, then, is not what appears fair or unfair to any one taxpayer or group of taxpayers. Some recognition of equity does exist, however, and explains part of the law. The concept of equity appears in tax provisions that alleviate the effect of multiple taxation and postpone the recognition of gain when the taxpayer lacks the ability or wherewithal to pay the tax. Provisions that mitigate the effect of the application of the annual accounting period concept and help taxpayers cope with the eroding results of inflation also reflect equity considerations.

Alleviating the Effect of Multiple Taxation

The income earned by a taxpayer may be subject to taxes imposed by different taxing authorities. If, for example, the taxpayer is a resident of New York City, income might generate Federal, state of New York, and city of New York income taxes. To compensate for this apparent inequity, the Federal tax law allows a taxpayer to claim a deduction for state and local income taxes. The deduction does not, however, neutralize the effect of multiple taxation, since the benefit derived depends on the taxpayer's Federal income tax rate. Only a tax credit, rather than a deduction, would eliminate the effects of multiple taxation on the same income.

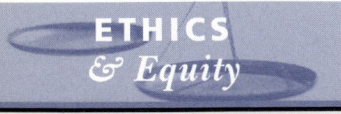

ETHICS & Equity   TREATING EVERYONE THE SAME

As noted in the text, a Federal income tax deduction for state and local income taxes paid is allowed to mitigate the effect of having the same income taxed more than once. But what if a state does not impose an income tax and, instead, derives comparable amounts of revenue from a general sales tax? Is it fair to deny a deduction to residents of this state just because the state imposes a tax on sales rather than on income?

Recent legislation resolved this purported inequity by allowing a Federal income tax deduction for state and local general sales taxes. However, a taxpayer who is subject to both state income and sales taxes must make a choice. One or the other, but not both, can be claimed as a deduction. Should the taxpayer have to choose?

Equity considerations can explain the Federal tax treatment of certain income from foreign sources. Since double taxation results when the same income is subject to both foreign and U.S. income taxes, the tax law permits the taxpayer to choose between a credit and a deduction for the foreign taxes paid.

The Wherewithal to Pay Concept

The **wherewithal to pay** concept recognizes the inequity of taxing a transaction when the taxpayer lacks the means with which to pay the tax. It is particularly suited to situations in which the taxpayer's economic position has not changed significantly as a result of the transaction.

An illustration of the wherewithal to pay concept is the provision of the tax law dealing with the treatment of gain resulting from an involuntary conversion. An involuntary conversion occurs when property is destroyed by a casualty or taken by a public authority through condemnation. If gain results from the conversion, it need not be recognized if the taxpayer replaces the property within a specified period of time. The replacement property must be similar or related in service or use to that involuntarily converted.

EXAMPLE 23

Some of the pasture land belonging to Ron, a rancher, is condemned by the state for use as a game preserve. The condemned pasture land cost Ron $120,000, but the state pays him $150,000 (its fair market value). Shortly thereafter, Ron buys more pasture land for $150,000. ∎

In Example 23, Ron has a realized gain of $30,000 [$150,000 (condemnation award) − $120,000 (cost of land)]. It would be inequitable to force Ron to pay a tax on this gain for two reasons. First, without disposing of the property acquired (the new land), Ron would be hard-pressed to pay the tax. Second, his economic position has not changed.

A warning is in order regarding the application of the wherewithal to pay concept. If the taxpayer's economic position changes in any way, tax consequences may result.

EXAMPLE 24

Assume the same facts as in Example 23, except that Ron reinvests only $140,000 of the award in new pasture land. Now, Ron has a taxable gain of $10,000. Instead of ending up with only replacement property, Ron now has $10,000 in cash. ∎

Mitigating the Effect of the Annual Accounting Period Concept

For purposes of effective administration of the tax law, all taxpayers must report to and settle with the Federal government at periodic intervals. Otherwise, taxpayers would remain uncertain as to their tax liabilities, and the government would have difficulty judging revenues and budgeting expenditures. The period selected for final settlement of most tax liabilities, in any event an arbitrary determination, is one year. At the close of each year, therefore, a taxpayer's position becomes complete for that particular year. Referred to as the annual accounting period concept, its effect is to divide each taxpayer's life, for tax purposes, into equal annual intervals.

The finality of the annual accounting period concept could lead to dissimilar tax treatment for taxpayers who are, from a long-range standpoint, in the same economic position.

EXAMPLE 25

José and Alicia, both sole proprietors, have experienced the following results during the past three years:

	Profit (or Loss)	
Year	José	Alicia
2009	$50,000	$150,000
2010	60,000	60,000
2011	60,000	(40,000)

Although José and Alicia have the same profit of $170,000 over the period from 2009 to 2011, the finality of the annual accounting period concept places Alicia at a definite disadvantage for tax purposes. The net operating loss procedure offers Alicia some relief by allowing her to apply some or all of her 2011 loss to the earlier profitable years (in this case, 2009). Thus, with a net operating loss carryback, Alicia is in a position to obtain a refund for some of the taxes she paid on the $150,000 profit reported for 2009. ∎

The same reasoning used to support the deduction of net operating losses can explain the special treatment the tax law accords to excess capital losses and excess charitable contributions.[28] Carryback and carryover procedures help mitigate the effect of limiting a loss or a deduction to the accounting period in which it was realized. With such procedures, a taxpayer may be able to salvage a loss or a deduction that might otherwise be wasted.

The installment method of recognizing gain on the sale of property allows a taxpayer to spread tax consequences over the payout period.[29] The harsh effect of taxing all the gain in the year of sale is thereby avoided. The installment method can also be explained by the wherewithal to pay concept since recognition of gain is tied to the collection of the installment notes received from the sale of the property. Tax consequences, then, tend to correspond to the seller's ability to pay the tax.

Coping with Inflation

Because of the progressive nature of the income tax, a wage adjustment to compensate for inflation can increase the income tax bracket of the recipient. Known as *bracket creep*, its overall impact is an erosion of purchasing power. Congress recognized this problem and began to adjust various income tax components, such as tax brackets, standard deduction amounts, and personal and dependency exemptions, through an indexation procedure. Indexation is based upon the rise in the consumer price index over the prior year.

POLITICAL CONSIDERATIONS

A large segment of the Federal tax law is made up of statutory provisions. Since these statutes are enacted by Congress, is it any surprise that political considerations influence tax law? For purposes of discussion, the effect of political considerations on the tax law is divided into the following topics: special interest legislation, political expediency situations, and state and local government influences.

Special Interest Legislation

There is no doubt that certain provisions of the tax law can largely be explained by the political influence some pressure groups have had on Congress. Is there any other realistic reason that, for example, prepaid subscription and dues income is not taxed until earned while prepaid rents are taxed to the landlord in the year received?

The American Jobs Creation Act of 2004 included several good examples of special interest legislation. One provision, sponsored by former Senator Zell Miller (D–Ga.), suspended the import duties on ceiling fans. The nation's largest seller of ceiling fans is Home Depot, which is based in Atlanta, Georgia. Another provision, sponsored by then House Speaker Dennis Hastert (R–Ill.), reduced the excise taxes on fishing tackle boxes. Representative Hastert's district includes Plano Molding, a major manufacturer of tackle boxes. The justification for this change was that it placed tackle boxes on a more level playing field with toolboxes (which are not subject to tax). Allegedly, fishermen had been buying and converting toolboxes to avoid the excise tax!

Special interest legislation is not necessarily to be condemned if it can be justified on economic, social, or some other utilitarian grounds. In most cases, however, it is objectionable in that it adds further complexity to an already cluttered tax law. At any rate, it is an inevitable product of our political system.

---

[28]The tax treatment of these items is discussed in Chapters 7, 10, and 16.

[29]Under the installment method, each payment received by the seller represents both a recovery of capital (the nontaxable portion) and profit from the sale (the taxable portion). The tax rules governing the installment method are discussed in Chapter 18.

Political Expediency Situations

Various tax reform proposals rise and fall in favor with the shifting moods of the American public. That Congress is sensitive to popular feeling is an accepted fact. Therefore, certain provisions of the tax law can be explained by the political climate at the time they were enacted.

Measures that deter more affluent taxpayers from obtaining so-called preferential tax treatment have always had popular appeal and, consequently, the support of Congress. A direct approach bars the benefit completely and explains such provisions as the imputed interest rules and the limitations on the deductibility of interest on investment indebtedness. More subtle are provisions that phase out tax breaks as income rises. Because taxpayers may be unaware of what is causing the shift to higher marginal tax rates, these phaseouts are often called "stealth taxes." The tax law contains several dozen such phaseout provisions. Examples include the earned income credit, child tax credit, lifetime learning credit, and the credit for first-time home purchases. At least for the immediate future, the use of these stealth taxes can be expected to increase.

Other changes explained at least partially by political expediency include the lowering of individual income tax rates, the increase in the personal and dependency exemptions, and the increase in the amount of the earned income credit.

State and Local Government Influences

Political considerations have played a major role in the nontaxability of interest received on state and local obligations. In view of the furor that has been raised by state and local political figures every time any modification of this tax provision has been proposed, one might well regard it as next to sacred.

Somewhat less apparent has been the influence state law has had in shaping our present Federal tax law. Such was the case with community property systems. The nine states with community property systems are Louisiana, Texas, New Mexico, Arizona, California, Washington, Idaho, Nevada, and Wisconsin. The rest of the states are classified as common law jurisdictions.[30] The difference between common law and community property systems centers around the property rights possessed by married persons. In a common law system, each spouse owns whatever he or she earns. Under a community property system, one-half of the earnings of each spouse is considered owned by the other spouse.

EXAMPLE 26

Al and Fran are husband and wife, and their only income is the $80,000 annual salary Al receives. If they live in New Jersey (a common law state), the $80,000 salary belongs to Al. If, however, they live in Arizona (a community property state), the $80,000 is divided equally, in terms of ownership, between Al and Fran. ■

At one time, the tax position of the residents of community property states was so advantageous that many common law states adopted community property systems. Needless to say, the political pressure placed on Congress to correct the disparity in tax treatment was considerable. To a large extent this was accomplished in the Revenue Act of 1948, which extended many of the community property tax advantages to residents of common law jurisdictions.

The major advantage extended was the provision allowing married taxpayers to file joint returns and compute their tax liability as if the income had been earned one-half by each spouse. This result is automatic in a community property state, since half of the income earned by one spouse belongs to the other spouse. The income-splitting benefits of a joint return are now incorporated as part of the tax rates applicable to married taxpayers. See Chapter 3.

---

[30]In Alaska, spouses can choose to have the community property rules apply.
Otherwise, property rights are determined under common law rules.

LO.8

Describe the role played by the IRS and the courts in the evolution of the Federal tax system.

INFLUENCE OF THE INTERNAL REVENUE SERVICE

The influence of the IRS is apparent in many areas beyond its role in issuing the administrative pronouncements that make up a considerable portion of our tax law. In its capacity as the protector of the national revenue, the IRS has been instrumental in securing the passage of much legislation designed to curtail the most flagrant tax avoidance practices (to close *tax loopholes*). As the administrator of the tax law, the IRS has sought and obtained legislation to make its job easier (to attain administrative feasibility).

The IRS as Protector of the Revenue

Innumerable examples can be given of provisions in the tax law that stem from the direct influence of the IRS. Usually, such provisions are intended to prevent a loophole from being used to avoid the tax consequences intended by Congress. Working within the letter of existing law, ingenious taxpayers and their advisers devise techniques that accomplish indirectly what cannot be accomplished directly. As a consequence, legislation is enacted to close the loopholes that taxpayers have located and exploited. Some tax law can be explained in this fashion and is discussed in the chapters to follow.

In addition, the IRS has secured from Congress legislation of a more general nature that enables it to make adjustments based on the substance, rather than the formal construction, of what a taxpayer has done. For example, one such provision permits the IRS to make adjustments to a taxpayer's method of accounting when the method used by the taxpayer does not clearly reflect income.[31]

EXAMPLE 27

Tina, a cash basis taxpayer, owns and operates a pharmacy. All drugs and other items acquired for resale, such as cosmetics, are charged to the purchases account and written off (expensed) for tax purposes in the year of acquisition. As this procedure does not clearly reflect income, it would be appropriate for the IRS to require that Tina establish and maintain an ending inventory account. ■

Administrative Feasibility

Some tax law is justified on the grounds that it simplifies the task of the IRS in collecting the revenue and administering the law. With regard to collecting the revenue, the IRS long ago realized the importance of placing taxpayers on a pay-as-you-go basis. Elaborate withholding procedures apply to wages, while the tax on other types of income may be paid at periodic intervals throughout the year. The IRS has been instrumental in convincing the courts that accrual basis taxpayers should in most cases pay taxes on prepaid income in the year received and not when earned. The approach may be contrary to generally accepted accounting principles, but it is consistent with the wherewithal to pay concept.

Of considerable aid to the IRS in collecting revenue are the numerous provisions that impose interest and penalties on taxpayers for noncompliance with the tax law. Provisions such as the penalties for failure to pay a tax or to file a return that is due, the negligence penalty for intentional disregard of rules and regulations, and various penalties for civil and criminal fraud serve as deterrents to taxpayer noncompliance.

One of the keys to an effective administration of our tax system is the audit process conducted by the IRS. To carry out this function, the IRS is aided by provisions that reduce the chance of taxpayer error or manipulation and therefore simplify the audit effort that is necessary. An increase in the amount of the standard deduction, for example, reduces the number of individual taxpayers who will choose the alternative of itemizing their personal deductions.[32] With fewer deductions to check, the audit function is simplified.[33]

---

[31]See Chapter 18.

[32]For a discussion of the standard deduction, see Chapter 3.

[33]The same justification was given by the IRS when it proposed to Congress the $100 limitation on personal casualty and theft losses. Imposition of the limitation eliminated many casualty and theft loss deductions and, as a consequence, saved the IRS considerable audit time. Later legislation, in addition to retaining the $100 feature, limits deductible losses to those in excess of 10% of a taxpayer's adjusted gross income. See Chapter 7.

INFLUENCE OF THE COURTS

In addition to interpreting statutory provisions and the administrative pronouncements issued by the IRS, the Federal courts have influenced tax law in two other respects.[34] First, the courts have formulated certain judicial concepts that serve as guides in the application of various tax provisions. Second, certain key decisions have led to changes in the Internal Revenue Code.

Judicial Concepts Relating to Tax

A leading tax concept developed by the courts deals with the interpretation of statutory tax provisions that operate to benefit taxpayers. The courts have established the rule that these relief provisions are to be narrowly construed against taxpayers if there is any doubt about their application.

Important in this area is the *arm's length* concept. Particularly in dealings between related parties, transactions may be tested by looking to whether the taxpayers acted in an arm's length manner. The question to be asked is: Would unrelated parties have handled the transaction in the same way?

EXAMPLE 28

Rex, the sole shareholder of Silver Corporation, leases property to the corporation for a yearly rent of $60,000. To test whether the corporation should be allowed a rent deduction for this amount, the IRS and the courts will apply the arm's length concept. Would Silver Corporation have paid $60,000 a year in rent if it had leased the same property from an unrelated party (rather than from Rex)? Suppose it is determined that an unrelated third party would have paid an annual rent for the property of only $50,000. Under these circumstances, Silver Corporation will be allowed a deduction of only $50,000. The other $10,000 it paid for the use of the property represents a nondeductible dividend. Accordingly, Rex will be treated as having received rent income of $50,000 and dividend income of $10,000. ■

Judicial Influence on Statutory Provisions

Some court decisions have been of such consequence that Congress has incorporated them into statutory tax law. For example, many years ago the courts found that stock dividends distributed to the shareholders of a corporation were not taxable as income. This result was largely accepted by Congress, and a provision in the tax statutes now covers the issue.

On occasion, however, Congress has reacted negatively to judicial interpretations of the tax law.

EXAMPLE 29

Nora leases unimproved real estate to Wade for 20 years. At a cost of $400,000, Wade erects a building on the land. The building is worth $150,000 when the lease terminates and Nora takes possession of the property. Does Nora have any income either when the improvements are made or when the lease terminates? In a landmark decision, a court held that Nora must recognize income of $150,000 upon the termination of the lease. ■

Congress felt that the result reached in Example 29 was inequitable in that it was not consistent with the wherewithal to pay concept. Consequently, the tax law was amended to provide that a landlord does not recognize any income either when the improvements are made (unless made in lieu of rent) or when the lease terminates.

---

[34]A great deal of case law is devoted to ascertaining congressional intent. The courts, in effect, ask: What did Congress have in mind when it enacted a particular tax provision?

1.8 SUMMARY

In addition to its necessary revenue-raising objective, the Federal tax law has developed in response to several other factors:

- *Economic considerations.* The emphasis here is on tax provisions that help regulate the economy and encourage certain activities and types of businesses.
- *Social considerations.* Some tax provisions are designed to encourage (or discourage) certain socially desirable (or undesirable) practices.
- *Equity considerations.* Of principal concern in this area are tax provisions that alleviate the effect of multiple taxation, recognize the wherewithal to pay concept, mitigate the effect of the annual accounting period concept, and recognize the eroding effect of inflation.
- *Political considerations.* Of significance in this regard are tax provisions that represent special interest legislation, reflect political expediency, and exhibit the effect of state and local law.
- *Influence of the IRS.* Many tax provisions are intended to aid the IRS in the collection of revenue and the administration of the tax law.
- *Influence of the courts.* Court decisions have established a body of judicial concepts relating to tax law and have, on occasion, led Congress to enact statutory provisions to either clarify or negate their effect.

These factors explain various tax provisions and thereby help in understanding why the tax law developed to its present state. The next step involves learning to work with the tax law, which is the subject of Chapter 2.

REFOCUS ON THE BIG PICTURE

FAMILY AND TAXES—A TYPICAL YEAR

The explanation given for the difference in the ad valorem taxes—the Carters' increase and the Walkers' decrease—seems reasonable (see Example 4). It is not likely that the Carters' increase was due to a *general* upward assessment in valuation, as the Walkers' taxes on their residence (located nearby) dropped. More business use of the Carters' residence (presuming Travis conducts his consulting practice from his home) might be responsible for the increase, but capital improvements appear to be a more likely cause.

The imposition of the use tax when Travis registered the new automobile illustrates one of the means by which a state can preclude the avoidance of its sales tax (see Example 5).

When gifts between family members are material in amount (e.g., an RV) and exceed the annual exclusion, a gift tax return needs to be filed (see Example 11). Even though no gift tax may be due because of the availability of the unified transfer tax credit, the filing of a return starts the running of the statute of limitations.

The imposition of the "jock tax" on nonathletes is unusual but not improper. The Carters must recognize that some of their income is subject to income taxes in two states and take advantage of whatever relief is available to mitigate the result (see Example 12).

Employment within and by the family group (e.g., children, other relatives, domestics) has become a priority item in the enforcement of Social Security tax and income tax withholdings. Thus, the Carters need to be aware of the need to cover their son, Martin (see Example 13).

Because of the double audit (i.e., both state and Federal) and the deficiency assessed, the Carters need to make sure that future returns do not contain similar errors (see Example 19). As the text suggests, taxpayers with prior deficiencies are among those whose returns may be selected for audit.

KEY TERMS

Ad valorem taxes, 1–7

Correspondence audit, 1–22

Employment taxes, 1–17

Estate tax, 1–12

Excise taxes, 1–9

FICA tax, 1–18

Field audit, 1–22

Financial Accounting Standards Board (FASB), 1–16

Flat tax, 1–20

Franchise tax, 1–19

FUTA tax, 1–18

Generally Accepted Accounting Principles (GAAP), 1–16

Gift tax, 1–13

Inheritance tax, 1–12

International Accounting Standards Board (IASB), 1–16

International Financial Reporting Standards (IFRS), 1–16

National sales tax, 1–20

Occupational fees, 1–19

Office audit, 1–22

Personalty, 1–8

Realty, 1–7

Revenue neutrality, 1–27

Sales tax, 1–10

Severance taxes, 1–11

Statute of limitations, 1–23

Sunset provision, 1–27

Use tax, 1–10

Value added tax (VAT), 1–20

Wherewithal to pay, 1–31

DISCUSSION QUESTIONS

1. **LO.1** Marvin is the executor and sole heir of his aunt's estate. The estate includes her furnished home, which Marvin is considering converting to rental property to generate additional cash flow. What are some of the tax problems that Marvin may confront?

   ISSUE ID

2. **LO.2** The effect of the Sixteenth Amendment to the U.S. Constitution was to validate the Federal income tax imposed on individuals. Do you agree?

3. **LO.2** World War II converted the Federal income tax into a *mass tax*. Explain.

4. **LO.2** How does the pay-as-you-go procedure apply to wage earners? To persons who have income from other than wages?

5. **LO.3** In terms of Adam Smith's canon of *economy*, how does the Federal income tax fare?

6. **LO.3** Using Adam Smith's canon of *certainty*, evaluate the Federal income tax.

7. **LO.3** Distinguish between taxes that are *proportional* and those that are *progressive*.

8. **LO.4** Several years ago, Ethan purchased the former parsonage of St. James Church to use as a personal residence. To date, Ethan has not received any ad valorem property tax bills from either the city or the county tax authorities.

   ISSUE ID

   a. What is a reasonable explanation for this oversight?
   b. What should Ethan do?

9. **LO.4** The Adams Independent School District wants to sell a parcel of unimproved land that it does not need. Its three best offers are as follows: from the State Department of Public Safety (DPS), $2.3 million; from the Second Baptist Church, $2.2 million; and from Baker Motors, $2.1 million. DPS would use the property for a new state highway patrol barracks; Second Baptist would start a church school; and Baker would open a car dealership. If you are the financial adviser for the school district, which offer would you prefer? Why?

   ISSUE ID

10. **LO.4** The commissioners for Colby County are actively negotiating with Eagle Industries regarding the location of a new manufacturing facility in the county. As Eagle is considering several other sites, a "generous tax holiday" may be needed to influence its choice. The local school district is opposed to any "generous tax holiday."
    a. In terms of a "generous tax holiday," what might the proposal entail?
    b. Why should the school district be opposed?

11. **LO.4** The Williams family made significant improvements to their personal residence and then converted it to a bed and breakfast facility. They were surprised when the property taxes on the residence were raised twice. Explain what probably happened.

12. **LO.4** Franklin County is in dire financial straits and is considering a number of sources for additional revenue. Evaluate the following possibilities in terms of anticipated taxpayer compliance:
    a. A property tax on business inventories.
    b. A tax on intangibles (i.e., stocks and bonds) held as investments.
    c. A property tax on boats used for recreational purposes.

13. **LO.4** Many excise taxes are imposed by *both* the Federal and state governments. Give several examples of this practice.

14. **LO.4** After his first business trip to a major city, Herman is alarmed when he reviews his credit card receipts. Both the hotel bill and the car rental charge are in excess of the price he was quoted. Was Herman overcharged, or is there an explanation for the excess amounts?

15. **LO.4** What is the difference between an excise tax and a general sales tax?
    a. Do all states impose a general sales tax?
    b. Does the Federal government impose a general sales tax?

16. **LO.4** Eileen, a resident of Wyoming, goes to Montana to purchase her new automobile. She does this because Wyoming imposes a sales tax while Montana does not. Has Eileen successfully avoided the Wyoming sales tax? Explain.

ISSUE ID

17. **LO.4** Velma lives in Wilson County, which is adjacent to Grimes County. Although the retail stores in both counties are comparable, Velma drives an extra 10 miles to do all of her shopping in Grimes County. Why might she do this?

ISSUE ID

18. **LO.4** During a social event, Muriel and Earl are discussing the home computer each recently purchased. Although the computers are identical makes and models, Muriel is surprised to learn that she paid a sales tax, while Earl did not. Comment as to why this could happen.

19. **LO.4** Distinguish between an estate tax and an inheritance tax.
    a. Do some states impose both? Neither?
    b. Which, if either, does the Federal government impose?

ISSUE ID

20. **LO.4** Jake (age 72) and Jessica (age 28) were recently married. To avoid any transfer taxes, Jake has promised to leave Jessica all of his wealth when he dies. Is Jake under some misconception about the operation of the Federal gift and estate taxes? Explain.

21. **LO.4** Address the following issues:
    a. What is the purpose of the unified transfer tax credit?
    b. Is the same amount available for both the Federal gift tax and the estate tax? Explain.
    c. Does the use of the credit for a gift affect the amount of credit available for the estate tax? Explain.

22. **LO.4** Miles and Trudy are husband and wife and have six married children and ten minor grandchildren. For tax year 2011, what is the maximum amount they can give to the family (including the sons- and daughters-in-law) without using any of their unified transfer tax credit?

23. **LO.4** In arriving at taxable income, how does the Federal income tax imposed on corporations differ from that imposed on individuals?

24. **LO.4** With reference to state income taxes, what is meant by the "piggyback" approach? "Decoupling" from this approach?

ISSUE ID

25. **LO.4** Mike Barr was an outstanding football player in college and expects to be drafted by the NFL in the first few rounds. Mike has let it be known that he would prefer to sign with a club located in Florida, Texas, or Washington. Mike sees no reason why he should have to pay state income tax on his player's salary! Is Mike under any delusions? Explain.

ISSUE ID

26. **LO.4, 5** A question on a state income tax return asks the taxpayer if he or she made any out-of-state Internet or mail-order catalog purchases during the year. The question requires a yes or no answer, and if the taxpayer answers yes, the amount of such purchases is to be listed.
    a. Does such an inquiry have any relevance to the state income tax? If not, why is it being asked?
    b. Your client, Harriet, wants to leave the question unanswered. As the preparer of her return, how do you respond?

27. **LO.4** As to those states that impose an income tax on individuals, comment on the following:
    a. Use of withholding procedures.
    b. Treatment of Federal income taxes paid.
    c. Due date for filing.
    d. Credit for income taxes paid to other states.

28. **LO.4** Many state income tax returns contain checkoff boxes that allow taxpayers to make donations to a multitude of local charitable causes. On what grounds has this procedure been criticized?

29. **LO.4** Many states have occasionally adopted amnesty programs that allow taxpayers to pay back taxes with reduced penalties.
    a. Besides the revenue generated, how are these programs advantageous?
    b. Could an amnesty program be used by a state that does not levy an income tax?
    c. Does the IRS utilize this approach?

30. **LO.4** Contrast FICA and FUTA as to the following:
    a. Purpose of the tax.
    b. Upon whom imposed.
    c. Governmental administration of the tax.
    d. Reduction of tax based on a merit rating system.

31. **LO.4** One of the tax advantages of hiring family members to work in your business is that FICA taxes are avoided. Do you agree with this statement? Explain.

32. **LO.4** Describe the nature and purpose of the following taxes:
    a. Severance taxes.
    b. Franchise taxes.
    c. Occupational fees.

33. **LO.4** Regarding the value added tax (VAT), comment on the following:
    a. Popularity of this type of tax.
    b. Nature of the tax.

34. **LO.4** Both a value added tax (VAT) and a national sales tax have been criticized as being *regressive* in their effect.
    a. Explain.
    b. How could this shortcoming be remedied in the case of a national sales tax?

35. **LO.4, 5** Serena operates a lawn maintenance service in Southern California. As most of her employees are itinerant, they are paid on a day-to-day basis. Because of cash-flow problems, Serena requires her customers to pay cash for the services she provides.   **ISSUE ID**
    a. What are some of the tax problems Serena might have?
    b. Assess Serena's chances of audit by the IRS.

36. **LO.5** Assess the probability of an audit in each of the following independent situations:
    a. As a result of a jury trial, Linda was awarded $3.5 million because of job discrimination. The award included $3 million for punitive damages.
    b. Mel operates a combination check-cashing service and pawnshop.
    c. Cindy has annual AGI in excess of $500,000.
    d. Pierre is the maître d' at a five-star restaurant and also manages the valet parking concession.
    e. Giselle is a cocktail waitress at an upscale night club. She has been audited several times in past years.
    f. Marcus was recently assessed a large *state* income tax deficiency by the state of California for his utilization of an abusive tax shelter.
    g. Guy, a professional gambler, recently broke up with his companion of 10 years and married her teenage daughter.
    h. Rick's only source of income is the wages he earns working on the assembly line of a lawn mower manufacturer.

37. **LO.5** With regard to the IRS audit process, comment on the following:
    a. Availability of an "informant's fee."
    b. DIF score.
    c. The audit is resolved by mail.
    d. The audit is conducted at the office of the IRS.

    e.   A "no change" RAR results.

    f.   Special agent joins the audit team.

38. **LO.5** Aldo has just been audited by the IRS. He does not agree with the agent's findings but feels he has only two choices: pay the proposed deficiency or resort to the courts. Do you agree with Aldo's conclusion? Why or why not?

39. **LO.5** What purpose is served by a statute of limitations? How is it relevant in the case of tax controversies?

40. **LO.5** Regarding the statute of limitations on additional assessments of tax by the IRS, determine the applicable period in each of the following situations. Assume a calendar year individual with no fraud or substantial omission involved.
    a.   The income tax return for 2010 was filed on February 23, 2011.
    b.   The income tax return for 2010 was filed on June 24, 2011.
    c.   The income tax return for 2010 was prepared on April 7, 2011, but was never filed. Through some misunderstanding between the preparer and the taxpayer, each expected the other to file the return.
    d.   The income tax return for 2010 was never filed because the taxpayer thought no additional tax was due.

41. **LO.5** Brianna, a calendar year taxpayer, files her income tax return for 2010 on February 4, 2011. Although she makes repeated inquiries, she does not receive her refund from the IRS until May 27, 2011. Is Brianna entitled to interest on the refund? Explain.

42. **LO.5, 6** On a Federal income tax return filed five years ago, Andy inadvertently omitted a large amount of gross income.
    a.   Andy seeks your advice as to whether the IRS is barred from assessing additional income tax in the event he is audited. What is your advice?
    b.   Would your advice differ if you are the person who prepared the return in question? Explain.
    c.   Suppose Andy asks you to prepare his current year's return. Would you do so? Explain.

43. **LO.5** Lori files her income tax return 45 days after the due date of the return without obtaining an extension from the IRS. Along with the return, she remits a check for $40,000, which is the balance of the tax she owes. Disregarding the interest element, what are Irene's penalties for failure to file and for failure to pay?

44. **LO.5** For tax year 2008, the IRS assesses a deficiency against Rhett for $500,000. Disregarding the interest component, what is Rhett's penalty if the deficiency is attributable to:
    a.   Negligence?
    b.   Fraud?

45. **LO.5, 6** In March 2011, Jim asks you to prepare his Federal income tax returns for tax years 2008, 2009, and 2010. In discussing this matter with him, you discover that he also has not filed for tax year 2007. When you mention this fact, Jim tells you that the statute of limitations precludes the IRS from taking any action as to this year.
    a.   Is Jim correct about the application of the statute of limitations? Why?
    b.   If Jim refuses to file for 2007, should you prepare returns for 2008 through 2010?

46. **LO.5, 6** The Benson CPA firm is considering utilizing an offshore service provider to prepare many of its tax returns. In this regard, what are the ethical considerations that must be taken into account?

47. **LO.7** In terms of tax reform policy, what do the following mean?
    a.   Revenue neutrality.
    b.   Pay-as-you-go or "paygo."
    c.   Sunset provision.

48. **LO.7** Some tax rules can be justified on multiple grounds (e.g., economic, social, etc.). In this connection, comment on the possible justification for the rules governing the following:
    a.   Energy conservation and pollution control.
    b.   Pension plans.
    c.   Education.
    d.   Home ownership.

49. **LO.7** Discuss the probable justification for each of the following provisions of the tax law:
    a. The § 179 election to expense certain business assets upon their acquisition.
    b. Favorable treatment accorded to research and development expenditures.
    c. A deduction allowed for income resulting from U.S. production (manufacturing) activities.
    d. The deduction allowed for contributions to qualified charitable organizations.
    e. An election that allows certain corporations to avoid the corporate income tax and pass losses through to their shareholders.
    f. A tax credit for amounts spent to furnish care for minor children while the parent works.

50. **LO.7** The state highway department condemns some of Chad's grazing land. The land cost Chad $20,000, and the condemnation award is the land's fair market value of $100,000. Shortly after the condemnation, Chad buys replacement grazing land. What is his recognized gain if the replacement land costs:
    a. $70,000?
    b. $110,000?
    c. $20,000?
    d. What, if any, is the justification for deferring the recognition of gain on an involuntary conversion?

51. **LO.7, 8** Discuss the probable justification for each of the following aspects of the tax law:
    a. Net operating losses of a current year can be carried back to profitable years.
    b. A taxpayer that sells property on an installment basis can recognize gain on the sale over the period the payments are received.
    c. Every year the tax brackets and the amounts of the standard deduction and dependency exemptions are adjusted by the IRS.
    d. Certain preferential tax treatment is phased out for more affluent taxpayers.
    e. The exclusion from Federal tax of certain interest income from state and local bonds.
    f. Prepaid income is taxed to the recipient in the year received and not in the year it is earned.
    g. The deduction for personal casualty losses is subject to dollar and percentage limitations.

52. **LO.8** A mother sells a valuable collection of antiques to her daughter for $1,000. What judicial concept might the IRS invoke to question this transaction?

53. **LO.8** Edward leases real estate to Janet for a period of 20 years. Janet makes capital improvements to the property. When the lease expires, Edward reclaims the property, including the improvements made by Janet.
    a. Under current law, at what point does Edward recognize income as a result of Janet's improvements?
    b. Has the law in part (a) always been the rule?
    c. What is the justification, if any, for the current rule?

Working with the Tax Law

LEARNING OBJECTIVES

After completing Chapter 2, you should be able to:

L0.1

Distinguish between the statutory, administrative, and judicial sources of the tax law and understand the purpose of each source.

L0.2

Locate and work with the appropriate tax law sources.

L0.3

Have an awareness of tax research tools.

L0.4

Understand the tax research process.

L0.5

Communicate the results of the tax research process in a client letter and a tax file memorandum.

L0.6

Apply tax research techniques and planning procedures.

L0.7

Be aware of taxation on the CPA examination.

OUTLINE

2.1 TAX SOURCES

LO.1

Distinguish between the statutory, administrative, and judicial sources of the tax law and understand the purpose of each source.

Understanding taxation requires a mastery of the sources of the *rules of tax law*. These sources include not only legislative provisions in the form of the Internal Revenue Code, but also congressional Committee Reports, Treasury Department Regulations, other Treasury Department pronouncements, and court decisions. Thus, the *primary sources* of tax information include pronouncements from all three branches of government: legislative, executive, and judicial.

In addition to being able to locate and interpret the sources of the tax law, a tax professional must understand the relative weight of authority within these sources. The tax law is of little significance, however, until it is applied to a set of facts and circumstances. This chapter, therefore, both introduces the statutory, administrative, and judicial sources of tax law and explains how the law is applied to individual and business transactions. It also explains how to apply research techniques and use planning procedures effectively.

A large part of tax research focuses on determining the intent of Congress. Although Congress often claims simplicity as one of its goals, a cursory examination of the tax law indicates that it has not been very successful in achieving this objective. Commenting on his 48-page tax return, author James Michener said, "It is unimaginable in that I graduated from one of America's better colleges, yet I am totally incapable of understanding tax returns." David Brinkley, the television news commentator, observed that "settling a dispute is difficult when our tax regulations are all written in a foreign tongue whose language flows like damp sludge leaking from a sanitary landfill."

Frequently, uncertainty in the tax law causes disputes between the Internal Revenue Service (IRS) and taxpayers. Due to these *gray areas* and the complexity of the tax law, a taxpayer may have more than one alternative for structuring a business transaction. In structuring business transactions and engaging in other tax planning activities, the tax adviser must be cognizant that the objective of tax planning is not necessarily to minimize the tax liability. Instead a taxpayer should maximize his or her after-tax return, which may include maximizing nontax as well as noneconomic benefits.

STATUTORY SOURCES OF THE TAX LAW

Origin of the Internal Revenue Code

Before 1939, the statutory provisions relating to Federal taxation were contained in the individual revenue acts enacted by Congress. Because dealing with many separate acts was inconvenient and confusing, in 1939 Congress codified all of the Federal tax laws. Known as the Internal Revenue Code of 1939, the codification arranged all Federal tax provisions in a logical sequence and placed them in a separate part of the Federal statutes. A further rearrangement took place in 1954 and resulted in the Internal Revenue Code of 1954, which continued in effect until 1986 when it was replaced by the Internal Revenue Code of 1986. Although Congress did not recodify the law in the Tax Reform Act (TRA) of 1986, the magnitude of the changes made by TRA of 1986 did provide some rationale for renaming the Federal tax law the Internal Revenue Code of 1986.

The following observations help clarify the codification procedure:

- Neither the 1939 nor the 1954 Code substantially changed the tax law existing on the date of its enactment. Much of the 1939 Code, for example, was incorporated into the 1954 Code; the major change was the reorganization and renumbering of the tax provisions.
- Although the 1986 Code resulted in substantial changes, only a minority of the statutory provisions were affected.[1]

---

[1] This point is important in assessing judicial decisions interpreting provisions of the Internal Revenue Code of 1939 and the Internal Revenue Code of 1954. If the same provision was included in the Internal Revenue Code of 1986 and has not been subsequently amended, the decision has continuing validity.

| TAX *in* the *NEWS* | TAX FREEDOM DAY |

In income tax history, 1913 was an important year. In that year, the Sixteenth Amendment to the Constitution was ratified:

> The Congress shall have power to tax and collect taxes on incomes, from whatever source derived, without apportionment among the several States, and without regard to any census or enumeration.

The first income tax legislation that definitely was constitutional was passed that same year.

According to the Tax Foundation, in 2010 Tax Freedom Day fell on April 9, one day later than in 2009, but one week earlier than in 2008. Tax Freedom Day is the date on which an average taxpayer through working has paid off his or her taxes for the year. Nevertheless, Americans still paid more in taxes in 2010 than they spent on food, clothing, and shelter combined. Of course, if you lived in Connecticut with the heaviest total tax burden, Tax Freedom Day fell on April 27. Alaska and Louisiana celebrated Tax Freedom Day the earliest—on March 26, the 85th day of the year.

Source: Tax Foundation, "America Celebrates Tax Freedom Day," www.taxfoundation.org/taxfreedomday.html

- Statutory amendments to the tax law are integrated into the Code. For example, the Tax Relief Reconciliation Act of 2001, the Job Creation and Worker Assistance Act of 2002, the Jobs and Growth Tax Relief Reconciliation Act (JGTRRA) of 2003, the Working Families Tax Relief Act of 2004, the American Jobs Creation Act of 2004, the Energy Tax Incentives Act of 2005, the Tax Increase Prevention Act of 2005 (TIPRA), the Pension Protection Act of 2006, the Tax Relief and Health Care Act of 2006, the Small Business and Work Opportunity Tax Act of 2007, the Economic Stimulus Act of 2008, the Food, Conservation, and Energy Act of 2008, the Housing Assistance Tax Act of 2008, the American Recovery and Reinvestment Tax Act of 2009, the Worker, Homeownership, and Business Assistance Act of 2009, the Hiring Incentives to Restore Employment Act of 2010, the Patient Protection and Affordable Care Act of 2010, the Health Care and Education Reconciliation Act of 2010, the Small Business Jobs Act of 2010, and the Tax Relief Act of 2010 all became part of the Internal Revenue Code of 1986. In view of the frequency with which tax legislation has been enacted in recent years, it appears that the tax law will continue to be amended frequently.

The Legislative Process

Federal tax legislation generally originates in the House of Representatives, where it is first considered by the House Ways and Means Committee. Tax bills originate in the Senate when they are attached as riders to other legislative proposals.[2] If acceptable to the House Ways and Means Committee, the proposed bill is referred to the entire House of Representatives for approval or disapproval. Approved bills are sent to the Senate, where they are considered by the Senate Finance Committee.

The next step is referral from the Senate Finance Committee to the entire Senate. Assuming no disagreement between the House and Senate, passage by the Senate results in referral to the President for approval or veto. If the bill is approved or if the President's veto is overridden, the bill becomes law and part of the Internal Revenue Code of 1986.

Both the House and the Senate passed the Food, Conservation, and Energy Act of 2008 on May 15, 2008. On May 21, 2008, President George Bush vetoed the bill, but both houses of Congress overwhelmingly voted on May 22, 2008, to override the President's veto. Thus, the tax provisions contained in this 2008 Act became part of the Internal Revenue Code of 1986.

House and Senate versions of major tax bills frequently differ. One reason bills are often changed in the Senate is that each individual senator has considerable latitude to make amendments when the Senate as a whole is voting on a bill referred to

[2]The Tax Equity and Fiscal Responsibility Act of 1982 originated in the Senate, and its constitutionality was unsuccessfully challenged in the courts. The Senate version of the Deficit Reduction Act of 1984 was attached as an amendment to the Federal Boat Safety Act.

it by the Senate Finance Committee.[3] In contrast, the entire House of Representatives either accepts or rejects what is proposed by the House Ways and Means Committee, and changes from the floor are rare. When the Senate version of the bill differs from that passed by the House, the Joint Conference Committee, which includes members of both the House Ways and Means Committee and the Senate Finance Committee, is called upon to resolve the differences. The deliberations of the Joint Conference Committee usually produce a compromise between the two versions, which is then voted on by both the House and the Senate. If both bodies accept the bill, it is referred to the President for approval or veto. Former Senator Daniel Patrick Moynihan observed that in the last hours of Congress, the White House and lawmakers often agree on a "1,200-page monster, we vote for it; nobody knows what is in it." Figure 2.1 summarizes the typical legislative process for tax bills.

The role of the Joint Conference Committee indicates the importance of compromise in the legislative process. As an example of the practical effect of the compromise process, consider Figure 2.2, which shows what happened with amendments to the first-time homebuyer credit in the American Recovery and Reinvestment Tax Act (ARRTA) of 2009.

Referrals from the House Ways and Means Committee, the Senate Finance Committee, and the Joint Conference Committee are usually accompanied by Committee Reports. These Committee Reports often explain the provisions of the proposed legislation and are therefore a valuable source for ascertaining the *intent of Congress*. What Congress had in mind when it considered and enacted tax legislation is, of course, the key to interpreting such legislation by taxpayers, the IRS, and the courts. Since Regulations normally are not issued immediately after a statute is enacted, taxpayers often look to Committee Reports to determine congressional intent.

Arrangement of the Code

The Internal Revenue Code of 1986 is found in Title 26 of the U.S. Code. In working with the Code, it helps to understand the format. Note, for example, the following partial table of contents:

In referring to a provision of the Code, the *key* is usually the Section number. In citing Section 2(a) (dealing with the status of a surviving spouse), for example, it is unnecessary to include Subtitle A, Chapter 1, Subchapter A, Part I. Merely mentioning Section 2(a) will suffice, since the Section numbers run consecutively and do not begin again with each new Subtitle, Chapter, Subchapter, or Part. Not all Code Section numbers are used, however. Notice that Part I ends with Section 5 and Part II starts with Section 11 (at present there are no Sections 6, 7, 8, 9, and 10).[4]

Tax practitioners commonly refer to some specific areas of income tax law by their Subchapters. Some of the more common Subchapter designations include Subchapter C ("Corporate Distributions and Adjustments"), Subchapter K ("Partners and Partnerships"), and Subchapter S ("Tax Treatment of S Corporations and Their Shareholders"). In the last situation in particular, it is much more convenient to describe the subject of the applicable Code provisions (Sections 1361–1379) as S corporation status rather than as the "Tax Treatment of S Corporations and Their Shareholders."

---

[3]During the passage of the Tax Reform Act of 1986, Senate leaders tried to make the bill *amendment proof* to avoid the normal amendment process.

[4]When the 1954 Code was drafted, some Section numbers were intentionally omitted so that later changes could be incorporated into the Code without disrupting its organization. When Congress does not leave enough space, subsequent Code Sections are given A, B, C, etc., designations. A good example is the treatment of §§ 280A through 280H.

FIGURE 2.1 Legislative Process for Tax Bills

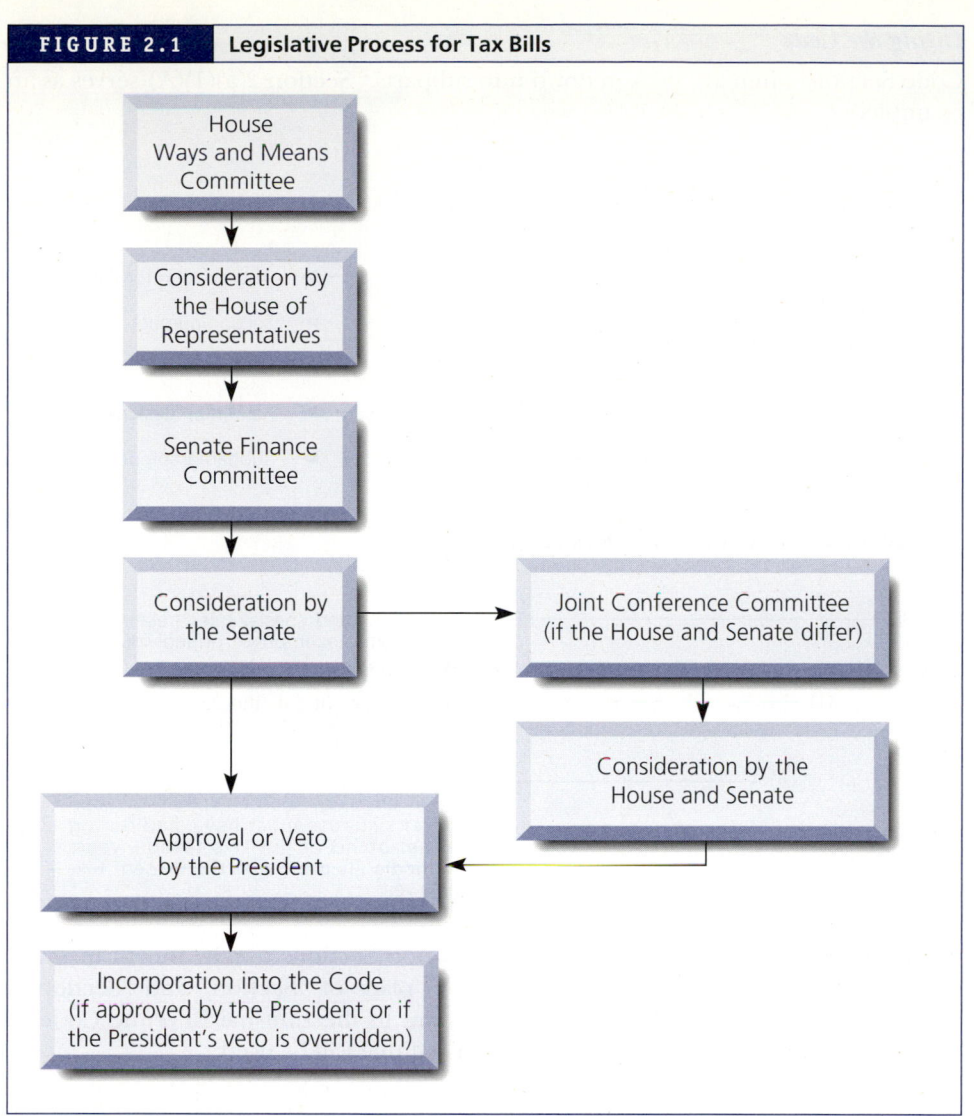

FIGURE 2.2 Example of Compromise in the Joint Conference Committee

Citing the Code

Code Sections often are broken down into subparts.[5] Section 2(a)(1)(A) serves as an example.

Broken down by content, § 2(a)(1)(A) becomes:

Throughout the text, references to the Code Sections are in the form given above. The symbols "§" and "§§" are used in place of "Section" and "Sections." Unless otherwise stated, all Code references are to the Internal Revenue Code of 1986. The following table summarizes the format that will be used:

Complete Reference	Text Reference
Section 2(a)(1)(A) of the Internal Revenue Code of 1986	§ 2(a)(1)(A)
Sections 1 and 2 of the Internal Revenue Code of 1986	§§ 1 and 2
Section 2 of the Internal Revenue Code of 1954	§ 2 of the Internal Revenue Code of 1954
Section 12(d) of the Internal Revenue Code of 1939[7]	§ 12(d) of the Internal Revenue Code of 1939

ADMINISTRATIVE SOURCES OF THE TAX LAW

The administrative sources of the Federal tax law can be grouped as follows: Treasury Department Regulations, Revenue Rulings and Revenue Procedures, and various other administrative pronouncements (see Exhibit 2.1). All are issued by either the U.S. Treasury Department or the IRS.

---

[5]Some Code Sections do not require subparts. See, for example, §§ 211 and 241.

[6]Some Code Sections omit the subsection designation and use the paragraph designation as the first subpart. See, for example, §§ 212(1) and 1222(1).

[7]Section 12(d) of the Internal Revenue Code of 1939 is the predecessor to § 2 of the Internal Revenue Code of 1954 and the Internal Revenue Code of 1986. Keep in mind that the 1954 Code superseded the 1939 Code and the 1986 Code has superseded the 1954 Code. Footnote 1 of this chapter explains why references to the 1939 or 1954 Code are included.

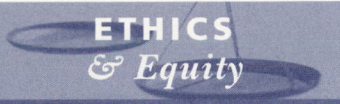

ETHICS & Equity

IS IT ETHICAL TO REPORT A TAX CHEAT?

The IRS makes it worthwhile to turn in someone who cheats on income taxes. The person who reports a cheater can receive up to 15 to 30 percent of any underpayment, up to a maximum of $10 million. The IRS's tip line is 1-800-829-0433, and the appropriate form to report a tax cheat is Form 3949A (Information Referral). The IRS estimates that taxpayers underpay their taxes by $345 billion each year. Is it ethical to report a tax cheat?

Treasury Department Regulations

Regulations are issued by the U.S. Treasury Department under authority granted by Congress.[8] Interpretive by nature, they provide taxpayers with considerable guidance on the meaning and application of the Code. Regulations may be issued in *proposed, temporary,* or *final* form. Regulations carry considerable authority as the official interpretation of tax statutes. They are an important factor to consider in complying with the tax law.

Since Regulations interpret the Code, they are arranged in the same sequence as the Code. A number is added at the beginning, however, to indicate the type of tax or administrative, procedural, or definitional matter to which they relate. For example, the prefix 1 designates the Regulations under the income tax law. Thus, the Regulations under Code § 2 are cited as Reg. § 1.2 with subparts added for further identification. The numbering patterns of these subparts often have no correlation with the Code subsections. The prefix 20 designates estate tax Regulations; 25 covers gift tax Regulations; 31 relates to employment taxes; and 301 refers to procedure and administration. This list is not all-inclusive.

New Regulations and changes to existing Regulations are usually issued in proposed form before they are finalized. The interval between the proposal of a Regulation and its finalization permits taxpayers and other interested parties to comment on the propriety of the proposal. **Proposed Regulations** under Code § 2, for example, are cited as Prop.Reg. § 1.2. The Tax Court indicates that Proposed Regulations carry little weight—no more than a position advanced in a written brief prepared by a litigating party before the Tax Court. **Finalized Regulations** have the force and effect of law.[9]

Sometimes the Treasury Department issues **Temporary Regulations** relating to matters where immediate guidance is important. These Regulations are issued without the comment period required for Proposed Regulations. Temporary Regulations have the same authoritative value as final Regulations and may be cited as precedents. Temporary Regulations must also be issued as Proposed Regulations and automatically expire within three years after the date of issuance.[10] Temporary Regulations and the simultaneously issued Proposed Regulations carry more weight than traditional Proposed Regulations. An example of a Temporary Regulation is Temp.Reg. § 1.482–7T(b)(4), which provides guidance for both prior and new cost-sharing arrangements.

Proposed, Temporary, and final Regulations are published in the *Federal Register*, in the *Internal Revenue Bulletin* (I.R.B.), and by major tax services. Final Regulations are issued as Treasury Decisions (TDs).

Regulations may also be classified as *legislative, interpretive,* or *procedural*. This classification scheme is discussed under Assessing the Validity of a Treasury Regulation later in the chapter.

---

[8]§ 7805.

[9]*F. W. Woolworth Co.*, 54 T.C. 1233 (1970); *Harris M. Miller,* 70 T.C. 448 (1978); and *James O. Tomerlin Trust,* 87 T.C. 876 (1986).

[10]§ 7805(e).

EXHIBIT 2.1	Administrative Sources	

Source	Location	Authority**
Regulations	*Federal Register**	Force and effect of law.
Temporary Regulations	*Federal Register** *Internal Revenue Bulletin* *Cumulative Bulletin*	May be cited as a precedent.
Proposed Regulations	*Federal Register** *Internal Revenue Bulletin* *Cumulative Bulletin*	Preview of final Regulations.
Revenue Rulings Revenue Procedures Treasury Decisions Actions on Decisions	*Internal Revenue Bulletin* *Cumulative Bulletin*	Do not have the force and effect of law.

General Counsel Memoranda
Technical Advice Memoranda
	Tax Analysts' *Tax Notes;* RIA's *Internal
	   Memoranda of the IRS;* CCH's *IRS Position
	   Reporter*
		May not be cited as a precedent.

Letter Rulings	Research Institute of America and Commerce Clearing House tax services	Applicable only to taxpayer addressed. No precedential force.

*Finalized, Temporary, and Proposed Regulations are published in soft-cover form by several publishers.

**Each of these sources may be substantial authority for purposes of the accuracy-related penalty in § 6662. Notice 90–20, 1990–1 C.B. 328.

Revenue Rulings and Revenue Procedures

Revenue Rulings are official pronouncements of the National Office of the IRS.[11] They typically provide one or more examples of how the IRS would apply a law to specific fact situations. Like Regulations, Revenue Rulings are designed to provide interpretation of the tax law. However, they do not carry the same legal force and effect as Regulations and usually deal with more restricted problems. Regulations are approved by the Secretary of the Treasury, whereas Revenue Rulings generally are not.

Although letter rulings (discussed below) are not the same as Revenue Rulings, a Revenue Ruling often results from a specific taxpayer's request for a letter ruling. If the IRS believes that a taxpayer's request for a letter ruling deserves official publication because of its widespread impact, the letter ruling will be converted into a Revenue Ruling and issued for the information and guidance of taxpayers, tax practitioners, and IRS personnel. Names, identifying descriptions, and money amounts are changed to conceal the identity of the requesting taxpayer. Revenue Rulings also arise from technical advice to District Offices of the IRS, court decisions, suggestions from tax practitioner groups, and various tax publications.

Revenue Procedures are issued in the same manner as Revenue Rulings but deal with the internal management practices and procedures of the IRS. Familiarity with these procedures can increase taxpayer compliance and help the IRS administer the tax laws more efficiently. A taxpayer's failure to follow a Revenue Procedure can result in unnecessary delay or, in a discretionary situation, can cause the IRS to decline to act on behalf of the taxpayer.

Both Revenue Rulings and Revenue Procedures serve an important function by providing *guidance* to IRS personnel and taxpayers in handling routine tax matters. Revenue Rulings and Revenue Procedures generally apply retroactively and may be revoked or modified by subsequent rulings or procedures, Regulations, legislation, or court decisions.

---

[11]§ 7805(a).

Revenue Rulings and Revenue Procedures are published weekly by the U.S. Government in the *Internal Revenue Bulletin* (I.R.B.). Semiannually, the bulletins for a six-month period are gathered together and published in a bound volume called the *Cumulative Bulletin* (C.B.).[12] The proper form for citing Revenue Rulings and Revenue Procedures depends on whether the item has been published in the *Cumulative Bulletin* or is only available in I.R.B. form. Consider, for example, the following transition:

Temporary Citation
{ Rev.Rul. 2010–19, I.R.B. No. 31, 174.
Explanation: Revenue Ruling Number 19, appearing on page 174 of the 31st weekly issue of the *Internal Revenue Bulletin* for 2010.

Permanent Citation
{ Rev.Rul. 2010–19, 2010–2 C.B. 174.
Explanation: Revenue Ruling Number 19, appearing on page 174 of Volume 2 of the *Cumulative Bulletin* for 2010.

Note that the page reference of 174 is the same for both the I.R.B. (temporary) and C.B. (permanent) versions of the ruling. The IRS numbers the pages of the I.R.B.'s consecutively for each six-month period so as to facilitate their conversion to C.B. form. Revenue Rulings and other tax resources may be found on Tax Almanac, a free online resource from Intuit at **www.taxalmanac.org**.

Revenue Procedures are cited in the same manner, except that "Rev.Proc." is substituted for "Rev.Rul." Some recent Revenue Procedures dealt with the following matters:

- Where and how to mail forms or returns that seek a prompt refund.
- Guidance on the U.S. and area medium gross income figures needed by issuers of qualified mortgage bonds and mortgage credit certificates.
- The 2011 inflation-adjusted amounts for Health Savings Accounts.

Letter Rulings

Letter rulings are issued for a fee upon a taxpayer's request and describe how the IRS will treat a *proposed* transaction for tax purposes. They apply only to the taxpayer who asks for and obtains the ruling, but post-1984 letter rulings may be substantial authority for purposes of the accuracy-related penalty.[13] Letter rulings can be useful to taxpayers who wish to be certain of how a transaction will be taxed before proceeding with it. Letter rulings also allow taxpayers to avoid unexpected tax costs. Although the procedure for requesting a ruling can be quite cumbersome, sometimes requesting a ruling is the most effective way to carry out tax planning. Nevertheless, the IRS limits the issuance of individual rulings to restricted, preannounced areas of taxation. The main reason the IRS will not rule in certain areas is that they involve fact-oriented situations. Thus, a ruling may not be obtained on many of the problems that are particularly troublesome for taxpayers.[14] The IRS issues more than 2,000 letter rulings each year.

The law now requires the IRS to make individual rulings available for public inspection after identifying details are deleted.[15] Published digests of private letter rulings can be found in *Private Letter Rulings* (published by RIA), BNA's *Daily Tax Reports*, and Tax Analysts *Tax Notes*. In addition, computerized databases of letter rulings are available through several private publishers.

---

[12]Usually, only two volumes of the *Cumulative Bulletin* are published each year. However, in the past, when Congress has enacted major tax legislation, other volumes have been published containing the congressional Committee Reports supporting the Revenue Act. See, for example, the two extra volumes for 1984 dealing with the Deficit Reduction Act of 1984. The 1984–3 *Cumulative Bulletin*, Volume 1, contains the text of the law itself; 1984–3, Volume 2, contains the Committee Reports. There are a total of four volumes of the *Cumulative Bulletin* for 1984: 1984–1; 1984–2; 1984–3, Volume 1; 1984–3, Volume 2.

[13]Notice 90–20, 1990–1 C.B. 328. In this regard, letter rulings differ from Revenue Rulings, which are applicable to *all* taxpayers. A letter ruling may later

lead to the issuance of a Revenue Ruling if the holding affects many taxpayers. In its Agents' Manual, the IRS indicates that letter rulings may be used as a guide with other research materials in formulating a District Office position on an issue. The IRS is required to charge a taxpayer a fee for letter rulings, determination letters, etc.

[14]Rev.Proc. 2011–1, I.R.B. No. 1, 1 contains a list of areas in which the IRS will not issue advance rulings. From time to time, subsequent Revenue Procedures are issued that modify or amplify Rev.Proc. 2011–1.

[15]§ 6110.

Letter rulings are issued multidigit file numbers, which indicate the year and week of issuance as well as the number of the ruling during that week. Consider, for example, Ltr.Rul. 201008049, which provides the tax consequences of the disposition of the assets of two Individual Retirement Accounts (IRAs) previously held by a decedent.

2010	08	049
Year 2010	8th week of issuance	49th ruling issued during the 8th week

Other Administrative Pronouncements

Treasury Decisions (TDs) are issued by the Treasury Department to promulgate new Regulations, amend or otherwise change existing Regulations, or announce the position of the Government on selected court decisions. Like Revenue Rulings and Revenue Procedures, TDs are published in the *Internal Revenue Bulletin* and subsequently transferred to the *Cumulative Bulletin.*

The IRS also publishes other administrative communications in the *Internal Revenue Bulletin* such as Announcements, Notices, IRs (News Releases), Legal Memoranda (ILMs), Chief Counsel Notices (CC), and Prohibited Transaction Exemptions.

Like letter rulings, **determination letters** are issued at the request of taxpayers and provide guidance on the application of the tax law. They differ from letter rulings in that the issuing source is the Area Director rather than the National Office of the IRS. Also, determination letters usually involve *completed* (as opposed to proposed) transactions. Determination letters are not published and are made known only to the party making the request.

The following examples illustrate the distinction between letter rulings and determination letters:

EXAMPLE 1

The shareholders of Red Corporation and Green Corporation want assurance that the consolidation of the corporations into Blue Corporation will be a nontaxable reorganization. The proper approach is to request that the National Office of the IRS issue a letter ruling concerning the income tax effect of the proposed transaction. ■

EXAMPLE 2

Chris operates a barber shop in which he employs eight barbers. To comply with the rules governing income tax and payroll tax withholdings, Chris wants to know whether the barbers working for him are employees or independent contractors. The proper procedure is to request a determination letter on their status from the appropriate Area Director. ■

Several internal memoranda that constitute the working law of the IRS now must be released. These General Counsel Memoranda (GCMs), Technical Advice Memoranda (TAMs), and Field Service Advices (FSAs) are not officially published, and the IRS indicates that they may not be cited as precedents by taxpayers.[16] However, these working documents do explain the IRS's position on various issues.

The National Office of the IRS releases **Technical Advice Memoranda (TAMs)** weekly. TAMs resemble letter rulings in that they give the IRS's determination of an issue. However, they differ in several respects. Letter rulings deal with proposed transactions and are issued to taxpayers at their request. In contrast, TAMs deal with completed transactions. Furthermore, TAMs arise from questions raised by IRS personnel during audits and are issued by the National Office of the IRS to its field personnel. TAMs are often requested for questions relating to exempt organizations

---

[16]These are unofficially published by the publishers listed in Exhibit 2.1. Such internal memoranda for post-1984 transactions may be substantial authority for purposes of the accuracy-related penalty. Notice 90–20, 1990–1 C.B. 328.

and employee plans. TAMs are not officially published and may not be cited or used as precedent.[17] They are assigned file numbers according to the same procedure used for letter rulings. For example, TAM 201005061 refers to the 61st TAM issued during the 5th week of 2010.

The Office of Chief Counsel prepares Field Service Advice (FSAs) to help IRS employees. They are issued in response to requests for advice, guidance, and analysis on difficult or significant tax issues. FSAs are not binding on either the taxpayer to whom they pertain or on the IRS. For example, FSA 200233016 states that § 269 may be used to disallow foreign tax credits and deductions that arise from a series of reorganizations if the underlying transaction's principal purpose is to secure tax benefits.

Field Service Advices are being replaced by a new form of field guidance called Technical Expedited Advice Memoranda (TEAMs). The purpose of TEAMs is to expedite legal guidance to field agents as disputes are developing. FSAs are reverting to their original purpose of case-specific development of facts.

A TEAM guidance differs from a TAM in several ways, including a mandatory pre-submission conference involving the taxpayer. In the event of a tentatively adverse conclusion for the taxpayer or the field, a conference of right is offered to the taxpayer and to the field; once the conference of right is held, no further conferences are offered.

JUDICIAL SOURCES OF THE TAX LAW

The Judicial Process in General

After a taxpayer has exhausted some or all of the remedies available within the IRS (i.e., no satisfactory settlement has been reached at the agent or at the Appeals Division level), the dispute can be taken to the Federal courts. The dispute is first considered by a **court of original jurisdiction** (known as a trial court) with any appeal (either by the taxpayer or the IRS) taken to the appropriate appellate court. In most situations, the taxpayer has a choice of any of *four trial courts:* a **Federal District Court**, the **U.S. Court of Federal Claims**, the **U.S. Tax Court**, or the **Small Cases Division** of the U.S. Tax Court. The trial and appellate court system for Federal tax litigation is illustrated in Figure 2.3.

The broken line between the U.S. Tax Court and the Small Cases Division indicates that there is no appeal from the Small Cases Division. The jurisdiction of the Small Cases Division is limited to cases involving amounts of $50,000 or less. The proceedings of the Small Cases Division are informal (e.g., no necessity for the taxpayer to be represented by a lawyer or other tax adviser). Special trial judges rather than Tax Court judges preside over these proceedings. The decisions of the Small Cases Division are not precedents for any other court decision and are not reviewable by any higher court. Proceedings can be more timely and less expensive in the Small Cases Division. Some of these cases can now be found on the U.S. Tax Court website.

American law, following English law, is frequently *made* by judicial decisions. Under the doctrine of *stare decisis*, each case (except in the Small Cases Division) has precedential value for future cases with the same controlling set of facts. Most Federal and state appellate court decisions and some decisions of trial courts are published. Published court decisions are organized by jurisdiction (Federal or state) and level of court (trial or appellate).

A decision of a particular court is called its holding. Sometimes a decision includes dicta or incidental opinions beyond the current facts. Such passing remarks, illustrations, or analogies are not essential to the current holding. Although the holding has precedential value under *stare decisis*, dicta are not binding on a future court.

---

[17]§ 6110(j)(3). Post-1984 TAMs may be substantial authority for purposes of avoiding the accuracy-related penalty. Notice 90–20, 1990–1 C.B. 328.

FIGURE 2.3   Federal Judicial System

Knowledge of several terms is important in understanding court decisions. The term *plaintiff* refers to the party requesting action in a court, and the *defendant* is the party against whom the suit is brought. Sometimes a court uses the terms *petitioner* and *respondent*. In general, "petitioner" is a synonym for "plaintiff," and "respondent" is a synonym for "defendant." At the trial court level, a taxpayer is normally the plaintiff (or petitioner), and the Government is the defendant (or respondent). If the taxpayer wins and the Government appeals as the new petitioner (or appellant), the taxpayer becomes the new respondent.

Trial Courts

The differences among the various trial courts (courts of original jurisdiction) can be summarized as follows:

- *Number of courts.* There is only one Court of Federal Claims and only one Tax Court, but there are many Federal District Courts. The taxpayer does not select the District Court that will hear the dispute but must sue in the one that has jurisdiction where the taxpayer resides.
- *Number of judges.* District Courts have various numbers of judges, but only one judge hears a case. The Court of Federal Claims has 16 judges, and the Tax Court has 19 regular judges. The entire Tax Court, however, reviews a case (the case is sent to court conference) only when more important or novel tax issues are involved. Most cases are heard and decided by one of the 19 judges.
- *Location.* The Court of Federal Claims meets most often in Washington, D.C., whereas a District Court meets at a prescribed seat for the particular district. Each state has at least one District Court, and many of the more populous states have more than one. Choosing the District Court usually minimizes the inconvenience and expense of traveling for the taxpayer and his or her counsel. Although the Tax Court is officially based in Washington, D.C., the various judges travel to different parts of the country and hear cases at predetermined locations and dates. This procedure eases the distance problem for the taxpayer, but it can mean a delay before the case comes to trial and is decided.
- *Jurisdiction of the Court of Federal Claims.* The Court of Federal Claims has jurisdiction over any claim against the United States that is based upon the

Constitution, any Act of Congress, or any regulation of an executive department. Thus, the Court of Federal Claims hears nontax litigation as well as tax cases. This forum appears to be more favorable for issues having an equitable or pro-business orientation (as opposed to purely technical issues) and for those requiring extensive discovery.[18]

- *Jurisdiction of the Tax Court and District Courts.* The Tax Court hears only tax cases and is the most popular forum. The District Courts hear a wide variety of nontax cases, including drug crimes and other Federal violations, as well as tax cases. Some Tax Court judges have been appointed from IRS or Treasury Department positions. For these reasons, some people suggest that the Tax Court has more expertise in tax matters.

- *Jury trial.* The only court in which a taxpayer can obtain a jury trial is a District Court. But since juries can only decide questions of fact and not questions of law, even taxpayers who choose the District Court route often do not request a jury trial. In that event, the judge will decide all issues. Note that a District Court decision is controlling only in the district in which the court has jurisdiction.

- *Payment of deficiency.* For the Court of Federal Claims or a District Court to have jurisdiction, the taxpayer must pay the tax deficiency assessed by the IRS and sue for a refund. A taxpayer who wins (assuming no successful appeal by the Government) recovers the tax paid plus appropriate interest. For the Tax Court, however, jurisdiction is usually obtained without first paying the assessed tax deficiency. In the event the taxpayer loses in the Tax Court (and does not appeal or an appeal is unsuccessful), the deficiency must be paid with appropriate interest. With the elimination of the deduction for personal (consumer) interest, the Tax Court route of delaying payment of the deficiency can become expensive. For example, to earn 7 percent after tax in 2011, a taxpayer with a 35 percent marginal tax rate would have to earn 10.77 percent. By paying the tax, a taxpayer limits underpayment interest and penalties on the underpayment.

- *Termination of running of interest.* A taxpayer who selects the Tax Court may deposit a cash bond to stop the running of interest. The taxpayer must deposit both the amount of the tax and any accrued interest. If the taxpayer wins and the deposited amount is returned, the Government does not pay interest on the deposit.

- *Appeals.* Appeals from a District Court or a Tax Court decision are to the U.S. Court of Appeals for the circuit in which the taxpayer resides. Appeals from the Court of Federal Claims go to the Court of Appeals for the Federal

---

[18]T. D. Peyser, "The Case for Selecting the Claims Court to Litigate a Federal Tax Liability," *The Tax Executive* (Winter 1988): 149.

CONCEPT SUMMARY   2.1

Federal Judicial System: Trial Courts

Issue	U.S. Tax Court	U.S. District Court	U.S. Court of Federal Claims
Number of judges per court	19*	Varies	16
Payment of deficiency before trial	No	Yes	Yes
Jury trial available	No	Yes	No
Types of disputes	Tax cases only	Most criminal and civil issues	Claims against the United States
Jurisdiction	Nationwide	Location of taxpayer	Nationwide
IRS acquiescence policy	Yes	Yes	Yes
Appeal route	U.S. Court of Appeals	U.S. Court of Appeals	U.S. Court of Appeals for the Federal Circuit

*There are also 14 special trial judges and 9 senior judges.

Circuit. Few Tax Court cases are appealed, and when appeals are made, most are filed by the taxpayer rather than the IRS.

- *Bankruptcy.* When a taxpayer files a bankruptcy petition, the IRS, like other creditors, is prevented from taking action against the taxpayer. Sometimes a bankruptcy court may settle a tax claim.

For a summary of the Federal trial courts, see Concept Summary 2.1.

Appellate Courts

The losing party can appeal a trial court decision to a **Circuit Court of Appeals**. The 11 geographic circuits, the circuit for the District of Columbia, and the Federal Circuit[19] appear in Figure 2.4. The appropriate circuit for an appeal depends on where the litigation originated. For example, an appeal from New York goes to the Second Circuit.

If the Government loses at the trial court level (District Court, Tax Court, or Court of Federal Claims), it need not (frequently does not) appeal. The fact that an appeal is not made, however, does not indicate that the IRS agrees with the result and will not litigate similar issues in the future. The IRS may decide not to appeal for a number of reasons. First, if the current litigation load is heavy, the IRS may decide that available personnel should be assigned to other, more important cases. Second, the IRS may determine that this case is not a good one to appeal. Perhaps the taxpayer is in a sympathetic position or the facts are particularly strong in his or her favor. In that event, the IRS may wait to test the legal issues involved with a taxpayer who has a much weaker case. Third, if the appeal is from a District Court or the Tax Court, the Court of Appeals of jurisdiction could have some bearing on whether the IRS chooses to go forward with an appeal. Based on past experience and precedent, the IRS may conclude that the chance for success on a particular issue might be more promising in another Court of Appeals. If so, the IRS will wait for a similar case to arise in a different jurisdiction.

The Federal Circuit at the appellate level provides the taxpayer with an alternative forum to the Court of Appeals for his or her home circuit. Appeals from both the Tax Court and the District Court go to a taxpayer's home circuit. When a particular

---

[19]The Court of Appeals for the Federal Circuit was created, effective October 1, 1982, by P.L. No. 97-164 (4/2/82) to hear decisions appealed from the Claims Court (now the Court of Federal Claims).

FIGURE 2.4	The Federal Courts of Appeals

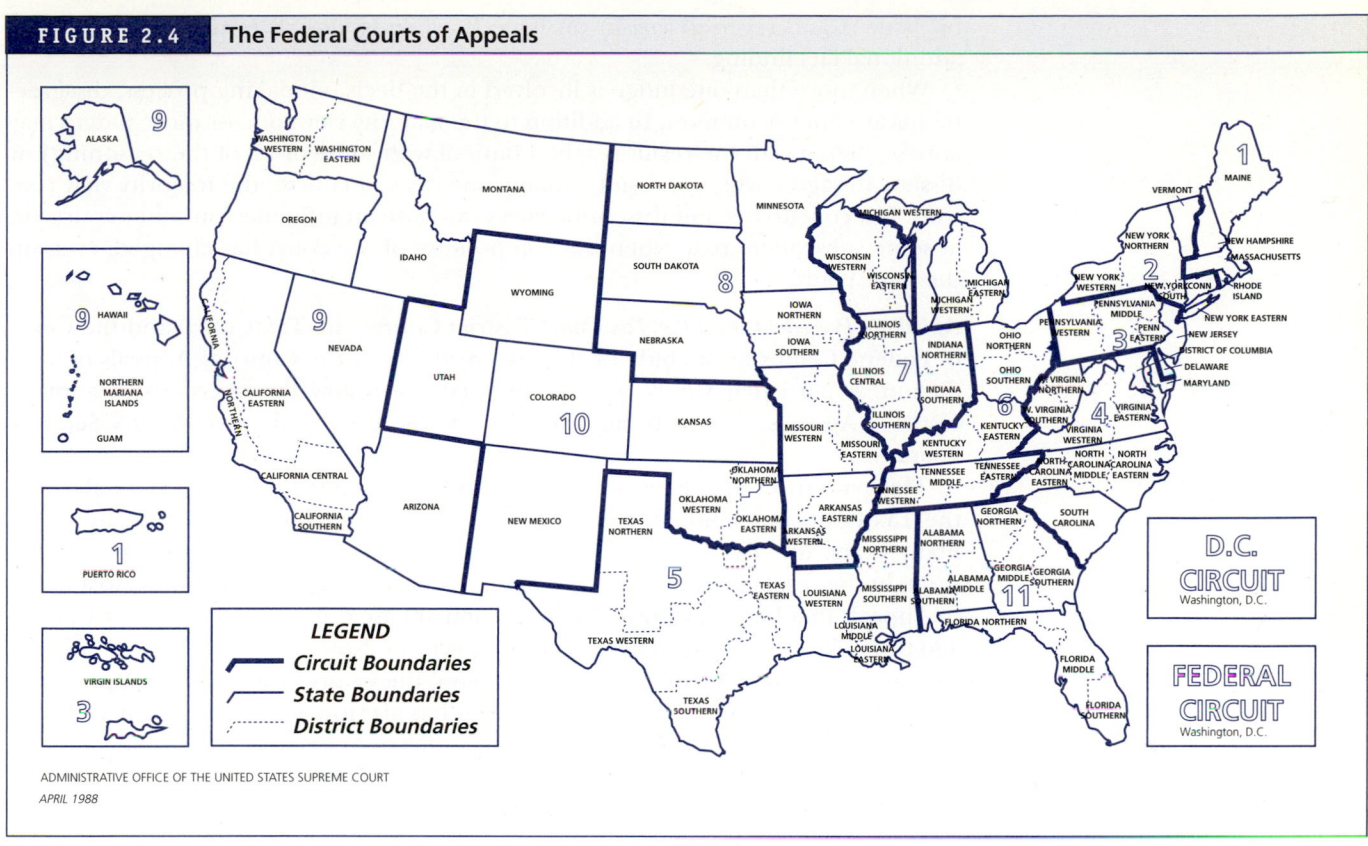

ADMINISTRATIVE OFFICE OF THE UNITED STATES SUPREME COURT
APRIL 1988

circuit has issued an adverse decision, the taxpayer may prefer the Court of Federal Claims route, since any appeal will be to the Federal Circuit.

The Appellate Process

The *role* of the appellate courts is limited to a review of the record of trial compiled by the trial courts. Thus, the appellate process usually involves a determination of whether the trial court applied the proper law in arriving at its decision. Rarely will an appellate court disturb a lower court's fact-finding determination.

Both the Code and the Supreme Court indicate that Federal appellate courts are bound by findings of facts unless they are clearly erroneous.[20] This aspect of the appellate process is illustrated by a decision of the Court of Appeals for the District of Columbia involving whether a taxpayer was engaged in an activity for profit under § 183.[21] This appeals court specifically held that the "Tax Court's findings of facts are binding on Federal courts of appeals unless clearly erroneous." The court applauded the Tax Court for the thoroughness of its factual inquiry but could "not place the stamp of approval upon its eventual legal outcome." In reversing and remanding the decision to the Tax Court, the appellate court said that "the language of § 183, its legislative history and the applicable Treasury regulation combine to demonstrate that the court's [Tax Court's] standard is erroneous as a matter of law." The appeals court held that this taxpayer's claims of deductibility were to be evaluated by proper legal standards.

An appeal can have any of a number of possible outcomes. The appellate court may approve (affirm) or disapprove (reverse) the lower court's finding, or it may send the case back for further consideration (remand). When many issues are involved, a mixed result is not unusual. Thus, the lower court may be affirmed (*aff'd*)

---

[20]§§ 7482(a) and (c). *Comm. v. Duberstein*, 60–2 USTC ¶9515, 5 AFTR 2d 1626, 80 S.Ct. 1190 (USSC, 1960). See Rule 52(a) of the Federal Rules of Civil Procedure.

[21]*Dreicer v. Comm.*, 81–2 USTC ¶9683, 48 AFTR 2d 5884, 665 F.2d 1292 (CA–DC, 1981).

on Issue A and reversed (*rev'd*) on Issue B, while Issue C is remanded (*rem'd*) for additional fact finding.

When more than one judge is involved in the decision-making process, disagreements are not uncommon. In addition to the majority view, one or more judges may concur (agree with the result reached but not with some or all of the reasoning) or dissent (disagree with the result). In any one case, of course, the majority view controls. But concurring and dissenting views can have an influence on other courts or, at some subsequent date when the composition of the court has changed, even on the same court.

Appellate Precedents and the Tax Court District Courts, the Tax Court, and the Court of Federal Claims must abide by the **precedents** set by the Court of Appeals of jurisdiction. A particular Court of Appeals need not follow the decisions of another Court of Appeals. All courts, however, must follow the decisions of the **U.S. Supreme Court**.

This pattern of appellate precedents raises an issue for the Tax Court. Because the Tax Court is a national court, it decides cases from all parts of the country. For many years, the Tax Court followed a policy of deciding cases based on what it thought the result should be, even though its decision might be appealed to a Court of Appeals that had previously decided a similar case differently. A number of years ago this policy was changed in the *Golsen*[22] decision. Now the Tax Court will decide a case as it feels the law should be applied *only* if the Court of Appeals of appropriate jurisdiction has not yet passed on the issue or has previously decided a similar case in accord with the Tax Court's decision. If the Court of Appeals of appropriate jurisdiction has previously held otherwise, the Tax Court will conform under the *Golsen* rule even though it disagrees with the holding.

EXAMPLE 3	Emily lives in Texas and sues in the Tax Court on Issue A. The Fifth Circuit Court of Appeals is the appellate court of appropriate jurisdiction. It has already decided, in a case involving similar facts but a different taxpayer, that Issue A should be resolved against the Government. Although the Tax Court feels that the Fifth Circuit Court of Appeals is wrong, under its *Golsen* policy it will render judgment for Emily. Shortly thereafter, Rashad, a resident of New York, in a comparable case, sues in the Tax Court on Issue A. Assume that the Second Circuit Court of Appeals, the appellate court of appropriate jurisdiction, has never expressed itself on Issue A. Presuming the Tax Court has not reconsidered its position on Issue A, it will decide against Rashad. Thus, it is entirely possible for two taxpayers suing in the same court to end up with opposite results merely because they live in different parts of the country. ∎

Appeal to the U.S. Supreme Court Appeal to the U.S. Supreme Court is by **Writ of Certiorari**. If the Court agrees to hear the case, it will grant the Writ (*Cert. granted*). Most often, it will deny jurisdiction (*Cert. denied*). For whatever reason or reasons, the Supreme Court rarely hears tax cases. The Court usually grants certiorari to resolve a conflict among the Courts of Appeals (e.g., two or more appellate courts have assumed opposing positions on a particular issue) or where the tax issue is extremely important. The granting of a Writ of Certiorari indicates that at least four members of the Supreme Court believe that the issue is of sufficient importance to be heard by the full Court.

Judicial Citations

LO.2

Locate and work with the appropriate tax law sources.

Having briefly described the judicial process, it is appropriate to consider the more practical problem of the relationship of case law to tax research. As previously noted, court decisions are an important source of tax law. The ability to cite and locate a case is, therefore, a must in working with the tax law. Judicial citations usually follow

---

[22]*Jack E. Golsen,* 54 T.C. 742 (1970).

a standard pattern: case name, volume number, reporter series, page or paragraph number, court (where necessary), and the year of the decision.

Judicial Citations—The U.S. Tax Court A good starting point is with the Tax Court. The Tax Court issues two types of decisions: Regular and Memorandum. The Chief Judge decides whether the opinion is issued as a Regular or Memorandum decision. The distinction between the two involves both substance and form. In terms of substance, *Memorandum* decisions deal with situations necessitating only the application of already established principles of law. *Regular* decisions involve novel issues not previously resolved by the court. In actual practice, however, this distinction is not always preserved. Not infrequently, Memorandum decisions will be encountered that appear to warrant Regular status and vice versa. At any rate, do not conclude that Memorandum decisions possess no value as precedents. Both represent the position of the Tax Court and, as such, can be relied on.

The Regular and Memorandum decisions issued by the Tax Court also differ in form. Memorandum decisions are made available but are not published by the government. Regular decisions are published by the U.S. Government in a series entitled *Tax Court of the United States Reports* (T.C.). Each volume of these *Reports* covers a six-month period (January 1 through June 30 and July 1 through December 31) and is given a succeeding volume number. But there is usually a time lag between the date a decision is rendered and the date it appears in bound form. A temporary citation may be necessary to help the researcher locate a recent Regular decision. Consider, for example, the temporary and permanent citations for *Larry G. Mitchell*, a decision filed on December 15, 2008:

Temporary Citation	{ *Larry G. Mitchell*, 131 T.C. ___, No. 15 (2008).
	Explanation: Page number left blank because not yet known.
Permanent Citation	{ *Larry G. Mitchell*, 131 T.C. 215 (2008).
	Explanation: Page number now available.

Both citations tell us that the case will ultimately appear in Volume 131 of the *Tax Court of the United States Reports*. But until this volume is bound and made available to the general public, the page number must be left blank. Instead, the temporary citation identifies the case as being the 15th Regular decision issued by the Tax Court since Volume 130 ended. With this information, the decision can easily be located in either of the special Tax Court services published by Commerce Clearing House (now owned by the Dutch company Wolters Kluwer) or Research Institute of America (formerly by Prentice-Hall). Once Volume 131 is released, the permanent citation can be substituted and the number of the case dropped. Starting in 1999, both Regular decisions and Memorandum decisions are published on the U.S. Tax Court website (**www.ustaxcourt.gov**).

Before 1943, the Tax Court was called the Board of Tax Appeals, and its decisions were published as the *United States Board of Tax Appeals Reports* (B.T.A.). These 47 volumes cover the period from 1924 to 1942. For example, the citation *Karl Pauli*, 11 B.T.A. 784 (1928), refers to the 11th volume of the *Board of Tax Appeals Reports*, page 784, issued in 1928.

If the IRS loses in a decision, it may indicate whether it agrees or disagrees with the results reached by the court by publishing an **acquiescence** ("A" or "*Acq.*") or **nonacquiescence** ("NA" or "*Nonacq.*"), respectively. Until 1991, acquiescences and nonacquiescences were published only for certain Regular decisions of the Tax Court, but the IRS has expanded its acquiescence program to include other civil tax cases where guidance is helpful. The acquiescence or nonacquiescence is published in the *Internal Revenue Bulletin* and the *Cumulative Bulletin* as an *Action on Decision*. The IRS can retroactively revoke an acquiescence.

Most often the IRS issues nonacquiescences to adverse decisions that are not appealed. In this manner, the Government indicates that it disagrees with the result reached, despite its decision not to seek review of the matter in an appellate court. A nonacquiescence provides a warning to taxpayers that a similar case cannot be settled administratively. A taxpayer will incur fees and expenses appealing within the IRS even though the IRS may be unwilling to litigate a fact pattern similar to a nonacquiescence decision.[23]

Although Memorandum decisions were not published by the U.S. Government until recently (they are now published on the U.S. Tax Court website), they were— and continue to be—published by Commerce Clearing House (CCH) and Research Institute of America (RIA [formerly by Prentice-Hall]). Consider, for example, the three different ways that *Nick R. Hughes* can be cited:

> *Nick R. Hughes*, T.C.Memo. 2009–94
> The 94th Memorandum decision issued by the Tax Court in 2009.
> *Nick R. Hughes*, 97 TCM 1488
> Page 1488 of Vol. 97 of the CCH *Tax Court Memorandum Decisions.*
> *Nick R. Hughes*, 2009 RIA T.C.Memo. ¶2009,094
> Paragraph 2009,094 of the RIA *T.C. Memorandum Decisions.*

Note that the third citation contains the same information as the first. Thus, ¶2009,094 indicates the following information about the case: year 2009, 94th T.C.Memo. decision. Before the Prentice-Hall Information Services division was incorporated into Research Institute of America, "P-H" was used instead of "RIA" for the third citation.[24]

U.S. Tax Court Summary Opinions relate to decisions of the Tax Court's Small Cases Division. These opinions are published commercially, and on the U.S. Tax Court website, with the warning that they may not be treated as precedent for any other case. For example, *Howard Slater*, filed on January 11, 2010, is cited as follows:

> *Howard Slater*, T.C. Summary Opinion 2010–1.

In 2005, the U.S. Supreme Court held that decisions of the Small Cases Division must be made public.

Judicial Citations—The U.S. District Court, Court of Federal Claims, and Courts of Appeals District Court, Court of Federal Claims, Courts of Appeals, and Supreme Court decisions dealing with Federal tax matters are reported in both the CCH *U.S. Tax Cases* (USTC) and the RIA *American Federal Tax Reports* (AFTR) series. Federal District Court decisions, dealing with *both* tax and nontax issues, also are published by West (owned by Thomson Reuters) in its *Federal Supplement Series* (F.Supp.). Volume 999, published in 1998, is the last volume of the *Federal Supplement Series*. It is followed by the *Federal Supplement Second Series* (F.Supp.2d). The following examples illustrate three different ways of citing a District Court case:

> *Turner v. U.S.*, 2004–1 USTC ¶60,478 (D.Ct. Tex., 2004).
> *Explanation:* Reported in the first volume of the *U.S. Tax Cases* published by Commerce Clearing House for calendar year 2004 (2004–1) and located at paragraph 60,478 (¶60,478).
>
> *Turner v. U.S.*, 93 AFTR 2d 2004–686 (D.Ct. Tex., 2004).
> *Explanation:* Reported in the 93rd volume of the second series of the *American Federal Tax Reports* (AFTR 2d) published by RIA and beginning on page 686.
>
> *Turner v. U.S.*, 306 F.Supp.2d 668 (D.Ct. Tex., 2004).
> *Explanation:* Reported in the 306th volume of the *Federal Supplement Second Series* (F.Supp.2d) published by West and beginning on page 668.

---

[23]G. W. Carter, "Nonacquiescence: Winning by Losing," *Tax Notes* (September 19, 1988): 1301–1307.

[24]In this text, the RIA citation for Memorandum decisions of the U.S. Tax Court is omitted. Thus, *Nick R. Hughes* will be cited as. 97 TCM 1488, T.C. Memo. 2009–94.

In all of the preceding citations, note that the name of the case is the same (Turner being the taxpayer), as is the reference to the Federal District Court of Texas (D.Ct. Tex.) and the year the decision was rendered (2004).[25]

Decisions of the Court of Federal Claims[26] and the Courts of Appeals are published in the USTCs, AFTRs, and a West reporter called the *Federal Second Series* (F.2d). Volume 999, published in 1993, is the last volume of the *Federal Second Series*. It is followed by the *Federal Third Series* (F.3d). Beginning with October 1982, the Court of Federal Claims decisions are published in another West reporter entitled the *Claims Court Reporter* (abbreviated Cl.Ct.). Beginning with Volume 27 on October 30, 1992, the name of the reporter changed to the *Federal Claims Reporter* (abbreviated as Fed.Cl.). The following examples illustrate the different forms:

Note that *Estate of Gribauskas v. Comm.* is a decision rendered by the Second Circuit Court of Appeals in 2003 (CA–2, 2003), while *Apollo Computer, Inc.* was issued by the Court of Federal Claims in 1994 (Fed.Cl., 1994).

Judicial Citations—The U.S. Supreme Court Like all other Federal tax decisions (except those rendered by the Tax Court), Supreme Court decisions are published by Commerce Clearing House in the USTCs and by RIA in the AFTRs. The U.S. Government Printing Office also publishes these decisions in the *United States Supreme Court Reports* (U.S.) as does West in its *Supreme Court Reporter* (S.Ct.) and the Lawyer's Co-operative Publishing Company in its *United States Reports, Lawyer's Edition* (L.Ed.). The following illustrates the different ways the same decision can be cited:

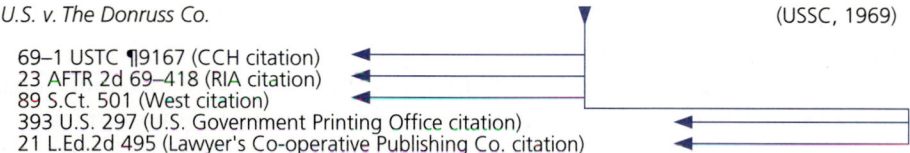

The parenthetical reference (USSC, 1969) identifies the decision as having been rendered by the U.S. Supreme Court in 1969. In this text, the citations of Supreme Court decisions will be limited to the CCH (USTC), RIA (AFTR), and West (S.Ct.) versions. For a summary, see Concept Summary 2.2.

OTHER SOURCES OF THE TAX LAW

Other sources of tax information that a tax practitioner may need to consult include tax treaties and tax periodicals.

---

[25]In this text, the case would be cited in the following form: *Turner v. U.S.*, 2004–1 USTC ¶60,478, 93 AFTR 2d 2004–686, 306 F.Supp.2d 668 (D.Ct. Tex., 2004). Prentice-Hall Information Services is now owned by Research Institute of America. Although recent volumes contain the RIA imprint, many of the older volumes continue to have the P-H imprint.

[26]Before October 29, 1992, the Court of Federal Claims was called the Claims Court. Before October 1, 1982, the Court of Federal Claims was called the Court of Claims.

GLOBAL
Tax Issues

TAX TREATIES

The United States has entered into treaties with most of the major countries of the world in order to eliminate possible double taxation. For example, nonresident alien students wishing to claim exemption from taxation are required to provide an information statement as set forth in several Revenue Procedures. The withholding agent must also certify the form.

Chinese students are required to prepare a four-part statement. Part 3 of the student's statement is as follows:

> I will receive compensation for personal services performed in the United States. This compensation qualifies for exemption from withholding of Federal income tax under the tax treaty between the United States and the People's Republic of China in an amount not in excess of $5,000 for any taxable year.

Tax Treaties

The United States signs certain tax treaties (sometimes called tax conventions) with foreign countries to render mutual assistance in tax enforcement and to avoid double taxation. Tax legislation enacted in 1988 provided that neither a tax law nor a tax treaty takes general precedence. Thus, when there is a direct conflict, the most recent item will take precedence. A taxpayer must disclose on the tax return any position where a treaty overrides a tax law.[27] There is a $1,000 penalty per failure to disclose for individuals and a $10,000 per failure penalty for corporations.[28]

Tax Periodicals

The use of tax periodicals can often shorten the research time needed to resolve a tax issue. If the article is relevant to the issue at hand, it may provide the references needed to locate the primary sources of the tax law that apply (e.g., citations to judicial decisions, Regulations, and other IRS pronouncements). Thus, the researcher obtains a "running start" in arriving at a solution to the problem.

Among the many indexes available for locating tax articles pertinent to a tax problem is Commerce Clearing House's *Federal Tax Articles*. This multivolume service includes a subject index, a Code Section number index, and an author's index.

Another is the *Index to Federal Tax Articles* (published by Warren, Gorham, and Lamont). Both of these indexes are updated periodically, but are available only in print form.

The following are some of the more useful tax periodicals:

Journal of Taxation
Journal of International Taxation
Practical Tax Strategies
Estate Planning
Corporate Taxation
Business Entities
ria.thomsonreuters.com/Journals

The Tax Executive
www.tei.org

The Tax Adviser
aicpa.org/pubs/taxadv

Tax Law Review
www.law.nyu.edu/llmjsd/tax/ taxlawreview/ECM_DLV_005627

Journal of the American Taxation Association
aaahq.org/ata/_ATAMenu/ ATAPubJATA.html

The ATA Journal of Legal Tax Research
aaahq.org/ata/_ATAMenu/ ATAPubJLTR.html

---

[27]§ 7852(d).   [28]Reg. §§ 301.6114–1, 301.6712–1, and 301.7701(b)(7).

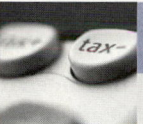

CONCEPT SUMMARY 2.2

Judicial Sources

Court	Location	Authority
U.S. Supreme Court	S.Ct. Series (West)	Highest authority
	U.S. Series (U.S. Gov't.)	
	L.Ed.2d (Lawyer's Co-op.)	
	AFTR (RIA)	
	USTC (CCH)	
U.S. Courts of Appeal	Federal 3d (West)	Next highest appellate court
	AFTR (RIA)	
	USTC (CCH)	
Tax Court (Regular decisions)	U.S. Gov't. Printing Office	Highest trial court*
	RIA/CCH separate services	
Tax Court (Memorandum decisions)	RIA T.C.Memo. (RIA)	Less authority than Regular T.C. decision
	TCM (CCH)	
U.S. Court of Federal Claims**	Federal Claims Reporter (West)	Similar authority as Tax Court
	AFTR (RIA)	
	USTC (CCH)	
U.S. District Courts	F.Supp.2d Series (West)	Lowest trial court
	AFTR (RIA)	
	USTC (CCH)	
Small Cases Division of Tax Court	U.S. Tax Court website***	No precedent value

*Theoretically, the Tax Court, Court of Federal Claims, and District Courts are on the same level of authority. But some people believe that since the Tax Court hears and decides tax cases from all parts of the country (i.e., it is a national court), its decisions may be more authoritative than a Court of Federal Claims or District Court decision.
**Before October 29, 1992, the U.S. Claims Court.
***Starting in 2001.

Oil, Gas & Energy Quarterly
**www.bus.lsu.edu/accounting/faculty/
lcrumbley/oilgas.html**

Journal of Passthrough Entities
TAXES—The Tax Magazine
tax.cchgroup.com/Books

Trusts and Estates
trustsandestates.com

Tax Notes
taxanalysts.com

2.2 WORKING WITH THE TAX LAW— TAX RESEARCH TOOLS

Tax law consists of a body of legislative (e.g., Code Sections, tax treaties), administrative (e.g., Regulations, Rulings), and judicial (e.g., court cases) pronouncements. Working with the tax law requires being able to effectively locate and use these sources. A key consideration is the time required to carry out this research and finding activity.

Unless the problem is simple (e.g., the Code Section is known, and there is a Regulation on point), the research process should begin with a tax service.

> **LO.3**
> Have an awareness of tax research tools.

COMMERCIAL TAX SERVICES

Due to various changes, categorizing tax services has become an almost impossible task. Previously, services could be classified as *annotated* (i.e., organized by Internal Revenue Code) or *topical* (i.e., organized by major topics), but this classification system is no longer appropriate for many tax services as their format has been modified. Often the change is due to the acquisition of what was a competing tax service. For example, the *United States Tax Reporter* (annotated) now has a version that contains the *Federal Tax Coordinator 2d* (topical).

Tax services also can no longer be distinguished based on whether they are available only in hard copy or online versions. Previously, for example, *Tax Management Portfolios* was solely a print publication. Now, like most other tax services, it is also accessible online.

In addition, the list of publishers producing the tax services is not the same. Not only have there been ownership changes (e.g., Research Institute of America [RIA] now owns Prentice-Hall [P-H]), but also new players have arrived. LexisNexis for example, through *Tax Center*, offers primary tax services such as the Code and Regulations as well as material obtained from the Matthew Bender and Kleinrock services. Westlaw, due to its common ownership by Thomson, offers the RIA products and also the Mertens service.

Many new tax services have become like automobiles with a version to fit every practitioner's needs and financial resources. At one extreme, an abbreviated version of the regular ("Standard") service (e.g., CCH and its two-volume *Federal Tax Guide*) is designed for those with minimal tax research needs. For others, the basic product can include "extras" (e.g., CCH and its *Federal Excise Tax Reporter*).

A partial list of the available commercial tax services includes:

- *Standard Federal Tax Reporter*, Commerce Clearing House.
- *CCH IntelliConnect*, Commerce Clearing House Internet service.
- *United States Tax Reporter*, Research Institute of America.
- RIA *Checkpoint*, Research Institute of America. The online version of *United States Tax Reporter* also can include the *Federal Tax Coordinator 2d*.
- ATX/Kleinrock *Tax Expert*, CCH/Wolters Kluwer Business services.
- *Tax Management Portfolios*, Bureau of National Affairs.
- *Mertens Law of Federal Income Taxation*, West Group.
- Westlaw services—compilations include access to *Tax Management Portfolios*, *Federal Tax Coordinator 2d*, and *Mertens*.
- *TaxCenter*, LexisNexis compilation of primary sources and various materials taken from CCH, Matthew Bender, Kleinrock, and Bureau of National Affairs.
- *Federal Research Library*, Tax Analysts (a nonprofit organization) databases dealing with explanations and commentaries on primary source materials.

USING ONLINE TAX SERVICES

Instructions on how to use a tax service are not particularly worthwhile unless a specific service is involved. Even here, instructions need to be followed by hands-on experience to be effective. For online versions of a tax service, however, following certain procedures can simplify the research process. Since a practitioner's time is valuable and several research services base usage charges on time spent, time is of the essence.

When the principal emphasis is on time, every shortcut helps. The following suggestions (most of which are familiar to any user of the Internet) may be helpful.[29]

---

[29]For a more complete discussion of the use of RIA *Checkpoint* and CCH *Tax Research NetWork* and Internet research in taxation, see Raabe, Whittenburg, Sanders, and Sawyers, *South-Western's Federal Tax Research*, 9th ed. (Cengage Learning South-Western, 2011), Chapters 6 and 7.

- Choose keywords for the search carefully. Words with a broad usage, such as *income*, are worthless when standing alone. If the researcher is interested in qualified dividend income, even *dividend income* is too broad because it will call up stock dividends, constructive dividends, liquidating dividends, and more. By using *qualified dividend income* at the outset, the search is considerably narrowed. In RIA *Checkpoint*, for example, these two modifications narrowed the search from over 10,000 items to 3,824 and finally to 884. Obviously, further contraction will be needed, but at least the researcher is starting with a considerably smaller number of potential items.

- Take advantage of *connectors* to place parameters on the search and further restrict the output. Although each service has its own set of connectors, many are used by several services. Thus, quotation marks around a phrase mean *exact phrase* in both RIA *Checkpoint* and CCH *NetWork* (e.g., "personal service corporation").

- Be selective in choosing a database. For example, if the research project does not involve case law, there is no point in including the judicial decision component in the search database. Doing so just adds to the output items and will necessitate further screening through a search modification.

- Use a table of contents, index, or citation approach when appropriate. Although the keyword approach is most frequently used, databases can be searched in other ways. Using the table of contents or index is the usual approach with print versions of a tax service. With the citation route, access may be through a statutory (e.g., Code Section), administrative (e.g., Rev.Rul.), or judicial citation (e.g., Tax Court), depending on the tax service. When a judicial citation is involved and only the taxpayer's last name is known, though, problems can arise. For example, how many responses would a taxpayer named Smith yield? Likewise, before a Code Section is used, consider its scope. How many items would § 162 retrieve? Nevertheless, the use of a table of contents, index, or citation approach can be a valuable time-saver under the right circumstances.

NONCOMMERCIAL ONLINE TAX SERVICES

The Internet provides a wealth of tax information in several popular forms, sometimes at no direct cost to the researcher. Using so-called browser software that often is distributed with new computer systems and their communication devices, the tax professional can access information provided around the world that can aid the research process.

- *Home pages (sites) on the Web* are provided by accounting and consulting firms, publishers, tax academics and libraries, and governmental bodies as a means of making information widely available or of soliciting subscriptions or consulting engagements. The best sites offer links to other sites and direct contact to the site providers. One of the best sites available to the tax practitioner is the Internal Revenue Service's home page, illustrated in Exhibit 2.2. This site offers downloadable forms and instructions, "plain English" versions of Regulations, and news update items. Exhibit 2.3 lists some of the websites that may be most useful to tax researchers and their Internet addresses as of press date. Particularly useful is the directory at **taxsites.com**, which provides links to accounting and tax sources (including international as well as payroll).

- *Newsgroups* provide a means by which information related to the tax law can be exchanged among taxpayers, tax professionals, and others who subscribe to the group's services. Newsgroup members can read the exchanges

EXHIBIT 2.2 | **The IRS's Home Page**

among other members and offer replies and suggestions to inquiries as desired. Discussions address the interpretation and application of existing law, analysis of proposals and new pronouncements, and reviews of tax software.

In many situations, solutions to research problems benefit from, or require, the use of various electronic tax research tools. A competent tax professional must become familiar and proficient with these tools and be able to use them to meet the expectations of clients and the necessities of work in the modern world.[30]

2.3 WORKING WITH THE TAX LAW— TAX RESEARCH

LO.4

Understand the tax research process.

Tax research is the method by which a tax practitioner, student, or professor determines the best available solution to a situation that possesses tax consequences. In other words, it is the process of finding a competent and professional conclusion to

---

[30]For a more detailed discussion of the use of electronic tax research in the modern tax practice, see Raabe, Whittenburg, Sanders, and Sawyers, *South-Western's Federal Tax Research*, 9th ed. (Cengage Learning South-Western, 2011).

EXHIBIT 2.3	Tax-Related Websites	

Website	Web Address at Press Date (usually preceded by http://www.)	Description
Accounting firms and professional organizations	For instance, the AICPA's page is at **aicpa.org**, Ernst and Young is at **ey.com**, and KPMG is at **kpmg.com**	Tax planning newsletters, descriptions of services offered and career opportunities, and exchange of data with clients and subscribers
Cengage Learning South-Western	**cengage.com/taxation/swft**	Informational updates, newsletters, support materials for students and adopters, and continuing education
Commercial tax publishers	For instance, **tax.com** and **cch.com**	Information about products and services available for subscription and newsletter excerpts
Court opinions	The site at **lexisone.com/lx1/caselaw/freecaselaw** covers some state, Federal circuit (last 10 years), and Supreme Court (all years) decisions but not the Tax Court	Provides a synopsis of result reached by the court
Internal Revenue Service	**irs.gov**	News releases, downloadable forms and instructions, tables, Circular 230, and e-mail
Tax Almanac	**taxalmanac.org**	Smorgasbord of tax research resources
Tax Analysts	**taxanalysts.com**	Policy-oriented readings on the tax law and proposals to change it, moderated bulletins on various tax subjects
Tax Foundation	**taxfoundation.org**	Nonprofit educational organization that promotes sound tax policy and measures tax burdens
Tax laws online	Regulations are at **law.cornell.edu/cfr** and the Code is at **uscode.house.gov/search/criteria.shtml** and **www4.law.cornell.edu/uscode**	
Tax Sites Directory	**taxsites.com**	References and links to tax sites on the Internet, including state and Federal tax sites, academic and professional pages, tax forms, and software
U.S. Tax Court decisions	**ustaxcourt.gov**	Recent U.S. Tax Court decisions

NOTE: Caution: addresses change frequently.

a tax problem. The problem may originate from completed or proposed transactions. In the case of a completed transaction, the objective of the research is to determine the tax result of what has already taken place. For example, was the expenditure incurred by the taxpayer deductible or not deductible for tax purposes? When dealing with proposed transactions, the tax research process is directed toward the determination of possible alternative tax consequences. To the extent that tax research leads to a choice of alternatives or otherwise influences the future actions of the taxpayer, it becomes the key to effective tax planning.

Tax research involves the following procedures:

- Identifying and refining the problem.
- Locating the appropriate tax law sources.
- Assessing the validity of the tax law sources.
- Arriving at the solution or at alternative solutions with due consideration given to nontax factors.

DATA WAREHOUSING REDUCES GLOBAL TAXES

Many global companies are using data warehouses to collect data, which can be analyzed and used to minimize their global tax liabilities. "You take all of your tax data and dump it into a data warehouse," says Michael S. Burke of KPMG's e-tax solutions. "Next, it's applying a tool to define user requirements—compliance, real time analysis, etc." The company can then manipulate all of this information to reduce compliance costs, facilitate planning for value added taxes, and minimize time spent dealing with international tax problems.

For example, a company wishes to implement an e-procurement technique that would save it $100 million in expenses and increase taxable income. That could mean that about $40 million in additional taxes would go to the U.S. Treasury and state treasuries. By looking at the tax laws worldwide, the company may decide to base the operation in Bermuda, Ireland, or the Philippines where the tax will be only $20 million. That's a savings of $20 million, which is not taxable.

Source: Adapted from Jay Weinstein, "Internet Tax Solutions Proliferate," *Global Finance*, January 2001, pp. 74–75.

- Effectively communicating the solution to the taxpayer or the taxpayer's representative.
- Following up on the solution (where appropriate) in light of new developments.

This process is depicted schematically in Figure 2.5. The broken lines reflect the steps of particular interest when tax research is directed toward proposed, rather than completed, transactions.

IDENTIFYING THE PROBLEM

Problem identification must start with a compilation of the relevant facts involved.[31] In this regard, *all* of the facts that may have a bearing on the problem must be gathered because any omission could modify the solution reached. To illustrate, consider what appears to be a very simple problem.

EXAMPLE 4

Early in December 2011, Fred and Megan review their financial and tax situation with their son, Sam, and daughter-in-law, Dana, who live with them. Fred and Megan are in the 28% tax bracket in 2011. Both Sam and Dana are age 21. Sam, a student at a nearby university, owns some publicly traded stock that he inherited from his grandmother. A current sale would result in approximately $8,000 of gross income ($19,000 amount realized − $11,000 adjusted basis). At this point, Fred and Megan provide about 55% of Sam and Dana's support. Although neither is now employed, Sam has earned $960 and Dana has earned $900. The problem: Should the stock be sold, and would the sale prohibit Fred and Megan from claiming Sam and Dana as dependents? Would the stock sale in 2011 result in a tax liability for Sam and Dana? ∎

REFINING THE PROBLEM

Initial reaction is that Fred and Megan in Example 4 could *not* claim Sam and Dana as dependents if the stock is sold, since Sam would then have gross income of more than the exemption amount under § 151(d).[32] However, after 2004, the test for whether a child qualifies for dependency status is first conducted under the

---

[31]For an excellent discussion of the critical role of facts in carrying out tax research, see R. L. Gardner, D. N. Stewart, and R. G. Worsham, *Tax Research*

Techniques, 8th ed. (New York: The American Institute of Certified Public Accountants, 2008), Chapter 2.

[32]§ 152(d)(2). See the related discussion in Chapter 3.

FIGURE 2.5	Tax Research Process

qualifying child requirements. Only if these requirements cannot be satisfied is the test for dependency status conducted under the *qualifying relative* requirements. The gross income test is applicable only under the qualifying relative status.[33] Thus, Sam could sell the stock without penalizing the parents with respect to the gross income test. Under the qualifying child provision, however, Sam must not have provided more than one-half of his own support.[34] Hence, the $19,000 of proceeds from the sale of the stock might lead to the failure of the not self-supporting requirement, depending on how much Sam spends for his support.

Assume, however, that further fact gathering reveals the following additional information:

- Sam does not really need to spend the proceeds from the sale of the stock.
- Sam receives a sizable portion of his own support from a scholarship.

With these new facts, additional research leads to § 152(f)(5) and Regulation § 1.152–1(c), which indicate that a scholarship received by a student is not included for purposes of computing whether Sam is self-supporting under the qualifying child provision. Further, if Sam does not spend the proceeds from the sale of the stock, the unexpended amount is not counted for purposes of the not self-supporting test. Thus, it appears that the parents would not be denied the dependency exemptions for Sam and Dana, as the qualifying child requirements appear to be satisfied for Sam and the qualifying relative requirements appear to be satisfied for Dana.

LOCATING THE APPROPRIATE TAX LAW SOURCES

Once the problem is clearly defined, what is the next step? Although the next step is a matter of individual judgment, most tax research begins with the index volume of a hard copy tax service or a keyword search on an online tax service as described

---

[33]Compare § 152(c) for qualifying child with § 152(d) for qualifying relative.   [34]§ 152(c)(1)(D).

earlier. If the problem is not complex, the researcher may bypass the tax service or online service and turn directly to the Internal Revenue Code and Treasury Regulations. For the beginner, the latter procedure saves time and will solve many of the more basic problems. If the researcher does not have a personal copy of the Code or Regulations, resorting to the appropriate volume(s) of a tax service will be necessary.[35]

ASSESSING THE VALIDITY OF THE TAX LAW SOURCES

Once a source has been located, the next step is to assess it in light of the problem at hand. Proper assessment involves careful interpretation of the tax law with consideration given to its relevance and validity. In connection with validity, an important step is to check for recent changes in the tax law.

Interpreting the Internal Revenue Code

The language of the Code often is difficult to comprehend fully. Contrary to many people's suspicions, the Code is not written deliberately to confuse. Unfortunately, though, it often has that effect. The Code is intended to apply to more than 200 million taxpayers, many of whom are willing to exploit any linguistic imprecision to their benefit—to find a "loophole" in popular parlance. Many of the Code's provisions are limitations or restrictions involving two or more variables. Expressing such concepts algebraically would be more direct; using words to accomplish this task instead is often quite cumbersome. Among the worst such attempts was former § 341(e) relating to so-called collapsible corporations. One sentence had more than 450 words (twice as many as in Abraham Lincoln's Gettysburg Address). Within this same subsection was another sentence of 300 words. Research has shown that in one-third of the conflicts reaching the Tax Court, the court could not discern the intent of Congress by simply reading the statute. Yet the overriding attitude of the Tax Court judges is that the statute comes first. Even when the statute is unworkable, the court will not rewrite the law.[36]

Assessing the Validity of a Treasury Regulation

Treasury Regulations are the official interpretation of the Code and are entitled to great deference. Occasionally, however, a court will invalidate a Regulation or a portion thereof on the grounds that the Regulation is contrary to the intent of Congress. Usually, the courts do not question the validity of Regulations because of the belief that "the first administrative interpretation of a provision as it appears in a new act often expresses the general understanding of the times or the actual understanding of those who played an important part when the statute was drafted."[37]

Keep the following observations in mind when assessing the validity of a Regulation:

- IRS agents must give the Code and the Regulations issued thereunder equal weight when dealing with taxpayers and their representatives.
- Proposed Regulations provide a preview of future final Regulations, but they are not binding on the IRS or taxpayers.
- In a challenge, the burden of proof is on the taxpayer to show that the Regulation varies from the language of the statute and has no support in the Committee Reports.
- If the taxpayer loses the challenge, a 20 percent negligence penalty may be imposed.[38] This accuracy-related penalty applies to any failure to make a

---

[35]Several of the major tax services publish paperback editions of the Code and Treasury Regulations that can be purchased at modest prices. These editions are usually revised twice each year. For an annotated and abridged version of the Code and Regulations that is published annually, see James E. Smith, *South-Western Federal Taxation: Internal Revenue Code of 1986 and Treasury Regulations: Annotated and Selected* (Cengage Learning South-Western, 2012).

[36]T. L. Kirkpatrick and W. B. Pollard, "Reliance by the Tax Court on the Legislative Intent of Congress," *The Tax Executive* (Summer 1986): 358–359.

[37]*Augustus v. Comm.*, 41–1 USTC ¶9255, 26 AFTR 612, 118 F.2d 38 (CA–6, 1941).

[38]§§ 6662(a) and (b)(1).

reasonable attempt to comply with the tax law and any disregard of rules and Regulations.[39]

- Final Regulations can be classified as procedural, interpretive, or legislative. **Procedural Regulations** neither establish tax laws nor attempt to explain tax laws. Procedural Regulations are *housekeeping-type instructions* indicating information that taxpayers should provide the IRS as well as information about the internal management and conduct of the IRS itself.

- Some **interpretive Regulations** rephrase and elaborate what Congress stated in the Committee Reports that were issued when the tax legislation was enacted. Such Regulations are *hard* and *solid* and almost impossible to overturn because they clearly reflect the intent of Congress. An interpretive Regulation is given less deference than a legislative Regulation, however. The Supreme Court has told lower courts to analyze Treasury Regulations carefully before accepting the Treasury's interpretation.[40]

- In some Code Sections, Congress has given the *Secretary or his delegate* the authority to prescribe Regulations to carry out the details of administration or to otherwise complete the operating rules. Under such circumstances, Congress effectively is delegating its legislative powers to the Treasury Department. Regulations issued pursuant to this type of authority possess the force and effect of law and are often called **legislative Regulations** (e.g., consolidated return Regulations).

- Courts tend to apply a legislative reenactment doctrine. A particular Regulation is assumed to have received congressional approval if the Regulation was finalized many years earlier and Congress has not amended the Code Section pertaining to that Regulation.

Assessing the Validity of Other Administrative Sources of the Tax Law

Revenue Rulings issued by the IRS carry less weight than Treasury Department Regulations. Revenue Rulings are important, however, in that they reflect the position of the IRS on tax matters. In any dispute with the IRS on the interpretation of tax law, therefore, taxpayers should expect agents to follow the results reached in any applicable Revenue Rulings. A 1986 Tax Court decision, however, indicated that Revenue Rulings "typically do not constitute substantive authority for a position."[41] Most Revenue Rulings apply retroactively unless a specific statement indicates the extent to which a ruling is to be applied without retroactive effect.[42]

Actions on Decisions further tell the taxpayer the IRS's reaction to certain court decisions. Recall that the IRS follows a practice of either acquiescing (agreeing) or nonacquiescing (not agreeing) with selected judicial decisions. A nonacquiescence does not mean that a particular court decision is of no value, but it does indicate that the IRS may continue to litigate the issue involved.

Assessing the Validity of Judicial Sources of the Tax Law

The judicial process as it relates to the formulation of tax law has already been described. How much reliance can be placed on a particular decision depends upon the following variables:

- The higher the level of the court that issued a decision, the greater the weight accorded to that decision. A decision rendered by a trial court (e.g., a Federal District Court) carries less weight than one issued by an appellate court (e.g., the Fifth Circuit Court of Appeals). Unless Congress changes the Code, decisions by the U.S. Supreme Court represent the last word on any tax issue.

---

[39]§ 6662(c).
[40]*U.S. v. Vogel Fertilizer Co.*, 82–1 USTC ¶9134, 49 AFTR 2d 82–491, 102 S.Ct. 821 (USSC, 1982); *National Muffler Dealers Assn., Inc.*, 79–1 USTC ¶9264, 43 AFTR 2d 79–828, 99 S.Ct. 1304 (USSC, 1979).
[41]*Nelda C. Stark*, 86 T.C. 243 (1986). See also *Ann R. Neuhoff*, 75 T.C. 36 (1980). For a different opinion, however, see *Industrial Valley Bank & Trust Co.*, 66 T.C. 272 (1976).
[42]Rev.Proc. 87–1, 1987–1 C.B. 503.

TAX in the NEWS

INTERNAL REVENUE CODE: INTERPRETATION PITFALLS

One author has noted 10 common pitfalls in interpreting the Code:

1. Determine the limitations and exceptions to a provision. Do not permit the language of the Code Section to carry greater or lesser weight than was intended.
2. Just because a Section fails to mention an item does not necessarily mean that the item is excluded.
3. Read definitional clauses carefully.
4. Do not overlook small words such as *and* and *or*. There is a world of difference between these two words.
5. Read the Code Section completely; do not jump to conclusions.
6. Watch out for cross-referenced and related provisions, since many Sections of the Code are interrelated.

7. At times Congress is not careful when reconciling new Code provisions with existing Sections. Conflicts among Sections, therefore, do arise.
8. Be alert for hidden definitions; terms in a particular Code Section may be defined in the same Section or in a separate Section.
9. Some answers may not be found in the Code; therefore, a researcher may have to consult the Regulations and/or judicial decisions.
10. Take careful note of measuring words such as *less than 50 percent*, *more than 50 percent*, and *at least 80 percent*.

Source: Adapted by permission from Henry G. Wong, "Ten Common Pitfalls in Reading the Internal Revenue Code," *Journal of Business Strategy* (July–August 1972): 30–33. Reprinted with permission from Emerald Publishing Limited.

- More reliance is placed on decisions of courts that have jurisdiction in the area where the taxpayer's legal residence is located. If, for example, a taxpayer lives in Texas, a decision of the Fifth Circuit Court of Appeals means more than one rendered by the Second Circuit Court of Appeals. This result occurs because any appeal from a U.S. District Court or the Tax Court would be to the Fifth Circuit Court of Appeals and not to the Second Circuit Court of Appeals.[43]

- A Tax Court Regular decision carries more weight than a Memorandum decision since the Tax Court does not consider Memorandum decisions to be binding precedents.[44] Furthermore, a Tax Court *reviewed* decision carries even more weight. All of the Tax Court judges participate in a reviewed decision.

- A Circuit Court decision where certiorari has been requested and denied by the U.S. Supreme Court carries more weight than a Circuit Court decision that was not appealed. A Circuit Court decision heard *en banc* (all the judges participate) carries more weight than a normal Circuit Court case.

- A decision that is supported by cases from other courts carries more weight than a decision that is not supported by other cases.

- The weight of a decision also can be affected by its status on appeal. For example, was the decision affirmed or overruled?

In connection with the last two variables, the use of a citator is invaluable to tax research.[45] A **citator** provides the history of a case, including the authority relied on (e.g., other judicial decisions) in reaching the result. Reviewing the references listed in the citator discloses whether the decision was appealed and, if so, with what result (e.g., affirmed, reversed, remanded). It also reveals other cases with the same or similar issues and how they were decided. Thus, a citator reflects on the validity of a case and may lead to other relevant judicial material.[46] If one intends to rely on a

---

[43]Before October 1, 1982, an appeal from the then-named U.S. Court of Claims (the other trial court) was directly to the U.S. Supreme Court.

[44]*Severino R. Nico, Jr.*, 67 T.C. 647 (1977).

[45]The major citators are published by Commerce Clearing House, RIA, Westlaw, and Shepard's Citations, Inc.

[46]The CCH version is available online through the CCH *NetWork* service; for RIA, use *Checkpoint.* Shepard's Internet version is part of LexisNexis.

TAX *in* the *NEWS* **THE AFTERMATH OF HEALTH CARE REFORM**

In the recently passed health care reform legislation, Congress gave the IRS vast new powers and duties, but no extra money and personnel. For example, one new provision will affect 30 million sole proprietors and S corporations, 2 million farms, and 1 million charities. National Taxpayer Advocate Nina Olson says "the agency is now responsible for the most extensive social benefit program the IRS has been asked to implement in recent history." She indicates that without "sufficient funding" the IRS will not be able to discharge its new duties. This situation provides a reminder of attorney Jonathan Blattmachr's comment that "the U.S. Code is the most political law in the world."

Source: Adapted from "Lost in Taxation," Review and Outlook, *Wall Street Journal,* July 17, 2010.

judicial decision to any significant degree, "running" the case through a citator is imperative.

Assessing the Validity of Other Sources

Primary sources of tax law include the Constitution, legislative history materials, statutes, treaties, Treasury Regulations, IRS pronouncements, and judicial decisions. In general, the IRS considers only primary sources to constitute substantial authority. However, a researcher might wish to refer to *secondary materials* such as legal periodicals, treatises, legal opinions, General Counsel Memoranda, and written determinations. In general, secondary sources are not authority.

Although the statement that the IRS regards only primary sources as substantial authority generally is true, there is one exception. In Notice 90–20,[47] the IRS expanded the list of substantial authority *for purposes of* the accuracy-related penalty in § 6662 to include a number of secondary materials (e.g., letter rulings, General Counsel Memoranda, the Bluebook). "Authority" does not include conclusions reached in treatises, legal periodicals, and opinions rendered by tax professionals.

A letter ruling or determination letter is substantial authority *only* for the taxpayer to whom it is issued, except as noted above with respect to the accuracy-related penalty.

Upon the completion of major tax legislation, the staff of the Joint Committee on Taxation (in consultation with the staffs of the House Ways and Means and Senate Finance Committees) often will prepare a General Explanation of the Act, commonly known as the Bluebook because of the color of its cover. The IRS will not accept this detailed explanation as having legal effect, except as noted above with respect to the accuracy-related penalty. The Bluebook does, however, provide valuable guidance to tax advisers and taxpayers until Regulations are issued. Some letter rulings and General Counsel Memoranda of the IRS cite Bluebook explanations.

ARRIVING AT THE SOLUTION OR AT ALTERNATIVE SOLUTIONS

Example 4 raised the question of whether a taxpayer would be denied dependency exemptions for a son and a daughter-in-law if the son sold some stock near the end of the year. A refinement of the problem supplies additional information:

• Sam and Dana anticipate filing a joint return.

Section 152(b)(2) indicates that a taxpayer is not permitted a dependency exemption for a married dependent if the married individual files a joint return. Initial reaction is that a joint return by Sam and Dana would be disastrous to the parents. However, more research uncovers two Revenue Rulings that provide an exception if neither the dependent nor the dependent's spouse is required to file a return but

---

[47]1990–1 C.B. 328; see also Reg. § 1.6661–3(b)(2).

FINANCIAL DISCLOSURE *Insights*

WHERE DOES GAAP COME FROM?

As this chapter has described, the tax law is developed by many entities including Congress and the legislators of other countries, the courts, and the IRS. Accounting principles also have many sources. Consequently, in reconciling the tax and financial accounting reporting of a transaction, the tax professional will need to know the hierarchy of authority of accounting principles, in particular, the level of importance to assign to a specific GAAP document. The diagram below presents the sources of GAAP, arranged in a general order of authority, from highest to lowest.

Professional research is conducted to find and analyze the sources of accounting reporting standards, in much the same way that a tax professional conducts research into an open tax question. In fact, many of the publishers that provide tax research materials also can be used to find GAAP and International Financial Reporting Standards (IFRS) documents. These include the Research Institute of America (RIA) and Commerce Clearing House (CCH). The Financial Standards Accounting Board (FASB) also makes its standards and interpretations available by subscription.

Highest Authority
- Financial Accounting Standards and Interpretations of the FASB.
- Pronouncements of bodies that preceded the FASB, such as the Accounting Principles Board (APB).

- FASB Technical Bulletins.
- Audit and Accounting Guides, prepared by the American Institute of CPAs (AICPA) and cleared by the FASB.
- Practice Bulletins, prepared by the American Institute of CPAs (AICPA) and cleared by the FASB.

- Interpretation Guides of the FASB Staff.
- Accounting Interpretations of the AICPA.
- IASB Accounting Standards
- FASB Concepts Standards.
- Widely accepted accounting practices, professional journals, accounting textbooks, and treatises.

does so solely to claim a refund of tax withheld. The IRS asserts that each spouse must have gross income of less than the exemption amount.[48] Therefore, if Sam sells the stock and he and Dana file a joint return, the parents would lose the dependency exemption for both Sam and Dana.

If the stock is not sold until January 2012, both dependency exemptions are available to the parents in 2011 even if Sam and Dana file a joint return. However, under § 151(d)(2) a personal exemption is not available to a taxpayer who can be claimed as a dependent by another taxpayer (whether actually claimed or not). Thus, if the parents can claim Sam and Dana as dependents, Sam and Dana would lose their personal exemptions on their tax return.

L0.5

Communicate the results of the tax research process in a client letter and a tax file memorandum.

COMMUNICATING TAX RESEARCH

Once the problem has been researched adequately, the researcher may need to prepare a memo, letter, or oral presentation setting forth the result. The form such a communication takes could depend on a number of considerations. For example, does the employer or professor recommend a particular procedure or format for tax research memos? Is the memo to be given directly to the client, or will it first go to the researcher's employer? Who is the audience for the oral presentation? How long should you talk? Whatever form it takes, a good tax research communication should contain the following elements:

---

[48]Rev.Rul. 54–567, 1954–2 C.B. 108; Rev.Rul. 65–34, 1965–1 C.B. 86.

- A clear statement of the issue.
- In more complex situations, a short review of the fact pattern that raises the issue.
- A review of the pertinent tax law sources (e.g., Code, Regulations, Revenue Rulings, judicial authority).
- Any assumptions made in arriving at the solution.
- The solution recommended and the logic or reasoning supporting it.
- The references consulted in the research process.

In short, a good tax research communication should tell the audience what was researched, the results of that research, and the justification for the recommendation made.[49]

Illustrations of the memos for the tax file and the client letter associated with Example 4 appear in Figure 2.6, Figure 2.7, and Figure 2.8.

2.4 WORKING WITH THE TAX LAW— TAX PLANNING

Tax research and tax planning are inseparable. The *primary* purpose of effective *tax planning* is to reduce the taxpayer's total tax bill. This statement does not mean that the course of action selected must produce the lowest possible tax under the circumstances. The minimization of tax liability must be considered in context with the legitimate business goals of the taxpayer.

A *secondary* objective of effective tax planning is to reduce or defer the tax in the current tax year. Specifically, this objective aims to accomplish one or more of the following: eradicating the tax entirely; eliminating the tax in the current year; deferring the receipt of income; converting ordinary income into capital gains; converting active to passive income; converting passive to active expense; proliferating taxpayers (i.e., forming partnerships and corporations or making lifetime gifts to family members); eluding double taxation; avoiding ordinary income; or creating, increasing, or accelerating deductions. However, this second objective should be approached with considerable reservation and moderation. For example, a tax election in one year may reduce taxes currently, but saddle future years with a disadvantageous tax position.

LO.6

Apply tax research techniques and planning procedures.

NONTAX CONSIDERATIONS

There is an honest danger that tax motivations may take on a significance that does not correspond to the true values involved. In other words, tax considerations may impair the exercise of sound business judgment by the taxpayer. Thus, the tax planning process can become a medium through which to accomplish ends that are socially and economically objectionable. All too often, planning seems to lean toward the opposing extremes of placing either too little or too much emphasis on tax considerations. The happy medium—a balance that recognizes the significance of taxes, but not beyond the point where planning detracts from the exercise of good business judgment—turns out to be the promised land that is too infrequently reached.

The remark is often made that a good rule is to refrain from pursuing any course of action that would not be followed were it not for certain tax considerations. This statement is not entirely correct, but it does illustrate the desirability of preventing business logic from being *sacrificed at the altar of tax planning.*

COMPONENTS OF TAX PLANNING

The popular perception of tax planning often is restricted to the adage "defer income and accelerate deductions." Although this timing approach does hold true and is important, meaningful tax planning involves considerably more.

[49]See Chapter 6 of the publication cited in Footnote 31. For oral presentations, see W. A. Raabe and G. E. Whittenburg, "Talking Tax: How to Make a Tax Presentation," *The Tax Adviser* (March 1997): 179–182.

FIGURE 2.6   Tax File Memorandum

August 16, 2011

TAX FILE MEMORANDUM

FROM: John J. Jones
SUBJECT: Fred and Megan Taxpayer
Engagement: Issues

Today I talked to Fred Taxpayer with respect to his August 12, 2011 letter requesting tax assistance. He wishes to know if his son, Sam, can sell stock worth $19,000 (basis = $11,000) without the parents losing the dependency exemptions for Sam and Sam's wife, Dana. Fred would also like to know the effect on Sam and Dana's tax liability in 2011 if the stock is sold.

Fred Taxpayer is married to Megan, and Sam is a full-time student at a local university. Sam inherited the stock from his grandmother about five years ago. If he sells the stock, he will save the proceeds from the sale. Sam does not need to spend the proceeds if he sells the stock because he receives a $5,500 scholarship that he uses for his own support (i.e., to pay for tuition, books, and fees). Although neither Sam nor Dana is currently employed, Sam has earned income of $960, and Dana has earned income of $900. Fred and Megan are in the 28% tax bracket and furnish approximately 55% of Sam and Dana's support.

ISSUES: If the stock is sold, would the sale prohibit Fred and Megan from claiming Sam and Dana as dependents? What is the effect on Sam and Dana's tax liability if the stock is sold in 2011? I told Fred that we would have an answer for him within two weeks.

Preferable to deferring income is complete *avoidance.* Consider, for example, the corporate employee who chooses nontaxable fringe benefits (e.g., group term life insurance, health insurance) over a fully taxable future pay increase.[50] Complete avoidance of gain recognition also occurs when the owner of appreciated property transfers it by death. Presuming a step-up in basis occurs, the built-in appreciation escapes the income tax forever.[51]

If the recognition of income cannot be avoided, its deferral will postpone income tax consequences. *Deferral* of income can take many forms. Besides like-kind exchanges and involuntary conversions, most retirement plans put off income tax consequences until the payout period. Deferral of gain recognition also can occur when appreciated property is transferred to a newly formed corporation or partnership.[52]

A corollary to the deferral of income is the acceleration of deductions. For example, an accrual basis, calendar year corporation desires an additional charitable deduction for 2011 but has a cash-flow problem. If the corporation authorizes the contribution in 2011 and pays it on or before March 15, 2012, the deduction can be claimed for 2011.[53] Taxes can be saved by *shifting* income to lower-bracket taxpayers. Gifts of appreciated property to lower-bracket family members can reduce the applicable capital gain rate on a later sale by 15 percentage points (from 15 percent to 0 percent).[54]

If income cannot be avoided, deferred, or shifted, the nature of the gain can be *converted.* By changing the classification of property, income taxes can be reduced.[55] Thus, a taxpayer who transfers appreciated inventory to a controlled corporation has converted ordinary income property to a capital asset. When the taxpayer's stock is later sold, preferential capital gain rates apply.

---

[50]See Examples 19, 20, and 23 in Chapter 5.
[51]See Examples 25 and 27 in Chapter 14.
[52]See Examples 20, 21, and 44 in Chapter 20, Chapter 19 in general (especially Example 12 in Chapter 19), and Section 4.6 in Chapter 4.
[53]See Example 6 in Chapter 20.
[54]See Section 14.4 in Chapter 14.
[55]See Example 53 in Chapter 4.

FIGURE 2.7	Tax File Memorandum

August 26, 2011

TAX FILE MEMORANDUM

FROM: John J. Jones
SUBJECT: Fred and Megan Taxpayer
         Engagement: Conclusions

See the Tax File Memorandum dated August 16, 2011, which contains the facts and identifies the tax issues.

Section 152(a) provides that in order for a taxpayer to take a dependency exemption, the potential dependent must satisfy either the qualifying child requirements or the qualifying relative requirements (see Chapter 3). Fred and Megan provide about 55% of the support of their son, Sam, and their daughter-in-law, Dana. If Sam should sell the stock in 2011, he would not need to spend the proceeds for support purposes (i.e., would save the proceeds). Thus, the stock sale would not affect his qualifying as not self-supporting under § 152(c)(1)(D). In calculating the percentage of support provided by Fred and Megan, a $5,500 scholarship received by Sam is not counted in determining the amount of support Sam provides for himself [see § 152(f)(5) and Reg. § 1.152–1(c)]. Note, however, that if the $5,500 had been provided by student loans, it would have been included in calculating support [*Philip J. McCauley*, 56 T.C. 48 (1971)].

Section 152(d)(1)(B) provides that in order to qualify for a dependency exemption as a qualifying relative, the potential dependent's gross income must be less than the exemption amount (i.e., $3,700 in 2011). Without the stock sale, the gross income of both Sam ($960) and Dana ($900) will be below the exemption amount in 2011. The $5,500 Sam receives as a scholarship is excluded from his gross income under § 117(a) because he uses the entire amount to pay for his tuition, books, and fees at a local university.

Although the gross income test is not applicable to Sam (as a qualifying child), it is applicable to Dana, the daughter-in-law (a qualifying relative). [See Concept Summary 3.1.] A key issue is whether the stock sale that will produce $8,000 of recognized gain for Sam and Dana will cause the gross income test to be violated for Dana. Since the $8,000 recognized gain is from the sale of Sam's separately owned asset and they do not live in a community property state, Dana should qualify as a dependent because her gross income would be only $900.

Sam must not be self-supporting under the qualifying child requirements. So, if the stock is sold, he must limit his spending of the sales proceeds such that he continues to be supported by his parents. Since he plans on not spending any of the sales proceeds, this should not be an issue.

The stock sale would result in the parents' loss of the dependency exemptions for Sam and Dana if they file a joint return for 2011 [see § 152(b)(2)]. The joint return requirement does not apply, however, if the dependent files a joint return solely to claim a refund and neither spouse had a tax liability on a separate return (Rev.Rul. 65–34, 1965–1 C.B. 86). However, sale of the stock would keep this exception from applying.

From a tax planning perspective, Sam can choose to sell the stock in 2011. However, if this choice is made, Sam and Dana need to file separate returns so as not to violate the absence of a joint return provision. Under these circumstances, the sale will not interfere with Fred and Megan's ability to claim dependency exemptions for Sam and Dana on their 2011 return. Note, however, that neither Sam nor Dana will be permitted to take a personal exemption deduction on their 2011 tax return since they are claimed as dependents on someone else's return [see § 151(d)(2)]. This disallowance of the personal exemption deduction will not produce any significant negative tax consequences for Dana since her tax liability would be $0. However, Sam's tax liability would now be $915 (see the kiddie tax in Chapter 3). Alternatively, Sam could delay the sale of the stock until 2012. In this case, Sam and Dana's tax liability in 2011 would be $0. The disallowance of the personal exemption deductions by Sam and Dana will not produce any negative tax consequences since both Sam and Dana's tax liability would be $0.

The conversion approach also can work in tax planning for losses. Properly structured, a loan to a corporation that becomes worthless can be an ordinary loss rather than the less desirable capital loss. Likewise, planning with § 1244 permits an investor in qualified small business stock to convert what would be a capital loss into an ordinary loss.[56]

Effective tax planning requires that careful consideration be given to the *choice of entity* used for conducting a business. The corporate form results in double taxation but permits shareholder-employees to be covered by fringe benefit programs. Partnerships and S corporations allow a pass-through of losses and other tax attributes, but transferring ownership interests as gifts to family members may be difficult.[57]

---

[56]See Example 8 in Chapter 7.   [57]See Sections 20.6 and 20.7 in Chapter 20.   AQ9

FIGURE 2.8	Client Letter

Hoffman, Smith, and Willis, CPAs
5191 Natorp Boulevard
Mason, Ohio 45040

August 30, 2011

Mr. and Ms. Fred Taxpayer
111 Boulevard
Williamsburg, Virginia 23185

Dear Mr. and Ms. Taxpayer:

This letter is in response to your request for us to review your family's financial and tax situation. Our conclusions are based upon the facts as outlined in your August 12th letter. Any change in the facts may affect our conclusions.

You provide over 50% of the support for your son, Sam, and his wife, Dana. The scholarship Sam receives is not included in determining support. If the stock is not sold, you will qualify for a dependency exemption for both Sam and Dana.

If the stock is sold, a gain of approximately $8,000 will result. If Sam and Dana then file a joint return, you would lose the dependency exemption for Sam as a qualifying child and would lose the dependency exemption for Dana as a qualifying relative. You can avoid the loss of these two dependency exemptions if Sam and Dana file separate returns. This would result in a tax liability of $0 for Dana and $915 for Sam.

From a family tax planning and tax avoidance perspective, Sam should not sell the stock in 2011. Delaying the stock sale will enable you to claim dependency exemptions for both Sam and Dana and will enable Sam and Dana to have a $0 tax liability for 2011.

Should you need more information or need to clarify our conclusions, do not hesitate to contact me.

Sincerely yours,

John J. Jones, CPA
Partner

Although the substance of a transaction, rather than its form, generally controls, this rule is not always the case with tax planning. *Preserving formalities* often is crucial to the result. Is an advance to a corporation a loan or a contribution to capital? The answer may well depend on the existence of a note. Along with preserving formalities, the taxpayer should keep records that support a transaction. Returning to the issue of loan versus contribution to capital, how is the advance listed on the books of the borrower? What do the corporate minutes say about the advance?

Lastly, effective tax planning requires *consistency* on the part of taxpayers. A shareholder who treats a corporate distribution as a return of capital cannot later avoid a stock basis adjustment by contending that the distribution was really a dividend.

In summary, the key components of tax planning include the following:

- *Avoid* the recognition of income (usually by resorting to a nontaxable source or nontaxable event).
- *Defer* the recognition of income (or accelerate deductions).
- *Convert* the classification of income (or deductions) to a more advantageous form (e.g., ordinary income into capital gain).
- *Choose* the business *entity* with the desired tax attributes.
- Preserve *formalities* by generating and maintaining supporting documentation.
- Act in a manner *consistent* with the intended objective.

TAX AVOIDANCE AND TAX EVASION

A fine line exists between legal tax planning and illegal tax planning—tax avoidance versus tax evasion. **Tax avoidance** is merely tax minimization through legal techniques. In this sense, tax avoidance is the proper objective of all tax planning. Tax evasion, while also aimed at the elimination or reduction of taxes, connotes the use of subterfuge and fraud as a means to an end. Popular usage—probably because of the common goals involved—has so linked these two concepts that many individuals are no longer aware of the true distinctions between them. Consequently, some taxpayers have been deterred from properly taking advantage of planning possibilities. The now classic words of Judge Learned Hand in *Commissioner v. Newman* reflect the true values the taxpayer should have:

> Over and over again courts have said that there is nothing sinister in so arranging one's affairs as to keep taxes as low as possible. Everybody does so, rich or poor; and all do right, for nobody owes any public duty to pay more than the law demands: taxes are enforced extractions, not voluntary contributions. To demand more in the name of morals is mere cant.[58]

As Denis Healy, a former British Chancellor, once said, "The difference between tax avoidance and tax evasion is the thickness of a prison wall."

The Government Accountability Office estimates that U.S. taxpayers spend at least $107 billion each year on tax compliance costs. The Treasury Department estimates that individuals spend at least 6.4 billion hours preparing Federal income tax returns. Small businesses, self-employed persons, and taxpayers with the highest marginal tax rates have the highest levels of tax evasion.[59]

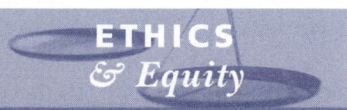
ETHICS & Equity

WHO DID NOT PAY HIS INCOME TAXES PROPERLY?

Representative Charles P. Rangel had to write six checks for a total of approximately $10,800 in back (Federal and state) taxes due on his 2005, 2006, and 2007 tax returns. Among other items, he overlooked paying income taxes on rent income on a beach house he owns in the Dominican Republic. Rangel was chairman of the tax writing committee—the House Ways and Means Committee. Apparently, penalties and interest were not included in the amount paid. What are your thoughts?

Source: Adapted from "Morality and Charles Rangel's Taxes," *Wall Street Journal* online, July 27, 2009.

FOLLOW-UP PROCEDURES

Because tax planning usually involves a proposed (as opposed to a completed) transaction, it is predicated upon the continuing validity of the advice based upon the tax research. A change in the tax law (either legislative, administrative, or judicial) could alter the original conclusion. Additional research may be necessary to test the solution in light of current developments (refer to the broken lines at the right in Figure 2.5).

TAX PLANNING—A PRACTICAL APPLICATION

Returning to the facts of Example 4, what could be done to protect the dependency exemptions for the parents? If Sam and Dana refrain from filing a joint return, both could be claimed by the parents.

---

[58]*Comm. v. Newman*, 47–1 USTC ¶9175, 35 AFTR 857, 159 F.2d 848 (CA–2, 1947).

[59]Adapted from J. A. Tackett, Joe Antenucci, and Fran Wolf, "A Criminological Perspective of Tax Evasion," *Tax Notes* (February 6, 2006): 654–658; L. E. Burman, "Tax Evasion, IRS Priorities, and the EITC," *Statement before the United States House of Representatives Committee on the Budget; On Waste, Fraud, and Abuse in Federal Mandatory Programs* (July 9, 2003).

An obvious tax planning tool is the installment method. Could the securities be sold using the installment method under § 453 so that most of the gain is deferred into the next year? Under the installment method, certain gains may be postponed and recognized as the cash proceeds are received. The problem is that the installment method is not available for stock traded on an established securities market.[60]

A little more research, however, indicates that Sam might be able to sell the stock and postpone the recognition of gain until the following year by selling short an equal number of substantially identical shares and covering the short sale in the subsequent year with the shares originally held. Selling short means that Sam sells borrowed stock (substantially identical) and repays the lender with the stock held on the date of the short sale. This *short against the box* technique would allow Sam to protect his $8,000 profit and defer the closing of the sale until the following year.[61] However, additional research indicates that 1997 tax legislation provides that the short against the box technique will no longer produce the desired postponement of recognized gain. That is, at the time of the short sale, Sam will have a recognized gain of $8,000 from a constructive sale. Note the critical role of obtaining the correct facts in attempting to resolve the proper strategy for the taxpayers.

Throughout this text, most chapters include observations on Tax Planning. Such observations are not all-inclusive but are intended to illustrate some of the ways in which the material covered can be effectively utilized to minimize taxes.

2.5 TAXATION ON THE CPA EXAMINATION

The CPA examination has changed from a paper-and-pencil exam to a computer-based exam with increased emphasis on information technology and general business knowledge. The 14-hour exam has four sections, and taxation is included in the 3-hour Regulations section.

The CPA examination is not curved to produce a designated pass rate. In theory, if all candidates are well prepared, they will all pass. Of course, if all are unprepared, all could fail. The likelihood of passing at least one section is greater for candidates who take more than one CPA examination section in a testing window.

As of January 1, 2011, the CPA examination has been reorganized so that all written communication tasks are concentrated in the Business Environment & Concepts section. Shorter simulations have replaced the longer simulations.

Each exam section includes both multiple-choice questions and two other sections that will have short task-based simulation (TBS) questions. The Regulations section is 60 percent Taxation and 40 percent Law & Professional Responsibilities (all areas other than Business Structure). The three-hour Regulations section has a new format. It now contains:

- Three multiple-choice question (MCQ) testlets consisting of 72 questions.
- One testlet (i.e., a group of questions prepared to appear together) containing six short task-based simulations with the research question in a new format.

A candidate may review and change answers within each testlet but cannot go back after exiting a testlet. Candidates take different, but equivalent exams.

Simulations are small case studies designed to test a candidate's tax knowledge and skills using real-life work-related situations. Simulations include a four-function pop-up calculator, a blank spreadsheet with some elementary functionality, and authoritative literature appropriate to the subject matter. The taxation database includes authoritative excerpts that are necessary to complete the tax case study

---

[60]See Chapter 18 for a discussion of installment sales.

[61]§§ 1233(a) and 1233(b)(2). See Chapter 16 for a discussion of short sales.

> ### TAX*in* the NEWS
>
> ## THE DISAPPEARING TAXPAYERS
>
> Should income taxes be increased, not decreased, especially on the bottom 50 percent of taxpayers? Should the tax base be expanded? Recent tax data lend credence to such unpopular opinions.
>
> In 2007, the top 50 percent of taxpayers paid 97.11 percent of Federal income taxes, and the bottom 50 percent paid only 2.89 percent. The top 10 percent paid 71.33 percent of Federal income taxes. For 2009, almost 47 percent of potential taxpayers paid no taxes, either because their income was too low or because they qualified for enough credits, exclusions, and deductions to eliminate their Federal income tax liability. More disturbing is the fact that the bottom 40 percent made a profit from the Federal income tax—our government sent them a payment. It would appear that these people are getting something for nothing.
>
> President Obama's making work pay credit and the expanded child tax credit and earned income tax credit have shifted the tax burden even further onto the top
>
> earners. Shifting the tax burden onto a smaller and smaller segment of high-income earners could be economically dangerous.
>
> Another problem is that the Internet is helping taxpayers to disappear. In a *New Yorker* magazine cartoon, two dogs are sitting in front of a computer screen: one tells the other, "On the Internet, nobody knows that you are a dog." Similarly, in order to collect a tax, the government must know who is liable to pay the tax. Taxpayers are becoming increasingly more difficult to identify as anonymous electronic money and uncrackable encryption techniques are developed.
>
> ***Sources:*** Adapted from Curtis S. Dubay, "The Rich Pay More Taxes: Top 20 Percent Pay Record Share of Income Taxes," The Heritage Foundation, **www.heritage.org/research/taxes/wm2420.cfm**; Stephen Ohlmacher, "Nearly Half of U.S. Households Escape Fed Income Tax," Yahoo! News, April 7, 2010.

simulations (e.g., Internal Revenue Code, Regulations, IRS publications, and Federal tax forms). Examples of such simulations follow.

EXAMPLE 5

The *tax citation type* simulation requires the candidate to research the Internal Revenue Code and enter a Code Section and subsection. For example, Amber Company is considering using the simplified dollar-value method of pricing its inventory for purposes of the LIFO method that is available to certain small businesses. What Code Section is the relevant authority in the Internal Revenue Code to which you should turn to determine whether the taxpayer is eligible to use this method? To be successful, the candidate needs to find § 474. ■

EXAMPLE 6

A *tax form completion* simulation requires the candidate to fill out a portion of a tax form. For example, Red Company is a limited liability company (LLC) for tax purposes. Complete the income section of the IRS Form 1065 for Red Company using the values found and calculated on previous tabs along with the following data:

Ordinary income from other partnerships	$ 5,200
Net gain (loss) from Form 4797	2,400
Management fee income	12,000

The candidate is provided with page 1 of Form 1065 on which to record the appropriate amounts.

Any field that requires an entry is a shaded rectangular cell. Some white rectangular cells will automatically calculate based on the entries in the shaded cell. ■

Candidates can learn more about the CPA examination at **www.cpa-exam.org**. This online tutorial site's topics include:

- Common tools.
- Navigation.
- Form completion.

- Numeric entry.
- Research questions.
- Authoritative literature search.
- Written communication.

The common tools are a calculator, spreadsheet, reminder flags, and examination clock. A 30- to 60-minute sample exam will familiarize a candidate with the types of questions on the examination.

KEY TERMS

Acquiescence, 2–17	Letter rulings, 2–9	Tax research, 2–24
Circuit Court of Appeals, 2–14	Nonacquiescence, 2–17	Technical Advice Memoranda (TAMs), 2–10
Citator, 2–30	Precedents, 2–16	Temporary Regulations, 2–7
Court of original jurisdiction, 2–11	Procedural Regulations, 2–29	U.S. Court of Federal Claims, 2–11
Determination letters, 2–10	Proposed Regulations, 2–7	U.S. Supreme Court, 2–16
Federal District Court, 2–11	Revenue Procedures, 2–8	U.S. Tax Court, 2–11
Finalized Regulations, 2–7	Revenue Rulings, 2–8	Writ of Certiorari, 2–16
Interpretive Regulations, 2–29	Small Cases Division, 2–11	
Legislative Regulations, 2–29	Tax avoidance, 2–37	

DISCUSSION QUESTIONS

1. **LO.1** What are the primary sources of tax information?

2. **LO.1** Taxpayers should always minimize their tax liability. Discuss this statement.

3. **LO.1** When did Congress first codify all of the Federal tax laws?

4. **LO.1** What happens when the House and Senate versions of major tax bills differ?

5. **LO.1** Why may Committee Reports be valuable to tax practitioners and taxpayers?

COMMUNICATIONS

6. **LO.2, 5** Butch Bishop operates a small international firm named Tile, Inc. A new treaty between the United States and France conflicts with a Section of the Internal Revenue Code. Butch asks you for advice. If he follows the treaty position, does he need to disclose this on his tax return? If he is required to disclose, are there any penalties for failure to disclose? Prepare a letter in which you respond to Butch. Tile's address is 100 International Drive, Tampa, FL 33620.

7. **LO.1, 2** Interpret this Regulation citation: Reg. § 1.162–5(a)(1).

8. **LO.1, 2** Explain how Regulations are arranged. How would the following Regulations be cited?
   a. Finalized Regulations under § 351.
   b. Proposed Regulations under § 2036.
   c. Temporary Regulations under § 482.
   d. Legislative Regulations under § 1504.

9. **LO.1, 4** Distinguish between legislative, interpretive, and procedural Regulations.

10. **LO.1** In the citation Rev.Rul. 76–175, 1976–1 C.B. 92, to what do the 175 and the 92 refer?

11. **LO.1, 4** Rank the following items from the lowest authority to the highest in the Federal tax law system:
    a. Interpretive Regulation.
    b. Legislative Regulation.
    c. Letter ruling.
    d. Revenue Ruling.
    e. Internal Revenue Code.
    f. Proposed Regulation.

12. **LO.1** Interpret each of the following citations:
    a. Prop.Reg. § 1.1001–3(h)(2).
    b. Rev.Proc. 2002–38, 2002–1 C.B. 1037.
    c. Ltr.Rul. 9015014.

13. **LO.1, 5** Sally Brown calls you on the phone. She says that she has found a 2001 letter ruling that agrees with a position she wishes to take on her tax return. She asks you about the precedential value of a letter ruling. Draft a memo for the tax files outlining what you told Sally.

    COMMUNICATIONS

14. **LO.1** Sri is considering writing the IRS to find out whether a possible stock redemption would be a qualified stock redemption. Outline some relevant tax issues Sri faces in determining whether to request a letter ruling.

    ISSUE ID

15. **LO.1** Where may private letter rulings be found?

16. **LO.1** What are the differences between Technical Advice Memoranda (TAMs) and Technical Expedited Advice Memoranda (TEAMs)?

17. **LO.1** Dwain receives a 90-day letter after his discussion with an appeals officer. He is not satisfied with the $92,000 settlement offer. Identify the relevant tax research issues facing Dwain.

    ISSUE ID

18. **LO.1** Which of the following would be considered advantages of the Small Cases Division of the Tax Court?
    a. Appeal to the U.S. Tax Court is possible.
    b. A hearing of a deficiency of $65,000 is considered on a timely basis.
    c. Taxpayer can handle the litigation without using a lawyer or certified public accountant.
    d. Taxpayer can use other Small Cases Division decisions for precedential value.
    e. The actual hearing is conducted informally.
    f. Travel time will probably be reduced.

19. **LO.1** List an advantage and a disadvantage of using the U.S. District Court as the trial court for Federal tax litigation.

20. **LO.1, 5** Caleb Toombs is considering litigating a tax deficiency of approximately $323,000 in the court system. He asks you to provide him with a short description of his alternatives indicating the advantages and disadvantages of each. Prepare your response to Caleb in the form of a letter. His address is 200 Mesa Drive, Tucson, AZ 85714.

    COMMUNICATIONS

21. **LO.1** List an advantage and a disadvantage of using the U.S. Tax Court as the trial court for Federal tax litigation.

22. **LO.1** A taxpayer lives in Michigan. In a controversy with the IRS, the taxpayer loses at the trial court level. Describe the appeal procedure under the following different assumptions:
    a. The trial court was the Small Cases Division of the U.S. Tax Court.
    b. The trial court was the U.S. Tax Court.
    c. The trial court was a U.S. District Court.
    d. The trial court was the U.S. Court of Federal Claims.

23. **LO.1** What is meant by the term *petitioner*?

24. **LO.1** An appellate court will often become involved in fact-finding determination. Discuss the validity of this statement.

25. **LO.1** For the U.S. Tax Court, U.S. District Court, and U.S. Court of Federal Claims, indicate the following:
    a. Number of regular judges per court.
    b. Availability of a jury trial.
    c. Whether the deficiency must be paid before the trial.

26. **LO.1** In which of the following states could a taxpayer appeal the decision of a U.S. District Court to the Ninth Circuit Court of Appeals?
    a. Alaska.
    b. Arkansas.
    c. Florida.
    d. New York.
    e. Kansas.

27. **LO.1** What precedents must each of these courts follow?
    a. U.S. Tax Court.
    b. U.S. Court of Federal Claims.
    c. U.S. District Court.

28. **LO.1** What determines the appropriate Circuit Court of Appeals for a particular taxpayer?

29. **LO.1, 4** In assessing the validity of a prior court decision, discuss the significance of the following on the taxpayer's issue:
    a. The decision was rendered by the U.S. District Court of Wyoming. Taxpayer lives in Wyoming.
    b. The decision was rendered by the U.S. Court of Federal Claims. Taxpayer lives in Wyoming.
    c. The decision was rendered by the Second Circuit Court of Appeals. Taxpayer lives in California.
    d. The decision was rendered by the U.S. Supreme Court.
    e. The decision was rendered by the U.S. Tax Court. The IRS has acquiesced in the result.
    f. Same as (e) except that the IRS has issued a nonacquiescence as to the result.

30. **LO.2** In the citation *Adelman v. U.S.*, 304 F.Supp. 599 (D.Ct. Cal., 1969), *aff'd* 440 F.2d 991 (CA–9, 1971), to what do the 304 and 991 refer? Which is the trial court citation?

31. **LO.2** Is there an automatic right to appeal to the U.S. Supreme Court? What is the process?

32. **LO.2** Referring to the citations only, determine which court issued these decisions.
    a. *Lucas v. Ox Fibre Brush Co.*, 281 U.S. 115 (1930).
    b. *Jack E. Golsen*, 54 T.C. 742 (1970).
    c. *Greg McIntosh*, T.C.Memo. 2001–144.
    d. *Magneson v. Comm.*, 753 F.2d 1490 (CA–9, 1985).
    e. *BB&T Corp. v. U.S.*, 97 AFTR 2d 2006–873 (D. Ct. N. Car., 2006).
    f. Rev.Rul. 2003–102, 2003–2 C.B. 559.

33. **LO.2** Interpret each of the following citations:
    a. 81 T.C. 782 (1983).
    b. 125 F.3d 120 (CA–3, 1997).
    c. 2005–2 USTC ¶ 50,575 (CA–2, 2005).
    d. 96 AFTR 2d 2005–6344 (CA–2, 2005).
    e. 330 F.Supp.2d 122 (D.Ct. Conn., 2004).

34. **LO.1, 2** Explain the following abbreviations:

a. CA–2.	f. *Cert. denied.*	k. F.3d.
b. Fed.Cl.	g. *acq.*	l. F.Supp.
c. *aff'd.*	h. B.T.A.	m. USSC.
d. *rev'd.*	i. USTC.	n. S.Ct.
e. *rem'd.*	j. AFTR.	o. D.Ct.

35. **LO.2** Give the Commerce Clearing House citation for the following courts:
    a. Small Cases Division of the Tax Court.
    b. Federal District Court.
    c. U.S. Supreme Court.
    d. U.S. Court of Federal Claims.
    e. Tax Court Memorandum decision.

36. **LO.2** Where can you locate a published decision of the U.S. Court of Federal Claims?

37. **LO.1, 2** Which of the following items can probably be found in the *Cumulative Bulletin*?
    a. Action on Decision.
    b. Small Cases Division of the U.S. Tax Court decision.
    c. Letter ruling.
    d. Revenue Procedure.
    e. Finalized Regulation.
    f. U.S. Court of Federal Claims decision.
    g. Senate Finance Committee Report.
    h. Acquiescences to Tax Court decisions.
    i. U.S. Circuit Court of Appeals decision.

38. **LO.3** Yvonne has to prepare a research paper discussing the tax aspects of alimony payments for her tax class. Explain to Yvonne how she can research this topic using hard copy.

39. **LO.4** Where can a researcher find the current Internal Revenue Code of 1986?

40. **LO.2, 4** You inherit a tax problem that was researched five months ago. You believe the answer is correct, but you are unfamiliar with the general area. How would you find some recent articles dealing with the subject area? How do you evaluate the reliability of the authority cited in the research report? How do you determine the latest developments pertaining to the research problem?

41. **LO.6** What is the difference between tax avoidance and tax evasion?

42. **LO.7** Describe simulation questions on the CPA exam.

PROBLEMS

43. **LO.1** In which Subchapter of the Internal Revenue Code would one find information about partnership taxation?
    a. Subchapter S.
    b. Subchapter C.
    c. Subchapter P.
    d. Subchapter K.
    e. Subchapter M.

44. **LO.1** In order to locate an IRS Revenue Procedure that was issued during the past week, which source would you consult?
    a. *Cumulative Bulletin.*
    b. *Federal Register.*
    c. *Internal Revenue Bulletin.*
    d. Internal Revenue Code.
    e. Some other source.

45. **LO.1** Which of the following items can be found in the *Federal Register*?
    a. Letter Ruling.
    b. Action on Decision.
    c. Revenue Ruling.
    d. Temporary Regulation.
    e. Technical Advice Memorandum.

46. **LO.1, 4** Rank the items below from the most reliable to the least reliable:
    a. Letter Ruling.
    b. Legislative Regulation.
    c. Code Section.
    d. Revenue Ruling.
    e. Proposed Regulation.
    f. Interpretive Regulation.
    g. Recent Temporary Regulation.

47. **LO.4** Using the legend provided, classify each of the following tax sources:

Legend
P = Primary tax source
S = Secondary tax source
B = Both
N = Neither

    a. Sixteenth Amendment to the U.S. Constitution.
    b. Tax treaty between the United States and France.
    c. Revenue Procedure.

     d.   General Counsel Memoranda (1989).

     e.   U.S. District Court decision.

     f.   *Tax Notes* article.

     g.   Temporary Regulations (issued 2006).

     h.   U.S. Tax Court Memorandum decision.

     i.   Small Cases Division of the U.S. Tax Court decision.

     j.   House Ways and Means Committee report.

48. **L0.1, 2** Using the legend provided, classify each of the following citations as to publisher:

Legend
RIA = Research Institute of America
CCH = Commerce Clearing House
W = West
U.S. = U.S. Government
O = Others

     a.   24 T.C. 818.

     b.   64 TCM 1594.

     c.   563 F.Supp. 379.

     d.   45 AFTR 2d 80–1487.

     e.   54–2 USTC ¶9714.

     f.   RIA T.C.Memo. Dec. ¶92726.

     g.   Announcement 2006–30, 2006–1 C.B. 879.

     h.   Rev.Rul. 71–381, 1971–2 C.B. 126.

     i.   104 S.Ct 1495.

     j.   348 U.S. 426.

49. **L0.6** Using the legend provided, classify each of the following statements:

Legend
A = Tax avoidance
E = Tax evasion
N = Neither

     a.   Monica writes a $1,000 check for a charitable contribution on December 28, 2011, but does not mail the check to the charitable organization until January 10, 2012. She takes a deduction in 2011.

     b.   Robert decides not to report interest income from a bank because the amount is only $11.75.

     c.   Jim pays property taxes on his home in December 2011 rather than waiting until February 2012.

     d.   Jane switches her investments from taxable corporate bonds to tax-exempt municipal bonds.

     e.   Ted encourages his mother to save most of her Social Security benefits so that he will be able to claim her as a dependent.

RESEARCH PROBLEMS

THOMSON REUTERS

Checkpoint® Student Edition

Note: Solutions to Research Problems can be prepared by using the **Checkpoint®
Student Edition** online research product, which is available to accompany this text. It is also possible to prepare solutions to the Research Problems by using tax research materials found in a standard tax library.

Research Problem 1. Under Code § 274(a), are lunches with lawyers and accountants to build up goodwill deductible?

Research Problem 2. Determine what is covered in the following Subchapters in Chapter 1, Subtitle A of the Internal Revenue Code of 1986:

a. A.
b. C.
c. E.
d. G.
e. L.
f. O.

Research Problem 3. What is covered in these Regulation prefixes?

a. Part 1.
b. Part 20.
c. Part 25.
d. Part 31.
e. Part 301.
f. Part 601.

Research Problem 4. Determine the missing data in these court decisions and rulings:

a. *Deputy v. DuPont*, 308 U.S. 488 (_____).
b. *Katz v. U.S.*, 67 AFTR 2d 91–733 (Cl.Ct., _____).
c. *General Electric Co. v. U.S.*, 83–2 USTC ¶ 9532 (_____, 1983).
d. *U.S. v. Scott*, 167 F.2d _____ (CA–8, 1948).
e. *Garrow v. Comm.*, 43 T.C. 890 (_____).
f. *Estate of Smith v. Comm.*, 36 TCM _____ (1977).
g. Rev.Rul. 69–_____, 1969–1 C.B. 100.
h. Rev.Rul. 60–226, 1960–1 C.B. _____.

Research Problem 5. Locate the July 2010 issue of *The Tax Adviser* and find the article by J. D. Zook and K. L. Zook. What are the title and page numbers of their article? How did the American Recovery and Reinvestment Act of 2009 modify the HOPE scholarship credit?

Research Problem 6. Most major airlines offer frequent-flyer programs that allow passengers to accumulate miles for each flight. Individuals may also earn frequent-flyer miles or other promotional benefits in other ways, such as through rental cars or hotels. These promotional benefits may generally be exchanged for upgraded seating, free travel, discounted travel, travel-related services, or other services or benefits. Are frequent-flyer miles taxable?

Research Problem 7. In the following tax publications matrix, place an X if a court decision can be found in the publication. There may be more than one X in a row for a particular court.

Court	U.S. Govt. Printing Office	West				Research Institute of America			Commerce Clearing House	
		Federal Supp.2d	Federal 3d	Federal Claims Reporter	S.Ct.	BTA Memo.	T.C.Memo.	AFTR	T.C. Memo.	USTC
U.S. Supreme Court										
Circuit Court of Appeals										
Court of Federal Claims										
District Court										
Tax Court (Regular decisions)										
Tax Court (Memo decisions)										
Board of Tax Appeals										
BTA Memo.										

Research Problem 8. When Oprah gave away Pontiac G6 sedans to her TV audience, was the value of the cars taxable? On Labor Day weekend in 2006, World Furniture Mall in Plano, Illinois, gave away $275,000 of furniture because the Chicago Bears shut out the Green Bay Packers in their football season opener at Lambeau Field in Green Bay (26–0). Was the

DECISION MAKING

free furniture in the form of a discount or rebate taxable, or should the furniture company hand the customers a Form 1099–MISC?

Research Problem 9. You are interviewing a client before preparing his tax return. He indicates that he did not list as income $96,000 received as a recovery for false imprisonment. What should you do with respect to this significant recovery?

Partial list of research aids:
CCA 200809001.
Daniel and Brenda Stadnyk, T.C.Memo. 2008–289.
Rev.Rul. 2007–14, 2007–1 C.B. 747.
§ 104.

INTERNET *activity*

Use the tax resources of the Internet to address the following questions. Do not restrict your search to the Web, but include a review of newsgroups and general reference materials, practitioner sites and resources, primary sources of the tax law, chat rooms and discussion groups, and other opportunities.

Research Problem 10. Go to **www.taxalmanac.org** and **www.Legalbitstream.com** on the Internet and find the following:
a. Letter Rulings.
b. Actions on Decisions
c. IRS Notices.
d. General Counsel Memoranda.
e. Technical Advice Memoranda.
f. Treasury Decisions.
g. Revenue Rulings.
h. Revenue Procedures.
i. IRS Announcements.
j. U.S. Tax Court Summary Decisions.
k. U.S. Tax Court Memorandum Decisions.

Research Problem 11. Go to the U.S. Tax Court Internet site:
a. What different types of cases can be found on the site?
b. What is a Summary Opinion? Find one.
c. What is a Memorandum Opinion? Find one.
d. Find the "Rules and Practices and Procedures."
e. Is the site user-friendly? E-mail suggested improvements to the webmaster.

Tax Formula and Tax Determination; An Overview of Property Transactions

LEARNING OBJECTIVES

After completing Chapter 3, you should be able to:

L0.1
Recognize and apply the components of the Federal income tax formula.

L0.2
Explain the standard deduction and evaluate its choice in arriving at taxable income.

L0.3
Apply the rules for arriving at personal exemptions.

L0.4
Explain the rules for determining dependency exemptions.

L0.5
List the filing requirements and choose the proper filing status.

L0.6
Demonstrate the proper procedures for determining the tax liability.

L0.7
Identify and report kiddie tax situations.

L0.8
Formulate the fundamentals of property transactions.

L0.9
Evaluate tax planning opportunities associated with the individual tax formula.

OUTLINE

FRAMEWORK 1040:

Tax Formula for Individuals

This chapter covers the boldfaced portions of the Tax Formula for Individuals that is introduced in Figure 3.1 on p. 3-3. Below those portions are the sections of Form 1040 where the results are reported.

Income (broadly conceived)...	$xx,xxx
Less: Exclusions	(x,xxx)
Gross income	$xx,xxx
Less: Deductions for adjusted gross income	(x,xxx)
Adjusted gross income...	$xx,xxx
Less: The greater of total itemized deductions *or* the standard deduction.................	(x,xxx)

FORM 1040 (P.1)

1 ☐ Single
2 ☐ Married filing jointly (even if only one had income)
3 ☐ Married filing separately. Enter spouse's SSN above and full name here. ▶

4 ☐ Head of household (with qualifying person). (See instructions.) If the qualifying person is a child but not your dependent, enter this child's name here. ▶
5 ☐ Qualifying widow(er) with dependent child

Personal and dependency exemptions..	(x,xxx)

FORM 1040 (P.2)

39a Check if: ☐ **You** were born before January 2, 1946,   ☐ Blind. ☐ **Spouse** was born before January 2, 1946,   ☐ Blind.   } Total boxes checked ▶ **39a** ☐

b If your spouse itemizes on a separate return or you were a dual-status alien, check here ▶   39b☐

40 **Itemized deductions** (from Schedule A) **or** your **standard deduction** (see instructions) . .

42 **Exemptions.** Multiply $3,650 by the number on line 6d . . . .

Taxable income	$ xx,xxx
Tax on taxable income (see Tax Tables or Tax Rate Schedules).........................	$ x,xxx
Less: Tax credits (including income taxes withheld and prepaid)........................	(xxx)
Tax due (or refund)...	$ xxx

THE BIG PICTURE   Tax Solutions for the Real World

A DIVIDED HOUSEHOLD

Polly maintains a household in which she lives with her unemployed husband (Nick), stepdaughter (Paige), and a family friend (Maude). She provides more than one-half of the support of both Paige and Maude. Maude was fatally injured in an automobile accident in February, and Polly paid for her hospitalization and funeral expenses. Paige, an accomplished gymnast, graduated from high school last year. Paige has a part-time job but spends most of her time training and looking for an athletic scholarship to the "right" college. In March, Nick left for parts unknown and has not been seen or heard from since. Polly was more surprised than distressed over Nick's unexpected departure. One reaction, however, was to sell her wedding rings to a cousin who was getting married. The rings cost $15,000 and were sold for their approximate value of $8,000.

Based on these facts, what are Polly's income tax concerns for the current year? **Read the chapter and formulate your response.**

The framework for the application of the Federal income tax to individuals is the tax formula. As Chapter 1 mentioned, the tax formula is an integral part of our U.S. tax system (i.e., local, state, and Federal), and Chapter 3 provides a summary of its components. In addition, several of its key components—the standard deduction, personal and dependency exemptions, and tax determination—are discussed at length in Chapter 3.

By introducing the tax formula, therefore, Chapter 3 establishes the framework for almost all of the rest of the text (i.e., Chapters 4 to 19). The formula and its impact on the chapters to follow are reflected in Figure 3.1. In integrating the formula with the

FIGURE 3.1	Tax Formula for Individuals (Components Integrated into the Text)	
		Text Discussion
Income (broadly conceived)	$xx,xxx	Chs. 3, 4
Less: **Exclusions**	(x,xxx)	Ch. 5
Gross income	$xx,xxx	Chs. 4, 16, 17
Less: **Deductions** *for* adjusted gross income	(x,xxx)	Chs. 6–9, 11, 16, 17
Adjusted gross income	$xx,xxx	
Less: The greater of—		
Total **itemized deductions**	(x,xxx)	Chs. 6, 9, 10, 11
or **standard deduction**		Ch. 3
Less: **Personal** and **dependency exemptions**	(x,xxx)	Ch. 3
Taxable income	$xx,xxx	Chs. 3, 12, 13
Tax on taxable income	$ x,xxx	Chs. 3, 12, 13
Less: **Tax credits**	(xxx)	Ch. 13
Tax due (or refund)	$ xxx	Chs. 3, 12, 13

chapters in the text, however, some liberties were taken. In the interest of simplicity, Figure 3.1 omits references to several chapters for the following reasons:

- Chapter 18 deals with the more sophisticated aspects of accounting periods and methods. The main consideration in this area is the distinction between the cash and accrual methods of accounting. The method used controls the recognition *or* deferral of *income* and *deductions* and, therefore, is discussed in Chapters 4 and 6.
- Chapter 19 deals with deferred compensation and cuts across several parts of the tax formula. Depending on the type of arrangement involved, gross income may be recognized (or deferred), or a deduction can materialize.

Chapter 3 also provides an overview of property transactions. When property is sold or otherwise disposed of, a gain or loss may result, which can affect the determination of taxable income. Although property transactions are covered in detail in Chapters 14–17, an understanding of certain basic concepts helps in working with some of the materials to follow. The concluding portion of this chapter furnishes an overview of property transactions, including the distinction between realized and recognized gain or loss, and the classification of such gain or loss (ordinary or capital) for income tax purposes.

In terms of the tax formula, net gains from property transactions that are recognized will affect the gross income component. If the gain is deferred (e.g., like-kind exchanges or involuntary conversions—see Chapter 15) or not recognized (i.e., sale of a residence—see Chapter 15), there is no immediate tax effect. Recognized losses from property transactions are treated as deductions *for* adjusted gross income (AGI).

3.1 TAX FORMULA

Given that the tax formula establishes the framework for the Federal income tax on individuals, a brief review of its components will be helpful in understanding the in-depth discussion that follows in this and subsequent chapters.

LO.1

Recognize and apply the components of the Federal income tax formula.

COMPONENTS OF THE TAX FORMULA

Income (Broadly Conceived)

In the tax formula, "income" is broadly conceived and includes all the taxpayer's income, both taxable and nontaxable. Although it is essentially equivalent to gross receipts, it does not include a return of capital or receipt of borrowed funds.

EXHIBIT 3.1   **Partial List of Exclusions from Gross Income**

Accident insurance proceeds	Meals and lodging (if furnished for employer's convenience)
Annuities (cost element)	Military allowances
Bequests	Minister's dwelling rental value allowance
Child support payments	
Cost-of-living allowance (for military)	Railroad retirement benefits (to a limited extent)
Damages for personal injury or sickness	
Gifts received	Scholarship grants (to a limited extent)
Group term life insurance, premium paid by employer (for coverage up to $50,000)	Social Security benefits (to a limited extent)
	Veterans' benefits
Inheritances	Welfare payments
Interest from state and local (i.e., municipal) bonds	Workers' compensation benefits
Life insurance paid on death	

EXAMPLE 1

Dan decides to quit renting and move into a new house. Consequently, the owner of the apartment building returns to Dan the $600 damage deposit he previously made. In order to make a down payment on the house, Dan sells stock for $20,000 (original cost of $8,000) and borrows $50,000 from a bank. Only the $12,000 gain from the sale of the stock is income to Dan. The $600 damage deposit and the $8,000 cost of the stock are a return of capital. The $50,000 bank loan is not income as Dan has an obligation to repay that amount. ∎

Exclusions

For various reasons, Congress has chosen to exclude certain types of income from the income tax base. The principal income exclusions are discussed in Chapter 5. A partial list of these exclusions is shown in Exhibit 3.1.

Gross Income

The Internal Revenue Code defines gross income broadly as "except as otherwise provided . . ., all income from whatever source derived."[1] The "except as otherwise provided" refers to exclusions. Gross income includes, but is not limited to, the items in the partial list in Exhibit 3.2. It does not include unrealized gains. Gross income is discussed in Chapters 4 and 5.

EXAMPLE 2

Beth received the following amounts during the year:

Salary	$30,000
Interest on savings account	900
Gift from her aunt	10,000
Prize won in state lottery	1,000
Alimony from ex-husband	12,000
Child support from ex-husband	6,000
Damages for injury in auto accident	25,000
Ten $50 bills in an unmarked envelope found in an airport lounge (airport authorities could not locate anyone who claimed ownership)	500
Federal income tax refund for last year's tax overpayment	120
Increase in the value of stock held for investment	5,000 ∎

---

[1] § 61(a).

EXHIBIT 3.2	Partial List of Gross Income Items

Alimony	Hobby income
Annuities (income element)	Interest
Awards	Jury duty fees
Back pay	Living quarters, meals (unless furnished for employer's convenience)
Bargain purchase from employer	
Bonuses	
Breach of contract damages	Mileage allowance
Business income	Military pay (unless combat pay)
Clergy fees	Notary fees
Commissions	Partnership income
Compensation for services	Pensions
Death benefits	Prizes
Debts forgiven	Professional fees
Director's fees	Punitive damages
Dividends	Rents
Embezzled funds	Rewards
Employee awards (in certain cases)	Royalties
Employee benefits (except certain fringe benefits)	Salaries
	Severance pay
Estate and trust income	Strike and lockout benefits
Farm income	Supplemental unemployment benefits
Fees	Tips and gratuities
Gains from illegal activities	Travel allowance (in certain cases)
Gains from sale of property	Treasure trove (found property)
Gambling winnings	Wages
Group term life insurance, premium paid by employer (for coverage over $50,000)	

Review Exhibits 3.1 and 3.2 to determine the amount Beth must include in the computation of taxable income and the amount she may exclude. Then check your answer in footnote 2.[2]

Deductions for Adjusted Gross Income

Individual taxpayers have two categories of deductions: (1) deductions *for* adjusted gross income (deductions to arrive at adjusted gross income) and (2) deductions *from* adjusted gross income.

Deductions *for* adjusted gross income (AGI) are sometimes known as *above-the-line* deductions because on the tax return they are taken before the "line" designating AGI. They are also referred to as *page 1 deductions* since they are claimed, either directly or indirectly (i.e., through supporting schedules), on page 1 of Form 1040. Deductions *for* AGI include, but are not limited to, the following:[3]

- Expenses incurred in a trade or business.
- One-half of self-employment tax.
- Unreimbursed moving expenses.
- Contributions to traditional Individual Retirement Accounts (IRAs) and certain other retirement plans.
- Fees for college tuition and related expenses.

---

[2]Beth must include $44,400 in computing taxable income ($30,000 salary + $900 interest + $1,000 lottery prize + $12,000 alimony + $500 found property). She can exclude $41,000 ($10,000 gift from aunt + $6,000 child support + $25,000 damages). The $120 Federal income tax refund is excluded because it represents an adjustment (i.e., overpayment) of a nondeductible expenditure made in the previous year. The unrealized gain on the stock held for investment also is not included in gross income. Such gain will be included in gross income only when it is realized upon disposition of the stock.

[3]§ 62.

CITIZENSHIP IS NOT TAX-FREE

Gross income from "whatever source derived" includes income from both U.S. and foreign sources. This approach to taxation, where the government taxes its citizens and residents on their worldwide income regardless of where earned, is referred to as a *global system*. Income earned by U.S. citizens outside the United States can be subject to additional taxes, however, because all countries maintain the right to tax income earned within their borders. Consequently, the U.S. tax law includes various mechanisms to alleviate the double taxation that arises when income is subject to tax in multiple jurisdictions. These mechanisms include the foreign tax deduction, the foreign tax credit, the foreign earned income exclusion for U.S. citizens and residents working abroad, and various tax treaty provisions.

Most industrialized countries use variants of the global system. An alternative approach is the *territorial system*, where a government taxes only the income earned within its borders. Hong Kong and Guatemala, for example, use a territorial approach.

- Contributions to Health Savings Accounts (HSAs).
- Penalty for early withdrawal from savings.
- Interest on student loans.
- Excess capital losses.
- Alimony payments.

The principal deductions *for* AGI are discussed in Chapters 6, 7, 8, 9, 11, 16, and 17.

Adjusted Gross Income (AGI)

AGI is an important subtotal that serves as the basis for computing percentage limitations on certain itemized deductions, such as medical expenses, charitable contributions, and certain casualty losses. For example, medical expenses are deductible only to the extent they exceed 7.5 percent of AGI, and charitable contribution deductions may not exceed 50 percent of AGI. These limitations might be described as a 7.5 percent *floor* under the medical expense deduction and a 50 percent *ceiling* on the charitable contribution deduction.

EXAMPLE 3

Keith earned a salary of $68,000 in the current year. He contributed $5,000 to his traditional Individual Retirement Account (IRA) and paid alimony of $3,000 to his ex-wife. His AGI is computed as follows:

Gross income		
Salary		$68,000
Less: Deductions *for* AGI		
IRA contribution	$5,000	
Alimony payment	3,000	(8,000)
AGI		$60,000

EXAMPLE 4

 Assume the same facts as in Example 3, and that Keith also had medical expenses of $5,800. Medical expenses may be included in itemized deductions to the extent they exceed 7.5% of AGI. In computing his itemized deductions, Keith may include medical expenses of $1,300 [$5,800 medical expenses − $4,500 (7.5% × $60,000 AGI)]. ∎

Itemized Deductions

As a general rule, personal expenditures are disallowed as deductions in arriving at taxable income. However, Congress allows specified personal expenses as

EXHIBIT 3.3	Partial List of Itemized Deductions

Medical expenses in excess of 7.5% of AGI
State and local income or sales taxes
Real estate taxes
Personal property taxes
Interest on home mortgage
Investment interest (to a limited extent)
Charitable contributions (within specified percentage limitations)
Casualty and theft losses in excess of 10% of AGI
Miscellaneous expenses (to the extent such expenses exceed 2% of AGI)
    Union dues
    Professional dues and subscriptions
    Certain educational expenses
    Tax return preparation fee
    Investment counsel fees
    Unreimbursed employee business expenses (after a percentage
      reduction for meals and entertainment)

itemized deductions. Such expenditures include medical expenses, certain taxes and interest, and charitable contributions.

In addition to these personal expenses, taxpayers are allowed itemized deductions for expenses related to (1) the production or collection of income and (2) the management of property held for the production of income.[4] These expenses, sometimes referred to as *nonbusiness expenses*, differ from trade or business expenses. Trade or business expenses, which are deductions *for* AGI, must be incurred in connection with a trade or business. Nonbusiness expenses, on the other hand, are expenses incurred in connection with an income-producing activity that does not qualify as a trade or business. Such expenses are itemized deductions.

EXAMPLE 5

Leo is the owner and operator of a video game arcade. All allowable expenses he incurs in connection with the arcade business are deductions *for* AGI. In addition, Leo has an extensive portfolio of stocks and bonds. Leo's investment activity is not treated as a trade or business. All allowable expenses that Leo incurs in connection with these investments are itemized deductions. ∎

Itemized deductions include, but are not limited to, the expenses listed in Exhibit 3.3. See Chapters 9 and 10 for a detailed discussion of itemized deductions.

Nondeductible Expenditures

Many expenditures are not deductible and, therefore, provide no tax benefit. Examples include, but are not limited to, the following:

- Personal living expenses, including any losses on the sale of personal use property.
- Hobby losses.
- Life insurance premiums.
- Expenses incident to jury duty.
- Gambling losses (in excess of gains).
- Child support payments.
- Fines and penalties.
- Political contributions.
- Certain passive losses.

---

[4]§ 212.

- Funeral expenses.
- Expenses paid on another's behalf.
- Capital expenditures.

If an expenditure is classified as nondeductible, the component of the tax formula affected will be either the deduction *for* AGI or the deduction *from* AGI. Thus, a traffic fine for speeding is nondeductible whether the taxpayer was using the automobile on a business trip (normally a deduction *for* AGI) or participating in a Habitat for Humanity project (normally a deduction *from* AGI).[5] Most of the nondeductible items listed above are discussed in Chapter 6. Passive loss limitations, however, are treated in Chapter 11.

Standard Deduction

In lieu of claiming itemized deductions, taxpayers will use the **standard deduction**. As discussed later in the chapter, the standard deduction varies depending on filing status, age, and blindness. Like personal and dependency exemptions (discussed later), the standard deduction is adjusted (i.e., indexed) each year for inflation.

Personal and Dependency Exemptions

Exemptions are allowed for the taxpayer, the taxpayer's spouse, and each dependent of the taxpayer. The exemption amount for 2011 is $3,700 (up from $3,650 in 2010).

Taxable Income

The determination of taxable income is illustrated below in Example 6.

EXAMPLE 6

Grace, age 25, is single and has her disabled and dependent mother living with her. Grace is a high school teacher and earned a $40,000 salary in 2011. Her other income consisted of $1,000 interest on a certificate of deposit (CD) and $500 interest on municipal bonds that she had received as a graduation gift in 2007. During 2011, she sustained a deductible capital loss of $1,000. Her itemized deductions are $8,800. Grace's taxable income for the year is computed as follows:

Income (broadly conceived)	
Salary	$40,000
Interest on a CD	1,000
Interest on municipal bonds	500
	$41,500
Less: Exclusion—Interest on municipal bonds	(500)
Gross income	$41,000
Less: Deduction *for* adjusted gross income—Capital loss	(1,000)
Adjusted gross income	$40,000
Less: The greater of total itemized deductions ($8,800) *or* the standard deduction for head of household ($8,500)	(8,800)
Personal and dependency exemptions (2 × $3,700)	(7,400)
Taxable income	$23,800

Note that the exclusion of $500 (i.e., interest from municipal bonds) is deducted in determining gross income. The loss of $1,000 from a property transaction is classified as a deduction *for* AGI. Grace chose to itemize her deductions *from* AGI as they exceed the standard deduction (see Table 3.1 later in the chapter for the derivation of the $8,500 amount). Grace's income tax is determined later in this chapter in Example 40.

[5]The use of a personal automobile in connection with a charitable activity would probably qualify for the charitable contribution deduction—a deduction *from* AGI.

Tax Due (or Refund)

The last step in applying the tax formula is the determination of tax due (or refund). Ascertain the appropriate filing status (single, head of household, etc.) and then apply the appropriate set of rates (i.e., Tax Rate Schedules or Tax Tables) to taxable income. Once the tax is derived, adjust for the various tax credits allowed (e.g., withholdings, earned income, research, foreign) to arrive at the additional tax due or any overpayment (i.e., refund) involved. Filing status and the use of the tax rates are discussed later in this chapter, while tax credits are the subject of Chapter 13.

TAX FORMULA—CORRELATION WITH FORM 1040

The structure of individual income tax returns (Forms 1040, 1040–A, or 1040–EZ) parallels the tax formula in Figure 3.1. Like the formula, the tax return places major emphasis on adjusted gross income (AGI), which appears on the bottom of page 1 and at the top of page 2 of Form 1040. In arriving at gross income (referred to as *total income*), *most* exclusions are not reported on the tax return. Deductions *for AGI* are summarized on page 1 of Form 1040. Deductions *from* AGI (referred to as "itemized deductions") are carried over from Schedule A to page 2 of Form 1040. The choice between the standard deduction and itemized deductions is made on page 2. This is followed by the deduction for personal and dependency exemptions to arrive at taxable income. Page 2 contains the tax determination aspects of the tax formula including any reduction allowed for available tax credits. The format of Form 1040 and its tie-in to the various supporting schedules containing components of the tax formula is graphically illustrated in Figure 6.1 of Chapter 6.

3.2 STANDARD DEDUCTION

A major component of the tax formula is the standard deduction. The effect of the standard deduction is to exempt part of a taxpayer's income from Federal income tax liability. In the past, Congress has attempted to set the tax-free amount represented by the standard deduction approximately equal to an estimated poverty level,[6] but it has not always been consistent in doing so.

> **LO.2**
>
> Explain the standard deduction and evaluate its choice in arriving at taxable income.

BASIC AND ADDITIONAL STANDARD DEDUCTION

The standard deduction is the sum of two components: the *basic* standard deduction and the *additional* standard deduction.[7] Table 3.1 lists the basic standard deduction allowed for taxpayers in each filing status. All taxpayers allowed a *full* standard deduction are entitled to the applicable amount listed in Table 3.1. The standard deduction amounts are subject to adjustment for inflation each year.

Certain taxpayers are not allowed to claim *any* standard deduction, and the standard deduction is *limited* for others. These provisions are discussed later in the chapter.

A taxpayer who is age 65 or over *or* blind qualifies for an *additional standard deduction* of $1,150 or $1,450, depending on filing status (see amounts in Table 3.2). Two additional standard deductions are allowed for a taxpayer who is age 65 or over *and* blind. The additional standard deduction provisions also apply for a qualifying spouse who is age 65 or over or blind, but a taxpayer may not claim an additional standard deduction for a dependent.

To determine whether to itemize, the taxpayer compares the *total* standard deduction (the sum of the basic standard deduction and any additional standard deductions) with total itemized deductions. Taxpayers are allowed to deduct the *greater* of itemized

---

[6]S.Rep. No. 92–437, 92nd Cong., 1st Sess., 1971, p. 54. Another purpose of the standard deduction was discussed in Chapter 1 under Influence of the Internal Revenue Service—Administrative Feasibility. The size of the standard deduction has a direct bearing on the number of taxpayers who are in a position to itemize deductions. Reducing the number of taxpayers who itemize also reduces the audit effort required from the IRS.

[7]§ 63(c)(1).

TABLE 3.1	Basic Standard Deduction Amounts		
		Standard Deduction Amount	
Filing Status		**2010**	**2011**
Single		$ 5,700	$ 5,800
Married, filing jointly		11,400	11,600
Surviving spouse		11,400	11,600
Head of household		8,400	8,500
Married, filing separately		5,700	5,800

TABLE 3.2	Amount of Each Additional Standard Deduction		
Filing Status		**2010**	**2011**
Single		$1,400	$1,450
Married, filing jointly		1,100	1,150
Surviving spouse		1,100	1,150
Head of household		1,400	1,450
Married, filing separately		1,100	1,150

deductions or the standard deduction. The choice is elective. Undoubtedly, some taxpayers claim the standard deduction because they do not want to bother completing the Schedule A required for itemizing deductions *from* AGI. Likewise, the choice is an annual one, and a taxpayer is not bound by what was done on returns filed for past years. For example, many taxpayers who have previously claimed the standard deduction will switch to itemizing after purchasing a home (because of the mortgage interest and property tax deductions). In other circumstances, the reverse could be true—the taxpayer will switch from itemizing to the standard deduction. As illustrated below, age can make a difference.

EXAMPLE 7

Prior to 2011, Sara, who is single, had always chosen to itemize. In 2011, however, she reaches age 65. Her itemized deductions for 2011 are $6,500, but her total standard deduction is $7,250 [$5,800 (basic standard deduction) + $1,450 (additional standard deduction)]. Sara should compute her taxable income for 2011 using the standard deduction ($7,250), since it exceeds her itemized deductions ($6,500). ∎

For 2008 and 2009, Congress provided special standard deductions that allowed a limited deduction for real property taxes and the sales taxes on automobile purchases. These provisions were designed to stimulate home ownership and the automobile industry and were available only to nonitemizers. Once expired, the special standard deductions were not renewed!

INDIVIDUALS NOT ELIGIBLE FOR THE STANDARD DEDUCTION

Although almost two-thirds of individuals choose the standard deduction in preference to itemizing their deductions *from* AGI, some taxpayers do not qualify. The following individual taxpayers are ineligible to use the standard deduction and must therefore itemize:[8]

---

[8]§ 63(c)(6).

- A married individual filing a separate return where either spouse itemizes deductions.
- A nonresident alien.
- An individual filing a return for a period of less than 12 months because of a change in the annual accounting period.

The death of an individual does not eliminate the standard deduction for the year of death; nor does the deduction have to be allocated to the pre-death portion of the year. If, for example, Sandy (age 80 and single) died on January 14, 2011, his executor would be able to claim a standard deduction of $7,250 [$5,800 (basic standard deduction) + $1,450 (additional standard deduction for age)] on his final income tax return (covering the period from January 1 to January 14, 2011). This presumes, of course, that the standard deduction is preferable to itemizing.

SPECIAL LIMITATIONS ON THE STANDARD DEDUCTION FOR DEPENDENTS

Special rules apply to the standard deduction and personal exemption of an individual who can be claimed as a dependent on another person's tax return.

When filing his or her own tax return, a *dependent's* basic standard deduction in 2011 is limited to the greater of $950 or the sum of the individual's earned income for the year plus $300.[9] However, if the sum of the individual's earned income plus $300 exceeds the normal standard deduction, the standard deduction is limited to the appropriate amount shown in Table 3.1. These limitations apply only to the basic standard deduction. A dependent who is 65 or over or blind or both is also allowed the additional standard deduction amount on his or her own return (refer to Table 3.2). These provisions are illustrated in Examples 8 through 11.

EXAMPLE 8

Susan, who is 17 years old and single, is claimed as a dependent on her parents' tax return. During 2011, she received $1,200 interest (unearned income) on a savings account. She also earned $400 from a part-time job. When Susan files her own tax return, her standard deduction is $950 (the greater of $950 or the sum of earned income of $400 plus $300). ∎

EXAMPLE 9

Assume the same facts as in Example 8, except that Susan is 67 years old and is claimed as a dependent on her son's tax return. In this case, when Susan files her own tax return, her standard deduction is $2,400 [$950 (the greater of $950 or the sum of earned income of $400 plus $300) + $1,450 (the additional standard deduction allowed because Susan is 65 or over)]. ∎

EXAMPLE 10

Peggy, who is 16 years old and single, earned $700 from a summer job and had no unearned income during 2011. She is claimed as a dependent on her parents' tax return. Her standard deduction is $1,000 (the greater of $950 or the sum of $700 earned income plus $300). ∎

EXAMPLE 11

Jack, who is a 20-year-old, single, full-time college student, is claimed as a dependent on his parents' tax return. He worked as a musician during the summer of 2011, earning $5,900. Jack's standard deduction is $5,800 (the greater of $950 or the sum of $5,900 earned income plus $300, but limited to the $5,800 standard deduction for a single taxpayer). ∎

---

[9]§ 63(c)(5). Both the $950 amount and the $300 amount are subject to adjustment for inflation each year. Neither amount was raised from that available in 2010.

3.3 PERSONAL EXEMPTIONS

LO.3

Apply the rules for arriving at personal exemptions.

The use of exemptions in the tax system is based in part on the idea that a taxpayer with a small amount of income should be exempt from income taxation. An exemption frees a specified amount of income from tax ($3,700 in 2011 and $3,650 in 2010). The exemption amount is indexed (adjusted) annually for inflation.

Exemptions that are allowed for the taxpayer and spouse are designated as **personal exemptions**. Those exemptions allowed for the care and maintenance of other persons are called dependency exemptions and are discussed in the next section.

An individual cannot claim a personal exemption if he or she is claimed as a dependent by another.

EXAMPLE 12

Assume the same facts as in Example 11. On his own income tax return,[10] Jack's taxable income is determined as follows:

Gross income	$ 5,900
Less: Standard deduction	(5,800)
Personal exemption	(–0–)
Taxable income	$ 100

Note that Jack is not allowed a personal exemption because he is claimed as a dependent by his parents. ∎

When a husband and wife file a joint return, they may claim two personal exemptions. However, when separate returns are filed, a married taxpayer cannot claim an exemption for his or her spouse *unless* the spouse has no gross income and is not claimed as the dependent of another taxpayer.[11]

The determination of marital status generally is made at the end of the taxable year, except when a spouse dies during the year. Spouses who enter into a legal separation under a decree of divorce or separate maintenance before the end of the year are considered to be unmarried at the end of the taxable year.

The amount of the exemption is not reduced due to the taxpayer's death. The same rule applies to dependency exemptions. As long as an individual qualified as a dependent at the time of death, the full amount of the exemption can be claimed.

For *Federal* tax purposes, the law does not recognize same-sex marriages. By virtue of the Defense of Marriage Act (Pub. L. No. 104–199), a marriage means a legal union only between a man and a woman as husband and wife.

3.4 DEPENDENCY EXEMPTIONS

LO.4

Explain the rules for determining dependency exemptions.

As is the case with personal exemptions, a taxpayer is permitted to claim an exemption of $3,700 in 2011 ($3,650 in 2010) for each person who qualifies as a dependent. A **dependency exemption** is available for either a qualifying child or a qualifying relative and must not run afoul of certain other rules (i.e., joint return, nonresident alien prohibitions).

 ## QUALIFYING CHILD

In the interest of uniformity, Congress has tried to establish a uniform definition of a qualifying child. The qualifying child definition applies to the following tax provisions:

- Dependency exemption.
- Head-of-household filing status.

---

[10]As noted on p. 3–21, Jack's situation is such that he will be required to file an income tax return.

[11]§ 151(b).

- Earned income tax credit.
- Child tax credit.
- Credit for child and dependent care expenses.

A **qualifying child** must meet the relationship, abode, age, and support tests.[12] For dependency exemption purposes, a qualifying child must also satisfy the joint return test and the citizenship or residency test.

Relationship Test

The relationship test includes a taxpayer's child (son, daughter), adopted child, stepchild, eligible foster child, brother, sister, half brother, half sister, stepbrother, stepsister, or a *descendant* of any of these parties (e.g., grandchild, nephew, niece). Note that *ancestors* of any of these parties (e.g., uncles and aunts) and in-laws (e.g., son-in-law, brother-in-law) *are not included.*

An adopted child includes a child lawfully placed with the taxpayer for legal adoption even though the adoption is not final. An eligible foster child is one who is placed with the taxpayer by an authorized placement agency or by a judgment decree or other order of any court of competent jurisdiction.

EXAMPLE 13

Maureen's household includes her mother, grandson, stepbrother, stepbrother's daughter, uncle, and sister. All meet the relationship test for a qualifying child except the mother and uncle. ∎

Abode Test

A qualifying child must live with the taxpayer for more than half of the year. For this purpose, temporary absences (e.g., school, vacation, medical care, military service, detention in a juvenile facility) are disregarded. Special rules apply in the case of certain kidnapped children.[13]

Age Test

A qualifying child must be under age 19 or under age 24 in the case of a student. A student is a child who, during any part of five months of the year, is enrolled full time at a school or government-sponsored on-farm training course.[14] The age test does not apply to a child who is disabled during any part of the year.[15] Also, an individual cannot be older than the taxpayer claiming him or her as a qualifying child (e.g., a brother cannot claim his older sister as a qualifying child).

EXAMPLE 14
THE BIG PICTURE

Return to the facts of *The Big Picture* on p. 3-2. Does Paige meet the requirements of a qualifying child as to Polly? Paige satisfies the relationship and abode tests, but the answer to the age test remains unclear. Since she is not a full-time student or disabled, she must be under 19 to meet the age test. Unfortunately, the facts given do not provide Paige's precise age. ∎

Support Test

In order to be a qualifying child, the individual must not be self-supporting (i.e., provide more than one-half of his or her own support). In the case of a child who is a full-time student, scholarships are not considered to be support.[16]

---

[12]§ 152(c).

[13]§ 152(f)(6).

[14]§ 152(f)(2).

[15]Within the meaning of § 22(e)(3). See the discussion of the credit for the elderly or disabled in Chapter 13.

[16]§ 152(f)(5).

TABLE 3.3	Tiebreaker Rules for Claiming Qualified Child

Persons Eligible to Claim Exemption	Person Prevailing
One of the persons is the parent.	Parent
Both persons are the parents, and the child lives longer with one parent.	Parent with the longer period of residence
Both persons are the parents, and the child lives with each the same period of time.	Parent with the higher adjusted gross income (AGI)
None of the persons is the parent.	Person with highest AGI

EXAMPLE 15

Shawn, age 23, is a full-time student and lives with his parents and an older cousin. During 2011, Shawn receives his support from the following sources: 30% from a part-time job, 30% from a scholarship, 20% from his parents, and 20% from the cousin. Shawn is not self-supporting and can be claimed by his parents as a dependent. (Note: Shawn cannot be a qualifying child as to his cousin due to the relationship test.) ∎

Tiebreaker Rules

In some situations, a child may be a qualifying child to more than one person. In this event, the tax law specifies which person has priority in claiming the dependency exemption.[17] Called "tiebreaker rules," these rules are summarized in Table 3.3 and are illustrated in the examples that follow.

EXAMPLE 16

Tim, age 15, lives in the same household with his mother and grandmother. As the parent, the mother has priority as to the dependency exemption. ∎

EXAMPLE 17

Jennifer, age 17, lives in the same household with her parents during the entire year. If her parents file separate returns, the one with the higher AGI has priority as to the dependency exemption. ∎

EXAMPLE 18

Assume the same facts as in Example 17, except that the father moves into an apartment in November (Jennifer remains with her mother). The mother has priority as to the dependency exemption (see Table 3.3). ∎

Resorting to the tiebreaker rules in Table 3.3 is not necessary if the person who would prevail does not claim the exemption. Thus, in Example 16, the mother can allow the grandmother to claim Tim as a dependent by not claiming him on her own return.

QUALIFYING RELATIVE

Besides the category of a qualifying child, there is a second category of dependency exemption designated as the **qualifying relative**.

A qualifying relative must meet the relationship, gross income, and support tests.[18] As in the case of the qualifying child category, qualifying relative status also requires that the joint return and nonresident alien restrictions be avoided (see Other Rules for Dependency Exemptions later in the chapter).

---

[17]§ 152(c)(4).   [18]§ 152(d).

Relationship Test

The relationship test for a qualifying relative is more expansive than for a qualifying child. Also included are the following relatives:

- Lineal ascendants (e.g., parents, grandparents).
- Collateral ascendants (e.g., uncles, aunts).
- Certain in-laws (e.g., son-, daughter-, father-, mother-, brother-, and sister-in-law).[19]

Children who do not satisfy the qualifying child definition may meet the qualifying relative criteria.

The relationship test also includes unrelated parties who live with the taxpayer (i.e., are members of the household). Member-of-the-household status is not available for anyone whose relationship with the taxpayer violates local law or anyone who was a spouse during any part of the year.[20] However, an ex-spouse can qualify as a member of the household in a year following that of the divorce.

As the relationship test indicates, the category designation of "qualifying relative" is somewhat misleading. As just noted, persons other than relatives can qualify as dependents. Furthermore, not all relatives will qualify—notice the absence of the "cousin" grouping.

> **EXAMPLE 19**
> **THE BIG PICTURE**
>
> Return to the facts of *The Big Picture* on p. 3-2. Although Maude is unrelated to Polly, she qualifies as Polly's dependent by being a member of the household. Since Maude is a dependent, Polly can also claim the medical expenses she paid on Maude's behalf. The funeral expenses are not deductible. Although Maude lived for only two months, the full amount of the dependency exemption is allowed and does not have to be apportioned. ■

Gross Income Test

A dependent's gross income must be *less* than the exemption amount—$3,700 in 2011 and $3,650 in 2010. Gross income is determined by the income that is taxable. In the case of scholarships, for example, include the taxable portion (e.g., amounts received for room and board) and exclude the nontaxable portion (e.g., amounts received for books and tuition).

2012—$3,800

> **EXAMPLE 20**
>
> Elsie provides more than half of the support of her son, Tom, who does not live with her. Tom, age 26, is a full-time student in medical school, earns $3,000 from a part-time job, and receives a $12,000 scholarship covering his tuition. Elsie may claim Tom as a dependent since he meets the gross income test and is a qualifying relative. (Note: Tom is not a qualifying child due to either the abode or the age test.) ■

cannot claim as a child but qualifying relative.

> **EXAMPLE 21**
>
> Aaron provides more than half of the support of his widowed aunt, Myrtle, who does not live with him. Myrtle's income for the year is as follows: dividend income of $1,100, earnings from pet sitting of $1,200, Social Security benefits of $6,000, and interest from City of Milwaukee bonds of $8,000. Since Myrtle's gross income is only $2,300 ($1,100 + $1,200), she meets the gross income test and can be claimed as Aaron's dependent. ■

> **EXAMPLE 22**
> **THE BIG PICTURE**
>
> Return to the facts of *The Big Picture* on p. 3-2. Assuming that Paige is not a qualifying child (see Example 14), can she be a qualifying relative for dependency exemption purposes? She meets the relationship and support tests, but what about the gross income test? If her income from her part-time job is less than $3,700, she does qualify and can be claimed by Polly as a dependent. ■

---

[19]Once established by marriage, in-law status continues to exist and survives divorce.

[20]§§ 152(d)(2)(H) and (f)(3).

Support Test

Over one-half of the support of the qualifying relative must be furnished by the taxpayer. Support includes food, shelter, clothing, toys, medical and dental care, education, and the like.[21] However, a scholarship (both taxable and nontaxable portions) received by a student is not included for purposes of computing whether the taxpayer furnished more than half of the child's support.

EXAMPLE 23	Hal contributed $3,400 (consisting of food, clothing, and medical care) toward the support of his nephew, Sam, who lives with him. Sam earned $1,500 from a part-time job and received a $2,000 scholarship to attend a local university. Assuming that the other dependency tests are met, Hal can claim Sam as a dependent since he has contributed more than half of Sam's support. The $2,000 scholarship is not included as support for purposes of this test. ∎

If the individual does not spend funds that have been received from any source, the unexpended amounts are not counted for purposes of the support test.

EXAMPLE 24	Emily contributed $3,000 to her father's support during the year. In addition, her father received $2,400 in Social Security benefits, $200 of interest, and wages of $600. Her father deposited the Social Security benefits, interest, and wages in his own savings account and did not use any of the funds for his support. Thus, the Social Security benefits, interest, and wages are not considered as support provided by Emily's father. Emily may claim her father as a dependent if the other tests are met. ∎

An individual's own funds, however, must be taken into account if applied toward support. In this regard, the source of the funds so used is immaterial.

EXAMPLE 25	Frank contributes $8,000 toward his parents' total support of $20,000. The parents, who do not live with Frank, obtain the other $12,000 from savings and a home equity loan on their residence. Although the parents have no income, their use of savings and borrowed funds are counted as part of their support. Because Frank does not satisfy the support test, he cannot claim his parents as dependents. ∎

Capital expenditures for items such as furniture, appliances, and automobiles are included in total support if the item does, in fact, constitute support.

EXAMPLE 26	Norm purchased a television set costing $650 and gave it to his mother who lives with him. The television set was placed in the mother's bedroom and was used exclusively by her. Norm should include the cost of the television set in determining the support of his mother. ∎

Multiple Support Agreements An exception to the support test involves a **multiple support agreement**. A multiple support agreement permits one of a group of taxpayers who furnish support for a qualifying relative to claim a dependency exemption for that individual even if no one person provides more than 50 percent of the support.[22] The group together must provide more than 50 percent of the support. Any person who contributed *more than 10 percent* of the support is entitled to claim the exemption if each person in the group who contributed more than 10 percent files a written consent. This provision frequently enables one of the children of aged dependent parents to claim an exemption when none of the children meets the 50 percent support test.

---

[21]A worksheet for determining support is provided in IRS Publication 501 (*Exemptions, Standard Deduction, and Filing Information*).   [22]§ 152(d)(3).

Each person who is a party to the multiple support agreement must meet all other requirements (except the support requirement) for claiming the exemption. A person who does not meet the relationship or member-of-the-household requirement, for instance, cannot claim the dependency exemption under a multiple support agreement. It does not matter if he or she contributes more than 10 percent of the individual's support.

EXAMPLE 27

Wanda, who resides with her son, Adam, received $12,000 from various sources during the year. This constituted her entire support for the year. She received support from the following:

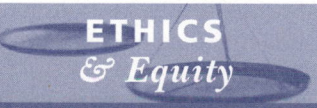

	Amount	Percentage of Total
Adam, a son	$ 5,760	48
Bob, a son	1,200	10
Carol, a daughter	3,600	30
Diane, a friend	1,440	12
	$12,000	100

If Adam and Carol file a multiple support agreement, either may claim the dependency exemption for Wanda. Bob may not claim Wanda because he did not contribute more than 10% of her support. Bob's consent is not required in order for Adam and Carol to file a multiple support agreement. Diane does not meet the relationship or member-of-the-household test and cannot be a party to the agreement. The decision as to who claims Wanda rests with Adam and Carol. It is possible for Carol to claim Wanda, even though Adam furnished more of Wanda's support. ∎

Each person who qualifies under the more-than-10 percent rule (except for the person claiming the exemption) must complete Form 2120 (Multiple Support Declaration) waiving the exemption. The person claiming the exemption must attach all Forms 2120 to his or her own return.

ETHICS & Equity   DISCOVERING LOST DEPENDENCY EXEMPTIONS

For the six years prior to his death in late 2011, Jesse lived with his daughter, Hannah. Because he had no source of income, Jesse was supported by equal contributions from Hannah and his two sons, Bill and Bob. At Jesse's funeral, his surviving children are amazed to discover that none of them has been claiming Jesse as a dependent. Upon the advice of the director of the funeral home, they decide to divide, among themselves, the dependency exemptions for the past six years. Multiple Forms 2120 are executed, and each of the three children files amended returns for different past years. As Jesse died before the end of the current year, no deduction is planned for 2011.

Comment on the tax expectations of the parties involved.

Children of Divorced or Separated Parents Another exception to the support test applies when parents with children are divorced or separated under a decree of separate maintenance. For unmarried parents, living apart (for the last six months of the year) will suffice. Special rules apply if the parents meet the following conditions:

• They would have been entitled to the dependency exemption(s) had they been married and filed a joint return.
• They have custody (either jointly or singly) of the child (or children) for more than half of the year.

Under the general rule, the parent having custody of the child (children) for the greater part of the year (i.e., the custodial parent) is entitled to the dependency exemption(s).[23] The general rule does not apply if a multiple support agreement is in effect. It also does not apply if the custodial parent issues a waiver in favor of the noncustodial parent.[24]

The waiver, Form 8332 (Release/Revocation of Release of Claim to Exemption for Child by Custodial Parent), can apply to a single year, a number of specified years, or all future years. The noncustodial parent must attach a copy of Form 8332 to his or her return.

OTHER RULES FOR DEPENDENCY EXEMPTIONS

In addition to fitting into either the qualifying child or the qualifying relative category, a dependent must meet the joint return and the citizenship or residency tests.

Joint Return Test

If a dependent is married, the supporting taxpayer (e.g., the parent of a married child) generally is not permitted a dependency exemption if the married individual files a joint return with his or her spouse.[25] The joint return rule does not apply, however, if the following conditions are met:

- The reason for filing is to claim a refund for tax withheld.
- No tax liability would exist for either spouse on separate returns.
- Neither spouse is required to file a return.

See Table 3.4 later in the chapter and the related discussion concerning income level requirements for filing a return.

EXAMPLE 28

Paul provides over half of the support of his son Quinn. He also provides over half of the support of Vera, who is Quinn's wife. During the year, both Quinn and Vera had part-time jobs. In order to recover the taxes withheld, they file a joint return. If Quinn and Vera are not required to file a return, Paul is allowed to claim both as dependents. ■

Citizenship or Residency Test

To be a dependent, the individual must be either a U.S. citizen, a U.S. resident, or a resident of Canada or Mexico for some part of the calendar year in which the taxpayer's tax year begins.[26]

Under an exception, an adopted child need not be a citizen or resident of the United States (or a contiguous country) as long as his or her principal abode is with a U.S. citizen.

EXAMPLE 29

Esther is a U.S. citizen who lives and works in Spain. She has adopted Benito, a four-year-old Italian national, who lives with her and is a member of her household. Although Benito does not meet the usual citizenship or residency test, he is covered by the exception. Benito is a qualifying child, and Esther can claim him as a dependent. ■

COMPARISON OF CATEGORIES FOR DEPENDENCY EXEMPTIONS

Concept Summary 3.1 sets forth the tests for the two categories of dependency exemptions. In contrasting the two categories, the following observations are in order:

- As to the relationship tests, the qualifying relative category is considerably more expansive. Besides including those prescribed under the qualifying child grouping, other relatives are added. Nonrelated persons who are members of the household are also included.

[23]Reg. § 1.152–4T.
[24]§§ 152(e)(2) and (5).
[25]§ 152(b)(2).
[26]§ 152(b)(3).

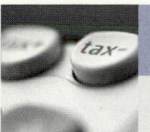

CONCEPT SUMMARY 3.1

Tests for Dependency Exemption

Category	
Qualifying Child	**Qualifying Relative**
Relationship[1]	Support
Abode[2]	Relationship[3] or member of household[2]
Age	Gross income
Support	Joint return[4]
Joint return[4]	Citizenship or residency[4]
Citizenship or residency[4]	

[1] Children and their descendants, and siblings and stepsiblings and their descendants.
[2] The rules for abode are the same as for member of the household.
[3] Children and their descendants, siblings and their children, parents and their ascendants, uncles and aunts, stepparents and stepsiblings, and certain in-laws.
[4] The joint return rules and the citizenship or residency rules are the same for each category.

- The support tests are entirely different. In the case of a qualifying child, support is not necessary. What is required is that the child not be self-supporting.
- The qualifying child category has no gross income limitation, whereas the qualifying relative category has no age restriction.

PHASEOUT OF EXEMPTIONS

Is there any reason why certain higher-income taxpayers should be denied some or all of the tax benefits of being able to claim as a deduction personal and dependency exemptions? Apparently, Congress originally thought so and enacted legislation that phased out any such deduction in stages. Congress later changed its mind and reduced the phaseout. Thus, during this period of indecisiveness in the tax law, higher-bracket taxpayers experienced years when they were losing their exemptions followed by years when the exemptions were being restored. As of 2010, the restoration is complete, and all taxpayers, regardless of income level, may *fully* deduct any personal and dependency exemptions to which they are entitled.[27]

Under a sunset provision (see Glossary in Appendix C for a definition), the phaseout of exemption deductions was scheduled to be reinstated beginning in 2011. However, the Tax Relief Act (TRA) of 2010 put off the reinstatement for two years (i.e., 2011 and 2012).

What does this history of phaseouts portend for the future? In this period of budget crises when new sources of revenue are at a premium, high-income taxpayers will be highly vulnerable. A future postponement by Congress of the phaseouts on personal and dependency exemptions should not be expected!

CHILD TAX CREDIT

In addition to providing a dependency exemption, a child of the taxpayer may also generate a tax credit. Called the **child tax credit**, the amount allowed is $1,000 through 2012 for each dependent child (including stepchildren and eligible foster children) under the age of 17.[28] For a more complete discussion of the child tax credit, see Chapter 13.

---

[27]The phaseouts and their later reduction are clearly set forth in § 151(d)(3).   [28]§ 24(a).

No government likes to admit that it is enacting new taxes or even raising the rates on existing taxes. Needless to say, this is particularly true of the U.S. Congress. But there are more subtle ways to raise revenue (or to curtail revenue loss). The most popular way is to use a so-called *stealth tax*. A stealth tax is not really a tax at all. Instead, it is a means of depriving higher-income taxpayers of the benefits of certain tax provisions thought to be available to all.

The heart and soul of the stealth tax is the phaseout approach. Thus, as income increases, the tax benefit thought to be derived from a particular relief provision decreases. Since the phaseout usually is gradual and not drastic, many affected taxpayers are unaware of what has happened.

The tax law is rampant with phaseouts. The following are a few notable examples of these stealth taxes, along with where each is discussed in the text:

- Earned income credit (Chapter 13).
- Spousal IRA deduction (Chapter 19).
- Child tax credit (Chapter 13).
- College tuition deduction (Chapter 9).
- Interest deduction on student loans (Chapter 10).
- American Opportunity college credit (Chapter 13).

As mentioned in the text, personal and dependency exemptions were once denied to higher-bracket taxpayers on a phaseout basis.

3.5 TAX DETERMINATION— FILING CONSIDERATIONS

LO.5

List the filing requirements and choose the proper filing status.

Once taxable income has been ascertained, a two-step process is used in determining income tax due (or refund available). First, certain procedural matters must be resolved. Second, the tax has to be computed and adjusted for available tax credits—see Figure 3.1 and the tax formula. This section deals with the procedural aspects—designated as filing considerations. The section to follow covers the computation procedures.

Under the category of filing considerations, the following questions need to be resolved:

- Is the taxpayer required to file an income tax return?
- If so, which form should be used?
- When and how should the return be filed?
- What is the taxpayer's filing status?

FILING REQUIREMENTS

General Rules

An individual must file a tax return if certain minimum amounts of gross income have been received. The general rule is that a tax return is required for every individual who has gross income that equals or exceeds the sum of the exemption amount plus the applicable standard deduction.[29] For example, a single taxpayer under age 65 must file a tax return in 2011 if gross income equals or exceeds $9,500 ($3,700 exemption plus $5,800 standard deduction). Table 3.4 lists the income levels[30] that require tax returns under the general rule and under certain special rules.

The additional standard deduction for being age 65 or older is considered in determining the gross income filing requirements. For example, note in Table 3.4 that the 2011 filing requirement for a single taxpayer age 65 or older is $10,950 ($5,800 basic standard deduction + $1,450 additional standard deduction + $3,700 exemption). However, the additional standard deduction for blindness is not taken

[29]The gross income amounts for determining whether a tax return must be filed are adjusted for inflation each year.

[30]§ 6012(a)(1).

TABLE 3.4	Filing Levels		
Filing Status		2010 Gross Income	2011 Gross Income
Single			
Under 65 and not blind		$ 9,350	$ 9,500
Under 65 and blind		9,350	9,500
65 or older		10,750	10,950
Married, filing joint return			
Both spouses under 65 and neither blind		$18,700	$19,000
Both spouses under 65 and one or both spouses blind		18,700	19,000
One spouse 65 or older		19,800	20,150
Both spouses 65 or older		20,900	21,300
Married, filing separate return			
All—whether 65 or older or blind		$ 3,650	$ 3,700
Head of household			
Under 65 and not blind		$12,050	$12,200
Under 65 and blind		12,050	12,200
65 or older		13,450	13,650
Qualifying widow(er)			
Under 65 and not blind		$15,050	$15,300
Under 65 and blind		15,050	15,300
65 or older		16,150	16,450

into account. The 2011 filing requirement for a single taxpayer under age 65 and blind is $9,500 ($5,800 basic standard deduction + $3,700 exemption).

A self-employed individual with net earnings of $400 or more from a business or profession must file a tax return regardless of the amount of gross income.

Even though an individual has gross income below the filing level amounts and therefore does not owe any tax, he or she must file a return to obtain a tax refund of amounts withheld. A return is also necessary to obtain the benefits of the earned income credit allowed to taxpayers with little or no tax liability. Chapter 13 discusses the earned income credit.

Filing Requirements for Dependents

Computation of the gross income filing requirement for an individual who can be claimed as a dependent on another person's tax return is subject to more complex rules. Such an individual must file a return if he or she has *any* of the following:

- Earned income only and gross income that is more than the total standard deduction (including any additional standard deduction) that the individual is allowed for the year.
- Unearned income only and gross income of more than $950 plus any additional standard deduction that the individual is allowed for the year.
- Both earned and unearned income and gross income of more than the larger of $950 or the sum of earned income plus $300 (but limited to the applicable basic standard deduction), plus any additional standard deduction that the individual is allowed for the year.

TAX *in* the NEWS

IRS VERSUS USCIS

Foreign persons who earn income within the United States may need to file a Federal income tax return, but may not have a Social Security number for filing purposes. If not, they can use a nine-digit Individual Tax Identification Number (ITIN) instead. The IRS issues ITINs upon the submission of an application and proof of identification (e.g., a driver's license). As the IRS does not require an applicant to show that he or she is in the United States legally, the ITINs are freely available to undocumented persons (i.e., illegal immigrants). The use of an ITIN also can enable the holder to carry out other financial transactions (e.g., establish a bank account, secure a credit card, obtain a loan).

Through its lax procedures in issuing ITINs, is the IRS indirectly encouraging, or at least condoning, the status of undocumented persons? Along this line, should the IRS require proof of legal presence in the United States before issuing an ITIN? Since the IRS and USCIS (U.S. Citizenship and Immigration Services) do not collaborate on the issuance of ITINs, is this another example of one Federal agency not cooperating with another?

The position of the IRS is that the current ITIN procedure brings in revenue that otherwise would not be forthcoming. Some undocumented workers want to comply with the law and pay the income taxes they owe. This practice should not be discouraged as the tax law applies with equal force to legal and illegal residents of the United States. Although a breakdown between legal and illegal residents is not available, the tax liability of ITIN filers from 1996 to 2003 was $50 billion.

Thus, the filing requirement for a dependent who has no unearned income is the total of the *basic* standard deduction plus any *additional* standard deduction, which includes both the additional deduction for blindness and the deduction for being age 65 or older. For example, the 2011 filing requirement for a single dependent who is under age 65 and not blind is $5,800, the amount of the basic standard deduction for 2011. The filing requirement for a single dependent under age 65 and blind is $7,250 ($5,800 basic standard deduction + $1,450 additional standard deduction).

Selecting the Proper Form

The 2011 tax forms had not been released at the date of publication of this text. The following comments apply to the 2010 forms. It is possible that some provisions will change for the 2011 forms.

Although a variety of forms are available to individual taxpayers, the use of some of these forms is restricted. For example, Form 1040EZ cannot be used if:

- Taxpayer claims any dependents;
- Taxpayer (or spouse) is 65 or older or blind; or
- Taxable income is $100,000 or more.

Taxpayers who desire to itemize deductions *from* AGI cannot use Form 1040–A, but must file Form 1040 (the long form).

The E-File Approach

In addition to traditional paper returns, the **e-file** program is an increasingly popular alternative. Here, the required tax information is transmitted to the IRS electronically either directly from the taxpayer (i.e., an "e-file online return") or indirectly through an electronic return originator (ERO). EROs are tax professionals who have been accepted into the electronic filing program by the IRS. Such parties hold themselves out to the general public as "authorized IRS e-file providers." Providers often are also the preparers of the return.

Through prearrangement with the IRS, approximately 20 software providers offer free e-filing services. These services are available only to taxpayers who have AGI of $58,000 or below. A list of these providers and their eligibility requirements can be obtained through the IRS website. Regardless of income, any taxpayer can use online Fillable Forms, which are an electronic version of IRS paper forms.

For direct online e-filing, a taxpayer must have a personal computer and purchase commercial tax preparation software with the capability of conveying the information via modem to an electronic return transmitter. Otherwise a taxpayer must use an authorized provider who makes the e-file transmission. Except as previously noted, the provider charges a fee for the e-filing service.

TAX *in the NEWS*

IRS STAYS UP-TO-DATE

As part of its commitment to modernization, the IRS has launched its first smartphone application, IRS2Go. This app is available free at the iTunes app store for the Apple iPhone or iTouch and at the Android Marketplace for an Android device. This first release of the IRS2Go app allows taxpayers to check their refund and to get tax updates, daily during tax filing season and periodically during the rest of the year.

And taxpayers can sign up to follow the IRS Twitter news feed, @IRSnews. The IRSnews tweets provide the latest Federal tax law changes and other important information. The IRS also uses tools such as YouTube at **www.youtube.com/irsvideos** and other social media channels to share the latest information.

All taxpayers and tax return preparers must attest to the returns they file. For most taxpayers, this attesting can be done through an electronic return signature using a personal identification number (a Self-Select PIN). Information on establishing a Self-Select PIN can be found in the instructions to Form 1040, Form 1040–A, or Form 1040–EZ, or at **www.irs.gov/efile**. If certain paper documents must be submitted, a one-page form must be completed and filed when the return is e-filed. Form 8453 (U.S. Individual Income Tax Transmittal for an IRS *e-file* Return) is used to submit required attachments for both self- and practitioner-prepared electronic returns. Or a practitioner PIN method may be used whereby the taxpayer authorizes a tax preparer to generate a PIN by signing Form 8879 (IRS e-file Signature Authorization).

The e-file approach has two major advantages. First, compliance with the format required by the IRS eliminates many errors that would otherwise occur. Second, the time required for processing a refund usually is reduced to three weeks or less.

When and Where to File

Tax returns of individuals are due on or before the fifteenth day of the fourth month following the close of the tax year. For the calendar year taxpayer, the usual filing date is on or before April 15 of the following year.[31] When the due date falls on a Saturday, Sunday, or legal holiday, the last day for filing falls on the next business day. If the return is mailed to the proper address with sufficient postage and is postmarked on or before the due date, it is deemed timely filed. The Code enables the IRS to prescribe rules governing the filing of returns using various private parcel delivery services (e.g., FedEx, UPS).[32]

If a taxpayer is unable to file the return by the specified due date, a six-month extension of time can be obtained by filing Form 4868 (Application for Automatic Extension of Time to File U.S. Individual Income Tax Return). Certain taxpayers who are members of the Armed Forces are allowed additional time for filing their Federal income tax returns.[33]

Although obtaining an extension excuses a taxpayer from a penalty for failure to file, it does not insulate against the penalty for failure to pay. If more tax is owed, the filing of Form 4868 should be accompanied by an additional remittance to cover the balance due. The failure to file and failure to pay penalties are discussed in Chapter 1.

The return should be sent or delivered to the Regional Service Center listed in the instructions for each type of return or contained in software applications.[34] Because of an IRS reorganization that began in October 2000 and is still ongoing, some taxpayers may be required to file at a different Service Center than in the past.

If an individual taxpayer needs to file an amended return (e.g., because of a failure to report income or to claim a deduction or tax credit), Form 1040X is filed. The form generally must be filed within three years of the filing date of the original return or within two years from the time the tax was paid, whichever is later.

---

[31]§ 6072(a).

[32]§ 7502(f).

[33]Reg. § 1.6081–4. See also *Your Federal Income Tax* (IRS Publication 17), Chapter 1.

[34]The Regional Service Centers and the geographic area each covers can also be found at **www.irs.gov/file**.

TAX in the NEWS

"CHARGE IT"—CONVENIENT BUT NOT CHEAP!

When a consumer uses a credit card to buy goods, the merchant pays a fee to the credit card company. When a credit card is used to pay income taxes, however, the law prevents the IRS from paying any such fee. Instead, the credit card company charges the user a "convenience fee" equal to 2.5 percent of the tax paid. The fee must be paid even if the user pays the credit card bill in full when it arrives. If, for example, John uses his Visa card to pay the $10,000 in taxes that he owes, he will be charged $250 (2.5% × $10,000) as a convenience fee. John will have to pay the $250 fee even if he pays Visa the $10,000 when billed. Furthermore, regular credit card interest (usually 15 percent or more) will be charged on extended time payments.

Clearly, then, using credit cards to pay income taxes, though convenient, is not without cost!

Mode of Payment

Usually, payment is made by check. In that event, the check should be made out to "United States Treasury."

The IRS has approved the use of MasterCard, American Express, Discover, and Visa to pay Federal taxes. The use of a credit card to pay taxes will result in a charge against the cardholder by the credit card company.

FILING STATUS

The amount of tax will vary considerably depending on which Tax Rate Schedule is used. This is illustrated in the following example.

EXAMPLE 30

The following amounts of tax are computed using the 2011 Tax Rate Schedules for a taxpayer (or taxpayers in the case of a joint return) with $60,000 of taxable income (see Appendix A).

Filing Status	Amount of Tax
Single	$11,125
Married, filing joint return	8,150
Married, filing separate return	11,125
Head of household	9,768

■

Besides the effect on the tax rates that will apply, filing status also has an impact on the amount of the standard deduction that is allowed—see Tables 3.1 and 3.2 earlier in the chapter.

Single Taxpayers

A taxpayer who is unmarried or separated from his or her spouse by a decree of divorce or separate maintenance and does not qualify for another filing status must use the rates for single taxpayers. Marital status is determined as of the last day of the tax year, except when a spouse dies during the year. In that case, marital status is determined as of the date of death. State law governs whether a taxpayer is considered married, divorced, or legally separated.

Under a special relief provision, however, married persons who live apart may be able to qualify as single. Married taxpayers who are considered single under the *abandoned spouse rules* are allowed to use the head-of-household rates. See the discussion of this filing status under Abandoned Spouse Rules later in the chapter.

Married Individuals

The joint return [Tax Rate Schedule Y, Code § 1(a)] was originally enacted in 1948 to establish equity between married taxpayers in common law states and those in

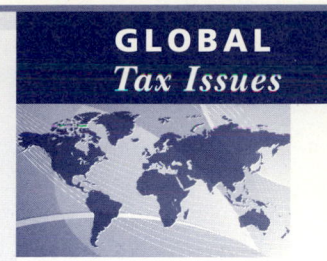

FILING A JOINT RETURN

John Garth is a U.S. citizen and resident, but he spends a lot of time in London where his employer sends him on frequent assignments. John is married to Victoria, a citizen and resident of the United Kingdom.

Can John and Victoria file a joint return for U.S. Federal income tax purposes? Although § 6013(a)(1) specifically precludes the filing of a joint return if one spouse is a nonresident alien, another Code provision permits an exception. Under § 6013(g), the parties can elect to treat the nonqualifying spouse as a "resident" of the United States. This election would allow John and Victoria to file jointly.

But should John and Victoria make this election? If Victoria has considerable income of her own (from non-U.S. sources), the election could be ill-advised. As a nonresident alien, Victoria's non-U.S. source income *would not* be subject to the U.S. income tax. If she is treated as a U.S. resident, however, her non-U.S. source income *will be subject to U.S. tax.* Under the U.S. global approach to taxation, all income (regardless of where earned) of anyone who is a *resident* or *citizen* of the United States is subject to tax.

community property states. Before the joint return rates were enacted, taxpayers in community property states were in an advantageous position relative to taxpayers in common law states because they could split their income. For instance, if one spouse earned $100,000 and the other spouse was not employed, each spouse could report $50,000 of income. Splitting the income in this manner caused the total income to be subject to lower marginal tax rates. Each spouse would start at the bottom of the rate structure.

Taxpayers in common law states did not have this income-splitting option, so their taxable income was subject to higher marginal rates. This inconsistency in treatment was remedied by the joint return provisions. The progressive rates in the joint return Tax Rate Schedule are constructed based on the assumption that income is earned equally by the two spouses.

If married individuals elect to file separate returns, each reports only his or her own income, exemptions, deductions, and credits, and each must use the Tax Rate Schedule applicable to married taxpayers filing separately. It is generally advantageous for married individuals to file a joint return, since the combined amount of tax is lower. However, special circumstances (e.g., significant medical expenses incurred by one spouse subject to the 7.5 percent limitation) may warrant the election to file separate returns. It may be necessary to compute the tax under both assumptions to determine the most advantageous filing status.

Marriage Penalty When Congress enacted the rate structure available to those filing joint returns, it generally favored married taxpayers. In certain situations, however, the parties would incur less tax if they were not married and filed separate returns. The additional tax that a joint return caused, commonly called the **marriage penalty**, usually developed when *both* spouses had large taxable incomes. Long aware of the inequity of the marriage penalty, Congress reduced the effect of the problem in JGTRRA of 2003. Beginning in 2003, the standard deduction available to married filers increased to 200 percent of that applicable to single persons. Furthermore and also beginning in 2003, the 15 percent bracket for joint filers increased to 200 percent of the size of that applicable to single filers.

Although changes in the tax rates and the standard deduction have reduced the marriage penalty, the Code places some limitations on married persons who file separate returns. Some examples of these limitations are listed below.

- If either spouse itemizes deductions, the other spouse must also itemize.
- The earned income credit and the credit for child and dependent care expenses cannot be claimed (see Chapter 13).

- No deduction is allowed for interest paid on qualified education loans (see Chapter 10).
- Only $1,500 of excess capital losses can be claimed (see Chapter 16).

In such cases, being single would be preferable to being married and filing separately.

Surviving Spouse The joint return rates also apply for two years following the death of one spouse, if the surviving spouse maintains a household for a dependent child. The child must be a son, stepson, daughter, or stepdaughter who qualifies as a dependent of the taxpayer. This is referred to as **surviving spouse** status.[35]

EXAMPLE 31

Fred dies in 2010 leaving Ethel with a dependent child. For the year of Fred's death (2010), Ethel files a joint return with Fred (presuming the consent of Fred's executor is obtained). For the next two years (2011 and 2012), Ethel, as a surviving spouse, may use the joint return rates. In subsequent years, Ethel may use the head-of-household rates if she continues to maintain a household as her home that is the domicile of the child. ■

Keep in mind, however, that for the year of death, the surviving spouse is treated as being married. Thus, a joint return can be filed if the deceased spouse's executor agrees. If not, the surviving spouse is forced into the status of married, filing separately.

Head of Household

Unmarried individuals who maintain a household for a dependent (or dependents) are generally entitled to use the **head-of-household** rates.[36] The tax liability using the head-of-household rates falls between the liability using the joint return Tax Rate Schedule and the liability using the Tax Rate Schedule for single taxpayers.

To qualify for head-of-household rates, a taxpayer must pay more than half the cost of maintaining a household as his or her home. The household must also be the principal home of a dependent. Except for temporary absences (e.g., school, hospitalization), the dependent must live in the taxpayer's household for over half the year.

A dependent must be either a qualifying child or a qualifying relative who meets the relationship test (other than a member-of-the-household test).[37]

EXAMPLE 32
THE BIG PICTURE

Return to the facts of *The Big Picture* on p. 3-2. Assuming that Polly can be treated as single (i.e., not married), can Maude qualify Polly for head-of-household filing status? The answer is no. Even though Maude can be claimed as Polly's dependent (see Example 19), she does not meet the relationship test. ■

EXAMPLE 33

Emma, a widow, maintains a household in which she and her aunt live. If the aunt qualifies as a dependent, Emma may file as head of household. Note that an aunt meets the relationship test. ■

A special rule allows taxpayers to avoid having to live with their parents. Head-of-household status still may be claimed if the taxpayer maintains a *separate home* for his or her *parent or parents* if at least one parent qualifies as a dependent of the taxpayer.[38]

EXAMPLE 34

Rick, an unmarried individual, lives in New York City and maintains a household in Detroit for his dependent parents. Rick may use the head-of-household rates even though his parents do not reside in his New York home. ■

---

[35]§ 2(a). The IRS label for surviving spouse status is "qualifying widow(er) with dependent child."
[36]§ 2(b).
[37]§ 2(b)(3)(B).
[38]§ 2(b)(1)(B).

TEMPORARY OR PERMANENT ABSENCE?

For several years, Minerva, a widow, has maintained a household in which she and her uncle, Luther, live. Because Luther has no income, he is supported by Minerva and claimed by her as a dependent. In June 2011, Luther is admitted to a medical facility for treatment of a mental disorder. In January 2012, Luther unexpectedly dies while still at the facility.

In completing her Federal income tax returns for both 2011 and 2012, Minerva intends to file as head of household and claim Luther as her dependent. Comment on the propriety of what Minerva plans to do.

Head-of-household status is not changed during the year by the death of the dependent. As long as the taxpayer provided more than half of the cost of maintaining the household prior to the dependent's death, head-of-household status is preserved.

Abandoned Spouse Rules

When married persons file separate returns, several unfavorable tax consequences result. For example, the taxpayer must use the Tax Rate Schedule for married taxpayers filing separately. To mitigate such harsh treatment for some taxpayers, Congress enacted provisions commonly referred to as the **abandoned spouse** rules. The IRS does not use the "abandoned spouse" terminology but considers the taxpayer to be treated as *not married* if the following conditions are satisfied:[39]

- The taxpayer does not file a joint return.
- The taxpayer paid more than one-half the cost of maintaining his or her home for the tax year.
- The taxpayer's spouse did not live in the home during the last six months of the tax year.
- The home was the principal residence of the taxpayer's son, daughter, stepson, stepdaughter, foster child, or adopted child for more than half the year, and the child can be claimed as a dependent.[40]

Thus, the net effect of being treated as unmarried and having the specified dependents is that the abandoned spouse qualifies for head-of-household filing status.

> **EXAMPLE 35**
> **THE BIG PICTURE**
>
> Return to the facts of *The Big Picture* on p. 3-2. Can Polly qualify as an abandoned spouse? Yes, if she can claim Paige as a dependent—either as a qualifying child (see Example 14) or as a qualifying relative (see Example 22). If so, Polly can use head-of-household filing status. If not, her filing status is married person filing separately. ∎

3.6 TAX DETERMINATION— COMPUTATION PROCEDURES

The computation of income tax due (or refund) involves applying the proper set of tax rates to taxable income and then adjusting for available credits. In certain cases, however, the application of the kiddie tax will cause a modification of the means by which the tax is determined.

> **LO.6**
> Demonstrate the proper procedures for determining the tax liability.

---

[39]§ 7703(b).
[40]§ 152(f)(1). The dependency requirement does not apply, however, if the taxpayer could have claimed a dependency exemption except for the fact that the exemption was claimed by the noncustodial parent under a written agreement.

TAX RATES

The basic tax rate structure is progressive, with current rates ranging from 10 percent to 35 percent. Prior to the Tax Relief Reconciliation Act of 2001, the rates ranged from 15 percent to 36 percent. The Act established 10 percent as the new lowest bracket. Later legislation lowered the top rate to 35 percent. The Tax Relief Act (TRA) of 2010 extended the 10 percent to 35 percent rate structure through 2012.[41] By way of comparison, the lowest rate structure, which was in effect in 1913–1915, ranged from 1 to 7 percent, and the highest, in effect during 1944–1945, ranged from 23 to 94 percent.

Tax Table Method

The tax liability is computed using either the Tax Table method or the Tax Rate Schedule method. Most taxpayers compute their tax using the **Tax Table**. Eligible taxpayers compute taxable income (as shown in Figure 3.1) and *must* determine their tax by reference to the Tax Table. The following taxpayers, however, may not use the Tax Table method:

- An individual who files a short period return (see Chapter 18).
- Individuals whose taxable income exceeds the maximum (ceiling) amount in the Tax Table. The 2010 Tax Table applies to taxable income below $100,000 for Form 1040.
- An estate or trust.

The IRS does not release the Tax Tables until late in the year to which they apply. The Tax Rate Schedules, however, are released at the end of the year preceding their applicability. To illustrate, the Tax Table for 2011 will be available at the end of 2011. The Tax Rate Schedules for 2011, however, were released at the end of 2010.[42] For purposes of estimating tax liability and making quarterly prepayments, the Tax Rate Schedules will usually need to be consulted. Based on its availability, the 2010 Tax Table will be used to illustrate the tax computation using the Tax Table method.

Although the Tax Table is derived by using the Tax Rate Schedules (discussed below), the tax calculated using the two methods may vary slightly. This variation occurs because the tax for a particular income range in the Tax Table is based on the midpoint amount.

EXAMPLE 36

Linda is single and has taxable income of $30,000 for calendar year 2010. To determine Linda's tax using the Tax Table (see Appendix A), find the $30,000 to $30,050 income

---

[41]A sunset provision applicable after 2012 will reinstate the pre-2001 rates of 15%, 28%, 31%, 36%, and 39.6%.

[42]The 2011 Tax Table was not available from the IRS at the date of publication of this text. The Tax Table for 2010 and the Tax Rate Schedules for 2010

and 2011 are reproduced in Appendix A. For quick reference, the rate schedules are also reproduced inside the front cover of this text.

| TABLE 3.5 | 2011 Tax Rate Schedule for Single Taxpayers |

If Taxable Income Is		The Tax Is:	Of the Amount Over
Over	**But Not Over**		
$ –0–	$ 8,500	10%	$ –0–
8,500	34,500	$ 850 + 15%	8,500
34,500	83,600	4,750 + 25%	34,500
83,600	174,400	17,025 + 28%	83,600
174,400	379,150	42,449 + 33%	174,400
379,150		110,016.50 + 35%	379,150

line. The tax of $4,085 is actually the tax the Tax Rate Schedule would yield on taxable income of $30,025 (i.e., the midpoint amount between $30,000 and $30,050). ∎

Tax Rate Schedule Method

As previously noted, the **Tax Rate Schedules** have undergone several reductions since 1970. However, a sunset provision that is to take effect after 2012 will restore the pre-2001 rates.[43] As the graduation of tax rates is highly political, the ultimate application of this sunset provision, and the modifications it may undergo, is problematical.

The 2011 rate schedule for single taxpayers is reproduced in Table 3.5. This schedule is used to illustrate the tax computations in Examples 37 and 38.

EXAMPLE 37

Pat is single and had $5,870 of taxable income in 2011. His tax is $587 ($5,870 × 10%). ∎

Several terms are used to describe tax rates. The rates in the Tax Rate Schedules are often referred to as *statutory* (or nominal) rates. The *marginal* rate is the highest rate that is applied in the tax computation for a particular taxpayer. In Example 37, the statutory rate and the marginal rate are both 10 percent.

EXAMPLE 38

Chris is single and had taxable income of $90,000 in 2011. Her tax is $18,817 [$17,025 + 28%($90,000 − $83,600)]. ∎

The *average* rate is equal to the tax liability divided by taxable income. In Example 38, Chris has statutory rates of 10 percent, 15 percent, 25 percent, and 28 percent, and a marginal rate of 28 percent. Chris's average rate is 21 percent ($18,817 tax liability ÷ $90,000 taxable income).

A tax is *progressive* (or graduated) if a higher rate of tax applies as the tax base increases. The progressive nature of the Federal income tax on individuals is illustrated by computing the tax in Example 38 utilizing each rate bracket.

Tax on first $8,500 at 10%	$ 850
Tax on $34,500 − $8,500 at 15%	3,900
Tax on $83,600 − $34,500 at 25%	12,275
Tax on $90,000 − $83,600 at 28%	1,792
Total tax on taxable income of $90,000	$18,817

A special computation limits the effective tax rate on qualified dividends (see Chapter 4) and net long-term capital gain (see Chapter 16).

---

[43]§ 1(i). See comment in footnote 41.

COMPUTATION OF NET TAXES PAYABLE OR REFUND DUE

The pay-as-you-go feature of the Federal income tax system requires payment of all or part of the taxpayer's income tax liability during the year. These payments take the form of Federal income tax withheld by employers or estimated tax paid by the taxpayer or both.[44] The payments are applied against the tax from the Tax Table or Tax Rate Schedules to determine whether the taxpayer will get a refund or pay additional tax.

Employers are required to withhold income tax on compensation paid to their employees and to pay this tax over to the government. The employer notifies the employee of the amount of income tax withheld on Form W–2 (Wage and Tax Statement). The employee should receive this form by January 31 after the year in which the income tax is withheld.

If taxpayers receive income that is not subject to withholding or income from which not enough tax is withheld, they may have to pay estimated tax. These individuals must file Form 1040–ES (Estimated Tax for Individuals) and pay in quarterly installments the income tax and self-employment tax estimated to be due (see Chapter 13 for a thorough discussion).

The income tax from the Tax Table or the Tax Rate Schedules is reduced first by the individual's tax credits. There is an important distinction between tax credits and tax deductions. Tax credits reduce the tax liability dollar-for-dollar. Tax deductions reduce taxable income on which the tax liability is based.

EXAMPLE 39

Gail is a taxpayer in the 25% tax bracket. As a result of incurring $1,000 in child care expenses (see Chapter 13 for details), she is entitled to a $200 child care credit ($1,000 child care expenses × 20% credit rate). She also contributed $1,000 to the American Cancer Society and included this amount in her itemized deductions. The child care credit results in a $200 reduction of Gail's tax liability for the year. The contribution to the American Cancer Society reduces taxable income by $1,000 and results in a $250 reduction in Gail's tax liability ($1,000 reduction in taxable income × 25% tax rate). ∎

Tax credits are discussed in Chapter 13. The following are several of the more common credits:

- Earned income credit.
- Credit for child and dependent care expenses.
- Credit for the elderly.
- Foreign tax credit.
- Child tax credit.
- Making work pay credit.

The making work pay credit is a refundable credit of up to $400 ($800 for married filing jointly) calculated at a rate of 6.2 percent of earned income.[45] It is phased out at a rate of 2 percent of modified adjusted gross income (MAGI)[46] over $75,000 ($150,000 for married filing jointly). Thus, it is completely phased out for a single taxpayer with MAGI of $95,000 [2% of $20,000 = $400] and on a joint return with MAGI of $190,000 [2% of $40,000 = $800]. The making work pay credit applies *only* for 2009 and 2010, but it is discussed at this point because it will be applicable in many of the Tax Return Problems appearing in the chapters that follow.

The computation of net taxes payable or refund due can be illustrated by returning to the facts of Example 6.

---

[44]§ 3402 for withholding; § 6654 for estimated payments.

[45]*Earned income* for this purpose includes employee compensation and net earnings from self-employment but excludes such items as interest, dividends, pension benefits, nontaxable income, and alimony.

[46]*Modified adjusted gross income* for this purpose is AGI less foreign income and income from certain possessions.

EXAMPLE 40

Grace is single and has her disabled and dependent mother living with her. Recall that Example 6 established that she has taxable income of $23,800. Further assume that Grace has the following: income tax withheld, $2,300; estimated tax payments, $600; and credit for dependent care expenses, $200. Grace's net tax payable is computed as follows:

Income tax (from 2011 Tax Rate Schedule, for head of household, Appendix A)		$ 2,963 (rounded)
Less: Tax credits and prepayments—		
Credit for dependent care expenses	$ 200	
Income tax withheld	2,300	
Estimated tax payments	600	(3,100)
Net taxes payable or (refund due if negative)		$ (137)

Note that since Grace maintains a home for a qualifying dependent relative, she can utilize head-of-household filing status. Her tax was computed using the Tax Rate Schedules. In actual practice, she would have used the Tax Tables—see footnote 42 as to why the rate schedules were used.

KIDDIE TAX—UNEARNED INCOME OF CHILDREN TAXED AT PARENTS' RATE

LO.7

Identify and report kiddie tax situations.

At one time, a dependent child could claim an exemption on his or her own return even if claimed as a dependent by the parents. This enabled a parent to shift investment income (such as interest and dividends) to a child by transferring ownership of the assets producing the income. The child would pay no tax on the income to the extent that it was sheltered by the child's exemption and standard deduction amounts.

Also, an additional tax motivation existed for shifting income from parents to children. Although a child's unearned income in excess of the exemption and standard deduction amounts was subject to tax, it was taxed at the child's rate, rather than the parents' rate.

To reduce the tax savings that result from shifting income from parents to children, the net **unearned income** (commonly called investment income) of certain children is taxed as if it were the parents' income. Unearned income includes such income as taxable interest, dividends, capital gains, rents, royalties, pension and annuity income, and income (other than earned income) received as the beneficiary of a trust. This provision, commonly referred to as the **kiddie tax**, applies to any child who is under age 19 (or under age 24 if a full-time student) and has unearned income of more than $1,900.[47] The kiddie tax does not apply if the child has earned income that exceeds half of his or her support, if the child is married and files a joint return, or if both parents are deceased.

Net Unearned Income

Net unearned income of a dependent child is computed as follows:

Unearned income
Less: $950
Less: The greater of
  - $950 of the standard deduction *or*
  - The amount of allowable itemized deductions directly connected with the production of the unearned income
Equals: Net unearned income

If net unearned income is zero (or negative), the child's tax is computed without using the parents' rate. If the amount of net unearned income (regardless of source) is positive, the net unearned income is taxed at the parents' rate. The $950 amounts in the preceding formula are subject to adjustment for inflation each year (these amounts were the same for 2010).

---

[47]§ 1(g)(2).

Tax Determination

If a child is subject to the kiddie tax, there are two options for computing the tax on the income. A separate return may be filed for the child, or the parents may elect to report the child's income on their own return. If a separate return is filed for the child, the tax on net unearned income (referred to as the *allocable parental tax*) is computed as though the income had been included on the parents' return. Form 8615 is used to compute the tax. The steps required in this computation are illustrated below.

EXAMPLE 41

Olaf and Olga have a child, Hans (age 10). In 2011, Hans received $3,000 of interest income and paid investment-related fees of $200. Olaf and Olga had $70,000 of taxable income, not including their child's investment income. The parents have no qualified dividends or capital gains. Olaf and Olga do not make the parental election.

1. Determine Hans's net unearned income

Gross income (unearned)	$ 3,000
Less: $950	(950)
Less: The greater of	
• $950 or	
• Investment expense ($200)	(950)
Equals: Net unearned income	$ 1,100

2. Determine allocable parental tax

Parents' taxable income	$70,000
Plus: Hans's net unearned income	1,100
Equals: Revised taxable income	$71,100
Tax on revised taxable income	$10,025
Less: Tax on parents' taxable income	(9,750)
Allocable parental tax	$ 275

3. Determine Hans's nonparental source tax

Hans's AGI	$ 3,000
Less: Standard deduction	(950)
Less: Personal exemption	(–0–)
Equals: Taxable income	$ 2,050
Less: Net unearned income	(1,100)
Nonparental source taxable income	$ 950
Equals: Tax ($950 × 10% rate)	$ 95

4. Determine Hans's total tax liability

Nonparental source tax (step 3)	$ 95
Allocable parental tax (step 2)	275
Total tax	$ 370

Election to Claim Certain Unearned Income on Parent's Return

If a child who is subject to the kiddie tax is required to file a tax return and meets all of the following requirements, the parent may elect to report the child's unearned income that exceeds $1,900 on the parent's own tax return:

- Gross income is from interest and dividends only.
- Gross income is more than $950 but less than $9,500.
- No estimated tax has been paid in the name and Social Security number of the child, and the child is not subject to backup withholding (see Chapter 13).

If the parental election is made, the child is treated as having no gross income and then is not required to file a tax return. The parental election is made by completing and filing Form 8814 (Parents' Election to Report Child's Interest and Dividends).

The parent(s) must also pay an additional tax equal to the smaller of $95 or 10 percent of the child's gross income over $950. Parents who have substantial itemized deductions based on AGI (see Chapter 10) may find that making the parental election increases total taxes for the family unit. Taxes should be calculated both with the parental election and without it to determine the appropriate choice.

Other Provisions

If parents have more than one child subject to the tax on net unearned income, the tax for the children is computed as shown in Example 41 and then allocated to the children based on their relative amounts of income. For children of divorced parents, the taxable income of the custodial parent is used to determine the allocable parental tax. This parent is the one who may elect to report the child's unearned income. For married individuals filing separate returns, the individual with the greater taxable income is the applicable parent.[48]

3.7 GAINS AND LOSSES FROM PROPERTY TRANSACTIONS—IN GENERAL

Gains and losses from property transactions are discussed in detail in Chapters 14 through 17. Because of their importance in the tax system, however, they are introduced briefly at this point.

> **LO.8**
> Formulate the fundamentals of property transactions.

When property is sold or otherwise disposed of, gain or loss may result. Such gain or loss has an effect on the income tax position of the party making the sale or other disposition when the *realized* gain or loss is *recognized* for tax purposes. Without realized gain or loss, there generally can be no recognized gain or loss. The concept of realized gain or loss is expressed as follows:

$$\text{Amount realized from the sale} - \text{Adjusted basis of the property} = \text{Realized gain (or loss)}$$

The amount realized is the selling price of the property less any costs of disposition (e.g., brokerage commissions) incurred by the seller. The adjusted basis of the property is determined as follows:

Cost (or other original basis) at date of acquisition[49]	
Add:	Capital additions
Subtract:	Depreciation (if appropriate) and other capital recoveries (see Chapter 8)
Equals:	Adjusted basis at date of sale or other disposition

All realized gains are recognized (taxable) unless some specific part of the tax law provides otherwise (see Chapter 15 dealing with certain nontaxable exchanges). Realized losses may or may not be recognized (deductible) for tax purposes, depending on the circumstances involved. Generally, losses realized from the disposition of personal use property (property neither held for investment nor used in a trade or business) are not recognized.

> **EXAMPLE 42**
>
> During the current year, Ted sells his sailboat (adjusted basis of $4,000) for $5,500. Ted also sells one of his personal automobiles (adjusted basis of $8,000) for $5,000. Ted's realized gain of $1,500 from the sale of the sailboat is recognized. On the other hand, the $3,000 realized loss on the sale of the automobile is not recognized and will not provide Ted with any deductible tax benefit. ∎

---

[48]See Chapter 31 of *Your Federal Income Tax* (IRS Publication 17).

[49]Cost usually means purchase price plus expenses related to the acquisition of the property and incurred by the purchaser (e.g., brokerage commissions). For the basis of property acquired by gift or inheritance and other basis rules, see Chapter 14.

Once it has been determined that the disposition of property results in a recognized gain or loss, the next step is to classify the gain or loss as capital or ordinary. Although ordinary gain is fully taxable and ordinary loss is fully deductible, the same may not hold true for capital gains and capital losses.

3.8 GAINS AND LOSSES FROM PROPERTY TRANSACTIONS—CAPITAL GAINS AND LOSSES

To obtain a good perspective on how the Federal income tax functions, some overview of property transactions is needed. This is particularly the case with capital gains and losses, which can generate unique tax consequences. For in-depth treatment of property transactions (including capital gains and losses), refer to Chapters 14 through 17. For now, the overview appearing below should suffice.

DEFINITION OF A CAPITAL ASSET

Capital assets are defined in the Code as any property held by the taxpayer *other than* property listed in § 1221. The list in § 1221 includes inventory, accounts receivable, and depreciable property or real estate used in a business. Thus, the sale or exchange of assets in these categories usually results in ordinary income or loss treatment (see Chapter 17).

EXAMPLE 43

Kelly owns a pizza parlor. During the current year, he sells an automobile that had been used as a pizza delivery car for three years. The sale resulted in a loss of $1,000. Because this automobile is property used in his business, Kelly has an ordinary loss deduction of $1,000, rather than a capital loss deduction. ■

The principal capital assets held by an individual taxpayer include assets held for personal (rather than business) use, such as a personal residence or an automobile, and assets held for investment purposes (e.g., corporate securities and land). Capital assets generally include collectibles, which are subject to somewhat unique tax treatment. **Collectibles** include art, antiques, gems, metals, stamps, some coins and bullion, and alcoholic beverages that are held as investments.

TAXATION OF NET CAPITAL GAIN

Net capital gains are classified and taxed as follows:

Classification	Maximum Rate
Short-term gains (held for one year or less)	35%
Long-term gains (held for more than one year)—	
Collectibles	28%
Certain depreciable property used in a trade or business (known as unrecaptured § 1250 gain and discussed in Chapter 17)	25%
All other long-term capital gains	15%, 5%, or 0%

The special tax rate applicable to long-term capital gains is called the alternative tax computation. It is to be used only if the taxpayer's regular tax rate *exceeds* the applicable alternative tax rate. The 5 percent and 0 percent rates, noted above, apply only if the taxpayer's regular tax bracket is 15 percent or less. If so and the sale or exchange took place prior to 2008, the rate is 5 percent. If the transaction takes place after 2007 and before 2013, the rate is 0 percent.[50]

EXAMPLE 44

During 2011, Polly is in the 15% tax bracket and has the following capital gains for the year:

Robin Corporation stock (held for 6 months)	$1,000
Crow Corporation stock (held for 13 months)	1,000

Polly's tax on these transactions is $150 ($1,000 × 15%) as to Robin and $0 ($1,000 × 0%) as to Crow. ■

EXAMPLE 45

Assume the same facts as in Example 44, except that Polly's regular tax bracket for the year is 33% (not 15%). Polly's tax on these transactions now becomes $330 ($1,000 × 33%) as to Robin and $150 ($1,000 × 15%) as to Crow. ■

DETERMINATION OF NET CAPITAL GAIN

In order to arrive at a net capital gain, capital losses must be taken into account. The capital losses are aggregated by holding period (short term and long term) and applied against the gains in that category. If excess losses result, they are then shifted to the category carrying the *highest* tax rate. A *net capital gain* will occur if the net long-term capital gain (NLTCG) exceeds the net short-term capital loss (NSTCL).

EXAMPLE 46

In the current year, Colin is in the 35% tax bracket and has the following capital transactions:

Penguin Corporation stock (held for 8 months)	$ 1,000
Owl Corporation stock (held for 10 months)	(3,000)
Stamp collection (held for 5 years)	2,000
Land (held as an investment for 3 years)	4,000

The Penguin Corporation short-term capital gain (STCG) of $1,000 is offset by the Owl Corporation short-term capital loss (STCL) of $3,000. The net STCL of $2,000 is then applied against the collectible gain of $2,000. The end result is a net long-term capital gain of $4,000 from the land sale. Colin's net capital gain is taxed at a 15% rate. Note that the stamp collection gain would have been taxed at a higher 28% rate had it not been offset by the excess short-term capital loss. ■

TREATMENT OF NET CAPITAL LOSS

For individual taxpayers, net capital loss can be used to offset ordinary income of up to $3,000 ($1,500 for married persons filing separate returns). If a taxpayer has both short- and long-term capital losses, the short-term category is used first to arrive at the $3,000. Any remaining net capital loss is carried over indefinitely until exhausted. When carried over, the excess capital loss retains its classification as short or long term.

EXAMPLE 47

In 2011, Tina has a short-term capital loss of $2,000, a long-term capital loss of $2,500, and no capital gains. She can deduct $3,000 ($2,000 short-term + $1,000 long-term) of this amount as an ordinary loss. The remaining $1,500 is carried over to 2012 as a long-term capital loss. ■

EXAMPLE 48
THE BIG PICTURE

Return to the facts of *The Big Picture* on p. 3-2. Polly's sale of her wedding rings resulted in a realized capital loss of $7,000 [$8,000 (selling price) − $15,000 (cost basis)]. However, because they were personal use property, Polly cannot deduct the loss. ■

---

[50]§ 1(h)(1) as amended by JGTRRA of 2003, further amended by TIPRA of 2005 and extended by TRA of 2010. After 2012, under a sunset provision, the long-term capital gain rates revert back to 20% and 10%. For recognized gains prior to May 6, 2003, the maximum rates were 20% and 10%.

TAX PLANNING:

3.9 MAXIMIZING THE USE OF THE STANDARD DEDUCTION

In most cases, the choice between using the standard deduction and itemizing deductions *from* AGI is a simple matter—pick whichever yields the larger tax benefit. Families in the initial stages of home ownership, for example, will invariably make the itemization choice due to the substantial mortgage interest and property tax payments involved. Older taxpayers, however, have paid for their homes and are enjoying senior citizen property tax exemptions. For them, the more attractive benefit is the additional standard deduction that can accompany the standard deduction choice.

In some cases, the difference between the standard deduction and itemizing may not be a significant amount. Here, taxes might be saved by alternating between the two options. The taxpayer does this by using the cash method to concentrate multiple years' deductions in a single year (e.g., church pledges for several years can be paid in one year). Then, the standard deduction is used in alternate years.

3.10 DEPENDENCY EXEMPTIONS

THE JOINT RETURN TEST

A married person can be claimed as a dependent only if that individual does not file a joint return with his or her spouse. If a joint return has been filed, the damage may be undone if separate returns are substituted on a timely basis (on or before the due date of the return).

| EXAMPLE 49 | While preparing a client's 2010 income tax return on April 1, 2011, the tax practitioner discovered that the client's daughter filed a joint return with her husband in late January of 2011. Presuming the daughter otherwise qualifies as the client's dependent, the exemption is not lost if she and her husband file separate returns on or before April 18, 2011. (Note: In 2011, April 15 falls on a Friday that is a Washington D.C. holiday. Thus, the usual filing date carries over to the next working day—Monday, April 18.) ∎ |

An initial election to file a joint return must be considered carefully in any situation in which the taxpayers might later decide to amend their return and file separately. As indicated above, separate returns may be substituted for a joint return only if the amended returns are filed on or before the normal due date of the return. If the taxpayers in Example 49 attempt to file separate returns after April 18, 2011, the returns will not be accepted, and the joint return election is binding.[51]

Keep in mind that the filing of a joint return is not fatal to the dependency exemption if the parties are filing solely to recover all income tax withholdings, they are not required to file a return, and no tax liability would exist on separate returns.

SUPPORT CONSIDERATIONS

The support of a qualifying child becomes relevant only if the child is self-supporting. In cases where the child has an independent source of funds, planning could help prevent an undesirable result. When a qualifying relative is involved, meeting the support test is essential, as the dependency exemption is not otherwise available.

| EXAMPLE 50 | In 2011, Imogene maintains a household that she shares with her son and mother. The son, Barry, is 23 years of age and a full-time student in law school. The mother, Gladys, is 68 years of age and active in charitable causes. Barry works part-time for a local law firm, while Gladys has income from investments. In resolving the support issue (or self-support in the |

---

[51]Reg. § 1.6013–1(a)(1).

case of Barry), compare Imogene's contribution with that made by Barry and Gladys.[52] In this connection, what Barry and Gladys do with their funds becomes crucial. The funds that are used for nonsupport purposes (e.g., purchase of investments) or not used at all (e.g., deposited in a bank) should not be considered. To the extent possible, control how much Barry and Gladys contribute to their own support. Records should be maintained showing the amount of support and its source. ■

Example 50 does not mention the possible application of the gross income test. Presuming Barry is a qualifying child, the amount he earns does not matter, as the gross income test does not apply. Gladys, however, comes under the qualifying relative category, where the gross income test applies. Therefore, for her to be claimed as a dependent, her income that is taxable will have to be less than $3,700.

COMMUNITY PROPERTY RAMIFICATIONS

In certain cases, state law can have an effect on the availability of a dependency exemption.

EXAMPLE 51

In 2011, Mitch provides more than half of the support of his son, Ross, and daughter-in-law, Connie, who live with him. Ross, age 22, is a full-time student, while Connie earns $4,000 from a part-time job. Ross and Connie do not file a joint return. All parties live in New York, a common law state. Mitch can claim Ross as a dependent, as he is a qualifying child. Connie is not a dependent because she does not meet the gross income test under the qualifying relative category. ■

EXAMPLE 52

Assume the same facts as in Example 51, except that all parties live in Arizona, a community property state. Now, Connie also qualifies as a dependent. Since Connie's gross income is only $2,000 (one-half of the community income), she satisfies the gross income test. ■

RELATIONSHIP TO THE DEDUCTION FOR MEDICAL EXPENSES

Generally, medical expenses are deductible only if they are paid on behalf of the taxpayer, his or her spouse, and their dependents. Since deductibility may rest on dependency status, planning is important in arranging multiple support agreements.

EXAMPLE 53

During the year, Zelda will be supported by her two sons (Vern and Vito) and her daughter (Maria). Each will furnish approximately one-third of the required support. If the parties decide that the dependency exemption should be claimed by the daughter under a multiple support agreement, any medical expenses incurred by Zelda should be paid by Maria. ■

In planning a multiple support agreement, take into account which of the parties is most likely to exceed the 7.5 percent limitation (see Chapter 10). In Example 53, for instance, Maria might be a poor choice if she and her family do not expect to incur many medical and drug expenses of their own.

One exception permits the deduction of medical expenses paid on behalf of someone who is not a spouse or a dependent. If the person could be claimed as a dependent *except* for the gross income or joint return test, the medical expenses are, nevertheless, deductible. For additional discussion, see Chapter 10.

ETHICS & Equity

A TAX BENEFIT FROM NONDEPENDENTS

During 2011, Kristen provides more than half of the support of her parents who do not live with her. She cannot claim them as dependents, however, because they have too much gross income and file a joint return. She pays $20,000 for her mother's dental implants and $12,000 for her father's knee replacement. From a tax standpoint, has Kristen acted wisely?

---

[52]As part of her support contribution to Barry and Gladys, Imogene can count the fair market value of the meals and lodging she provides.

3.11 TAKING ADVANTAGE OF TAX RATE DIFFERENTIALS

It is natural for taxpayers to be concerned about the tax rates they are paying. How does a tax practitioner communicate information about rates to clients? There are several possibilities.

The marginal rate (refer to Examples 37 and 38) provides information that can help a taxpayer evaluate a particular course of action or structure a transaction in the most advantageous manner. For example, a taxpayer who is in the 15 percent bracket this year and expects to be in the 28 percent bracket next year should, if possible, defer payment of deductible expenses until next year to maximize the tax benefit of the deduction.

A note of caution is in order with respect to shifting income and expenses between years. Congress has recognized the tax planning possibilities of such shifting and has enacted many provisions to limit a taxpayer's ability to do so. Some of these limitations on the shifting of income are discussed in Chapters 4, 5, and 18. Limitations that affect a taxpayer's ability to shift deductions are discussed in Chapters 6 through 11 and in Chapter 18.

A taxpayer's *effective rate* can be an informative measure of the effectiveness of tax planning. The effective rate is computed by dividing the taxpayer's tax liability by the total amount of income. A low effective rate can be considered an indication of effective tax planning.

One way of lowering the effective rate is to exclude income from the tax base. For example, a taxpayer might consider investing in tax-free municipal bonds rather than taxable corporate bonds. Although pre-tax income from corporate bonds is usually higher, after-tax income may be higher if the taxpayer invests in tax-free municipals.

Another way of lowering the effective rate is to make sure that the taxpayer's expenses and losses are deductible. For example, losses on investments in passive activities may not be deductible (see Chapter 11). Therefore, a taxpayer who plans to invest in an activity that will produce a loss in the early years should take steps to ensure that the business is treated as active rather than passive. Active losses are deductible while passive losses are not.

3.12 INCOME OF CERTAIN CHILDREN

Taxpayers can use several strategies to avoid or minimize the effect of the rules that tax the unearned income of certain children at the parents' rate. With the cutoff age being 19 (under 24 for full-time students), many children are vulnerable to the application of the kiddie tax. Parents should consider giving a younger child assets that defer taxable income until the child reaches a nonvulnerable age. For example, U.S. government Series EE savings bonds can be used to defer income until the bonds are cashed in (see Chapter 4).

Growth stocks typically pay little in the way of dividends. However, the profit on an astute investment may more than offset the lack of dividends. The child can hold the stock until he or she reaches a safe age. If the stock is sold then at a profit, the profit is taxed at the child's low rates.

Taxpayers in a position to do so can employ their children in their business and pay them a reasonable wage for the work they actually perform (e.g., light office help, such as filing). The child's earned income is sheltered by the standard deduction, and the parents' business is allowed a deduction for the wages. The kiddie tax rules have no effect on earned income, even if it is earned from the parents' business.

REFOCUS ON THE BIG PICTURE

A DIVIDED HOUSEHOLD

Of major concern to Polly is her filing status. If she qualifies as an abandoned spouse, she is entitled to file as head of household. If not, she is considered to be a married person filing separately. Moreover, in order to be an abandoned spouse, Polly must be able to claim Paige as a dependent. To be a dependent, Paige must meet the requirements of a qualifying child *or* a qualifying relative.

For qualifying child purposes, Paige must meet either the age (i.e., under age 19) or the full-time student (under age 24) test. (A disabled child exception seems highly unlikely.) Because Paige currently is not a full-time student, is she under age 19? If so, she is a qualifying child (see Example 14). If Paige is not a qualifying child, is she a qualifying relative? Here, the answer depends on meeting the gross income test (see Example 22). How much did Paige earn from her part-time job? If her earnings are under $3,700, she satisfies the gross income test. Thus, if Paige can be claimed as a dependent under either the qualifying child or the qualifying relative category, Polly is an abandoned spouse entitled to head-of-household filing status (see Example 35). If not, she is a married person filing separately.

Maude can be claimed as Polly's dependent because she is a member of the household. It does not matter that she died in February, and the dependency exemption amount need not be apportioned and is allowed in full. Because Maude is her dependent, Polly can claim the medical expenses she paid on Maude's behalf. The funeral expenses, however, are not deductible (see Example 19).

Does Maude qualify Polly for head-of-household filing status? No—although she is a dependent, Maude does not meet the relationship test (see Example 32).

The sale of the wedding rings results in a capital loss of $7,000 ($8,000 – $15,000). Because the loss is for personal use property, it cannot be claimed for tax purposes (see Example 48).

What If?

Assume that Nick left for parts unknown in August (not March). Now Polly cannot qualify as an abandoned spouse. Her spouse lived in the home during part of the last six months of the year. Consequently, Polly is treated as married and cannot qualify for head-of-household filing status. She must file as a married person filing separately. The change in when Nick left will not affect the dependency issue regarding Paige, however.

KEY TERMS

Abandoned spouse, 3–27	Itemized deductions, 3–7	Qualifying relative, 3–14
Child tax credit, 3–19	Kiddie tax, 3–31	Standard deduction, 3–8
Collectibles, 3–34	Marriage penalty, 3–25	Surviving spouse, 3–26
Dependency exemption, 3–12	Multiple support agreement, 3–16	Tax Rate Schedules, 3–29
E-file, 3–22	Personal exemptions, 3–12	Tax Table, 3–28
Head of household, 3–26	Qualifying child, 3–13	Unearned income, 3–31

DISCUSSION QUESTIONS

1. **LO.1** Rearrange the following items to show the correct formula for arriving at *taxable income* of individuals under the Federal income tax:
   a. Deductions *for* AGI.
   b. Income (broadly conceived).
   c. Taxable income.

d.   Adjusted gross income.
e.   Personal and dependency exemptions.
f.   Gross income.
g.   Exclusions.
h.   The greater of the standard deduction or itemized deductions.

2.   **LO.1, 5, 8, 9** During the year, Lucy is involved in the following transactions:
   • Won money gambling on a recent trip to a casino.
   • Paid a traffic ticket received while double parking to attend a business meeting.
   • Contributed to the mayor's reelection campaign. The mayor had promised Lucy to have some of her land rezoned. The mayor was reelected and got Lucy's land rezoned.
   • Borrowed money from a bank to make a down payment on a residence.
   • Sold a houseboat and a camper on eBay. Both were personal use items, and the gain from one offset the loss from the other.
   • Her dependent aunt died on January 3 of the year.
   • Paid for dependent aunt's funeral expenses.
   • Paid premiums on her dependent son's life insurance policy.

   What are the possible income tax ramifications of these transactions?

3.   **LO.1** Which of the following items are *inclusions* in gross income?
   a.   During the year, stock the taxpayer purchased as an investment doubled in value.
   b.   Amount an off-duty motorcycle police officer received for escorting a funeral procession.
   c.   While his mother was in the hospital, the taxpayer sold her jewelry and gave the money to his girlfriend.
   d.   Child support payments received.
   e.   A damage deposit the taxpayer recovered when he vacated the apartment he had rented.
   f.   Interest received by the taxpayer on an investment in bonds issued by IBM.
   g.   Amounts received by the taxpayer, a baseball "Hall of Famer," for autographing sports equipment (e.g., balls, gloves).
   h.   Jury duty fees received.

4.   **LO.1** Which of the following items are *exclusions* from gross income?
   a.   Alimony payments received.
   b.   Damages award received by the taxpayer—all were for punitive damages.
   c.   A new golf cart won in a church raffle.
   d.   Amount collected on a loan previously made to a college friend.
   e.   Insurance proceeds paid to the taxpayer on the death of her uncle—she was the designated beneficiary under the policy.
   f.   Interest income on City of Miami bonds.
   g.   Scholarship award that covers the taxpayer's college tuition.
   h.   Reward paid by the IRS for information provided that led to the conviction of the taxpayer's former employer for tax evasion.
   i.   A box store refund of $200 that the taxpayer received when she discovered an overcharge on the purchase of home appliances.
   j.   An envelope containing $8,000 found (and unclaimed) by the taxpayer in a bus station.

5.   **LO.1** Harold, a U.S. citizen, accepts employment overseas. He was careful to choose a country that does not impose an income tax. Has Harold avoided an income tax completely? Explain.

6.   **LO.1** One class of deductions is variously described as *deductions for AGI, above-the-line deductions*, and *page 1 deductions*. Explain the meaning of the various designations.

7.   **LO.1, 8, 9** In late 2011, the Polks come to you for tax advice. They are considering selling some stock investments for a loss and making a contribution to a traditional IRA. In reviewing their situation, you note that they have large medical expenses and a casualty loss, neither of which is covered by insurance. What advice would you give to the Polks?

8.   **LO.2** In choosing between the standard deduction and itemizing deductions *from* AGI, what effect, if any, does each of the following have?
   a.   The age of the taxpayer(s).
   b.   Taxpayer's filing status (e.g., single, married, filing jointly).

c. The taxpayers have paid off the mortgage on their personal residence.
d. Because of their senior citizen exemption, the taxpayers had to pay $3,000 less in property taxes on their personal residence.
e. Whether married taxpayers decide to file separate returns.
f. The taxpayer's uninsured personal residence was recently destroyed by fire.
g. The number of personal and dependency exemptions the taxpayer can claim.

9. **LO.2** In connection with the standard deduction alternative, comment on the following:
   a. Percentage of taxpayers who chose the standard deduction rather than itemize.
   b. Status of a taxpayer who dies before year-end.
   c. Types of standard deductions available.
   d. When not available.

10. **LO.2, 3, 5** Mel, age 76 and a widower, is being claimed as a dependent by his daughter. How does this situation affect the following?
   a. Mel's own individual filing requirement.
   b. Mel's personal exemption.
   c. The standard deduction allowed to Mel.
   d. The availability of any additional standard deduction.

11. **LO.2** Bernice and Drew are dependents of their parents, and each has income of $2,000 for the year. Bernice's standard deduction for the year is $950, while Drew's is $2,300. As their income is the same, what causes the difference in the amount of the standard deduction?   **ISSUE ID**

12. **LO.4** Kirby, age 18, lives with her parents in a household maintained by them. As an actress, she earns $600,000 during the year, which, after taxes, is placed in a trust for her. Can Kirby be claimed as a dependent by her parents?   **ISSUE ID**

13. **LO.4** Patsy maintains a household that includes a son (age 30) and a cousin (age 28). She can claim the cousin as a dependent but not her son. Explain.   **ISSUE ID**

14. **LO.4** Heather, age 12, lives in the same household with her mother, grandmother, and uncle.
   a. Who can qualify for the dependency exemption?
   b. Who takes preference?

15. **LO.4** Under what circumstances, if any, can a taxpayer claim an ex-spouse as a dependent? What about claiming the ex-spouse's relatives as dependents?

16. **LO.4** Joshua and his two sisters provide more than half of the support of their mother, who has significant health problems. After comparing notes, Joshua tells his sisters to split the dependency exemption between them as the deduction will result in a greater tax benefit.
   a. What is Joshua referring to?
   b. Do you see any flaw in Joshua's advice?
   c. Why has Joshua concluded that his sisters will derive a greater tax benefit?

17. **LO.4** Jerry and Arlene were divorced in 2010. In 2011, Arlene has custody of their children, but Jerry provides nearly all of their support. Who is entitled to claim the children as dependents?   **ISSUE ID**

18. **LO.4** Marcus maintains a household in which his 18-year-old married daughter and her husband live. Although Marcus provides most of their support, he does not claim them as dependents because they file a joint return. Is Marcus correct?

19. **LO.4** Alberto, who is single, is a U.S. citizen and resident. He provides almost all of the support of his parents and two aunts, who are citizens and residents of Mexico. Alberto's parents and aunts are seriously considering moving to and becoming residents of El Salvador. Would such a move have any impact on Alberto? Why or why not?   **ISSUE ID**

20. **LO.5, 9** Jack and Joyce, who are married, had itemized deductions of $7,500 and $500, respectively, during 2011. Jack suggests that they file separately—he will itemize his deductions *from* AGI, and she will claim the standard deduction.   **ISSUE ID**
   a. Evaluate Jack's suggestion.
   b. What should they do?

21. **LO.5** Oliver is a U.S. citizen employed by a multinational corporation at its London office. Oliver is married to Regina, a British citizen, and they reside in England. Regina receives substantial rent income from real estate she owns in western Europe.   **ISSUE ID**

    a.   Must Oliver file a U.S. income tax return?

    b.   Under what circumstances might Regina be considered a resident of the United States? Would such a classification be advantageous? Disadvantageous?

22. **LO.4, 5** Comment on the availability of head-of-household filing status for 2011 in each of the following situations:

    a.   Taxpayer lives alone but maintains the household of his parents. In July 2011, the parents use their savings to purchase a Lexus automobile for $51,000.

    b.   Taxpayer maintains a home in which she and her father live. The father enters a nursing facility for treatment for a mental disorder.

    c.   Taxpayer, a single parent, maintains a home in which she and her unmarried son live. The son, age 18, earns $4,000 from a part-time job.

    d.   Assume the same facts as in (c) except that the son is age 20, not 18.

    e.   Taxpayer lives alone but maintains the household where her dependent daughter lives.

    f.   Taxpayer maintains a household that includes an unrelated friend who qualifies as his dependent.

23. **LO.5** In many cases, a surviving spouse ultimately becomes a head of household for filing status purposes. Explain this statement.

24. **LO.7** In connection with the kiddie tax, comment on the following:

    a.   Justification for the tax.

    b.   Earned income versus unearned income.

    c.   Age coverage.

    d.   Exceptions to the kiddie tax.

    e.   Effect of parental election.

    f.   Parents are divorced.

    g.   Parents file separate returns.

25. **LO.8** During the year, Hernando has the following transactions:

- Gain on the sale of stock held as an investment for 10 months.
- Gain on the sale of land held as an investment for 4 years.
- Gain on the sale of a houseboat owned for 2 years and used for family vacations.
- Loss on the sale of a reconditioned motorcycle owned for 3 years and used for recreational purposes.

How should Hernando treat these transactions for income tax purposes?

ISSUE ID

26. **LO.8** Several years ago, Milton and Arlene inherited equal shares of their father's coin collection. When they sold the collection this year, Milton paid a tax based on 28% on his profit while Arlene's tax rate was only 25%. Presuming each had the same amount of gain, explain the difference in result.

27. **LO.8** During the year, Brandi had the following transactions: a long-term capital gain from the sale of land; a short-term capital loss from the sale of stock; and a long-term capital gain from the sale of a gun collection.

    a.   How are these transactions treated for income tax purposes?

    b.   Does this treatment favor the taxpayer or the IRS? Explain.

PROBLEMS

28. **LO.1** Compute the taxable income for 2011 in each of the following independent situations:

    a.   Drew and Meg, ages 40 and 41, are married and file a joint return. In addition to four dependent children, they have AGI of $65,000 and itemized deductions of $12,000.

    b.   Sybil, age 40, is single and supports her dependent parents who live with her and also supports her grandfather who is in a nursing home. She has AGI of $80,000 and itemized deductions of $8,000.

    c.   Scott, age 49, is an abandoned spouse. His household includes two unmarried stepsons who qualify as his dependents. He has AGI of $75,000 and itemized deductions of $9,500.

    d.   Amelia, age 33, is a surviving spouse and maintains a household for her three dependent children. She has AGI of $58,000 and itemized deductions of $10,200.

e.   Dale, age 42, is divorced but maintains the home in which he and his daughter, Jill, live. Jill is single and qualifies as Dale's dependent. Dale has AGI of $64,000 and itemized deductions of $9,900.

Note: Problems 29 and 30 can be solved by referring to Figure 3.1, Exhibits 3.1 through 3.3, Tables 3.1 and 3.2, and the discussion under Deductions for Adjusted Gross Income in this chapter.

29. **LO.1, 8** Compute the taxable income for 2011 for Curtis on the basis of the following information. His filing status is single.

Salary	$80,000
Interest income from bonds issued by City of San Diego	3,000
Alimony payments made	3,600
Contribution to traditional IRA	5,000
Gift from grandparents	26,000
Capital loss from stock investment	3,000
Amount lost in football office pool (sports gambling is against the law where Curtis lives)	1,500
Number of potential dependents (two nephews, who live in another state)	?
Age	39

30. **LO.1** Compute the taxable income for 2011 for Mattie on the basis of the following information. Mattie is married but has not seen or heard from her husband since 2009.

Salary	$ 70,000
Interest on bonds issued by AT&T Corporation	3,000
Interest on CD issued by Wells Fargo Bank	2,000
Cash dividend received on Chevron common stock	2,200
Life insurance proceeds paid on death of aunt (Mattie was the designated beneficiary of the policy)	100,000
Inheritance received on death of aunt	200,000
Casey (a cousin) repaid a loan Mattie made to him in 2007 (no interest was provided for)	5,000
Itemized deductions (state income tax, property taxes on residence, interest on home mortgage, charitable contributions)	10,200
Number of dependents (children, ages 17 and 18, mother-in-law, age 60)	3
Age	40

31. **LO.2** Determine the amount of the standard deduction allowed for 2011 in the following independent situations. In each case, assume the taxpayer is claimed as another person's dependent.

a.   Edward, age 18, has income as follows: $600 interest from a certificate of deposit and $5,900 from repairing cars.

b.   Sarah, age 18, has income as follows: $400 cash dividends from a stock investment and $4,600 from handling a paper route.

c.   Colin, age 16, has income as follows: $900 interest on a bank savings account and $800 for painting a neighbor's fence.

d.   Kara, age 15, has income as follows: $300 cash dividends from a stock investment and $600 from grooming pets.

e.   Kay, age 67 and a widow, has income as follows: $400 from a bank savings account and $3,100 from baby-sitting.

32. **LO.4** Using the legend provided below, classify each statement as to the taxpayer for dependency exemption purposes.

Legend
QC = Could be a qualifying child
QR = Could be a qualifying relative
B = Could satisfy the definition of *both* a qualifying child *and* a qualifying relative
N = Could not satisfy the definition of *either* a qualifying child *or* a qualifying relative

    a.   Taxpayer's son has gross income of $7,000.

    b.   Taxpayer's niece has gross income of $3,000.

    c.   Taxpayer's mother lives with him.

    d.   Taxpayer's daughter is age 25 and disabled.

    e.   Taxpayer's daughter is age 18, has gross income of $8,000, and does not live with him.

    f.   Taxpayer's cousin lives with her.

    g.   Taxpayer's brother does not live with her.

    h.   Taxpayer's sister, has dropped out of school, is age 20, and lives with him.

    i.   Taxpayer's nephew is age 20 and a full-time student.

    j.   Taxpayer's grandson does not live with her and has gross income of $7,000.

33. **LO.3, 4** For tax year 2011, determine the number of personal and dependency exemptions in each of the following independent situations:

    a.   Leo and Amanda (ages 48 and 46) are husband and wife and furnish more than 50% of the support of their two children, Elton (age 18) and Trista (age 24). During the year, Elton earns $4,500 providing transportation for elderly persons with disabilities, and Trista receives a $5,000 scholarship for tuition at the law school she attends.

    b.   Audry (age 65) was divorced 10 years ago. She maintains a household in which she, her ex-husband, Clint, and his mother, Olive, live and furnishes more than 50% of their support. Olive is age 82 and blind.

    c.   Crystal, age 45, furnishes more than 50% of the support of her married son, Andy (age 18), and his wife, Paige (age 19), who live with her. During the year, Andy earned $8,000 from a part-time job. All parties live in Arizona (a community property state).

    d.   Assume the same facts as in (c), except that all parties live in New York (a common law state).

34. **LO.3, 4** Compute the number of personal and dependency exemptions in each of the following independent situations:

    a.   Reginald, a U.S. citizen and resident, contributes 100% of the support of his parents who are citizens of Canada and live there.

    b.   Pablo, a U.S. citizen and resident, contributes 100% of the support of his parents who are citizens of Mexico. Pablo's father is a resident of Mexico, and his mother is a legal resident of the United States.

    c.   Marlena, a U.S. citizen and resident, contributes 100% of the support of her parents who are citizens and residents of Germany.

    d.   Elena is a U.S. citizen and a resident of Italy. Her household includes Mario, a four-year-old adopted son who is a citizen of Spain.

35. **LO.3, 4** Determine how many personal and dependency exemptions would be available in each of the following independent situations. Specify whether any such exemptions would come under the qualifying child or the qualifying relative category.

    a.   Andy maintains a household that includes a cousin (age 12), a niece (age 18), and a son (age 26). All are full-time students. Andy furnishes all of their support.

    b.   Minerva provides all of the support of a family friend's son (age 20) who lives with her. She also furnishes most of the support of her stepmother who does not live with her.

    c.   Raul, a U.S. citizen, lives in Costa Rica. Raul's household includes an adopted daughter, Helena, who is age 9 and a citizen of Costa Rica. Raul provides all of Helena's support.

    d.   Karen maintains a household that includes her ex-husband, her mother-in-law, and her brother-in-law (age 23 and not a full-time student). Karen provides more than half of all of their support. Karen is single and was divorced in the current year.

36. **LO.4** During 2011, Jenny, age 14, lives in a household with her father, uncle, and grandmother. The household is maintained by the uncle. The parties, all of whom file separate returns, have AGI as follows: father ($30,000), uncle ($50,000), and grandmother ($40,000).

    a.   Who is eligible to claim Jenny as a dependent?

    b.   Who has preference as to the exemption?

37. **LO.3, 4** Determine the number of personal and dependency exemptions for 2011 in each of the following independent situations:

a. Marcus (age 68) and Alice (age 65 and blind) file a joint return. They furnish more than 50% of the support of a cousin, Ida, who lives with them. Ida (age 20) is a full-time student and earns $5,000 during the year tutoring special needs children.

b. Penny (age 45) is single and maintains a household in which she and her nephew, Clint, live. Clint (age 18) earns $4,900 from doing yard work, but receives more than 50% of his support from Penny.

c. Trent (age 38) is single and lives alone. He provides more than 50% of the support of his parents (ages 69 and 70) who are in a nursing home.

d. Jack and Carol were divorced in 2007, and Carol has custody of their three children (ages 5, 7, and 9). Jack does not furnish more than half of their support, and the divorce decree is silent as to the dependency exemptions. Carol signs a Form 8332.

38. **LO.4, 9** Isaiah and Inez (ages 88 and 89) live in an assisted care facility and for years 2010 and 2011 received their support from the following sources:

	Percentage of Support
Social Security benefits	17%
Daughter	21
Nephew	30
Cousin	11
Sister	10
Family friend (not related)	11

a. Which persons are eligible to claim the dependency exemptions under a multiple support agreement?

b. Must Isaiah and Inez be claimed by the same person(s) for both 2010 and 2011?

c. Who, if anyone, can claim their medical expenses?

39. **LO.3, 7** Taylor, age 18, is claimed as a dependent by her parents. For 2011, she has the following income: $4,000 wages from a summer job; $1,900 interest from a money market account; and $1,000 interest from City of Boston bonds.

a. What is Taylor's taxable income for 2011?

b. What is Taylor's tax for 2011? (Her parents file a joint return and have taxable income of $120,000 [no dividends or capital gains].)

40. **LO.4, 9** Walter and Nancy provide 60% of the support of their daughter (age 18) and son-in-law (age 22). The son-in-law (John) is a full-time student at a local university, while the daughter (Irene) holds various part-time jobs from which she earns $11,000. Walter and Nancy engage you to prepare their tax return for 2011. During a meeting with them in late March of 2012, you learn that John and Irene have filed a joint return. What tax advice would you give based on the following assumptions:

ISSUE ID

DECISION MAKING

a. All parties live in Louisiana (a community property state).

b. All parties live in New Jersey (a common law state).

41. **LO.1, 2, 3, 4, 5, 6** Miles (age 42) is a surviving spouse and provides all of the support of his four minor children who live with him. He also maintains the household in which his parents live and furnished 60% of their support. Besides interest on City of Miami bonds in the amount of $1,500, Miles's father received $2,400 from a part-time job. Miles has a salary of $90,000, a short-term capital loss of $4,000, a cash prize of $2,000 from a church raffle, and itemized deductions of $9,500. Using the Tax Rate Schedules, compute the 2011 tax liability for Miles.

42. **LO.1, 2, 3, 4, 5, 6** Morgan (age 45) is single and provides more than 50% of the support of Rosalyn (a family friend), Flo (a niece, age 18), and Jerold (a nephew, age 18). Both Rosalyn and Flo live with Morgan, but Jerold (a French citizen) lives in Canada. Morgan earns a salary of $95,000, contributes $5,000 to a traditional IRA, and receives sales proceeds of $15,000 for an RV that cost $60,000 and was used for vacations. She has $8,200 in itemized deductions. Using the Tax Rate Schedules, compute the 2011 tax liability for Morgan.

43. **LO.1, 3, 7** Ava, age 18, is claimed as a dependent on her parents' 2011 return, on which they report taxable income of $100,000 (no qualified dividends or capital gains). Ava

earned $2,900 pet sitting and $3,000 in interest on a savings account. What are Ava's taxable income and tax liability for 2011?

44. **L0.1, 3, 7** Terri, age 16, is claimed as a dependent on her parents' 2011 return. During the year, Terri earned $5,000 in interest income and $3,000 from part-time jobs.
    a.   What is Terri's taxable income?
    b.   How much of Terri's income is taxed at her rate? At her parents' rate?
    c.   Can the parental election be made? Why or why not?

45. **L0.5** Which of the following individuals are required to file a tax return for 2011? Should any of these individuals file a return even if filing is not required? Why?
    a.   Patricia, age 19, is a self-employed single individual with gross income of $4,500 from an unincorporated business. Business expenses amounted to $4,300.
    b.   Mike is single and is 67 years old. His gross income from wages was $10,800.
    c.   Ronald is a dependent child under age 19 who received $5,100 in wages from a part-time job.
    d.   Sam is married and files a joint return with his spouse, Lana. Both Sam and Lana are 67 years old. Their combined gross income was $21,400.

46. **L0.5** Which of the following taxpayers must file a Federal income tax return for 2011?
    a.   Ben, age 19, is a full-time college student. He is claimed as a dependent by his parents. He earned $5,000 wages during the year.
    b.   Anita, age 12, is claimed as a dependent by her parents. She earned interest income of $1,200 during the year.
    c.   Earl, age 16, is claimed as a dependent by his parents. He earned wages of $2,700 and interest of $1,100 during the year.
    d.   Ellen, age 17, is claimed as a dependent by her parents. She earned interest of $300 during the year. In addition, she earned $550 during the summer operating her own business at the beach, where she painted caricatures of her customers.

DECISION MAKING

47. **L0.5, 6, 9** Corey and Addison are engaged and plan to get married. During 2011, Corey is a full-time student and earns $8,000 from a part-time job. With this income, student loans, savings, and nontaxable scholarships, he is self-supporting. For the year, Addison is employed and has wages of $60,000. How much income tax, if any, can Addison save if she and Corey marry in 2011 and file a joint return?

48. **L0.5** In each of the following *independent* situations, determine Winston's filing status for 2011. Winston is not married.
    a.   Winston lives alone, but he maintains a household in which his parents live. The mother qualifies as Winston's dependent, but the father does not.
    b.   Winston lives alone but maintains a household in which his married daughter, Karin, lives. Both Karin and her husband (Winston's son-in-law) qualify as Winston's dependents.
    c.   Winston maintains a household in which he and a family friend, Ward, live. Ward qualifies as Winston's dependent.

49. **L0.4, 5** Christopher died in 2009 and is survived by his wife, Chloe, and their 18-year-old son, Dylan. Chloe is the executor of Christopher's estate and maintains the household in which she and Dylan live. All of their support is furnished by Chloe while Dylan saves his earnings. Dylan's status for 2009–2011 is as follows:

Year	Earnings	Student Status
2009	5,000	Yes
2010	7,000	No
2011	6,000	Yes

What is Chloe's filing status for:
    a.   2009?
    b.   2010?
    c.   2011?

50. **L0.3, 4, 5** Nadia died in 2010 and is survived by her husband, Jerold (age 44), her married son, Travis (age 22), and her daughter-in-law, Macy (age 18). Jerold is the

executor of his wife's estate. He maintains the household where he, Travis, and Macy live and furnished all of their support. During 2010 and 2011, Travis is a full-time student, while Macy earns $7,000 each year from a part-time job. Travis and Macy do not file jointly during either year. What is Jerold's filing status for 2010 and 2011 if all parties reside in:

a. Idaho (a community property state)?
b. Kansas (a common law state)?

51. **LO.8** During the year, Ophelia had the following transactions involving capital assets:

Gain on the sale of unimproved land (held as an investment for 3 years)	$ 3,000
Loss on the sale of a camper (purchased 2 years ago and used for family vacations)	(5,000)
Loss on the sale of ADM stock (purchased 9 months ago as an investment)	(1,000)
Gain on the sale of a fishing boat and trailer (acquired 11 months ago at an auction and used for recreational purposes)	2,000

a. If Ophelia is in the 35% bracket, how much income tax results?
b. If Ophelia is in the 15% bracket and 2011 is the year when these sales occurred?

52. **LO.8** During the year, Chester had the following transactions involving capital assets:

Gain on the sale of an arrowhead collection (acquired as an investment at different times but all pieces have been held for more than one year)	$ 6,000
Loss on the sale of IBM Corporation stock (purchased 11 months ago as an investment)	(4,000)
Gain on the sale of a city lot (acquired 5 years ago as an investment)	2,000

a. If Chester is in the 33% bracket, how much income tax results?
b. If Chester is in the 15% bracket and 2011 is the year involved?

53. **LO.9** Each year, the Hundleys normally have itemized deductions of $9,500, including a $3,600 pledge payment to their church. Upon the advice of a friend, they do the following: in early January 2011, they pay their pledge for 2010; during 2011, they pay the pledge for 2011; and in late December 2011, they prepay their pledge for 2012.
a. Explain what the Hundleys are trying to accomplish.
b. What will be the tax saving if their marginal tax bracket is 25% for all three years? (Assume the standard deduction amounts for 2011 and 2012 are the same.)

DECISION MAKING

CUMULATIVE PROBLEMS

54. Lance H. and Wanda B. Dean are married and live at 431 Yucca Drive, Santa Fe, NM 87501. Lance works for the convention bureau of the local Chamber of Commerce, while Wanda is employed part-time by a law firm as a paralegal.
  During 2010, the Deans had the following receipts:

TAX RETURN PROBLEM

H&R BLOCK
At Home

Salaries ($60,000 for Lance, $41,000 for Wanda)		$101,000
Interest income—		
City of Albuquerque general purpose bonds	$1,000	
Ford Motor Company bonds	1,100	
Ally Bank certificate of deposit	400	2,500
Child support payments from John Allen		7,200
Annual gifts from Lance's parents		26,000
Settlement from Roadrunner Touring Company		90,000
Lottery winnings		600
Federal income tax refund (for tax year 2009)		400

  Wanda was previously married to John Allen. When they divorced several years ago, Wanda was awarded custody of their two children, Penny and Kyle. (Note: Wanda has never issued a Form 8332 waiver.) Under the divorce decree, John was obligated to pay alimony and child support—the alimony payments were to terminate if Wanda remarried.

In July, while going to lunch in downtown Santa Fe, Wanda was injured by a tour bus. As the driver was clearly at fault, the owner of the bus, Roadrunner Touring Company, paid her medical expenses (including a one-week stay in a hospital). To avoid a lawsuit, Roadrunner also transferred to her $90,000 in settlement of the personal injuries she sustained.

The Deans keep track of their lottery winnings but have no idea what their losses are.

The Deans had the following expenditures for 2010:

Medical expenses (not covered by insurance)		$8,100
Taxes—		
Property taxes on personal residence	$3,600	
State of New Mexico income tax (includes amount withheld from wages during 2010)	4,200	7,800
Interest on home mortgage		6,000
Paid church pledge		3,600
Life insurance premiums (policy on Lance's life)		1,200
Contribution to traditional IRA (on Wanda's behalf)		5,000
Traffic fines		300
Contribution to the reelection campaign fund of the mayor of Santa Fe		300
Funeral expenses for Wayne Boyle		5,100

The life insurance policy was taken out by Lance several years ago and designates Wanda as the beneficiary. As a part-time employee, Wanda is excluded from coverage under her employer's pension plan. Consequently, she provides for her own retirement with a traditional IRA obtained at a local trust company. Because the mayor is a member of the local Chamber of Commerce, Lance felt compelled to make the political contribution.

The Deans' household includes the following, for whom they provide more than half of the support:

	Social Security Number	Birth Date
Lance Dean (age 42)	123–45–6786	12/16/1968
Wanda Dean (age 40)	123–45–6787	08/08/1970
Penny Allen (age 19)	123–45–6788	10/09/1991
Kyle Allen (age 17)	123–45–6789	05/03/1993
Wayne Boyle (age 70)	123–45–6785	06/15/1940

Penny graduated from high school on May 9, 2010, and is undecided about college. During 2010, she earned $8,500 (placed in a savings account) playing a harp in the lobby of a local hotel. Wayne is Wanda's widower father who died on January 10, 2010. For the past few years, Wayne qualified as a dependent of the Deans.

Federal income tax withheld is $5,200 (Lance) and $3,100 (Wanda). The proper amount of Social Security and Medicare tax was withheld.

Determine the Federal income tax for 2010 for the Deans on a joint return by completing the appropriate forms. They do not wish to contribute to the Presidential Election Campaign Fund. If an overpayment results, it is to be refunded to them. Suggested software: H&R BLOCK At Home.

TAX RETURN PROBLEM

DECISION MAKING

COMMUNICATIONS

55. Ellen M. Rand, age 48, is a widow whose husband, Clint, died on May 9, 2008. She lives at 384 Meadowlark Land, Overland Park, KS 66204. She is employed as a business manager for a local medical clinic. During 2010, she had the following receipts:

Salary		$85,000
Interest income—		
Money market account at Prosperity Bank	$ 240	
Savings account at Lawrence State Bank	1,900	
City of Wichita general purpose bonds	2,400	4,540

Inheritance from Mary	$ 40,000
Life insurance proceeds	100,000
Amount from sale of Kansas City lot	60,000
Proceeds from estate sale	18,000
Fees for jury duty service	400

Ellen inherited securities worth $40,000 from her maiden aunt, Mary, who died in 2010. Ellen also was the designated beneficiary of an insurance policy on Mary's life with a maturity value of $100,000. The lot in Kansas City was purchased by Ellen and Clint on May 2, 2003, for $65,000 and held as an investment. As the neighborhood has deteriorated, Ellen decided to cut her losses and sold the lot on January 5, 2010, for $60,000. The estate sale consisted largely of items belonging to Clint and Mary (e.g., camper, boat, furniture, fishing and hunting equipment). Ellen estimates that the property sold originally cost at least twice the $18,000 she received and has declined or stayed the same in value since Clint and Mary died.

Ellen's expenditures for 2010 include the following:

Medical expenses (including $9,500 for dental)		$10,500
Taxes—		
State of Kansas income tax (includes withholdings during 2010)	$3,800	
Property taxes on personal residence	4,200	8,000
Interest on home mortgage		4,500
Contribution to church (paid pledges for 2010 and 2011)		4,800

Ellen and her dependents are covered by her employer's health insurance policy. However, she is subject to a deductible, and dental care is not included. The $9,500 dental charge was for Herbert's implants. Herbert is Ellen's widowed father who lives with her (see below). Ellen normally pledges $2,400 ($200 per month) each year to her church. On December 5, 2010, upon the advice of her pastor, she prepaid her pledge for 2011.

Ellen's household, all of whom she supports, includes the following:

	Social Security Number	Birth Date
Ellen Rand (age 48)	123-45-6787	08/30/1962
Herbert Martin (age 70)	123-45-6780	01/13/1940
Neil Rand (age 23)	123-45-6783	07/18/1987
Donna Rand (age 22)	123-45-6784	02/16/1988

Herbert, Ellen's father, receives a modest Social Security benefit. Neil, a son, is a full-time student in dental school and earns $4,500 as a part-time dental assistant. Donna, a daughter, does not work and is engaged to be married.

Part 1—Tax Computation
Using the appropriate forms and schedules, compute Ellen's income tax for 2010. In addition to Federal income tax of $6,200 withheld from her wages, Ellen applied her 2009 overpayment of $300 to her 2010 tax liability. As was true in the past, she wants any 2010 overpayment handled in the same way. Assume that the proper amounts of Social Security and Medicare taxes were withheld. Ellen does not wish to contribute to the Presidential Election Campaign Fund. Suggested software: H&R BLOCK At Home.

Part 2—Follow-up Advice
In early 2011, the following take place:

- Herbert decides he wants to live with one of his sons and moves to Florida.
- Neil graduates from dental school and joins an existing practice in Kansas City.
- Donna marries, and she and her husband move in with his parents.
- Using the insurance proceeds she received on Mary's death, Ellen pays off the mortgage on her personal residence.

Ellen believes these events may have an effect on her tax position for 2011. Therefore, she requests your advice.

Write a letter to Ellen explaining in general terms the changes that will occur for tax purposes. Assume Ellen's salary and other factors not mentioned (e.g., property and state income taxes) will remain the same. Use the Tax Rate Schedules in projecting Ellen's tax for 2011.

RESEARCH PROBLEMS

THOMSON REUTERS

Checkpoint® Student Edition

Note: Solutions to Research Problems can be prepared by using the **Checkpoint**® **Student Edition** online research product, which is available to accompany this text. It is also possible to prepare solutions to the Research Problems by using tax research materials found in a standard tax library.

COMMUNICATIONS

Research Problem 1. Don and Mary Dewey are successful professionals and have a combined AGI of approximately $400,000. Their household includes two children: Debra (age 16) and Van (age 23). Van is not a student but works at a part-time job where he earns $16,000. Don has heard that it might be beneficial if Van, rather than Don and Mary, claims Debra as a qualified child for income tax purposes. At a local Chamber of Commerce meeting, he asks you to advise him on this matter. Send a letter to Don at 4321 Mount Vernon Road, Dover, DE 19901, advising him about the advantages of such a choice and whether it is feasible. In your letter, discuss the relevance of Code §§ 24, 32, 151, and 152.

Research Problem 2. Bernice and Nate were divorced on July 7, 2010. Under the divorce decree, Bernice received full custody of their three children, and Nate was awarded the dependency exemptions for them. After the trial was over, Nate had Bernice sign a Form 8332 (Release/Revocation of Release of Claim to Exemption for Child by Custodial Parent) releasing her rights to the dependency exemptions for the next five years. In early April 2011, Bernice realizes the tax costs of losing the deduction for the dependency exemptions. Besides contacting Nate, who is already delinquent in his child support payments, does she have any way out?

COMMUNICATIONS

Research Problem 3. Sophia Durbin maintains a household in which she, her son (Ryan), and her widowed mother-in-law (Isabella) live. Since 2009, she also has provided more than half of their support. Sophia's husband, Karl, left for parts unknown in April 2009 and, except for one postcard, has not been heard from since. The postcard (no return address included) was received by Sophia in March 2010 and announced that he planned to claim both Ryan and Isabella as dependents on his own tax return.

Ryan (age 19 in December 2009) graduated from high school on May 6, 2009, and plans to start college in 2011. Until then, he is working as much as possible to save for college expenses. He earned $8,000 in 2009 and $17,000 in 2010. Isabella's income is negligible and originates from nontaxable sources (e.g., Social Security benefits, interest on municipal bonds).

For tax year 2009, Sophia filed her Federal income tax return as married filing separately and claimed no exemptions for dependents. She has not yet filed for 2010. Being somewhat perplexed with her situation, she comes to you for advice in early March 2011.

a. Write a letter to Sophia Durbin addressing her concerns. She lives at 1310 Ash Street, Kearney, NE 68849.

b. Prepare a memo for your firm's client files that lists and discusses the legal basis for the advice rendered.

DECISION MAKING

Research Problem 4. John and Janet Baker are husband and wife and maintain a household in which the following persons live: Calvin and Florence Carter; Darin, Andrea, and Morgan Baker.

- Calvin and Florence are Janet's parents who are retired. During the year, they receive $19,000 in nontaxable funds (e.g., disability income, interest on municipal bonds, Social Security benefits). Of this amount, $8,000 is spent equally between them for clothing, transportation, and recreation (e.g., vacation), and the balance of $11,000 is invested in tax-exempt securities. Janet paid $1,000 for her mother's dental work and paid the $1,200 premium on an insurance policy her father owned on his own life. Calvin also had medical expenses, but he insisted on paying for them with his own funds.

- Darin is the Bakers' 18-year-old son who is not a student but operates a pool-cleaning service on a part-time basis. During the year, he earns $14,000 from the business, which he places in a savings account for later college expenses.
- Andrea is the Bakers' 19-year-old daughter who does not work or go to school. Tired of the inconvenience of borrowing and sharing the family car, during the year she purchased a Camaro for $21,000. Andrea used funds from a savings account she had established several years ago with an inheritance from her paternal grandfather.
- Morgan is the Bakers' 23-year-old daughter. To attend graduate school at a local university, she applied for and obtained a student loan of $20,000. She uses the full amount to pay her college tuition.

The Bakers' fair rental value of their residence, including utilities, is $14,000 while their total food expense for the household is $10,500.

a. How many dependency exemptions will the Bakers be entitled to claim for the year? Explain your answer.
b. From a planning standpoint, how might the Bakers have improved the tax result?

Partial list of research aids:
Reg. §§ 1.152–1(a) and –1(c).
Your Federal Income Tax (IRS Pub. 17), Ch. 3

Use the tax resources of the Internet to address the following questions. Do not restrict your search to the Web, but include a review of newsgroups and general reference materials, practitioner sites and resources, primary sources of the tax law, chat rooms and discussion groups, and other opportunities.

Research Problem 5. Locate IRS Form 2120 and answer the following questions.

a. Who must sign the form?
b. Who must file the form?
c. Can it be used for someone who is not related to the taxpayer?

Research Problem 6. What purpose is served by IRS Form 8857? In this regard, see IRS Publication 971.

Research Problem 7. A nonresident alien earns money in the United States that is subject to Federal income tax. What guidance does the IRS provide on what tax form needs to be used and on when it should be filed? In terms of the proper filing date, does it matter whether the earnings were subject to income tax withholding?

Research Problem 8. When taxpayers pay their income taxes by means of a credit or debit card, they are charged "convenience fees" by the issuer of the card. Are these fees deductible for income tax purposes? (Note: The IRS issued a notice clarifying its position on this matter.)

Research Problem 9. Locate IRS Forms 8615 and 8814. What do these forms have in common? What purpose is served by each?

Gross Income

Part 2 presents the income component of the basic tax model. Included in this presentation are the determination of what is income and the statutory exclusions that are permitted in calculating gross income. Because the taxpayer's accounting method and accounting period affect when income is reported, an introductory discussion of these topics is also included.

Gross Income: Concepts and Inclusions

OUTLINE

FRAMEWORK 1040:
Tax Formula for Individuals

This chapter covers the boldfaced portions of the Tax Formula for Individuals that was introduced in Figure 3.1 on p. 3-3. Below those portions are the sections of Form 1040 where the results are reported.

Income (broadly conceived)	$xx,xxx
Less: Exclusions	(x,xxx)
Gross Income	$xx,xxx

FORM 1040 (p. 1)

7	Wages, salaries, tips, etc. Attach Form(s) W-2	
8a	**Taxable** interest. Attach Schedule B if required	
b	**Tax-exempt** interest. **Do not** include on line 8a	8b
9a	Ordinary dividends. Attach Schedule B if required	
b	Qualified dividends	9b
11	Alimony received	
12	Business income or (loss). Attach Schedule C or C-EZ	
20a	Social security benefits 20a	b Taxable amount
21	Other income. List type and amount	

Less: Deductions for adjusted gross income	(x,xxx)
Adjusted gross income	$ xx,xxx
Less: The greater of total itemized deductions *or* the standard deduction	(x,xxx)
Personal and dependency exemptions	(x,xxx)
Taxable income	$ xx,xxx
Tax on taxable income (see Tax Tables or Tax Rate Schedules)	$ x,xxx
Less: Tax credits (including income taxes withheld and prepaid)	(xxx)
Tax due (or refund)	$ xxx

THE BIG PICTURE   Tax Solutions for the Real World

CALCULATION OF GROSS INCOME

At the beginning of the year, Dr. Cliff Payne opened his dental practice as a sole proprietorship. He previously had worked at a large dental clinic where he was a salaried employee. For his new business, he selected a December 31 year-end. He also entered into a contract to have a building constructed for his medical practice. In addition, now that he has completed his medical education and repaid all of his education loans, he used $12,000 of extra money to purchase some stock.

Dr. Payne's financial reporting system provides him with the following information regarding the income from his dental practice for the first year of operation.

Revenues (amounts billed patients for dental services)	$385,000
Accounts receivable: January 1	–0–
Accounts receivable: December 31	52,000

The accounts receivable represent the amounts he has billed patients that will be paid by the patients, paid by insurance companies, or charged off as uncollectible bad debts.

During the year, Sam Jones, a contractor who owed Dr. Payne $4,000 for dental services, satisfied the account by installing solar panels on the roof of Dr. Payne's new medical building.

As an undergraduate student at State University, Cliff took an accounting course. He originally had planned to major in accounting and go to work for one of the Big 4 Accounting Firms, but decided that he liked science courses better than accounting and business courses. From his accounting course, he remembers that the accrual method of accounting provides a better measure of the income and expenses of a business. Using the information provided by his financial reporting system, he concludes that the gross income for Federal income tax purposes is the $385,000 that he billed his patients for the dental services rendered.

Has Dr. Payne correctly calculated the gross income of this dental practice? **Read the chapter and formulate your response.**

M r. Zarin lost over $2.5 million of his own money gambling. The casino then allowed him to gamble on credit. After several months, his liability to the casino totaled more than $3.4 million. Following protracted negotiations, the casino agreed to settle its claim against Mr. Zarin for a mere $500,000. Although Mr. Zarin had paid for gambling losses of $3 million, the IRS had the audacity to ask him to pay tax on $2.9 million, that is, the amount the casino marked down his account.[1] Mr. Zarin undoubtedly had difficulty understanding how he could be deemed to have income in this situation.

Given an understanding of the income tax formula, though, one can see how the "free" gambling Mr. Zarin enjoyed could constitute income. The starting point in the formula is the determination of gross income rather than "net income." Once gross income is determined, the next step is to determine the allowable deductions. In Mr. Zarin's way of thinking, these steps were collapsed.

This chapter is concerned with the first step in the computation of taxable income—the determination of gross income. Questions that are addressed include the following:

- What: What is income?
- When: In which tax period is the income recognized?
- Who: Who must include the item of income in gross income?

The Code provides an all-inclusive definition of gross income in § 61. Chapter 5 presents items of income that are specifically excluded from gross income (exclusions).

4.1 GROSS INCOME—WHAT IS IT?

DEFINITION

Section 61(a) of the Internal Revenue Code defines the term **gross income** as follows:

> Except as otherwise provided in this subtitle, gross income means all income from whatever source derived.

This definition is derived from the language of the Sixteenth Amendment to the Constitution.

Supreme Court decisions have made it clear that all sources of income are subject to tax unless Congress specifically excludes the type of income received:

> The starting point in all cases dealing with the question of the scope of what is included in "gross income" begins with the basic premise that the purpose of Congress was to use the full measure of its taxing power.[2]

Although at this point we know that *income* is to be broadly construed, we still do not have a satisfactory definition of the term *income*. Congress left it to the judicial and administrative branches to thrash out the meaning of income.

> **LO.1**
>
> Explain the concepts of gross income and realization and distinguish between the economic, accounting, and tax concepts of gross income.

---

[1] *Zarin v. Comm.*, 90–2 USTC ¶50,530, 66 AFTR 2d 90–5679, 916 F.2d 110 (CA–3, 1990).

[2] *James v. U.S.*, 61–1 USTC ¶9449, 7 AFTR 2d 1361, 81 S.Ct. 1052 (USSC, 1961).

GLOBAL Tax Issues

FROM "ALL SOURCES" IS A BROAD DEFINITION

When § 61 refers to "income from whatever source derived," the taxing authorities are reaching far beyond the borders of the United States. Although one interpretation of "source" in this context is type of income (wages, interest, etc.), a broader interpretation revolves around the place where the income is generated. In this context, citizens and residents of the United States are subject to taxation on income earned from sources both inside and outside the country. This "worldwide income" tax base can cause potential double taxation problems, with other countries also taxing income earned within their borders, but mechanisms such as the foreign tax credit can alleviate these tax burdens.

Recently, some U.S. corporations have relocated to other countries to avoid the higher U.S. tax rates on income earned abroad. Congress is considering ways of stopping this "flight of capital."

RECOVERY OF CAPITAL DOCTRINE

The Constitution grants Congress the power to tax income but does not define the term. Because the Constitution does not define income, it would seem that Congress could simply tax gross receipts. Although Congress does allow certain deductions, none are constitutionally required. However, the Supreme Court has held that there is no income subject to tax until the taxpayer has recovered the capital invested.[3] This concept is known as the **recovery of capital doctrine**.

In its simplest application, this doctrine means that sellers can reduce their gross receipts (selling price) by the adjusted basis of the property sold.[4] This net amount, in the language of the Code, is gross income.

EXAMPLE 1 THE BIG PICTURE	Return to the facts of *The Big Picture* on p. 4-2. Dr. Payne sells common stock for $15,000. He had purchased the stock for $12,000. Dr. Payne's gross receipts are $15,000. This amount consists of a $12,000 recovery of capital and $3,000 of gross income. ∎

Collections on annuity contracts and installment payments received from sales of property must be allocated between recovery of capital and income. Annuities are discussed in this chapter, and installment sales are discussed in Chapter 18.

ECONOMIC AND ACCOUNTING CONCEPTS

The term **income** is used in the Code but is not separately defined. Thus, the courts were required to interpret "the commonly understood meaning of the term which must have been in the minds of the people when they adopted the Sixteenth Amendment to the Constitution."[5] Early in the development of the income tax law, a choice had to be made between two competing models: economic income and accounting income. In determining the definition of income, the Supreme Court rejected the economic concept of income.

Economists measure income (**economic income**) by first determining the fair market value of the individual's net assets (assets minus liabilities) at the beginning and end of the year (change in net worth). Then, to arrive at economic income, this change in net worth is added to the goods and services that person actually consumed during the period. Economic income also includes imputed values for such items as the rental value of an owner-occupied home and the value of food a taxpayer might grow for personal consumption.[6]

---

[3]*Doyle v. Mitchell Bros. Co.*, 1 USTC ¶17, 3 AFTR 2979, 38 S.Ct. 467 (USSC, 1916).
[4]For a definition of "adjusted basis," see the Glossary in Appendix C.
[5]*Merchants Loan and Trust Co. v. Smietanka*, 1 USTC ¶42, 3 AFTR 3102, 41 S.Ct. 386 (USSC, 1921).

[6]See Henry C. Simons, *Personal Income Taxation* (Chicago: University of Chicago Press, 1933), Chapters 2–3.

TAX *in* the NEWS

THE GENERAL WELFARE EXCEPTION

The broad concept of gross income and the government's role in promoting the general welfare sometimes are in conflict. For example, if the government makes payments to persons based on their need, it does not make sense for the government to extract a tax from those same individuals and thus reduce the relief it intended to confer. Therefore, the courts and the IRS have created the "general welfare exception," which excludes from gross income certain types of governmental payments that might otherwise be taxable under the broad gross income concept. To qualify for this exception, the payments must be:

- Made from a governmental welfare fund.
- Based on need.
- Not made as a payment for services.

The exception has been applied to a wide range of government payments including Federal grants to rebuild homes destroyed by Hurricane Katrina and to make mortgage payments for persons suffering severe hardship. It also applies to grants by state governments to motivate the purchase of appliances with an Energy Star rating.

Sources: Adapted from Robert W. Woods, "Updating General Welfare Exception Authorities," 123 *Tax Notes*, June 22, 2009, p. 1443; Rev.Rul. 2009–19, I.R.B. No. 28, 111.

EXAMPLE 2

Helen, who is Dr. Payne's aunt, has economic income as follows:

Fair market value of Helen's assets on December 31, 2011	$220,000	
Less liabilities on December 31, 2011	(40,000)	
Net worth on December 31, 2011		$ 180,000
Fair market value of Helen's assets on January 1, 2011	$200,000	
Less liabilities on January 1, 2011	(80,000)	
Net worth on January 1, 2011		(120,000)
Increase in net worth		$ 60,000
Consumption		
Food, clothing, and other personal expenditures		25,000
Imputed rental value of the home Helen owns and occupies		12,000
Economic income		$ 97,000

The need to value assets annually would make compliance with the tax law burdensome and would cause numerous controversies between the taxpayer and the IRS over valuation. In addition, using market values to determine income for tax purposes could result in liquidity problems. The taxpayer's assets may increase in value even though they are not readily convertible into the cash needed to pay the tax (e.g., commercial real estate). Thus, the IRS, Congress, and the courts have rejected the economic concept of income as impractical.

In contrast, the accounting concept of income is founded on the realization principle.[7] According to this principle, income (**accounting income**) is not recognized until it is realized. For realization to occur, (1) an exchange of goods or services must take place between the accounting entity and some independent, external group, and (2) in the exchange the accounting entity must receive assets that are capable of being objectively valued. Thus, income is recognized when an employee embezzles his employer's funds, when the income from an illegal business is realized, and when a person discovers buried treasure.[8] On the other hand, the appreciation in the market value of an asset owned is not realized and thus is not included in gross income until the asset is sold. Income is not realized when an individual creates assets for her own use (e.g., vegetables grown in a personal garden) because there is no exchange transaction with another party.

---

[7]See the American Accounting Association Committee Report on the "Realization Concept," *The Accounting Review* (April 1965): 312–322.

[8]*Rutkin v. U.S.*, 52–1 USTC ¶9260, 41 AFTR 2d 596, 72 S.Ct. 571 (USSC, 1952); Rev.Rul. 61, 1953–1 C.B. 17.

The Supreme Court expressed an inclination toward the accounting concept of income when it adopted the realization requirement in *Eisner v. Macomber*:

> Income may be defined as the gain derived from capital, from labor, or from both combined, provided it is understood to include profit gained through a sale or conversion of capital assets. . . . Here we have the essential matter: not a gain accruing to capital; not a *growth* or *increment* of value *in* investment; but a gain, a profit, something of exchangeable value, *proceeding from* the property, *severed from* the capital however invested or employed, and *coming in*, being "*derived*"—that is, *received* or *drawn by* the recipient for his separate use, benefit and disposal—*that is*, income derived from the property.[9]

In summary, *income* represents an increase in wealth recognized for tax purposes only upon realization.

COMPARISON OF THE ACCOUNTING AND TAX CONCEPTS OF INCOME

Although income tax rules frequently parallel financial accounting measurement concepts, differences do exist. Of major significance, for example, is the fact that unearned (prepaid) income received by an accrual basis taxpayer often is taxed in the year of receipt. For financial accounting purposes, such prepayments are not treated as income until earned.[10] Because of this and other differences, many corporations report financial accounting income that is substantially different from the amounts reported for tax purposes (see Reconciliation of Corporate Taxable Income and Accounting Income in Chapter 20).

The Supreme Court provided an explanation for some of the variations between accounting and taxable income in a decision involving inventory and bad debt adjustments:

> The primary goal of financial accounting is to provide useful information to management, shareholders, creditors, and others properly interested; the major responsibility of the accountant is to protect these parties from being misled. The primary goal of the income tax system, in contrast, is the equitable collection of revenue. . . . Consistently with its goals and responsibilities, financial accounting has as its foundation the principle of conservatism, with its corollary that 'possible errors in measurement [should] be in the direction of understatement rather than overstatement of net income and net assets.' In view of the Treasury's markedly different goals and responsibilities, understatement of income is not destined to be its guiding light.

---

[9]1 USTC ¶32, 3 AFTR 3020, 40 S.Ct. 189 (USSC, 1920).

[10]Similar differences exist in the deduction area.

... Financial accounting, in short, is hospitable to estimates, probabilities, and reasonable certainties; the tax law, with its mandate to preserve the revenue, can give no quarter to uncertainty.[11]

FORM OF RECEIPT

Gross income is not limited to cash received. "It includes income realized in any form, whether in money, property, or services. Income may be realized [and recognized], therefore, in the form of services, meals, accommodations, stock or other property, as well as in cash."[12]

Ostrich Corporation allows Bill, an employee, to use a company car for his vacation. Bill realizes income equal to the rental value of the car for the time and mileage. ∎	**EXAMPLE 3**

Terry owes $10,000 on a mortgage. The creditor accepts $8,000 in full satisfaction of the debt. Terry realizes income of $2,000 from retiring the debt.[13] ∎	**EXAMPLE 4**

Return to the facts of *The Big Picture* on p. 4-2. When Sam Jones performed the services in satisfaction of his $4,000 account, Dr. Payne realized income equal to the value of the services of $4,000. ∎	**EXAMPLE 5** **THE BIG PICTURE**

ETHICS & Equity

A BUSINESS MADE POSSIBLE BY eBAY

Each Saturday morning Ted makes the rounds of the local yard sales. He has developed a keen eye for bargains, but he cannot use all the items he thinks are "real bargains." Ted has found a way to share the benefits of his talent with others. If Ted spots something priced at $40 that he knows is worth $100, for example, he will buy it and list it on eBay for $70. Ted does not include his gain in his gross income because he reasons that he is performing a valuable service for others (both the original sellers and the future buyers) and sacrificing profit he could receive. "Besides," according to Ted, "the IRS does not know about these transactions." Should Ted's ethical standards depend on his perception of his own generosity and the risk that his income-producing activities will be discovered by the IRS? Discuss.

---

[11]*Thor Power Tool Co. v. Comm.*, 79–1 USTC ¶9139, 43 AFTR 2d 79–362, 99 S.Ct. 773 (USSC, 1979).

[12]Reg. § 1.61–1(a).

[13]Reg. § 1.61–12. See *U.S. v. Kirby Lumber Co.*, 2 USTC ¶814, 10 AFTR 458, 52 S.Ct. 4 (USSC, 1931). Exceptions to this general rule are discussed in Chapter 5.

4.2 YEAR OF INCLUSION

LO.2

Describe the cash and accrual methods of accounting and the related effects of the choice of taxable year.

TAXABLE YEAR

The annual accounting period or **taxable year** is a basic component of our tax system.[14] Generally, an entity must use the *calendar year* to report its income. However, a *fiscal year* (a period of 12 months ending on the last day of any month other than December) can be elected if the taxpayer maintains adequate books and records. This fiscal year option generally is not available to partnerships, S corporations, and personal service corporations, as discussed in Chapter 18.[15]

Determining the particular year in which the income will be taxed is important for determining when the tax must be paid and the present value of the tax. Assuming the tax rates do not change between years, the longer payment of the tax can be postponed, the lower the present value of the tax. The year each item of income is subject to tax can also affect the total tax liability over the entity's lifetime. This is true for the following reasons:

- With a progressive rate system, a taxpayer's marginal tax rate can change from year to year.
- Congress may change the tax rates.
- The relevant rates may change because of a change in the entity's status (e.g., a person may marry or a business may be incorporated).
- Several provisions in the Code are dependent on the taxpayer's gross income for the year (e.g., whether the person can be claimed as a dependent, as discussed in Chapter 3).

ACCOUNTING METHODS

The year an item of income is subject to tax often depends upon which acceptable **accounting method** the taxpayer regularly employs.[16] The three primary methods of accounting are (1) the cash receipts and disbursements method, (2) the accrual method, and (3) the hybrid method. Most individuals use the cash receipts and disbursements method of accounting, whereas most larger corporations use the accrual method. The Regulations require the accrual method for determining purchases and sales when inventory is an income-producing factor.[17] Some businesses employ a hybrid method that is a combination of the cash and accrual methods of accounting.

In addition to these overall accounting methods, a taxpayer may choose to spread the gain from an installment sale of property over the collection periods by using the *installment method* of income recognition. Contractors may either spread profits from contracts over the periods in which the work is done (the *percentage of completion method*) or defer all profit until the year in which the project is completed (the *completed contract method*, which can be used only in limited circumstances).[18]

The IRS has the power to prescribe the accounting method to be used by the taxpayer. Section 446(b) grants the IRS broad powers to determine if the accounting method used *clearly reflects income.*

> If no method of accounting has been regularly used by the taxpayer, or *if the method used does not clearly reflect income, the computation of taxable income shall be made under such method as, in the opinion of the Secretary ... does clearly reflect income.*

A change in the method of accounting requires the consent of the IRS.[19]

---

[14]See Accounting Periods in Chapter 18.

[15]§§ 441(a) and (d).

[16]See Accounting Methods in Chapter 18.

[17]Reg. § 1.446–1(c)(2)(i). Other circumstances in which the accrual method must be used are presented in Chapter 18. For the small business exception to the inventory requirement, see Rev.Proc. 2002–28, 2002–1 C.B. 815.

[18]§§ 453 and 460. See Chapter 18 for limitations on the use of the installment method and the completed contract method.

[19]§ 446(e). See Chapter 18.

Cash Receipts Method

Under the **cash receipts method**, property or services received are included in the taxpayer's gross income in the year of actual or constructive receipt by the taxpayer or agent, regardless of whether the income was earned in that year.[20] The income received need not be reduced to cash in the same year. All that is necessary for income recognition is that property or services received have a fair market value—a cash equivalent.[21] Thus, a cash basis taxpayer who receives a note in payment for services has income in the year of receipt equal to the fair market value of the note. However, a creditor's mere promise to pay (e.g., an account receivable), with no supporting note, usually is not considered to have a fair market value.[22] Thus, the cash basis taxpayer defers income recognition until the account receivable is collected.

EXAMPLE 6

Dana, an accountant, reports her income by the cash method. In 2011, she performed an audit for Orange Corporation and billed the client for $5,000, which was collected in 2012. In 2011, Dana also performed an audit for Blue Corporation. Because of Blue's precarious financial position, Dana required Blue to issue an $8,000 secured negotiable note in payment of the fee. The note had a fair market value of $6,000. Dana collected $8,000 on the note in 2012. Dana's gross income for the two years is as follows:

	2011	2012
Fair market value of note received from Blue	$6,000	
Cash received		
From Orange on account receivable		$ 5,000
From Blue on note receivable		8,000
Less: Recovery of capital		(6,000)
Total gross income	$6,000	$ 7,000

Generally, a check received is considered a cash equivalent. Thus, a cash basis taxpayer must recognize the income when the check is received. This is true even if the taxpayer receives the check after banking hours. An exception to this rule is that if the person paying with the check requests that the check not be cashed until a subsequent date, the cash basis income is deferred until the date the check can be cashed.[23]

Accrual Method

Under the **accrual method**, an item is generally included in the gross income for the year in which it is earned, regardless of when the income is collected. The income is earned when (1) all the events have occurred that fix the right to receive such income and (2) the amount to be received can be determined with reasonable accuracy.[24]

Generally, the taxpayer's rights to the income accrue when title to property passes to the buyer or the services are performed for the customer or client.[25] If the rights to the income have accrued but are subject to a potential refund claim (e.g., under a product warranty), the income is reported in the year of sale, and a deduction is allowed in subsequent years when actual claims accrue.[26]

Where the taxpayer's rights to the income are being contested (e.g., when a contractor fails to meet specifications), the year in which the income is subject to tax

---

[20]*Julia A. Strauss*, 2 B.T.A. 598 (1925). See the Glossary in Appendix C for a discussion of the terms "cash equivalent doctrine" and "constructive receipt."

[21]Reg. §§ 1.446–1(a)(3) and (c)(1)(i).

[22]*Bedell v. Comm.*, 1 USTC ¶359, 7 AFTR 8469, 30 F.2d 622 (CA–2, 1929).

[23]*Charles F. Kahler*, 18 T.C. 31 (1952); *Bright v. U.S.*, 91–1 USTC ¶50,142, 67 AFTR 2d 91–673, 926 F.2d 383 (CA–5, 1991).

[24]Reg. § 1.451–1(a).

[25]*Lucas v. North Texas Lumber Co.*, 2 USTC ¶484, 8 AFTR 10276, 50 S.Ct. 184 (USSC, 1930).

[26]*Brown v. Helvering*, 4 USTC ¶1222, 13 AFTR 851, 54 S.Ct. 356 (USSC, 1933).

depends upon whether payment has been received. If payment has not been received, no income is recognized until the claim is settled. Only then is the right to the income established.[27] However, if the payment is received before the dispute is settled, the court-made **claim of right doctrine** requires the taxpayer to recognize the income in the year of receipt.[28]

EXAMPLE 7 THE BIG PICTURE	Return to the facts of *The Big Picture* on p. 4-2. On completing the construction of Dr. Payne's medical office building in 2011, the contractor submitted a bill. Dr. Payne refused to pay the bill, however, claiming that the contractor had not met specifications. The contractor did not reach a settlement with Dr. Payne until 2012. No income accrues to the contractor until 2012. If Dr. Payne had paid for the work and then filed suit for damages, the contractor could not defer the income (the income would be taxable in 2011). ∎

The measure of accrual basis income is generally the amount the taxpayer has a right to receive. Unlike the cash basis, the fair market value of the customer's obligation is irrelevant in measuring accrual basis income.

EXAMPLE 8	Assume the same facts as in Example 6, except that Dana is an accrual basis taxpayer. Dana must recognize $13,000 ($8,000 + $5,000) gross income in 2011, the year her rights to the income accrued. ∎

Hybrid Method

The **hybrid method** is a combination of the accrual method and the cash method. Generally, when the hybrid method is used, inventory is a material income-producing factor. Therefore, the Regulations require that the accrual method be used for determining sales and cost of goods sold. In this circumstance, to simplify record keeping, the taxpayer accounts for inventory using the accrual method and uses the cash method for all other income and expense items (e.g., dividend and interest income). The hybrid method is primarily used by small businesses.

EXCEPTIONS APPLICABLE TO CASH BASIS TAXPAYERS

Constructive Receipt

Income that has not actually been received by the taxpayer is taxed as though it had been received—the income is constructively received—under the following conditions:

- The amount is made readily available to the taxpayer.
- The taxpayer's actual receipt is not subject to substantial limitations or restrictions.[29]

The rationale for the **constructive receipt** doctrine is that if the income is available, the taxpayer should not be allowed to postpone the income recognition. For instance, a taxpayer is not permitted to defer income for December services by refusing to accept payment until January. However, determining whether the income is *readily available* and whether *substantial limitations or restrictions exist* necessitates a factual inquiry that leads to a judgment call.[30] The following are some examples of the application of the constructive receipt doctrine.

---

[27]*Burnet v. Sanford and Brooks*, 2 USTC ¶636, 9 AFTR 603, 51 S.Ct. 150 (USSC, 1931).

[28]*North American Oil Consolidated Co. v. Burnet*, 3 USTC ¶943, 11 AFTR 16, 52 S.Ct. 613 (USSC, 1932).

[29]Reg. § 1.451–2(a).

[30]*Baxter v. Comm.*, 87–1 USTC ¶9315, 59 AFTR 2d 87–1068, 816 F.2d 493 (CA–9, 1987).

EXAMPLE 9

Ted is a member of a barter club. In 2011, Ted performed services for other club members and earned 1,000 points. Each point entitles him to $1 in goods and services sold by other members of the club; the points can be used at any time. In 2012, Ted exchanged his points for a new high-definition TV. Ted must recognize $1,000 gross income in 2011 when the 1,000 points were credited to his account.[31] ∎

EXAMPLE 10
THE BIG PICTURE

Return to the facts of *The Big Picture* on p. 4-2. On December 31, Dr. Payne has $10,000 in patients' checks that have not been deposited. They include a check for $3,000 from a patient who asked Dr. Payne not to deposit the check until after January 4 of next year, because her account did not contain sufficient funds to pay the debt. Under the cash method, Dr. Payne must recognize $7,000 income from the $7,000 in checks on hand in the current year because the checks are a cash equivalent that is actually received. The income from the $3,000 check is neither actually nor constructively received in the current year because an insufficient account means that the funds are not available.[32] ∎

EXAMPLE 11

Rick owns interest coupons that mature on December 31. The coupons can be converted to cash at any bank at maturity. Thus, the income is constructively received by Rick on December 31, even though Rick failed to cash in the coupons until the following year.[33] Dove Company mails a dividend check to Rick on December 31, 2011. Rick does not receive the check until January 2012. Rick does not realize gross income until 2012.[34] ∎

The constructive receipt doctrine does not reach income that the taxpayer is not yet entitled to receive even though the taxpayer could have contracted to receive the income at an earlier date.

EXAMPLE 12
THE BIG PICTURE

Return to the facts of *The Big Picture* on p. 4-2. Assume that Dr. Payne elected to use the cash basis of accounting. If he allowed patients to pay by credit card, Dr. Payne would receive immediate credit in his bank account for 96% of the charge. The other 4% would be retained by the credit card issuer. To avoid the 4% charge, Dr. Payne chose not to accept credit card payments. Instead, he established a policy of requiring all bills to be paid within 30 days after the dental services were provided. He communicated this policy to patients before he performed the services. At the end of the year, several patients who owed a combined $2,000 offered to pay with credit cards, but his office rejected their offers.

The $2,000 was not constructively received at the end of the year. Although Dr. Payne could have received payment by credit card in the current year, he contracted to receive payment at a later date before the dental services were performed. Moreover, the 4% charge by the credit card company would be a "substantial limitation." [35] ∎

Income set apart or made available is not constructively received if its actual receipt is subject to *substantial restrictions*. The life insurance industry has used substantial restrictions as a cornerstone for designing life insurance contracts with favorable tax features. Ordinary life insurance policies provide (1) current protection—an amount payable in the event of death—and (2) a savings feature—a cash surrender value payable to the policyholder if the policy is terminated during the policyholder's life. The annual increase in cash surrender value is not taxable because the policyholder must cancel the policy to actually receive the increase in value. Because the cancellation requirement is a substantial restriction, the policyholder does not constructively receive the annual increase in cash surrender value.[36]

---

[31]Rev.Rul. 80–52, 1980–1 C.B. 100.

[32]*L. M. Fischer*, 14 T.C. 792 (1950).

[33]Reg. § 1.451–2(b).

[34]Reg. § 1.451–2(b).

[35]*Cowden v. Comm.*, 61–1 USTC ¶9382, 7 AFTR 2d 1160, 289 F.2d 20 (CA–5, 1961).

[36]*Theodore H. Cohen*, 39 T.C. 1055 (1963).

Employees often receive from their employers property subject to substantial restrictions. Generally, no income is recognized until the restrictions lapse.[37]

EXAMPLE 13

Carlos is a key employee of Red, Inc. The corporation gives stock with a value of $10,000 to Carlos. The stock cannot be sold, however, for five years. Carlos is not required to recognize income until the restrictions lapse at the end of five years. ∎

ETHICS & Equity

DISCOUNTS FOR CASH

Independent contractors are one source of the "tax gap." Sometimes, especially when working for an individual rather than a corporation, an independent contractor does not receive a W–2 or Form 1099 from the employer or customer. In these situations, some independent contractors will give a discount if paid in cash. The apparent reason for this discount is that the independent contractor does not intend to report the income and is concerned that with a check, the IRS is more likely to discover the unreported income. Evaluate the behavior of the independent contractor and that of the customer who pays in cash.

Original Issue Discount

Lenders frequently make loans that require a payment at maturity of more than the amount of the original loan. The difference between the amount due at maturity and the amount of the original loan is actually interest but is referred to as **original issue discount**. Under the general rules of tax accounting, the cash basis lender would not report the original issue discount as interest income until the year the amount is collected, although an accrual basis borrower would deduct the interest as it is earned. However, the Code puts the lender and borrower on parity by requiring that the original issue discount be reported when it is earned, regardless of the taxpayer's accounting method.[38] The interest "earned" is calculated by the effective interest rate method.

EXAMPLE 14

On January 1, 2011, Mark, a cash basis taxpayer, pays $82,645 for a 24-month certificate. The certificate is priced to yield 10% (the effective interest rate) with interest compounded annually. No interest is paid until maturity, when Mark receives $100,000. Thus, Mark's gross income from the certificate is $17,355 ($100,000 − $82,645). Mark's income earned each year is calculated as follows:

2011(.10 × $82,645) =	$ 8,264
2012 [.10 × ($82,645 + $8,264)] =	9,091
	$17,355

∎

The original issue discount rules do not apply to U.S. savings bonds (discussed in the following paragraphs) or to obligations with a maturity date of one year or less from the date of issue.[39] See Chapter 16 for additional discussion of the tax treatment of original issue discount.

Series E and Series EE Bonds

Certain U.S. government savings bonds (Series E before 1980 and Series EE after 1979) are issued at a discount and are redeemable for fixed amounts that increase at stated intervals. No interest payments are actually made. The difference between the purchase price and the amount received on redemption is the bondholder's interest income from the investment.

---

[37]§ 83(a). See also the discussion of Restricted Property Plans in Chapter 19.
[38]§§ 1272(a)(3) and 1273(a).
[39]§ 1272(a)(2).

GLOBAL *Tax Issues*

TAX CREDIT NEUTRALIZES FOREIGN INCOME TAXES

When a U.S. taxpayer invests in a foreign country, that investment income is subject to tax in the United States and may also be subject to tax in the foreign country. However, the taxpayer is allowed a credit on his or her U.S. Federal income tax return for income taxes paid to the foreign country. The credit system allows the taxpayer to treat the taxes paid to the foreign country as though they were paid to the United States. If the foreign taxes paid are less than the U.S. tax on the income, the foreign taxes have cost the taxpayer nothing. On the other hand, if the foreign taxes are greater than the U.S. tax on the income, the credit is limited to the amount of the U.S. tax on the income. In this case, the taxes paid by the taxpayer will exceed what they would have been if the income had been earned in the United States.

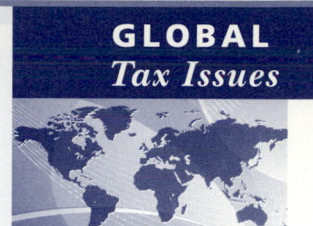

The income from these savings bonds is generally deferred until the bonds are redeemed or mature. Furthermore, Series E bonds previously could be exchanged within one year of their maturity date for Series HH bonds, and the interest on the Series E bonds could be further deferred until maturity of the Series HH bonds.[40] Thus, U.S. savings bonds have attractive income deferral features not available with corporate bonds and certificates of deposit issued by financial institutions.

Of course, the deferral feature of government bonds issued at a discount is not an advantage if the investor has insufficient income to be subject to tax as the income accrues. In fact, the deferral may work to the investor's disadvantage if the investor has other income in the year the bonds mature or the bunching of the bond interest into one tax year creates a tax liability. Fortunately, U.S. government bonds have a provision for these investors. A cash basis taxpayer can elect to include in gross income the annual increment in redemption value.[41]

EXAMPLE 15

Kate purchases Series EE U.S. savings bonds for $500 (face value of $1,000) on January 2 of the current year. If the bonds are redeemed during the first six months, no interest is paid. At December 31, the redemption value is $519.60.

If Kate elects to report the interest income annually, she must report interest income of $19.60 for the current year. If she does not make the election, she will report no interest income for the current year. ∎

When a taxpayer elects to report the income from the bonds on an annual basis, the election applies to all such bonds the taxpayer owns at the time of the election and to all such securities acquired subsequent to the election. A change in the method of reporting the income from the bonds requires permission from the IRS.

Amounts Received under an Obligation to Repay

The receipt of funds with an obligation to repay that amount in the future is the essence of borrowing. Because the taxpayer's assets and liabilities increase by the same amount, no income is realized when the borrowed funds are received. Because amounts paid to the taxpayer by mistake and customer deposits are often classified as borrowed funds, receipt of these funds is not a taxable event.

EXAMPLE 16

A landlord receives a damage deposit from a tenant. The landlord does not recognize income until the deposit is forfeited because the landlord has an obligation to repay the deposit if no damage occurs.[42] However, if the deposit is in fact a prepayment of rent, it is taxed in the year of receipt. ∎

---

[40]Treas. Dept. Circulars No. 1–80 and No. 2–80, 1980–1 C.B. 714, 715. Note that interest is paid at semiannual intervals on the Series HH bonds and must be included in income as received. Refer to Chapter 5 for a discussion of the savings bond interest exclusion. This exchange opportunity applied through August 31, 2004.

[41]§ 454(a).

[42]*John Mantell*, 17 T.C. 1143 (1952).

EXCEPTIONS APPLICABLE TO ACCRUAL BASIS TAXPAYERS

Prepaid Income

For financial reporting purposes, advance payments received from customers are reflected as prepaid income and as a liability of the seller. However, for tax purposes, the prepaid income often is taxed in the year of receipt.

EXAMPLE 17

In December 2011, a tenant pays his January 2012 rent of $1,000. The accrual basis landlord must include the $1,000 in her 2011 gross income for tax purposes, although the unearned rent income is reported as a liability on the landlord's December 31, 2011 financial accounting balance sheet. ∎

Taxpayers have repeatedly argued that deferral of income until it is actually earned properly matches revenues and expenses. Moreover, a proper matching of income with the expenses of earning the income is necessary to clearly reflect income, as required by the Code. The IRS responds that § 446(b) grants it broad powers to determine whether an accounting method clearly reflects income. The IRS further argues that generally accepted financial accounting principles should not dictate tax accounting for prepaid income because of the practical problems of collecting Federal revenues. Collection of the tax is simplest in the year the taxpayer receives the cash from the customer or client.

After a number of years of continual disputes between the IRS and taxpayers, in 1971 the IRS relented and modified its rules on the prepaid income issue in some situations, as explained below.

Deferral of Advance Payments for Goods

Generally, a taxpayer can elect to defer recognition of income from *advance payments for goods* if the method of accounting for the sale is the same for tax and financial reporting purposes.[43]

EXAMPLE 18

Brown Company will ship goods only after payment for the goods has been received. In December 2011, Brown received $10,000 for goods that were not shipped until January 2012. Brown can elect to report the income for tax purposes in 2012, assuming the company reports the income in 2012 for financial reporting purposes. ∎

Deferral of Advance Payments for Services

Revenue Procedure 2004–34[44] permits an accrual basis taxpayer to defer recognition of income for *advance payments for services* to be performed after the end of the tax year of receipt. The portion of the advance payment that relates to services performed in the tax year of receipt is included in gross income in the tax year of receipt. The portion of the advance payment that relates to services to be performed after the tax year of receipt is included in gross income in the *tax year following the tax year of receipt* of the advance payment.

EXAMPLE 19

Yellow Corporation, an accrual basis calendar year taxpayer, sells its services under 12-month, 24-month, and 36-month contracts. The corporation provides services to each customer every month. On May 1, 2011, Yellow Corporation sold the following customer contracts:

---

[43]Reg. § 1.451–5(b). See Reg. § 1.451–5(c) for exceptions to this deferral opportunity. The financial accounting conformity requirement is not applicable to contractors who use the completed contract method.

[44]2004–1 C.B. 991.

Length of Contract	Total Proceeds
12 months	$3,000
24 months	4,800
36 months	7,200

Yellow may defer until 2012 all of the income that will be earned after 2011.

Length of Contract	Income Recorded in 2011	Income Recorded in 2012
12 months	$2,000 ($3,000 × 8/12)	$1,000 ($3,000 × 4/12)
24 months	1,600 ($4,800 × 8/24)	3,200 ($4,800 × 16/24)
36 months	1,600 ($7,200 × 8/36)	5,600 ($7,200 × 28/36)

Revenue Procedure 2004–34 does not apply to prepaid rent or prepaid interest. Advance payments for these items are always taxed in the year of receipt.

4.3 INCOME SOURCES

PERSONAL SERVICES

LO.3

Identify who should pay the tax on a particular item of income in various situations.

It is a well-established principle of taxation that income from personal services must be included in the gross income of the person who performs the services. This principle was first established in a Supreme Court decision, *Lucas v. Earl.*[45] Mr. Earl entered into a binding agreement with his wife under which Mrs. Earl was to receive one-half of Mr. Earl's salary. Justice Holmes used the celebrated **fruit and tree metaphor** to explain that the fruit (income) must be attributed to the tree from which it came (Mr. Earl's services). A mere **assignment of income** does not shift the liability for the tax.

Services of an Employee

Services performed by an employee for the employer's customers are considered performed by the employer. Thus, the employer is taxed on the income from the services provided to the customer, and the employee is taxed on any compensation received from the employer.[46]

EXAMPLE 20

Dr. Shontelle incorporates her medical practice and enters into a contract to work for the corporation for a salary. All patients contract to receive their services from the corporation, and those services are provided through the corporation's employee, Dr. Shontelle. The corporation must include the patients' fees in its gross income. Dr. Shontelle must include her salary in her gross income. The corporation is allowed a deduction for the reasonable salary paid to Dr. Shontelle (see the discussion of unreasonable compensation in Chapter 6). ■

Services of a Child

In the case of a child, the Code specifically provides that amounts earned from personal services must be included in the child's gross income. This result applies even though the income is paid to other persons (e.g., the parents).[47]

---

[45]2 USTC ¶496, 8 AFTR 10287, 50 S.Ct. 241 (USSC, 1930).

[46]*Sargent v. Comm.*, 91–1 USTC ¶50,168, 67 AFTR 2d 91–718, 929 F.2d 1252 (CA–8, 1991).

[47]§ 73. For circumstances in which the child's unearned income is taxed at the parents' rate, see Kiddie Tax—Unearned Income of Children Taxed at Parents' Rate in Chapter 3.

INCOME FROM PROPERTY

Income from property (interest, dividends, rent) must be included in the gross income of the *owner* of the property. If a father clips interest coupons from bonds shortly before the interest payment date and gives the coupons to his son, the interest will still be taxed to the father. A father who assigns rents from rental property to his daughter will be taxed on the rent since he retains ownership of the property.[48]

Often income-producing property is transferred after income from the property has accrued, but before the income is recognized under the transferor's method of accounting. The IRS and the courts have developed rules to allocate the income between the transferor and the transferee.

Interest

According to the IRS, interest accrues daily. Therefore, the interest for the period that includes the date of the transfer is allocated between the transferor and transferee based on the number of days during the period that each owned the property.

| EXAMPLE 21 | Floyd, a cash basis taxpayer, gave his son, Seth, bonds with a face amount of $10,000 and an 8% stated annual interest rate. The gift was made on January 31, 2011, and the interest was paid on December 31, 2011. Floyd must recognize $68 in interest income ($8\% \times \$10,000 \times {}^{31}/_{365}$). Seth will recognize $732 in interest income ($800 − $68). ∎ |

When the transferor must recognize the income from the property depends upon the method of accounting and the manner in which the property was transferred. In the case of a gift of income-producing property, the donor must recognize his or her share of the accrued income at the time it would have been recognized had the donor continued to own the property.[49] However, if the transfer is a sale, the transferor must recognize the accrued income at the time of the sale. This results because the accrued interest will be included in the sales proceeds.

| EXAMPLE 22 | Assume the same facts as in Example 21, except that the interest that was payable as of December 31 was not actually or constructively received by the bondholders until January 3, 2012. As a cash basis taxpayer, Floyd generally does not recognize interest income until it is received. If Floyd had continued to own the bonds, the interest would have been included in his 2012 gross income, the year it would have been received. Therefore, Floyd must include the $68 accrued income in his gross income as of January 3, 2012.

Further assume that Floyd sold identical bonds on the date of the gift. The bonds sold for $9,900, including accrued interest. On January 31, 2011, Floyd must recognize the accrued interest of $68 on the bonds sold. Thus, the selling price of the bonds is $9,832 ($9,900 − $68). ∎ |

Dividends

A corporation is taxed on its earnings, and the shareholders are taxed on the dividends paid to them from the corporation's after-tax earnings. The dividend can take the form of an actual dividend or a constructive dividend (e.g., shareholder use of corporate assets).

Partial relief from the double taxation of dividends has been provided in the Jobs and Growth Tax Relief Reconciliation Act of 2003 and extended by the Tax Increase Prevention Act of 2005 (TIPRA). Generally, dividends received in taxable years beginning after 2002 are taxed at the same marginal rate that is applicable to a net capital gain.[50] Thus, individuals otherwise subject to the 10 or 15 percent marginal tax rate paid only a 5 percent tax on qualified dividends received in 2007, and in

---

[48]*Galt v. Comm.*, 54–2 USTC ¶9457, 46 AFTR 633, 216 F.2d 41 (CA–7, 1954); *Helvering v. Horst*, 40–2 USTC ¶9787, 24 AFTR 1058, 61 S.Ct. 144 (USSC, 1940).

[49]Rev.Rul. 72–312, 1972–1 C.B. 22.

[50]§ 1(h)(11).

2008–2012 such individuals are eligible for a 0 percent tax on qualified dividends received. Individuals subject to the 25, 28, 33, or 35 percent marginal tax rate pay a 15 percent tax on qualified dividends received. Thus, dividends receive favorable treatment as compared to interest income. Such favorable treatment of dividends is scheduled to expire for dividends received after December 31, 2012.

Note that qualified dividends are not treated as capital gains in the gains and losses netting process; thus, they are *not* reduced by capital losses. Qualified dividend income is merely taxed at the rates that would apply to the taxpayer if he or she had an excess of net long-term capital gain over net short-term capital loss.

Because the beneficial tax rate is intended to mitigate double taxation, only certain dividends are eligible for the beneficial treatment. Excluded are certain dividends from foreign corporations, dividends from tax-exempt entities, and dividends that do not satisfy the holding period requirement.

A dividend from a foreign corporation is eligible for qualified dividend status only if one of the following requirements is met: (1) the foreign corporation's stock is traded on an established U.S. securities market, or (2) the foreign corporation is eligible for the benefits of a comprehensive income tax treaty between its country of incorporation and the United States.

To satisfy the holding period requirement, the stock on which the dividend is paid must have been held for more than 60 days during the 121-day period beginning 60 days before the ex-dividend date.[51] The purpose of this requirement is to prevent the taxpayer from buying the stock shortly before the dividend is paid, receiving the dividend, and then selling the stock at a loss (a capital loss) after the stock goes ex-dividend. A stock's price often declines after the stock goes ex-dividend.

EXAMPLE 23

In June 2011, Green Corporation pays a dividend of $1.50 on each share of its common stock. Madison and Daniel, two unrelated shareholders, each own 1,000 shares of the stock. Consequently, each receives $1,500 (1,000 shares × $1.50). Assume Daniel satisfies the 60/121-day holding period rule, but Madison does not. The $1,500 Daniel receives is subject to preferential 15%/0% treatment in 2011. The $1,500 Madison receives, however, is not. Because Madison did not comply with the holding period rule, her dividend is not a *qualified dividend* and is taxed at ordinary income rates. ■

EXAMPLE 24

Assume that both Madison and Daniel in Example 23 are in the 35% tax bracket. Consequently, Madison pays a tax of $525 (35% × $1,500) on her dividend, while Daniel pays a tax of $225 (15% × $1,500) on his. The $300 saving that Daniel enjoys underscores the advantages of a qualified dividend received before January 1, 2013. ■

Unlike interest, dividends do not accrue on a daily basis because the declaration of a dividend is at the discretion of the corporation's board of directors. Generally, dividends are taxed to the person who is entitled to receive them—the shareholder of record as of the corporation's record date.[52] Thus, if a taxpayer sells stock after a dividend has been declared but before the record date, the dividend generally will be taxed to the purchaser.

If a donor makes a gift of stock to someone (e.g., a family member) after the declaration date but before the record date, the Tax Court has held that the donor does not shift the dividend income to the donee. The *fruit* has sufficiently ripened as of the declaration date to tax the dividend income to the donor of the stock.[53] In a similar set of facts, the Fifth Circuit Court of Appeals concluded that the dividend income should be included in the gross income of the donee (the owner at the

---

[51]The ex-dividend date is the date before the record date on which the corporation finalizes the list of shareholders who will receive the dividends.

[52]Reg. § 1.61–9(c). The record date is the cutoff for determining the shareholders who are entitled to receive the dividend.

[53]*M. G. Anton*, 34 T.C. 842 (1960).

record date). In this case, the taxpayer gave stock to a qualified charity (a charitable contribution) after the declaration date and before the record date.[54]

EXAMPLE 25

On June 20, the board of directors of Black Corporation declares a $10 per share dividend. The dividend is payable on June 30, to shareholders of record on June 25. As of June 20, Maria owned 200 shares of Black Corporation's stock. On June 21, Maria sold 100 of the shares to Norm for their fair market value and gave 100 of the shares to Sam (her son). Both Norm and Sam are shareholders of record as of June 25. Norm (the purchaser) will be taxed on $1,000 since he is entitled to receive the dividend. However, Maria (the donor) will be taxed on the $1,000 received by Sam (the donee) because the gift was made after the declaration date of the dividend. ∎

ETHICS & Equity   ENHANCING LOTTERY WINNINGS

Some family members have net losses from gambling, which can be used only to reduce gambling gains. Another family member has a substantial gain from winning the lottery.

Suppose that the winner gives the winning ticket to the family members with gambling losses, thereby creating what is tantamount to tax-exempt income. Evaluate this proposal.

INCOME RECEIVED BY AN AGENT

Income received by the taxpayer's agent is considered to be received by the taxpayer. A cash basis principal must recognize the income at the time it is received by the agent.[55]

EXAMPLE 26

Jack, a cash basis taxpayer, delivered cattle to the auction barn in late December. The auctioneer, acting as the farmer's agent, sold the cattle and collected the proceeds in December. The auctioneer did not pay Jack until the following January. Jack must include the sales proceeds in his gross income for the year the auctioneer received the funds. ∎

INCOME FROM PARTNERSHIPS, S CORPORATIONS, TRUSTS, AND ESTATES

A **partnership** is not a separate taxable entity. Rather, the partnership merely files an information return (Form 1065), which serves to provide the data necessary for determining the character and amount of each partner's distributive share of the partnership's income and deductions. Each partner must then report his or her distributive share of the partnership's income and deductions for the partnership's tax year ending within or with the partner's tax year. The income must be reported by each partner in the year it is earned, even if such amounts are not actually distributed to the partners. Because a partner pays tax on income as the partnership earns it, a distribution by the partnership to the partner is treated under the recovery of capital rules.[56]

EXAMPLE 27

Tara owns a one-half interest in the capital and profits of T & S Company (a calendar year partnership). For tax year 2011, the partnership earned revenue of $150,000 and had operating expenses of $80,000. During the year, Tara withdrew from her capital account $2,500 per month (for a total of $30,000). For 2011, Tara must report $35,000 as her share of the partnership's profits [½ × ($150,000 − $80,000)] even though she received distributions of only $30,000. ∎

---

[54]*Caruth Corp. v. U.S.*, 89–1 USTC ¶9172, 63 AFTR 2d 89–716, 865 F.2d 644 (CA–5, 1989).

[55]Rev.Rul. 79–379, 1979–2 C.B. 204.

[56]§ 706(a) and Reg. § 1.706–1(a)(1). For further discussion, see Chapter 20.

TAX *in*
the NEWS

THE ATTORNEY'S FEE WAS THE PLAINTIFF'S INCOME

Mr. Banks sued his employer for employment discrimination and received a settlement. Banks's attorney received approximately one-third of the settlement, and Banks reasoned that he should include only the remaining amount in his gross income.

The U.S. Supreme Court disagreed. The Court applied "assignment of income" and "principal-agent" reasoning to conclude that Banks was required to include the entire settlement amount in his gross income. The Court considered the lawsuit a property interest. Banks controlled the lawsuit and diverted some of the proceeds to the attorney; that is, Banks assigned a portion of his income to the attorney. The Court rejected Banks's argument that he and the attorney were partners pursuing the lawsuit. Instead, the Court concluded that Banks and his attorney maintained a "quintessential principal-agent relationship," with the attorney-agent pursuing the rights of his principal, Banks. Under well-settled principles of tax law, the amount received as a result of the agent's efforts nevertheless belonged to Banks, the principal. According to the Court, the tax treatment of the amount due the attorney would have to be addressed through the tax deduction rules. For Mr. Banks, this deduction was classified as a miscellaneous itemized deduction subject to the 2 percent floor under § 67. After the Supreme Court decision, Congress modified § 67 to allow the deduction as a deduction *for* AGI.

Contrary to the general provision that a corporation must pay tax on its income, a *small business corporation* may elect to be taxed similarly to a partnership. Thus, the shareholders, rather than the corporation, pay the tax on the corporation's income.[57] The electing corporation is referred to as an **S corporation**. Generally, the shareholders report their proportionate shares of the corporation's income and deductions for the year, whether or not the corporation actually makes any distributions to the shareholders.

The *beneficiaries of estates and trusts* generally are taxed on the income earned by the estates or trusts that is actually distributed or required to be distributed to them.[58] Any income not taxed to the beneficiaries is taxable to the estate or trust.

ETHICS
& Equity

THE HONEST AND DISHONEST PARTNERS

Suppose that a partner in a professional practice collects a large fee from a client but does not tell the other partners. The partner subsequently loses the fee gambling. Later the IRS discovers the partner's diversion of the partnership's income. Because the fee was earned by the partnership, each of the partners was required to report a share of the diverted income, although the dishonest partner received all the benefit of the income. The other partners' legal remedy is to collect from their dishonest partner. If the efforts to collect are unsuccessful, the partners' tax remedy is a bad debt deduction when the receivable is determined to be worthless.

Is it fair that the honest partners must pay income tax on funds they unintentionally "loaned" to their dishonest colleague?

INCOME IN COMMUNITY PROPERTY STATES

General

State law in Louisiana, Texas, New Mexico, Arizona, California, Washington, Idaho, Nevada, and Wisconsin is based upon a community property system. In Alaska, spouses can choose to have the community property rules apply. All other states have a common law property system. The basic difference between common law and community property systems centers around the property rights of married persons.

---

[57]§§ 1361(a) and 1366. For further discussion, see Chapter 20.

[58]§§ 652(a) and 662(a). For further discussion of the taxation of income from partnerships, S corporations, trusts, and estates, see *South-Western Federal Taxation: Corporations, Partnerships, Estates, and Trusts,* Chapters 10, 11, 12, and 20.

Questions about community property income most frequently arise when the husband and wife file separate returns.

Under a **community property** system, all property is deemed either to be separately owned by the spouse or to belong to the marital community. Property may be held separately by a spouse if it was acquired before marriage or received by gift or inheritance following marriage. Otherwise, any property is deemed to be community property. For Federal tax purposes, each spouse is taxed on one-half of the income from property belonging to the community.

The laws of Texas, Louisiana, Wisconsin, and Idaho distinguish between separate property and the income it produces. In these states, the income from separate property belongs to the community. Accordingly, for Federal income tax purposes, each spouse is taxed on one-half of the income. In the remaining community property states, separate property produces separate income that the owner-spouse must report on his or her Federal income tax return.

What appears to be income, however, may really represent a recovery of capital. A recovery of capital and gain realized on separate property retain their identity as separate property. Items such as nontaxable stock dividends, royalties from mineral interests, and gains and losses from the sale of property take on the same classification as the assets to which they relate.

EXAMPLE 28

Bob and Jane are husband and wife and reside in California. Among other transactions during the year, the following occurred:

- Nontaxable stock dividend received by Jane on stock that was given to her after her marriage by her mother.
- Gain of $10,000 on the sale of unimproved land purchased by Bob before his marriage.
- Oil royalties of $15,000 from a lease Jane acquired after marriage with her separate funds.

Since the stock dividend was distributed on stock held by Jane as separate property, it also is her separate property. The same result occurs for the oil royalties Jane receives. All of the proceeds from the sale of the unimproved land (including the gain of $10,000) are Bob's separate property. ∎

In all community property states, income from personal services (e.g., salaries, wages, income from a professional partnership) is generally treated as if one-half is earned by each spouse.

EXAMPLE 29

Fred and Wilma are married but file separate returns. Fred received $25,000 salary and $300 taxable interest on a savings account he established in his name. The deposits to the savings account were made from Fred's salary that he earned since the marriage. Wilma collected $2,000 taxable dividends on stock she inherited from her father. Wilma's gross income is computed as follows under three assumptions as to the state of residency of the couple:

	California	Texas	Common Law States
Dividends	$ 2,000	$ 1,000	$2,000
Salary	12,500	12,500	–0–
Interest	150	150	–0–
	$14,650	$13,650	$2,000

∎

Community Property Spouses Living Apart

The general rules for taxing the income from services performed by residents of community property states can create complications and even inequities for spouses who are living apart.

TAX in the NEWS

TAX LAW AND MARITAL PROPERTY

Before the joint return rules were enacted in 1948, married couples in community property states were treated more favorably than couples living in the other states. This result occurred because in the community property states the couple's income was taxed as though each spouse earned one-half of their combined income, whereas in the other states each spouse paid tax on only his or her own income. Thus, if one spouse earned most of the income, as was the case in most households, the income for the couple that did not live in a community property state would be subjected to higher marginal tax rates than the income of an identical couple living in a community property state. In effect, half the income in the community property states was shifted from the higher-income earner to the lower-income spouse.

Some states changed their marital property laws from a common law system to a community property system, primarily so that their residents could enjoy the Federal tax benefits of residents of community property states. In 1948, Congress enacted the joint return rules so that such state actions would be unnecessary.

EXAMPLE 30

Cole and Debra were married but living apart for the first nine months of 2011 and were divorced as of October 1, 2011. In December 2011, Cole married Emily, who was married but living apart from Frank before their divorce in June 2011. Cole and Frank had no income from personal services in 2011.

Cole brought into his marriage to Emily a tax liability on one-half of Debra's earnings for the first nine months of the year. However, Emily left with Frank a tax liability on one-half of her earnings for the first six months of 2011. ■

Congress has developed a simple solution to the many tax problems of community property spouses living apart. A spouse (or former spouse) is taxed only on his or her actual earnings from personal services if the following conditions are met:[59]

- The individuals live apart for the entire year.
- They do not file a joint return with each other.
- No portion of the earned income is transferred between the individuals.

EXAMPLE 31

Jim and Lori reside in a community property state, and both are gainfully employed. On July 1, 2011, they separated, and on June 30, 2012, they were divorced. Assuming their only source of income is wages, one-half of such income for each year is earned by June 30, and they did not file a joint return for 2011, each should report the following gross income:

	Jim's Separate Return	Lori's Separate Return
2011	One-half of Jim's wages	One-half of Jim's wages
	One-half of Lori's wages	One-half of Lori's wages
2012	All of Jim's wages	All of Lori's wages

The results would be the same if Jim or Lori married another person in 2012, except that the newlyweds would probably file a joint return. ■

The IRS may absolve from liability an *innocent spouse* who does not live apart for the entire year and files a separate return but omits his or her share of the community income received by the other spouse. To qualify for the innocent spouse relief, the taxpayer must not know or must have no reason to know of the omitted community income. Even if all of these requirements cannot be satisfied, the IRS has additional statutory authority to absolve the innocent spouse from tax liability. If, under

---

[59]§ 66.

the facts and circumstances, it is inequitable to hold the spouse liable for any unpaid tax, the IRS can absolve the spouse from tax liability.

4.4 ITEMS SPECIFICALLY INCLUDED IN GROSS INCOME

LO.4

Apply the Internal Revenue Code provisions on alimony, loans made at below-market interest rates, annuities, prizes and awards, group term life insurance, unemployment compensation, and Social Security benefits.

The general principles of gross income determination (discussed in the previous sections) as applied by the IRS and the courts have on occasion yielded results Congress found unacceptable. Consequently, Congress has provided more specific rules for determining the gross income from certain sources. Some of these special rules appear in §§ 71–90 of the Code.

ALIMONY AND SEPARATE MAINTENANCE PAYMENTS

When a married couple divorce or become legally separated, state law generally requires a division of the property accumulated during the marriage. In addition, one spouse may have a legal obligation to support the other spouse. The Code distinguishes between the support payments (alimony or separate maintenance) and the property division in terms of the tax consequences.

Alimony and separate maintenance payments are *deductible* by the party making the payments and are *includible* in the gross income of the party receiving the payments.[60] Thus, income is shifted from the income earner to the income beneficiary, who is better able to pay the tax on the amount received.

EXAMPLE 32

Pete and Tina are divorced, and Pete is required to pay Tina $15,000 of alimony each year. Pete earns $31,000 a year. The tax law presumes that because Tina receives the $15,000, she is better able than Pete to pay the tax on that amount. Therefore, Tina must include the $15,000 in her gross income, and Pete is allowed to deduct $15,000 from his gross income. ■

A transfer of property *other than cash* to a former spouse under a divorce decree or agreement is not a taxable event. The transferor is not entitled to a deduction and does not recognize gain or loss on the transfer. The transferee does not recognize income and has a cost basis equal to the transferor's basis.[61]

EXAMPLE 33

Paul transfers stock to Rosa as part of a 2011 divorce settlement. The cost of the stock to Paul is $12,000, and the stock's value at the time of the transfer is $15,000. Rosa later sells the stock for $16,000. Paul is not required to recognize gain from the transfer of the stock to Rosa, and Rosa has a realized and recognized gain of $4,000 ($16,000 − $12,000) when she sells the stock. ■

In the case of *cash payments*, however, it is often difficult to distinguish payments under a support obligation (alimony) and payments for the other spouse's property (property settlement). In 1984, Congress developed objective rules to classify the payments.

Post-1984 Agreements and Decrees

Payments made under post-1984 agreements and decrees are *classified as alimony* only if the following conditions are satisfied:

1. The payments are in cash.
2. The agreement or decree does not specify that the payments are not alimony.

---

[60]§§ 71 and 215.

[61]§ 1041, added to the Code in 1984 to repeal the rule of *U.S. v. Davis*, 62–2 USTC ¶9509, 9 AFTR 2d 1625, 82 S.Ct. 1190 (USSC, 1962). Under the *Davis* rule, which applied to pre-1985 divorces, a property transfer incident to divorce was a taxable event.

TAX *in* the NEWS | **A VOLUNTARY PAYMENT IS NOT ALIMONY**

When Mr. Benzin and his wife were divorced, the final agreement specified that neither party would be required to pay for the maintenance of the other party. Five years later Mr. Benzin retired and began receiving a pension. He was financially comfortable, but his former spouse was in need. He concluded that the "right thing to do" would be to share some of his wealth with his ex-wife. Therefore, he began sending her $475 a month and deducted it on his return as alimony paid. The Tax Court concluded that the payments were not alimony because they were not pursuant to the divorce agreement. Although this was bad news for Mr. Benzin, it was good news for his former spouse because she is not required to include the payments in her gross income as alimony.

Source: Donald A. Benzin, T.C. Summary Opinion 2009–198.

3. The payor and payee are not members of the same household at the time the payments are made.
4. There is no liability to make the payments for any period after the death of the payee.[62]

Requirement 1 simplifies the law by clearly distinguishing alimony from a property division; that is, if the payment is not in cash, it must be a property division. Requirement 2 allows the parties to determine by agreement whether or not the payments will be alimony. The prohibition on cohabitation—requirement 3—is aimed at assuring the alimony payments are associated with duplicative living expenses (maintaining two households).[63] Requirement 4 is an attempt to prevent alimony treatment from being applied to what is, in fact, a payment for property rather than a support obligation. That is, a seller's estate generally will receive payments for property due after the seller's death. Such payments after the death of the payee could not be for the payee's support.

Front-Loading

As a further safeguard against a property settlement being disguised as alimony, special rules apply to post-1986 agreements if payments in the first or second year exceed $15,000. If the change in the amount of the payments exceeds statutory limits, **alimony recapture** results to the extent of the excess alimony payments. In the *third* year, the payor must include the excess alimony payments for the first and second years in gross income, and the payee is allowed a deduction for these excess alimony payments. The recaptured amount is computed as follows:[64]

$$R = D + E$$

$$D = B - (C + \$15,000)$$

$$E = A - \left(\frac{B - D + C}{2} + \$15,000\right)$$

R = amount recaptured in Year 3 tax return
D = recapture from Year 2
E = recapture from Year 1
A, B, C = payments in the first (A), second (B), and third (C) calendar years of the agreement or decree, where $D \geq 0$, $E \geq 0$

The recapture formula provides an objective technique for determining alimony recapture. Thus, at the time of the divorce, the taxpayers can ascertain the tax consequences. The general concept is that if the alimony payments decrease by more than

---

[62]§ 71(b)(1). This set of alimony rules can also apply to pre-1985 agreements and decrees if both parties agree in writing. The rules applicable to pre-1985 agreements and decrees are not discussed in this text.

[63]*Alexander Washington*, 77 T.C. 601 (1981) at 604.
[64]§ 71(f).

CONCEPT SUMMARY 4.1

Tax Treatment of Payments and Transfers Pursuant to Post-1984 Divorce Agreements and Decrees

	Payor	Recipient
Alimony	Deduction from gross income.	Included in gross income.
Alimony recapture	Included in gross income of the third year.	Deducted from gross income of the third year.
Child support	Not deductible.	Not includible in gross income.
Property settlement	No income or deduction.	No income or deduction; basis for the property is the same as the transferor's basis.

$15,000 between years in the first three years, there will be alimony recapture with respect to the decrease in excess of $15,000 each year. This rule is applied for the change between Year 2 and Year 3 (D in the above formula). However, rather than making the same calculation for Year 2 payments versus Year 1 payments, the Code requires that the *average* of the payments in Years 2 and 3 be compared with the Year 1 payments (E in the preceding formula). For this purpose, revised alimony for Year 2 (alimony deducted for Year 2 minus the alimony recapture for Year 2) is used.

EXAMPLE 34

Wes and Rita are divorced in 2011. Under the agreement, Rita is to receive $50,000 in 2011, $20,000 in 2012, and nothing thereafter. The payments are to cease upon Rita's death or remarriage. In 2013, Wes must include an additional $32,500 in gross income for alimony recapture, and Rita is allowed a deduction for the same amount.

$$D = \$20,000 - (\$0 + \$15,000) = \$5,000$$

$$E = \$50,000 - \left(\frac{\$20,000 - \$5,000 + \$0}{2} + \$15,000\right) = \$27,500$$

$$R = \$5,000 + \$27,500 = \$32,500$$

Note that for 2011 Wes deducts alimony of $50,000, and Rita includes $50,000 in her gross income. For 2012, the amount of the alimony deduction for Wes is $20,000, and Rita's gross income from the alimony is $20,000.

If instead Wes paid $50,000 of alimony in 2011 and nothing for the following years, $35,000 would be recaptured in 2013.

$$D = \$0 - (\$0 + \$15,000) = -\$15,000, \text{ but } D \text{ must be } \geq \$0$$

$$E = \$50,000 - \left(\frac{\$0 - \$0 + \$0}{2} + \$15,000\right) = \$35,000$$

$$R = \$0 + \$35,000 = \$35,000$$

Alimony recapture does not apply if the decrease in payments is due to the death of either spouse or the remarriage of the payee.[65] Recapture is not applicable because these events typically terminate alimony under state laws. In addition, the recapture rules do not apply to payments where the amount is contingent (e.g., a percentage of income from certain property or a percentage of the payor spouse's compensation), the payments are to be made over a period of three years or longer (unless death, remarriage, or other contingency occurs), and the contingencies are beyond the payor's control.[66]

---

[65]§ 71(f)(5)(A).   [66]§ 71(f)(5)(C).

EXAMPLE 35

Under a 2011 divorce agreement, Ed is to receive an amount equal to one-half of Nina's income from certain rental properties for 2011–2014. Payments are to cease upon the death of Ed or Nina or upon the remarriage of Ed. Ed receives $50,000 in 2011 and $50,000 in 2012; in 2013, however, the property is vacant, and Ed receives nothing. Nina, who deducted alimony in 2011 and 2012, is not required to recapture any alimony in 2013 because the payments were contingent. ∎

Child Support

A taxpayer does not realize income from the receipt of child support payments made by his or her former spouse. This result occurs because the money is received subject to the duty to use the money for the child's benefit. The payor is not allowed to deduct the child support payments because the payments are made to satisfy the payor's legal obligation to support the child.

In many cases, it is difficult to determine whether an amount received is alimony or child support. If the amount of the payments would be reduced upon the happening of a contingency related to a child (e.g., the child attains age 21 or dies), the amount of the future reduction in the payment is deemed child support.[67]

EXAMPLE 36

A divorce agreement provides that Matt is required to make periodic alimony payments of $500 per month to Grace. However, when Matt and Grace's child reaches age 21, marries, or dies (whichever occurs first), the payments will be reduced to $300 per month. Grace has custody of the child. Since the required contingency is the cause for the reduction in the payments, from $500 to $300, child support payments are $200 per month, and alimony is $300 per month. ∎

IMPUTED INTEREST ON BELOW-MARKET LOANS

As discussed earlier in the chapter, generally no income is recognized unless it is realized. Realization generally occurs when the taxpayer performs services or sells goods and thus becomes entitled to a payment from the other party. It follows that no income is realized if the goods or services are provided at no charge. Under this interpretation of the realization requirement, before 1984, interest-free loans were used to shift income between taxpayers.

EXAMPLE 37

Veneia (daughter) is in the 20% (combined Federal and state rates) tax bracket and has no investment income. Kareem (father) is in the 50% (combined Federal and state rates) tax bracket and has $400,000 in a money market account earning 5% interest. Kareem would like Veneia to receive and pay tax on the income earned on the $400,000. Because Kareem would also like to have access to the $400,000 should he need the money, he does not want to make an outright gift of the money, nor does he want to commit the money to a trust.

Before 1984, Kareem could achieve his goals as follows. He could transfer the money market account to Veneia in exchange for her $400,000 non-interest-bearing note, payable on Kareem's demand. As a result, Veneia would receive the income, and the family's taxes would be decreased by $6,000.

Decrease in Kareem's tax—	
$(.05 \times \$400,000).50 =$	($10,000)
Increase in Veneia's tax—	
$(.05 \times \$400,000).20 =$	4,000
Decrease in the family's taxes	($ 6,000)

∎

---

[67]§ 71(c)(2).

Under the 1984 amendments to the Code, Kareem in Example 37 is required to recognize **imputed interest** income.[68] Veneia is deemed to have incurred interest expense equal to Kareem's imputed interest income. Veneia's interest may be deductible on her return as investment interest if she itemizes deductions (see Chapter 10). To complete the fictitious series of transactions, Kareem is then deemed to have given Veneia the amount of the imputed interest she did not pay. The gift received by Veneia is not subject to income tax (see Chapter 5), although Kareem may be subject to the gift tax (unified transfer tax) on the amount deemed given to Veneia (refer to Chapter 1).

Imputed interest is calculated using the rate the Federal government pays on new borrowings and is compounded semiannually. This Federal rate is adjusted monthly and is published by the IRS.[69] Actually, there are three Federal rates: short-term (not over three years and including demand loans), mid-term (over three years but not over nine years), and long-term (over nine years).[70]

EXAMPLE 38

Assume the Federal rate applicable to the loan in Example 37 is 3.5% through June 30 and 4% from July 1 through December 31. Kareem made the loan on January 1, and the loan is still outstanding on December 31. Kareem must recognize interest income of $15,140, and Veneia has interest expense of $15,140. Kareem is deemed to have made a gift of $15,140 to Veneia.

Interest calculations:	
January 1–June 30—.035($400,000) (½ year)	$ 7,000
July 1–December 31—.04($400,000 + $7,000) (½ year)	8,140
	$15,140

■

If interest is charged on the loan but is less than the Federal rate, the imputed interest is the difference between the amount that would have been charged at the Federal rate and the amount actually charged.

EXAMPLE 39

Assume the same facts as in Example 38, except that Kareem charged 3% interest, compounded annually.

Interest at the Federal rate	$ 15,140
Less interest charged (.03 × $400,000)	(12,000)
Imputed interest	$ 3,140

■

The imputed interest rules apply to the following *types* of below-market loans:[71]

1. Gift loans (made out of love, affection, or generosity, as in Example 37).
2. Compensation-related loans (employer loans to employees).
3. Corporation-shareholder loans (a corporation's loans to its shareholders).
4. Tax avoidance loans and other loans that significantly affect the borrower's or lender's Federal tax liability (discussed in the following paragraphs).

The effects of the first three types of loans on the borrower and lender are summarized in Concept Summary 4.2.

Tax Avoidance and Other Below-Market Loans

In addition to the three specific types of loans that are subject to the imputed interest rules, the Code includes a catchall provision for *tax avoidance loans* and other arrangements that have a significant effect on the tax liability of the borrower or lender. The Conference Report provides the following example of an arrangement that might be subject to the imputed interest rules.[72]

---

[68]§ 7872(a)(1).
[69]§§ 7872(b)(2) and (f)(2).
[70]§ 1274(d).

[71]§ 7872(c).
[72]H. Rep. No. 98–861, 98th Cong., 2d Sess., 1984, p. 1023.

CONCEPT SUMMARY 4.2

Effect of Certain Below-Market Loans on the Lender and Borrower

Type of Loan		Lender	Borrower
Gift	Step 1	Interest income	Interest expense
	Step 2	Gift made	Gift received
Compensation-related	Step 1	Interest income	Interest expense
	Step 2	Compensation expense	Compensation income
Corporation to shareholder	Step 1	Interest income	Interest expense
	Step 2	Dividend paid	Dividend income

EXAMPLE 40

Annual dues for the Good Health Club are $400. In lieu of paying dues, a member can make a $4,000 deposit, refundable at the end of one year. The club can earn $400 interest on the deposit.

If interest were not imputed, an individual with $4,000 could, in effect, earn tax-exempt income on the deposit. That is, rather than invest the $4,000, earn $400 in interest, pay tax on the interest, and then pay $400 in dues, the individual could avoid tax on the interest by making the deposit. Thus, income and expenses are imputed as follows: interest income and nondeductible health club fees for the club member; income from fees and interest expense for the club. ■

Many commercially motivated transactions could be swept into this other below-market loans category. However, the Temporary Regulations have carved out a frequently encountered exception for customer prepayments. If the prepayments are included in the recipient's income under the recipient's method of accounting, the payments are not considered loans and, thus, are not subject to the imputed interest rules.[73]

Exceptions and Limitations

No interest is imputed on total outstanding *gift loans* of $10,000 or less between individuals, unless the loan proceeds are used to purchase income-producing property.[74] This exemption eliminates from these complex provisions immaterial amounts that do not result in apparent shifts of income. However, if the proceeds of such a loan are used to purchase income-producing property, the limitations discussed in the following paragraphs apply instead.

On loans of $100,000 or less between individuals, the imputed interest cannot exceed the borrower's net investment income for the year (gross income from all investments less the related expenses).[75] As discussed previously, one of the purposes of the imputed interest rules is to prevent high-income taxpayers from shifting income to relatives in a lower marginal bracket. This shifting of investment income is considered to occur only to the extent the borrower has net investment income. Thus, the income imputed to the lender is limited to the borrower's net investment income. As a further limitation, or exemption, if the borrower's net investment income for the year does not exceed $1,000, no interest is imputed on loans of $100,000 or less. However, these limitations for loans of $100,000 or less do not apply

---

[73]Prop.Reg. § 1.7872–2(b)(1)(i).
[74]§ 7872(c)(2).

[75]§ 7872(d).

LOANS TO EXECUTIVES PROHIBITED

Interest-free loans have become a popular form of compensation for executives. Several examples of multimillion-dollar loans have come to light as a result of recent bankruptcies by large corporations. The board of directors often justifies the loans as necessary to enable the executive to purchase a residence or to buy stock in the company.

Loans by publicly held corporations to their executives are now generally prohibited by Federal law. The Sarbanes-Oxley Act of 2002 (Public Law No. 107–294) places a general prohibition on loans by corporations to their executives. However, an exception permits corporate loans to finance the acquisition of a personal residence for an executive.

---

if a principal purpose of a loan is tax avoidance. In such a case, interest is imputed, and the imputed interest is not limited to the borrower's net investment income.[76]

EXAMPLE 41

Vicki made interest-free gift loans as follows:

Borrower	Amount	Borrower's Net Investment Income	Purpose
Susan	$ 8,000	$ –0–	Education
Dan	9,000	500	Purchase of stock
Bonnie	25,000	–0–	Purchase of a business
Megan	90,000	15,000	Purchase of a residence
Olaf	120,000	–0–	Purchase of a residence

Assume that tax avoidance is not a principal purpose of any of the loans. The loan to Susan is not subject to the imputed interest rules because the $10,000 exception applies. The $10,000 exception does not apply to the loan to Dan because the proceeds were used to purchase income-producing assets. However, under the $100,000 exception, the imputed interest is limited to Dan's investment income ($500). Since the $1,000 exception also applies to this loan, no interest is imputed.

No interest is imputed on the loan to Bonnie because the $100,000 exception applies. Interest is imputed on the loan to Megan based on the lesser of (1) the borrower's $15,000 net investment income or (2) the interest as calculated by applying the Federal rate to the outstanding loan. None of the exceptions apply to the loan to Olaf because the loan was for more than $100,000.

Assume the relevant Federal rate is 10% and the loans were outstanding for the entire year. Vicki would recognize interest income, compounded semiannually, as follows:

Loan to Megan:	
First 6 months (.10 × $90,000 × ½ year)	$ 4,500
Second 6 months (.10 × $94,500 × ½ year)	4,725
	$ 9,225
Loan to Olaf:	
First 6 months (.10 × $120,000 × ½ year)	$ 6,000
Second 6 months (.10 × $126,000 × ½ year)	6,300
	$12,300
Total imputed interest ($9,225 + $12,300)	$21,525

---

[76]*Deficit Reduction Tax Bill of 1984: Explanation of the Senate Finance Committee* (April 2, 1984), p. 484.

CONCEPT SUMMARY 4.3

Exceptions to the Imputed Interest Rules for Below-Market Loans

Exception	Eligible Loans	Ineligible Loans and Limitations
De minimis—aggregate loans of $10,000 or less	Gift loans	Proceeds used to purchase income-producing assets.
	Employer-employee	Principal purpose is tax avoidance.
	Corporation-shareholder	Principal purpose is tax avoidance.
Aggregate loans of $100,000 or less	Between individuals	Principal purpose is tax avoidance. For all other loans, interest is imputed to the extent of the borrower's net investment income if that income exceeds $1,000.

As with gift loans, there is a $10,000 exemption for *compensation-related loans* and *corporation-shareholder loans*. However, the $10,000 exception does not apply if tax avoidance is one of the principal purposes of a loan.[77] This vague tax avoidance standard makes practically all compensation-related and corporation-shareholder loans suspect. Nevertheless, the $10,000 exception should apply when an employee's borrowing was necessitated by personal needs (e.g., to meet unexpected expenses) rather than tax considerations.

These exceptions to the imputed interest rules are summarized in Concept Summary 4.3.

INCOME FROM ANNUITIES

Annuity contracts generally require the purchaser (the annuitant) to pay a fixed amount for the right to receive a future stream of payments. Typically, the issuer of the contract is an insurance company and will pay the annuitant a cash value if the annuitant cancels the contract. The insurance company invests the amounts received from the annuitant, and the income earned serves to increase the cash value of the annuity. No income is recognized by the annuitant at the time the cash value of the annuity increases because the taxpayer has not actually received any income. The income is not constructively received because, generally, the taxpayer must cancel the policy to receive the increase in value (the increase in value is subject to substantial restrictions).

> **EXAMPLE 42**
>
> Jean, age 50, pays $30,000 for an annuity contract that is to pay her $500 per month beginning when she reaches age 65 and continuing until her death. If Jean should cancel the policy after one year, she would receive $30,200. The $200 increase in value is not includible in Jean's gross income as long as she does not actually receive the $200. ∎

The tax accounting problem associated with receiving payments under an annuity contract is one of apportioning the amounts received between recovery of capital and income.

> **EXAMPLE 43**
>
> In 2011, Tom purchased for $15,000 an annuity intended as a source of retirement income. In 2013, when the cash value of the annuity is $17,000, Tom collects $1,000 on the contract. Is the $1,000 gross income, recovery of capital, or a combination of recovery of capital and income? ∎

---

[77]§ 7872(c)(3).

The statutory solution to this problem depends upon whether the payments began before or after the annuity starting date and upon when the policy was acquired.

Collections before the Annuity Starting Date

Generally, an annuity contract specifies a date on which monthly or annual payments will begin—the annuity starting date. Often the contract will also allow the annuitant to collect a limited amount before the starting date. The amount collected may be characterized as either an actual withdrawal of the increase in cash value or a loan on the policy. In 1982, Congress changed the rules applicable to these withdrawals and loans.

Collections (including loans) equal to or less than the post–August 13, 1982 increases in cash value must be included in gross income. Amounts received in excess of post–August 13, 1982 increases in cash value are treated as a recovery of capital until the taxpayer's cost has been entirely recovered. Additional amounts are included in gross income.[78]

The taxpayer may also be subject to a penalty on early distributions of 10 percent of the income recognized. The penalty generally applies if the amount is received before the taxpayer reaches age 59½ or is disabled.[79] The early distribution penalty is deemed necessary to prevent taxpayers from using annuities as a way of avoiding the original issue discount rules. That is, the investment in the annuity earns a return that is not taxed until it is collected under the annuity rules, whereas the interest on a certificate of deposit is taxed each year as the income accrues. Thus, the annuity offers a tax advantage (deferral of income) that Congress does not want exploited.

EXAMPLE 44

Jack, age 50, purchased an annuity contract for $30,000 in 2009. In 2011, when the cash value of the contract has increased to $33,000, Jack withdraws $4,000. He must recognize $3,000 of income ($33,000 cash value − $30,000 cost) and must pay a penalty of $300 ($3,000 × 10%). The remaining $1,000 is a recovery of capital and reduces Jack's basis in the annuity contract to $29,000. ∎

Collections on and after the Annuity Starting Date

The annuitant can exclude from income (as a recovery of capital) the proportion of each payment that the investment in the contract bears to the expected return under the contract. The *exclusion amount* is calculated as follows:

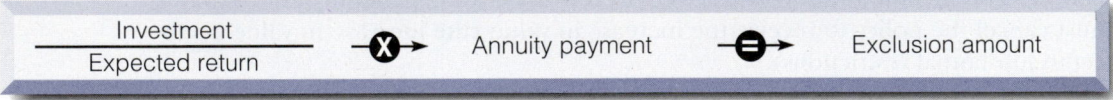

$$\frac{\text{Investment}}{\text{Expected return}} \quad \boxed{\times} \rightarrow \quad \text{Annuity payment} \quad \boxed{=} \rightarrow \quad \text{Exclusion amount}$$

The *expected return* is the annual amount to be paid to the annuitant multiplied by the number of years the payments will be received. The payment period may be fixed (a *term certain*) or for the life of one or more individuals. When payments are for life, the taxpayer generally must use the annuity table published by the IRS to determine the expected return (see Table 4.1). This is an actuarial table that contains life expectancies.[80] The expected return is calculated by multiplying the appropriate multiple (life expectancy) by the annual payment.

EXAMPLE 45

The taxpayer, age 60, purchases an annuity from an insurance company for $90,000. She is to receive $500 per month for life. Her life expectancy (from Table 4.1) is 24.2

---

[78]§ 72(e)(3); Reg. § 1.72–9.

[79]§ 72(q).

[80]The life expectancies in Table 4.1 apply for annuity investments made on or after July 1, 1986. See *General Rules for Pensions and Annuities*, IRS Publication 939 (Rev. April 2003), p. 25. See also *Pension and Annuity Income*, IRS Publication 575 (Rev. 2009).

TABLE 4.1	Ordinary Life Annuities: One Life—Expected Return Multiples

Age	Multiple	Age	Multiple	Age	Multiple
5	76.6	42	40.6	79	10.0
6	75.6	43	39.6	80	9.5
7	74.7	44	38.7	81	8.9
8	73.7	45	37.7	82	8.4
9	72.7	46	36.8	83	7.9
10	71.7	47	35.9	84	7.4
11	70.7	48	34.9	85	6.9
12	69.7	49	34.0	86	6.5
13	68.8	50	33.1	87	6.1
14	67.8	51	32.2	88	5.7
15	66.8	52	31.3	89	5.3
16	65.8	53	30.4	90	5.0
17	64.8	54	29.5	91	4.7
18	63.9	55	28.6	92	4.4
19	62.9	56	27.7	93	4.1
20	61.9	57	26.8	94	3.9
21	60.9	58	25.9	95	3.7
22	59.9	59	25.0	96	3.4
23	59.0	60	24.2	97	3.2
24	58.0	61	23.3	98	3.0
25	57.0	62	22.5	99	2.8
26	56.0	63	21.6	100	2.7
27	55.1	64	20.8	101	2.5
28	54.1	65	20.0	102	2.3
29	53.1	66	19.2	103	2.1
30	52.2	67	18.4	104	1.9
31	51.2	68	17.6	105	1.8
32	50.2	69	16.8	106	1.6
33	49.3	70	16.0	107	1.4
34	48.3	71	15.3	108	1.3
35	47.3	72	14.6	109	1.1
36	46.4	73	13.9	110	1.0
37	45.4	74	13.2	111	.9
38	44.4	75	12.5	112	.8
39	43.5	76	11.9	113	.7
40	42.5	77	11.2	114	.6
41	41.5	78	10.6	115	.5

years from the annuity starting date. Thus, her expected return is $500 × 12 × 24.2 = $145,200, and the exclusion amount is $3,719 [($90,000 investment/$145,200 expected return) × $6,000 annual payment]. The $3,719 is a nontaxable return of capital, and $2,281 is included in gross income. ∎

The *exclusion ratio* (investment ÷ expected return) applies until the annuitant has recovered his or her investment in the contract. Once the investment is recovered, the entire amount of subsequent payments is taxable. If the annuitant dies before recovering the investment, the unrecovered cost (adjusted basis) is deductible in the year the payments cease (usually the year of death).[81]

---

[81]§ 72(b).

TABLE 4.2	Number of Anticipated Monthly Annuity Payments under the Simplified Method	

Age	Number of Anticipated Monthly Payments
55 and under	360
56–60	310
61–65	260
66–70	210
71 and over	160

EXAMPLE 46

Assume the taxpayer in Example 45 receives annuity payments for 25.2 years (302 months). For the last 12 months $[302 - (12 \times 24.2) = 12]$, the taxpayer will include $500 each month in gross income. If instead the taxpayer dies after 36 months, she is eligible for a $78,843 deduction on her final tax return.

Cost of the contract	$ 90,000
Cost previously recovered	
$90,000/$145,200 × 36($500) =	(11,157)
Deduction	$ 78,843

Simplified Method for Annuity Distributions from Qualified Retirement Plans

A simplified method is required for allocating basis to the annuity payments received under a qualified retirement plan. The portion of each annuity payment that is excluded as a return of capital is the employee's investment in the contract divided by the number of anticipated monthly payments determined in accordance with Table 4.2.[82]

EXAMPLE 47

Andrea, age 62, receives an annuity distribution of $500 per month for life from her qualified retirement plan beginning in January 2011. Her investment in the contract is $100,100. The excludible amount of each payment is $385 ($100,100 investment/260 monthly payments). Thus, $115 ($500 − $385) of each annuity payment is included in Andrea's gross income. ∎

The rules for annuity payments received after the basis has been recovered by the annuitant and for the annuitant who dies before the basis is recovered are the same as under the exclusion ratio method discussed earlier.

PRIZES AND AWARDS

The fair market value of prizes and awards (other than scholarships exempted under § 117, to be discussed subsequently) must be included in gross income.[83] Therefore, TV giveaway prizes, magazine publisher prizes, door prizes, and awards from an employer to an employee in recognition of performance are fully taxable to the recipient.

A narrow exception permits a prize or award to be excluded from gross income if *all* of the following requirements are satisfied:

• The prize or award is received in recognition of religious, charitable, scientific, educational, artistic, literary, or civic achievement (e.g., Nobel Prize, Pulitzer Prize, faculty teaching award).

[82]§ 72(d).   [83]§ 74.

- The recipient transfers the prize or award to a qualified governmental unit or nonprofit organization.
- The recipient was selected without any action on his or her part to enter the contest or proceeding.
- The recipient is not required to render substantial future services as a condition for receiving the prize or award.[84]

Because the transfer of the property to a qualified governmental unit or nonprofit organization ordinarily would be a charitable contribution (an itemized deduction as presented in Chapter 10), the exclusion produces beneficial tax consequences in the following situations:

- The taxpayer does not itemize deductions and thus would receive no tax benefit from the charitable contribution.
- The taxpayer's charitable contributions exceed the annual statutory ceiling on the deduction.
- Including the prize or award in gross income would reduce the amount of deductions the taxpayer otherwise would qualify for because of gross income limitations (e.g., the gross income test for a dependency exemption, the adjusted gross income limitation in calculating the medical expense deduction).

The taxpayer can avoid including prizes and awards in gross income by refusing to accept the prize or award.

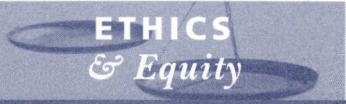

ETHICS & Equity   **TAX EFFECTS OF A DONATED PRIZE**

The Allen family wins an expensive flat panel television at their church raffle. The TV retails for $4,200, but the church paid the wholesale price of $3,400 (one of its members owns an appliance store). Because the Allens already have enough TVs, they donate their prize to the church and claim a $4,200 charitable contribution deduction on their income tax return. Have the Allens acted properly? Wisely?

Another exception is provided for certain *employee achievement awards* in the form of tangible personal property (e.g., a gold watch). The awards must be made in recognition of length of service or safety achievement. Generally, the ceiling on the excludible amount for an employee is $400 per taxable year. However, if the award is a qualified plan award, the ceiling on the exclusion is $1,600 per taxable year.[85]

GROUP TERM LIFE INSURANCE

For many years, the IRS did not attempt to tax the value of life insurance protection provided to an employee by the employer. Some companies took undue advantage of the exclusion by providing large amounts of insurance protection for executives. Therefore, Congress enacted § 79, which created a limited exclusion for **group term life insurance**. The premiums on the first $50,000 of group term life insurance protection are excludible from the employee's gross income.

The benefits of this exclusion are available only to employees. Proprietors and partners are not considered employees. The Regulations generally require broad-scale coverage of employees to satisfy the *group* requirement (e.g., shareholder-employees would not constitute a qualified group). The exclusion applies only to term insurance (protection for a period of time but with no cash surrender value) and not to ordinary life insurance (lifetime protection plus a cash surrender value that can be drawn upon before death).

---

[84]§ 74(b).   [85]§§ 74(c) and 274(j).

TABLE 4.3	Uniform Premiums for $1,000 of Group Term Life Insurance Protection

Attained Age on Last Day of Employee's Tax Year	Cost per $1,000 of Protection for One-Month Period*
Under 25	$ .05
25–29	.06
30–34	.08
35–39	.09
40–44	.10
45–49	.15
50–54	.23
55–59	.43
60–64	.66
65–69	1.27
70 and above	2.06

*Reg. § 1.79–3, effective for coverage after June 30, 1999.

As mentioned, the exclusion applies to the first $50,000 of group term life insurance protection. For each $1,000 of coverage in excess of $50,000, the employee must include the amounts indicated in Table 4.3 in gross income.[86]

EXAMPLE 48

Finch Corporation has a group term life insurance policy with coverage equal to the employee's annual salary. Keith, age 52, is president of the corporation and receives an annual salary of $75,000. Keith must include $69 in gross income from the insurance protection for the year.

$$\frac{\$75,000 - \$50,000}{\$1,000} \times \$0.23 \times 12 \text{ months} = \$69$$

Generally, the amount that must be included in gross income, computed from Table 4.3, is much less than the price an individual would pay an insurance company for the same amount of protection. Thus, even the excess coverage provides some tax-favored income for employees when group term life insurance coverage in excess of $50,000 is desirable.

If the plan discriminates in favor of certain key employees (e.g., officers), the key employees are not eligible for the exclusion. In such a case, the key employees must include in gross income the *greater* of actual premiums paid by the employer or the amount calculated from the Uniform Premiums in Table 4.3. The other employees are still eligible for the $50,000 exclusion and continue to use the Uniform Premiums table to compute the income from excess insurance protection.[87]

UNEMPLOYMENT COMPENSATION

The unemployment compensation program is sponsored and operated by the states and Federal government to provide a source of income for people who have been employed and are temporarily (hopefully) out of work. In a series of rulings over a period of 40 years, the IRS exempted unemployment benefits from tax. These payments were considered social benefit programs for the promotion of the general welfare. After experiencing dissatisfaction with the IRS's treatment of unemployment compensation, Congress amended the Code to provide that the benefits are taxable.[88]

---

[86]Reg. § 1.79–3(d)(2).
[87]§ 79(d).

[88]§ 85.

In the American Recovery and Reinvestment Tax Act (ARRTA) of 2009, Congress provided that the first $2,400 of unemployment compensation in 2009 is excluded from gross income. Congress chose not to extend this exclusion relief in 2010 tax legislation.

SOCIAL SECURITY BENEFITS

If a taxpayer's income exceeds a specified base amount, as much as 85 percent of Social Security retirement benefits must be included in gross income. The taxable amount of benefits is determined through the application of one of two formulas that utilize a unique measure of income—*modified adjusted gross income (MAGI)*.[89] MAGI is, generally, the taxpayer's adjusted gross income from all sources (other than Social Security) plus the foreign earned income exclusion and any tax-exempt interest income.

In the formulas, two sets of base amounts are established. The first set is as follows:

- $32,000 for married taxpayers who file a joint return.
- $0 for married taxpayers who do not live apart for the entire year but file separate returns.
- $25,000 for all other taxpayers.

The second set of base amounts is as follows:

- $44,000 for married taxpayers who file a joint return.
- $0 for married taxpayers who do not live apart for the entire year but file separate returns.
- $34,000 for all other taxpayers.

If MAGI plus one-half of Social Security benefits exceeds the first set of base amounts, but not the second set, the taxable amount of Social Security benefits is the *lesser* of the following:

- .50(Social Security benefits).
- .50[MAGI + .50(Social Security benefits) − first base amount].

EXAMPLE 49

A married couple with adjusted gross income of $30,000, no tax-exempt interest, and $11,000 of Social Security benefits who file jointly must include $1,750 of the benefits in gross income. This works out as the lesser of the following:

1. .50($11,000) = $5,500.
2. .50[$30,000 + .50($11,000) − $32,000] = .50($3,500) = $1,750.

If instead the couple had adjusted gross income of $15,000 and their Social Security benefits totaled $5,000, none of the benefits would be taxable, since .50[$15,000 + .50($5,000) − $32,000] is not a positive number. ■

If MAGI plus one-half of Social Security benefits exceeds the second set of base amounts, the taxable amount of Social Security benefits is the *lesser* of 1 or 2 below:

1. .85(Social Security benefits).
2. Sum of:
   a. .85[MAGI + .50(Social Security benefits) − second base amount], and
   b. Lesser of:
      - Amount included through application of the first formula.
      - $4,500 ($6,000 for married filing jointly).

[89]§ 86. The rationale for taxing 85% of the Social Security benefits is as follows: For the average Social Security recipient, 15% of the amount received is a recovery of amounts that the individual paid into the program, and the remainder of the benefits is financed by the employer's contribution and interest earned by the Social Security trust fund.

TAX in the NEWS

SOCIAL SECURITY BENEFITS AS A SOURCE OF FEDERAL REVENUE

Recipients' Social Security benefits are indexed for inflation, but the base amounts used in the formula to calculate the taxable portion of the benefits are not indexed. The $25,000 and $32,000 base amounts were established in 1984. If they were indexed for inflation, these nontaxable amounts would have doubled by 2010. Thus, as income and Social Security benefits rise with inflation, taxable income increases more than the related increase in "real" benefits.

EXAMPLE 50

A married couple who file jointly have adjusted gross income of $72,000, no tax-exempt interest, and $12,000 of Social Security benefits. Their includible Social Security benefits will be $10,200.

Include the lesser of the following:

1. .85($12,000) = $10,200.
2. Sum of:
   a. .85[$72,000 + .50($12,000) − $44,000] = $28,900, and
   b. Lesser of:
      - Amount calculated by the first formula, which is the lesser of:
        − .50($12,000) = $6,000.
        − .50[$72,000 + .50($12,000) − $32,000] = $23,000.
      - $6,000.

The sum equals $34,900 ($28,900 + $6,000). Since 85% of the Social Security benefits received is less than this amount, $10,200 is included in the couple's gross income. ∎

LO.5

Identify tax planning strategies for minimizing gross income.

TAX PLANNING:

The materials in this chapter have focused on the following questions:

- What is income?
- When is the income recognized?
- Who is the taxpayer?

Planning strategies suggested by these materials include the following:

- Maximize economic benefits that are not included in gross income.
- Defer the recognition of income.
- Shift income to taxpayers who are in a lower marginal tax bracket.

Some specific techniques for accomplishing these strategies are discussed in the following paragraphs.

4.5 NONTAXABLE ECONOMIC BENEFITS

Home ownership is the prime example of economic income from capital that is not subject to tax. If the taxpayer uses his or her capital to purchase investments, but pays rent on a personal residence, the taxpayer would pay the rent from after-tax income. However, if the taxpayer purchases a personal residence instead of the investments, he or she would give up gross income from the forgone investments in exchange for the rent savings. The savings in rent enjoyed as a result of owning the home are not subject to tax. Thus, the homeowner will have substituted nontaxable for taxable income.

4.6 TAX DEFERRAL

GENERAL

Since deferred taxes are tantamount to interest-free loans from the government, the deferral of taxes is a worthy goal of the tax planner. However, the tax planner must also consider the tax rates for the years the income is shifted from and to. For example, a one-year deferral of income from a year in which the taxpayer's tax rate was 28 percent to a year in which the tax rate will be 35 percent would not be advisable if the taxpayer expects to earn less than a 7 percent after-tax return on the deferred tax dollars.

The taxpayer can often defer the recognition of income from appreciated property by postponing the event triggering realization (the final closing on a sale or exchange of property). If the taxpayer needs cash, obtaining a loan by using the appreciated property as collateral may be the least costly alternative. When the taxpayer anticipates reinvesting the proceeds, a sale may be inadvisable.

EXAMPLE 51

Ira owns 100 shares of Pigeon Company common stock with a cost of $20,000 and a fair market value of $50,000. Although the stock's value has increased substantially in the past three years, Ira thinks the growth days are over. If he sells the Pigeon stock, Ira will invest the proceeds from the sale in other common stock. Assuming Ira's marginal tax rate on the sale is 15%, he will have only $45,500 [$50,000 − .15($50,000 − $20,000)] to reinvest. The alternative investment must substantially outperform Pigeon in the future in order for the sale to be beneficial. ■

SELECTION OF INVESTMENTS

Because no tax is due until a gain has been recognized, the law favors investments that yield appreciation rather than annual income.

EXAMPLE 52

Vera can buy a corporate bond or an acre of land for $10,000. The bond pays $1,000 of interest (10%) each year, and Vera expects the land to increase in value 10% each year for the next 10 years. She is in the 40% (combined Federal and state) tax bracket for ordinary income and 26% for qualifying capital gains. Assuming the bond would mature or the land would be sold in 10 years and Vera would reinvest the interest at a 10% before-tax return, she would accumulate the following amount at the end of 10 years.

		Bond	Land
Original investment		$10,000	$10,000
Annual income	$1,000		
Less tax	(400)		
	$ 600		
Compound amount reinvested for 10 years at 6% after-tax	×13.18	7,908	
		$17,908	
Compound amount, 10 years at 10%			× 2.59
			$25,900
Less tax on sale: 26%($25,900 − $10,000)			(4,134)
			$21,766

Therefore, the value of the deferral that results from investing in the land rather than in the bond is $3,858 ($21,766 − $17,908). ■

Series EE bonds can also be purchased for long-term deferrals of income. In situations where the taxpayer's goal is merely to shift income one year into the future, bank certificates of deposit are useful tools. If the maturity period is one year or less, all interest is reported in the year of maturity. Time certificates are especially useful for a taxpayer who realizes an unusually large gain from the sale of property in one year (and thus is in a high tax bracket) but expects his or her gross income to be less the following year.

CASH BASIS

The timing of income from services can often be controlled through the use of the cash method of accounting. Although taxpayers are somewhat constrained by the constructive receipt doctrine (they cannot turn their backs on income), seldom will customers and clients offer to pay before they are asked. The usual lag between billings and collections (e.g., December's billings collected in January) will result in a continuous deferring of some income until the last year of operations. A salaried individual approaching retirement may contract with the employer before the services are rendered to receive a portion of compensation in the lower tax bracket retirement years.

PREPAID INCOME

For the accrual basis taxpayer who receives advance payments from customers, the transactions should be structured to avoid payment of tax on income before the time the income is actually earned. Revenue Procedure 2004–34 provides the guidelines for deferring the tax on prepayments for services, and Regulation § 1.451–5 provides the guidelines for deferrals on sales of goods. In addition, both cash and accrual basis taxpayers can sometimes defer income by stipulating that the payments are deposits rather than prepaid income. For example, a landlord should require an equivalent damage deposit rather than prepayment of the last month's rent under the lease.

4.7 SHIFTING INCOME TO RELATIVES

The tax liability of a family can be minimized by shifting income from higher- to lower-bracket family members. This can be accomplished through gifts of income-producing property. Furthermore, in many cases, income can be shifted with no negative effect on the family's investment plans.

EXAMPLE 53

Adam, who is in the 28% tax bracket, would like to save for his children's education. All of the children are under 19 years of age and are dependents of Adam. Adam could transfer income-producing properties to the children, and the children could each receive up to $950 of income each year (refer to Chapter 3) with no tax liability. The next $950 would be taxed at the child's tax rate. After a child has more than $1,900 of unearned income, there is no tax advantage to shifting more income to the child (because the income will be taxed at the parents' rate) until the child is 19 years old (or age 24 if a full-time student), when all income will be taxed according to the child's tax rate. ■

The Uniform Gifts to Minors Act, a model law adopted by all states (but with some variations among the states), facilitates income shifting. Under the Act, a gift of intangibles (e.g., bank accounts, stocks, bonds, life insurance contracts) can be made to a minor but with an adult serving as custodian. Usually, a parent who makes the gift is also named as custodian. The state laws allow the custodian to sell or redeem and reinvest the principal and to accumulate or distribute the income, practically at the custodian's discretion provided there is no commingling of the child's income with the parent's property. Thus, the parent can give appreciated securities to the child, and the donor custodian can then sell the securities and reinvest the proceeds, thereby shifting both the gain and the annual income to the child. Such planning is limited by the tax liability calculation provision for a child under the age of 19 (or age 24 if a full-time student) (refer to Chapter 3).

U.S. government bonds (Series EE) can be purchased by parents for their children. When this is done, the children generally should file a return and elect to report the income on the accrual basis.

EXAMPLE 54

Abby pays $7,500 for Series EE bonds in 2011 and immediately gives them to Wade (her son), who will enter college the year of original maturity of the bonds. The bonds have a maturity value of $10,000. Wade elects to report the annual increment in redemption value as income for each year the bonds are held. The first year the increase is $250, and Wade includes that amount in his gross income. If Wade has no other income, no tax will be due on the $250 bond interest, since such an amount will be more than offset by his available standard deduction. The following year, the increment is $260, and Wade includes this amount in income. Thus, over the life of the bonds, Wade will include $2,500 in income ($10,000 − $7,500), none of which will result in a tax liability, assuming he has no other income. However, if the election had not been made, Wade would be required to include $2,500 in income on the bonds in the year of original maturity, if they were redeemed as planned. This amount of income might result in a tax liability. ■

In some cases, it may be advantageous for the child not to make the accrual election. For example, a child under age 19 (or age 24 if a full-time student) with investment income of more than $1,900 each year and parents in the 25, 28, 33, or 35 percent tax bracket would probably benefit from deferring the tax on the savings bond interest. The child would also benefit from the use of the usually lower tax rate (rather than subjecting the income to the parents' tax rate) if the bonds mature after the child is age 19 or older (or age 24 or older if a full-time student).

4.8 ACCOUNTING FOR COMMUNITY PROPERTY

The classification of income as community or separate property becomes important when either of two events occurs:

- Husband and wife, married taxpayers, file separate income tax returns for the year.
- Husband and wife obtain a divorce and therefore have to file separate returns for the year (refer to Chapter 3).

For planning purposes, it behooves married persons to keep track of the source of income (community or separate). To be in a position to do this effectively when income-producing assets are involved, it may be necessary to distinguish between separate and community property.[90]

4.9 ALIMONY

The person making the alimony payments favors a divorce settlement that includes a provision for deductible alimony payments. On the other hand, the recipient prefers that the payments do not qualify as alimony. If the payor is in a higher tax bracket than the recipient, both parties may benefit by increasing the payments and structuring them so that they qualify as alimony.

EXAMPLE 55

Carl and Polly are negotiating a divorce settlement. Carl has offered to pay Polly $10,000 each year for 10 years, but payments would cease upon Polly's death. Polly is willing to accept the offer if the agreement will specify that the cash payments are not alimony. Carl is in the 35% tax bracket, and Polly's marginal rate is 15%.

If Carl and Polly agree that Carl will pay Polly $12,000 of alimony each year, both will have improved after-tax cash flows.

[90]Being able to distinguish between separate and community property is crucial to the determination of a property settlement incident to a divorce. It also is vital in the estate tax area (refer to Chapter 1) since the surviving wife's or husband's share of the community property is not included in the gross estate of the deceased spouse.

	Annual Cash Flows	
	Carl	**Polly**
Nonalimony payments	($10,000)	$10,000
Alimony payments	($12,000)	$12,000
Tax effects		
.35($12,000)	4,200	
.15($12,000)		(1,800)
After-tax cash flows	($ 7,800)	$10,200
Benefit of alimony option	$ 2,200	$ 200

Both parties benefit at the government's expense if the $12,000 alimony option is used. ■

REFOCUS ON THE BIG PICTURE

CALCULATION OF GROSS INCOME

Using the accrual method of accounting, Dr. Cliff Payne has correctly calculated the gross income of his sole proprietorship. He will report the $385,000 amount on Schedule C of Form 1040.

What If?

From a tax planning perspective, what can Dr. Payne do to decrease his gross income from his first year of operating his dental practice and thereby produce better financial results for him?

Rather than electing to use the accrual method of accounting, Dr. Payne should elect the cash method of accounting since his dental practice is a service entity rather than a merchandising entity. His gross income for Federal income tax purposes under the cash method is calculated as follows:

Revenues	$385,000
Plus: Accounts receivable: January 1	–0–
Less: Accounts receivable: December 31	(52,000)
Gross income	$333,000

Electing to use the cash method of accounting enables Dr. Payne to defer paying Federal income taxes on the unpaid accounts receivable. Furthermore, each year that Dr. Payne has accounts receivable at the end of the tax year, that income is continuously deferred. Thus, if his accounts receivable remain at $52,000 at the end of each tax year, by using the cash method of accounting rather than the accrual method, he will defer that amount of income until he terminates his practice.

KEY TERMS

Accounting income, 4–5

Accounting method, 4–8

Accrual method, 4–9

Alimony and separate maintenance payments, 4–22

Alimony recapture, 4–23

Annuity, 4–29

Assignment of income, 4–15

Cash receipts method, 4–9

Claim of right doctrine, 4–10

Community property, 4–20

Constructive receipt, 4–10

Economic income, 4–4

Fruit and tree metaphor, 4–15

Gross income, 4–3

Group term life insurance, 4–33

Hybrid method, 4–10

Imputed interest, 4–26

Income, 4–4

Original issue discount, 4–12

Partnership, 4–18

Recovery of capital doctrine, 4–4

S corporation, 4–19

Taxable year, 4–8

DISCUSSION QUESTIONS

1. **LO.1** According to the Supreme Court, what are the goals of financial accounting and tax accounting in regard to measuring annual income?

2. **LO.1** Why do the tax laws employ the realization principle to measure income rather than the economists' concept of income?

3. **LO.1** Allen visits Reno, Nevada, once each year to gamble. This year his gambling loss was $25,000. He commented to you, "At least I didn't have to pay for my airfare and hotel room. The casino paid that because I am such a good customer. That was worth at least $3,000." What are the relevant tax issues for Allen?   **ISSUE ID**

4. **LO.1** Ben works full-time, and his hobby is gardening. He spent $1,400 on seeds and fertilizer to grow enough vegetables to last him the entire year. Should Ben be required to recognize income equal to the fair market value of the vegetables in excess of their cost?

5. **LO.1** Howard buys wrecked cars and stores them on his property. Recently, he purchased a 1990 Ford Taurus for $400. If he can sell all of the usable parts, his total proceeds from the Taurus would be over $2,500. As of the end of the year, he has sold only the radio for $75, and he does not know how many, if any, of the remaining parts will ever be sold. What are Howard's income recognition issues?   **ISSUE ID**

6. **LO.2, 3** On December 31, 2011, an employee received a $6,000 check from her employer's client. The check was payable to the employer, but the employee did not receive it until after the bank had closed. The employee did not remit the funds to the employer until January 2, 2012. When is the cash basis employer required to include the $6,000 in gross income?

7. **LO.2** Why does the constructive receipt doctrine apply to cash basis taxpayers, but not to accrual basis taxpayers?

8. **LO.2** On December 31, 2011, Maurice received a $5,000 check from his employer's client. The check was payable to the employer, but Maurice did not receive the check until after the bank was closed. The bank would not reopen until January 2012. Maurice remitted the check to the employer late on December 31. Identify the cash basis employer's income recognition issues?   **ISSUE ID**

9. **LO.2** In 2011, Sandra, a cash basis taxpayer, purchased a certificate of deposit for $943 that will be redeemed in 2013 for $1,000. Is Sandra required to recognize any income from the certificate in 2011 and 2012?

10. **LO.2** A Series EE U.S. government savings bond accrues 3.5% interest each year. The bond matures in three years, at which time the principal and interest will be paid. The bank will pay the taxpayer at a 3.5% interest rate each year if he agrees to leave money on deposit for three years. What tax advantage does the Series EE bond offer that is not available with the bank deposit?

11. **LO.2** Why is it often advantageous to the taxpayer to use the cash method of accounting rather than the accrual method?

12. **LO.3, 5** Wade paid $7,000 for an automobile that needed substantial repairs. He worked nights and weekends to restore the car and spent $2,400 on parts for it. He knows he can sell the car for $13,000. His daughter's college tuition is due in a few days. Would it matter, after taxes, whether Wade sells the car and pays the tuition, or whether he gives the car to his daughter and she sells it for $13,000 and pays her tuition?

13. **LO.3** Anita, a cash basis taxpayer, sued her former employer for wage discrimination. Her attorney agreed to pursue the case on a contingent fee basis—the attorney would receive one-third of any settlement or court award. The parties reached a settlement, and the attorney for Anita's former employer wrote a check payable to Anita for $320,000 and a check payable to her attorney for $160,000. Anita reasons that she and the attorney were partners in the lawsuit who shared profits two-thirds and one-third. Therefore, she includes $320,000 in her gross income. Is Anita's analysis correct? Explain.

14. **LO.3** Rex is a partner with a 40% interest in the partnership profits. In 2011, the partnership generated $400,000 of taxable income, and Rex withdrew $120,000. In 2012,

the partnership had $500,000 of taxable income, and Rex was able to withdraw $200,000. What is Rex's gross income from the partnership in 2011 and 2012?

15. **LO.3, 5** Mike and Debbie were residents of Texas. In 2011, Debbie left Mike, and he has been unable to find her even though he hired a private investigator to do so. Mike and Debbie are still married at year-end. Both Debbie and Mike were employed, and each had substantial investments. They did not have any children. How will Debbie's absence complicate Mike's 2011 income tax return?

16. **LO.4** What are the tax consequences if the alimony recapture rules apply to a cash payment to a former spouse?

17. **LO.4** Why is a married couple's cost of assets (adjusted basis) for appreciated assets relevant in negotiating their divorce agreement?

18. **LO.4, 5** William and Abigail, who live in San Francisco, have been experiencing problems with their marriage. They have a three-year-old daughter, April, who stays with William's parents during the day since both William and Abigail are employed. Abigail worked to support William while he attended medical school, and now she has been accepted by a medical school in Mexico. Abigail has decided to divorce William and attend medical school. April will stay in San Francisco because of her strong attachment to her grandparents and because they can provide her with excellent day care. Abigail knows that William will expect her to contribute to the cost of raising April. Abigail also feels that, to finance her education, she must receive cash for her share of the property they accumulated during their marriage. In addition, she feels she should receive some reimbursement for her contribution to William's support while he was in medical school. She expects the divorce proceedings will take several months. Identify the relevant tax issues for Abigail.

19. **LO.4, 5** Patrick and Eva are planning to divorce. Patrick has offered to pay Eva $12,000 each year for 10 years, until their daughter reaches age 21, or to transfer to her common stock he owns with a fair market value of $100,000 in satisfaction of Eva's share of the marital property. What factors should Eva and Patrick consider in deciding between these two options?

20. **LO.4, 5** Brenda loaned her son Bart $250,000 to purchase a new home. Brenda did not charge interest on the loan. Brenda was required to recognize imputed interest income, and Bart had imputed home mortgage interest expense that he deducted as an itemized deduction. Would Brenda's and Bart's combined total income taxes likely increase or decrease as a result of the imputed interest?

21. **LO.4** The Rose Corporation made a $1 million interest-free loan to John Rose, the corporation's controlling shareholder. Mr. Rose is also the corporation's chief executive officer. Why would the corporation prefer to characterize the loan as a compensation-related loan rather than a corporation-shareholder loan?

22. **LO.2, 4** Brad is the president of the Yellow Corporation. He and other members of his family control the corporation. Brad has a temporary need for $50,000, and the corporation has excess cash. He could borrow the money from a bank at 9%, and Yellow is earning 6% on its temporary investments. Yellow has made loans to other employees on several occasions. Therefore, Brad is considering borrowing $50,000 from the corporation. He will repay the loan principal in two years plus interest at 5%. Identify the relevant tax issues for Brad and the Yellow Corporation.

23. **LO.4** On July 1, 1998, when Betty was 65 years old, she purchased an annuity contract for $108,000. The annuity was to pay Betty $9,000 on June 30 each year for the remainder of her life. Betty died on March 31, 2011. What are the effects of the annuity on Betty's gross income and taxable income for 2011?

24. **LO.4** An employer provides all of his employees with life insurance protection equal to twice the employee's annual salary. Melba, who is age 39, has an annual salary of $40,000. Is Melba required to recognize income even though she is still alive at the end of the year and thus nothing has been collected on the life insurance policy?

25. **LO.4** Eve is age 67 and unmarried. She receives $12,000 a year in Social Security benefits and $20,000 from a taxable pension. She is in the 15% marginal tax bracket on her Federal income tax return. She claims the standard deduction. She is considering selling

stock she has held for more than one year. Her cost of the stock is $6,000, and its fair market value is $13,000. She has no other gains or losses for the year. She has asked you to estimate the tax consequences of selling the stock.

PROBLEMS

26. **LO.1** Determine the taxpayer's current-year (1) economic income and (2) gross income for tax purposes from the following events:
    a. Sue, a coach, was paid $950,000 to terminate her coaching contract.
    b. Elliot, a six-year-old child, was paid $10,000 for appearing in a television commercial. His parents put the funds into a savings account for the child's education.
    c. Valery's land increased in value by $100,000 when he was successful in having the zoning changed from residential to commercial.
    d. Winn purchased a lottery ticket for $5 and won $900,000.
    e. Larry spent $600 to raise vegetables that he and his family consumed. The cost of the vegetables in a store would have been $2,400.

27. **LO.1, 5** Andy recently completed medical school and is beginning his medical practice. Most of his patients are covered by health insurance with a co-pay requirement (e.g., the patient pays $10, and the insurance company is billed for the remainder). It takes approximately two months to collect from the health insurance plan. What advice can you provide Andy regarding the selection of a tax accounting method?

ISSUE ID

28. **LO.1, 2, 5** A taxpayer is considering three alternative investments of $10,000. Assume the taxpayer is in the 28% marginal tax bracket for ordinary income and 15% for qualifying capital gains in all tax years. The selected investment will be liquidated at the end of five years. The alternatives are:

DECISION MAKING

    • A taxable corporate bond yielding 5% before tax, and the interest can be reinvested at 5% before tax.
    • A Series EE bond that will have a maturity value of $12,200 (a 4% before-tax rate of return).
    • Land that will increase in value.

    The gain on the land will be classified and taxed as a long-term capital gain. The income from the bonds is taxed as ordinary income. How much must the land increase in value to yield a greater after-tax return than either of the bonds?

    Given: Compound amount of $1 and compound value of annuity payments at the end of five years:

Interest Rate	$1 Compounded for 5 Years	$1 Annuity Compounded for 5 Years
5%	$1.28	$5.53
4%	1.22	5.42
3.6%	1.19	5.37

29. **LO.1** Determine the taxpayer's gross income for tax purposes in each of the following situations:
    a. Deb, a cash basis taxpayer, traded a corporate bond with accrued interest of $300 for corporate stock with a fair market value of $11,000 at the time of the exchange. Deb's cost of the bond was $10,000. The value of the stock had increased to $12,000 by the end of the year.
    b. Deb needed $10,000 to make a down payment on her house. She instructed her broker to sell some stock to raise the $10,000. Deb's cost of the stock was $3,000. Based on her broker's advice, instead of selling the stock, she borrowed the $10,000 using the stock as collateral for the debt.
    c. Deb's boss gave her two tickets to the Rabid Rabbits rock concert because she met her sales quota. At the time she received the tickets, they had a face price of $200 and were selling on eBay for $350 each. On the date of the concert, the tickets were selling for $400 each. Deb and her son attended the concert.

30. **LO.1, 2** Determine Amos Seagull's gross income in each of the following cases:
    a. In the current year, Seagull Corporation purchased an automobile for $25,000. The company was to receive a $1,500 rebate from the manufacturer. However, the corporation directed that the rebate be paid to Amos, the corporation's sole shareholder.
    b. Amos sold his corporation. In addition to the selling price of the stock, he received $50,000 for a covenant not to compete—an agreement that he will not compete with his former business for five years.
    c. Amos and his neighbor got into an argument over Amos's dog. The neighbor built a fence to keep the dog out of his yard. The fence cost $2,000 but added $3,000 to the value of Amos's property.

31. **LO.2, 5** Al is a medical doctor who conducts his practice as a sole proprietor. During 2011, he received cash of $280,000 for medical services. Of the amount collected, $40,000 was for services provided in 2010. At the end of 2011, Al had accounts receivable of $60,000, all for services rendered in 2011. In addition, at the end of the year, Al received $12,000 as an advance payment from a health maintenance organization (HMO) for services to be rendered in 2012. Compute Al's gross income for 2011:
    a. Using the cash basis of accounting.
    b. Using the accrual basis of accounting.
    c. Advise Al on which method of accounting he should use.

32. **LO.2** Selma operates a contractor's supply store. She maintains her books using the cash method. At the end of the year, her accountant computes her accrual basis income that is used on her tax return. For 2011, Selma had cash receipts of $1.5 million, which included $300,000 collected on accounts receivable from 2010 sales. It also included the proceeds of a $100,000 bank loan. At the end of 2011, she had $350,000 in accounts receivable from customers, all from 2011 sales.
    a. Compute Selma's accrual basis gross receipts for 2011.
    b. Selma paid cash for all of the purchases. The total amount paid for merchandise in 2011 was $1.2 million. At the end of 2010, she had merchandise on hand with a cost of $100,000. At the end of 2011, the cost of merchandise on hand was $300,000. Compute Selma's gross income from merchandise sales for 2011.

33. **LO.2, 3, 5** Your client is a new partnership, ARP Associates, which is an engineering consulting firm. Generally, ARP bills clients for services at the end of each month. Client billings are about $50,000 each month. On average, it takes 45 days to collect the receivables. ARP's expenses are primarily for salary and rent. Salaries are paid on the last day of each month, and rent is paid on the first day of each month. The partnership has a line of credit with a bank, which requires monthly financial statements. These must be prepared using the accrual method. ARP's managing partner, Amanda Sims, has suggested that the firm should also use the accrual method for tax purposes and thus reduce accounting fees by $600. Assume the partners are in the 35% (combined Federal and state) marginal tax bracket. Write a letter to your client explaining why you believe it would be worthwhile for ARP to file its tax return on the cash basis even though its financial statements are prepared on the accrual basis. ARP's address is 100 James Tower, Denver, CO 80208.

34. **LO.2** Color Paint Shop, Inc. (459 Ellis Avenue, Harrisburg, PA 17111), is an accrual basis taxpayer that paints automobiles. During the year, the company painted Samuel's car and was to receive a $1,000 payment from his insurance company. Samuel was not satisfied with the work, however, and the insurance company refused to pay. In December 2011, Color and Samuel agreed that Color would receive $800 for the work, subject to final approval by the insurance company. In the past, Color had come to terms with customers only to have the insurance company negotiate an even lesser amount. In May 2012, the insurance company reviewed the claim and paid the $800 to Color. An IRS agent thinks that Color, as an accrual basis taxpayer, should report $1,000 of income in 2011, when the work was done, and then deduct a $200 loss in 2012. Prepare a memo to Susan Apple, a tax partner for whom you are working, with the recommended treatment for the disputed income.

35. **LO.2** Determine the effects of the following on a cash basis taxpayer's gross income for 2011 and 2012.
    a. On the morning of December 31, 2011, the taxpayer received a $1,500 check from a customer. The taxpayer did not cash the check until January 3, 2012.

b. The same as part (a), except the customer asked the taxpayer not to cash the check until January 3, 2012, after the customer's salary check could be deposited.

c. The same as part (a), except the check was not received until after the bank had closed on December 31, 2011.

36. **LO.2** Marlene, a cash basis taxpayer, invests in Series EE U.S. government savings bonds and bank certificates of deposit (CDs). Determine the tax consequences of the following on her 2011 gross income.

a. On July 1, 2011, she purchased a CD for $10,000. The CD matures on June 30, 2013, and will pay $10,816, thus yielding a 4% annual return.

b. On December 31, 2011, she cashed in a CD and received $11,025. She purchased the CD on January 1, 2010, and the yield to maturity was 5%.

c. On September 30, 2011, she cashed in Series EE bonds for $10,000. She purchased the bonds in 2001 for $7,025. The yield to maturity on the bonds was 4.5%.

37. **LO.2** Drake Appliance Company, an accrual basis taxpayer, sells home appliances and service contracts. Determine the effect of each of the following transactions on the company's 2011 gross income assuming that the company uses any available options to defer its taxes.

a. In December 2010, the company received a $1,200 advance payment from a customer for an appliance that Drake special ordered from the manufacturer. The appliance did not arrive from the manufacturer until January 2011, and Drake immediately delivered it to the customer. The sale was reported in 2011 for financial accounting purposes.

b. In October 2011, the company sold a 6-month service contract for $240. The company also sold a 36-month service contract for $1,260 in July 2011.

c. On December 31, 2011, the company sold an appliance for $1,200. The company received $500 cash and a note from the customer for $700 and $260 interest, to be paid at the rate of $40 a month for 24 months. Because of the customer's poor credit record, the fair market value of the note was only $600. The cost of the appliance was $750.

38. **LO.2, 5** Freda is a cash basis taxpayer. In 2011, she negotiated her salary for 2012. Her employer offered to pay her a total of $250,000 for the year. Freda countered that she would accept $10,000 each month for the 12 months in 2012 and the remaining $130,000 in January 2013. The employer accepted Freda's terms for 2012 and 2013.

a. Did Freda actually or constructively receive $250,000 in 2012?

b. What could explain Freda's willingness to spread her salary over a longer period of time?

39. **LO.2, 5** The Bluejay Apartments is a new development and is in the process of structuring its lease agreements. The company would like to set the damage deposits high enough that tenants will keep the apartments in good condition. The company is actually more concerned about damage than about tenants not paying their rent.

a. Discuss the tax effects of the following alternatives:
  - $1,000 damage deposit with no rent prepayment.
  - $500 damage deposit and $500 rent for the final month of the lease.
  - $1,000 rent for the final two months of the lease and no damage deposit.

b. Which option do you recommend?

DECISION MAKING

40. **LO.3** Rusty has been experiencing serious financial problems. His annual salary was $100,000, but a creditor garnished his salary for $20,000, so the employer paid the creditor (rather than Rusty) the $20,000. To prevent creditors from attaching his investments, Rusty gave his investments to his 21-year-old daughter, Rebecca. Rebecca received $5,000 in dividends and interest from the investments during the year. Rusty transferred some cash to a Swiss bank account that paid him $6,000 interest during the year. Rusty did not withdraw the interest from the Swiss bank account. Rusty also hid some of his assets in his wholly owned corporation that received $150,000 rent income but had $160,000 in related expenses, including a $20,000 salary paid to Rusty. Rusty reasons that his gross income should be computed as follows:

Salary received	$ 80,000
Loss from rental property ($150,000 − $160,000)	(10,000)
Gross income	$ 70,000

Compute Rusty's correct gross income for the year, and explain any differences between your calculation and Rusty's.

41. **LO.2, 3** Troy, a cash basis taxpayer, is employed by Eagle Corporation, also a cash basis taxpayer. Troy is a full-time employee of the corporation and receives a salary of $60,000 per year. He also receives a bonus equal to 10% of all collections from clients he serviced during the year. Determine the tax consequences of the following events to the corporation and to Troy:

a. On December 31, 2011, Troy was visiting a customer. The customer gave Troy a $10,000 check payable to the corporation for appraisal services Troy performed during 2011. Troy did not deliver the check to the corporation until January 2012.

b. The facts are the same as in (a), except that the corporation is an accrual basis taxpayer and Troy deposited the check on December 31, but the bank did not add the deposit to the corporation's account until January 2012.

c. The facts are the same as in (a), except that the customer told Troy to hold the check until January 2012 when the customer could make a bank deposit that would cover the check.

42. **LO.3, 4** Fran, Gary, and Heidi each have a one-third interest in the capital and profits of the FGH Partnership. Each partner had a capital account of $50,000 at the beginning of the tax year. The partnership profits for the tax year were $240,000. Changes in their capital accounts during the tax year were as follows:

	Fran	Gary	Heidi	Total
Beginning balance	$ 50,000	$ 50,000	$ 50,000	$150,000
Withdrawals	(25,000)	(35,000)	(10,000)	(70,000)
Additional contributions	–0–	–0–	5,000	5,000
Allocation of profits	80,000	80,000	80,000	240,000
Ending balance	$105,000	$ 95,000	$125,000	$325,000

In arriving at the $240,000 of partnership profits, the partnership deducted $1,800 ($600 for each partner) in premiums paid for group term life insurance on the partners. Fran and Gary are 39 years old, and Heidi is 35 years old. Other employees are also eligible for group term life insurance equal to their annual salary. These premiums of $10,000 have been deducted in calculating the partnership profits of $240,000. Compute each partner's gross income from the partnership for the tax year.

43. **LO.3, 5** In 2011, Alva received dividends on her stocks as follows:

Amur Corporation (a French corporation whose stock is traded on an established U.S. securities market)	$55,000
Blaze, Inc., a Delaware corporation	25,000
Grape, Inc., a Virginia corporation	12,000

a. Alva purchased the Grape stock four years ago, and she purchased the Amur stock two years ago. She purchased the Blaze stock 15 days before it went ex-dividend and sold it 20 days later at a $22,000 loss. Alva had no other capital gains and losses for the year. She is in the 35% marginal tax bracket. Compute Alva's tax on her dividend income for 2011.

b. Alva's daughter, who is age 25 and who is not Alva's dependent, had taxable income of $6,000, which included $1,000 of dividends on Grape, Inc. stock. The daughter had purchased the stock two years ago. Compute the daughter's tax liability on the dividends.

c. Alva can earn 5% before-tax interest on a corporate bond or a 4% dividend on a preferred stock. Assuming the appreciation in value is the same, which investment produces the greater after-tax income?

d. The same as part (c), except Alva's daughter is to make the investment.

44. **LO.3** Liz and Doug were divorced on July 1 of the current year after 10 years of marriage. Their current year's income received before the divorce was as follows:

Doug's salary	$41,000
Liz's salary	55,000
Rent on apartments purchased by Liz 15 years ago	8,000
Dividends on stock Doug inherited from his mother 4 years ago	1,900
Interest on a savings account in Liz's name funded with her salary	2,400

Allocate the income to Liz and Doug assuming they live in:
a. California.
b. Texas.

45. **LO.4** Nell and Kirby are in the process of negotiating their divorce agreement. What should be the tax consequences to Nell and Kirby if the following, considered individually, became part of the agreement?
   a.   In consideration for her one-half interest in their personal residence, Kirby will transfer to Nell stock with a value of $200,000. Kirby's cost of the stock was $150,000, and the value of the personal residence is $400,000. They purchased the residence three years ago for $300,000.
   b.   Nell will receive $1,000 per month for the lesser of 120 months or the number of months she lives after the divorce becomes final.
   c.   Nell is to have custody of their 12-year-old son, Bobby. She is to receive $1,200 per month until Bobby (1) dies or (2) attains age 21 (whichever occurs first). After either of these events occurs, Nell will receive only $300 per month for the remainder of her life.

46. **LO.4** Karen and Al are in the process of negotiating a divorce. They have tentatively agreed on all the terms, and Karen is to pay Al $240,000 over a three-year period. Furthermore, the payments are to be spread over the three years in amounts that will qualify as alimony and minimize alimony recapture. Al desires to receive as much of the $240,000 as soon as possible because if he dies or remarries within the three years, the payments will cease. Which of the two following patterns of payments will result in the least alimony recapture in year 3?

Year	Option 1: Amount Paid	Option 2: Amount Paid
1	$100,000	$100,000
2	70,000	90,000
3	70,000	50,000
Total	$240,000	$240,000

47. **LO.4** Alicia and Rafel are in the process of negotiating a divorce agreement. They both worked during the marriage and contributed an equal amount to the marital assets. They own a home with a fair market value of $400,000 (cost of $300,000) that is subject to a mortgage for $250,000. They have lived in the home for 12 years. They also have investment assets with a cost of $160,000 and a fair market value of $410,000. Thus, the net worth of the couple is $560,000 ($400,000 − $250,000 + $410,000). The holding period for the investments is longer than one year. Alicia would like to continue to live in the house. Therefore, she has proposed that she receive the residence subject to the mortgage, a net value of $150,000. In addition, she would receive $17,600 each year for the next 10 years, which has a present value (at 6% interest) of $130,000. Rafel would receive the investment assets. If Rafel accepts this plan, he must sell one-half of the investments so that he can purchase a home. Assume that you are counseling Alicia. Explain to Alicia whether the proposed agreement would be "fair" on an after-tax basis.

DECISION MAKING

48. **LO.4, 5** Roy decides to buy a personal residence and goes to the bank for a $150,000 loan. The bank tells him he can borrow the funds at 7% if his father will guarantee the debt. Roy's father, Hal, owns CDs currently yielding 6%. The Federal rate is 5%. Hal is willing to do either of the following:

- Cash in the CDs and lend Roy the funds at 6% interest.
- Guarantee the loan for Roy.

DECISION MAKING

Hal will consider lending the funds to Roy at an even lower interest rate, depending on the tax consequences. Hal is in the 35% marginal tax bracket. Roy, whose only source of income is his salary, is in the 15% marginal tax bracket. The interest Roy pays on the mortgage will be deductible by him. Considering only the tax consequences, which option will maximize the family's after-tax wealth?

49. **LO.2, 4** On June 30, 2011, Ridge borrowed $62,000 from his employer. On July 1, 2011, Ridge used the money as follows:

Interest-free loan to Ridge's controlled corporation (operated by Ridge on a part-time basis)	$31,000
Interest-free loan to Tab (Ridge's son)	11,000
National Bank of Grundy 5% CD ($14,700 due at maturity, June 30, 2012)	14,000
National Bank of Grundy 5.5% CD ($6,678 due at maturity, June 30, 2013)	6,000
	$62,000

Ridge's employer did not charge him interest. The applicable Federal rate was 5% throughout the relevant period. Tab had investment income of $800 for the year, and he used the loan proceeds to pay medical school tuition. There were no other outstanding loans between Ridge and Tab. What are the effects of the preceding transactions on Ridge's taxable income for 2011?

50. **LO.4** Indicate whether the imputed interest rules should apply in the following situations. Assume all the loans were made at the beginning of the tax year unless otherwise indicated.
    a. Mike loaned his sister $90,000 to buy a new home. Mike did not charge interest on the loan. The Federal rate was 5%. Mike's sister had $900 of investment income for the year.
    b. Sam's employer maintains an emergency loan fund for its employees. During the year, Sam's wife was very ill, and he incurred unusually large medical expenses. He borrowed $8,500 from his employer's emergency loan fund for six months. The Federal rate was 5.5%. Sam and his wife had no investment income for the year.
    c. Jody borrowed $25,000 from her controlled corporation for six months. She used the funds to pay her daughter's college tuition. The corporation charged Jody 4% interest. The Federal rate was 5%. Jody had $3,500 of investment income for the year.
    d. Kait loaned her son, Jake, $60,000 for six months. Jake used the $60,000 to pay off college loans. The Federal rate was 5%, and Kait did not charge Jake any interest. Jake had dividend and interest income of $2,100 for the tax year.

51. **LO.4** Vito is the sole shareholder of Vito, Inc. He is also employed by the corporation. On June 30, 2011, Vito borrowed $8,000 from Vito, Inc., and on July 1, 2012, he borrowed an additional $4,000. Both loans were due on demand. No interest was charged on the loans, and the Federal rate was 8% for all relevant dates. Vito used the money to purchase a boat, and he had $1,100 of investment income. Determine the tax consequences to Vito and Vito, Inc., in each of the following situations:
    a. The loans are considered employer-employee loans.
    b. The loans are considered corporation-shareholder loans.

52. **LO.4** Tess retires after 30 years of service with her employer. She is 66 years old and has contributed $37,800 to her employer's qualified pension fund. She elects to receive her retirement benefits as an annuity of $3,000 per month for the remainder of her life.
    a. Assume that Tess retires in June 2011 and collects six annuity payments this year. What is her gross income from the annuity payments in the first year?
    b. Assume that Tess lives 30 years after retiring. What is her gross income from the annuity payments in the twenty-ninth year?
    c. Assume that Tess dies after collecting 180 payments. She collected six payments in the year of her death. What are Tess's gross income and deductions from the annuity contract in the year of her death?

53. **LO.4** For each of the following, determine the amount that should be included in gross income:
    a. Don was selected as the most valuable player in the World Series. In recognition of this, he was awarded a sports car worth $75,000 and $100,000 in cash.

b. Wanda won the Mrs. America beauty contest. She received various prizes valued at $200,000. None of the $200,000 was for a scholarship or travel expenses.

c. Jacob was awarded the Nobel Prize in Medicine. He donated the $1.4 million check he received to City University, his alma mater.

54. **LO.4** The LMN Partnership has a group term life insurance plan. Each partner has $150,000 protection, and each employee has protection equal to twice his or her annual salary. Employee Alice (age 36) has $85,000 of insurance under the plan, and partner Kay (age 54) has $150,000 of coverage. Because the plan is a "group plan," it is impossible to determine the cost of coverage for an individual employee or partner.

a. Assuming the plan is nondiscriminatory, how much must Alice and Kay each include in gross income as a result of the partnership paying the insurance premiums?

b. Assume that the partnership is incorporated. Kay becomes a shareholder and an employee who receives a $75,000 annual salary. The corporation provides Kay with $150,000 of group term life insurance coverage under a nondiscriminatory plan. What is Kay's gross income as a result of the corporation paying the insurance premiums?

55. **LO.2, 4** Herbert was employed for the first six months of 2011 and earned $90,000 in salary. During the next six months, he collected $8,800 of unemployment compensation, borrowed $12,000 (using his personal residence as collateral), and withdrew $2,000 from his savings account (including $60 interest). He received dividends of $550. His luck was not all bad, for in December he won $1,500 in the lottery on a $5 ticket. Calculate Herbert's gross income.

56. **LO.4, 5** Linda and Don are married and file a joint return. In 2011, they received $12,000 in Social Security benefits and $35,000 in taxable pension benefits and interest.

DECISION MAKING

a. Compute the couple's adjusted gross income on a joint return.

b. Don would like to know whether they should sell for $100,000 (at no gain or loss) a corporate bond that pays 8% in interest each year and use the proceeds to buy a $100,000 nontaxable State of Virginia bond that will pay $6,000 in interest each year.

c. If Linda in (a) works part-time and earns $30,000, how much would Linda and Don's adjusted gross income increase?

57. **LO.4** Melissa, who is 70 years old, is unmarried and has no dependents. Her annual income consists of a taxable pension of $20,000, $12,000 in Social Security benefits, and $3,000 of dividend income. She does not itemize her deductions. She is in the 15% marginal income tax bracket. She is considering getting a part-time job that would pay her $10,000 a year.

a. What would be Melissa's after-tax income from the part-time job, considering Social Security and Medicare tax (7.65%) as well as Federal income tax on the earnings of $10,000?

b. What would be the effective tax rate (increase in tax/increase in income) on the additional income from the part-time job?

c. Assume instead that Melissa's only income is a taxable pension of $18,000 and $12,000 in Social Security benefits. She is considering selling land for $10,000 that she purchased as an investment in 2007 for $3,000. Her marginal tax rate on ordinary income is 15%. What would be the effective tax rate on the gain from the sale of the land?

58. **LO.3, 4** Donna does not think she has an income tax problem but would like to discuss her situation with you just to make sure she will not get hit with an unexpected tax liability. Base your suggestions on the following relevant financial information:

a. Donna's share of the SAT Partnership income is $150,000, but none of the income can be distributed because the partnership needs the cash for operations.

b. Donna's Social Security benefits totaled $8,400, but Donna loaned the cash received to her nephew.

c. Donna assigned to a creditor the right to collect $1,200 interest on some bonds she owned.

d. Donna and her husband lived together in California until September, when they separated. Donna has heard rumors that her husband had substantial gambling winnings since they separated.

CUMULATIVE PROBLEMS

59. Daniel B. Butler and Freida C. Butler, husband and wife, file a joint return. The Butlers live at 625 Oak Street in Corbin, KY 27521. Dan's Social Security number is 111–11–1111, and Freida's is 123–45–6789. Dan was born on January 15, 1962, and Freida was born on August 20, 1962.

During 2010, Dan and Freida furnished over half of the total support of each of the following individuals, all of whom still live at home:

a. Gina, their daughter, age 22, a full-time student, who married on December 21, 2010, has no income of her own, and for 2010 did not file a joint return with her husband, Casey, who earned $10,600 during 2010. Gina's Social Security number is 123–45–6788.

b. Sam, their son, age 20, who had gross income of $6,300 in 2010, dropped out of college in October 2010. He had graduated from high school in May 2010. Sam's Social Security number is 123–45–6787.

c. Ben, their oldest son, age 26, is a full-time graduate student with gross income of $5,200. Ben's Social Security number is 123–45–6786.

Dan was employed as a manager by WJJJ, Inc. (employer identification number 11–1111111, 604 Franklin Street, Corbin, KY 27521), and Freida was employed as a salesperson for Corbin Realty, Inc. (employer identification number 98–7654321, 899 Central Street, Corbin, Ky 27521). Information from the W–2 Forms provided by the employers is presented below. Dan and Freida use the cash method.

Line	Description	Dan	Freida
1	Wages, tips, other compensation	$86,000	$65,000
2	Federal income tax withheld	$12,000	$11,400
3	Social Security wages	$86,000	$65,000
4	Social Security tax withheld	$5,332	$4,030
5	Medicare wages and tips	$86,000	$65,000
6	Medicare tax withheld	$1,247	$943
15	State	Kentucky	Kentucky
16	State wages, tips, etc.	$86,000	$65,000
17	State income tax withheld	$2,900	$2,700

Freida sold a house on December 30, 2010, and will be paid a commission of $3,100 (not included in the $65,000 reported on the W–2) on the January 10, 2011 closing date.

Other income (as reported on 1099 Forms) for 2010 consisted of the following:

Dividends on CSX stock (qualified)	$3,500
Interest on savings at Second Bank	1,600
Interest on City of Corbin bonds	900
Interest on First Bank CD	383

The $383 from First Bank was original issue discount. Dan and Freida collected $15,000 on the First Bank CD that matured on September 30, 2010. The CD was purchased on October 1, 2008, for $14,000, and the yield to maturity was 3.5%.

Dan received a Schedule K–1 from the Falcon Partnership, which showed his distributive share as $9,000. In addition to the above information, Dan and Freida's itemized deductions included the following:

Paid on 2009 Kentucky income tax	$ 400
Personal property tax paid	600
Real estate taxes paid	1,800
Interest on home mortgage (Corbin S&L)	4,900
Cash contributions to the Boy Scouts	975

Sales tax from the sales tax table is $1,860. Dan and Freida made Federal estimated tax payments of $8,000.

Part 1—Tax Computation

Compute Dan and Freida's 2010 Federal income tax payable (or refund due). If you use tax forms for your computations, you will need Form 1040 and Schedules A, B, and E. Suggested software: H&R BLOCK At Home.

Part 2—Tax Planning

Dan plans to reduce his work schedule and work only halftime for WJJJ in 2011. He has been writing songs for several years and wants to devote more time to developing a career as a songwriter. Because of the uncertainty in the music business, however, he would like you to make all computations assuming he will have no income from songwriting in 2011. To make up for the loss of income, Freida plans to increase the amount of time she spends selling real estate. She estimates she will be able to earn $70,000 in 2011. Assume all other income and expense items will be approximately the same as they were in 2010. Assume Sam will be enrolled in college as a full-time student for the summer and fall semesters. Will the Butlers have more or less disposable income (after Federal income tax) in 2011? Write a letter to the Butlers that contains your advice and prepare a memo for the tax files.

60. Cecil C. Seymour is a 66-year-old widower. He had income for 2011 as follows:

TAX COMPUTATION PROBLEM

Pension from former employer	$36,000
Interest income from Alto National Bank	5,500
Interest income on City of Alto bonds	4,500
Dividends received from IBM	2,000
Collections on annuity contract he purchased from Great Life Insurance	5,400
Social Security benefits	12,000
Rent income on townhouse	7,600

The cost of the annuity was $54,000, and Cecil was expected to receive a total of 240 monthly payments of $450. Cecil has received 22 payments through 2011.

Cecil's 40-year-old daughter, Sarah C. Seymour, borrowed $60,000 from Cecil on January 2, 2011. She used the money to start a new business. Cecil does not charge her interest because she could not afford to pay it, but he does expect to eventually collect the principal. Sarah is living with Cecil until the business becomes profitable. Except for housing, Sarah provides her own support from her business and $1,600 in dividends on stocks that she inherited from her mother.

Other relevant information is presented below:

- Cecil's Social Security number: 123–45–6785
- Address: 3840 Springfield Blvd., Alto, GA 30754
- Sarah's Social Security number: 123–45–6784
- Expenses on rental townhouse:

Utilities	$2,800
Maintenance	1,000
Depreciation	2,000
Real estate taxes	750
Insurance	700

- State income taxes paid: $3,500
- County personal property taxes paid: $2,100
- Payments on estimated 2011 Federal income tax: $5,900
- Charitable contributions of cash to Alto Baptist Church: $6,400
- Federal interest rate: 6%
- Sales taxes paid: $912

Compute Cecil's 2011 Federal income tax payable (or refund due).

RESEARCH PROBLEMS

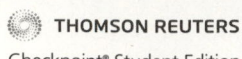

THOMSON REUTERS

Checkpoint® Student Edition

Note: Solutions to Research Problems can be prepared by using the **Checkpoint®** **Student Edition** online research product, which is available to accompany this text. It is also possible to prepare solutions to the Research Problems by using tax research materials found in a standard tax library.

COMMUNICATIONS

Research Problem 1. Tranquility Funeral Home, Inc., your client, is an accrual basis taxpayer that sells preneed funeral contracts. Under these contracts, the customer pays in advance for goods and services to be provided at the contract beneficiary's death. These payments are refundable at the contract purchaser's request, pursuant to state law, at any time until the goods and services are furnished. Tranquility, consistent with its financial accounting reporting, includes the payments in income for the year the funeral service is provided. The IRS agent insists that the payments are prepaid income subject to tax in the year of receipt. Your client believes the amounts involved are customer deposits. Write a letter to Tranquility that contains your advice about how the issue should be resolved. The client's address is 400 Rock Street, Memphis, TN 38152.

Research Problem 2. Your client was the beneficiary of an annuity contract purchased by her stepmother. When the stepmother died, the insurance company paid the client $400,000 and sent her a Form 1099 indicating that the taxable portion (i.e., the amount in excess of the investment in the contract) was $50,000. However, according to the client, her father fraudulently convinced her that he was the intended beneficiary. She gave her father a check equal to the amount she had received from the insurance company. She did not report any of the annuity proceeds in her income tax return. She later discovered the fraud and filed a lawsuit to collect from her father. The IRS has examined your client's return and has taken the position that she must include the $50,000 in her gross income.

Evaluate the IRS's position.

Research Problem 3. Clint, your client, is considering a job that would require him to live in Alaska for two years. He has heard that residents of Alaska receive a payment each year from the state's "permanent fund," which is funded from mineral royalties. He would like to know whether the amounts received from the permanent fund must be included in his Federal taxable income.

Partial list of research aids:
IRS Publication 17, *Your Federal Income Tax.*

Research Problem 4. Employees of Alleghany Aggregates Company pay their employee travel expenses and are reimbursed by the company. Employees who travel by airline accumulate frequent-flyer miles, which the employees use for personal travel (e.g., vacations, visits to relatives). Are the employees required to include the value of the frequent-flyer miles in their gross income?

INTERNET *activity*

Use the tax resources of the Internet to address the following questions. Do not restrict your search to the Web, but include a review of newsgroups and general reference materials, practitioner sites and resources, primary sources of the tax law, chat rooms and discussion groups, and other opportunities.

Research Problem 5. Determine the applicable Federal rate for purposes of below-market loans. Use this figure to complete Problem 49 for this chapter.

COMMUNICATIONS

Research Problem 6. Go to the web page of a consulting firm that offers counseling services to individuals as they negotiate the terms of a divorce. What specific tax-related services do these firms offer? Send an e-mail message to one of these firms suggesting that it add a specific service or revise its web page to emphasize other tax-related services for its clients.

Gross Income: Exclusions

LEARNING OBJECTIVES

After completing Chapter 5, you should be able to:

L0.1

Understand that statutory authority is required to exclude an item from gross income.

L0.2

Identify the circumstances under which various items are excludible from gross income.

L0.3

Determine the extent to which receipts can be excluded under the tax benefit rule.

L0.4

Describe the circumstances under which income must be reported from the discharge of indebtedness.

L0.5

Identify tax planning strategies for obtaining the maximum benefit from allowable exclusions.

OUTLINE

FRAMEWORK 1040:
Tax Formula for Individuals

This chapter covers the boldfaced portions of the Tax Formula for Individuals that was introduced in Figure 3.1 on p. 3-3. Below those portions are the sections of Form 1040 where the results are reported.

Income (broadly conceived) .... $xx,xxx
Less: Exclusions .... (x,xxx)

FORM 1040 (p. 1)			
8b	**Tax-exempt** interest. **Do not** include on line 8a . . .	8b	

Gross income .... $xx,xxx

FORM 1040 (p. 1)	
10	Taxable refunds, credits, or offsets of state and local income taxes . . . .
19	Unemployment compensation . . . .
21	Other income. List type and amount _____

Less: Deductions for adjusted gross income . . . . (x,xxx)
Adjusted gross income. . . . . $xx,xxx
Less: The greater of total itemized deductions *or* the standard deduction. . . . . (x,xxx)
     Personal and dependency exemptions . . . . (x,xxx)
Taxable income . . . . $xx,xxx
Tax on taxable income (see Tax Tables or Tax Rate Schedules) . . . . $ x,xxx
Less: Tax credits (including income taxes withheld and prepaid) . . . . (xxx)
Tax due (or refund) . . . . $ xxx

THE BIG PICTURE   Tax Solutions for the Real World

EXCLUSIONS

Paul is a graduate student in the last semester of an accounting program at State University. This past summer he was an intern with a CPA firm, working in the compliance area. Paul was paid well enough for his work as an intern that he was able to pay for his meals and lodging and to save some for school. The CPA firm was so pleased with Paul's work that at the conclusion of his internship, he was given a bonus of $1,500 more than the firm had agreed to pay him. The extra amount was intended to help with his graduate school expenses. The CPA firm has offered him a full-time job after he completes his graduate program in December.

The university has awarded Paul a graduate assistantship that waives his tuition of $6,000 per semester and pays him $500 per month. Paul is required to teach a principles of accounting course each semester. Paul has used the $500 per month for books and for room and board.

In November, Paul was crossing a street in the pedestrian crosswalk when a delivery van struck him. The driver of the truck had a blood alcohol level of .12. Paul suffered a severe injury to his right arm that has delayed his starting date for work by three months. The delivery company's insurance company settled the case by paying damages, itemized as follows:

Compensatory damages:	
Medical expenses	$ 30,000
Injury to Paul's right arm	100,000
Pain and suffering	50,000
Loss of income	15,000
Legal fees	25,000
Punitive damages	160,000
	$380,000

Paul's mother was with him in the crosswalk. Fortunately, the van did not hit her, and she was not physically injured. But she did suffer emotional distress and received $25,000 in the settlement.

Besides being Paul's girlfriend, you also are a senior accounting major and have a keen interest in taxation. You tell Paul that you will look into the tax consequences of the settlement. **Read the chapter and formulate your response.**

5.1 ITEMS SPECIFICALLY EXCLUDED FROM GROSS INCOME

Chapter 4 discussed the concepts and judicial doctrines that affect the determination of gross income. If an income item is within the all-inclusive definition of gross income, the item can be excluded only if the taxpayer can locate specific authority for doing so. Chapter 5 focuses on the exclusions Congress has authorized. These exclusions are listed in Exhibit 5.1.

Tax advisers spend countless hours trying to develop techniques to achieve tax-exempt status for income. Employee benefits planning is greatly influenced by the availability of certain types of exclusions. Taxes play an important role in employee benefits, as well as in other situations, because attaining an exclusion is another means of enhancing after-tax income. For example, for a person whose combined Federal and state marginal tax rate is 40 percent, $1.00 of tax-exempt income is equivalent to $1.67 [$1 ÷ (1 − .4)] in income subject to taxation. The tax adviser's optimal strategy is to attach the right labels or provide the right wording to render income nontaxable without affecting the economics of the transaction.

Consider the case of an employee who is in the 28 percent marginal tax bracket and is paying $3,000 a year for health insurance. If the employer provided this protection in a manner that qualified for exclusion treatment but reduced the employee's salary by $3,000, the employee's after-tax and after-insurance income would increase at no additional cost to the employer.

Salary received to use to purchase health insurance	$ 3,000
Less: Taxes ($3,000 × 28%)	(840)
Cash available to purchase health insurance	$ 2,160
Less: Cost of health insurance	(3,000)
Excess of cost of health insurance over cash available	($ 840)

Thus, the employee in this case is $840 better off with a salary reduction of $3,000 and employer-provided health insurance. The employee may still decide that the $3,000 salary is preferable if, for example, the employee has access to health insurance through a spouse's employer. Understanding the tax influence, however, does enable the employee to make a more informed choice.

EXHIBIT 5.1   **Summary of Principal Exclusions from Gross Income**

1. Donative items
   Gifts, bequests, and inheritances (§ 102)
   Life insurance proceeds paid by reason of death (§ 101)
   Accelerated death benefits [§ 101(g)]
   Survivor benefits for public safety officer killed in the line of duty [§ 101(h)]
   Scholarships (§ 117)
2. Personal and welfare items
   Injury or sickness payments (§ 104)
   Public assistance payments (Rev.Rul. 71–425, 1971–2 C.B. 76)
   Amounts received under insurance contracts for certain living expenses (§ 123)
   Reimbursement for the costs of caring for a foster child (§ 131)
   Disaster relief payments (§ 139)
3. Wage and salary supplements
   a. Fringe benefits
      Accident and health benefits (§§ 105 and 106)
      Health Savings Accounts [§ 106(d)]
      Lodging and meals furnished for the convenience of the employer (§ 119)
      Rental value of parsonages (§ 107)
      Employee achievement awards [§ 74(c)]
      Employer contributions to employee group term life insurance (§ 79)
      Cafeteria plans (§ 125)
      Educational assistance payments (§ 127)
      Child or dependent care (§ 129)
      Services provided to employees at no additional cost to the employer (§ 132)
      Employee discounts (§ 132)
      Working condition and *de minimis* fringes (§ 132)
      Athletic facilities provided to employees (§ 132)
      Qualified transportation fringe (§ 132)
      Qualified moving expense reimbursement (§ 132)
      Qualified retirement planning services (§ 132)
      Tuition reductions granted to employees of educational institutions (§ 117)
      Child adoption expenses (§ 137)
      Long-term care insurance (§ 7702B)
   b. Military benefits
      Combat pay (§ 112)
      Housing, uniforms, and other benefits (§ 134)
   c. Foreign earned income (§ 911)
4. Investor items
   Interest on state and local government obligations (§ 103)
   Improvements by tenant to landlord's property (§ 109)
   Fifty percent, 75 percent, or 100 percent exclusion for gain from sale of certain small business stock (§ 1202)
5. Benefits for the elderly
   Social Security benefits (except in the case of certain higher-income taxpayers) (§ 86)
6. Other benefits
   Income from discharge of indebtedness (§ 108)
   Recovery of a prior year's deduction that yielded no tax benefit (§ 111)
   Gain from the sale of personal residence (§ 121)
   Educational savings bonds (§ 135)
   Qualified tuition program (§ 529)
   Coverdell Education Savings Account (§ 530)
   Lessee construction allowances for short-term leases (§ 110)
   Conservation cost-sharing payments (§ 126)

TAX in the NEWS

TOUGH ECONOMIC TIMES RAISE TOUGH TAX ISSUES

Individuals and businesses that were victims of the recent economic downturn received assistance in many different forms. The Federal government's "Cash for Clunkers" program benefited customers, automobile dealers, and automobile manufacturers. Various government programs assisted homeowners who could not meet their mortgage payments. Under one program, mortgage holders adjusted the terms of the loans so that homeowners could afford to make the mortgage payments and thereby avoid foreclosure. Clearly, under the broad concept of gross income, all of the beneficiaries of these programs experienced an increase in wealth. In many cases, however, assessing a tax seemed inappropriate under the circumstances; that is, the law and justice seemed to be at odds. Reconciliation could be achieved only by fitting the benefit received within one

of the existing categories of tax-exempt income or by creating new exclusions.

In a recent ruling, the IRS found a nonstatutory basis for excluding payments received by homeowners to assist them in meeting their mortgage obligations. Under the Federal Homeowner Affordability and Stability Plan, homeowners who had a record of meeting their mortgage payments but were currently experiencing financial difficulties were given cash payments to be applied toward their mortgages. The IRS ruled that "payments under governmental social benefit programs for the promotion of the general welfare and not for services rendered ... are not includible in the recipient's gross income."

Source: Rev.Rul. 2009–19, I.R.B. No. 28, 111 (June 23, 2009).

5.2 STATUTORY AUTHORITY

Sections 101 through 150 provide the authority for excluding specific items from gross income. In addition, other exclusions are scattered throughout the Code. Each exclusion has its own legislative history and reason for enactment. Certain exclusions are intended as a form of indirect welfare payments. Other exclusions prevent double taxation of income or provide incentives for socially desirable activities (e.g., nontaxable interest on certain U.S. government bonds where the owner uses the funds for educational expenses).

In some cases, Congress has enacted exclusions to rectify the effects of judicial decisions. For example, the Supreme Court held that the fair market value of improvements (not made in lieu of rent) made by a tenant to the landlord's property should be included in the landlord's gross income upon termination of the lease.[1] The landlord was required to include the value of the improvements in gross income even though the property had not been sold or otherwise disposed of. Congress provided relief in this situation by enacting § 109, which defers taxing the value of the improvements until the property is sold.[2]

At times Congress responds to specific events. For example, in 2001 Congress enacted § 139 to ensure that victims of a *qualified disaster* (disaster resulting from a terrorist attack, presidentially declared disaster, common carrier accident of a catastrophic nature) would not be required to include payments received for living expenses, funeral expenses, and property damage resulting from the disaster in gross income.

> **LO.1**
> Understand that statutory authority is required to exclude an item from gross income.

5.3 GIFTS AND INHERITANCES

GENERAL

Beginning with the Income Tax Act of 1913 and continuing to the present, Congress has allowed the recipient of a gift to exclude the value of the property from gross income. The exclusion applies to gifts made during the life of the donor (*inter vivos*

> **LO.2**
> Identify the circumstances under which various items are excludible from gross income.

---

[1] *Helvering v. Bruun,* 40–1 USTC ¶9337, 24 AFTR 652, 60 S.Ct. 631 (USSC, 1940).

[2] If the tenant made the improvements in lieu of rent, the value of the improvements is not eligible for exclusion.

TAX *in*
the NEWS

BEGGING AS A TAX-DISFAVORED OCCUPATION

In five recent decisions, the Tax Court ruled that amounts received from begging are nontaxable gifts. In a reversal of the normal roles, the beggars contended that the amounts received were earned income while the IRS argued that the taxpayers had merely received gifts. The beggars wanted the fruit of their efforts to be treated as earned income in order to qualify them for the earned income credit (see Chapter 13 for the discussion of the earned income credit).

gifts) and transfers that take effect upon the death of the donor (bequests and inheritances).[3] However, as discussed in Chapter 4, the recipient of a gift of income-producing property is subject to tax on the income subsequently earned from the property. Also, as discussed in Chapter 1, the donor or the decedent's estate may be subject to gift or estate taxes on the transfer.

In numerous cases, gifts are made in a business setting. For example, a salesperson gives a purchasing agent free samples; an employee receives cash from his or her employer on retirement; a corporation makes payments to employees who were victims of a natural disaster; a corporation makes a cash payment to a deceased employee's spouse. In these and similar instances, it is frequently unclear whether the payment was a gift or represents compensation for past, present, or future services.

The courts have defined a **gift** as "a voluntary transfer of property by one to another without adequate [valuable] consideration or compensation therefrom."[4] If the payment is intended to be for services rendered, it is not a gift, even though the payment is made without legal or moral obligation and the payor receives no economic benefit from the transfer. To qualify as a gift, the payment must be made "out of affection, respect, admiration, charity or like impulses."[5] Thus, the cases on this issue have been decided on the basis of the donor's intent.

In a landmark case, *Comm. v. Duberstein*,[6] the taxpayer (Duberstein) received a Cadillac from a business acquaintance. Duberstein had supplied the businessman with the names of potential customers with no expectation of compensation. The Supreme Court concluded:

> . . . despite the characterization of the transfer of the Cadillac by the parties [as a gift] and the absence of any obligation, even of a moral nature, to make it, it was at the bottom a recompense for Duberstein's past service, or an inducement for him to be of further service in the future.

Duberstein was therefore required to include the fair market value of the automobile in gross income.

GIFTS TO EMPLOYEES

In the case of cash or other property *received by an employee* from his or her employer, Congress has eliminated any ambiguity. Transfers from an employer to an employee cannot be excluded as a gift.[7] However, victims of a qualified disaster who are reimbursed by their employers for living expenses, funeral expenses, and property damage can exclude the payments from gross income under § 139, as previously discussed.

EMPLOYEE DEATH BENEFITS

Frequently, an employer makes payments (**death benefits**) to a deceased employee's surviving spouse, children, or other beneficiaries. If the decedent had a nonforfeitable right to the payments (e.g., the decedent's accrued salary), the amounts are generally

---

[3]§ 102.
[4]*Estate of D. R. Daly*, 3 B.T.A. 1042 (1926).
[5]*Robertson v. U.S.*, 52–1 USTC ¶9343, 41 AFTR 1053, 72 S.Ct. 994 (USSC, 1952).

[6]60–2 USTC ¶9515, 5 AFTR 2d 1626, 80 S.Ct. 1190 (USSC, 1960).
[7]§ 102(c).

TAX *in* the NEWS — AN INSURABLE INTEREST?

One of the tenets of insurance law is that the beneficiary of a life insurance policy must have an interest in the well-being of the person whose life is being insured that is substantial enough that insuring against the death of that person does not amount to a mere wager. In other words, the beneficiary must benefit in some way from the well-being of the insured and not merely be betting that the insured is going to die.

The principle of insurable interest is at the heart of a number of lawsuits involving "stranger-originated" life insurance policies that are now before the courts. Such policies typically come about when insurance agents and investors persuade an elderly person to take out a substantial life insurance policy. The insured person in turn sells the policy to the investors who then pay the premiums and collect the insurance when the person dies. Often there is little or no connection between the investors and the insured person.

In one case, both the beneficiary of the policy and the family of the decedent are suing American International

Group (AIG) to collect on a $15 million life insurance policy on a 74-year-old woman who drowned in her bathtub. The beneficiary of the policy, who was also the last person to see the decedent alive, claims that he took out the policy because the decedent was a director of his media company and that the insurance was simply "key person" insurance. AIG has refused to pay out the insurance on the ground that the beneficiary lacked an insurable interest in the decedent's life. Meanwhile, the decedent's family has entered the suit. They agree that the beneficiary lacked an insurable interest, but say that since AIG accepted the premiums, it should pay out the insurance proceeds—but to the family, not the beneficiary on the policy.

Source: Adapted from Leslie Scism and Mark Maremont, "More Life Insurance Was Sought on Woman," *Wall Street Journal*, April 14, 2010, p. A3.

EXAMPLE 2

Gold Corporation purchases a life insurance policy to cover its key employee. If the proceeds were taxable, the corporation would require more insurance coverage to pay the tax as well as to cover the economic loss of the employee. ∎

Thus, in general, Congress concluded that making life insurance proceeds exempt from income tax was a good policy.

ACCELERATED DEATH BENEFITS

Generally, if the owner of a life insurance policy cancels the policy and receives the cash surrender value, the taxpayer must recognize gain equal to the excess of the amount received over premiums paid on the policy (a loss is not deductible). The gain is recognized because the general exclusion provision for life insurance proceeds applies only to life insurance proceeds paid upon the death of the insured. If the taxpayer cancels the policy and receives the cash surrender value, the life insurance policy is treated as an investment by the insured.

In a limited circumstance, however, the insured is permitted to receive the benefits of the life insurance contract without having to include the gain in gross income. Under the **accelerated death benefits** provisions, exclusion treatment is available for insured taxpayers who are either terminally ill or chronically ill.[12] A terminally ill taxpayer can collect the cash surrender value of the policy from the insurance company or assign the policy proceeds to a qualified third party. The resultant gain, if any, is excluded from the insured's gross income. A *terminally ill* individual is one whom a medical doctor certifies as having an illness that is reasonably expected to cause death within 24 months.

In the case of a chronically ill patient, no gain is recognized if the proceeds of the policy are used for the long-term care of the insured. A person is *chronically ill* if he or she is certified as being unable to perform without assistance certain activities of daily living. These exclusions for the terminally ill and the chronically ill are available only to the insured. Thus, a person who purchases a life insurance policy from the insured does not qualify.

---

[12]§ 101(g).

TAX *in* the NEWS — FREQUENT-FLYER MILES WILL NOT BE TAXED

IRS officials believe that when a taxpayer receives frequent-flyer miles in connection with business travel, the taxpayer has received income. This is clearly true if the taxpayer has deducted the cost of the airline ticket. Under the tax benefit rule, the frequent-flyer miles should be included in gross income as a recovery of a prior deduction. If the employer pays for the business travel but the employee is awarded the frequent-flyer miles, the employee has obviously received additional compensation.

Nevertheless, the IRS has announced (Announcement 2002–18) that it will not attempt to tax frequent-flyer miles. The major consideration in creating this nonstatutory exemption was the complexity that would result from attempting to tax the miles. Distinguishing the miles awarded for personal travel (nontaxable reduction in the cost of ticket) from the business miles would be difficult. Furthermore, the valuation issues would be horrendous.

taxable to the recipient just the same as if the employee had lived and collected the payments. But when the employer makes voluntary payments, the gift issue arises. Generally, the IRS considers such payments to be compensation for prior services rendered by the deceased employee.[8] However, some courts have held that payments to an employee's surviving spouse or other beneficiaries are gifts if the following are true:[9]

- The payments were made to the surviving spouse and children rather than to the employee's estate.
- The employer derived no benefit from the payments.
- The surviving spouse and children performed no services for the employer.
- The decedent had been fully compensated for services rendered.
- Payments were made pursuant to a board of directors' resolution that followed a general company policy of providing payments for families of deceased employees (but not exclusively for families of shareholder-employees).

When all of the above conditions are satisfied, the payment is presumed to have been made *as an act of affection or charity*. When one or more of these conditions is not satisfied, the surviving spouse and children may still be deemed the recipients of a gift if the payment is made in light of the survivors' financial needs.[10]

5.4 LIFE INSURANCE PROCEEDS

GENERAL RULE

Life insurance proceeds paid to the beneficiary because of the death of the insured are exempt from income tax.[11]

> **EXAMPLE 1**
>
> Mark purchases an insurance policy on his life and names his wife, Linda, as the beneficiary. Mark pays $45,000 in premiums. When he dies, Linda collects the insurance proceeds of $200,000. The $200,000 is exempt from Federal income tax. ∎

Congress chose to exempt life insurance proceeds for the following reasons:

- For family members, life insurance proceeds serve much the same purpose as a nontaxable inheritance.
- In a business context (as well as in a family situation), life insurance proceeds replace an economic loss suffered by the beneficiary.

---

[8]Rev.Rul. 62–102, 1962–2 C.B. 37.

[9]*Estate of Sydney J. Carter v. Comm.*, 72–1 USTC ¶9129, 29 AFTR 2d 332, 453 F.2d 61 (CA–2, 1972), and the cases cited there.

[10]*Simpson v. U.S.*, 58–2 USTC ¶9923, 2 AFTR 2d 6036, 261 F.2d 497 (CA–7, 1958), *cert. denied* 79 S.Ct. 724 (USSC, 1958).

[11]§ 101(a).

EXAMPLE 3

Tom owned a term life insurance policy at the time he was diagnosed as having a terminal illness. After paying $5,200 in premiums, he sold the policy to Amber Benefits, Inc., a company that is authorized by the State of Virginia to purchase such policies. Amber paid Tom $50,000. When Tom died six months later, Amber collected the face amount of the policy, $75,000. Tom is not required to include the $44,800 gain ($50,000 − $5,200) on the sale of the policy in his gross income. Assume Amber pays additional premiums of $4,000 during the six-month period. When Amber collects the life insurance proceeds of $75,000, it must include the $21,000 gain [$75,000 proceeds − ($50,000 cost + $4,000 additional premiums paid)] in gross income. ■

ETHICS & Equity

SHOULD THE TERMINALLY ILL PAY SOCIAL SECURITY TAXES?

The rationale for excluding accelerated death benefits from the gross income of the terminally ill is that they often use the funds to pay medical expenses and other costs associated with dying and do not have the ability to pay tax on the gain from the accelerated receipt of the life insurance proceeds. Yet the wages of a terminally ill person who is employed (or profits of a self-employed person) are subject to Social Security taxes. The Social Security taxes are intended to pay for retirement benefits, but a terminally ill person is unlikely to collect any Social Security benefits.

Several bills have been introduced in Congress to exempt the terminally ill from the Social Security tax. Evaluate the equity of the current tax treatment versus that in the proposed legislation.

TRANSFER FOR VALUABLE CONSIDERATION

A life insurance policy (other than one associated with accelerated death benefits) may be transferred after it is issued by the insurance company. If the policy is *transferred for valuable consideration*, the insurance proceeds are includible in the gross income of the transferee to the extent the proceeds received exceed the amount paid for the policy by the transferee plus any subsequent premiums paid.

EXAMPLE 4

Adam pays premiums of $4,000 for an insurance policy in the face amount of $10,000 upon the life of Beth and subsequently transfers the policy to Carol for $6,000. On Beth's death, Carol receives the proceeds of $10,000. The amount that Carol can exclude from gross income is limited to $6,000 plus any premiums she paid subsequent to the transfer. ■

The Code, however, provides four exceptions to the rule illustrated in the preceding example. These exceptions permit exclusion treatment for transfers to the following:

1. A partner of the insured.
2. A partnership in which the insured is a partner.
3. A corporation in which the insured is an officer or shareholder.
4. A transferee whose basis in the policy is determined by reference to the transferor's basis.

The first three exceptions facilitate the use of insurance contracts to fund buy-sell agreements.

EXAMPLE 5

Rick and Sam are equal partners who have an agreement that allows either partner to purchase the interest of a deceased partner for $50,000. Neither partner has sufficient cash to actually buy the other partner's interest, but each has a life insurance policy on his own life in the amount of $50,000. Rick and Sam could exchange their policies (usually at little or no taxable gain), and upon the death of either partner, the surviving partner could collect tax-free insurance proceeds. The proceeds could then be used to purchase the decedent's interest in the partnership. ■

The fourth exception applies to policies that were transferred pursuant to a tax-free exchange or were received by gift.[13]

Investment earnings arising from the reinvestment of life insurance proceeds are generally subject to income tax. Often the beneficiary will elect to collect the insurance proceeds in installments. The annuity rules (discussed in Chapter 4) are used to apportion the installment payment between the principal element (excludible) and the interest element (includible).[14]

5.5 SCHOLARSHIPS

GENERAL INFORMATION

Payments or benefits received by a student at an educational institution may be (1) compensation for services, (2) a gift, or (3) a scholarship. If the payments or benefits are received as compensation for services (past or present), the fact that the recipient is a student generally does not render the amounts received nontaxable.[15]

EXAMPLE 6
THE BIG PICTURE

Return to the facts of *The Big Picture* on p. 5-2. State University waives tuition for all graduate teaching assistants. The tuition waived is intended as compensation for services and is therefore included in the graduate assistant's gross income.

Therefore, the $6,000 Paul received in the form of a tuition waiver each semester is compensation for his services. The $500 he received each month also is compensation for services. The fact that he used the funds for educational expenses does not change the tax treatment of the compensation. ∎

As discussed earlier, gifts are not includible in gross income.

The **scholarship** rules are intended to provide exclusion treatment for education-related benefits that cannot qualify as gifts but are not compensation for services. According to the Regulations, "a scholarship is an amount paid or allowed to, or for the benefit of, an individual to aid such individual in the pursuit of study or research."[16] The recipient must be a candidate for a degree at an educational institution.[17]

EXAMPLE 7

Terry enters a contest sponsored by a local newspaper. Each contestant is required to submit an essay on local environmental issues. The prize is one year's tuition at State University. Terry wins the contest. The newspaper has a legal obligation to Terry (as contest winner). Thus, the benefits are not a gift. However, since the tuition payment aids Terry in pursuing her studies, the payment is a scholarship. ∎

A scholarship recipient may exclude from gross income the amount used for tuition and related expenses (fees, books, supplies, and equipment required for courses), provided the conditions of the grant do not require that the funds be used for other purposes.[18] Amounts received for room and board are *not* excludible and are treated as earned income for purposes of calculating the standard deduction for a taxpayer who is another taxpayer's dependent.[19]

---

[13]See the discussion of gifts in Chapter 14 and tax-free exchanges in Chapters 15 and 20.

[14]Reg. §§ 1.72–7(c)(1) and 1.101–7T.

[15]Reg. § 1.117–2(a). See *C. P. Bhalla*, 35 T.C. 13 (1960), for a discussion of the distinction between a scholarship and compensation. See also *Bingler v. Johnson*, 69–1 USTC ¶9348, 23 AFTR 2d 1212, 89 S.Ct. 1439 (USSC, 1969).

For potential exclusion treatment, see the subsequent discussion of qualified tuition reductions.

[16]Prop.Reg. § 1.117–6(c)(3)(i).

[17]§ 117(a).

[18]§ 117(b).

[19]Prop.Reg. § 1.117–6(h).

EXAMPLE 8

Kelly receives a scholarship of $9,500 from State University to be used to pursue a bachelor's degree. She spends $4,000 on tuition, $3,000 on books and supplies, and $2,500 for room and board. Kelly may exclude $7,000 ($4,000 + $3,000) from gross income. The $2,500 spent for room and board is includible in Kelly's gross income.

   The scholarship is Kelly's only source of income. Her parents provide more than 50% of Kelly's support and claim her as a dependent. Kelly's standard deduction of $2,800 ($2,500 + $300) exceeds her $2,500 gross income. Thus, she has no taxable income. ∎

TIMING ISSUES

Frequently, the scholarship recipient is a cash basis taxpayer who receives the money in one tax year but pays the educational expenses in a subsequent year. The amount eligible for exclusion may not be known at the time the money is received. In that case, the transaction is held *open* until the educational expenses are paid.[20]

EXAMPLE 9

In August 2011, Sanjay received $10,000 as a scholarship for the academic year 2011–2012. Sanjay's expenditures for tuition, books, and supplies were as follows:

August–December 2011	$3,000
January–May 2012	4,500
	$7,500

Sanjay's gross income for 2012 includes $2,500 ($10,000 − $7,500) that is not excludible as a scholarship. None of the scholarship is included in his gross income in 2011. ∎

DISGUISED COMPENSATION

Some employers make scholarships available solely to the children of key employees. The tax objective of these plans is to provide a nontaxable fringe benefit to the executives by making the payment to the child in the form of an excludible scholarship. However, the IRS has ruled that the payments are generally includible in the gross income of the parent-employee.[21]

QUALIFIED TUITION REDUCTION PLANS

Employees (including retired and disabled former employees) of nonprofit educational institutions are allowed to exclude a tuition waiver from gross income if the waiver is pursuant to a **qualified tuition reduction plan**.[22] The plan may not discriminate in favor of highly compensated employees. The exclusion applies to the employee, the employee's spouse, and the employee's dependent children. The exclusion also extends to tuition reductions granted by any nonprofit educational institution to employees of any other nonprofit educational institution (reciprocal agreements).

EXAMPLE 10

ABC University allows the dependent children of XYZ University employees to attend ABC University with no tuition charge. XYZ University grants reciprocal benefits to the children of ABC University employees. The dependent children can also attend tuition-free the university where their parents are employed. Employees who take advantage of these benefits are not required to recognize gross income. ∎

   Generally, the exclusion is limited to *undergraduate* tuition waivers. However, in the case of teaching or research assistants, graduate tuition waivers may also qualify for exclusion treatment. According to the Proposed Regulations, the exclusion is limited to the value of the benefit in excess of the employee's reasonable

---

[20]Prop.Reg. § 1.117–6(b)(2).   [22]§ 117(d).
[21]Rev.Rul. 75–448, 1975–2 C.B. 55; *Richard T. Armantrout*, 67 T.C. 996 (1977).

compensation.[23] Thus, a tuition reduction that is a substitute for cash compensation cannot be excluded.

EXAMPLE 11

Susan is a graduate research assistant. She receives a $5,000 salary for 500 hours of service over a nine-month period. This pay, $10 per hour, is reasonable compensation for Susan's services. In addition, Susan receives a waiver of $6,000 for tuition. Susan may exclude the tuition waiver from gross income. ■

5.6 COMPENSATION FOR INJURIES AND SICKNESS

DAMAGES

A person who suffers harm caused by another is often entitled to compensatory damages. The tax consequences of the receipt of damages depend on the type of harm the taxpayer has experienced. The taxpayer may seek recovery for (1) a loss of income, (2) expenses incurred, (3) property destroyed, or (4) personal injury.

Generally, reimbursement for a loss of income is taxed the same as the income replaced (see the exception under Personal Injury below). The recovery of an expense is not income, unless the expense was deducted. Damages that are a recovery of the taxpayer's previously deducted expenses are generally taxable under the tax benefit rule, discussed later in this chapter.

A payment for damaged or destroyed property is treated as an amount received in a sale or exchange of the property. Thus, the taxpayer has a realized gain if the damages payments received exceed the property's basis. Damages for personal injuries receive special treatment under the Code.

Personal Injury

The legal theory of personal injury damages is that the amount received is intended "to make the plaintiff [the injured party] whole as before the injury."[24] It follows that if the damages payments received were subject to tax, the after-tax amount received would be less than the actual damages incurred and the injured party would not be "whole as before the injury."

In terms of personal injury damages, a distinction is made between compensatory damages and punitive damages. Under specified circumstances, compensatory damages may be excluded from gross income. Under no circumstances may punitive damages be excluded from gross income.

Compensatory damages are intended to compensate the taxpayer for the damages incurred. Only those compensatory damages received on account of *physical personal injury or physical sickness* can be excluded from gross income.[25] Such exclusion treatment includes amounts received for loss of income associated with the physical personal injury or physical sickness. Compensatory damages awarded on account of emotional distress are not received on account of physical injury or physical sickness and thus cannot be excluded (except to the extent of any amount received for medical care) from gross income. Likewise, any amounts received for age discrimination or injury to one's reputation cannot be excluded.

Punitive damages are amounts the person who caused the harm must pay to the victim as punishment for outrageous conduct. Punitive damages are not intended to compensate the victim, but rather to punish the party who caused the harm. Thus, it follows that amounts received as punitive damages may actually place the victim in a better economic position than before the harm was experienced. Logically, punitive damages are thus included in gross income.

---

[23]Prop.Reg. § 1.117–6(d).
[24]*C. A. Hawkins,* 6 B.T.A. 1023 (1928).

[25]§ 104(a)(2).

TAX in the NEWS

THE TAX ON A WHISTLEBLOWER'S DAMAGES AWARD DECLARED UNCONSTITUTIONAL—FOR A SHORT WHILE

When an employer retaliated against a whistleblowing employee who had reported various alleged infractions, the employee was awarded compensatory damages for emotional distress and damage to her professional reputation. In *Murphy v. IRS*, the U.S. Court of Appeals for the D.C. Circuit recently held that the award was not includible in gross income, but rather was a recovery of capital. The court concluded that Congress exceeded the bounds of its constitutional authority when it enacted a statute that taxes as income damages received for nonphysical injury. Most commentators thought that the Supreme Court would reverse the decision because the taxpayer had no capital invested in the emotions that gave rise to the damages award.

Rather than filing a Writ of Certiorari with the Supreme Court, the government petitioned the Court of Appeals for the D.C. Circuit to rehear the case. In the rehearing, the court changed its mind. It rejected all of "Murphy's arguments in all aspects." So the full amount of the award Murphy received must be included in gross income.

EXAMPLE 12
THE BIG PICTURE

Return to the facts of *The Big Picture* on p. 5-2. The damages Paul received were awarded as a result of a physical personal injury. Therefore, all of the compensatory damages can be excluded. Note that even the compensation for the loss of income of $15,000 can be excluded. The punitive damages Paul received, however, must be included in his gross income.

Paul's mother did not suffer a personal physical injury or sickness. Therefore, the $25,000 she received must be included in her gross income. ∎

WORKERS' COMPENSATION

State workers' compensation laws require the employer to pay fixed amounts for specific job-related injuries. The state laws were enacted so that the employee will not have to go through the ordeal of a lawsuit (and possibly not collect damages because of some defense available to the employer) to recover the damages. Although the payments are intended, in part, to compensate for a loss of future income, Congress has specifically exempted workers' compensation benefits from inclusion in gross income.[26]

ACCIDENT AND HEALTH INSURANCE BENEFITS

The income tax treatment of accident and health insurance benefits depends on whether the policy providing the benefits was purchased by the taxpayer or the taxpayer's employer. Benefits collected under an accident and health insurance policy *purchased by the taxpayer* are excludible. In this case, benefits collected under the taxpayer's insurance policy are excluded even though the payments are a substitute for income.[27]

EXAMPLE 13

Bonnie purchases a medical and disability insurance policy. The insurance company pays Bonnie $1,000 per week to replace wages she loses while in the hospital. Although the payments serve as a substitute for income, the amounts received are tax-exempt benefits collected under Bonnie's insurance policy. ∎

EXAMPLE 14

Joe's injury results in a partial paralysis of his left foot. He receives $20,000 for the injury from his accident insurance company under a policy he had purchased. The $20,000 accident insurance proceeds are tax-exempt. ∎

---

[26]§ 104(a)(1).   [27]§ 104(a)(3).

CONCEPT SUMMARY 5.1

Taxation of Damages

Type of Claim	Taxation of Award or Settlement
Breach of contract (generally loss of income)	Taxable.
Property damages	Recovery of cost; gain to the extent of the excess over basis. A loss is deductible for business property and investment property to the extent of basis over the amount realized. A loss may be deductible for personal use property (see discussion of casualty losses in Chapter 7).
Personal injury	
Physical	All compensatory amounts are excluded unless previously deducted (e.g., medical expenses). Amounts received as punitive damages are included in gross income.
Nonphysical	Compensatory damages and punitive damages are included in gross income.

ETHICS & Equity — TAX TREATMENT OF DAMAGES NOT RELATED TO PHYSICAL PERSONAL INJURY

An individual who prevails in a personal injury claim for something other than a physical injury or sickness must include the amount of the award or settlement in gross income. In contrast, an award or settlement for a physical personal injury or sickness can be excluded (except for punitive damages) from gross income. Should damages awarded for a physical personal injury or sickness be treated more favorably than damages awarded for emotional distress or other nonphysical personal injuries such as age and sex discrimination?

A different set of rules applies if the accident and health insurance protection was *purchased by the individual's employer*, as discussed in the following section.

5.7 EMPLOYER-SPONSORED ACCIDENT AND HEALTH PLANS

Congress encourages employers to provide employees, retired former employees, and their dependents with **accident and health benefits**, disability insurance, and long-term care plans. The *premiums* are deductible by the employer and excluded from the employee's income.[28] Although § 105(a) provides the general rule that the employee has includible income when he or she collects the insurance *benefits*, two exceptions are provided.

Section 105(b) generally excludes payments received for medical care of the employee, spouse, and dependents. However, if the payments are for expenses that do

---

[28] § 106, Reg. § 1.106–1, and Rev.Rul. 82–196, 1982–1 C.B. 106.

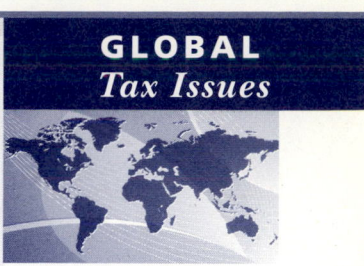

GLOBAL
Tax Issues

WHEN JOBS LEAVE THE COUNTRY, SO DO THE HEALTH INSURANCE BENEFITS

Firms in the textile industry generally provided health insurance coverage for their employees. As textile mills in the United States close and production is moved to foreign countries, often the U.S. employees lose their health insurance as well as their jobs. If and when the former textile worker finds new employment, the new employer may not provide health insurance. In addition, the pay on the new job is often so low that the worker cannot afford to purchase health insurance, which may cost over $500 per month.

Among the factors contributing to increased foreign competition for the domestic textile industry are the North American Free Trade Agreement of 1993, the Caribbean Basin Initiative of 2000, and the opening up of trade with China.

not meet the Code's definition of medical care,[29] the amount received must be included in gross income. In addition, the taxpayer must include in gross income any amounts received for medical expenses that were deducted by the taxpayer on a prior return.

EXAMPLE 15

In 2011, Tab's employer-sponsored health insurance plan pays $4,000 for hair transplants that do not meet the Code's definition of medical care. Tab must include the $4,000 in his gross income for 2011. ■

Section 105(c) excludes payments for the permanent loss or the loss of the use of a member or function of the body or the permanent disfigurement of the employee, spouse, or a dependent. Payments that are a substitute for salary (e.g., related to the period of time absent) are includible.

EXAMPLE 16

Jill loses an eye in an automobile accident unrelated to her work. As a result of the accident, Jill incurs $2,000 of medical expenses, which she deducts on her return. She collects $10,000 from an accident insurance policy carried by her employer. The benefits are paid according to a schedule of amounts that vary with the part of the body injured (e.g., $10,000 for loss of an eye, $20,000 for loss of a hand). Because the payment is for loss of a *member or function of the body*, the $10,000 is excluded from gross income. Jill is absent from work for a week as a result of the accident. Her employer provides her with insurance for the loss of income due to illness or injury. Jill collects $500, which is includible in gross income. ■

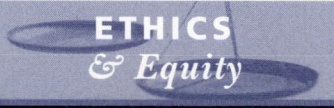

ETHICS
& Equity   THE HEALTH CARE EXCLUSIONS AFFECT PROGRESSIVITY OF THE TAX

Employer-provided health insurance and medical reimbursement plans are usually provided to employees in the middle- and higher-income classes. The lower-income groups frequently have jobs that do not provide health care benefits. Furthermore, those taxpayers in the higher tax brackets can benefit more in terms of absolute dollars of tax savings from the exclusions than can lower-income employees. To provide equity to the lower-income taxpayers who do receive health insurance benefits from their employers, should the health benefit exclusion be replaced with a tax credit?

---

[29]See the discussion of medical care in Chapter 10.

MEDICAL REIMBURSEMENT PLANS

In lieu of providing the employee with insurance coverage for hospital and medical expenses, the employer may agree to reimburse the employee for these expenses. The amounts received through the insurance coverage (insured plan benefits) are excluded from income under § 105 (as previously discussed). Unfortunately in terms of cost considerations, the insurance companies that issue this type of policy usually require a broad coverage of employees. An alternative is to have a plan that is not funded with insurance (a self-insured arrangement). The benefits received under a self-insured plan can be excluded from the employee's income if the plan does not discriminate in favor of highly compensated employees.[30]

There is also an alternative means of accomplishing a medical reimbursement plan. The employer can purchase a medical insurance plan with a high deductible (e.g., the employee is responsible for the first $2,400 of the family's medical expenses) and then make contributions to the employee's **Health Savings Account (HSA)**.[31] The employer can make contributions each month up to the maximum contribution of 100 percent of the deductible amount. The monthly deductible amount is limited to one-twelfth of $3,050 under a high-deductible plan for self-only coverage. The monthly amount for an individual who has family coverage is limited to one-twelfth of $6,150 under a high-deductible plan. Withdrawals from the HSA must be used to reimburse the employee for the medical expenses paid by the employee that are not covered under the high-deductible plan. The employee is not taxed on the employer's contributions to the HSA, the earnings on the funds in the account, or the withdrawals made for medical expenses.[32]

LONG-TERM CARE INSURANCE BENEFITS

Generally, **long-term care insurance,** which covers expenses such as the cost of care in a nursing home, is treated the same as accident and health insurance benefits. Thus, the employee does not recognize income when the employer pays the premiums. This exclusion is subject to annual limits as follows:

Insured's Age before Close of Tax Year	2010	2011
40 or less	$ 330	$ 340
41 to 50	620	640
51 to 60	1,230	1,270
61 to 70	3,290	3,390
More than 70	4,110	4,240

When benefits are received from the policy, whether the employer or the individual purchased the policy, the exclusion from gross income is limited to the greater of the following amounts:

- $300 in 2011 (indexed amount for 2010 was $290) for each day the patient receives the long-term care.
- The actual cost of the care.

The above amount is reduced by any amounts received from other third parties (e.g., damages received).[33]

EXAMPLE 17

Hazel, who suffers from Alzheimer's disease, is a patient in a nursing home for the last 30 days of 2011. While in the nursing home, she incurs total costs of $7,600. Medicare

---

[30]§ 105(h).
[31]§§ 106(d) and 223. See additional coverage in Chapter 10.

[32]§§ 106(d), 223(b), and 223(d). The amounts for 2010 were $3,050 and $6,150.
[33]§§ 7702B and § 213(d)(10).

pays $3,200 of the costs. Hazel receives $6,000 from her long-term care insurance policy (which pays $200 per day while she is in the facility).

The amount that Hazel may exclude is calculated as follows:

Greater of:		
Daily statutory amount of $300 ($300 × 30 days)	$9,000	
Actual cost of the care	7,600	$ 9,000
Less: Amount received from Medicare		(3,200)
Amount of exclusion		$ 5,800

Therefore, Hazel must include $200 ($6,000 − $5,800) of the long-term care benefits received in her gross income. ∎

The exclusion for long-term care insurance is not available if it is provided as part of a cafeteria plan or a flexible spending plan.

5.8 MEALS AND LODGING

FURNISHED FOR THE CONVENIENCE OF THE EMPLOYER

As discussed in Chapter 4, income can take any form, including meals and lodging. However, § 119 excludes from income the value of meals and lodging provided to the employee and the employee's spouse and dependents under the following conditions:[34]

- The meals and/or lodging are *furnished* by the employer, on the employer's *business premises*, for the *convenience of the employer.*
- In the case of lodging, the *employee is required* to accept the lodging as a condition of employment.

The courts have construed both of these requirements strictly.

Furnished by the Employer

The following two questions have been raised with regard to the *furnished by the employer* requirement:

- Who is considered an *employee?*
- What is meant by *furnished?*

The IRS and some courts have reasoned that because a partner is not an employee, the exclusion does not apply to a partner. However, the Tax Court and the Fifth Circuit Court of Appeals have ruled in favor of the taxpayer on this issue.[35]

The Supreme Court held that a cash meal allowance was ineligible for the exclusion because the employer did not actually furnish the meals.[36] Similarly, one court denied the exclusion where the employer paid for the food and supplied the cooking facilities but the employee prepared the meal.[37]

On the Employer's Business Premises

The *on the employer's business premises* requirement, applicable to both meals and lodging, has resulted in much litigation. The Regulations define business premises as simply "the place of employment of the employee."[38] Thus, the Sixth Circuit Court of Appeals held that a residence, owned by the employer and occupied

---

[34]§ 119(a). The meals and lodging are also excluded from FICA and FUTA tax. *Rowan Companies, Inc. v. U.S.,* 81–1 USTC ¶9479, 48 AFTR 2d 81–5115, 101 S.Ct. 2288 (USSC, 1981).

[35]Rev.Rul. 80, 1953–1 C.B. 62; *Comm. v. Doak,* 56–2 USTC ¶9708, 49 AFTR 1491, 234 F.2d 704 (CA–4, 1956); but see *G. A. Papineau,* 16 T.C. 130 (1951); *Armstrong v. Phinney,* 68–1 USTC ¶9355, 21 AFTR 2d 1260, 394 F.2d 661 (CA–5, 1968).

[36]*Comm. v. Kowalski,* 77–2 USTC ¶9748, 40 AFTR 2d 6128, 98 S.Ct. 315 (USSC, 1977).

[37]*Tougher v. Comm.,* 71–1 USTC ¶9398, 27 AFTR 2d 1301, 441 F.2d 1148 (CA–9, 1971).

[38]Reg. § 1.119–1(c)(1).

by an employee, two blocks from the motel that the employee managed was not part of the business premises.[39] However, the Tax Court considered an employer-owned house across the street from the hotel that was managed by the taxpayer to be on the business premises of the employer.[40] Apparently, the closer the lodging to the business operations, the more likely the convenience of the employer is served.

For the Convenience of the Employer

The *convenience of the employer* test is intended to focus on the employer's motivation for furnishing the meals and lodging rather than on the benefits received by the employee. If the employer furnishes the meals and lodging primarily to enable the employee to perform his or her duties properly, it does not matter that the employee considers these benefits to be a part of his or her compensation.

The Regulations give the following examples in which the tests for excluding meals are satisfied:[41]

- A restaurant requires its service staff to eat their meals on the premises during the busy lunch and breakfast hours.
- A bank furnishes meals on the premises for its tellers to limit the time the employees are away from their booths during the busy hours.
- A worker is employed at a construction site in a remote part of Alaska. The employer must furnish meals and lodging due to the inaccessibility of other facilities.

If more than half of the employees to whom meals are furnished receive their meals for the convenience of the employer, then all such employee meals are treated as provided for the convenience of the employer.[42] Thus, in this situation, all employees are treated the same (either all of the employees are allowed exclusion treatment, or none of the employees can exclude the meals from gross income).

EXAMPLE 18

Allison's Restaurant has a restaurant area and a bar. Nine employees work in the restaurant and three work in the bar. All of the employees are provided one meal per day. In the case of the restaurant workers, the meals are provided for the convenience of the employer. The meals provided to the bar employees do not satisfy the convenience of the employer requirement. Because more than half of the employees receive their meal for the convenience of the employer, all 12 employees qualify for exclusion treatment. ∎

Required as a Condition of Employment

The *employee is required to accept* test applies only to lodging. If the employee's use of the housing would serve the convenience of the employer, but the employee is not required to use the housing, the exclusion is not available.

EXAMPLE 19

VEP, a utilities company, has all of its service personnel on 24-hour call for emergencies. The company encourages its employees to live near the plant so that the employees can respond quickly to emergency calls. Company-owned housing is available rent-free. Only 10 of the employees live in the company housing because it is not suitable for families.

Although the company-provided housing serves the convenience of the employer, it is not required. Therefore, the employees who live in the company housing cannot exclude its value from gross income. ∎

---

[39] *Comm. v. Anderson,* 67–1 USTC ¶9136, 19 AFTR 2d 318, 371 F.2d 59 (CA–6, 1966).

[40] *J. B. Lindeman,* 60 T.C. 609 (1973).

[41] Reg. § 1.119–1(f).

[42] § 119(b)(4).

In addition, if the employee has the *option* of cash or lodging, the *required* test is not satisfied.

	EXAMPLE 20

Khalid is the manager of a large apartment complex. The employer gives Khalid the option of rent-free housing (value of $6,000 per year) or an additional $5,000 per year. Khalid selects the housing option. Therefore, he must include $6,000 in gross income. ∎

OTHER HOUSING EXCLUSIONS

Employees of Educational Institutions

An employee of an educational institution may be able to exclude the value of campus housing provided by the employer. Generally, the employee does not recognize income if he or she pays annual rents equal to or greater than 5 percent of the appraised value of the facility. If the rent payments are less than 5 percent of the value of the facility, the deficiency must be included in gross income.[43]

	EXAMPLE 21

Swan University provides on-campus housing for its full-time faculty during the first three years of employment. The housing is not provided for the convenience of the employer. Professor Edith pays $3,000 annual rent for the use of a residence with an appraised value of $100,000 and an annual rental value of $12,000. Edith must recognize $2,000 of gross income [.05($100,000) − $3,000 = $2,000] for the value of the housing provided to her. ∎

Ministers of the Gospel

Ministers of the gospel and other religious leaders can exclude (1) the rental value of a home furnished as compensation; (2) a rental allowance paid to them as compensation, to the extent the allowance is used to rent or provide a home; or (3) the rental value of a home owned by the minister.[44] The housing or housing allowance must be provided as compensation for the conduct of religious worship, the administration and maintenance of religious organizations, or the performance of teaching and administrative duties at theological seminaries.

	EXAMPLE 22

Pastor Bill is allowed to live rent-free in a house owned by the congregation. The annual rental value of the house is $6,000 and is provided as part of the pastor's compensation for ministerial services. Assistant Pastor Olga is paid a $4,500 cash housing allowance. She uses the $4,500 to pay rent and utilities on a home she and her family occupy. Neither Pastor Bill nor Assistant Pastor Olga is required to recognize gross income associated with the housing or housing allowance. ∎

Military Personnel

Military personnel are allowed housing exclusions under various circumstances. Authority for these exclusions generally is found in Federal laws that are not part of the Internal Revenue Code.[45]

5.9 OTHER EMPLOYEE FRINGE BENEFITS

SPECIFIC BENEFITS

Congress has enacted exclusions to encourage employers to (1) finance and make available child care facilities, (2) provide athletic facilities for employees, (3) finance

---

[43]§ 119(d).
[44]§ 107 and Reg. § 1.107–1.

[45]H. Rep. No. 99–841, 99th Cong., 2d Sess., p. 548 (1986). See also § 134.

certain employees' education, and (4) pay or reimburse child adoption expenses. These provisions are summarized as follows:

- The employee does not have to include in gross income the value of child and dependent care services paid for by the employer and incurred to enable the employee to work. The exclusion cannot exceed $5,000 per year ($2,500 if married and filing separately). For a married couple, the annual exclusion cannot exceed the earned income of the spouse who has the lesser amount of earned income. For an unmarried taxpayer, the exclusion cannot exceed the taxpayer's earned income.[46]

- The value of the use of a gymnasium or other athletic facilities by employees, their spouses, and their dependent children may be excluded from an employee's gross income. The facilities must be on the employer's premises, and substantially all of the use of the facilities must be by employees and their family members.[47]

- Qualified employer-provided educational assistance (tuition, fees, books, and supplies) at the undergraduate and graduate level is excludible from gross income. The exclusion does not cover meals, lodging, and transportation costs. In addition, it does not cover educational payments for courses involving sports, games, or hobbies. The exclusion is subject to an annual employee statutory ceiling of $5,250.[48]

- The employee can exclude from gross income up to $13,360 of expenses incurred to adopt a child where the adoption expenses are paid or reimbursed by the employer under a qualified adoption assistance program.[49] The limit on the exclusion is the same even if the child has special needs (is not physically or mentally capable of caring for himself or herself). However, for a child with special needs, the $13,360 exclusion from gross income applies even if the actual adoption expenses are less than that amount. The exclusion is phased out as adjusted gross income increases from $185,210 to $225,210.

CAFETERIA PLANS

Generally, if an employee is offered a choice between cash and some other form of compensation, the employee is deemed to have constructively received the cash even when the noncash option is elected. Thus, the employee has gross income regardless of the option chosen.

An exception to this constructive receipt treatment is provided under the **cafeteria plan** rules. Under such a plan, the employee is permitted to choose between cash and nontaxable benefits (e.g., group term life insurance, health and accident protection, and child care). If the employee chooses the otherwise nontaxable benefits, the cafeteria plan rules enable the benefits to remain nontaxable.[50] Cafeteria plans provide tremendous flexibility in tailoring the employee pay package to fit individual needs. Some employees (usually the younger group) prefer cash, while others (usually the older group) will opt for the fringe benefit program. However, Congress excluded long-term care insurance from the excludible benefits that can be provided under a cafeteria plan.[51] Thus, the employer must provide these benefits separate from the cafeteria plan.

EXAMPLE 23	Hawk Corporation offers its employees (on a nondiscriminatory basis) a choice of any one or all of the following benefits:

---

[46]§ 129. The exclusion applies to the same types of expenses that, if they were paid by the employee (and not reimbursed by the employer), would be eligible for the credit for child and dependent care expense discussed in Chapter 13.

[47]§ 132(j)(4).

[48]§ 127.

[49]§ 137.

[50]§ 125.

[51]§ 125(f).

Benefit	Cost
Group term life insurance	$ 200
Hospitalization insurance for family members	2,400
Child care payments	1,800
	$4,400

If a benefit is not selected, the employee receives cash equal to the cost of the benefit. Kay, an employee, has a spouse who works for another employer that provides hospitalization insurance but no child care payments. Kay elects to receive the group term life insurance, the child care payments, and $2,400 of cash. Only the $2,400 must be included in Kay's gross income. ■

FLEXIBLE SPENDING PLANS

Flexible spending plans (often referred to as flexible benefit plans) operate much like cafeteria plans. Under these plans, the employee accepts lower cash compensation in return for the employer agreeing to pay certain costs that the employer can pay without the employee recognizing gross income. For example, assume the employer's health insurance policy does not cover dental expenses. The employee could estimate his or her dental expenses for the upcoming year and agree to a salary reduction equal to the estimated dental expenses. The employer then pays or reimburses the employee for the actual dental expenses incurred, with a ceiling of the amount of the salary reduction. If the employee's actual dental expenses are less than the reduction in cash compensation, the employee cannot recover the difference. Hence, these plans are often referred to as *use or lose* plans. As is the case for cafeteria plans, flexible spending plans cannot be used to pay long-term care insurance premiums.

Under recently issued IRS rules for these *use or lose* plans, the taxpayer has until the fifteenth day of the third month after the end of the plan year to use the funds for qualified expenses (a two and one-half month grace period). Employers have generally amended their plans to provide that payments made during the grace period will be taken first from the balance in the flexible spending account at the beginning of the plan year.

GENERAL CLASSES OF EXCLUDED BENEFITS

An employer can confer numerous forms and types of economic benefits on employees. Under the all-inclusive concept of income, the benefits are taxable unless one of the provisions previously discussed specifically excludes the item from gross income. The amount of the income is the fair market value of the benefit. This reasoning can lead to results that Congress considers unacceptable, as illustrated in the following example.

EXAMPLE 24

Vern is employed in New York as a ticket clerk for Trans National Airlines. He has a sick mother in Miami, Florida, but has no money for plane tickets. Trans National has daily flights from New York to Miami that often leave with empty seats. The cost of a round-trip ticket is $400, and Vern is in the 25% tax bracket. If Trans National allows Vern to fly without charge to Miami, under the general gross income rules, Vern has income equal to the value of a ticket. Therefore, Vern must pay $100 tax (.25 × $400) on a trip to Miami. Because Vern does not have $100, he cannot visit his mother, and the airplane flies with another empty seat. ■

If Trans National in Example 24 will allow employees to use resources that would otherwise be wasted, why should the tax laws interfere with the employee's decision to take advantage of the available benefit? Thus, to avoid the undesirable results that occur in Example 24 and in similar situations, as well as to create uniform rules for fringe benefits, Congress established seven broad classes of nontaxable employee benefits:[52]

- No-additional-cost services.
- Qualified employee discounts.
- Working condition fringes.
- *De minimis* fringes.
- Qualified transportation fringes.
- Qualified moving expense reimbursements.
- Qualified retirement planning services.

No–Additional-Cost Services

Example 24 illustrates the **no-additional-cost service** type of fringe benefit. The services will be nontaxable if all of the following conditions are satisfied:

- The employee receives services, as opposed to property.
- The employer does not incur substantial additional cost, including forgone revenue, in providing the services to the employee.
- The services are offered to customers in the ordinary course of the business in which the employee works.[53]

EXAMPLE 25

Assume that Vern in Example 24 can fly without charge only if the airline cannot fill the seats with paying customers. That is, Vern must fly on standby. Although the airplane may burn slightly more fuel because Vern is on the airplane and Vern may receive the same meal or snacks as paying customers, the additional costs would not be substantial. Thus, the trip could qualify as a no-additional-cost service.

On the other hand, assume that Vern is given a reserved seat on a flight that is frequently full. The employer would be forgoing revenue to allow Vern to fly. This forgone revenue would be a substantial additional cost, and thus the benefit would be taxable. ▪

Note that if Vern were employed in a hotel owned by Trans National, the receipt of the airline ticket would be taxable because Vern did not work in that line of business. However, the Code allows the exclusion for reciprocal benefits offered by employers in the same line of business.

EXAMPLE 26

Grace is employed as a desk clerk for Plush Hotels, Inc. The company and Chain Hotels, Inc., have an agreement that allows any of their employees to stay without charge in either company's resort hotels during the off-season. If Grace takes advantage of the plan by staying in a Chain Hotel, she is not required to recognize income. ▪

---

[52]See, generally, § 132.

[53]Reg. § 1.132–2.

The no-additional-cost exclusion extends to the employee's spouse and dependent children and to retired and disabled former employees. In the Regulations, the IRS has conceded that partners who perform services for the partnership are employees for purposes of the exclusion.[54] (As discussed earlier in the chapter, the IRS's position is that partners are not employees for purposes of the § 119 meals and lodging exclusion.) However, the exclusion is not allowed to highly compensated employees unless the benefit is available on a nondiscriminatory basis.

Qualified Employee Discounts

When the employer sells goods or services (other than no-additional-cost benefits just discussed) to the employee for a price that is less than the price charged regular customers, the employee realizes income equal to the discount. However, the discount, referred to as a **qualified employee discount**, can be excluded from the gross income of the employee, subject to the following conditions and limitations:

- The exclusion is not available for real property (e.g., a house) or for personal property of the type commonly held for investment (e.g., common stocks).
- The property or services must be from the same line of business in which the employee works.
- In the case of *property*, the exclusion is limited to the *gross profit component* of the price to customers.
- In the case of *services*, the exclusion is limited to 20 percent of the customer price.[55]

EXAMPLE 27

Silver Corporation, which operates a department store, sells a television set to a store employee for $300. The regular customer price is $500, and the gross profit rate is 25%. The corporation also sells the employee a service contract for $120. The regular customer price for the contract is $150. The employee must include $75 in gross income.

Customer price for property	$ 500
Less: Gross profit (25%)	(125)
	$ 375
Employee price	(300)
Income	$ 75
Customer price for service	$ 150
Less: 20 percent	(30)
	$ 120
Employee price	(120)
Income	$ –0–

EXAMPLE 28

Assume the same facts as in Example 27, except that the employee is a clerk in a hotel operated by Silver Corporation. Because the line of business requirement is not met, the employee must recognize $200 income ($500 − $300) from the purchase of the television and $30 income ($150 − $120) from the service contract. ■

As in the case of no-additional-cost benefits, the exclusion applies to employees (including service partners), employees' spouses and dependent children, and retired and disabled former employees. However, the exclusion does not apply to highly compensated individuals unless the discount is available on a nondiscriminatory basis.

Working Condition Fringes

Generally, an employee is not required to include in gross income the cost of property or services provided by the employer if the employee could deduct the cost of

---

[54]Reg. § 1.132–1(b).
[55]§ 132(c).

those items if he or she had actually paid for them.[56] These benefits are called **working condition fringes**.

EXAMPLE 29

Mitch is a CPA employed by an accounting firm. The employer pays Mitch's annual dues to professional organizations. Mitch is not required to include the payment of the dues in gross income because if he had paid the dues, he would have been allowed to deduct the amount as an employee business expense (as discussed in Chapter 9). ∎

In many cases, this exclusion merely avoids reporting income and an offsetting deduction. However, in two specific situations, the working condition fringe benefit rules allow an exclusion where the expense would not be deductible if paid by the employee:

- Automobile salespeople are allowed to exclude the value of certain personal use of company demonstrators (e.g., commuting to and from work).[57]
- The employee business expense would be eliminated by the 2 percent floor on miscellaneous itemized deductions under § 67 (see Chapter 10).

Unlike the other fringe benefits discussed previously, working condition fringes can be made available on a discriminatory basis and still qualify for the exclusion.

De Minimis *Fringes*

As the term suggests, **de minimis fringe** benefits are so small that accounting for them is impractical.[58] The House Report contains the following examples of *de minimis* fringes:

- The typing of a personal letter by a company secretary, occasional personal use of a company copying machine, occasional company cocktail parties or picnics for employees, occasional supper money or taxi fare for employees because of overtime work, and certain holiday gifts of property with a low fair market value are excluded.
- Subsidized eating facilities (e.g., an employees' cafeteria) operated by the employer are excluded if located on or near the employer's business premises, if revenue equals or exceeds direct operating costs, and if nondiscrimination requirements are met.

When taxpayers venture beyond the specific examples contained in the House Report and the Regulations, there is obviously much room for disagreement as to what is *de minimis*. However, note that except in the case of subsidized eating facilities, the *de minimis* fringe benefits can be granted in a manner that favors highly compensated employees.

Qualified Transportation Fringes

The intent of the exclusion for **qualified transportation fringes** is to encourage the use of mass transit for commuting to and from work. Qualified transportation fringes encompass the following transportation benefits provided by the employer to the employee:[59]

1. Transportation in a commuter highway vehicle between the employee's residence and the place of employment.
2. A transit pass.
3. Qualified parking.
4. Qualified bicycle commuting reimbursement.

Statutory dollar limits are placed on the amount of the exclusion. Categories (1) and (2) above are combined for purposes of applying the limit. In this case, the

---

limit on the exclusion for 2010 was $230 and for 2011 is $230. Category (3) has a separate limit. For qualified parking, the limit on the exclusion for 2011 is $230 per month ($230 in 2010). Both of these dollar limits are indexed annually for inflation.

A *commuter highway vehicle* is any highway vehicle with a seating capacity of at least six adults (excluding the driver). In addition, at least 80 percent of the vehicle's use must be for transporting employees between their residences and place of employment.

Qualified parking includes the following:

- Parking provided to an employee on or near the employer's business premises.
- Parking provided to an employee on or near a location from which the employee commutes to work via mass transit, in a commuter highway vehicle, or in a carpool.

The *qualified bicycle commuting reimbursement* enables an employee to exclude up to $20 per month received from an employer as reimbursement for the cost of commuting by bicycle (i.e., bicycle purchase, improvement, repair, and storage).

Qualified transportation fringes may be provided directly by the employer or may be in the form of cash reimbursements.

EXAMPLE 30

Gray Corporation's offices are located in the center of a large city. The company pays for parking spaces to be used by the company officers. Steve, a vice president, receives $250 of such benefits each month. The parking space rental qualifies as a qualified transportation fringe. Of the $250 benefit received each month by Steve, $230 is excludible from gross income. The balance of $20 is included in his gross income. The same result would occur if Steve paid for the parking and was reimbursed by his employer. ■

Qualified Moving Expense Reimbursements

Qualified moving expenses that are reimbursed or paid by the employer are excludible from gross income. A qualified moving expense is one that would be deductible under § 217. See the discussion of moving expenses in Chapter 9.

Qualified Retirement Planning Services

Qualified retirement planning services include any retirement planning advice or information that an employer who maintains a qualified retirement plan provides to an employee or the employee's spouse.[60] Congress decided to exclude the value of such services from gross income because they are a key part of retirement income planning. Such an exclusion should motivate more employers to provide retirement planning services to their employees.

Nondiscrimination Provisions

For no-additional-cost services, qualified employee discounts, and qualified retirement planning services, if the plan is discriminatory in favor of highly compensated employees, these key employees are denied exclusion treatment. However, the non-highly compensated employees who receive benefits from the plan can still enjoy exclusion treatment for the no-additional-cost services, qualified employee discounts, and qualified retirement planning services.[61]

EXAMPLE 31

Dove Company's officers are allowed to purchase goods from the company at a 25% discount. Other employees are allowed only a 15% discount. The company's gross profit margin on these goods is 30%.

Peggy, an officer in the company, purchased goods from the company for $750 when the price charged to customers was $1,000. Peggy must include $250 in gross income because the plan is discriminatory.

---

[60]§§ 132(a)(7) and (m). [61]§§ 132(j)(1) and 132(m)(2).

Leo, an employee of the company who is not an officer, purchased goods for $850 when the customer price was $1,000. Leo is not required to recognize gross income because he received a qualified employee discount. ∎

De minimis (except in the case of subsidized eating facilities) and working condition fringe benefits can be provided on a discriminatory basis. The *de minimis* benefits are not subject to tax because the accounting problems that would be created are out of proportion to the amount of additional tax that would result. A nondiscrimination test would simply add to the compliance problems. In the case of working condition fringes, the types of services required vary with the job. Therefore, a nondiscrimination test probably could not be satisfied, although usually there is no deliberate plan to benefit a chosen few. Likewise, the qualified transportation fringe and the qualified moving expense reimbursement can be provided on a discriminatory basis.

TAXABLE FRINGE BENEFITS

If the fringe benefits cannot qualify for any of the specific exclusions or do not fit into any of the general classes of excluded benefits, the taxpayer must recognize gross income equal to the fair market value of the benefits. Obviously, problems are frequently encountered in determining values. The IRS has issued extensive Regulations addressing the valuation of personal use of an employer's automobiles and meals provided at an employer-operated eating facility.[62]

If a fringe benefit plan discriminates in favor of highly compensated employees, generally those employees are not allowed to exclude the benefits they receive that other employees do not enjoy. However, the highly compensated employees, as well as the other employees, are generally allowed to exclude the nondiscriminatory benefits.[63]

EXAMPLE 32

MED Company has a medical reimbursement plan that reimburses officers for 100% of their medical expenses, but reimburses all other employees for only 80% of their medical expenses. Cliff, the president of the company, was reimbursed $1,000 during the year for medical expenses. Cliff must include $200 in gross income [(1 − .80) × $1,000 = $200]. Mike, an employee who is not an officer, received $800 (80% of his actual medical expenses) under the medical reimbursement plan. None of the $800 is includible in his gross income. ∎

5.10 FOREIGN EARNED INCOME

A U.S. citizen is generally subject to U.S. tax on his or her income regardless of the income's geographic origin. The income may also be subject to tax in the foreign country, and thus the taxpayer must carry a double tax burden. Out of a sense of fairness and to encourage U.S. citizens to work abroad (so that exports might be increased), Congress has provided alternative forms of relief from taxes on foreign earned income. The taxpayer can elect *either* (1) to include the foreign income in his or her taxable income and then claim a credit for foreign taxes paid or (2) to exclude the foreign earnings from his or her U.S. gross income (the **foreign earned income exclusion**).[64] The foreign tax credit option is discussed in Chapter 13, but as is apparent from the following discussion, most taxpayers will choose the exclusion.

---

[62]Reg. § 1.61–21(d). Generally, the income from the personal use of the employer's automobile is based on the lease value of the automobile (what it would have cost the employee to lease the automobile). Meals are valued at 150% of the employer's direct costs (e.g., food and labor) of preparing the meals.

[63]§§ 79(d), 105(h), 127(b)(2), and 132(j)(1). See the discussion of the term "highly compensated employee" in Chapter 19.

[64]§ 911(a).

Foreign earned income consists of the earnings from the individual's personal services rendered in a foreign country (other than as an employee of the U.S. government). To qualify for the exclusion, the taxpayer must be either of the following:

- A bona fide resident of the foreign country (or countries).
- Present in a foreign country (or countries) for at least 330 days during any 12 consecutive months.[65]

EXAMPLE 33

Sandra's trips to and from a foreign country in connection with her work were as follows:

Arrived in Foreign Country	Arrived in United States
March 10, 2010	February 1, 2011
March 7, 2011	June 1, 2011

During the 12 consecutive months ending on March 10, 2011, Sandra was present in the foreign country for at least 330 days (365 days less 28 days in February and 7 days in March 2011). Therefore, all income earned in the foreign country through March 10, 2011, is eligible for the exclusion. The income earned from March 11, 2011, through May 31, 2011, is also eligible for the exclusion because Sandra was present in the foreign country for 330 days during the 12 consecutive months ending on May 31, 2011. ∎

The exclusion is *limited* to an indexed amount of $92,900 for 2011 ($91,500 in 2010). For married persons, both of whom have foreign earned income, the exclusion is computed separately for each spouse. Community property rules do not apply (the community property spouse is not deemed to have earned one-half of the other spouse's foreign earned income). If all the days in the tax year are not qualifying days, then the taxpayer must compute the maximum exclusion on a daily basis ($92,900 divided by the number of days in the entire year and multiplied by the number of qualifying days).

EXAMPLE 34

Keith qualifies for the foreign earned income exclusion. He was present in France for all of 2011. Keith's salary for 2011 is $100,000. Since all of the days in 2011 are qualifying days, Keith can exclude $92,900 of his $100,000 salary.

Assume instead that only 335 days were qualifying days. Then, Keith's exclusion is limited to $85,264, computed as follows:

$$\$92,900 \times \frac{335 \text{ days in foreign country}}{365 \text{ days in the year}} = \$85,264$$

∎

Some tax policy experts believe that the nation's benefits from the foreign earned income exclusion are not worth the loss of revenues. Rather than eliminating the exclusion, Congress recently decreased its benefit by requiring a special tax computation. The tax on the taxable income after the foreign earned income exclusion is calculated using the tax rate that would apply if the excluded foreign earned income were included in gross income.

EXAMPLE 35

In 2011, Carol, who is not married, had taxable income of $89,450 after excluding $83,600 of foreign earned income. Without the benefit of the exclusion, Carol's taxable income would have been $173,050 ($83,600 + $89,450). The tax on the taxable income of $89,450 is calculated using the marginal rate applicable to income between $83,600 and $173,050, which is 28%. Therefore, Carol's tax liability is $25,046 (.28 × $89,450). ∎

---

[65]§ 911(d). For the definition of resident, see Reg. § 1.871–2(b). Under the Regulations, a taxpayer is not a resident if he or she is there for a definite period (e.g., until completion of a construction contract).

CONCEPT SUMMARY 5.2

General Classes of Excluded Benefits

Benefit	Description and Examples	Coverage Allowed	Effect of Discrimination
1. No-additional-cost services	The employee takes advantage of the employer's excess capacity (e.g., free passes for airline employees).	Current, retired, and disabled employees; their spouses and dependent children; spouses of deceased employees. Partners are treated as employees.	No exclusion for highly compensated employees.
2. Qualified discounts on goods	The employee is allowed to purchase the employer's merchandise at a price that is not less than the employer's cost.	Same as (1) above.	Same as (1) above.
3. Qualified discounts on services	The employee is allowed a discount (maximum of 20%) on services the employer offers to customers.	Same as (1) above.	Same as (1) above.
4. Working condition fringes	Expenses paid by the employer that would be deductible if paid by the employee (e.g., a mechanic's tools). Also, includes auto salesperson's use of a car held for sale.	Current employees, partners, directors, and independent contractors.	No effect.
5. *De minimis* items	Expenses so immaterial that accounting for them is not warranted (e.g., occasional supper money, personal use of the copy machine).	*Any recipient* of a fringe benefit.	No effect.
6. Qualified transportation fringes	Transportation benefits provided by the employer to employees including commuting in a commuter highway vehicle, a transit pass, qualified parking, and qualified bicycle commuting.	Current employees.	No effect.
7. Qualified moving expense reimbursements	Qualified moving expenses that are paid or reimbursed by the employer. A qualified moving expense is one that would be deductible under § 217.	Current employees.	No effect.
8. Qualified retirement planning services	Qualified retirement planning services that are provided by the employer.	Current employees and spouses.	Same as (1) above.

In addition to the exclusion for foreign earnings, the *reasonable housing costs* incurred by the taxpayer and the taxpayer's family in a foreign country in excess of a base amount may be excluded from gross income. The base amount is 16 percent of the statutory amount (indexed amount for 2011 is $92,900) assuming all of the days are qualifying days for the foreign earned income exclusion. The housing costs exclusion is limited to 30 percent of the statutory amount (as indexed) for the foreign earned income exclusion.[66]

---

[66]§ 911(c).

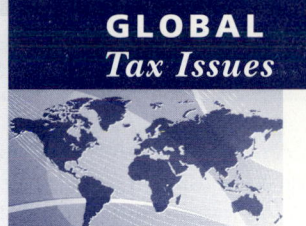

U.S. TAXPAYERS ABROAD ARE GONE BUT NOT FORGOTTEN

GLOBAL *Tax Issues*

U.S. citizens and residents working and living abroad create unique compliance issues for the IRS. These individuals are potentially liable for U.S. taxes and must file U.S. tax returns, even if they earn less than the § 911 foreign earned income exclusion amount. However, in practical terms, many of these individuals are outside the enforcement net of the IRS. In recent years, the IRS has taken several steps to improve compliance, including taxpayer education, simplification of the filing burden, and increased enforcement efforts.

As previously mentioned, the taxpayer may elect to include the foreign earned income in gross income and claim a credit (an offset against U.S. tax) for the foreign tax paid. The credit alternative may be advantageous if the individual's foreign earned income far exceeds the excludible amount so that the foreign taxes paid exceed the U.S. tax on the amount excluded. However, once an election is made, it applies to all subsequent years unless affirmatively revoked. A revocation is effective for the year of the change and the four subsequent years.

5.11 INTEREST ON CERTAIN STATE AND LOCAL GOVERNMENT OBLIGATIONS

At the time the Sixteenth Amendment was ratified by the states, there was some question as to whether the Federal government possessed the constitutional authority to tax interest on state and local government obligations. Taxing such interest was thought to violate the doctrine of intergovernmental immunity in that the tax would impair the state and local governments' ability to finance their operations.[67] Thus, interest on state and local government obligations was specifically exempted from Federal income taxation.[68] However, the Supreme Court has concluded that there is no constitutional prohibition against levying a nondiscriminatory Federal income tax on state and local government obligations.[69] Nevertheless, currently the statutory exclusion still exists.

Obviously, the exclusion of the interest reduces the cost of borrowing for state and local governments. A taxpayer in the 35 percent tax bracket requires only a 5.2 percent yield on a tax-exempt bond to obtain the same after-tax income as a taxable bond paying 8 percent interest [$5.2\% \div (1 - .35) = 8\%$].

The current exempt status applies solely to state and local government bonds. Thus, income received from the accrual of interest on a condemnation award or an overpayment of state income tax is fully taxable.[70] Nor does the exemption apply to gains on the sale of tax-exempt securities.

EXAMPLE 36

Megan purchases State of Virginia bonds for $10,000 on July 1, 2010. The bonds pay $400 interest each June 30th and December 31st. On March 31, 2011, Megan sells the bonds for $10,500 plus $200 accrued interest. Megan must recognize a $500 gain ($10,500 − $10,000), but the $200 accrued interest is exempt from taxation. ∎

Although the Internal Revenue Code excludes from Federal gross income the interest on state and local government bonds, the interest on U.S. government bonds is not excluded from the Federal tax base. Congress has decided, however, that if the

---

[67] *Pollock v. Farmer's Loan & Trust Co.*, 3 AFTR 2602, 15 S.Ct. 912 (USSC, 1895).

[68] § 103(a).

[69] *South Carolina v. Baker III*, 88–1 USTC ¶9284, 61 AFTR 2d 88–995, 108 S.Ct. 1355 (USSC, 1988).

[70] *Kieselbach v. Comm.*, 43–1 USTC ¶9220, 30 AFTR 370, 63 S.Ct. 303 (USSC, 1943); *U.S. Trust Co. of New York v. Anderson*, 3 USTC ¶1125, 12 AFTR 836, 65 F.2d 575 (CA–2, 1933).

To Qualify for the Foreign Earned Income Exclusion, You Must Work in a "Country"

Mr. Arnett found out that to qualify for the foreign earned income exclusion, it is not sufficient that where you work is "foreign"—you must also work in a country. Mr. Arnett worked in Antarctica for the requisite period of time, but the court concluded that the term "foreign country" means a territory under the sovereignty of a government other than that of the United States. Under various treaties, Antarctica is not under the sovereignty of any government.

Therefore, Mr. Arnett did not qualify for the foreign earned income exclusion. Apparently, the exclusion would also be denied to a person working in outer space (i.e., at the International Space Station).

Source: *Arnett v. Comm.*, 99 AFTR 2d 2007–492, 473 F.3d 790 (CA–7, 2007).

Federal government is not to tax state and local bond interest, the state and local governments are prohibited from taxing interest on U.S. government bonds.[71] While this parity between the Federal and state and local governments exists in regard to taxing each others' obligations, the states are free to tax one another's obligations. Thus, some states exempt the interest on the bonds they issue, but tax the interest on bonds issued by other states.[72]

EXAMPLE 37

Aaron is a resident of Virginia. He owns U.S. government bonds that paid him $800 interest during the current year. He also invests in American States Bond Fund, which reports to Aaron that his share of Virginia interest income is $300 and his share of interest income from other states is $600. Aaron must include the $800 in his Federal gross income. Virginia exempts from Virginia taxation the interest on the Virginia bonds, but taxes the interest on bonds issued by other states. Therefore, Aaron must include $600 of interest from other states in his Virginia gross income. ■

5.12 DIVIDENDS

GENERAL INFORMATION

A *dividend* is a payment to a shareholder with respect to his or her stock (see Chapter 4). Dividends to shareholders are taxable only to the extent the payments are made from *either* the corporation's *current earnings and profits* (similar to net income per books) or its *accumulated earnings and profits* (similar to retained earnings per books).[73] Distributions that exceed earnings and profits are treated as a nontaxable recovery of capital and reduce the shareholder's basis in the stock. Once the shareholder's basis is reduced to zero, any subsequent distributions are taxed as capital gains (see Chapter 14).[74]

Some payments are frequently referred to as dividends but are not considered dividends for tax purposes:

- Dividends received on deposits with savings and loan associations, credit unions, and banks are actually interest (a contractual rate paid for the use of money).
- Patronage dividends paid by cooperatives (e.g., for farmers) are rebates made to the users and are considered reductions in the cost of items

---

[71] 31 U.S.C.A. § 742.

[72] The practice of a state exempting interest on its bonds from tax but taxing the interest on bonds issued by other states was upheld by the Supreme Court in 2008. See the "Tax in the News" on p. 5–31.

[73] § 316(a). Refer to the discussion of the beneficial tax rates for qualified dividends in Chapter 4.

[74] § 301(c). See Chapter 5, *South-Western Federal Taxation: Corporations, Partnerships, Estates, and Trusts,* for a detailed discussion of corporate distributions.

TAX *in*
the NEWS

U.S. SUPREME COURT RULES ON STATE TAXATION OF OTHER STATES' INTEREST

Like many other states, Kentucky exempts from taxation interest earned on its own state bonds, but taxes its residents on interest income received from bonds issued by other states. A married couple residing in Kentucky challenged the law as unconstitutionally discriminating against interstate commerce by treating Kentucky bonds more favorably than the bonds issued by other states. The U.S. Supreme Court ruled in favor of Kentucky, thus permitting the state (and the 41 other states with similar laws) to tax the out-of-state bond interest while exempting Kentucky bond interest.

This is a very important case because many taxpayers invest in state and local bond funds. These funds often purchase bonds issued by several states. Although the interest from all of the state bonds is generally exempt from Federal income tax, the investor may owe state income tax to the state of residence on the interest received on the bonds of other states. Thus, the bond fund must inform the investor of the amount of interest income earned from the bonds issued by the various states.

Source: *Department of Revenue of Kentucky v. Davis*, 128 S.Ct. 1801 (USSC, 2008).

purchased from the association. The rebates are usually made after year-end (after the cooperative has determined whether it has met its expenses) and are apportioned among members on the basis of their purchases.

- Mutual insurance companies pay dividends on unmatured life insurance policies that are considered rebates of premiums.
- Shareholders in a mutual investment fund are allowed to report as capital gains their proportionate share of the fund's gains realized and distributed. The capital gain and ordinary income portions are reported on the Form 1099 that the fund supplies its shareholders each year.

STOCK DIVIDENDS

When a corporation issues a simple stock dividend (e.g., common stock issued to common shareholders), the shareholder has merely received additional shares that represent the same total investment. Thus, the shareholder does not realize income.[75] However, if the shareholder has the *option* of receiving either cash or stock in the corporation, the individual realizes gross income whether he or she receives stock or cash.[76] A taxpayer who elects to receive the stock could be deemed to be in constructive receipt of the cash he or she has rejected.[77] However, the amount of the income in this case is the value of the stock received, rather than the cash the shareholder has rejected. See Chapter 14 for a detailed discussion of stock dividends.

5.13 EDUCATIONAL SAVINGS BONDS

The cost of a college education has risen dramatically during the past 15 years. According to U.S. Department of Education estimates, the cost of attending a publicly supported university for four years now commonly exceeds $60,000. For a private university, the cost often exceeds $200,000. Consequently, Congress has attempted to assist low- to middle-income parents in saving for their children's college education.

---

[75]*Eisner v. Macomber*, 1 USTC ¶32, 3 AFTR 3020, 40 S.Ct. 189 (USSC, 1920); § 305(a).

[76]§ 305(b).

[77]Refer to the discussion of constructive receipt in Chapter 4.

The assistance is in the form of an interest income exclusion on **educational savings bonds**.[78] The interest on Series EE U.S. government savings bonds may be excluded from gross income if the bond proceeds are used to pay qualified higher education expenses. The exclusion applies only if both of the following requirements are satisfied:

• The savings bonds are issued after December 31, 1989.
• The savings bonds are issued to an individual who is at least 24 years old at the time of issuance.

The exclusion is not available for a married couple who file separate returns.

The redemption proceeds must be used to pay qualified higher education expenses. *Qualified higher education expenses* consist of tuition and fees paid to an eligible educational institution for the taxpayer, spouse, or dependent. In calculating qualified higher education expenses, the tuition and fees paid are reduced by excludible scholarships and veterans' benefits received. If the redemption proceeds (both principal and interest) exceed the qualified higher education expenses, only a pro rata portion of the interest will qualify for exclusion treatment.

EXAMPLE 38

Tracy's redemption proceeds from qualified savings bonds during the taxable year are $6,000 (principal of $4,000 and interest of $2,000). Tracy's qualified higher education expenses are $5,000. Since the redemption proceeds exceed the qualified higher education expenses, only $1,667 [($5,000/$6,000) × $2,000] of the interest is excludible. ∎

The exclusion is limited by the application of the wherewithal to pay concept. That is, once the modified adjusted gross income exceeds a threshold amount, the phaseout of the exclusion begins. *Modified adjusted gross income* (*MAGI*) is adjusted gross income prior to the § 911 foreign earned income exclusion and the educational savings bond exclusion. The threshold amounts are adjusted for inflation each year. For 2011, the phaseout begins at $71,100 ($106,650 on a joint return).[79] The phaseout is completed when MAGI exceeds the threshold amount by more than $15,000 ($30,000 on a joint return). The otherwise excludible interest is reduced by the amount calculated as follows:

$$\frac{\text{MAGI} - \$71,100}{\$15,000} \times \frac{\text{Excludible interest}}{\text{before phaseout}} = \frac{\text{Reduction in}}{\text{excludible interest}}$$

On a joint return, $106,650 is substituted for $71,100 (in 2011), and $30,000 is substituted for $15,000.

EXAMPLE 39

Assume the same facts as in Example 38, except that Tracy's MAGI for 2011 is $80,000. The phaseout results in Tracy's interest exclusion being reduced by $989 {[($80,000 − $71,100)/$15,000] × $1,667 }. Therefore, Tracy's exclusion is $678 ($1,667 − $989). ∎

5.14 QUALIFIED TUITION PROGRAMS (§ 529 PLANS)

Nearly all, if not all, states have created programs whereby parents can in effect prepay their child's college tuition. The prepayment serves as a hedge against future increases in tuition. Generally, if the child does not attend college, the parents are refunded their payments plus interest. Upon first impression, these prepaid tuition programs resemble the below-market loans discussed in Chapter 4. That is, assuming the tuition increases, the parent receives a reduction in the child's tuition in exchange for the use of the funds. However, Congress has created an exclusion provision for these programs.[80]

---

[78]§ 135.
[79]The indexed amounts for 2010 were $70,100 and $105,100.

[80]§ 529. For another way to beneficially fund educational costs, see the discussion of Coverdell Education Savings Accounts (CESAs) in Chapter 19 (§ 530).

Under a **qualified tuition program (§ 529 plan)**, the amounts contributed must be used for qualified higher education expenses. These expenses include tuition, fees, books, supplies, room and board, and equipment required for enrollment or attendance at a college, university, or certain vocational schools. Under ARRTA of 2009, the allowable expenses are extended to computers and computer technology, including software that provides access to the Internet. Qualified higher education expenses also include the expenses for special needs services that are incurred in connection with the enrollment and attendance of special needs students.

The earnings of the contributed funds, including the discount on tuition charged to participants, are not included in Federal gross income provided that the contributions and earnings are used for qualified higher education expenses. Some states also exclude these educational benefits from state gross income.

EXAMPLE 40

Agnes paid $20,000 into a qualified tuition program to be used for her son's college tuition. When her son graduated from high school, the fund balance had increased to $30,000 as a result of interest credited to the account. The interest was not included in Agnes's gross income. During the current year, $7,500 of the balance in the fund was used to pay the son's tuition and fees. None of this amount is included in either Agnes's or the son's gross income. ■

If the parent receives a refund (e.g., child does not attend college), the excess of the amount refunded over the amount contributed by the parent is included in the parent's gross income.

Qualified tuition programs have been expanded to apply to private educational institutions as well as public educational institutions. Distributions made after December 31, 2003, from such a plan maintained by an entity other than the state for qualified higher education expenses are eligible for exclusion from gross income.

5.15 TAX BENEFIT RULE

LO.3

Determine the extent to which receipts can be excluded under the tax benefit rule.

Generally, if a taxpayer obtains a deduction for an item in one year and in a later year recovers all or a portion of the prior deduction, the recovery is included in gross income in the year received.[81]

EXAMPLE 41

A taxpayer deducted as a loss a $1,000 receivable from a customer when it appeared the amount would never be collected. The following year, the customer paid $800 on the receivable. The taxpayer must report the $800 as gross income in the year it is received. ■

However, the § 111 **tax benefit rule** provides that no income is recognized upon the recovery of a deduction, or the portion of a deduction, that did not yield a tax benefit in the year it was taken. If the taxpayer in Example 41 had no tax liability in the year of the deduction (e.g., itemized deductions and personal exemptions exceeded adjusted gross income), the recovery would be partially or totally excluded from gross income in the year of the recovery.[82]

EXAMPLE 42

Ali filed his 2010 income tax return as a single individual. His AGI for 2010 was $48,000. He had $6,200 in itemized deductions, including $1,200 in state income tax. His personal exemption was $3,650. In 2011, he received a $700 refund of the state income taxes that he paid in 2010. Because the standard deduction in 2010 was $5,700, the $1,200 of state income taxes Ali paid in 2010 yielded a tax benefit of only $500 ($6,200 itemized deduction − $5,700 standard deduction) in 2010. Under the tax benefit rule, only $500 of the state income tax refund is included in gross income in 2011. ■

---

[81]§ 111(a).   [82]Itemized deductions are discussed in Chapter 10.

ONE WAY TO AVOID BANKRUPTCY

Many businesses rely heavily on debt obligations (e.g., notes, bonds) to finance their operations. If these obligations come due when other credit sources are scarce and refinancing is not possible, the debtor's default could lead to bankruptcy. To avoid bankruptcy, the debtor may be able to purchase the obligation at a discount. Unfortunately, the discount component constitutes forgiveness of debt and generates income to the debtor.

In ARRTA of 2009, Congress recognized the problem and provides some relief to the business debtor. For repurchases of debt after December 31, 2008, and before January 1, 2011, the debtor may defer income recognition to 2014. Even better, such recognition can be spread over five years. Evidently, Congress is trying to provide the tax incentive that will encourage the repurchase option and discourage the bankruptcy approach.

5.16 INCOME FROM DISCHARGE OF INDEBTEDNESS

LO.4

Describe the circumstances under which income must be reported from the discharge of indebtedness.

A transfer of appreciated property (fair market value is greater than adjusted basis) in satisfaction of a debt is an event that triggers the realization of income. The transaction is treated as a sale of the appreciated property followed by payment of the debt.[83] Foreclosure by a creditor is also treated as a sale or exchange of the property.[84]

EXAMPLE 43

Juan owes State Bank $100,000 on an unsecured note. He satisfies the note by transferring to the bank common stock with a basis of $60,000 and a fair market value of $100,000. Juan must recognize a $40,000 gain on the transfer. Juan also owes the bank $50,000 on a note secured by land. When Juan's basis in the land is $20,000 and the land's fair market value is $50,000, the bank forecloses on the loan and takes title to the land. Juan must recognize a $30,000 gain on the foreclosure. ■

In some cases, creditors will not exercise their right of foreclosure and will even forgive a portion of the debt to assure the vitality of the debtor. In such cases, the debtor realizes income from discharge of indebtedness.

EXAMPLE 44

Brown Corporation is unable to meet the mortgage payments on its factory building. Both the corporation and the mortgage holder are aware of the depressed market for industrial property in the area. Foreclosure would only result in the creditor's obtaining unsalable property. To improve Brown Corporation's financial position and thus improve Brown's chances of obtaining the additional credit necessary for survival from other lenders, the creditor agrees to forgive all amounts past due and to reduce the principal amount of the mortgage. ■

Generally, the income realized by the debtor from the forgiveness of a debt is taxable.[85] A similar debt discharge (produced by a different creditor motivation) associated with personal use property is illustrated in Example 45.

EXAMPLE 45

In 2006, Joyce borrowed $60,000 from National Bank to purchase her personal residence. Joyce agreed to make monthly principal and interest payments for 15 years. The interest rate on the note was 7%. In 2011, when the balance on the note has been

---

[83]Reg. § 1.1001–2(a).

[84]*Estate of Delman v. Comm.*, 73 T.C. 15 (1979).

[85]*U.S. v. Kirby Lumber Co.*, 2 USTC ¶814, 10 AFTR 458, 52 S.Ct. 4 (USSC, 1931), codified in § 61(a)(12).

| TAX *in* the NEWS | HOPE FOR EXCLUSION OF CREDIT CARD DEBT FORGIVENESS |

The airwaves are full of advertisements about how credit card debt can be reduced without actually paying the debt. Generally, the reduction in the debt creates income from discharge of indebtedness. But in a recent petition to the U.S. Supreme Court, the taxpayers unveiled a new theory for excluding the gain from income. The taxpayers argued that the interest portion of the debt forgiven was not tax-able because it was an adjustment to the purchase price that the credit card issuer charged. Another theory that will undoubtedly be tested in the context of consumer debt adjustments is that the cancellation of the debt is not tax-able income under the tax benefit rule. That is, because the expenditure that created the debt was not deductible, the recovery should not be taxable.

reduced through monthly payments to $48,000, the bank offers to accept $45,000 in full settlement of the note. The bank makes the offer because interest rates have increased to 11%. Joyce accepts the bank's offer. As a result, Joyce must recognize $3,000 ($48,000 − $45,000) of gross income.[86] ∎

The following discharge of indebtedness situations are subject to special treatment:[87]

1. Creditors' gifts.
2. Discharges under Federal bankruptcy law.
3. Discharges that occur when the debtor is insolvent.
4. Discharge of the farm debt of a solvent taxpayer.
5. Discharge of **qualified real property business indebtedness**.
6. A seller's cancellation of the buyer's indebtedness.
7. A shareholder's cancellation of the corporation's indebtedness.
8. Forgiveness of certain loans to students.
9. Discharge of indebtedness on the taxpayer's principal residence that occurs between January 1, 2007, and January 1, 2013, and is the result of the financial condition of the debtor.

If the creditor reduces the debt as an act of *love, affection,* or *generosity,* the debtor has simply received a nontaxable gift (situation 1). Rarely will a gift be found to have occurred in a business context. A businessperson may settle a debt for less than the amount due, but as a matter of business expediency (e.g., high collection costs or disputes as to contract terms) rather than generosity.[88]

In situations 2, 3, 4, 5, and 9, the Code allows the debtor to reduce his or her basis in the assets by the realized gain from the discharge.[89] Thus, the realized gain is merely deferred until the assets are sold (or depreciated). Similarly, in situation 6 (a price reduction), the debtor reduces the basis in the specific assets financed by the seller.[90]

A shareholder's cancellation of the corporation's indebtedness to him or her (situation 7) usually is considered a tax-free contribution of capital to the corporation by the shareholder. Thus, the corporation's paid-in capital is increased, and its liabilities are decreased by the same amount.[91]

Many states make loans to students on the condition that the loan will be forgiven if the student practices a profession in the state upon completing his or her studies. The amount of the loan that is forgiven (situation 8) is excluded from gross income.[92]

---

[86]Rev.Rul. 82–202, 1982–1 C.B. 35.

[87]§§ 108 and 1017.

[88]*Comm. v. Jacobson,* 49–1 USTC ¶9133, 37 AFTR 516, 69 S.Ct. 358 (USSC, 1949).

[89]§§ 108(a), (c), (e), and (g). Note that § 108(b) provides that other tax attributes (e.g., net operating loss) will be reduced by the realized gain from the debt discharge prior to the basis adjustment unless the taxpayer elects to apply the basis adjustment first.

[90]§ 108(e)(5).

[91]§ 108(e)(6).

[92]§ 108(f).

TAX PLANNING:

5.17 LIFE INSURANCE

The present law excludes certain types of economic gains from taxation. Therefore, taxpayers may find tax planning techniques helpful in obtaining the maximum benefits from the exclusion of such gains. Following are some of the tax planning opportunities made available by the exclusions described in this chapter.

Life insurance offers several favorable tax attributes. As discussed in Chapter 4, the annual increase in the cash surrender value of the policy is not taxable (because no income has been actually or constructively received). By borrowing on the policy's cash surrender value, the owner can actually receive the policy's increase in value in cash but without recognizing income.

5.18 EMPLOYEE BENEFITS

Generally, employees view accident and health insurance, as well as life insurance, as necessities. Employees can obtain group coverage at much lower rates than individuals would have to pay for the same protection. Premiums paid by the employer can be excluded from the employees' gross income. Because of the exclusion, employees will have a greater after-tax and after-insurance income if the employer pays a lower salary but also pays the insurance premiums.

EXAMPLE 46

Pat receives a salary of $30,000. The company has group insurance benefits, but Pat is required to pay his own premiums as follows:

Hospitalization and medical insurance	$1,400
Term life insurance ($30,000 coverage)	200
Disability insurance	400
	$2,000

To simplify the analysis, assume Pat's tax rate on income is 25%. After paying taxes of $7,500 (.25 × $30,000) and $2,000 for insurance, Pat has $20,500 ($30,000 − $7,500 − $2,000) for his other living needs.

If Pat's employer reduced Pat's salary by $2,000 (to $28,000) but paid his insurance premiums, Pat's tax liability would be only $7,000 ($28,000 × .25). Thus, Pat would have $21,000 ($28,000 − $7,000) to meet his other living needs. The change in the compensation plan would save Pat $500 ($21,000 − $20,500). ∎

Similarly, employees must often incur expenses for child care and parking. The employee can have more income for other uses if the employer pays these costs for the employee but reduces the employee's salary by the cost of the benefits.

The use of cafeteria plans has increased dramatically in recent years. These plans allow employees to tailor their benefits to meet their individual situations. Thus, where both spouses in a married couple are working, duplications of benefits can be avoided, and other needed benefits can often be added. If less than all of the employee's allowance is spent, the employee can receive cash.

The meals and lodging exclusion enables employees to receive from their employer what they ordinarily must purchase with after-tax dollars. Although the requirements that the employee live and take his or her meals on the employer's premises limit the tax planning opportunities, the exclusion is an important factor in the employee's compensation in certain situations (e.g., hotels, motels, restaurants, farms, and ranches).

The employees' discount provision is especially important for manufacturers and wholesalers. Employees of manufacturers can avoid tax on the manufacturer's, wholesaler's, and retailer's markups. The wholesaler's employees can avoid tax on an amount equal to the wholesale and retail markups.

It should be recognized that the exclusion of benefits is generally available only to employees. Proprietors and partners must pay tax on the same benefits their employees receive tax-free. By incorporating and becoming an employee of the corporation, the former proprietor or partner can also receive these tax-exempt benefits. Thus, the availability of employee benefits is a consideration in the decision to incorporate.

5.19 INVESTMENT INCOME

Tax-exempt state and local government bonds are almost irresistible investments for many high-income taxpayers. To realize the maximum benefit from the exemption, the investor can purchase zero-coupon bonds. Like Series EE U.S. government savings bonds, these investments pay interest only at maturity. The advantage of the zero-coupon feature for a tax-exempt bond is that the investor can earn tax-exempt interest on the accumulated principal and interest. If the investor purchases a bond that pays the interest each year, the interest received may be such a small amount that an additional tax-exempt investment cannot be made. In addition, reinvesting the interest may entail transaction costs (broker's fees). The zero-coupon feature avoids these problems.

Series EE U.S. government savings bonds can earn tax-exempt interest if the bond proceeds are used for qualified higher education expenses. Many taxpayers can foresee these expenditures being made for their children's educations. In deciding whether to invest in the bonds, however, the investor must take into account the income limitations for excluding the interest from gross income.

REFOCUS ON THE BIG PICTURE

EXCLUSIONS

You have looked into Paul's tax situation and have the following information for him:

- *Compensation.* The amount Paul was paid for his internship is compensation for services rendered and must be included in his gross income. This includes both his base pay and the $1,500 bonus.
- *Graduate assistantship.* The tuition waiver of $6,000 and the related payments of $500 per month are also intended as a form of compensation. So Paul must include both of these in his gross income.
- *Damages.* Damages awards that relate to personal physical injury or sickness can be excluded from gross income if the payments are for compensatory damages. So all of the compensatory damages of $220,000 can be excluded from gross income. The punitive damages of $160,000 must be included in Paul's gross income. Likewise, the compensatory damages of $25,000 received by Paul's mother must be included in her gross income since emotional distress does not qualify as personal physical injury or sickness.

What If?

From a tax planning perspective, can Paul do anything to reduce the amount of the punitive damages settlement that he must include in his gross income?

As things now stand (i.e., a completed settlement), Paul cannot reduce the $160,000 punitive damages amount he must include in gross income. However, proper tax planning might have enabled Paul to reduce the amount includible in gross income. Note that both the amount of the damages and the labels attached to the damages are negotiated. If a larger portion of the settlement had been assigned to compensatory damages rather than punitive damages, Paul could have reduced the amount he must include in his gross income.

KEY TERMS

Accelerated death benefits, 5–8	Foreign earned income exclusion, 5–26	Qualified real property business indebtedness, 5–35
Accident and health benefits, 5–14	Gift, 5–6	
Cafeteria plan, 5–20	Health Savings Account (HSA), 5–16	Qualified transportation fringes, 5–24
Compensatory damages, 5–12	Life insurance proceeds, 5–7	Qualified tuition program (§ 529 plan), 5–33
Death benefits, 5–6	Long-term care insurance, 5–16	Qualified tuition reduction plan, 5–11
De minimis fringe, 5–24	No-additional-cost service, 5–22	Scholarship, 5–10
Educational savings bonds, 5–32	Punitive damages, 5–12	Tax benefit rule, 5–33
Flexible spending plans, 5–21	Qualified employee discount, 5–23	Working condition fringes, 5–24

DISCUSSION QUESTIONS

1. **LO.2** Uncle Tom promised John, "Come and take care of me and I will leave you the farm when I die." John took care of Uncle Tom for the five years preceding his death. When Uncle Tom died, in accordance with his will, John received the farm. Can John exclude the value of the farm from his gross income as a gift or inheritance, or has he received compensation income?

2. **LO.2** Albert was a flood victim and had to spend a considerable amount to restore his home after the flood. His church held a special collection and gave him $1,500. Also, his employer gave him $1,000 to help him in "his time of need." How much gross income must Albert recognize from the receipt of the $2,500?

3. **LO.1, 2** Twenty college fraternity brothers each placed $2,500 in a mutual fund account. They agreed that upon the death of a fraternity brother, his beneficiary would receive $20,000 that was to be paid from the mutual fund account. The beneficiary of the last remaining fraternity brother would receive the balance remaining in the account. The mutual fund did very well. Earl was the last to die, at age 92, and his beneficiary received $250,000. Can the $250,000 be excluded from the beneficiary's gross income?

4. **LO.2** Janice was a cash basis taxpayer. At the time of her death, she was owed $30,000 in accrued salary. She also owned several thousand shares of stock in her corporate employer. Her cost of the stock was $25,000. Her employer was required to purchase the stock on Janice's death for $150,000. To fund the agreement, the employer had purchased an insurance policy on Janice's life that cost $60,000. The insurance company paid the employer the life insurance proceeds of $150,000 on Janice's death. Wayne, as the sole beneficiary of Janice's estate, received the $180,000 from Janice's estate, which included Janice's $30,000 of accrued salary. What are the employer's and Wayne's gross income from these transactions?

5. **LO.2** Matt is a waiter in a restaurant. His usual tip is 20% of the price of the meal. A customer, whose meal cost $5, left a $100 bill as a tip. Matt is sure the customer thought he had left a $1 bill. Nevertheless, Matt believes he can exclude the entire amount (or at least $99) from his gross income because it was received as a gift rather than as compensation for services rendered. Is Matt correct?

6. **LO.2** Carey is a self-employed landscaper. He contracted to maintain Ted's lawn for $150 per month. Ted was very pleased with Carey's work and at the end of the year paid Carey an additional $500. Does the fact that Ted had no legal obligation to make the payment mean that Carey can exclude the $500 from gross income as a gift?

7. **LO.2** Lime Finance Company requires its customers to purchase a credit life insurance policy associated with the loans it makes. Lime is the beneficiary of the policy to the extent of the remaining balance on the loan at the time of the customer's death. In 2010, Lime wrote off as uncollectible a $5,000 account receivable from Wally, which included $1,500 of accrued interest. When Wally died in 2011, the life insurance policy was still in force, and Lime received $3,500. Is the $3,500 of life insurance proceeds received by Lime included in its gross income?

8. **LO.2** Sarah, who has a terminal illness, cashed in her life insurance policy (cost of $24,000 and proceeds of $50,000) to go on an around-the-world cruise. Ed paid $24,000 of life insurance premiums before cashing in his life insurance policy for the $50,000 cash surrender value. He decided he could invest the money and earn a higher rate of return. Tom's wife died, and Tom collected $50,000 as the beneficiary on a group term life insurance policy purchased by her employer. Determine the amounts that Sarah, Ed, and Tom should include in their gross income.

9. **LO.2** Joe is a graduate student who works as a resident adviser (RA) in the college dormitory. As compensation for serving as an RA, he is not charged the $2,200 other students pay for their dormitory rooms for the fall 2011 semester. As an RA, he is required to live in the dormitory. He is also paid $1,500 for being available to dormitory residents at all hours during the fall semester. Joe also has a scholarship that pays him $12,000 to be used for his tuition for the academic year. He uses the scholarship proceeds

to pay $6,000 of tuition in August 2011. In January 2012, he pays $6,000 for his spring semester tuition. What is Joe's gross income for 2011?

10. **LO.2** Billy fell off a bar stool and hurt his back. As a result, he was unable to work for three months. He sued the bar owner and collected $100,000 for the physical injury and $50,000 for the loss of income. Billy also collected $15,000 from an income replacement insurance policy purchased by his employer. Amber was away from work for three months following heart bypass surgery. Amber collected $30,000 under an income replacement insurance policy she had purchased. Are the amounts received by Billy and Amber treated the same under the tax law?

11. **LO.2** Wes was a major league baseball pitcher before a career-ending injury caused by a negligent driver. Wes sued the driver and collected $15 million as compensation for lost estimated future income as a pitcher and $10 million as punitive damages. Sam was also a major league baseball pitcher and earned $25 million for pitching. Do the amounts that Wes and Sam received have the same effect on their gross income? Explain.

12. **LO.2** Holly was injured while working in a factory and received $12,000 as workers' compensation while she was unable to work because of the injury. Jill, who was self-employed, was also injured and unable to work. Jill collected $12,000 on an insurance policy she had purchased to replace her loss of income while she was unable to work. How much are Holly and Jill each required to include in their gross income?

13. **LO.2** Melba's employer provides a flexible spending plan for medical and dental expenses not covered by insurance. Melba contributed $1,500 during 2011, but by the end of December 2011, she still had $300 remaining in the account. Melba intended to get new eyeglasses, but was too busy during the holiday season. Is Melba required to forfeit the balance in her flexible spending account?

DECISION MAKING

14. **LO.2, 5** Casey is in the 15% marginal tax bracket, and Jean is in the 35% marginal tax bracket. Their employer is experiencing financial difficulties and cannot continue to pay for the company's health insurance plan. The annual premiums are approximately $7,000 per employee. The employer has proposed to either (1) require the employee to pay the premiums or (2) reduce each employee's pay by $8,000 per year with the employer paying the premium. Which option is less objectionable to Casey, and which is less objectionable to Jean?

15. **LO.2** What is the difference between a "cafeteria plan" and an employee "flexible spending plan"?

16. **LO.2** Ted works for Sage Motors, an automobile dealership. All employees can buy a car at the company's cost plus 2%. The company does not charge employees the $175 transfer service fee that nonemployees must pay. Ted purchased an automobile for $24,480 ($24,000 + $480). The company's cost was $24,000. The price for a nonemployee would have been $27,775 ($27,600 + $175 transfer service fee). What is Ted's gross income from the purchase of the automobile?

17. **LO.2, 5** Ted has been offered a job where his salary would be $150,000 and he would also receive health insurance coverage. Another potential employer has offered to match the first offer but would not provide any health insurance coverage. Ted can purchase health insurance for $8,000 per year. Assume that Ted is in the 28% marginal tax bracket and does not itemize his deductions. How much salary must the second potential employer pay so that Ted's financial status will be the same under both offers?

18. **LO.2, 5** Eagle Life Insurance Company pays its employees $.30 per mile for driving their personal automobiles to and from work. The company reimburses each employee who rides the bus $100 a month for the cost of a pass. Tom collected $100 for his automobile mileage, and Ted received $100 as reimbursement for the cost of a bus pass.
    a. What are the effects of the above on Tom's and Ted's gross income?
    b. Assume that Tom and Ted are in the 28% marginal tax bracket and the actual before-tax cost for Tom to drive to and from work is $.30 per mile. What are Tom's and Ted's after-tax costs of commuting to and from work?

ISSUE ID

19. **LO.2** Several of Egret Company's employees have asked the company to create a hiking trail that employees could use during their lunch hours. The company owns vacant land that is being held for future expansion but would have to spend approximately $50,000 if

it were to make a trail. Nonemployees would be allowed to use the facility as part of the company's effort to build strong community support. What are the relevant tax issues for the employees?

20. **LO.2** The Azure Company has the opportunity to purchase a building located next to its office. Azure would use the building as a day care center for the children of its employees and an exercise facility for the employees. Occasionally, portions of the building could be used for employees' family events such as reunions, birthday parties, and anniversaries. The company would like to know if the planned uses of the building would fit into a beneficially taxed employee compensation plan.

21. **LO.2** For a U.S. citizen, what are the possible beneficial tax consequences of working in a foreign country in terms of the calculation of gross income?

22. **LO.2, 5** Tammy, a resident of Virginia, is considering purchasing a corporate bond that yields 7% before tax. She is in the 35% Federal marginal tax bracket and the 5% marginal state tax bracket. She is aware that State of Virginia bonds of comparable risk are yielding 4.6% and State of North Carolina bonds are yielding 4.7%. Which of the three options will provide the greatest after-tax return to Tammy?

DECISION MAKING

23. **LO.3** In 2011, Montgomery County experienced a budget surplus. The County is considering using a portion of the surplus to rebate part of the real estate taxes paid by county real estate owners. What would be the income tax consequences to the real estate owners of receiving the rebate in 2012?

24. **LO.2** Andrea entered into a § 529 qualified tuition program for the benefit of her daughter, Joanna. Andrea contributed $15,000 to the fund. The fund balance had accumulated to $25,000 by the time Joanna was ready to enter college. However, Joanna received a scholarship that paid for her tuition, fees, books, supplies, and room and board. Therefore, Andrea withdrew the funds from the § 529 plan and bought Joanna a new car.
    a. What are the tax consequences to Andrea of withdrawing the funds?
    b. Assume instead that Joanna's scholarship did not cover her room and board, which cost $7,500 per academic year. During the current year, $7,500 of the fund balance was used to pay for Joanna's room and board. The remaining amount was left in the § 529 plan to cover her room and board for future academic years. What are the tax consequences to Andrea and to Joanna of using the $7,500 to pay for the room and board?

25. **LO.3** Molly is a cash basis taxpayer. In 2011, she earned only $6,500, which was less than her standard deduction and personal exemption. In January 2012, Molly's employer determined that he had miscalculated her December 2011 bonus and that she should have received an additional $1,000 of compensation in 2011. The employer paid Molly the $1,000 in 2012. If Molly had received the $1,000 in 2011, it would not have resulted in any tax liability because her gross income would still have been less than her standard deduction and personal exemption. In 2012, Molly had over $30,000 in taxable income. Does the tax benefit rule apply to Molly's situation? Explain.

26. **LO.4** Harry was experiencing financial difficulties and could not make the mortgage payments on his home. The mortgage holder agreed to reduce the debt principal by $50,000 because the real estate market was depressed. Assuming that Harry is not bankrupt or insolvent, would the tax consequences differ under the following circumstances?

    • The mortgage is held by the person who sold him the property.
    • The mortgage is held by the financial institution that made the loan for the purchase of his residence.

27. **LO.4** Harry has experienced financial difficulties as a result of his struggling business. He has been behind on his mortgage payments for the last six months. The mortgage holder, who is a friend of Harry's, has offered to accept $80,000 in full payment of the $100,000 owed on the mortgage and payable over the next 10 years. The interest rate of the mortgage is 7%, and the market rate is now 8%. What tax issues are raised by the creditor's offer?

ISSUE ID

28. **LO.2** Ed, an employee of the Natural Color Company, suffered from a rare disease that was very expensive to treat. The local media ran several stories about Ed's problems, and the family received more than $10,000 in gifts from individuals to help pay the medical bills. Ed's employer provided hospital and medical insurance for its employees, but the policy did not cover Ed's illness. When it became apparent that Ed could not pay all of his medical expenses, the hospital canceled the $25,000 Ed owed at the time of his death. After Ed's death, his former employer paid Ed's widow $12,000 in "her time of need." Ed's widow also collected $50,000 on a group term life insurance policy paid for by Ed's employer. What are Ed's and his widow's gross income?

29. **LO.2** Determine the gross income of the beneficiaries in the following cases:
    a. Justin lost his job when his employer moved the plant to China. His employer gave Justin $15,000 to help him in his transition to a new job, even though the employer was not legally obligated to make the payment.
    b. Trina was injured while working. She collected $1,200 in workers' compensation and $1,500 on a loss of income policy she had purchased.
    c. Coral Corporation collected $1 million on a key person life insurance policy when its chief executive died. The corporation had paid the premiums on the policy of $77,000.
    d. Juan collected $50,000 on a life insurance policy when his wife, Leona, died. The policy was provided by Leona's employer, and the premiums were excluded from Leona's gross income as group term life insurance.
    e. Juan in part (d) above collected Leona's accrued vacation pay of $6,000 from her employer.

DECISION MAKING

30. **LO.2, 5** Laura was recently diagnosed with cancer and has begun chemotherapy treatments. A cancer specialist has stated that Laura has less than one year to live. She has incurred a lot of medical bills and other general living expenses and is in need of cash. Therefore, she is considering selling stock that cost $35,000 and has a fair market value of $50,000. This amount would be sufficient to pay her medical bills. However, she has read about a company (the Vital Benefits Company) that would purchase her life insurance policy for $50,000. She has paid $30,000 in premiums on the policy.
    a. Considering only the tax effects, would selling the stock or selling the life insurance policy result in more beneficial tax treatment?
    b. Assume that Laura is a dependent child and that her mother owns the stock and the life insurance policy, which is on the mother's life. Which of the alternative means of raising the cash would result in more beneficial tax treatment?

31. **LO.2** What is the taxpayer's gross income in each of the following situations?
    a. Darrin received a salary of $50,000 in 2011 from his employer, Green Construction Associates, Inc. In July 2011, Green gave each employee $2,500 as a bonus for exceeding the monthly sales goals.
    b. Megan received $10,000 from her employer to help her pay the college expenses of her daughter.
    c. Blake received $15,000 from his deceased wife's employer in "recognition of her 30 years of faithful service to the company."
    d. Clint collected $50,000 as the beneficiary of a group term life insurance policy for which his deceased wife's employer had paid the premiums.

32. **LO.2** Donald was killed in an accident while he was on the job in 2011. His employer had provided Donald with group term life insurance of $160,000 (twice his annual salary), which was payable to his widow, Darlene. Premiums on this policy totaling $2,700 have been included in Donald's gross income under § 79. Darlene received the $160,000 as a lump sum in 2011. Darlene also received Donald's accrued bonus of $20,000. In addition, Donald had purchased a $100,000 life insurance policy (premiums totaled $70,000) that paid $200,000 in the event of accidental death. The proceeds were payable to Darlene, who elected to receive installment payments of $25,000 each year for a 20-year period. She received her first installment this year. What is Darlene's gross income from the above in 2011?

33. **LO.2** Ray and Carin are partners in an accounting firm. The partners have entered into an arm's length agreement requiring Ray to purchase Carin's partnership interest from

Carin's estate if she dies before Ray. The price is set at 120% of the book value of Carin's partnership interest at the time of her death. Ray purchased an insurance policy on Carin's life to fund this agreement. After Ray had paid $45,000 in premiums, Carin was killed in an automobile accident, and Ray collected $800,000 of life insurance proceeds. Ray used the life insurance proceeds to purchase Carin's partnership interest.

a.   What amount should Ray include in his gross income from receiving the life insurance proceeds?

b.   The insurance company paid Ray $16,000 interest on the life insurance proceeds during the period Carin's estate was in administration. During this period, Ray had left the insurance proceeds with the insurance company. Is this interest taxable?

c.   When Ray paid $800,000 for Carin's partnership interest, priced as specified in the agreement, the fair market value of Carin's interest was $1 million. How much should Ray include in his gross income from this bargain purchase?

34. **LO.2** Sally was an all-state soccer player during her junior and senior years in high school. She accepted an athletic scholarship from State University. The scholarship provided the following:

Tuition and fees	$15,000
Housing and meals	7,500
Books and supplies	2,000

a.   Determine the effect of the scholarship on Sally's gross income.

b.   Sally's brother, Willy, was not a gifted athlete, but he received $17,000 from their father's employer as a scholarship during the year. The employer grants the children of all executives a scholarship equal to annual tuition, fees, books, and supplies. Determine the effect of the scholarship on Willy's and his father's gross income.

35. **LO.2** Adrian was awarded an academic scholarship to State University for the 2011–2012 academic year. He received $6,000 in August and $7,000 in December 2011. Adrian had enough personal savings to pay all expenses as they came due. Adrian's expenditures for the relevant period were as follows:

Tuition, August 2011	$3,600
Tuition, January 2012	3,700
Room and board	
August–December 2011	3,000
January–May 2012	2,400
Books and educational supplies	
August–December 2011	1,100
January–May 2012	1,200

Determine the effect on Adrian's gross income for 2011 and 2012.

36. **LO.2** Leigh sued an overzealous bill collector and received the following settlement:

Damage to her automobile the collector attempted to repossess	$ 3,300
Physical damage to her arm caused by the collector	15,000
Loss of income while her arm was healing	6,000
Punitive damages	80,000

a.   What effect does the settlement have on Leigh's gross income?

b.   Assume Leigh also collected $25,000 of damages for slander to her personal reputation caused by the bill collector misrepresenting the facts to Leigh's employer and other creditors. Is this $25,000 included in Leigh's gross income?

37. **LO.2** Determine the effect on gross income in each of the following cases:

a.   Eloise received $150,000 in settlement of a sex discrimination case against her former employer.

b.   Nell received $10,000 for damages to her personal reputation. She also received $40,000 in punitive damages.

c.   Orange Corporation, an accrual basis taxpayer, received $50,000 from a lawsuit filed against its auditor who overcharged for services rendered in a previous year.

d.   Beth received $10,000 in compensatory damages and $30,000 in punitive damages in a lawsuit she filed against a tanning parlor for severe burns she received from using its tanning equipment.

e.   Joanne received compensatory damages of $75,000 and punitive damages of $300,000 from a cosmetic surgeon who botched her nose job.

38. **LO.2** Rex, age 45, is an officer of Blue Company, which provides him with the following nondiscriminatory fringe benefits in 2011:

●   Hospitalization insurance premiums for Rex and his dependents. The cost of the coverage for Rex is $2,700 per year, and the additional cost for his dependents is $3,600 per year. The plan has a $2,000 deductible, but his employer contributed $1,500 to Rex's Health Savings Account. Rex withdrew only $800 from the HSA, and the account earned $50 interest during the year.

●   Long-term care insurance premiums for Rex, at a cost of $3,600 per year.

●   Insurance premiums of $840 for salary continuation payments. Under the plan, Rex will receive his regular salary in the event he is unable to work due to illness. Rex collected $4,500 on the policy to replace lost wages while he was ill during the year.

●   Rex is a part-time student working on his bachelor's degree in engineering. His employer reimbursed his $5,200 tuition under a plan available to all full-time employees.

Determine the amount Rex must include in gross income.

COMMUNICATIONS

39. **LO.2** The UVW Union and HON Corporation are negotiating contract terms. Assume the union members are in the 28% marginal tax bracket and all benefits are provided on a nondiscriminatory basis. Write a letter to the UVW Union members explaining the tax consequences of the options discussed below. The union's address is 905 Spruce Street, Washington, D.C. 20227.

a.   The company would impose a $100 deductible on medical insurance benefits. Most employees incur more than $100 each year in medical expenses.

b.   Employees would get an additional paid holiday with the same annual income (the same pay but less work).

c.   An employee who did not need health insurance (because the employee's spouse works and receives family coverage) would be allowed to receive the cash value of the coverage.

DECISION MAKING

40. **LO.2, 5** Mauve Corporation has a group hospitalization insurance plan that has a $200 deductible amount for hospital visits and a $15 deductible for doctor visits and prescriptions. The deductible portion paid by employees who have children has become substantial for some employees. The company is considering adopting a medical reimbursement plan or a flexible benefits plan to cover the deductible amounts. Either of these plans can be tailored to meet the needs of the employees. What are the cost considerations to the employer that should be considered in choosing between these plans?

41. **LO.2** Belinda spent the last 60 days of 2011 in a nursing home. The cost of the services provided to her was $15,000. Medicare paid $8,500 toward the cost of her stay. Belinda also received $10,500 of benefits under a long-term care insurance policy she purchased. What is the effect on Belinda's gross income?

42. **LO.2** Tim is the vice president of western operations for Maroon Oil Company and is stationed in San Francisco. He is required to live in an employer-owned home, which is three blocks from his company office. The company-provided home is equipped with high-speed Internet access and several telephone lines. Tim receives telephone calls and e-mails that require immediate attention any time of day or night because the company's business is spread all over the world. A full-time administrative assistant resides in the house to assist Tim with the urgent business matters. Tim often uses the home for entertaining customers, suppliers, and employees. The fair market value of comparable housing is $9,000 per month. Tim is also provided with free parking at his company's office. The value of the parking is $350 per month. Calculate the amount associated with the company-provided housing and free parking that Tim must include in his gross income.

43. **LO.2** Does the taxpayer recognize gross income in the following situations?

a.   Ava is a filing clerk at a large insurance company. She is permitted to leave the premises for her lunch, but she always eats in the company's cafeteria because doing so is much less expensive than purchasing a comparable meal at a nearby restaurant. On average, she pays $3 for a lunch that would cost $8 at a restaurant. However, if the prices in the cafeteria were not so low and the food was not so delicious, she would probably bring her lunch at a cost of $2 per day.

b.   Scott is a resident adviser (RA) in a college dormitory and is provided with lodging in the dormitory. He is not required to pay the $300 per month that a room costs other students. In addition, he is paid $100 per month.

c.   Ira recently moved to accept a job. For the first month on the new job, Ira was searching for a home to purchase or rent. During this time, his employer permitted Ira to live in an apartment the company maintains for customers during the buying season. The month that Ira occupied the apartment was not during the buying season, however, and the apartment would not otherwise have been occupied.

44.   **LO.2, 5** Bertha is considering taking an early retirement offered by her employer. She would receive $2,600 per month, indexed for inflation. However, she would no longer be able to use the company's health facilities, and she would be required to pay her hospitalization insurance of $8,000 each year. Bertha and her husband will file a joint return and take the standard deduction. She currently receives a salary of $50,000 a year, and her employer pays for all of her hospitalization insurance. If she retires, Bertha would not be able to use her former employer's exercise facilities because of the commuting distance. She would like to continue to exercise, however, and will therefore join a health club at a cost of $50 per month. Also, if she retires, she will spend approximately $300 less each month for commuting and clothing. Bertha and her husband have other sources of income and are in and will remain in the 25% marginal tax bracket. She currently pays Social Security and Medicare taxes of 7.65% on her salary, but her retirement pay would not be subject to this tax. She will earn about $11,000 a year from a part-time job if she retires from the company. Bertha would like to know whether she should accept the early retirement offer.

DECISION MAKING

45.   **LO.2, 5** Finch Construction Company provides the carpenters it employs with all of the required tools. However, the company believes that this practice has led to some employees not taking care of the tools and to the mysterious disappearance of some tools. The company is considering requiring all of its employees to provide their own tools. Each employee's salary would be increased by $1,500 to compensate for the additional cost. Write a letter to Finch's management explaining the tax consequences of this plan to the carpenters. Finch's address is 300 Harbor Drive, Vermillion, SD 57069.

COMMUNICATIONS

46.   **LO.2, 5** Bluebird, Inc., does not provide its employees with any tax-exempt fringe benefits. The company is considering adopting a hospital and medical benefits insurance plan that will cost approximately $7,500 per employee. In order to adopt this plan, the company may have to reduce salaries and/or lower future salary increases. Bluebird is in the 35% (combined Federal and state rates) bracket. Bluebird is also responsible for matching the Social Security and Medicare taxes withheld on employees' salaries. The benefits insurance plan will not be subject to the Social Security and Medicare taxes, and the company is not eligible for the small business credit for health insurance. The employees generally fall into three marginal tax rate groups:

Income Tax	Social Security and Medicare Tax	Total
.15	.0765	.2265
.25	.0765	.3265
.35	.0145	.3645

The company has asked you to assist in its financial planning for the benefits insurance plan by computing the following:

a.   How much taxable compensation is the equivalent of $7,500 of exempt compensation for each of the three classes of employees?

b.   What is the company's after-tax cost of the taxable compensation computed in (a) above?

c.   What is the company's after-tax cost of the exempt compensation?

d.   Briefly explain your conclusions from the above analysis.

47. **LO.2, 5** Rosa's employer has instituted a flexible benefits program. Rosa will use the plan to pay for her daughter's dental expenses and other medical expenses that are not covered by health insurance. Rosa is in the 25% marginal tax bracket and estimates that the medical and dental expenses not covered by health insurance will be within the range of $3,000 to $5,000. Her employer's plan permits her to set aside as much as $5,000 in the flexible benefits account. Rosa does not itemize her deductions.

    a. Rosa puts $3,000 into her flexible benefits account, and her actual expenses are $5,000. What is her cost of underestimating the expenses?

    b. Rosa puts $5,000 into her flexible benefits account, and her actual expenses are only $3,000. What is her cost of overestimating her expenses?

    c. What is Rosa's cost of underfunding as compared to the cost of overfunding the flexible benefits account?

    d. Does your answer in part (c) suggest that Rosa should fund the account closer to the low end or to the high end of her estimates?

48. **LO.2** Sparrow Corporation would like you to review its employee fringe benefits program with regard to the tax consequences of the plan for the company's president (Polly), who is also the majority shareholder:

    a. The company has a qualified retirement plan. The company pays the cost of employees attending a retirement planning seminar. The employee must be within 10 years of retirement, and the cost of the seminar is $1,500 per attendee.

    b. The company owns a parking garage that is used by customers, employees, and the general public. Only the general public is required to pay for parking. The charge to the general public for Polly's parking for the year would have been $3,000 (a $250 monthly rate).

    c. All employees are allowed to use the company's fixed charge long-distance telephone services, as long as the privilege is not abused. Although no one has kept track of the actual calls, Polly's use of the telephone had a value (what she would have paid on her personal telephone) of approximately $600.

    d. The company owns a condominium at the beach, which it uses to entertain customers. Employees are allowed to use the facility without charge when the company has no scheduled events. Polly used the facility 10 days during the year. Her use had a rental value of $1,000.

    e. The company is in the household moving business. Employees are allowed to ship goods without charge whenever there is excess space on a truck. Polly purchased a dining room suite for her daughter. Company trucks delivered the furniture to the daughter. Normal freight charges would have been $750.

    f. The company has a storage facility for household goods. Officers are allowed a 20% discount on charges for storing their goods. All other employees are allowed a 10% discount. Polly's discounts for the year totaled $900.

49. **LO.2** George is a U.S. citizen who is employed by Hawk Enterprises, a global company. Beginning on June 1, 2011, George began working in London. He worked there until January 31, 2012, when he transferred to Paris. He worked in Paris the remainder of 2012. His salary for the first five months of 2011 was $100,000, and it was earned in the United States. His salary for the remainder of 2011 was $175,000, and it was earned in London. George's 2012 salary from Hawk was $300,000, with part being earned in London and part being earned in Paris. What is George's gross income in 2011 and 2012 (assume the 2012 indexed amount is the same as the 2011 indexed amount)?

50. **LO.2, 3** Determine Hazel's gross income from the following receipts for the year:

Gain on sale of Augusta County bonds	$800
Interest on U.S. government savings bonds	400
Interest on state income tax refund	200
Interest on Augusta County bonds	700
Patronage dividend from Potato Growers Cooperative	350

The patronage dividend was received in March of the current year for amounts paid for her garden and lawn supplies.

51. **LO.2** In January 2011, Ezra purchased 1,000 shares of Gold Utility Mutual Fund for $20,000. In June, Ezra received an additional 50 shares as a dividend, in lieu of receiving $600 in cash dividends. In December, the company declared a two-for-one stock dividend. Ezra received an additional 1,050 shares, but there was no option to receive

cash. At the time of the stock dividend in December and at the end of the year, the fund shares were trading for $8 per share. Also, at the end of the year, the fund offered to buy outstanding shares for $9. Ezra did not sell any shares during the year.

   a.   What is Ezra's gross income from the 50 shares received in June?

   b.   What is Ezra's gross income from the receipt of the 1,050 shares as a two-for-one stock dividend?

   c.   Should Ezra be required to recognize gross income in 2011 even though the value of his investment at the end of the year was less than the fair market value at the beginning of the year?

52. **LO.2** Tonya, who lives in Virginia, inherited a $10,000 State of Virginia bond in 2011. Her marginal Federal tax rate is 35%, and her marginal state tax rate is 5%. The Virginia bond pays 4% interest, which is not subject to Virginia income tax. She can purchase a corporate bond of comparable risk that will yield 6% or a U.S. government bond that pays 5.6% interest. Tonya does not itemize her deductions. Which investment will provide the greatest after-tax yield?

DECISION MAKING

53. **LO.2** Lynn Swartz's husband died three years ago. Her parents have an income of over $200,000 a year and want to assure that funds will be available for the education of Lynn's 8-year-old son, Eric. Lynn is currently earning $45,000 a year. Lynn's parents have suggested that they start a savings account for Eric. They have calculated that if they invest $4,000 a year for the next 8 years, at the end of 10 years sufficient funds will be available for Eric's college expenses. Lynn realizes that the tax treatment of the investments could significantly affect the amount of funds available for Eric's education. She asked you to write a letter to her advising her about options available to her parents and to her for Eric's college education. Lynn's address is 100 Myrtle Cove, Fairfield, CT 06432.

DECISION MAKING
COMMUNICATIONS

54. **LO.2** Starting in 2002, Chuck and Luane have been purchasing Series EE bonds in their name to use for the higher education of their daughter (Susie, who currently is age 18). During the year, they cash in $12,000 of the bonds to use for freshman year tuition, fees, and room and board. Of this amount, $5,000 represents interest. Of the $12,000, $8,000 is used for tuition and fees, and $4,000 is used for room and board. Their AGI, before the educational savings bond exclusion, is $112,000.

   a.   Determine the tax consequences for Chuck and Luane, who will file a joint return, and for Susie.

   b.   Assume that Chuck and Luane purchased the bonds in Susie's name. Determine the tax consequences for Chuck and Luane and for Susie.

   c.   How would your answer for (a) change if Chuck and Luane file separate returns?

55. **LO.2** Albert established a qualified tuition program for each of his twins, Kim and Jim. He started each fund with $20,000 when the children were five years old. Albert made no further contributions to his children's plans. Thirteen years later, both children have graduated from high school. Kim's fund has accumulated to $45,000 while Jim's has accumulated to $42,000. Kim decides to attend a state university, which will cost $60,000 for four years (tuition, fees, room and board, and books). Jim decides to go to work instead of going to college. During the current year, $7,500 is used from Kim's plan to pay the cost of her first semester in college. Since Jim is not going to go to college now or in the future, Albert withdraws the $42,000 plan balance and gives it to Jim to start his new life after high school.

   a.   During the period since the plans were established, should Albert or the twins have been including the annual plan earnings in gross income?

   b.   What are the tax consequences to Kim and Albert of the $7,500 being used for the first semester's higher education costs?

   c.   Because of her participation in the qualified tuition program, Kim received a 10% reduction in tuition charges, so less than $7,500 was withdrawn from her account. Is either Albert or Kim required to include the value of this discount in gross income?

   d.   What are the tax consequences to Albert and Jim of Jim's qualified tuition program being closed?

56. **LO.3** How does the tax benefit rule apply in the following cases?

   a.   In 2009, the Orange Furniture Store, an accrual method taxpayer, sold furniture on credit for $1,000 to Sammy. The cost of the furniture was $600. In 2010, Orange took a bad debt deduction for the $1,000. Orange was in the 35% marginal tax bracket in

2010. In 2011, Sammy inherited some money and paid Orange the $1,000. Orange was in the 15% marginal tax bracket in 2011.

b. In 2010, Marvin, a cash basis taxpayer, took a $2,000 itemized deduction for state income taxes paid. This increased his itemized deductions to a total that was $1,200 more than the standard deduction. In 2011, Marvin received a $2,100 refund when he filed his 2010 state income tax return. Marvin was in the 15% marginal tax bracket in 2010, but was in the 35% marginal tax bracket in 2011.

c. In 2010, Barb, a cash basis taxpayer, was in an accident and incurred $7,000 in medical expenses, which she claimed as an itemized deduction for medical expenses. Because of the 7.5%-of-AGI reduction, the expense reduced her taxable income by only $5,000. In 2011, Barb collected $15,000 from the person who caused the accident that resulted in her personal injury. Barb was in the 15% marginal tax bracket in both 2010 and 2011.

DECISION MAKING

57. **LO.4, 5** Fran, who is in the 35% tax bracket, recently collected $100,000 on a life insurance policy she carried on her father. She currently owes $120,000 on her personal residence and $120,000 on business property. National Bank holds the mortgage on both pieces of property and has agreed to accept $100,000 in complete satisfaction of either mortgage. The interest rate on the mortgages is 8%, and both mortgages are payable over 10 years. What would be the tax consequences of each of the following alternatives, assuming Fran currently deducts the mortgage interest on her tax return?
a. Retire the mortgage on the residence.
b. Retire the mortgage on the business property.

Which alternative should Fran select?

58. **LO.4** Vic, who was experiencing financial difficulties, was able to adjust his debts as follows:
a. His father agreed to cancel a $25,000 debt. Vic's father told him, "I am not going to treat you any better than I treat your brothers and sisters; therefore, the $25,000 is coming out of your inheritance from me."
b. The Land Company, which had sold land to Vic for $80,000, reduced the mortgage on the land by $12,000.
c. The Subprime Bank reduced the principal of the mortgage on his principal residence by $9,000.

Determine the tax consequences to Vic.

CUMULATIVE PROBLEMS

59. **LO.4** Alfred E. Old and Beulah A. Crane, each age 42, married on September 7, 2009. Alfred and Beulah will file a joint return for 2010. Alfred's Social Security number is 111–11–1111. Beulah's Social Security number is 123–45–6789, and she adopted "Old" as her married name. They live at 211 Brickstone Drive, Atlanta, GA 30304.

Alfred was divorced from Sarah Old in March 2008. Under the divorce agreement, Alfred is to pay Sarah $1,250 per month for the next 10 years or until Sarah's death, whichever occurs first. Alfred pays Sarah $20,000 in 2010. In addition, in January 2010, Alfred pays Sarah $50,000, which is designated as being for her share of the marital property. Also, Alfred is responsible for all prior years' income taxes. Sarah's Social Security number is 123–45–6788.

Alfred's salary for 2010 is $150,000, and his employer, Cherry, Inc. (Federal I.D. No. 98–7654321), provides him with group term life insurance equal to twice his annual salary. His employer withheld $24,900 for Federal income taxes and $8,000 for state income taxes. The following amounts were withheld for FICA taxes: $6,622 ($106,800 × 6.2%) for Social Security and $2,175 ($150,000 × 1.45%) for Medicare.

Beulah recently graduated from law school and is employed by Legal Aid Society, Inc. (Federal I.D. No. 11–1111111), as a public defender. She receives a salary of $40,000 in 2010. Her employer withheld $7,500 for Federal income taxes and $2,400 for state income taxes. The following amounts were withheld for FICA taxes: $2,480 ($40,000 × 6.2%) for Social Security and $580 ($40,000 × 1.45%) for Medicare.

Beulah has $3,000 in qualified dividends on Yellow Corporation stock she inherited. Alfred and Beulah receive a $1,600 refund on their 2009 state income taxes. They itemized deductions on their 2009 Federal income tax return (total = $15,000). Alfred and Beulah pay $4,500 interest and $1,450 property taxes on their personal residence in 2010. Their charitable contributions total $2,100 (all to their church). They paid sales taxes of $1,400 for which they maintain the receipts.

Compute the Olds' net tax payable (or refund due) for 2010. If you use tax forms for your solution, you will need Form 1040 and Schedules A and B. Suggested software: H&R BLOCK At Home.

60. Martin S. Albert (Social Security number 111–11–1111) is 39 years old and is married to Michele R. Albert (Social Security number 123–45–6789). The Alberts live at 512 Ferry Road, Newport News, VA 23601. They file a joint return and have two dependent children (Charlene, age 17, and Jordan, age 18). Charlene's Social Security number is 123–45–6788, and Jordan's Social Security number is 123–45–6787. In 2011, Martin and Michele had the following transactions:

    a. Martin received $115,000 in salary from Red Steel Corporation, where he is a construction engineer. Withholding for Federal income tax was $10,750. The amounts withheld for FICA tax were as follows: $4,486 ($106,800 × 4.2%) for Social Security and $1,668 ($115,000 × 1.45%) for Medicare. Martin worked in Mexico from January 1, 2010, until February 15, 2011. His $115,000 salary for 2011 includes $16,000 he earned for January and one-half of February 2011 while working in Mexico.

    b. Martin and Michele received $800 in qualified dividends on Green, Inc. stock and $400 interest on Montgomery County (Virginia) school bonds.

    c. Martin received $2,300 interest from a Bahamian bank account.

    d. Michele received 50 shares of Applegate Corporation common stock as a stock dividend. The shares had a fair market value of $2,000 at the time Michele received them, and she did not have the option of receiving cash.

    e. Martin and Michele received a $900 refund on their 2010 Virginia income taxes. Their itemized deductions in 2010 totaled $12,500.

    f. Martin paid $6,000 alimony to his former wife, Rose T. Morgan (Social Security number 123–45–6786).

    g. Martin and Michele kept the receipts for their sales taxes paid of $1,100.

    h. Martin and Michele's itemized deductions were as follows:

        • State income tax paid and withheld totaled $5,100.
        • Real estate taxes on their principal residence were $3,400.
        • Mortgage interest on their principal residence was $2,500.
        • Cash contributions to the church totaled $2,800.

Part 1—Tax Computation
Compute the Alberts' net tax payable (or refund due) for 2011.

Part 2—Tax Planning
The Alberts are considering buying another house. Their house mortgage payments would increase by $500 (to $1,500) per month, which includes a $250 increase in interest and a $100 increase in property tax. The Alberts would like to know how much the mortgage payments would increase net of any change in their income tax. Write a letter to the Alberts that contains your advice.

TAX COMPUTATION PROBLEM

DECISION MAKING

COMMUNICATIONS

RESEARCH PROBLEMS

Note: Solutions to Research Problems can be prepared by using the Checkpoint® Student Edition online research product, which is available to accompany this text. It is also possible to prepare solutions to the Research Problems by using tax research materials found in a standard tax library.

THOMSON REUTERS
Checkpoint® Student Edition

Research Problem 1. Murray reported to the Environmental Protection Agency that his employer was illegally dumping chemicals into a river. His charges were true, and Murray's employer was fined. In retaliation, Murray's employer fired him and made deliberate efforts to prevent Murray from obtaining other employment. Murray sued the employer claiming that his reputation had been damaged. Murray won his lawsuit and received an award for "damages to his personal and professional reputation and for his mental suffering." Now he would like to know whether the award is taxable. He argues that he was awarded damages as a recovery of his human capital and a recovery of capital is not income. Therefore, the Federal government does not have the power to tax the award.

Research Problem 2. The employees of the City of Greenville must make mandatory contributions to the City's postretirement health benefit plan. The employees' contributions are placed in a trust and are used exclusively for the employees' benefits. The employees believe that since they are required to make the contributions from their base salaries, the result should be the same as if the employer made the contribution and had reduced their salaries by the amount of the contributions. Therefore, the employees believe they should be permitted to exclude the payments from gross income. The employees have asked you to research the issue.

Research Problem 3. Kristina will soon graduate from law school with more than $40,000 in student loans. She would like to work as a public defender, but the pay is not enough to allow her to meet her living expenses and repay the student loans. Her law school offers a "debt forgiveness program" for graduates who enter public service, including working as a public defender. Under the program, the school will pay the student's debt, but the graduate will owe an equal amount to the program. However, if the graduate remains in public service for at least four years, the debt is forgiven. Kristina would like to know the tax consequences if she decides to utilize this program.

Research Problem 4. Aubrey Brown is a decorated veteran of the Vietnam War. As a result of his exposure to Agent Orange during the war, Aubrey developed lung cancer and is unable to work. He received $12,000 of Social Security disability payments in the current year. He reasons that the payments should be excluded from his gross income because the payments are compensation for the physical injury he suffered as a result of his service in the armed forces. Is Aubrey correct?

Partial list of research aids:
Rev.Rul. 77–318, 1977–2 C.B. 45.
Reimels v. Comm., 2006–1 USTC ¶50,147, 97 AFTR 2d 2006–820, 436 F.3d 344 (CA–2, 2006).

Use the tax resources of the Internet to address the following questions. Do not restrict your search to the Web, but include a review of newsgroups and general reference materials, practitioner sites and resources, primary sources of the tax law, chat rooms and discussion groups, and other opportunities.

INTERNET *activity*

COMMUNICATIONS

Research Problem 5. Go to the IRS site on the Internet and download instructions and Regulations relative to educational savings bonds and qualified tuition programs. Summarize one of the key provisions in these materials in outline format.

Research Problem 6. Employers often use the Internet as a means of attracting applications from potential employees. Locate an Internet site offering employment opportunities, ideally one provided by a well-known corporation. How does the employer promote its fringe benefit and cafeteria plan packages? Compare and contrast several such sites.

Deductions

Part 3 presents the deduction component of the basic tax model. Deductions are classified as business versus nonbusiness, "for" versus "from," employee versus employer, active versus passive, and reimbursed versus unreimbursed. The effect of each of these classifications is analyzed. The presentation includes not only the deductions that are permitted, but also limitations and disallowances associated with deductions. Because deductions can exceed gross income, the treatment of losses is also included.

Deductions and Losses: In General

LEARNING OBJECTIVES

After completing Chapter 6, you should be able to:

L0.1
Differentiate between deductions *for* and *from* adjusted gross income and understand the relevance of the differentiation.

L0.2
Describe the cash and accrual methods of accounting.

L0.3
Apply the Internal Revenue Code deduction disallowance provisions associated with the following: public policy limitations, political activities, excessive executive compensation, investigation of business opportunities, hobby losses, vacation home rentals, payment of others' expenses, personal expenditures, capital expenditures, related-party transactions, and expenses related to tax-exempt income.

L0.4
Identify tax planning opportunities for maximizing deductions and minimizing the disallowance of deductions.

 For the latest in changes to tax legislation, visit **www.cengage.com/taxation/swft.**

FRAMEWORK 1040:
Tax Formula for Individuals

This chapter covers the boldfaced portions of the Tax Formula for Individuals that was introduced in Figure 3.1 on p. 3-3. Below those portions are the sections of Form 1040 where the results are reported.

Income (broadly conceived)	$xx,xxx
Less: Exclusions	(x,xxx)
Gross income	$xx,xxx
Less: Deductions for adjusted gross income	**(x,xxx)**

FORM 1040 (p. 1)

12	Business income or (loss). Attach Schedule C or C-EZ	

Adjusted gross income	$xx,xxx
Less: The greater of total **itemized deductions** *or* the standard deduction	**(x,xxx)**

FORM 1040 (p. 2)

40	**Itemized deductions** (from Schedule A) **or** your **standard deduction** (see instructions)	

Personal and dependency exemptions	(x,xxx)
Taxable income	$xx,xxx
Tax on taxable income (see Tax Tables or Tax Rate Schedules)	$ x,xxx
Less: Tax credits (including income taxes withheld and prepaid)	(xxx)
Tax due (or refund)	$ xxx

THE BIG PICTURE   Tax Solutions for the Real World

CALCULATION OF DEDUCTIBLE EXPENSES

Dr. Cliff Payne extracts the following information from his financial reporting system associated with his dental practice.

Salaries including FICA (unpaid at year-end of $5,000)	$120,000
Building rent	24,000
Depreciation of dental equipment and office furnishings and equipment	52,000
Insurance (malpractice and of dental equipment and office furnishings and equipment)	22,000
Dental supplies (ending inventory of $7,000)	16,000
Office supplies (ending inventory of $1,500)	3,000
Contribution to U.S. Senate campaign fund of Barbara Boxer	1,000
Contribution to U.S. Senate campaign fund of Carly Fiorina	1,000
Legal expenses associated with patient lawsuit (jury decision for defendant)	4,000
Draw by Dr. Payne for living expenses ($5,000 monthly)	60,000

Dr. Payne calculates the deductible expenses that he can report on Schedule C of Form 1040 as follows:

Salaries including FICA	$120,000
Building rent	24,000
Depreciation of dental equipment and office furnishings and equipment	52,000
Insurance (malpractice and of dental equipment and office furnishings and equipment)	22,000
Dental supplies ($16,000 − $7,000)	9,000
Office supplies ($3,000 − $1,500)	1,500
Contribution to U.S. Senate campaign fund of Barbara Boxer	–0–
Contribution to U.S. Senate campaign fund of Carly Fiorina	–0–
Legal expenses associated with patient lawsuit (jury decision for defendant)	4,000
Draw by Dr. Payne for living expenses ($5,000 monthly)	60,000
	$292,500

Dr. Payne's close relatives include the following:

Terry	mother
Jack	father
Camille	mother-in-law
Walter	father-in-law
Pauline	sister (age 15)
Neal	brother (age 16)

Has Dr. Payne correctly calculated the business expenses for his dental practice? **Read the chapter and formulate your response.**

6.1 CLASSIFICATION OF DEDUCTIBLE EXPENSES

LO.1
Differentiate between deductions *for* and *from* adjusted gross income and understand the relevance of the differentiation.

The tax law has an all-inclusive definition of income; that is, income from whatever source derived is includible in gross income. Income cannot be excluded unless there is a specific statement to that effect in the Internal Revenue Code.

Similarly, deductions are disallowed unless a specific provision in the tax law permits them. The inclusive definition of income and the exclusive definition of deductions may not seem fair to taxpayers, but it is the structure of the tax law.

The courts have held that, whether and to what extent deductions are allowed depends on legislative grace.[1] In other words, any exclusions from income and all deductions are gifts from Congress!

It is important to classify deductible expenses as **deductions for adjusted gross income** (AGI) or **deductions from adjusted gross income**. Deductions *for* AGI can be claimed whether or not the taxpayer itemizes. Deductions *from* AGI result in a tax benefit only if they exceed the taxpayer's standard deduction. If itemized deductions (*from* AGI) are less than the standard deduction, they provide no tax benefit.

---

[1] *New Colonial Ice Co. v. Helvering*, 4 USTC ¶1292, 13 AFTR 1180, 54 S.Ct. 788 (USSC, 1934).

EXAMPLE 1

Steve is a self-employed CPA. Ralph is one of Steve's employees. During the year, Steve and Ralph incur the following expenses:

	Steve	Ralph
Dues to American Institute of CPAs and State Society of CPAs	$ 400	$ 300
Subscriptions to professional journals	500	200
Registration fees for tax conferences	800	800
	$1,700	$1,300

Steve does not reimburse any of his employees for dues, subscriptions, or educational programs.

Steve's expenses are classified as a deduction *for* AGI. Therefore, he can deduct the $1,700 on his Federal income tax return. Ralph's expenses are classified as deductions *from* AGI. Ralph will be able to benefit from the $1,300 of expenses on his Federal income tax return only if he itemizes deductions. If he takes the standard deduction instead, the $1,300 of expenses will have no effect on the calculation of his taxable income. Even if Ralph does itemize deductions, he must reduce the $1,300 of expenses, which are classified as miscellaneous itemized deductions, by 2% of his AGI. As this example illustrates, whether a deduction is classified as *for* AGI or *from* AGI can affect the benefit the taxpayer receives from the deduction. ■

See Concept Summary 6.3 later in the chapter for the classification of deductions as deductions *for* AGI or as deductions *from* AGI.

Deductions *for* AGI are also important in determining the *amount* of itemized deductions because many itemized deductions are limited to amounts in excess of specified percentages of AGI. Examples of itemized deductions that are limited by AGI are medical expenses and personal casualty losses. Itemized deductions that are deductible only to the extent that they exceed a specified percentage of AGI are increased when AGI is decreased. Likewise, when AGI is increased, these itemized deductions are decreased.

EXAMPLE 2

Tina earns a salary of $20,000 and has no other income. She itemizes deductions during the current year. Medical expenses for the year are $1,800. Since medical expenses are deductible only to the extent they exceed 7.5% of AGI, Tina's medical expense deduction is $300 [$1,800 − (7.5% × $20,000)]. If Tina had a $2,000 deduction *for* AGI, her medical expense deduction would be $450 [$1,800 − (7.5% × $18,000)], or $150 more. If the $2,000 deduction was *from* AGI, her medical expense deduction would remain $300 since AGI is unchanged. ■

DEDUCTIONS FOR ADJUSTED GROSS INCOME

To understand how deductions of individual taxpayers are classified, it is necessary to examine the role of § 62. The purpose of § 62 is to classify various deductions as deductions *for* AGI. It does not provide the statutory authority for taking the deduction. For example, § 212 allows individuals to deduct expenses attributable to income-producing property. Section 212 expenses that are attributable to rents or royalties are classified as deductions *for* AGI. Likewise, a deduction for trade or business expenses is allowed by § 162. These expenses are classified as deductions *for* AGI.

If a deduction is not listed in § 62, it is an itemized deduction, not a deduction *for* AGI. Following is a *partial* list of the items classified as deductions *for* AGI by § 62:

- Expenses attributable to a trade or business carried on by the taxpayer. A trade or business does not include the performance of services by the taxpayer as an employee.
- Expenses incurred by a taxpayer in connection with the performance of services as an employee if the expenses are reimbursed and other conditions are satisfied.

- Deductions that result from losses on the sale or exchange of property by the taxpayer.
- Deductions attributable to property held for the production of rents and royalties.
- The deduction for payment of alimony.
- The deduction for one-half of the self-employment tax paid by a self-employed taxpayer.
- The deduction for the medical insurance premiums paid by a self-employed taxpayer for coverage of the taxpayer, spouse, and any dependents.
- Certain contributions to pension, profit sharing, and annuity plans of self-employed individuals.
- The deduction for certain retirement savings allowed by § 219 (e.g., traditional IRAs).
- The penalty imposed on premature withdrawal of funds from time savings accounts or deposits.
- The deduction for moving expenses.
- The deduction for interest paid on student loans.
- The deduction for qualified tuition and related expenses under § 222 (refer to Chapter 9).
- The deduction for up to $250 for teacher supplies for elementary and secondary school teachers (refer to Chapter 9).

These items are covered in detail in various chapters in the text.

ITEMIZED DEDUCTIONS

The Code defines itemized deductions as the deductions allowed other than "the deductions allowable in arriving at adjusted gross income."[2] Thus, if a deduction is not properly classified as a deduction *for* AGI, then it is classified as an itemized deduction.

Section 212 Expenses

Section 212 allows deductions for ordinary and necessary expenses paid or incurred for the following:

- The production or collection of income.
- The management, conservation, or maintenance of property held for the production of income.
- Expenses paid in connection with the determination, collection, or refund of any tax.

Section 212 expenses related to rent and royalty income are deductions *for* AGI. Expenses paid in connection with the determination, collection, or refund of taxes related to the income of sole proprietorships, rents and royalties, or farming operations are deductions *for* AGI. All other § 212 expenses are itemized deductions (deductions *from* AGI). For example, investment-related expenses (e.g., safe deposit box rentals) are deductible as itemized deductions attributable to the production of investment income.[3]

Deductible Personal Expenses

Taxpayers are allowed to deduct certain expenses that are primarily personal in nature. These expenses, which generally are not related to the production of income, are deductions *from* AGI (itemized deductions). Some of the more frequently encountered deductions in this category include the following:

- Contributions to qualified charitable organizations (not to exceed a specified percentage of AGI).
- Medical expenses (in excess of 7.5 percent of AGI).
- Certain state and local taxes (e.g., real estate taxes and state and local income or sales taxes).

---

[2]§ 63(d).

[3]§ 62(a)(4) and Reg. § 1.212–1(g).

- Personal casualty losses (in excess of an aggregate floor of 10 percent of AGI and a $100 floor per casualty).[4]
- Certain personal interest (e.g., mortgage interest on a personal residence).

Itemized deductions are discussed in detail in Chapter 10.

TRADE OR BUSINESS EXPENSES AND PRODUCTION OF INCOME EXPENSES

Section 162(a) permits a deduction for all ordinary and necessary expenses paid or incurred in carrying on a trade or business. These include reasonable salaries paid for services, expenses for the use of business property, and one-half of self-employment taxes paid (see Chapter 13). Such expenses are deducted *for* AGI.

It is sometimes difficult to determine whether an expenditure is deductible as a trade or business expense. The term "trade or business" is not defined in the Code or Regulations, and the courts have not provided a satisfactory definition. It is usually necessary to ask one or more of the following questions to determine whether an item qualifies as a trade or business expense:

- Was the use of the particular item related to a business activity? For example, if funds are borrowed for use in a business, the interest is deductible as a business expense.
- Was the expenditure incurred with the intent to realize a profit or to produce income? For example, expenses in excess of the income from raising horses are not deductible if the activity is classified as a personal hobby rather than a trade or business.
- Were the taxpayer's operation and management activities extensive enough to indicate the carrying on of a trade or business?

Section 162 *excludes* the following items from classification as trade or business expenses:

- Charitable contributions or gifts.
- Illegal bribes and kickbacks and certain treble damage payments.
- Fines and penalties.

A bribe paid to a domestic official is not deductible if it is illegal under the laws of the United States. Foreign bribes are deductible unless they are unlawful under the Foreign Corrupt Practices Act of 1977.[5]

Ordinary and Necessary Requirement

The terms **ordinary and necessary** are found in both §§ 162 and 212. To be deductible, any trade or business expense must be "ordinary and necessary." In addition, compensation for services must be "reasonable" in amount.

Many expenses that are necessary are *not* ordinary. Neither "ordinary" nor "necessary" is defined in the Code or Regulations. The courts have held that an expense is *necessary* if a prudent businessperson would incur the same expense and the expense is expected to be appropriate and helpful in the taxpayer's business.[6]

EXAMPLE 3

Pat purchased a manufacturing concern that had just been adjudged bankrupt. Because the business had a poor financial rating, Pat satisfied some of the obligations to employees and outside salespeople incurred by the former owners. Pat had no legal obligation to pay these debts, but felt this was the only way to keep salespeople and employees. The Second Circuit Court of Appeals found that the payments were necessary in that they were both appropriate and helpful. However, the court held that the payments were *not* ordinary but were in the nature of capital expenditures to build a reputation.[7] Therefore, no deduction was allowed. ∎

[4]For 2009 the $100 floor was increased to $500.
[5]§ 162(c)(1).
[6]*Welch v. Helvering*, 3 USTC ¶1164, 12 AFTR 1456, 54 S.Ct. 8 (USSC, 1933).
[7]*Dunn and McCarthy, Inc. v. Comm.*, 43–2 USTC ¶9688, 31 AFTR 1043, 139 F.2d 242 (CA–2, 1943).

An expense is *ordinary* if it is normal, usual, or customary in the type of business conducted by the taxpayer and is not capital in nature.[8] However, an expense need not be recurring to be deductible as ordinary.

EXAMPLE 4

Albert engaged in a mail-order business. The post office judged that his advertisements were false and misleading. Under a fraud order, the post office stamped "fraudulent" on all letters addressed to Albert's business and returned them to the senders. Albert spent $30,000 on legal fees in an unsuccessful attempt to force the post office to stop. The legal fees (though not recurring) were ordinary business expenses because they were normal, usual, or customary in the circumstances.[9] ∎

For § 212 deductions, the law requires that expenses bear a reasonable and proximate relationship to (1) the production or collection of income or to (2) the management, conservation, or maintenance of property held for the production of income.[10]

EXAMPLE 5
THE BIG PICTURE

Return to the facts of *The Big Picture* on p. 6-2. Dr. Payne owns a small portfolio of investments, including 10 shares of Hawk, Inc. common stock worth $1,000. He incurred $350 in travel expenses to attend the annual shareholders' meeting where he voted his 10 shares against the current management group. No deduction is permitted because a 10-share investment is insignificant in value in relation to the travel expenses incurred.[11] ∎

Reasonableness Requirement

The Code refers to **reasonableness** solely with respect to salaries and other compensation for services.[12] But the courts have held that for any business expense to be ordinary and necessary, it must also be reasonable in amount.[13]

What constitutes reasonableness is a question of fact. If an expense is unreasonable, the excess amount is not allowed as a deduction. The question of reasonableness generally arises with respect to closely held corporations where there is no separation of ownership and management.

Transactions between the shareholders and the closely held company may result in the disallowance of deductions for excessive salaries and rent expense paid by the corporation to the shareholders. The courts will view an unusually large salary in light of all relevant circumstances and may find that the salary is reasonable despite its size.[14] If excessive payments for salaries and rents are closely related to the percentage of stock owned by the recipients, the payments are generally treated as dividends.[15] Since dividends are not deductible by the corporation, the disallowance results in an increase in the corporate taxable income. Deductions for reasonable salaries will not be disallowed *solely* because the corporation has paid insubstantial portions of its earnings as dividends to its shareholders.

EXAMPLE 6

Sparrow Corporation, a closely held C corporation, is owned equally by Lupe, Carlos, and Ramon. The company has been highly profitable for several years and has not paid dividends. Lupe, Carlos, and Ramon are key officers of the company, and each receives a salary of $200,000. Salaries for similar positions in comparable companies average only $100,000. Amounts paid the owners in excess of $100,000 may be deemed unreasonable, and, if so, a total of $300,000 in salary deductions by Sparrow is disallowed. The disallowed amounts are treated as dividends rather than salary income to Lupe,

---

[8] *Deputy v. DuPont*, 40–1 USTC ¶9161, 23 AFTR 808, 60 S.Ct. 363 (USSC, 1940).

[9] *Comm. v. Heininger*, 44–1 USTC ¶9109, 31 AFTR 783, 64 S.Ct. 249 (USSC, 1943).

[10] Reg. § 1.212–1(d).

[11] *J. Raymond Dyer*, 36 T.C. 456 (1961).

[12] § 162(a)(1).

[13] *Comm. v. Lincoln Electric Co.*, 49–2 USTC ¶9388, 38 AFTR 411, 176 F.2d 815 (CA–6, 1949).

[14] *Kennedy, Jr. v. Comm.*, 82–1 USTC ¶9186, 49 AFTR 2d 82–628, 671 F.2d 167 (CA–6, 1982), *rev'g* 72 T.C. 793 (1979).

[15] Reg. § 1.162–8.

Carlos, and Ramon because the payments are proportional to stock ownership. Salaries are deductible by the corporation, but dividends are not. ∎

BUSINESS AND NONBUSINESS LOSSES

Section 165 provides for a deduction for losses not compensated for by insurance. As a general rule, deductible losses of individual taxpayers are limited to those incurred in a trade or business or in a transaction entered into for profit. Individuals are also allowed to deduct losses that are the result of a casualty. Casualty losses include, but are not limited to, those caused by fire, storm, shipwreck, and theft. See Chapter 7 for a further discussion of this topic. Deductible personal casualty losses are reduced by $100 per casualty, and the aggregate of all personal casualty losses is reduced by 10 percent of AGI. A personal casualty loss is an itemized deduction. See Concept Summary 6.3 near the end of the chapter for the classification of expenses.

REPORTING PROCEDURES

All deductions *for* and *from* AGI wind up on pages 1 and 2 of Form 1040. All deductions *for* AGI are reported on page 1. The last line on page 1 is adjusted gross income.

The first item on page 2 is also adjusted gross income. Itemized deductions are entered next, followed by the deduction for personal and dependency exemptions. The result is taxable income.

Most of the deductions *for* AGI on page 1 originate on supporting schedules. Examples include business expenses (Schedule C); rent, royalty, partnership, and fiduciary deductions (Schedule E); and farming expenses (Schedule F). Other deductions *for* AGI, such as traditional IRAs, Keogh retirement plans, and alimony, are entered directly on page 1 of Form 1040.

All itemized deductions on page 2 are carried over from Schedule A. Some Schedule A deductions originate on other forms. Examples include investment interest, noncash charitable contributions in excess of $500, casualty losses, and unreimbursed employee expenses.

Form 1040 becomes a summary of the detailed information entered on the other schedules and forms. See Figure 6.1.

See Concept Summary 6.3 later in the chapter for the classification of deductions as deductions *for* AGI or as deductions *from* AGI.

6.2 DEDUCTIONS AND LOSSES— TIMING OF EXPENSE RECOGNITION

LO.2

Describe the cash and accrual methods of accounting.

IMPORTANCE OF TAXPAYER'S METHOD OF ACCOUNTING

A taxpayer's **accounting method** is a major factor in determining taxable income. The method used determines when an item is includible in income and when an item is deductible on the tax return. Usually, the taxpayer's regular method of record keeping is used for income tax purposes.[16] The taxing authorities do not require uniformity among all taxpayers. They do require that the method used clearly reflect income and that items be handled consistently.[17] The most common methods of accounting are the cash method and the accrual method. If a taxpayer owns multiple businesses, it may be possible to use the cash method for some and the accrual method for others.

Throughout the portions of the Code dealing with deductions, the phrase "paid or incurred" is used. *Paid* refers to the cash basis taxpayer who gets a deduction only in the year of payment. *Incurred* concerns the accrual basis taxpayer who obtains the

---

[16]§ 446(a).

[17]§§ 446(b) and (e); Reg. § 1.446–1(a)(2).

FIGURE 6.1   Format of Form 1040

deduction in the year in which the liability for the expense becomes certain (refer to Chapter 4).

CASH METHOD REQUIREMENTS

The expenses of cash basis taxpayers are deductible only when they are actually paid with cash or other property. Promising to pay or issuing a note does not satisfy the actually paid requirement.[18] However, the payment can be made with borrowed funds. At the time taxpayers charge expenses on their credit cards, they are allowed to claim the deduction. They are deemed to have simultaneously borrowed money from the credit card issuer and constructively paid the expenses.[19]

Although the cash basis taxpayer must have actually or constructively paid the expense, payment does not assure a current deduction. Cash basis and accrual basis taxpayers cannot take a current deduction for capital expenditures except through amortization, depletion, or depreciation over the life (actual or statutory) of the asset. The Regulations set forth the general rule that an expenditure that creates an

---

[18]*Page v. Rhode Island Trust Co., Exr.*, 37–1 USTC ¶9138, 19 AFTR 105, 88 F.2d 192 (CA–1, 1937).

[19]Rev.Rul. 78–39, 1978–1 C.B. 73. See also Rev.Rul. 80–335, 1980–2 C.B. 170, which applies to pay-by-phone arrangements.

asset having a useful life that extends substantially beyond the end of the tax year must be capitalized.[20]

EXAMPLE 7

John, a calendar year and cash basis taxpayer, rents property from Carl. On July 1, 2011, John pays $24,000 rent for the 24 months ending June 30, 2013. The prepaid rent extends 18 months after the close of the tax year—substantially beyond the year of payment. Therefore, John must capitalize the prepaid rent and amortize the expense on a monthly basis. His deduction for 2011 is $6,000. ∎

The Tax Court and the IRS took the position that an asset that will expire or be consumed by the end of the tax year following the year of payment must be pro-rated. The Ninth Circuit Court of Appeals held that such expenditures are currently deductible, however, and the Supreme Court apparently concurs (the one-year rule for prepaid expenses).[21]

EXAMPLE 8

Assume the same facts as in Example 7 except that John is required to pay only 12 months' rent in 2011. He pays $12,000 on July 1, 2011. The entire $12,000 is deductible in 2011. ∎

The payment must be required, not a voluntary prepayment, to obtain the current deduction under the one-year rule.[22] The taxpayer must also demonstrate that allowing the current deduction will not result in a material distortion of income. Generally, the deduction will be allowed if the item is recurring or was made for a business purpose rather than to manipulate income.[23]

As Chapter 18 explains, not all taxpayers are allowed to use the cash method.[24] For example, in most cases the taxpayer is required to use the accrual method for sales and cost of goods sold if inventories are an income-producing factor of the business.

ACCRUAL METHOD REQUIREMENTS

The period in which an accrual basis taxpayer can deduct an expense is determined by applying the *all events test* and the *economic performance test*. A deduction cannot be claimed until (1) all the events have occurred to create the taxpayer's liability and (2) the amount of the liability can be determined with reasonable accuracy. Once these requirements are satisfied, the deduction is permitted only if economic performance has occurred. The economic performance test is met only when the service, property, or use of property giving rise to the liability is actually performed for, provided to, or used by the taxpayer.[25]

EXAMPLE 9

On December 22, 2011, Chris's entertainment business sponsored a jazz festival in a rented auditorium at a local college. His business is responsible for cleaning up the auditorium after the festival and for reinstalling seats that were removed so more people could attend the festival. Since the college is closed over the Christmas holidays, the company hired by Chris to perform the work did not begin these activities until January 2, 2012. The cost to Chris is $1,200. Chris cannot deduct the $1,200 until 2012, when the services are performed. ∎

---

[20]Reg. § 1.461–1(a).

[21]*Zaninovich v. Comm.*, 80–1 USTC ¶9342, 45 AFTR 2d 80–1442, 616 F.2d 429 (CA–9, 1980), *rev'g* 69 T.C. 605 (1978). Cited by the Supreme Court in *Hillsboro National Bank v. Comm.*, 83–1 USTC ¶9229, 51 AFTR 2d 83–874, 103 S.Ct. 1134 (USSC, 1983).

[22]*Bonaire Development Co. v. Comm.*, 82–2 USTC ¶9428, 50 AFTR 2d 82–5167, 679 F.2d 159 (CA–9, 1982).

[23]*Keller v. Comm.*, 84–1 USTC ¶9194, 53 AFTR 2d 84–663, 725 F.2d 1173 (CA–8, 1984), *aff'g* 79 T.C. 7 (1982).

[24]§ 448.

[25]§ 461(h).

An exception to the economic performance requirements allows certain *recurring items* to be deducted if the following conditions are met:

- The item is recurring in nature and is treated consistently by the taxpayer.
- Either the accrued item is not material, or accruing it results in better matching of income and expenses.
- All the events have occurred that determine the fact of the liability, and the amount of the liability can be determined with reasonable accuracy.
- Economic performance occurs within a reasonable period (but not later than 8½ months after the close of the taxable year).[26]

EXAMPLE 10

Rick, an accrual basis, calendar year taxpayer, entered into a monthly maintenance contract during the year. He makes a monthly accrual at the end of every month for this service and pays the fee sometime between the first and fifteenth of the following month when services are performed. The amount involved is immaterial, and all the other tests are met. The December 2011 accrual is deductible in 2011 even though the service is performed on January 12, 2012. ∎

EXAMPLE 11

Rita, an accrual basis, calendar year taxpayer, shipped merchandise sold on December 30, 2011, via Greyhound Van Lines on January 2, 2012, and paid the freight charges at that time. Since Rita reported the sale of the merchandise in 2011, the shipping charge should also be deductible in 2011. This procedure results in a better matching of income and expenses. ∎

Reserves for estimated expenses (frequently employed for financial accounting purposes) generally are not allowed for tax purposes because the economic performance test cannot be satisfied.

EXAMPLE 12

Blackbird Airlines is required by Federal law to test its engines after 3,000 flying hours. Aircraft cannot return to flight until the tests have been conducted. An unrelated aircraft maintenance company does all of the company's tests for $1,500 per engine. For financial reporting purposes, the company accrues an expense based upon $.50 per hour of flight and credits an allowance account. The actual amounts paid for maintenance are offset against the allowance account. For tax purposes, the economic performance test is not satisfied until the work has been done. Therefore, the reserve method cannot be used for tax purposes. ∎

6.3 DISALLOWANCE POSSIBILITIES

LO.3

Apply the Internal Revenue Code deduction disallowance provisions associated with the following: public policy limitations, political activities, excessive executive compensation, investigation of business opportunities, hobby losses, vacation home rentals, payment of others' expenses, personal expenditures, capital expenditures, related-party transactions, and expenses related to tax-exempt income.

The tax law provides for the disallowance of certain types of expenses. Without specific restrictions in the tax law, taxpayers might attempt to deduct certain items that in reality are personal expenditures. For example, specific tax rules are provided to determine whether an expenditure is for trade or business purposes or related to a personal hobby.

Certain disallowance provisions are a codification or extension of prior court decisions. After the courts denied deductions for payments considered to be in violation of public policy, the tax law was changed to provide specific authority for the disallowance of these deductions. Discussions of specific disallowance provisions in the tax law follow.

---

[26]§ 461(h)(3)(A).

PUBLIC POLICY LIMITATION

Justification for Denying Deductions

The courts developed the principle that a payment that is in violation of public policy is not a necessary expense and is not deductible.[27] Although a bribe or fine may be appropriate and helpful, and even contribute to the profitability of an activity, the courts held that to allow such expenses would frustrate clearly defined public policy. A deduction would dilute the effect of the penalty since the government would be indirectly subsidizing a taxpayer's wrongdoing.

Accordingly, the IRS was free to restrict deductions if, in its view, the expenses were contrary to public policy. But since the law did not explain which actions violated public policy, taxpayers often had to go to court to determine whether their expense fell into this category.

Furthermore, the public policy doctrine could be arbitrarily applied in cases where no clear definition had emerged. To solve these problems, Congress enacted legislation that attempts to limit the use of the doctrine. Under the legislation, deductions are disallowed for certain specific types of expenditures that are considered contrary to public policy:

- Bribes and kickbacks, including those associated with Medicare or Medicaid (in the case of foreign bribes and kickbacks, only if the payments violate the U.S. Foreign Corrupt Practices Act of 1977).
- Fines and penalties paid to a government for violation of law.

EXAMPLE 13

Brown Corporation, a moving company, consistently loads its trucks with weights in excess of the limits allowed by state law. The additional revenue more than offsets the fines levied. The fines are for a violation of public policy and are not deductible. ■

- Two-thirds of the treble damage payments made to claimants resulting from violation of the antitrust law.[28]

To be disallowed, the bribe or kickback must be illegal under either Federal or state law and must also subject the payor to a criminal penalty or the loss of a license or privilege to engage in a trade or business. For a bribe or kickback that is illegal under state law, a deduction is denied only if the state law is generally enforced.

EXAMPLE 14

During the year, Keith, an insurance salesman, paid $5,000 to Karen, a real estate broker. The payment represented 20% of the commissions Keith earned from customers referred by Karen. Under state law, the splitting of commissions by an insurance salesperson is an act of misconduct that could warrant a revocation of the salesperson's license. Keith's $5,000 payments to Karen are not deductible provided the state law is generally enforced. ■

Legal Expenses Incurred in Defense of Civil or Criminal Penalties

To deduct legal expenses, the taxpayer must be able to show that the origin and character of the claim are directly related to a trade or business, an income-producing activity, or the determination, collection, or refund of a tax. Personal legal expenses are not deductible. Thus, legal fees incurred in connection with a criminal defense are deductible only if the crime is associated with the taxpayer's trade or business or income-producing activity.[29]

EXAMPLE 15

Debra, a financial officer of Blue Corporation, incurs legal expenses in connection with her defense in a criminal indictment for evasion of Blue's income taxes. Debra may

---

[27]*Tank Truck Rentals, Inc. v. Comm.*, 58–1 USTC ¶9366, 1 AFTR 2d 1154, 78 S.Ct. 507 (USSC, 1958).

[28]§§ 162(c), (f), and (g).

[29]*Comm. v. Tellier*, 66–1 USTC ¶9319, 17 AFTR 2d 633, 86 S.Ct. 1118 (USSC, 1966).

BRIBES THAT ARE DEDUCTIBLE?

GLOBAL
Tax Issues

Under the Foreign Corrupt Practices Act of 1977, a payment that is a common business practice in the country where it is made is legal and is not disallowed as a bribe.

According to a study published by the Brookings Institution, bribes, patronage, and other forms of public corruption are major sources of Greece's ballooning debt. Such costs deprive Greece of at least 8 percent of its GDP each year. In 2009, 13.5 percent of Greek households paid at least one bribe, amounting to 1,355 euros on average (about $1,900 in 2010 dollars). Ordinary citizens hand out "little envelopes" to get driver's licenses, doctor's appointments, and building permits. Such envelopes are also used to reduce taxes owed to the government. Some tax offices apparently operate under the "4-4-2" system, a name derived from a soccer tactic. For example, if an individual or company owes the government 10,000 euros, it is distributed as follows: pay 4,000 to the tax inspector, keep 4,000, and pay 2,000 to the government.

In this environment, bribes of government officials would probably be deductible under the provisions of the Foreign Corrupt Practices Act.

Source: Adapted from Marcus Walker, "Tragic Flaw: Graft Feeds Greek Crisis," *Wall Street Journal*, April 16, 2010, p. A1.

---

deduct her legal expenses because she is deemed to be in the trade or business of being an executive. The legal action impairs her ability to conduct this business activity.[30] ∎

Deductible legal expenses associated with the following are deductible *for* AGI:

- Ordinary and necessary expenses incurred in connection with a trade or business.
- Ordinary and necessary expenses incurred in conjunction with rental or royalty property held for the production of income.

All other deductible legal expenses are deductible *from* AGI. For example, legal expenses generally are deductible *from* AGI if they are for fees for tax advice relative to the preparation of an individual's income tax return. Contrast this with the deduction *for* classification of legal fees for tax advice relative to the preparation of the portion of the tax return for a sole proprietor's trade or business (Schedule C) or an individual's rental or royalty income (Schedule E).

Expenses Relating to an Illegal Business

The usual expenses of operating an illegal business (e.g., a numbers racket) are deductible.[31] However, § 162 disallows a deduction for fines, bribes to public officials, illegal kickbacks, and other illegal payments.

EXAMPLE 16

Sam owns and operates an illegal gambling establishment. In connection with this activity, he has the following expenses during the year:

Rent	$ 60,000
Payoffs to the police	40,000
Depreciation on equipment	100,000
Wages	140,000
Interest	30,000
Criminal fines	50,000
Illegal kickbacks	10,000
Total	$430,000

---

[30]Rev.Rul. 68–662, 1968–2 C.B. 69.

[31]*Comm. v. Sullivan*, 58–1 USTC ¶9368, 1 AFTR 2d 1158, 78 S.Ct. 512 (USSC, 1958).

All of the usual expenses (rent, depreciation, wages, and interest) are deductible; payoffs, fines, and kickbacks are not deductible. Of the $430,000 spent, $330,000 is deductible and $100,000 is not. ■

An exception applies to expenses incurred in illegal trafficking in drugs.[32] *Drug dealers* are not allowed a deduction for ordinary and necessary business expenses incurred in their business. In arriving at gross income from the business, however, dealers may reduce total sales by the cost of goods sold.[33] In this regard, no distinction is made between legal and illegal businesses in calculating gross income. Treating cost of goods sold as a negative income item rather than as a deduction item produces the unseemly result that a drug dealer's taxable income is reduced by cost of goods sold.

ETHICS & Equity   TOO MUCH OF A GOOD THING

Clark, a prospective new client, visits your office on March 12, 2011. He wants you to prepare a Form 1120S for 2010 for his washateria, Wash Clean, an S corporation. Clark owns at least six different businesses in your community and has a reputation of being a risk taker and an "operator." He provides you with the financial data prepared monthly for Wash Clean by a local bookkeeping service. He hopes to file the S corporation return by March 15 "to avoid any problems with the IRS." Clark also is the president of the Chamber of Commerce.

In preparing the Form 1120S, you note that the net income for Wash Clean far exceeds that of several other washateria clients. About a month ago, one of your golfing companions mentioned that he had heard that Wash Clean was laundering more than clothes.

You have all the data you need to complete the Form 1120S for Wash Clean. Should you do so?

POLITICAL CONTRIBUTIONS AND LOBBYING ACTIVITIES

Political Contributions

Generally, no business deduction is permitted for direct or indirect payments for political purposes.[34] Historically, the government has been reluctant to accord favorable tax treatment to business expenditures for political purposes. Allowing deductions might encourage abuses and enable businesses to have undue influence upon the political process.

Lobbying Expenditures

Lobbying expenses incurred in attempting to influence state or Federal legislation or the actions of certain high-ranking public officials (e.g., the President, Vice President, cabinet-level officials, and the two most senior officials in each agency of the executive branch) are not deductible.[35] The disallowance also applies to a pro rata portion of the membership dues of trade associations and other groups that are used for lobbying activities.

---

[32]§ 280E.

[33]Reg. § 1.61–3(a). Gross income is defined as sales minus cost of goods sold. Thus, while § 280E prohibits any deductions for drug dealers, it does not modify the normal definition of gross income.

[34]§ 276.

[35]§ 162(e).

GLOBAL Tax Issues

GERMANY'S EXECUTIVE PAY LIMITS

The pay of top executives of major U.S. corporations has become a controversial issue that is frequently discussed in the media and at shareholders' meetings. Nevertheless, all of this attention has had little success at reducing the compensation of top executives or narrowing the pay gap between those executives and the average worker.

In Germany, the government is getting involved in the executive pay controversy. The lower house of the German parliament, the Bundestag, has approved a law that will place restraints on executive pay. The goal is to encourage firms to focus on long-term, rather than short-term, performance.

The law extends the period that board members must hold their stock options before cashing them in from two years to four years. Compensation oversight boards will be subject to increased liability if they approve excessive executive compensation. Disclosure of executive compensation will be mandatory unless 75 percent of the shareholders vote against such disclosure.

Source: Adapted from Klaus Lauer, Dave Graham, and Victoria Main, "Germany Passes Law Imposing Limits on Executive Pay," *Reuters,* June 18, 2009.

EXAMPLE 17

Egret Company pays a $10,000 annual membership fee to the Free Trade Group, a trade association for plumbing wholesalers. The trade association estimates that 70% of its dues are allocated to lobbying activities. Thus, Egret Company's deduction is limited to $3,000 ($10,000 × 30%). ∎

There are three exceptions to the disallowance of lobbying expenses. An exception is provided for influencing local legislation (e.g., city and county governments). Second, the disallowance provision does not apply to activities devoted solely to monitoring legislation. Third, a *de minimis* exception is provided for annual in-house expenditures (lobbying expenses other than those paid to professional lobbyists or any portion of dues used by associations for lobbying) if such expenditures do not exceed $2,000. If the in-house expenditures exceed $2,000, none of the in-house expenditures can be deducted.

EXCESSIVE EXECUTIVE COMPENSATION

Prior to tax legislation enacted in 2008, the deduction of executive compensation was subject to only two limitations. As discussed earlier in this chapter, the compensation of shareholder-employees of closely held corporations is subject to the reasonableness requirement. The second limitation, the so-called millionaires' provision, applies to publicly held corporations (a corporation that has at least one class of stock registered under the Securities Exchange Act of 1934).[36]

The millionaires' provision does not limit the amount of compensation that can be paid to an employee. Instead, it limits the amount the employer can deduct for the compensation of a covered executive to $1 million annually. Covered employees include the chief executive officer and the four other most highly compensated officers.

Employee compensation *excludes* the following:

- Commissions based on individual performance.
- Certain performance-based compensation based on company performance according to a formula approved by a board of directors compensation

---

[36] § 162(m).

| TAX *in* the *NEWS* | RECENT INROADS ON THE DEDUCTIBILITY OF EXECUTIVE COMPENSATION |

Under the Emergency Economic Stabilization Act of 2008, Congress established the Troubled Asset Relief Program (TARP) to help bail out ailing financial institutions. Under TARP, the government is authorized to make direct purchases or sponsored-auction purchases of troubled assets. For the participating companies standards are set on the deductibility of executive compensation (e.g., for CEOs, CFOs, and other key officers). In direct purchase situations, the IRS is empowered to establish compensation parameters. In auction cases, however, a cap of $500,000 is imposed. Also affected are golden parachutes (i.e., severance bonuses paid to executives in change of ownership or control situations).

Nontax legislation has imposed other limits on compensation that can be paid by TARP recipients. These provisions are being administered by the so-called compensation czar, the Treasury Department's special master for TARP executive compensation. His powers include veto authority over the compensation paid by seven companies that received huge sums of Federal aid under TARP. He must approve or review the compensation paid to senior executive officers and the 100 highest-paid employees.

committee (composed solely of two or more outside directors) and by shareholder vote. The performance attainment must be certified by this compensation committee.

- Payments to tax-qualified retirement plans.
- Payments that are excludible from the employee's gross income (e.g., certain fringe benefits).

The third limitation, which was added by 2008 tax legislation, applies only to covered executives of companies receiving Troubled Asset Relief Program (TARP) assistance. In this case, the deduction for compensation paid to a covered executive is limited to $500,000. The exception to the statutory limit under the aforementioned millionaires' provision for performance-based compensation does not apply to the $500,000 limit. Covered employees are somewhat similar to those under the millionaires' provision and include the chief executive officer, the chief financial officer, and the three other most highly compensated officers.

INVESTIGATION OF A BUSINESS

Investigation expenses are expenses paid or incurred to determine the feasibility of entering a new business or expanding an existing business. They include such costs as travel, engineering and architectural surveys, marketing reports, and various legal and accounting services. How such expenses are treated for tax purposes depends on a number of variables, including the following:

- The current business, if any, of the taxpayer.
- The nature of the business being investigated.
- The extent to which the investigation has proceeded.
- Whether or not the acquisition actually takes place.

If the taxpayer is in a business the *same as or similar to* that being investigated, all investigation expenses are deductible in the year paid or incurred. The tax result is the same whether or not the taxpayer acquires the business being investigated.[37]

---

[37]§ 195. *York v. Comm.*, 58–2 USTC ¶9952, 2 AFTR 2d 6178, 261 F.2d 421 (CA–4, 1958).

CONCEPT SUMMARY 6.1

Costs of Investigating a Business

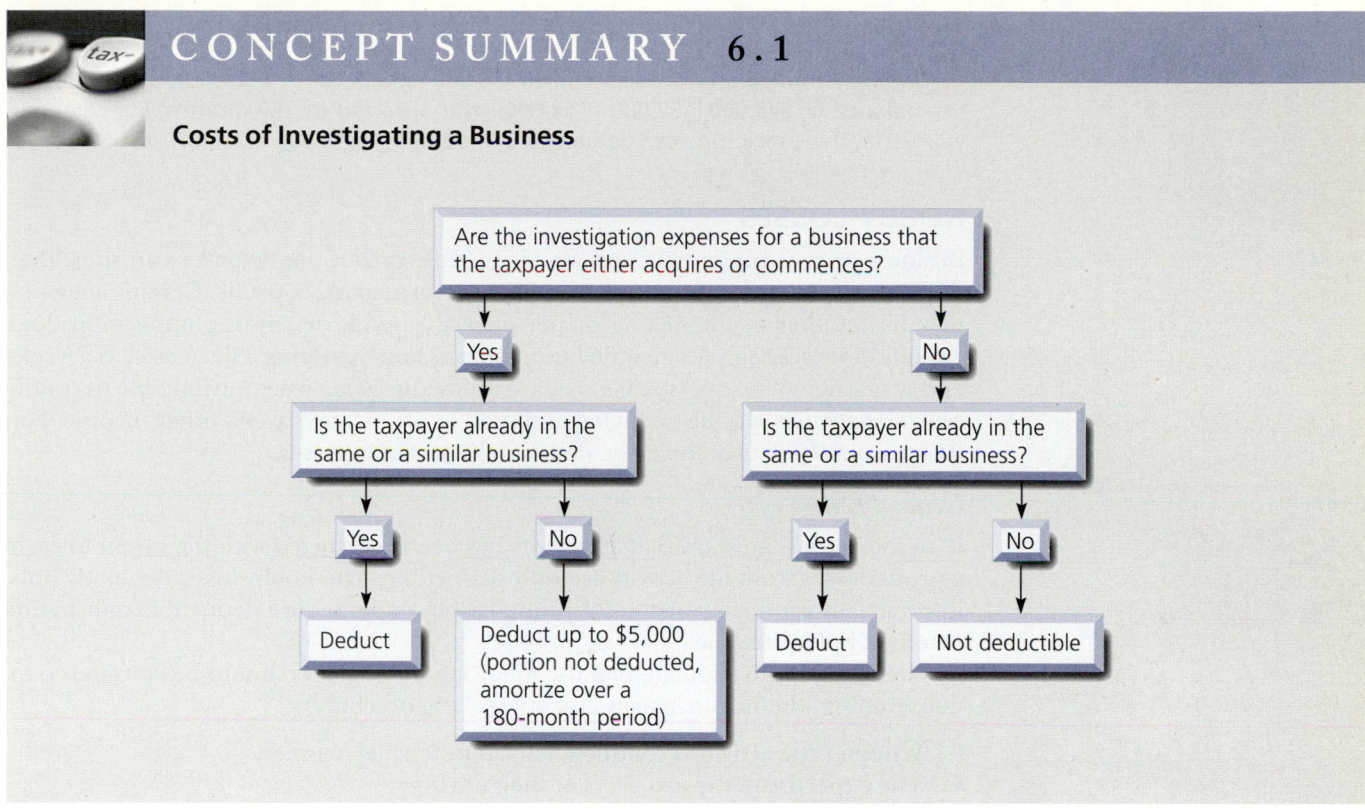

Return to the facts of *The Big Picture* on p. 6-2. Dr. Payne's mother, Terry, an accrual basis sole proprietor, owns and operates three motels in Georgia. In the current year, Terry incurs expenses of $8,500 in investigating the possibility of acquiring several additional motels located in South Carolina. The $8,500 is deductible in the current year whether or not Terry acquires the motels in South Carolina. ■

EXAMPLE 18
THE BIG PICTURE

When the taxpayer is *not* in a business that is the same as or similar to the one being investigated, the tax result depends on whether the new business is acquired. If the business is not acquired, all investigation expenses generally are nondeductible.[38]

Lynn, a retired merchant, incurs expenses in traveling from Rochester, New York, to California to investigate the feasibility of acquiring several auto care centers. If no acquisition takes place, none of the expenses are deductible. ■

EXAMPLE 19

If the taxpayer is *not* in a business that is the same as or similar to the one being investigated and actually acquires the new business, the expenses must be capitalized as startup expenses. At the election of the taxpayer, the first $5,000 of the expenses can be immediately deducted. Any excess expenses can be amortized over a period of 180 months (15 years). In arriving at the $5,000 immediate deduction allowed, a dollar-for-dollar reduction must be made for those expenses in excess of $50,000.[39]

Tina owns and operates 10 restaurants located in various cities throughout the Southeast. She travels to Atlanta to discuss the acquisition of an auto dealership. In addition, she incurs legal and accounting costs associated with the potential acquisition. After

EXAMPLE 20

---

[38]Rev.Rul. 57–418, 1957–2 C.B. 143; *Morton Frank*, 20 T.C. 511 (1953); and *Dwight A. Ward*, 20 T.C. 332 (1953).

[39]§ 195(b). For startup expenses incurred in taxable years beginning in 2010 only, up to $10,000 could be deducted immediately and the phaseout began at $60,000.

incurring total investigation costs of $52,000, she acquires the auto dealership on October 1, 2011.

Tina may immediately deduct $3,000 [$5,000 − ($52,000 − $50,000)] and amortize the balance of $49,000 ($52,000 − $3,000) over a period of 180 months. For calendar year 2011, therefore, Tina can deduct $3,817 [$3,000 + ($49,000 × 3/180)]. ■

HOBBY LOSSES

Business or investment expenses are deductible only if the taxpayer can show that the activity was entered into for the purpose of making a profit. Certain activities may have either profit-seeking or personal attributes, depending upon individual circumstances. Examples include raising horses and operating a farm used as a weekend residence. While personal losses are not deductible, losses attributable to profit-seeking activities may be deducted and used to offset a taxpayer's other income. For this reason, the tax law limits the deductibility of **hobby losses**.

General Rules

If an individual can show that an activity has been conducted with the intent to earn a profit, losses from the activity are fully deductible. The hobby loss rules apply only if the activity is not engaged in for profit. Hobby expenses are deductible only to the extent of hobby income.[40]

The Regulations stipulate that the following nine factors should be considered in determining whether an activity is profit seeking or a hobby:[41]

- Whether the activity is conducted in a businesslike manner.
- The expertise of the taxpayers or their advisers.
- The time and effort expended.
- The expectation that the assets of the activity will appreciate in value.
- The taxpayer's previous success in conducting similar activities.
- The history of income or losses from the activity.
- The relationship of profits earned to losses incurred.
- The financial status of the taxpayer (e.g., if the taxpayer does not have substantial amounts of other income, this may indicate that the activity is engaged in for profit).
- Elements of personal pleasure or recreation in the activity.

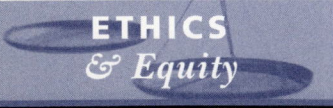
ETHICS *& Equity*   **WHEN IS A DAIRY FARM A TRADE OR BUSINESS?**

Randolph has been an orthopedic surgeon in New Orleans for 15 years. He would like to devote less time to his medical practice, spend more time with his family, and pay less income tax. His net income from his medical practice has been about $500,000 per year for the past five years.

Randolph grew up on a dairy farm in southeastern Louisiana. He has many fond memories of his childhood and believes a farm would be an excellent environment for his three children.

Randolph purchases a dairy farm across Lake Pontchartrain from New Orleans. He hires two full-time employees to handle the milking operations and other part-time employees as needed. In addition, Randolph and his family participate in performing various activities on the farm.

Randolph commutes to New Orleans four days a week to continue his medical practice. Because he is devoting less time to the practice, his net income decreases to $400,000. Randolph has a loss of $75,000 for the dairy farm that he attributes to depressed milk prices and his inexperience at running the farm. He considers the medical practice and the dairy farm to be separate trades or businesses. Therefore, on the Federal income tax return, the $75,000 net loss is offset against the $400,000 net income. Assume that the net income and net loss from the medical practice and the dairy farm, respectively, remain approximately the same for the next four years.

Is the position adopted by Randolph defensible? Discuss.

---

[40]§ 183(b)(2).   [41]Reg. §§ 1.183–2(b)(1) through (9).

The presence or absence of a factor is not by itself determinative of whether the activity is profit seeking or a hobby. Rather, the decision is a subjective one that is based on an analysis of the facts and circumstances.

Presumptive Rule of § 183

The Code provides a rebuttable presumption that an activity is profit seeking if the activity shows a profit in at least three of any five prior consecutive years.[42] If the activity involves horses, a profit in at least two of seven consecutive years meets the presumptive rule. If these profitability tests are met, the activity is presumed to be a trade or business rather than a personal hobby. In this situation, the IRS bears the burden of proving that the activity is personal rather than trade or business related.

EXAMPLE 21
THE BIG PICTURE

Return to the facts of *The Big Picture* on p. 6-2. Recall that Camille and Walter are Dr. Payne's mother- and father-in-law. Camille, who is an executive for a large corporation, is paid a salary of $800,000. Walter is a collector of antiques. Several years ago, he opened an antique shop in a local shopping center and spends most of his time buying and selling antiques. He occasionally earns a small profit from this activity but more frequently incurs substantial losses. If Walter's losses are business related, they are fully deductible against Camille's salary income on a joint return. In resolving this issue, consider the following:

- Initially determine whether Walter's antique activity has met the three-out-of-five years profit test.
- If the presumption is not met, the activity may nevertheless qualify as a business if Walter can show that the intent is to engage in a profit-seeking activity. It is not necessary to show actual profits.
- Attempt to fit the operation within the nine criteria prescribed in the Regulations and listed previously. These criteria are the factors considered in trying to rebut the § 183 presumption. ∎

Determining the Amount of the Deduction

If an activity is deemed to be a hobby, the expenses are deductible only to the extent of the gross income from the hobby. These expenses must be deducted in the following order:

- Amounts deductible under other Code sections without regard to the nature of the activity, such as property taxes and home mortgage interest.
- Amounts deductible under other Code sections if the activity had been engaged in for profit, but only if those amounts do not affect adjusted basis. Examples include maintenance, utilities, and supplies.
- Amounts that affect adjusted basis and would be deductible under other Code sections if the activity had been engaged in for profit.[43] Examples include depreciation, amortization, and depletion.

These deductions are deductible *from* AGI as itemized deductions to the extent they exceed 2 percent of AGI.[44] If the taxpayer uses the standard deduction rather than itemizing, all hobby loss deductions are wasted.

[42]§ 183(d).
[43]Reg. § 1.183–1(b)(1).
[44]Reg. § 1.67–1T(a)(1)(iv) and Rev.Rul. 75–14, 1975–1 C.B. 90.

EXAMPLE 22

Jim, the vice president of an oil company, has AGI of $80,000. He decides to pursue painting in his spare time. He uses a home studio, comprising 10% of the home's square footage. During the current year, Jim incurs the following expenses:

Frames	$ 350
Art supplies	300
Fees paid to models	1,000
Home studio expenses:	
Total property taxes	900
Total home mortgage interest	10,000
Depreciation on 10% of home	500
Total home maintenance and utilities	3,600

During the year, Jim sold paintings for a total of $3,200. If the activity is held to be a hobby, Jim is allowed deductions as follows:

Gross income		$ 3,200
Deduct: Taxes and interest (10% of $10,900)		(1,090)
Remainder		$ 2,110
Deduct: Frames	$ 350	
Art supplies	300	
Models' fees	1,000	
Maintenance and utilities (10%)	360	(2,010)
Remainder		$ 100
Deduct: Depreciation ($500, but limited to $100)		(100)
Net income		$ –0–

Jim includes the $3,200 of income in AGI, making his AGI $83,200. The taxes and interest are itemized deductions, deductible in full. The remaining $2,110 of expenses are reduced by 2% of his AGI ($1,664), so the net deduction is $446. Since the property taxes and home mortgage interest are deductible anyway, the net effect is a $2,754 ($3,200 less $446) increase in taxable income. ■

EXAMPLE 23

Assume that Jim's activity in Example 22 is held to be a business. The business is located in a small office building he owns. Expenses are property taxes of $90, mortgage interest of $1,000, frames of $350, art supplies of $300, models' fees of $1,000, maintenance and utilities of $360, and depreciation of $500. Under these circumstances, Jim could deduct expenses totaling $3,600. All these expenses would be trade or business expenses deductible *for* AGI. His reduction in AGI would be as follows:

Gross income		$ 3,200
Less: Taxes and interest	$1,090	
Other business expenses	2,010	
Depreciation	500	(3,600)
Reduction in AGI		($ 400)

RENTAL OF VACATION HOMES

Restrictions on the deductions allowed for part-year rentals of personal **vacation homes** were written into the law to prevent taxpayers from deducting essentially personal expenses as rental losses. Many taxpayers who owned vacation homes had formerly treated the homes as rental property and generated rental losses as deductions *for* AGI. For example, a summer cabin would be rented for 2 months per year, used for vacationing for 1 month, and left vacant the rest of the year. The taxpayer would then deduct 11 months' depreciation, utilities, maintenance, etc., as rental expenses, resulting in a rental loss. Section 280A eliminates this treatment by allowing deductions on residences used primarily for personal purposes only to the extent of the income generated. Only a break-even situation is allowed; no losses can be deducted.

There are three possible tax treatments for residences used for both personal and rental purposes. The treatment depends upon the *relative time* the residence is used for personal purposes versus rental use.

Primarily Personal Use

If the residence is *rented* for *fewer than 15 days* in a year, it is treated as a personal residence. The rent income is excluded from gross income, and mortgage interest and real estate taxes are allowed as itemized deductions, as with any personal residence.[45] No other expenses (e.g., depreciation, utilities, maintenance) are deductible. Although this provision exists primarily for administrative convenience, several bills have been introduced in Congress that would have repealed this exclusion from gross income.

---

[45]§ 280A(g).

EXAMPLE 24
THE BIG PICTURE

Return to the facts of *The Big Picture* on p. 6-2. Camille, Dr. Payne's mother-in-law, owns a vacation cottage on the lake. During the current year, she rented it for $1,600 for two weeks, lived in it two months, and left it vacant the remainder of the year. The year's expenses amounted to $6,000 mortgage interest expense, $500 property taxes, $1,500 utilities and maintenance, and $2,400 depreciation. Since the property was not rented for at least 15 days, the income is excluded, the mortgage interest and property tax expenses are itemized deductions, and the remaining expenses are nondeductible personal expenses. ∎

Primarily Rental Use

If the residence is *rented* for 15 days or more in a year and is *not used* for personal purposes for more than the greater of (1) 14 days or (2) 10 percent of the total days rented, the residence is treated as rental property.[46] The expenses must be allocated between personal and rental days if there are any personal use days during the year. The deduction of the expenses allocated to rental days can exceed rent income and result in a rental loss. The loss may be deductible, subject to the at-risk and passive activity loss rules (discussed in Chapter 11).

EXAMPLE 25
THE BIG PICTURE

Assume instead that Camille in Example 24 used the cottage for 12 days and rented it for 48 days for $4,800. Since she rented the cottage for 15 days or more but did not use it for more than 14 days, the cottage is treated as rental property. The expenses must be allocated between personal and rental days.

	Percentage of Use	
	Rental 80%	Personal 20%
Income	$ 4,800	$ –0–
Expenses		
Mortgage interest ($6,000)	($ 4,800)	($1,200)
Property taxes ($500)	(400)	(100)
Utilities and maintenance ($1,500)	(1,200)	(300)
Depreciation ($2,400)	(1,920)	(480)
Total expenses	($ 8,320)	($2,080)
Rental loss	($ 3,520)	$ –0–

Camille deducts the $3,520 rental loss *for* AGI (assuming she satisfies the at-risk and passive activity loss rules, discussed in Chapter 11). She also has an itemized deduction for property taxes of $100 associated with the personal use. The mortgage interest of $1,200 associated with the personal use is not deductible as an itemized deduction because the cottage is not a qualified residence (qualified residence interest) for this purpose (see Chapter 10). The portion of utilities and maintenance and depreciation attributable to personal use is not deductible. ∎

EXAMPLE 26
THE BIG PICTURE

Assume instead that Camille in Example 24 rented the cottage for 200 days and lived in it for 19 days. The cottage is primarily rental use since she rented it for 15 days or more and did not use it for personal purposes for more than 20 days (10% of the rental days). The expenses must be allocated between personal and rental days as illustrated in Example 25. ∎

---

[46]§ 280A(d) and Prop.Reg. § 1.280A–3(c).

Personal/Rental Use

If the residence is rented for 15 days or more in a year *and* is used for personal purposes for more than the greater of (1) 14 days or (2) 10 percent of the total days rented, it is treated as a personal/rental use residence. The expenses must be allocated between personal days and rental days. Expenses are allowed only to the extent of rent income.

Assume instead that Camille in Example 24 rented the property for 30 days and lived in it for 30 days. The residence is classified as personal/rental use property since she used it more than 14 days and rented it for 15 days or more. The expenses must be allocated between rental use and personal use, and the rental expenses are allowed only to the extent of rent income. ∎	**EXAMPLE 27** **THE BIG PICTURE**

If a residence is classified as personal/rental use property, the expenses that are deductible anyway (e.g., real estate taxes and mortgage interest) must be deducted first. If a positive net income results, otherwise nondeductible expenses that do not affect adjusted basis (e.g., maintenance, utilities, insurance) are allowed next. Finally, if any positive balance remains, depreciation is allowed. Any disallowed expenses allocable to rental use are carried forward and used in future years subject to the same limitations.

Expenses must be allocated between personal and rental days before the limits are applied. The courts have held that real estate taxes and mortgage interest, which accrue ratably over the year, are allocated on the basis of 365 days.[47] The IRS, however, disagrees and allocates real estate taxes and mortgage interest on the basis of total days of use.[48] Other expenses (utilities, maintenance, depreciation, etc.) are allocated on the basis of total days used.

EXAMPLE 28

Jason rents his vacation home for 60 days and lives in the home for 30 days. The limitations on personal/rental use residences apply. Jason's gross rent income is $10,000. For the entire year (not a leap year), the real estate taxes are $2,190; his mortgage interest expense is $10,220; utilities and maintenance expense equals $2,400; and depreciation is $9,000. Using the IRS approach, these amounts are deductible in this specific order:

Gross income	$10,000
Deduct: Taxes and interest ($^{60}/_{90} \times$ $12,410)	(8,273)
Remainder to apply to rental operating expenses and depreciation	$ 1,727
Deduct: Utilities and maintenance ($^{60}/_{90} \times$ $2,400)	(1,600)
Balance	$ 127
Deduct: Depreciation ($^{60}/_{90} \times$ $9,000 = $6,000 but limited to above balance)	(127)
Net rent income	$ –0–

The nonrental use portion of real estate taxes and mortgage interest ($4,137 in this case) is deductible if the taxpayer elects to itemize (see Chapter 10). The personal use portion of utilities, maintenance, and depreciation is not deductible in any case. Jason has a carryover of $5,873 ($6,000 − $127) of the unused depreciation. Also note that the basis of the property is not reduced by the $5,873 depreciation not allowed because of the above limitation. (See Chapter 14 for a discussion of the reduction in basis for depreciation allowed or allowable.) ∎

EXAMPLE 29

Using the court's approach in allocating real estate taxes and mortgage interest, Jason, in Example 28, would have this result:

---

[47]*Bolton v. Comm.*, 82–2 USTC ¶9699, 51 AFTR 2d 83–305, 694 F.2d 556 (CA–9, 1982).   [48]Prop.Reg. § 1.280A–3(d)(4).

CONCEPT SUMMARY 6.2

Vacation/Rental Home

*Allocated on the basis of 365 (366 in a leap year) days (court) or total days of use (IRS).
**Allocated on the basis of total days of use.

See Concept Summary 6.2 for a summary of the vacation home rules.

EXPENDITURES INCURRED FOR TAXPAYER'S BENEFIT OR TAXPAYER'S OBLIGATION

To be deductible, an expense must be incurred for the taxpayer's benefit or arise from the taxpayer's obligation. An individual cannot claim a tax deduction for the payment of the expenses of another individual.

EXAMPLE 32

During the current year, Fred pays the property taxes on his son Vern's home. Neither Fred nor Vern can take a deduction for the amount paid for Vern's property taxes. Fred is not entitled to a deduction because the property taxes are not his obligation. Vern cannot claim a deduction because he did not pay the property taxes. The tax result would have been more favorable had Fred made a cash gift to Vern and let him pay the property taxes. Then Vern could have deducted the property taxes. Fred likely would not be liable for any gift taxes depending upon the amount involved due to the annual exclusion (see Chapter 1). A deduction would have been created with no cash difference to the family. ■

One exception to this disallowance rule is the payment of medical expenses for a dependent. Such expenses are deductible by the payor subject to the normal rules that limit the deductibility of medical expenses (see Chapter 10).[50]

DISALLOWANCE OF PERSONAL EXPENDITURES

Section 262 states that "except as otherwise expressly provided in this chapter, no deduction shall be allowed for personal, living, or family expenses." To justify a deduction, an individual must be able to identify a particular section of the Code that sanctions the deduction (e.g., charitable contributions, medical expenses). Sometimes the character of a particular expenditure is not easily determined. For example, the legal fee associated with a property settlement that results in one party retaining ownership of a family business is not deductible. Likewise, the legal fee paid to resolve the title to income-producing property is not deductible.

The IRS has clarified the issue of the deduction of legal fees incurred in connection with a divorce.[51] To be deductible, an expense must relate solely to tax advice in a divorce proceeding. For example, legal fees attributable to the determination of dependency exemptions of children are deductible if the fees are distinguishable from the general legal fees incurred in obtaining a divorce. Other examples are the costs of creating a trust to make periodic alimony payments and the determination of the tax consequences of a property settlement. Therefore, it is advisable to request an itemization of attorney's fees to substantiate a deduction for the tax-related amounts.

EXAMPLE 33

THE BIG PICTURE

Return to the facts of *The Big Picture* on p. 6-2. Terry and Jack, Dr. Payne's parents, are divorced near the end of the current tax year. They had been married for 28 years and have two dependent children, Pauline (age 15), and Neal (age 16). (Dr. Payne is no longer his parents' dependent.) As part of the divorce agreement, Jack paid all of the legal fees, which amounted to $24,300. The invoice from the divorce lawyer listed the following charges:

Child custody agreement and determination of amount of monthly child support	$ 3,000
Divorce decree proceedings	10,000
County court filing costs	1,800
Property settlement determination	6,000
Tax consequences of property settlement	2,000
Tax consequences of child custody and child support payments and tax filing status	1,500

Only the $3,500 ($2,000 + $1,500) paid by Jack for the charges relating to tax advice is deductible. ■

DISALLOWANCE OF DEDUCTIONS FOR CAPITAL EXPENDITURES

The Code specifically disallows a deduction for "any amount paid out for new buildings or for permanent improvements or betterments made to increase the value of any property or estate."[52] The Regulations further define capital expenditures to include those expenditures that add to the value or prolong the life of property or adapt

---

[50]§ 213(a).
[51]Rev.Rul. 72–545, 1972–2 C.B. 179.

[52]§ 263(a)(1).

the property to a new or different use.[53] Incidental repairs and maintenance of the property are not capital expenditures and can be deducted as ordinary and necessary business expenses. Repairing a roof is a deductible expense, but replacing a roof is a capital expenditure subject to depreciation deductions over its recovery period. The tune-up of a delivery truck is an expense; a complete overhaul probably is a capital expenditure.

Capitalization versus Expense

When an expenditure is capitalized rather than expensed, the deduction is at best deferred and at worst lost forever. Although an immediate tax benefit for a large cash expenditure is lost, the cost may be deductible in increments over a longer period of time.

If the expenditure is for a tangible asset that has an ascertainable life, it is capitalized and may be deducted as depreciation (or cost recovery) over the life of the asset (for depreciation) or over a statutory period (for cost recovery under either ACRS or MACRS).[54] Land is not subject to depreciation (or cost recovery) since it does not have an ascertainable life.

EXAMPLE 34

Stan purchased a prime piece of land located in an apartment-zoned area. Stan paid $500,000 for the property, which had an old but usable apartment building on it. He immediately had the building demolished at a cost of $100,000. The $500,000 purchase price and the $100,000 demolition costs must be capitalized, and the basis of the land is $600,000. Since land is a nondepreciable asset, no deduction is allowed. ∎

If the expenditure is for an intangible asset (e.g., copyright, patent, covenant not to compete, goodwill), the capitalized expenditure can be amortized, regardless of whether or not the intangible asset has an ascertainable life. Intangible assets, referred to as § 197 intangibles, are amortized over a 15-year statutory period using the straight-line method. See Chapter 8 for additional discussion of the amortization of intangibles.

TRANSACTIONS BETWEEN RELATED PARTIES

The Code places restrictions on the recognition of gains and losses from **related-party transactions**. Without these restrictions, relationships created by birth, marriage, and business would provide endless possibilities for engaging in financial transactions that produce tax savings with no real economic substance or change. For example, to create an artificial loss, a wife could sell investment property to her husband at a loss and deduct the loss on their joint return. Her husband could then hold the asset indefinitely, and the family would sustain no real economic loss. A complex set of laws has been designed to eliminate such possibilities.

Losses

The Code provides for the disallowance of any "losses from sales or exchanges of property ... directly or indirectly" between related parties.[55] When the property is subsequently sold to a nonrelated party, any gain recognized is reduced by the loss previously disallowed. Any disallowed loss not used by the related-party buyer to offset the recognized gain on a subsequent sale or exchange to an unrelated party is permanently lost.

---

[53]Reg. § 1.263(a)–1(b).   [55]§ 267(a)(1).
[54]See Chapter 8 for the discussion of depreciation and cost recovery.

| EXAMPLE 35 | Freida sells common stock with a basis of $10,000 to her son, Bill, for its fair market value of $8,000. Bill sells the stock several years later for $11,000. Freida's $2,000 loss is disallowed upon the sale to Bill, and only $1,000 of gain ($11,000 selling price − $8,000 basis − $2,000 disallowed loss) is taxable to him upon the subsequent sale. ∎ |

| EXAMPLE 36 | George sells common stock with a basis of $10,500 to his son, Ray, for its fair market value of $8,000. Ray sells the stock eight months later to an unrelated party for $9,000. Ray's gain of $1,000 ($9,000 selling price − $8,000 basis) is not recognized because of George's previously disallowed loss of $2,500. Note that the offset may result in only partial tax benefit upon the subsequent sale (as in this case). If the property had not been transferred to Ray, George could have recognized a $1,500 loss upon the subsequent sale to the unrelated party ($10,500 basis − $9,000 selling price). ∎ |

| EXAMPLE 37 | Pete sells common stock with a basis of $10,000 to an unrelated third party for its fair market value of $8,000. Pete's son repurchased the same stock in the market on the same day for $8,000. The $2,000 loss is not allowed because the transaction is an indirect sale between related parties.[56] ∎ |

Unpaid Expenses and Interest

The law prevents related taxpayers from engaging in tax avoidance schemes where one related taxpayer uses the accrual method of accounting and the other uses the cash basis. An accrual basis, closely held corporation, for example, could borrow funds from a cash basis individual shareholder. At the end of the year, the corporation would accrue and deduct the interest, but the cash basis lender would not recognize interest income since no interest had been paid. Section 267 specifically defers the deduction of the accruing taxpayer until the recipient taxpayer must include it in income; that is, when it is actually paid to the cash basis taxpayer. This *matching* provision applies to interest as well as other expenses, such as salaries and bonuses.

This deduction deferral provision does not apply if both of the related taxpayers use the accrual method or both use the cash method. Likewise, it does not apply if the related party reporting income uses the accrual method and the related party taking the deduction uses the cash method.

Relationships and Constructive Ownership

Section 267 operates to disallow losses and defer deductions only between related parties. Losses or deductions generated by similar transactions with an unrelated party are allowed. *Related parties* include the following:

- Brothers and sisters (whether whole, half, or adopted), spouse, ancestors (parents, grandparents), and lineal descendants (children, grandchildren) of the taxpayer.
- A corporation owned more than 50 percent (directly or indirectly) by the taxpayer.
- Two corporations that are members of a controlled group.
- A series of other complex relationships between trusts, corporations, and individual taxpayers.

Constructive ownership provisions are applied to determine whether the taxpayers are related. Under these provisions, stock owned by certain relatives or related entities is *deemed* to be owned by the taxpayer for purposes of applying the loss and expense deduction disallowance provisions. A taxpayer is deemed to own not only his or her stock but also the stock owned by lineal descendants, ancestors, brothers and sisters or half-brothers and half-sisters, and spouse. The taxpayer is also

[56]*McWilliams v. Comm.*, 47–1 USTC ¶9289, 35 AFTR 1184, 67 S.Ct. 1477 (USSC, 1947).

deemed to own his or her proportionate share of stock owned by any partnership, corporation, estate, or trust of which the taxpayer is a member. An individual is deemed to own any stock owned, directly or indirectly, by his or her partner. However, constructive ownership by an individual of the partnership's and the other partner's shares does not extend to the individual's spouse or other relatives (no double attribution).

EXAMPLE 38

The stock of Sparrow Corporation is owned 20% by Ted, 30% by Ted's father, 30% by Ted's mother, and 20% by Ted's sister. On July 1 of the current year, Ted loaned $10,000 to Sparrow Corporation at 8% annual interest, principal and interest payable on demand. For tax purposes, Sparrow uses the accrual basis, and Ted uses the cash basis. Both are on a calendar year. Since Ted is deemed to own the 80% owned by his parents and sister, he directly and constructively owns 100% of Sparrow Corporation. If the corporation accrues the interest within the taxable year, no deduction can be taken until payment is made to Ted. ■

SUBSTANTIATION REQUIREMENTS

The tax law is built on a voluntary compliance system. Taxpayers file their tax returns, report income and take deductions to which they are entitled, and pay their taxes through withholding or estimated tax payments during the year. The taxpayer has the burden of proof for substantiating expenses deducted on the returns and must retain adequate records. Upon audit, the IRS will disallow any undocumented or unsubstantiated deductions. These requirements have resulted in numerous conflicts between taxpayers and the IRS.

In the case of charitable contributions, Congress has enacted stringent substantiation requirements. All cash contributions, for example, must be supported by receipts (e.g., canceled checks).[57] Single donations of $250 or more of both cash and property require an acknowledgment from the charity. Substantial donations of property (i.e., $500 or more) necessitate the filing of Form 8283 and may have to be supported by appraisals—see Chapter 10 for further details.

Specific and *more stringent* rules for deducting travel, entertainment, and gift expenses are discussed in Chapter 9. Certain mixed-use (both personal and business use) and listed property are also subject to the adequate records requirement (discussed in Chapter 8).

EXPENSES AND INTEREST RELATING TO TAX-EXEMPT INCOME

Certain income, such as interest on municipal bonds, is tax-exempt.[58] The law also allows the taxpayer to deduct expenses incurred for the production of income.[59] Deduction disallowance provisions, however, make it impossible to make money at the expense of the government by excluding interest income and deducting interest expense.[60]

EXAMPLE 39

Sandy, a taxpayer in the 35% bracket, purchased $100,000 of 6% municipal bonds. At the same time, she used the bonds as collateral on a bank loan of $100,000 at 8% interest. A positive cash flow would result from the tax benefit as follows:

Cash paid out on loan	($8,000)
Cash received from bonds	6,000
Tax savings from deducting interest expense (35% of $8,000 interest expense)	2,800
Net positive cash flow	$ 800

■

[57]Rev.Proc. 92–71, 1992–2 C.B. 437, addresses circumstances where checks are not returned by a financial institution or where electronic transfers are made.
[58]§ 103.
[59]§ 212.
[60]§ 265.

To eliminate the possibility illustrated in Example 39, the Code specifically disallows as a deduction the expenses of producing tax-exempt income. Interest on any indebtedness incurred or continued to purchase or carry tax-exempt obligations also is disallowed.

Judicial Interpretations

It is often difficult to show a direct relationship between borrowings and investment in tax-exempt securities. Suppose, for example, that a taxpayer borrows money, adds it to existing funds, buys inventory and stocks, then later sells the inventory and buys municipal bonds. A series of transactions such as these can completely obscure any connection between the loan and the tax-exempt investment. One solution would be to disallow interest on any debt to the extent that the taxpayer holds any tax-exempt securities. This approach would preclude individuals from deducting part of their home mortgage interest if they owned any municipal bonds. The law was not intended to go to such extremes. As a result, judicial interpretations have tried to be reasonable in disallowing interest deductions.

In one case, a company used municipal bonds as collateral on short-term loans to meet seasonal liquidity needs.[61] The court disallowed the interest deduction on the grounds that the company could predict its seasonal liquidity needs. The company could anticipate the need to borrow the money to continue to carry the tax-exempt securities. The same company *was* allowed an interest deduction on a building mortgage, even though tax-exempt securities it owned could have been sold to pay off the mortgage. The court reasoned that short-term liquidity needs would have been impaired if the tax-exempt securities were sold. Furthermore, the court ruled that carrying the tax-exempt securities bore no relationship to the long-term financing of a construction project.

| EXAMPLE 40 | In January of the current year, Alan borrowed $100,000 at 8% interest. He used the loan proceeds to purchase 5,000 shares of stock in White Corporation. In July, he sold the stock for $120,000 and reinvested the proceeds in City of Denver bonds, the income from which is tax-exempt. Assuming the $100,000 loan remained outstanding throughout the entire year, Alan cannot deduct the interest attributable to the period in which he held the bonds. ∎ |

TAX PLANNING:

6.4 TIME VALUE OF TAX DEDUCTIONS

LO.4

Identify tax planning opportunities for maximizing deductions and minimizing the disallowance of deductions.

Cash basis taxpayers often have the ability to make early payments for their expenses at the end of the tax year. This may permit the payments to be deducted currently instead of in the following tax year. In view of the time value of money, a tax deduction this year may be worth more than the same deduction next year. Before employing this strategy, the taxpayer must consider next year's expected income and tax rates and whether a cash-flow problem may develop from early payments. Thus, the time value of money as well as tax rate changes must be considered when an expense can be paid and deducted in either of two years.

| EXAMPLE 41 | Jena pledged $50,000 to her church's special building fund. She can make the contribution in December 2011 or January 2012. Jena is in the 35% tax bracket in 2011, and in the 28% bracket in 2012. She itemizes in both years. Assume Jena's discount rate is 8%. |

---

[61] *The Wisconsin Cheeseman, Inc. v. U.S.,* 68–1 USTC ¶9145, 21 AFTR 2d 383, 388 F.2d 420 (CA–7, 1968).

If she takes the deduction in 2011, she saves $4,536 ($17,500 − $12,964), due to the decrease in the tax rates and the time value of money.

	2011	2012
Contribution	$50,000	$50,000
Tax bracket	.35	.28
Tax savings	$17,500	$14,000
Discounted @ 8%	1.0	.926
Savings in present value	$17,500	$12,964

6.5 UNREASONABLE COMPENSATION

In substantiating the reasonableness of a shareholder-employee's compensation, an internal comparison test is sometimes useful. If it can be shown that nonshare-holder-employees and shareholder-employees in comparable positions receive comparable compensation, it is indicative that compensation is not unreasonable.

Another possibility is to demonstrate that the shareholder-employee has been underpaid in prior years. For example, the shareholder-employee may have agreed to take a less-than-adequate salary during the unprofitable formative years of the business. The expectation is that the "postponed" compensation would be paid in later, more profitable years. The agreement should be documented, if possible, in the corporate minutes.

Keep in mind that in testing for reasonableness, the *total* pay package must be considered. Look at all fringe benefits or perquisites, such as contributions by the corporation to a qualified pension plan. Even though those amounts are not immediately available to the covered shareholder-employee, they must be taken into account.

6.6 EXCESSIVE EXECUTIVE COMPENSATION

With the $1 million limit ($500,000 for TARP recipients) on the deduction of compensation of covered employees, many corporations and their executives must engage in additional tax planning. Previously, concerns over the deductibility of compensation related primarily to closely held corporations. The $1 million limit applies specifically to publicly held corporations. In many instances, it is now necessary for these corporations to restructure the compensation packages of their top executives in order to deduct payments in excess of $1 million. Opportunities include compensation payable on a commission basis, certain other performance-based compensation, payments to qualified retirement plans, and payments that are excludible fringe benefits.

6.7 SHIFTING DEDUCTIONS

Taxpayers should manage their obligations to avoid the loss of a deduction. Deductions can be shifted among family members, depending upon which member makes the payment. For example, a father buys a condo for his daughter and puts the title in both names. The taxpayer who makes the payment gets the deduction for the property taxes. If the condo is owned by the daughter only and her father makes the payment, neither is entitled to a deduction. In this case, the father should make a cash gift to the daughter who then makes the payment to the taxing authority.

CONCEPT SUMMARY   6.3

Classification of Expenses

Expense Item	Deductible		Not Deductible	Applicable Code §
	For AGI	From AGI		
Investment expenses				
Rent and royalty	X			§ 62(a)(4)
All other investments		X[4]		§ 212
Employee expenses				
Commuting expenses			X	§ 262
Travel and transportation[1]		X[4,5]		§ 162(a)(2)
Reimbursed expenses[1]	X			§ 62(a)(2)(A)
Moving expenses	X			§ 62(a)(15)
Entertainment[1]		X[4,5]		§ 162(a)
Teacher supplies	X[11]	X[4]		§ 62(a)(2)(D)
All other employee expenses[1]		X[4,5]		§ 162(a)
Certain expenses of performing artists	X			§ 62(a)(2)(B)
Trade or business expenses	X			§§ 162 and 62(a)(1)
Casualty losses				
Business	X			§ 165(c)(1)
Personal		X[6]		§ 165(c)(3)
Tax determination				
Collection or refund expenses	X[8]	X		§§ 212 and 62(a)(1) or (4)
Bad debts	X			§§ 166 and 62(a)(1) or (3)
Medical expenses		X[7]		§ 213
Charitable contributions		X		§ 170
Taxes				
Trade or business	X			§§ 162, 164, and 62(a)(1)
Personal taxes				
Real property		X		§ 164(a)(1)
Personal property		X		§ 164(a)(2)
State and local income *or* sales		X		§§ 164(a)(3) and (b)(5)
Investigation of a business[2]	X			§§ 162 and 62(a)(1)
Interest				
Business	X			§§ 162, 163, and 62(a)(1)
Personal	X[9]	X[3]	X[10]	§§ 163(a), (d), and (h)
Qualified tuition and related expenses	X			§§ 62(a)(18) and 222
All other personal expenses			X	§ 262

[1]Deduction for AGI if reimbursed, an adequate accounting is made, and employee is required to repay excess reimbursements.
[2]Provided certain criteria are met.
[3]Subject to the excess investment interest and the qualified residence interest provisions.
[4]Subject (in the aggregate) to a 2%-of-AGI floor imposed by § 67.
[5]Only 50% of meals and entertainment are deductible.
[6]Subject to a $100 floor per event and a 10%-of-AGI floor per tax year.
[7]Subject to a 7.5%-of-AGI floor.
[8]Only the portion relating to business, rental, or royalty income or losses.
[9]Only the portion relating to student loans.
[10]Other personal interest is disallowed.
[11]Subject to a statutory limit of $250.

6.8 HOBBY LOSSES

To demonstrate that an activity has been entered into for the purpose of making a profit, a taxpayer should treat the activity as a business. The business should engage in advertising, use business letterhead stationery, and maintain a business phone.

If a taxpayer's activity earns a profit in three out of five consecutive years, the presumption is that the activity is engaged in for profit. It may be possible for a cash basis taxpayer to meet these requirements by timing the payment of expenses or the receipt of revenues. The payment of certain expenses incurred before the end of the year might be made in the following year. The billing of year-end sales might be delayed so that collections are received in the following year.

Keep in mind that the three-out-of-five-years rule under § 183 is not absolute. All it does is shift the presumption. If a profit is not made in three out of five years, the losses may still be allowed if the taxpayer can show that they are due to the nature of the business. For example, success in artistic or literary endeavors can take a long time. Also, depending on the state of the economy, even full-time farmers and ranchers are often unable to show a profit. How can one expect a part-time farmer or rancher to do so?

Merely satisfying the three-out-of-five-years rule does not guarantee that a taxpayer is automatically home free. If the three years of profits are insignificant relative to the losses of other years, or if the profits are not from the ordinary operation of the business, the taxpayer is vulnerable. The IRS may still be able to establish that the taxpayer is not engaged in an activity for profit.

EXAMPLE 42

Ashley had the following gains and losses in an artistic endeavor:

2007	($ 50,000)
2008	(65,000)
2009	400
2010	200
2011	125

Under these circumstances, the IRS might try to overcome the presumption. ■

If Ashley in Example 42 could show conformity with the factors enumerated in the Regulations or could show evidence of business hardships (e.g., injury, death, or illness), the government cannot override the presumption.[62]

6.9 CAPITAL EXPENDITURES

On the sale of a sole proprietorship where the sales price exceeds the fair market value of the tangible assets and stated intangible assets, a planning opportunity may exist for both the seller and the buyer. The seller's preference is for the excess amount to be allocated to goodwill. Goodwill is a capital asset, whereas a covenant not to compete produces ordinary income treatment (see Chapter 16).

Because both a covenant and goodwill are amortized over a statutory 15-year period, the tax results of a covenant and goodwill are the same for the buyer. However, the buyer should recognize that an allocation to goodwill rather than a covenant may provide a tax benefit to the seller. Therefore, the seller and buyer, in negotiating the sales price, should factor in the tax benefit to the seller of having the excess amount labeled goodwill rather than a covenant not to compete. Of course, if the noncompetition aspects of a covenant are important to the buyer, part of the excess amount can be assigned to a covenant.

[62]*Faulconer, Sr. v. Comm.*, 84–2 USTC ¶9955, 55 AFTR 2d 85–302, 748 F.2d 890 (CA–4, 1984), *rev'g* 45 TCM 1084, T.C.Memo. 1983–165.

REFOCUS ON THE BIG PICTURE

CALCULATION OF DEDUCTIBLE BUSINESS EXPENSES AND TAX PLANNING

Using the accrual method of accounting, Dr. Payne has correctly calculated the deductible business expenses of his dental practice except for the $60,000 deduction he shows for his monthly $5,000 draw for living expenses. Since the dental practice is operated as a sole proprietorship, Dr. Payne will report the net income (gross income − deductible business expenses) of the practice on his Form 1040. So a deduction for his monthly draw is not permitted. The $232,500 ($292,500 − $60,000) amount will be reported by Dr. Payne on Schedule C of Form 1040.

Several of the items included in Dr. Payne's calculation of deductible business expenses require clarification. Political contributions ($1,000 + $1,000) cannot be deducted. The dental supplies expense and the office supplies expense must be reduced by the amount of the ending inventory (i.e., $7,000 and $1,500, respectively) since Dr. Payne is using the accrual method of accounting.

What If?

From a tax planning perspective, should Dr. Payne calculate his deductible business expenses using the accrual method of accounting or the cash method?

In Chapter 4, we concluded that Dr. Payne could minimize his Federal income tax liability if he used the cash method of accounting. If the cash method is used for reporting the gross income of a Schedule C business, then the cash method must be used for reporting the deductible business expenses that will appear on Schedule C of Form 1040. So the correct amount of deductible business expenses for his dental practice using the cash method of accounting is calculated as follows:

Salaries including FICA ($120,000 − $5,000)	$115,000
Building rent	24,000
Depreciation of dental equipment and office furnishings and equipment	52,000
Insurance (malpractice and of dental equipment and office furnishings and equipment)	22,000
Dental supplies	16,000
Office supplies	3,000
Contribution to U.S. Senate campaign fund of Barbara Boxer	–0–
Contribution to U.S. Senate campaign fund of Carly Fiorina	–0–
Legal expenses associated with patient lawsuit (jury decision for defendant)	4,000
Draw by Dr. Payne for living expenses	–0–
	$236,000

KEY TERMS

DISCUSSION QUESTIONS

1. **LO.1** "All income must be reported and all deductions are allowed unless specifically disallowed in the Code." Discuss.

2. **LO.1** Michael has AGI of $60,000 and deductions of $6,500. Does it matter to Michael whether the deductions are *for* or *from* AGI? Why or why not?

3. **LO.1** Billy earned $13,000 at the K-M Resort Golf Club during the summer prior to his senior year in college. He wants to make a contribution to a traditional IRA, but the amount is dependent on whether it reduces his taxable income. If Billy is going to claim the standard deduction, how much should he contribute to a traditional IRA?

4. **LO.1** Classify each of the following expenditures as a deduction *for* AGI, a deduction *from* AGI, or not deductible:
   a. Allison pays qualified moving expenses.
   b. Emalie gives cash to the Girl Scouts.
   c. Amos pays monthly alimony to his former spouse.
   d. Arnold pays real estate taxes levied by the county on his personal residence.
   e. April pays the premiums for insurance on her personal residence.
   f. Lonnie pays property taxes levied by the city on his SUV (used exclusively for business).

5. **LO.1** Classify each of the following expenditures as a deduction *for* AGI, a deduction *from* AGI, or not deductible:
   a. Amos contributes to his H.R. 10 plan (i.e., a retirement plan for a self-employed individual).
   b. Keith pays child support to his former wife, Renee, for the support of their son, Chris.
   c. Judy pays professional dues that are reimbursed by her employer.
   d. Ted pays $500 as the monthly mortgage payment on his personal residence. Of this amount, $100 represents a payment on principal, and $400 represents an interest payment.
   e. Lynn pays a moving company for moving her household goods to Detroit where she is starting a new job. She is not reimbursed by her employer.
   f. Ralph pays property taxes on his personal residence.

6. **LO.1** Larry and Susan each invest $10,000 in separate investment activities. They each incur deductible expenses of $800 associated with their respective investments. Explain why Larry's expenses might be properly classified as deductions *from* AGI (itemized deductions) and Susan's expenses might be appropriately classified as deductions *for* AGI.

7. **LO.1** Nanette is a third-grade teacher. Potential deductions are charitable contributions of $520, personal property taxes on her car of $225, and various supplies purchased for use in her classroom of $225 (none reimbursed by her school). How will these items affect Nanette's Federal income tax return?

8. **LO.1** Mabel, a machinist employed by Silver Airlines, owns 100 shares of Silver Airlines stock. Silver has 900,000 shares of stock outstanding. Mabel spends $1,500 to travel to Denver for Silver's annual meeting. Her expenses would have been $750 more, but she was permitted to fly free on Silver. She attended both days of the shareholders' meeting and actively participated. What are the tax consequences of the trip for Mabel?

9. **LO.1** In the determination of whether a business expense is deductible, the reasonableness requirement applies only to salaries. Evaluate this statement.

10. **LO.1** Dave uses the second floor of a building for his residence and the first floor for his business. The uninsured building is destroyed by fire. Are the tax consequences the same for each part of the building?

11. **LO.1** Mary Kate owns a building that she leases to an individual who operates a grocery store. Rent income is $10,000 and rental expenses are $6,000. On what Form 1040 schedule or schedules are the income and expenses reported?

12. **LO.2** Under the cash method of accounting, the taxpayer can deduct expenses when they are paid. Evaluate this statement.

13. **LO.2** Aubry, a cash basis and calendar year taxpayer, decides to reduce his taxable income for 2011 by buying $65,000 worth of supplies for his business on December 27, 2011. The supplies will be used up in 2012.
    a.   Can Aubry deduct the expenditure for 2011?
    b.   Would your answer in part (a) change if Aubry bought the supplies because the seller was going out of business and offered a significant discount on the price?

14. **LO.2** What is the significance of the all events and economic performance tests?

15. **LO.2** Why is the reserve method not allowed to be used for Federal income tax purposes?

16. **LO.3** Are any bribes or kickbacks deductible?

17. **LO.3** Ted is an agent for an airline manufacturer and is negotiating a sale with a representative of the U.S. government and with a representative of a developing country. Ted's company has sufficient capacity to handle only one of the orders. Both orders will have the same contract price. Ted believes that if his employer will authorize a $500,000 payment to the representative of the foreign country, he can guarantee the sale. He is not sure that he can obtain the same result with the U.S. government. Identify the relevant tax issues for Ted.

18. **LO.3** Stuart, an insurance salesman, is arrested for allegedly robbing a convenience store. He hires an attorney who is successful in getting the charges dropped. Is the attorney's fee deductible?

19. **LO.3** Linda operates a drug-running operation. Which of the following expenses she incurs can reduce taxable income?
    a.   Bribes paid to border guards.
    b.   Salaries to employees.
    c.   Price paid for drugs purchased for resale.
    d.   Kickbacks to police.
    e.   Rent on an office.
    f.   Depreciation on office furniture and equipment.
    g.   Tenant's casualty insurance.
    h.   Utilities.

20. **LO.3** Gordon anticipates that being positively perceived by the individual who is elected mayor will be beneficial for his business. Therefore, he contributes to the campaigns of both the Democratic and the Republican candidates. The Republican candidate is elected mayor. Can Gordon deduct any of the political contributions he made?

21. **LO.3** Carmine, Inc., a tobacco manufacturer, incurs certain expenditures associated with political contributions and lobbying activities. Which of these expenditures can be deducted?

Payments to Washington, D.C. law firm to lobby members of Congress	$800,000
Payments to Washington, D.C. law firm to lobby the head of the FDA	25,000
Payments to Richmond law firm to lobby members of the state legislature	50,000
Payments to Lexington law firm to lobby members of the Lexington City Council	5,000
Political contribution to Committee to Reelect the Mayor of Lexington	6,000

22. **LO.3** Agnes, an executive of a large corporation, receives a salary of $1.5 million. Taylor, who is an executive of another large corporation, receives a salary of $1.3 million. Agnes's corporation is permitted to deduct all of her salary while Taylor's corporation is permitted to deduct only part of his. Neither corporation is a TARP recipient. Assuming both salaries are reasonable, explain the result.

23. **LO.3** What is the significance of a taxpayer's occupation in the deductibility of expenses incurred in investigating another business?

24. **LO.3** Al has been working for an advertising agency during the two years since he graduated from college with a double major in marketing and art. In his spare time, Al enjoys painting landscapes. He sold his first painting in February at an art festival and has sold three more since then through contacts made at the festival. What are the tax

consequences of the sales income and the related expenses (e.g., art supplies, cost of travel to the art festival, advertising in the art festival program folder):

a.   If Al's art activity is classified as a hobby?

b.   If Al's art activity is classified as a trade or business?

25. **LO.3** Are there any circumstances under which taxpayers can rent their personal residence and not be required to report the rent income received? Does this have an effect on the deductions allowed?

26. **LO.3** Under what circumstances may a taxpayer deduct a rental loss associated with a vacation home?

27. **LO.3** Karen and Andy own a beach house. They have an agreement with a rental agent to rent it up to 200 days per year. For the past three years, the agent has been successful in renting it for 200 days. Karen and Andy use the beach house for one week during the summer and one week during Thanksgiving. Their daughter, Sarah, a college student, has asked if she and some friends can use the beach house for the week of spring break. Advise Karen and Andy how they should respond and identify any relevant tax issues.

ISSUE ID

28. **LO.3** Hank was transferred from Phoenix to North Dakota on March 1 of the current year. He immediately put his home in Phoenix up for rent. The home was rented May 1 to November 30 and was vacant during the month of December. It was rented again on January 1 for six months. What expenses, if any, can Hank deduct on his return? Which deductions are *for* AGI and which ones are *from* AGI?

29. **LO.3** Ray loses his job as a result of a corporate downsizing. Consequently, he falls behind on the mortgage payments on his personal residence. His friend Ted would like to make the delinquent mortgage payments for him.

DECISION MAKING

a.   Could the payments be structured so that Ray can deduct the mortgage interest?

b.   Could the payment arrangement deny both Ray and Ted a mortgage interest deduction?

c.   Could the payments be structured so that Ted could deduct the mortgage interest?

30. **LO.3** Edna incurs various legal fees in obtaining a divorce. Which types of expenses associated with the divorce are deductible by Edna, and which are not?

31. **LO.3** Ella owns 60% of the stock of Peach, Inc. The stock has declined in value since she purchased it five years ago. She is going to sell 5% of the stock to a relative. Ella is also going to make a gift of 10% of the stock to another relative. Identify the relevant tax issues for Ella.

ISSUE ID

32. **LO.3** Jarret owns City of Savannah bonds with an adjusted basis of $150,000. During the year, he receives interest payments of $4,500. Jarret partially financed the purchase of the bonds by borrowing $100,000 at 5% interest. Jarret's interest payments on the loan this year are $4,800, and his principal payments are $1,400.

a.   Should Jarret report any interest income this year?

b.   Can Jarret deduct any interest expense this year?

PROBLEMS

33. **LO.1** Amber is a self-employed tax attorney. She and Jon, her employee, attend a conference in Dallas sponsored by the American Institute of CPAs. The following expenses are incurred during the trip:

	Amber	Jon
Conference registration	$500	$500
Airfare	900	600
Taxi fares	75	–0–
Lodging in Dallas	700	300

a. Amber pays for all these expenses. Calculate the effect of these expenses on Amber's AGI.

b. Would your answer to part (a) change if the American Bar Association had sponsored the conference?

DECISION MAKING

34. **LO.1** Daniel is single and has the following income and expenses in 2011:

Salary income	$60,000
Net rent income	6,000
Dividend income	3,500
Payment of alimony	12,000
Mortgage interest on residence	4,900
Property tax on residence	1,200
Contribution to traditional IRA	5,000
Contribution to United Church	2,100
Loss on the sale of real estate (held for investment)	2,000
Medical expenses	3,250
State income tax	300
Federal income tax	7,000

a. Calculate Daniel's AGI.

b. Should Daniel itemize his deductions *from* AGI or take the standard deduction?

35. **LO.1** Julie is a student and earns $9,000 working part-time at the college ice cream shop in 2011. She has no other income. Her medical expenses for the year totaled $2,700. During the year, she suffered a casualty loss of $3,500 when her apartment burned. Julie contributed $1,950 to her church. On the advice of her parents, Julie is trying to decide whether to contribute $1,000 to the traditional IRA her parents have set up for her. What effect would the IRA contribution have on Julie's itemized deductions?

36. **LO.1** Drew and his wife Cassie own all of the stock of Thrush. Cassie is the president and Drew is the vice president. Cassie and Drew are paid salaries of $400,000 and $300,000, respectively, each year. They consider the salaries to be reasonable based on a comparison with salaries paid for comparable positions in comparable companies. They project Thrush's taxable income for next year, before their salaries, to be $800,000. They decide to place their four teenage children on the payroll and to pay them total salaries of $100,000. The children will each work about five hours per week for Thrush.

a. What are Drew and Cassie trying to achieve by hiring the children?

b. Calculate the tax consequences of hiring the children on Thrush, and on Drew and Cassie's family.

37. **LO.1** This has not been a good year for Betsy. During the year, she had losses from the following sales:

Personal use sailboat	$ 6,000
Personal residence	30,000
Rental house	12,000
Orange, Inc. stock	4,000
City of James bonds	2,000

a. What is the amount of Betsy's deductible losses?

b. Classify the deductible losses as deductions *for* or *from* AGI.

38. **LO.2** The income statement for Monroe's business shows the following revenues and expenses for 2011, the initial year of operations:

Sales revenue (including $19,000 credit sales uncollected at year-end)	$106,000
Wage expenses (including $3,000 unpaid at year-end)	32,000
Office expenses (supplies, copying, etc.)	2,000
Bad debt expense (of the $4,000 reserve established, $500 was written off as being currently uncollectible)	4,000
Utilities and telephone expense*	6,400
Insurance expense*	3,500
Rent expense (January 1, 2011–January 31, 2012)	9,750

*Amount incurred is the same as the amount paid.

a. Calculate Monroe's AGI using the accrual method.
b. Calculate Monroe's AGI using the cash method.

39. **LO.2** Maud, a calendar year taxpayer, is the owner of a sole proprietorship that uses the cash method. On February 1, 2011, she leases an office building to use in her business for $120,000 for an 18-month period. In order to obtain this favorable lease rate, she pays the $120,000 at the inception of the lease. How much rent expense may Maud deduct on her 2011 tax return?

40. **LO.2** Duck, an accrual basis corporation, sponsored a rock concert on December 29, 2011. Gross receipts were $300,000. The following expenses were incurred and paid as indicated:

Expense		Payment Date
Rental of coliseum	$ 25,000	December 21, 2011
Cost of goods sold:		
Food	30,000	December 30, 2011
Souvenirs	60,000	December 30, 2011
Performers	100,000	January 5, 2012
Cleaning of coliseum	10,000	February 1, 2012

Since the coliseum was not scheduled to be used again until January 15, the company with which Duck had contracted did not actually perform the cleanup until January 8–10, 2012.

Calculate Duck's net income from the concert for tax purposes for 2011.

41. **LO.3** Doug incurred and paid the following expenses during the year:

- $50 for a ticket for running a red light while he was commuting to work.
- $100 for a ticket for parking in a handicapped parking space.
- $200 to an attorney to represent him in traffic court as to the two tickets.
- $500 to an attorney to draft an agreement with a tenant for a one-year lease on an apartment that Doug owns.
- $1,000 to an attorney to negotiate a reduction in his child support payments.
- $2,500 to an attorney to negotiate a reduction in his qualified alimony payments to a former spouse.

Calculate the amount of Doug's deductible expenses.

42. **LO.3** Trevor, a friend of yours from high school, works as a waiter at the ST Café. He asks you to help him prepare his Federal income tax return. When you inquire about why his bank deposits substantially exceed his tip income, he confides to you that on the side he is a "bookie." Trevor then provides you with the following documented income and expenses for the year:

Tip income	$16,000
Gambling income	52,000
Gambling expenses	
Payouts to winners	29,000
Employee compensation	8,000
Bribe to police officer who is aware of Trevor's bookie activity	7,500

a. How will these items affect Trevor's AGI?
b. His taxable income?
c. If Trevor's business was an illegal drug operation and the cost of the illegal drugs sold was $6,200, how would your answers to parts (a) and (b) differ?

43. **LO.3** You are a senior government major. Two of the five seats on city council are up for election. Friends, knowing your interest in local politics, encourage you to run for city council. You are elected by a two-to-one majority. You received campaign contributions from the following:

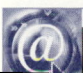

Your parents	$1,000
Government professor who is your faculty adviser	500
Friends who are classmates	750
Other friends	400

All of these funds were used for legitimate campaign purposes (e.g., signs, ads in local newspaper). How much of the campaign contributions can be deducted by the donors?

DECISION MAKING

COMMUNICATIONS

44. **LO.3, 4** Amber, a publicly held corporation (not a TARP recipient), currently pays its president an annual salary of $900,000. In addition, it contributes $20,000 annually to a defined contribution pension plan for him. As a means of increasing company profitability, the board of directors decides to increase the president's compensation. Two proposals are being considered. Under the first proposal, the salary and pension contribution for the president would be increased by 30%. Under the second proposal, Amber would implement a performance-based compensation program that is projected to provide about the same amount of additional compensation and pension contribution for the president.
    a. Evaluate the alternatives from the perspective of Amber, Inc.
    b. Prepare a letter to Amber's board of directors that contains your recommendations. Address the letter to the board chairperson, Agnes Riddle, whose address is 100 James Tower, Cleveland, OH 44106.

45. **LO.3** Vermillion, Inc., a publicly held corporation (not a TARP recipient), pays the following salaries to its executives:

	Salary	Bonus	Retirement Plan Contribution
CEO	$2,000,000	$100,000	$80,000
Executive vice president	1,800,000	90,000	72,000
Treasurer	1,600,000	–0–	64,000
Marketing vice president	1,500,000	75,000	60,000
Operations vice president	1,400,000	70,000	56,000
Distribution vice president	1,200,000	60,000	48,000
Research vice president	1,100,000	–0–	44,000
Controller	800,000	–0–	32,000

Vermillion normally does not pay bonuses, but after reviewing the results of operations for the year, the board of directors decided to pay a 5% bonus to selected executives. What is the amount of these payments that Vermillion may deduct?

46. **LO.3** Joan, the owner of a very successful restaurant chain in the Southeast, is exploring the possibility of expanding the chain into a city in the Northeast. She incurs $28,000 of expenses associated with this investigation. Based on the regulatory environment for restaurants in the city, she decides not to expand. During the year, she also investigates opening a hotel that will be part of a national hotel chain. Her expenses for this are $53,000. The hotel begins operations on July 1. Determine the amount that Joan can deduct in the current year for investigating these two businesses.

47. **LO.3** Terry traveled to a neighboring state to investigate the purchase of two hardware stores. His expenses included travel, legal, accounting, and miscellaneous expenses. The total was $52,000. He incurred the expenses in June and July 2011. Under the following circumstances, what can Terry deduct in 2011?
    a. Terry was in the hardware store business and did not acquire the two hardware stores.
    b. Terry was in the hardware store business and acquired the two hardware stores and began operating them on October 1, 2011.
    c. Terry did not acquire the two hardware stores and was not in the hardware store business.
    d. Terry acquired the two hardware stores, but was not in the hardware store business when he acquired them. Operations began on October 1, 2011.

48. **LO.3** Sonam makes pottery in her spare time. She sold $17,000 worth of pottery during the year and incurred expenses as follows:

Supplies	$14,000
Depreciation on business property	4,000
Advertising	2,000
Booth at arts and crafts fair	500

Her AGI, without considering the effect of the sales of the pottery, is $100,000. Calculate Sonam's AGI if the activity is:
a. A hobby.
b. A business.

49. **LO.3** Sandra, an orthodontist, is single and has net earnings of $90,000 from her practice. In addition, she collects antique books that she buys and sells at antique shows. She participates in six to eight weekend shows per year. Her income and expenses for the current year are as follows:

Revenue from sale of antique books	$22,000
Expenses	
Cost of goods sold	12,000
Show registration costs	3,000
Advertising	1,000
Dealer's license—annual fee	500
Insurance	900
Depreciation of display cases	1,200

Sandra has no other items that would affect her AGI. Itemized deductions consisting of taxes, interest, and charitable contributions are $19,000. Calculate Sandra's taxable income if the antique book activity is classified as:
a. A hobby.
b. A business.

50. **LO.3** Adelene, who lives in a winter resort area, rented her personal residence for 14 days while she was visiting Brussels. Rent income was $5,000. Related expenses for the year were as follows:

Real property taxes	$ 3,800
Mortgage interest	7,500
Utilities	3,700
Insurance	2,500
Repairs	2,100
Depreciation	15,000

Determine the effect on Adelene's AGI.

51. **LO.3** During the year (not a leap year), Anna rented her vacation home for 30 days, used it personally for 20 days, and left it vacant for 315 days. She had the following income and expenses:

Rent income	$ 7,000
Expenses	
Real estate taxes	2,500
Interest on mortgage	9,000
Utilities	2,400
Repairs	1,000
Roof replacement (a capital expenditure)	12,000
Depreciation	7,500

a. Compute Anna's net rent income or loss and the amounts she can itemize on her tax return, using the court's approach to allocating property taxes and interest.
b. How would your answer in part (a) differ using the IRS's method of allocating property taxes and interest?

52. **LO.3** How would your answer in Problem 51 differ if Anna had rented the house for 87 days and had used it personally for 13 days?

53. **LO.1, 3** Chee, single, age 40, had the following income and expenses during the year (not a leap year):

Income	
Salary	$43,000
Rental of vacation home (rented 60 days, used personally 60 days, vacant 245 days)	4,000
Municipal bond interest	2,000
Dividend from General Electric	400
Expenses	
Interest	
On home mortgage	8,400
On vacation home	4,758
On loan used to buy municipal bonds	3,100
Property tax on home	2,200
Property tax on vacation home	1,098
State income tax	3,300
State sales tax	900
Charitable contributions	1,100
Tax return preparation fee	300
Utilities and maintenance on vacation home	2,600
Depreciation on rental 50% of vacation home	3,500

Calculate Chee's taxable income for the year before personal exemptions.

DECISION MAKING

54. **LO.1, 3, 4** Velma and Clyde operate a retail sports memorabilia shop. For the current year, sales revenue is $50,000 and expenses are as follows:

Cost of goods sold	$19,000
Advertising	1,000
Utilities	2,000
Rent	4,000
Insurance	1,500
Wages to Boyd	7,000

Velma and Clyde pay $7,000 in wages to Boyd, a part-time employee. Since this amount is $1,000 below the minimum wage, Boyd threatens to file a complaint with the appropriate Federal agency. Although Velma and Clyde pay no attention to Boyd's threat, Chelsie (Velma's mother) gives Boyd a check for $1,000 for the disputed wages. Both Velma and Clyde ridicule Chelsie for wasting money when they learn what she has done. The retail shop is the only source of income for Velma and Clyde.
   a.   Calculate Velma and Clyde's AGI.
   b.   Can Chelsie deduct the $1,000 payment on her tax return?
   c.   How could the tax position of the parties be improved?

55. **LO.3, 4** Max is purchasing a sole proprietorship business from Darlene. The amount being paid exceeds the fair market value of the identifiable assets of the business by $930,000. Advise Max on the tax consequences of the $930,000 being allocated to goodwill versus it being allocated to a nine-year covenant not to compete.

DECISION MAKING

56. **LO.3, 4** Jay's sole proprietorship has the following assets:

	Basis	Fair Market Value
Cash	$ 10,000	$ 10,000
Accounts receivable	18,000	18,000
Inventory	25,000	30,000
Patent	22,000	40,000
Land	50,000	75,000
	$125,000	$173,000

The building in which Jay's business is located is leased. The lease expires at the end of the year.

Jay is age 70 and would like to retire. He expects to be in the 35% tax bracket. Jay is negotiating the sale of the business with Lois, a key employee. They have agreed on the fair market value of the assets, as indicated above, and agree the total purchase price should be about $200,000.

a. Advise Jay regarding how the sale should be structured.
b. Advise Lois regarding how the purchase should be structured.
c. What might they do to achieve an acceptable compromise?

57. **L0.3, 4** Eleanor Saxon sold stock (basis of $65,000) to her brother, Ridge, for $61,000, the fair market value.

a. What are the tax consequences to Eleanor?
b. What are the tax consequences to Ridge if he later sells the stock for $66,000? For $58,000? For $62,000?
c. Write a letter to Eleanor in which you inform her of the tax consequences if she sells the stock to Ridge for $61,000 and explain how a sales transaction could be structured that would produce better tax consequences for her. Eleanor's address is 32 Country Lane, Lawrence, KS 66045.

58. **L0.3** The Robin Corporation is owned as follows:

Isabelle	26%
Peter, Isabelle's husband	19%
Sonya, Isabelle's mother	15%
Reggie, Isabelle's father	25%
Quinn, an unrelated party	15%

Robin is on the accrual basis, and Isabelle and Peter are on the cash basis. Isabelle and Peter each loaned the Robin Corporation $40,000 out of their separate funds. On December 31, 2011, Robin accrued interest at 7% on both loans. The interest was paid on February 4, 2012. What is the tax treatment of this interest expense/income to Isabelle, Peter, and Robin?

59. **L0.3** For each of the following independent transactions, calculate the recognized gain or loss to the seller and the adjusted basis to the buyer.

a. Bonnie sells Parchment, Inc. stock (adjusted basis $17,000) to Phillip, her brother, for its fair market value of $12,000.
b. Amos sells land (adjusted basis $85,000) to his nephew, Boyd, for its fair market value of $70,000.
c. Susan sells a tax-exempt bond (adjusted basis $20,000) to her wholly owned corporation for its fair market value of $19,000.
d. Ron sells a business truck (adjusted basis $20,000) that he uses in his sole proprietorship to his cousin, Agnes, for its fair market value of $18,500.
e. Martha sells her partnership interest (adjusted basis $175,000) in Pearl Partnership to her adult daughter, Kim, for $220,000.

60. **L0.3** Chris has a brokerage account and buys on the margin, which resulted in an interest expense of $18,000 during the year. Income generated through the brokerage account was as follows:

Municipal interest	$20,000
Taxable dividends and interest	80,000

How much investment interest can Chris deduct?

61. **L0.1** Lee incurred the following expenses in the current tax year. Indicate, in the spaces provided, whether each expenditure is deductible *for* AGI, *from* AGI, or not deductible.

		Deductible		Not
	Expense Item	For AGI	From AGI	Deductible
a.	Lee's personal medical expenses	___	___	___
b.	Lee's dependent daughter's medical expenses	___	___	___
c.	Real estate taxes on Lee's rental property	___	___	___
d.	Real estate taxes on Lee's personal residence	___	___	___
e.	Real estate taxes on daughter's personal residence	___	___	___
f.	Lee's state income taxes	___	___	___
g.	Interest on Lee's rental property mortgage	___	___	___
h.	Interest on Lee's personal residence mortgage	___	___	___
i.	Interest on daughter's personal residence mortgage	___	___	___
j.	Interest on Lee's business loans	___	___	___
k.	Lee's charitable contributions	___	___	___
l.	Depreciation on Lee's rental property	___	___	___
m.	Depreciation on auto used in Lee's business	___	___	___
n.	Depreciation on Lee's personal use auto	___	___	___
o.	Depreciation on daughter's personal use auto	___	___	___

CUMULATIVE PROBLEMS

TAX RETURN PROBLEM

62. Roberta Santos, age 41, is single and lives at 120 Sanborne Avenue, Springfield, IL 60740. Her Social Security number is 123–45–6789. Roberta has been divorced from her former husband, Wayne, for three years. She has a son, Jason, who is age 17, and a daughter, June, who is age 18. Jason's Social Security number is 111–11–1111 and June's is 123–45–6788. Roberta does not wish to contribute $3 to the Presidential Election Campaign Fund.

Roberta, an advertising executive, earned a salary of $75,000 in 2010. Her employer withheld $8,500 in Federal income tax, $3,100 in state income tax, and the appropriate amount of FICA tax: $4,650 for Social Security tax and $1,087.50 for Medicare tax.

Roberta has legal custody of Jason and June. The divorce decree provides that Roberta is to receive the dependency deductions for the children. Jason lives with his father during summer vacation. Wayne indicates that his expenses for Jason are $10,500. Roberta can document that she spent $6,500 for Jason's support during 2010. In prior years, Roberta gave a signed Form 8332 to Wayne regarding Jason. For 2010, she has decided not to do so. Roberta provides all of June's support.

Roberta's mother died on January 7, 2010. Roberta inherited assets worth $625,000 from her mother. As the sole beneficiary of her mother's life insurance policy, Roberta received insurance proceeds of $300,000. Her mother's cost basis for the life insurance policy was $120,000. Roberta's favorite aunt gave her $13,000 for her birthday in October.

On November 8, 2010, Roberta sells for $20,000 Amber stock that she had purchased for $24,000 from her first cousin, Walt, on December 5, 2005. Walt's cost basis for the stock was $26,000, and the stock was worth $23,000 on December 5, 2005. On December 1, 2010, Roberta sold Falcon stock for $13,500. She had acquired the stock on July 2, 2007, for $7,000.

An examination of Roberta's records reveals that she received the following:

- Interest income of $2,000 from First Savings Bank.
- Groceries valued at $750 from a local grocery store for being the 100,000th customer.
- Qualified dividend income of $1,800 from Amber.
- Interest income of $3,750 on City of Springfield school bonds.
- Alimony of $15,000 from Wayne.

- Distribution of $4,800 from ST Partnership. Her distributive share of the partnership passive taxable income was $5,300.

From her checkbook records, she determines that she made the following payments during 2010:

- Charitable contributions of $3,500 to First Presbyterian Church and $1,500 to the American Red Cross (proper receipts obtained).
- Mortgage interest on her residence of $7,800.
- Property taxes of $3,100 on her residence and $1,100 on her car.
- Estimated Federal income taxes of $3,800 and estimated state income taxes of $1,000.
- Medical expenses of $5,000 for her and $800 for Jason. In December her medical insurance policy reimbursed $1,500 of her medical expenses.
- A $1,000 ticket for parking in a handicapped space.
- Attorney's fees of $500 associated with unsuccessfully contesting the parking ticket.
- Contribution of $250 to the campaign of a candidate for governor.
- Since she did not maintain records of the sales tax she paid, she calculates the amount from the sales tax table to be $994.

Calculate Roberta's net tax payable or refund due for 2010. If you use tax forms, you will need Form 1040 and Schedules A, B, D, and E. Suggested software: H&R BLOCK At Home.

63. John and Mary Jane Sanders are married, filing jointly. Their address is 204 Shoe Lane, Blacksburg, VA 24061. They are expecting their first child in early 2012. John's salary in 2011 was $90,000, from which $20,200 of Federal income tax and $4,700 of state income tax were withheld. Mary Jane made $50,000 and had $3,000 of Federal income tax and $3,100 of state income tax withheld. The appropriate amount of FICA tax was withheld for John and for Mary Jane: for John, Social Security tax of $3,780 and Medicare tax of $1,305; for Mary Jane, Social Security tax of $2,100 and Medicare tax of $725. John's Social Security number is 111–11–1111, and Mary Jane's Social Security number is 123–45–6789.

> **TAX COMPUTATION PROBLEM**
>
> **DECISION MAKING**
>
> **COMMUNICATIONS**

John and Mary Jane are both covered by their employer's medical insurance policies with three-fourths of the premiums being paid by the employers. The total premiums were $6,000 for John and $4,200 for Mary Jane. Mary Jane received medical benefits of $6,200 under the plan. John was not ill during 2011.

John makes child support payments of $12,000 for his son, Rod, who lives with June, John's former spouse, except for two months in the summer when he visits John and Mary Jane. At the time of the divorce, John worked for a Fortune 500 company and received a salary of $250,000. As a result of corporate downsizing, he lost his job.

Mary Jane's father lived with them until his death in November. His only sources of income were salary of $1,900, unemployment compensation benefits of $3,500, and Social Security benefits of $3,200. Of this amount, he deposited $4,800 in a savings account. The remainder of his support of $9,000, which included funeral expenses of $5,100, was provided by John and Mary Jane.

Other income received by the Sanderses was as follows:

Interest on certificates of deposit	$3,500
Share of S corporation taxable income (distributions from the S corporation to Mary Jane were $600)	1,200
Award received by Mary Jane from employer for outstanding suggestion for cutting costs	1,500

John has always wanted to operate his own business. In October 2011, he incurred expenses of $10,000 in investigating the establishment of a retail computer franchise. With the birth of their child expected next year, however, he decides to forgo self-employment for at least a couple of years.

John and Mary Jane made charitable contributions of $4,000 during the year and paid an additional $1,200 in state income taxes in 2011 upon filing their 2010 state income tax return. Their deductible home mortgage interest was $7,500, and their property taxes came to $4,500. They paid sales taxes of $1,700 for which they have receipts.

Part 1—Tax Computation
Calculate John and Mary Jane's tax (or refund) due for 2011.

Part 2—Tax Planning

Assume that the Sanderses come to you for advice in December 2011. John has learned that he will receive a $30,000 bonus. He wants to know if he should take it in December 2011 or in January 2012. Mary Jane will quit work on December 31 to stay home with the baby. Their itemized deductions will decrease by $3,100 because Mary Jane will not have state income taxes withheld. Mary Jane will not receive the employee award in 2012. She expects the medical benefits received to be $9,000. The Sanderses expect all of their other income items to remain the same in 2012. Write a letter to John and Mary Jane that contains your advice and prepare a memo for the tax files.

RESEARCH PROBLEMS

THOMSON REUTERS

Checkpoint® Student Edition

Note: Solutions to Research Problems can be prepared by using the **Checkpoint®** **Student Edition** online research product, which is available to accompany this text. It is also possible to prepare solutions to the Research Problems by using tax research materials found in a standard tax library.

Research Problem 1. Robin, Inc., acquired all the assets of Sparrow, Inc. In addition, Robin assumed certain liabilities of Sparrow. Robin agreed that it would be legally responsible for any judgment in a patent infringement claim being litigated against Sparrow. Experts' opinions indicated that the likelihood that a contingent liability would result was remote (i.e., between 0% and 5%).

After a trial, a jury concluded that patent infringement had occurred and awarded a judgment of $5 million. Robin paid the $5 million and deducted it as an ordinary and necessary business expense. Upon audit, the IRS reclassified the $5 million payment and treated it as a capital expenditure under § 263. Evaluate the positions taken by Robin and by the IRS.

COMMUNICATIONS

Research Problem 2. Gray Chemical Company manufactured pesticides that were toxic. Over the course of several years, the toxic waste contaminated the air and water around the company's plant. Several employees suffered toxic poisoning, and the Environmental Protection Agency cited the company for violations. In court, the judge found Gray guilty and imposed fines of $15 million. The company voluntarily set up a charitable fund for the purpose of bettering the environment and funded it with $8 million. The company incurred legal expenses in setting up the foundation and defending itself in court. The court reduced the fine from $15 million to $7 million.

Gray Chemical Company deducted the $8 million paid to the foundation and the legal expenses incurred. The IRS disallowed both deductions on the grounds that the payment was, in fact, a fine and in violation of public policy.

Gray's president, Ted Jones, has contacted you regarding the deductibility of the $7 million fine, the $8 million payment to the foundation, and the legal fees. Write a letter to Mr. Jones that contains your advice and prepare a memo for the tax files. Gray's address is 200 Lincoln Center, Omaha, NE 68182.

Partial list of research aids:
§§ 162(a) and (f).
Reg. § 1.162–21(b).

Research Problem 3. Rex and Agnes Harrell purchased a beach house at Duck, North Carolina, in early 2009. Although they intended to use the beach house occasionally for recreational purposes, they also planned to rent it through the realty agency that had handled the purchase in order to help pay the mortgage payments, property taxes, and maintenance costs. Rex is a surgeon, and Agnes is a counselor.

The beach house was in need of substantial repairs. Rather than hiring a contractor, Rex and Agnes decided they would make the repairs themselves. During both high school and college, Rex had worked summers in construction. In addition, he had taken an advanced course in woodworking and related subjects from a local community college several years ago.

During 2009, according to a log maintained by the Harrells, they occupied the beach house 38 days and rented it 49 days. The log also indicated that on 24 of the 38 days that they occupied the beach house, one or both of them were engaged in work on the beach house. Their two teenage children were with them on all of these days, but did not help with the work being done. On their 2009 income tax return, Rex and Agnes, who filed a joint return, treated the beach house as a rental property and deducted a pro rata share of the property taxes, mortgage interest, utilities, maintenance and repairs, and depreciation in determining their net loss from the beach home. An IRS agent has limited the deductions to the rent income. He contends that the 14-day personal use provision was exceeded and that many of the alleged repairs were capital expenditures. Advise the Harrells on how they should respond to the IRS.

Research Problem 4. In early 2009, Walter Hodges began investigating the real estate market with the intention of acquiring real estate for investment or rental. He had not previously been involved in any real estate rental or investment ventures.

Walter started marketing his business via business cards, flyers, and word of mouth in spring 2009. At the same time, he completed a business plan for buying, remodeling, and renting property.

In October 2009, Walter paid $25,000 for training classes designed to provide real estate investment skills. He obtained a loan for his business of $45,000 from the U.S. Small Business Administration in November 2009. During the same month, he obtained an employer ID number from the IRS. In December 2009, he opened a checking account and obtained a credit card in the name of the business.

Walter attempted to purchase several properties during the last half of 2009, but was unsuccessful until he acquired property on December 30, 2009. He listed the property for rent in early January 2010 and was successful in renting it in March 2010.

On his Form 1040 for 2009, Walter prepared a Schedule C on which he showed a business loss of $29,000. He included the cost of the training classes, automobile expenses, meals and entertainment, computer and software expenses, and supplies.

The IRS has disallowed Walter's $29,000 deduction on the grounds that he was not yet in a trade or business during 2009. Evaluate the position taken by the IRS.

Research Problem 5. Bill Robinson is a physician whose specialty is obstetrics and gynecology (Ob/Gyn). He and his wife Joy have lived in Richmond Hill, Georgia, for more than 15 years. Due to the high cost of his medical malpractice insurance, Bill decided to discontinue the "delivering babies" part of his practice. Joy is employed as an administrator with a home health agency.

In order to partially offset the loss of income associated with the curtailment of Bill's medical practice, Joy became a salesperson for several direct marketing companies. Her activities varied in that one of the companies sold beauty products while another marketed a tax product that supposedly would increase a taxpayer's deductions by at least $5,000. The direct marketing companies required that Joy purchase a certain amount of inventory each month. Joy received a commission based on the amount of her sales. In addition, Joy received part of the commissions earned by other people that she signed up to work for the direct marketing companies (i.e., she was an "upline distributor," and the recruits were "downline distributors").

Fortunately, Joy was able to retain her administrative position and do her direct marketing activities in the evenings and on weekends. She estimated she worked about 15 to 20 hours per week in these direct marketing activities. She prepared 30- and 90-day sales reports and kept a record of her expenses. For the first five years as a direct seller, she had losses of more than $20,000 each year. She reported and deducted these losses on a Schedule C.

The IRS audits the Robinsons' joint income tax return and disallows as a hobby the loss reported by Joy on her Schedule C.

Joy contends that her direct marketing activity is a trade or business and supports this position with the following facts:

- She conducted her direct marketing activity as a trade or business. For each of her direct selling activities, she prepared a business plan that included goals regarding the number of customers she would attract and the sales she would achieve.
- She worked about 15 to 20 hours per week in the direct marketing activities with 60% of the time being devoted to signing up downline distributors (primarily family members or friends at a lunch or dinner that she paid for). Unfortunately, most of her success in this area has been short-lived (i.e., nearly all of her signees quit within six months).
- She invested in the business by purchasing inventory.
- She obtained tax advice on her direct marketing activities from a CPA.

- She hired a CPA to evaluate the legality of the tax product she was selling.
- She occasionally sought advice on sales, product training, and recruiting others from her upline distributor.

Evaluate the controversy by applying the nine factors in Reg. §§ 1.183–2(b)(1) through (9).

Research Problem 6. Medical Benefits, Inc., was established pursuant to the California Public Benefit Corporation Law. Its articles of incorporation provided that it was "organized and operated exclusively for charitable, educational, and scientific purposes." According to Medical Benefits, it operated with a dual purpose. Its primary purpose was to provide caregiving services to its members. Its secondary purpose was to furnish its members with medical marijuana and instructions for using it to benefit their health pursuant to the California Compassionate Use Act of 1996. Recipients paid Medical Benefits a membership fee in consideration of the right to receive caregiving services and the right to receive medical marijuana.

Medical Benefits was tax-exempt in California but not for Federal purposes. Medical Benefits' annual revenues and expenses were approximately the same amount (i.e., a break-even result). Consequently, any Federal tax liability was either $0 or minimal.

According to the IRS, all of Medical Benefits' deductions should be disallowed. Therefore, its Federal tax liability should be calculated based solely on its revenues. The basis for the disallowance is § 280E (Expenditures in Connection with the Illegal Sale of Drugs). Since Medical Benefits was "trafficking in controlled substances," no deductions are permitted.

Evaluate the positions taken by Medical Benefits and the IRS.

INTERNET *activity*

Use the tax resources of the Internet to address the following questions. Do not restrict your search to the Web, but include a review of newsgroups and general reference materials, practitioner sites and resources, primary sources of the tax law, chat rooms and discussion groups, and other opportunities.

Research Problem 7. Locate and read a recent judicial or administrative ruling regarding the deductibility of hobby losses. Look for rulings that deal with horse breeding, professional sports teams, or art collecting activities. Which criteria did the ruling emphasize in upholding or reversing the taxpayer's deduction for such losses?

Research Problem 8. The $1 million maximum compensation deduction does not seem to have deterred large corporations from remunerating their executives at very high levels. What techniques are being used to work around the millionaires' provision? Are executives taking pay cuts, or are their salaries being deferred or changed in nature due to § 162(m)?

CHAPTER

7

Deductions and Losses: Certain Business Expenses and Losses

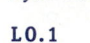

LEARNING OBJECTIVES

After completing Chapter 7, you should be able to:

L0.1
Determine the amount, classification, and timing of the **bad debt deduction**.

L0.2
Understand the tax treatment of **worthless securities** including §1244 stock.

L0.3
Distinguish between deductible and nondeductible **losses of individuals**.

L0.4
Identify a casualty and determine the amount, classification, and timing of **casualty and theft losses**.

L0.5
Recognize and apply the alternative tax treatments for **research and experimental expenditures**.

L0.6
Calculate the **domestic production activities deduction**.

L0.7
Determine the amount of the **net operating loss** and recognize the impact of the carryback and carryover provisions.

L0.8
Identify **tax planning opportunities** in deducting certain business expenses, business losses, and personal losses.

OUTLINE

7.1 Bad Debts, 7-3
Specific Charge-Off Method, 7-4
Business versus Nonbusiness Bad Debts, 7-4
Loans between Related Parties, 7-5

7.2 Worthless Securities, 7-7
Small Business Stock, 7-7

7.3 Losses of Individuals, 7-8
Events That Are Not Casualties, 7-8
Theft Losses, 7-9
When to Deduct Casualty Losses, 7-9
Measuring the Amount of Loss, 7-11
Statutory Framework for Deducting
    Losses of Individuals, 7-13
Personal Casualty Gains and Losses, 7-14

7.4 Research and Experimental Expenditures, 7-15
Expense Method, 7-16
Deferral and Amortization Method, 7-16

7.5 Domestic Production Activities Deduction, 7-17
Operational Rules, 7-17
Eligible Taxpayers, 7-19

7.6 Net Operating Losses, 7-19
Carryback and Carryover Periods, 7-21
Computation of the Net Operating Loss, 7-22
Recomputation of Tax Liability for Year to
    Which Net Operating Loss Is Carried, 7-24
Calculation of the Remaining Net Operating Loss, 7-25

TAX PLANNING, 7-26
7.7 Tax Consequences of the *Groetzinger* Case, 7-26
7.8 Documentation of Related-Taxpayer Loans, Casualty Losses, and Theft Losses, 7-26
7.9 Worthless Securities, 7-26
7.10 Small Business Stock, 7-27
7.11 Casualty Losses, 7-27
7.12 Net Operating Losses, 7-28

For the latest in changes to tax legislation, visit **www.cengage.com/taxation/swft.**

FRAMEWORK 1040:
Tax Formula for Individuals

This chapter covers the boldfaced portions of the Tax Formula for Individuals that was introduced in Figure 3.1 on p. 3-3. Below those portions are the sections of Form 1040 where the results are reported.

Income (broadly conceived)	$xx,xxx
Less: Exclusions	(x,xxx)
Gross income	$xx,xxx
Less: Deductions for adjusted gross income	**(x,xxx)**

FORM 1040 (p. 1)

12	Business income or (loss). Attach Schedule C or C-EZ	
35	Domestic production activities deduction. Attach Form 8903	

Adjusted gross income	$xx,xxx
Less: The greater of total **itemized deductions** *or* the standard deduction	**(x,xxx)**

FORM 1040 (p. 2)

40	**Itemized deductions** (from Schedule A) **or** your **standard deduction** (see instructions)

Personal and dependency exemptions	(x,xxx)
Taxable income	$xx,xxx
Tax on taxable income (see tax Tables or Tax Rate Schedules)	$ x,xxx
Less: Tax credits (including income taxes withheld and prepaid)	(xxx)
Tax due (or refund)	$ xxx

THE BIG PICTURE   **Tax Solutions for the Real World**

LOSSES

Martha is nearing the end of a year that she would like to forget. Several years ago she loaned a friend $25,000 to enable him to start a business. The friend had made scheduled payments of $7,000 ($1,000 of this was interest) when he unexpectedly died in January. At the time of his death, he was insolvent. Martha's attempts to collect on the debt were fruitless.

Last October Martha invested $50,000 in the stock of a pharmaceutical company that previously had been profitable. However, as a result of losing a patent infringement suit, the company declared bankruptcy in May of this year. Martha is notified by the bankruptcy trustee that she can expect to receive nothing from the company.

Martha has owned and operated a bookstore as a sole proprietorship for the past 10 years. The bookstore previously has produced annual profits of about $75,000. Due to a chain bookstore opening down the street, Martha's bookstore sustained a net loss of $180,000 this year.

In September, a hurricane caused a large oak tree to blow over onto Martha's house. The cost of removing the tree and making repairs was $32,000. Martha received a check for $25,000 from her insurance company in final settlement of the claim. Her adjusted basis for the house was $280,000.

Can you help to relieve Martha's feeling of hopelessness by making her aware of beneficial loss provisions in the tax law? **Read the chapter and formulate your response.**

Working with the tax formula for individuals requires the proper classification of items that are deductible *for* adjusted gross income (AGI) and items that are deductions *from* AGI (itemized deductions). Business expenses and losses, discussed in this chapter, are reductions of gross income to arrive at the taxpayer's AGI. Expenses and losses incurred in connection with a transaction entered into for profit and attributable to rents and royalties are deducted *for* AGI. All other expenses and losses incurred in connection with a transaction entered into for profit are deducted *from* AGI.

The situation of Robert P. Groetzinger provides an interesting insight into the importance of the proper classification for the individual taxpayer. Groetzinger terminated his employment with a private company and devoted virtually all of his working time to pari-mutuel wagering on dog races. He had no other profession or employment, and his only sources of income, apart from his gambling winnings, were interest, dividends, and sales from investments. During the tax year in question, he went to the track six days a week and devoted 60 to 80 hours per week to preparing and making wagers on his own account.

The tax question that this case presents is whether Groetzinger's gambling activities constitute a trade or business. If the gambling is a trade or business, his gambling losses are deductions *for* AGI. If the gambling activity is not a trade or business, the losses are itemized deductions, and Groetzinger's taxes increase by $2,142.[1]

Deductible losses on personal use property are deducted as an itemized deduction. Itemized deductions are deductions *from* AGI. While the general coverage of itemized deductions is in Chapter 10, casualty and theft losses on personal use property are discussed in this chapter.

In determining the amount and timing of the deduction for bad debts, proper classification is again important. A business bad debt is classified as a deduction *for* AGI, and a nonbusiness bad debt is classified as a short-term capital loss.

Other topics discussed in Chapter 7 are research and experimental expenditures, the domestic production activities deduction, and the net operating loss deduction.

7.1 BAD DEBTS

If a taxpayer sells goods or provides services on credit and the account receivable subsequently becomes worthless, a **bad debt** deduction is permitted only if income arising from the creation of the account receivable was previously included in income.[2] No deduction is allowed, for example, for a bad debt arising from the sale of a product or service when the taxpayer is on the cash basis because no income is reported until the cash has been collected. Permitting a bad debt deduction for a cash basis taxpayer would amount to a double deduction because the expenses of the product or service rendered are deducted when payments are made to suppliers and to employees, or at the time of the sale.

> **LO.1**
> Determine the amount, classification, and timing of the bad debt deduction.

EXAMPLE 1

Tracy, an individual, is a sole proprietor. She operates a business named Executive Accounting and Tax Services. Last year, Pat hired Tracy to help him with the accounting for his small business. Tracy also prepared the S corporation income tax return for the business and Pat's personal income tax return. Tracy billed Pat $8,000 for the services she performed. Pat has never paid the bill, his business no longer exists, and his whereabouts are unknown.

If Tracy is an accrual basis taxpayer, she includes the $8,000 in income when the services are performed. When she determines that Pat's account will not be collected, she deducts the $8,000 as a bad debt expense.

If Tracy is a cash basis taxpayer, she does not include the $8,000 in income until payment is received. When she determines that Pat's account will not be collected, she cannot deduct the $8,000 as a bad debt expense because it was never recognized as income. ■

[1]*Groetzinger v. Comm.*, 85–2 USTC ¶9622, 56 AFTR 2d 85–5683, 771 F.2d 269 (CA–7, 1985).   [2]Reg. § 1.166–1(e).

A bad debt can also result from the nonrepayment of a loan made by the taxpayer or from purchased debt instruments.

SPECIFIC CHARGE-OFF METHOD

Taxpayers (other than certain financial institutions) may use only the **specific charge-off method** in accounting for bad debts. Certain financial institutions are allowed to use the **reserve method** for computing deductions for bad debts.

A taxpayer using the specific charge-off method may claim a deduction when a specific business debt becomes either partially or wholly worthless or when a specific nonbusiness debt becomes wholly worthless.[3] For the business debt, the taxpayer must satisfy the IRS that the debt is partially worthless and must demonstrate the amount of worthlessness.

If a business debt previously deducted as partially worthless becomes totally worthless in a future year, only the remainder not previously deducted can be deducted in the future year.

In the case of total worthlessness, a deduction is allowed for the entire amount in the year the debt becomes worthless. The amount of the deduction depends on the taxpayer's basis in the bad debt. If the debt arose from the sale of services or products and the face amount was previously included in income, that amount is deductible. If the taxpayer purchased the debt, the deduction is equal to the amount the taxpayer paid for the debt instrument.

One of the more difficult tasks is determining if and when a bad debt is worthless. The loss is deductible only in the year of partial or total worthlessness for business debts and only in the year of total worthlessness for nonbusiness debts. Legal proceedings need not be initiated against the debtor when the surrounding facts indicate that such action will not result in collection.

| EXAMPLE 2 | In 2009, Ross loaned $1,000 to Kay, who agreed to repay the loan in two years. In 2011, Kay disappeared after the note became delinquent. If a reasonable investigation by Ross indicates that he cannot find Kay or that a suit against Kay would not result in collection, Ross can deduct the $1,000 in 2011. ∎ |

Bankruptcy is generally an indication of at least partial worthlessness of a debt. Bankruptcy may create worthlessness before the settlement date. If this is the case, the deduction may be taken in the year of worthlessness.

| EXAMPLE 3 | In Example 2, assume that Kay filed for personal bankruptcy in 2010 and that the debt is a business debt. At that time, Ross learned that unsecured creditors (including Ross) were ultimately expected to receive 20 cents on the dollar. In 2011, settlement is made and Ross receives only $150. He should deduct $800 ($1,000 loan − $200 expected settlement) in 2010 and $50 in 2011 ($200 balance − $150 proceeds). ∎ |

If a receivable has been written off (deducted) as uncollectible during the current tax year and is subsequently collected during the current tax year, the write-off entry is reversed. If a receivable has been written off (deducted) as uncollectible, the collection of the receivable in a later tax year may result in income being recognized. Income will result if the deduction yielded a tax benefit in the year it was taken. See Examples 41 and 42 in Chapter 5.

BUSINESS VERSUS NONBUSINESS BAD DEBTS

A **nonbusiness bad debt** is a debt unrelated to the taxpayer's trade or business either when it was created or when it became worthless. The nature of a debt depends on whether the lender was engaged in the business of lending money or whether there is a proximate relationship between the creation of the debt and the lender's trade or business.

---

[3] § 166(a) and Reg. § 1.166.

CONCEPT SUMMARY 7.1

Specific Charge-Off Method

Expense deduction and account write-off	The expense arises and the write-off takes place when a specific business account becomes either partially or wholly worthless or when a specific nonbusiness account becomes wholly worthless.
Recovery of accounts previously written off	If the account recovered was written off during the current taxable year, the write-off entry is reversed. If the account recovered was written off during a previous taxable year, income is created subject to the tax benefit rule.

The use to which the borrowed funds are put by the debtor is of no consequence. Loans to relatives or friends are the most common type of nonbusiness bad debt.

EXAMPLE 4
THE BIG PICTURE

Return to the facts of *The Big Picture* on p. 7-2. Martha loaned her friend, Jamil, $25,000. Jamil used the money to start a business, which subsequently failed. When Jamil died after having made payments of $7,000 on the loan, he was insolvent. Even though the proceeds of the loan were used in a business, the loan is a nonbusiness bad debt because the business was Jamil's, not Martha's. ■

The distinction between a business bad debt and a nonbusiness bad debt is important. A **business bad debt** is deductible as an ordinary loss in the year incurred, whereas a nonbusiness bad debt is always treated as a short-term capital loss. Thus, regardless of the age of a nonbusiness bad debt, the deduction may be of limited benefit due to the limitations on capital loss deductibility in any one year. The maximum amount of a net short-term capital loss that an individual can deduct against ordinary income in any one year is $3,000 (see Chapter 16 for a detailed discussion). Although no deduction is allowed when a nonbusiness bad debt is partially worthless, the taxpayer is entitled to deduct the net amount of the loss upon final settlement.

The following example is an illustration of business bad debts adapted from the Regulations.[4]

EXAMPLE 5

In 2010, Leif sold his business but retained a claim (note or account receivable) against Bob. The claim became worthless in 2011. Leif's loss is treated as a business bad debt because the debt was created in the conduct of his former trade or business. Leif is accorded business bad debt treatment even though he was holding the note as an investor and was no longer in a trade or business when the claim became worthless. ■

The nonbusiness bad debt provisions are *not* applicable to corporations. It is assumed that any loans made by a corporation are related to its trade or business. Therefore, any bad debts of a corporation are business bad debts.

LOANS BETWEEN RELATED PARTIES

Loans between related parties (especially family members) raise the issue of whether the transaction was a *bona fide* loan or a gift. The Regulations state that a bona fide debt arises from a debtor-creditor relationship based on a valid and enforceable obligation to pay a fixed or determinable sum of money. Thus, individual circumstances must be examined to determine whether advances between related parties are gifts or loans. Some considerations are these:

---

[4]Reg. § 1.166–5(d).

GLOBAL Tax Issues

WRITING OFF BAD DEBTS

As a result of the recession, English banks and building societies were forced to write off £3.5 billion (about $5.5 billion) between April and June of 2010. This was equivalent to writing off around £40 million every day. The largest part of the bad debts—£2.1 billion—was the result of credit card debt.

Source: Adapted from Becky Barrow, "Banks Are Writing Off Pounds 40m a Day in Bad Debts," *Daily Mail London,* September 1, 2010, p. 4.

- Was a note properly executed?
- Was there a reasonable rate of interest?
- Was collateral provided?
- What collection efforts were made?
- What was the intent of the parties?

CONCEPT SUMMARY 7.2

Bad Debt Deductions

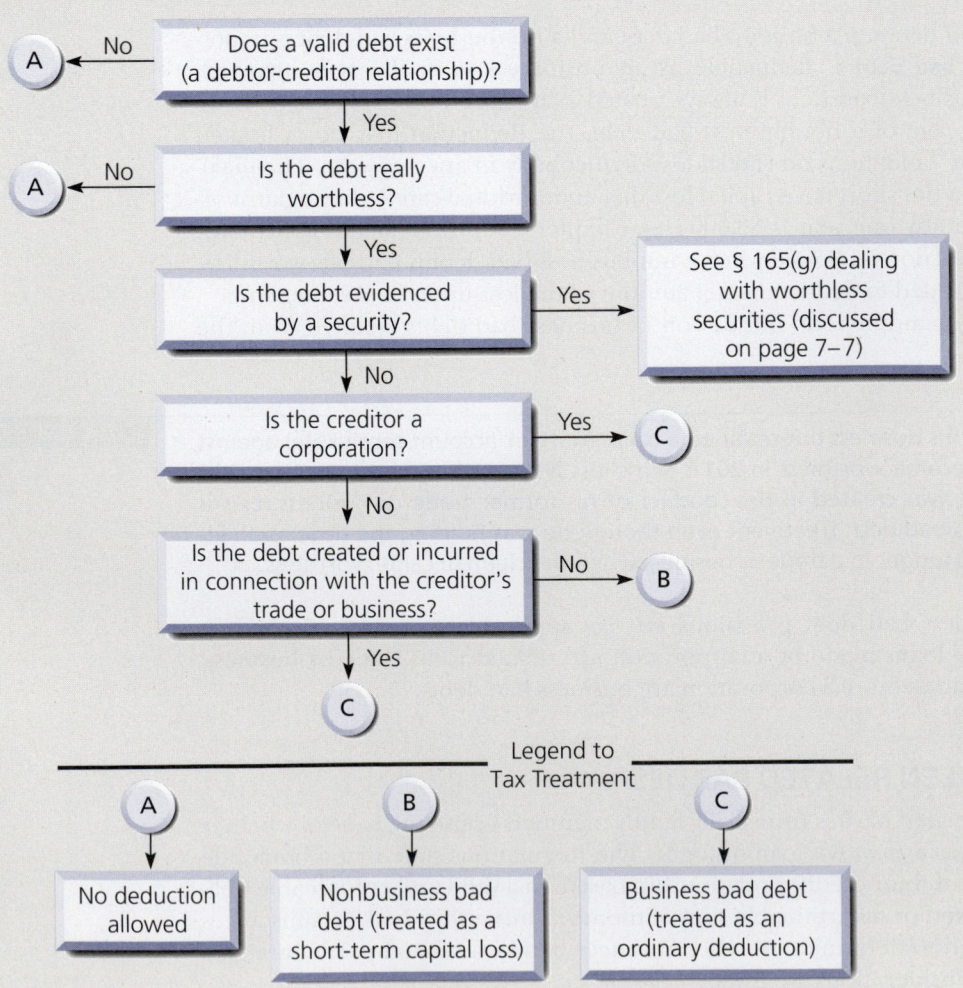

EXAMPLE 6

Lana loans $2,000 to her widowed mother for an operation. Lana's mother owns no property and is not employed, and her only income consists of Social Security benefits. No note is issued for the loan, no provision for interest is made, and no repayment date is mentioned. In the current year, Lana's mother dies, leaving no estate. Assuming the loan is not repaid, Lana cannot take a deduction for a nonbusiness bad debt because the facts indicate that no debtor-creditor relationship existed. ∎

7.2 WORTHLESS SECURITIES

A loss is allowed for securities that become *completely* worthless during the year (**worthless securities**).[5] Such securities are shares of stock, bonds, notes, or other evidence of indebtedness issued by a corporation or government. The losses generated are treated as capital losses deemed to have occurred on the *last day* of the taxable year. By treating the loss as having occurred on the last day of the taxable year, a loss that would otherwise have been classified as short term (if the date of worthlessness was used) may be classified as a long-term capital loss. Capital losses may be of limited benefit due to the $3,000 capital loss limitation.[6]

LO.2

Understand the tax treatment of worthless securities including § 1244 stock.

EXAMPLE 7
THE BIG PICTURE

Return to the facts of *The Big Picture* on p. 7-2. Assume that Martha is a calendar year taxpayer. She owned stock in Owl Corporation (a publicly held company). She acquired the stock as an investment on October 1, 2010, at a cost of $50,000. On May 31, 2011, the stock became worthless as the company declared bankruptcy. Since the stock is deemed to have become worthless as of December 31, 2011, Martha has a capital loss from an asset held for 15 months (a long-term capital loss). ∎

SMALL BUSINESS STOCK

The general rule is that shareholders receive capital gain or loss treatment upon the sale or exchange of stock. However, it is possible to receive an ordinary loss deduction if the loss is sustained on **small business stock** (**§ 1244 stock**). This loss could arise from a sale of the stock or from the stock becoming worthless. Only *individuals*[7] who acquired the stock *from* the corporation are eligible to receive ordinary loss treatment under § 1244. The ordinary loss treatment is limited to $50,000 ($100,000 for married individuals filing jointly) per year. Losses on § 1244 stock in excess of the statutory limits receive capital loss treatment.

The corporation must meet certain requirements for the loss on § 1244 stock to be treated as an *ordinary*—rather than a capital—loss. The major requirement is that the total amount of money and other property received by the corporation for stock as a contribution to capital (or paid-in surplus) does not exceed $1 million. The $1 million test is made at the time the stock is issued. Section 1244 stock can be common or preferred stock. Section 1244 applies only to losses. If § 1244 stock is sold at a gain, the Section is not applicable, and the gain is capital gain.

EXAMPLE 8

Iris, a single individual, was looking for an investment that would give some diversity to her stock portfolio. A friend suggested she acquire some stock in Eagle Corporation, a new start-up company. On July 1, 2009, Iris purchased 100 shares of Eagle Corporation for $100,000. At the time Iris acquired her stock from Eagle Corporation, the corporation had $700,000 of paid-in capital. Hence, the stock qualified as § 1244 stock. On June 20, 2011, Iris sold all of her Eagle stock for $20,000. Because the Eagle stock is § 1244 stock, Iris has $50,000 of ordinary loss and $30,000 of long-term capital loss. ∎

---

[5]§ 165(g).
[6]§ 1211(b).

[7]The term "individuals" for this purpose includes a partnership but not a trust or an estate.

7.3 Losses of Individuals

LO.3

Distinguish between deductible and nondeductible losses of individuals.

An individual may deduct the following losses under § 165(c):

- Losses incurred in a trade or business.
- Losses incurred in a transaction entered into for profit.
- Losses caused by fire, storm, shipwreck, or other casualty or by theft.

An individual taxpayer may deduct losses to property used in the taxpayer's trade or business or losses to property used in a transaction entered into for profit. Examples include a loss on property used in a proprietorship, a loss on property held for rent, or a loss on stolen bearer bonds. Note that an individual's losses on property used in a trade or business or on transactions entered into for profit are not limited to losses caused by fire, storm, shipwreck, or other casualty or by theft.

An individual taxpayer suffering losses from damage to nonbusiness property can deduct only those losses attributable to fire, storm, shipwreck, or other casualty or theft. Although the meaning of the terms *fire, storm, shipwreck,* and *theft* is relatively free from dispute, the term *other casualty* needs further clarification. It means casualties analogous to fire, storm, or shipwreck. The term also includes accidental loss of property provided the loss qualifies under the same rules as any other casualty. These rules are that the loss must result from an event that is (1) identifiable; (2) damaging to property; and (3) sudden, unexpected, and unusual in nature.

A *sudden event* is one that is swift and precipitous and not gradual or progressive. An *unexpected event* is an event that is ordinarily unanticipated and occurs without the intent of the individual who suffers the loss. An *unusual event* is one that is extraordinary and nonrecurring and does not commonly occur during the activity in which the taxpayer was engaged when the destruction occurred.[8] Examples include hurricanes, tornadoes, floods, storms, shipwrecks, fires, auto accidents, mine cave-ins, sonic booms, and vandalism. Weather that causes damage (drought, for example) must be unusual and severe for the particular region. Damage must be to the taxpayer's property to qualify as a **casualty loss**.

A taxpayer can take a deduction for a casualty loss from an automobile accident only if the damage was not caused by the taxpayer's willful act or willful negligence.

EXAMPLE 9

Ted parks his car on a hill and fails to set the brake properly and to curb the wheels. As a result of Ted's negligence, the car rolls down the hill and is damaged. The repairs to Ted's car should qualify for casualty loss treatment since Ted's act of negligence appears to be simple rather than willful. ∎

EVENTS THAT ARE NOT CASUALTIES

LO.4

Identify a casualty and determine the amount, classification, and timing of casualty and theft losses.

Not all acts of God are treated as casualty losses for income tax purposes. Because a casualty must be sudden, unexpected, and unusual, progressive deterioration (such as erosion due to wind or rain) is not a casualty because it does not meet the suddenness test.

Examples of nonsudden events that generally do not qualify as casualties include disease and insect damage. When the damage was caused by termites over a period of several years, some courts have disallowed a casualty loss deduction.[9] On the other hand, some courts have held that termite damage over periods of up to 15 months after infestation constituted a sudden event and was, therefore, deductible as a casualty loss.[10] Despite the existence of some judicial support for the deductibility of termite damage as a casualty loss, the current position of the IRS is that termite damage is not deductible.[11]

Other examples of events that are not casualties are losses resulting from a decline in value rather than an actual loss of the property. No loss was allowed where the taxpayer's home declined in value as a result of a landslide that destroyed

---

[8]Rev.Rul. 72–592, 1972–2 C.B. 101.

[9]*Fay v. Helvering,* 41–2 USTC ¶9494, 27 AFTR 432, 120 F.2d 253 (CA–2, 1941); *U.S. v. Rogers,* 41–1 USTC ¶9442, 27 AFTR 423, 120 F.2d 244 (CA–9, 1941).

[10]*Rosenberg v. Comm.,* 52–2 USTC ¶9377, 42 AFTR 303, 198 F.2d 46 (CA–8, 1952); *Shopmaker v. U.S.,* 54–1 USTC ¶9195, 45 AFTR 758, 119 F.Supp. 705 (D.Ct. Mo., 1953).

[11]Rev.Rul. 63–232, 1963–2 C.B. 97.

TAX in the NEWS

TAINTED CHINESE DRYWALL

A study published by the Consumer Product Safety Commission (CPSC) concluded that there was a strong association between tainted Chinese drywall and a gas smelling like rotten eggs, caused by high levels of sulfur in the drywall. As a consequence of the study, lawmakers and the CPSC asked the Internal Revenue Service to decide if taxpayers incurring this problem could claim a casualty loss deduction on their tax returns.

An IRS spokesperson indicated that the Service would consider granting a tax deduction if the homeowner could prove that the Chinese drywall caused sudden, unusual, and unexpected damage to the taxpayer's home. A key to claiming a deduction is expert documentation.

Source: Adapted from Isaac Wolf, "IRS: Tax Deduction May Go to Homeowners with Tainted Chinese Drywall," *Scripps Howard News Service*, December 3, 2009.

---

neighboring homes but did no actual damage to the taxpayer's home.[12] Similarly, a taxpayer was allowed a loss for the actual flood damage to his property but not for the decline in market value due to the property's being flood-prone.[13]

THEFT LOSSES

Theft includes, but is not necessarily limited to, larceny, embezzlement, and robbery.[14] Theft does not include misplaced items.[15]

Theft losses are computed like other casualty losses (discussed in the following section), but the *timing* for recognition of the loss differs. A theft loss is deducted in the year of discovery, not the year of the theft (unless, of course, the discovery occurs in the same year as the theft). If, in the year of the discovery, a claim exists (e.g., against an insurance company) and there is a reasonable expectation of recovering the adjusted basis of the asset from the insurance company, no deduction is permitted.[16] If, in the year of settlement, the recovery is less than the asset's adjusted basis, a partial deduction may be available. If the recovery is greater than the asset's adjusted basis, gain may be recognized.

EXAMPLE 10

Keith's new sailboat, which he uses for personal purposes, was stolen from the storage marina in December 2010. He discovered the loss on June 3, 2011, and filed a claim with his insurance company that was settled on January 30, 2012. Assuming there is a reasonable expectation of full recovery, no deduction is allowed in 2011. A partial deduction may be available in 2012 if the actual insurance proceeds are less than the lower of the fair market value or the adjusted basis of the asset. (Loss measurement rules are discussed later in this chapter.) ■

WHEN TO DEDUCT CASUALTY LOSSES

General Rule

Generally, a casualty loss is deducted in the year the loss occurs. However, no casualty loss is permitted if a reimbursement claim with a *reasonable prospect of full recovery* exists.[17] If the taxpayer has a partial claim, only part of the loss can be claimed in the year of the casualty, and the remainder is deducted in the year the claim is settled.

EXAMPLE 11

Brian's new sailboat was completely destroyed by fire in 2011. Its cost and fair market value were $10,000. Brian's only claim against the insurance company was on a $7,000 policy and was not settled by year-end. The following year, 2012, Brian settled with the insurance company for $6,000. He is entitled to a $3,000 deduction in 2011 and a $1,000 deduction in 2012. If Brian held the sailboat for personal use, the $3,000 deduction in 2011 is reduced

---

[12]*H. Pulvers v. Comm.*, 69–1 USTC ¶9222, 23 AFTR 2d 69–678, 407 F.2d 838 (CA–9, 1969).

[13]*S. L. Solomon*, 39 TCM 1282, T.C.Memo. 1980–87.

[14]Reg. § 1.165–8(d).

[15]*Mary Francis Allen*, 16 T.C. 163 (1951).

[16]Reg. §§ 1.165–1(d)(2) and 1.165–8(a)(2).

[17]Reg. § 1.165–1(d)(2)(i).

GLOBAL Tax Issues

NOTIFICATION OF CASUALTY LOSSES

Tropical storm Ondoy and Typhoon Pepeng hit Manila on September 26 and October 2, 2009, respectively. These were two of the most devastating storms ever to hit the Philippines. In response to the anticipated losses caused by these storms, the Philippines Bureau of Internal Revenue issued a Revenue Memorandum Order that provided guidelines for reporting losses. The order gave affected taxpayers less than 45 days to file a Sworn Declaration of Loss and all the supporting documents. Unless they filed a Sworn Declaration of Loss, taxpayers could not claim a casualty loss on their tax returns.

Source: Adapted from José Jaffy Y. Azarraga, "Taxwise or Otherwise," *Business World Manila,* April 29, 2010.

first by $100 and then by 10% of his 2011 AGI. The $1,000 deduction in 2012 is reduced by 10% of his 2012 AGI (see the following discussion on the $100 and 10% floors). ■

If a taxpayer receives reimbursement for a casualty loss sustained and deducted in a previous year, an amended return is not filed for that year. Instead, the taxpayer must include the reimbursement in gross income on the return for the year in which it is received to the extent that the previous deduction resulted in a tax benefit.

EXAMPLE 12

Fran had a deductible casualty loss of $5,000 on her 2010 tax return. Fran's taxable income for 2010 was $60,000. In June 2011, Fran is reimbursed $3,000 for the prior year's casualty loss. Fran includes the entire $3,000 in gross income for 2011 because the deduction in 2010 produced a tax benefit. ■

Disaster Area Losses

An exception to the general rule for the time of deduction is allowed for **disaster area losses**, which are casualties sustained in an area designated as a disaster area by the President of the United States.[18] In such cases, the taxpayer may *elect* to treat the loss as having occurred in the taxable year immediately *preceding* the taxable year in which the disaster actually occurred. The rationale for this exception is to provide immediate relief to disaster victims in the form of accelerated tax benefits.

If the due date, plus extensions, for the prior year's return has not passed, a taxpayer makes the election to claim the disaster area loss on the prior year's tax return. If the disaster occurs after the prior year's return has been filed, it is necessary to file either an amended return or a refund claim. In any case, the taxpayer must show clearly that such an election is being made.

Disaster loss treatment also applies in the case of a personal residence that has been rendered unsafe for use as a residence because of a disaster. This provision applies when, within 120 days after the President designates the area as a disaster area, the state or local government where the residence is located orders the taxpayer to demolish or relocate the residence.[19]

EXAMPLE 13
THE BIG PICTURE

Return to the facts of *The Big Picture* on p. 7-2. On September 28, 2011, Martha's personal residence was damaged when a hurricane caused an oak tree to fall onto the house. The amount of her uninsured loss was $7,000. Because of the extent of the damage in the area, the President of the United States designated the area a disaster area. Because Martha's loss is a disaster area loss, she may elect to file an amended return for 2010 and take the loss in that year. If Martha elects this course of action, the amount of the loss will be reduced first by $100 (the materiality amount in 2010) and then by 10% of her 2010 AGI. If Martha forgoes the election, she may take the loss on her 2011 income tax return. The amount of the loss will be reduced first by $100 (the materiality amount in 2011) and then by 10% of her 2011 AGI. ■

---

[18]§ 165(h).   [19]§ 165(k).

MEASURING THE AMOUNT OF LOSS

Amount of Loss

The rules for determining the amount of a loss depend in part on whether business use, income-producing use, or personal use property was involved. Another factor that must be considered is whether the property was partially or completely destroyed.

If business property or property held for the production of income (e.g., rental property) is *completely destroyed*, the loss is equal to the adjusted basis of the property at the time of destruction.

EXAMPLE 14

Vicki's automobile, which was used only for business purposes, was destroyed by fire. Vicki had unintentionally allowed her insurance coverage to expire. The fair market value of the automobile was $9,000 at the time of the fire, and its adjusted basis was $10,000. Vicki is allowed a loss deduction of $10,000 (the basis of the automobile). The $10,000 loss is a deduction *for* AGI. ■

A different measurement rule applies for *partial destruction* of business property and income-producing property and for *partial* or *complete destruction* of personal use property. In these situations, the loss is the *lesser* of the following:

- The adjusted basis of the property.
- The difference between the fair market value of the property before the event and the fair market value immediately after the event.

EXAMPLE 15

Kelly's uninsured automobile, which was used only for business purposes, was damaged in an accident. At the date of the accident, the fair market value of the automobile was $12,000, and its adjusted basis was $9,000. After the accident, the automobile was appraised at $4,000. Kelly's loss deduction is $8,000 (the lesser of the adjusted basis or the decrease in fair market value). The $8,000 loss is a deduction *for* AGI. ■

The deduction for the loss of property that is part business and part personal must be computed separately for the business portion and the personal portion.

Any insurance recovery reduces the loss for business, production of income, and personal use losses. In fact, a taxpayer may realize a gain if the insurance proceeds exceed the amount of the loss. Chapter 17 discusses the treatment of net gains and losses on business property and income-producing property.

A taxpayer is not permitted to deduct a casualty loss for damage to insured personal use property unless a *timely insurance claim* is filed with respect to the damage to the property. This rule applies to the extent that any insurance policy provides for full or partial reimbursement for the loss.[20]

Generally, an appraisal before and after the casualty is needed to measure the amount of the loss. However, the *cost of repairs* to the damaged property is acceptable as a method of establishing the loss in value provided the following criteria are met:

- The repairs are necessary to restore the property to its condition immediately before the casualty.
- The amount spent for such repairs is not excessive.
- The repairs do not extend beyond the damage suffered.
- The value of the property after the repairs does not, as a result of the repairs, exceed the value of the property immediately before the casualty.[21]

Reduction for $100 and 10 Percent-of-AGI Floors

The amount of the loss for personal use property must be further reduced by a $100 *per event* floor and a 10 percent-of-AGI *aggregate* floor.[22] The $100 floor applies separately to each casualty and applies to the entire loss from each casualty (e.g., if a

---

[20]§ 165(h)(5)(E).
[21]Reg. § 1.165–7(a)(2)(ii).
[22]§ 165(c)(3).

TAX in the NEWS

A PROPOSAL FOR CHANGING THE CASUALTY LOSS LIMITS

On July 24, 2008, Senate Finance Committee Chairman Max Baucus introduced legislation aimed at promoting American jobs, developing clean energy, and providing families with targeted tax relief and incentives. Under the proposal, the 10 percent-of-AGI rule for casualty losses would be waived, and the $100 floor would be permanently raised to $500. The bill would also allow nonitemizers to take the loss as an addition to the standard deduction. To date, this bill has not become law. Since Baucus is the chair of the Senate Finance Committee, it will be interesting to see if it is enacted.

Source: Adapted from U.S. Senate Documents.

storm damages both a taxpayer's residence and automobile, only $100 is subtracted from the total amount of the loss). The losses are then added together, and the total is reduced by 10 percent of the taxpayer's AGI. The resulting loss is the taxpayer's itemized deduction for casualty and theft losses.

EXAMPLE 16

Rocky, who had AGI of $30,000, was involved in a motorcycle accident in 2011. His motorcycle, which was used only for personal use and had a fair market value of $12,000 and an adjusted basis of $9,000, was completely destroyed. He received $5,000 from his insurance company. Rocky's casualty loss deduction is $900 [$9,000 basis − $5,000 insurance recovery − $100 floor − $3,000 (.10 × $30,000 AGI)]. The $900 casualty loss is an itemized deduction (*from* AGI). ∎

When a nonbusiness casualty loss is spread between two taxable years because of the *reasonable prospect of recovery* doctrine, the loss in the second year is not reduced by the $100 floor. This result occurs because this floor is imposed per event and has already reduced the amount of the loss in the first year. However, the loss in the second year is still subject to the 10 percent floor based on the taxpayer's second-year AGI (refer to Example 11).

Taxpayers who suffer qualified disaster area losses can elect to deduct the losses in the year preceding the year of occurrence. The disaster loss is treated as having occurred in the preceding taxable year. Hence, the 10 percent-of-AGI floor is determined by using the AGI of the year for which the deduction is claimed.[23]

Multiple Losses

The rules for computing loss deductions where multiple losses have occurred are explained in Examples 17 and 18.

EXAMPLE 17

During the year, Tim had the following casualty losses:

Asset	Adjusted Basis	Fair Market Value of Asset		Insurance Recovery
		Before the Casualty	**After the Casualty**	
A	$900	$600	$–0–	$400
B	300	800	250	100

Assets A and B were used in Tim's business at the time of the casualty. The following losses are allowed:

Asset A: $500. The complete destruction of a business asset results in a deduction of the adjusted basis of the property (reduced by any insurance recovery) regardless of the asset's fair market value.

Asset B: $200. The partial destruction of a business (or personal use) asset results in a deduction equal to the lesser of the adjusted basis ($300) or the decline in value ($550), reduced by any insurance recovery ($100).

---

[23]§ 165(i).

Both the Asset A and Asset B losses are deductions *for* AGI. The $100 floor and the 10%-of-AGI floor do not apply because the assets are business assets. ∎

EXAMPLE 18

In 2011, Emily had AGI of $20,000 and the following casualty losses:

		Fair Market Value of Asset		
Asset	Adjusted Basis	Before the Casualty	After the Casualty	Insurance Recovery
A	$1,900	$1,400	$ –0–	$200
B	2,500	4,000	1,000	–0–
C	800	400	100	250

Assets A, B, and C were held for personal use, and the losses to these three assets are from three different casualties. The loss for each asset is computed as follows:

Asset A: $1,100. The lesser of the adjusted basis of $1,900 or the $1,400 decline in value, reduced by the insurance recovery of $200, minus the $100 floor.

Asset B: $2,400. The lesser of the adjusted basis of $2,500 or the $3,000 decline in value, minus the $100 floor.

Asset C: $0. The lesser of the adjusted basis of $800 or the $300 decline in value, reduced by the insurance recovery of $250, minus the $100 floor.

Emily's itemized casualty loss deduction for the year is $1,500:

Asset A loss	$ 1,100
Asset B loss	2,400
Asset C loss	–0–
Total loss	$ 3,500
Less: 10% of AGI (10% × $20,000)	(2,000)
Itemized casualty loss deduction	$ 1,500

∎

STATUTORY FRAMEWORK FOR DEDUCTING LOSSES OF INDIVIDUALS

Casualty and theft losses incurred by an individual in connection with a trade or business are deductible *for* AGI.[24] These losses are not subject to the $100 per event and the 10 percent-of-AGI limitations. Casualty and theft losses incurred by an employee in connection with a trade or business are deductible *for* AGI if the loss is reimbursed by the employer. If the loss is not reimbursed, the loss is deductible *from* AGI as a miscellaneous itemized deduction subject to the 2 percent-of-AGI floor. These losses are not subject to the $100 per event and the 10 percent-of-AGI limitations.

Casualty and theft losses incurred by an individual in a transaction entered into for profit are not subject to the $100 per event and the 10 percent-of-AGI limitations. If these losses are attributable to rents or royalties, the deduction is *for* AGI.[25] However, if these losses are not connected with property held for the production of rents and royalties, they are deductions *from* AGI. More specifically, these losses are classified as other miscellaneous itemized deductions. An example of this type of loss would be the theft of a security. However, theft losses of investment property are not subject to the 2 percent-of-AGI floor on certain miscellaneous itemized deductions (explained in Chapters 9 and 10).

Casualty and theft losses attributable to personal use property are subject to the $100 per event and the 10 percent-of-AGI limitations. These losses are itemized deductions, but they are not subject to the 2 percent-of-AGI floor.[26]

---

[24]§ 62(a)(1).
[25]§ 62(a)(4).
[26]§ 67(b)(3).

CONCEPT SUMMARY   7.3

Casualty Gains and Losses

	Business Use or Income-Producing Property	Personal Use Property
Event creating the loss	Any event.	Casualty or theft.
Amount	The lesser of the decline in fair market value or the adjusted basis, but always the adjusted basis if the property is totally destroyed.	The lesser of the decline in fair market value or the adjusted basis.
Insurance	Insurance proceeds received reduce the amount of the loss.	Insurance proceeds received (or for which there is an unfiled claim) reduce the amount of the loss.
$100 floor	Not applicable.	Applicable per event.
Gains and losses	Gains and losses are netted (see detailed discussion in Chapter 17).	Personal casualty and theft gains and losses are netted.
Gains exceeding losses		The gains and losses are treated as gains and losses from the sale of capital assets.
Losses exceeding gains		The gains—and the losses to the extent of gains— are treated as ordinary items in computing AGI. The losses in excess of gains, to the extent they exceed 10% of AGI, are itemized deductions.

PERSONAL CASUALTY GAINS AND LOSSES

If a taxpayer has personal casualty and theft gains as well as losses, a special set of rules applies for determining the tax consequences. A **personal casualty gain** is the recognized gain from a casualty or theft of personal use property. A **personal casualty loss** for this purpose is a casualty or theft loss of personal use property after the application of the $100 floor. A taxpayer who has both gains and losses for the taxable year must first net (offset) the personal casualty gains and personal casualty losses. If the gains exceed the losses, the gains and losses are treated as gains and losses from the sale of capital assets. The capital gains and losses are short term or long term, depending on the period the taxpayer held each of the assets. In the netting process, personal casualty and theft gains and losses are not netted with the gains and losses on business and income-producing property.

EXAMPLE 19

During the year, Cliff had the following personal casualty gains and losses (after deducting the $100 floor):

Asset	Holding Period	Gain or (Loss)
A	Three months	($ 300)
B	Three years	(2,400)
C	Two years	3,200

Cliff computes the tax consequences as follows:

Personal casualty gain	$ 3,200
Personal casualty loss ($300 + $2,400)	(2,700)
Net personal casualty gain	$ 500

Cliff treats all of the gains and losses as capital gains and losses and has the following:

Short-term capital loss (Asset A)	$ 300
Long-term capital loss (Asset B)	2,400
Long-term capital gain (Asset C)	3,200

If personal casualty losses exceed personal casualty gains, all gains and losses are treated as ordinary items. The gains—and the losses to the extent of gains—are treated as ordinary income and ordinary loss in computing AGI. Losses in excess of gains are deducted as itemized deductions to the extent the losses exceed 10 percent of AGI.[27]

EXAMPLE 20

During the year, Hazel had AGI of $20,000 and the following personal casualty gain and loss (after deducting the $100 floor):

Asset	Holding Period	Gain or (Loss)
A	Three years	($2,700)
B	Four months	200

Hazel computes the tax consequences as follows:

Personal casualty loss	($2,700)
Personal casualty gain	200
Net personal casualty loss	($2,500)

Hazel treats the gain and the loss as ordinary items. The $200 gain and $200 of the loss are included in computing AGI. Hazel's itemized deduction for casualty losses is computed as follows:

Casualty loss in excess of gain ($2,700 − $200)	$ 2,500
Less: 10% of AGI (10% × $20,000)	(2,000)
Itemized deduction	$ 500

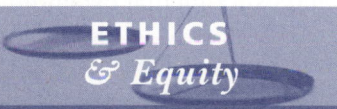

THE AMOUNT OF A CASUALTY LOSS

In the case of a casualty loss to personal use property, the loss is allowed only to the extent that it exceeds $100 and the net casualty loss for the tax year exceeds 10 percent of AGI. The amount of the loss allowed is the lesser of (1) the decline in the fair market value of the property as a result of the casualty or (2) the adjusted basis of the property.

George and Mabel purchased their house 60 years ago for $100,000. Shortly after they moved in, they purchased an oak tree for $10 and planted it in front of their new home. Earlier this year, a severe windstorm passed through their neighborhood and uprooted the oak tree. No damage was done to their house. After the storm, George had the property appraised. The appraiser told George that the value of the property had declined by $10,000 because of the loss of the oak tree. George also contacted a nursery and was told that it would cost at least $20,000 to replace the oak with a tree much smaller than the one that was destroyed. George is considering claiming a loss deduction of at least $20,000 for the destroyed oak tree. Evaluate George's plan.

7.4 RESEARCH AND EXPERIMENTAL EXPENDITURES

Section 174 covers the treatment of research and experimental expenditures. The Regulations define **research and experimental expenditures** as follows:

> all such costs incident to the development of an experimental or pilot model, a plant process, a product, a formula, an invention, or similar property, and the improvement of already existing property of the type mentioned. The

L0.5

Recognize and apply the alternative tax treatments for research and experimental expenditures.

---

[27]§ 165(h).

term does not include expenditures such as those for the ordinary testing or inspection of materials or products for quality control or those for efficiency surveys, management studies, consumer surveys, advertising, or promotions.[28]

Expenses in connection with the acquisition or improvement of land or depreciable property are not research and experimental expenditures. Rather, they increase the basis of the land or depreciable property. However, depreciation on a building used for research may be a research and experimental expense. Only the depreciation that is a research and experimental expense (not the cost of the asset) is subject to the three alternatives discussed below.

The law permits the following *three alternatives* for the handling of research and experimental expenditures:

- Expensed in the year paid or incurred.
- Deferred and amortized.
- Capitalized.

If the costs are capitalized, a deduction is not available until the research project is abandoned or is deemed worthless. Since many products resulting from research projects do not have a definite and limited useful life, a taxpayer should ordinarily elect to write off the expenditures immediately or to defer and amortize them. It is generally preferable to elect an immediate write-off of the research expenditures because of the time value of the tax deduction.

The law also provides for a research activities credit. The credit amounts to 20 percent of certain research and experimental expenditures.[29] (The credit is discussed more fully in Chapter 13.)

EXPENSE METHOD

A taxpayer can elect to expense all of the research and experimental expenditures incurred in the current year and all subsequent years. The consent of the IRS is not required if the method is adopted for the first taxable year in which such expenditures were paid or incurred. Once the election is made, the taxpayer must continue to expense all qualifying expenditures unless a request for a change is made to, and approved by, the IRS. In certain instances, a taxpayer may incur research and experimental expenditures before actually engaging in any trade or business activity. In such instances, the Supreme Court has applied a liberal standard of deductibility and permitted a deduction in the year of incurrence.[30]

DEFERRAL AND AMORTIZATION METHOD

Alternatively, research and experimental expenditures may be deferred and amortized if the taxpayer makes an election.[31] Under the election, research and experimental expenditures are amortized ratably over a period of not less than 60 months. A deduction is allowed beginning with the month in which the taxpayer first realizes benefits from the experimental expenditure. The election is binding, and a change requires permission from the IRS.

EXAMPLE 21

Gold Corporation decides to develop a new line of adhesives. The project begins in 2011. Gold incurs the following expenses in 2011 in connection with the project:

Salaries	$25,000
Materials	8,000
Depreciation on machinery	6,500

---

[28]Reg. § 1.174–2(a)(1).

[29]§ 41. See the information in Chapter 13 on the termination date for the research activities credit.

[30]*Snow v. Comm.*, 74–1 USTC ¶9432, 33 AFTR 2d 74–1251, 94 S.Ct. 1876 (USSC, 1974).

[31]§ 174(b)(2).

Gold incurs the following expenses in 2012 in connection with the project:

Salaries	$18,000
Materials	2,000
Depreciation on machinery	5,700

The benefits from the project will be realized starting in March 2013. If Gold Corporation elects a 60-month deferral and amortization period, there is no deduction prior to March 2013, the month benefits from the project begin to be realized. The deduction for 2013 is $10,867, computed as follows:

Salaries ($25,000 + $18,000)	$43,000
Materials ($8,000 + $2,000)	10,000
Depreciation ($6,500 + $5,700)	12,200
Total	$65,200
$65,200 × (10 months/60 months) =	$10,867

The option to treat research and experimental expenditures as deferred expense is usually employed when a company does not have sufficient income to offset the research and experimental expenses. Rather than create net operating loss carryovers that might not be utilized because of the 20-year limitation on such carryovers, the deferral and amortization method may be used. The deferral of research and experimental expenditures should also be considered if the taxpayer expects higher tax rates in the future.

7.5 DOMESTIC PRODUCTION ACTIVITIES DEDUCTION

The American Jobs Creation Act of 2004 was enacted to replace certain tax provisions that our world trading partners regarded as allowing unfair advantage to U.S. exports. Among other changes, the Act created a deduction based on the income from manufacturing activities (designated as *production activities*).[32] The **domestic production activities deduction (DPAD)** is contained in § 199.

> **LO.6**
> Calculate the domestic production activities deduction.

OPERATIONAL RULES

Calculation of the Domestic Production Activities Deduction

For tax years beginning in 2010 and thereafter, the DPAD is based on the following formula:[33]

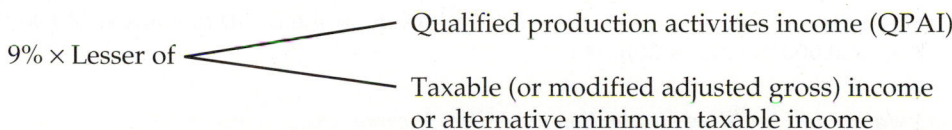

9% × Lesser of
- Qualified production activities income (QPAI)
- Taxable (or modified adjusted gross) income or alternative minimum taxable income

For tax years beginning in 2005 or 2006, the 9 percent factor was 3 percent. For tax years beginning in 2007, 2008, and 2009, the 9 percent factor was 6 percent.

Taxable income is determined without regard to the DPAD. In the case of an individual (a sole proprietorship or an owner of a flow-through entity), **modified adjusted gross income** is substituted for taxable income.[34]

The taxable income limitation is determined after the application of any net operating loss (NOL) deduction for the tax year (NOLs are explained in detail later in the chapter). Thus, a company with an NOL carryforward for a tax year is ineligible for the DPAD if the carryforward eliminates current taxable income. Further,

---

[32]Section 101 of the *American Jobs Creation Act of 2004*, Public Law No. 108-357 (October 22, 2004).

[33]§ 199(a).

[34]§ 199(d)(2). Generally, modified AGI is AGI prior to the effect of § 199.

a taxpayer that has an NOL carryback may lose part or all of the DPAD benefit for that year. As taxable income is reduced by the NOL carryback, there is a corresponding reduction in the DPAD. If qualified production activities income (QPAI) cannot be used in a particular year due to the taxable income limitation (see the above formula), it is lost forever. (The calculation of QPAI is explained in the next section.)

EXAMPLE 22

Opal, Inc., manufactures and sells costume jewelry. It also sells costume jewelry purchased from other manufacturers. During 2011, Opal had a *profit* of $200,000 (QPAI) from the sale of its own manufactured jewelry and a *loss* of $50,000 from the sale of the purchased jewelry. Based on this information, Opal's QPAI is $200,000, and its taxable income is $150,000 ($200,000 − $50,000). Opal's DPAD becomes $13,500 [9% of the lesser of $200,000 (QPAI) or $150,000 (taxable income)]. ∎

EXAMPLE 23

Assume the same facts as in Example 22, except that Opal also has an NOL carryover from 2010 of $300,000. As taxable income for 2011 is zero ($200,000 − $50,000 − $300,000), there is no DPAD. ∎

Another important limitation is that the amount of the DPAD cannot exceed 50 percent of certain **W–2 wages** paid by the taxpayer during the tax year.[35] The purpose of this limitation is to preserve U.S. manufacturing jobs and to discourage their outsourcing. An employer's W–2 wages include the sum of the aggregate amount of wages and elective deferrals required to be included on the W–2 wage statements for certain employees during the employer's taxable year. Elective deferrals include those amounts deferred under § 457 plans and Roth contributions (see Chapter 19). An employer previously included wages paid to all workers during a tax year and not just the wages of the employees engaged in qualified production activities. However, as a result of a recent statutory change, an employer is permitted to include only those W–2 wages paid to employees engaged in qualified production activities.

EXAMPLE 24

In 2011, Red, Inc., a calendar year taxpayer, has QPAI of $2 million and taxable income of $2.1 million. Since Red outsources much of its work to independent contractors, its W–2 wage base, which for Red is related entirely to production activities, is $80,000. Although Red's DPAD normally would be $180,000 [9% of the lesser of $2 million (QPAI) or $2.1 million (taxable income)], it is limited to $40,000 [50% of $80,000 (W–2 wages)]. ∎

EXAMPLE 25

Assume the same facts as in Example 24, except that Red also pays salaries of $50,000 related to its *nonproduction* activities. Because these wages are not paid to employees engaged in production activities, the wage limitation on the DPAD remains at $40,000 [50% of $80,000 ($80,000 + $0)]. ∎

Calculation of Qualified Production Activities Income

Qualified production activities income (QPAI) is the excess of **domestic production gross receipts (DPGR)** over the sum of:

- The cost of goods sold allocated to such receipts.
- Other deductions, expenses, or losses directly allocated to such receipts.
- The ratable portion of deductions, expenses, and losses not directly allocable to such receipts or another class of income.[36]

QPAI is determined on an item-by-item basis—not on a division-by-division or a transaction-by-transaction basis. Because all items must be netted in the calculation, the final QPAI amount can be either positive or negative. The effect of the netting rule is to preclude taxpayers from selecting only profitable product lines or profitable transactions when calculating QPAI.

---

[35]§ 199(b). [36]§ 199(c).

TAX in the NEWS   **REPEAL OF § 199 FOR OIL PRODUCERS**

Senator Max Baucus has added an amendment to a small business lending bill that would repeal § 199 (the domestic production activities deduction) for the top five U.S. oil-producing firms. Baucus believes that these firms no longer need this incentive because they have been highly profitable in recent years. The American Petroleum Institute claims that its studies show that the repeal would result in lower oil production and the loss of thousands of jobs. It will be interesting to see if this repeal provision is enacted in this or subsequent legislation.

Source: Adapted from Mike Godfrey, "U.S. Oil Warns against Tax Hike," Tax-News.com, August 18, 2010.

EXAMPLE 26

A taxpayer manufactures pants and shirts with the following QPAI results: $5 for one pair of pants and a negative $2 for one shirt. Because the two items are netted, the QPAI amount that controls is $3 ($5 − $2). ■

Five specific categories of DPGR qualify for the DPAD:[37]

- The lease, license, sale, exchange, or other disposition of qualified production property (QPP) that was manufactured, produced, grown, or extracted (MPGE) in the United States.
- Qualified films largely created in the United States.
- The production of electricity, natural gas, or potable water.
- Construction (but not self-construction) performed in the United States.
- Engineering and architectural services for domestic construction.

The sale of food and beverages prepared by a taxpayer at a retail establishment and the transmission or distribution of electricity, natural gas, or potable water are specifically excluded from the definition of DPGR.

ELIGIBLE TAXPAYERS

The deduction is available to a variety of taxpayers including individuals, partnerships, S corporations, C corporations, cooperatives, estates, and trusts. For a pass-through entity (e.g., partnerships, S corporations), the deduction flows through to the individual owners. In the case of a sole proprietor, a deduction *for* AGI results and is claimed on Form 1040, line 35 on page 1. A Form 8903 must be attached to support the deduction.

For additional information on the DPAD, see Chapter 3 in *South-Western Federal Taxation: Corporations, Partnerships, Estates, and Trusts.*

7.6 NET OPERATING LOSSES

The requirement that every taxpayer file an annual income tax return (whether on a calendar year or a fiscal year) may result in certain inequities for taxpayers who experience cyclical patterns of income or expense. Inequities result from the application of a progressive rate structure to taxable income determined on an annual basis. A **net operating loss (NOL)** in a particular tax year would produce no tax benefit if the Code did not provide for the carryback and carryforward of such losses to profitable years.

LO.7

Determine the amount of the net operating loss and recognize the impact of the carryback and carryover provisions.

EXAMPLE 27

Juanita has a business and realizes the following taxable income or loss over a five-year period: Year 1, $50,000; Year 2, ($30,000); Year 3, $100,000; Year 4, ($200,000); and Year 5, $380,000. She is married and files a joint return. Hubert also has a business and has a taxable income pattern of $60,000 every year. He, too, is married and files a joint return. Note that both Juanita and Hubert have total taxable income of $300,000 over

---

[37]§ 199(c)(4).

FINANCIAL DISCLOSURE *Insights*

TAX LOSSES AND THE DEFERRED TAX ASSET

To some people, a current-year net operating loss (NOL) represents a failure of an entity's business model, but others see it as an immediate tax refund. But when an NOL hits the balance sheet as a deferred tax asset, the story is not over. The NOL creates or increases a deferred tax asset that may or may not be used in future financial accounting reporting periods: the key question for a financial analyst is whether the entity will generate enough net revenue in future years that can be offset by the NOL carryover amount.

When a business entity holds a loss carryforward, for every reporting period its management must assess whether the loss is likely to be used to create cash flow in the future, as the loss carryforward offsets operating or other profits from future years. When it is more likely than not that a loss carryforward *will not be realized*, GAAP requires that a valuation allowance be created to reduce the deferred tax asset to a lower amount that is expected to be realized in the future. The valuation allowance is a contra-asset account (like accumulated depreciation on a fixed asset) against the deferred tax asset.

A valuation allowance against an NOL carryforward might be created when there is doubt as to the level of the entity's future net profits. The valuation allowance is reduced or eliminated, though, when it appears that the NOL will be fully realized due to any of the following:

- Future years' net income from operations or other activities.
- New product orders or contracts for the business.
- The reversal of other temporary book-tax differences.
- An effective use of tax planning strategies.

Evidence that a loss carryforward might not be realized in the future includes the following.

- A series of operating losses in previous years for the reporting entity.
- A history of the entity's tax losses expiring unused.
- Open transactions, such as lawsuits and regulatory challenges, that might reduce the business's future profits.

The current version of IFRS does not allow for a valuation allowance. Under IAS 12, a deferred tax asset is recorded only when it is "probable" (a higher standard than GAAP's "more likely than not") that the deferred tax amount will be realized, and then only to the extent of that probable amount. Thus, no offsetting valuation allowance is needed.

the five-year period. Assume there is no provision for carryback or carryover of NOLs. Juanita and Hubert would have the following five-year tax bills:

Year	Juanita's Tax	Hubert's Tax
1	$ 6,650	$ 8,150
2	–0–	8,150
3	17,250	8,150
4	–0–	8,150
5	102,872	8,150
	$126,772	$40,750

NOTE: The computation of tax is made without regard to any NOL benefit. Rates applicable to 2011 are used to compute the tax.

Even though Juanita and Hubert realized the same total taxable income ($300,000) over the five-year period, Juanita had to pay taxes of $126,772, while Hubert paid taxes of only $40,750. ∎

To provide partial relief from this inequitable tax treatment, a deduction is allowed for NOLs.[38] This provision permits NOLs for any one year to be offset against taxable income of other years. The NOL provision is intended as a form of relief for business income and losses. Thus, only losses from the operation of a trade or business (or profession), casualty and theft losses, or losses from the confiscation

[38]§ 172.

of a business by a foreign government can create an NOL. In other words, a salaried individual with itemized deductions and personal exemptions in excess of gross income is not permitted to deduct the excess amounts as an NOL. On the other hand, a personal casualty loss is treated as a business loss and can therefore create (or increase) an NOL for an individual.

CARRYBACK AND CARRYOVER PERIODS

General Rules

An NOL generally must be applied initially to the two taxable years preceding the year of the loss (unless an election is made not to carry the loss back at all). It is carried first to the second prior year, and then to the immediately preceding tax year (or until used up). If the loss is not fully used in the carryback period, it must be carried forward to the first year after the loss year, and then forward to the second, third, etc., year after the loss year. The carryover period is 20 years. A loss sustained in 2011 is used in this order: 2009, 2010, 2012 through 2031.

A three-year carryback period is available for any portion of an individual's NOL resulting from a casualty or theft loss. The three-year carryback rule also applies to NOLs that are attributable to presidentially declared disasters that are incurred by a small business. A small business is one whose average annual gross receipts for a three-year period are $5 million or less.

A 5-year carryback period and a 20-year carryover period are allowed for a farming loss. A taxpayer may elect to waive the special five-year carryback period. If this election is made, the general two-year carryback period applies. A farming loss is the amount of the NOL for the taxable year if only income and deductions attributable to the farming business are taken into account. However, the amount of the farming loss cannot exceed the amount of the taxpayer's NOL for the taxable year. To determine the amount of the carryback and carryover, a farming loss for any taxable year is treated as a separate NOL for such year and applied after the remaining portion of the NOL for the year is taken into account.

EXAMPLE 28

For the year 2011, the taxpayer and spouse have an NOL of $50,000. The $50,000 NOL includes a $40,000 loss that is attributable to a farming business. Only the $40,000 loss attributable to the farming business can be carried back five years. The loss not attributable to the farming business can be carried back only two years. ∎

If the loss is being carried to a preceding year, an amended return is filed on Form 1040X, or a quick refund claim is filed on Form 1045. In either case, a refund of taxes previously paid is requested. Form 1045 is an application for a tentative refund. The IRS normally will process Form 1045 and pay the refund within 90 days of the date it is filed. When the loss is carried forward, the current return shows an NOL deduction for the prior year's loss.

Sequence of Use of NOLs

When the taxpayer has NOLs in two or more years, the rule is always to use the earliest year's loss first until it is completely absorbed. The later years' losses can then be used until they also are absorbed or lost. Thus, one year's return could show NOL carryovers from two or more years. Each loss is computed and applied separately.

Election to Forgo Carryback

A taxpayer can *irrevocably elect* not to carry back an NOL to any of the prior years. In that case, the loss is available as a carryover for 20 years. The election is made if it is to the taxpayer's tax advantage. For example, a taxpayer might be in a low marginal tax bracket in the carryback years but expect to be in a high marginal tax bracket in future years. Therefore, it would be to the taxpayer's advantage to use the NOL to offset income in years when the tax rate is high rather than use it when the tax rate is relatively low.

EXAMPLE 29

For 2011, taxpayer and spouse have an NOL of $10,000. The NOL may be carried back and applied against taxable income first in 2009 and then in 2010. Any remaining NOL is carried forward to years 2012 through 2031. If, however, the taxpayer and spouse elect to forgo the carryback period, the NOL initially is carried to 2012 and then to years 2013 through 2031. ∎

ETHICS
& Equity

NOL CARRYOVER

John timely filed his 2007 and 2008 Federal income tax returns, reporting AGI of $90,000 and $100,000, respectively. For the years 2009 and 2010, John had NOLs of $25,000 and $40,000, respectively. Because John had NOLs for 2009 and 2010, he did not file tax returns for those years. In 2011, John has taxable income, so he is considering using his NOLs from 2009 and 2010 to offset his income for 2011. Evaluate John's plan.

COMPUTATION OF THE NET OPERATING LOSS

Since the NOL provisions apply solely to business-related losses, certain adjustments must be made so that the loss more closely resembles the taxpayer's *economic* loss. The required adjustments for corporate taxpayers are usually insignificant because a corporation's tax loss is generally similar to its economic loss. However, in computing taxable income, individual taxpayers are allowed deductions for such items as personal and dependency exemptions and itemized deductions that do not reflect actual business-related economic losses.

To arrive at the NOL for an individual, taxable income must be adjusted by adding back the following items:[39]

1. No deduction is allowed for personal and dependency exemptions. These amounts do not reflect economic, or business, outlays and hence must be added back.
2. The NOL carryover or carryback from another year is not allowed in the computation of the current year's NOL.
3. Capital losses and nonbusiness deductions are limited in determining the current year's NOL. These limits are as follows:
    a. The excess of nonbusiness capital losses over nonbusiness capital gains must be added back.
    b. The excess of nonbusiness deductions over the sum of nonbusiness income and *net* nonbusiness capital gains must be added back. *Net nonbusiness capital gains* are the excess of nonbusiness capital gains over

---

[39]§ 172(d); Reg. § 1.172–3(a).

nonbusiness capital losses. *Nonbusiness income* is income that is not attributable to, or derived from, a taxpayer's trade or business. It includes items such as dividends, investment interest, alimony received, and Social Security income. *Nonbusiness deductions* are those deductions that are not attributable to, or derived from, a taxpayer's trade or business. Examples are Individual Retirement Account (IRA) deductions, alimony paid deductions, most itemized deductions except for personal casualty and theft losses and losses incurred in a transaction entered into for profit, and employee business expense deductions.

A taxpayer who does not itemize deductions computes the excess of nonbusiness deductions over nonbusiness income by substituting the standard deduction for total itemized deductions.

c. The excess of business capital losses over the sum of business capital gains and the excess of nonbusiness income and net nonbusiness capital gains over nonbusiness deductions must be added back.

d. The add-back for net nonbusiness capital losses and excess business capital losses does not include net capital losses not included in the current-year computation of taxable income because of the capital loss limitation provisions (discussed in Chapter 16).

The capital loss and nonbusiness deduction limits are illustrated in Examples 30 through 33.

EXAMPLE 30

For 2011, taxpayer and spouse have $6,000 of nonbusiness capital losses and $4,000 of nonbusiness capital gains. They must add back $2,000 ($6,000 − $4,000) in determining the excess of nonbusiness capital losses over nonbusiness capital gains. ∎

EXAMPLE 31

For 2011, taxpayer and spouse have $2,600 of nonbusiness capital gains, $1,000 of nonbusiness capital losses, $2,000 of interest income, and no itemized deductions. They must add back $8,000 {$11,600 standard deduction − [$2,000 interest income + $1,600 ($2,600 − $1,000) net nonbusiness capital gains]}. Note that, in this example, there is no excess of nonbusiness capital losses over nonbusiness capital gains. ∎

EXAMPLE 32

For 2011, taxpayer and spouse have $2,600 of nonbusiness capital gains, $1,000 of nonbusiness capital losses, $15,000 of interest income, $14,500 of itemized deductions (none of which are personal casualty and theft losses), $4,000 of business capital losses, and $1,000 of business capital gains. They must add back $900 {$4,000 business capital losses − [$1,000 business capital gains + ($15,000 nonbusiness income + $1,600 net nonbusiness capital gains − $14,500 nonbusiness deductions)]}. Note that, in this example, there is no excess of nonbusiness capital losses over nonbusiness capital gains, nor is there an excess of nonbusiness deductions over the sum of nonbusiness income and net nonbusiness capital gains. ∎

EXAMPLE 33

For 2011, taxpayer and spouse have $2,600 of nonbusiness capital gains, $3,000 of nonbusiness capital losses, $13,000 of interest income, $15,000 of itemized deductions (none of which are personal casualty and theft losses), $8,000 of business capital losses, and $4,000 of business capital gains. They must add back $2,000 ($15,000 − $13,000), the excess of nonbusiness deductions over nonbusiness income, and $3,000, the excess of combined capital losses. Because of the capital loss limitations, only $3,000 of the loss would have been used in computing taxable income for the year. ∎

Example 34 illustrates the computation of an NOL.

EXAMPLE 34

James opened a retail store in 2010 and experienced an NOL of $185 for that year. James had no taxable income for 2008 or 2009. James is married, has no dependents, and files a joint return. For 2011, James and his wife have the following taxable income:

Gross income from the business	$ 67,000	
Less: Business expenses	(73,000)	($ 6,000)
Salary from a part-time job		875
Interest on savings account		525
Nonbusiness long-term capital gain		1,000
NOL carryover from 2010		(185)
Net loss on rental property		(100)
Adjusted gross income		($ 3,885)
Less: Itemized deductions		
Interest expense	$ 4,600	
Taxes	7,300	
Casualty loss	2,000	
Total itemized deductions		(13,900)
Exemptions (2 × $3,700)		(7,400)
Taxable income		($25,185)

James's NOL is computed as follows:

Taxable income				($25,185)
Add:				
Net operating loss from 2010			$ 185	
Personal exemptions (2)			7,400	
Excess of nonbusiness deductions over nonbusiness income				
Total itemized deductions		$13,900		
Less: Casualty loss		(2,000)		
		$11,900		
Less: Interest	$ 525			
Less: Long-term capital gain	1,000	(1,525)	10,375	17,960
Net operating loss				($ 7,225)

The NOL can be thought of as follows:

Business loss	($ 6,000)
Rental loss	(100)
Casualty loss	(2,000)
Salary income	875
Net operating loss	($ 7,225)

RECOMPUTATION OF TAX LIABILITY FOR YEAR TO WHICH NET OPERATING LOSS IS CARRIED

When an NOL is carried back to a nonloss year, the taxable income and income tax for the carryback year must be recomputed by including the NOL as a deduction *for* AGI. Several deductions (such as medical expenses and charitable contributions) are based on the amount of AGI. When an NOL is carried back, all such deductions *except* the charitable contributions deduction must be recomputed on the basis of the new AGI after the NOL has been applied. The deduction for charitable contributions is determined without regard to any NOL carryback but with regard to any other modification affecting AGI. Furthermore, any tax credits limited by or based upon the tax must be recomputed, based on the recomputed tax.

EXAMPLE 35

Peggy sustains an NOL of $11,000 in 2011. Because Peggy had no taxable income in 2009, the loss is carried back to 2010. For 2010, the joint income tax return of Peggy and her husband was as follows:

Salary income	$15,000
Dividends (not qualified dividends)	4,000
Net short-term capital gain	1,400
Adjusted gross income	$20,400

Itemized deductions		
Charitable contributions	$3,700	
Medical [$1,600 − ($20,400 × 7.5%)]	70	
Interest	5,700	
Taxes	2,420	(11,890)
Exemptions (2 × $3,650)		(7,300)
Taxable income		$ 1,210
Tax (married filing jointly)		$ 121

Peggy's new tax liability for the carryback year is computed as follows:

Adjusted gross income		$20,400
Less: Net operating loss		(11,000)
Recomputed adjusted gross income		$ 9,400
Itemized deductions		
Charitable contributions	$3,700	
Medical [$1,600 − ($9,400 × 7.5%)]	895	
Interest	5,700	
Taxes	2,420	(12,715)
Exemptions (2 × $3,650)		(7,300)
Recomputed taxable income		($10,615)
Tax		$ −0−
Tax originally paid and refund claim		$ 121	∎

CALCULATION OF THE REMAINING NET OPERATING LOSS

After computing the amount of the refund claim for the initial carryback year, it is then necessary to determine the extent to which any NOL remains to carry over to future years. The amount of this carryover loss is the excess of the NOL over the taxable income of the year to which the loss is being applied. However, the taxable income of the year to which the loss is being applied must be determined with the following *modifications*:

- No deduction is allowed for excess capital losses over capital gains.
- No deduction is allowed for the NOL that is being carried back. However, deductions are allowed for NOLs occurring before the loss year.
- Any deductions claimed that are based on or limited by AGI must be determined after making the preceding adjustments. However, charitable contributions do not take into account any NOL carryback.
- No deduction is allowed for personal and dependency exemptions.

EXAMPLE 36

Referring to the facts in Example 35, the NOL carryover from 2010 available for future years is ($2,490), computed as follows:

Salary income		$15,000
Dividends (not qualified dividends)		4,000
Net short-term capital gain		1,400
Adjusted gross income		$20,400
Itemized deductions		
Charitable contributions	$3,700	
Medical [$1,600 − ($20,400 × 7.5%)]	70	
Interest	5,700	
Taxes	2,420	(11,890)
Exemptions (not allowed)		−0−
Modified taxable income		$ 8,510
Net operating loss		($11,000)
Modified taxable income		8,510
Net operating loss to carry forward		($ 2,490)

Since the ending figure is negative, it represents the NOL remaining to carry over to 2012 or later years. ∎

CONCEPT SUMMARY 7.4

Computation of Net Operating Loss

Taxable income shown on the return
Add back:

1. Personal and dependency exemptions.
2. Net operating loss carryover or carryback from another year.
3. The excess of nonbusiness capital losses over nonbusiness capital gains.
4. The excess of nonbusiness deductions over the sum of nonbusiness income plus *net* nonbusiness capital gains.

5. The excess of business capital losses over the sum of business capital gains plus the excess of nonbusiness income and *net* nonbusiness capital gains over nonbusiness deductions. The add-back from the total of items 3 and 5 will not exceed $3,000 because of the capital loss limitation rules.

Equals the net operating loss

TAX PLANNING:

7.7 TAX CONSEQUENCES OF THE *GROETZINGER* CASE

In the *Groetzinger* case discussed earlier in the chapter, the court established that the appropriate tests for determining if gambling is a trade or business are whether an individual engages in gambling full-time in good faith, with regularity, and for the production of income as a livelihood, and not as a mere hobby. The court held that Robert Groetzinger satisfied the tests because of his constant and large-scale effort. Skill was required and was applied. He did what he did for a livelihood, though with less than successful results. His gambling was not a hobby, a passing fancy, or an occasional bet for amusement. Therefore, his gambling was a trade or business, and hence, he was able to deduct his gambling losses *for* AGI. If the court had ruled that Groetzinger's gambling was not a trade or business, his gambling losses would have been limited to his gambling winnings and would have been classified as itemized deductions.

7.8 DOCUMENTATION OF RELATED-TAXPAYER LOANS, CASUALTY LOSSES, AND THEFT LOSSES

Since non-bona fide loans between related taxpayers may be treated as gifts, adequate documentation is needed to substantiate a bad debt deduction if the loan subsequently becomes worthless. Documentation should include proper execution of the note (legal form) and the establishment of a bona fide purpose for the loan. In addition, it is desirable to stipulate a reasonable rate of interest and a fixed maturity date.

Since a theft loss is not permitted for misplaced items, a loss should be documented by a police report and evidence of the value of the property (e.g., appraisals, pictures of the property, newspaper clippings). Similar documentation of the value of property should be provided to support a casualty loss deduction because the amount of loss is measured, in part, by the decline in fair market value of the property.

Casualty loss deductions must be reported on Form 4684.

7.9 WORTHLESS SECURITIES

To be deductible, a security must be completely worthless. To obtain the deduction, the taxpayer must prove that the security was not worthless in a prior year and that

---

TAX *in*
the **NEWS**   **WHEN IS A SECURITY WORTHLESS?**

Usually, losses that have not been documented by the marketplace cannot be deducted (i.e., unrealized losses). An exception exists for securities that are completely worthless. But proving complete worthlessness can sometimes be difficult. Just because a company declares bankruptcy does not necessarily prove that its stock is completely worthless because in some cases the stock can recover. Determining whether this can happen requires an analysis of the relevant facts and circumstances. Even though a stock may be selling for a fraction of a penny (i.e., it has some value), some tax advisers argue that if the stock's selling price would be less than the broker's commission for selling the stock, a deduction can be taken at that time.

---

the security was worthless in the year claimed. Because of the subjectivity associated with this burden of proof, the only safe practice is to claim a loss for the earliest year when it may possibly be allowed and to renew the claim in subsequent years if there is any reasonable chance that it will be applicable to the income for those years.[40] Fortunately, the statute of limitations for worthless securities is seven years.[41]

7.10 SMALL BUSINESS STOCK

Because § 1244 limits the amount of loss classified as ordinary loss on a yearly basis, a taxpayer might maximize the benefits of § 1244 by selling the stock in more than one taxable year. The result could be that the losses in any one taxable year would not exceed the § 1244 limits on ordinary loss.

> **EXAMPLE 37**
>
> Mitch, a single individual, purchased small business stock in 2009 for $150,000 (150 shares at $1,000 per share). On December 20, 2011, the stock is worth $60,000 (150 shares at $400 per share). Mitch wants to sell the stock at this time. Mitch earns a salary of $80,000 a year, has no other capital transactions, and does not expect any in the future. If Mitch sells all of the small business stock in 2011, his recognized loss will be $90,000 ($60,000 − $150,000). The loss will be characterized as a $50,000 ordinary loss and a $40,000 long-term capital loss. In computing taxable income for 2011, Mitch could deduct the $50,000 ordinary loss but could deduct only $3,000 of the capital loss. The remainder of the capital loss could be carried over and used in future years subject to the $3,000 limitation if Mitch has no capital gains. If Mitch sells 82 shares in 2011, he will recognize an ordinary loss of $49,200 [82 × ($1,000 − $400)]. If Mitch then sells the remainder of the shares in 2012, he will recognize an ordinary loss of $40,800 [68 × ($1,000 − $400)]. Mitch could deduct the $49,200 ordinary loss in computing 2011 taxable income and the $40,800 ordinary loss in computing 2012 taxable income. ∎

7.11 CASUALTY LOSSES

A special election is available for taxpayers who sustain casualty losses in an area designated by the President as a disaster area. This election affects only the timing, not the calculation, of the deduction. The deduction can be taken in the year before the year in which the loss occurred. Thus, for a loss occurring between January 1 and December 31, 2011, an individual can take the deduction on the 2010 return. The benefit, of course, is a faster refund (or reduction in tax). It will also be advantageous

---

[40] *Young v. Comm.*, 41–2 USTC ¶9744, 28 AFTR 365, 123 F.2d 597 (CA–2, 1941).   [41] § 6511(d)(1).

FINANCIAL DISCLOSURE *Insights*

VALUATION ALLOWANCES FOR NOLS

Financial analysts use the valuation allowance system to help them determine the entity's expected future cash flows. Some critics of the GAAP rules for valuation allowances maintain that they enable management to manipulate profits and earnings per share in an arbitrary fashion.

Only a few of the largest business entities, supported by going-concern assumptions and access to worldwide debt and equity capital, need to record sizable valuation allowances. But smaller entities and those in volatile industries are more likely to present questions as to their future profitability, and the valuation allowances may be found in those financial reports somewhat more often.

In a recent reporting year, for instance, the following telecommunications businesses reported valuation allowances related to expectations that their NOLs (for Federal and/or state taxing jurisdictions) would expire unused.

	Deferred Tax Assets ($000)	Valuation Allowance ($000)
Verizon	$10,750	$2,700
Bell South	2,100	1,100
AT&T	11,400	1,050
SBC Communications	3,900	150

Establishing a valuation allowance does not affect the entity's internal cash balances, but it might have an effect on the stock price. Valuation allowances can be "released" by management when evidence develops that the carryforwards are likely to be used in the future, for example, if profitability has improved and appears to be sustainable. For instance, the homebuilder Toll Brothers created a large valuation allowance when the real estate market collapsed, but it will release the allowance when housing prices stabilize and increase. Several corporations estimated that the health care reform legislation would force them to create sizable valuation allowances, because the mandated expenditures would reduce future profitability.

Reduction in Deferred Tax Assets Due to Health Care Reform ($ million): Estimate	
AT&T	$1,000
John Deere	150
Caterpillar	100
3M	90
Norfolk Southern	27

to carry the loss back if the taxpayer's tax rate in the carryback year is higher than the tax rate in the year of the loss.

To find out if an event qualifies as a disaster area loss, one can look in any of the major tax services, the Weekly Compilation of Presidential Documents, or the *Internal Revenue Bulletin*.

7.12 NET OPERATING LOSSES

In certain instances, it may be advisable for a taxpayer to elect not to carry back an NOL. For an individual, the benefits from the loss carryback could be scaled down or lost due to the economic adjustments that must be made to taxable income for the year to which the loss is carried. For example, a taxpayer should attempt to minimize the number of taxable years to which an NOL is carried. The more years to which the NOL is applied, the more benefits are lost from adjustments for items such as personal and dependency exemptions.

The election not to carry back the loss might also be advantageous if there is a disparity in marginal tax rates applicable to different tax years.

EXAMPLE 38

Abby sustained an NOL of $10,000 in Year 3. Her marginal tax bracket in Year 1 was 15%. In Year 4, however, she expects her bracket to be 35% due to a large profit she will make on a business deal. If Abby carries her loss back, her refund will be $1,500 (15% × $10,000). If she elects not to carry it back to Year 1 but chooses, instead, to carry it forward, her savings will be $3,500 (35% × $10,000). Even considering the time value of an immediate tax refund, Abby appears to be better off using the carryover approach. ∎

REFOCUS ON THE BIG PICTURE

LOSSES

Martha can receive tax benefits associated with her unfortunate occurrences during the current tax year. Some of the losses, however, will provide a greater tax benefit than others as a result of different tax provisions governing the amount and the classification of the losses.

Bad Debt

Based on the facts provided, it appears that Martha's loan to her friend was a bona fide debt. Otherwise, nothing would be deductible. The amount of the deduction is the unpaid principal balance of $19,000 ($25,000 − $6,000). Unfortunately, since the bad debt is a nonbusiness bad debt, it is classified as a short-term capital loss. (See Example 4.)

Loss from Investment

The $50,000 loss is deductible. However, it appears that the loss should be classified as a long-term capital loss rather than as a short-term capital loss. Although the actual holding period was not greater than one year (October through May), the disposal date for the stock (qualifies as a worthless security) is deemed to be the last day of the tax year (October of last year through end of December of the current year). The loss does not appear to qualify for ordinary loss treatment under § 1244. (See Example 7.)

Loss from Bookstore

The $180,000 loss from the bookstore is reported on Schedule C of Form 1040. It is an ordinary loss, and it qualifies for NOL treatment. Therefore, Martha can carry the $180,000 net loss back and offset it against the net income of the bookstore for the past two years. Any amount not offset (probably about $30,000) can be carried forward for the next 20 years. The carryback will produce a claim for a tax refund.

Casualty Loss

The loss on the damage to Martha's personal residence is classified as a personal casualty loss. Using the cost of repairs method, the amount of the casualty loss is $7,000 ($32,000 − $25,000). However, this amount must be reduced by the statutory materiality amounts of $100 and 10 percent of AGI.

If the President classified the area in which Martha's house is located as a disaster area, Martha has the option of deducting the casualty loss on the prior year's tax return. (See Example 13.)

KEY TERMS

Bad debt, 7-3	Net operating loss (NOL), 7-19	Section 1244 stock, 7-7
Business bad debt, 7-5	Nonbusiness bad debt, 7-4	Small business stock (§ 1244 stock), 7-7
Casualty loss, 7-8	Personal casualty gain, 7-14	Specific charge-off method, 7-4
Disaster area losses, 7-10	Personal casualty loss, 7-14	Theft losses, 7-9
Domestic production activities deduction (DPAD), 7-17	Qualified production activities income (QPAI), 7-18	W–2 wages, 7-18
Domestic production gross receipts (DPGR), 7-18	Research and experimental expenditures, 7-15	Worthless securities, 7-7
Modified adjusted gross income, 7-17	Reserve method, 7-4	

1. **LO.1** Explain how a purchased debt instrument can give rise to a bad debt deduction.

2. **LO.1** Ron sells his business accounts receivable of $100,000 to Mike for $70,000 (70% of the actual accounts receivable). Mike later determines that he will be able to collect only $6,000 of a $10,000 receivable. Discuss the amount and classification of Mike's bad debt deduction.

3. **LO.1** Discuss when a bad debt deduction can be taken for a nonbusiness debt.

4. **LO.1** During the past tax year, Jane identified $50,000 as a nonbusiness bad debt. In that tax year, Jane had $100,000 of taxable income, of which $5,000 consisted of short-term capital gains. During the current tax year, Jane collected $10,000 of the amount she had previously identified as a bad debt. Discuss Jane's tax treatment of the $10,000 received in the current tax year.

5. **LO.1** Bob owns a collection agency. He purchases uncollected accounts receivable from other businesses at 60% of their face value and then attempts to collect these accounts. Discuss the treatment of any account Bob is unable to collect.

6. **LO.1** Discuss the treatment of a business bad debt when the business also has long-term capital gains.

ISSUE ID

7. **LO.1** Many years ago, Jack purchased 400 shares of Canary stock. During the current year, the stock became worthless. It was determined that the company "went under" because several corporate officers embezzled a large amount of company funds. Identify the relevant tax issues for Jack.

8. **LO.2** Sean is in the business of buying and selling stocks and bonds. He has a bond of Green Corporation for which he paid $200,000. The bond is currently worth only $50,000. Discuss whether Sean can take a $150,000 loss for a business bad debt or for a worthless security.

9. **LO.2** Discuss the tax treatment of the sale of § 1244 stock at a loss.

10. **LO.3, 4** Jim discovers that one of his business warehouses has extensive termite damage. Discuss whether he may take a deduction for the damage to the building.

11. **LO.3, 4** The value of Mary's personal residence has declined significantly because of a recent forest fire in the area where she lives. Mary's house suffered no actual damage during the fire, but because much of the surrounding area was destroyed, the value of all of the homes in the area declined substantially. Discuss whether Mary can take a casualty loss for the decline in value of her residence caused by the fire.

12. **LO.4** Discuss at what point in time a casualty loss generally is recognized.

13. **LO.4** Mary's diamond ring was stolen in 2010. She originally paid $8,000 for the ring, but it was worth considerably more at the time of the theft. Mary filed an insurance claim for the stolen ring, but the claim was denied. Because the insurance claim was denied, Mary took a casualty loss for the stolen ring on her 2010 tax return. In 2010, Mary had AGI of $40,000. In 2011, the insurance company had a "change of heart" and sent Mary a check for $5,000 for the stolen ring. Discuss the proper tax treatment of the $5,000 Mary received from the insurance company in 2011.

14. **LO.4** Discuss the measurement rule for partial or complete destruction of personal use property.

15. **LO.4** Discuss the tax consequences of not making an insurance claim when insured personal use property is subject to a loss.

16. **LO.4** Discuss the circumstances under which the cost of repairs to the damaged property can be used to measure the amount of a casualty loss.

17. **LO.4** Discuss the treatment of a loss on rental property under the following facts:

Basis	$700,000
FMV before the loss	900,000
FMV after the loss	–0–

18. **LO.4** Hazel sustained a loss on the theft of a painting. She had paid $50,000 for the painting, but it was worth $40,000 at the time of the theft. Evaluate the tax consequences of treating the painting as investment property or as personal use property.

19. **LO.4** When casualty losses exceed casualty gains, only the amount of the casualty loss in excess of casualty gains is subject to the 10%-of-AGI floor. Discuss the significance of netting losses against gains in this manner rather than having the entire casualty loss be subject to the 10%-of-AGI floor.

20. **LO.4** Kelly decided to invest in Lime, Inc. common stock after reviewing Lime's public disclosures, including recent financial statements and a number of press releases issued by Lime. On August 7, 2009, Kelly purchased 60,000 shares of Lime for $210,000. In May 2010, Lime entered into a joint venture with Cherry, Inc. In November 2010, the joint venture failed, and Lime's stock began to decline in value. In December 2010, Cherry filed a lawsuit against Lime for theft of corporate opportunity and breach of fiduciary responsibility. In February 2011, Lime filed a countersuit against Cherry for fraud and misappropriation of funds. At the end of December 2011, Kelly's stock in Lime was worth $15,000. Identify the relevant tax issues for Kelly.

ISSUE ID

21. **LO.3, 4** In 2008, John opened an investment account with Randy Hansen who held himself out to the public as an investment adviser and securities broker. John contributed $200,000 to the account in 2008. John provided Randy with a power of attorney to use the $200,000 to purchase and sell securities on John's behalf. John instructed Randy to reinvest any gains and income earned. In the years 2008, 2009, and 2010, John received statements of the amount of income earned by his account and included these amounts in his gross income for these years. In 2011, it was discovered that Randy's purported investment advisory and brokerage activity was in fact a fraudulent investment arrangement known as a "Ponzi" scheme. In reality, John's account balance was zero, the money having been used by Randy in his scheme. Identify the relevant tax issues for John.

ISSUE ID

22. **LO.5** Green Corporation made extensive modifications to a portion of a building so that it could be used to conduct product research. Discuss whether the modification costs would qualify as research and experimental expenditures.

23. **LO.5** Discuss under what circumstances a company would elect to amortize research and experimental expenditures rather than use the expense method.

24. **LO.6** Amos began a business, Silver, Inc., on July 1, 2008. The business extracts and processes silver ore. During 2011, Amos becomes aware of the domestic production activities deduction (DPAD) and would like to take advantage of this deduction. Identify the relevant tax issues for Silver, Inc.

ISSUE ID

25. **LO.6** The DPAD is unlike other deductions and is designed to provide a tax benefit in a somewhat unique manner. Explain this statement.

26. **LO.6** Discuss the impact of an NOL on the DPAD.

27. **LO.7** Discuss whether an itemized employee business expense deduction can create an NOL for an individual taxpayer.

28. **LO.7** Discuss how the carryback period for a loss attributable to a farming business differs from the carryback period for a regular NOL.

29. **LO.7** Discuss whether itemized deductions can create an NOL.

30. **LO.7** Discuss the effect of an NOL carryback on a charitable contribution.

31. **LO.7** Thomas believes that he has an NOL for the current year and wants to carry it back to a previous year and receive a tax refund. In determining his NOL, Thomas offset his business income by alimony payments he made to his ex-wife, contributions he made to his traditional Individual Retirement Account (IRA), and moving expenses he incurred. His reason for using these items in the NOL computation is that each item is a deduction *for* AGI. Identify the relevant tax issues for Thomas.

ISSUE ID

PROBLEMS

COMMUNICATIONS

32. **L0.1** Several years ago John Johnson, who is not in the lending business, loaned Sara $30,000 to purchase an automobile to be used for personal purposes. In August of the current year, Sara filed for bankruptcy, and John was notified that he could not expect to receive more than $4,000. As of the end of the current year, John has received $1,000. John has contacted you about the possibility of taking a bad debt deduction for the current year.

    Write a letter to John that contains your advice as to whether he can claim a bad debt deduction for the current year. Also, prepare a memo for the tax files. John's address is 100 Tyler Lane, Erie, PA 16563.

33. **L0.1** Monty loaned his friend Ned $20,000 three years ago. Ned signed a note and made payments on the loan. Last year, when the remaining balance was $11,000, Ned filed for bankruptcy and notified Monty that he would be unable to pay the balance on the loan. Monty treated the $11,000 as a nonbusiness bad debt. Last year Monty had no capital gains and taxable income of $12,000. During the current year, Ned paid Monty $5,000 in satisfaction of the debt. Determine Monty's tax treatment for the $5,000 received in the current year.

34. **L0.1** Sally is in the business of purchasing accounts receivable. Last year, Sally purchased an account receivable with a face value of $80,000 for $60,000. During the current year, Sally settled the account, receiving $55,000. Determine the maximum amount of the bad debt deduction for Sally for the current year.

35. **L0.1, 2** Mable and Jack file a joint return. For the current year, they had the following items:

Salaries	$ 90,000
Loss on sale of § 1244 stock acquired two years ago	105,000
Gain on sale of § 1244 stock acquired six months ago	20,000
Nonbusiness bad debt	19,000

Determine their AGI for the current year.

DECISION MAKING

36. **L0.2, 8** Mary, a single taxpayer, purchased 10,000 shares of § 1244 stock several years ago at a cost of $20 per share. In November of the current year, Mary received an offer to sell the stock for $12 per share. She has the option of either selling all of the stock now or selling half of the stock now and half of the stock in January of next year. Mary will receive a salary of $80,000 for the current year and $90,000 next year. Mary will have long-term capital gains of $8,000 for the current year and $10,000 next year. If Mary's goal is to minimize her AGI for the two years, determine whether she should sell all of her stock this year or half of her stock this year and half next year.

37. **L0.4** During 2011, someone broke into Jacob's personal residence and took the following items:

Asset	Adjusted Basis	FMV before	FMV after	Insurance Recovery
Business computer	$12,000	$10,000	–0–	$7,000
Bearer bonds	30,000	32,000	–0–	–0–
Silverware	7,000	10,000	–0–	2,000
Cash	8,000	8,000	–0–	–0–

Jacob is an employee and used the computer 100% of the time in his employment. Although his homeowner's insurance policy paid Jacob $7,000 for the stolen computer, Jacob's employer did not reimburse Jacob for any of the remainder of his loss. Jacob's AGI for the year, before considering any of the above items, is $50,000. Determine the total deduction for the stolen items on Jacob's 2011 tax return.

DECISION MAKING

38. **L0.3, 4, 8** Olaf owns a 500-acre farm in Minnesota. A tornado hit the area and destroyed a farm building and some farm equipment and damaged a barn. Fortunately for Olaf, the tornado occurred after he had harvested his corn crop. Applicable information is as follows:

Item	Adjusted Basis	FMV before	FMV after	Insurance Proceeds
Building	$90,000	$ 70,000	$ –0–	$70,000
Equipment	40,000	50,000	–0–	25,000
Barn	90,000	120,000	70,000	25,000

Because of the extensive damage caused by the tornado, the President designated the area as a disaster area.

Olaf, who files a joint return with his wife, Anna, had $174,000 of taxable income last year. Their taxable income for the current year, excluding the loss from the tornado, is $250,000.

Determine the amount of Olaf and Anna's loss and the year in which they should take the loss.

39. **LO.3, 4** Heather owns a two-story building. The building is used 60% for business use and 40% for personal use. During 2011, a fire caused major damage to the building and its contents. Heather purchased the building for $800,000 and has taken depreciation of $150,000 on the business portion. At the time of the fire, the building had a fair market value of $900,000. Immediately after the fire, the fair market value was $200,000. The insurance recovery on the building was $600,000. The contents of the building were insured for any loss at fair market value. The business assets had an adjusted basis of $220,000 and a fair market value of $175,000. These assets were totally destroyed. The personal use assets had an adjusted basis of $50,000 and a fair market value of $65,000. These assets were also totally destroyed. If Heather's AGI is $100,000 before considering the effects of the fire, determine her itemized deduction as a result of the fire. Also determine Heather's AGI.

40. **LO.3, 4** On July 24 of the current year, Sam Smith was involved in an accident with his business use automobile. Sam had purchased the car for $30,000. The automobile had a fair market value of $20,000 before the accident and $8,000 immediately after the accident. Sam has taken $20,000 of depreciation on the car. The car is insured for the fair market value of any loss. Because of Sam's history, he is afraid that if he submits a claim, his policy will be canceled. Therefore, he is considering not filing a claim. Sam believes that the tax loss deduction will help mitigate the loss of the insurance reimbursement. Sam's current marginal tax rate is 35%.

Write a letter to Sam that contains your advice with respect to the tax and cash-flow consequences of filing versus not filing a claim for the insurance reimbursement for the damage to his car. Also, prepare a memo for the tax files. Sam's address is 450 Colonel's Way, Warrensburg, MO 64093.

DECISION MAKING

COMMUNICATIONS

41. **LO.5** Blue Corporation, a manufacturing company, decided to develop a new line of merchandise. The project began in 2011. Blue had the following expenses in connection with the project:

	2011	2012
Salaries	$500,000	$600,000
Materials	90,000	70,000
Insurance	8,000	11,000
Utilities	6,000	8,000
Cost of inspection of materials for quality control	7,000	6,000
Promotion expenses	11,000	18,000
Advertising	–0–	20,000
Equipment depreciation	15,000	14,000
Cost of market survey	8,000	–0–

The new product will be introduced for sale beginning in July 2013. Determine the amount of the deduction for research and experimental expenditures for 2011, 2012, and 2013 if:

    a.   Blue Corporation elects to expense the research and experimental expenditures.

    b.   Blue Corporation elects to amortize the research and experimental expenditures over 60 months.

42. **LO.6** Sarah Ham, operating as a sole proprietor, manufactures printers in the United States. For 2011, the proprietorship has QPAI of $300,000. Sarah's modified AGI was $350,000. The W–2 wages paid by the proprietorship to employees engaged in the qualified domestic production activity were $90,000. Calculate Sarah's DPAD for 2011.

43. **LO.6** Barbara, a calendar year taxpayer, owns and operates a company that manufactures toys. For 2011, she has modified AGI of $600,000 and QPAI of $550,000. Ignoring the W–2 wage limitation, calculate Barbara's DPAD.

44. **LO.6** Red Corporation manufactures hand tools in the United States. For the current year, the QPAI derived from the manufacture of hand tools was $1 million. Red's taxable income for the current year was $1.5 million. Last year, Red had an NOL of $800,000, which Red elected to carry forward. Calculate Red's DPAD for the current year.

45. **LO.6** Green Corporation manufactures skirts and blouses in the United States. The DPGR derived from the manufacture of one skirt is $12, and the DPGR from one blouse is $10. The cost of goods sold is $5 for one skirt and $6 for one blouse. Other allocated costs are $1 for one skirt and $5 for one blouse. What amount of QPAI is available to Green for calculating the DPAD?

DECISION MAKING

46. **LO.6** In 2011, Rose, Inc., has QPAI of $4 million and taxable income of $3 million. Rose pays independent contractors $500,000. Rose's W–2 wages are $600,000, but only $400,000 of the wages are paid to employees engaged in qualified domestic production activities.

    a.   Calculate the DPAD for Rose, Inc., for 2011.

    b.   What suggestions could you make to enable Rose to increase its DPAD?

47. **LO.7** Sam, age 45, is single. For 2011, he has the following items:

Business income	$70,000
Business expenses	65,000
Alimony paid	12,000
Interest income	3,000
Itemized deductions	4,000

    a.   Determine Sam's taxable income for 2011.

    b.   Determine Sam's NOL for 2011.

48. **LO.7** Mary, a single taxpayer with two dependent children, has the following items of income and expense during 2011:

Gross receipts from business	$144,000
Business expenses	180,000
Alimony received	22,000
Interest income	3,000
Itemized deductions (no casualty or theft)	28,000

    a.   Determine Mary's taxable income for 2011.

    b.   Determine Mary's NOL for 2011.

49. **LO.7** Gus, who is married and files a joint return, owns a grocery store. In 2011, his gross sales were $276,000, and operating expenses were $320,000. Other items on his 2011 return were as follows:

Nonbusiness capital gains (short term)	$20,000
Nonbusiness capital losses (long term)	9,000
Itemized deductions (no casualty or theft)	18,000
Ordinary nonbusiness income	8,000
Salary from part-time job	10,000

During the year 2009, Gus had no taxable income. In 2010, Gus had taxable income of $21,800 computed as follows:

Net business income		$60,000
Interest income		2,000
Adjusted gross income		$62,000
Less: Itemized deductions		
Charitable contributions of $40,000, limited to 50% of AGI	$31,000	
Medical expenses of $6,550, limited to the amount in excess of 7.5% of AGI ($6,550 − $4,650)	1,900	
Total itemized deductions		(32,900)
Exemptions (2 × $3,650)		(7,300)
Taxable income		$21,800

a. What is Gus's 2011 NOL?
b. Determine Gus's recomputed taxable income for 2010.
c. Determine the amount of Gus's 2011 NOL to be carried forward to 2012.

50. **LO.7** During 2011, Rick and his wife, Sara, had the following items of income and expense to report:

Gross receipts from farming business	$400,000
Farming expenses	525,000
Interest income from bank savings accounts	8,000
Sara's salary	50,000
Long-term capital gain on stock held as an investment	4,000
Itemized deductions (no casualty or theft)	15,000

a. Assuming Rick and Sara file a joint return, what is their taxable income for 2011?
b. What is the amount of Rick and Sara's farming loss for 2011?
c. What is the amount of Rick and Sara's NOL for 2011?
d. To what years can Rick and Sara's NOL be carried?

51. **LO.7** Assume that in addition to the information in Problem 50, Rick and Sara had no taxable income for the years 2006, 2007, 2008, and 2009 and $4,400 of taxable income for 2010 computed as follows:

Salary		$25,000
Capital loss		(1,000)
Adjusted gross income		$24,000
Less: Itemized deductions		
Charitable contributions of $20,000, limited to 50% of AGI	$12,000	
Medical expenses of $2,100, limited to the amount in excess of 7.5% of AGI ($2,100 − $1,800)	300	
Total itemized deductions		(12,300)
Exemptions (2 × $3,650)		(7,300)
Taxable income		$ 4,400

a. Determine Rick and Sara's recomputed taxable income for 2010.
b. Determine the amount of Rick and Sara's 2011 NOL to be carried forward to 2012.

52. **LO.7** During 2011, Ron and his wife, Sue, had the following items of income and expense to report:

Farming income	$300,000
Farming expenses	350,000
Interest income	6,000
Medical expenses (after 7.5%-of-AGI reduction)	12,000
Casualty loss (after $100 reduction and 10%-of-AGI reduction)	20,000

a. Determine Ron and Sue's taxable income for 2011.
b. Determine Ron and Sue's NOL for 2011.

c. Determine Ron and Sue's farming loss for 2011.
d. To what years can Ron and Sue's NOL be carried?

53. **L0.7** Robert and Susan Reid had an NOL of $30,000 in 2011. They had no taxable income for the year 2009 and $14,950 of taxable income for 2010 computed as follows:

Salary		$50,000
Capital loss		(4,000)
Adjusted gross income		$46,000
Less: Itemized deductions		
Charitable contributions of $24,000, limited to 50% of AGI	$23,000	
Medical expenses of $4,200, limited to the amount in excess of 7.5% of AGI ($4,200 − $3,450)	750	
Total itemized deductions		(23,750)
Exemptions (2 × $3,650)		(7,300)
Taxable income		$14,950

Write a letter to Robert and Susan informing them of the amount of the remaining NOL to be carried forward if the loss is applied against the 2010 taxable income. Also, prepare a memo for the tax files. Their address is 201 Jerdone Avenue, Conway, SC 29526.

54. **L0.7** Pete and Polly are married and file a joint return. They had the following income and deductions for 2011:

Salary	$50,000
Interest from savings account	5,000
Itemized deductions (no casualty or theft)	8,000
2010 NOL carried to 2011	60,000

a. What is Pete and Polly's taxable income for 2011?
b. What is Pete and Polly's NOL for 2011?
c. What is Pete and Polly's NOL to be carried to 2012?

55. **L0.1, 2, 7** Soong, single and age 32, had the following items for the tax year 2011:

- Salary of $30,000.
- Interest income from U.S. government bonds of $2,000.
- Dividends from a foreign corporation of $500.
- Sale of small business § 1244 stock on October 20, 2011, for $20,000. The stock had been acquired two years earlier for $65,000.
- Business bad debt of $4,000.
- Nonbusiness bad debt of $5,000.
- Sale of small business § 1244 stock on November 12, 2011, for $4,000. The stock had been acquired on June 5, 2011, for $800.
- Sale of preferred stock on December 4, 2011, for $40,000. The stock was acquired four years ago for $18,000.
- Total itemized deductions of $20,000 (no casualty or theft).

a. Determine Soong's NOL for 2011.
b. Assuming Soong has had taxable income for each of the last five years, determine the carryback year to which the 2011 NOL should be applied.

56. **L0.1, 3** Nell, single and age 38, had the following income and expense items in 2011:

Nonbusiness bad debt	$ 6,000
Business bad debt	2,000
Nonbusiness long-term capital gain	4,000
Nonbusiness short-term capital loss	3,000
Salary	50,000
Interest income	3,000

Determine Nell's AGI for 2011.

57. **LO.1, 4** Assume that in addition to the information in Problem 56, Nell had the following items in 2011:

Personal casualty gain on an asset held for four months	$10,000
Personal casualty loss on an asset held for two years	1,000

Determine Nell's AGI for 2011.

58. **LO.1, 4, 7** Assume that in addition to the information in Problems 56 and 57, Nell had the following items in 2011:

Personal casualty loss on an asset held for five years	$60,000
Interest expense on home mortgage	15,000

Determine Nell's taxable income and NOL for 2011.

59. **LO.1, 2, 3, 4, 7** Jed, age 55, is married with no children. During 2011, Jed had the following income and expense items:

   a.   Three years ago, Jed loaned a friend $10,000 to help him purchase a new car. In June of the current year, Jed learned that his friend had been declared bankrupt and had left the country. There is no possibility that Jed will ever collect any of the $10,000.

   b.   In April of last year, Jed purchased some stock for $5,000. In March of the current year, the company was declared bankrupt, and Jed was notified that his shares of stock were worthless.

   c.   Several years ago, Jed purchased some § 1244 stock for $120,000. This year, he sold the stock for $30,000.

   d.   In July of this year, Jed sold some land that he had held for two years for $60,000. He had originally paid $42,000 for the land.

   e.   Jed received $40,000 of interest income from State of Minnesota bonds.

   f.   In September, Jed's home was damaged by an earthquake. Jed's basis in his home was $430,000. The value of the home immediately before the quake was $610,000. After the quake, the home was worth $540,000. Because earthquake damage was an exclusion on Jed's homeowner's insurance policy, he received no insurance recovery.

   g.   Jed received a salary of $80,000.

   h.   Jed paid home mortgage interest of $14,000.

   If Jed files a joint return for 2011, determine his NOL for the year.

CUMULATIVE PROBLEMS

60. Jane Smith, age 40, is single and has no dependents. She is employed as a legal secretary by Legal Services, Inc. She owns and operates Typing Services located near the campus of Florida Atlantic University at 1986 Campus Drive. Jane is a material participant in the business. She is a cash basis taxpayer. Jane lives at 2020 Oakcrest Road, Boca Raton, FL 33431. Jane's Social Security number is 123–45–6789. Jane indicates that she wishes to designate $3 to the Presidential Election Campaign Fund. During 2010, Jane had the following income and expense items:

   a. $100,000 salary from Legal Services, Inc.

   b. $20,000 gross receipts from her typing services business.

   c. $700 interest income from Acme National Bank.

   d. $1,000 Christmas bonus from Legal Services, Inc.

   e. $60,000 life insurance proceeds on the death of her sister.

   f. $5,000 check given to her by her wealthy aunt.

   g. $100 won in a bingo game.

   h.   Expenses connected with the typing service:

Office rent	$7,000
Supplies	4,400
Utilities and telephone	4,680
Wages to part-time typists	5,000
Payroll taxes	500
Equipment rentals	3,000

   i. $9,500 interest expense on a home mortgage (paid to San Jose Savings and Loan).

TAX RETURN PROBLEM

DECISION MAKING

COMMUNICATIONS

H&R BLOCK
At Home

j. $15,000 fair market value of silverware stolen from her home by a burglar on October 12, 2010. Jane had paid $14,000 for the silverware on July 1, 2001. She was reimbursed $1,500 by her insurance company.

k. Jane had loaned $2,100 to a friend, Joan Jensen, on June 3, 2007. Joan declared bankruptcy on August 14, 2010, and was unable to repay the loan. Assume the loan is a bona fide debt.

l. Legal Services, Inc., withheld Federal income tax of $18,000 and FICA tax of $7,376 {Social Security tax of $5,978 [($101,000 − $4,580) × 6.2%] + Medicare tax of 1,398 [($101,000 − $4,580) × 1.45%]}.

m. Alimony of $10,000 received from her former husband, Ted Smith.

n. Interest income of $800 on City of Boca Raton bonds.

o. Jane made estimated Federal tax payments of $1,000.

p. Sales taxes from the sales tax table of $964.

q. Charitable contributions of $2,500.

Part 1—Tax Computation

Compute Jane Smith's 2010 Federal income tax payable (or refund due). If you use tax forms for your computations, you will need Forms 1040 and 4684 and Schedules A, C, and D. Suggested software: H&R BLOCK At Home.

Part 2—Tax Planning

In 2011, Jane plans to continue her job with Legal Services, Inc. Therefore, items a, d, and l will recur in 2011. Jane plans to continue her typing services business (refer to item b) and expects gross receipts of $26,000. She projects that all business expenses (refer to item h) will increase by 10%, except for office rent, which, under the terms of her lease, will remain the same as in 2010. Items e, f, g, j, and k will not recur in 2011. Items c, i, m, n, p, and q will be approximately the same as in 2010.

Jane would like you to compute the minimum amount of estimated tax she will have to pay for 2011 so that she will not have to pay any additional tax upon filing her 2011 Federal income tax return. Write a letter to Jane that contains your advice and prepare a memo for the tax files.

TAX COMPUTATION PROBLEM

61. Alan Rice, age 45, and his wife, Ruth, live at 230 Wood Lane, Salt Lake City, UT 84201. Alan's Social Security number is 111–11–1111. Ruth's Social Security number is 123–45–6789. Alan and Ruth are cash basis taxpayers and had the following items for the year 2011:

- Salary of $95,000.
- Business bad debt of $28,000 from uncollected rent.
- Sale of § 1244 stock resulting in a loss of $25,000. The stock was acquired nine months earlier.
- Rental income of $52,000.
- Rental expenses of $28,000.
- Casualty loss on rental property of $12,000.
- Personal casualty loss (from one event) of $25,000.
- Other itemized deductions of $17,000.
- NOL carryover from 2010 of $18,000.
- Federal income tax withheld of $6,000.

Compute Alan and Ruth's 2011 Federal income tax payable (or refund due).

RESEARCH PROBLEMS

Note: Solutions to Research Problems can be prepared by using the **Checkpoint®** **Student Edition** online research product, which is available to accompany this text. It is also possible to prepare solutions to the Research Problems by using tax research materials found in a standard tax library.

Research Problem 1. During 2011, John was the chief executive officer and a shareholder of Maze, Inc. He owned 60% of the outstanding stock of Maze. In 2008, John and Maze, as co-borrowers, obtained a $100,000 loan from United National Bank. This loan was secured by John's personal residence. Though Maze was listed as a co-borrower, John repaid the loan in full in 2011. On Maze's Form 1120 tax returns, no loans from shareholders were reported. Discuss whether John is entitled to a bad debt deduction for the amount of the payment on the loan.

Partial list of research aids:
U.S. v. Generes, 405 U.S. 93 (1972).
Dale H. Sundby, T.C.Memo. 2003–204.
Arrigoni v. Comm., 73 T.C. 792 (1980).
Estate of Herbert M. Rapoport, T.C.Memo. 1982–584.
Clifford L. Brody and Barbara J. DeClerk, T.C. Summary Opinion, 2004–149.

Research Problem 2. Henry Hansen is a real estate developer. He was successful for many years. Three years ago, however, the real estate market crashed, and Henry reported losses for the two following tax years. The IRS disputed these losses and assessed tax deficiencies of $300,000 and $200,000 for the two years in question. In March of the current year, Henry offered to resolve all issues relating to those two years by paying the IRS $250,000 or $125,000 for each year. In April of the current year, the Commissioner accepted Henry's offer without discussion or negotiation. Henry now finds that he has an NOL for last year. If he carries the NOL back to the two years for which he has reached a settlement with the IRS, the stipulated tax deficiency will be eliminated. Discuss whether Henry will be allowed to carry his NOL back to the two prior years for which he has reached a settlement.

Research Problem 3. Jeb Simmons operated an illegal gambling business out of his home. While executing a search warrant, the local sheriff seized gambling paraphernalia and $200,000 in cash. Subsequently, Jeb voluntarily consented to forfeit to the state the cash that had been seized in connection with the execution of the search warrant. Write a letter to Jeb advising him as to whether he can claim a loss under § 165 for the seized cash. Also, prepare a memo for the tax files. Jeb's address is 100 Honey Lane, Macon, GA 62108.

COMMUNICATIONS

Research Problem 4. In 2004, John Burns started a tax preparation service as a sole proprietorship. In 2006, he incorporated the business as Tax Services, Inc. (TSI). TSI issued both John and his wife Delores 1,000 shares of stock at $10 per share. John routinely paid cash for various TSI business expenses. John did not demand or receive repayment for any of the expenses he paid on behalf of TSI. John did, however, keep records to document these expenses. In 2011, John and Delores dissolved TSI. Discuss whether John is entitled to a business bad debt deduction for the expenses he paid on behalf of TSI.

Research Problem 5. In June of the current year, Bob attended a party at a friend's house. Because of the amount of alcohol Bob consumed at the party, he asked a friend to drive him home. Several hours after arriving home, Bob decided to drive to his parents' home. On the way there, he failed to negotiate a turn, and his car slid off the road and rolled. The car was extensively damaged from the rollover, but Bob was not severely injured. At the time of the accident, Bob's blood-alcohol level was slightly over the state legal limit. Hence, he was cited and arrested for driving under the influence of alcohol (DUI). Bob's automobile insurance carrier denied his loss claim in accordance with the terms of his policy because of his DUI citation and arrest. As a result of the accident, Bob's car suffered $35,000 of damages. Discuss whether Bob is entitled to a casualty loss deduction on his current year's tax return.

Use the tax resources of the Internet to address the following questions. Do not restrict your search to the Web, but include a review of newsgroups and general reference materials, practitioner sites and resources, primary sources of the tax law, chat rooms and discussion groups, and other opportunities.

INTERNET *activity*

Research Problem 6. Find a newspaper article that discusses tax planning for casualty losses when a disaster area designation is made. Does the article convey the pertinent tax rules correctly? Then list all of the locations identified by the President as Federal disaster areas in the last two years.

Research Problem 7. Scan several publications that are read by owners of small businesses. Some of the articles in these publications address tax-related issues such as how to structure a new business. Do these articles do an adequate job of conveying the benefits of issuing § 1244 small business stock? Prepare a short memo explaining the use of § 1244 stock and post it to a newsgroup that is frequented by inventors, engineers, and others involved in startup corporations.

COMMUNICATIONS

Depreciation, Cost Recovery, Amortization, and Depletion

LEARNING OBJECTIVES

After completing Chapter 8, you should be able to:

LO.1

Understand the rationale for the cost consumption concept and identify the relevant time periods for depreciation, ACRS, and MACRS.

LO.2

Determine the amount of cost recovery under MACRS.

LO.3

Recognize when and how to make the § 179 expensing election, calculate the amount of the deduction, and apply the effect of the election in making the MACRS calculation.

LO.4

Identify listed property and apply the deduction limitations on listed property and on luxury automobiles.

LO.5

Determine when and how to use the alternative depreciation system (ADS).

LO.6

Be aware of the major characteristics of ACRS.

LO.7

Identify intangible assets that are eligible for amortization and calculate the amount of the deduction.

LO.8

Determine the amount of depletion expense including being able to apply the alternative tax treatments for intangible drilling and development costs.

LO.9

Perform the reporting procedures for cost recovery.

LO.10

Identify tax planning opportunities for cost recovery, amortization, and depletion.

OUTLINE

 For the latest in changes to tax legislation, visit **www.cengage.com/taxation/swft**.

FRAMEWORK 1040:

Tax Formula for Individuals

This chapter covers the boldfaced portions of the Tax Formula for Individuals that was introduced in Figure 3.1 on p. 3-3. Below those portions are the sections of Form 1040 where the results are reported.

Income (broadly conceived)	$xx,xxx
Less: Exclusions	(x,xxx)
Gross income	$xx,xxx
Less: Deductions for adjusted gross income	**(x,xxx)**

FORM 1040 (P.1)

12	Business income or (loss). Attach Schedule C or C-EZ . . . .

Adjusted gross income	$xx,xxx
Less: The greater of total itemized deductions *or* the standard deduction	(x,xxx)
Personal and dependency exemptions	(x,xxx)
Taxable income	$xx,xxx
Tax on taxable income (see Tax Tables or Tax Rate Schedules)	$ x,xxx
Less: Tax credits (including income taxes withheld and prepaid)	(xxx)
Tax due (or refund)	$ xxx

THE BIG PICTURE   Tax Solutions for the Real World

CALCULATION OF DEPRECIATION EXPENSE AND TAX PLANNING

Dr. Cliff Payne purchases and places in service in his dental practice the following fixed assets during the current year:

Office furniture and fixtures	$ 70,000
Computers and peripheral equipment	67,085
Dental equipment	475,000

Using his financial reporting system, he concludes that the depreciation expense on Schedule C of Form 1040 is $91,298.

Office furniture and fixtures ($70,000 × 14.29%)	$10,003
Computers and peripheral equipment ($67,085 × 20%)	13,417
Dental equipment ($475,000 × 14.29%)	67,878
	$91,298

In addition, during the current year, Dr. Payne purchased another personal residence for $300,000 and converted his original residence to rental property. He also purchased a condo for $170,000 near his office that he is going to rent.

Has Dr. Payne correctly calculated the depreciation expense for his dental practice? Will he be able to deduct any depreciation expense for his rental properties? **Read the chapter and formulate your response.**

8.1 OVERVIEW

GENERAL

LO.1

Understand the rationale for the cost consumption concept and identify the relevant time periods for depreciation, ACRS, and MACRS.

The Internal Revenue Code provides for a deduction for the consumption of the cost of an asset through depreciation, cost recovery, amortization, or depletion. These deductions are applications of the recovery of capital doctrine (discussed in Chapter 4). The concept of depreciation is based on the premise that the asset acquired (or improvement made) benefits more than one accounting period. Otherwise, the expenditure is deducted in the year incurred—see Chapter 6 and the discussion of capitalization versus expense.

Congress completely overhauled the **depreciation** rules in 1981 tax legislation by creating the accelerated **cost recovery** system (ACRS). Substantial modifications were made to ACRS in 1986 tax legislation (MACRS). These changes to the depreciation rules and the time frames involved are noted in Concept Summary 8.1. A knowledge of all of the depreciation and cost recovery rules may be needed as Example 1 illustrates for cost recovery.

EXAMPLE 1

The Brown Company owns a building purchased in 1986 that has a 19-year cost recovery life. In 2011, the business purchased a computer. To compute the cost recovery for 2011, Brown used the ACRS rules for the building and the MACRS rules for the computer. For 2011, there would be no additional cost recovery for the building because the basis of the building at the beginning of 2011 would be $0. ■

The statutory changes that have taken place since 1980 have widened the gap that exists between the accounting and tax versions of depreciation. The tax rules that existed prior to 1981 were much more compatible with generally accepted accounting principles.

This chapter initially focuses on the MACRS rules.[1] Because they cover more recent property acquisitions (i.e., after 1986), their use is more widespread. The ACRS rules, however, are reviewed in Concept Summary 8.5 and briefly discussed on p. 8–22. The pre-1981 rules are covered in Appendix G. The chapter concludes with a discussion of the amortization of intangible property and startup expenditures and the depletion of natural resources.

Taxpayers may write off the cost of certain assets that are used in a trade or business or held for the production of income. A write-off may take the form of depreciation (or cost recovery), depletion, or amortization. Tangible assets, other than natural resources, are *depreciated*. Natural resources, such as oil, gas, coal, and timber, are *depleted*. Intangible assets, such as copyrights and patents, are *amortized*. Generally, no write-off is allowed for an asset that does not have a determinable useful life.

CONCEPTS RELATING TO DEPRECIATION

Nature of Property

Property includes both realty (real property) and personalty (personal property). Realty generally includes land and buildings permanently affixed to the land. Personalty is defined as any asset that is not realty.[2] Personalty includes furniture, machinery, equipment, and many other types of assets. Do not confuse personalty (or personal property) with *personal use* property. Personal use property is any property (realty or personalty) that is held for personal use rather than for use in a trade or business or an income-producing activity. Write-offs are not allowed for personal use assets.

In summary, both realty and personalty can be either business use/income-producing property or personal use property. Examples include a residence (realty that is personal use), an office building (realty that is business use), a dump truck (personalty

---

[1] § 168. The terms "depreciation" and "cost recovery" are used interchangeably in the text and in § 168.

[2] Refer to Chapter 1 for a further discussion.

CONCEPT SUMMARY 8.1

Depreciation and Cost Recovery: Relevant Time Periods

System	Date Property Is Placed in Service
Pre-1981 depreciation	Before January 1, 1981, and *certain* property placed in service after December 31, 1980.
Original accelerated cost recovery system (ACRS)	After December 31, 1980, and before January 1, 1987.
Modified accelerated cost recovery system (MACRS)	After December 31, 1986.

that is business use), and regular wearing apparel (personalty that is personal use). It is imperative that this distinction between the *classification* of an asset (realty or personalty) and the *use* to which the asset is put (business or personal) be understood.

Assets used in a trade or business or for the production of income are eligible for cost recovery if they are subject to wear and tear, decay or decline from natural causes, or obsolescence. Assets that do not decline in value on a predictable basis or that do not have a determinable useful life (e.g., land, stock, antiques) are not eligible for cost recovery.

Placed in Service Requirement

The key date for the commencement of depreciation is the date an asset is placed in service. This date, and not the purchase date of an asset, is the relevant date. This distinction is particularly important for an asset that is purchased near the end of the tax year, but not placed in service until after the beginning of the following tax year.

Cost Recovery Allowed or Allowable

The basis of cost recovery property must be reduced by the cost recovery allowed and by not less than the allowable amount. The *allowed* cost recovery is the cost recovery actually taken, whereas the *allowable* cost recovery is the amount that could have been taken under the applicable cost recovery method. If the taxpayer does not claim any cost recovery on property during a particular year, the basis of the property must still be reduced by the amount of cost recovery that should have been deducted (the allowable cost recovery).

EXAMPLE 2

On March 15, 2011, Jack purchased a copier, to use in his business, for $10,000. The copier is five-year property, and Jack elected to use the straight-line method of cost recovery. Jack made the election because the business was a new undertaking and Jack reasoned that in the first few years of the business, a large cost recovery deduction was not needed. Because the business was doing poorly, Jack did not even take any cost recovery deductions in years 3 and 4. In years 5 and 6, Jack took the proper amount of cost recovery. Therefore, the allowed cost recovery (cost recovery actually deducted) and the allowable cost recovery are as follows:

	Cost Recovery Allowed	Cost Recovery Allowable
Year 1	$1,000	$1,000
Year 2	2,000	2,000
Year 3	–0–	2,000
Year 4	–0–	2,000
Year 5	2,000	2,000
Year 6	1,000	1,000

If Jack sold the copier for $800 in year 7, he would recognize an $800 gain ($800 amount realized − $0 adjusted basis) because the adjusted basis of the copier is zero. ■

DEPRECIATION DEDUCTIONS NOT BEING TAKEN

Property investors in Townsville, Australia, are not taking $60 million to $90 million in tax depreciation benefits each year. These amounts are not being taken because taxpayers assume that depreciation can be taken only on new properties. The Australian Tax Office allows depreciation on older properties as well as on renovations or improvements completed after 1992.

Source: Adapted from Alexis Gillham, "Appreciate Value of Depreciation," *Townsville Bulletin*, June 16, 2010, p. 18.

Cost Recovery Basis for Personal Use Assets Converted to Business or Income-Producing Use

If personal use assets are converted to business or income-producing use, the basis for cost recovery and for loss is the *lower* of the adjusted basis or the fair market value at the time the property was converted. As a result of this lower-of-basis rule, losses that occurred while the property was personal use property will not be recognized for tax purposes through the cost recovery of the property.

EXAMPLE 3
THE BIG PICTURE

Return to the facts of *The Big Picture* p. 8-2. Five years ago Dr. Payne had purchased a personal residence for $250,000. In the current year, with the housing market down, Dr. Payne found a larger home that he acquired for his personal residence. Because of the downturn in the housing market, however, he was not able to sell his original residence and recover his purchase price of $250,000. The residence was appraised at $180,000. Instead of continuing to try to sell the original residence, Dr. Payne converted it to rental property. The basis for cost recovery of the rental property is $180,000 because the fair market value is less than the adjusted basis. The $70,000 decline in value is deemed to be personal (since it occurred while the property was held for personal use by Dr. Payne) and therefore nondeductible. ∎

8.2 MODIFIED ACCELERATED COST RECOVERY SYSTEM (MACRS)

Under the **modified accelerated cost recovery system (MACRS)**, the cost of an asset is recovered over a predetermined period that is generally shorter than the useful life of the asset or the period the asset is used to produce income. The MACRS rules were designed to encourage investment, improve productivity, and simplify the law and its administration.

MACRS provides separate cost recovery tables for realty (real property) and personalty (personal property). Write-offs are not available for land because it does not have a determinable useful life. Cost recovery allowances for real property, other than land, are based on recovery lives specified in the law. The IRS provides tables that specify cost recovery allowances for personalty and for realty.

LO.2

Determine the amount of cost recovery under MACRS.

PERSONALTY: RECOVERY PERIODS AND METHODS

Classification of Property

The general effect of TRA of 1986 was to lengthen asset lives compared with those used under ACRS. MACRS provides that the cost recovery basis of eligible personalty (and certain realty) is recovered over 3, 5, 7, 10, 15, or 20 years. Property is classified by recovery period under MACRS as follows (see Exhibit 8.1 for examples):[3]

---

[3]§ 168(e).

EXHIBIT 8.1	Cost Recovery Periods: MACRS Personalty

Class of Property	Examples
3-year	Tractor units for use over-the-road.
	Any horse that is not a racehorse and is more than 12 years old at the time it is placed in service.
	Any racehorse that is more than 2 years old at the time it is placed in service.
	Breeding hogs.
	Special tools used in the manufacturing of motor vehicles such as dies, fixtures, molds, and patterns.
5-year	Automobiles and taxis.
	Light and heavy general-purpose trucks.
	Buses.
	Trailers and trailer-mounted containers.
	Typewriters, calculators, and copiers.
	Computers and peripheral equipment.
	Breeding and dairy cattle.
	Rental appliances, furniture, carpets, etc.
7-year	Office furniture, fixtures, and equipment.
	Breeding and work horses.
	Agricultural machinery and equipment.
	Railroad track.
10-year	Vessels, barges, tugs, and similar water transportation equipment.
	Assets used for petroleum refining or for the manufacture of grain and grain mill products, sugar and sugar products, or vegetable oils and vegetable oil products.
	Single-purpose agricultural or horticultural structures.
15-year	Land improvements.
	Assets used for industrial steam and electric generation and/or distribution systems.
	Assets used in the manufacture of cement.
	Assets used in pipeline transportation.
	Electric utility nuclear production plant.
	Municipal wastewater treatment plant.
20-year	Farm buildings except single-purpose agricultural and horticultural structures.
	Gas utility distribution facilities.
	Water utilities.
	Municipal sewer.

3-year 200% class . . . . ADR midpoints of 4 years and less.[4] Excludes automobiles and light trucks. Includes racehorses more than 2 years old and other horses more than 12 years old.

5-year 200% class . . . . ADR midpoints of more than 4 years and less than 10 years, adding automobiles, light trucks, qualified technological equipment, renewable energy and biomass properties that are small power production facilities, research and experimentation property, semiconductor manufacturing equipment, and computer-based central office switching equipment.

[4] Rev. Proc. 87–56, 1987–2 C.B. 674 is the source for the ADR midpoint lives.

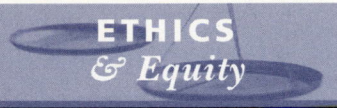

ETHICS
& Equity

CAPITALIZATION VERSUS EXPENSING

Joe Carter owns 15 apartment buildings. During the year, Joe replaced the carpeting in many of the apartments. Because the costs associated with replacing the carpeting are relatively small in comparison with the gross rents, Joe is considering expensing the costs as repairs and maintenance. Evaluate the appropriateness of Joe's plan.

7-year 200% class	ADR midpoints of 10 years and more and less than 16 years, adding property with no ADR midpoint not classified elsewhere. Includes railroad track and office furniture, fixtures, and equipment.
10-year 200% class	ADR midpoints of 16 years and more and less than 20 years, adding single-purpose agricultural or horticultural structures, any tree or vine bearing fruits or nuts.
15-year 150% class	ADR midpoints of 20 years and more and less than 25 years, including sewage treatment plants, and telephone distribution plants and comparable equipment used for the two-way exchange of voice and data communications.
20-year 150% class	ADR midpoints of 25 years and more, other than real property with an ADR midpoint of 27.5 years and more, and including sewer pipes.

Accelerated depreciation is allowed for these six MACRS classes of property. Two hundred percent declining-balance is used for the 3-, 5-, 7-, and 10-year classes, with a switchover to straight-line depreciation when it yields a larger amount. One hundred and fifty percent declining-balance is allowed for the 15- and 20-year classes, with an appropriate straight-line switchover.[5] The appropriate computation methods and conventions are built into the tables, so it is not necessary to calculate the appropriate percentages. To determine the amount of the cost recovery allowances, simply identify the asset by class and go to the appropriate table for the percentage. The MACRS percentages for personalty appear in Table 8.1 *(all tables are located at the end of the chapter prior to the problem materials).*

Taxpayers may *elect* the straight-line method to compute cost recovery allowances for each of these classes of property. Certain property is not eligible for accelerated cost recovery and must be depreciated under an alternative depreciation system (ADS). Both the straight-line election and ADS are discussed later in the chapter.

MACRS views property as placed in service in the middle of the first year (the **half-year convention**).[6] Thus, for example, the statutory recovery period for three-year property begins in the middle of the year an asset is placed in service and ends three years later. In practical terms, this means that taxpayers must wait an extra year to recover the cost of depreciable assets. That is, the actual write-off periods are 4, 6, 8, 11, 16, and 21 years. MACRS also allows for a half-year of cost recovery in the year of disposition or retirement.

EXAMPLE 4

Kareem acquires a five-year class asset on April 10, 2011, for $30,000. Kareem's cost recovery deduction for 2011 is $6,000, computed as follows:

MACRS cost recovery
  [$30,000 × .20 (Table 8.1)] $6,000   ■

EXAMPLE 5

Assume the same facts as in Example 4 and that Kareem disposes of the asset on March 5, 2013. Kareem's cost recovery deduction for 2013 is $2,880 [$30,000 × ½ × .192 (Table 8.1)]. ■

---

[5]§ 168(b).   [6]§ 168(d)(4)(A).

Additional First–Year Depreciation

The Economic Stimulus Act of 2008 provided for **additional first-year depreciation** on qualified property acquired after December 31, 2007, and before January 1, 2009, and placed in service before January 1, 2009. The American Recovery and Reinvestment Tax Act of 2009 extended additional first-year depreciation for an additional year (qualified property acquired and placed in service before January 1, 2010). The Small Business Jobs Act of 2010 extended additional first-year depreciation for one more year (qualified property acquired and placed in service before January 1, 2011). The provision allows for an additional 50 percent cost recovery in the year the asset is placed in service. The term *qualified property* includes most types of *new* property other than buildings. The term *new* means original or first use of the property. Property that is used but new to the taxpayer does not qualify.[7]

The Tax Relief Act of 2010 extends additional first-year depreciation for 2011 and increases the percentage from 50 percent to 100 percent. The act also extends additional first-year depreciation for 2012, but at the 50 percent rate. The effective date for 100 percent additional first-year depreciation is for qualified property placed in service after September 8, 2010 and before January 1, 2012. The effective date for 50 percent additional first-year depreciation is for qualified property placed in service after December 31, 2011 and before January 1, 2013.

The additional first-year depreciation is taken in the year in which the qualifying property is placed in service and may be claimed in addition to the otherwise available depreciation deduction. For property placed in service in 2011, the adjusted basis of the property after additional first-year depreciation is deducted is $0. So no standard cost recovery deduction under MACRS would be available. However, for property placed in service in 2012, after calculating the additional first-year depreciation, the standard cost recovery allowance under MACRS is calculated by multiplying the cost recovery basis (original cost recovery basis less additional first-year depreciation) by the percentage that reflects the applicable cost recovery method and the applicable cost recovery convention. A taxpayer may make an election to not take additional first-year depreciation.

Examples 6 and 7 reflect the tax treatment for 2011.

EXAMPLE 6

Morgan acquires and places in service a five-year class asset on March 20, for $50,000. Morgan's total cost recovery deduction depends on whether the asset was placed in service on March 20, 2011 or March 20, 2012 as indicated below.

March 20, 2011:

> Under additional first-year depreciation, $50,000 is deducted. So the total cost recovery is $50,000 and the adjusted basis is $0.

March 20, 2012:

50% additional first-year depreciation ($50,000 × .50)	$25,000
MACRS cost recovery [($50,000 − $25,000) × .20 (Table 8.1)]	5,000
Total cost recovery	$30,000

[7]§ 168(k).

EXAMPLE 7

Assume the same facts as in Example 6 and that Morgan disposes of the asset on October of the year following acquisition. Morgan's cost recovery deduction for the asset placed in service in 2011 (100% additional first-year depreciation was deducted in 2011) is $0. Morgan's cost recovery deduction for the asset placed in service in 2012 (50% additional first-year depreciation was deducted in 2011) is $2,400 [$25,000 × ½ × .192 (Table 8.1)]. ▪

Mid-Quarter Convention

If more than 40 percent of the value of property other than eligible real estate (see Realty: Recovery Periods and Methods for a discussion of eligible real estate) is placed in service during the last quarter of the year, a **mid-quarter convention** applies.[8] Under this convention, property acquisitions are grouped by the quarter they were acquired for cost recovery purposes. Acquisitions during the first quarter are allowed 10.5 months (three and one-half quarters) of cost recovery; the second quarter, 7.5 months (two and one-half quarters); the third quarter, 4.5 months (one and one-half quarters); and the fourth quarter, 1.5 months (one-half quarter). The percentages are shown in Table 8.2.

EXAMPLE 8

Silver Corporation acquires the following new five-year class property in 2011 and elects not to take additional first-year depreciation.

Property Acquisition Dates	Cost
February 15	$ 200,000
July 10	400,000
December 5	600,000
Total	$1,200,000

If Silver Corporation uses the statutory percentage method, the cost recovery allowances for the first two years are computed as indicated below. Since more than 40% ($600,000/$1,200,000 = 50%) of the acquisitions are in the last quarter, the mid-quarter convention applies.

2011

	Mid-Quarter Convention Depreciation	Total Depreciation
February 15	$200,000 × .35 (Table 8.2)	$ 70,000
July 10	$400,000 × .15	60,000
December 5	$600,000 × .05	30,000
		$160,000

2012

	Mid-Quarter Convention Depreciation	Total Depreciation
February 15	$200,000 × .26 (Table 8.2)	$ 52,000
July 10	$400,000 × .34	136,000
December 5	$600,000 × .38	228,000
		$416,000

▪

When property to which the mid-quarter convention applies is disposed of, the property is treated as though it were disposed of at the midpoint of the quarter. Hence, in the quarter of disposition, cost recovery is allowed for one-half of the quarter.

[8] § 168(d)(3).

CONCEPT SUMMARY 8.2

Statutory Percentage Method under MACRS

	Personal Property	Real Property*
Convention	Half-year or mid-quarter	Mid-month
Cost recovery deduction in the year of disposition	Half-year for year of disposition or half-quarter for quarter of disposition	Half-month for month of disposition

*Straight-line method must be used.

EXAMPLE 9

Assume the same facts as in Example 8, except that Silver Corporation sells the $400,000 asset on November 30 of 2012. The cost recovery allowance for 2012 is computed as follows:

February 15	$200,000 × .26 (Table 8.2)	$ 52,000
July 10	$400,000 × .34 × (3.5/4)	119,000
December 5	$600,000 × .38	228,000
Total		$399,000

REALTY: RECOVERY PERIODS AND METHODS

Under MACRS, the cost recovery period for residential rental real estate is 27.5 years, and the straight-line method is used for computing the cost recovery allowance. **Residential rental real estate** includes property where 80 percent or more of the gross rental revenues are from nontransient dwelling units (e.g., an apartment building). Hotels, motels, and similar establishments are not residential rental property. Low-income housing is classified as residential rental real estate. Nonresidential real estate has a recovery period of 39 years (31.5 years for such property placed in service before May 13, 1993) and is also depreciated using the straight-line method.[9]

Some items of real property are not treated as real estate for purposes of MACRS. For example, single-purpose agricultural structures are in the 10-year MACRS class. Land improvements are in the 15-year MACRS class.

All eligible real estate is depreciated using the **mid-month convention**.[10] Regardless of when during the month the property is placed in service, it is deemed to have been placed in service at the middle of the month. This allows for one-half month's cost recovery for the month the property is placed in service. If the property is disposed of before the end of the recovery period, one-half month's cost recovery is permitted for the month of disposition regardless of the specific date of disposition.

Cost recovery is computed by multiplying the applicable rate (Table 8.6) by the cost recovery basis.

EXAMPLE 10

Alec acquired a building on April 1, 1996, for $800,000. If the building is classified as residential rental real estate, the cost recovery deduction for 2011 is $29,088 (.03636 × $800,000). If the building is sold on October 7, 2011, the cost recovery deduction for 2011 is $23,028 [.03636 × (9.5/12) × $800,000]. (See Table 8.6 for percentage.) ∎

EXAMPLE 11

Jane acquired a building on March 2, 1993, for $1 million. If the building is classified as nonresidential real estate, the cost recovery deduction for 2011 is $31,750 (.03175 × $1,000,000). If the building is sold on January 5, 2011, the cost recovery deduction for 2011 is $1,323 [.03175 × (.5/12) × $1,000,000]. (See Table 8.6 for percentage.) ∎

---

[9]§§ 168(b), (c), and (e).   [10]§ 168(d)(1).

EXAMPLE 12

Mark acquired a building on November 19, 2011, for $1.2 million. If the building is classified as nonresidential real estate, the cost recovery deduction for 2011 is $3,852 [.00321 × $1,200,000 (Table 8.6)]. The cost recovery deduction for 2012 is $30,768 [.02564 × $1,200,000 (Table 8.6)]. If the building is sold on May 21, 2012, the cost recovery deduction for 2012 is $11,538 [.02564 × (4.5/12) × $1,200,000 (Table 8.6)]. ∎

STRAIGHT-LINE ELECTION

Although MACRS requires straight-line depreciation for all eligible real estate as previously discussed, the taxpayer may *elect* to use the straight-line method for personal property.[11] The property is depreciated using the class life (recovery period) of the asset with a half-year convention or a mid-quarter convention, whichever is applicable. The election is available on a class-by-class and year-by-year basis. The percentages for the straight-line election with a half-year convention appear in Table 8.3.

EXAMPLE 13

Terry acquires a new 10-year class asset on August 4, 2011, for $100,000. He elects the straight-line method of cost recovery. Terry's cost recovery deduction for 2011 is $5,000 ($100,000 × .050). His cost recovery deduction for 2012 is $10,000 ($100,000 × .100). (See Table 8.3 for percentages.) ∎

EXAMPLE 14

Assume the same facts as in Example 13, except that Terry sells the asset on November 21, 2012. His cost recovery deduction for 2012 is $5,000 [$100,000 × .100 × (½) (Table 8.3)]. ∎

FARM PROPERTY

When tangible personal property is used in a farming business, generally the cost of the asset is recovered under MACRS using the 150 percent declining-balance method.[12] However, the MACRS straight-line method is required for any tree or vine bearing fruits or nuts.[13] The cost of real property used in the farming business is recovered over the normal periods (27.5 years and 39 years) using the straight-line method. A farming business is defined as the trade or business of farming, which includes operating a nursery or sod farm and the raising or harvesting of trees bearing fruit, nuts, or other crops, or ornamental trees.[14] The applicable cost recovery method is also affected if the taxpayer elects to not have the uniform capitalization rules apply to the farming business.[15] Under the uniform capitalization rules, the costs of property produced or acquired for resale must be capitalized. When this election is made, the cost recovery method required is the alternative depreciation system (ADS) straight-line method (discussed further later in the chapter). This method must be applied to all assets placed in service in any taxable year during which the election is in effect. Even though this election is made and the straight-line method must be used, it does not prevent the taxpayer from electing to expense personalty under § 179.[16] Exhibit 8.2 shows examples of cost recovery periods for farming assets.

EXAMPLE 15

James purchased new farm equipment on July 10, 2011, for $80,000. If James does not elect to expense any of the cost under § 179, his cost recovery deduction for 2011 is $8,568 [(.1071 × $80,000) (Table 8.4)]. ∎

EXAMPLE 16

Assume the same facts as in Example 15, except that James has made an election to not have the uniform capitalization rules apply. His 2011 cost recovery deduction is $4,000 [(.05 × $80,000)(Table 8.5)]. ∎

---

[11]§ 168(b)(5).

[12]§ 168(b)(2)(B).

[13]§§ 168(b)(3)(E) and 168(e)(3)(D)(ii).

[14]§ 263A(e)(4).

[15]§ 263A(d)(3)(A).

[16]Reg. § 1.263A–4(d)(4)(ii).

EXHIBIT 8.2	Cost Recovery Periods for Farming Assets		
		Recovery Period in Years	
Assets		**MACRS**	**ADS**
Agricultural structures (single purpose)		10	15
Cattle (dairy or breeding)		5	7
Farm buildings		20	25
Farm machinery and equipment		7	10
Fences (agricultural)		7	10
Horticultural structures (single purpose)		10	15
Trees or vines bearing fruit or nuts		10	20
Truck (heavy duty, unloaded weight 13,000 pounds or more)		5	6
Truck (actual weight less than 13,000 pounds)		5	5

LEASEHOLD IMPROVEMENT PROPERTY

When the lessor is the owner of leasehold improvement property, the cost recovery period is the statutorily prescribed life. The recovery period for residential rental real estate is 27.5 years, and the recovery period for nonresidential real estate is 39 years. For these real property leasehold improvements, the straight-line method is used. If the improvement is tangible personal property, the shorter MACRS lives and accelerated methods are used.

When lessor-owned leasehold improvements are disposed of or abandoned by the lessor because of the termination of the lease, the property will be treated as disposed of by the lessor, and hence, a loss can be taken for the unrecovered basis.[17]

EXAMPLE 17

On April 7, 2011, Mary signed a 10-year lease with John on a building to be used for her business. The lease period begins on May 1, 2011, and ends on April 30, 2021. Prior to the signing of the lease, John paid $300,000 to have a unique storefront added to the building. John's cost recovery deduction for 2011 for the addition is $4,815 [(.01605 × $300,000) (Table 8.6)]. ∎

EXAMPLE 18

Assume the same facts as in Example 17. John's cost recovery deduction for 2021 is $2,244 {[.02564 × (3.5/12) × $300,000] (Table 8.6)}. At the end of the lease, John has to remove the unique storefront, so he can lease the building to other tenants. John's loss as a result of the termination of the lease and the removal of the unique storefront is $223,713 computed as follows:

Cost	$300,000
Less: Cost recovery	
2011 (Example 17)	(4,815)
2012–2020 (.02564 × $300,000 × 9 years)	(69,228)
2021	(2,244)
Loss (unrecovered cost)	$223,713

∎

The costs of leasehold improvements made to leased property and owned by the lessee are recovered in accordance with the general cost recovery rules. This means that the cost recovery period is determined without regard to the lease term. Any unrecovered basis in the leasehold improvement property not retained by the lessee is deducted in the year the lease is terminated.

The Tax Relief Act of 2010 extends 15-year straight-line cost recovery for *qualified* leasehold improvement property. The Act also allows for 100 percent additional

---

[17]§ 163(i)(8)(B).

first-year depreciation for a qualified leasehold improvement to an interior portion of a building which is nonresidential real property. The improvement must be made under or pursuant to a lease by the lessee or lessor and placed in service more than 3 years after the date the building was first placed in service.

ELECTION TO EXPENSE ASSETS

Section 179 (Election to Expense Certain Depreciable Business Assets) permits the taxpayer to elect to write off up to $500,000 in 2010 and 2011) of the acquisition cost of *tangible personal property* used in a trade or business. Amounts that are expensed under § 179 may not be capitalized and depreciated. The **§ 179 expensing** election is an annual election and applies to the acquisition cost of property placed in service that year. The immediate expense election generally is not available for real property or for property used for the production of income.[18]

In addition, any elected § 179 expense is taken *before* additional first-year depreciation is computed. The base for calculating the standard MACRS deduction is net of the § 179 expense and the additional first-year depreciation (100 percent for assets placed in service in 2011 and 50 percent for assets placed in service in 2012).

> **LO.3**
>
> Recognize when and how to make the § 179 expensing election, calculate the amount of the deduction, and apply the effect of the election in making the MACRS calculation.

EXAMPLE 19

Kelly acquires machinery (five-year class asset) on February 1, 2011, at a cost of $525,000 and elects to expense $500,000 under § 179. Kelley takes the statutory percentage cost recovery (see Table 8.1 for percentage) for 2011. As a result, the total deduction for the year is calculated as follows:

§ 179 expense	$500,000
100% additional first-year depreciation [($525,000 − $500,000) × 100%]	$ 25,000
Standard MACRS calculation [($525,000 − $500,000 − $25,000) × 20%]	–0–
	$525,000 ∎

Annual Limitations

Two additional limitations apply to the amount deductible under § 179. First, the ceiling amount on the deduction is reduced dollar-for-dollar when § 179 property placed in service during the taxable year exceeds $2 million in 2010 and 2011. Second, the amount expensed under § 179 cannot exceed the aggregate amount of taxable income derived from the conduct of any trade or business by the taxpayer. Taxable income of a trade or business is computed without regard to the amount expensed under § 179. Any § 179 expensed amount in excess of taxable income is carried forward to future taxable years and added to other amounts eligible for expensing. The § 179 amount eligible for expensing in a carryforward year is limited to the *lesser* of (1) the statutory dollar amount ($500,000 in 2011) reduced by the cost of § 179 property placed in service in excess of $2 million in the carryforward year or (2) the business income limitation in the carryforward year.

EXAMPLE 20

Jill owns a computer service and operates it as a sole proprietorship. In 2011, she will net $80,000 before considering any § 179 deduction. If Jill spends $2.3 million on new equipment, her § 179 expense deduction is computed as follows:

§ 179 deduction before adjustment	$500,000
Less: Dollar limitation reduction ($2,300,000 − $2,000,000)	(300,000)
Remaining § 179 deduction	$200,000
Business income limitation	$ 80,000
§ 179 deduction allowed	$ 80,000
§ 179 deduction carryforward ($200,000 − $80,000)	$120,000 ∎

---

[18]The § 179 amount allowed is per taxpayer, per year. On a joint return, the statutory amount applies to the couple. If the taxpayers are married and file separate returns, each spouse is eligible for 50% of the statutory amount.

CONCEPT SUMMARY 8.3

Straight-Line Election under MACRS

	Personal Property	Real Property*
Convention	Half-year or mid-quarter	Mid-month
Cost recovery deduction in the year of disposition	Half-year for year of disposition or half-quarter for quarter of disposition	Half-month for month of disposition
Elective or mandatory	Elective	Mandatory
Breadth of election	Class by class	

*Straight-line method must be used.

The Small Business Jobs Act of 2010 expands the definition of property qualifying for § 179 to include certain real property.[19] The real property included is qualified leasehold improvement property, qualified restaurant property, and qualified retail improvement property. The maximum amount of qualified real property that may be expensed is $250,000. In addition, § 179 deductions in 2011 attributable to qualified real property that are disallowed under the trade or business income limitation may not be carried over to 2012. Any amounts that are not used in 2011 are treated as property placed in service in 2011 for purposes of computing cost recovery. If a taxpayer does not elect to include qualified real property as § 179 property, then it is excluded from the definition of § 179 property.

EXAMPLE 21

During 2011, Green Corporation purchased § 179 equipment costing $200,000 and qualifying leasehold improvement property costing $350,000. Green has no other asset purchases during 2011 and is not subject to the taxable income limitation. The maximum § 179 deduction Green can claim for 2011 is $450,000 ($200,000 with respect to the equipment and $250,000 with respect to the qualifying leasehold improvements). ∎

EXAMPLE 22

During 2011, Red Corporation purchased and placed in service $1.9 million of § 179 equipment and $200,000 of qualifying leasehold improvement property. If Red elects to treat the qualified leasehold improvement property as § 179 property, the § 179 deduction is limited to $400,000 [$500,000 − ($2,100,000 − $2,000,000)]. If Red does not elect to treat the qualifying leasehold improvement property as § 179 property, the § 179 deduction will be $500,000. ∎

Effect on Basis

The basis of the property for cost recovery purposes is reduced by the § 179 amount after it is adjusted for property placed in service in excess of $2 million. This adjusted amount does not reflect any business income limitation.

EXAMPLE 23

Assume the same facts as in Example 20 and that the new equipment is five-year class property. Jill elects not to take additional first-year depreciation. After considering the § 179 deduction, Jill's cost recovery deduction for 2011 (see Table 8.1 for percentage) is calculated as follows:

Standard MACRS calculation
[($2,300,000 − $200,000) × .20]   <u>$420,000</u> ∎

---

[19]Section 179 property includes qualified real property only if an election is made to treat the qualified real property as § 179 property.

FINANCIAL DISCLOSURE *Insights*

TAX AND BOOK DEPRECIATION

A common book-tax difference relates to the depreciation amounts that are reported for GAAP and Federal income tax purposes. Typically, tax depreciation deductions are accelerated; that is, they are claimed in earlier reporting periods than is the case for financial accounting purposes. Almost every tax law change since 1980 has included depreciation provisions that accelerate the related deductions relative to the expenses allowed under GAAP. Accelerated cost recovery deductions represent a means by which the

taxing jurisdiction infuses the business with cash flow created by the reduction in the year's tax liabilities.

For instance, recently about one-quarter of General Electric's deferred tax liabilities related to depreciation differences. For Toyota's and Ford's depreciation differences, that amount was about one-third. And for the trucking firm Ryder Systems, depreciation differences accounted for all but 1 percent of the deferred tax liabilities.

Conversion to Personal Use

Conversion of the expensed property to personal use at any time results in recapture income (see Chapter 17). A property is converted to personal use if it is not used predominantly in a trade or business. Regulations provide for the mechanics of the recapture.[20]

BUSINESS AND PERSONAL USE OF AUTOMOBILES AND OTHER LISTED PROPERTY

Limits exist on MACRS deductions for automobiles and other listed property that are used for both personal and business purposes.[21] If the listed property is *predominantly used* for business, the taxpayer is allowed to use the *statutory percentage method* to recover the cost. In cases where the property is *not predominantly used* for business, the cost is recovered using the *straight-line method*.

Listed property includes the following:

- Any passenger automobile.
- Any other property used as a means of transportation.
- Any property of a type generally used for purposes of entertainment, recreation, or amusement.
- Any computer or peripheral equipment, with the exception of equipment used exclusively at a regular business establishment, including a qualifying home office.
- Any other property specified in the Regulations.

> **LO.4**
> Identify listed property and apply the deduction limitations on listed property and on luxury automobiles.

Automobiles and Other Listed Property Used Predominantly in Business

For listed property to be considered as *predominantly used in business*, its *business usage* must exceed 50 percent.[22] The use of listed property for production of income does not qualify as business use for purposes of the more-than-50 percent test. However, both production of income and business use percentages are used to compute the cost recovery deduction.

EXAMPLE 24

On September 1, 2011, Emma places in service listed five-year recovery property. The property cost $10,000. She elects not to take additional first-year depreciation. If Emma uses the property 40% for business and 25% for the production of income, the property is not considered as predominantly used for business. The cost is recovered using straight-line cost recovery. Emma's cost recovery allowance for the year is $650 ($10,000 × 10% × 65%). If, however, Emma uses the property 60% for business and 25% for the production of income, the property is considered as used predominantly for business. Therefore, she may use the statutory percentage method. Emma's cost recovery allowance for the year is $1,700 ($10,000 × .200 × 85%). ■

---

[20]Reg. § 1.179–1(e).

[21]§ 280F.

[22]§ 280F(b)(3).

The method for determining the percentage of business usage for listed property is specified in the Regulations. The Regulations provide that for automobiles a mileage-based percentage is to be used. Other listed property is to use the most appropriate unit of time (e.g., hours) the property is actually used (rather than available for use).[23]

Limits on Cost Recovery for Automobiles

The law places special limitations on the cost recovery deduction for passenger automobiles. These statutory dollar limits were imposed on passenger automobiles because of the belief that the tax system was being used to underwrite automobiles whose cost and luxury far exceeded what was needed for their business use.

A *passenger automobile* is any four-wheeled vehicle manufactured for use on public streets, roads, and highways with an unloaded gross vehicle weight (GVW) rating of 6,000 pounds or less.[24] This definition specifically excludes vehicles used directly in the business of transporting people or property for compensation such as taxicabs, ambulances, hearses, and trucks and vans as prescribed by the Regulations.

The following limits apply to the cost recovery deductions for passenger automobiles for 2010:[25]

Year	Recovery Limitation*
1	$3,060
2	4,900
3	2,950
Succeeding years until the cost is recovered	1,775

* The indexed amounts for 2011 were not available at the time of this writing.

For an automobile placed in service in 2009, the limitation for subsequent years' cost recovery will be based on the limits for the year the automobile was placed in service. Hence, the limit for the third year's cost recovery for an automobile placed in service in 2009 is $2,850 and not a limit published in 2011.[26]

In the event that a passenger automobile used predominantly for business qualifies for additional first-year depreciation (i.e., new property), the first-year recovery limitation is increased by $8,000. Therefore, for acquisitions made in 2011, the initial-year cost recovery limitation increases from $3,060 to $11,060 ($3,060 + $8,000).

There are also separate cost recovery limitations for trucks and vans and for electric automobiles. Because these limitations are applied in the same manner as those imposed on passenger automobiles, these additional limitations are not discussed further in this chapter.

---

[23]Reg. § 1.280F–6T(e).

[24]§ 280F(d)(5).

[25]§ 280F(a)(1). Since the 2011 indexed amounts were not available at the time of this writing, the 2010 amounts are used in the Examples and in the Problem Materials.

[26]Cost recovery limitations for prior years can be found in IRS Publication 463.

The limits are imposed before any percentage reduction for personal use. In addition, the limitation in the first year includes any amount the taxpayer elects to expense under § 179.[27] If the passenger automobile is used partly for personal use, the personal use percentage is ignored for the purpose of determining the unrecovered cost available for deduction in later years.

EXAMPLE 25

On July 1, 2011, Dan places in service a new automobile that cost $40,000. He does not elect § 179 expensing. The car is always used 80% for business and 20% for personal. Dan chooses the MACRS 200% declining-balance method of cost recovery (see the 5-year column in Table 8.1). The depreciation computation for 2011–2016 is summarized below if Dan elects not to take additional first-year depreciation.

Year	MACRS Amount	Recovery Limitation	Depreciation Allowed
2011	$6,400 ($40,000 × 20% × 80%)	$2,448 ($3,060 × 80%)	$2,448
2012	$10,240 ($40,000 × 32% × 80%)	$3,920 ($4,900 × 80%)	$3,920
2013	$6,144 ($40,000 × 19.2% × 80%)	$2,360 ($2,950 × 80%)	$2,360
2014	$3,686 ($40,000 × 11.52% × 80%)	$1,420 ($1,775 × 80%)	$1,420
2015	$3,686 ($40,000 × 11.52% × 80%)	$1,420 ($1,775 × 80%)	$1,420
2016	$1,843 ($40,000 × 5.76% × 80%)	$1,420 ($1,775 × 80%)	$1,420

The cost recovery allowed is the lesser of the MACRS amount or the recovery limitation. If Dan continues to use the car after 2016, his cost recovery is limited to the lesser of the recoverable basis or the recovery limitation (i.e., $1,775 × business use percentage). For this purpose, the recoverable basis is computed as if the full recovery limitation was allowed even if it was not. Thus, the recoverable basis as of January 1, 2017, is $23,765 ($40,000 − $3,060 − $4,900 − $2,950 − $1,775 − $1,775 − $1,775). ■

If Dan takes additional first-year depreciation, the calculated amount of additional first-year depreciation is $32,000 ($40,000 × 100% × 80%). However, the recovery limitation in 2011 would be $8,848 [($8,000 + $3,060) × 80%].

The cost recovery limitations are maximum amounts. If the regular calculation produces a lesser amount of cost recovery, the lesser amount is used.

EXAMPLE 26

On April 2, 2011, Gail places in service a used automobile that cost $10,000. The car is always used 70% for business and 30% for personal use. Therefore, the cost recovery allowance for 2011 is $1,400 ($10,000 × 20% × 70%), which is less than $2,142 ($3,060 × 70%). ■

Note that the cost recovery limitations apply *only* to passenger automobiles and not to other listed property.

Special Limitation

The American Jobs Creation Act of 2004 (AJCA) placed a limit of $25,000 on the § 179 deduction for certain vehicles not subject to the statutory dollar limits on cost recovery deductions that are imposed on passenger automobiles. The limit applies

---

[27]§ 280F(d)(1).

to sport utility vehicles (SUVs) with an unloaded GVW rating of more than 6,000 pounds and not more than 14,000 pounds.[28]

EXAMPLE 27

During 2011, Jay acquires and places in service an SUV that cost $70,000 and has a GVW of 8,000 pounds. Jay uses the vehicle 100% of the time for business use. The total deduction for 2011 with respect to the SUV is $70,000, computed as follows:

§ 179 expense	$25,000
100% additional first-year depreciation [($70,000 − $25,000) × 100%]	45,000
Standard MACRS calculation [($70,000 − $25,000 − $45,000) × .20 (Table 8.1)]	–0–
	$70,000 ∎

Automobiles and Other Listed Property Not Used Predominantly in Business

The cost of listed property that does not pass the more-than-50 percent business usage test in the year the property is placed in service must be recovered using the straight-line method.[29] In addition, such property does not qualify for additional first-year depreciation. The straight-line method to be used is that required under the alternative depreciation system (explained later in the chapter). This system requires a straight-line recovery period of five years for automobiles. However, even though the straight-line method is used, the cost recovery allowance for passenger automobiles cannot exceed the dollar limitations.

EXAMPLE 28

On July 27, 2011, Fred places in service an automobile that cost $20,000. The auto is used 40% for business and 60% for personal use. The cost recovery allowance for 2011 is $800 [$20,000 × 10% (Table 8.5) × 40%]. ∎

EXAMPLE 29

Assume the same facts as in Example 28, except that the automobile cost $50,000. The cost recovery allowance for 2011 is $1,224 [$50,000 × 10% (Table 8.5) = $5,000 (limited to $3,060) × 40%]. ∎

If the listed property fails the more-than-50 percent business usage test, the straight-line method must be used for the remainder of the property's life. This applies even if at some later date the business usage of the property increases to more than 50 percent. Even though the straight-line method must continue to be used, however, the amount of cost recovery will reflect the increase in business usage.

EXAMPLE 30

Assume the same facts as in Example 28, except that in 2012, Fred uses the automobile 70% for business and 30% for personal use. Fred's cost recovery allowance for 2012 is $2,800 [$20,000 × 20% (Table 8.5) × 70%], which is less than 70% of the second-year limit. ∎

Change from Predominantly Business Use

If the business use percentage of listed property falls to 50 percent or lower after the year the property is placed in service, the property is subject to *cost recovery recapture*. The amount required to be recaptured and included in the taxpayer's return as ordinary income is the excess cost recovery.

Excess cost recovery is the excess of the cost recovery deduction taken in prior years using the statutory percentage method over the amount that would have been allowed if the straight-line method had been used since the property was placed in service.[30]

---

[28]§ 179(b)(6).
[29]§ 280F(b)(1).

[30]§ 280F(b)(2).

EXAMPLE 31

Seth purchased a new car on January 22, 2011, at a cost of $20,000. Business usage was 80% in 2011, 70% in 2012, 40% in 2013, and 60% in 2014. Seth elects not to take additional first-year depreciation. Seth's excess cost recovery to be recaptured as ordinary income in 2013 is computed as follows:

2011

MACRS [($20,000 × .20 × .80) (limited to $3,060 × .80)]	$ 2,448
Straight-line [($20,000 × .10 × .80) (limited to $3,060 × .80)]	(1,600)
Excess	$ 848

2012

MACRS [($20,000 × .32 × .70) (limited to $4,900 × .70)]	$ 3,430
Straight-line [($20,000 × .20 × .70) (limited to $4,900 × .70)]	(2,800)
Excess	$ 630

2013

2011 excess	$ 848
2012 excess	630
Ordinary income recapture	$ 1,478

■

After the business usage of the listed property drops below the more-than-50 percent level, the straight-line method must be used for the remaining life of the property.

EXAMPLE 32

Assume the same facts as in Example 31. Seth's cost recovery allowance for the years 2013 and 2014 would be $1,180 and $1,065, computed as follows:

2013—$1,180	[($20,000 × 20% × .40) limited to $2,950 × 40%]
2014—$1,065	[($20,000 × 20% × .60) limited to $1,775 × 60%]

■

Leased Automobiles

A taxpayer who leases a passenger automobile must report an *inclusion amount* in gross income. The inclusion amount is computed from an IRS table for each taxable year for which the taxpayer leases the automobile. The purpose of this provision is to prevent taxpayers from circumventing the cost recovery dollar limitations by leasing, instead of purchasing, an automobile.

The dollar amount of the inclusion is based on the fair market value of the automobile and is prorated for the number of days the auto is used during the taxable year. The prorated dollar amount is then multiplied by the business and income-producing usage percentage to determine the amount to be included in gross income.[31] The

[31]Reg. § 1.280F–7(a).

CONCEPT SUMMARY   8.4

Listed Property Cost Recovery

Legend to Tax Treatment

A   Straight-line cost recovery reduced by the personal use percentage.

B   Straight-line cost recovery subject to the recovery limitations ($3,060, $4,900, $2,950, $1,775) and reduced by the personal use percentage.

C   Statutory percentage cost recovery reduced by the personal use percentage.

D   Statutory percentage cost recovery subject to the recovery limitations ($3,060, $4,900, $2,950, $1,775) and reduced by the personal use percentage.

---

taxpayer deducts the lease payments, multiplied by the business and income-producing usage percentage. The net effect is that the annual deduction for the lease payment is reduced by the inclusion amount.

EXAMPLE 33

On April 1, 2011, Jim leases and places in service a passenger automobile worth $40,000. The lease is to be for a period of five years. During the taxable years 2011 and 2012, Jim uses the automobile 70% for business and 30% for personal use. Assuming the dollar amounts from the IRS table for 2011 and 2012 are $50 and $109, Jim must include $26 in gross income for 2011 and $76 for 2012, computed as follows:

2011	$50 × (275/365) × 70% = $26
2012	$109 × (366/366) × 70% = $76

In addition, Jim can deduct 70% of the lease payments each year because this is the business use percentage. ∎

Substantiation Requirements

Listed property is now subject to the substantiation requirements of § 274. This means that the taxpayer must prove the business usage as to the amount of expense or use, the time and place of use, the business purpose for the use, and the business relationship to the taxpayer of persons using the property. Substantiation requires adequate records or sufficient evidence corroborating the taxpayer's statement. However, these substantiation requirements do not apply to vehicles that, by reason of their nature, are not likely to be used more than a *de minimis* amount for personal purposes.[32]

---

[32]§§ 274(d) and (i).

ALTERNATIVE DEPRECIATION SYSTEM (ADS)

The **alternative depreciation system (ADS)** must be used for the following:[33]

LO.5

Determine when and how to use the alternative depreciation system (ADS).

- To calculate the portion of depreciation treated as an alternative minimum tax (AMT) adjustment for purposes of the corporate and individual AMT (see Chapters 12 and 20).[34]
- To compute depreciation allowances for property for which any of the following is true:
  - *Used predominantly outside the United States.*
  - *Leased or otherwise used by a tax-exempt entity.*
  - *Financed with the proceeds of tax-exempt bonds.*
  - *Imported from foreign countries that maintain discriminatory trade practices or otherwise engage in discriminatory acts.*
- To compute depreciation allowances for earnings and profits purposes (see Chapter 20).

In general, ADS depreciation is computed using straight-line recovery without regard to salvage value. However, for purposes of the AMT, depreciation of personal property is computed using the 150 percent declining-balance method with an appropriate switch to the straight-line method.

The taxpayer must use the half-year or the mid-quarter convention, whichever is applicable, for all property other than eligible real estate. The mid-month convention is used for eligible real estate. The applicable ADS rates are found in Tables 8.4, 8.5, and 8.7.

The recovery periods under ADS are as follows:[35]

- The ADR midpoint life for property that does not fall into any of the following listed categories.
- Five years for qualified technological equipment, automobiles, and light-duty trucks.
- Twelve years for personal property with no class life.
- Forty years for all residential rental property and all nonresidential real property.

Taxpayers may *elect* to use the 150 percent declining-balance method to compute the regular income tax rather than the 200 percent declining-balance method that is available for personal property. Hence, if the election is made, there will be no difference between the cost recovery for computing the regular income tax and the AMT.[36]

EXAMPLE 34

On March 1, 2011, Abby purchases computer-based telephone central office switching equipment for $80,000. Abby elects not to take additional first-year depreciation. If Abby uses statutory percentage cost recovery (assuming no § 179 election), the cost recovery allowance for 2011 is $16,000 [$80,000 × 20% (Table 8.1, five-year class property)]. If Abby elects to use ADS 150% declining-balance cost recovery for the regular income tax (assuming no § 179 election), the cost recovery allowance for 2011 is $12,000 [$80,000 × 15% (Table 8.4, five-year class property)]. ∎

In lieu of depreciation under the regular MACRS method, taxpayers may *elect* straight-line under ADS for property that qualifies for the regular MACRS method. The election is available on a class-by-class and year-by-year basis for property other than eligible real estate. The election for eligible real estate is on a property-by-property

---

[33]§ 168(g).

[34]This AMT adjustment applies for real and personal property placed in service before January 1, 1999. However, it will continue to apply for personal property placed in service after December 31, 1998, if the taxpayer uses the 200% declining-balance method for regular income tax purposes. See Chapter 12.

[35]The class life for certain properties described in § 168(e)(3) is specially determined under § 168(g)(3)(B).

[36]For personal property placed in service before January 1, 1999, taxpayers making the election are required to use the ADS recovery periods in computing cost recovery for the regular income tax. The ADS recovery periods generally are longer than the regular recovery periods under MACRS.

CONCEPT SUMMARY 8.5

Characteristics of ACRS

Property	Accounting Convention	Life	Method
Personalty	Half-year or mid-quarter	3, 5, 7, 10, 15, or 20 years	Accelerated or straight-line
Realty	Mid-month	15, 18, or 19 years	Accelerated or straight-line

basis. One reason for making this election is to avoid a difference between deductible depreciation and earnings and profits depreciation.

EXAMPLE 35

Polly acquires an apartment building on March 17, 2011, for $700,000. She takes the maximum cost recovery allowance for determining taxable income. Polly's cost recovery allowance for computing 2011 taxable income is $20,153 [$700,000 × .02879 (Table 8.6)]. However, Polly's cost recovery for computing her earnings and profits is only $13,853 [$700,000 × .01979 (Table 8.7)]. ■

8.3 ACCELERATED COST RECOVERY SYSTEM (ACRS)

LO.6

Be aware of the major characteristics of ACRS.

The major characteristics of the **accelerated cost recovery system (ACRS)** are listed in Concept Summary 8.5. Note that for personalty, except for 20-year property, the recovery period expired (all of the cost recovery basis has been recovered) prior to 2005. For 20-year property, the recovery period expired during 2005. For realty, the recovery period also expired during 2005.

8.4 AMORTIZATION

LO.7

Identify intangible assets that are eligible for amortization and calculate the amount of the deduction.

Taxpayers can claim an **amortization** deduction on intangible assets called "amortizable § 197 intangibles." The amount of the deduction is determined by amortizing the adjusted basis of such intangibles ratably over a 15-year period beginning in the month in which the intangible is acquired.[37]

An *amortizable § 197 intangible* is any § 197 intangible acquired after August 10, 1993, and held in connection with the conduct of a trade or business or for the production of income. Section 197 intangibles include goodwill and going-concern value, franchises, trademarks, and trade names. Covenants not to compete, copyrights, and patents are also included if they are acquired in connection with the acquisition of a business. Generally, self-created intangibles are not § 197 intangibles. The 15-year amortization period applies regardless of the actual useful life of an amortizable § 197 intangible. No other depreciation or amortization deduction is permitted with respect to any amortizable § 197 intangible except those permitted under the 15-year amortization rules.

EXAMPLE 36

On June 1, 2011, Neil purchased and began operating the Falcon Café. Of the purchase price, $90,000 is correctly allocated to goodwill. The deduction for amortization for 2011 is $3,500 [($90,000/15) × (7/12)]. ■

[37]§ 197(a).

TAX in the NEWS

AMORTIZING A FRANCHISE

Tom Ricketts has made an offer to purchase the Chicago Cubs for $845 million from the Tribune Company. The deal makes sense for Ricketts because the tax breaks will enable him to save $100 million. Section 197 of the Internal Revenue Code allows the cost of a franchise to be amortized over 15 years. Dividing the $845 million purchase price by 15 years produces a $56.3 million deduction against income each year for the next 15 years. If the projected income for the Cubs is about $45 million a year, the $56 million would shelter all of the income and no tax would be due.

Source: Adapted from Josh Peter, "Buying Cubs Could Be a Steal for Ricketts," *Yahoo! Sports,* September 16, 2010.

ETHICS & Equity

ALLOCATION OF PURCHASE PRICE TO COVENANT NOT TO COMPETE

Red Corporation and Bernie Jones, an officer of the corporation, signed an agreement that called for $400,000 to be paid to Bernie for the redemption of his stock in Red Corporation and for a covenant not to compete. When Bernie and the corporation negotiated the agreement, neither side called for the $400,000 to be allocated between the stock and the covenant not to compete. The agreement itself specifically stated that the amount to be paid was for the purchase of Bernie's stock. Nothing in the agreement allocated a portion of the payment to the covenant not to compete. Now that the transaction has been completed, Red Corporation is considering unilaterally allocating a portion of the payment to the covenant not to compete so that the allocated amount can be capitalized and amortized under § 197. Evaluate the appropriateness of Red Corporation's plan.

Startup expenditures are also partially amortizable under § 195. This treatment is available only by election.[38] A taxpayer must make this election no later than the time prescribed by law for filing the return for the taxable year in which the trade or business begins.[39] If no election is made, the startup expenditures must be capitalized.[40]

The elective treatment for startup expenditures allows the taxpayer to deduct the lesser of (1) the amount of startup expenditures with respect to the trade or business or (2) $5,000, reduced, but not below zero, by the amount by which the startup expenditures exceed $50,000. Any startup expenditures not deducted may be amortized ratably over a 180-month period beginning in the month in which the trade or business begins.[41]

EXAMPLE 37

Green Corporation begins business on August 1, 2011. The corporation has startup expenditures of $47,000. If Green Corporation elects § 195, the total amount of startup expenditures that Green Corporation may deduct in 2011 is $6,167, computed as follows:

Deductible amount	$5,000
Amortizable amount {[($47,000 − $5,000)/180] × 5 months}	1,167
Total deduction	$6,167

■

---

[38]§ 195(b).
[39]§ 195(d).
[40]§ 195(a).

[41]§§ 195(b)(1)(A) and (B). For 2010, the $5,000 was increased to $10,000, and the $50,000 was increased to $60,000.

EXAMPLE 38

Assume the same facts as in Example 37, except that the startup expenditures are $53,000. The total deduction for the year 2011 is $3,417, computed as follows:

Deductible amount [$5,000 − ($53,000 − $50,000)]	$2,000
Amortizable amount {[($53,000 − $2,000)/180] × 5 months}	1,417
Total deduction	$3,417

Expenditures that are subject to capitalization and elective amortization under § 195 as startup expenditures generally must satisfy two requirements.[42] First, the expenditures must be paid or incurred in connection with any one of the following:

- The creation of an active trade or business.
- The investigation of the creation or acquisition of an active trade or business.
- Any activity engaged in for profit in anticipation of such activity becoming an active trade or business.

Second, such costs must be the kinds of costs that would be currently deductible if paid or incurred in connection with the operation of an existing trade or business in the same field as that entered into by the taxpayer.

The costs of creating a new active trade or business could include advertising; salaries and wages; travel and other expenses incurred in lining up prospective distributors, suppliers, or customers; and salaries and fees for executives, consultants, and professional services. Costs that relate to either created or acquired businesses could include expenses incurred for the analysis or survey of potential markets, products, labor supply, transportation facilities, and the like. Startup expenditures do not include any amount with respect to which a deduction is allowable under § 163(a) (interest), § 164 (taxes), and § 174 (research and experimental expenditures).[43]

Other assets that could be subject to amortization include research and experimental expenditures under § 174 (see Chapter 7) and organizational expenses under § 248 (see Chapter 20).

ETHICS & Equity

BUSINESS EXPENSE OR STARTUP EXPENSE?

Mark works as a writer for a local newspaper. Ten years ago he wrote a book about gardening. The book was a moderate success, and he ended up making about $15,000 from sales of the book. During the current year, Mark had $20,000 of expenses in connection with writing a book dealing with soccer. The expenses were for travel, meals, lodging, and research. Mark is considering expensing these items in the current year as trade and business expenses rather than capitalizing and amortizing them as startup expenses. Evaluate the appropriateness of Mark's plan.

8.5 DEPLETION

LO.8

Determine the amount of depletion expense including being able to apply the alternative tax treatments for intangible drilling and development costs.

Natural resources (e.g., oil, gas, coal, gravel, timber) are subject to **depletion**, which is simply a form of depreciation applicable to natural resources. Land generally cannot be depleted.

The owner of an interest in the natural resource is entitled to deduct depletion. An owner is one who has an economic interest in the property.[44] An economic interest requires the acquisition of an interest in the resource in place and the receipt of income from the extraction or severance of that resource. Like depreciation, depletion is a deduction *for* adjusted gross income.

---

[42]§§ 195(c)(1)(A) and (B).
[43]§ 195(c).

[44]Reg. § 1.611–1(b).

TAX *in* *the* NEWS	DEPLETION OF LANDFILL SITES

Landfill operators are allowed a depletion allowance, which is a deduction in computing Federal taxable income. The depletion deduction is the value of the air space that is being filled up. The value of the air space is the product of some of the goodwill costs, some of the land costs, and all of the engineering, siting, and construction costs.

Although all natural resources are subject to depletion, oil and gas wells are used as an example in the following paragraphs to illustrate the related costs and issues.

In developing an oil or gas well, the producer must make four types of expenditures:

- Natural resource costs.
- Intangible drilling and development costs.
- Tangible asset costs.
- Operating costs.

Natural resources are physically limited, and the costs to acquire them (e.g., oil under the ground) are, therefore, recovered through depletion. Costs incurred in making the property ready for drilling such as the cost of labor in clearing the property, erecting derricks, and drilling the hole are **intangible drilling and development costs (IDC)**. These costs generally have no salvage value and are a lost cost if the well is dry. Costs for tangible assets such as tools, pipes, and engines are capital in nature. These costs must be capitalized and recovered through depreciation (cost recovery). Costs incurred after the well is producing are operating costs. These costs would include expenditures for such items as labor, fuel, and supplies. Operating costs are deductible when incurred (on the accrual basis) or when paid (on the cash basis).

The expenditures for depreciable assets and operating costs pose no unusual problems for producers of natural resources. The tax treatment of depletable costs and intangible drilling and development costs is quite a different matter.

INTANGIBLE DRILLING AND DEVELOPMENT COSTS (IDC)

Intangible drilling and development costs can be handled in one of two ways at the option of the taxpayer. They can be *either* charged off as an expense in the year in which they are incurred *or* capitalized and written off through depletion. The taxpayer makes the election in the first year such expenditures are incurred either by taking a deduction on the return or by adding them to the depletable basis. No formal statement of intent is required. Once made, the election is binding on both the taxpayer and the IRS for all such expenditures in the future. If the taxpayer fails to make the election to expense IDC on the original timely filed return the first year such expenditures are incurred, an automatic election to capitalize them has been made and is irrevocable.

As a general rule, it is more advantageous to expense IDC. The obvious benefit of an immediate write-off (as opposed to a deferred write-off through depletion) is not the only advantage. Since a taxpayer can use percentage depletion, which is calculated without reference to basis (see Example 42), the IDC may be completely lost as a deduction if they are capitalized.

DEPLETION METHODS

There are two methods of calculating depletion: cost and percentage. Cost depletion can be used on any wasting asset (and is the only method allowed for timber). Percentage depletion is subject to a number of limitations, particularly for oil and gas deposits. Depletion should be calculated both ways, and the method that results in the larger deduction should be used. The choice between cost depletion and percentage depletion is an annual decision. Thus, the taxpayer can use cost depletion in one year and percentage depletion in the following year.

GLOBAL *Tax Issues*

IS AN ADDITIONAL NATURAL RESOURCE TAX GOOD FOR AUSTRALIA?

How can the Australian Federal government reap billions of dollars of new revenue? It proposes to do so by imposing additional taxes on the natural resource industry. Under the proposal, taxes will be increased on wealthy mining companies while those on smaller companies will be reduced.

Imposing additional taxes would supposedly result in two benefits. First, additional revenue would be provided to the Federal government. Second, corporate taxes could be cut, enabling Australia to be more globally competitive.

Opponents such as Scott Driscoll, national president of the United Retail Foundation, believe that these supposed benefits will never materialize. Xstrata PLC, the Anglo-Swiss mining giant has indicated its disappointment with the tax-overhaul plan. According to Xstrata CEO Mick Davis, under the plan Australia would have the highest taxes on the mineral sector of any country in the world when the 40 percent tax on profits is included.

Source: Adapted from Rachel Pannett, "Australia Plans New Resource Tax," *Wall Street Journal,* May 3, 2010, p. A15; and Neil Sands, "Xstrata Objects to Australian Tax," *Wall Street Journal,* May 3, 2010, p. B3.

Cost Depletion

Cost depletion is determined by using the adjusted basis of the asset.[45] The basis is divided by the estimated recoverable units of the asset (e.g., barrels, tons) to arrive at the depletion per unit. The depletion per unit then is multiplied by the number of units sold (*not* the units produced) during the year to arrive at the cost depletion allowed. Cost depletion, therefore, resembles the units-of-production method of calculating depreciation.

EXAMPLE 39

On January 1, 2011, Pablo purchases the rights to a mineral interest for $1 million. At that time, the remaining recoverable units in the mineral interest are estimated to be 200,000. The depletion per unit is $5 [$1,000,000 (adjusted basis) ÷ 200,000 (estimated recoverable units)]. If during the year 60,000 units are mined and 25,000 are sold, the cost depletion is $125,000 [$5 (depletion per unit) × 25,000 (units sold)]. ∎

If the taxpayer later discovers that the original estimate was incorrect, the depletion per unit for future calculations must be redetermined based on the revised estimate.[46]

EXAMPLE 40

Assume the same facts as in Example 39. In 2012, Pablo realizes that an incorrect estimate was made. The remaining recoverable units now are determined to be 400,000. Based on this new information, the revised depletion per unit is $2.1875 [$875,000 (adjusted basis) ÷ 400,000 (estimated recoverable units)]. Note that the adjusted basis is the original cost ($1,000,000) reduced by the depletion claimed in 2011 ($125,000). If 30,000 units are sold in 2012, the depletion for the year is $65,625 [$2.1875 (depletion per unit) × 30,000 (units sold)]. ∎

Percentage Depletion

Percentage depletion (also referred to as statutory depletion) is a specified percentage provided for in the Code. The percentage varies according to the type of mineral interest involved. A sample of these percentages is shown in Exhibit 8.3. The rate is applied to the gross income from the property, but in no event may percentage

---

[45]§ 612.   [46]§ 611(a).

EXHIBIT 8.3	Sample of Percentage Depletion Rates

22% Depletion

Cobalt	Sulfur
Lead	Tin
Nickel	Uranium
Platinum	Zinc

15% Depletion

Copper	Oil and gas
Gold	Oil shale
Iron	Silver

14% Depletion

Borax	Magnesium carbonates
Calcium carbonates	Marble
Granite	Potash
Limestone	Slate

10% Depletion

Coal	Perlite
Lignite	Sodium chloride

5% Depletion

Gravel	Pumice
Peat	Sand

depletion exceed 50 percent of the taxable income from the property before the allowance for depletion.[47]

EXAMPLE 41

Assuming gross income of $100,000, a depletion rate of 22%, and other expenses relating to the property of $60,000, the depletion allowance is determined as follows:

Gross income	$100,000
Less: Other expenses	(60,000)
Taxable income before depletion	$ 40,000
Depletion allowance [the lesser of $22,000 (22% × $100,000) or $20,000 (50% × $40,000)]	(20,000)
Taxable income after depletion	$ 20,000

The adjusted basis of the property is reduced by $20,000, the depletion allowed. If the other expenses had been only $55,000, the full $22,000 could have been deducted, and the adjusted basis would have been reduced by $22,000. ∎

Note that percentage depletion is based on a percentage of the gross income from the property and makes no reference to cost. Thus, when percentage depletion is used, it is possible to deduct more than the original cost of the property. If percentage depletion is used, however, the adjusted basis of the property (for computing

---

[47]§ 613(a). Special rules apply for certain oil and gas wells under § 613A (e.g., the 50% ceiling is replaced with a 100% ceiling, and the percentage depletion may not exceed 65% of the taxpayer's taxable income from all sources before the allowance for depletion).

cost depletion) must be reduced by the amount of percentage depletion taken until the adjusted basis reaches zero. See Example 46.

Effect of Intangible Drilling Costs on Depletion

The treatment of IDC has an effect on the depletion deduction in two ways. If the costs are capitalized, the basis for cost depletion is increased. As a consequence, the cost depletion is increased. If IDC are expensed, they reduce the taxable income from the property. This reduction may result in application of the provision that limits depletion to 50 percent (100 percent for certain oil and gas wells) of taxable income before deducting depletion.

EXAMPLE 42

Iris purchased the rights to an oil interest for $1 million. The recoverable barrels were estimated to be 200,000. During the year, 50,000 barrels were sold for $2 million. Regular expenses amounted to $800,000, and IDC were $650,000. If the IDC are capitalized, the depletion per unit is $8.25 ($1,000,000 + $650,000 ÷ 200,000 barrels), and the following taxable income results:

Gross income	$2,000,000
Less: Expenses	(800,000)
Taxable income before depletion	$1,200,000
Cost depletion ($8.25 × 50,000) = $412,500	
Percentage depletion (15% × $2,000,000) = $300,000	
Greater of cost or percentage depletion	(412,500)
Taxable income	$ 787,500

If the IDC are expensed, the taxable income is $250,000, calculated as follows:

Gross income	$2,000,000
Less: Expenses, including IDC	(1,450,000)
Taxable income before depletion	$ 550,000
Cost depletion [($1,000,000 ÷ 200,000 barrels) × 50,000 barrels] = $250,000	
Percentage depletion (15% of $2,000,000 = $300,000, limited to 100% of $550,000 taxable income before depletion) = $300,000	
Greater of cost or percentage depletion	(300,000)
Taxable income	$ 250,000

∎

For further restrictions on the use or availability of the percentage depletion method, see § 613.

8.6 REPORTING PROCEDURES

LO.9

Perform the reporting procedures for cost recovery.

Sole proprietors engaged in a business should file a Schedule C, Profit or Loss from Business, to accompany Form 1040. Schedule C for 2010 is presented because the 2011 form was not yet available.

The top part of page 1 requests certain key information about the taxpayer (e.g., name, address, Social Security number, principal business activity, and the accounting method used). Part I provides for the reporting of items of income. If the business requires the use of inventories and the computation of cost of goods sold (see Chapter 18 for when this is necessary), Part III must be completed and the cost of goods sold amount transferred to line 4 of Part I.

Part II allows for the reporting of deductions. Some of the deductions discussed in this chapter and their location on the form are depletion (line 12) and depreciation (line 13). Other expenses (line 27) include those items not already covered (see lines 8–26). An example would be research and experimental expenditures.

If depreciation is claimed, it should be supported by completing Form 4562. Form 4562 for 2010 is presented because the 2011 form was not yet available. The amount listed on line 22 of Form 4562 is then transferred to line 13 of Part II of Schedule C.

EXAMPLE 43

Thomas Andrews, Social Security number 111–11–1111, was employed as an accountant until May 2010, when he opened his own practice. His address is 279 Mountain View, Ogden, UT 84201. Andrews keeps his books on the cash basis and had the following revenue and business expenses in 2010:

a.   Revenue from accounting practice, $192,000.
b.   Insurance, $5,000.
c.   Office supplies, $4,000.
d.   Office rent, $16,000.
e.   Copier lease payments, $3,000.
f.   Licenses, $2,000.
g.   New furniture and fixtures were acquired on May 10, for $142,000. Thomas elects § 179 expensing and uses the statutory percentage cost recovery method.

Andrews would report the above information on Schedule C and Form 4562 as illustrated on the following pages. ■

TAX PLANNING:

8.7 COST RECOVERY

LO.10

Identify tax planning opportunities for cost recovery, amortization, and depletion.

Cost recovery schedules should be reviewed annually for possible retirements, abandonments, and obsolescence.

EXAMPLE 44

An examination of the cost recovery schedule of Eagle Company reveals the following:

• Asset A was abandoned when it was discovered that the cost of repairs would be in excess of the cost of replacement. Asset A had an adjusted basis of $3,000.
• Asset J became obsolete this year, at which point, its adjusted basis was $8,000.

Assets A and J should be written off for an additional expense of $11,000 ($3,000 + $8,000). ■

Because of the deductions for cost recovery, interest, and ad valorem property taxes, investments in real estate can be highly attractive. In figuring the economics of such investments, one should be sure to take into account any tax savings that result.

EXAMPLE 45
THE BIG PICTURE

Return to the facts of *The Big Picture* on p. 8-2. In early January 2010, Dr. Payne purchased residential rental property for $170,000 (of which $20,000 was allocated to the land and $150,000 to the building). He made a down payment of $25,000 and assumed the seller's mortgage for the balance. Under the mortgage agreement, monthly payments of $1,000 are required and are applied toward interest, taxes, insurance, and principal. Since the property was already occupied, Dr. Payne continued to receive rent of $1,200 per month from the tenant. He actively participates in this activity and hence comes under the special rule for a rental real estate activity with respect to the limitation on passive activity losses (refer to Chapter 11). He is in the 28% tax bracket.
   During 2011, Dr. Payne's expenses were as follows:

Interest	$10,000
Taxes	800
Insurance	1,000
Repairs and maintenance	2,200
Depreciation ($150,000 × .03636)	5,454
Total	$19,454

The deductible loss from the rental property is computed as follows:

Rent income ($1,200 × 12 months)	$ 14,400
Less expenses (see above)	(19,454)
Net loss	($ 5,054)

But what is Dr. Payne's overall position for the year when the tax benefit of the loss is taken into account? Considering just the cash intake and outlay, it is summarized below:

Intake—		
Rent income	$14,400	
Tax savings [28% (income tax bracket) × $5,054		
(loss from the property)]	1,415	$ 15,815
Outlay—		
Mortgage payments ($1,000 × 12 months)	$12,000	
Repairs and maintenance	2,200	(14,200)
Net cash benefit		$ 1,615

It should be noted, however, that should Dr. Payne cease being an active participant in the rental activity, the passive activity loss rules would apply, and he could lose the current period benefit of the loss.

Another consideration when making decisions with respect to cost recovery is whether fast or slow cost recovery will be more beneficial for the taxpayer. If the taxpayer's goal is to recover the cost of fixed assets as quickly as possible, the following strategies should be used:

- When constructing a facility, try to avoid "fixture" classification. Refer to the discussion in Chapter 1 on p. 1–7.
- When electing § 179 expensing, choose assets with longer lives.
- Choose accelerated cost recovery methods where available.

If a taxpayer has a new business with little income or a business with a net operating loss carryover, the taxpayer's goal may be to slow down cost recovery. In such a situation, the taxpayer should:

- Elect not to take additional first-year depreciation.
- Choose the straight-line cost recovery method.
- Make no election under § 179.
- Defer placing assets in service in the current tax year or postpone capital outlays until future tax years.

8.8 AMORTIZATION

When a business is purchased, goodwill and covenants not to compete are both subject to a statutory amortization period of 15 years. Therefore, the purchaser does not derive any tax benefits when part of the purchase price is assigned to a covenant rather than to goodwill.

Thus, from the purchaser's perspective, bargaining for a covenant should be based on legal rather than tax reasons. Note, however, that from the seller's perspective, goodwill is a capital asset and the covenant is an ordinary income asset.

Since the amortization period for both goodwill and a covenant is 15 years, the purchaser may want to attempt to minimize these amounts if the purchase price can be assigned to assets with shorter lives (e.g., inventory, receivables, and personalty). Conversely, the purchaser may want to attempt to maximize these amounts if part of the purchase price will otherwise be assigned to assets with longer recovery periods (e.g., realty) or to assets not eligible for cost recovery (e.g., land).

Form **4562**	**Depreciation and Amortization**	OMB No. 1545-0172
Department of the Treasury Internal Revenue Service (99)	**(Including Information on Listed Property)** ▶ See separate instructions.　　▶ Attach to your tax return.	20**10** Attachment Sequence No. **67**

Name(s) shown on return	Business or activity to which this form relates	Identifying number
Thomas Andrews	*Accounting services*	*111-11-1111*

Part I　Election To Expense Certain Property Under Section 179

Note: *If you have any listed property, complete Part V before you complete Part I.*

1	Maximum amount (see instructions)	**1**	
2	Total cost of section 179 property placed in service (see instructions)	**2**	*142,000*
3	Threshold cost of section 179 property before reduction in limitation (see instructions)	**3**	
4	Reduction in limitation. Subtract line 3 from line 2. If zero or less, enter -0-	**4**	*-0-*
5	Dollar limitation for tax year. Subtract line 4 from line 1. If zero or less, enter -0-. If married filing separately, see instructions	**5**	*142,000*

6	**(a)** Description of property	**(b)** Cost (business use only)	**(c)** Elected cost	
	Furniture and Fixtures	*142,000*	*142,000*	

7	Listed property. Enter the amount from line 29	**7**	
8	Total elected cost of section 179 property. Add amounts in column (c), lines 6 and 7	**8**	*142,000*
9	Tentative deduction. Enter the **smaller** of line 5 or line 8	**9**	*142,000*
10	Carryover of disallowed deduction from line 13 of your 2009 Form 4562	**10**	*-0-*
11	Business income limitation. Enter the smaller of business income (not less than zero) or line 5 (see instructions)	**11**	*142,000*
12	Section 179 expense deduction. Add lines 9 and 10, but do not enter more than line 11	**12**	*142,000*
13	Carryover of disallowed deduction to 2011. Add lines 9 and 10, less line 12 ▶	**13**	

Note: *Do not use Part II or Part III below for listed property. Instead, use Part V.*

Part II　Special Depreciation Allowance and Other Depreciation (Do not include listed property.**)** (See instructions.)

14	Special depreciation allowance for qualified property (other than listed property) placed in service during the tax year (see instructions)	**14**	
15	Property subject to section 168(f)(1) election	**15**	
16	Other depreciation (including ACRS)	**16**	

Part III　MACRS Depreciation (Do not include listed property.**)** (See instructions.)

Section A

17	MACRS deductions for assets placed in service in tax years beginning before 2010	**17**	
18	If you are electing to group any assets placed in service during the tax year into one or more general asset accounts, check here . . . . ▶ ☐		

Section B—Assets Placed in Service During 2010 Tax Year Using the General Depreciation System

(a) Classification of property	**(b)** Month and year placed in service	**(c)** Basis for depreciation (business/investment use only—see instructions)	**(d)** Recovery period	**(e)** Convention	**(f)** Method	**(g)** Depreciation deduction
19a　3-year property						
b　5-year property						
c　7-year property						
d 10-year property						
e 15-year property						
f 20-year property						
g 25-year property			25 yrs.		S/L	
h Residential rental property			27.5 yrs.	MM	S/L	
			27.5 yrs.	MM	S/L	
i Nonresidential real property			39 yrs.	MM	S/L	
				MM	S/L	

Section C—Assets Placed in Service During 2010 Tax Year Using the Alternative Depreciation System

20a Class life					S/L
b 12-year			12 yrs.		S/L
c 40-year			40 yrs.	MM	S/L

Part IV　Summary (See instructions.)

21	Listed property. Enter amount from line 28	**21**	
22	**Total.** Add amounts from line 12, lines 14 through 17, lines 19 and 20 in column (g), and line 21. Enter here and on the appropriate lines of your return. Partnerships and S corporations—see instructions	**22**	*142,000*
23	For assets shown above and placed in service during the current year, enter the portion of the basis attributable to section 263A costs **23**		

For Paperwork Reduction Act Notice, see separate instructions.	Cat. No. 12906N	Form **4562** (2010)

SCHEDULE C
(Form 1040)

Department of the Treasury
Internal Revenue Service (99)

Profit or Loss From Business

(Sole Proprietorship)

▶ **Partnerships, joint ventures, etc., generally must file Form 1065 or 1065-B.**
▶ **Attach to Form 1040, 1040NR, or 1041.**   ▶ **See Instructions for Schedule C (Form 1040).**

OMB No. 1545-0074

20**10**

Attachment
Sequence No. **09**

Name of proprietor	Social security number (SSN)
Thomas Andrews	*111–11–1111*

A Principal business or profession, including product or service (see instructions)

B Enter code from pages C-9, 10, & 11
▶

C Business name. If no separate business name, leave blank.
Andrews Accounting Services

D Employer ID number (EIN), if any

E Business address (including suite or room no.) ▶ *279 Mountain View*
City, town or post office, state, and ZIP code   *Ogden, UT 84201*

F Accounting method: **(1)** ☒ Cash   **(2)** ☐ Accrual   **(3)** ☐ Other (specify) ▶ _____

G Did you "materially participate" in the operation of this business during 2010? If "No," see instructions for limit on losses   ☒ Yes   ☐ No

H If you started or acquired this business during 2010, check here   . . . . ▶ ☐

Part I   Income

1	Gross receipts or sales. **Caution.** See instructions and check the box if: • This income was reported to you on Form W-2 and the "Statutory employee" box on that form was checked, or • You are a member of a qualified joint venture reporting only rental real estate income not subject to self-employment tax. Also see instructions for limit on losses. ▶ ☐	1	*192,000*
2	Returns and allowances	2	
3	Subtract line 2 from line 1	3	*192,000*
4	Cost of goods sold (from line 42 on page 2) . .	4	
5	**Gross profit.** Subtract line 4 from line 3 . . .	5	*192,000*
6	Other income, including federal and state gasoline or fuel tax credit or refund (see instructions)	6	
7	**Gross income.** Add lines 5 and 6 . . . . ▶	7	*192,000*

Part II   Expenses. Enter expenses for business use of your home **only** on line 30.

8	Advertising	8		18	Office expense	18	*4,000*
9	Car and truck expenses (see instructions)	9		19	Pension and profit-sharing plans .	19	
10	Commissions and fees .	10		20	Rent or lease (see instructions):		
11	Contract labor (see instructions)	11		a	Vehicles, machinery, and equipment	20a	*3,000*
12	Depletion	12		b	Other business property . . .	20b	*16,000*
13	Depreciation and section 179 expense deduction (not included in Part III) (see instructions)	13	*142,000*	21	Repairs and maintenance . . .	21	
				22	Supplies (not included in Part III) .	22	
				23	Taxes and licenses	23	*2,000*
				24	Travel, meals, and entertainment:		
				a	Travel	24a	
14	Employee benefit programs (other than on line 19) . .	14		b	Deductible meals and entertainment (see instructions) . .	24b	
15	Insurance (other than health)	15	*5,000*	25	Utilities	25	
16	Interest:			26	Wages (less employment credits) .	26	
a	Mortgage (paid to banks, etc.)	16a		27	Other expenses (from line 48 on page 2)	27	
b	Other	16b					
17	Legal and professional services	17					

28	**Total expenses** before expenses for business use of home. Add lines 8 through 27 . . . . . . ▶	28	*172,000*
29	Tentative profit or (loss). Subtract line 28 from line 7	29	*20,000*
30	Expenses for business use of your home. Attach **Form 8829**	30	
31	**Net profit or (loss).** Subtract line 30 from line 29. • If a profit, enter on both **Form 1040, line 12,** and **Schedule SE, line 2,** or on **Form 1040NR, line 13** (if you checked the box on line 1, see instructions). Estates and trusts, enter on **Form 1041, line 3.** • If a loss, you **must** go to line 32.	31	*20,000*
32	If you have a loss, check the box that describes your investment in this activity (see instructions). • If you checked 32a, enter the loss on both **Form 1040, line 12,** and **Schedule SE, line 2,** or on **Form 1040NR, line 13** (if you checked the box on line 1, see the line 31 instructions). Estates and trusts, enter on **Form 1041, line 3.** • If you checked 32b, you **must** attach **Form 6198.** Your loss may be limited.	32a ☐ All investment is at risk. 32b ☐ Some investment is not at risk.	

For Paperwork Reduction Act Notice, see your tax return instructions.   Cat. No. 11334P   Schedule C (Form 1040) 2010

8.9 DEPLETION

While a basis remains in a depletable asset, cost depletion or percentage depletion, whichever method produces the larger deduction, will be used. When the basis of the asset is exhausted, percentage depletion can still be taken.

EXAMPLE 46

Assume the following facts for Melissa:

Remaining depletable basis	$ 11,000
Gross income (10,000 units)	100,000
Expenses (other than depletion)	30,000

Since cost depletion is limited to the basis of $11,000 and if the percentage depletion is $22,000 (assume a 22% rate), Melissa would choose the latter. Her basis is then reduced to zero. In future years, however, she can continue to take percentage depletion since percentage depletion is taken without reference to the remaining basis. ■

The election to expense intangible drilling and development costs is a one-time election. Once the election is made to either expense or capitalize the IDC, it is binding on all future expenditures. The permanent nature of the election makes it extremely important for the taxpayer to determine which treatment will provide the greater tax advantage. (Refer to Example 42 for an illustration of the effect of using the two different alternatives for a given set of facts.)

8.10 COST RECOVERY TABLES

Summary of Tables

Table 8.1 Modified ACRS statutory percentage table for personalty.
   Applicable depreciation methods: 200 or 150 percent declining-balance switching to straight-line.
   Applicable recovery periods: 3, 5, 7, 10, 15, 20 years.
   Applicable convention: half-year.

Table 8.2 Modified ACRS statutory percentage table for personalty.
   Applicable depreciation method: 200 percent declining-balance switching to straight-line.
   Applicable recovery periods: 3, 5, 7 years.
   Applicable convention: mid-quarter.

Table 8.3 Modified ACRS optional straight-line table for personalty.
   Applicable depreciation method: straight-line.
   Applicable recovery periods: 3, 5, 7, 10, 15, 20 years.
   Applicable convention: half-year.

Table 8.4 Alternative minimum tax declining-balance table for personalty.
   Applicable depreciation method: 150 percent declining-balance switching to straight-line.
   Applicable recovery periods: 3, 5, 7, 9.5, 10, 12 years.
   Applicable convention: half-year.

Table 8.5 Alternative depreciation system straight-line table for personalty.
   Applicable depreciation method: straight-line.
   Applicable recovery periods: 5, 10, 12 years.
   Applicable convention: half-year.

Table 8.6 Modified ACRS straight-line table for realty.
   Applicable depreciation method: straight-line.
   Applicable recovery periods: 27.5, 31.5, 39 years.
   Applicable convention: mid-month.

Table 8.7 Alternative depreciation system straight-line table for realty.
   Applicable depreciation method: straight-line.
   Applicable recovery period: 40 years.
   Applicable convention: mid-month.

TABLE 8.1	MACRS Accelerated Depreciation for Personal Property Assuming Half-Year Convention

For Property Placed in Service after December 31, 1986

Recovery Year	3-Year (200% DB)	5-Year (200% DB)	7-Year (200% DB)	10-Year (200% DB)	15-Year (150% DB)	20-Year (150% DB)
1	33.33	20.00	14.29	10.00	5.00	3.750
2	44.45	32.00	24.49	18.00	9.50	7.219
3	14.81*	19.20	17.49	14.40	8.55	6.677
4	7.41	11.52*	12.49	11.52	7.70	6.177
5		11.52	8.93*	9.22	6.93	5.713
6		5.76	8.92	7.37	6.23	5.285
7			8.93	6.55*	5.90*	4.888
8			4.46	6.55	5.90	4.522
9				6.56	5.91	4.462*
10				6.55	5.90	4.461
11				3.28	5.91	4.462
12					5.90	4.461
13					5.91	4.462
14					5.90	4.461
15					5.91	4.462
16					2.95	4.461
17						4.462
18						4.461
19						4.462
20						4.461
21						2.231

*Switchover to straight-line depreciation.

TABLE 8.2	MACRS Accelerated Depreciation for Personal Property Assuming Mid-Quarter Convention

For Property Placed in Service after December 31, 1986 (Partial Table*)

Recovery Year	First Quarter	3-Year Second Quarter	Third Quarter	Fourth Quarter
1	58.33	41.67	25.00	8.33
2	27.78	38.89	50.00	61.11

Recovery Year	First Quarter	5-Year Second Quarter	Third Quarter	Fourth Quarter
1	35.00	25.00	15.00	5.00
2	26.00	30.00	34.00	38.00

Recovery Year	First Quarter	7-Year Second Quarter	Third Quarter	Fourth Quarter
1	25.00	17.85	10.71	3.57
2	21.43	23.47	25.51	27.55

*The figures in this table are taken from the official tables that appear in Rev.Proc. 87–57, 1987–2 C.B. 687. Because of their length, the complete tables are not presented.

TABLE 8.3	MACRS Straight-Line Depreciation for Personal Property Assuming Half-Year Convention*

For Property Placed in Service after December 31, 1986

MACRS Class	% First Recovery Year	Other Recovery Years		Last Recovery Year	
		Years	%	Year	%
3-year	16.67	2–3	33.33	4	16.67
5-year	10.00	2–5	20.00	6	10.00
7-year	7.14	2–7	14.29	8	7.14
10-year	5.00	2–10	10.00	11	5.00
15-year	3.33	2–15	6.67	16	3.33
20-year	2.50	2–20	5.00	21	2.50

*The official table contains a separate row for each year. For ease of presentation, certain years are grouped in this table. In some instances, this will produce a difference of .01 for the last digit when compared with the official table.

TABLE 8.4	Alternative Minimum Tax: 150% Declining-Balance Assuming Half-Year Convention

For Property Placed in Service after December 31, 1986 (Partial Table*)

Recovery Year	3-Year 150%	5-Year 150%	7-Year 150%	9.5-Year 150%	10-Year 150%	12-Year 150%
1	25.00	15.00	10.71	7.89	7.50	6.25
2	37.50	25.50	19.13	14.54	13.88	11.72
3	25.00**	17.85	15.03	12.25	11.79	10.25
4	12.50	16.66**	12.25**	10.31	10.02	8.97
5		16.66	12.25	9.17**	8.74**	7.85
6		8.33	12.25	9.17	8.74	7.33**
7			12.25	9.17	8.74	7.33
8			6.13	9.17	8.74	7.33
9				9.17	8.74	7.33
10				9.16	8.74	7.33
11					4.37	7.32
12						7.33
13						3.66

*The figures in this table are taken from the official table that appears in Rev.Proc. 87–57, 1987–2 C.B. 687. Because of its length, the complete table is not presented.

**Switchover to straight-line depreciation.

TABLE 8.5	ADS Straight-Line for Personal Property Assuming Half-Year Convention

For Property Placed in Service after December 31, 1986 (Partial Table)*

Recovery Year	5-Year Class	10-Year Class	12-Year Class
1	10.00	5.00	4.17
2	20.00	10.00	8.33
3	20.00	10.00	8.33
4	20.00	10.00	8.33
5	20.00	10.00	8.33
6	10.00	10.00	8.33
7		10.00	8.34
8		10.00	8.33
9		10.00	8.34
10		10.00	8.33
11		5.00	8.34
12			8.33
13			4.17

*The figures in this table are taken from the official table that appears in Rev.Proc. 87–57, 1987–2 C.B. 687. Because of its length, the complete table is not presented. The tables for the mid-quarter convention also appear in Rev.Proc. 87–57.

TABLE 8.6	MACRS Straight-Line Depreciation for Real Property Assuming Mid-Month Convention*

For Property Placed in Service after December 31, 1986: 27.5-Year Residential Real Property

Recovery Year(s)	The Applicable Percentage Is (Use the Column for the Month in the First Year the Property Is Placed in Service):											
	1	2	3	4	5	6	7	8	9	10	11	12
1	3.485	3.182	2.879	2.576	2.273	1.970	1.667	1.364	1.061	0.758	0.455	0.152
2–18	3.636	3.636	3.636	3.636	3.636	3.636	3.636	3.636	3.636	3.636	3.636	3.636
19–27	3.637	3.637	3.637	3.637	3.637	3.637	3.637	3.637	3.637	3.637	3.637	3.637
28	1.970	2.273	2.576	2.879	3.182	3.485	3.636	3.636	3.636	3.636	3.636	3.636
29	0.000	0.000	0.000	0.000	0.000	0.000	0.152	0.455	0.758	1.061	1.364	1.667

For Property Placed in Service after December 31, 1986, and before May 13, 1993: 31.5-Year Nonresidential Real Property

Recovery Year(s)	The Applicable Percentage Is (Use the Column for the Month in the First Year the Property Is Placed in Service):											
	1	2	3	4	5	6	7	8	9	10	11	12
1	3.042	2.778	2.513	2.249	1.984	1.720	1.455	1.190	0.926	0.661	0.397	0.132
2–19	3.175	3.175	3.175	3.175	3.175	3.175	3.175	3.175	3.175	3.175	3.175	3.175
20–31	3.174	3.174	3.174	3.174	3.174	3.174	3.174	3.174	3.174	3.174	3.174	3.174
32	1.720	1.984	2.249	2.513	2.778	3.042	3.175	3.175	3.175	3.175	3.175	3.175
33	0.000	0.000	0.000	0.000	0.000	0.000	0.132	0.397	0.661	0.926	1.190	1.455

For Property Placed in Service after May 12, 1993: 39-Year Nonresidential Real Property

Recovery Year(s)	The Applicable Percentage Is (Use the Column for the Month in the First Year the Property Is Placed in Service):											
	1	2	3	4	5	6	7	8	9	10	11	12
1	2.461	2.247	2.033	1.819	1.605	1.391	1.177	0.963	0.749	0.535	0.321	0.107
2–39	2.564	2.564	2.564	2.564	2.564	2.564	2.564	2.564	2.564	2.564	2.564	2.564
40	0.107	0.321	0.535	0.749	0.963	1.177	1.391	1.605	1.819	2.033	2.247	2.461

*The official tables contain a separate row for each year. For ease of presentation, certain years are grouped in these tables. In some instances, this will produce a difference of .001 for the last digit when compared with the official tables.

TABLE 8.7	ADS Straight-Line for Real Property Assuming Mid-Month Convention

For Property Placed in Service after December 31, 1986

Recovery Year	Month Placed in Service											
	1	2	3	4	5	6	7	8	9	10	11	12
1	2.396	2.188	1.979	1.771	1.563	1.354	1.146	0.938	0.729	0.521	0.313	0.104
2–40	2.500	2.500	2.500	2.500	2.500	2.500	2.500	2.500	2.500	2.500	2.500	2.500
41	0.104	0.312	0.521	0.729	0.937	1.146	1.354	1.562	1.771	1.979	2.187	2.396

REFOCUS ON THE BIG PICTURE

CALCULATION OF DEPRECIATION EXPENSE AND TAX PLANNING

Regardless of whether the accrual method or the cash method of accounting is used, MACRS must be used in calculating the depreciation expense for fixed assets for tax purposes. Evidently, Dr. Payne's financial reporting system uses MACRS because $91,298 is the correct amount of depreciation expense. The computers and peripheral equipment are five-year property. The office furniture and fixtures and the dental equipment are seven-year property. Based on the IRS cost recovery tables, the following percentages are used in calculating depreciation expense for the first year of each asset's life:

5-year property	20.00%
7-year property	14.29%

Dr. Payne will also be able to deduct depreciation on the house he converted from personal use to rental use and on the rental house that he purchased.

What If?

From a tax planning perspective, what can Dr. Payne do to increase the amount of depreciation expense associated with the purchase of these fixed assets and thereby reduce the amount of business net income reported on Schedule C of Form 1040 for his dental practice?

In addition to the standard MACRS deduction using the aforementioned percentages for 2011, § 179 provides for the limited expensing of fixed assets. This provision applies to personalty, but does not apply to realty (e.g., buildings). The maximum amount that can be deducted under this limited expensing provision is subject to several overall limits. First, the total amount deducted cannot exceed $500,000. Second, the $500,000 amount is reduced dollar-for-dollar for § 179 asset purchases placed in service during the tax year once such purchases exceed $2 million. Finally, the § 179 deduction for a tax year cannot exceed the taxable income from the trade or business.

If Dr. Payne elects § 179 treatment for some of the fixed asset purchases of his dental practice, he could reduce the Schedule C net income of his dental practice to $0. The remaining amount of the $612,085 purchases of § 179 assets not deducted in the current year would be eligible for MACRS depreciation in future years.

For future reference associated with similar fixed asset purchases for his business, the sequence of calculating the deduction is as follows:

- § 179 limited expensing.
- Additional first-year depreciation.
- Standard MACRS cost recovery.

KEY TERMS

Accelerated cost recovery system (ACRS), 8–22

Additional first-year depreciation, 8–8

Alternative depreciation system (ADS), 8–21

Amortization, 8–22

Cost depletion, 8–26

Cost recovery, 8–3

Depletion, 8–24

Depreciation, 8–3

Half-year convention, 8–7

Intangible drilling and development costs (IDC), 8–25

Listed property, 8–15

Mid-month convention, 8–10

Mid-quarter convention, 8–9

Modified accelerated cost recovery system (MACRS), 8–5

Percentage depletion, 8–26

Residential rental real estate, 8–10

Section 179 expensing, 8–13

Startup expenditures, 8–23

DISCUSSION QUESTIONS

1. **LO.1** Discuss whether property that is classified as personalty is subject to cost recovery.

2. **LO.1** If a taxpayer does not take any cost recovery on an asset during the year, what will be the impact on the basis of the asset?

3. **LO.1** Discuss whether land improvements are eligible for cost recovery.

ISSUE ID

4. **LO.2** At the beginning of the current year, Henry purchased a ski resort for $10 million. Henry does not own the land on which the resort is located. The Federal government owns the land, and Henry has the right to operate the resort on the land pursuant to Special Use Permits, which are terminable at will by the Federal government, and Term Special Use Permits, which allow the land to be used for a fixed number of years. In preparing the income tax return for the current year, Henry properly allocated $2 million of the purchase price to the costs of constructing mountain roads, slopes, and trails. Since the acquisition, Henry has spent an additional $1 million on maintaining the mountain roads, slopes, and trails. Identify the relevant tax issues for Henry.

5. **LO.2** Discuss whether the date an asset is purchased important in determining whether the mid-quarter convention applies for personalty.

6. **LO.2** Discuss the actual recovery period for the cost of an asset if the half-year convention applies.

7. **LO.2** Discuss the computation of cost recovery in the year an asset is placed in service when the half-year convention is being used.

8. **LO.2** Discuss whether the acquisition of real property affects the 40% test to determine whether the mid-quarter convention must be used.

9. **LO.2** Discuss the computation of cost recovery in the year of sale of an asset when the mid-quarter convention is being used.

10. **LO.2** Discuss the mid-month convention.

11. **LO.2** Robert purchased and placed in service $100,000 of seven-year class assets on August 10 of the current year. He also purchased and placed in service $500,000 of five-year class assets on November 15 of the current year. He elects not to take additional first-year depreciation. If Robert elects to use the MACRS straight-line method of cost recovery on the seven-year class assets, discuss the calculation of cost recovery for the five-year class assets.

12. **LO.2** Discuss the general cost recovery method and period for new farm machinery placed in service in 2011.

13. **LO.2** Discuss the applicable convention for farming assets if an election is made to not have the uniform capitalization rules apply.

ISSUE ID

14. **LO.2** Jim owns a very large ranch. A large part of his business is the production and raising of breeding cattle. Jim understands that under MACRS he is entitled to cost recovery on breeding cattle. Identify the relevant tax issues for Jim with respect to taking cost recovery on his self-produced breeding cattle.

15. **LO.2** Discuss the cost recovery periods and methods to be used on leasehold improvement property owned by the lessor.

16. **LO.2** Discuss the cost recovery periods and methods to be used on qualified leasehold improvement property owned by the lessee.

17. **LO.2** Discuss the tax treatment for the unrecovered basis in leasehold property owned by the lessee when the lease terminates.

18. **LO.3** Discuss whether § 179 expensing may be taken on qualified leasehold improvement real property.

19. **LO.3** Explain how the § 179 limited expensing deduction affects the computation of MACRS cost recovery.

20. **LO.3** Discuss the treatment of a § 179 expensing carryforward.

21. **LO.3** Discuss the definition of *taxable income* as it is used in limiting the § 179 expensing amount.

22. **LO.2, 3** A professional consulting business sells professional tools and equipment and provides associated services, such as repair and maintenance, to its customer base. The company's employees include technicians, who are required to provide and maintain their own tools and equipment for performing the repairs and maintenance work. The company will reimburse a technician for amounts spent to purchase tools and equipment eligible for a § 179 deduction up to a set amount each year. Any costs for tools and equipment that exceed the set amount will not be reimbursed. John is a technician for the company. During the current year, he purchased equipment that qualifies for the § 179 deduction. John paid $50,000 for the equipment and was reimbursed the set amount of $40,000. Identify the relevant tax issues for John with respect to § 179 and the computation of his taxable income. **ISSUE ID**

23. **LO.3, 4** Discuss the implications of an automobile used in a trade or business having a gross vehicle weight (GVW) exceeding 6,000 pounds.

24. **LO.4** Discuss how the limits on cost recovery apply to listed property.

25. **LO.4** Discuss the purpose of the lease inclusion amount and explain how it is determined with respect to leased passenger automobiles.

26. **LO.7** Explain the amortization period of a § 197 intangible if the actual useful life is less than 15 years.

27. **LO.7** Harold and Bart own 75% of the stock of Orange Motors. The other 25% of the stock is owned by Jeb. Orange Motors entered into an agreement with Harold and Bart to acquire all of their stock in Orange Motors. In addition, Harold and Bart signed a noncompete agreement with Orange Motors. Under the terms of the noncompete agreement, Orange will pay Harold and Bart $15,000 each per year for four years. Identify the relevant tax issues for Orange Motors. **ISSUE ID**

28. **LO.7** Discuss the amortization of startup expenditures.

29. **LO.7** In May 2011, George began searching for a trade or business to acquire. In anticipation of finding a suitable aquisition, George hired an investment banker to evaluate three potential businesses. He also hired a law firm to begin drafting regulatory approval documents for a target company. Eventually, George decided to purchase all the assets of Blue Corporation. Blue Corporation and George entered into an acquisition agreement on December 1, 2011. Identify the relevant tax issues for George. **ISSUE ID**

30. **LO.8** Discuss how the cost of mineral rights enters into the calculation of percentage depletion.

PROBLEMS

31. **LO.1, 2** On November 4, 2009, Blue Company acquired an asset (27.5-year residential real property) for $200,000 for use in its business. In 2009 and 2010, respectively, Blue took $642 and $5,128 of cost recovery. These amounts were incorrect because Blue

applied the wrong percentages (i.e., those for 39-year rather than 27.5-year). Blue should have taken $910 and $7,272 cost recovery in 2009 and 2010. On January 1, 2011, the asset was sold for $180,000. Calculate the gain or loss on the sale of the asset in 2011.

32. **LO.1, 2** José purchased a house for $300,000 in 2008. He used the house as his personal residence. In March 2011, when the fair market value of the house was $250,000, he converted the house to rental property. What is José's cost recovery for 2011?

33. **LO.2** Orange Corporation acquired new office furniture on August 15, 2011, for $130,000. Orange did not elect immediate expensing under § 179. Orange elects not to take additional first-year depreciation. Determine Orange's cost recovery for 2011.

34. **LO.2** Weston acquires a used office machine (seven-year class asset) on November 2, 2011, for $75,000. This is the only asset acquired by Weston during the year. He does not elect immediate expensing under § 179. On September 15, 2012, Weston sells the machine.
    a. Determine Weston's cost recovery for 2011.
    b. Determine Weston's cost recovery for 2012.

35. **LO.2** Juan acquires a new five-year class asset on March 14, 2011, for $150,000. This is the only asset acquired by Juan during the year. He does not elect immediate expensing under § 179. He elects not to take additional first-year depreciation. On July 15, 2012, Juan sells the asset.
    a. Determine Juan's cost recovery for 2011.
    b. Determine Juan's cost recovery for 2012.

36. **LO.2** Debra acquired the following new assets during the current year:

Date	Asset	Cost
April 11	Furniture	$40,000
July 28	Trucks	40,000
November 3	Computers	70,000

Determine the cost recovery for the current year. Debra does not elect immediate expensing under § 179. She elects not to take additional first-year depreciation.

37. **LO.2** On August 2, 2011, Wendy purchased a new office building for $3.2 million. On October 1, 2011, she began to rent out office space in the building. On July 15, 2015, Wendy sold the office building.
    a. Determine Wendy's cost recovery for 2011.
    b. Determine Wendy's cost recovery for 2015.

38. **LO.2** On April 3, 2011, Terry purchased and placed in service a building. The building cost $2 million. An appraisal determined that 25% of the total cost was attributed to the value of the land. The bottom floor of the building is leased to a retail business for $32,000. The other floors of the building are rental apartments with an annual rent of $160,000. Determine Terry's cost recovery for 2011.

39. **LO.2** On May 5, 2011, Christy purchased and placed in service a hotel. The hotel cost $2.8 million. Calculate Christy's cost recovery for 2011. For 2021.

40. **LO.2** Janice acquired an apartment building on June 4, 2011, for $1.6 million. The value of the land is $300,000. Janice sold the apartment building on November 29, 2017.
    a. Determine Janice's cost recovery for 2011.
    b. Determine Janice's cost recovery for 2017.

41. **LO.2** On April 20, 2011, Ralph purchased new equipment to be used in his farming business. The cost of the equipment is $150,000. Ralph does not elect immediate expensing under § 179; nor does he elect to not have the uniform capitalization rules apply. Compute Ralph's cost recovery for 2011.

42. **LO.2** During the month of March 2011, Sam constructed agricultural fences on his farm. The cost of the fencing was $70,000. Sam does not elect immediate expensing under § 179, but an election to not have the uniform capitalization rules apply is in effect. Compute Sam's cost recovery for 2011.

43. **LO.2** As a condition of leasing a 10-year-old warehouse, Martha had to make capital improvements to the building to accommodate the lessee. These improvements cost Martha $300,000. The improvements were completed and the 10-year lease commenced on October 28, 2011. Martha elects not to deduct any amount under § 179 nor take additional first-year depreciation. Determine Martha's cost recovery for 2011 with respect to the leasehold improvement.

44. **LO.2** On January 1, 2004, Jim leased a building to be used in his business as an office building. The lease will terminate on December 31, 2011. On February 2, 2005, Jim made a capital improvement to the building. The cost of the leasehold improvement to Jim was $80,000. Jim has no legal rights in the capital improvement after the termination of the lease. Determine Jim's loss in 2011, if any, with respect to the leasehold improvement as a result of the termination of the lease.

45. **LO.2, 3, 10** Lori, who is single, purchased five-year class property for $150,000 and seven-year class property for $400,000 on May 20, 2011. Lori expects the taxable income derived from her business (without regard to the amount expensed under § 179) to be about $800,000. Lori wants to elect immediate § 179 expensing, but she doesn't know which asset she should expense under § 179. She elects not to take additional first-year depreciation.

    a. Determine Lori's total deduction if the § 179 expense is first taken with respect to the five-year class asset.
    b. Determine Lori's total deduction if the § 179 expense is first taken with respect to the seven-year class asset.
    c. What is your advice to Lori?

46. **LO.2, 3** Olga is the proprietor of a small business. In 2011, the business income, before consideration of any cost recovery or § 179 deduction, is $750,000. Olga spends $2,050,000 on new seven-year class assets and elects to take the § 179 deduction on them. She elects not to take additional first-year depreciation. Olga's cost recovery deduction for 2011, except for the cost recovery with respect to the new seven-year assets, is $95,000. Determine Olga's total cost recovery for 2011 with respect to the seven-year class assets and the amount of any § 179 carryforward.

47. **LO.2, 3, 10** On June 5, 2011, Dan purchased and placed in service a seven-year class asset costing $150,000. On July 10, Dan placed in service qualified leasehold improvement property on a commercial building that cost $350,000. Dan does not take additional first-year depreciation. Determine Dan's total cost recovery deduction with respect to these two assets.

48. **LO.3, 4** John Johnson is considering acquiring an automobile at the beginning of 2011 that he will use 100% of the time as a taxi. The purchase price of the automobile is $35,000. John has heard of cost recovery limits on automobiles and wants to know how much of the $35,000 he can deduct in the first year. Write a letter to John in which you present your calculations. Also, prepare a memo for the tax files. John's address is 100 Morningside, Clinton, MS 39058.

49. **LO.2, 4** On October 15, 2011, Jon purchased and placed in service a used car. The purchase price was $25,000. This was the only business use asset Jon acquired in 2011. He used the car 80% of the time for business and 20% for personal use. Jon used the statutory percentage method of cost recovery. Calculate the total deduction Jon may take for 2011 with respect to the car.

50. **LO.4** On June 5, 2011, Leo purchased and placed in service a new car that cost $20,000. The business use percentage for the car is always 100%. He elects not to take additional first-year depreciation. Compute Leo's cost recovery deduction in 2011 and 2012.

51. **LO.2, 3, 4** On March 15, 2011, Helen purchased and placed in service a new Escalade. The purchase price was $62,000, and the vehicle had a rating of 6,500 GVW. The vehicle was used 100% for business.

    a. Calculate the maximum total deduction Helen may take with respect to the vehicle in 2011.
    b. How would your answer above change if Helen elected not to take additional first-year depreciation?

52. **LO.2, 4** On May 28, 2011, Mary purchased and placed in service a new $20,000 car. The car was used 60% for business, 20% for production of income, and 20% for personal use in 2011. In 2012, the usage changed to 40% for business, 30% for production of income, and 30% for personal use. Mary did not elect immediate expensing under § 179. She elects not to take additional first-year depreciation. Compute the cost recovery and any cost recovery recapture in 2012.

DECISION MAKING

53. **LO.2, 4, 10** Sally purchased a new computer (five-year property) on June 1, 2011, for $4,000. Sally could use the computer 100% of the time in her business, or she could allow her family to also use the computer. Sally estimates that if her family uses the computer, the business use will be 45% and the personal use will be 55%. Determine the tax cost to Sally, in the year of acquisition, of allowing her family to use the computer. Assume that Sally would not elect § 179 limited expensing and that her marginal tax rate is 28%. She elects not to take additional first-year depreciation.

DECISION MAKING

COMMUNICATIONS

54. **LO.2, 4, 10** Dennis Harding is considering acquiring a new automobile that he will use 100% for business. The purchase price of the automobile would be $35,000. If Dennis leased the car for five years, the lease payments would be $375 per month. Dennis will acquire the car on January 1, 2011. The inclusion dollar amounts from the IRS table for the next five years are $40, $87, $130, $156, and $179. Dennis desires to know the effect on his adjusted gross income of purchasing versus leasing the car for the next five years. He elects not to take additional first-year depreciation. Write a letter to Dennis and present your calculations. Also, prepare a memo for the tax files. His address is 150 Avenue I, Memphis, TN 38112.

55. **LO.2, 5** In 2011, Muhammad purchased a new computer for $16,000. The computer is used 100% for business. Muhammad did not make a § 179 election with respect to the computer. He elects not to take additional first-year depreciation. If Muhammad uses the statutory percentage method, determine his cost recovery deduction for 2011 for computing taxable income and for computing his alternative minimum tax.

DECISION MAKING

56. **LO.2, 5, 10** Jamie purchased $100,000 of new office furniture for her business in June of the current year. Jamie understands that if she elects to use ADS to compute her regular income tax, there will be no difference between the cost recovery for computing the regular income tax and the AMT. Jamie wants to know the *regular* income tax cost, after three years, of using ADS rather than MACRS. Assume that Jamie does not elect § 179 limited expensing and that her marginal tax rate is 28%. She elects not to take additional first-year depreciation.

DECISION MAKING

COMMUNICATIONS

57. **LO.2, 7, 10** Mike Saxon is negotiating the purchase of a business. The final purchase price has been agreed upon, but the allocation of the purchase price to the assets is still being discussed. Appraisals on a warehouse range from $1.2 million to $1.5 million. If a value of $1.2 million is used for the warehouse, the remainder of the purchase price, $800,000, will be allocated to goodwill. If $1.5 million is allocated to the warehouse, goodwill will be $500,000. Mike wants to know what effect each alternative will have on cost recovery and amortization during the first year. Under the agreement, Mike will take over the business on January 1 of next year. Write a letter to Mike in which you present your calculations and recommendation. Also, prepare a memo for the tax files. Mike's address is 200 Rolling Hills Drive, Shavertown, PA 18708.

58. **LO.7** Oleander Corporation, a calendar year entity, begins business on March 1, 2011. The corporation has startup expenditures of $54,000. If Oleander elects § 195 treatment, determine the total amount of startup expenditures that it may deduct in 2011.

59. **LO.7** Martha was considering starting a new business. During her preliminary investigations, she incurred the following expenditures:

Salaries	$20,000
Travel	18,000
Interest on short-term note	2,000
Professional fees	13,000

Martha begins the business on June 1 of the current year. If Martha elects § 195 treatment, determine her startup expenditure deduction for the current year.

60. **LO.8** Wes acquired a mineral interest during the year for $10 million. A geological survey estimated that 250,000 tons of the mineral remained in the deposit. During the year, 80,000 tons were mined, and 45,000 tons were sold for $12 million. Other expenses amounted to $5 million. Assuming the mineral depletion rate is 22%, calculate Wes's lowest taxable income.

61. **LO.8, 10** Chris purchased an oil interest for $2 million. Recoverable barrels were estimated to be 500,000. During the year, 120,000 barrels were sold for $3.84 million, regular expenses (including cost recovery) were $1.24 million, and IDC were $1 million. Calculate Chris's taxable income under the expensing and capitalization methods of handling IDC.

DECISION MAKING

CUMULATIVE PROBLEMS

62. Janice Morgan, age 32, is single and has no dependents. She is a freelance writer. In January 2010, Janice opened her own office located at 2751 Waldham Road, Pleasantville, NM 17196. She called her business Writers Anonymous. Janice is a cash basis taxpayer. She lives at 132 Stone Avenue, Pleasantville, NM 17196. Her Social Security number is 123–45–6789. Janice desires to contribute to the Presidential Election Campaign Fund.

TAX RETURN PROBLEM

During 2010, Janice had the following income and expense items connected with her business:

Income from sale of articles	$105,000
Rent	16,500
Utilities	7,900
Supplies	1,800
Insurance	5,000
Travel (including meals of $1,200)	3,500

Janice purchased and placed in service the following fixed assets for her business:

- Furniture and fixtures (new) costing $17,000 on January 10, 2010.
- Computer equipment (new) costing $40,000 on July 28, 2010.

Janice did not elect immediate expensing under § 179. She elected not to take additional first-year depreciation.

Janice's itemized deductions are as follows:

State income tax	$3,000
Home mortgage interest paid to First Bank	6,000
Property taxes on home	1,500
Charitable contributions	1,200

Janice did not keep a record of the sales tax she paid. The amount from the sales tax table is $437.

Janice has interest income of $5,000 on certificates of deposit at Second Bank. Janice makes estimated tax payments of $17,000 for 2010.

Compute Janice Morgan's 2010 Federal income tax payable (or refund due). If you use tax forms for your computations, you will need Form(s) 1040 and 4562 and Schedules A, B, C, and SE. Suggested software: H&R BLOCK At Home.

63. John Smith, age 31, is single and has no dependents. At the beginning of 2011, John started his own excavation business and named it Earth Movers. John lives at 1045 Center Street, Lindon, UT, and his business is located at 381 State Street, Lindon, UT. The zip code for both addresses is 84059. John's Social Security number is 111–11–1111, and the business identification number is 11–1111111. John is a cash basis taxpayer. During 2011, John had the following items in connection with his business:

TAX COMPUTATION PROBLEM

DECISION MAKING

COMMUNICATIONS

Fees for services	$912,000
Building rental expense	36,000
Office furniture and equipment rental expense	9,000

Office supplies	$ 2,500
Utilities	4,000
Salary for secretary	34,000
Salary for equipment operators	42,000
Payroll taxes	7,000
Fuel and oil for the equipment	21,000
Purchase of three new front-end loaders on January 15, 2011, for $600,000. John made the election under § 179.	600,000
Purchase of a new dump truck on January 18, 2011	85,000

During 2011, John had the following additional items:

Interest income from First National Bank	$ 10,000
Dividends from ExxonMobil	9,500
Quarterly estimated tax payments	11,500

John elected not to take additional first-year depreciation.

On October 8, 2011, John inherited IBM stock from his Aunt Mildred. John had been her favorite nephew. According to the data provided by the executor of Aunt Mildred's estate, the stock was valued for estate tax purposes at $110,000. John is considering selling the IBM stock for $115,000 on December 29, 2011, and using $75,000 of the proceeds to purchase an Acura ZDX. He would use the car 100% for business. John wants to know what effect these transactions would have on his 2011 adjusted gross income.

Write a letter to John in which you present your calculations. Also, prepare a memo for the tax files.

RESEARCH PROBLEMS

THOMSON REUTERS
Checkpoint® Student Edition

Note: Solutions to Research Problems can be prepared by using the **Checkpoint® Student Edition** online research product, which is available to accompany this text. It is also possible to prepare solutions to the Research Problems by using tax research materials found in a standard tax library.

COMMUNICATIONS

Research Problem 1. Harry Pickart, one of your clients, operates a business that rents aircraft parts to motion picture studios for use in film production. Harry purchased most of the aircraft parts at auctions held throughout the United States. At those auctions, Harry usually acquired the parts in large quantities because he speculated that he would be able to use at least some of them in his rental business. After the conclusion of a film production, the movie studio returns the aircraft parts it rented from Harry. The parts are often returned in damaged condition or with pieces missing. Harry sometimes attempts to repair a damaged part so that it can be rented again. After being subjected to wear and tear from use, however, a part deteriorates over time, which varies depending on the particular part and its treatment by the studios during rental. Harry believes that all of the aircraft parts have a useful life of less than four years and, therefore, are entitled to be classed as three-year property. Write a letter to Harry that contains your advice on whether the aircraft parts can be depreciated over three years. Also, prepare a memo for the tax files. Harry's mailing address is P.O. Box 100, Sun River, OR 97600.

Research Problem 2. Acme Motors sells and leases automobiles. Acme administers a leasing program for its employees. The lease terminates automatically if the employee (lessee) ceases to be employed by Acme. The leases are solely for the personal use of the automobile by the lessees and do not involve use of the automobile in the employee's employment-related activities for Acme. The leased vehicles are registered and titled in Acme's name, and Acme pays all registration fees, insurance, and maintenance costs. Acme wants to know whether the leased vehicles are exempt from the depreciation limitations of § 280F for purposes of computing its taxable income.

Research Problem 3. Blue Power and Light Corporation is an energy company. It produces electricity, sells wholesale and retail electricity, and delivers electricity to customers. Blue also provides street and highway lighting and area lighting for public and private entities. The equipment used to provide street and area lighting is called street-lights. Blue wants to know the appropriate asset class to determine the cost recovery deduction for the street-lights.

Research Problem 4. Juan owns a business that acquires exotic automobiles that are high-technology, state-of-the-art vehicles with unique design features or equipment. The exotic automobiles are not licensed or set up to be used on the road. Rather, the cars are used exclusively for car shows or related promotional photography. Juan would like to know whether he can take a cost recovery deduction with respect to the exotic automobiles on his Federal income tax return.

Partial list of research aids:
Bruce Selig, 70 TCM 1125, T.C.Memo. 1995–519.

Research Problem 5. George Black operates a winery and vineyards. In the process of growing grapes, trellis systems are used to support the grape vines. The primary structural components that affix the trellis to the earth are the end and in-line posts, which are rammed 2 to 3 feet into the ground and secured by metal stakes and/or mechanically screwed-in anchors. George would like to know how the trellis system will be classified for purposes of computing cost recovery.

Use the tax resources of the Internet to address the following questions. Do not restrict your search to the Web, but include a review of newsgroups and general reference materials, practitioner sites and resources, primary sources of the tax law, chat rooms and discussion groups, and other opportunities.

INTERNET
activity

Research Problem 6. Locate a financial calculator program that assesses the wisdom of buying versus leasing a new car. Install the program on your computer and become familiar with it. Use the program to work through Problem 54 in this chapter.

Research Problem 7. Changes to depreciation systems often are discussed by policy makers and observers of the tax system. Outline the terms and policy objectives of one of the changes currently proposed by the Treasury, a member of Congress, or a tax policy think tank.

COMMUNICATIONS

Deductions: Employee and Self-Employed–Related Expenses

LEARNING OBJECTIVES

After completing Chapter 9, you should be able to:

LO.1
Distinguish between employee and self-employed status.

LO.2
Recognize deductible transportation expenses.

LO.3
Describe how travel expenses are treated.

LO.4
Determine the moving expense deduction.

LO.5
Differentiate between deductible and nondeductible education expenses.

LO.6
Explain how entertainment and meal expenses are treated.

LO.7
Identify other employee expenses.

LO.8
Compare various deductions for contributions to retirement accounts.

LO.9
Demonstrate the difference between accountable and nonaccountable employee plans.

LO.10
Apply the limitations on miscellaneous itemized deductions.

LO.11
Discuss tax planning ideas related to employee business expenses.

OUTLINE

For the latest in changes to tax legislation, visit **www.cengage.com/taxation/swft.**

FRAMEWORK 1040:
Tax Formula for Individuals

This chapter covers the boldfaced portions of the Tax Formula for Individuals that was introduced in Figure 3.1 on p. 3-3. Below those portions are the sections of Form 1040 where the results are reported.

Income (broadly conceived).	$xx,xxx
Less: Exclusions	(x,xxx)
Gross income	$xx,xxx
Less: Deductions for adjusted gross income	**(x,xxx)**

FORM 1040 (p. 1)

12	Business income or (loss). Attach Schedule C or C-EZ	. . . .
23	Educator expenses .	. . . .
24	Certain business expenses of reservists, performing artists, and fee-basis government officials. Attach Form 2106 or 2106-EZ	
26	Moving expenses. Attach Form 3903	. . . .
32	IRA deduction .	. . . .
34	Tuition and fees. Attach Form 8917	. . . .

Adjusted gross income.	$xx,xxx
Less: The greater of total **itemized deductions** *or* the standard deduction	**(x,xxx)**

FORM 1040 (p. 2)

40	**Itemized deductions** (from Schedule A) **or** your **standard deduction** (see instructions) . .

Personal and dependency exemptions	(x,xxx)
Taxable income	$xx,xxx
Tax on taxable income (see Tax Tables or Tax Rate Schedules)	$ x,xxx
Less: Tax credits (including income taxes withheld and prepaid)	(xxx)
Tax due (or refund)	$ xxx

THE BIG PICTURE   Tax Solutions for the Real World

THE FIRST JOB

After an extensive search, Morgan, a recent college graduate with a major in finance, has accepted a job with Kite Corporation. The job is in sales and will require travel and some entertainment (i.e., business lunches). She will be based in a major metropolitan area in another state. Kite has no available space in the locale, so she will have to maintain her own work facility. In addition to her salary, Morgan will receive a travel allowance. However, Kite has made it clear that the allowance *will not* cover all of her travel expenses.

Morgan is delighted with the new job since it will enable her to maintain a flexible work schedule. Furthermore, working out of her own apartment avoids a time-consuming and costly commute.

What are some of the income tax problems presented by this situation? **Read the chapter and formulate your response.**

Considering the large number of taxpayers affected, the tax treatment of job-related expenses is unusually complex. To resolve this matter in a systematic fashion, a number of key questions must be asked:

- Is the taxpayer an *employee* or *self-employed*?
- If an employee, what expenses *qualify* as deductions?
- How are the expenses that qualify *classified* for tax purposes?
- To the extent the expenses are classified as deductions *from* AGI, are they subject to any *limitation*?

Once these questions have been posed and answered, the chapter considers various planning procedures available to maximize the deductibility of employee and self-employed expenses.

9.1 EMPLOYEE VERSUS SELF-EMPLOYED

When one person performs services for another, the person performing the service is either an employee or self-employed (an **independent contractor**). Failure to recognize employee status can have serious consequences. Tax deficiencies as well as interest and penalties may result.

The problem is likely to intensify since businesses are increasingly relying on the services of self-employed persons for numerous reasons. Unlike employees, self-employed persons do not have to be included in various fringe benefit programs (e.g., group term life insurance) and retirement plans. Since they are not covered by FICA and FUTA (see Chapter 1), these payroll costs are avoided. The IRS is very much aware of the tendency of businesses to wrongly classify workers as self-employed rather than as employees.

In terms of tax consequences, employment status also makes a great deal of difference to the persons who perform the services. Expenses of self-employed taxpayers, to the extent allowable, are classified as deductions *for* AGI and are reported on Schedule C (Profit or Loss From Business) of Form 1040.[1] With the exception of reimbursement under an accountable plan (see later in the chapter), expenses of employees are deductions *from* AGI. They are reported on Form 2106 (Employee Business Expenses) and Schedule A (Itemized Deductions) of Form 1040.[2]

Most persons classified as employees are common law employees. The common law employee classification originated in judicial case law and is summarized in various IRS pronouncements.[3] Revenue Ruling 87–41, for example, lists 20 factors that can be used in determining whether a worker is a common law employee or an independent contractor (and, thus, self-employed).[4]

But when does a common law employee-employer relationship exist? Such a relationship exists when the employer has the right to specify the end result and the ways and means by which that result is to be attained.[5] An employee is subject to the will and control of the employer with respect not only to what shall be done but also to how it shall be done. If the individual is subject to the direction or control of another only to the extent of the end result but not as to the means of accomplishment, an employee-employer relationship does not exist.

Certain factors indicate an employee-employer relationship. These include the performance of the following by the employer:

- Furnishing of tools or equipment and a place to work.
- Providing support services including the hiring of assistants to help do the work.
- Making training available to provide needed job skills.

L0.1

Distinguish between employee and self-employed status.

---

[1]Under certain conditions, a Schedule C–EZ can be substituted. Also, a Schedule SE (Self-Employment Tax) must be filed.

[2]In certain cases, a Form 2106–EZ (Unreimbursed Employee Business Expenses) can be substituted.

[3]See, for example, *Employer's Supplemental Tax Guide* (IRS Publication 15-A).

[4]1987–1 C.B. 296.

[5]Reg. § 31.3401(c)–(1)(b).

- Allowing participation in various workplace fringe benefits (e.g., accident and health plans, group life insurance, retirement plans).
- Paying for services based on time rather than the task performed.

For their part, independent contractors are more likely than employees to have unreimbursed business expenses, a significant investment in tools and work facilities, and less permanency in their business relationships. Independent contractors, moreover, anticipate a profit from their work, make their services available to the relevant marketplace, and are paid a flat fee on a per-job basis. Although the right to discharge may depend on any contractual arrangement between the parties, employees generally are easier to terminate than independent contractors.

In resolving employment status, each case must be tested on its own merits. Keep in mind, however, that the right to control the means and methods of accomplishment is the definitive test that leads to a common law employee result.

| EXAMPLE 1 | Arnold is a lawyer whose major client accounts for 60% of his billings. He does the routine legal work and income tax returns at the client's request. He is paid a monthly retainer in addition to amounts charged for extra work. Arnold is a self-employed individual. Even though most of his income comes from one client, he still has the right to determine how the end result of his work is attained. ■ |

| EXAMPLE 2 | Ellen is a lawyer hired by Arnold to assist him in the performance of services for the client mentioned in Example 1. Ellen is under Arnold's supervision; he reviews her work and pays her an hourly fee. Ellen is an employee of Arnold. ■ |

When one taxpayer holds multiple jobs, it is possible to have dual status as both an employee and an independent contractor (i.e., self-employed).

| EXAMPLE 3 | Dr. Davis, DDS, is a full-time employee at the Robin University Health Center. In the evenings and on weekends, he shares a practice with another dentist who works the Monday through Friday daytime shifts. Dr. Davis is both employed and self-employed. ■ |

Certain workers who *are not* common law employees are treated as employees for employment tax purposes. Known as **statutory employees**, this group includes certain drivers (e.g., nondairy beverage distributors, laundry and dry cleaning pickup service), life insurance sales agents, home workers, and other sales persons. These employees are allowed to claim their business-related expenses as deductions *for* AGI by using Schedule C. The wages or commissions paid to statutory employees are not subject to Federal income tax withholding but are subject to Social Security tax.[6]

If a taxpayer wants clarification as to whether employee or independent contractor status exists, a ruling from the IRS can be obtained by filing Form SS–8 (Determination of Worker Status for Purposes of Federal Employment Taxes and Income Tax Withholding). An adverse ruling is appealable to the U.S. Tax Court.[7]

9.2 EMPLOYEE EXPENSES—IN GENERAL

Once the employment relationship is established, employee expenses fall into one of the following categories:

- Transportation.
- Travel.
- Moving.

---

[6]§ 3121(d)(3). See Circular E, *Employer's Tax Guide* (IRS Publication 15), for further discussion of statutory employees.

[7]§ 7436.

- Education.
- Entertainment.
- Other.

These expenses are discussed below in the order presented.

Keep in mind, however, that these expenses are not necessarily limited to employees. A deduction for business transportation, for example, is equally available to taxpayers who are self-employed.

9.3 TRANSPORTATION EXPENSES

QUALIFIED EXPENDITURES

An employee may deduct unreimbursed employment-related transportation expenses as an itemized deduction *from* AGI. **Transportation expenses** include only the cost of transporting the employee from one place to another in the course of employment when the employee is *not* away from home *in travel status*. Such costs include taxi fares, automobile expenses, tolls, and parking.

> **LO.2**
>
> Recognize deductible transportation expenses.

Commuting Expenses

Commuting between home and one's place of employment is a personal, nondeductible expense. The fact that one employee drives 30 miles to work and another employee walks six blocks is of no significance.

> **EXAMPLE 4**
>
> Geraldo is employed by Sparrow Corporation. He drives 22 miles each way to work. The 44 miles he drives each workday are nondeductible commuting expenses. ∎

The rule that disallows a deduction for commuting expenses has several exceptions. An employee who uses an automobile to transport heavy tools to work and who otherwise would not drive to work is allowed a deduction, but only for the additional costs incurred to transport the work implements. Additional costs are those exceeding the cost of commuting by the same mode of transportation without the tools. For example, the rental of a trailer for transporting tools is deductible, but the expenses of operating the automobile generally are not deductible. The Supreme Court has held that a deduction is permitted only when the taxpayer can show that the automobile would not have been used without the necessity to transport tools or equipment.[8]

Another exception is provided for an employee who has a second job. The expenses of getting from one job to another are deductible. If the employee goes home between jobs, the deduction is based on the distance between jobs.

> **EXAMPLE 5**
>
> In the current year, Cynthia holds two jobs, a full-time job with Blue Corporation and a part-time job with Wren Corporation. During the 250 days that she works (adjusted for weekends, vacation, and holidays), Cynthia customarily leaves home at 7:30 A.M. and drives 30 miles to the Blue Corporation plant, where she works until 5:00 P.M. After dinner at a nearby café, Cynthia drives 20 miles to Wren Corporation and works from 7:00 to 11:00 P.M. The distance from the second job to Cynthia's home is 40 miles. Her deduction is based on 20 miles (the distance between jobs). ∎

If the taxpayer is required to incur a transportation expense to travel between work stations, that expense is deductible.

---

[8]*Fausner v. Comm.*, 73–2 USTC ¶9515, 32 AFTR 2d 73–5202, 93 S.Ct. 2820 (USSC, 1973).

EXAMPLE 6

Norman is the local manager for a national chain of fast-food outlets. Each workday he drives from his home to his office to handle administrative matters. Most of his day, however, is then spent making the rounds of the retail outlets, after which he drives home. The costs incurred in driving to his office and driving home from the last outlet are nondeductible commuting expenses. The other transportation costs are deductible. ■

Likewise, the commuting costs from home to a temporary work station and from the temporary work station to home are deductible.

EXAMPLE 7

Vivian works for a firm in downtown Denver and commutes to work. She occasionally works in a customer's office. On one such occasion, Vivian drove directly to the customer's office, a round-trip distance from her home of 40 miles. She did not go into her office, which is a 52-mile round-trip. Her mileage for going to and from the temporary work station is deductible. ■

Also deductible is the reasonable travel cost between the general working area and a temporary work station outside that area.

EXAMPLE 8

Sam, a building inspector in Minneapolis, regularly inspects buildings for building code violations for his employer, a general contractor. During one busy season, the St. Paul inspector became ill, and Sam was required to inspect several buildings in St. Paul. The expenses for transportation for the trips to St. Paul are deductible. ■

What constitutes the general working area depends on the facts and circumstances of each situation. Furthermore, if an employee customarily works on several temporary assignments in a localized area, that localized area becomes the regular place of employment. Transportation from home to these locations becomes a personal, nondeductible commuting expense.

If a taxpayer has an office in the home that qualifies as a principal place of business, the transportation between home and various work locations is not a commuting expense.

EXAMPLE 9
THE BIG PICTURE

Return to the facts of *The Big Picture* on p. 9-2. Because Morgan will have an office in her home, the apartment will be her principal place of business. Thus, any transportation from her home to business sites *will not* be disallowed as a commuting expense. ■

COMPUTATION OF AUTOMOBILE EXPENSES

A taxpayer has two choices in determining automobile expenses: the automatic mileage method and the actual cost method. If a mixed-use automobile is involved, only the expenses attributable to the business use are deductible. The percentage of business use is usually arrived at by comparing the business mileage with total mileage—both business and personal.

Automatic Mileage Method

Also called the standard mileage method, the **automatic mileage method** is convenient in that it simplifies record keeping. The rate allowed per mile takes into account average operating expenses (such as gas and oil, repairs, and depreciation). Consequently, the taxpayer only has to multiply the automatic mileage rate by the miles driven to compute the deduction for business transportation.

For 2011, the deduction is based on 51 cents per mile for business miles.[9] For 2010, the business mileage rate was 50 cents. In some past years, however, the rate set did not remain the same for the entire year. Due to sizable fluctuations in fuel prices, a

---

[9]Rev.Proc. 2010–51, I.R.B. No. 51, 883 and Notice 2010–88, I.R.B. No. 51, 882.

different rate was set for the last part of the year. The possibility of such a change makes it important that the taxpayer be able to identify when the mileage took place. The automatic mileage rate for deductible education expenses is the same as for business; 19 cents per mile is allowed for moving (discussed later in this chapter) and medical purposes, and the rate for the charitable contribution deduction is 14 cents a mile (as to medical and charitable deductions, see Chapter 10). Parking fees and tolls are allowed in addition to expenses computed using the automatic mileage method.

Generally, a taxpayer may elect either method for any particular year. However, the following restrictions apply:

- The vehicle must be owned or leased by the taxpayer.
- The vehicle is not used for hire (e.g., taxicab).
- If five or more vehicles are in use (for business purposes) at the *same* time (not alternately), a taxpayer may not use the automatic mileage method.
- A basis adjustment is required if the taxpayer changes from the automatic mileage method to the actual operating cost method. Depreciation is considered allowed for the business miles in accordance with the following schedule for the most recent five years:

Year	Rate per Mile
2011	22 cents
2010	23 cents
2009	21 cents
2008	21 cents
2007	19 cents

EXAMPLE 10

Tim purchased his automobile in 2008 for $36,000. It is used 90% for business purposes. Tim drove the automobile for 10,000 business miles in 2010; 8,500 business miles in 2009; and 6,000 business miles in 2008. At the beginning of 2011, the basis of the business portion is $27,055.

Depreciable basis ($36,000 × 90%)	$32,400
Less depreciation:	
2010 (10,000 miles × 23 cents)	(2,300)
2009 (8,500 miles × 21 cents)	(1,785)
2008 (6,000 miles × 21 cents)	(1,260)
Adjusted business basis 1/1/2011	$27,055

- Use of the automatic mileage method in the first year the auto is placed in service is considered an election to exclude the auto from the MACRS method of depreciation (discussed in Chapter 8).
- A taxpayer may not switch to the automatic mileage method if the MACRS statutory percentage method or the election to expense under § 179 has been used.

Actual Cost Method

Under this method, the actual cost of operating the automobile is used to compute the deduction. Actual costs include the following expenses:

- Gas and oil, lubrication.
- Depreciation (or lease payments).
- Insurance.
- Dues to auto clubs.
- Repairs.
- Tires and other parts.
- Licenses and registration fees.
- Parking and tolls.

As noted in Chapter 8, the allowance for depreciation (or lease payments) is subject to limitations when mixed-use vehicles are involved (see Example 24 on p. 8–15). Interest on car loans is not deductible if the taxpayer is an employee, but it can qualify as a business expense if the taxpayer is self-employed.[10] Sales taxes paid on the purchase of a car are added to the cost of the car and recovered by means of the depreciation deduction. In mixed-use situations, the portion of the sales tax attributable to personal use may, in some cases, be claimed as a deduction *from* AGI (see Chapter 10 and the choice required between state and local income and sales taxes).

Except for parking and tolls, none of the expenses noted previously can be separately claimed under the automatic mileage method. A deduction for parking tickets and other traffic violations is not allowed under either method due to the public policy limitation (see Chapter 6).

EXAMPLE 11
THE BIG PICTURE

Return to the facts of *The Big Picture* on p. 9-2. During Morgan's senior year in college, her parents gave her one of the family cars—a 2008 Chevrolet Impala. Morgan has no idea as to the car's original cost or the odometer reading at the time the car was registered in her name. She has, however, kept track of the miles driven for business since she accepted her new job. Morgan should use the automatic mileage method in claiming business use of the car. ■

9.4 TRAVEL EXPENSES

L0.3

Describe how travel expenses are treated.

DEFINITION OF TRAVEL EXPENSES

An itemized deduction is allowed for unreimbursed travel expenses related to a taxpayer's employment. **Travel expenses** are more broadly defined in the Code than are transportation expenses. Travel expenses include transportation expenses and meals and lodging while away from home in the pursuit of a trade or business. Meals cannot be lavish or extravagant under the circumstances. Transportation expenses (as previously discussed) are deductible even though the taxpayer is not away from home. A deduction for travel expenses is available only if the taxpayer is away from his or her tax home. Travel expenses also include reasonable laundry and incidental expenses.

AWAY-FROM-HOME REQUIREMENT

The crucial test for the deductibility of travel expenses is whether the employee is away from home overnight. "Overnight" need not be a 24-hour period, but it must be a period substantially longer than an ordinary day's work and must require rest, sleep, or a relief-from-work period.[11] A one-day business trip is not travel status, and meals and lodging for such a trip are not deductible.

Temporary Assignments

The employee must be away from home for a temporary period. If the taxpayer-employee is reassigned to a new post for an indefinite period of time, that new post becomes his or her tax home. *Temporary* indicates that the assignment's termination is expected within a reasonably short period of time. The position of the IRS is that the tax home is the business location, post, or station of the taxpayer. Thus, travel expenses are not deductible if a taxpayer is reassigned for an indefinite period and does not move his or her place of residence to the new location.

EXAMPLE 12

Malcolm's employer opened a branch office in San Diego. Malcolm was assigned to the new office for three months to train a new manager and to assist in setting up the new

---

[10]An interest deduction could be available if the purchase of the auto was financed with a home equity loan. See the discussion of itemized deductions in Chapter 10.

[11]*U.S. v. Correll*, 68–1 USTC ¶9101, 20 AFTR 2d 5845, 88 S.Ct. 445 (USSC, 1967); Rev.Rul. 75–168, 1975–1 C.B. 58.

TAX in the NEWS

TURNING A SATURDAY LEISURE DAY INTO A BUSINESS DAY

The high cost of air travel together with the substantial discount allowed for a Saturday night stayover may offer travelers an opportunity to do some sightseeing or shopping on business trips. The extra meals and lodging expenses for the nonbusiness day are deductible if the cost is less than the additional cost of flying without a Saturday stay. For the employee, any reimbursement for such costs is nontaxable. Thus, the Saturday is treated as a business day even though no business activity takes place.

Source: Private Letter Ruling (Ltr.Rul.) 9237014.

---

office. He tried commuting from his home in Los Angeles for a week and decided that he could not continue driving several hours a day. He rented an apartment in San Diego, where he lived during the week. He spent weekends with his wife and children at their home in Los Angeles. Malcolm's rent, meals, laundry, incidentals, and automobile expenses in San Diego are deductible. To the extent that Malcolm's transportation expense related to his weekend trips home exceeds what his cost of meals and lodging would have been, the excess is personal and nondeductible. ■

EXAMPLE 13

Assume that Malcolm in Example 12 was transferred to the new location to become the new manager permanently. His wife and children continued to live in Los Angeles until the end of the school year. Malcolm is no longer "away from home" because the assignment is not temporary. His travel expenses are not deductible. ■

To curtail controversy in this area, the Code specifies that a taxpayer "*shall not* be treated as *temporarily* away from home during any period of employment if such period exceeds 1 year."[12]

Determining the Tax Home

Under ordinary circumstances, determining the location of a taxpayer's tax home does not present a problem. The tax home is the area in which the taxpayer derives his or her source of income.

It is possible for a taxpayer never to be away from his or her tax home. In other words, the tax home follows the taxpayer. Thus, all meals and lodging remain personal and are not deductible.

EXAMPLE 14

Jim is single and works full-time as a long-haul truck driver. He lists his mother's home as his address and stays there during holidays. However, he contributes nothing toward its maintenance. Since Jim has no regular place of duty or place where he regularly lives, his tax home is where he works (i.e., on the road). As an itinerant (transient), he is never away from home, and all of his meals and lodging while on the road are personal and not deductible. ■

The result reached in Example 14 is justified on the grounds that there is no duplication of living expenses in the case of itinerant taxpayers.[13]

When a taxpayer has more than one place of business or work, the main one is considered to be the tax home. This is determined by considering the time spent, the level of activity involved, and the income earned at each job.

EXAMPLE 15

Art, a physical therapist, lives with his family in Lancaster (Pennsylvania). For seven months of each year, he is employed by the New Orleans Saints football team at a

---

[12]§ 162(a).

[13]Rev.Rul. 73–539, 1973–2 C.B. 37 and *James O. Henderson*, 70 TCM 1407, T.C.Memo. 1995–559, *aff'd* by 98–1 USTC ¶50,375, 81 AFTR 2d 98–1748, 143 F.3d 497 (CA–9, 1998).

salary of $150,000. During this period, he rents an apartment in New Orleans. In the offseason, he works for the Lancaster YMCA at a salary of $15,000. Art's tax home is clearly New Orleans and not Lancaster. Consequently, his living expenses while in New Orleans (i.e., food, lodging) are not deductible. ∎

RESTRICTIONS ON TRAVEL EXPENSES

The possibility always exists that taxpayers will attempt to treat vacation or pleasure travel as deductible business travel. To prevent such practices, the law contains restrictions on certain travel expenses.

Conventions

For travel expenses to be deductible, a convention must be directly related to the taxpayer's trade or business.[14]

EXAMPLE 16

Dr. Hill, a pathologist who works for a hospital in Ohio, travels to Las Vegas to attend a two-day session on recent developments in estate planning. No deduction is allowed for Dr. Hill's travel expenses. ∎

EXAMPLE 17

Assume the same facts as in Example 16, except that the convention deals entirely with recent developments in pathology. Now, a travel deduction is allowed. ∎

If the proceedings of the convention are videotaped, the taxpayer must attend convention sessions to view the videotaped materials along with other participants. This requirement does not disallow deductions for costs (other than travel, meals, and entertainment) of renting or using videotaped materials related to business.

EXAMPLE 18

A CPA is unable to attend a convention at which current developments in taxation are discussed. She pays $200 for videotapes of the lectures and views them at home later. The $200 is an itemized deduction if the CPA is an employee. If she is self-employed, the $200 is a deduction *for* AGI. ∎

The Code places stringent restrictions on the deductibility of travel expenses of the taxpayer's spouse or dependent.[15] Generally, the accompaniment by the spouse or dependent must serve a bona fide business purpose, and the expenses must be otherwise deductible.

EXAMPLE 19

Assume the same facts as in Example 17 with the additional fact that Dr. Hill is accompanied by Mrs. Hill. Mrs. Hill is not employed, but possesses secretarial skills and takes notes during the proceedings. No deduction is allowed for Mrs. Hill's travel expenses. If, however, Mrs. Hill is a nurse trained in pathology and is employed by Dr. Hill as his assistant, her travel expenses become deductible. ∎

Education

Travel as a form of education is not deductible.[16] If, however, the education qualifies as a deduction, the travel involved is allowed.

EXAMPLE 20

Greta, a German teacher, travels to Germany to maintain general familiarity with the language and culture. No travel expense deduction is allowed. ∎

EXAMPLE 21

Jean-Claude, a scholar of French literature, travels to Paris to do specific library research that cannot be done elsewhere and to take courses that are offered only at the

---

[14]§ 274(h)(1).

[15]§ 274(m)(3).

[16]§ 274(m)(2).

Sorbonne. The travel costs are deductible, assuming that the other requirements for deducting education expenses (discussed later in the chapter) are met. ■

COMBINED BUSINESS AND PLEASURE TRAVEL

To be deductible, travel expenses need not be incurred in the performance of specific job functions. Travel expenses incurred in attending a professional convention are deductible by an employee if attendance is connected with services as an employee. For example, an employee of a law firm can deduct travel expenses incurred in attending a meeting of the American Bar Association.

Domestic Travel

Travel deductions have been used in the past by persons who claimed a tax deduction for what was essentially a personal vacation. As a result, several provisions have been enacted to govern deductions associated with combined business and pleasure trips. If the business/pleasure trip is from one point in the United States to another point in the United States, the transportation expenses are deductible only if the trip is *primarily for business.*[17] If the trip is primarily for pleasure, no transportation expenses qualify as a deduction. Meals, lodging, and other expenses are allocated between business and personal days.

In the current year, Hana travels from Seattle to New York primarily for business. She spends five days conducting business and three days sightseeing and attending shows. Her plane and taxi fare amounts to $1,160. Her meals amount to $200 per day, and lodging and incidental expenses are $350 per day. She can deduct the transportation charges of $1,160, since the trip is primarily for business (five days of business versus three days of sightseeing). Meals are limited to five days and are subject to the 50% cutback (discussed later in the chapter) for a total of $500 [5 days × ($200 × 50%)], and other expenses are limited to $1,750 (5 days × $350). If Hana is an employee, the unreimbursed travel expenses are miscellaneous itemized deductions. ■	**EXAMPLE 22**

Assume Hana goes to New York for a two-week vacation. While there, she spends several hours renewing acquaintances with people in her company's New York office. Her transportation expenses are not deductible. ■	**EXAMPLE 23**

Foreign Travel

When the trip is *outside the United States,* special rules apply. Transportation expenses must be allocated between business and personal unless (1) the taxpayer is away from home for seven days or less *or* (2) less than 25 percent of the time was for personal purposes. No allocation is required if the taxpayer has no substantial control over arrangements for the trip or the desire for a vacation is not a major factor in taking the trip. If the trip is primarily for pleasure, no transportation charges are deductible. Days devoted to travel are considered business days. Weekends, legal holidays, and intervening days are considered business days, provided that both the preceding and succeeding days were business days.[18]

In the current year, Robert takes a trip from New York to Japan primarily for business purposes. He is away from home from June 10 through June 19. He spends three days vacationing and seven days conducting business (including two travel days). His airfare is $4,000, his meals amount to $200 per day, and lodging and incidental expenses are $300 per day. Since Robert is away from home for more than seven days and more than	**EXAMPLE 24**

---

[17]Reg. § 1.162–2(b)(1).

[18]§ 274(c) and Reg. § 1.274–4. For purposes of the seven-days-or-less exception, the departure travel day is not counted.

25% of his time is devoted to personal purposes, only 70% (7 days business/10 days total) of the transportation is deductible. His deductions are as follows:

Transportation (70% × $4,000)		$2,800
Lodging ($300 × 7)		2,100
Meals ($200 × 7)	$ 1,400	
Less: 50% cutback (discussed later)	(700)	700
Total		$5,600 ∎

EXAMPLE 25

Assume the same facts as in Example 24. Robert is gone the same period of time but spends only two days (rather than three) vacationing. Now no allocation of transportation is required. Since the pleasure portion of the trip is less than 25% of the total, all of the airfare qualifies for the travel deduction. ∎

9.5 Moving Expenses

LO.4

Determine the moving expense deduction.

Moving expenses are deductible for moves in connection with the commencement of work at a new principal place of work.[19] Both employees and self-employed individuals can deduct these expenses. To be eligible for a moving expense deduction, a taxpayer must meet two basic tests: distance and time.

DISTANCE TEST

To meet the distance test, the taxpayer's new job location must be at least 50 miles farther from the taxpayer's old residence than the old residence was from the former place of employment. In this regard, the location of the new residence is not relevant. This eliminates a moving deduction for taxpayers who purchase a new home in the same general area without changing their place of employment. Those who accept a new job in the same general area as the old job location are also eliminated.

EXAMPLE 26

Harry is permanently transferred to a new job location. The distance from Harry's former home to his new job (80 miles) exceeds the distance from his former home to his old job (30 miles) by at least 50 miles. Harry has met the distance test for a moving expense deduction. (See the following diagram.)

If Harry is not employed before the move, his new job must be at least 50 miles from his former residence. In this instance, Harry has met the distance test if he was not previously employed. ∎

TIME TEST

To meet the time test, an employee must be employed on a full-time basis at the new location for 39 weeks in the 12-month period following the move. If the taxpayer is a self-employed individual, he or she must work in the new location for 78 weeks

---

during the next two years. The first 39 weeks must be in the first 12 months. The time test is disregarded if the taxpayer dies, becomes disabled, or is discharged (other than for willful misconduct) or transferred by the new employer.

A taxpayer might not be able to meet the 39-week test by the due date of the tax return for the year of the move. For this reason, two alternatives are allowed. The taxpayer can take the deduction in the year the expenses are incurred, even though the 39-week test has not been met. If the taxpayer later fails to meet the test, either (1) the income of the following year is increased by an amount equal to the deduction previously claimed for moving expenses, or (2) an amended return is filed for the year of the move. The second alternative is to wait until the test is met and then file an amended tax return for the year of the move.

TREATMENT OF MOVING EXPENSES

What Is Included

"Qualified" moving expenses include *reasonable* expenses of:

- Moving household goods and personal effects.
- Traveling from the former residence to the new place of residence.

For this purpose, *traveling* includes lodging, but not meals, for the taxpayer and members of the household.[20] The taxpayer can elect to use actual auto expenses (no depreciation is allowed) or the automatic mileage method. In this case, moving expense mileage is limited in 2011 to 19 cents per mile for each car. The automatic mileage rate for 2010 was 16.5 cents per mile. These expenses are also limited by the reasonableness standard. For example, if one moves from Texas to Florida via Maine and takes six weeks to do so, the transportation and lodging must be allocated between personal and moving expenses.

EXAMPLE 27

Jill is transferred by her employer from the Atlanta office to the San Francisco office. In this connection, she spends the following amounts:

Cost of moving furniture	$4,800
Transportation	700
Meals	450
Lodging	600

Jill's total qualified moving expense is $6,100 ($4,800 + $700 + $600). ∎

The moving expense deduction is allowed regardless of whether the employee is transferred by the existing employer or is employed by a new employer. It is allowed if the employee moves to a new area and obtains employment or switches from self-employed status to employee status (and vice versa). The moving expense deduction is also allowed if an individual is unemployed before obtaining employment in a new area.

What Is Not Included

In addition to meals while en route, the moving expense deduction does *not* include the following costs:

- New car tags and driver's licenses.
- Loss on the sale of a residence or penalty for breaking a lease.
- Forfeiture of security deposits and loss from disposing of club memberships.
- Pre-move house-hunting expenses.
- Temporary living expenses.

Also not deductible are the costs of moving servants and others who are not members of the household.

---

[20]§ 217(b).

GLOBAL *Tax Issues*

EXPATRIATES AND THE MOVING EXPENSE DEDUCTION

Expatriates, U.S. persons who accept work assignments overseas, enjoy several favorable tax advantages regarding foreign moves. First, the cost of storing household goods qualifies as a moving expense. This could lead to a major tax saving since expatriates do not ship most of their household effects to the foreign location. Furthermore, the cost of storage, particularly in a climate-controlled facility, is not insignificant.

The second advantage expatriates could enjoy is an exemption from the time test. Those who return to the United States to retire are absolved from the 39-week or 78-week work requirement. Thus, the return home expenses are treated as qualified moving expenses.

Source: Internal Revenue Code § 217(i).

How Treated

Qualified moving expenses that are paid (or reimbursed) by the employer are not reported as part of the gross income of the employee.[21] Moving expenses that are paid (or reimbursed) by the employer and are not qualified moving expenses are included in the employee's gross income and are not deductible.

The employer is responsible for allocating the reimbursement between the qualified and nonqualified moving expenses. Reimbursed qualified moving expenses are separately stated on the Form W–2 given to the employee for the year involved. Qualified moving expenses that are not reimbursed and those of self-employed taxpayers are deductions *for* AGI.[22]

EXAMPLE 28
THE BIG PICTURE

Return to the facts of *The Big Picture* on p. 9-2. Even though this is her first job, Morgan will be entitled to a moving expense deduction. This presumes that she is not reimbursed by Kite Corporation for these expenses. She should not forget that the mileage on her auto (at the rate of 19 cents per mile) also is allowed. Her deduction is *for* AGI and can be claimed even if she chooses the standard deduction option. ∎

Form 3903 is used to report the details of the moving expense deduction if the employee is not reimbursed or a self-employed person is involved.

9.6 EDUCATION EXPENSES

L0.5

Differentiate between deductible and nondeductible education expenses.

GENERAL REQUIREMENTS

An employee can deduct expenses incurred for education (**education expenses**) as ordinary and necessary business expenses provided the expenses are incurred for either of two reasons:

- To maintain or improve existing skills required in the present job.
- To meet the express requirements of the employer or the requirements imposed by law to retain his or her employment status.

Education expenses are *not* deductible if the education is for either of the following purposes (except as discussed below under A Limited Deduction Approach):

- To meet the minimum educational standards for qualification in the taxpayer's existing job.
- To qualify the taxpayer for a new trade or business.[23]

---

[21]§§ 132(a)(6) and (g).
[22]§ 62(a)(15).
[23]Reg. §§ 1.162–5(b)(2) and (3).

> **TAX in the NEWS**
>
> ## IS AN MBA DEGREE DEDUCTIBLE?
>
> Education that maintains or improves existing skills is deductible, but education that qualifies a taxpayer for a new field is not. But how do these basic rules apply to a conventional (i.e., nonspecialized) MBA degree? Does being a manager or a consultant require an MBA degree? Generally, the answer has always been that it does not. In this regard, therefore, the education does not create a new skill, so its cost should be deductible.
>
> Several recent holdings, however, have found that an MBA degree can lead to qualifying for a new trade or business. But these holdings involved situations where the education resulted in a job change and satisfied different minimum requirements set by the employer. In one case, for example, the taxpayer moved from the position of investment analyst to become an investment banker, and the latter position required an MBA degree. Under these circumstances, the cost of the education was held to be nondeductible.
>
> But barring a change to a job where the degree is required, the cost of an MBA degree should be deductible as merely improving existing managerial skills.
>
> *Source: Daniel R. Allemeier, Jr., 90 TCM 197, T.C.Memo. 2005–207.*

Fees incurred for professional qualification exams (the bar exam, for example) and fees for review courses (such as a CPA review course) are not deductible.[24] If the education incidentally results in a promotion or raise, the deduction still can be taken as long as the education maintained and improved existing skills and did not qualify a person for a new trade or business. A change in duties is always fatal to the deduction if the new duties involve the same general work. For example, the IRS has ruled that a practicing dentist's education expenses incurred to become an orthodontist are deductible.[25]

REQUIREMENTS IMPOSED BY LAW OR BY THE EMPLOYER FOR RETENTION OF EMPLOYMENT

Taxpayers are permitted to deduct education expenses if additional courses are required by the employer or are imposed by law. Many states require a minimum of a bachelor's degree and a specified number of additional courses to retain a teaching job. In addition, some public school systems have imposed a master's degree requirement and require teachers to make satisfactory progress toward a master's degree in order to keep their positions. If the required education is the minimum degree required for the job, no deduction is allowed.

A taxpayer classified as a staff accountant who went back to school to obtain a bachelor's degree in accounting was not allowed to deduct the expenses. Although some courses tended to maintain and improve his existing skills in his entry-level position, the degree was the minimum requirement for his job.[26]

Expenses incurred for education required by law for various professions will also qualify for deduction.

> **EXAMPLE 29**
>
> In order to satisfy the State Board of Public Accountancy rules for maintaining her CPA license, Nancy takes an auditing course sponsored by a local college. The cost of the education is deductible. ∎

MAINTAINING OR IMPROVING EXISTING SKILLS

The "maintaining or improving existing skills" requirement in the Code has been difficult for both taxpayers and the courts to interpret. For example, a business executive may be permitted to deduct the costs of obtaining an MBA on the grounds that the advanced management education is undertaken to maintain and improve

---

[24]Reg. § 1.212–1(f) and Rev.Rul. 69–292, 1969–1 C.B. 84.
[25]Rev.Rul. 74–78, 1974–1 C.B. 44.

[26]Reg. § 1.162–5(b)(2)(iii) Example (2); *Collin J. Davidson*, 43 TCM 743, T.C.Memo. 1982–119. But see the subsequent discussion of § 222 (i.e., the deduction for higher education qualified tuition and related expenses).

existing management skills. The executive is eligible to deduct the costs of specialized, nondegree management courses that are taken for continuing education or to maintain or improve existing skills. Expenses incurred by the executive to obtain a law degree are not deductible, however, because the education constitutes training for a new trade or business. The Regulations deny a self-employed accountant a deduction for expenses relating to law school.[27]

CLASSIFICATION OF SPECIFIC ITEMS

Education expenses include books, tuition, typing, and transportation (e.g., from the office to night school) and travel (e.g., meals and lodging while away from home at summer school).

EXAMPLE 30

Bill, who holds a bachelor of education degree, is a secondary education teacher in the Charleston school system. The school board recently raised its minimum education requirement for new teachers from four years of college training to five. A grandfather clause allows teachers with only four years of college to continue to qualify if they show satisfactory progress toward a graduate degree. Bill enrolls at the University of South Carolina and takes two graduate courses. His unreimbursed expenses for this purpose are as follows:

Books and tuition	$3,600
Lodging while in travel status (June–August)	2,150
Meals while in travel status	1,100
Laundry while in travel status	220
Transportation	900

Bill has an itemized deduction as follows:

Books and tuition	$3,600
Lodging	2,150
Meals less 50% cutback (see below)	550
Laundry	220
Transportation	900
	$7,420

■

A LIMITED DEDUCTION APPROACH

One of the major shortcomings of the education deduction, previously discussed, is that it is unavailable for taxpayers obtaining a basic skill. Thus, a taxpayer working for an accounting firm cannot deduct the cost of earning a bachelor's degree in accounting. Under 2001 tax legislation, this shortcoming has been partly resolved with the **deduction for qualified tuition and related expenses**.

A deduction *for* AGI is allowed for qualified tuition and related expenses involving higher education (i.e., postsecondary). The deduction is the lesser of the qualifying amount spent or the maximum amount allowed by § 222. The maximum deductions allowed are shown in Table 9.1. Note that the limitations are based on the taxpayer's MAGI and filing status.[28] Although a phaseout is provided for, note its short and drastic effect. Only two steps are involved ($65,000/$80,000 for single and $130,000/$160,000 for married), and the benefit of § 222 *disappears completely* after the second step. Thus, a married couple with MAGI of $160,000 would lose the entire deduction if they earned an additional $1. The § 222 limitations are not indexed for inflation.[29]

---

[27]Reg. § 1.162–5(b)(3)(ii) Example (1).

[28]MAGI is modified adjusted gross income as defined in § 222(b)(2)(C). Examples of some of these modifications include the adding back to regular AGI of the foreign earned income exclusion and the domestic production activities deduction. See *Tax Benefits for Education* (IRS Publication 970).

[29]Section 222 expired at the end of 2009, but has been extended through 2011.

TABLE 9.1	Limitations for Qualified Tuition Deduction	
Filing Status	**MAGI Limit**	**Maximum Deduction Allowed**
Single	$ 65,000 ⎱	$4,000
Married	130,000 ⎰	
Single	65,001 to 80,000*	2,000
Married	130,001 to 160,000*	2,000

*No deduction at all is available if MAGI exceeds this amount.

Various aspects of the higher education tuition deduction are summarized below:

- Qualified tuition and related expenses include whatever is required for enrollment at the institution. Usually, student activity fees, books, and room and board are not included.[30]
- The expense need not be employment related, although it can be.
- The deduction is available for a taxpayer's spouse or anyone who can be claimed as a dependent and is an eligible student.
- The deduction is not available for married persons who file separate returns.
- To avoid a "double benefit," the deduction must be coordinated with other education provisions (e.g., American Opportunity and lifetime learning credits). Along this same line, no deduction is allowed for a taxpayer who qualifies as another's dependent.[31]
- The deduction *for* AGI classification avoids the 2 percent-of-AGI floor on miscellaneous itemized deductions. As noted later in the chapter, this is the fate suffered by other education-related employee expenses.

Return to the facts of *The Big Picture* on p. 9-2. After starting her new job, Morgan enrolls in the night program of a local law school and begins attending classes. Although Morgan does not plan to practice law, she feels that a law degree would advance her career. Except for the tuition she pays (see the discussion of § 222), none of her expenses relating to the education will be deductible.[32] ■

EXAMPLE 31
THE BIG PICTURE

The deduction for qualified tuition and related expenses can be determined by completing Form 8917 (Tuition and Fees Deduction). The form should be attached to Form 1040 (or Form 1040-A).

---

[30]Section 222(d) refers to § 25A(f), which deals with the American Opportunity and lifetime learning credits (see Chapter 13). Student activity fees and prescribed course-related books could be allowed if they are a condition for enrollment.

[31]§ 222(c).

[32]*Steven Galligan*, 83 TCM 1859, T.C.Memo. 2002–150.

MAXIMIZING THE TUITION DEDUCTION

Blake maintains a household that includes his daughter Bianca who is 23 years old and a full-time student. Using funds from a savings account she inherited from her aunt, Bianca pays for her $5,000 college tuition. For the year, Blake properly claims Bianca as a dependent (under the qualifying child category) and, making use of § 222, deducts $4,000 of the tuition. On her own income tax return, Bianca also uses § 222 to deduct the $1,000 balance of the $5,000 tuition. What are the parties trying to accomplish? Have they acted properly? Explain.

OTHER PROVISIONS DEALING WITH EDUCATION

Although this chapter deals with employment-related expenses, mention should be made of various other tax provisions that deal with education. Because the encouragement of education is a desirable social goal, Congress has not been hesitant in enacting laws that provide tax incentives. The incentives come in the form of income exclusions, deductions (both *for* AGI and *from* AGI), and various credits. The paragraphs that follow summarize these benefits.

Similar to the § 222 deduction for qualified tuition and related expenses just discussed is a deduction for interest on student loans.[33] Also treated as a deduction *for* AGI, a maximum of up to $2,500 per year is allowed.

In the area of exclusions from gross income are Coverdell Education Savings Accounts (CESAs).[34] The maximum annual contribution to a CESA is $2,000. Although no deduction is allowed for contributions, earnings on these funds accumulate free of tax. Distributions also are nontaxable if used for tuition and related expenses.

Qualified tuition programs (commonly referred to as "§ 529 plans") have the same objective as CESAs—to help pay for a beneficiary's (usually a dependent family member's) education. The tax consequences are also similar, with no deduction allowed for any contribution to the plan and no tax imposed on income accumulations.[35] Since the plan must be sponsored by a state or a private university, the terms and conditions set forth in the plan will vary accordingly.

Another exclusion from gross income comes in the form of educational assistance programs.[36] Sponsored by employers, such programs cover up to $5,250 per year of an employee's education costs (e.g., tuition, fees, books, supplies), which can be at the undergraduate or graduate level.

Last but not least in the area of exclusions are certain scholarship awards.[37] Exclusion treatment is available for scholarships covering tuition and related expenses but not for those providing room and board.

In the area of tax credits, taxpayers benefit significantly from two provisions: the American Opportunity credit (formerly the HOPE scholarship credit) and the lifetime learning credit.[38] Both cover tuition and related expenses but not room and board costs. The American Opportunity credit allows no more than $2,500 per year for the first four years of college, while the lifetime learning credit permits up to $2,000 (20 percent of qualifying costs up to $10,000) per year with no time constraints. Concept Summary 9.1 reviews the tax consequences of the various provisions dealing with education and indicates where they are discussed in the text.

LO.6

Explain how entertainment and meal expenses are treated.

9.7 ENTERTAINMENT AND MEAL EXPENSES

Many taxpayers attempt to deduct personal entertainment expenses as business expenses. For this reason, the tax law restricts the deductibility of entertainment

---

[33]§ 221.

[34]§ 530.

[35]The major advantage of one of the two types of § 529 plans is protection against increasing tuition cost. The plan freezes the tuition that will be charged to the current amount.

[36]§ 127.

[37]§ 117.

[38]§ 25A.

CONCEPT SUMMARY 9.1

Tax Consequences of Provisions Dealing with Education

Provision	Tax Effect	Income Phaseout[a]	Code	Text
			Reference	
Educational savings bonds	*Exclusion* for interest on U.S. Series EE bonds used for higher education	Yes	§ 135	Ch. 5, p. 5-31
Qualified tuition program	No deduction; *exclusion* for distributions	No	§ 529	Ch. 5, p. 5-32
Educational assistance plans	*Exclusion* of up to $5,250 for employer-provided assistance	No[b]	§ 127	Ch. 5, p. 5-20
Scholarships	*Exclusion* allowed for education costs (excluding room and board)	No	§ 117	Ch. 5, p. 5-10
Qualified tuition reduction plan	*Exclusion* as to tuition waivers for employees (and dependents) of nonprofit educational institutions	No[b]	§ 117(d)	Ch. 5, p. 5-11
Coverdell Education Savings Account (CESA)	No deduction; *exclusion* for distributions	Yes	§ 530	Ch. 19, p. 19-25
Premature distributions from IRAs	If used for qualified higher education, income recognized but penalty waived	—	§ 72(t)	Ch. 19, p. 19-28
Qualified tuition and related expenses	*Deduction for* AGI; up to $4,000	Yes	§ 222	Ch. 9, p. 9-16
Educator expenses	*Deduction for* AGI; up to $250	No	§ 62(a)(2)(D)	Ch. 9, p. 9-26
Interest on student loans	*Deduction for* AGI; up to $2,500 per year	Yes	§ 221	Ch. 10, p. 10-15
Job-related education expenses	*Deduction from* AGI for an *employee* and subject to 2%-of-AGI floor; *deduction for* AGI for *self-employed*	No	§ 162	Ch. 9, p. 9-14
American Opportunity credit	Formerly the HOPE credit; extended to 4 years of postsecondary education; up to $2,500 per year	Yes	§ 25A(i)	Ch. 13, p. 13-24
Lifetime learning credit	20% of qualifying expenses (not to exceed $10,000 per year)	Yes	§ 25(A)(c)	Ch. 13, p. 13-24

[a] The phaseout of benefits occurs when income reaches a certain level. The phaseout amounts vary widely, depend on filing status (i.e., single, married filing jointly), and are based on MAGI (modified AGI).
[b] The availability of the benefit cannot be discriminatory (i.e., cannot favor higher-income taxpayers).

expenses. The Code contains strict record-keeping requirements and provides restrictive tests for the deduction of certain types of **entertainment expenses**.

CUTBACK ADJUSTMENT

During the administration of Jimmy Carter, considerable controversy arose regarding the "three martini" business lunch. By virtue of allowing a tax deduction, should the tax law be subsidizing a practice that contained a significant element of personal pleasure? One possible remedy for the situation was to disallow any deduction for business entertainment, but this option was regarded as being too harsh. Instead the *cutback* rule was instituted. Rather than disallowing *all* of the deduction, allow only a certain percentage, and the rest of the expenditure would be cut back. Currently, only 50 percent of meal and entertainment expenses are allowed as a deduction.[39] The limitation applies in the context of both employment and self-

---
[39]§ 274(n).

employment status. Although the 50 percent cutback can apply to either the employer or the employee, it will not apply twice. The cutback applies to the one who really pays (economically) for the meals or entertainment.

EXAMPLE 32	Jane, an employee of Pato Corporation, entertains one of her clients. If Pato Corporation does not reimburse Jane, she is subject to the cutback adjustment. If, however, Pato Corporation reimburses Jane (or pays for the entertainment directly), Pato suffers the cutback. ▪

In certain situations, however, a full 50 percent cutback seems unfair. If, for example, the hours of service are regulated (by the U.S. Department of Transportation) and away-from-home meals are frequent and necessary, the "three martini" business lunch type of abuse is unlikely. Consequently, the cutback rule is mitigated for the following types of employees:

- Certain air transportation employees, such as flight crews, dispatchers, mechanics, and control tower operators.
- Interstate truck and bus drivers.
- Certain railroad employees, such as train crews and dispatchers.
- Certain merchant mariners.

Effective for 2008 and thereafter, 80 percent of the cost of meals is allowed as a deduction.

What Is Covered

Transportation expenses are not affected by the cutback rule—only meals and entertainment. The cutback also applies to taxes and tips relating to meals and entertainment. Cover charges, parking fees at an entertainment location, and room rental fees for a meal or cocktail party are also subject to the 50 percent rule.

EXAMPLE 33	Joe pays a $40 cab fare to meet his client for dinner. The meal costs $150, and Joe leaves a $30 tip. His deduction is $130 [($150 + $30) × 50% + $40 cab fare]. ▪

What Is Not Covered

The cutback rule has a number of exceptions. One exception covers the case where the full value of the meals or entertainment is included in the compensation of the employee (or independent contractor).

EXAMPLE 34	Myrtle wins an all-expense-paid trip to Europe for selling the most insurance for her company during the year. Her employer treats this trip as additional compensation to Myrtle. The cutback adjustment does not apply to the employer. ▪

Another exception applies to meals and entertainment in a subsidized eating facility or where the *de minimis* fringe benefit rule is met (see Chapter 5).

EXAMPLE 35	General Hospital has an employee cafeteria on the premises for its doctors, nurses, and other employees. The cafeteria operates at cost. The cutback rule does not apply to General Hospital. ▪

EXAMPLE 36	Canary Corporation gives a ham, a fruitcake, and a bottle of wine to each employee at year-end. Since the *de minimis* fringe benefit exclusion applies to business gifts of packaged foods and beverages, their *full* cost is deductible by Canary. ▪

A similar exception applies to employer-paid recreational activities for employees (e.g., the annual Christmas party or spring picnic).[40]

CLASSIFICATION OF EXPENSES

Entertainment expenses are categorized as follows: those *directly related* to business and those *associated with* business.[41] Directly related expenses are related to an actual business meeting or discussion. These expenses are distinguished from entertainment expenses that are incurred to promote goodwill, such as maintaining existing customer relations. To obtain a deduction for directly related entertainment, it is not necessary to show that actual benefit resulted from the expenditure as long as there was a reasonable expectation of benefit. To qualify as directly related, the expense should be incurred in a clear business setting. If there is little possibility of engaging in the active conduct of a trade or business due to the nature of the social facility, it is difficult to qualify the expenditure as directly related to business.

Expenses associated with, rather than directly related to, business entertainment must serve a specific business purpose, such as obtaining new business or continuing existing business. These expenditures qualify only if the expenses directly precede or follow a bona fide business discussion. Entertainment occurring on the same day as the business discussion meets the test.

RESTRICTIONS UPON DEDUCTIBILITY

Business Meals

Any business meal is deductible only if the following are true:[42]

- The meal is directly related to or associated with the active conduct of a trade or business.
- The expense is not lavish or extravagant under the circumstances.
- The taxpayer (or an employee) is present at the meal.

A business meal with a business associate or customer is not deductible unless business is discussed before, during, or after the meal. This requirement is not intended to disallow the deduction for a meal consumed while away from home on business.

> **EXAMPLE 37**
>
> Lacy travels to San Francisco for a business convention. She pays for dinner with three colleagues and is not reimbursed by her employer. They do not discuss business. She can deduct 50% of the cost of her meal. However, she cannot deduct the cost of her colleagues' meals. ■

The taxpayer or an employee must be present at the business meal for the meal to be deductible. An independent contractor who renders significant services to the taxpayer is treated as an employee.

> **EXAMPLE 38**
>
> Lance, a party to a contract negotiation, buys dinner for other parties to the negotiation but does not attend the dinner. No deduction is allowed. ■

Club Dues

The Code provides: "No deduction shall be allowed . . . for amounts paid or incurred for membership in any club organized for business, pleasure, recreation, or other social purpose."[43] Although this prohibition seems quite broad, the IRS does allow a deduction for dues to clubs whose primary purpose is public service and community volunteerism (e.g., Kiwanis, Lions, Rotary).

Even though dues are not deductible, actual entertainment at a club may qualify.

---

[40]§ 274(e)(4).
[41]§ 274(a)(1)(A).

[42]§ 274(k).
[43]§ 274(a)(3).

EXAMPLE 39

During the current year, Vincent spent $1,400 on business lunches at the Lakeside Country Club. The annual membership fee was $6,000, and Vincent used the facility 60% of the time for business. Presuming the lunches meet the business meal test, Vincent may claim $700 (50% × $1,400) as a deduction. None of the club dues are deductible. ■

Ticket Purchases for Entertainment

A deduction for the cost of a ticket for an entertainment activity is limited to the face value of the ticket.[44] This limitation is applied before the 50 percent rule. The face value of a ticket includes any tax. Under this rule, the excess payment to a scalper for a ticket is not deductible. Similarly, the fee to a ticket agency for the purchase of a ticket is not deductible.

Expenditures for the rental or use of a luxury skybox at a sports arena in excess of the face value of regular tickets are disallowed as deductions. If a luxury skybox is used for entertainment that is directly related to or associated with business, the deduction is limited to the face value of nonluxury box seats. All seats in the luxury skybox are counted, even when some seats are unoccupied.

The taxpayer may also deduct stated charges for food and beverages under the general rules for business entertainment. The deduction for skybox seats, food, and beverages is limited to 50 percent of cost.

EXAMPLE 40

In the current year, Jay Company pays $12,000 to rent a 10-seat skybox at City Stadium for three football games. Nonluxury box seats at each event range in cost from $55 to $120 a seat. In September, a Jay representative and eight clients use the skybox for the first game. The entertainment follows a bona fide business discussion, and Jay spends $490 for food and beverages during the game. The deduction for the first sports event is as follows:

Food and beverages	$ 490
Deduction for seats ($120 × 10 seats)	1,200
Total entertainment expense	$1,690
50% limitation	× .50
Deduction	$ 845

■

Business Gifts

Business gifts are deductible to the extent of $25 per donee per year.[45] An exception is made for gifts costing $4 or less (e.g., pens with the employee's or company's name on them) or promotional materials. Such items are not treated as business gifts subject to the $25 limitation. In addition, incidental costs such as engraving of jewelry and nominal charges for gift-wrapping, mailing, and delivery are not included in the cost of the gift in applying the limitation. Gifts to superiors and employers are not deductible.

The $25 limitation on business gifts cannot be circumvented by having the donor's spouse join in the gift or by making multiple gifts that include the customer's family.

An activity that can be considered either a gift or entertainment generally will be classified as entertainment. However, packaged food or beverages intended for later consumption are treated as a gift. Tickets to a theater performance or sporting event can be treated as *either* entertainment or a gift if the taxpayer *does not* accompany the client. However, if the taxpayer also attends (see Example 40), the gift option is not available.

Records must be maintained to substantiate business gifts.

---

[44]§ 274(l).   [45]§ 274(b)(1).

9.8 OTHER EMPLOYEE EXPENSES

OFFICE IN THE HOME

Employees and self-employed individuals are not allowed a deduction for **office in the home expenses** unless a portion of the residence is used *exclusively* on a *regular basis* as either of the following:

- The principal place of business for any trade or business of the taxpayer.
- A place of business used by clients, patients, or customers.

Employees must meet an additional test: The use must be for the *convenience of the employer* rather than merely being "appropriate and helpful."[46]

The precise meaning of "principal place of business" has been the subject of considerable controversy.[47] Congress ultimately resolved the issue by amending the Code.[48] The term "principal place of business" now includes a place of business that satisfies the following requirements:

- The office is used by the taxpayer to conduct administrative or management activities of a trade or business.
- There is no other fixed location of the trade or business where the taxpayer conducts these activities.

> **L0.7**
> Identify other employee expenses.

> **EXAMPLE 41**
>
> Dr. Smith is a self-employed anesthesiologist. During the year, he spends 30 to 35 hours per week administering anesthesia and postoperative care to patients in three hospitals, none of which provides him with an office. He also spends two or three hours per day in a room in his home that he uses exclusively as an office. He does not meet patients there, but he performs a variety of tasks related to his medical practice (e.g., contacting surgeons, bookkeeping, reading medical journals). A deduction will be allowed since Dr. Smith uses the office in the home to conduct administrative or management activities of his trade or business, and there is no other fixed location where these activities can be carried out. ∎

The exclusive use requirement means that part of the home must be used solely for business purposes. An exception allows mixed use (both business and personal) of the home if a licensed day-care business is involved.

> **EXAMPLE 42**
>
> Troy is self-employed and maintains an office in his home for business purposes. The office is also used by his wife to pay the family bills and by his children to do homework assignments. Troy does not satisfy the exclusive use requirement, and no office in the home deduction is allowed. ∎

> **EXAMPLE 43**
>
> Muriel operates a licensed day-care center in her home. The children use the living room as a play area during the day, and Muriel and her family use it for personal purposes in the evening and on weekends. The mixed use of the living room does not disqualify Muriel from an office in the home deduction. ∎

In arriving at the office in the home deduction, relevant expenses are categorized as direct or indirect. Direct expenses benefit only the business part of the home (e.g., the office is repainted) and are deducted in full. Indirect expenses are for maintaining and operating the home. Since they benefit both business and personal use, an allocation between the two is necessary. The allocation is made based on the

---

[46]§ 280A(c)(1).

[47]See the restrictive interpretation arrived at in *Comm. v. Soliman*, 93–1 USTC ¶50,014, 71 AFTR 2d 93–463, 113 S.Ct. 701 (USSC, 1993).

[48]§ 280A(c)(1) as modified by the Tax Reform Act of 1997.

floor space involved—divide the business area by the total home area to arrive at the business percentage.

The allowable home office expenses cannot exceed the gross income from the business less all other business expenses attributable to the activity. Furthermore, the home office expenses that are allowed as itemized deductions anyway (e.g., mortgage interest and real estate taxes) must be deducted first. All home office expenses of an employee are miscellaneous itemized deductions, except those (such as interest and taxes) that qualify as other personal itemized deductions. Home office expenses of a self-employed individual are trade or business expenses and are deductible *for* AGI.

WHOSE OFFICE IS IT?

Gene and Mary are married, and both work at home. Gene is self-employed, while Mary is employed. They have set aside 20 percent of the living area of their residence for an office that they both use. On a joint return for the year, the full office in the home expenses are deducted on Gene's Schedule C (Profit or Loss From Business), while Mary's Form 2106 (Employee Business Expenses) contains no such deduction. What are the parties trying to accomplish? Have they acted properly?

Any disallowed home office expenses are *carried forward* and used in future years subject to the same limitations.

EXAMPLE 44

Rick is a certified public accountant employed by a regional CPA firm as a tax manager. He operates a separate business in which he refinishes furniture in his home. For this business, he uses two rooms in the basement of his home exclusively and regularly. The floor space of the two rooms constitutes 10% of the floor space of his residence. Gross income from the business totals $8,000. Expenses of the business (other than home office expenses) are $6,500. Rick incurs the following home office expenses:

Real property taxes on residence	$ 4,000
Interest expense on residence	7,500
Operating expenses of residence	2,000
Depreciation on residence (based on 10% business use)	250

Rick's deductions are determined as follows:

Business income		$ 8,000
Less: Other business expenses		(6,500)
		$ 1,500
Less: Allocable taxes ($4,000 × 10%)	$400	
Allocable interest ($7,500 × 10%)	750	(1,150)
		$ 350
Allocable operating expenses of the residence ($2,000 × 10%)		(200)
		$ 150
Allocable depreciation ($250, limited to remaining income)		(150)
		$ –0–

Rick has a carryover of $100 (the unused excess depreciation). Because he is self-employed, the allocable taxes and interest ($1,150), the other deductible office expenses ($200 + $150), and $6,500 of other business expenses are deductible *for* AGI. ■

The office in the home deduction includes an allocable portion of the depreciation on the personal residence. To arrive at this depreciation, use the MACRS percentage for 39-year nonresidential real property. Except for the first and last years (i.e., 1 and 40), the applicable percentage is 2.564 percent—see Table 8.6 in Chapter 8.

The furnishings of the office are handled separately and are either expensed under § 179 or depreciated in accordance with the rules set forth in Chapter 8—see Exhibit 8.1 and Table 8.1.

An office in the home deduction is also available to those who rent (rather than own) their home. If the taxpayer does not own the property, the applicable percentage of business use is applied to the rent being paid.

EXAMPLE 45
THE BIG PICTURE

Return to the facts of *The Big Picture* on p. 9-2. The portion of Morgan's rent, utilities, renters' insurance, and the like allocable to her office will qualify for the deduction. Because she will be working in an apartment where space is limited, she must be careful to meet the exclusive-use requirement for the area set aside. For the furnishings she acquires (e.g., desk, file cabinet), Morgan may prefer to forgo expensing (§ 179) and claim depreciation instead. This way the tax deduction is deferred to later, higher-income years. ■

To claim the office in the home deduction, use Form 8829 (Expenses for Business Use of Your Home). For further information on the deduction, see the instructions for Form 8829 and *Business Use of Your Home* (Publication 587) issued by the IRS.

MISCELLANEOUS EMPLOYEE EXPENSES

Miscellaneous employee expenses include those costs that are job related and are not otherwise covered elsewhere. As the focus here is on their deductibility, this discussion presumes that such expenses have not been reimbursed by the employer under an accountable plan arrangement (discussed later in the chapter).

Expenses related to maintaining job status make up a significant category of miscellaneous expenses. They include such costs as union dues, membership dues to professional organizations, subscriptions to trade publications and professional journals, and various license fees paid to government agencies and other regulatory bodies.

Special Clothing

To be deductible, special clothing must be both specifically required as a condition of employment and not adaptable for regular wear. For example, a police officer's uniform must be worn when "on duty" but is not suitable for "off-duty" activities. Its cost, therefore, is deductible. When special clothing qualifies for deductibility, so does the cost of its maintenance (i.e., alterations, laundry, dry cleaning).

Whether the out-of-pocket cost of military uniforms is deductible depends on the duty status of the taxpayer. If a member of the National Guard (or reserves) is not on active duty, then the cost of the uniform qualifies for deductibility. For those on active duty, the cost of regular uniforms does not qualify because the uniforms are suitable for ordinary street wear. Even for those on active duty, some apparel, such as ceremonial attire (dress blues) or combat gear, will qualify because it is not adaptable for regular wear.

The cost of clothing possessing *safety* features to prevent workplace injuries will qualify. This includes such items as safety glasses, shoes (e.g., "steel-toed"), special gloves, lab coats, and "hard hats." The tolerance of the IRS in the area of safety clothing is partially attributable to its lack of suitability for personal use.

Job Hunting

The expenses incurred in seeking employment can be deductible under certain conditions. The search must involve the same trade or business as the taxpayer's current position. No deduction is allowed for the cost of obtaining the first job. An unemployed person, however, can qualify for the deduction if there has not been a significant time lapse since the last job. In terms of deductibility, it does not matter whether the job search is successful. Nor does a change in jobs have to result. Costs that qualify include job counseling, compilation and distribution of biographical data (such as work history), and unreimbursed travel for job interviews.

EXAMPLE 46
THE BIG PICTURE

Return to the facts of *The Big Picture* on p. 9-2. Recall that Morgan conducted an extensive job search before obtaining her position with Kite Corporation. Because this is her first job, the expenses she incurred in the search are not deductible. ■

Educator Expenses

Many teachers purchase school supplies for classroom use and are not reimbursed by their employer. These out-of-pocket expenses can be deducted only if the teacher itemizes his or her deductions *from* AGI, and even then they are subject to the 2 percent-of-AGI floor (see later in this chapter). Thus, these restrictions can reduce or eliminate any tax benefit available to the teacher. Recent legislation provides *modest* relief for such out-of-pocket expenses by allowing elementary and secondary school teachers to claim up to $250 for school supplies as a deduction *for* AGI.[49] Eligible educators must work at least 900 hours during a school year as a teacher, instructor, counselor, principal, or aide at either public or private elementary and secondary schools. Covered costs include unreimbursed expenses for books, supplies, computer and other equipment, and supplementary materials used in the classroom.

EXAMPLE 47

Hortense is a full-time teacher at Hoover Elementary. During 2011, she spends $1,200 for school supplies for her fourth grade class. Under an accountable plan (see later in the chapter), Hoover reimburses her for $400 of these supplies. As to the $800 balance, Hortense may claim $250 as a deduction *for* AGI and $550 as a miscellaneous itemized deduction (subject to the 2%-of-AGI floor). ■

9.9 CONTRIBUTIONS TO RETIREMENT ACCOUNTS

LO.8

Compare various deductions for contributions to retirement accounts.

Pension considerations are an essential feature of any compensation arrangement. As noted in Chapter 1, providing retirement security for employees can be justified on both economic and social grounds. Because the public sector (i.e., Social Security) will not provide sufficient retirement security for recipients, the private sector must fill the need. Congress has given the private sector the necessary incentive by enacting various measures that provide significant tax advantages for retirement plans. These plans fall into two major classifications: those available to employees and those available to self-employed persons.

---

[49]§ 62(a)(2)(D). This provision expired at the end of 2007, but was extended through 2009 and now has been extended through 2011.

EMPLOYEE IRAs

Pension plans covering employees follow one of two income tax approaches. Most plans allow an *exclusion* for the contributions the employee makes to the plan. The employee's income tax return shows nothing regarding the contribution—no income, exclusion, or deduction. This is the case even if the contribution is funded entirely (or partially) by means of a salary reduction.[50]

The other income tax approach is followed by the **traditional IRA**. Here, the contributing employee is allowed a deduction *for* AGI. The amount, a maximum of $5,000 for 2011, is reported as a deduction on Form 1040.[51] As with the exclusion variety of pension plan, nothing is taxed to the employee-participant until distributions from the traditional IRA occur. Consequently, all of these types of retirement plans carry the advantage of deferring the taxation of income. As described in Chapter 19, all retirement plans are subject to various rules regarding coverage requirements, degree of vesting, excessive contributions, and premature distributions. Generally, these rules are less stringent for traditional IRAs.

The traditional IRA is to be distinguished from the **Roth IRA**, which takes a radically different tax approach. No tax benefit (i.e., exclusion or deduction) results from the initial contribution to a Roth IRA. Instead, later distributions (including postcontribution earnings) are recovered tax-free.[52]

SELF-EMPLOYED KEOGH (H.R. 10) PLANS

Self-employed taxpayers can also participate in retirement plans with tax-favored benefits. Known as Keogh (or H.R. 10) plans, these arrangements follow the deduction approach of traditional IRAs.[53] The amount contributed under a plan is a deduction *for* AGI and is reported as a deduction on Form 1040. The plan established by a self-employed taxpayer who has employees must meet stringent requirements to ensure that it provides similar retirement benefits for the group. The law is structured to ensure that employees share an owner-employer's ability to defer taxes.

Retirement plans for self-employed taxpayers and other small businesses are not restricted to H.R. 10 plans. Other options include solo or individual § 401(k) plans, simplified employee pension (SEP) plans, and savings incentive match plans for employees (SIMPLEs).[54] The operational rules governing all of these plans are covered in Chapter 19.

9.10 CLASSIFICATION OF EMPLOYEE EXPENSES

The classification of employee expenses depends on whether they are reimbursed by the employer under an accountable plan. If so, then they are not reported by the employee at all. In effect, therefore, this result is equivalent to treating the expenses as deductions *for* AGI. If the expenses are reimbursed under a nonaccountable plan or are not reimbursed at all, then they are classified as deductions *from* AGI and can be claimed only if the employee-taxpayer itemizes. An exception is made for moving expenses and the employment-related expenses of a qualified performing artist.[55] Here, deduction *for* AGI classification is allowed.

For classification purposes, therefore, the difference between accountable and nonaccountable plans is significant.

> **LO.9**
> Demonstrate the difference between accountable and nonaccountable employee plans.

---

[50]See, for example, §§ 401(k), 403(b), and 457.
[51]§§ 219 and 408.
[52]§ 408A.

[53]§ 401(c).
[54]Relevant Code Sections are § 408(k) for SEPs and § 408(p) for SIMPLEs..
[55]As defined in § 62(b).

ACCOUNTABLE PLANS

In General

An **accountable plan** requires the employee to satisfy these two requirements:

- Adequately account for (substantiate) the expenses. An employee renders an *adequate accounting* by submitting a record, with receipts and other substantiation, to the employer.[56]
- Return any excess reimbursement or allowance. An "excess reimbursement or allowance" is any amount that the employee does not adequately account for as an ordinary and necessary business expense.

Substantiation

The law provides that no deduction is allowed for any travel, entertainment, business gift, or listed property (automobiles, computers) expenditure unless properly substantiated by adequate records. The records should contain the following information:[57]

- The amount of the expense.
- The time and place of travel or entertainment (or date of gift).
- The business purpose of the expense.
- The business relationship of the taxpayer to the person entertained (or receiving the gift).

This means the taxpayer must maintain an account book or diary in which the above information is recorded at the time of the expenditure. Documentary evidence, such as itemized receipts, is required to support any expenditure for lodging while traveling away from home and for any other expenditure of $75 or more. If a taxpayer fails to keep adequate records, each expense must be established by a written or oral statement of the exact details of the expense and by other corroborating evidence.[58]

| EXAMPLE 48 | Bertha has travel expenses substantiated only by canceled checks. The checks establish the date, place, and amount of the expenditure. Because neither the business relationship nor the business purpose is established, the deduction is disallowed.[59] ∎ |

| EXAMPLE 49 | Dwight has travel and entertainment expenses substantiated by a diary showing the time, place, and amount of the expenditure. His oral testimony provides the business relationship and business purpose. However, since he has no receipts, any expenditures of $75 or more are disallowed.[60] ∎ |

Deemed Substantiation

In lieu of reimbursing actual expenses for travel away from home, many employers reduce their paperwork by adopting a policy of reimbursing employees with a *per diem* allowance, a flat dollar amount per day of business travel. Of the substantiation requirements listed previously, the *amount* of the expense is proved, or *deemed substantiated*, by using such a per diem allowance or reimbursement procedure. The amount of expenses that is deemed substantiated is equal to the lesser of the per diem allowance or the amount of the Federal per diem rate.

The regular Federal per diem rate is the highest amount that the Federal government will pay to its employees for lodging, meals, and incidental expenses[61] while in travel status away from home in a particular area. The rates are different for different locations.[62]

[56]Reg. § 1.162–17(b)(4).

[57]§ 274(d).

[58]Reg. § 1.274–5T(c)(3).

[59]*William T. Whitaker*, 56 TCM 47, T.C.Memo. 1988–418.

[60]*W. David Tyler*, 43 TCM 927, T.C.Memo. 1982–160.

[61]Incidental expenses include tips and fees to porters, bellhops, hotel maids, etc. For travel away from home, the term does *not* include expenses for laundry and dry cleaning of clothing, lodging taxes, and telephone calls.

[62]*Per Diem Rates* (IRS Publication 1542) contains the list and amounts for the year. This publication is available only on the Internet at **www.irs.gov**. A print edition is no longer published. Links to per diem rates can also be found at **www.gsa.gov**.

The use of the standard Federal per diem rates for meals and incidental expenses constitutes an adequate accounting. Employees and self-employed persons can use these standard allowances instead of deducting the actual cost of daily meals and incidental expenses, even if not reimbursed. There is no standard lodging allowance, however.

Only the amount of the expense is considered substantiated under the deemed substantiated method. The other substantiation requirements must be provided: place, date, business purpose of the expense, and the business relationship of the parties involved.

NONACCOUNTABLE PLANS

A **nonaccountable plan** is one in which an adequate accounting or return of excess amounts, or both, is not required. All reimbursements of expenses are reported in full as wages on the employee's Form W–2. Any allowable expenses are deductible in the same manner as are unreimbursed expenses.

Unreimbursed Employee Expenses

Unreimbursed employee expenses are treated in a straightforward manner. Meals and entertainment expenses are subject to the 50 percent limit. Total unreimbursed employee business expenses are usually reported as miscellaneous itemized deductions subject to the 2 percent-of-AGI floor (see below). If the employee could have received, but did not seek, reimbursement for whatever reason, none of the employment-related expenses are deductible.

Failure to Comply with Accountable Plan Requirements

An employer may have an accountable plan and require employees to return excess reimbursements or allowances, but an employee may fail to follow the rules of the plan. In that case, the expenses and reimbursements are subject to nonaccountable plan treatment.

REPORTING PROCEDURES

The reporting requirements range from no reporting at all (accountable plans when all requirements are met) to the use of some or all of the following forms: Form W–2 (Wage and Tax Statement), Form 2106 (Employee Business Expenses) or Form 2106–EZ (Unreimbursed Employee Business Expenses), and Schedule A (Itemized Deductions) for nonaccountable plans and unreimbursed employee expenses.

Reimbursed employee expenses that are adequately accounted for under an accountable plan are deductible *for* AGI on Form 2106. Allowed excess expenses, expenses reimbursed under a nonaccountable plan, and unreimbursed expenses are deductible *from* AGI on Schedule A, subject to the 2 percent-of-AGI floor.

When a reimbursement under an accountable plan is paid in separate amounts relating to designated expenses such as meals or entertainment, no problem arises. The reimbursements and expenses are reported as such on the appropriate forms. If the reimbursement is made in a single amount, an allocation must be made to determine the appropriate portion of the reimbursement that applies to meals and entertainment and to other employee expenses.

EXAMPLE 50

Elizabeth, who is employed by Green Company, had AGI of $42,000. During the year, she incurred $2,000 of transportation and lodging expense and $1,000 of meals and entertainment expense, all fully substantiated. Elizabeth received $1,800 reimbursement under an accountable plan. The reimbursement rate that applies to meals and entertainment is 33.33% ($1,000 meals and entertainment expense/$3,000 total expenses). Thus, $600 ($1,800 × 33.33%) of the reimbursement applies to meals and entertainment, and $1,200($1,800 − $600) applies to transportation and lodging. Elizabeth's itemized deduction consists of the $800 ($2,000 total − $1,200 reimbursement) of unreimbursed transportation and lodging expenses and $400 ($1,000 − $600) of unreimbursed meal and entertainment expenses as follows:

Transportation and lodging	$ 800
Meals and entertainment ($400 × 50%)	200
Total (reported on Form 2106)	$1,000
Less: 2% of $42,000 AGI (see limitation discussed below)	(840)
Deduction (reported on Schedule A)	$ 160

In summary, Elizabeth reports $3,000 of expenses and the $1,800 reimbursement on Form 2106 and $160 as a miscellaneous itemized deduction on Schedule A. ∎

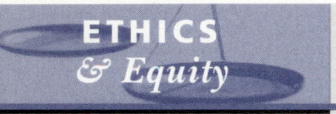

A SANITIZED EXPENSE ACCOUNT

Donald is a star traveling salesperson for Cardinal Supply, a nationwide wholesaler of sporting goods equipment. He also has a reputation with management of being very conservative in his use of company funds. Because of these traits—salesmanship and frugality—Donald has received frequent promotions and bonuses.

Unknown to the company, Donald is quite generous when entertaining customers. He feels that his high level of "wine and dine" is largely responsible for his outstanding sales record. In the expense account he submits to the company, Donald omits the excessive portion. He is not sure that the company would reimburse him for the extra costs, and he wants to maintain his reputation for frugality. On his own tax return, however, Donald deducts the portion of the expenses that were not included in his expense account.

What difficulties, if any, do you anticipate with what Donald is doing?

9.11 LIMITATIONS ON ITEMIZED DEDUCTIONS

L0.10

Apply the limitations on miscellaneous itemized deductions.

Many itemized deductions, such as medical expenses and charitable contributions, are subject to limitations expressed as a percentage of AGI. These limitations may be expressed as floors or ceilings and are discussed in Chapter 10.

MISCELLANEOUS ITEMIZED DEDUCTIONS SUBJECT TO THE 2 PERCENT FLOOR

Certain miscellaneous itemized deductions, including most *unreimbursed employee business expenses*, are aggregated and then reduced by 2 percent of AGI.[63] Expenses subject to the 2 percent floor include the following:

- All § 212 expenses, except expenses of producing rent and royalty income (refer to Chapter 6).
- All unreimbursed employee expenses (after the 50 percent reduction, if applicable) except moving.
- Professional dues and subscriptions.
- Union dues and work uniforms.
- Employment-related education expenses (except for § 222 qualified tuition and related expenses).

[63]§ 67.

TAX *in* the NEWS	RELIEF FOR MEMBERS OF THE ARMED FORCES RESERVES

In the Military Family Tax Relief Act of 2003, Congress provided various tax benefits for reservists, one of which deals with the classification of travel expenses. Members of the Reserves or National Guard who travel to drills and other service-related activities may claim the expenses as deductions *for* AGI. Previously, the expenses were not deductible unless the taxpayer itemized. (As miscellaneous itemized deductions, they were subject to the 2 percent-of-AGI floor.) To qualify for the deduction *for* AGI classification, the trip must be more than 100 miles from home and include an overnight stay. Any deduction is limited to the Federal per diem rates applicable to the area involved.

Source: Armed Forces' Tax Guide (IRS Publication 3), p. 5.

- Malpractice insurance premiums.
- Expenses of job hunting (including employment agency fees and résumé-writing expenses).
- Home office expenses of an employee or outside salesperson.
- Legal, accounting, and tax return preparation fees.
- Hobby expenses (up to hobby income).
- Investment expenses, including investment counsel fees, subscriptions, and safe deposit box rental.
- Custodial fees relating to income-producing property or a traditional IRA or a Keogh plan.
- Any fees paid to collect interest or dividends.
- Appraisal fees establishing a casualty loss or charitable contribution.

MISCELLANEOUS ITEMIZED DEDUCTIONS NOT SUBJECT TO THE 2 PERCENT FLOOR

Certain miscellaneous itemized deductions, including the following, are not subject to the 2 percent floor:

- Impairment-related work expenses of handicapped individuals.
- Gambling losses to the extent of gambling winnings.
- Certain terminated annuity payments.

EXAMPLE 51

Ted, who has AGI of $40,000, has the following miscellaneous itemized deductions:

Gambling losses (to extent of gains)	$2,200
Tax return preparation fees	500
Unreimbursed employee transportation	600
Professional dues and subscriptions	360
Safe deposit box rental	90

Ted's itemized deductions are as follows:

Deduction not subject to 2% floor (gambling losses)		$2,200
Deductions subject to 2% floor ($500 + $600 + $360 + $90)	$1,550	
Less 2% of AGI	(800)	750
Total miscellaneous itemized deductions		$2,950

If instead Ted's AGI is $80,000, the floor is $1,600 (2% of $80,000), and he cannot deduct any expenses subject to the 2% floor. ■

TAX PLANNING:

9.12 SELF-EMPLOYED INDIVIDUALS

LO.11

Discuss tax planning ideas related to employee business expenses.

Some taxpayers have the flexibility to be classified as either employees or self-employed individuals. Examples include real estate agents and direct sellers. These taxpayers should carefully consider all factors and not automatically assume that self-employed status is preferable.

It is advantageous to deduct one's business expenses *for* AGI and avoid the 2 percent floor. However, a self-employed individual may have higher expenses, such as local gross receipts taxes, license fees, franchise fees, personal property taxes, and occupation taxes. In addition, the record-keeping and filing requirements can be quite burdensome.

One of the most expensive considerations is the Social Security tax versus the self-employment tax. For an employee in 2011, for example, the Social Security tax applies at a rate of 4.2 percent on a base amount of wages of $106,800, and the Medicare tax applies at a rate of 1.45 percent with no limit on the base amount. For self-employed persons, the rate, but not the base amount, for each tax doubles. Even though a deduction *for* AGI is allowed for part of the self-employment tax paid, an employee and a self-employed individual are not in the same tax position on equal amounts of earnings. The self-employment tax is explained in Chapter 13. For the applicability of these taxes to employees, see Chapter 1.

If a taxpayer misclassifies workers as self-employed, rather than employees, one of the penalties for being wrong is the liability for the employment taxes that should have been paid. But this penalty for misclassifying workers will be avoided if *all* three of the following requirements are met:

- The employer has a reasonable basis for *not* treating the workers as employees. Reasonable basis means reliance on any of the following—
  - *A judicial precedent, published ruling, or technical advice.*
  - *A past IRS audit that resulted in no employment tax assessment.*
  - *A longstanding practice of independent contractor status in the same industry.*
- The employer has consistently treated the workers as independent contractors.
- The employer has filed Form 1099 MISC (Miscellaneous Income) for each worker (when such filing was required).

Satisfaction of these requirements will help an employer avoid disputes with the IRS over workers' employment status.[64]

---

[64]This safe harbor for withholding purposes originated in § 530 of the Revenue Act of 1978. See IRS *Headliner* vol. 152 (March 27, 2006).

9.13 SHIFTING DEDUCTIONS BETWEEN EMPLOYER AND EMPLOYEE

An employee can avoid the 2 percent floor for employee business expenses. Typically, an employee incurs travel and entertainment expenses in the course of employment. The employer gets the deduction if it reimburses the employee, and the employee gets the deduction *for* AGI. An adequate accounting must be made, and excess reimbursements cannot be kept by the employee.

9.14 TRANSPORTATION AND TRAVEL EXPENSES

Adequate detailed records of all transportation and travel expenses should be kept. Since the regular mileage allowance often is modest in amount, a new, expensive automobile used primarily for business may generate a higher expense based on actual cost. In using the actual cost method, include the business portion of depreciation, repairs and maintenance, automobile club dues, insurance, gasoline and oil, and other related costs. The cost of gasoline, when coupled with the poor mileage performance of some vehicles, can be a significant factor. If the taxpayer is located in a metropolitan area, automobile insurance is more expensive. For the self-employed taxpayer, the business portion of finance charges (i.e., interest on car loans) can be included.

Once a method is chosen, a later change may be possible. Conversion from the automatic mileage method to the actual cost method is allowed if a basis adjustment is made for depreciation deemed taken (see Example 10). Conversion from the actual cost method to the automatic mileage method is possible only if the taxpayer has not used the MACRS statutory percentage method or claimed § 179 limited expensing.

If a taxpayer wishes to sightsee or vacation on a business trip, it would be beneficial to schedule business on both a Friday and a Monday to turn the weekend into business days for allocation purposes. It is especially crucial to schedule appropriate business days when foreign travel is involved.

ETHICS & Equity — WALKING TO SOCCER PRACTICE

Mel Wilson is married and has three children, ages 9, 12, and 14. Mel works in the city, but the family lives in the suburbs. Mrs. Wilson does not work outside the home. The Wilsons own only one automobile and for tax purposes classify it as being used 95 percent for business use and 5 percent for personal use. Do you envision any problems with this allocation? Would it matter whether the Wilsons base their deduction on the actual cost method or the automatic mileage method?

9.15 MOVING EXPENSES

Persons who retire and move to a new location incur personal nondeductible moving expenses. If the retired person accepts a full-time job in the new location, the moving expenses are deductible.

EXAMPLE 52

At the time of his retirement from the national office of a major accounting firm, Gordon had an annual salary of $420,000. He moves from New York City to Seattle to retire. To qualify for the moving expense deduction, Gordon accepts a full-time teaching position at a Seattle junior college at an annual salary of $15,000. If Gordon satisfies the 39-week test, his moving expenses are deductible. The disparity between the two salaries (previous and current) is of no consequence. ∎

9.16 EDUCATION EXPENSES

Education expenses are treated as nondeductible personal items unless the individual is employed or is engaged in a trade or business. A temporary leave of absence for further education is one way to reasonably assure that the taxpayer is still qualified, even if a full-time student. An individual was permitted to deduct education expenses even though he resigned from his job, returned to school full-time for two years, and accepted another job in the same field upon graduation. The court held that the student had merely suspended active participation in his field.[65]

If the time out of the field is too long, educational expense deductions will be disallowed. For example, a teacher who left the field for four years to raise her child and curtailed her employment searches and writing activities was denied a deduction. She was not actively engaged in the trade or business of being an educator.[66]

To secure the deduction, an individual should arrange his or her work situation to preserve employee or business status.

The deduction for qualified tuition and related expenses provides some relief from the current restrictions on the deduction of education expenses by employees. First, the education expense does not have to be work related. Second, it is a deduction *for* (not *from*) AGI. Unfortunately, the deduction possesses severe shortcomings: not only is the annual amount allowed quite modest, but it may be unavailable to certain taxpayers. It is not available, for example, to those who exceed an AGI ceiling or to someone who can be claimed as a dependent of another.

Before selecting the § 222 deduction approach, however, consider the possible availability of the American Opportunity (formerly the HOPE credit) or the lifetime learning credit under § 25A.[67] As credits provide a dollar-for-dollar reduction of tax liability, these provisions could yield a greater tax benefit than deductions *for* AGI. But these credits may not be available to higher-income taxpayers.

9.17 ENTERTAINMENT AND MEAL EXPENSES

Proper documentation of expenditures is essential because of the strict record-keeping requirements and the restrictive tests that must be met. For example, documentation that consists solely of credit card receipts and canceled checks may be inadequate to substantiate the business purpose and business relationship.[68] Taxpayers should maintain detailed records of amounts, time, place, business purpose, and business relationships. A credit card receipt details the place, date, and amount of the expense. A notation made on the receipt of the names of the person(s) attending, the business relationship, and the topic of discussion should constitute proper documentation.

Associated with or goodwill entertainment is not deductible unless a business discussion is conducted immediately before or after the entertainment. Furthermore, a business purpose must exist for the entertainment. Taxpayers should arrange for a business discussion before or after such entertainment. They must provide documentation of the business purpose, such as obtaining new business from a prospective customer.

Unreimbursed meals and entertainment are subject to the 50 percent cutback rule in addition to the 2 percent floor. Consequently, the procedure of negotiating a salary reduction, as discussed in the next section, is even more valuable to the taxpayer.

9.18 UNREIMBURSED EMPLOYEE BUSINESS EXPENSES

The 2 percent floor for unreimbursed employee business expenses offers a tax planning opportunity for married couples. If one spouse has high miscellaneous

---

[65]*Stephen G. Sherman*, 36 TCM 1191, T.C.Memo. 1977–301.

[66]*Brian C. Mulherin*, 42 TCM 834, T.C.Memo. 1981–454; *George A. Baist*, 56 TCM 778, T.C.Memo. 1988–554.

[67]These credits are briefly mentioned on page 18 in this chapter and are discussed at greater length in Chapter 13.

[68]*Kenneth W. Guenther*, 54 TCM 382, T.C.Memo. 1987–440.

expenses subject to the floor, it may be beneficial for the couple to file separate returns. If they file jointly, the 2 percent floor is based on the incomes of both. Filing separately lowers the reduction to 2 percent of only one spouse's income.

Other provisions of the law should be considered, however. For example, filing separately could cost a couple losses of up to $25,000 from self-managed rental units under the passive activity loss rules (discussed in Chapter 11).

Another possibility is to negotiate a salary reduction with one's employer in exchange for the 100 percent reimbursement of employee expenses. The employee is better off because the 2 percent floor does not apply. The employer is better off because certain expense reimbursements are not subject to Social Security and other payroll taxes.

REFOCUS ON THE BIG PICTURE

THE FIRST JOB

The first issue that might arise as a result of Morgan's new job is the dependency exemption possibility. If Morgan was living at home and accepted the job late in the year, she could qualify as a dependent of her parents. If so, they might also be able to claim the qualified tuition deduction (or the lifetime learning credit). If, however, her employment began early in the year, she could not be a qualifying child (due to the self-supporting limitation) or a qualifying relative (due to the gross income limitation)—see Chapter 3.

Although Morgan's "extensive search" for employment indicates that she may have incurred job hunting expenses, such expenses are not deductible in a *first job* setting (see Example 46). Her qualified moving expenses, however, are not so restricted. Moving expenses are deductions *for* AGI (see Example 28).

Under the circumstances, Morgan is justified in claiming an office in the home deduction. The deduction would include a portion of the rent paid for the apartment, depreciation on office equipment, and other operating expenses (e.g., utilities). She must be careful not to violate the "exclusive use" restriction (see Example 45).

As she is required to travel as part of her job, Morgan will use her car for business. Thus, she will need to make a choice between the automatic mileage method and the actual cost method (see Example 11). Since her tax home is in her apartment, she will have no nondeductible commuting expenses (see Example 9).

If she renders an adequate accounting (and has to return any excess) to Kite Corporation, then her allowance need not be reported on her Federal income tax return. Nonreimbursed amounts, however, will have to be allocated between meals and entertainment (subject to the 50 percent cutback adjustment) and other employment-related expenses. The balance is an itemized deduction subject to the 2 percent-of-AGI floor.

If she does not render an adequate accounting, the full allowance is included in her gross income. All of the meals and entertainment expenses are subject to the 50 percent cutback adjustment, and the total of all employment-related expenses is an itemized deduction subject to the 2 percent-of-AGI floor.

If Morgan started the job with Kite Corporation late in the year, it is unlikely that she will be in a position to itemize her deductions *from* AGI. Instead, she will claim the standard deduction.

Morgan must maintain adequate substantiation regarding all of these employment-related transactions. Detailed records are particularly important in arriving at the office in the home deduction and the business use of an automobile (under the actual cost method). If Morgan does not render an accounting to Kite, records are crucial in supporting the travel and entertainment expenses.

KEY TERMS

Accountable plan, 9–28

Automatic mileage method, 9–6

Deduction for qualified tuition and related expenses, 9–16

Education expenses, 9–14

Entertainment expenses, 9–19

Independent contractor, 9–3

Moving expenses, 9–12

Nonaccountable plan, 9–29

Office in the home expenses, 9–23

Roth IRA, 9–27

Statutory employees, 9–4

Traditional IRA, 9–27

Transportation expenses, 9–5

Travel expenses, 9–8

DISCUSSION QUESTIONS

ISSUE ID

1. **LO.1, 9** Kirk and Yvette are married and file a joint return. Their return for 2010 included a Form 2106 for each of them. Their return for 2011, however, included a Form 2106 for Kirk and a Schedule C for Yvette. In terms of employment status, what probably occurred?

ISSUE ID

2. **LO.1, 9** Yolanda is employed but is not reimbursed by her employer for her job-related expenses. If Yolanda always claims the standard deduction, she can never deduct any of these expenses. Do you agree with this conclusion? Explain.

3. **LO.1** Milton performs services for Junco Company. In determining whether Milton is an employee or an independent contractor, discuss the relevance of each of the independent factors listed below:
   a. Milton acquired his job skills at Junco's training program.
   b. Milton sets his own work schedule.
   c. Milton uses the tools provided by Junco.
   d. Milton furnishes his own assistants.
   e. The services are performed at Milton's workplace.
   f. Junco issues a Form W–2 to Milton at year-end.
   g. Milton is paid on an hourly basis.
   h. Milton reports his unreimbursed expenses on a Form 2106.

DECISION MAKING

4. **LO.1** Bernard operates a hair styling salon as a sole proprietor. Because his shop has several extra work stations that are not being used, he is considering renting these to other stylists, but he wants to avoid any employer-employee relationship with them. Advise Bernard on the type of working arrangement he should set up to ensure that any new stylists will be classified as independent contractors and not as employees.

ISSUE ID

5. **LO.2, 11** Garth recently purchased a new automobile for which he plans mixed use (i.e., both business and personal). In the next few years, he intends to use the actual cost method to maximize the depreciation deduction on the car and, thereafter, to convert to the automatic mileage method. He expects that this approach will maximize his tax benefits from the business use of the car. Are there any flaws in Garth's plan?

DECISION MAKING

6. **LO.2, 11** Kristen has just purchased a new automobile that she plans to use about 70% of the time for business. As to the difference between the actual cost method and the automatic mileage method, advise Kristen on the tax treatment of the following items:
   a. State and local sales tax on the purchase of the auto.
   b. Business parking.
   c. Interest on auto loan.
   d. Depreciation.
   e. Auto insurance and automobile club dues.
   f. Toll charges while on family vacation trip.
   g. Periodic oil changes and rotation of tires.
   h. Fines for traffic violations incurred during business use.

ISSUE ID

7. **LO.2** In 2009, Emma purchased an automobile, which she uses for both business and personal purposes. Although Emma does not keep records as to operating expenses (e.g., gas, oil, repairs), she can prove the percentage of business use and the miles driven each year. In March 2011, Emma seeks your advice as to what income tax benefit, if any, she can derive from the use of her automobile. What would you suggest?

8. **LO.2, 3** Explain the difference between *travel* expenses and *transportation* expenses.

9. **LO.3** Lance, who practices law in New York City, leaves his office on Tuesday at 4:00 A.M., flies to Los Angeles, makes a court appearance at 1:00 P.M., and flies back to New York that same day.
    a.   Was Lance away from home for income tax purposes?
    b.   What difference does it make?

10. **LO.3** Dr. Werner is a full-time professor of accounting at Pelican University. During the year, he teaches continuing education programs for CPA groups in several cities. He also serves as an expert witness in numerous lawsuits involving accounting fraud. Comment on the possible tax treatment of Dr. Werner's job-related expenses.

    ISSUE ID

11. **LO.3** Bill and Jean Wilder attend a three-day seminar in Chicago on current developments in taxation. Bill is a partner in a law firm in Memphis specializing in tax practice, while his wife, Jean, is a paralegal with the same firm. Comment on the deductibility of the Wilders' expenses in attending the seminar.

12. **LO.3** Rick is scheduled to go to London on business and would like to do some sightseeing while there. A colleague advises him that to maximize his deductible expenses he should plan the business and personal portions of the trip carefully and maximize the use of weekends and holidays. What is meant by this advice?

    DECISION MAKING

13. **LO.4** In order to qualify for the moving expense deduction, a taxpayer must satisfy a time test.
    a.   What is the time test?
    b.   When might the taxpayer be excused from satisfying the time test?

14. **LO.4** Provide some examples (at least three) of moving expenses that are not "qualified" and, therefore, not deductible.

15. **LO.5, 10** Jamie has an undergraduate degree in finance and is employed full-time by a bank. She is taking courses at a local university leading to an MBA degree.
    a.   Is the cost of this education deductible to her?
    b.   If so, are any limitations imposed on the deduction?

16. **LO.5, 10** In connection with § 222 (deduction for qualified tuition and related expenses), comment on the relevance of the following:
    a.   A dentist enrolls in medical school.
    b.   The standard deduction is claimed.
    c.   Enrollment at a college requires the payment of a student activity fee.
    d.   The lifetime learning credit is claimed.
    e.   The taxpayer is married and has MAGI of $160,001.
    f.   Miscellaneous itemized deductions exceed 2% of AGI.
    g.   The tuition is paid by the taxpayer who qualifies as a dependent of his parents.
    h.   The taxpayer is married and files a separate return.

17. **LO.5, 10** The Federal income tax contains many provisions that encourage education. In this regard, give examples of various benefits available in the form of:
    a.   Exclusions from gross income.
    b.   Deductions.
    c.   Credits.

18. **LO.6** In each of the following situations, indicate whether there is a cutback adjustment.
    a.   Each year the employer awards its top salesperson an expense-paid trip to Jamaica.
    b.   The employer has a cafeteria for its employees where meals are furnished at cost.
    c.   The employer sponsors an annual Labor Day picnic for its employees.
    d.   Every Christmas, the employer gives each employee a fruit cake.
    e.   The taxpayer, an airline pilot, pays for meals and lodging during a layover between flights.
    f.   The taxpayer pays a cover charge to take key clients to a nightclub.
    g.   The taxpayer gives business gifts to her clients at Christmas.
    h.   The taxpayer purchases tickets in order to take clients to an athletic event.

19. **LO.6** At the last minute, a law firm purchases 10 tickets to the Super Bowl in order to entertain certain key clients. Comment on some possible tax ramifications of this situation.

    ISSUE ID

20. **LO.7** In connection with the office in the home deduction, comment on the following:
    a. When justified if the taxpayer is an employee.
    b. The exclusive use requirement.
    c. The distinction between *direct* and *indirect* expenses.
    d. Taxpayer is self-employed and claims the standard deduction.
    e. The deduction is not available to taxpayers who do not own their home (e.g., live in rented apartments).
    f. The treatment of expenses that exceed the gross income from the business.
    g. The treatment of expenses that might otherwise be deductible (e.g., interest on home mortgage).

ISSUE ID

21. **LO.4, 7** Trent, a resident of Florida, attends Vanderbilt University. After graduation, he moves to Dallas where he begins a job search. Shortly thereafter, he accepts a position with a local radio station as an announcer. Trent's college degree is in management. Presuming no reimbursement, what employment-related expenses might Trent be eligible to deduct?

22. **LO.8** Regarding the tax implications of various retirement plans, comment on the following:
    a. The difference between Keogh (H.R. 10) and traditional deductible IRA plans.
    b. The difference between traditional IRA and Roth IRA plans.

23. **LO.9** What tax return reporting procedures must be followed by an employee under the following circumstances?
    a. Expenses and reimbursements are equal under an accountable plan.
    b. Reimbursements at the appropriate Federal per diem rate exceed expenses, and an adequate accounting is made to the employer.
    c. Expenses exceed reimbursements under a nonaccountable plan.

DECISION MAKING

24. **LO.6, 9, 10, 11** Kim recently graduated from college and is interviewing for a position in marketing. Crane Corporation has offered her a job as a sales representative that will require extensive travel and entertainment but provide valuable experience. Under the offer, she has two options: a salary of $48,000 and she absorbs all expenses; a salary of $35,000 and Crane reimburses for all expenses. Crane assures Kim that the $13,000 difference in the two options will be adequate to cover the expenses incurred. What issues should have an impact on Kim's choice?

ISSUE ID

DECISION MAKING

25. **LO.4, 11** Ralph plans to retire and move to New Mexico. Discuss Ralph's deduction for moving expenses under the following circumstances:
    a. He is a self-employed physician living and practicing in York, Pennsylvania.
    b. He is a geologist for a major oil company living and working in Nigeria (Africa).
    c. What suggestions, if any, do you have that would improve Ralph's tax position under each assumption?

26. **LO.10** Comment on the deductibility of each of the following items:
    a. Gambling losses that are less than gambling gains. Taxpayer is not a professional gambler.
    b. Expenses incurred in applying for the CFO (chief financial officer) position of a grocery chain. Taxpayer, an auditor with a CPA firm, did not get the job.
    c. Club dues for the Coronado Club. Taxpayer, a lawyer, uses the luncheon club exclusively for business.
    d. Cost of visual aids prepared by a college professor for use in a graduate seminar.
    e. Cost of dry cleaning uniforms (including alterations by a tailor). Taxpayer is the doorman at a New York City hotel.
    f. Cost of safety shoes. Taxpayer is a self-employed stone mason.
    g. Cost of noncredit CPA exam review program. Taxpayer just graduated from business school and is employed by an accounting firm.
    h. Expenses incurred by taxpayer, a member of the Vermont National Guard, to participate in a two-day training session conducted in Pennsylvania.

PROBLEMS

27. **LO.2, 3** During the year, Judith holds two jobs. After an eight-hour day at the first job, she works three hours at the second job. On Fridays of each week, she returns home for dinner before going to the second job. On the other days (Monday through Thursday),

she goes directly from the first job to the second job, stopping along the way for a meal. The mileage involved is as follows:

Home to first job	20
First job to second job	18
Home to second job	29

    a.   Assuming Judith works 48 weeks during the year, how much of her mileage is deductible?

    b.   Can Judith deduct the dinners she purchased? Why or why not?

28. **LO.2, 5** Byron is employed by an accounting firm and uses his automobile in connection with his work. During the month of August 2011, he works at the office for 5 days and participates in the audit of a key client for 18 days. In the audit situation, Byron goes directly from his home to the client's office. On all other days, he drives to his employer's office. On four Saturdays in August, he drives from his home to a local university where he attends classes in a part-time MBA program. Relevant mileage is as follows:

Home to office	12
Office to audit client	13
Home to audit client	9
Home to university	16

Using the automatic mileage method, what is Byron's deduction for the month?

29. **LO.2** Jeri is the regional sales manager for a fast-food chain. She starts her working day by driving from home to the regional office, works there for several hours, and then visits the three sales outlets in her region. Relevant mileage is as follows:

Home to regional office	10
Regional office to sales outlet #1	11
Sales outlet #1 to sales outlet #2	13
Sales outlet #2 to sales outlet #3	12
Sales outlet #3 to home	15

If Jeri uses the automatic mileage method and works on 240 days in 2011, what is her deduction for the year?

30. **LO.2** On July 1, 2009, Rex purchases a new automobile for $40,000. He uses the car 80% for business and drives the car as follows: 8,000 miles in 2009; 19,000 miles in 2010; and 20,000 miles in 2011. Determine Rex's basis in the auto as of January 1, 2012, under the following assumptions.

    a.   Rex uses the automatic mileage method.

    b.   Rex uses the actual cost method. [Assume that no § 179 expensing is claimed and that 200% declining-balance cost recovery with the half-year convention is used—see Chapter 8. The recovery limitation for 2009 is as follows: $2,960 (first year), $4,800 (second year), $2,850 (third year).]

31. **LO.3** Carla, the regional manager for a national retail drug chain, is based in Atlanta. During March and April of this year, she has to replace temporarily the district manager in Jackson (Mississippi). During this period, Carla flies to Jackson on Sunday night, spends the week at the district office, and returns home to Atlanta on Friday afternoon. The cost of returning home is $650, while the cost of spending the weekend in Jackson would have been $500.

    a.   Presuming no reimbursement by her employer, how much, if any, of these weekend expenses may Carla deduct?

    b.   Would your answer in (a) change if the amounts involved are reversed (i.e., the trip home cost $500; staying in Jackson would have been $650)?

32. **LO.3, 6** In June of this year, Dr. and Mrs. Bret Spencer traveled to Denver to attend a three-day conference sponsored by the American Society of Implant Dentistry. Bret, a practicing oral surgeon, participated in scheduled technical sessions dealing with the latest developments in surgical procedures. On two days, Mrs. Spencer attended group meetings where various aspects of family tax planning were discussed. On the other day, she went sightseeing. Mrs. Spencer does not work for her husband, but she does their tax

returns and handles the family investments. Expenses incurred in connection with the conference are summarized below:

Airfare (two tickets)	$2,000
Lodging (single and double occupancy are the same rate—$250 each day)	750
Meals ($200 × 3 days)*	600
Conference registration fee (includes $120 for Family Tax Planning sessions)	620
Car rental	300

*Split equally between Dr. and Mrs. Spencer.

How much, if any, of these expenses can the Spencers deduct?

33. **L0.1, 3, 6** Louise works for a clothing manufacturer as a dress designer. She travels to New York City to attend three days of fashion shows and then spends three days sightseeing. Her expenses are as follows;

Airfare	$1,400
Lodging (6 nights)	1,800
Meals (6 days)	1,200
Airport transportation	120

[Assume lodging/meals are the same amount for the business and personal portion of the trip (e.g., $200 per day for meals).]

a. Presuming no reimbursement, how much can Louise deduct as to the trip?
b. Would the tax treatment of Louise's deduction differ if she was an independent contractor (rather than an employee)? Explain.

34. **L0.3** On Thursday, Justin flies from Baltimore (his home office) to Cadiz (Spain). He conducts business on Friday and Tuesday; vacations on Saturday, Sunday, and Monday (a legal holiday in Spain); and returns to Baltimore on Thursday. Justin was scheduled to return home on Wednesday, but all flights were canceled due to bad weather. Therefore, he spent Wednesday watching floor shows at a local casino.

a. For tax purposes, what portion of Justin's trip is regarded as being for business?
b. Suppose Monday had not been a legal holiday. Would this change your answer in (a)?
c. Under either (a) or (b), how much of Justin's airfare qualifies as a deductible business expense?

DECISION MAKING

35. **L0.3** Monica travels from her office in Boston to Lisbon, Portugal, on business. Her absence of 13 days was spent as follows:

Thursday	Depart for and arrive at Lisbon
Friday	Business transacted
Saturday and Sunday	Vacationing
Monday through Friday	Business transacted
Saturday and Sunday	Vacationing
Monday	Business transacted
Tuesday	Depart Lisbon and return to office in Boston

a. For tax purposes, how many days has Monica spent on business?
b. What difference does it make?
c. Could Monica have spent more time than she did vacationing on the trip without loss of existing tax benefits? Explain.

36. **L0.4** Marlo, a financial planner, decides to quit his job with an investment bank in Columbia, South Carolina, and establish a private practice in Albuquerque, New Mexico. In connection with the move, he incurs the following expenses:

Moving van charge	$4,300
Lodging during move	520
Meals during move	360
Loss on sale of residence in Columbia	4,000
Mileage for personal autos	3,400 miles

How much of these expenses, if any, can Marlo deduct?

37. **LO.4, 7** Upon losing his job as a plant manager in Quincy (Massachusetts), Anthony incurs $6,200 in job search expenses. Having no success in finding new employment in the same type of work, Anthony moves to Clearwater (Florida) and begins a charter boat business. His expenses in connection with the move are summarized below:

Penalty for breaking lease on Quincy rented residence	$2,800
Forfeiture of membership in Quincy Country Club	2,200
Packing and moving van charges	7,100
Lodging during move (3 nights)	380
Meals during move	360
Mileage (for two automobiles)	2,400 miles

How much of these expenses may Anthony deduct?

38. **LO.4** After being downsized by his former employer, in November 2010 Wayne moves from Minnesota to Alabama to accept a new job. When filing his Federal income tax return for 2010, Wayne deducts the $14,000 in moving expenses he incurred (none of which were reimbursed by either his former or new employer). On June 6, 2011, Wayne's employment terminates. What are the tax consequences if the termination occurred because:
   a. Wayne was killed by a drunk driver?
   b. Wayne was downsized by the new employer?
   c. Wayne was fired by the new employer because he assaulted a client?
   d. Wayne quit because he inherited a large amount of money and decided he did not want to work anymore?

39. **LO.5** Eric is employed as a full-time high school teacher. The school district where he works recently instituted a policy requiring all of its teachers to start working on a master's degree. Pursuant to this new rule, Eric spent most of the summer of 2011 taking graduate courses at an out-of-town university. His expenses are as follows:

Tuition	$6,300
Books and course materials	1,300
Lodging	1,500
Meals	2,200
Laundry and dry cleaning	280
Campus parking	250

In addition, Eric drove his personal automobile 1,900 miles in connection with the education. He uses the automatic mileage method.
   a. How much, if any, of these expenses might qualify as deductions *for* AGI?
   b. How much, if any, of these expenses might qualify as deductions *from* AGI?

40. **LO.5** In each of the following independent situations, determine how much, if any, qualifies as a deduction *for* AGI under § 222 (qualified tuition and related expenses):
   a. Sophia is single and is employed as an architect. During 2011, she spends $3,900 in tuition to attend law school at night. Her MAGI is $64,000.
   b. John is single and is employed as a pharmacist. During 2011, he spends $2,300 ($2,100 for tuition and $200 for books) to take a course in herbal supplements at a local university. His MAGI is $70,000.
   c. Hailey is married and is employed as a bookkeeper. She spends $5,200 for tuition and $900 for books and supplies pursuing a bachelor's degree in accounting. Her MAGI is $40,000 on the separate return she files.
   d. How much, if any, of the above amounts *not allowed under* § 222 might otherwise qualify as a deduction *from* AGI?

41. **LO.5** In each of the following independent situations, determine how much, if any, qualifies as a deduction *for* AGI under § 222 (qualified tuition and related expenses):
   a. Carmen is a divorced mother with MAGI of $66,000. She pays $4,800 to enroll her dependent son at a local college.
   b. The Bells have MAGI of $80,000 and file a joint return. They spend $4,100 to enroll their dependent daughter at a state college. The $4,100 includes $3,800 for tuition and $300 for a student activity fee.

c. Charles is single and has MAGI of $100,000. He pays $5,000 in tuition for his dependent mother to attend graduate school.

d. Benjamin is single and is claimed as a dependent by his parents. He pays $3,000 from his savings for tuition at a junior college.

42. **LO.6, 9** Dexter is a licensed commercial pilot who works for Kite Charter Jet Service. Typically, Dexter, who lives near the airport, flies a charter out of Frankfort, Kentucky, to either Las Vegas or Reno, spends several nights there, and then returns home with the same group. Kite provides Dexter with a travel allowance of $1,700 per month but requires no accountability. For the current calendar year, Dexter had the following job-related expenses:

Meals	$ 8,000
Lodging	11,000
Transportation (taxis, limos)	600
Uniforms	1,100
Dry cleaning of uniforms	300
Annual physical exam	1,000

The uniforms are required to be worn on the job. The Federal Aviation Administration requires the annual physical exam for the maintenance of a commercial pilot's license. How may Dexter treat these expenses for Federal income tax purposes?

43. **LO.6** Snipe Associates paid $70,000 for a 20-seat skybox at Veterans Stadium for eight professional football games. Regular seats to these games range from $80 to $200 each. At one game, an employee of Snipe entertained 18 clients. Snipe furnished food and beverages for the event at a cost of $1,000. The game was preceded by a bona fide business discussion, and all expenses are adequately substantiated.

a. How much may Snipe deduct for this event?

b. What, if any, is the deduction if no representative from Snipe attended the game?

c. What if there was no bona fide business discussion either preceding or after the event?

44. **LO.6** During the current year, Paul, the vice president of a bank, made gifts in the following amounts:

To Sarah (Paul's personal assistant) at Christmas	$36
To Darryl (a key client)—$3 was for gift-wrapping	53
To Darryl's wife (a homemaker) on her birthday	20
To Veronica (Paul's boss) at Christmas	30

In addition, on professional assistants' day, Paul takes Sarah to lunch at a cost of $82. Presuming Paul has adequate substantiation and is not reimbursed, how much can he deduct?

45. **LO.7** Christine is employed full-time as an accountant for a national hardware chain. She also has a private consulting practice, which provides tax advice and financial planning to the general public. For this purpose, she maintains an office in her home. Expenses relating to her home are as follows:

Real property taxes	$3,900
Interest on home mortgage	4,000
Operating expenses of home	1,100
Depreciation allocated to 20% business use	1,600

Christine's income from consulting is $16,000, and the related expenses are $5,000.

a. What is Christine's office in the home deduction?

b. Suppose that Christine also spent $3,000 to repaint and replace the carpet in the office. How do these additional costs change the answer to part (a)?

c. Suppose that Christine's income from consulting is only $8,000 (not $16,000). How does this change the answer to part (a)?

46. **LO.7** Melanie is a full-time teacher of the fifth grade at Tern Academy. During the year, she spends $1,300 for classroom supplies. Upon the submission of adequate substantiation, Tern reimburses her for $600 of these expenses—the maximum amount of reimbursement allowed for supplies under school policy. [The reimbursement is not shown as income (box 1) on the Form W–2 Tern sends to Melanie.] What are the income tax consequences of the $1,300 if Melanie:

a.   Claims the standard deduction?
b.   Chooses to itemize her deductions *from* AGI?

47. **LO.3, 6, 9** Tim has AGI of $92,000 during the year and the following expenses related to his employment:

Lodging while in travel status	$4,000
Meals during travel	3,800
Business transportation	5,200
Entertainment of clients	3,600
Professional dues and subscriptions	1,000

Tim is reimbursed $13,000 under his employer's accountable plan. What are his deductions *for* and *from* AGI?

48. **LO.3, 6, 9** During the year, Brenda has the following expenses related to her employment:

DECISION MAKING

Airfare	$8,500
Meals	4,000
Lodging	4,900
Transportation while in travel status (taxis, limos)	940
Entertainment of clients	8,000

Although Brenda renders an adequate accounting to her employer, she is reimbursed for only $12,000 of the above expenses. What are Brenda's tax consequences based on the following assumptions?
a.   The $12,000 reimbursement does not designate which expenses are covered.
b.   The reimbursement specifically covers *only* the meals and entertainment expenses.
c.   The reimbursement covers any of the expenses *other than* meals and entertainment.
d.   If Brenda has a choice of reimbursement procedures [parts (a), (b), or (c) above], which should she select and why?

49. **LO.6, 9, 10** Audry, age 38 and single, earns a salary of $59,000. She has interest income of $1,600 and has a $2,000 long-term capital loss from the sale of a stock investment. Audry incurs the following employment-related expenses during the year:

Transportation	$5,500
Meals	2,800
Lodging	4,200
Entertaining clients	2,200
Professional dues and subscriptions	300

Under an accountable plan, Audry receives reimbursements of $4,500 from her employer. Calculate her AGI and itemized employee business expenses.

50. **LO.5, 7, 10** B. J. and Carolyn Grace are full-time employees. B. J. is an elementary school teacher, and Carolyn is a registered nurse at a hospital. During 2011, they incur the following employment-related expenses:

School supplies for use in the classroom	$1,400
Emergency room uniforms	800
Union dues (teachers association)	200
Job hunting expenses (Carolyn obtained another nursing position but decided not to change jobs)	1,300
Continuing education correspondence courses (required to maintain nursing license)	380
Professional dues and subscriptions	1,100

None of these expenses are reimbursed by the employers.

For the year, the Graces file a joint return reflecting salary income of $90,000. They also have gambling income of $6,000 and gambling losses of $7,000 (fully substantiated). They pay $400 to have their tax return prepared. They have other itemized deductions (i.e., interest on home mortgage, property taxes on personal residence, state income taxes, charitable contributions) of $14,500. Determine the total amount of itemized deductions allowed to the Graces for tax year 2011.

51. **LO.1, 2, 4, 5, 7, 10** Complete the following table by classifiying each of the independent expenditures (assume no reimbursement takes place).

Expense Item	Deductible *for* AGI	Deductible *from* AGI	Not Deductible
a. Moving expense of an employee	_____	_____	_____
b. Moving expense of a self-employed taxpayer	_____	_____	_____
c. Gambling losses in excess of gambling gains incurred by a retired taxpayer	_____	_____	_____
d. Cost of taking the bar exam	_____	_____	_____
e. Tax return preparation fee incurred by an employed plumber	_____	_____	_____
f. Safety glasses purchased by an employed pipefitter	_____	_____	_____
g. Club dues to Rotary Club paid by self-employed dentist	_____	_____	_____
h. Dues to auto club (e.g., AAA) for taxpayer who uses the automatic mileage method	_____	_____	_____
i. Nursing refresher course for taxpayer who retired from nursing five years ago	_____	_____	_____

CUMULATIVE PROBLEMS

TAX RETURN PROBLEM

H&R BLOCK
At Home

52. Kirk B. and Trudy N. Ward (ages 44 and 42) are husband and wife and live at 4321 Peak Avenue, Denver, CO 80202. Kirk is a regional sales manager for Eagle Industries, a national wholesaler of plumbing and heating supplies, while Trudy is a part-time dental hygienist for a chain of dental clinics.

- Kirk is classified by Eagle as a statutory employee with compensation for 2010 (based on commissions) of $92,000. He is expected to maintain his own office and pay for all business expenses from this amount. Eagle does not require him to render an accounting. It does not withhold for Federal and state income taxes but does withhold and account for the payroll taxes incurred (e.g., Social Security and Medicare). Kirk is covered by Eagle's noncontributory medical plan but has chosen not to participate in its § 401(k) retirement plan.

    Kirk's employment-related expenses for 2010 are summarized below:

Airfare	$7,700
Lodging	5,200
Meals (during travel status)	4,800
Entertainment	3,200
Ground transportation (e.g., limos, rental cars, taxis)	900
Business gifts	600
Office supplies (includes postage, overnight delivery, copying)	1,200

    The entertainment involved business meals for purchasing agents, store owners, and building contractors. The business gifts consisted of $50 gift certificates to a national steak house. These were sent by Kirk during the Christmas holidays to 12 of his major customers.

    In addition, Kirk drove his 2008 Ford Expedition 12,000 miles for business (3,000 for personal) during 2010. He purchased the Expedition on March 15, 2008, and has always used the automatic (standard) mileage method for tax purposes.

    Parking and tolls relating to business use total $280 for 2010. (Assume the mileage on the Ford took place evenly during the year.)

- When the Wards purchased their present residence in March 2008, they devoted 300 of the 3,000 square feet of living space to an office for Kirk. The property cost $340,000 ($40,000 of which is attributable to the land) and has since appreciated in value. Expenses during 2010 relating to the residence (see below for mortgage interest and property taxes) are as follows:

Insurance	$2,400
Repairs and maintenance	900
Utilities	4,500
Carpeting (office area only)	1,500

  In terms of depreciation, the Wards use the MACRS percentage tables applicable to 39-year nonresidential real property.

- Trudy works part-time as a substitute for whichever hygienist is ill or on vacation or when one of the clinics is particularly busy (e.g., prior to the beginning of the school year). Besides her transportation, she has to provide and maintain her own uniforms. Her expenses for 2010 appear below:

Uniforms (including laundry charges of $240)	$610
State and city occupational licenses	240
Professional journal and membership dues in the American Dental Hygiene Association	310
Correspondence study course (taken online) dealing with teeth whitening procedures	400

  In addition, Trudy drove the family Chevrolet Suburban 1,800 miles going from her home to and from work assignments.

  Her Form W–2 for the year shows earnings of $41,000 and income tax withholdings of $4,000 (Federal) and $1,000 (state) and the proper amount of payroll taxes (Social Security and Medicare). Since Trudy is a part-time employee, she is not included in her employer's medical or retirement plans.

- Besides the items already mentioned, the Wards had the following receipts during 2010:

Interest income—		
State of Idaho general-purpose bonds	$1,400	
Ford Motor Company bonds	600	
Wells Fargo Bank CD	900	$ 2,900
Federal income tax refund for tax year 2009		180
Life insurance proceeds paid by Falcon Assurance Corporation		100,000
Inheritance of savings account from Louise Ward		100,000
Sales proceeds from two ATVs		8,000

  For several years, the Wards' household has included Kirk's divorced mother, Louise, who has been claimed as their dependent. In late November 2010, Louise unexpectedly died in her sleep of a coronary arrest. Unknown to them, Louise had a life insurance policy and a savings account (with Kirk as the designated beneficiary of each). In 2009, the Wards purchased two ATVs for $12,000. After several near mishaps, they decided the sport was too dangerous. In 2010, they sold the ATVs to their neighbor.

  Additional expenditures for 2010 include:

Funeral expenses for Louise Ward		$ 6,500
Taxes—		
Real property taxes on personal residence	$5,200	
Colorado state income tax due (paid in April 2010 for tax year 2009)	310	5,510
Mortgage interest on personal residence		6,200
Paid church pledge		2,400
Contributions to traditional IRAs for Trudy and Kirk ($5,000 + $5,000)		10,000

In 2010, the Wards made quarterly estimated tax payments of $1,400 (Federal) and $500 (state) for a total of $5,600 (Federal) and $2,000 (state).

Compute the Wards' Federal income tax payable or refund due, assuming they file a joint income tax return for 2010. If they have overpaid, they want the amount refunded. They do not want to contribute to the Presidential Election Campaign Fund. Suggested Software: H&R BLOCK At Home. Social Security numbers are as follows: 123–45–6787 (Louise); 123–45–6788 (Trudy); and 123–45–6789 (Kirk). Kirk's business code number is 421700.

TAX COMPUTATION PROBLEM

53. Gloria L. Carson, age 35, is single and lives alone at 430 Poplar Street, Apartment 300, Memphis, TN 38101. Gloria is the regional manager for STAFIT, a national chain of weight control and physical fitness centers.

- STAFIT pays Gloria an annual salary of $70,000 plus an expense allowance of $25,000. STAFIT requires no accounting as to the expense allowance and expects Gloria to use the funds as needed to absorb her employment-related expenses (including maintaining an office in her home). She participates in STAFIT's contributory health and § 401(k) plans. In 2011, she paid in $2,400 for the medical insurance and contributed $8,000 to the § 401(k) retirement plan.
- Gloria's employment-related expenses for 2011 include the following:

Airfare	$4,200
Lodging	3,900
Meals (while in travel status)	4,200
Entertainment	1,000
Business gifts	600
Ground transportation while in travel status (e.g., rental cars, limos, taxis)	300
Subscriptions to trade journals	120
Online correspondence course on Pilates exercises	280

The gifts consisted of fruit baskets [$25 (cost) + $2 (wrapping) + $3 (shipping)] that Gloria sent to 20 key managers at Christmas. Gloria took the correspondence course to help her evaluate the Pilates programs offered at the STAFIT centers.

- Of the 1,600 square feet of living space in Gloria's apartment, she has devoted 400 square feet for exclusive use as an office. Expenses in connection with her apartment during 2011 are as follows:

Insurance (renter's casualty and theft coverage)	$ 1,200
Rent	12,000
Utilities	3,600
Wallpapering (office area only)	1,800

- Gloria owns a Chrysler 300 that she purchased June 29, 2009, for $32,000 (no trade-in involved). The car is used 80% for business and 20% for personal purposes. Depreciation has been claimed under the MACRS 200% declining-balance method, and no § 179 election was made in the year of purchase. (For depreciation information, see Chapter 8 in the text and the IRS Instructions to Form 4562, Part V.) During 2011, Gloria drove 14,000 miles. Expenses relating to the car are:

Gasoline	$ 1,950
Repairs and maintenance	310
Auto club dues	250
Insurance	3,000
Interest on car loan	1,200
Traffic fines (all during business use)	420
Parking and tolls (all during business use)	580

- Gloria provides more than half of the support of her parents, Doyle and Grace Carson, who live in their own house in Franklin, Tennessee. In addition to Social Security benefits, the parents have a small amount of interest from municipal bonds. Besides some medical expenses (see below), Gloria also pays the premiums of $1,800 on Doyle's life insurance policy.

- Gloria had the following additional receipts in 2011:

Proceeds from the sale of land	$15,000
Fees for serving on a jury	600
TV set won in a church raffle	1,500
Cash found in a parking lot	1,000

The land sale consisted of a city lot located in Nashville (Tennessee) purchased by Gloria as an investment on April 9, 2002. She paid $20,000 for the property in the hope of future appreciation. When she was offered $15,000 for the lot, Gloria accepted and transferred title on January 6, 2011. In connection with the jury duty, Gloria incurred unreimbursed expenses (e.g., parking) of $80. The TV set cost the church $1,500 but has a retail value of $2,200. Since Gloria already owns a TV, she declined to accept the prize. While shopping at a mall during the Christmas season, Gloria found an unmarked envelope in the parking lot containing 20 $50 bills. Gloria decided to keep the money as she saw no realistic way of locating the true owner.

- Other expenditures for 2011 are summarized below:

Medical and dental expenses not covered by insurance	$6,800
Net gambling loss	1,200
State and local general sales tax	3,300
Paid church pledges for 2010 and 2011	3,600
Fee paid for preparation of 2010 Federal income tax return	500
Contribution to the reelection campaign fund of the mayor of Memphis	100

The medical expenses include $5,000 paid for dental implants received by Grace. During 2011, Gloria had gambling winnings of $600 and losses of $1,800. The $1,200 represents the end result after offsetting gains against losses. Gloria keeps a record of all of her purchases and can, therefore, substantiate the $3,300 sales tax amount. Gloria pledges $1,800 a year to her church. On January 4, 2011, she paid the pledges for 2010 and 2011.

Relevant Social Security numbers are 123–45–6786 (Gloria); 123–45–6784 (Doyle); and 123–45–6785 (Grace). Gloria's employer withheld $4,600 for Federal income tax purposes, and she applied her $450 overpayment for 2010 toward the 2011 tax liability.

Compute Gloria's Federal income tax payable or refund for 2011.

RESEARCH PROBLEMS

Note: Solutions to Research Problems can be prepared by using the **Checkpoint®** **Student Edition** online research product, which is available to accompany this text. It is also possible to prepare solutions to the Research Problems by using tax research materials found in a standard tax library.

THOMSON REUTERS
Checkpoint® Student Edition

Research Problem 1. Aaron, a resident of Minnesota, has been a driver for Green Delivery Service for the past six years. For this purpose, he leases a truck from Green, and his compensation is based on a percentage of the income resulting from his pickup and delivery services. Green allows its drivers to choose their 10-hour shifts and does not exercise any control on how these services are carried out (e.g., the route to be taken or the order in which parcels are delivered or picked up). Under Green's operating agreement with its drivers, Green can terminate the arrangement after 30 days' notice. In practice, however, Green allows its truckers to quit immediately without giving advance notice. The agreement also labels the drivers as independent contractors. Green maintains no health or retirement plans for its drivers, and each year it reports their income by issuing Forms 1099–MISC (and not Forms W–2). Green requires its drivers to maintain a commercial driver's license and be in good standing with the state highway law enforcement division.

Citing the employment tax Regulations in §§ 31.3121(d)–1(c)(2) and 31.3306(i)–1(b), an IRS agent contends that Aaron is an independent contractor and, therefore, is subject to the self-employment tax. Based on *Peno Trucking, Inc.* (93 TCM 1027, T.C.Memo. 2007–66), Aaron disagrees and contends that he is an employee (i.e., not self-employed). Who is correct and why?

Research Problem 2. Richard Harding is the sheriff of Howard County, Indiana. In addition to the usual law enforcement duties, the sheriff has the responsibility of maintaining the detention facility (i.e., county jail). Further, he must furnish meals for all prisoners in accordance with certain nutritional standards prescribed by the state. Although the sheriff must absorb the cost of the meals, the county provides a personal allowance.

During the year, Sheriff Harding received a salary of $35,000 (as reported on a Form W–2 issued by Howard County). He spent $90,000 on prisoner meals and received meal allowances of $110,000. On his income tax return, he reported the salary as employee income, but listed the allowances and meals on a Schedule C. Thus, he treated himself as self-employed by claiming the cost of the meals as a deduction *for* AGI.

Upon audit, the IRS determined that the Schedule C treatment was improper. Harding was not in a separate trade or business of providing meals, but was merely carrying out his employment-related duties. The costs of the meals are employee business expenses deductible only as miscellaneous itemized deductions on Schedule A. As such, they are subject to the 2%-of-AGI floor.

Is Sheriff Harding or the IRS correct? Why?

Research Problem 3. Tony Martin has worked for many years as a mechanic for Eagle Airlines at its repair facility in the Minneapolis–St. Paul airport. In early 2008, Eagle downsized its Minnesota staff and eliminated Tony's job. Using his union seniority, Tony was able to obtain a similar position by "bumping" a mechanic in Chicago. A few months later, Eagle continued the downsizing, and Tony ended up at LaGuardia (New York). After one final "bump" to Anchorage, Tony ran out of seniority and was finally terminated by Eagle.

During his work assignments in Chicago, New York, and Anchorage, Tony kept his family and residence in the Minneapolis area. Consequently, he deducted all of his out-of-town expenses (e.g., meals, lodging) as being work related. The IRS disallowed the deduction contending that Tony was not in travel status for tax purposes. Which party should prevail?

COMMUNICATIONS

Research Problem 4. Rick Beam has been an independent sales representative for various textile manufacturers for many years. His products consist of soft goods, such as tablecloths, curtains, and drapes. Rick's customers are clothing store chains, department stores, and smaller specialty stores. The employees of these companies who are responsible for purchasing merchandise are known as buyers. These companies generally prohibit their buyers from accepting gifts from manufacturers' sales representatives.

Each year Rick gives cash gifts (never more than $25) to most of the buyers who are his customers. Generally, he cashes a large check in November and gives the money personally to the buyers around Christmas. Rick says, "This is one of the ways that I maintain my relationship with my buyers." He maintains adequate substantiation of all the gifts.

Rick's deductions for these gifts have been disallowed by the IRS, based on § 162(c)(2). Rick is confused and comes to you, a CPA, for advice.

a. Write a letter to Rick concerning his tax position on this issue. Rick's address is 948 Octavia Street, Baton Rouge, LA 70821.

b. Prepare a memo for your files supporting the advice you have given.

INTERNET
activity

Use the tax resources of the Internet to address the following questions. Do not restrict your search to the Web, but include a review of newsgroups and general reference materials, practitioner sites and resources, primary sources of the tax law, chat rooms and discussion groups, and other opportunities.

Research Problem 5. What are the guidelines regarding the deductibility of luxury water travel (e.g., cruise ships) for business purposes? Refer to Chapter 1 of IRS Publication No. 463.

Research Problem 6. In reporting the transactions of a self-employed taxpayer, when can a Schedule C–EZ be used instead of the regular Schedule C of Form 1040?

Research Problem 7. Determine whether your city qualifies for the "high-cost" travel per diem allowances provided by the IRS.

Research Problem 8. Using the IRS website, retrieve Notice 989 (as revised on 8/12/09). What is the purpose of this IRS Notice?

Deductions and Losses: Certain Itemized Deductions

LEARNING OBJECTIVES

After completing Chapter 10, you should be able to:

LO.1

Distinguish between deductible and nondeductible personal expenses.

LO.2

Define medical expenses and compute the medical expense deduction.

LO.3

Contrast deductible taxes with nondeductible fees, licenses, and other charges.

LO.4

Understand the Federal income tax treatment of state and local income taxes and sales taxes.

LO.5

Distinguish between deductible and nondeductible interest and apply the appropriate limitations to deductible interest.

LO.6

Understand charitable contributions and their related measurement problems and percentage limitations.

LO.7

List the business and personal expenditures that are deductible either as miscellaneous itemized deductions or as other itemized deductions.

LO.8

Identify tax planning strategies that can maximize the benefit of itemized deductions.

OUTLINE

FRAMEWORK 1040:

Tax Formula for Individuals

This chapter covers the boldfaced portions of the Tax Formula for Individuals that was introduced in Figure 3.1 on p. 3-3. Below those portions are the sections of Form 1040 where the results are reported.

Income (broadly conceived)... $xx,xxx

Less: Exclusions .... (x,xxx)

Gross income .... $xx,xxx

Less: Deductions for adjusted gross income .... (x,xxx)

Adjusted gross income... $xx,xxx

Less: The greater of total **itemized deductions** *or* the standard deduction ....**(x,xxx)**

FORM 1040 (p. 2)
40   **Itemized deductions** (from Schedule A) **or** your **standard deduction** (see instructions)   .   .

    Personal and dependency exemptions .... (x,xxx)

Taxable income .... $xx,xxx

Tax on taxable income (see Tax Tables or Tax Rate Schedules) .... $ x,xxx

Less: Tax credits (including income taxes withheld and prepaid) .... (xxx)

Tax due (or refund) .... $ xxx

THE BIG PICTURE   Tax Solutions for the Real World

IMPACT OF ITEMIZED DEDUCTIONS ON MAJOR PURCHASES

John and Susan Williamson, a young professional couple, have been renting an apartment since they were married. Their income has grown as they've become more established in their careers, and they now feel that the time has come to purchase their own home. John and Susan's current monthly rent is $2,000, but they are willing to spend $2,500 per month on an after-tax basis if necessary for their first home.

After months of house hunting, they have found the perfect home, but they fear it may be too expensive. If they acquire a standard mortgage to finance the purchase of the home, the total cash outlay during the first year of ownership would be $42,000 ($2,000 principal payments, $37,000 interest payments, $3,000 real estate taxes). Alternatively, if they use their retirement and taxable investments to secure the home financing, they could qualify for a lower interest rate and thereby reduce the interest charge from $37,000 to $35,000. They expect their Federal taxable income to range between $160,000 and $185,000 for the year. John and Susan have not itemized their deductions in prior years because the amount of their qualifying personal expenditures has fallen just short of the standard deduction amount. The Williamsons live in a state that imposes an income tax at a flat rate of 6 percent.

Can John and Susan Williamson afford to pursue their dream of home ownership? **Read the chapter and formulate your response.**

10.1 GENERAL CLASSIFICATION OF EXPENSES

As a general rule, the deduction of personal expenditures is disallowed by § 262 of the Code. However, Congress has chosen to allow certain personal expenditures to be deducted as itemized deductions. Personal expenditures that are deductible as itemized deductions include medical expenses, certain taxes, mortgage interest, investment interest, and charitable contributions. These expenditures and other personal expenditures that are allowed as itemized deductions are covered in this chapter. Though certain exceptions exist (e.g., alimony and traditional IRA contributions are deductible *for* AGI), personal expenditures not specifically allowed as itemized deductions by the tax law are nondeductible.

Allowable itemized deductions are deductible *from* AGI in arriving at taxable income if the taxpayer elects to itemize. The election to itemize is appropriate when total itemized deductions exceed the standard deduction based on the taxpayer's filing status.[1]

> **L0.1**
>
> Distinguish between deductible and nondeductible personal expenses.

EXAMPLE 1
THE BIG PICTURE

Return to the facts of *The Big Picture* on p. 10-2. John and Susan Williamson will discover that with the purchase of a home, they will be able to itemize their deductions for the first time instead of claiming the standard deduction. Assuming the home mortgage interest expense and real estate taxes meet the requirements discussed in this chapter, they will be deducted *from* AGI because their total would exceed the amount of the standard deduction for a married couple filing a joint return. Further, other qualifying expenditures, such as state income taxes or sales tax and charitable contributions, likewise will be deductible as itemized deductions, providing an explicit tax benefit to the Williamsons. ■

10.2 MEDICAL EXPENSES

GENERAL REQUIREMENTS

Medical expenses paid for the care of the taxpayer, spouse, and dependents are allowed as an itemized deduction to the extent the expenses are not reimbursed. The **medical expense** deduction is limited to the amount by which such expenses *exceed* 7.5 percent of the taxpayer's AGI. Beginning in 2013, the 7.5 percent threshold is scheduled to become 10 percent.

> **L0.2**
>
> Define medical expenses and compute the medical expense deduction.

EXAMPLE 2

During the year, Iris had medical expenses of $4,800, of which $1,000 was reimbursed by her insurance company. If her AGI for the year is $40,000, the itemized deduction for medical expenses is limited to $800 [($4,800 − $1,000) − (7.5% × $40,000)]. ■

MEDICAL EXPENSES DEFINED

The term *medical care* includes expenditures incurred for the "diagnosis, cure, mitigation, treatment, or prevention of disease, or for the purpose of affecting any structure or function of the body."[2] A *partial* list of deductible and nondeductible medical items appears in Exhibit 10.1.

A medical expense does not have to relate to a particular ailment to be deductible. Since the definition of medical care is broad enough to cover preventive measures, the cost of periodic physical and dental exams qualifies even for a taxpayer in good health.

Amounts paid for unnecessary *cosmetic surgery* are not deductible medical expenses. However, if cosmetic surgery is deemed necessary, it is deductible as a medical expense. Cosmetic surgery is necessary when it ameliorates (1) a deformity arising from a congenital abnormality, (2) a personal injury, or (3) a disfiguring disease.

---

[1] See §§ 63(c) and (d), respectively, for the definitions of the terms "standard deduction" and "itemized deductions."

[2] § 213(d)(1)(A).

TAX *in* the NEWS — THE PRESIDENT AND VICE PRESIDENT ITEMIZE

Approximately two-thirds of all individual taxpayers take the standard deduction each year rather than itemize. President Barack H. Obama and Vice President Joseph R. Biden are among the one-third who itemize. Both the President and the Vice President, who file joint returns with their wives, released their 2009 income tax returns to the public in 2010. Their itemized deductions, along with certain other information from their tax returns, are shown to the right.

	President Obama	Vice President Biden
Gross income	$5,623,690	$333,182
Adjusted gross income	$5,505,409	$333,182
Itemized deductions:		
Medical expenses	$ –0–	$ –0–
Taxes	186,910	31,038
Interest	52,195	30,349
Charitable contributions	329,100	4,820
Job expenses and other miscellaneous deductions	–0–	–0–
Total itemized deductions	$ 568,205	$ 66,207

EXAMPLE 3

Art, a calendar year taxpayer, paid $11,000 to a plastic surgeon for a face lift. Art, age 75, merely wanted to improve his appearance. The $11,000 does not qualify as a medical expense since the surgery was unnecessary. In contrast, Marge's face is disfigured as a result of a serious automobile accident. The cost of restorative cosmetic surgery is deductible as a medical expense. ■

The cost of care in a *nursing home or home for the aged*, including meals and lodging, can be included in deductible medical expenses if the primary reason for being in the home is to get medical care. If the primary reason for being there is personal,

---

EXHIBIT 10.1   Examples of Deductible and Nondeductible Medical Expenses

Deductible	Nondeductible
Medical (including dental, mental, and hospital) care	Funeral, burial, or cremation expenses
Prescription drugs and insulin	Nonprescription drugs (except insulin)
Special equipment	Bottled water
Wheelchairs	Toiletries, cosmetics
Crutches	Diaper service, maternity clothes
Artificial limbs	Programs for the *general* improvement of health
Eyeglasses (including contact lenses)	Weight reduction
Hearing aids	Health spas
Transportation for medical care	Social activities (e.g., dancing and swimming lessons)
Medical and hospital insurance premiums	Unnecessary cosmetic surgery
Long-term care insurance premiums (subject to limitations)	
Cost of alcohol and drug rehabilitation	
Certain costs to stop smoking	
Weight reduction programs related to obesity	

any costs for medical or nursing care can be included in deductible medical expenses, but the cost of meals and lodging must be excluded.[3]

EXAMPLE 4

Norman has a chronic heart ailment. In October, his family decides to place Norman in a nursing home equipped to provide medical and nursing care facilities. Total nursing home expenses amount to $15,000 during the year. Of this amount, $4,500 is directly attributable to medical and nursing care. Since Norman is in need of significant medical and nursing care and is placed in the facility primarily for this purpose, all $15,000 of the nursing home costs are deductible (subject to the 7.5% floor). ∎

Tuition expenses of a dependent at a special school may be deductible as a medical expense. The cost of medical care can include the expenses of a special school for a mentally or physically handicapped individual. The deduction is allowed if a principal reason for sending the individual to the school is the school's special resources for alleviating the infirmities. In this case, the cost of meals and lodging, in addition to the tuition, is a proper medical expense deduction.[4]

EXAMPLE 5

Jason's daughter Marcia attended public school through the seventh grade. Because Marcia was a poor student, she was examined by a psychiatrist who diagnosed a problem that created a learning disability. Upon the recommendation of the psychiatrist, Marcia is enrolled in a private school so that she can receive individual attention. The school has no special program for students with learning disabilities and does not provide special medical treatment. The expense related to Marcia's attendance is not deductible as a medical expense. The cost of any psychiatric care, however, qualifies as a medical expense. ∎

Example 5 shows that the recommendation of a physician does not automatically make the expenditure deductible.

CAPITAL EXPENDITURES FOR MEDICAL PURPOSES

Some examples of *capital expenditures* for medical purposes are swimming pools if the taxpayer does not have access to a neighborhood pool and air conditioners if they do not become permanent improvements (e.g., window units).[5] Other examples include dust elimination systems,[6] elevators,[7] and vans specially designed for wheelchair-bound taxpayers. These expenditures are medical in nature if they are incurred as a medical necessity upon the advice of a physician, the facility is used primarily by the patient alone, and the expense is reasonable.

Capital expenditures normally are adjustments to basis and are not deductible. However, both a capital expenditure for a permanent improvement and expenditures made for the operation or maintenance of the improvement may qualify as medical expenses. If a capital expenditure qualifies as a medical expense, the allowable cost is deductible in the year incurred. Although depreciation is required for most other capital expenditures, it is not required for capital expenditures for medical purposes.

A capital improvement that ordinarily would not have a medical purpose qualifies as a medical expense if it is directly related to prescribed medical care and is deductible to the extent that the expenditure *exceeds* the increase in value of the related property. Appraisal costs related to capital improvements are also deductible, but not as medical expenses. These costs are expenses incurred in the determination of the taxpayer's tax liability.[8]

EXAMPLE 6

Fred is afflicted with heart disease. His physician advises him to install an elevator in his residence so he will not be required to climb the stairs. The cost of installing the elevator

---

[3]Reg. § 1.213–1(e)(1)(v).

[4]*Donald R. Pfeifer*, 37 TCM 816, T.C.Memo. 1978–189. Also see Rev.Rul. 78–340, 1978–2 C.B. 124.

[5]Reg. § 1.213–1(e)(1)(iii).

[6]Ltr.Rul. 7948029.

[7]*Riach v. Frank*, 62–1 USTC ¶9419, 9 AFTR 2d 1263, 302 F.2d 374 (CA–9, 1962).

[8]§ 212(3).

is $3,000, and the increase in the value of the residence is determined to be only $1,700. Therefore, $1,300 ($3,000 − $1,700) is deductible as a medical expense. Additional utility costs to operate the elevator and maintenance costs are deductible as medical expenses as long as the medical reason for the capital expenditure continues to exist. ■

The full cost of certain home-related capital expenditures incurred to enable a *physically handicapped* individual to live independently and productively qualifies as a medical expense. Qualifying costs include expenditures for constructing entrance and exit ramps to the residence, widening hallways and doorways to accommodate wheelchairs, installing support bars and railings in bathrooms and other rooms, and adjusting electrical outlets and fixtures.[9] These expenditures are subject to the 7.5 percent floor only, and the increase in the home's value is deemed to be zero.

MEDICAL EXPENSES INCURRED FOR SPOUSE AND DEPENDENTS

In computing the medical expense deduction, a taxpayer may include medical expenses for a spouse and for a person who was a dependent at the time the expenses were paid or incurred. Of the requirements that normally apply in determining dependency status,[10] neither the gross income nor the joint return test applies in determining dependency status for medical expense deduction purposes.

EXAMPLE 7

Ernie (age 22) is married and a full-time student at a university. During the year, Ernie incurred medical expenses that were paid by Matilda (Ernie's mother). She provided more than half of Ernie's support for the year. Even if Ernie files a joint return with his wife, Matilda may claim the medical expenses she paid for him. Matilda would combine Ernie's expenses with her own before applying the 7.5% floor. ■

For *divorced persons* with children, a special rule applies to the noncustodial parent. The noncustodial parent may claim any medical expenses he or she pays even though the custodial parent claims the children as dependents.

EXAMPLE 8

Irv and Joan were divorced last year, and Joan was awarded custody of their child, Keith. During the current year, Irv pays $2,500 of Keith's medical bills. Together, Irv and Joan provide more than half of Keith's support. Even though Joan claims Keith as a dependent, Irv can combine the $2,500 of medical expenses that he pays for Keith with his own when calculating his medical expense deduction. ■

TRANSPORTATION, MEAL, AND LODGING EXPENSES FOR MEDICAL TREATMENT

Payments for transportation to and from a point of treatment for medical care are deductible as medical expenses (subject to the 7.5 percent floor). Transportation expenses for medical care include bus, taxi, train, or plane fare, charges for ambulance service, and out-of-pocket expenses for the use of an automobile. A mileage allowance of 19 cents per mile[11] for 2011 may be used instead of actual out-of-pocket automobile expenses. Whether the taxpayer chooses to claim out-of-pocket automobile expenses or the 19 cents per mile automatic mileage option, related parking fees and tolls can also be deducted. The cost of meals while en route to obtain medical care is not deductible.

A deduction is also allowed for the transportation expenses of a parent who must accompany a child who is receiving medical care or for a nurse or other person giving assistance to a person who is traveling to get medical care and cannot travel alone.

A deduction is allowed for lodging while away from home for medical care if the following requirements are met:[12]

---

[9]For a complete list of the items that qualify, see Rev.Rul. 87–106, 1987–2 C.B. 67.
[10]Refer to Chapter 3 for discussion of these requirements.

[11]This amount is adjusted periodically. The allowance was 16.5 cents for 2010.
[12]§ 213(d)(2).

- The lodging is primarily for and essential to medical care.
- Medical care is provided by a doctor in a licensed hospital or a similar medical facility (e.g., a clinic).
- The lodging is not lavish or extravagant under the circumstances.
- There is no significant element of personal pleasure, recreation, or vacation in the travel away from home.

The deduction for lodging expenses included as medical expenses cannot exceed $50 *per* night for *each* person. The deduction is allowed not only for the patient but also for a person who must travel with the patient (e.g., a parent traveling with a child who is receiving medical care).

EXAMPLE 9

Herman, a resident of Winchester, Kentucky, is advised by his family physician that Martha, Herman's dependent and disabled mother, needs specialized treatment for her heart condition. Consequently, Herman and Martha fly to Cleveland, Ohio, where Martha receives the therapy at a heart clinic on an outpatient basis. Expenses in connection with the trip are as follows:

Round-trip airfare ($250 each)	$500
Lodging in Cleveland for two nights ($60 each per night)	240

Herman's medical expense deduction for transportation is $500, and his medical expense deduction for lodging is $200 ($50 per night per person). Because Martha is disabled, it is assumed that his accompanying her is justified. ■

No deduction is allowed for the cost of meals unless they are part of the medical care and are furnished at a medical facility. When allowable, such meals are not subject to the 50 percent limit applicable to business meals.

ETHICS & Equity

TRAVEL EXPENSES: MEDICAL OR PERSONAL?

Ron, who lives in Phoenix, has a chronic heart problem. He flies to Rochester, Minnesota, several times each year for checkups and treatment at the Mayo Clinic, which has one of the most highly rated heart treatment programs in the United States. On each trip, he visits his two children, who live in Rochester with his ex-wife. Is Ron justified in deducting the cost of his airline tickets and his lodging in Rochester as a medical expense?

AMOUNTS PAID FOR MEDICAL INSURANCE PREMIUMS

Medical insurance premiums are included with other medical expenses subject to the 7.5 percent floor. Premiums paid by the taxpayer under a group plan or an individual plan are included as medical expenses. If an employer pays all or part of the taxpayer's medical insurance premiums, the amount paid by the employer is not included in gross income by the employee. Likewise, the premium is not included in the employee's medical expenses.

If a taxpayer is *self-employed,* insurance premiums paid for medical coverage are deductible as a *business* expense (*for* AGI).[13] The deduction *for* AGI is allowed for premiums paid on behalf of the taxpayer, the taxpayer's spouse, and dependents of the taxpayer. The deduction is not allowed to any taxpayer who is eligible to participate in a subsidized health plan maintained by any employer of the taxpayer or of the taxpayer's spouse. Premiums paid for medical insurance coverage of *employees* are deductible as business expenses.

---

[13]§ 162(l).

| EXAMPLE 10 | Ellen, a sole proprietor of a restaurant, has two dependent children. During the year, she paid health insurance premiums of $8,400 for her own coverage and $7,000 for coverage of her two children. Ellen can deduct $15,400 as a business deduction (*for* AGI) in computing her taxable income. ∎ |

Taxpayers may also include premiums paid on qualified long-term care insurance contracts in medical expenses, subject to limitations based on the age of the insured. For 2011, the per-person limits range from $340 for taxpayers age 40 and under to $4,240 for taxpayers over age 70. See IRS Publication 502 for details relating to requirements for deducting costs associated with qualified long-term care insurance contracts.[14]

YEAR OF DEDUCTION

Regardless of a taxpayer's method of accounting, medical expenses are deductible only in the year *paid*. In effect, this places all individual taxpayers on a cash basis as far as the medical expense deduction is concerned. One exception, however, is allowed for deceased taxpayers. If the medical expenses are paid within one year from the day following the day of death, they can be treated as being paid at the time they were *incurred*. Thus, such expenses may be reported on the final income tax return of the decedent or on earlier returns if incurred before the year of death.

No current deduction is allowed for payment for medical care to be rendered in the future unless the taxpayer is under an obligation to make the payment. Whether an obligation to make the payment exists depends upon the policy of the physician or the institution furnishing the medical care.

| EXAMPLE 11 | Upon the recommendation of his regular dentist, in December 2011 Gary consults Dr. Smith, a prosthodontist, who specializes in crown and bridge work. Dr. Smith tells Gary that he can do the restorative work for $12,000 and that he requires all new patients to prepay 40% of the total cost of the procedure. Accordingly, Gary pays $4,800 in December 2011. The balance of $7,200 is paid when the work is completed in January 2012. Under these circumstances, the qualifying medical expense deductions are $4,800 for 2011 and $7,200 in 2012. The result would be the same even if Gary prepaid the full $12,000 in 2011. ∎ |

REIMBURSEMENTS

If medical expenses are reimbursed in the same year as paid, no problem arises. The reimbursement merely reduces the amount that would otherwise qualify for the medical expense deduction. But what happens if the reimbursement occurs in a later year than the expenditure? In computing casualty losses, any reasonable prospect of recovery must be considered (refer to Chapter 7). For medical expenses, however, any expected reimbursement is disregarded in measuring the amount of the deduction. Instead, the reimbursement is accounted for separately in the year in which it occurs.

Under the *tax benefit rule*, a taxpayer who receives an insurance reimbursement for medical expenses deducted in a previous year might have to include the reimbursement in gross income in the year of receipt. However, a taxpayer who did not itemize deductions in the year the expenses were paid did not receive a tax benefit and is *not* required to include a reimbursement in gross income.

The tax benefit rule applies to reimbursements if the taxpayer itemized deductions in the previous year. In this case, the taxpayer may be required to report some or all of the medical expense reimbursement in income in the year the reimbursement is received. Under the tax benefit rule, the taxpayer must include the reimbursement in income up to the amount of the deductions that decreased taxable income in the earlier year.

---

[14]The amounts for 2010 were $330 for taxpayers age 40 and under and $4,110 for taxpayers over age 70.

EXAMPLE 12

Homer had AGI of $60,000 for 2011. He was injured in a car accident and paid $4,300 for hospital expenses and $700 for doctor bills. Homer also incurred medical expenses of $600 for his dependent child. In 2012, Homer was reimbursed $650 by his insurance company for the medical expenses attributable to the car accident. His deduction for medical expenses in 2011 is computed as follows:

Hospitalization	$ 4,300
Bills for doctor's services	700
Medical expenses for dependent	600
Total	$ 5,600
Less: 7.5% of $60,000	(4,500)
Medical expense deduction (assuming Homer itemizes his deductions)	$ 1,100

Assume that Homer would have elected to itemize his deductions even if he had no medical expenses in 2011. If the reimbursement for medical care had occurred in 2011, the medical expense deduction would have been only $450 [$5,600 (total medical expenses) − $650 (reimbursement) − $4,500 (floor)], and Homer would have paid more income tax.

Since the reimbursement was made in a subsequent year, Homer will include $650 in gross income for 2012. If Homer had not itemized in 2011, he would *not* include the $650 reimbursement in 2012 gross income because he would have received no tax benefit for the medical expenses in 2011. ■

HEALTH SAVINGS ACCOUNTS

Qualifying individuals may make deductible contributions to a **Health Savings Account (HSA)**. An HSA is a qualified trust or custodial account administered by a qualified HSA trustee, which can be a bank, insurance company, or other IRS-approved trustee. The HSA funds are used to pay for the individual's medical expenses in excess of the deductible amount under a high-deductible policy.[15]

A taxpayer can use an HSA in conjunction with a high-deductible medical insurance policy to help reduce the overall cost of medical coverage. Converting from a low-deductible to a high-deductible plan can generally save an individual 20 to 40 percent in premiums. The high-deductible policy provides coverage for extraordinary medical expenses (in excess of the deductible), and expenses not covered by the policy can be paid with funds withdrawn tax-free from the HSA.

EXAMPLE 13

Sanchez, who is married and has three dependent children, carries a high-deductible medical insurance policy with a deductible of $4,400. He establishes an HSA and contributes the maximum allowable amount to the HSA in 2011. During 2011, the Sanchez family incurs medical expenses of $7,000. The high-deductible policy covers $2,600 of the expenses ($7,000 expenses − $4,400 deductible). Sanchez may withdraw $4,400 from the HSA to pay the medical expenses not covered by the high-deductible policy. ■

High-Deductible Plans

High-deductible policies are less expensive than low-deductible policies, so taxpayers with low medical costs can benefit from the lower premiums and use funds from the HSA to pay costs not covered by the high-deductible policy. A plan must meet two requirements to qualify as a high-deductible plan.[16]

1. The annual deductible in 2011 is not less than $1,200 for self-only coverage ($2,400 for family coverage).
2. The annual limit in 2011 on total out-of-pocket costs (excluding premiums) under the plan does not exceed $5,950 for self-only coverage ($11,900 for family coverage).

---

[15]§ 223.   [16]§ 223(c)(2).

Tax Treatment of HSA Contributions and Distributions

To establish an HSA, a taxpayer contributes funds to a tax-exempt trust.[17] As illustrated in the preceding example, funds can be withdrawn from an HSA to pay medical expenses that are not covered by the high-deductible policy. The following general tax rules apply to HSAs:

1. Contributions made by the taxpayer to an HSA are deductible from gross income to arrive at AGI (deduction *for* AGI). Thus, the taxpayer does not need to itemize in order to take the deduction.
2. Earnings on HSAs are not subject to taxation unless distributed, in which case taxability depends on the way the funds are used.[18]
   - Distributions from HSAs are excluded from gross income if they are used to pay for medical expenses not covered by the high-deductible policy.
   - Distributions that are not used to pay for medical expenses are included in gross income and are subject to an additional 10 percent penalty if made before age 65, death, or disability. Such distributions made by reason of death or disability and distributions made after the HSA beneficiary becomes eligible for Medicare are taxed but not penalized.

HSAs have at least two other attractive features. First, an HSA is portable. Taxpayers who switch jobs can take their HSAs with them. Second, more people than ever before can qualify to set up an HSA. Generally, anyone under age 65 who has a high-deductible plan and is not covered by another policy that is not a high-deductible plan can establish an HSA.

Deductible Amount

The annual deduction for contributions to an HSA is limited to the sum of the monthly limitations. The monthly limitation is calculated for each month that the individual is an eligible individual. The monthly deduction is not allowed after the individual becomes eligible for Medicare coverage.

The amount of the monthly limitation for an individual who has self-only coverage in 2011 is one-twelfth of $3,050, while the monthly limitation for an individual who has family coverage in 2011 is one-twelfth of $6,150. These amounts are subject to annual cost-of-living adjustments.[19] An eligible taxpayer who has attained age 55 by the end of the tax year may make an additional annual contribution in 2011 of up to $1,000. This additional amount is referred to as a *catchup* contribution.

EXAMPLE 14	Liu, who is married and self-employed, carries a high-deductible medical insurance policy with family coverage and an annual deductible of $4,000. In addition, he has established an HSA. Liu's maximum annual contribution to the HSA in 2011 is $6,150. ∎

EXAMPLE 15 — During 2011, Adam, who is self-employed, made 12 monthly payments of $875 for an HSA contract that provides medical insurance coverage with a $3,600 deductible. The plan covers Adam, his wife, and two children. Of the $875 monthly fee, $400 was for the high-deductible policy and $475 was deposited into an HSA. The deductible monthly contribution to the HSA is calculated as follows:

Maximum annual deduction for family coverage	$ 6,150
Monthly limitation (1/12 of $6,150)	$512.50

[17] § 223(d).
[18] § 223(f).
[19] § 223(b)(2). The annual limits also were $3,050 and $6,150 in 2010. Section 223(b)(8) allows a taxpayer who is an eligible member of a high-deductible plan as of the first day of December (for a calendar year taxpayer) to be *treated* as an eligible member of the plan for the entire year. Therefore, for example, if a calendar year taxpayer enrolls in an HSA by December 2011, the limit on the contribution is $3,050 (or $6,150 in the event of family coverage) and not the sum of the monthly limits.

Because Adam is self-employed, he can deduct $4,800 of the amount paid for the high-deductible policy ($400 per month × 12 months) as a deduction *for* AGI (refer to Example 10). In addition, he can deduct the $5,700 ($475 × 12) paid to the HSA as a deduction *for* AGI. Note that the $5,700 HSA deduction does not exceed the $6,150 ceiling. ∎

10.3 TAXES

A deduction is allowed for certain state and local taxes paid or accrued by a taxpayer.[20] The deduction was created to relieve the burden of multiple taxes upon the same source of revenue.

LO.3

Contrast deductible taxes with nondeductible fees, licenses, and other charges.

DEDUCTIBILITY AS A TAX

A distinction must be made between a tax and a fee, since fees are not deductible unless incurred as an ordinary and necessary business expense or as an expense in the production of income. The IRS has defined a tax as follows:

> A tax is an enforced contribution exacted pursuant to legislative authority in the exercise of taxing power, and imposed and collected for the purpose of raising revenue to be used for public or governmental purposes, and not as payment for some special privilege granted or service rendered. Taxes are, therefore, distinguished from various other contributions and charges imposed for particular purposes under particular powers or functions of the government. In view of such distinctions, the question whether a particular contribution or charge is to be regarded as a tax depends upon its real nature.[21]

Accordingly, fees for dog licenses, automobile inspections, automobile titles and registration, hunting and fishing licenses, bridge and highway tolls, drivers' licenses, parking meter deposits, and postage are not deductible if personal in nature. These items, however, could be deductible if incurred as a business expense or for the production of income. Deductible and nondeductible taxes are summarized in Exhibit 10.2.

PROPERTY TAXES

State, local, and foreign taxes on real property are generally deductible only by the person upon whom the tax is imposed. Deductible personal property taxes must be *ad valorem* (assessed in relation to the value of the property). Therefore, a motor vehicle tax based on weight, model, year, and horsepower is not an ad valorem tax. However, a tax based on value and other criteria may qualify in part.

EXAMPLE 16
THE BIG PICTURE

Return to the facts of *The Big Picture* on p.10-2 Assuming that the Williamsons proceed with the purchase of a home, the real estate taxes they pay will be deductible *from* AGI because they qualify to itemize their deductions. However, if they also pay a personal property tax on their automobile, the payment may be only partially deductible. In their state, the government imposes a motor vehicle registration tax on 4% of the value of the vehicle plus 40 cents per hundredweight. The Williamsons own a car having a value of $20,000 and weighing 3,000 pounds. They pay an annual registration fee of $812. Of this amount, $800 (4% of $20,000) is deductible as a personal property tax. The remaining $12, based on the weight of the car, is not deductible. ∎

Assessments for Local Benefits

As a general rule, real property taxes do not include taxes assessed for local benefits because such assessments tend to increase the value of the property (e.g., special assessments for streets, sidewalks, curbing, and other similar improvements). A

[20]Most deductible taxes are listed in § 164, while nondeductible items are included in § 275.

[21]Rev.Rul. 57–345, 1957–2 C.B. 132, and Rev.Rul. 70–622, 1970–2 C.B. 41.

EXHIBIT 10.2	Deductible and Nondeductible Taxes

Deductible	Nondeductible
State, local, and foreign real property taxes	Federal income taxes
	FICA taxes imposed on employees
State and local personal property taxes	Employer FICA taxes paid on domestic household workers
State and local income taxes *or* sales/use taxes*	Estate, inheritance, and gift taxes
	Federal, state, and local excise taxes (e.g., gasoline, tobacco, spirits)
Foreign income taxes	Foreign income taxes if the taxpayer chooses the foreign tax credit option
	Taxes on real property to the extent such taxes are to be apportioned and treated as imposed on another taxpayer

*Currently, the sales/use tax alternative is available through 2011.

taxpayer was denied a deduction for the cost of a new sidewalk (relative to a personal residence), even though the construction was required by the city and the sidewalk may have provided an incidental benefit to the public welfare.[22] Such assessments are added to the adjusted basis of the taxpayer's property.

Apportionment of Real Property Taxes between Seller and Purchaser

Real estate taxes for the entire year are apportioned between the buyer and seller on the basis of the number of days the property was held by each during the real property tax year. This apportionment is required whether the tax is paid by the buyer or the seller or is prorated according to the purchase agreement. It is the apportionment that determines who is entitled to deduct the real estate taxes in the year of sale. The required apportionment prevents the shifting of the deduction for real estate taxes from the buyer to the seller, or vice versa. In making the apportionment, the assessment date and the lien date are disregarded.[23]

EXAMPLE 17

A county's real property tax year runs from January 1 to December 31. Susan, the owner on January 1 of real property located in the county, sells the real property to Bob on June 30 (assume this year is not a leap year). Bob owns the real property from June 30 through December 31. The tax for the real property tax year, January 1 through December 31, is $3,650. The portion of the real property tax treated as imposed upon Susan, the seller, is $1,800 [(180/365) × $3,650, January 1 through June 29], and $1,850 [(185/365) × $3,650, June 30 through December 31] of the tax is treated as imposed upon Bob, the purchaser. ■

If the actual real estate taxes are not prorated between the buyer and seller as part of the purchase agreement, adjustments are required. The adjustments are necessary to determine the amount realized by the seller and the adjusted basis of the property to the buyer. If the buyer pays the entire amount of the tax, he or she has, in effect, paid the seller's portion of the real estate tax and has therefore paid more for the property than the actual purchase price. Thus, the amount of real estate tax that is apportioned to the seller (for Federal income tax purposes) and paid by the

---

[22]*Erie H. Rose*, 31 TCM 142, T.C.Memo. 1972–39; Reg. § 1.164–4(a).

[23]For most years, the apportionment is based on a 365-day year. However, in a leap year (i.e., a year that is evenly divisible by 4), the taxes are prorated over 366 days. In making the apportionment, the date of sale counts as a day the property is owned by the buyer.

buyer is added to the buyer's adjusted basis. The seller must increase the amount realized on the sale by the same amount.

Seth sells real estate on October 3 for $400,000. The buyer, Wilma, pays the real estate taxes of $3,650 for the calendar year, which is the real estate property tax year. Assuming this is not a leap year, $2,750 (for 275 days) of the real estate taxes is apportioned to and is deductible by the seller, Seth, and $900 (for 90 days) of the taxes is deductible by Wilma. The buyer has, in effect, paid Seth's real estate taxes of $2,750 and has therefore paid $402,750 for the property. Wilma's basis is increased to $402,750, and the amount realized by Seth from the sale is increased to $402,750. ■

The opposite result occurs if the seller (rather than the buyer) pays the real estate taxes. In this case, the seller reduces the amount realized from the sale by the amount that has been apportioned to the buyer. The buyer is required to reduce his or her adjusted basis by a corresponding amount.

Ruth sells real estate to Butch for $400,000 on October 3. While Ruth held the property, she paid the real estate taxes of $3,650 for the calendar year, which is the real estate property tax year. Although Ruth paid the entire $3,650 of real estate taxes, $900 of that amount is apportioned to Butch, based on the number of days he owned the property, and is therefore deductible by him. The effect is that the buyer, Butch, has paid only $399,100 ($400,000 − $900) for the property. The amount realized by Ruth, the seller, is reduced by $900, and Butch reduces his basis in the property to $399,100. ■

STATE AND LOCAL INCOME TAXES AND SALES TAXES

L0.4

Understand the Federal income tax treatment of state and local income taxes and sales taxes.

The position of the IRS is that state and local income taxes imposed upon an individual are deductible only as itemized deductions, even if the taxpayer's sole source of income is from a business, rents, or royalties.

Cash basis taxpayers are entitled to deduct state income taxes withheld by the employer in the year the taxes are withheld. In addition, estimated state income tax payments are deductible in the year the payment is made by cash basis taxpayers even if the payments relate to a prior or subsequent year.[24] If the taxpayer overpays state income taxes because of excessive withholdings or estimated tax payments, the refund received is included in gross income of the following year to the extent that the deduction reduced taxable income in the prior year.

Leona, a cash basis, unmarried taxpayer, had $800 of state income tax withheld during 2011. Additionally in 2011, Leona paid $100 that was due when she filed her 2010 state income tax return and made estimated payments of $300 on her 2011 state income tax. When Leona files her 2011 Federal income tax return in April 2012, she elects to itemize deductions, which amount to $7,500, including the $1,200 of state income tax payments and withholdings, all of which reduce her taxable income.

As a result of overpaying her 2011 state income tax, Leona receives a refund of $200 early in 2012. She will include this amount in her 2012 gross income in computing her Federal income tax. It does not matter whether Leona received a check from the state for $200 or applied the $200 toward her 2012 state income tax. ■

[24]Rev.Rul. 71–190, 1971–1 C.B. 70. See also Rev.Rul. 82–208, 1982–2 C.B. 58, where a deduction is not allowed when the taxpayer cannot, in good faith, reasonably determine that there is additional state income tax liability.

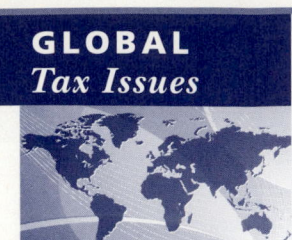

GLOBAL Tax Issues

DEDUCTIBILITY OF FOREIGN TAXES

Josef, a citizen of the United States who works primarily in New York, also works several months each year in Austria. He owns a residence in Austria and pays income taxes to Austria on the income he earns there. Both the property tax he pays on his Austrian residence and the income tax he pays on his Austrian income are deductible in computing U.S. taxable income. However, if Josef deducts the Austrian income tax, he may not claim the foreign tax credit with respect to this tax (see Chapter 13).

Itemized Deduction for Sales Taxes Paid

Individuals can elect to deduct either their state and local income taxes *or* their sales/use taxes paid as an itemized deduction on Schedule A of Form 1040. The annual election can reflect actual sales/use tax payments *or* an amount from an IRS table (see Appendix A). The amount from the table may be increased by sales tax paid on the purchase of motor vehicles, boats, and other specified items. Most likely, the sales tax deduction will be elected by those living in states with no individual income tax. At the time of this writing, this deduction alternative is available through 2011.

10.4 INTEREST

LO.5

Distinguish between deductible and nondeductible interest and apply the appropriate limitations to deductible interest.

A deduction for interest has been allowed since the income tax law was enacted in 1913. Despite its long history of congressional acceptance, the interest deduction has been one of the most controversial areas in the tax law. The controversy centered around the propriety of allowing the deduction of interest charges for the purchase of consumer goods and services and interest on borrowings used to acquire investments (investment interest). Personal (consumer) interest is not deductible. This includes credit card interest, interest on car loans, and any other interest that is not interest on qualified student loans, home mortgage interest, investment interest, or business interest. Interest on qualified student loans, **qualified residence** (home mortgage) **interest**, and investment interest continue to be deductible, subject to the limits discussed on the following pages.

ALLOWED AND DISALLOWED ITEMS

The Supreme Court has defined *interest* as compensation for the use or forbearance of money.[25] The general rule permits a deduction for interest paid or accrued within the taxable year on indebtedness.

Interest on Qualified Student Loans

Taxpayers who pay interest on a qualified student loan may be able to deduct the interest as a deduction *for* AGI. The deduction is allowable only to the extent that the proceeds of the loan are used to pay qualified education expenses. Such payments must be made to qualified educational institutions. See IRS Publication 970, *Tax Benefits for Education*, for details.

The maximum annual deduction for qualified student loan interest is $2,500. However, in 2011 the deduction is phased out for taxpayers with modified AGI

---

[25] *Old Colony Railroad Co. v. Comm.*, 3 USTC ¶880, 10 AFTR 786, 52 S.Ct. 211 (USSC, 1932).

(MAGI) between $60,000 and $75,000 ($120,000 and $150,000 on joint returns). The deduction is not allowed for taxpayers who are claimed as dependents or for married taxpayers filing separately.[26]

The numerator in the phaseout computation is equal to MAGI minus the floor of the phaseout range (i.e., $60,000 or $120,000, depending on filing status). The denominator is equal to the amount in the phaseout range (e.g., $150,000 − $120,000 = $30,000 for married taxpayers filing jointly).

In 2011 Curt and Rita, who are married and file a joint return, paid $3,000 of interest on a qualified student loan. Their MAGI was $135,000. Their maximum potential deduction for qualified student interest is $2,500, but it must be reduced by $1,250 as a result of the phaseout rules.

$$\$2,500 \text{ interest} \times (\$135,000 \text{ MAGI} - \$120,000 \text{ phaseout floor})/$$
$$\$30,000 \text{ phaseout range} = \$1,250 \text{ reduction}$$

Curt and Rita would be allowed a student loan interest deduction of $1,250 ($2,500 maximum deduction − $1,250 reduction = $1,250 deduction *for* AGI). ∎

Qualified Residence Interest

Qualified residence interest is interest paid or accrued during the taxable year on indebtedness (subject to limitations) *secured* by any property that is a qualified residence of the taxpayer. Qualified residence interest falls into two categories: (1) interest on acquisition indebtedness and (2) interest on home equity loans. Before discussing each of these categories, however, the term *qualified residence* must be defined.

A *qualified residence* includes the taxpayer's principal residence and one other residence of the taxpayer or spouse. The *principal residence* is one that meets the requirement for nonrecognition of gain upon sale under § 121 (see Chapter 15). The *one other residence*, or second residence, refers to one that is used as a residence if not rented or, if rented, meets the requirements for a personal residence under the rental of vacation home rules (refer to Chapter 6). A taxpayer who has more than one second residence can make the selection each year as to which one is the qualified second residence. A residence includes, in addition to a house in the ordinary sense, cooperative apartments, condominiums, and mobile homes and boats that have living quarters (sleeping accommodations and toilet and cooking facilities).

Although in most cases interest paid on a home mortgage is fully deductible, there are limitations.[27] Interest paid or accrued during the tax year on aggregate **acquisition indebtedness** of $1 million or less ($500,000 for married persons filing separate returns) is deductible as qualified residence interest. *Acquisition indebtedness* refers to amounts incurred in acquiring, constructing, or substantially improving a qualified residence of the taxpayer.

Return to the facts of *The Big Picture* on p. 10-2. Because John and Susan Williamson will need to borrow at least a portion of the purchase price of a new home, a standard mortgage likely will qualify as acquisition indebtedness because the borrowed funds are used to acquire a principal residence. However, the interest on the acquisition indebtedness will be fully deductible only if the amount of the mortgage is $1 million or less (assuming John and Susan file a joint return) and the mortgage is secured by the home, which is the typical case. Recall that the Williamsons are also

---

[26]§ 221. See § 221(b)(2)(C) for the definition of MAGI. For 2010, the MAGI threshold amounts also were $60,000 and $75,000 ($120,000 and $150,000 on joint returns).

[27]§ 163(h)(3).

considering what appears to be a less expensive route of using their retirement and taxable investments to secure the debt. If they choose this alternative, the interest will not be deductible as qualified residence interest because the loan would not be acquisition indebtedness (i.e., the loan would not be secured by the home). ■

Qualified residence interest also includes interest on **home equity loans**. These loans utilize the personal residence of the taxpayer as security, typically in the form of a second mortgage. Because the funds from home equity loans can be used for personal purposes (e.g., auto purchases, medical expenses), what would otherwise have been nondeductible consumer interest becomes deductible qualified residence interest.

However, interest is deductible only on the portion of a home equity loan that does not exceed the *lesser of*:

* The fair market value of the residence, reduced by the acquisition indebtedness, *or*
* $100,000 ($50,000 for married persons filing separate returns).

EXAMPLE 23	Larry owns a personal residence with a fair market value of $450,000 and an outstanding first mortgage of $420,000. Therefore, his equity in his home is $30,000 ($450,000 − $420,000). Larry issues a second mortgage on the residence and in return borrows $15,000 to purchase a new family automobile. All interest on the $435,000 of first and second mortgage debt is treated as qualified residence interest. ■
EXAMPLE 24	Leon and Pearl, married taxpayers, took out a mortgage on their home for $290,000 in 1994. In March of the current year, when the home has a fair market value of $400,000 and they owe $195,000 on the mortgage, Leon and Pearl take out a home equity loan for $120,000. They use the funds to purchase a boat to be used for recreational purposes. The boat, which does not have living quarters, does not qualify as a personal residence. On a joint return, Leon and Pearl can deduct all of the interest on the first mortgage since it is acquisition indebtedness. Of the $120,000 home equity loan, only the interest on the first $100,000 is deductible. The interest on the remaining $20,000 is not deductible because it exceeds the statutory ceiling of $100,000. ■

Interest Paid for Services

Mortgage loan companies commonly charge a fee, often called a loan origination fee, for finding, placing, or processing a mortgage loan. Loan origination fees are typically nondeductible amounts included in the basis of the acquired property. Other fees, sometimes called **points** and expressed as a percentage of the loan amount, are paid to reduce the interest rate charged over the term of the loan. Essentially, the payment of points is a prepayment of interest and is considered compensation to a lender solely for the use or forbearance of money. To be deductible, points must be in the nature of interest and cannot be a form of service charge or payment for specific services.[28]

Points must be capitalized and are amortized and deductible ratably over the life of the loan. A special exception, however, permits the purchaser of a principal residence to deduct qualifying points in the year of payment.[29] The exception also covers points paid to obtain funds for home improvements.

Points paid to *refinance* an existing home mortgage cannot be immediately deducted, but must be capitalized and amortized as an interest deduction over the life of the new loan.[30]

---

[28]Rev.Rul. 69–188, 1969–1 C.B. 54.
[29]§ 461(g)(2).

[30]Rev.Rul. 87–22, 1987–1 C.B. 146.

EXAMPLE 25

Sandra purchased her residence several years ago, obtaining a 30-year mortgage at an annual interest rate of 8%. In the current year, Sandra refinances the mortgage in order to reduce the interest rate to 5%. To obtain the refinancing, she has to pay points of $2,600. The $2,600 paid comes under the usual rule applicable to points. The $2,600 must be capitalized and amortized over the life of the mortgage. ∎

Points paid by the seller for a buyer are, in effect, treated as an adjustment to the price of the residence, and the buyer is treated as having used cash to pay the points that were paid by the seller. A buyer may deduct seller-paid points in the tax year in which they are paid if several conditions are met. Refer to Revenue Procedure 94–27 for a complete list of these conditions.[31]

Mortgage Insurance Payments

Mortgage insurance is an additional cost that some taxpayers incur when purchasing a home. To protect their interests, mortgage lenders may require this coverage if the homebuyer cannot afford to make a down payment of at least 20 percent. The borrower pays the premiums on the policy, but the lender is the beneficiary who receives reimbursement in the event of foreclosure. Under current law, mortgage insurance premiums are deductible as interest if they relate to a qualified residence of the taxpayer. However, the deduction begins to phase out for taxpayers with AGI in excess of $100,000 ($50,000 for married taxpayers filing separately).[32]

Prepayment Penalty

When a mortgage or loan is paid off in full in a lump sum before its term (early), the lending institution may require an additional payment of a certain percentage applied to the unpaid amount at the time of prepayment. This is known as a prepayment penalty and is considered to be interest (e.g., personal, qualified residence, investment) in the year paid. The general rules for deductibility of interest also apply to prepayment penalties.

Investment Interest

Taxpayers frequently borrow funds that they use to acquire investment assets. Congress, however, has limited the deductibility of interest on funds borrowed for the purpose of purchasing or continuing to hold investment property. Under this limitation, the deduction for investment interest expense may not exceed the net investment income for the year. A complete discussion of investment interest occurs in Chapter 11 in the context of the limitations that taxpayers face when dealing with assets held for investment purposes.

Interest Paid to Related Parties

Nothing prevents the deduction of interest paid to a related party as long as the payment actually took place and the interest meets the requirements for deductibility. Recall from Chapter 6 that a special rule for related taxpayers applies when the debtor uses the accrual basis and the related creditor is on the cash basis. If this rule is applicable, interest that has been accrued but not paid at the end of the debtor's tax year is not deductible until payment is made and the income is reportable by the cash basis recipient.

---

[31]Rev.Proc. 94–27, 1994–1 C.B. 613.

[32]§§ 163(h)(3)(E)(i) and (ii). The deduction is fully phased out when AGI exceeds $109,000 ($54,500 for married taxpayers filing separately). The deduction thresholds are not subject to indexation for inflation. This provision is scheduled to expire after 2011.

CONCEPT SUMMARY   10.1

Deductibility of Personal, Student Loan, Mortgage, and Investment Interest

Type	Deductible	Comments
Personal (consumer) interest	No	Includes any interest that is not qualified residence interest, qualified student loan interest, investment interest, or business interest. Examples include interest on car loans and credit card debt.
Qualified student loan interest	Yes	Deduction *for* AGI; subject to limitations.
Qualified residence interest on acquisition indebtedness	Yes	Deductible as an itemized deduction; limited to indebtedness of $1 million.
Qualified residence interest on home equity indebtedness	Yes	Deductible as an itemized deduction; limited to indebtedness equal to lesser of $100,000 or FMV of residence minus acquisition indebtedness.
Investment interest (*not* related to rental or royalty property)	Yes	Itemized deduction; limited to net investment income for the year; disallowed interest can be carried over to future years. See Chapter 11 for a complete discussion of investment interest.
Investment interest (related to rental or royalty property)	Yes	Deduction *for* AGI; limited to net investment income for the year; disallowed interest can be carried over to future years. See Chapter 11 for a complete discussion of investment interest.

Tax-Exempt Securities

The tax law provides that no deduction is allowed for interest on debt incurred to purchase or carry tax-exempt securities.[33] A major problem for the courts has been to determine what is meant by the words *to purchase or carry*. Refer to Chapter 6 for a detailed discussion of these issues.

RESTRICTIONS ON DEDUCTIBILITY AND TIMING CONSIDERATIONS

Taxpayer's Obligation

Allowed interest is deductible if the related debt represents a bona fide obligation for which the taxpayer is liable.[34] Thus, for interest to be deductible, both the debtor and the creditor must intend for the loan to be repaid. Intent of the parties can be especially crucial between related parties such as a shareholder and a closely held corporation. In addition, an individual may not deduct interest paid on behalf of another taxpayer. For example, a shareholder may not deduct interest paid by the corporation on his or her behalf.[35] Likewise, a husband may not deduct interest paid on his wife's property if he files a separate return, except in the case of qualified residence interest. If both husband and wife consent in writing, either the husband or the wife may deduct the allowed interest on the principal residence and one other residence.

Time of Deduction

Generally, interest must be paid to secure a deduction unless the taxpayer uses the accrual method of accounting. Under the accrual method, interest is deductible ratably over the life of the loan.

---

[33]§ 265(a)(2).

[34]*Arcade Realty Co.*, 35 T.C. 256 (1960).

[35]*Continental Trust Co.*, 7 B.T.A. 539 (1927).

EXAMPLE 26

On November 1, 2011, Ramon borrows $1,000 to purchase appliances for a rental house. The loan is payable in 90 days at 12% interest. On the due date in January 2012, Ramon pays the $1,000 note and interest amounting to $30. Ramon can deduct the accrued portion ($2/_3 \times \$30 = \$20$) of the interest in 2011 only if he is an accrual basis taxpayer. Otherwise, the entire amount of interest ($30) is deductible in 2012. ∎

Prepaid Interest

Accrual method reporting is imposed on cash basis taxpayers for interest prepayments that extend beyond the end of the taxable year.[36] Such payments must be allocated to the tax years to which the interest payments relate. These provisions are intended to prevent cash basis taxpayers from *manufacturing* tax deductions before the end of the year by prepaying interest.

CLASSIFICATION OF INTEREST EXPENSE

Whether interest is deductible *for* AGI or as an itemized deduction (*from* AGI) depends on whether the indebtedness has a business, investment, or personal purpose. If the indebtedness is incurred in relation to a business (other than performing services as an employee) or for the production of rent or royalty income, the interest is deductible *for* AGI. If the indebtedness is incurred for personal use, such as qualified residence interest, any deduction allowed is taken *from* AGI and is reported on Schedule A of Form 1040 if the taxpayer elects to itemize. Note, however, that interest on a student loan is a deduction *for* AGI. If the taxpayer is an employee who incurs debt in relation to his or her employment, the interest is considered to be personal, or consumer, interest. Business expenses appear on Schedule C of Form 1040, and expenses related to rents or royalties are reported on Schedule E.

If a taxpayer deposits money in a certificate of deposit (CD) that has a term of one year or less and the interest cannot be withdrawn without penalty, the full amount of the interest must still be included in income, even though part of the interest is forfeited due to an early withdrawal. However, the taxpayer will be allowed a deduction *for* AGI as to the forfeited amount.

10.5 CHARITABLE CONTRIBUTIONS

Section 170 allows individuals and corporations to deduct contributions made to qualified *domestic* organizations. Contributions to qualified charitable organizations serve certain social welfare needs and thus relieve the government of the cost of providing these needed services to the community.

The **charitable contribution** provisions are among the most complex in the tax law. To determine the amount deductible as a charitable contribution, several important questions must be answered:

- What constitutes a charitable contribution?
- Was the contribution made to a qualified organization?
- When is the contribution deductible?
- What record-keeping and reporting requirements apply to charitable contributions?
- How is the value of donated property determined?
- What special rules apply to contributions of property that has increased in value?
- What percentage limitations apply to the charitable contribution deduction?
- What rules apply to amounts in excess of percentage limitations (carryovers)?

These questions are addressed in the sections that follow.

LO.6

Understand charitable contributions and their related measurement problems and percentage limitations.

---

[36]§ 461(g)(1).

TAX *in* the *NEWS*	**PAYING FOR THE RIGHT TO SIT**

Generally, the value of a charitable contribution is reduced by any benefits received by the taxpayer. An exception provides that 80 percent of the amount paid for rights to preferred seating at college and university athletic events can be deducted, even though a benefit is received in return.

UCLA's renovated basketball arena is scheduled to reopen in 2012. Interested individuals can purchase the right to a courtside seat for $500,000. To retain the right after the first year costs a mere $17,000.

Source: Adapted from "The Count," *Wall Street Journal,* July 2, 2009, p. D6.

CRITERIA FOR A GIFT

A *charitable contribution* is defined as a gift made to a qualified organization.[37] The major elements needed to qualify a contribution as a gift are a donative intent, the absence of consideration, and acceptance by the donee. Consequently, the taxpayer has the burden of establishing that the transfer was made from motives of *disinterested generosity* as established by the courts.[38] This test is quite subjective and has led to problems of interpretation (refer to the discussion of gifts in Chapter 5).

Benefit Received Rule

When a donor derives a tangible benefit from a contribution, he or she cannot deduct the value of the benefit.

> **EXAMPLE 27**

Ralph purchases a ticket at $100 for a special performance of the local symphony (a qualified charity). If the price of a ticket to a symphony concert is normally $35, Ralph is allowed only $65 as a charitable contribution. Even if Ralph does not attend the concert, the deduction is limited to $65. However, if Ralph does not accept the ticket from the symphony, he can deduct the full $100. ■

An exception to this benefit rule provides for the deduction of an automatic percentage of the amount paid for the right to purchase athletic tickets from colleges and universities.[39] Under this exception, 80 percent of the amount paid to or for the benefit of the institution qualifies as a charitable contribution deduction.

> **EXAMPLE 28**

Janet donates $500 to State University's athletic department. The payment guarantees that she will have preferred seating on the 50-yard line at football games. Subsequently, Janet buys four $35 game tickets. Under the exception to the benefit rule, she is allowed a $400 (80% of $500) charitable contribution deduction for the taxable year.

If, however, Janet's $500 donation includes four $35 tickets, that portion [$140 ($35 × 4)] and the remaining portion of $360 ($500 − $140) are treated as separate amounts. Thus, Janet is allowed a charitable contribution deduction of $288 (80% of $360). ■

Contribution of Services

No deduction is allowed for a contribution of one's services to a qualified charitable organization. However, unreimbursed expenses related to the services rendered may be deductible. For example, the cost of a uniform (without general utility) that is required to be worn while performing services may be deductible, as are certain out-of-pocket transportation costs incurred for the benefit of the charity. In lieu of these out-of-pocket costs for an automobile, a standard mileage rate of 14 cents per

---

[37]§ 170(c).

[38]*Comm. v. Duberstein,* 60–2 USTC ¶9515, 5 AFTR 2d 1626, 80 S.Ct. 1190 (USSC, 1960).

[39]§ 170(l).

TAX *in the* **NEWS**	**A CHARITABLE CONTRIBUTION DEDUCTION FOR BURNING DOWN YOUR HOUSE?**

Sometimes taxpayers purchase a less than desirable house, intending to tear it down and build a new home on the land. The demolition and removal costs, however, are not deductible. Instead, they must be capitalized as part of the cost of the new home.

An alternative is to donate the old house to the local police and fire departments for training purposes. First, the police SWAT team will practice beating down doors to "rescue" persons at risk. Then the fire department will intentionally set fire to the building to give the firefighters practice in putting out fires. Not only do members of the police and fire departments benefit from the training, but the homeowner avoids the cost of destroying and removing the house because it's been burned to ashes. This strategy seems like a "win-win" proposition.

Some clever taxpayers, however, have strived for even greater benefits. In some cases, they have sought to claim a charitable contribution for the gift of the house. Such deductions raise a number of questions, though. For example, what was the value of the house at the time of the gift, and was the benefit received by the taxpayer equal to or greater than the value transferred to the police and fire departments? An even more important issue is how the IRS will react to such a charitable contribution deduction. Thus far, the IRS has not been happy about such arrangements!

Source: Adapted from Meghan Barr, "Burning Down the House? IRS Nixes Tax Deductions," Associated Press, September 25, 2009.

mile is allowed.[40] Deductions are permitted for transportation, reasonable expenses for lodging, and the cost of meals while away from home incurred in performing the donated services. The travel expenses are not deductible if the travel involves a significant element of personal pleasure, recreation, or vacation.[41]

EXAMPLE 29

Grace, a delegate representing her church in Miami, Florida, travels to a two-day national meeting in Denver, Colorado, in February. After the meeting, Grace spends two weeks at a nearby ski resort. Under these circumstances, none of the transportation, meals, or lodging is deductible because the travel involved a significant element of personal pleasure, recreation, or vacation. ∎

Nondeductible Items

In addition to the benefit received rule and the restrictions placed on contributions of services, the following items may *not* be deducted as charitable contributions:

- Dues, fees, or bills paid to country clubs, lodges, fraternal orders, or similar groups.
- Cost of raffle, bingo, or lottery tickets.
- Cost of tuition.
- Value of blood given to a blood bank.
- Donations to homeowners associations.
- Gifts to individuals.
- Rental value of property used by a qualified charity.

QUALIFIED ORGANIZATIONS

To be deductible, a contribution must be made to one of the following organizations:[42]

- A state or possession of the United States or any subdivisions thereof.
- A corporation, trust, community chest, fund, or foundation that is situated in the United States and is organized and operated exclusively for religious, charitable, scientific, literary, or educational purposes or for the prevention of cruelty to children or animals.

---

[40]§ 170(i).
[41]§ 170(j).

[42]§ 170(c).

- A veterans' organization.
- A fraternal organization operating under the lodge system.
- A cemetery company.

The IRS publishes a list of organizations that have applied for and received tax-exempt status under § 501 of the Code.[43] This publication is updated frequently and may be helpful in determining if a gift has been made to a qualifying charitable organization.

Because gifts made to needy individuals are not deductible, a deduction will not be permitted if a gift is received by a donee in an individual capacity rather than as a representative of a qualifying organization.

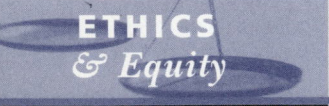

ETHICS & Equity

AN INDIRECT ROUTE TO A CONTRIBUTION DEDUCTION

In July, a plane crashed into a residential community in Middleboro, destroying and damaging many homes. Tanya's church, a qualified charitable organization, initiated a fundraising drive to help the Middleboro citizens whose homes had been affected. Tanya donated $50,000 to First Middleboro Church and suggested to the pastor that $25,000 of her contribution should be given to her sister, Tanesha, whose home had suffered extensive damage. The pastor appointed a committee to award funds to needy citizens. The committee solicited applications from the community and awarded Tanesha $15,000. Discuss whether Tanya is justified in deducting $50,000 as a charitable contribution.

TIME OF DEDUCTION

A charitable contribution generally is deducted in the year the payment is made. This rule applies to both cash and accrual basis individuals. (An interesting exception to this rule arose following the devastating earthquake in Haiti in early 2010. To encourage Americans to assist the victims affected by the earthquake in Haiti, Congress provided that an otherwise qualifying charitable contribution made after January 11, 2010 and before March 1, 2010 could be deducted on a taxpayer's 2009 income tax return rather than on the 2010 return.) A contribution is ordinarily deemed to have been made on the delivery of the property to the donee. For example, if a gift of securities (properly endorsed) is made to a qualified charitable organization, the gift is considered complete on the day of delivery or mailing. However, if the donor delivers the certificate to his or her bank or broker or to the issuing corporation, the gift is considered complete on the date the stock is transferred on the books of the corporation.

A contribution made by check is considered delivered on the date of mailing. Thus, a check mailed on December 31, 2011, is deductible on the taxpayer's 2011 tax return. If the contribution is charged on a credit card, the date the charge is made determines the year of deduction.

RECORD-KEEPING AND VALUATION REQUIREMENTS

Record-Keeping Requirements

No deduction is allowed for a charitable contribution made to a qualified organization unless the taxpayer gathers (and, in some cases, supplies to the IRS) the appropriate documentation and substantiation. The specific type of documentation required depends on the amount of the contribution and whether the contribution is made in cash or noncash property.[44] In addition, special rules may apply to gifts of certain types of property (e.g., used automobiles) where Congress has noted taxpayer abuse in the past. Further, for certain gifts of noncash property, Form 8283 (Noncash Charitable Contributions) must be attached to the taxpayer's return.

---

[43]Although this *Cumulative List of Organizations*, IRS Publication 78, may be helpful, qualified organizations are not required to be listed. Not all organizations that qualify are listed in this publication. The list is available on the Web at **www.irs.gov**.

[44]The specific documentation thresholds and requirements are provided in § 170(f).

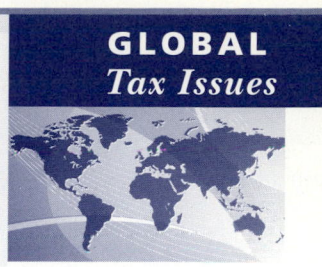

CHOOSE THE CHARITY WISELY

GLOBAL *Tax Issues*

Ibrahim, a U.S. citizen of Turkish descent, was distressed by the damage caused by a major earthquake in Turkey. He donated $100,000 to the Earthquake Victims' Relief Fund, a Turkish charitable organization that was set up to help victims of the earthquake. Ahmed, also a U.S. citizen of Turkish descent, donated $100,000 to help with the relief effort. However, Ahmed's contribution went to his mosque, which sent the proceeds of a fund drive to the Earthquake Victims' Relief Fund in Turkey. Ibrahim's contribution is not deductible, but Ahmed's is. Why? Contributions to charitable organizations are not deductible unless the organization is a U.S. charity.

The required substantiation must be obtained before the earlier of (1) the due date (including extensions) of the return for the year the contribution is claimed or (2) the date the return is filed. Failure to comply with the reporting rules may result in disallowance of the charitable contribution deduction. Additionally, significant overvaluation exposes the taxpayer to stringent penalties.

Common documentation and substantiation requirements are summarized in Concept Summary 10.2.

Valuation Requirements

Property donated to a charity is generally valued at fair market value at the time the gift is made. The Code and Regulations give very little guidance on the measurement of the fair market value except to say, "The fair market value is the price at which the property would change hands between a willing buyer and a willing seller, neither being under any compulsion to buy or sell and both having reasonable knowledge of relevant facts."

Generally, charitable organizations do not attest to the fair market value of the donated property. Nevertheless, as noted in Concept Summary 10.2, the taxpayer must maintain reliable written evidence of the donation.

LIMITATIONS ON CHARITABLE CONTRIBUTION DEDUCTION

In General

The potential charitable contribution deduction is the total of all donations, both money and property, that qualify for the deduction. After this determination is made, the actual amount of the charitable contribution deduction that is allowed for individuals for the tax year is limited as follows:

- If the qualifying contributions for the year total 20 percent or less of AGI, they are fully deductible.
- If the qualifying contributions are more than 20 percent of AGI, the deductible amount may be limited to either 20 percent, 30 percent, or 50 percent of AGI, depending on the type of property given and the type of organization to which the donation is made.
- In any case, the maximum charitable contribution deduction may not exceed 50 percent of AGI for the tax year.

To understand the complex rules for computing the amount of a charitable contribution deduction, it is necessary to understand the distinction between capital gain property and ordinary income property. In addition, it is necessary to understand when the 50 percent, 30 percent, and 20 percent limitations apply. If a taxpayer's contributions for the year exceed the applicable percentage limitations, the excess contributions may be carried forward and deducted during a five-year carryover period. These topics are discussed in the sections that follow.

Ordinary Income Property

Ordinary income property is any property that, if sold, will result in the recognition of ordinary income. The term includes inventory for sale in the taxpayer's trade or

CONCEPT SUMMARY 10.2

Documentation and Substantiation Requirements for Charitable Contributions

Cash gifts	• A deduction is allowed only if the taxpayer has a proper receipt (e.g., bank record such as a canceled check, written statement from the charity) showing the name of the charitable organization and the date and amount of the contribution.
	• A written statement from the charity is required if a payment is for more than $75 and is partly a contribution and partly for goods or services. The statement must provide an estimate of the value of the goods and services received by the donor.
Noncash gifts (e.g., household items)	• A receipt from the charity must be kept for any gift of property other than money. Clothes or other household items are deductible if they are in "good used condition or better" at the time of the gift.
	• If the items are not in good used condition or better and their value is $500 or more, a deduction is allowed if a "qualified appraisal" is included with the return.
Used automobiles	• The deduction is generally limited to the amount the charity receives on the sale of the car. The taxpayer should obtain a statement from the charity documenting the sales price of the automobile. However, FMV may be deducted if it is $500 or less.
Cash or noncash gifts of $250 or more	• Written acknowledgment from the charity (or certain payroll records in the case of gifts made by payroll deductions) is required to deduct a single cash or property contribution of $250 or more. The acknowledgment must include the amount of money and a description of any other property contributed, whether the charity provided any goods or services in return for the contribution, and a description and estimated value of the goods or services provided.
Noncash gifts of more than $500	• Additional substantiation (e.g., how the property was acquired and its basis) is required on the tax return if donated noncash property is valued at more than $500. Qualified appraisals may be required if noncash contributions exceed $5,000 in value.
Antiques, paintings, jewelry, and other "tangible personal property"	• The deduction is equal to the property's appreciated FMV only if the charity puts the property to "a use related to its tax-exempt purpose." Otherwise, the deduction is limited to the property's cost. The taxpayer should obtain a statement from the charity documenting the property's use.

business, a work of art created by the donor, and a manuscript prepared by the donor. It also includes, *for purposes of the charitable contribution calculation,* a capital asset held by the donor for less than the required holding period for long-term capital gain treatment (long term is a period longer than one year). To the extent that disposition of property results in the recognition of ordinary income due to the recapture of depreciation, it is ordinary income property.[45]

If ordinary income property is contributed, the deduction is equal to the fair market value of the property less the amount of ordinary income that would have been reported if the property were sold. In most instances, the deduction is limited to the adjusted basis of the property to the donor.

EXAMPLE 30

Tim donates stock in White Corporation to a university on May 1, 2011. Tim had purchased the stock for $2,500 on March 3, 2011, and the stock had a value of $3,600 when he made the donation. Since he had not held the property long enough to meet the long-term capital gain requirement, Tim would have recognized a short-term capital gain of $1,100 if he had sold the property. Since short-term capital gain property is

[45]For a more complete discussion of the difference between ordinary income and capital gain property, see Chapter 16.

treated as ordinary income property for charitable contribution purposes, Tim's charitable contribution deduction is limited to the property's adjusted basis of $2,500 ($3,600 − $1,100). ∎

In Example 30, suppose the stock had a fair market value of $2,300 (rather than $3,600) when it was donated to charity. Because the fair market value now is less than the adjusted basis, the charitable contribution deduction is $2,300.

Capital Gain Property

Capital gain property is any property that would have resulted in the recognition of long-term capital gain or § 1231 gain if the property had been sold by the donor.[46] As a general rule, the deduction for a contribution of capital gain property is equal to the fair market value of the property.

Three major exceptions disallow the deductibility of the appreciation on capital gain property. One exception concerns certain private foundations. Private foundations are organizations that traditionally do not receive their funding from the general public (e.g., the Bill and Melinda Gates Foundation). Generally, foundations fall into two categories: operating and nonoperating. A private *operating* foundation is one that spends substantially all of its income in the active conduct of the charitable undertaking for which it was established. Other private foundations are *nonoperating* foundations. Often, only the private foundation knows its status (operating or nonoperating) for sure, and the status can change from year to year.

If capital gain property is contributed to a private *nonoperating* foundation, the taxpayer must reduce the contribution by the long-term capital gain that would have been recognized if the property had been sold at its fair market value. The effect of this provision is to limit the deduction to the property's adjusted basis.[47]

EXAMPLE 31

Walter purchased land for $8,000 on January 1, 1998, and has held it as an investment since then. This year, when the land is worth $20,000, he donates it to a private nonoperating foundation. Walter's charitable contribution is $8,000 ($20,000 − $12,000), the land's basis. ∎

If, in Example 31, Walter had donated the land to either a public charity or a private operating foundation, his charitable contribution would be $20,000, the fair market value of the land.

A second exception applying to capital gain property relates to *tangible personalty*. Tangible personalty is all property that is not realty (land and buildings) and does not include intangible property such as stock or securities. If tangible personalty is contributed to a public charity such as a museum, church, or university, the charitable deduction may have to be reduced. The amount of the reduction is the long-term capital gain that would have been recognized if the property had been sold for its fair market value. In general, the reduction is required if the property is put to an *unrelated use*. The term *unrelated use* means a use that is unrelated to the exempt purpose or function of the charitable organization. For example, a piece of artwork donated to the American Red Cross is unlikely to be put to a related use. Instead, the Red Cross would likely sell the art to generate funds that would then be used to support its mission of providing assistance to individuals who have been struck by disasters.

This reduction generally will not apply if the property is, in fact, not put to an unrelated use or if, at the time of the contribution, it was reasonable to anticipate that the property would not be put to an unrelated use by the donee.[48]

---

[46]See General Scheme of Taxation in Chapter 16 for a discussion of holding periods.

[47]§ 170(e)(1)(B)(ii). However, § 170(e)(5) provides that taxpayers who donate *qualified appreciated stock* to private nonoperating foundations may deduct the fair market value of the stock. Qualified appreciated stock is stock for which market quotations are readily available on an established securities market.

[48]§ 170(e)(1)(B)(i) and Reg. § 1.170A–4(b)(3)(ii)(b). In certain situations, if the donee disposes of the property within three years of the contribution, the donor is required to recapture the appreciation element of the deduction unless the donee certifies that it put the property to a related use or intended to put the property to a related use.

EXAMPLE 32

Myrtle contributes a Picasso painting, for which she paid $20,000, to a local museum. She had owned the painting for four years. It had a value of $30,000 at the time of the donation. The museum displays the painting for five years and subsequently sells it for $50,000. The charitable contribution is $30,000. It is not reduced by the unrealized appreciation since the painting is not put to an unrelated use even though it is later sold by the museum. ∎

A third exception applying to capital gain property disallows a deduction for the appreciation on several types of intellectual property. Patents, certain copyrights, trademarks, trade names, trade secrets, know-how, and some software are subject to this rule, which limits the contribution to the lesser of the taxpayer's basis in the property or the property's fair market value. As a consequence of this exception, if many of these types of intellectual property are donated by their creator, the charitable contribution deduction will be relatively small because the creator usually has a low basis for them.

Fifty Percent Ceiling

Contributions made to public charities may not exceed 50 percent of an individual's AGI for the year. Excess contributions may be carried over to the next five years. The 50 percent ceiling on contributions applies to public charities such as churches, schools, hospitals, and Federal, state, or local governmental units. The 50 percent ceiling also applies to contributions to private operating foundations and certain private nonoperating foundations.

In the remaining discussion of charitable contributions, public charities and private foundations (both operating and nonoperating) that qualify for the 50 percent ceiling will be referred to as *50 percent organizations.*

Thirty Percent Ceiling

A 30 percent ceiling applies to contributions of cash and ordinary income property to private nonoperating foundations that are not 50 percent organizations. The 30 percent ceiling also applies to contributions of appreciated capital gain property to 50 percent organizations unless the taxpayer makes a special election (see below).

In the event the contributions for any one tax year involve both 50 percent and 30 percent property, the allowable deduction comes first from the 50 percent property.

EXAMPLE 33

During the year, Lisa makes the following donations to her church: cash of $2,000 and unimproved land worth $30,000. Lisa had purchased the land four years ago for $22,000 and held it as an investment. Therefore, it is capital gain property. Lisa's AGI for the year is $60,000. Disregarding percentage limitations, Lisa's potential deduction is $32,000 [$2,000 (cash) + $30,000 (fair market value of land)].

In applying the percentage limitations, however, the *current* deduction for the land is limited to $18,000 [30% (limitation applicable to capital gain property) × $60,000 (AGI)]. Thus, the total current deduction is $20,000 ($2,000 cash + $18,000 land). Note that the total deduction does not exceed $30,000, which is 50% of Lisa's AGI. ∎

Under a special election, a taxpayer may choose to forgo a deduction of the appreciation on capital gain property. Referred to as the *reduced deduction election*, this enables the taxpayer to move from the 30 percent limitation to the 50 percent limitation.

EXAMPLE 34

Assume the same facts as in Example 33, except that Lisa makes the reduced deduction election. Now the deduction becomes $24,000 [$2,000 (cash) + $22,000 (basis in land)] because both donations fall under the 50% limitation. Thus, by making the election, Lisa has increased her current charitable contribution deduction by $4,000 [$24,000 − $20,000 (Example 33)]. ∎

Although the reduced deduction election appears attractive, it should be considered carefully. The election sacrifices a deduction for the appreciation on capital gain property that might eventually be allowed. Note that in Example 33, the potential deduction was $32,000, yet in Example 34 only $24,000 is allowed. The reason

CONCEPT SUMMARY 10.3

Determining the Deduction for Contributions of Appreciated Property by Individuals

If the Type of Property Contributed Is:	And the Property Is Contributed to:	The Contribution Is Measured by:	But the Deduction Is Limited to:
1. Capital gain property	A 50% organization	Fair market value of the property	30% of AGI
2. Ordinary income property	A 50% organization	The basis of the property*	50% of AGI
3. Capital gain property (and the property is tangible personal property put to an unrelated use by the donee)	A 50% organization	The basis of the property*	50% of AGI
4. Capital gain property (and the reduced deduction is elected)	A 50% organization	The basis of the property	50% of AGI
5. Capital gain property	A private nonoperating foundation that is not a 50% organization	The basis of the property*	The lesser of: 1. 20% of AGI 2. 50% of AGI minus other contributions to 50% organizations

*If the fair market value of the property is less than the adjusted basis (i.e., the property has declined in value instead of appreciating), the fair market value is used.

the potential deduction is decreased by $8,000 ($32,000 − $24,000) is that no carry-over is allowed for the amount sacrificed by the election.

Twenty Percent Ceiling

A 20 percent ceiling applies to contributions of appreciated capital gain property to private nonoperating foundations that are not 50 percent organizations.

Contribution Carryovers

Contributions that exceed the percentage limitations for the current year can be carried over for five years. In the carryover process, such contributions do not lose their identity for limitation purposes. Thus, if the contribution originally involved 30 percent property, the carryover will continue to be classified as 30 percent property in the carryover year.

EXAMPLE 35

Assume the same facts as in Example 33. Because only $18,000 of the $30,000 value of the land is deducted in the current year, the balance of $12,000 may be carried over to the following year. But the carryover will still be treated as capital gain property and is subject to the 30%-of-AGI limitation. ■

In applying the percentage limitations, current charitable contributions must be claimed first before any carryovers can be considered. If carryovers involve more than one year, they are utilized in a first-in, first-out order.

10.6 MISCELLANEOUS ITEMIZED DEDUCTIONS

In general, no deduction is allowed for personal, living, or family expenses.[49] How-ever, a taxpayer may incur a number of expenditures related to employment. If an employee or outside salesperson incurs unreimbursed business expenses or expenses that are reimbursed under a nonaccountable plan, including travel and

> **LO.7**
> List the business and personal expenditures that are deductible either as miscellaneous itemized deductions or as other itemized deductions.

---

[49]§ 262.

transportation, the expenses are deductible as **miscellaneous itemized deductions.**[50] Certain other expenses also fall into the special category of miscellaneous itemized deductions. Some are deductible only if, in total, they exceed 2 percent of the taxpayer's AGI. These miscellaneous itemized deductions include (but are not limited to) the following:

- Professional dues to membership organizations.
- Uniforms or other clothing that cannot be used for normal wear.
- Fees incurred for the preparation of one's tax return or fees incurred for tax litigation before the IRS or the courts.
- Job-hunting costs.
- Fee paid for a safe deposit box used to store papers and documents relating to taxable income-producing investments.
- Investment expenses that are deductible under § 212 as discussed in Chapter 6.
- Appraisal fees to determine the amount of a casualty loss or the fair market value of donated property.
- Hobby losses up to the amount of hobby income (refer to Chapter 6).
- Unreimbursed employee expenses (refer to Chapter 9).

Certain employee business expenses that are reimbursed are not itemized deductions, but are deducted *for* AGI. Employee business expenses are discussed in depth in Chapter 9.

10.7 OTHER MISCELLANEOUS DEDUCTIONS

Certain expenses and losses do not fall into any category of itemized deductions already discussed but are nonetheless deductible. The following expenses and losses are deductible on line 28 of Schedule A as Other Miscellaneous Deductions.

- Gambling losses up to the amount of gambling winnings.
- Impairment-related work expenses of a handicapped person.
- Federal estate tax on income in respect of a decedent.
- Deduction for repayment of amounts under a claim of right if more than $3,000 (discussed in Chapter 18).
- The unrecovered investment in an annuity contract when the annuity ceases by reason of death, discussed in Chapter 4.

Unlike the expenses and losses discussed previously under Miscellaneous Itemized Deductions, the above expenses and losses are not subject to the 2 percent-of-AGI floor.

10.8 COMPREHENSIVE EXAMPLE OF SCHEDULE A

Harry and Jean Brown, married filing jointly, had the following transactions for 2010:

Medicines that required a prescription	$ 430
Doctor and dentist bills paid and not reimbursed	2,120
Medical insurance premium payments	1,200
Contact lenses	170
Transportation for medical purposes on March 1, 2010 (321 miles × 16.5 cents/mile + $10.00 parking)	63
State income tax withheld (This amount exceeds the sales tax from the sales tax table.)	1,900

---

[50]Actors and performing artists who meet certain requirements are not subject to this rule. See § 62(a)(2)(B).

Real estate taxes	$1,580
Interest paid on qualified residence mortgage	2,340
Qualifying charitable contributions paid by check	860
Transportation in performing charitable services (800 miles × 14 cents/mile + $7.00 parking and tolls)	119
Unreimbursed employee expenses (from Form 2106)	870
Tax return preparation	150
Safe deposit box (used for keeping investment documents and tax records)	170

The Browns' AGI is $40,000. Their completed 2010 Schedule A on the following page reports itemized deductions totaling $8,172. Schedule A for 2010 is used for illustration purposes because the 2011 form was not available at the date of this printing.

10.9 OVERALL LIMITATION ON CERTAIN ITEMIZED DEDUCTIONS

Recall from the discussion in Chapter 3 that certain higher income taxpayers were subject to a phaseout of personal and dependency exemptions that is no longer in effect as of the beginning of 2010. A similar phaseout provision also formerly applied to certain itemized deductions where a limitation was placed on their full deductibility. Phaseouts of this type are sometimes referred to as "stealth taxes." The Tax in the News on p. 10-31 illustrates the effect of the limitation on President and Mrs. Obamas' 2009 income tax return, which required them to pay $18,685 more in Federal income taxes than they would have paid had their itemized deductions been fully deductible. That limitation does not apply to individual taxpayers for tax years beginning after 2009, and now taxpayers may *fully* deduct any itemized deductions to which they are entitled.[51] However, many believe that in future years, higher income taxpayers could again be subject to an overall limitation on the deductibility of itemized deductions as Congress searches for ways to reduce significant Federal budget deficits.

ETHICS & Equity

BETWEEN A ROCK AND A HARD PLACE

Robert Ryan, a candidate for governor, has released his income tax return to the public. As Ryan's former tax adviser, you examine the return closely and realize that a considerable amount of his income was not reported on the return. You confide to a friend in the tabloid newspaper business that you are aware that a candidate for high public office has filed a fraudulent tax return. Your friend assures you that you will be able to sell your story for at least $25,000 to a tabloid and still remain anonymous. Another friend, a CPA, argues that you should inform Ryan and give him an opportunity to correct the problem. You tell your friend that you are concerned that Ryan will be very vindictive if you approach him about the issue. Which course of action will you choose?

---

[51]§ 68. In 2009, before the provision's expiration, the limitation applied to taxpayers whose AGI exceeded $166,800 ($83,400 for married taxpayers filing separately). Section 68(g) provides for its termination for tax years beginning after December 31, 2009.

SCHEDULE A (Form 1040) Department of the Treasury Internal Revenue Service (99)	**Itemized Deductions** ► Attach to Form 1040. ► See Instructions for Schedule A (Form 1040).	OMB No. 1545-0074 20**10** Attachment Sequence No. **07**

Name(s) shown on Form 1040 — *Harry and Jean Brown*

Your social security number: *111   11   1111*

Medical and Dental Expenses		**Caution.** Do not include expenses reimbursed or paid by others.			
	1	Medical and dental expenses (see instructions)	**1**	*3,983*	
	2	Enter amount from Form 1040, line 38 | **2** *40,000*			
	3	Multiply line 2 by 7.5% (.075)	**3**	*3,000*	
	4	Subtract line 3 from line 1. If line 3 is more than line 1, enter -0-	**4**		*983*
Taxes You Paid	5	State and local **(check only one box):**			
	a	[X] Income taxes, **or** ⎱	**5**	*1,900*	
	b	☐ General sales taxes ⎰			
	6	Real estate taxes (see instructions)	**6**	*1,580*	
	7	New motor vehicle taxes from line 11 of the worksheet on back (for certain vehicles purchased in 2009). Skip this line if you checked box 5b	**7**		
	8	Other taxes. List type and amount ► _____	**8**		
	9	Add lines 5 through 8	**9**		*3,480*
Interest You Paid **Note.** Your mortgage interest deduction may be limited (see instructions).	10	Home mortgage interest and points reported to you on Form 1098	**10**	*2,340*	
	11	Home mortgage interest not reported to you on Form 1098. If paid to the person from whom you bought the home, see instructions and show that person's name, identifying no., and address ► _____ _____	**11**		
	12	Points not reported to you on Form 1098. See instructions for special rules	**12**		
	13	Mortgage insurance premiums (see instructions)	**13**		
	14	Investment interest. Attach Form 4952 if required. (See instructions.)	**14**		
	15	Add lines 10 through 14	**15**		*2,340*
Gifts to Charity If you made a gift and got a benefit for it, see instructions.	16	Gifts by cash or check. If you made any gift of $250 or more, see instructions	**16**	*860*	
	17	Other than by cash or check. If any gift of $250 or more, see instructions. You **must** attach Form 8283 if over $500 . . .	**17**	*119*	
	18	Carryover from prior year	**18**		
	19	Add lines 16 through 18	**19**		*979*
Casualty and Theft Losses	20	Casualty or theft loss(es). Attach Form 4684. (See instructions.)	**20**		
Job Expenses and Certain Miscellaneous Deductions	21	Unreimbursed employee expenses—job travel, union dues, job education, etc. Attach Form 2106 or 2106-EZ if required. (See instructions.) ► _____	**21**	*870*	
	22	Tax preparation fees	**22**	*150*	
	23	Other expenses—investment, safe deposit box, etc. List type and amount ► _____ *Safe deposit box* _____	**23**	*170*	
	24	Add lines 21 through 23	**24**	*1,190*	
	25	Enter amount from Form 1040, line 38 | **25** *40,000*			
	26	Multiply line 25 by 2% (.02)	**26**	*800*	
	27	Subtract line 26 from line 24. If line 26 is more than line 24, enter -0-	**27**		*390*
Other Miscellaneous Deductions	28	Other—from list in instructions. List type and amount ► _____ _____	**28**		
Total Itemized Deductions	29	Add the amounts in the far right column for lines 4 through 28. Also, enter this amount on Form 1040, line 40	**29**		*8,172*
	30	If you elect to itemize deductions even though they are less than your standard deduction, check here . . . . ► ☐			

For Paperwork Reduction Act Notice, see Form 1040 instructions.   Cat. No. 17145C   Schedule A (Form 1040) 2010

TAX *in*
the **NEWS**   **THE FIRST FAMILY AND ITEMIZED DEDUCTION PHASEOUTS**

In 2010, President Barack H. and Michelle L. Obama itemized deductions on their 2009 tax return (refer to Tax in the News, p. 10–4). Because of their income level, their itemized deductions were reduced, as shown in the column to the right.

The top marginal rate of 35 percent applied to the Obamas' taxable income in 2009. Therefore, the phaseout of itemized deductions cost them $18,685 in additional Federal income tax ($53,386 reduction × 35% marginal tax rate).

While this phaseout provision expired after 2009 and is not currently part of the law (i.e., does not apply for 2011 and 2012), many commentators expect it could return sooner than 2013 once Congress begins to focus on ways to reduce the large budget deficit.

Itemized Deductions	
Medical expenses	$ –0–
Taxes	186,910
Interest	52,195
Charitable contributions	329,100
Job expenses and most other miscellaneous deductions	–0–
Total itemized deductions	$568,205
Reduction due to phaseout [($5,505,409 AGI − $166,800) × .03 × ⅓]	(53,386)
Itemized deductions allowed	$514,819

TAX PLANNING:

10.10 EFFECTIVE UTILIZATION OF ITEMIZED DEDUCTIONS

Since an individual may use the standard deduction in one year and itemize deductions in another year, it is frequently possible to obtain maximum benefit by shifting itemized deductions from one year to another. For example, if a taxpayer's itemized deductions and the standard deduction are approximately the same for each year of a two-year period, the taxpayer should use the standard deduction in one year and shift itemized deductions (to the extent permitted by law) to the other year. The individual could, for example, prepay a church pledge for a particular year to shift the deduction to the current year or avoid paying end-of-the-year medical expenses to shift the deduction to the following year.

LO.8

Identify tax planning strategies that can maximize the benefit of itemized deductions.

10.11 UTILIZATION OF MEDICAL DEDUCTIONS

When a taxpayer anticipates that medical expenses will approximate the percentage floor, much might be done to generate a deductible excess. Any of the following procedures can help build a deduction by the end of the year:

- Incur the obligation for needed dental work or have needed work carried out.[52] Orthodontic treatment, for example, may have been recommended for a member of the taxpayer's family.
- Have elective remedial surgery that may have been postponed from prior years (e.g., tonsillectomies, vasectomies, correction of hernias, hysterectomies).
- Incur the obligation for capital improvements to the taxpayer's personal residence recommended by a physician (e.g., an air filtration system to alleviate a respiratory disorder).

---

[52]Prepayment of medical expenses does not generate a current deduction unless the taxpayer is under an obligation to make the payment.

As an aid to taxpayers who may experience temporary cash-flow problems at the end of the year, the use of credit cards is deemed to be payment for purposes of timing the deductibility of charitable and medical expenses.

EXAMPLE 36

On December 13, 2011, Marge (a calendar year taxpayer) purchases two pairs of prescription contact lenses and one pair of prescribed orthopedic shoes for a total of $450. These purchases are separately charged to Marge's credit card. On January 6, 2012, Marge receives her statement containing these charges and makes payment shortly thereafter. The purchases are deductible as medical expenses in the year charged (2011) and not in the year the account is settled (2012). ∎

Recognizing which expenditures qualify for the medical deduction also may be crucial to exceeding the percentage limitations.

EXAMPLE 37

Mortimer employs Lana (an unrelated party) to care for his incapacitated and dependent mother. Lana is not a trained nurse but spends approximately one-half of the time performing nursing duties (e.g., administering injections and providing physical therapy) and the rest of the time doing household chores. An allocable portion of Lana's wages that Mortimer pays (including the employer's portion of FICA taxes) qualifies as a medical expense. ∎

10.12 TIMING THE PAYMENT OF DEDUCTIBLE TAXES

It is sometimes possible to defer or accelerate the payment of certain deductible taxes, such as state income tax, real property tax, and personal property tax. For instance, the final installment of estimated state income tax is generally due after the end of a given tax year. Accelerating the payment of the final installment could result in larger itemized deductions for the current year.

EXAMPLE 38

Jenny, who is single, expects to have itemized deductions of $5,500 in 2011 and $2,500 in 2012. She plans to pay $900 as the final installment on her 2011 estimated state income tax, which is due on January 15, 2012. The standard deduction for 2011 is $5,800 for single taxpayers. If Jenny does not pay the final installment until 2012, she will not itemize in either 2011 or 2012. However, if she pays the final installment in December 2011, her itemized deductions will be $6,400 ($5,500 + $900) in 2011, and she will benefit from itemizing. ∎

10.13 PROTECTING THE INTEREST DEDUCTION

Although the deductibility of prepaid interest by a cash basis taxpayer has been severely restricted, a notable exception allows a deduction for points paid by the buyer to obtain financing for the purchase or improvement of a principal residence in the year of payment. However, such points must actually be paid by the taxpayer obtaining the loan and must represent a charge for the use of money. It has been held that points paid from the mortgage proceeds do not satisfy the payment requirement.[53] Also, the portion of the points attributable to service charges does not represent deductible interest.[54] Taxpayers financing home purchases or improvements usually should direct their planning toward avoiding these two hurdles to immediate deductibility.

---

[53]*Alan A. Rubnitz*, 67 T.C. 621 (1977). Seller-paid points may also be deductible by the buyer under the provisions of Rev.Proc. 94–27, cited in footnote 31.

[54]*Donald L. Wilkerson*, 70 T.C. 240 (1978).

In rare instances, a taxpayer may find it desirable to forgo the immediate expensing of points in the year paid. Instead, it could prove beneficial to capitalize the points and write them off as interest expense over the life of the mortgage.

EXAMPLE 39

Gerald purchases a home on December 15, 2011, for $380,000 with $120,000 cash and a 15-year mortgage of $260,000 financed by the Greater Metropolis National Bank. Gerald pays two points in addition to interest allocated to the period from December 15 until December 31, 2011, at an annual rate of 6%. Since Gerald does not have enough itemized deductions to exceed the standard deduction for 2011, he should elect to capitalize the points and amortize them over 15 years. In this instance, Gerald would deduct $346.67 for 2012, as part of his qualified residence interest expense [$5,200 (two points) divided by 15 years], if he elects to itemize that year. ∎

Because personal (consumer) interest is not deductible, taxpayers should consider making use of home equity loans. Recall that these loans utilize the personal residence of the taxpayer as security. The funds from these loans can be used for personal purposes (e.g., auto loans, vacations). By making use of home equity loans, therefore, what would have been nondeductible consumer interest becomes deductible qualified residence interest.

10.14 ASSURING THE CHARITABLE CONTRIBUTION DEDUCTION

For a charitable contribution deduction to be available, the recipient must be a qualified charitable organization. Sometimes the mechanics of how the contribution is carried out can determine whether a deduction results.

EXAMPLE 40

Fumiko wants to donate $5,000 to her church's mission in Kobe, Japan. In this regard, she considers three alternatives:

1. Send the money directly to the mission.
2. Give the money to her church with the understanding that it is to be passed on to the mission.
3. Give the money directly to the missionary in charge of the mission who is currently in the United States on a fund-raising trip.

If Fumiko wants to obtain a deduction for the contribution, she should choose alternative 2. A direct donation to the mission (alternative 1) is not deductible because the mission is a foreign charity. A direct gift to the missionary (alternative 3) does not comply since an individual cannot be a qualified charity for income tax purposes.[55] ∎

A clearly established rule provides that a donor may not claim a charitable contribution to the extent that a benefit is received in return. For example, if $100 is paid to attend a charity ball and a reasonable value of that privilege is $35, the charitable contribution is $65. However, consider the following circumstances.

EXAMPLE 41

In response to a solicitation from the University Medical Association, Rich and Lucile pay $200, which allows them to attend a fund-raising benefit event. The charity mails them a ticket and a statement indicating that for a contribution at the $200 level, $140 may be deducted because the value of the benefit provided to the donor equals $60. If Rich and Lucile accept the ticket, whether they attend the benefit or not, their deduction is $140. However, if they *return* the ticket to the charity for resale (e.g., they know their schedule will prevent them from

[55] *Thomas E. Lesslie*, 36 TCM 495, T.C.Memo. 1977–111.

TAX *in*
the NEWS

GETTING THE BIGGEST BANG FOR THE BUCK WHEN SUPPORTING CHARITY

Individuals are often motivated to support a charitable organization's goals for numerous reasons: they want to help by providing food and shelter to those in need, responding to natural disasters, or delivering other basic goods or services to the needy. But in a world of limited resources, donors also must choose *which* organization(s) to support from among many worthwhile causes because it is impossible to support all of them in a meaningful way. So what factors might be helpful to a prospective donor in deciding how to deploy limited charitable dollars?

- All other things being equal, a deductible gift is better than a nondeductible gift. Therefore, to ensure a charitable contribution deduction, the donor should be certain that the recipient is a qualified domestic organization. Check with the

IRS to verify that a particular charity is qualified (**www.irs.gov**).
- The donor may want to know whether the charitable organization is efficient in using the resources at its disposal in meeting its objectives. To compare the relative efficiency of charities on a scale of 0 to 10, check with Charity Navigator (**www.charitynavigator.org**).
- Is the organization efficient in its fund-raising efforts, or does the charity typically incur a large amount of fund-raising expenditures relative to the resources it generates? This type of information is reflected in a grade assigned by the American Institute of Philanthropy (**www.charitywatch.org**).

---

attending), the charitable contribution deduction equals the entire amount paid for the ticket. ■

When making noncash donations, the type of property chosen can have decided implications in determining the amount, if any, of the deduction.

EXAMPLE 42

Sam wants to give $60,000 in value to his church in some form other than cash. In this connection, he considers four alternatives:

1. Stock held for two years as an investment with a basis of $100,000 and a fair market value of $60,000.
2. Stock held for five years as an investment with a basis of $10,000 and a fair market value of $60,000.
3. The rent-free use for a year of a building that normally leases for $5,000 a month.
4. A valuable stamp collection held as an investment and owned for 10 years with a basis of $10,000 and a fair market value of $60,000. The church plans to sell the collection if and when it is donated.

Alternative 1 is ill-advised as the subject of the gift. Even though Sam would obtain a deduction of $60,000, he would forgo the potential loss of $40,000 that would be recognized if the property were sold.[56] Alternative 2 makes good sense since the deduction still is $60,000 and none of the $50,000 of appreciation that has occurred must be recognized as income. Alternative 3 yields no deduction at all and is not a wise choice. Alternative 4 involves tangible personalty that the recipient does not plan to use. As a result, the amount of the deduction is limited to $10,000, the stamp collection's basis.[57] ■

For property transfers (particularly real estate), the ceiling limitations on the amount of the deduction allowed in any one year (50 percent, 30 percent, or 20 percent of AGI, as the case may be) could be a factor to take into account. With proper planning, donations can be controlled to stay within the limitations and therefore avoid the need for a carryover of unused charitable contributions.

---

[56]*LaVar M. Withers*, 69 T.C. 900 (1978).

[57]No reduction of appreciation is necessary in alternative 2 since stock is intangible property and not tangible personalty.

EXAMPLE 43

Andrew wants to donate a tract of unimproved land held as an investment to Eastern University (a qualified charitable organization). The land has been held for six years and has a current fair market value of $300,000 and a basis to Andrew of $50,000. Andrew's AGI for the current year is estimated to be $200,000, and he expects much the same for the next few years. In the current year, he deeds (transfers) an undivided one-fifth interest in the real estate to the university. ■

What has Andrew in Example 43 accomplished for income tax purposes? In the current year, he will be allowed a charitable contribution deduction of $60,000 ($\frac{1}{5} \times \$300,000$), which will be within the applicable limitation of AGI (30% × $200,000). Presuming no other charitable contributions for the year, Andrew has avoided the possibility of a carryover. In future years, Andrew can arrange donations of undivided interests in the real estate to stay within the bounds of the percentage limitations. The only difficulty with this approach is the need to revalue the real estate each year before the donation, since the amount of the deduction is based on the fair market value of the interest contributed at the time of the contribution.

EXAMPLE 44

Tiffany dies in October 2011. In completing her final income tax return for 2011, Tiffany's executor determines the following information: AGI of $104,000 and a donation by Tiffany to her church of stock worth $60,000. Tiffany had purchased the stock two years ago for $50,000 and held it as an investment. Tiffany's executor makes the reduced deduction election and, as a consequence, claims a charitable contribution deduction of $50,000. With the election, the potential charitable contribution deduction of $50,000 ($60,000 − $10,000) is less than the 50% ceiling of $52,000 ($104,000 × 50%). If the executor had not made the election, the potential charitable contribution deduction of $60,000 would have been reduced by the 30% ceiling to $31,200 ($104,000 × 30%). No carryover of the $28,800 ($60,000 − $31,200) would have been available because Tiffany's 2011 income tax return is her final return. ■

REFOCUS ON THE BIG PICTURE

ITEMIZED DEDUCTIONS CAN REDUCE THE AFTER-TAX COST OF MAJOR PURCHASES

Because the Federal tax law provides that qualified residence interest and real estate taxes are deductible by individual taxpayers, the after-tax cost of a home purchase will be reduced by the tax savings associated with these itemized tax deductions (see Example 1). Given the Williamsons' projected taxable income, they are in the 28 percent Federal tax bracket and the 6 percent state tax bracket (i.e., aggregate marginal tax bracket of 34 percent). As a result, the after-tax cost of financing the purchase of the home will be:

Nondeductible principal payments	$ 2,000
Deductible qualified residence interest and real estate taxes [($37,000 + $3,000) × (1 − .34)]	26,400
Total	$28,400
After-tax monthly cost ($28,400 ÷ 12)	$ 2,367

Because the Williamsons will be able to itemize their deductions if they purchase a new home and will be able to deduct most of their monthly house payment, the home purchase will be affordable (see Examples 16 and 22).

What If?

What if the Williamsons use the less expensive route to finance the purchase of their home by using their retirement and taxable portfolio as security for the loan? What

CONTINUED

may at first appear to be a cost-effective approach ends up being more costly when considering the impact of the tax law. With this approach, the interest expense is not deductible because it is not qualified residence interest (see Example 22); further, it is not deductible as investment interest (see Chapter 11). Therefore, the after-tax cost of financing the home using this approach makes the home unaffordable.

Nondeductible principal and interest payments	$37,000
Deductible real estate taxes [$3,000 × (1 − .34)]	1,980
Total	$38,980
After-tax monthly cost ($38,980 ÷ 12)	$ 3,248

KEY TERMS

Acquisition indebtedness, 10–15	Home equity loans, 10–16	Ordinary income property, 10–23
Capital gain property, 10–25	Medical expense, 10–3	Points, 10–16
Charitable contribution, 10–19	Miscellaneous itemized deductions, 10–28	Qualified residence interest, 10–14
Health Savings Account (HSA), 10–9		

DISCUSSION QUESTIONS

1. **LO.1, 2** Erin, who prepared her own income tax return for the current year, failed to claim a deduction for her contribution to a traditional Individual Retirement Account (IRA). Her AGI, as reported on the incorrect return, was $100,000, and her medical expenses were $10,000.
   a. Will the correction of this omission affect the amount of medical expenses Erin can deduct? Explain. *yeas .*
   b. Will Erin's medical expense deduction increase or decrease when she corrects her return? *Increase*

2. **LO.2** Roberta incurred the following expenditures during the year:
   - Medical insurance premiums.
   - Life insurance premiums.
   - Nonprescription calcium supplements to prevent osteoporosis.
   - Fees for an alcohol rehabilitation program.
   - Contact lenses.
   - Travel expenses to obtain treatment at the Mayo Clinic in Minnesota.

   Which of these expenses can Roberta include as medical expenses for purposes of computing her medical expense deduction?

3. **LO.2** Joe was in an accident and required cosmetic surgery for injuries to his nose. He also had the doctor do additional surgery to reshape his chin, which had not been injured. Will the cosmetic surgery to Joe's nose qualify as a medical expense? Will the cosmetic surgery to Joe's chin qualify as a medical expense? Explain.

DECISION MAKING

4. **LO.2, 8** Frank, a widower, had a serious stroke and is no longer capable of caring for himself. He has three sons, all of whom live in different states. Because they are unable to care for Frank in their homes, his sons have placed him in a nursing home equipped to provide medical and nursing care. Total nursing home expenses amount to $36,000 per year. Of this amount, $15,000 is directly attributable to medical and nursing care. Frank's

Social Security benefits are used to pay for $10,000 of the nursing home charges. He has no other income. His sons plan to split the remaining medical expenses equally.

a. What portion of the nursing home charges is potentially deductible as a medical expense?

b. Can you provide Frank's sons with a tax planning idea for maximizing the deduction for his medical expenses?

5. **LO.2** Nathan, who is physically handicapped, paid $10,000 for the installation of wheelchair ramps, support bars, and railings in his personal residence. These improve-ments increased the value of his personal residence by $2,500. How much of Nathan's expenditure qualifies as a medical expense deduction (subject to the 7.5% floor)? Explain.

6. **LO.2** Bob and June were divorced in 2009. In July 2011, their daughter, Harriet, broke her leg while playing soccer. Harriet lives with June, and June claims her as a dependent. Bob pays for the medical expenses related to Harriet's injury. Can Bob claim the medical expenses he pays for Harriet on his tax return?

7. **LO.2** David, a sole proprietor of a bookstore, pays a $7,500 premium for medical insurance for himself and his family. Joan, an employee of a small firm that doesn't provide her with medical insurance, pays medical insurance premiums of $8,000 for herself. How does the tax treatment differ for David and Joan?

8. **LO.2** Arturo, a calendar year taxpayer, paid $16,000 in medical expenses and sustained a $20,000 casualty loss in 2011. He expects $12,000 of the medical expenses and $14,000 of the casualty loss to be reimbursed by insurance companies in 2012. Before considering any limitations on these deductions, how much can Arturo include in determining his itemized deductions for 2011?

9. **LO.2** Hubert, a self-employed taxpayer, is married and has two children. He has asked you to explain the tax and nontax advantages of creating a Health Savings Account (HSA) for himself and his family.

10. **LO.2** A local ophthalmologist's advertising campaign included a certificate for free LASIK eye surgery for the lucky winner of a drawing. Ahmad held the winning ticket, which was drawn in December 2010. Ahmad had no vision problems and was uncertain what he should do with the prize. In February 2011, Ahmad's daughter, who lives with his former wife, was diagnosed with a vision problem that could be treated with either prescription glasses or LASIK surgery. The divorce decree requires that Ahmad pay for all medical expenses incurred for his daughter. Identify the relevant tax issues for Ahmad.

ISSUE ID

11. **LO.3** Diego sold his personal residence to Dinah on July 1, 2011. He had paid real property taxes on March 1, 2011, the due date for property taxes for 2011.

a. How will Diego's payment affect his deduction for property taxes in 2011?

b. Will Diego's payment of the taxes have any effect on Dinah's itemized deductions for 2011?

c. What other tax or financial effects will Diego's payment of the taxes have on either party?

ISSUE ID

12. **LO.5, 8** Julia owns a principal residence in California, a condo in New York City, and a houseboat in Florida. All of the properties have mortgages on which Julia pays interest. What are the limitations on Julia's mortgage interest deduction? What strategy should Julia consider to maximize her mortgage interest deduction?

DECISION MAKING

13. **LO.5, 8** Mason Gregg's car was destroyed by a flood. Unfortunately, his insurance had lapsed two days before he incurred the loss. Mason uses his car for both business and personal use. Mason, who is self-employed, does not have adequate savings to replace the car and must borrow money to purchase a new car. He is considering taking out a home equity loan, at a 5% interest rate, to obtain funds for the purchase. Margaret, his wife, would prefer not to do so because they paid off their mortgage recently and she does not want to incur any obligations related to their home. She would prefer to sell some of their stock in Bluebird, Inc., to raise funds to purchase the new car. Mason does not want to sell the stock because it has declined in value since they purchased it and he is convinced that its price will increase within the next two years. Mason has suggested that they obtain conventional financing for the purchase from their bank, which charges 7% interest on car loans. Identify the tax issues related to each of the three alternatives Mason and Margaret are considering.

ISSUE ID

14. **LO.5** Ed borrows $20,000 and purchases an automobile. Jack borrows $20,000 to purchase a diamond engagement ring for his fiancée. Ed qualifies for an interest deduction on the amount he borrowed, but Jack does not. Can you offer any explanation for the difference?

15. **LO.5** Thomas purchased a personal residence from Rachel. In order to sell the residence, Rachel agreed to pay $5,500 in points related to Thomas's mortgage. Discuss the deductibility of the points.

16. **LO.5** Ellen borrowed $50,000 from her parents for a down payment on the purchase of a new home. She paid interest of $3,200 in 2009, $0 in 2010, and $9,000 in 2011. The IRS disallowed the deduction. Can you offer any explanation for the disallowance?

17. **LO.6** To dissuade his pastor from resigning and taking a position with a larger church, Michael, an ardent leader of the congregation, gives the pastor a new car. Is the cost of the car deductible by Michael as a charitable contribution? Explain.

18. **LO.6** Paula contributed Orange Corporation common stock to the United Way, a qualified charitable organization. In addition, she contributed tables and chairs from her proprietorship's inventory to the high school in her city. Should Paula's charitable contribution deduction for these contributions be determined by the basis or fair market value of the contributed items?

19. **LO.6** Nancy, who is a professor at State University, does some of her writing and class preparation at home at night. Her department provides faculty members with a $1,500 allowance for a desktop computer for use at school, but does not ordinarily provide computers for use at home. In order to have a computer for use at school and at home, Nancy has asked the department to provide her with a notebook computer that costs $2,500. The head of her department is willing to provide the standard $1,500 allowance and will permit Nancy to purchase the $2,500 notebook computer if she makes a donation of $1,000 to the department. If she acquires the notebook computer, Nancy's home use of the computer will be approximately 60% for business and 40% for personal use not related to her job. Discuss the tax issues that Nancy should consider in deciding whether to acquire the notebook computer under these conditions.

20. **LO.6** Fran traveled to San Francisco during the year to do volunteer work for one week for the Salvation Army. She normally receives $1,500 salary per week at her job and is planning to deduct the $1,500 as a charitable contribution. In addition, Fran incurred the following costs in connection with the trip: $400 for transportation, $1,600 for lodging, and $550 for meals. What is Fran's deduction associated with this charitable activity?

21. **LO.6, 8** William, a high school teacher, earns about $50,000 each year. In December 2011, he won $1 million in the state lottery. William plans to donate $100,000 to his church. He has asked you, his tax adviser, whether he should donate the $100,000 in 2011 or 2012. Identify the tax issues related to William's decision.

22. **LO.6, 8** The "Top Four Games," which involves four of the top golfers on the PGA Tour, is held each year on the weekend after Thanksgiving. Total prize money amounts to $1 million, and the leading money winner also receives an automobile as a prize. Twenty percent of the money won by each player goes to charity. In addition, on the par three holes, the winner of the hole receives the keys to an automobile, which goes to the player's favorite charity. Identify the relevant tax issues for the players. Consider the following possibilities with respect to the car won by the leading money winner: (1) keep the car for personal use and sell his or her present car; (2) sell the new car; (3) give the car to a friend or relative; (4) donate the car to charity; or (5) give the car to his or her caddy.

23. **LO.6, 8** Colin had AGI of $180,000 in 2011. He contributed stock in White, Inc. (a publicly traded corporation), to the United Way, a qualified charitable organization. The stock was worth $105,000 on the date it was contributed. Colin had acquired it as an investment two years ago at a cost of $84,000.
    a. What is the total amount that Colin can deduct as a charitable contribution, assuming he carries over any disallowed contribution from 2011 to future years?
    b. What is the maximum amount that Colin can deduct as a charitable contribution in 2011?
    c. What factors should Colin consider in deciding how to treat the contribution for Federal income tax purposes?
    d. Assume Colin dies in December 2011. What advice would you give the executor of his estate with regard to possible elections that can be made relative to the contribution?

PROBLEMS

24. **LO.2** Doug and Karen are married and together have AGI of $80,000 in 2011. They have two dependents and file a joint return. They pay $3,000 for a high-deductible health insurance policy and contribute $2,400 to a qualified Health Savings Account. During the year, they paid the following amounts for medical care: $7,500 in doctor and dentist bills and hospital expenses, and $1,700 for prescription drugs. In November 2011, they received an insurance reimbursement of $2,100 for hospitalization. They expect to receive an additional reimbursement of $1,000 in January 2012. Determine the maximum deduction allowable for medical expenses in 2011.

25. **LO.2** Andy had AGI of $80,000 for 2011. He was injured in a rock-climbing accident and paid $5,200 for hospital expenses and $2,800 for doctor bills. Andy also incurred medical expenses of $2,400 for his child, Jodi, who lives with his former wife, Pearl, and is claimed as a dependent by her. In 2012, Andy was reimbursed $2,600 by his insurance company for the medical expenses attributable to the rock-climbing accident.
    a. Compute Andy's deduction for medical expenses in 2011.
    b. Assume that Andy would have elected to itemize his deductions even if he had no medical expenses in 2011. How much, if any, of the $2,600 reimbursement must be included in gross income in 2012?
    c. Assume that Andy's other itemized deductions in 2011 were $5,300 and that he filed as a head of household. How much of the $2,600 reimbursement must he include in gross income in 2012?

26. **LO.2** Jung suffers from heart problems and, upon the recommendation of a physician, has an elevator installed in his personal residence. In connection with the elevator, Jung incurs and pays the following amounts during the current year:

Elevator and cost of installation	$7,500
Increase in utility bills due to the elevator	400
Cost of certified appraisal	300

    The system has an estimated useful life of 10 years. The appraisal was to determine the value of Jung's residence with and without the system. The appraisal states that the system increased the value of Jung's residence by $1,500. How much of these expenses qualifies for the medical expense deduction in the current year?

27. **LO.2** For calendar year 2011, Jean was a self-employed consultant with no employees. She had $80,000 net profit from consulting and paid $7,000 in medical insurance premiums on a policy covering 2011. How much of these premiums may Jean deduct as a deduction *for* AGI, and how much may she deduct as an itemized deduction (subject to the 7.5% floor)?

28. **LO.2** During the current year, Susan incurred and paid the following expenses for Beth (her daughter), Ed (her father), and herself:

Surgery for Beth	$4,500
Red River Academy charges for Beth:	
Tuition	5,100
Room, board, and other expenses	4,800
Psychiatric treatment	5,100
Doctor bills for Ed	2,200
Prescription drugs for Susan, Beth, and Ed	780
Insulin for Ed	540
Nonprescription drugs for Susan, Beth, and Ed	570
Charges at Heartland Nursing Home for Ed:	
Medical care	5,000
Lodging	2,700
Meals	2,650

    Beth qualifies as Susan's dependent, and Ed would also qualify except that he receives $7,400 of taxable retirement benefits from his former employer. Beth's psychiatrist recommended Red River Academy because of its small classes and specialized psychiatric treatment program that is needed to treat Beth's illness. Ed, who is a paraplegic and diabetic, entered Heartland in October. Heartland offers the type of care that he requires.

Upon the recommendation of a physician, Susan has an air filtration system installed in her personal residence. She suffers from severe allergies. In connection with this equipment, Susan incurs and pays the following amounts during the year:

Filtration system and cost of installation	$6,500
Increase in utility bills due to the system	700
Cost of certified appraisal	360

The system has an estimated useful life of 10 years. The appraisal was to determine the value of Susan's residence with and without the system. The appraisal states that the system increased the value of Susan's residence by $2,200. Ignoring the 7.5% floor, what is the total of Susan's expenses that qualifies for the medical expense deduction?

ISSUE ID

29. **LO.2** In May, Rebecca's daughter, Susan, sustained a serious injury that made it impossible for her to continue living alone. Susan, who is a novelist, moved back into Rebecca's home after the accident. Susan has begun writing a new novel based on her recent experiences. To accommodate Susan, Rebecca incurred significant remodeling expenses (widening hallways, building a separate bedroom and bathroom, making kitchen appliances accessible to Susan). In addition, Rebecca had an indoor swimming pool constructed so Susan could do rehabilitation exercises prescribed by her physician.

In September, Susan underwent major reconstructive surgery in Denver. The surgery was performed by Dr. Rama Patel, who specializes in treating injuries of the type sustained by Susan. Rebecca drove Susan from Champaign, Illinois, to Denver, a total of 1,100 miles, in Susan's specially equipped van. They left Champaign on Tuesday morning and arrived in Denver on Thursday afternoon. Rebecca incurred expenses for gasoline, highway tolls, meals, and lodging while traveling to Denver. Rebecca stayed in a motel near the clinic for eight days while Susan was hospitalized. Identify the relevant tax issues based on this information and prepare a list of questions that you would need to ask Rebecca and Susan in order to advise them as to the resolution of any issues you have identified.

30. **LO.2** During 2011, Felicia, who is self-employed, paid $500 per month for an HSA plan that provides medical insurance coverage with a $2,900 deductible. The plan covers Felicia, her husband, and three children. Of the $500 monthly payment, $200 was for the high-deductible policy and $300 was deposited into an HSA. How much of the amount paid for the high-deductible policy can Felicia deduct as a deduction *for* AGI?

COMMUNICATIONS

31. **LO.3** In 2004, Angela purchased a personal residence from Victor. She paid $300,000 for the residence. Victor paid real estate taxes of $9,125 for the real estate property tax year, of which $5,500 was allocable to the portion of the year that Angela owned the residence. Angela sold the residence to Earl for $350,000 on December 8, 2011. Earl paid real estate taxes of $10,220 for the real estate property tax year, of which $9,576 was allocable to the portion of the year that Angela owned the residence. Angela has provided you with the above information and asked that you determine her basis in the residence at the date of sale, the amount realized for the residence, her realized gain on the sale, and her property tax deduction for 2011. Write a letter to Angela Henson, who lives at 17250 Calistoga Drive, El Dorado, KS 67042, to communicate your answers.

32. **LO.4** Dylan is a self-employed, calendar year taxpayer. He reports on the cash basis. Dylan made the following estimated state income tax payments:

Date	Amount
January 18, 2011	$1,800 (4th payment for 2010)
April 15, 2011	2,250 (1st payment for 2011)
June 15, 2011	2,250 (2nd payment for 2011)
September 15, 2011	2,250 (3rd payment for 2011)
January 17, 2012	2,250 (4th payment for 2011)

Dylan had a tax overpayment of $1,200 on his 2010 state income tax return and, rather than requesting a refund, had the overpayment applied to his 2011 state income taxes. What is the amount of Dylan's state income tax itemized deduction for his 2011 Federal income tax return?

33. **LO.5** In 2002, Roland, who is single, purchased a personal residence for $340,000 and took out a mortgage of $200,000 on the property. In May of the current year, when the residence had a fair market value of $440,000 and Roland owed $140,000 on the mortgage, he took out a home equity loan for $220,000. He used the funds to purchase a recreational vehicle, which he uses 100% for personal use. What is the maximum amount on which Roland can deduct home equity interest?

34. **LO.5** Ron and Tom are equal owners in Robin Corporation. On July 1, 2011, each lends the corporation $30,000 at an annual interest rate of 10%. Ron and Tom are brothers. Both shareholders are on the cash method of accounting, and Robin Corporation is on the accrual method. All parties use the calendar year for tax purposes. On June 30, 2012, Robin repays the loans of $60,000 together with the specified interest of $6,000.
    a. How much of the interest can Robin Corporation deduct in 2011? In 2012?
    b. When is the interest included in Ron and Tom's gross income?

35. **LO.6** Nadia donates $4,000 to Eastern University's athletic department. The payment guarantees that Nadia will have preferred seating near the 50-yard line.
    a. Assume Nadia subsequently buys four $100 game tickets. How much can she deduct as a charitable contribution to the university's athletic department?
    b. Assume that Nadia's $4,000 donation includes four $100 tickets. How much can she deduct as a charitable contribution to the university's athletic department?

36. **LO.6** Rachel had AGI of $100,000 in 2011. She donated Bronze Corporation stock with a basis of $9,000 to a qualified charitable organization on July 5, 2011.
    a. What is the amount of Rachel's deduction, assuming that she purchased the stock on December 3, 2010, and the stock had a fair market value of $16,000 when she made the donation?
    b. Assume the same facts as in (a), except that Rachel purchased the stock on July 1, 2008.
    c. Assume the same facts as in (a), except that the stock had a fair market value of $5,000 (rather than $16,000) when Rachel donated it to the charity.

37. **LO.6, 8** Pedro contributes a painting to an art museum in October of this year. He has owned the painting for 12 years, and it is worth $130,000 at the time of the donation. Pedro's adjusted basis for the painting is $90,000, and his AGI for the year is $250,000. Pedro has asked you whether he should make the reduced deduction election for this contribution. Write a letter to Pedro Valdez at 1289 Greenway Avenue, Foster City, CA 94404 and advise him on this matter.

DECISION MAKING

COMMUNICATIONS

38. **LO.6** During the year, Ricardo made the following contributions to a qualified public charity:

Cash	$220,000
Stock in Seagull, Inc. (a publicly traded corporation)	280,000

Ricardo acquired the stock in Seagull, Inc., as an investment five years ago at a cost of $120,000. Ricardo's AGI is $840,000.
    a. What is Ricardo's charitable contribution deduction?
    b. How are excess amounts, if any, treated?

39. **LO.8** Ramon had AGI of $180,000 in 2011. He contributed stock in Charlton, Inc. (a publicly traded corporation), to the American Heart Association, a qualified charitable organization. The stock was worth $105,000 on the date it was contributed. Ramon had acquired it as an investment two years ago at a cost of $84,000.
    a. Assuming that Ramon carries over any disallowed contribution from 2011 to future years, what is the total amount that he can deduct as a charitable contribution?
    b. What is the maximum amount that Ramon can deduct as a charitable contribution in 2011?
    c. What factors should Ramon consider in deciding how to treat the contribution for Federal income tax purposes?
    d. Assume Ramon dies in December 2011. What advice would you give the executor of his estate with regard to possible elections that can be made relative to the contribution?

DECISION MAKING

40. **L0.6** On December 30, 2011, Roberta purchased four tickets to a charity ball sponsored by the city of San Diego for the benefit of underprivileged children. Each ticket cost $200 and had a fair market value of $35. On the same day as the purchase, Roberta gave the tickets to the minister of her church for personal use by his family. At the time of the gift of the tickets, Roberta pledged $4,000 to the building fund of her church. The pledge was satisfied by a check dated December 31, 2011, but not mailed until January 3, 2012.
    a. Presuming Roberta is a cash basis and calendar year taxpayer, how much can she deduct as a charitable contribution for 2011?
    b. Would the amount of the deduction be any different if Roberta is an accrual basis taxpayer? Explain.

DECISION MAKING

COMMUNICATIONS

41. **L0.6, 8** In December each year, Eleanor Young contributes 10% of her gross income to the United Way (a 50% organization). Eleanor, who is in the 28% marginal tax bracket, is considering the following alternatives for satisfying the contribution.

	Fair Market Value
(1) Cash donation	$23,000
(2) Unimproved land held for six years ($3,000 basis)	23,000
(3) Blue Corporation stock held for eight months ($3,000 basis)	23,000
(4) Gold Corporation stock held for two years ($28,000 basis)	23,000

Eleanor has asked you to help her decide which of the potential contributions listed above will be most advantageous taxwise. Evaluate the four alternatives and write a letter to Eleanor to communicate your advice to her. Her address is 2622 Bayshore Drive, Berkeley, CA 94709.

DECISION MAKING

COMMUNICATIONS

42. **L0.2, 3, 4, 5, 7, 8** Manuel and Rosa Garcia, both age 47, are married and have no dependents. They have asked you to advise them whether they should file jointly or separately in 2011. They present you with the following information:

	Manuel	Rosa	Joint
Salary	$40,000		
Business net income		$100,000	
Interest income	1,500	2,300	$2,200
Deductions *for* AGI	3,000	14,000	
Medical expenses	10,000	600	
State income tax	800	2,000	
Real estate tax			3,400
Mortgage interest			5,200
Unreimbursed employee expenses	1,100		

If they file separately, Manuel and Rosa will split the real estate tax and mortgage interest deductions equally. Write Manuel and Rosa a letter in which you make and explain a recommendation on filing status for 2011. Manuel and Rosa reside at 2003 Highland Drive, Durham, NC 27707.

43. **L0.2, 3, 4, 5, 6, 7** Kelsey, who is a head of household with one dependent, had AGI of $315,000 for 2011. She incurred the following expenses and losses during the year:

Medical expenses before the 7.5%-of-AGI limitation	$25,000
State and local income taxes	4,300
State sales tax	1,205
Real estate taxes	3,705
Home mortgage interest	4,400
Credit card interest	820
Charitable contribution	3,800
Casualty loss before 10% limitation (after $100 floor)	38,000
Unreimbursed employee expenses subject to the 2%-of-AGI limitation	7,100

Calculate Kelsey's allowable itemized deductions for the year.

44. **LO.2, 3, 4, 5, 6, 7** For calendar year 2011, Stuart and Pamela Gibson file a joint return reflecting AGI of $264,000. Their itemized deductions are as follows:

Medical expenses	$25,300
Casualty loss after $100 floor (not covered by insurance)	28,600
Home mortgage interest	11,000
Credit card interest	800
Property taxes on home	14,300
Charitable contributions	18,700
State income tax	16,500
Tax return preparation fees	1,200

Calculate the amount of itemized deductions the Gibsons may claim for the year.

CUMULATIVE PROBLEMS

45. Alice J. and Bruce M. Byrd are married taxpayers who file a joint return. Their Social Security numbers are 123–45–6789 and 111–11–1111, respectively. Alice's birthday is September 21, 1963, and Bruce's is June 27, 1962. They live at 473 Revere Avenue, Ames, MA 01850. Alice is the office manager for Ames Dental Clinic, 433 Broad Street, Ames, MA 01850 (employer identification number 98–7654321). Bruce is the manager of a Super Burgers fast-food outlet owned and operated by Plymouth Corporation, 1247 Central Avenue, Hauppauge, NY 11788 (employer identification number 11–1111111).

The following information is shown on their Wage and Tax Statements (Form W–2) for 2010.

Line	Description	Alice	Bruce
1	Wages, tips, other compensation	$52,600	$61,500
2	Federal income tax withheld	4,180	5,990
3	Social Security wages	52,600	61,500
4	Social Security tax withheld	3,261	3,813
5	Medicare wages and tips	52,600	61,500
6	Medicare tax withheld	763	892
15	State	Massachusetts	Massachusetts
16	State wages, tips, etc.	52,600	61,500
17	State income tax withheld	2,280	2,990

The Byrds provide over half of the support of their two children, Cynthia (born January 25, 1986, Social Security number 123–45–6788) and John (born February 7, 1990, Social Security number 123–45–6786). Both children are full-time students and live with the Byrds except when they are away at college. Cynthia earned $3,700 from a summer internship in 2010, and John earned $3,400 from a part-time job.

During 2010, the Byrds furnished 60% of the total support of Bruce's widower father, Sam Byrd (born March 6, 1934, Social Security number 123–45–6787). Sam lived alone and covered the rest of his support with his Social Security benefits. Sam died in November, and Bruce, the beneficiary of a policy on Sam's life, received life insurance proceeds of $600,000 on December 28.

The Byrds had the following expenses relating to their personal residence during 2010:

Property taxes	$4,720
Qualified interest on home mortgage	9,130
Repairs to roof	4,780
Utilities	3,810
Fire and theft insurance	2,290

The following facts relate to medical expenses for 2010:

Medical insurance premiums	$4,380
Doctor bill for Sam incurred in 2009 and not paid until 2010	7,760
Operation for Sam	7,310

Prescription medicines for Sam	$ 860
Hospital expenses for Sam	2,850
Reimbursement from insurance company, received in 2010	3,000

The medical expenses for Sam represent most of the 60% Bruce contributed toward his father's support.

Other relevant information follows:

- When they filed their 2009 state return in 2010, the Byrds paid additional state income tax of $950.
- During 2010, Alice and Bruce attended a dinner dance sponsored by the Ames Police Disability Association (a qualified charitable organization). The Byrds paid $400 for the tickets. The cost of comparable entertainment would normally be $160.
- The Byrds contributed $4,800 to Ames Presbyterian Church and gave used clothing (cost of $1,100 and fair market value of $450) to the Salvation Army. All donations are supported by receipts and are in very good condition.
- In 2010, the Byrds received interest income of $2,695, which was reported on a Form 1099–INT from Second National Bank.
- Alice's employer requires that all employees wear uniforms to work. During 2010, Alice spent $482 on new uniforms and $211 on laundry charges.
- Bruce paid $320 for an annual subscription to the *Journal of Franchise Management.*
- Neither Alice's nor Bruce's employer reimburses for employee expenses.
- The Byrds do not keep the receipts for the sales taxes they paid and had no major purchases subject to sales tax.
- Alice and Bruce paid no estimated Federal income tax. Neither Alice nor Bruce wishes to designate $3 to the Presidential Election Campaign Fund.

Part 1—Tax Computation

Compute net tax payable or refund due for Alice and Bruce Byrd for 2010. If they have overpaid, they want the amount to be refunded to them. If you use tax forms for your computations, you will need Forms 1040 and 2106 and Schedules A, B, and M. Suggested software: H&R BLOCK At Home.

Part 2—Tax Planning

Alice and Bruce are planning some significant changes for 2011. They have provided you with the following information and asked you to project their taxable income and tax liability for 2011.

The Byrds will invest the $600,000 of life insurance proceeds in short-term certificates of deposit (CDs) and use the interest for living expenses during 2011. They expect to earn total interest of $21,000 on the CDs.

Bruce has been promoted to regional manager, and his salary for 2011 will be $85,000. He estimates that state income tax withheld will increase by $4,000 and the Social Security tax withheld will be $3,570.

Alice, who has been diagnosed with a serious illness, will take a leave of absence from work during 2011. The estimated cost for her medical treatment is $14,500, of which $5,500 will be reimbursed by their insurance company in 2011.

John will graduate from college in December 2010 and will take a job in New York City in January 2011. His starting salary will be $37,500.

Assume all the information reported in 2010 will be the same in 2011 unless other information has been presented above.

TAX COMPUTATION PROBLEM

46. Paul and Donna Decker are married taxpayers, ages 44 and 42, who file a joint return for 2011. The Deckers live at 1121 College Avenue, Carmel, IN 46032. Paul is an assistant manager at Carmel Motor Inn, and Donna is a teacher at Carmel Elementary School. They present you with W–2 forms that reflect the following information:

	Paul	Donna
Salary	$60,000	$61,000
Federal tax withheld	7,000	7,200
State income tax withheld	950	1,000
FICA (Social Security and Medicare) withheld	3,390	3,447
Social Security numbers	111–11–1111	123–45–6789

Donna is the custodial parent of two children from a previous marriage who reside with the Deckers through the school year. The children, Larry and Jane Parker, reside with their father, Bob, during the summer. Relevant information for the children follows:

	Larry	Jane
Age	17	18
Social Security numbers	123–45–6788	123–45–6787
Months spent with Deckers	9	9

Under the divorce decree, Bob pays child support of $200 per month per child during the nine months the children live with the Deckers. Bob says he spends $225 per month per child during the three summer months they reside with him. Donna and Paul can document that they provide $3,000 support per child per year. The divorce decree is silent as to which parent can claim the exemptions for the children.

In August, Paul and Donna added a suite to their home to provide more comfortable accommodations for Hannah Snyder (123–45–6786), Donna's mother, who had moved in with them in February 2010 after the death of Donna's father. Not wanting to borrow money for this addition, Paul sold 300 shares of Acme Corporation stock for $50 per share on May 3, 2011, and used the proceeds of $15,000 to cover construction costs. The Deckers had purchased the stock on April 29, 2006, for $30 per share. They received dividends of $800 on the jointly owned stock a month before the sale.

Hannah, who is 66 years old, received $7,500 in Social Security benefits during the year, of which she gave the Deckers $2,500 to use toward household expenses and deposited the remainder in her personal savings account. The Deckers determine that they have spent $3,000 of their own money for food, clothing, medical expenses, and other items for Hannah. They do not know what the rental value of Hannah's suite would be, but they estimate it would be at least $300 per month.

Interest paid during the year included the following:

Home mortgage interest (paid to Carmel Federal Savings & Loan)	$8,000
Interest on an automobile loan (paid to Carmel National Bank)	1,490
Interest on Citibank Visa card	870

In July, Paul hit a submerged rock while boating. Fortunately, he was thrown from the boat, landed in deep water, and was uninjured. However, the boat, which was uninsured, was destroyed. Paul had paid $25,000 for the boat in June 2010, and its value was appraised at $18,000 on the date of the accident.

The Deckers paid doctor and hospital bills of $9,000 and were reimbursed $2,100 by their insurance company. They spent $700 for prescription drugs and medicines and $2,810 for premiums on their health insurance policy. They have filed additional claims of $1,200 with their insurance company and have been told they will receive payment for that amount in January 2012. Included in the amounts paid for doctor and hospital bills were payments of $380 for Hannah and $850 for the children.

Additional information of potential tax consequence follows:

Real estate taxes paid	$3,700
Sales taxes paid (per table)	1,379
Contributions to church	4,500
Appraised value of books donated to public library	750
Paul's unreimbursed employee expenses to attend hotel management convention:	
Airfare	840
Hotel	270
Meals	125
Registration fee	340
Refund of state income tax for 2010 (the Deckers itemized on their 2010 Federal tax return)	1,600

Compute net tax payable or refund due for the Deckers for 2011. Ignore the child tax credit in your computations. If they have overpaid, the amount is to be credited toward their taxes for 2012.

RESEARCH PROBLEMS

THOMSON REUTERS
Checkpoint® Student Edition

Note: Solutions to Research Problems can be prepared by using the **Checkpoint**® **Student Edition** online research product, which is available to accompany this text. It is also possible to prepare solutions to the Research Problems by using tax research materials found in a standard tax library.

COMMUNICATIONS

Research Problem 1. After several years of a difficult marriage, Donald and Marla agreed to a divorce. As part of the property settlement, Marla transferred to Donald corporate stock, a commercial building, and a personal residence. Donald transferred other property to Marla, but the fair market value of the property was $600,000 less than the fair market value of the property Marla had transferred to him. To make the settlement equal, Donald agreed to pay Marla $600,000, payable over 10 years at 8% interest. For several years, Donald deducted the interest on his Federal income tax return as investment interest. Upon audit, the IRS disallowed the interest deduction, classifying it as nondeductible personal interest. Donald believes the interest is deductible and has asked you to find support for the deduction. Write a letter indicating your findings to Donald Jansen, 104 South Fourth Street, Dalton, GA 30720.

Partial list of research aids:
U.S. v. Gilmore, 63–1 USTC ¶9285, 11 AFTR 2d 758, 83 S.Ct. 623 (USSC, 1963).
John L. Seymour, 109 T.C. 279 (1997).

Research Problem 2. Jane suffers from a degenerative spinal disorder. Her physician said that swimming could help prevent the onset of permanent paralysis and recommended the installation of a swimming pool at her residence for her use. Jane's residence had a market value of approximately $500,000 before the swimming pool was installed. The swimming pool was built, and an appraiser estimated that the value of Jane's home increased by $98,000 because of the addition.

    The pool cost $194,000, and Jane claimed a medical expense deduction of $96,000 ($194,000 − $98,000) on her tax return. Upon audit of the return, the IRS determined that an adequate pool should have cost $70,000 and would increase the value of her home by only $31,000. Thus, the IRS claims that Jane is entitled to a deduction of only $39,000 ($70,000 − $31,000).

a. Is there any ceiling limitation on the amount deductible as a medical expense?
b. Can capital expenditures be deducted as medical expenses?
c. What is the significance of a "minimum adequate facility"? Should aesthetic or architectural qualities be considered in this determination?

COMMUNICATIONS

Research Problem 3. In January, Ron, a firefighter, was injured in the line of duty as a result of interference by a homeowner. He incurred medical expenses of $6,500 related to his injuries. Ron sued the homeowner and was awarded damages of $26,500 in December. The court indicated that $6,500 of the award was for payment of Ron's medical expenses and $20,000 was for punitive damages. Ron has prepared his income tax return for the year and has asked you to review it. You notice that Ron has not reported any part of the award as income and has included the medical expenses in computing his itemized deductions. Write a brief memorandum to the tax files that summarizes the advice you should give Ron.

Research Problem 4. Tom and Mary Smith, whose son was found murdered in a parking garage, offered a $100,000 reward for the city police to use to obtain information leading to the arrest and conviction of the murderer. As a result of the reward, a person who had overheard the murderer telling a friend about the crime reported the conversation to the police. The murderer was arrested and convicted, and the Smiths contributed the money to the police department, which gave the reward to the informant. Can the Smiths treat the payment as an itemized deduction?

COMMUNICATIONS

Research Problem 5. Marcia, a shareholder in a corporation with stores in five states, donated stock with a basis of $10,000 to a qualified charitable organization in 2010. Although the stock of the corporation was not traded on a public stock exchange, many shares had been sold over the past several years. Based on the average selling price for the stock in 2010, Marcia deducted $95,000 on her 2010 tax return. Marcia received a notice from the IRS that the $95,000 deduction had been reduced to $10,000 because she had not obtained a qualified appraisal or attached a summary of her appraisal to her tax return. Marcia has asked you to advise her on this matter. Write a letter containing your conclusions to Ms. Marcia Meyer, 1311 Santos Court, San Bruno, CA 94066.

Partial list of research aids:
Reg. § 1.170A–13(c)(2).

Use the tax resources of the Internet to address the following questions. Do not restrict your search to the Web, but include a review of newsgroups and general reference materials, practitioner sites and resources, primary sources of the tax law, chat rooms and discussion groups, and other opportunities.

INTERNET
activity

Research Problem 6. Find the IRS website and print a copy of Schedule A. If the 2011 Schedule A is available, compare it with the 2010 Schedule A in the text (p. 10–30) and discuss any changes.

Research Problem 7. Search the Internet for stories about major charitable contributions by individuals, including Bill Gates, Warren Buffett, Steve Jobs, and at least one other individual. Briefly discuss any tax issues that are related to the contributions.

Investor Losses

LEARNING OBJECTIVES

After completing Chapter 11, you should be able to:

LO.1

Discuss tax shelters and the reasons for at-risk and passive loss limitations.

LO.2

Explain the at-risk limitation.

LO.3

Describe how the passive loss rules limit deductions for losses, and identify the taxpayers subject to these restrictions.

LO.4

Discuss the definition of passive activities and the rules for identifying an activity.

LO.5

Analyze and apply the tests for material participation.

LO.6

Understand the nature of rental activities under the passive loss rules.

LO.7

Recognize the relationship between the at-risk and passive activity limitations.

LO.8

Discuss the special treatment available to real estate activities.

LO.9

Determine the proper tax treatment upon the disposition of a passive activity.

LO.10

Identify restrictions placed on the deductibility of other investor losses and deductions, including those that apply to investment interest.

LO.11

Suggest tax planning strategies to minimize the effect of the passive loss limitations.

OUTLINE

Income (broadly conceived)	$xx,xxx
Less: Exclusions	(x,xxx)
Gross Income	$xx,xxx
Less: Deductions for adjusted gross income	**(x,xxx)**

> **FORM 1040 (p. 1)**
>
> **12** Business income or (loss). Attach Schedule C or C-EZ . . . .
> **13** Capital gain or (loss). Attach Schedule D if required. If not required, check here ▶ ☐
> **14** Other gains or (losses). Attach Form 4797 . . . .
> **17** Rental real estate, royalties, partnerships, S corporations, trusts, etc. Attach Schedule E

Adjusted gross income.	$xx,xxx
Less: The greater of total **itemized deductions** *or* the standard deduction	**(x,xxx)**

> **FORM 1040 (p. 2)**
>
> **40** **Itemized deductions** (from Schedule A) **or** your **standard deduction** (see instructions) . .

Personal and dependency exemptions	(x,xxx)
Taxable income	$xx,xxx
Tax on taxable income (see tax Tables or Tax Rate Schedules)	$ x,xxx
Less: Tax credits (including income taxes withheld and prepaid)	(xxx)
Tax due (or refund).	$ xxx

THE BIG PICTURE   Tax Solutions for the Real World

INVESTOR LOSS LIMITATIONS AFFECT THE VIABILITY OF CERTAIN INVESTMENT OPPORTUNITIES

Trudy and Jim Reswick are considering ways to enhance their financial security. In fact, they are willing to borrow a substantial sum so that they can make an appropriate investment.

Currently, Trudy and Jim's sole source of income is their salaries from full-time jobs, totaling $100,000. Their most significant asset is their personal residence (fair market value of $500,000 with a mortgage of $350,000). Their broker suggests that the Reswicks borrow $100,000 at 8 percent and use the proceeds to make *one* of the following investments:

- A high-growth, low-yield portfolio of marketable securities. The portfolio's value is expected to grow 10 percent each year.
- An interest in a limited partnership that owns and operates orange groves in Florida. The limited partnership interest is expected to generate tax losses of $25,000 in each of the next five years, after which profits are expected. The broker predicts that after taking into account the tax benefit from the losses, the Reswicks would average an annual 10 percent return over a 10-year period.
- An interest in a local limited partnership that owns and rents apartments to college students. This limited partnership interest also would generate losses of $25,000 per year for five years, after which profits would follow. These expected profits and losses would produce an average annual total return of 10 percent over a 10-year period.

Trudy and Jim want to choose the alternative that produces the best after-tax return over a 10-year planning horizon. They are aware, however, that tax restrictions may limit the advantages of some of these investment options. In this connection, evaluate each option. **Read the chapter and formulate your response.**

s discussed in Chapter 6, a tax deduction for an expense or a loss is not allowed unless specifically provided for by Congress. For example, losses can be recognized and deducted in the case of certain unprofitable investments only because the Code so provides. Such losses can arise from the operation of an activity or upon its ultimate disposition. For most individual taxpayers, deductible investor losses come within the scope of § 165(c)(2) relating to transactions entered into for profit.[1] In many situations, the tax law limits the *amount* or *timing* of a deduction or loss, or even changes its *nature* (i.e., ordinary rather than capital). Thus, for various reasons, Congress has imposed restrictions on the deductibility of investor losses. This, in turn, may affect the viability of the investment itself.

11.1 THE TAX SHELTER PROBLEM

Before Congress enacted legislation to reduce their effectiveness, **tax shelters** provided a popular way to avoid or defer taxes, as they could generate deductions and other benefits to offset income from other sources. Because of the tax avoidance potential of many tax shelters, they were attractive to wealthy taxpayers in high income tax brackets. Many tax shelters merely provided an opportunity for "investors" to buy deductions and credits in ventures that were not expected to generate a profit, even in the long run.

Although it may seem odd that a taxpayer would intentionally invest in an activity that was designed to produce losses, there is a logical explanation. The typical tax shelter operated as a partnership and relied heavily on nonrecourse financing.[2] Accelerated depreciation and interest expense deductions generated large losses in the early years of the activity. At the very least, the tax shelter deductions deferred the recognition of any net income from the venture until the activity was sold. In the best of situations, the investor could realize additional tax savings by offsetting other income (e.g., salary, interest, and dividends) with deductions flowing from the tax shelter. Ultimately, the sale of the investment would result in capital gain. The following examples illustrate what was possible *before* Congress enacted legislation to curb tax shelter abuses.

> **LO.1**
>
> Discuss tax shelters and the reasons for at-risk and passive loss limitations.

EXAMPLE 1

Bob, who earned a salary of $400,000 as a business executive and dividend income of $15,000, invested $20,000 for a 10% interest in a cattle-breeding tax shelter. Through the use of $800,000 of nonrecourse financing and available cash of $200,000, the partnership acquired a herd of an exotic breed of cattle costing $1 million. Depreciation, interest, and other deductions related to the activity resulted in a loss of $400,000, of which Bob's share was $40,000. Bob was allowed to deduct the $40,000 loss, even though he had invested and stood to lose only $20,000 if the investment became worthless. The net effect of the $40,000 deduction from the partnership was that a portion of Bob's salary and dividend income was "sheltered," and as a result, he was required to calculate his tax liability on only $375,000 of income [$415,000 (salary and dividends) − $40,000 (deduction)] rather than $415,000. If this deduction were available under current law and if Bob was in a combined Federal and state income tax bracket of 40%, this deduction would generate a tax savings of $16,000 ($40,000 × 40%) in the first year alone! ∎

---

[1] If the losses are incurred in connection with a trade or business, § 165(c)(1) applies.

[2] Nonrecourse debt is an obligation for which the borrower is not personally liable. An example of nonrecourse debt is a liability on real estate acquired by a partnership without the partnership or any of the partners assuming any liability for the mortgage. The acquired property generally is pledged as collateral for the loan.

A review of Example 1 shows that the taxpayer took a *two-for-one* write-off ($40,000 deduction, $20,000 investment). In the heyday of these types of tax shelters, promoters often promised *multiple* write-offs for the investor.

The first major provision aimed at tax shelters was the **at-risk limitation**. Its objective is to limit a taxpayer's deductions to the amount "at risk," which is the amount the taxpayer stands to lose if the investment becomes worthless.

EXAMPLE 2

Returning to the facts of Example 1, under the current at-risk rules Bob would be allowed to deduct $20,000 (i.e., the amount that he could lose if the business failed). This deduction would reduce his other income, and as a result, Bob would have to report only $395,000 of income ($415,000 − $20,000). The remaining nondeductible $20,000 loss and any future losses flowing from the partnership would be suspended under the at-risk rules and would be deductible in the future only as his at-risk amount increased. ■

The second major attack on tax shelters came with the passage of the passive activity loss rules. These rules are intended to halt an investor's ability to benefit from the mismatching of an entity's expenses and income that often occurs in the early years of the business. Congress observed that despite the at-risk limitations, investors could still deduct losses flowing from an entity and thereby defer their tax liability on other income. In effect, the passive activity rules have, to a great degree, limited the tax benefits arising from such investments. Now, ventures where investors are not involved in the day-to-day operations of the business are generally referred to as passive investments, or *passive activities*, rather than tax shelters.

The **passive loss** rules require the taxpayer to segregate all income and losses into three categories: active, passive, and portfolio. In general, the passive loss limits disallow the deduction of passive losses against active or portfolio income, even when the taxpayer is at risk to the extent of the loss. In general, passive losses can only offset passive income.

EXAMPLE 3

Returning to the facts of Example 1, the passive activity loss rules further restrict Bob's ability to claim the $20,000 tax deduction shown in Example 2. Because Bob is a passive investor and does not materially participate in any meaningful way in the activities of the cattle-breeding operation, the $20,000 loss allowed under the at-risk rules is disallowed under the passive loss rules. The passive loss is disallowed because Bob does not generate any passive income that could absorb his passive loss. Further, his salary (active income) and dividends (portfolio income) cannot be used to absorb any of the passive loss. Consequently, Bob's current-year taxable income must reflect his nonpassive income of $415,000, and he receives no current benefit from his share of the partnership loss. However, all is not lost because Bob's share of the entity's loss is *suspended*; it is carried forward and can be deducted in the future when he has passive income or sells his interest in the activity. ■

The nature of the at-risk limits and the passive activity loss rules and their impact on investors are discussed in the pages that follow. An interesting consequence of these rules is that now investors evaluating potential investments must consider mainly the economics of the venture instead of the tax benefits or tax avoidance possibilities that an investment may generate.

11.2 AT-RISK LIMITS

LO.2

Explain the at-risk limitation.

The at-risk provisions limit the deductibility of losses from business and income-producing activities. These provisions, which apply to individuals and closely held corporations, are designed to prevent taxpayers from deducting losses in excess of their actual economic investment in an activity. In the case of an S corporation or a

CONCEPT SUMMARY 11.1

Calculation of At-Risk Amount

Increases to a taxpayer's at-risk amount:

- Cash and the adjusted basis of property contributed to the activity.
- Amounts borrowed for use in the activity for which the taxpayer is personally liable or has pledged as security property not used in the activity.
- Taxpayer's share of amounts borrowed for use in the activity that are qualified nonrecourse financing.
- Taxpayer's share of the activity's income.

Decreases to a taxpayer's at-risk amount:

- Withdrawals from the activity.
- Taxpayer's share of the activity's deductible loss.
- Taxpayer's share of any reductions of debt for which recourse against the taxpayer exists or reductions of qualified nonrecourse debt.

partnership, the at-risk limits apply at the owner level. Under the at-risk rules, a taxpayer's deductible loss from an activity for any taxable year is limited to the amount the taxpayer has at risk at the end of the taxable year (the amount the taxpayer could actually lose in the activity).

While the amount at risk generally vacillates over time, the initial amount considered at risk consists of the following:[3]

- The amount of cash and the adjusted basis of property contributed to the activity by the taxpayer.
- Amounts borrowed for use in the activity for which the taxpayer is personally liable or has pledged as security property not used in the activity.

This amount generally is increased each year by the taxpayer's share of income and is decreased by the taxpayer's share of losses and withdrawals from the activity. In addition, because general partners are jointly and severally liable for recourse debts of the partnership, their at-risk amounts are increased when the partnership increases its debt and are decreased when the partnership reduces its debt. However, a taxpayer generally is not considered at risk with respect to borrowed amounts if either of the following is true:

- The taxpayer is not personally liable for repayment of the debt (e.g., nonrecourse debt).
- The lender has an interest (other than as a creditor) in the activity.

An important exception provides that in the case of an activity involving the holding of real property, a taxpayer is considered at risk for his or her share of any *qualified nonrecourse financing* that is secured by real property used in the activity.[4]

Subject to the passive activity rules discussed later in the chapter, a taxpayer may deduct a loss as long as the at-risk amount is positive. However, once the at-risk amount is exhausted, any remaining loss cannot be deducted until a later year. Any losses disallowed for any given taxable year by the at-risk rules may be deducted in the first succeeding year in which the rules do not prevent the deduction—that is, when there is, and to the extent of, a positive at-risk amount.

EXAMPLE 4

In 2011, Sue invests $40,000 in an oil partnership that, by the use of nonrecourse loans, spends $60,000 on deductible intangible drilling costs applicable to her interest.

---

[3]§ 465(b)(1).   [4]Section 465(b)(6) defines qualified nonrecourse financing.

Assume Sue's interest in the partnership is subject to the at-risk limits but is not subject to the passive loss limits. Since Sue has only $40,000 of capital at risk, she cannot deduct more than $40,000 against her other income and must reduce her at-risk amount to zero ($40,000 at-risk amount − $40,000 loss deducted). The nondeductible loss of $20,000 ($60,000 loss generated − $40,000 loss allowed) can be carried over to 2012. ■

EXAMPLE 5

In 2012, Sue has taxable income of $15,000 from the oil partnership and invests an additional $10,000 in the venture. Her at-risk amount is now $25,000 ($0 beginning balance + $15,000 taxable income + $10,000 additional investment). This enables Sue to deduct the carryover loss and requires her to reduce her at-risk amount to $5,000 ($25,000 at-risk amount − $20,000 carryover loss allowed). ■

An additional complicating factor is that previously allowed losses must be recaptured to the extent the at-risk amount is reduced below zero.[5] That is, previous losses that were allowed must be offset by the recognition of enough income to bring the at-risk amount up to zero. This rule applies in such situations as when the amount at risk is reduced below zero by distributions to the taxpayer or when the status of indebtedness changes from recourse to nonrecourse.

11.3 PASSIVE LOSS LIMITS

CLASSIFICATION AND IMPACT OF PASSIVE INCOME AND LOSSES

LO.3
Describe how the passive loss rules limit deductions for losses, and identify the taxpayers subject to these restrictions.

The passive loss rules operate by requiring taxpayers to classify their income and losses into various categories. Then the rules limit the extent to which losses in the passive category can be used to offset income in the other categories.

Classification

The passive loss rules require income and losses to be classified into one of three categories: active, passive, or portfolio. **Active income** includes the following:

- Wages, salary, commissions, bonuses, and other payments for services rendered by the taxpayer.
- Profit from a trade or business in which the taxpayer is a material participant.
- Gain on the sale or other disposition of assets used in an active trade or business.
- Income from intangible property if the taxpayer's personal efforts significantly contributed to the creation of the property.

    Portfolio income includes the following:

- Interest, dividends, annuities, and royalties not derived in the ordinary course of a trade or business.
- Gain or loss from the disposition of property that produces portfolio income or is held for investment purposes.

    Section 469 provides that income or loss from the following activities is treated as *passive:*

- Any trade or business or income-producing activity in which the taxpayer does not materially participate.
- Subject to certain exceptions, all rental activities, whether the taxpayer materially participates or not.

---

[5] § 465(e).

Although the Code defines rental activities as passive activities, several exceptions allow losses from certain real estate rental activities to offset nonpassive (active or portfolio) income. These exceptions are discussed under Special Passive Activity Rules for Real Estate Activities later in the chapter.

General Impact

Losses or expenses generated by passive activities can be deducted only to the extent of income from all of the taxpayer's passive activities. Any excess may not be used to offset income from active sources or portfolio income. Instead, any unused passive losses are suspended and carried forward to future years to offset passive income generated in those years. Otherwise, suspended losses may be used only when a taxpayer disposes of his or her entire interest in an activity. In that event, all current and suspended losses related to the activity may offset active and portfolio income.

EXAMPLE 6

Kim, a physician, earns $150,000 from her full-time practice. She also receives $10,000 in dividends and interest from various portfolio investments, and her share of loss from a passive investment not limited by the at-risk rules is $60,000. Because the loss is a passive loss, it is not deductible against her other income. The loss is suspended and is carried over to the future. If Kim has passive income from this investment or from other passive investments in the future, she can offset the suspended loss against that passive income. If she does not have passive income to offset this suspended loss in the future, she will be allowed to offset the loss against other types of income when she eventually disposes of the passive activity. ■

Impact of Suspended Losses

When a taxpayer disposes of his or her entire interest in a passive activity, the actual economic gain or loss from the investment, including any suspended losses, can finally be determined. As a result, under the passive loss rules, upon a fully taxable disposition, any overall loss realized from the activity by the taxpayer is recognized and can be offset against any income.

A fully taxable disposition generally involves a sale of the property to a third party at arm's length and thus, presumably, for a price equal to the property's fair market value. Gain recognized upon a transfer of an interest in a passive activity generally is treated as passive and is first offset by the suspended losses from that activity.

EXAMPLE 7

Rex sells an apartment building, a passive activity, with an adjusted basis of $100,000 for $180,000. In addition, he has suspended losses of $60,000 associated with the building. His total gain, $80,000, and his taxable gain, $20,000, are calculated as follows:

Net sales price	$ 180,000
Less: Adjusted basis	(100,000)
Total gain	$ 80,000
Less: Suspended losses	(60,000)
Taxable gain (passive)	$ 20,000

■

If current and suspended losses of the passive activity exceed the gain realized or if the sale results in a realized loss, the amount of

- any loss from the activity for the tax year (including losses suspended in the activity disposed of)

in excess of

- net income or gain for the tax year from all passive activities (without regard to the activity disposed of) is treated as a loss that is not from a passive activity. In computing the loss from the activity for the year of disposition, any gain or loss recognized is included.

EXAMPLE 8

Dean sells an apartment building, a passive activity, with an adjusted basis of $100,000 for $150,000. In addition, he has current and suspended losses of $60,000 associated with the building and has no other passive activities. His total gain of $50,000 and his deductible loss of $10,000 are calculated as follows:

Net sales price	$ 150,000
Less: Adjusted basis	(100,000)
Total gain	$ 50,000
Less: Suspended losses	(60,000)
Deductible loss (not passive)	($ 10,000)

The $10,000 deductible loss is offset against Dean's active and portfolio income. ∎

Carryovers of Suspended Losses

In the above examples, it was assumed that the taxpayer had an interest in only one passive activity, and as a result, the suspended loss was related exclusively to the activity that was disposed of. Taxpayers often own interests in more than one activity, however, and in that case, any suspended losses must be allocated among the activities in which the taxpayer has an interest. The allocation to an activity is made by multiplying the disallowed passive activity loss from all activities by the following fraction:

$$\frac{\text{Loss from activity}}{\text{Sum of losses for taxable year from all activities having losses}}$$

EXAMPLE 9

Diego has investments in three passive activities with the following income and losses for 2010:

Activity A	($ 30,000)
Activity B	(20,000)
Activity C	25,000
Net passive loss	($ 25,000)
Net passive loss allocated to:	
Activity A ($25,000 × $30,000/$50,000)	($ 15,000)
Activity B ($25,000 × $20,000/$50,000)	(10,000)
Total suspended losses	($ 25,000)

∎

Suspended losses are carried over indefinitely and are offset in the future against any passive income from the activities to which they relate.[6]

EXAMPLE 10

Assume the same facts as in Example 9 and that Activity A produces $10,000 of income in 2011. Of the suspended loss of $15,000 from 2010 for Activity A, $10,000 is offset against the income from this activity. If Diego sells Activity A in early 2012, then the remaining $5,000 suspended loss is used in determining his taxable gain or loss. ∎

Passive Credits

Credits arising from passive activities are limited in much the same way as passive losses. Passive credits can be utilized only against regular tax attributable to

---

[6] § 469(b).

passive income,[7] which is calculated by comparing the tax on all income (including passive income) with the tax on income excluding passive income.

EXAMPLE 11

Sam owes $50,000 of tax, disregarding net passive income, and $80,000 of tax, considering both net passive and other taxable income (disregarding the credits in both cases). The amount of tax attributable to the passive income is $30,000. ∎

Sam in the preceding example can claim a maximum of $30,000 of passive activity credits; the excess credits are carried over. These passive activity credits (such as the low-income housing credit and rehabilitation credit—discussed in Chapter 13) can be used only against the *regular* tax attributable to passive income. If a taxpayer has a net loss from passive activities during a given year, no credits can be used.

Carryovers of Passive Credits

Tax credits attributable to passive activities can be carried forward indefinitely much like suspended passive losses. Unlike passive losses, however, passive credits are lost forever when the activity is disposed of in a taxable transaction where loss is recognized. Credits are allowed on dispositions only when there is sufficient tax on passive income to absorb them.

EXAMPLE 12

Alicia sells a passive activity for a gain of $10,000. The activity had suspended losses of $40,000 and suspended credits of $15,000. The $10,000 gain is offset by $10,000 of the suspended losses, and the remaining $30,000 of suspended losses is deductible against Alicia's active and portfolio income. The suspended credits are lost forever because the sale of the activity did not generate any tax. ∎

EXAMPLE 13

If Alicia in Example 12 had realized a $100,000 gain on the sale of the passive activity, the suspended credits could have been used to the extent of the regular tax attributable to the net passive income.

Gain on sale	$100,000
Less: Suspended losses	(40,000)
Taxable gain	$ 60,000

If the tax attributable to the taxable gain of $60,000 is $15,000 or more, the entire $15,000 of suspended credits can be used. If the tax attributable to the gain is less than $15,000, the excess of the suspended credits over the tax attributable to the gain is lost forever. ∎

When a taxpayer has sufficient regular tax liability from passive activities to trigger the use of suspended credits, the credits lose their character as passive credits. They are reclassified as regular tax credits and made subject to the same limits as other credits (discussed in Chapter 13).

Passive Activity Changes to Active

If a formerly passive activity becomes an active one, suspended losses are allowed to the extent of income from the now active business.[8] If any of the suspended loss remains, it continues to be treated as a loss from a passive activity. The excess suspended loss can be deducted from passive income or carried over to the next tax

---

[7]§ 469(d)(2).   [8]§ 469(f).

year and deducted to the extent of income from the now active business in the succeeding year(s). The activity must continue to be the same activity.

TAXPAYERS SUBJECT TO THE PASSIVE LOSS RULES

The passive loss rules apply to individuals, estates, trusts, personal service corporations, and closely held C corporations.[9] Passive income or loss from investments in S corporations or partnerships (see Chapter 20) flows through to the owners, and the passive loss rules are applied at the owner level.

Personal Service Corporations

Application of the passive loss limitations to personal service corporations is intended to prevent taxpayers from sheltering personal service income by creating personal service corporations and acquiring passive activities at the corporate level.

EXAMPLE 14

Two tax accountants, who earn an aggregate of $200,000 a year in their individual practices, agree to work together in a newly formed personal service corporation. Shortly after its formation, the corporation invests in a passive activity that produces a $200,000 loss during the year. Because the passive loss rules apply to personal service corporations, the corporation may not deduct the $200,000 loss against the $200,000 of active income. ∎

Determination of whether a corporation is a **personal service corporation** is based on rather broad definitions. A personal service corporation is a regular (or C) corporation that meets *both* of the following conditions:

- The principal activity is the performance of personal services.
- Such services are substantially performed by employee-owners.

Generally, personal service corporations include those in the fields of health, law, engineering, architecture, accounting, actuarial science, performing arts, and consulting.[10] A corporation is treated as a personal service corporation if more than 10 percent of the stock (by value) is held by employee-owners.[11] An employee is treated as an employee-owner if he or she owns stock on *any day* during the taxable year.[12] For these purposes, shareholder status and employee status do not have to occur on the same day.

Closely Held C Corporations

Application of the passive loss rules to closely held (non-personal service) C corporations is also intended to prevent individuals from incorporating to avoid the passive loss limitations. A corporation is classified as a **closely held corporation** if at any time during the taxable year more than 50 percent of the value of its outstanding stock is owned, directly or indirectly, by or for five or fewer individuals. Closely held C corporations (other than personal service corporations) may use passive losses to offset *active* income, but not portfolio income.

EXAMPLE 15

Silver Corporation, a closely held (non-personal service) C corporation, has $500,000 of passive losses from a rental activity, $400,000 of active income, and $100,000 of portfolio income. The corporation may offset $400,000 of the $500,000 passive loss against the $400,000 of active business income, but may not offset the remainder against the $100,000 of portfolio income. Thus, $100,000 of the passive loss is suspended ($500,000 passive loss − $400,000 offset against active income). ∎

---

[9]§ 469(a).
[10]§ 448(d)(2)(A).

[11]§ 469(j)(2).
[12]§ 269A(b)(2).

TAX *in* the *NEWS*

IF YOU CAN'T TRUST YOUR TAX PREPARER, WHO CAN YOU TRUST?

Many taxpayers choose to remain ignorant of the tax law because they assume that by paying a "professional" to complete their returns, they have shifted all responsibility to someone else. But they do so at their own risk. Failure to have at least a general understanding of the tax rules that apply to one's return can be a big mistake and can lead to various tax penalties.

One such taxpayer invested in several partnerships that engaged in horse activities in California. Being fully employed in New York, he did not participate in the partnerships' activities and had no knowledge of their business operations. When he received the tax information from the partnerships about his investments, he simply turned over the statements to his tax preparer who included the infor-

mation on the return filed. Essentially, the tax return reflected the taxpayer's losses from the horse activities, even though they are disallowed under the passive loss rules.

When the IRS discovered the error, the taxpayer pleaded ignorance and blamed the tax preparer. He claimed that he had been "duped by a charlatan" and pleaded for mercy. The Tax Court showed no compassion and held that the taxpayer owed additional taxes, interest, and penalties (*Ralph P. Cunningham,* 98 TCM 143, T.C.Memo. 2009–194). Perhaps the result would have been different if the taxpayer had a better understanding of the tax law in general and the passive activity rules in particular. Reliance on a tax preparer is not an excuse for blindly signing a tax return without understanding its content.

Application of the passive loss limitations to closely held C corporations prevents taxpayers from transferring their portfolio investments to such corporations in order to offset passive losses against portfolio income.

PASSIVE ACTIVITIES DEFINED

Section 469 specifies that the following types of activities are to be treated as passive:

- Any trade or business or income-producing activity in which the taxpayer does not materially participate.
- Subject to certain exceptions, all rental activities.

To understand the meaning of the term *passive activity* and the impact of the rules, one must address the following issues, each of which is the subject of statutory or administrative guidance:

- What constitutes an activity?
- What is meant by material participation?
- When is an activity a rental activity?

Even though guidance is available to help the taxpayer deal with these issues, their resolution is anything but simple.

> **LO.4**
> Discuss the definition of passive activities and the rules for identifying an activity.

Identification of an Activity

Identifying what constitutes an activity is a necessary first step in applying the passive loss limitations. Taxpayers who are involved in complex business operations need to determine whether a given segment of their overall business operations constitutes a separate activity or is to be treated as part of a single activity. Proper treatment is necessary in order to determine whether income or loss from an activity is active or passive.

EXAMPLE 16

Ben owns a business with two separate departments. Department A generates net income of $120,000, and Department B generates a net loss of $95,000. Ben participates for 700 hours in the operations of Department A and for 100 hours in

Department B. If Ben is allowed to treat the departments as components of a single activity, he can offset the $95,000 loss from Department B against the $120,000 of income from Department A. ■

EXAMPLE 17

Assume the same facts as in the previous example. If Ben is required to treat each department as a separate activity, the tax result is not as favorable. Because he is a material participant in Department A (having devoted 700 hours to it), the $120,000 profit is active income. However, he is not considered a material participant in Department B (100 hours), and the $95,000 loss is a passive loss. Therefore, Ben cannot offset the $95,000 passive loss from Department B against the $120,000 of active income from Department A. (A complete discussion of the material participation rules follows.) ■

Recall that on the disposition of a passive activity, a taxpayer is allowed to offset suspended losses from the activity against other types of income. Therefore, identifying what constitutes an activity is of crucial importance for this purpose too.

EXAMPLE 18

Linda owns a business with two departments. Department A has a net loss of $125,000 in the current year, and Department B has a $70,000 net loss. She disposes of Department B at the end of the year. Assuming Linda is allowed to treat the two departments as separate passive activities, she can offset the passive loss from Department B against other types of income in the following order: gain from disposition of the passive activity, other passive income, and nonpassive income. This treatment leaves her with a suspended loss of $125,000 from Department A. If Departments A and B are treated as components of the same activity, however, on the disposal of Department B, its $70,000 net loss would be suspended along with the other $125,000 of suspended loss of the activity. ■

The rules used to delineate what constitutes an activity for purposes of the passive loss limitations are provided in the Regulations.[13] These guidelines state that, in general, a taxpayer can treat one or more trade or business activities or rental activities as a single activity if those activities form an *appropriate economic unit* for measuring gain or loss. To determine what ventures form an appropriate economic unit, all of the relevant facts and circumstances must be considered. Taxpayers may use any reasonable method in applying the facts and circumstances. The following example, adapted from the Regulations, illustrates the application of the general rules for grouping activities.[14]

EXAMPLE 19

George owns a men's clothing store and an Internet café in Chicago. He also owns a men's clothing store and an Internet café in Milwaukee. Reasonable methods of applying the facts and circumstances test may result in any of the following groupings:

- All four activities may be grouped into a single activity because of common ownership and control.
- The clothing stores may be grouped into an activity, and the Internet cafés may be grouped into a separate activity.
- The Chicago activities may be grouped into an activity, and the Milwaukee activities may be grouped into a separate activity.
- Each of the four activities may be treated as a separate activity. ■

Regrouping of Activities Taxpayers should carefully consider all tax factors in deciding how to group their activities. Once activities have been grouped, they cannot be

[13]Reg. § 1.469–4.   [14]Reg. § 1.469–4(c)(3).

regrouped unless the original grouping was clearly inappropriate or there has been a material change in the facts and circumstances. The Regulations also grant the IRS the right to regroup activities when both of the following conditions exist:[15]

* The taxpayer's grouping fails to reflect one or more appropriate economic units.
* One of the primary purposes of the taxpayer's grouping is to avoid the passive loss limitations.

Special Grouping Rules for Rental Activities Two rules deal specifically with the grouping of rental activities. These provisions are designed to prevent taxpayers from grouping rental activities, which are generally passive, with other businesses in a way that would result in a tax advantage.

First, a rental activity may be grouped with a trade or business activity only if one activity is insubstantial in relation to the other. That is, the rental activity must be insubstantial in relation to the trade or business activity, or the trade or business activity must be insubstantial in relation to the rental activity. The Regulations provide no clear guidelines as to the meaning of "insubstantial."[16]

Schemers, a firm of CPAs, owns a building in downtown Washington, D.C., in which they conduct their public accounting practice. The firm also rents space on the street level of the building to several retail establishments. Of the total revenue generated by the firm, 95% is associated with the public accounting practice, and 5% is related to the rental operation. It is likely that the rental activity would be considered insubstantial relative to the accounting practice and the two ventures could be grouped as one nonrental activity. This grouping could be advantageous to the firm, particularly if the rental operation generates a loss! Alternatively, treating the rental operation as a *separate* activity may be advantageous if this operation produces (passive) income. The passive income could then be used to absorb otherwise nondeductible passive losses. ■	**EXAMPLE 20**

Second, taxpayers generally may not treat an activity involving the rental of real property and an activity involving the rental of personal property as a single activity.

Material Participation

If an individual taxpayer materially participates in a nonrental trade or business activity, any loss from that activity is treated as an active loss that can offset active or portfolio income. If a taxpayer does not materially participate, however, the loss is treated as a passive loss, which can only offset passive income. Therefore, controlling whether a particular activity is treated as active or passive is an important part of the tax strategy of a taxpayer who owns an interest in one or more businesses. Consider the following examples.

L0.5

Analyze and apply the tests for material participation.

Dewayne, a corporate executive, earns a salary of $600,000 per year. In addition, he owns a separate business in which he participates. The business produces a loss of $100,000 during the year. If Dewayne materially participates in the business, the $100,000 loss is an active loss that may offset his active income from his corporate employer. If he does not materially participate, the loss is passive and is suspended. Dewayne may use the suspended loss in the future only when he has passive income or disposes of the activity. ■	**EXAMPLE 21**

Kay, an attorney, earns $350,000 a year in her law practice. She owns interests in two activities, A and B, in which she participates. Activity A, in which she does *not* materially participate, produces a loss of $50,000. Kay has not yet met the material participation standard for Activity B, which produces income of $80,000. However, she can meet	**EXAMPLE 22**

---

[15]Reg. § 1.469–4(f).   [16]Reg. § 1.469–4(d).

the material participation standard if she spends an additional 50 hours in Activity B during the year. Should Kay attempt to meet the material participation standard for Activity B? If she continues working in Activity B and becomes a material participant, the $80,000 of income from the activity is *active*, and the $50,000 passive loss from Activity A must be suspended. A more favorable tax strategy is for Kay to *not meet* the material participation standard for Activity B, thus making the income from that activity passive. This enables her to offset the $50,000 passive loss from Activity A against the passive income from Activity B. ■

It is possible to devise numerous scenarios in which the taxpayer could control the tax outcome by increasing or decreasing his or her participation in different activities. Examples 21 and 22 demonstrate some of the possibilities. The conclusion reached in most analyses of this type is that taxpayers will benefit by having profitable activities classified as passive so that any passive losses can be used to offset that passive income. If the activity produces a loss, however, the taxpayer will benefit if it is classified as active so that the loss is not subject to the passive loss limitations.

As discussed previously, a nonrental trade or business in which a taxpayer owns an interest must be treated as a passive activity unless the taxpayer materially participates. As the Staff of the Joint Committee on Taxation explained, a material participant is one who has "a significant nontax economic profit motive" for taking on activities and selects them for their economic value. In contrast, a passive investor mainly seeks a return from a capital investment (including a possible reduction in taxes) as a supplement to an ongoing source of livelihood.[17] Even if the concept or the implication of being a material participant is clear, the precise meaning of the term **material participation** can be vague. As enacted, § 469 requires a taxpayer to participate on a *regular, continuous, and substantial* basis in order to be a material participant. In many situations, however, it is difficult or impossible to gain any assurance that this nebulous standard is met.

In response to this dilemma, Temporary Regulations[18] provide seven tests that are intended to help taxpayers cope with these issues. Material participation is achieved by meeting any *one* of the tests. These tests can be divided into three categories:

* Tests based on current participation.
* Tests based on prior participation.
* Test based on facts and circumstances.

Tests Based on Current Participation The first four tests are quantitative tests that require measurement, in hours, of the taxpayer's participation in the activity during the year.

1. *Does the individual participate in the activity for more than 500 hours during the year?*

The purpose of the 500-hour requirement is to restrict deductions from the types of trade or business activities Congress intended to treat as passive activities. The 500-hour standard for material participation was adopted for the following reasons:[19]

* Few investors in traditional tax shelters devote more than 500 hours a year to such an investment.
* The IRS believes that income from an activity in which the taxpayer participates for more than 500 hours a year should not be treated as passive.

[17] *General Explanation of the Tax Reform Act of 1986* ("Blue Book"), prepared by The Staff of the Joint Committee on Taxation, May 4, 1987, H.R. 3838, 99th Cong., p. 212.

[18] Temp.Reg. § 1.469–5T(a). The Temporary Regulations are also Proposed Regulations. Temporary Regulations have the same effect as final Regulations. Refer to Chapter 2 for a discussion of the different categories of Regulations.
[19] T.D. 8175, 1988–1 C.B. 191.

2. *Does the individual's participation in the activity for the taxable year constitute substantially all of the participation in the activity of all individuals (including nonowner employees) for the year?*

> **EXAMPLE 23**
>
> Ned, a physician, operates a separate business in which he participates for 80 hours during the year. He is the only participant and has no employees in the separate business. Ned meets the material participation standard of Test 2. If he had employees, it could be difficult to apply Test 2, because the Temporary Regulations do not define the term *substantially all*. ■

3. *Does the individual participate in the activity for more than 100 hours during the year, and is the individual's participation in the activity for the year not less than the participation of any other individual (including nonowner employees) for the year?*

> **EXAMPLE 24**
>
> Adam, a college professor, owns a separate business in which he participates 110 hours during the year. He has an employee who works 90 hours during the year. Adam meets the material participation standard under Test 3, but probably does not meet it under Test 2 because his participation is only 55% of the total participation. It is unlikely that 55% would meet the *substantially all* requirement of Test 2. ■

Tests 2 and 3 are included because the IRS recognizes that the operation of some activities does not require more than 500 hours of participation during the year.

4. *Is the activity a significant participation activity for the taxable year, and does the individual's aggregate participation in all significant participation activities during the year exceed 500 hours?*

A **significant participation activity** is a trade or business in which the individual's participation exceeds 100 hours during the year. This test treats taxpayers as material participants if their aggregate participation in several significant participation activities exceeds 500 hours. Test 4 thus accords the same treatment to an individual who devotes an aggregate of more than 500 hours to several significant participation activities as to an individual who devotes more than 500 hours to a single activity.

> **EXAMPLE 25**
>
> Mike owns five different businesses. He participates in each activity during the year as follows:
>
> | Activity | Hours of Participation |
> | --- | --- |
> | A | 110 |
> | B | 140 |
> | C | 120 |
> | D | 150 |
> | E | 100 |
>
> Activities A, B, C, and D are significant participation activities, and Mike's aggregate participation in those activities is 520 hours. Therefore, Activities A, B, C, and D are not treated as passive activities. Activity E is not a significant participation activity (not more than 100 hours), so it is not included in applying the 500-hour test. Activity E is treated as a passive activity, unless Mike meets one of the other material participation tests for that activity. ■

> **EXAMPLE 26**
>
> Assume the same facts as in the previous example, except that Activity A does not exist. All of the activities are now treated as passive under Test 4. Activity E is not counted in applying the more-than-500-hour test, so Mike's aggregate participation in significant participation activities is 410 hours (140 in Activity B + 120 in Activity C + 150 in

Activity D). He could meet the significant participation test for Activity E by participating for one more hour in the activity. This would cause Activities B, C, D, and E to be treated as nonpassive activities. However, before deciding whether to participate for at least one more hour in Activity E, Mike should assess how the participation would affect his overall tax liability. ∎

Tests Based on Prior Participation   Tests 5 and 6 are based on material participation in prior years. Under these tests, a taxpayer who is no longer a participant in an activity can continue to be *classified* as a material participant. The IRS takes the position that material participation in a trade or business for a long period of time is likely to indicate that the activity represents the individual's principal livelihood, rather than a passive investment. Consequently, withdrawal from the activity, or reduction of participation to the point where it is not material, does not change the classification of the activity from active to passive.

  5. *Did the individual materially participate in the activity for any 5 taxable years (whether consecutive or not) during the 10 taxable years that immediately precede the taxable year?*

EXAMPLE 27

Dawn, who owns a 50% interest in a restaurant, was a material participant in the operations of the restaurant from 2005 through 2009. She retired at the end of 2009 and is no longer involved in the restaurant except as an investor. Dawn will be treated as a material participant in the restaurant in 2010. Even if she does not become involved in the restaurant as a material participant again, she will continue to be treated as a material participant in 2011, 2012, 2013, and 2014. In 2015 and later years, Dawn's share of income or loss from the restaurant will be classified as passive unless she materially participates in those years. ∎

  6. *Is the activity a personal service activity, and did the individual materially participate in the activity for any three preceding taxable years (whether consecutive or not)?*

As indicated above, the material participation standards differ for personal service activities and other businesses. An individual who was a material participant in a personal service activity for *any three years* prior to the taxable year continues to be treated as a material participant after withdrawal from the activity.

EXAMPLE 28

Evan, a CPA, retires from the EFG Partnership after working full-time in the partnership for 30 years. As a retired partner, he will continue to receive a share of the profits of the firm for the next 10 years, even though he will not participate in the firm's operations. Evan also owns an interest in a passive activity that produces a loss for the year. Because he continues to be treated as a material participant in the EFG Partnership, his income from the partnership is active income. Therefore, he is not allowed to offset the loss from his passive investment against the income from the EFG Partnership. ∎

Test Based on Facts and Circumstances   Test 7 assesses the facts and circumstances to determine whether the taxpayer has materially participated.

  7. *Based on all the facts and circumstances, did the individual participate in the activity on a regular, continuous, and substantial basis during the year?*

Unfortunately, the Temporary Regulations provide little guidance as to the meaning of regular, continuous, and substantial participation.[20] However, a part of the Temporary Regulations has been reserved for further development of this test. For

---

[20]Temp.Reg. § 1.469–5T(b)(2).

the time being, taxpayers should rely on Tests 1 through 6 in determining whether the material participation standards have been met.

Participation Defined Participation generally includes any work done by an individual in an activity that he or she owns. Participation does not include work if it is of a type not customarily done by owners *and* if one of its principal purposes is to avoid the disallowance of passive losses or credits. Also, work done in an individual's capacity as an investor (e.g., reviewing financial reports in a nonmanagerial capacity) is not counted in applying the material participation tests. However, participation by an owner's spouse counts as participation by the owner.[21]

EXAMPLE 29

Tom, who is a partner in a CPA firm, owns a computer store that has operated at a loss during the year. In order to offset this loss against the income from his CPA practice, Tom would like to avoid having the computer business classified as a passive activity. Through December 15, he has worked 400 hours in the business in management and selling activities. During the last two weeks of December, he works 80 hours in management and selling activities and 30 hours doing janitorial chores. Also during the last two weeks in December, Tom's wife participates 40 hours as a salesperson. She has worked as a salesperson in the computer store in prior years, but has not done so during the current year. If any of Tom's work is of a type not customarily done by owners *and* if one of its principal purposes is to avoid the disallowance of passive losses or credits, it is not counted in applying the material participation tests. It is likely that Tom's 480 hours of participation in management and selling activities will count as participation, but the 30 hours spent doing janitorial chores will not. However, the 40 hours of participation by his wife will count, and as a result, Tom will qualify as a material participant under the more-than-500-hour rule (480 + 40 = 520). ∎

ETHICS & Equity

A LOVERS' TRIANGLE AND THE PASSIVE LOSS RULES

The troubled marriage of John and Eleanor finally reached an impasse, and they mutually agreed to divorce. Shortly after the divorce was finalized, John married Kristen. The three have known each other for years from working together to harvest the grapes of a vineyard owned by John. Prior to the divorce, each had worked 200 hours in the vineyard in the current year. The investment generates a loss for the current year, and John wants to classify the loss as active rather than passive. In order for the loss to be classified as active, the participation of John and his spouse together must exceed 500 hours. John claims that meeting that threshold is not a problem. He worked 200 hours, and Eleanor, who was his wife when the work was done, worked 200 hours. Kristen, who files a joint return with John, also worked 200 hours. John feels it is proper to aggregate Eleanor and Kristen's participation with his own. This approach makes the loss deductible in full. "Besides," says John, "there is nothing in the law that says I can't do this." As John's tax return preparer, how do you react?

Limited Partners A *limited* partner is one whose liability to third-party creditors of the partnership is limited to the amount the partner has invested in the partnership. Such a partnership must have at least one *general* partner, who is fully liable in an individual capacity for the debts of the partnership to third parties. Generally, a *limited partner* is not considered a material participant unless he or she qualifies under Test 1, 5, or 6 in the above list. However, a *general partner* may qualify as a material participant by meeting any of the seven tests. If a general partner also owns a limited interest in the same limited partnership, all interests are treated as a general interest.[22]

---

[21]Temp.Reg. § 1.469–5T(f)(3).   [22]§ 469(h)(2) and Temp.Reg. § 1.469–5T(e)(3)(ii).

TAX*in* the *NEWS*

ARE NEBRASKA FARMERS SIMILAR TO OWNERS OF OTHER LLCS AND LLPS?

A major advantage for limited partners in a limited partnership is that their personal exposure to potential business losses is restricted to their investments in the partnership. Further, from an operational perspective, a typical limited partner is truly a passive investor since he or she does not participate in the business or its management. As a result, the Temporary Regulations presume that a limited partner is not a material participant unless the individual qualifies under Test 1, 5, or 6.

As limited liability companies (LLCs) and limited liability partnerships (LLPs) have grown in popularity in the United States, however, the question has arisen as to whether owners of interests in these business forms who *are* active in the businesses should be presumed to not be material participants under the usual rules applicable to limited partners. In a recent Tax Court decision [*Paul D. Garnett*, 132 T.C. 368 (2009)], Nebraska chicken and pig farmers who operated

their businesses as LLCs and LLPs and played active roles were considered more akin to general partners. The court held that their material participation status should be determined by an analysis of the particular facts and circumstances of the situation and the material participation rules in general. The implication of this decision is that many taxpayers who are participants in LLCs or LLPs may be in a position to avoid the passive loss rules altogether merely by applying the general material participation tests found in the Temporary Regulations.

Since the Tax Court ruled in *Garnett*, judges in other cases have ruled similarly [*James R. Thompson v. U.S.*, 2009–2 USTC ¶50,501, 104 AFTR 2d 2009–5381, 87 Fed.Cl. 728 (Fed.Cl., 2009); *Lee E. Newell*, 99 TCM 1107, T.C.Memo. 2010–23]. With judicial pressure on the IRS's position building, many tax professionals expect a response from the IRS soon.

LO.6

Understand the nature of rental activities under the passive loss rules.

Rental Activities Defined

Subject to certain exceptions, all rental activities are to be treated as passive activities.[23] A **rental activity** is defined as any activity where payments are received principally for the use of tangible (real or personal) property.[24] Importantly, an activity that is classified as a rental activity is subject to the passive activity loss rules, even if the taxpayer involved is a material participant.

EXAMPLE 30

Sarah owns a fleet of automobiles that are held for rent and spends an average of 60 hours a week in the activity. Assuming that her automobile business is classified as a rental activity, it is automatically subject to the passive activity rules, even though Sarah spends more than 500 hours a year in its operation. ∎

Temporary Regulations, however, provide exceptions for certain situations where activities involving rentals of real and personal property are *not* to be *treated* as rental activities.[25]

EXAMPLE 31

Dan owns a DVD rental business. Because the average period of customer use is seven days or less, Dan's DVD business is not treated as a rental activity. ∎

The fact that Dan's DVD business in the previous example is not treated as a rental activity does not necessarily mean that it is classified as a nonpassive activity. Instead, the DVD business is treated as a trade or business activity subject to the material participation standards. If Dan is a material participant, the business is treated as active. If he is not a material participant, it is treated as a passive activity.

Thus, activities covered by any of the following six exceptions provided by the Temporary Regulations are not *automatically* treated as nonpassive activities merely

---

[23]§ 469(c)(2).
[24]§ 469(j)(8).
[25]Temp.Reg. § 1.469–1T(e)(3)(ii).

because they would not be classified as rental activities. Instead, the activities are subject to the material participation tests.

1. *The average period of customer use of the property is seven days or less.*

Under this exception, activities involving the short-term use of tangible property such as automobiles, DVDs, tuxedos, tools, and other such property are not treated as rental activities. The provision also applies to short-term rentals of hotel or motel rooms.

This exception is based on the presumption that a person who rents property for seven days or less is generally required to provide *significant services* to the customer. Providing such services supports a conclusion that the person is engaged in a service business rather than a rental business.

2. *The average period of customer use of the property is 30 days or less, and the owner of the property provides significant personal services.*

For longer-term rentals, the presumption that significant services are provided is not automatic, as it is in the case of the seven-day exception. Instead, the taxpayer must be able to *prove* that significant personal services are rendered in connection with the activity. Relevant facts and circumstances include the frequency with which such services are provided, the type and amount of labor required to perform the services, and the value of the services relative to the amount charged for the use of the property. Significant personal services include only services provided by *individuals*.[26]

3. *The owner of the property provides extraordinary personal services. The average period of customer use is of no consequence in applying this test.*

Extraordinary personal services are services provided by individuals where the customers' use of the property is incidental to their receipt of the services. For example, a patient's use of a hospital bed is incidental to his or her receipt of medical services. Another example is the use of a boarding school's dormitory, which is incidental to the scholastic services received.

4. *The rental of the property is treated as incidental to a nonrental activity of the taxpayer.*

Rentals of property incidental to a nonrental activity are not considered a passive activity. The Temporary Regulations provide that the following rentals are not passive activities:[27]

- *Property held primarily for investment.* This occurs where the principal purpose for holding the property is the expectation of gain from the appreciation of the property and the gross rent income is less than 2 percent of the lesser of (1) the unadjusted basis or (2) the fair market value of the property.

EXAMPLE 32

Ramon invests in vacant land for the purpose of realizing a profit on its appreciation. He leases the land during the period it is held. The land's unadjusted basis is $250,000, and the fair market value is $350,000. The lease payments are $4,000 per year. Because gross rent income is less than 2% of $250,000, the activity is not a rental activity. ∎

- *Property used in a trade or business.* This occurs where the property is owned by a taxpayer who is an owner of the trade or business using the rental property. The property must also have been used in the trade or business during the year or during at least two of the five preceding taxable years. The 2 percent test above also applies in this situation.

EXAMPLE 33

A farmer owns land with an unadjusted basis of $250,000 and a fair market value of $350,000. He used it for farming purposes in 2009 and 2010. In 2011, he leases the land to another farmer for $4,000. The activity is not a rental activity. ∎

---

[26]Temp.Reg. § 1.469–1T(e)(3)(iv).   [27]Temp.Regs. §§ 1.469–1T(e)(3)(vi)(B) through (D).

- *Lodging rented for the convenience of an employer.* If an employer provides lodging for an employee incidental to the employee's performance of services in the employer's trade or business, no rental activity exists.

These rules were written to prevent taxpayers from converting active or portfolio income into passive income for the purpose of offsetting other passive losses.

5. *The taxpayer customarily makes the property available during defined business hours for nonexclusive use by various customers.*

EXAMPLE 34

Pat is the owner-operator of a public golf course. Some customers pay daily greens fees each time they use the course, while others purchase weekly, monthly, or annual passes. The golf course is open every day from sunrise to sunset, except on certain holidays and on days when the course is closed due to inclement weather conditions. Pat is not engaged in a rental activity, regardless of the average period customers use the course. ■

6. *The property is provided for use in an activity conducted by a partnership, S corporation, or joint venture in which the taxpayer owns an interest.*

EXAMPLE 35

Joe, a partner in the Skyview Partnership, contributes the use of a building to the partnership. The partnership has net income of $30,000 during the year, of which Joe's share is $10,000. Unless the partnership is engaged in a rental activity, none of Joe's income from the partnership is income from a rental activity. ■

INTERACTION OF THE AT-RISK AND PASSIVE ACTIVITY LIMITS

LO.7

Recognize the relationship between the at-risk and passive activity limitations.

The determination of whether a loss is suspended under the passive loss rules is made *after* application of the at-risk rules, as well as other provisions relating to the measurement of taxable income. A loss that is not allowed for the year because the taxpayer is not at risk with respect to it is suspended under the at-risk provision and not under the passive loss rules. Further, a taxpayer's basis is reduced by deductions (e.g., depreciation) even if the deductions are not currently usable because of the passive loss rules.

EXAMPLE 36

Jack's adjusted basis in a passive activity is $10,000 at the beginning of 2010. His loss from the activity in 2010 is $4,000. Since Jack has no passive activity income, the $4,000 cannot be deducted. At year-end, Jack has an adjusted basis and an at-risk amount of $6,000 in the activity and a suspended passive loss of $4,000. ■

EXAMPLE 37

Jack in Example 36 has a loss of $9,000 in the activity in 2011. Since the $9,000 exceeds his at-risk amount ($6,000) by $3,000, that $3,000 loss is disallowed by the at-risk rules. If Jack has no passive activity income, the remaining $6,000 is suspended under the passive activity rules. At year-end, he has:

- A $3,000 loss suspended under the at-risk rules.
- $10,000 of suspended passive losses.
- An adjusted basis and an at-risk amount in the activity of zero.   ■

EXAMPLE 38

Jack in Example 37 realizes $1,000 of passive income from the activity in 2012. Because the $1,000 increases his at-risk amount, $1,000 of the $3,000 unused loss is reclassified as a passive loss. If he has no other passive income, the $1,000 income is offset by $1,000 of suspended passive losses. At the end of 2012, Jack has:

- No taxable passive income.
- $2,000 ($3,000 − $1,000) of unused losses under the at-risk rules.

- $10,000 of (reclassified) suspended passive losses ($10,000 + $1,000 of reclassified unused at-risk losses − $1,000 of passive losses offset against passive income).
- An adjusted basis and an at-risk amount in the activity of zero. ∎

EXAMPLE 39

In 2013, Jack has no gain or loss from the activity in Example 38. He contributes $5,000 more to the passive activity. Because the $5,000 increases his at-risk amount, the $2,000 of losses suspended under the at-risk rules is reclassified as passive. Jack gets no passive loss deduction in 2013. At year-end, he has:

- No suspended losses under the at-risk rules.
- $12,000 of suspended passive losses ($10,000 + $2,000 of reclassified suspended at-risk losses).
- An adjusted basis and an at-risk amount of $3,000 ($5,000 additional investment − $2,000 of reclassified losses). ∎

EXAMPLE 40
THE BIG PICTURE

Return to the facts of *The Big Picture* on p. 11-2. If the Reswicks invest in the orange grove limited partnership, the at-risk rules would not limit the deductibility of the $25,000 losses until after year 4. Ample at-risk basis will exist until the close of that year (i.e., the at-risk basis is reduced from $100,000 by $25,000 over each of the first four years of the investment). However, the passive loss rules prohibit deductions for the losses in the first four years of the investment (assuming the Reswicks do not have passive income from other sources). Therefore, based on the facts provided, none of the suspended losses would be deductible until year 6 when the orange grove is expected to begin producing profits. ∎

SPECIAL PASSIVE ACTIVITY RULES FOR REAL ESTATE ACTIVITIES

LO.8
Discuss the special treatment available to real estate activities.

The passive loss limits contain two exceptions related to real estate activities. These exceptions allow all or part of real estate rental losses to offset active or portfolio income, even though the activity otherwise is defined as a passive activity.

Material Participation in a Real Property Rental Trade or Business

The first exception relates to a special rule for material participation in a real estate rental trade or business. Losses from real estate rental activities are *not* treated as passive losses for certain real estate professionals.[28] To qualify for nonpassive treatment, a taxpayer must satisfy both of the following requirements:

- More than half of the personal services that the taxpayer performs in trades or businesses are performed in real property trades or businesses in which the taxpayer materially participates.
- The taxpayer performs more than 750 hours of services in these real property trades or businesses as a material participant.

Taxpayers who do not satisfy the above requirements must continue to treat losses from real estate rental activities as passive losses.

EXAMPLE 41

During the current year, Della performs personal service activities as follows: 900 hours as a personal financial planner, 550 hours in a real estate development business, and 600 hours in a real estate rental activity. Any loss Della incurs in either real estate activity will not be subject to the passive loss rules. Being a nonrental business, the development business is deemed active under the more-than-500-hour rule. The real estate rental activity is active since more than 50% of her personal services are devoted to real property trades or businesses (i.e., the development and rental businesses), and her

---

[28]§ 469(c)(7).

Often, ignoring what may seem to be trivial can turn out to be disastrous. As noted in the text, gains or losses from rental property are generally classified as passive. If the taxpayer is a real estate professional, however, the gains or losses arising from the property are treated as active. Being classified as a real estate professional can be attractive, but to receive such treatment, the taxpayer must be a material participant in the real property trades or businesses.

If a taxpayer owns three rental properties and devotes 200 hours to each property, does the taxpayer qualify as a material participant? The answer can vary. For example, to be treated as a material participant under the 500-hour rule, the taxpayer would have to elect to aggregate the three real estate rental interests and treat them as a single activity.

By so doing, the taxpayer is treated as having participated for 600 hours in this "single" activity and, thus, is a material participant [see Reg. § 1.469–9(e)]. If the taxpayer does not make the election, however, the material participation standard is evaluated on a property-by-property basis (i.e., the taxpayer has devoted only 200 hours to each activity).

An explicit election to aggregate the activities is required—taxpayers cannot assume that the IRS will understand their intentions. Several taxpayers learned this lesson recently when they failed to avoid the passive loss rules because they did not make their intentions clear. See *Anjum Shiekh* (99 TCM 1526, T.C.Memo. 2010–126) and *Donald W. Trask* (99 TCM 1335, T.C.Memo. 2010–78) for examples of taxpayers who wish they could redo their tax returns.

---

material participation in those real estate activities exceeds 750 hours. Thus, any losses from either real estate activity can offset active and portfolio sources of income. ■

As discussed earlier, a spouse's work is taken into consideration in satisfying the material participation requirement. However, the hours worked by a spouse are *not* taken into account when ascertaining whether a taxpayer has worked for more than 750 hours in real property trades or businesses during a year.[29] Services performed by an employee are not treated as being related to a real estate trade or business unless the employee performing the services owns more than a 5 percent interest in the employer. Additionally, a closely held C corporation may also qualify for the passive loss relief if more than 50 percent of its gross receipts for the year are derived from real property trades or businesses in which it materially participates.

Real Estate Rental Activities

The second exception is more significant in that it is not restricted to real estate professionals. This exception allows individuals to deduct up to $25,000 of losses from real estate rental activities against active and portfolio income.[30] The potential annual $25,000 deduction is reduced by 50 percent of the taxpayer's AGI in excess of $100,000. Thus, the entire deduction is phased out at $150,000 of AGI. If married individuals file separately, the $25,000 deduction is reduced to zero unless they lived apart for the entire year. If they lived apart for the entire year, the loss amount is $12,500 each, and the phaseout begins at $50,000. AGI for purposes of the phaseout is calculated without regard to IRA deductions, Social Security benefits, interest deductions on education loans, and net losses from passive activities.

To qualify for the $25,000 exception, a taxpayer must meet the following requirements:[31]

- Actively participate in the real estate rental activity.
- Own 10 percent or more (in value) of all interests in the activity during the entire taxable year (or shorter period during which the taxpayer held an interest in the activity).

---

[29]§ 469(c)(7)(B) and Reg. § 1.469–9.
[30]§ 469(i).

[31]§ 469(i)(6).

The difference between *active participation* and *material participation* is that the former can be satisfied without regular, continuous, and substantial involvement in operations as long as the taxpayer participates in making management decisions in a significant and bona fide sense. In this context, relevant management decisions include such decisions as approving new tenants, deciding on rental terms, and approving capital or repair expenditures.

EXAMPLE 42
THE BIG PICTURE

Return to the facts of *The Big Picture* on p. 11-2. If the Reswicks invest in the apartment rental limited partnership, their $25,000 loss would be deductible under the real estate rental activities exception. This assumes they actively participate and own at least a 10% interest in the partnership. The loss will be deductible in each of the first four years of their investment before exhausting their at-risk basis, even if they do not have passive income from other sources. ∎

The $25,000 allowance is available after all active participation rental losses and gains are netted and applied to other passive income. If a taxpayer has a real estate rental loss in excess of the amount that can be deducted under the real estate rental exception, that excess is treated as a passive loss.

EXAMPLE 43

Brad, who has $90,000 of AGI before considering rental activities, has $85,000 of losses from a real estate rental activity in which he actively participates. He also actively participates in another real estate rental activity from which he has $25,000 of income. He has other passive income of $36,000. Of the net rental loss of $60,000, $36,000 is absorbed by the passive income, leaving $24,000 that can be deducted against active or portfolio income because of the availability of the $25,000 allowance. ∎

The $25,000 offset allowance is an aggregate of both deductions and credits in deduction equivalents. The deduction equivalent of a passive activity credit is the amount of deductions that reduces the tax liability for the taxable year by an amount equal to the credit.[32] A taxpayer with $5,000 of credits and a tax bracket of 25 percent would have a deduction equivalent of $20,000 ($5,000 ÷ 25%).

If the total deduction and deduction equivalent exceed $25,000, the taxpayer must allocate the allowance on a pro rata basis, first among the losses (including real estate rental activity losses suspended in prior years) and then to credits in the following order: (1) credits other than rehabilitation and low-income housing credits, (2) rehabilitation credits, and (3) low-income housing credits.

EXAMPLE 44

Kevin is an active participant in a real estate rental activity that produces $8,000 of income, $26,000 of deductions, and $1,500 of credits. Kevin, who is in the 25% tax bracket, may deduct the net passive loss of $18,000 ($8,000 − $26,000). After deducting the loss, he has an available deduction equivalent of $7,000 ($25,000 − $18,000 passive loss). Therefore, the maximum amount of credits that he may claim is $1,750 ($7,000 × 25%). Since the actual credits are less than this amount, Kevin may claim the entire $1,500 credit. ∎

EXAMPLE 45

Kelly, who is in the 25% tax bracket, is an active participant in three separate real estate rental activities. The relevant tax results for each activity are as follows:

- Activity A: $20,000 of losses.
- Activity B: $10,000 of losses.
- Activity C: $4,200 of credits.

---

[32]§ 469(j)(5).

Kelly's deduction equivalent from the credits is $16,800 ($4,200 ÷ 25%). Therefore, the total passive deductions and deduction equivalents are $46,800 ($20,000 + $10,000 + $16,800), which exceeds the maximum allowable amount of $25,000. Consequently, Kelly must allocate pro rata first from among losses and then from among credits. Deductions from losses are limited as follows:

- Activity A {$25,000 × [$20,000 ÷ ($20,000 + $10,000)]} = $16,667.
- Activity B {$25,000 × [$10,000 ÷ ($20,000 + $10,000)]} = $8,333.

Since the amount of passive deductions exceeds the $25,000 maximum, the deduction balance of $5,000 and passive credits of $4,200 must be carried forward. Kelly's suspended losses and credits by activity are as follows:

	Total	A	B	C
			Activity	
Allocated losses	$ 30,000	$ 20,000	$10,000	$ –0–
Allocated credits	4,200	–0–	–0–	4,200
Utilized losses	(25,000)	(16,667)	(8,333)	–0–
Suspended losses	5,000	3,333	1,667	–0–
Suspended credits	4,200	–0–	–0–	4,200

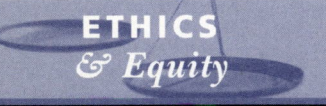

ETHICS & Equity

HOW ACTIVE IS ACTIVE?

Last year, George and Louise purchased several rental units near the university hoping to benefit from their expected appreciation and cash flow. Because George and Louise both have full-time jobs, they are unable to spend time managing the facilities. Consequently, they contracted with a well-regarded property manager to attract renters, collect the rents, and respond to service calls. After the close of the year, the property manager provided George and Louise with an accounting of the revenues and expenses related to the operation of the units. Though the results showed a positive cash flow, the impact of depreciation and mortgage interest expenses led to a net tax loss.

Not wanting to forgo claiming a loss on their income tax return, George and Louise chose to claim the loss under the real estate rental activity exception. Have George and Louise acted properly?

LO.9

Determine the proper tax treatment upon the disposition of a passive activity.

DISPOSITIONS OF PASSIVE INTERESTS

Recall from an earlier discussion that if a taxpayer disposes of an entire interest in a passive activity, any suspended losses (and in certain cases, suspended credits) may be utilized when calculating the final economic gain or loss on the investment. In addition, if a loss ultimately results, that loss can offset other types of income. However, the consequences may differ if the activity is disposed of in a transaction that is other than a fully taxable transaction. The following discusses the treatment of suspended passive losses in other types of dispositions.

Disposition of a Passive Activity at Death

A transfer of a taxpayer's interest in an activity by reason of the taxpayer's death results in suspended losses being allowed (to the decedent) to the extent they exceed the amount, if any, of the step-up in basis allowed.[33] Suspended losses are lost to the extent of the amount of the basis increase. The losses allowed generally are reported on the final return of the deceased taxpayer.

[33]§ 469(g)(2).

CONCEPT SUMMARY 11.2

Passive Activity Loss Rules: General Concepts

What is the fundamental passive activity rule?	Passive activity losses may be deducted only against passive activity income and gains. Losses not allowed are suspended and used in future years.
Who is subject to the passive activity rules?	Individuals.
	Estates.
	Trusts.
	Personal service corporations.
	Closely held C corporations.
What is a passive activity?	Trade or business or income-producing activity in which the taxpayer does not materially participate during the year, or rental activities, subject to certain exceptions, regardless of the taxpayer's level of participation.
What is an activity?	One or more trade or business or rental activities that comprise an appropriate economic unit.
How is an appropriate economic unit determined?	Based on a reasonable application of the relevant facts and circumstances.
What is material participation?	In general, the taxpayer participates on a regular, continuous, and substantial basis. More specifically, when the taxpayer meets the conditions of one of the seven tests provided in the Regulations.
What is a rental activity?	In general, an activity where payments are received for the use of tangible property. More specifically, a rental activity that does not meet one of the six exceptions provided in the Regulations. Special rules apply to rental real estate.

EXAMPLE 46

A taxpayer dies with passive activity property having an adjusted basis of $40,000, suspended losses of $10,000, and a fair market value at the date of the decedent's death of $75,000. The increase (i.e., step-up) in basis (see Chapter 14) is $35,000 (fair market value at date of death in excess of adjusted basis). None of the $10,000 suspended loss is deductible by either the decedent or the beneficiary. The suspended losses ($10,000) are lost because they do not exceed the step-up in basis ($35,000). ■

EXAMPLE 47

A taxpayer dies with passive activity property having an adjusted basis of $40,000, suspended losses of $10,000, and a fair market value at the date of the decedent's death of $47,000. Since the step-up in basis is only $7,000 ($47,000 − $40,000), the suspended losses allowed are limited to $3,000 ($10,000 suspended loss at time of death − $7,000 increase in basis). The $3,000 loss available to the decedent is reported on the decedent's final income tax return. ■

Disposition of a Passive Activity by Gift

In a disposition of a taxpayer's interest in a passive activity by gift, the suspended losses are added to the basis of the property.[34]

EXAMPLE 48

A taxpayer makes a gift of passive activity property having an adjusted basis of $40,000, suspended losses of $10,000, and a fair market value at the date of the gift of $100,000. The taxpayer cannot deduct the suspended losses in the year of the disposition. However, the suspended losses transfer with the property and are added to the adjusted basis of the property in the hands of the donee. ■

---

[34]§ 469(j)(6).

When a passive activity is transferred by gift, the suspended losses become permanently nondeductible to both the donor and the donee. Nonetheless, a tax *benefit* may be available to the donee for another reason. Due to the increase in the property's basis, greater depreciation deductions can result, and there will be less gain (or more loss) on a subsequent sale of the property. The side benefits of increased basis do not materialize if the recipient is a charity, as such organizations generally are not subject to income taxation.

Installment Sale of a Passive Activity

An installment sale of a taxpayer's entire interest in a passive activity triggers the recognition of the suspended losses.[35] The losses are allowed in each year of the installment obligation in the ratio that the gain recognized in each year bears to the total gain on the sale.

EXAMPLE 49

Stan sells his entire interest in a passive activity for $100,000. His adjusted basis in the property is $60,000. If he uses the installment method, his gross profit ratio is 40% ($40,000/$100,000). If Stan receives a $20,000 down payment, he will recognize a gain of $8,000 (40% of $20,000). If the activity has a suspended loss of $25,000, Stan will deduct $5,000 [($8,000 ÷ $40,000) × $25,000] of the suspended loss in the first year. ■

Nontaxable Exchange of a Passive Activity

In a nontaxable exchange of a passive investment, the taxpayer keeps the suspended losses, which generally become deductible when the acquired property is sold. If the activity of the old and the new property is the same, suspended losses can be used before the activity's disposition.

EXAMPLE 50

A taxpayer exchanges a duplex for a limited partnership interest in a § 721 nonrecognition transaction (see Chapter 20 for details). The suspended losses from the duplex are not deductible until the limited partnership interest is sold. Two different activities exist: a real estate rental activity and a limited partnership activity. If the taxpayer had continued to own the duplex and the duplex had future taxable income, the suspended losses would have become deductible before the time of disposition. ■

EXAMPLE 51

In a § 1031 nontaxable exchange (see Chapter 15 for details), a taxpayer exchanges a duplex for an apartment building. The suspended losses from the duplex are deductible against future taxable income of the apartment building, because the same activity exists. ■

11.4 INVESTMENT INTEREST

LO.10

Identify restrictions placed on the deductibility of other investor losses and deductions, including those that apply to investment interest.

Taxpayers frequently borrow funds that they use to acquire investment assets. When the interest expense is large relative to the income from the investments, substantial tax benefits could result. Congress has therefore limited the deductibility of interest on funds borrowed for the purpose of purchasing or continuing to hold investment property. The deduction for **investment interest** expense is *now* limited to net investment income for the year.

Investment income is gross income from interest, dividends (see below), annuities, and royalties not derived in the ordinary course of a trade or business. However, income from a passive activity and income from a real estate activity in which the taxpayer actively participates are not included in investment income.

---

[35]§ 469(g)(3).

EXAMPLE 52
THE BIG PICTURE

Return to the facts of *The Big Picture* on p. 11-2. If the Reswicks invest in the high-growth, low-yield portfolio of marketable securities, most of the investment return will consist of appreciation, which will not be taxed until the securities are sold. Relatively little of the current return will consist of currently taxable interest and dividend income. Assume that the interest and dividend income for the year from these securities equals $500 and that all of it is treated as investment income. If the investment interest expense on the $100,000 loan is $8,000, only $500 of this interest will be deductible this year (i.e., the deduction for the investment interest is limited to the $500 of net investment income). ■

The following types of income are not included in investment income unless the taxpayer *elects* to do so.

- Net capital gain attributable to the disposition of (1) property producing the types of income just enumerated or (2) property held for investment purposes.
- Qualified dividends that are taxed at the same marginal rate that is applicable to a net capital gain.

A taxpayer may include net capital gain and qualified dividends as investment income by electing to do so on Form 4952. The election is available only if the taxpayer agrees to reduce amounts qualifying for the 15 percent (0 percent for low-income taxpayers) rates that otherwise apply to net capital gain (see Chapter 16) and qualified dividends (refer to Chapter 4) by an equivalent amount.

EXAMPLE 53

Terry incurred $13,000 of interest expense related to her investments during the year. Her investment income included $4,000 of interest, $2,000 of qualified dividends, and a $5,000 net capital gain on the sale of investment securities. If Terry does not make the election to include the net capital gain and qualified dividends in investment income, her investment income for purposes of computing the investment income limitation is $4,000 (interest income). If she does make the election, her investment income is $11,000 ($4,000 interest + $2,000 qualified dividends + $5,000 net capital gain). ■

Net investment income is the excess of investment income over investment expenses. Investment expenses are those deductible expenses directly connected with the production of investment income. Investment expenses *do not* include interest expense. When investment expenses fall into the category of miscellaneous itemized deductions that are subject to the 2 percent-of-AGI floor (refer to Chapter 10), some may not enter into the calculation of net investment income because of the floor.

EXAMPLE 54

Gina has AGI of $80,000, which includes qualified dividends of $15,000 and interest income of $3,000. Besides investment interest expense, she paid $3,000 of city ad valorem property tax on stocks and bonds and had the following miscellaneous itemized expenses:

Safe deposit box rental (to hold investment securities)	$ 120
Investment counsel fee	1,200
Unreimbursed business travel	850
Uniforms	600
Total miscellaneous itemized expenses	$2,770

Before Gina can determine her investment expenses for purposes of calculating net investment income, those miscellaneous expenses that are not investment expenses are disallowed before any investment expenses are disallowed under the 2%-of-AGI floor. This is accomplished by selecting the *lesser* of the following:

1. The amount of investment expenses included in the total of miscellaneous itemized deductions subject to the 2%-of-AGI floor.
2. The amount of miscellaneous expenses deductible after the 2%-of-AGI rule is applied.

The amount under item 1 is $1,320 [$120 (safe deposit box rental) + $1,200 (investment counsel fee)]. The item 2 amount is $1,170 [$2,770 (total of miscellaneous expenses) − $1,600 (2% of $80,000 AGI)].

Then, Gina's investment expenses are calculated as follows:

Deductible miscellaneous deductions investment expense (the lesser of item 1 or item 2)	$1,170
Plus: Ad valorem tax on investment property	3,000
Total investment expenses	$4,170

Gina elects to include the qualified dividends in investment income. Gina's net investment income is $13,830 ($18,000 investment income − $4,170 investment expenses). ∎

After net investment income is determined, deductible investment interest expense can be calculated.

EXAMPLE 55

Continuing with the facts in the previous example, given that Gina's current net investment income is $13,830, her deductible investment interest expense is limited to $13,830 this year. Therefore, if Gina incurred investment interest of $16,000 this year, only $13,830 would be deductible currently. ∎

The amount of investment interest disallowed is carried over to future years. In Example 55, therefore, the amount that is carried over to the following year is $2,170 ($16,000 investment interest expense − $13,830 allowed). No limit is placed on the length of the carryover period. The investment interest expense deduction is determined by completing Form 4952.

11.5 OTHER INVESTMENT LOSSES

The investment activities summarized below are discussed elsewhere in this text (see the references provided).

- Sales of securities held as investments for less than basis yield capital losses. These losses can offset capital gains. In the case of individual taxpayers, excess losses are applied against ordinary income up to $3,000 (§ 1211). Any remaining excess capital losses are carried over for use in future years (§ 1212). See Chapter 16 for additional discussion.
- Securities held as an investment that become worthless produce capital losses. The losses are usually long term since they are treated as occurring on the last day of the year in which the securities become worthless [§ 165(g)(1)]. Because the securities must be completely worthless, determining the year when this takes place often is difficult. See Chapter 7 for additional discussion.
- Losses on small business stock (i.e., stock that qualifies under § 1244) are treated as ordinary losses up to a maximum of $100,000. Thus, the limitations placed on capital losses (see above) are avoided. See Chapter 7 for additional discussion.
- As discussed in Chapter 6, vacation homes that are rented for part of the year may generate investment losses depending on the extent of the rental period as compared to time devoted to personal use (§ 280A). If sufficient rental activity takes place, the facility may be treated as rental property. As such, any losses could be subject to the passive loss rules. See the discussion earlier in this chapter.

TAX in the NEWS   **FAVORABLE TREATMENT AVAILABLE FOR VICTIMS OF PONZI-STYLE SCAMS**

Due to the recent economic recession, millions of people have lost considerable amounts of wealth. In addition, some taxpayers have had to relearn the old adage that "if something appears to be too good to be true, then it just may be." These taxpayers were victims not just of the economic downturn, but also of outright fraud: they were duped by Ponzi-style operators masquerading as investment advisers.

For the thousands of taxpayers who entrusted their investments to Bernard Madoff and suffered severe financial losses, such losses would normally be subject to capital loss treatment. This is typically the result when investment losses arise from sales, exchanges, or worthlessness. Instead, the IRS has provided that such losses will qualify for business theft loss treatment [Rev.Rul. 2009–9 and Rev.Proc. 2009–20 (2009–1 C.B. 735 and 749)]. The implication of this treatment

is significant: the losses will be fully deductible against ordinary income without regard to the $100 floor and 10 percent-of-AGI limitation typically applicable to casualty and theft losses or the 2 percent-of-AGI limitation applicable to miscellaneous itemized deductions. Moreover, because these losses are classified as business theft losses, any losses not deductible in the year of the loss may be carried back and carried forward under the net operating loss (NOL) rules, producing an immediate tax refund *or* a lower tax liability in future years.

Unfortunately, qualifying for theft loss treatment rather than capital loss treatment will not make these fraud victims whole. Nonetheless, the tax benefits associated with this favorable tax treatment help mitigate the financial losses sustained.

- When an activity is classified as a hobby, any losses resulting are limited to the income from the activity [§ 183(b)(2)]. If the activity is not a hobby (i.e., a profit motive controls), however, full deduction of the losses is allowed [§§ 162 and 212(2)]. See the relevant discussion of hobby losses in Chapter 6.

TAX PLANNING:
11.6 UTILIZING PASSIVE LOSSES

Perhaps the biggest challenge individuals face with the passive loss rules is to recognize the potential impact of the rules and then to structure their affairs to minimize this impact. Taxpayers who have passive activity losses (PALs) should adopt a strategy of generating passive activity income that can be sheltered by existing passive losses. One approach is to buy an interest in a passive activity that is generating income (referred to as passive income generators, or PIGs). Then the PAL can offset income from the PIG. From a tax perspective, it would be foolish to buy a loss-generating passive activity unless one has other passive income to shelter or the activity is rental real estate that can qualify for the $25,000 exception or the exception available to real estate professionals.

If a taxpayer does invest in an activity that produces losses subject to the passive loss rules, the following strategies may help to minimize the loss of current deductions:

- If money is borrowed to finance the purchase of a passive activity, the associated interest expense is generally treated as part of any passive loss. Consequently, by increasing the amount of cash used to purchase the passive investment, the investor will need less debt and will incur less interest expense. By incurring less interest expense, a possible suspended passive loss deduction is reduced.
- If the investor does not have sufficient cash readily available for the larger down payment, it can be obtained by borrowing against the equity in his or her personal residence. The interest expense on such debt will be deductible under the qualified residence interest provisions (see Chapter 10) and will not

> **LO.11**
> Suggest tax planning strategies to minimize the effect of the passive loss limitations.

be subject to the passive loss limitations. Thus, the taxpayer avoids the passive loss limitation and secures a currently deductible interest expense.

Often unusable passive losses accumulate and provide no current tax benefit because the taxpayer has no passive income. When the taxpayer disposes of the entire interest in a passive activity, however, any suspended losses from that activity are used to reduce the taxable gain. If any taxable gain still remains, it can be offset by losses from other passive activities. As a result, the taxpayer should carefully select the year in which a passive activity is disposed of. It is to the taxpayer's advantage to wait until sufficient passive losses have accumulated to offset any gain recognized on the asset's disposition.

EXAMPLE 56

Bill, a calendar year taxpayer, owns interests in two passive activities: Activity A, which he plans to sell in December of this year at a gain of $100,000; and Activity B, which he plans to keep indefinitely. Current and suspended losses associated with Activity B total $60,000, and Bill expects losses from the activity to be $40,000 next year. If Bill sells Activity A this year, the $100,000 gain can be offset by the current and suspended losses of $60,000 from Activity B, producing a net taxable gain of $40,000. However, if Bill delays the sale of Activity A until January of next year, the $100,000 gain will be fully offset by the $100,000 of losses generated by Activity B ($60,000 current and prior losses + $40,000 next year's loss). Consequently, by postponing the sale by one month, he could avoid recognizing $40,000 of gain that would otherwise result. ■

Taxpayers with passive losses should consider the level of their involvement in all other trades or businesses in which they have an interest. If they show that they do not materially participate in a profitable activity, the activity becomes a passive activity. Any income generated by the profitable business then could be sheltered by current and suspended passive losses. Family partnerships in which certain members do not materially participate would qualify. The silent partner in any general partnership engaged in a trade or business would also qualify.

EXAMPLE 57

Gail has an investment in a limited partnership that produces annual passive losses of approximately $25,000. She also owns a newly acquired interest in a convenience store where she works. Her share of the store's income is $35,000. If she works enough to be classified as a material participant, her $35,000 share of income is treated as active income. This results in $35,000 being subject to tax every year, while her $25,000 loss is suspended. However, if Gail reduces her involvement at the store so that she is not a material participant, the $35,000 of income receives passive treatment. Consequently, the $35,000 of income can be offset by the $25,000 passive loss, resulting in only $10,000 being subject to tax. Thus, by reducing her involvement, Gail ensures that the income from the profitable trade or business receives passive treatment and can then be used to absorb passive losses from other passive activities. ■

Because of the restrictive nature of the passive activity loss rules, it may be advantageous for a taxpayer to use a vacation home enough to convert it to a second residence. This would enable all of the qualified interest and real estate taxes to be deducted without limitation. However, this strategy would lead to the loss of other deductions, such as repairs, maintenance, and insurance. See Examples 24 and 27 and the related discussion in Chapter 6.

As this chapter has shown, the passive loss rules can have a dramatic effect on a taxpayer's ability to claim passive losses currently. As a result, it is important to keep accurate records of all sources of income and losses, particularly any suspended passive losses and credits and the activities to which they relate, so that their potential tax benefit will not be lost.

REFOCUS ON THE BIG PICTURE

The objective for most investors should be to maximize after-tax wealth from among investment alternatives. This requires an understanding of the relevant tax restrictions that apply to certain expenses and losses arising from various investment choices. The after-tax returns from the three alternatives the Reswicks are considering may be affected by the at-risk, passive activity, and investment interest limitations.

The high-growth, low-yield portfolio is expected to generate very little if any current dividend income (i.e., net investment income). Nonetheless, if the broker's prediction is correct, the market value of the securities will grow by approximately 10 percent a year. However, the annual $8,000 interest expense on the debt incurred to purchase the securities may not be deductible as investment interest due to the lack of net investment income. Unless investment income is generated from this or some other source, the interest will not be deductible until the securities are sold (see Example 52). To the extent the interest is deducted as investment interest, the gain on the portfolio's sale will not be subject to preferential capital gains rates (see Example 53). As a result, the net after-tax return will be impaired because of the investment interest limitation.

The net returns from the other two investment choices will be diminished by the at-risk and passive activity loss rules in addition to the investment interest limitation. The projected 10 percent return is apparently contingent on the investor being able to utilize the current tax losses as they arise. These benefits will be deferred because the at-risk and passive activity loss rules delay the timing of the deductions. For example, in the case of the orange grove investment, none of the passive losses are deductible until year 6 when the investment is expected to produce passive income (see Example 40). In the real estate rental venture, however, Jim and Trudy could deduct the $25,000 passive loss under the exception for rental real estate for the first four years (see Example 42); the at-risk rules would limit any additional losses in year 5 to the at-risk amount. Consequently, since the at-risk and passive loss rules limit the tax losses flowing to the Reswicks, the after-tax return will not be nearly as high as their broker predicts.

What If?

If the Reswicks decide that the investment in marketable securities is their best option, could they modify their plan so that they avoid the restriction imposed by the investment interest limitation? Jim and Trudy's net after-tax return would improve if the interest cost of financing their investment could be deducted as incurred. They could finance their investment by borrowing up to $100,000 against the equity in their home (see Chapter 10). The interest on the home equity loan would be fully deductible, and consequently the after-tax return from their investment would increase. Furthermore, any gain recognition would be deferred until the securities are sold, and the tax on the gain would be subject to the preferential capital gains rate.

INVESTOR LOSS LIMITATIONS CAN SIGNIFICANTLY AFFECT INVESTMENT RETURNS

KEY TERMS

DISCUSSION QUESTIONS

1. **LO.1** Congress has passed two major provisions to limit a taxpayer's ability to use tax shelters to reduce or defer Federal income tax. What are these provisions?

2. **LO.2** Toni invested $80,000 for a 35% interest in a partnership in which she is not a material participant. The partnership borrowed $150,000 from a bank on a recourse loan and used the proceeds to acquire a building. What is Toni's at-risk amount?

3. **LO.2** List some events that increase and decrease an investor's at-risk amount. What are some strategies that a taxpayer can employ to increase the at-risk amount in order to claim a higher deduction for losses?

4. **LO.2, 3** In the current year, Dick invested $16,000 in a cattle-feeding operation that used nonrecourse notes to purchase $120,000 of feed, which was fed to the cattle and expensed. If his share of the expense was $24,000, how much can Dick deduct this year?

5. **LO.3** Explain the meaning of the terms *active income, portfolio income,* and *passive income.*

6. **LO.3** Alberto owns an interest in an activity that produces a $75,000 loss during the year. Would he generally prefer to have the activity classified as active or passive? Discuss.

7. **LO.3** Kim owns an interest in an activity that produces $100,000 of income during the year. Would Kim prefer to have the activity classified as active or passive? Discuss.

8. **LO.3** Upon a taxable disposition of a passive activity, the taxpayer can utilize any suspended losses and credits related to that activity. Do you agree? Explain.

9. **LO.3** A passive activity that Lucile acquired several years ago has resulted in losses. How will these passive losses affect Lucile's taxable income when she disposes of the activity?

10. **LO.3** Discuss whether the passive loss rules apply to the following: individuals, closely held C corporations, S corporations, partnerships, and personal service corporations.

11. **LO.3** New-Tech Services, Inc., which provides consulting services to inventors, is owned by four engineers, all of whom work full-time for the corporation. The corporation has eight other full-time employees, all on the clerical staff. The corporation has invested in a passive activity that produces a $60,000 loss this year. Can New-Tech deduct the loss in the current year? Explain.

12. **LO.4** What factors are relevant in determining whether activities constitute an appropriate economic unit?

13. **LO.4** Discuss what constitutes a passive activity.

14. **LO.4** The Regulations prohibit grouping rental activities in certain circumstances. Discuss these rules.

15. **LO.5** What is the significance of the term *material participation*? Why is the extent of a taxpayer's participation in an activity important in determining whether a loss from the activity is deductible or nondeductible?

16. **LO.5** Why did the IRS adopt the more-than-500-hour standard for material participation?

17. **LO.5** Doug, a high school teacher, operates four separate businesses and participates less than 500 hours in each. If all four businesses incur losses during the year, are there any circumstances under which Doug may treat the losses as active?

18. **LO.5, 11** Keith, a physician, operates a separate business that he acquired nine years ago. If he participates 90 hours in the business and it incurs a loss of $20,000, under what circumstances can Keith claim an active loss?

19. **LO.2, 3, 5** Rita retired from public accounting after a long and successful career of 45 years. As part of her retirement package, she continues to share in the profits and losses of the firm, albeit at a lower rate than when she was working full-time. Because Rita wants to stay busy during her retirement years, she has invested and works in a local hardware business, operated as a partnership. Unfortunately, the business has recently gone through a slump and has not been generating profits. Identify relevant tax issues for Rita.

20. **LO.5** Some types of work are counted in applying the material participation standards, and some types are not counted. Discuss and give examples of each type.

21. **LO.5** Even though Sylvia is a full-time employee at a major software developer, she has never given up her love of pottery. For many years, she has spent evenings and weekends working to develop a profitable pottery business by making original pieces to sell to the general public. How should Sylvia treat the income or loss generated by her pottery venture? What are the tax issues?   **ISSUE ID**

22. **LO.5** Sean, a limited partner in Ivy Nursery, is informed that his portion of the entity's current loss is $18,000. As a limited partner, can Sean assume that his share of the partnership loss is a passive loss?

23. **LO.6** In general, the definition of passive activity includes rental activities. However, certain activities involving rentals of real and personal property are not *treated* as rental activities. Explain.

24. **LO.4, 5, 6** How is *passive activity* defined in the Code, and what aspects of the definition have been clarified by final or Temporary Regulations?

25. **LO.5, 6, 8** Laura owns an apartment building and a DVD rental business. She participates for more than 500 hours in the operations of each activity. Are the businesses active or passive?

26. **LO.8** Tami incurs a loss of $75,000 on a real estate rental activity during the current year. Under what circumstances can Tami treat the entire loss as nonpassive?

27. **LO.2, 3, 4, 5, 6, 7** In the current year, Doug and Debbie Lee, both successful attorneys, made a cash investment in a limited partnership interest in a California almond grove. In addition to the cash generated from the investors, the venture borrowed a substantial sum to purchase assets necessary for its operation. The Lees' investment adviser told them that their share of the tax loss in the first year alone would be in excess of their initial cash investment. This result would be followed by several more years of losses. They feel confident that their interest in the almond grove is a sound investment. Identify the tax issues facing the Lees.   **ISSUE ID**

28. **LO.4** Since his college days, Charles has developed an entrepreneurial streak. After working in his family's grocery business, he starts several ventures on his own. Even though Charles is independently wealthy, he is looking forward to working in each of the ventures. He plans to "drop in" on the businesses from time to time between personal trips to Europe and the Caribbean. As of the end of the year, he has established computer software stores in Dayton (Ohio), Austin, and Seattle; bagel bakeries in Albany, Athens (Georgia), and Tallahassee; and mountain bike and ski rental shops in small towns in Vermont, West Virginia, Colorado, and California. Identify the tax issues facing Charles.   **ISSUE ID**

29. **LO.5, 8** Nancy owns an interest in a hobby shop that has six full-time employees; during the year, she works 400 hours in the shop. Nancy also owns an apartment building with no employees in which she works 950 hours. Is either activity a passive activity? Explain.

30. **LO.8** Brad owns a small townhouse complex that generates a loss during the year. Under what circumstances can Brad deduct a loss from the rental activity, and what limitations apply?

31. **LO.5, 8** Under the passive loss rules, what are the differences between *material participation* and *active participation*?

32. **LO.8, 11** Robert owns rental property that generally produces positive taxable income and cash flow. This year, however, Robert's current loss is $5,000. Before considering the effect of the depreciation deduction, however, the property would have generated a $1,500 profit. Robert's AGI for the year is $170,000. He asks you about the treatment of his loss for the current year. Robert also mentions that he has been considering either selling the property (within the next five years) or exchanging it for other rental property. Identify the tax issues.   **ISSUE ID**

PROBLEMS

33. **LO.2** In the current year, Lionel invests $20,000 for an interest in a partnership engaged in the wholesale distribution of plumbing supplies. Lionel is a material participant, and his share of the partnership loss is $25,000. Discuss the tax treatment of Lionel's share of the loss, and compute his at-risk basis.

COMMUNICATIONS

34. **LO.2** In the current year, Bill Parker (54 Oak Drive, St. Paul, MN 55162) is considering making an investment of $60,000 in Best Choice Partnership. The prospectus provided by Bill's broker indicates that the partnership investment is not a passive activity and that Bill's share of the entity's loss in the current year will likely be $40,000, while his share of the partnership loss next year will probably be $25,000. Write a letter to Bill in which you indicate how the losses would be treated for tax purposes in the current and next years.

DECISION MAKING

35. **LO.2, 11** Heather wishes to invest $40,000 in a relatively safe venture and has discovered two alternatives that would produce the following reportable ordinary income and loss over the next three years:

Year	Alternative 1 Income (Loss)	Alternative 2 Income (Loss)
1	($ 24,000)	($48,000)
2	(24,000)	32,000
3	72,000	40,000

She is interested in the after-tax effects of these alternatives over a three-year horizon. Assume that Heather's investment portfolio produces sufficient passive income to offset any potential passive loss that may arise from these alternatives, that her cost of capital is 8% (the present value factors are 0.92593, 0.85734, and 0.79383), that she is in the 25% tax bracket, that each investment alternative possesses equal growth potential, and that each alternative exposes her to comparable financial risk. In addition, assume that in the loss years for each alternative, there is no cash flow from or to the investment (i.e., the loss is due to depreciation), while in those years when the income is positive, cash flows to Heather equal the amount of the income. Based on these facts, compute the present value of these two investment alternatives and determine which option Heather should choose.

36. **LO.1, 3** Hazel has investments in two nonrental passive activities: Activity A, acquired seven years ago and profitable until the current year, and Activity B, acquired this year. Currently, Hazel's shares of the activities' losses are $10,000 from Activity A and $6,000 from Activity B. What is the total of Hazel's suspended losses from these activities?

37. **LO.1, 3** In 2006, Gene acquired an interest in a partnership in which he is not a material participant. The partnership was profitable through 2009, and Gene's basis in this partnership interest at the beginning of 2010 was $60,000. Gene's share of the partnership loss was $45,000 in 2010, and his share of the partnership income is $25,000 in 2011. How much can Gene deduct for 2010 and 2011?

38. **LO.3** Ken, a CPA, earns $200,000 from his accounting practice in the current year. He receives $20,000 in dividends and interest during the year. In addition, he incurs a loss of $50,000 from an investment in a passive activity acquired three years ago. What is Ken's net income for the current year after considering the passive investment?

DECISION MAKING

39. **LO.3, 11** Emily has $100,000 that she wishes to invest and is considering the following two options:

- Option A: Investment in Redbird Mutual Fund, which is expected to produce interest income of $8,000 per year.
- Option B: Investment in Cardinal Limited Partnership (buys, sells, and operates wine vineyards). Emily's share of the partnership's ordinary income and loss over the next three years would be:

Year	Income (Loss)
1	($ 8,000)
2	(2,000)
3	34,000

Emily is interested in the after-tax effects of these alternatives over a three-year horizon. Assume that Emily's investment portfolio produces ample passive income to offset any passive losses that may be generated. Her cost of capital is 8% (the present value factors are 0.92593, 0.85734, and 0.79383), and she is in the 28% tax bracket. The two investment alternatives possess equal growth potential and comparable financial risk. Based on these facts, compute the present value of these two investment alternatives and determine which option Emily should choose.

40. **LO.3** Ray acquired an activity several years ago, and in the current year, it generates a loss of $50,000. Ray has AGI of $140,000 before considering the loss from the activity. If the activity is a bakery and Ray is not a material participant, what is his AGI?

41. **LO.3, 11** Larry owns two passive investments, Activity A and Activity B. He plans to dispose of Activity A, either in the current year or next year. Celene has offered to buy Activity A this year for an amount that would produce a taxable passive gain to Larry of $100,000. However, if the sale, for whatever reason, is not made to Celene, Larry feels that he could find a buyer who would pay about $6,000 less than Celene. Passive losses and gains generated (and expected to be generated) by Activity B follow:

DECISION MAKING

Two years ago	($ 35,000)
Last year	(35,000)
This year	(5,000)
Next year	(19,000)
Future years	Minimal profits

All of Activity B's losses are suspended. Should Larry close the sale of Activity A with Celene this year, or should he wait until next year and sell to another buyer? Larry is in the 28% tax bracket.

42. **LO.3** Sarah has investments in four passive activity partnerships purchased several years ago. Last year, the income and losses were as follows:

Activity	Income (Loss)
A	$ 10,000
B	(5,000)
C	(25,000)
D	(20,000)

In the current year, she sold her interest in Activity D for a $19,000 gain. Activity D, which had been profitable until last year, had a current loss of $1,000. How will the sale of Activity D affect Sarah's taxable income in the current year?

43. **LO.3** Leon sells his interest in a passive activity for $100,000. Determine the tax effect of the sale based on each of the following independent facts:
   a. Adjusted basis in this investment is $35,000. Losses from prior years that were not deductible due to the passive loss restrictions total $40,000.
   b. Adjusted basis in this investment is $75,000. Losses from prior years that were not deductible due to the passive loss restrictions total $40,000.
   c. Adjusted basis in this investment is $75,000. Losses from prior years that were not deductible due to the passive loss restrictions total $40,000. In addition, suspended credits total $10,000.

44. **LO.3** In the current year, Blue, Inc., earns $300,000 from operations and receives $28,000 in dividends and interest on various portfolio investments. Blue also pays $150,000 to acquire a 20% interest in a passive activity that produces a $150,000 loss.
   a. Assuming Blue is a personal service corporation, how will these transactions affect its taxable income?
   b. Same as (a), except that Blue is closely held but not a personal service corporation.

45. **LO.3** Orange, Inc., earns $250,000 from operations in the current year. Orange also receives $18,000 in dividends and interest on various portfolio investments. During the year, Orange pays $150,000 to acquire a 30% interest in a passive activity that produces a $200,000 loss. How will these facts affect Orange's taxable income, assuming the corporation is:

a.   A personal service corporation?

b.   A closely held (non-personal service) C corporation?

DECISION MAKING

COMMUNICATIONS

46. **LO.3, 4, 5, 9, 11** Greg Horne (431 Maple Avenue, Cincinnati, OH 45229), a syndicated radio talk show host, earns an annual salary of $400,000. He works approximately 30 hours per week in this job, which leaves him time to participate in several businesses newly acquired in 2011. He owns a movie theater and a drugstore in Cincinnati, a movie theater and a drugstore in Indianapolis, and a drugstore in Louisville. A preliminary analysis on December 1, 2011, shows the following projected income and losses and time spent for these various businesses.

	Income (Loss)
Cincinnati movie theater (95 hours)	$ 56,000
Cincinnati drugstore (140 hours)	(89,000)
Indianapolis movie theater (90 hours)	34,000
Indianapolis drugstore (170 hours)	(41,000)
Louisville drugstore (180 hours)	(15,000)

Greg has full-time employees in each of the five businesses. Write a letter to Greg suggesting a grouping method and other strategies that will provide the greatest tax advantage. As Greg is not knowledgeable about tax law, provide a nontechnical explanation.

DECISION MAKING

COMMUNICATIONS

47. **LO.2, 3, 7, 11** Kristin Graf (123 Baskerville Mill Road, Jamison, PA 18929) is trying to decide how to invest a $10,000 inheritance. One option is to make an additional investment in Rocky Road Excursions in which she has an at-risk basis of $0, suspended losses under the at-risk rules of $7,000, and suspended passive losses of $1,000. If Kristin makes this investment, her share of the expected profits this year would be $8,000. If her investment stays the same, her share of profits from Rocky Road Excursions would be $1,000. Another option is to invest $10,000 as a limited partner in the Ragged Mountain Winery; this investment would produce passive income of $9,000. Write a letter to Kristin to review the tax consequences of each alternative. Kristin is in the 28% tax bracket.

DECISION MAKING

48. **LO.2, 3, 7, 11** The end of the year is approaching, and Maxine has begun to focus on ways of minimizing her income tax liability. Several years ago, she purchased an investment in Teal Limited Partnership, which is subject to both the at-risk and the passive activity loss rules. (Last year, Maxine sold a different investment that was subject to these rules but produced passive income.) She believes that her investment in Teal has good long-term economic prospects. However, it has been generating tax losses for several years in a row. In fact, when she was discussing last year's income tax return with her tax accountant, he said that unless "things change" with respect to her investments, she would not be able to deduct losses this year.

a.   What was the accountant referring to in his comment?

b.   You learn that Maxine's current at-risk basis in her investment is $1,000 and her share of the current loss is expected to be $13,000. Based on these facts, how will her loss be treated?

c.   After reviewing her situation, Maxine's financial adviser suggests that she invest at least an additional $12,000 in Teal in order to ensure a full loss deduction in the current year. How do you react to his suggestion?

d.   What would you suggest Maxine consider as she attempts to maximize her current-year deductible loss?

49. **LO.2, 3, 7** A number of years ago, Lee acquired a 20% interest in the BlueSky Partnership for $60,000. The partnership was profitable through 2010, and Lee's amount at risk in the partnership interest was $120,000 at the beginning of 2011. BlueSky incurred a loss of $400,000 in 2011 and reported income of $200,000 in 2012. Assuming Lee is not a material participant, how much of his loss from BlueSky Partnership is deductible in 2011 and 2012? Consider both the at-risk and the passive loss rules.

50. **LO.2, 3, 5, 7** Last year, Fran invested $40,000 for an interest in a partnership in which she is a material participant. Her share of the partnership loss for last year was $50,000. In the current year, Fran's share of the partnership's income is $30,000. What is the effect on her taxable income for the current year?

51. **LO.2, 3, 5, 7** Jonathan, a physician, earns $200,000 from his practice. He also receives $18,000 in dividends and interest on various portfolio investments. During the year, he pays $45,000 to acquire a 20% interest in a partnership that produces a $300,000 loss. Compute Jonathan's AGI, assuming that:
    a.   He does not participate in the operations of the partnership.
    b.   He is a material participant in the operations of the partnership.

52. **LO.2, 3, 7** Five years ago, Gerald invested $150,000 in a passive activity, his sole investment venture. On January 1, 2010, his amount at risk in the activity was $30,000. His shares of the income and losses were as follows:

Year	Income (Loss)
2010	($ 40,000)
2011	(30,000)
2012	50,000

How much can Gerald deduct in 2010 and 2011? What is his taxable income from the activity in 2012? Consider the at-risk rules as well as the passive loss rules.

53. **LO.3, 8** Beth acquired an activity four years ago. The loss from the activity is $35,000 in the current year. She has AGI of $120,000 before considering the loss from the activity. The activity is an apartment building, and Beth is an active participant. What is her AGI after considering the activity?

54. **LO.3, 8** Several years ago, Rachel acquired an apartment building that currently generates a loss of $35,000. She has AGI of $120,000 before considering the loss. If Rachel is not an active participant in the activity, what is the effect of the loss on her AGI?

55. **LO.3, 8, 11** Bonnie and Adam are married with no dependents and live in New Hampshire (not a community property state). Since Adam has large medical expenses, they seek your advice about filing separately to save taxes. Their income and expenses for 2011 are as follows:

DECISION MAKING

Bonnie's salary	$ 44,000
Adam's salary	30,000
Interest income (joint)	1,500
Rental loss from actively managed rental property	(23,000)
Adam's unreimbursed medical expenses	9,500
All other itemized deductions:*	
Bonnie	10,000
Adam	3,500

*None subject to limitations

Determine whether Bonnie and Adam should file jointly or separately for 2011.

56. **LO.3, 8, 11** Mary and Charles have owned a beach cottage on the New Jersey shore for several years and have always used it as a family retreat. When they acquired the property, they had no intentions of renting it. Because family circumstances have changed, they are considering using the cottage for only two weeks a year and renting it for the remainder of the year. Their AGI approximates $80,000 per year, and they are in the 30% tax bracket (combined Federal and state). Interest and real estate taxes total $8,000 per year and are expected to continue at this level in the foreseeable future. If Mary and Charles rent the property, their *incremental* revenue and expenses are projected to be:

DECISION MAKING

Rent income	$ 20,000
Rental commissions	(3,000)
Maintenance expenses	(8,000)
Depreciation expense	(10,000)

If the cottage is converted to rental property, they plan to be actively involved in key rental and maintenance decisions. Given the tax effects of converting the property to rental use, would the cash flow from renting the property be enough to meet the $12,000 annual mortgage payment?

57. **LO.3, 8** During the current year, Gene, a CPA, performs services as follows: 1,800 hours in his tax practice and 50 hours in an apartment leasing operation in which he has a 15% interest. Because of his oversight duties, Gene is considered to be an active participant. He expects that his share of the loss realized from the apartment leasing operation will be $30,000 while his tax practice will show profit of approximately $80,000. Gene is single and has no other income. Discuss the character of the income and losses generated by these activities.

58. **LO.3, 8** Ida, who has AGI of $80,000 before considering rental activities, is active in three separate real estate rental activities and is in the 28% tax bracket. She has $12,000 of losses from Activity A, $18,000 of losses from Activity B, and income of $10,000 from Activity C. She also has $2,100 of tax credits from Activity A. Calculate her deductions and credits allowed and the suspended losses and credits.

59. **LO.8** Ella has $105,000 of losses from a real estate rental activity in which she actively participates. She has other rental income of $25,000 and other passive income of $32,000. How much rental loss can Ella deduct against active and portfolio income (ignoring the at-risk rules)? Does she have any suspended losses to carry over?

60. **LO.9** Faye dies owning an interest in a passive activity property with an adjusted basis of $240,000, suspended losses of $42,000, and a fair market value of $270,000. What, if any, can be deducted on her final income tax return?

61. **LO.9** In 2010, Nina gave her son a passive activity (adjusted basis of $100,000, fair market value of $180,000, and suspended losses of $25,000). In 2011, the son realizes income of $12,000 from the passive activity. What are the tax effects to Nina and her son in 2010 and 2011?

62. **LO.9** Tonya sells a passive activity in the current year for $150,000. Her adjusted basis in the activity is $50,000, and she uses the installment method of reporting the gain. The activity has suspended losses of $12,000. Tonya receives $60,000 in the year of sale. What is her gain? How much of the suspended losses can she deduct?

DECISION MAKING

COMMUNICATIONS

63. **LO.10, 11** In 2011, Rachel Tweardy incurs $29,250 of interest expense related to her investments. Her investment income includes $7,000 of interest, $5,500 of qualified dividends, and a $12,750 net capital gain on the sale of securities. Rachel asks you to compute the amount of her deduction for investment interest, taking into consideration any options she might have. In addition, she wants your suggestions as to any tax planning alternatives that are available. Write a letter to her that contains your advice. Rachel lives at 11934 Briarpatch Drive, Midlothian, VA 23113.

64. **LO.10** Helen borrowed $100,000 to acquire a parcel of land to be held for investment purposes. During 2011, she paid interest of $11,000 on the loan. She had AGI of $75,000 for the year. Other items related to Helen's investments include the following:

Investment income	$10,000
Long-term capital gain on sale of stock	7,500
Investment counsel fees	2,000

Helen is unmarried and elects to itemize her deductions. She has no miscellaneous itemized deductions other than the investment counsel fees.
a. Determine Helen's investment interest deduction for 2011.
b. Discuss the treatment of the portion of Helen's investment interest that is disallowed in 2011.

RESEARCH PROBLEMS

THOMSON REUTERS
Checkpoint® Student Edition

Note: Solutions to Research Problems can be prepared by using the **Checkpoint® Student Edition** online research product, which is available to accompany this text. It is also possible to prepare solutions to the Research Problems by using tax research materials found in a standard tax library.

Research Problem 1. George and Judy Cash own a 30-foot yacht that is moored at Oregon Inlet on the Outer Banks of North Carolina. The yacht is offered for rent to tourists during March through November every year. George and Judy live too far away to be involved in the yacht's routine operation and maintenance. They are, however, able to perform certain periodic tasks, such as cleaning and winterizing it. Routine daily management, operating, and chartering responsibilities have been contracted to "Captain Mac." George and Judy are able to document spending 120 hours on the yacht chartering activities during the year. Determine how any losses resulting from the activity are treated under the passive activity loss rules.

Research Problem 2. Lane Mitchell (77 Lakeview Drive, Salt Lake City, UT 84109) is a married individual who files a separate return for the taxable year. He is employed full-time as an accountant and also owns an interest in a minor league baseball team. He does no work in connection with the baseball activity and anticipates that it will produce a loss. He pays his wife to work as an office receptionist in connection with the activity. Her work requires an average of 20 hours a week. Write a letter to Lane and explain whether he will be allowed to deduct his share of the loss from the activity.

Research Problem 3. David Drayer (2632 Holkham Drive, Lewisburg, PA 17837) is the lead partner in a local accounting firm whose practice consists of tax consulting and compliance. The firm also serves clients by providing write-up and payroll processing services. As his firm has grown, David has developed various ways to build its business.

David and his wife, Judy, created DJ Partnership to purchase an office building where David moved his practice. Because the building is larger than what the practice currently needs, space is rented to other tax practitioners. In addition to providing office space, the partnership offers professional and administrative services on an exclusive basis to the tenants. These services include secretarial support, telephone answering service, tax professionals available for special projects, access to a tax research library, computer hardware technology, and miscellaneous administrative support. DJ Partnership considers its primary activity to be providing professional and administrative services to its tenants rather than being a lessor.

Because of the attractiveness of the services offered to its tenants, the building is fully leased. In the first year, Judy works full-time at the partnership, and David commits about 550 hours to its operations. For the first year, the partnership incurs a tax loss of $60,000. Without considering the impact of the loss, David and Judy's AGI is $175,000. Write a letter to David in which you provide advice on the deductibility of the $60,000 loss for Federal income tax purposes. Because David is a professional, feel free to make use of technical language in your letter.

Partial list of research aids:
Reg. § 1.469–1T(e)(3)(ii).

Research Problem 4. Ida Ross has decided to purchase a new home in a retirement community for $400,000. She has $50,000 in cash for the down payment, but needs to borrow the remaining $350,000 to finance the purchase. Her financial adviser, Marc, suggests that rather than seeking a conventional mortgage, she should borrow the funds from State Bank using her portfolio of appreciated securities as collateral. Selling the securities to generate $350,000 in cash would lead to a substantial tax on the capital gain recognized. Therefore, a better strategy would be to borrow against her securities and then claim a deduction for the interest paid on the loan. How do you react to the financial adviser's strategy?

Partial list of research aids:
Temp.Reg. § 1.163–8T(c).

Use the tax resources of the Internet to address the following questions. Do not restrict your search to the Web, but include a review of newsgroups and general reference materials, practitioner sites and resources, primary sources of the tax law, chat rooms and discussion groups, and other opportunities.

INTERNET *activity*

Research Problem 5. Download and print a copy of Form 6198 and its instructions. Use these materials to complete the requirements of Problem 33.

Research Problem 6. Scan the materials offered in several newsgroups frequented by tax advisers and consultants. In what context are "tax shelters" still discussed by these professionals? Do these advisers and consultants adequately take into account the rules of §§ 465 and 469?

Special Tax Computation Methods, Payment Procedures, and Tax Credits

Part 4 presents several topics that relate to the theme of tax liability determination. The taxpayer must calculate the tax liability in accordance with the basic tax formula and also in accordance with the tax formula for the alternative minimum tax (AMT). The basic tax formula was presented in Part 1, and the AMT formula is covered in Part 4. Tax credits reduce the amount of the calculated tax liability. The specific procedures for the timing of the payment of the tax liability are also discussed.

Alternative Minimum Tax

LEARNING OBJECTIVES

After completing Chapter 12, you should be able to:

LO.1
Explain the rationale for the alternative minimum tax (AMT).

LO.2
Understand the formula for computing the AMT for individuals.

LO.3
Identify the adjustments made in calculating the AMT.

LO.4
Identify the tax preferences that are included in calculating the AMT.

LO.5
Apply the formula for computing the AMT and illustrate Form 6251.

LO.6
Describe the role of the AMT credit in the alternative minimum tax structure.

LO.7
Understand the basic features of the corporate AMT.

LO.8
Identify tax planning opportunities to minimize the AMT.

OUTLINE

For the latest in changes to tax legislation, visit **www.cengage.com/taxation/swft.**

FRAMEWORK 1040:

Tax Formula for Individuals

This chapter covers the boldfaced portions of the Tax Formula for Individuals that was introduced in Figure 3.1 on p. 3-3. Below those portions are the sections of Form 1040 where the results are reported.

Income (broadly conceived)..	\$xx,xxx
Less: Exclusions	(x,xxx)
Gross Income	\$xx,xxx
Less: Deductions for adjusted gross income	(x,xxx)
Adjusted gross income..	\$xx,xxx
Less: The greater of total itemized deductions *or* the standard deduction	(x,xxx)
Personal and dependency exemptions	(x,xxx)
Taxable income	**\$xx,xxx**
Tax on taxable income (see Tax Tables or Tax Rate Schedules).........................	\$ x,xxx
Less: Tax credits (including income taxes withheld and prepaid)........................	(xxx)
Tax due (or refund)...	**\$ xxx**

FORM 1040 (p. 2)

45	**Alternative minimum tax** (see instructions). Attach Form 6251	

THE BIG PICTURE   Tax Solutions for the Real World

THE PRESENCE OR ABSENCE OF THE AMT

Bob and Carol are unmarried individuals who have been engaged for four months. They work for the same employer and earn identical compensation. They have the same amount of gross income, including the same amount of investment income, which consists solely of interest income; they have similar investments in tax-exempt bonds that produce identical amounts of interest income. They also have the same amount of deductions.

Bob's tax return is prepared by Adam, and Carol's tax return is prepared by Eve. While discussing their tax liability one day at lunch, Carol is dismayed to learn that she paid $15,000 more in Federal income taxes than Bob did for the tax year. Carol meets with Eve that evening. Eve reviews Carol's tax return and assures her that her tax liability was properly calculated.

The above events raise a number of interesting questions for Bob and Carol that can be answered after completing this chapter. Why didn't Bob and Carol have the same tax liability? Were both tax returns properly prepared? Should Carol consider replacing her tax return preparer Eve with Adam? Is it possible and/or desirable for Carol to file an amended return? Should Bob do anything? **Read the chapter and formulate your response.**

Τ he tax law contains many incentives that are intended to influence the economic and social behavior of taxpayers (refer to Chapter 1). Some taxpayers have been able to take advantage of enough of these incentives to avoid or minimize any liability for Federal income tax. Although these taxpayers were reducing taxes legally, Congress became concerned about the inequity that results when taxpayers with substantial economic incomes can avoid paying any income tax. Such inequity undermines respect for the entire tax system.[1] To attempt to alleviate this inequity, the **alternative minimum tax (AMT)** was enacted as a backup to the regular income tax.

The individual AMT is discussed in the first part of this chapter. The corporate AMT is similar to the individual AMT, but differs in several important ways. Details of the corporate AMT are presented in the last part of the chapter.

> **L0.1**
>
> Explain the rationale for the alternative minimum tax (AMT).

12.1 INDIVIDUAL ALTERNATIVE MINIMUM TAX

AMT FORMULA FOR ALTERNATIVE MINIMUM TAXABLE INCOME (AMTI)

The AMT is separate from, but parallel to, the regular income tax system.[2] Most income and expense items are treated the same way for both regular income tax and AMT purposes. For example, a taxpayer's salary is included in computing taxable income and is also included in alternative minimum taxable income (AMTI). Alimony paid is allowed as a deduction *for* AGI for both regular income tax and AMT purposes. Certain itemized deductions, such as charitable contributions and gambling losses, are allowed for both regular income tax and AMT purposes.

On the other hand, some income and expense items are treated differently for regular income tax and AMT purposes. For example, interest income on bonds issued by state, county, or local governments is *excluded* in computing taxable income. However, interest on such bonds may be *included* in computing AMTI if the bonds are private activity bonds. The deduction for personal and dependency exemptions is *allowed* for regular income tax purposes, but is *disallowed* for AMT purposes.

In other cases, certain items are considered in both the regular income tax and AMT computations, but the amounts are different. For example, the completed contract method can be used to report income from some long-term contracts for regular income tax purposes, but the percentage of completion method is required for AMT purposes. Thus, the amount of income included in taxable income will differ from the amount included in AMTI. Depreciation is allowed as a deduction for both regular income tax and AMT purposes, but the *amount* of the regular income tax deduction may be different from the amount of the AMT deduction. Medical expenses are deductible in calculating both taxable income and AMTI, but the floor on the deduction is different.

The parallel but separate nature of the AMT means that AMTI will differ from taxable income. It is possible to compute AMTI by direct application of the AMT provisions, using the following formula:

> Gross income computed by applying the AMT rules
> **Minus:** Deductions computed by applying the AMT rules
> **Equals:** AMTI before tax preferences
> **Plus:** Tax preferences
> **Equals:** Alternative minimum taxable income

> **L0.2**
>
> Understand the formula for computing the AMT for individuals.

---

[1] *General Explanation of the Tax Reform Act of 1986 ("Blue Book")*, prepared by The Staff of the Joint Committee on Taxation, May 4, 1987, H.R. 3838, 99th Cong., pp. 432–433.

[2] § 55.

FIGURE 12.1	Alternative Minimum Taxable Income (AMTI) Formula

Taxable income
Plus: Positive AMT adjustments
Minus: Negative AMT adjustments
Equals: Taxable income after AMT adjustments
Plus: Tax preferences
Equals: Alternative minimum taxable income

While the direct approach for computing AMTI appears quite logical, both the tax law and the tax forms provide a very different approach. Both of these use taxable income (for Form 6251, taxable income *before* the deduction for personal exemptions and dependency deductions) as the starting point for computing AMTI, as shown in Figure 12.1. This indirect approach for computing AMTI is analogous to the indirect approach used in calculating a net operating loss.

The purpose of the AMT formula is to *reconcile* taxable income to AMTI. This reconciliation is similar to a bank reconciliation, which reconciles a checkbook balance to a bank balance by considering differences between the depositor's records and the bank's records. The reconciliation of taxable income to AMTI is accomplished by entering reconciling items to account for differences between regular income tax provisions and AMT provisions. These reconciling items are referred to as **AMT adjustments** or **tax preferences**. *Adjustments* can be either positive or negative, as shown in the formula in Figure 12.1. Tax preferences are always positive.

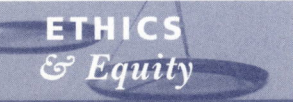

ETHICS & Equity

IMPACT OF THE AMT ON ACCELERATING EXPENSES

Maurice, a single, cash method taxpayer, projects his taxable income for 2011 to be about $300,000. For AMT purposes, he has positive adjustments and tax preferences of $200,000. He anticipates that his taxable income and positive adjustments and preferences will be about the same for 2012. He is evaluating several proposed transactions that could affect his 2011 tax liability.

One proposal involves an office building for which he is currently negotiating a lease. The lease has a starting date of July 1, 2011, provides for annual rent of $24,000, and carries an 18-month prepayment clause. Though Maurice favors a five-year lease, his tax adviser has suggested an 18-month period with an option to renew for 42 months. The adviser points out the tax advantage of being able to deduct the

$36,000 of rent at the inception of the lease. The projected tax liability under each option would be as follows:

	18-Month Lease	5-Year Lease
Regular income tax liability	$ 72,017	$ 79,937
AMT	54,403	53,203
Total	$126,420	$133,140

After comparing these results, Maurice takes his adviser's suggestion.

Is it appropriate for Maurice to avoid taxes in this manner? Is it wise?

Adjustments

Most adjustments relate to *timing differences* that arise because of *separate* regular income tax and AMT treatments. Adjustments that are caused by timing differences will eventually *reverse;* that is, positive adjustments will be offset by negative adjustments in the future, and vice versa.[3]

---

[3]§ 56.

For example, **circulation expenditures** can give rise to a timing difference that requires an AMT adjustment. For regular income tax purposes, circulation expenditures can be deducted in the year incurred. For AMT purposes, however, circulation expenditures must be deducted over a three-year period. This difference in treatment will be used to illustrate the role of adjustments in the formula for computing AMTI.

EXAMPLE 1

Bob had taxable income of $100,000 in 2011. In computing taxable income, he deducted $30,000 of circulation expenditures incurred in 2011. Bob's allowable deduction for AMT purposes was only $10,000. Therefore, an AMT adjustment was required in 2011 as follows:

Taxable income		$100,000
+ AMT adjustment:		
Circulation expenditures deducted for regular income tax purposes	$ 30,000	
Circulation expenditures allowed for AMT purposes	(10,000)	
Positive adjustment		20,000
= AMTI before tax preferences		$120,000
+ Tax preferences		–0–
AMTI		$120,000

Analysis of this computation shows that the allowable AMT deduction is $20,000 less than the allowable regular income tax deduction. Therefore, AMTI is $20,000 greater than taxable income. This is accomplished by entering a positive AMT adjustment of $20,000. ■

EXAMPLE 2

Assume that Bob from Example 1 has taxable income of $95,000 in 2012. He is allowed to deduct $10,000 of circulation expenditures for AMT purposes, but is not allowed a deduction for regular income tax purposes because all $30,000 was deducted in 2011. Therefore, a *negative* AMT adjustment is required.

Taxable income		$ 95,000
– AMT adjustment:		
Circulation expenditures deducted for regular income tax purposes	$ –0–	
Circulation expenditures allowed for AMT purposes	(10,000)	
Negative adjustment		(10,000)
= AMTI before tax preferences		$ 85,000
+ Tax preferences		–0–
AMTI		$ 85,000

Analysis of this computation shows that the allowable AMT deduction is $10,000 more than the allowable regular income tax deduction. Therefore, AMTI is $10,000 less than taxable income. This is accomplished by entering a negative AMT adjustment of $10,000. ■

As noted previously, timing differences eventually reverse. Therefore, total positive adjustments will be offset by total negative adjustments with respect to a particular item.

EXAMPLE 3

Refer to Examples 1 and 2. The difference in regular income tax and AMT treatments of circulation expenditures will result in AMT adjustments over a three-year period.

Year	Regular Income Tax Deduction	AMT Deduction	AMT Adjustment
2011	$30,000	$10,000	+$20,000
2012	–0–	10,000	–10,000
2013	–0–	10,000	–10,000
Total	$30,000	$30,000	$ –0–

TAX *in* the *NEWS*

WILL THE AMT BE FIXED?

At the present time, many taxpayers are wondering whether the AMT will continue to apply and, if so, whether Congress will do anything to prevent its reach from expanding. Currently, the AMT affects about 4 million taxpayers, but that number could soon grow to potentially as many as 26 million taxpayers, including many middle-income taxpayers.

Certainly, the AMT seems unlikely to go away. Senator Charles Grassley of Iowa, the ranking Republican on the Senate Finance Committee, observes that "Congress has done nothing to curb the AMT's growth." Grassley says that although most members of Congress "agree that something

needs to be done quickly, the discussion doesn't go any further than that."

A major reason that the AMT appears to be here to stay is that the AMT has become an important source of government revenue. In the recent past and in the current year, Congress has applied a "patch," increasing the AMT exemption amounts for individual taxpayers, to prevent the AMT from applying to more than approximately 4 million taxpayers. It is likely that Congress will continue to apply such patches.

Source: Adapted from Tom Herman, "Ask Dow Jones," *Tampa Tribune,* June 27, 2010, p. B4.

As the last column illustrates, if positive and negative AMT adjustments with respect to a particular item are caused by a timing difference, they will eventually net to zero. ∎

The adjustments for circulation expenditures and other items are discussed in detail under AMT Adjustments.

Although most adjustments relate to timing differences, there are exceptions. See the subsequent discussion of such items under Itemized Deductions. Adjustments that do not relate to timing differences result in a permanent difference between taxable income and AMTI.

Tax Preferences

Some deductions and exclusions allowed to taxpayers for regular income tax purposes provide extraordinary tax savings. Congress has chosen to single out these items, which are referred to as tax preferences.[4] The AMT is designed to take back all or part of the tax benefits derived through the use of preferences in the computation of taxable income for regular income tax purposes. This is why taxable income, which is the starting point in computing AMTI, is increased by tax preference items. The effect of adding these preference items is to disallow for *AMT purposes* those preferences that were allowed in the regular income tax computation. Tax preferences include the following items, which are discussed in detail under AMT Preferences:

- Percentage depletion in excess of the property's adjusted basis.
- Excess intangible drilling costs reduced by 65 percent of the net income from oil, gas, and geothermal properties.
- Interest on certain private activity bonds.
- Excess of accelerated over straight-line depreciation on real property placed in service before 1987.
- Excess of accelerated over straight-line depreciation on *leased* personal property placed in service before 1987.
- Excess of amortization allowance over depreciation on pre-1987 certified pollution control facilities.
- Seven percent of the exclusion from gross income associated with gains on the sale of certain small business stock under § 1202.

[4]§ 57.

FIGURE 12.2	Alternative Minimum Tax Formula for Individuals

Regular taxable income
Plus or minus: Adjustments
Equals: Taxable income after AMT adjustments
Plus: Tax preferences
Equals: Alternative minimum taxable income
Minus: Exemption
Equals: Alternative minimum tax base
Times: 26% or 28% rate
Equals: Tentative minimum tax before foreign tax credit
Minus: Alternative minimum tax foreign tax credit
Equals: Tentative minimum tax
Minus: Regular tax liability*
Equals: Alternative minimum tax (if amount is positive)

*This is the regular tax liability for the year reduced by any allowable foreign tax credit.

AMT FORMULA: OTHER COMPONENTS

To convert AMTI to AMT, other formula components including the exemption, rates, credit, and regular tax liability must be considered. The impact of each of these components is depicted in the AMT formula in Figure 12.2.

The relationship between the regular tax liability and the tentative AMT is key to the AMT formula. If the regular tax liability exceeds tentative AMT, then the AMT is zero. If the tentative AMT exceeds the regular tax liability, the amount of the excess is the AMT. In essence, the taxpayer will pay whichever tax liability is greater—that calculated using the regular income tax rules or that calculated using the AMT rules. However, both the tax law and Form 6251 adopt this excess approach with the taxpayer paying the regular tax liability plus any AMT.

EXAMPLE 4

Anna, an unmarried individual, has regular taxable income of $100,000. She has positive adjustments of $40,000 and tax preferences of $25,000. Calculate her AMT for 2011. Anna's regular tax liability is $21,617. Her AMT is calculated as follows:

Taxable income (TI)	$100,000
Plus: Adjustments	40,000
Equals: TI after AMT adjustments	$140,000
Plus: Tax preferences	25,000
Equals: AMTI	$165,000
Minus: AMT exemption ($48,450 − $13,125)	(35,325)*
Equals: AMT base	$129,675
Times: AMT rate	× 26%
Equals: Tentative AMT	$ 33,716
Minus: Regular tax liability	(21,617)
Equals: AMT	$ 12,099

*Discussed under Exemption Amount.

Anna will pay the IRS a total of $33,716, consisting of her regular tax liability of $21,617 plus her AMT of $12,099. ∎

Exemption Amount

The exemption amount can be thought of as a materiality provision. As such, it enables a taxpayer with a small amount of positive adjustments and tax preferences to avoid being subject to the burden of the AMT.

The *initial* exemption amount in 2011 is $74,450 for married taxpayers filing joint returns, $48,450 for single taxpayers, and $37,225 for married taxpayers filing separate returns.[5] However, the exemption is *phased out* at a rate of 25 cents on the dollar when AMTI exceeds these levels:

- $112,500 for single taxpayers.
- $150,000 for married taxpayers filing jointly.
- $75,000 for married taxpayers filing separately.

The phaseout of the exemption amount is an application of the wherewithal to pay concept. As the income level increases, so does the taxpayer's ability to pay income taxes.

The following example explains the calculation of the phaseout of the AMT exemption.

EXAMPLE 5

Hugh, who is single, has AMTI of $192,500 for the year. His $48,450 initial exemption amount is reduced by $20,000 [($192,500 − $112,500) × 25% phaseout rate]. Hugh's AMT exemption is $28,450 ($48,450 exemption − $20,000 reduction). ∎

The following table shows the beginning and end of the AMT exemption phaseout range for each filing status.

| | | Phaseout | |
Status	Exemption	Begins at	Ends at
Married, joint	$74,450*	$150,000	$447,800
Single or head of household	48,450*	112,500	306,300
Married, separate	37,225*	75,000	223,900

*See footnote 5.

AMT Rate Schedule

A graduated, two-tier AMT rate schedule applies to noncorporate taxpayers. A 26 percent rate applies to the first $175,000 of the AMT base ($87,500 for married, filing separately), and a 28 percent rate applies to the AMT base in excess of $175,000 ($87,500 for married, filing separately).[6] Any net capital gain and qualified dividend income included in the AMT base are taxed at the favorable alternative tax rates for capital gains (15 percent or 0 percent) rather than at the AMT statutory rates. See the discussion of the alternative tax on capital gains in Chapter 16.

Regular Tax Liability

The AMT is equal to the tentative minimum tax minus the *regular tax liability*. In most cases, the regular tax liability is equal to the amount of tax from the Tax Table or Tax Rate Schedules decreased by any foreign tax credit allowable for regular income tax purposes. The foreign tax credit is allowed as a reduction of the tentative minimum tax.

In an AMT year, the taxpayer's total tax liability is equal to the tentative minimum tax (refer to Figure 12.2). The tentative minimum tax consists of two potential components: the regular tax liability and the AMT. The disallowance of credits does not affect a taxpayer's total liability in an AMT year. However, it does decrease the amount of the AMT and, as a consequence, reduces the minimum tax credit (discussed subsequently) available to be carried forward.

It is also possible that taxpayers who have adjustments and preferences but *do not pay* AMT will lose the benefit of some or all of their nonrefundable credits. This

[5]§ 55(d). For tax years beginning in 2012 and thereafter, the exemption amount is scheduled to be reduced to $45,000 for married taxpayers filing jointly, $33,750 for single or head-of-household taxpayers, and $22,500 for married taxpayers filing separately. However, the general consensus is that

Congress is highly likely to extend the increased exemption amounts for 2012. For 2010, the exemption amounts are $72,450, $47,450, and $36,225 respectively.

[6]§ 55(b)(1).

result occurs because a taxpayer may claim many nonrefundable credits only to the extent that his or her regular tax liability exceeds the tentative minimum tax.

EXAMPLE 6

Vern has total nonrefundable *business* credits of $10,000, regular tax liability of $33,000, and tentative minimum tax of $25,000. He can claim only $8,000 of the nonrefundable credits in the current year ($33,000 − $8,000 = $25,000). The disallowed $2,000 credit is eligible for carryback and carryover. ∎

For tax years 2000–2011, all nonrefundable personal credits can offset both the regular income tax (less foreign tax credit) and the AMT.[7]

AMT ADJUSTMENTS

Direction of Adjustments

> **LO.3**
> Identify the adjustments made in calculating the AMT.

It is necessary to determine not only the amount of an adjustment, but also whether the adjustment is positive or negative. Careful study of Example 3 reveals the following pattern with regard to *deductions:*

- If the deduction allowed for regular income tax purposes exceeds the deduction allowed for AMT purposes, the difference is a positive adjustment.
- If the deduction allowed for AMT purposes exceeds the deduction allowed for regular income tax purposes, the difference is a negative adjustment.

Conversely, the direction of an adjustment attributable to an *income* item can be determined as follows:

- If the income reported for regular income tax purposes exceeds the income reported for AMT purposes, the difference is a negative adjustment.
- If the income reported for AMT purposes exceeds the income reported for regular income tax purposes, the difference is a positive adjustment.

Circulation Expenditures

For regular income tax purposes, circulation expenditures, other than those the taxpayer elects to charge to a capital account, may be expensed in the year incurred.[8] These expenditures include expenses incurred to establish, maintain, or increase the circulation of a newspaper, magazine, or other periodical.

Circulation expenditures are not deductible in the year incurred for AMT purposes. In computing AMTI, these expenditures must be capitalized and amortized ratably over the three-year period beginning with the year in which the expenditures were made.[9]

The AMT adjustment for circulation expenditures is the amount expensed for regular income tax purposes minus the amount that can be amortized for AMT purposes. The adjustment can be either positive or negative (refer to Examples 1, 2, and 3). A taxpayer can avoid the AMT adjustments for circulation expenditures by electing to write off the expenditures over a three-year period for regular income tax purposes.[10]

Depreciation of Post-1986 Real Property

The AMT depreciation adjustment for real property applies only to real property placed in service before January 1, 1999. Real property placed in service after December 31, 1998, uses the same MACRS recovery periods (see Table 8.6) for calculating the AMT as for calculating the regular income tax. Therefore, for such property, the AMT conforms to the regular income tax.

---

[7]§ 26(a)(2). Congress is likely to extend this provision for 2012.
[8]§ 173(a).

[9]§ 56(b)(2)(A)(i).
[10]§ 59(e)(2)(A).

For real property placed in service after 1986 (MACRS property) and before January 1, 1999, AMT depreciation is computed under the alternative depreciation system (ADS), which uses the straight-line method over a 40-year life. The depreciation lives for regular income tax purposes are 27.5 years for residential rental property and 39 years for all other real property.[11] The difference between AMT depreciation and regular income tax depreciation is treated as an adjustment in computing the AMT. The differences will be positive during the regular income tax life of the asset because the cost is written off over a shorter period for regular income tax purposes. For example, during the 27.5-year income tax life of residential real property, the regular income tax depreciation will exceed the AMT depreciation because AMT depreciation is computed over a 40-year period.

Table 8.6 is used to compute regular income tax depreciation on real property placed in service after 1986. For AMT purposes, depreciation on real property placed in service after 1986 and before January 1, 1999, is computed under the ADS (refer to Table 8.7).

EXAMPLE 7

In January 1998, Sara placed in service a residential building that cost $100,000. Regular income tax depreciation, AMT depreciation, and the AMT adjustment are as follows:

	Depreciation		
Year	Regular Income Tax	AMT	AMT Adjustment
1998	$ 3,485[a]	$ 2,396[b]	$ 1,089
1999	3,636[c]	2,500[d]	1,136
2000	3,636	2,500	1,136
2001	3,636	2,500	1,136
2002	3,636	2,500	1,136
2003	3,636	2,500	1,136
2004	3,636	2,500	1,136
2005	3,636	2,500	1,136
2006	3,636	2,500	1,136
2007	3,636	2,500	1,136
2008	3,636	2,500	1,136
2009	3,636	2,500	1,136
2010	3,636	2,500	1,136
2011	3,636	2,500	1,136
Total	$50,753	$34,896	$15,857

[a]$100,000 cost × 3.485% (Table 8.6) = $3,485.
[b]$100,000 cost × 2.396% (Table 8.7) = $2,396.
[c]$100,000 cost × 3.636% (Table 8.6) = $3,636.
[d]$100,000 cost × 2.500% (Table 8.7) = $2,500.

Note that if the building had been placed in service in 1999 or thereafter, there would have been no AMT depreciation adjustment for the tax year it was placed in service or for subsequent years. The depreciation for the tax year the building was placed in service would have been $3,485 ($100,000 × 3.485%) for both regular income tax purposes and AMT purposes. ∎

After real property placed in service before January 1, 1999, has been held for the entire depreciation period for regular income tax purposes, the asset will be fully depreciated. However, the depreciation period under the ADS is 41 years due to application of the half-year convention, so depreciation will continue for AMT purposes. This causes negative adjustments after the property has been fully depreciated for regular income tax purposes.

[11]The 39-year life generally applies to nonresidential real property placed in service on or after May 13, 1993.

EXAMPLE 8

Assume the same facts as in the previous example for the building placed in service in 1998, and compute the AMT adjustment for 2026 (the twenty-ninth year of the asset's life). Regular income tax depreciation is zero (refer to Table 8.6). AMT depreciation is $2,500 ($100,000 cost × 2.500% from Table 8.7). Therefore, Sara has a negative AMT adjustment of $2,500 ($0 regular income tax depreciation − $2,500 AMT depreciation). ∎

After real property is fully depreciated for both regular income tax and AMT purposes, the positive and negative adjustments that have been made for AMT purposes will net to zero.

Depreciation of Post–1986 Personal Property

For most personal property placed in service after 1986 (MACRS property), the MACRS deduction for regular income tax purposes is based on the 200 percent declining-balance method with a switch to straight-line when that method produces a larger depreciation deduction for the asset. Refer to Table 8.1 for computing regular income tax depreciation.

For AMT purposes, the taxpayer must use the ADS for such property placed in service before January 1, 1999. This method is based on the 150 percent declining-balance method with a similar switch to straight-line for all personal property.[12] Refer to Table 8.4 for percentages to be used in computing AMT depreciation.

All personal property placed in service after 1986 may be taken into consideration in computing one net adjustment. Using this netting process, the AMT adjustment for a tax year is the difference between the total MACRS depreciation for all personal property computed for regular income tax purposes and the total ADS depreciation computed for AMT purposes. When the total of MACRS deductions exceeds the total of ADS deductions, the amount of the adjustment is positive. When the total of ADS deductions exceeds the total of MACRS deductions, the adjustment for AMTI is negative.

The MACRS deduction for personal property is larger than the ADS deduction in the early years of an asset's life. However, the ADS deduction is larger in the later years. This is so because ADS lives (based on class life) are longer than MACRS lives (based on recovery period).[13] Over the ADS life of the asset, the same amount of depreciation is deducted for both regular income tax and AMT purposes. In the same manner as other timing adjustments, the AMT adjustments for depreciation will net to zero over the ADS life of the asset.

The taxpayer may elect to use the ADS for regular income tax purposes. If this election is made, no AMT adjustment is required because the depreciation deduction is the same for regular income tax and for the AMT. The election eliminates the burden of maintaining two sets of tax depreciation records.

Tax legislation enacted in 1997 either reduced or eliminated the AMT adjustment for the depreciation of personal property. Prior to the effective date of this legislation, the difference between regular income tax depreciation and AMT depreciation was caused by longer recovery periods for the AMT (class life versus MACRS recovery periods) and more accelerated depreciation methods for the regular income tax (200 percent declining balance rather than 150 percent declining balance). The statute now provides that the MACRS recovery periods are to be used in calculating AMT depreciation. Thus, if the taxpayer elects to use the 150 percent declining-balance method for regular income tax purposes, there are no AMT adjustments. Conversely, if the taxpayer uses the 200 percent declining-balance method for regular income tax purposes, there is an AMT adjustment for depreciation. Note, however, that this AMT recovery period conformity provision applies

---

[12]§ 56(a)(1).

[13]Class lives and recovery periods are established for all assets in Rev.Proc. 87–56, 1987–2 C.B. 674.

only to property placed in service after December 31, 1998. Thus, the adjustment continues to apply for personal property placed in service before January 1, 1999.

Pollution Control Facilities

For regular income tax purposes, the cost of certified pollution control facilities may be amortized over a period of 60 months. For AMT purposes, the cost of these facilities placed in service after 1986 and before January 1, 1999, must be depreciated under the ADS over the appropriate class life, determined as explained above for depreciation of post-1986 property.[14] The required adjustment for AMTI is equal to the difference between the amortization deduction allowed for regular income tax purposes and the depreciation deduction computed under the ADS. The adjustment may be positive or negative.

Tax legislation enacted in 1997 reduced the AMT adjustment for pollution control facilities for property placed in service after December 31, 1998. This reduction is achieved by providing conformity in the recovery periods used for regular income tax purposes and AMT purposes (MACRS recovery periods).

Expenditures Requiring 10-Year Write-off for AMT Purposes

Certain expenditures that may be deducted in the year incurred for regular income tax purposes must be written off over a 10-year period for AMT purposes. These rules apply to (1) mining exploration and development costs and (2) research and experimental expenditures.

In computing taxable income, taxpayers are allowed to deduct certain mining exploration and development expenditures. The deduction is allowed for expenditures paid or incurred during the taxable year for exploration (ascertaining the existence, location, extent, or quality of a deposit or mineral) and for development of a mine or other natural deposit, other than an oil or gas well.[15] Mining development expenditures are expenses paid or incurred after the existence of ores and minerals in commercially marketable quantities has been disclosed.

For AMT purposes, however, mining exploration and development costs must be capitalized and amortized ratably over a 10-year period.[16] The AMT adjustment for mining exploration and development costs that are expensed is equal to the amount expensed minus the allowable expense if the costs had been capitalized and amortized ratably over a 10-year period. This provision does not apply to costs relating to an oil or gas well.

E X A M P L E   9

In 2011, Audrey incurs $150,000 of mining exploration expenditures and deducts this amount for regular income tax purposes. For AMT purposes, these mining exploration expenditures must be amortized over a 10-year period. Audrey must make a positive adjustment for AMTI of $135,000 ($150,000 allowed for regular income tax − $15,000 for AMT) for 2011, the first year. In each of the next nine years for AMT purposes, Audrey is required to make a negative adjustment of $15,000 ($0 allowed for regular income tax − $15,000 for AMT). ∎

To avoid the AMT adjustments for mining exploration and development costs, a taxpayer may elect to write off the expenditures over a 10-year period for regular income tax purposes.[17]

Similar rules apply to the computation of the adjustment for research and experimental expenditures.

Use of Completed Contract Method of Accounting

For a long-term contract, taxpayers are required to use the percentage of completion method for AMT purposes.[18] However, in limited circumstances, taxpayers can use the

---

[14] § 56(a)(5).
[15] §§ 617(a) and 616(a).
[16] § 56(a)(2).

[17] §§ 59(e)(2)(D) and (E).
[18] § 56(a)(3).

completed contract method for regular income tax purposes.[19] Thus, a taxpayer recognizes a different amount of income for regular income tax purposes than for AMT purposes. The resulting AMT adjustment is equal to the difference between income reported under the percentage of completion method and the amount reported using the completed contract method. The adjustment can be either positive or negative, depending on the amount of income recognized under the different methods.

A taxpayer can avoid an AMT adjustment on long-term contracts by using the percentage of completion method for regular income tax purposes rather than the completed contract method.

Incentive Stock Options

Incentive stock options (ISOs) are granted by employers to help attract new personnel and retain those already employed. At the time an ISO is granted, the employer corporation sets an option price for the corporate stock. If the value of the stock increases during the option period, the employee can obtain stock at a favorable price by exercising the option. Employees are generally restricted as to when they can dispose of stock acquired under an ISO (e.g., a certain length of employment may be required). Therefore, the stock may not be freely transferable until some specified period has passed. See Chapter 19 for details regarding ISOs.

The exercise of an ISO does not increase regular taxable income.[20] However, for AMT purposes, the excess of the fair market value of the stock over the exercise price (the *spread*) is treated as an adjustment in the first taxable year in which the rights in the stock are freely transferable or are not subject to a substantial risk of forfeiture.[21]

EXAMPLE 10

In 2009, Manuel exercised an ISO that had been granted by his employer, Gold Corporation. Manuel acquired 1,000 shares of Gold stock for the option price of $20 per share. The stock became freely transferable in 2011 when the fair market value was $55 per share. The fair market value of the stock at the date of exercise was $50 per share. For AMT purposes, Manuel has a positive adjustment of $30,000 ($50,000 fair market value − $20,000 option price) for 2011. The transaction does not affect regular taxable income in 2009 or 2011. ■

No adjustment is required if the taxpayer exercises the option and disposes of the stock in the same tax year because the bargain element gain is reported for both regular income tax and AMT purposes in the same tax year.

The regular income tax basis of stock acquired through exercise of ISOs is different from the AMT basis. The regular income tax basis of the stock is equal to its cost, whereas the AMT basis is equal to the fair market value on the date the options are exercised. Consequently, the gain or loss upon disposition of the stock is different for regular income tax purposes and AMT purposes.

EXAMPLE 11

Assume the same facts as in the previous example and that Manuel sells the stock for $60,000 in 2013. His gain for regular income tax purposes is $40,000 ($60,000 amount realized − $20,000 regular income tax basis). For AMT purposes, the gain is $10,000 ($60,000 amount realized − $50,000 AMT basis). Therefore, Manuel has a $30,000 negative adjustment in computing AMT in 2013 ($40,000 regular income tax gain − $10,000 AMT gain). Note that the $30,000 negative adjustment upon disposition in 2013 offsets the $30,000 positive adjustment when the stock became freely transferable in 2011. ■

---

[19]See Chapter 18 for a detailed discussion of the completed contract and percentage of completion methods of accounting.
[20]§ 421(a).
[21]§ 56(b)(3).

Adjusted Gain or Loss

When property is sold during the year or a casualty occurs to business or income-producing property, gain or loss reported for regular income tax may be different from gain or loss determined for the AMT. This difference occurs because the adjusted basis of the property for AMT purposes must reflect any current and prior AMT adjustments for the following:[22]

- Depreciation.
- Circulation expenditures.
- Research and experimental expenditures.
- Mining exploration and development costs.
- Amortization of certified pollution control facilities.

A negative gain or loss adjustment is required if:

- the gain for AMT purposes is less than the gain for regular income tax purposes;
- the loss for AMT purposes is more than the loss for regular income tax purposes; or
- a loss is computed for AMT purposes and a gain is computed for regular income tax purposes.

Otherwise, the AMT gain or loss adjustment is positive.

EXAMPLE 12

Assume the same facts as in Example 7, except that Sara sells the building on December 20, 2011, for $105,000. When Sara sells the building, she has two tax consequences. She must determine her depreciation adjustment for 2011 and the gain (or loss) resulting from the sale.

As to the depreciation adjustment for 2011, the regular income tax depreciation for 2011 is $3,485 [($100,000 cost × 3.636% from Table 8.6) × (11.5/12)]. AMT depreciation for 2011 is $2,396 [($100,000 × 2.500% from Table 8.7) × (11.5/12)]. Sara's positive AMT adjustment for 2011 is $1,089 ($3,485 regular income tax depreciation − $2,396 AMT depreciation).

In computing gain (or loss), the adjusted basis of the building is different for regular income tax purposes than for AMT purposes. The adjusted basis for each purpose is determined as follows:

	Regular Income Tax	AMT
Cost	$100,000	$100,000
Less: Depreciation for 1998–2010 (see Example 7)	(47,117)	(32,396)
Depreciation for 2011 (see prior paragraph)	(3,485)	(2,396)
Adjusted basis	$ 49,398	$ 65,208

Having arrived at adjusted basis, recognized gain is computed for each purpose.

	Regular Income Tax	AMT
Amount realized	$105,000	$105,000
Adjusted basis	(49,398)	(65,208)
Recognized gain	$ 55,602	$ 39,792

Because the regular income tax and AMT gain on the sale of the building differ, Sara must make a negative AMT adjustment of $15,810 ($55,602 regular income tax gain −

$39,792 AMT gain). Note that this negative adjustment offsets the $15,810 total of the 14 positive adjustments for depreciation. ∎

Passive Activity Losses

Losses on passive activities are not deductible in computing either the regular income tax or the AMT. This does not, however, eliminate the possibility of adjustments attributable to passive activities.

The rules for computing taxable income differ from the rules for computing AMTI. It follows, then, that the rules for computing a loss for regular income tax purposes differ from the AMT rules for computing a loss. Therefore, any *passive loss* computed for regular income tax purposes may differ from the passive loss computed for AMT purposes.[23]

EXAMPLE 13

Soong acquired two passive activities in 2011. He received net passive income of $10,000 from Activity A and had no AMT adjustments or preferences in connection with the activity. Activity B had gross income of $27,000 and operating expenses (not affected by AMT adjustments or preferences) of $19,000. Soong claimed MACRS depreciation of $20,000 for Activity B; depreciation under the ADS would have been $15,000. In addition, Soong deducted $10,000 of percentage depletion in excess of basis. The following comparison illustrates the differences in the computation of the passive loss for regular income tax and AMT purposes for Activity B.

	Regular Income Tax	AMT
Gross income	$ 27,000	$ 27,000
Deductions:		
Operating expenses	($ 19,000)	($ 19,000)
Depreciation	(20,000)	(15,000)
Depletion	(10,000)	–0–
Total deductions	($ 49,000)	($ 34,000)
Passive loss	($ 22,000)	($ 7,000)

Because the adjustment for depreciation ($5,000) applies and the preference for depletion ($10,000) is not taken into account in computing AMTI, the regular income tax passive activity loss of $22,000 for Activity B is reduced by these amounts, resulting in a passive activity loss of $7,000 for AMT purposes. ∎

For regular income tax purposes, Soong would offset the $10,000 of net passive income from Activity A with $10,000 of the passive loss from Activity B. For AMT purposes, he would offset the $10,000 of net passive income from Activity A with the $7,000 passive activity loss allowed from Activity B, resulting in passive activity income of $3,000. Thus, in computing AMTI, Soong makes a positive passive loss adjustment of $3,000 [$10,000 (passive activity loss allowed for regular income tax) − $7,000 (passive activity loss allowed for the AMT)]. To avoid duplication, the AMT adjustment for depreciation and the preference for depletion are *not* reported separately. They are accounted for in determining the AMT passive loss adjustment.

EXAMPLE 14

Assume the same facts as in the previous example. For regular income tax purposes, Soong has a suspended passive loss of $12,000 [$22,000 (amount of loss) − $10,000 (used in 2011)]. This suspended passive loss can offset passive income in the future or can offset active or portfolio income when Soong disposes of the loss activity (refer to Chapter 11). For AMT purposes, Soong's suspended passive loss is $0 [$7,000 (amount of loss) − $7,000 (amount used in 2011)]. ∎

---

[23]See Chapter 11.

Alternative Tax Net Operating Loss Deduction

In computing taxable income, taxpayers are allowed to deduct net operating loss (NOL) carryovers and carrybacks (refer to Chapter 7). The regular income tax NOL must be modified, however, in computing AMTI. The starting point in computing the **alternative tax NOL deduction (ATNOLD)** is the NOL computed for regular income tax purposes. The regular income tax NOL is then modified for AMT adjustments and tax preferences with the result being the ATNOLD. Thus, preferences and adjustment items that have benefited the taxpayer in computing the regular income tax NOL are added back, thereby reducing or eliminating the ATNOLD.[24]

EXAMPLE 15

In 2011, Max incurred an NOL of $100,000. Max had no AMT adjustments, but his deductions included tax preferences of $18,000. His ATNOLD carryback to 2009 is $82,000 ($100,000 regular income tax NOL − $18,000 tax preferences deducted in computing the NOL). ∎

In Example 15, if the adjustment was not made to the regular income tax NOL, the $18,000 in tax preference items deducted in 2011 would have the effect of reducing AMTI in the year (or years) the 2011 NOL is utilized. This would weaken the entire concept of the AMT.

A ceiling exists on the amount of the ATNOLD that can be deducted in the carryback or carryforward year. The deduction is limited to 90 percent of AMTI (before the ATNOLD) for the carryback or carryforward year.

EXAMPLE 16

Assume the same facts as in the previous example. Max's AMTI (before the ATNOLD) in 2009 is $90,000. Therefore, of the $82,000 ATNOLD carried back to 2009 from 2011, only $81,000 ($90,000 × 90%) can be used in recalculating the 2009 AMT. The unused $1,000 of 2011 ATNOLD is now carried to 2010 for use in recalculating the 2010 AMT. ∎

A taxpayer who has an ATNOLD that is carried back or over to another year must use the ATNOLD against AMTI in the carryback or carryforward year even if the regular income tax, rather than the AMT, applies.

EXAMPLE 17

Emily's ATNOLD for 2012 (carried over from 2011) is $10,000. AMTI before considering the ATNOLD is $25,000. If Emily's regular income tax exceeds the AMT, the AMT does not apply. Nevertheless, Emily's ATNOLD of $10,000 is "used up" in 2012 and is not available for carryover to a later year. ∎

For regular income tax purposes, the NOL generally can be carried back 2 years and forward 20 years. However, the taxpayer may elect to forgo the 2-year carryback. These rules generally apply to the ATNOLD as well, except that the election to forgo the 2-year carryback is available for the ATNOLD only if the taxpayer elected it for the regular income tax NOL.

Itemized Deductions

Most of the itemized deductions that are allowed for regular income tax purposes are allowed for AMT purposes. Itemized deductions that are allowed for AMT purposes include the following:

- Casualty losses.
- Gambling losses.
- Charitable contributions.
- Medical expenses in excess of 10 percent of AGI.

[24]§ 56(a)(4).

- Estate tax on income in respect of a decedent.
- Qualified interest.

Taxes (state, local, and foreign income taxes, sales taxes, and property taxes) and miscellaneous itemized deductions that are subject to the 2 percent-of-AGI floor are not allowed in computing AMT.[25] A positive AMT adjustment in the total amount of the regular income tax deduction for each is required.

If the taxpayer's gross income includes the recovery of any tax deducted as an itemized deduction for regular income tax purposes, a negative AMT adjustment in the amount of the recovery is allowed for AMTI purposes.[26] For example, state, local, and foreign income taxes can be deducted for regular income tax purposes, but cannot be deducted in computing AMTI. Because of this, any refund of such taxes from a prior year is not included in AMTI. Therefore, in calculating AMTI, the taxpayer must make a negative adjustment for an income tax refund that has been included in computing regular taxable income. Under the tax benefit rule, a tax refund is included in regular taxable income to the extent that the taxpayer obtained a tax benefit by deducting the tax in a prior year.

Medical Expenses The rules for determining the AMT deductions for medical expenses are sufficiently complex to require further explanation. For regular income tax purposes, medical expenses are deductible to the extent they exceed 7.5 percent of AGI. However, for AMT purposes, medical expenses are deductible only to the extent they exceed 10 percent of AGI.[27]

EXAMPLE 18

Joann incurred uninsured medical expenses of $16,000 in 2011. She had AGI of $100,000 for the year. Her AMT adjustment for medical expenses is computed as follows:

	Regular Income Tax	AMT
Medical expenses incurred	$16,000	$ 16,000
Less reduction:		
$100,000 AGI × 7.5%	(7,500)	
$100,000 AGI × 10%		(10,000)
Medical expense deduction	$ 8,500	$ 6,000

Joann's AMT adjustment for medical expenses is $2,500 ($8,500 regular income tax deduction − $6,000 AMT deduction). ∎

Interest in General The AMT itemized deduction allowed for interest expense includes only qualified housing interest[28] and investment interest[29] to the extent of net investment income that is included in the determination of AMTI. Any interest that is deducted in calculating the regular income tax that is not permitted in calculating the AMT is treated as a positive adjustment.

In computing regular taxable income, taxpayers who itemize can deduct the following types of interest (refer to Chapter 10):

- Qualified residence interest.
- Investment interest, subject to the investment interest limitations (discussed under Investment Interest below).
- Qualified interest on student loans.

Housing Interest Under current regular income tax rules, taxpayers who itemize can deduct *qualified residence interest* on up to two residences. The deduction is

---

[25]§ 56(b)(1)(A).
[26]§ 56(b)(1)(D).
[27]§ 56(b)(1)(B).
[28]§ 56(b)(1)(C)(i).
[29]§ 56(b)(1)(C)(v).

limited to interest on acquisition indebtedness up to $1 million and home equity indebtedness up to $100,000. Acquisition indebtedness is debt that is incurred in acquiring, constructing, or substantially improving a qualified residence of the taxpayer and is secured by the residence. Home equity indebtedness is indebtedness secured by a qualified residence of the taxpayer, but does not include acquisition indebtedness.

EXAMPLE 19

Gail, who used the proceeds of a mortgage to acquire a personal residence, paid mortgage interest of $112,000 in 2011. Of this amount, $14,000 is attributable to acquisition indebtedness in excess of $1 million. For regular income tax purposes, Gail may deduct mortgage interest of $98,000 ($112,000 total − $14,000 disallowed). ∎

The mortgage interest deduction for AMT purposes is limited to *qualified housing interest*, rather than *qualified residence interest*. Qualified housing interest includes only interest incurred to acquire, construct, or substantially improve the taxpayer's principal residence and such interest on one other qualified dwelling used for personal purposes. A home equity loan qualifies only if it meets the definition of qualified housing interest, which frequently is not the case. When additional mortgage interest is incurred (e.g., a mortgage refinancing), interest paid is deductible as qualified housing interest for AMT purposes only if:

- The proceeds are used to acquire or substantially improve a qualified residence.
- Interest on the prior loan was qualified housing interest.
- The amount of the loan was not increased.

A positive AMT adjustment is required in the amount of the difference between qualified *residence* interest allowed as an itemized deduction for regular income tax purposes and qualified *housing* interest allowed in the determination of AMTI.

Investment Interest Investment interest is deductible for regular income tax purposes and for AMT purposes to the extent of qualified net investment income.

EXAMPLE 20

For the year, Dan had net investment income of $16,000 before deducting investment interest. He incurred investment interest expense of $30,000 during the year. His investment interest deduction is $16,000. ∎

Even though investment interest is deductible for both regular income tax and AMT purposes, an adjustment is required if the amount of investment interest deductible for regular income tax purposes differs from the amount deductible for AMT purposes. For example, an adjustment will arise if proceeds from a home equity loan are used to purchase investments. Interest on a home equity loan is deductible as qualified residence interest for regular income tax purposes, but is not deductible for

AMT purposes unless the proceeds are used to acquire or substantially improve a quali-fied residence. For AMT purposes, however, interest on a home equity loan is deducti-ble as investment interest expense if proceeds from the loan are used for investment purposes.

To determine the AMT adjustment for investment interest expense, it is necessary to compute the investment interest deduction for both regular income tax and AMT purposes. This computation is illustrated in the following example.

EXAMPLE 21

Tom had $20,000 interest income from corporate bonds and $5,000 dividends from pre-ferred stock. He reported the following amounts of investment income for regular income tax and AMT purposes:

	Regular Income Tax	AMT
Corporate bond interest	$20,000	$20,000
Preferred stock dividends	5,000	5,000
Net investment income	$25,000	$25,000

Tom incurred investment interest expense of $10,000 related to the corporate bonds. He also incurred $4,000 interest on a home equity loan and used the proceeds of the loan to purchase preferred stock. For regular income tax purposes, this $4,000 is de-ductible as qualified residence interest. His *investment* interest expense for regular income tax and AMT purposes is computed below:

	Regular Income Tax	AMT
To carry corporate bonds	$10,000	$10,000
On home equity loan to carry preferred stock	–0–	4,000
Total investment interest expense	$10,000	$14,000

Investment interest expense is deductible to the extent of net investment income. Because the amount deductible for regular income tax purposes ($10,000) differs from the amount deductible for AMT purposes ($14,000), an AMT adjustment is required. The adjustment is computed as follows:

AMT deduction for investment interest expense	$ 14,000
Regular income tax deduction for investment interest expense	(10,000)
Negative AMT adjustment	$ 4,000

As discussed subsequently under AMT Preferences, the interest on private activity bonds usually is a tax preference for AMT purposes. Such interest can also affect the calculation of the AMT investment interest deduction in that it is included in the cal-culation of net investment income.

Other Adjustments

The standard deduction and the personal and dependency exemption also give rise to AMT adjustments.[30] The standard deduction is not allowed as a deduction in com-puting AMTI. Although a person who does not itemize is rarely subject to the AMT, it is possible. In such a case, the taxpayer is required to enter a positive adjustment for the standard deduction in computing the AMT.

The personal and dependency exemption amount deducted for regular income tax purposes is not allowed in computing AMT. Therefore, taxpayers must enter a positive AMT adjustment for the personal and dependency exemption amount claimed in

---

[30]§ 56(b)(1)(E).

computing the regular income tax. A separate exemption (see Exemption Amount) is allowed for AMT purposes. To allow both the regular income tax exemption amount and the AMT exemption amount would result in extra benefits for taxpayers.

EXAMPLE 22	Eli, who is single, has no dependents and does not itemize deductions. He earned a salary of $109,500 in 2011. Based on this information, Eli's taxable income for 2011 is $100,000 ($109,500 − $5,800 standard deduction − $3,700 exemption). ∎
EXAMPLE 23	Assume the same facts as in Example 22. In addition, assume Eli's tax preferences for the year totaled $150,000. Eli's AMTI is $259,500 ($100,000 taxable income + $5,800 adjustment for standard deduction + $3,700 adjustment for exemption + $150,000 tax preferences). ∎

ETHICS & Equity

LARGE FAMILIES AND THE AMT

The taxpayers claimed 12 personal exemption and dependency deductions (taxpayer, spouse, and 10 children) on their Federal income tax return. The taxpayers' itemized deductions included medical and dental expenses and state and local income and property taxes.

Under the regular income tax calculation, the taxpayers' taxable income was a negative amount. However, applying the AMT adjustments for personal and dependency exemptions, medical and dental expenses, and state and local income and property taxes resulted in the taxpayers being subject to the AMT.

The taxpayers are members of a religious denomination that encourages large families. The tax return they filed showed a $0 Federal income tax liability and did not include a Form 6251. According to the taxpayers, the AMT should not apply to them for the following reasons:

- Congress did not intend for a large family in itself to be a causative factor producing an AMT.
- They had no tax preferences.
- The AMT burdened the taxpayers' free exercise of religion.
- The AMT violated their equal protection and due process rights.

Both the Tax Court and the Third Circuit Court of Appeals rejected these arguments and held that the taxpayers were subject to the AMT.

Should taxpayers who have large families and no tax preferences be subject to the AMT? Was this the intended objective of the AMT?

Source: Adapted from *Klaassen v. Comm.*, 99–1 USTC ¶50,418, 83 AFTR 2d 99–1750, 182 F.3d 932 (CA–3, 1999), *aff'g* 76 TCM 20, T.C.Memo. 1998–241.

AMT PREFERENCES

Identify the tax preferences that are included in calculating the AMT.

Percentage Depletion

Congress originally enacted the percentage depletion rules to provide taxpayers with incentives to invest in the development of specified natural resources. Percentage depletion is computed by multiplying a rate specified in the Code times the gross income from the property (refer to Chapter 8).[31] The percentage rate is based on the type of mineral involved. The basis of the property is reduced by the amount of depletion taken until the basis reaches zero. However, once the basis of the property reaches zero, taxpayers are allowed to continue taking percentage depletion deductions. Thus, over the life of the property, depletion deductions may greatly exceed the cost of the property.

The percentage depletion preference is equal to the excess of the regular income tax deduction for percentage depletion over the adjusted basis of the property at the end of the taxable year.[32] Basis is determined without regard to the depletion

---

[31]§ 613(a).

[32]§ 57(a)(1). Note that the preference label does not apply to percentage depletion on oil and gas wells for independent producers and royalty owners as defined in § 613A(c).

deduction for the taxable year. This preference item is figured separately for each piece of property for which the taxpayer is claiming depletion.

Kim owns a mineral property that qualifies for a 22% depletion rate. The basis of the property at the beginning of the year is $10,000. Gross income from the property for the year is $100,000. For regular income tax purposes, Kim's percentage depletion deduction (assume it is not limited by taxable income from the property) is $22,000. For AMT purposes, Kim has a tax preference of $12,000 ($22,000 − $10,000). ∎

Intangible Drilling Costs

In computing the regular income tax, taxpayers are allowed to deduct certain intangible drilling and development costs in the year incurred, although such costs are normally capital in nature (refer to Chapter 8). The deduction is allowed for costs incurred in connection with oil and gas wells and geothermal wells.

For AMT purposes, excess intangible drilling costs (IDC) for the year are treated as a preference.[33] The preference for excess IDC is computed as follows:

IDC expensed in the year incurred
Minus: Deduction if IDC were capitalized and amortized over 10 years
Equals: Excess of IDC expense over amortization
Minus: 65% of net oil and gas and geothermal income
Equals: Tax preference item

Ben, who incurred IDC of $50,000 during the year, elected to expense that amount. His net oil and gas income for the year was $60,000. Ben's tax preference for IDC is $6,000 [($50,000 IDC − $5,000 amortization) − (65% × $60,000 income)]. ∎

A taxpayer can avoid the preference for IDC by electing to write off the expenditures over a 10-year period for regular income tax purposes.

Interest on Private Activity Bonds

Income from private activity bonds is not included in taxable income, and expenses related to carrying such bonds are not deductible for regular income tax purposes. However, interest on private activity bonds usually is included as a preference in computing AMTI. Therefore, expenses incurred in carrying the bonds are offset against the interest income in computing the tax preference.[34] However, interest on private activity bonds issued after December 31, 2008, and before January 1, 2011, is not treated as a tax preference.

The Code contains a lengthy, complex definition of private activity bonds.[35] In general, **private activity bonds** are bonds issued by states or municipalities with more than 10 percent of the proceeds being used for private business use. For example, a bond issued by a city whose proceeds are used to construct a factory that is leased to a private business at a favorable rate is a private activity bond.

The vast majority of tax-exempt bonds issued by states and municipalities are not classified as private activity bonds. Therefore, the interest income from such bonds is not a tax preference item.

Return to the facts of *The Big Picture* on p. 12-2. Bob and Carol both have invested substantial amounts in private activity bonds. All of the private activity bonds that each of them owns were issued in 2010. Consequently, a tax preference does not result for either Carol or Bob. ∎

Depreciation

For real property and leased personal property placed in service before 1987, there is an AMT preference for the excess of accelerated depreciation over straight-line

---

[33]§ 57(a)(2).
[34]§ 57(a)(5).

[35]§ 141.

depreciation.[36] However, examination of the cost recovery tables for pre-1987 real property (refer to Chapter 8) reveals that from the eighth year on, accelerated depreciation will not exceed straight-line depreciation. Consequently, taxpayers no longer have preferences attributable to pre-1987 real property.

Accelerated depreciation on pre-1987 leased personal property was computed using specified ACRS percentages. AMT depreciation was based on the straight-line method, which was computed using the half-year convention, no salvage value, and a longer recovery period.[37] As a result, in the early years of the life of the asset, the cost recovery allowance used in computing the regular income tax was greater than the straight-line depreciation deduction allowed in computing AMT. The excess depreciation was treated as a tax preference item. For all leased personal property placed in service before 1987 (3-year, 5-year, 10-year, and 15-year public utility property), the cost recovery period has expired. Since there is no excess depreciation, there is no tax preference for AMT purposes.

The preference item for excess depreciation on leased personal property is figured separately for each piece of property. No preference is reported in the year the taxpayer disposes of the property.

Fifty Percent Exclusion for Certain Small Business Stock

Fifty percent of the gain on the sale of certain small business stock normally is excludible from gross income for regular income tax purposes. However, for 2009 and 2010, the 50 percent is increased to 75 percent. For 2011, the 75 percent is increased to 100 percent. Seven percent of the excluded amount is a tax preference for AMT purposes.[38]

The adjustments and preferences to taxable income in arriving at AMTI are set forth in Concept Summary 12.1.

L0.5

Apply the formula for computing the AMT and illustrate Form 6251.

ILLUSTRATION OF THE AMT COMPUTATION

The computation of the AMT is illustrated in the following example.

EXAMPLE 27

Hans Sims, who is single, had taxable income for 2011 as follows:

Salary		$ 92,000
Interest		8,000
Adjusted gross income		$100,000
Less itemized deductions:		
Medical expenses ($17,500 − 7.5% of $100,000 AGI)[a]	$10,000	
State income taxes	4,000	
Interest[b]		
Home mortgage (for qualified housing)	20,000*	
Investment interest	3,300*	
Contributions (cash)	5,000*	
Casualty losses ($14,000 − 10% of $100,000 AGI)	4,000*	(46,300)
		$ 53,700
Less personal exemption		(3,700)
Taxable income		$ 50,000

[a]Total medical expenses were $17,500, reduced by 7.5% of AGI, resulting in an itemized deduction of $10,000. However, for AMT purposes, the reduction is 10%, which leaves an AMT itemized deduction of $7,500 ($17,500 − 10% of $100,000 AGI). Therefore, an adjustment of $2,500 ($10,000 − $7,500) is required for medical expenses disallowed for AMT purposes.

[b]In this illustration, all interest is deductible in computing AMTI. Qualified housing interest is deductible. Investment interest ($3,300) is deductible to the extent of net investment income included in the minimum tax base. For this purpose, the $8,000 of interest income is treated as net investment income.

---

[36]§ 57(a)(6).

[37]The specified lives for AMT purposes are 5 years for 3-year property, 8 years for 5-year property, 15 years for 10-year property, and 22 years for 15-year property.

[38]§ 57(a)(7).

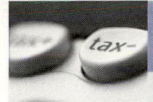

CONCEPT SUMMARY 12.1

AMT Adjustments and Preferences for Individuals

Adjustments	Positive	Negative	Both*
Circulation expenditures			X
Depreciation of post-1986 real property			X
Depreciation of post-1986 personal property			X
Pollution control facilities			X
Mining exploration and development costs			X
Research and experimental expenditures			X
Completed contract method			X
Incentive stock options	X**		
Adjusted gain or loss			X
Passive activity losses			X
Alternative tax NOL deduction			X
Itemized deductions:			
Medical expenses	X		
State income tax or sales tax	X		
Property tax on realty	X		
Property tax on personalty	X		
Miscellaneous itemized deductions	X		
Tax benefit rule for state income tax refund		X	
Qualified interest on student loans	X		
Qualified residence interest that is not qualified housing interest	X		
Qualified residence interest that is AMT investment interest	X	X	
Private activity bond interest that is AMT investment interest		X	
Standard deduction	X		
Personal exemptions and dependency deductions	X		

Preferences

	Positive	Negative	Both*
Percentage depletion in excess of adjusted basis	X		
Intangible drilling costs	X		
Private activity bond interest income	X***		
Depreciation on pre-1987 leased personal property	X		
§ 1202 exclusion for certain small business stock	X		

*Timing differences.
**While the adjustment is a positive adjustment, the AMT basis for the stock is increased by the amount of the positive adjustment.
***Interest on private activity bonds issued after December 31, 2008, and before January 1, 2011, is not treated as a tax preference.

Deductions marked by an asterisk are allowed as *alternative minimum tax itemized deductions*, and AMT adjustments are required for the other itemized deductions. Thus, adjustments are required for state income taxes and for medical expenses to the extent the medical expenses deductible for regular income tax purposes are not deductible in computing AMT (see note [a]). In addition to the items that affected taxable income, Hans had $35,000 interest on private activity bonds (an exclusion tax preference normally, but not for such bonds issued in 2009 or 2010) and a $35,000 spread on an ISO. Assume the private activity bonds were issued in 2010. AMTI is computed as follows:

Taxable income	$ 50,000
Plus: Adjustments	
State income taxes	4,000
Medical expenses (see note [a])	2,500
Incentive stock options	35,000
Personal exemption	3,700
Plus: Tax preference (interest on private activity bonds)	–0–
Equals: AMTI	$ 95,200
Minus: AMT exemption	(48,450)
Equals: Minimum tax base	$ 46,750
Times: AMT rate	× 26%
Equals: Tentative AMT	$ 12,155
Minus: Regular income tax on taxable income	(8,625)
Equals: AMT	$ 3,530

The solution to Example 27 is also presented on Form 6251. Though this example is for 2011, 2010 tax forms are used because the 2011 tax forms were not available at the time of this writing.

Note that the $3,700 personal exemption amount is a positive adjustment in the Example 27 solution, but does not appear as an adjustment in Form 6251. This difference occurs because line 1 of Form 6251 includes the amount from line 41 of Form 1040. Line 41 of Form 1040 is taxable income before the deduction for personal and dependency exemptions.

AMT CREDIT

LO.6

Describe the role of the AMT credit in the alternative minimum tax structure.

As discussed previously, timing differences give rise to adjustments to the minimum tax base. In later years, the timing differences reverse, as was illustrated in several of the preceding examples. To provide equity for the taxpayer when timing differences reverse, the regular income tax liability may be reduced by a tax credit for prior years' minimum tax liability attributable to timing differences. The **alternative minimum tax credit** may be carried over indefinitely. Therefore, there is no need to keep track of when the minimum tax credit arose.[39]

EXAMPLE 28

Assume the same facts as in Example 3. Also assume that in 2011, Bob paid AMT as a result of the $20,000 positive adjustment arising from the circulation expenditures. In 2012, $10,000 of the timing difference reverses, resulting in regular taxable income that is $10,000 greater than AMTI. Because Bob has already paid AMT as a result of the write-off of circulation expenditures, he is allowed an AMT credit in 2012. The AMT credit can offset Bob's regular income tax liability in 2012 to the extent that his regular income tax liability exceeds his tentative AMT. ∎

The AMT credit is applicable only for the AMT that results from timing differences. It is not available in connection with **AMT exclusions**, which represent permanent differences rather than timing differences between the regular income tax liability and the AMT. These AMT exclusions include the following:

- The standard deduction.
- Personal exemptions.
- Medical expenses, to the extent deductible for regular income tax purposes but not deductible in computing AMT.

[39]§ 53.

Form **6251**	**Alternative Minimum Tax—Individuals**	OMB No. 1545-0074
Department of the Treasury Internal Revenue Service (99)	▶ See separate instructions. ▶ Attach to Form 1040 or Form 1040NR.	**20**10 Attachment Sequence No. **32**

Name(s) shown on Form 1040 or Form 1040NR	Your social security number
Hans Sims	*111-11-1111*

Part I **Alternative Minimum Taxable Income** (See instructions for how to complete each line.)

1	If filing Schedule A (Form 1040), enter the amount from Form 1040, line 41, and go to line 2. Otherwise, enter the amount from Form 1040, line 38, and go to line 6. (If less than zero, enter as a negative amount.)	**1**	*53,700*
2	Medical and dental. Enter the **smaller** of Schedule A (Form 1040), line 4, **or** 2.5% (.025) of Form 1040, line 38. If zero or less, enter -0-	**2**	*2,500*
3	Taxes from Schedule A (Form 1040), lines 5, 6, and 8	**3**	*4,000*
4	Enter the home mortgage interest adjustment, if any, from line 6 of the worksheet on page 2 of the instructions	**4**	
5	Miscellaneous deductions from Schedule A (Form 1040), line 27	**5**	
6	If filing Schedule L (Form 1040A or 1040), enter as a negative amount the sum of lines 6 and 17 from that schedule	**6**	( )
7	Tax refund from Form 1040, line 10 or line 21	**7**	( )
8	Investment interest expense (difference between regular tax and AMT)	**8**	
9	Depletion (difference between regular tax and AMT)	**9**	
10	Net operating loss deduction from Form 1040, line 21. Enter as a positive amount	**10**	
11	Alternative tax net operating loss deduction	**11**	( )
12	Interest from specified private activity bonds exempt from the regular tax	**12**	
13	Qualified small business stock (7% of gain excluded under section 1202)	**13**	
14	Exercise of incentive stock options (excess of AMT income over regular tax income)	**14**	*35,000*
15	Estates and trusts (amount from Schedule K-1 (Form 1041), box 12, code A)	**15**	
16	Electing large partnerships (amount from Schedule K-1 (Form 1065-B), box 6)	**16**	
17	Disposition of property (difference between AMT and regular tax gain or loss)	**17**	
18	Depreciation on assets placed in service after 1986 (difference between regular tax and AMT)	**18**	
19	Passive activities (difference between AMT and regular tax income or loss)	**19**	
20	Loss limitations (difference between AMT and regular tax income or loss)	**20**	
21	Circulation costs (difference between regular tax and AMT)	**21**	
22	Long-term contracts (difference between AMT and regular tax income)	**22**	
23	Mining costs (difference between regular tax and AMT)	**23**	
24	Research and experimental costs (difference between regular tax and AMT)	**24**	
25	Income from certain installment sales before January 1, 1987.	**25**	( )
26	Intangible drilling costs preference	**26**	
27	Other adjustments, including income-based related adjustments	**27**	
28	**Alternative minimum taxable income.** Combine lines 1 through 27. (If married filing separately and line 28 is more than $219,900, see page 8 of the instructions.)	**28**	*95,200*

Part II **Alternative Minimum Tax (AMT)**

29 Exemption. (If you were under age 24 at the end of 2010, see page 8 of the instructions.)

IF your filing status is . . .	AND line 28 is not over . . .	THEN enter on line 29 . . .		
Single or head of household	$112,500	$47,450		
Married filing jointly or qualifying widow(er)	150,000	72,450	}	
Married filing separately.	75,000	36,225		**29** *48,450*

If line 28 is **over** the amount shown above for your filing status, see page 8 of the instructions.

30	Subtract line 29 from line 28. If more than zero, go to line 31. If zero or less, enter -0- here and on lines 33 and 35 and skip the rest of Part II	**30**	*46,750*
31	• If you are filing Form 2555 or 2555-EZ, see page 9 of the instructions for the amount to enter. • If you reported capital gain distributions directly on Form 1040, line 13; you reported qualified dividends on Form 1040, line 9b; **or** you had a gain on both lines 15 and 16 of Schedule D (Form 1040) (as refigured for the AMT, if necessary), complete Part III on the back and enter the amount from line 54 here. • All others: If line 30 is $175,000 or less ($87,500 or less if married filing separately), multiply line 30 by 26% (.26). Otherwise, multiply line 30 by 28% (.28) and subtract $3,500 ($1,750 if married filing separately) from the result.	**31**	*12,155*
32	Alternative minimum tax foreign tax credit (see page 9 of the instructions)	**32**	
33	Tentative minimum tax. Subtract line 32 from line 31	**33**	*12,155*
34	Tax from Form 1040, line 44 (minus any tax from Form 4972 and any foreign tax credit from Form 1040, line 47). If you used Schedule J to figure your tax, the amount from line 44 of Form 1040 must be refigured without using Schedule J (see page 11 of the instructions)	**34**	*8,625*
35	**AMT.** Subtract line 34 from line 33. If zero or less, enter -0-. Enter here and on Form 1040, line 45	**35**	*3,530*

For Paperwork Reduction Act Notice, see your tax return instructions.   Cat. No. 13600G   Form **6251** (2010)

THE AMT NIGHTMARE

Nina Olson is the National Taxpayer Advocate for the IRS. She is required to report to Congress annually on the problems facing taxpayers. In a recent report, she identified complexity as the most serious problem and called for a "simpler tax code."

In discussing the complexity of the Code, she described the AMT as a nightmare. Not only does the taxpayer have to compute regular tax liability with all its complexity, but the AMT requires that the computation be done twice. In Olson's opinion, the AMT is a "hideously complex parallel tax structure." Obviously, she does not think it should be retained in achieving a "simpler tax code."

Source: Adapted from Nina E. Olson, "We Still Need a Simpler Tax Code," *Wall Street Journal*, April 10, 2009, p. A13.

- Other itemized deductions not allowable for AMT purposes, including miscellaneous itemized deductions, taxes, and interest expense.
- Excess percentage depletion.
- Tax-exempt interest on specified private activity bonds.

EXAMPLE 29

Don, who is single, has zero taxable income for 2011. He also has positive timing adjustments of $300,000 and AMT exclusions of $100,000. His AMT base is $400,000 because his AMT exemption is phased out completely due to the level of AMTI. Don's tentative AMT is $108,500 [($175,000 × 26% AMT rate) + ($225,000 × 28% AMT rate)]. ∎

To determine the amount of AMT credit to carry over, the AMT must be recomputed reflecting only the AMT exclusions and the AMT exemption amount.

EXAMPLE 30

Assume the same facts as in the previous example. If there had been no positive timing adjustments for the year, Don's tentative AMT would have been $13,403 [($100,000 AMT exclusions − $48,450 exemption) × 26% AMT rate]. Don may carry over an AMT credit of $95,097 ($108,500 AMT − $13,403 related to AMT exclusions) to 2012 and subsequent years. ∎

12.2 CORPORATE ALTERNATIVE MINIMUM TAX

LO.7

Understand the basic features of the corporate AMT.

The AMT applicable to corporations is similar to that applicable to noncorporate taxpayers. However, there are several important differences:

- The corporate AMT rate is 20 percent versus a top rate of 28 percent for noncorporate taxpayers.[40]
- The AMT exemption for corporations is $40,000 reduced by 25 percent of the amount by which AMTI exceeds $150,000.[41]
- Tax preferences applicable to noncorporate taxpayers are also applicable to corporate taxpayers, but some adjustments differ (shown later in the chapter).

Although there are computational differences, the corporate AMT and the noncorporate AMT have the identical objective: to force taxpayers who are more profitable than their taxable income reflects to pay additional tax. The formula for determining the corporate AMT appears in Figure 12.3.

To compute the corporate AMT using tax forms, Form 4626 (Alternative Minimum Tax—Corporations) is applicable. Any tax so determined should be carried over to Schedule J of Form 1120 (U.S. Corporation Income Tax Return).

---

[40]§ 55(b)(1)(B).   [41]§§ 55(d)(2) and (3).

FIGURE 12.3	AMT Formula for Corporations

Taxable income
Plus: Income tax NOL deduction
Plus or minus: AMT adjustments
Plus: Tax preferences
Equals: AMTI before ATNOLD
Minus: ATNOLD (limited to 90% of AMTI before ATNOLD)
Equals: AMTI
Minus: Exemption
Equals: AMT base
Times: 20% rate
Equals: Tentative minimum tax before AMT foreign tax credit
Minus: AMT foreign tax credit
Equals: Tentative minimum tax
Minus: Regular tax liability before credits minus regular foreign tax credit
Equals: AMT if positive

REPEAL OF AMT FOR SMALL CORPORATIONS

Tax legislation enacted in 1997 repealed the AMT for small corporations for tax years beginning after December 31, 1997. For this purpose, a corporation is classified as a small corporation if it had average annual gross receipts of not more than $5 million for the three-year period beginning after December 1993. A corporation will continue to be classified as a small corporation if its average annual gross receipts for the three-year period preceding the current tax year and any intervening three-year periods do not exceed $7.5 million. However, if a corporation ever fails the gross receipts test, it is ineligible for small corporation classification in future tax years.[42]

Tax legislation enacted in 1998 provided an additional opportunity for a corporation to be classified as a small corporation. A corporation will automatically be classified as a small corporation in the first tax year of existence.[43]

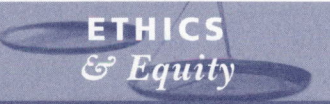

ETHICS & Equity — AMT AND SMALL CORPORATIONS

Abigail is the controller of a medium-size company specializing in the construction of single-family homes. As such, she prepares the corporate tax return.

The corporation expects its gross revenue in each of its first three years of operations to be approximately $15 million and to increase thereafter by 15 percent annually. Abigail is aware that the corporation is eligible for the small corporation exception to the AMT in its first year but will not be thereafter.

The corporation uses the completed contract method of accounting for 2011. After 2011, however, Abigail has the corporation switch to the percentage of completion method.

Evaluate what Abigail has done.

AMT ADJUSTMENTS

Adjustments Applicable to Individuals and Corporations

The following adjustments that were discussed in connection with the individual AMT also apply to the corporate AMT:

- Excess of MACRS over ADS depreciation on real and personal property placed in service after 1986.

---

[42]§§ 55(e)(1)(A) and (B). An estimated 3 million corporations (95% of incorporated businesses) qualify for this exemption.

[43]§ 55(e)(1)(C).

- Pollution control facilities placed in service after 1986 (AMT requires ADS depreciation over the asset's ADR life if placed in service before January 1, 1999, and over the MACRS recovery period if placed in service after December 31, 1998; 60-month amortization is allowed for regular income tax purposes).
- Mining and exploration expenditures (AMT requires amortization over 10 years versus immediate expensing allowed for regular income tax purposes).
- Income on long-term contracts (AMT requires percentage of completion method; completed contract method is allowed in limited circumstances for regular income tax purposes).
- Dispositions of assets (if gain or loss for AMT purposes differs from gain or loss for regular income tax purposes).
- Allowable ATNOLD (which cannot exceed 90 percent of AMTI before deduction for ATNOLD).

Adjustment Applicable Only to Corporations

An AMT adjustment applicable only to corporations is the adjusted current earnings (ACE) adjustment.[44] The **ACE adjustment** generally applies to all corporations[45] and has a significant impact on both tax and financial accounting.

Corporations are subject to an AMT adjustment equal to 75 percent of the excess of ACE over AMTI before the ACE adjustment.[46] Historically, the government has not required conformity between tax accounting and financial accounting. For many years, the only *direct* conformity requirement was that a corporation that used the LIFO method for tax accounting also had to use LIFO for financial accounting.[47] Through the ACE adjustment, Congress is *indirectly* imposing a conformity requirement on corporations. Though a corporation may still choose to use different methods for tax and financial accounting purposes, it may no longer be able to do so without incurring AMT as a result of the ACE adjustment. Thus, a corporation may incur AMT not only because of specifically targeted adjustments and preferences, but also as a result of any methods that cause ACE to exceed AMTI before the ACE adjustment.

The ACE adjustment can be either a positive or a negative amount. AMTI is increased by 75 percent of the excess of ACE over unadjusted AMTI. Or AMTI is reduced by 75 percent of the excess of unadjusted AMTI over ACE. The negative adjustment is limited to the aggregate of the positive adjustments under ACE for prior years, reduced by the previously claimed negative adjustments. See Concept Summary 12.2. Thus, the ordering of the timing differences is crucial because any lost negative adjustment is permanent. Unadjusted AMTI is AMTI without the ACE adjustment or the ATNOLD.[48]

EXAMPLE 31	A calendar year corporation has the following data:

	2010	2011	2012
Pre-adjusted AMTI	$3,000	$3,000	$3,100
Adjusted current earnings	4,000	3,000	2,000

In 2010, because ACE exceeds unadjusted AMTI by $1,000, $750 (75% × $1,000) is included as a positive adjustment to AMTI. No adjustment is necessary for 2011. As unadjusted AMTI exceeds ACE by $1,100 in 2012, there is a potential negative adjustment to AMTI of $825 ($1,100 × 75%). Since the total increases to AMTI for prior years

[44]§ 56(c).

[45]The ACE adjustment does not apply to S corporations. § 56(g)(6).

[46]§ 56(g).

[47]§ 472(c).

[48]§§ 56(g)(1) and (2).

CONCEPT SUMMARY 12.2

Determining the ACE Adjustment*

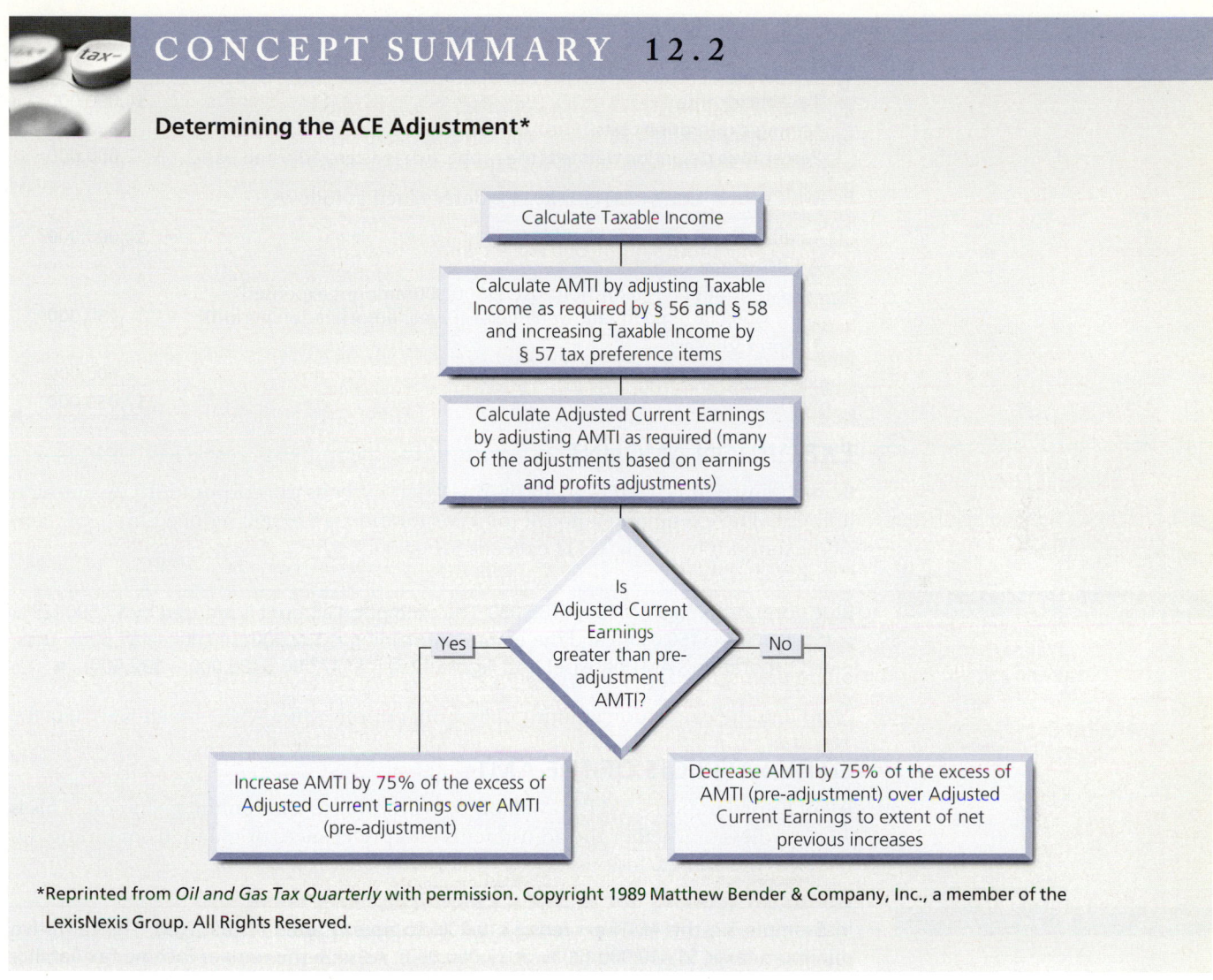

Calculate Taxable Income

Calculate AMTI by adjusting Taxable Income as required by § 56 and § 58 and increasing Taxable Income by § 57 tax preference items

Calculate Adjusted Current Earnings by adjusting AMTI as required (many of the adjustments based on earnings and profits adjustments)

Is Adjusted Current Earnings greater than pre-adjustment AMTI?

Yes

No

Increase AMTI by 75% of the excess of Adjusted Current Earnings over AMTI (pre-adjustment)

Decrease AMTI by 75% of the excess of AMTI (pre-adjustment) over Adjusted Current Earnings to extent of net previous increases

*Reprinted from *Oil and Gas Tax Quarterly* with permission. Copyright 1989 Matthew Bender & Company, Inc., a member of the LexisNexis Group. All Rights Reserved.

equal $750 and there are no previously claimed negative adjustments, only $750 of the potential negative adjustment reduces AMTI for 2012. Further, $75 of the negative amount is lost forever. ∎

ACE should not be confused with current earnings and profits (see Chapter 20). Although many items are treated in the same manner, certain variations exist. For example, Federal income taxes, deductible in computing earnings and profits, are not deductible in determining ACE.

The starting point for computing ACE is AMTI, which is defined as regular taxable income after AMT adjustments (other than the ATNOLD and ACE adjustments) and tax preferences. The resulting figure is adjusted for several items in order to arrive at ACE.[49]

TAX PREFERENCES

AMTI includes designated tax preference items. In some cases, this has the effect of subjecting nontaxable income to the AMT. Tax preference items that apply to individuals also apply to corporations.

---

[49]For additional coverage of the calculation of ACE, refer to Chapter 3 in *South-Western Federal Taxation: Corporations, Partnerships, Estates, and Trusts.*   The instructions for Form 4626 illustrate the ACE adjustment on p. 6 and provide a worksheet for its computation on p. 11.

EXAMPLE 32

The following information applies to Brown Corporation (a calendar year taxpayer) for 2011:

Taxable income	$4,000,000
Mining exploration costs	500,000
Percentage depletion claimed (the property has a zero adjusted basis)	2,600,000

Brown Corporation's AMTI for 2011 is determined as follows:

Taxable income	$4,000,000
Adjustments:	
Excess mining exploration costs [$500,000 (amount expensed) −	
$50,000 (amount allowed over a 10-year amortization period)]	450,000
Tax preferences:	
Excess depletion	2,600,000
AMTI	$7,050,000

EXEMPTION AMOUNT

The tentative AMT is 20 percent of AMTI that exceeds the corporation's exemption amount. The exemption amount for a corporation is $40,000 reduced by 25 percent of the amount by which AMTI exceeds $150,000.

EXAMPLE 33

Blue Corporation has AMTI of $180,000. The exemption amount is reduced by $7,500 [25% × ($180,000 − $150,000)], and the amount remaining is $32,500 ($40,000 − $7,500). Thus, Blue Corporation's AMT base (refer to Figure 12.3) is $147,500 ($180,000 − $32,500). ■

Note that the exemption amount phases out entirely when AMTI reaches $310,000.

OTHER ASPECTS OF THE AMT

All of a corporation's AMT is available for carryover as a minimum tax credit. This is so regardless of whether the adjustments and preferences originate from timing differences or AMT exclusions.

EXAMPLE 34

In Example 32, the AMTI exceeds $310,000, so no exemption is allowed. The tentative minimum tax is $1,410,000 (20% of $7,050,000). Assume the regular income tax liability is $1,360,000, and the AMT liability is $50,000 ($1,410,000 − $1,360,000). The amount of the minimum tax credit carryover is $50,000, which is all of the current year's AMT. ■

TAX PLANNING:

12.3 AVOIDING PREFERENCES AND ADJUSTMENTS

LO.8

Identify tax planning opportunities to minimize the AMT.

Several strategies and elections are available to help taxpayers avoid having preferences and adjustments.

- A taxpayer who is in danger of incurring AMT liability usually should not invest in tax-exempt private activity bonds unless doing so makes good investment sense. Any AMT triggered by interest on private activity bonds reduces the yield on an investment in the bonds. Other tax-exempt bonds or taxable corporate bonds might yield a better after-tax return. However, for private activity bonds *issued* after December 31, 2008, and before January 1, 2011, the interest earned is not an AMT tax preference.
- A taxpayer may elect to expense certain costs in the year incurred or to capitalize and amortize the costs over some specified period. The decision should be based on the present discounted value of after-tax cash flows under the available alternatives. Costs subject to elective treatment include circulation expenditures, mining exploration and development costs, and research and experimental expenditures.

TAX*in*
the NEWS

SIMPLIFYING THE CODE AND ELIMINATING THE AMT

In 2010, two U.S. senators, Democrat Ron Wyden of Oregon and Republican Judd Gregg of New Hampshire, introduced tax legislation entitled the "Bipartisan Tax Fairness and Simplification Act." Their principal objective was to simplify the Code. Among the ways this would be accomplished are the following:

- Establish a 24 percent flat corporate tax rate.
- Provide tax relief for families making up to $200,000.
- Reduce the number of tax rates for individuals from six to three (rates of 15, 25, and 35 percent).

- Nearly triple the amount of the standard deduction.
- Permit small businesses (gross annual receipts of up to $1 million) to expense inventory and equipment purchases.
- Repeal many special interest tax breaks.
- Repeal the AMT.

Source: Website of Senator Ron Wyden.

12.4 CONTROLLING THE TIMING OF PREFERENCES AND ADJUSTMENTS

The AMT exemption often keeps items of tax preference from being subject to the AMT. To use the AMT exemption effectively, taxpayers should avoid bunching preferences and positive adjustments in any one year. To avoid this bunching, taxpayers should attempt to control the timing of such items when possible.

12.5 TAKING ADVANTAGE OF THE AMT/ REGULAR TAX RATE DIFFERENTIAL

A taxpayer who cannot avoid triggering the AMT in a given year can usually save taxes by taking advantage of the rate differential between the AMT and the regular income tax.

EXAMPLE 35

Peter, a real estate dealer who expects to be in the 35% regular income tax bracket in 2012, is subject to the AMT in 2011 at the 26% rate. He is considering the sale of a parcel of land (inventory) at a gain of $100,000. If he sells the land in 2012, he will have to pay tax of $35,000 ($100,000 gain × 35% regular income tax rate). However, if he sells the land in 2011, he will pay tax of $26,000 ($100,000 gain × 26% AMT rate). Thus, accelerating the sale into 2011 will save Peter $9,000 ($35,000 − $26,000) in tax. ■

EXAMPLE 36

Cora, who expects to be in the 35% tax bracket in 2012, is subject to the AMT in 2011 at the 26% rate. She is going to contribute $10,000 in cash to her alma mater, State University. If Cora makes the contribution in 2012, she will save tax of $3,500 ($10,000 contribution × 35% regular income tax rate). However, if she makes the contribution in 2011, she will save tax of $2,600 ($10,000 contribution × 26% AMT rate). Thus, deferring the contribution until 2012 will save Cora $900 ($3,500 − $2,600) in tax. ■

This deferral/acceleration strategy should be considered for any income or expenses where the taxpayer can control the timing. This strategy applies to corporations as well as to individuals.

REFOCUS ON THE BIG PICTURE

THE PRESENCE OR ABSENCE OF THE AMT

Bob contacts Adam, his tax return preparer, and explains in an excited voice that he believes that he underpaid his Federal income tax liability for 2011 by $15,000. He is worried about the negative effects of any underpayment if it is discovered during an IRS audit, including the effect on his future marriage to Carol. Adam reviews Bob's tax return and assures him that it was properly prepared. Bob indicates that Carol has provided him with a copy of her tax return. He asks Adam to compare the returns and then explain the tax liability difference to him. He faxes a copy of Carol's return to Adam.

Adam examines the two tax returns and discovers that the difference relates to the treatment of the interest earned on the tax-exempt bonds. Both Bob and Carol own tax-exempt bonds, including private activity bonds that usually are subject to the AMT. However, Carol's accountant, Eve, apparently overlooked the fact that interest on private activity bonds is not a tax preference for private activity bonds issued in 2010. So the $15,000 AMT that was reported on Carol's Form 6251 is in error. Bob "texts" the good news to Carol that she is eligible for a Federal income tax refund.

KEY TERMS

ACE adjustment, 12–28

Alternative minimum tax (AMT), 12–3

Alternative minimum tax credit, 12–24

Alternative tax NOL deduction (ATNOLD), 12–16

AMT adjustments, 12–4

AMT exclusions, 12–24

Circulation expenditures, 12–5

Incentive stock options (ISOs), 12–13

Private activity bonds, 12–21

Tax preferences, 12–4

DISCUSSION QUESTIONS

1. **LO.1** Priscilla was recently promoted and received a substantial raise. She talks to her tax adviser about the potential tax ramifications. After making some projections, her adviser welcomes her to the AMT club. Priscilla believes that it is unfair that she must pay more than the regular income tax, as she is a "HENRY" (high earner not rich yet) with substantial college-related debts. Explain to Priscilla the purpose of the AMT and why it applies to her.

2. **LO.2** Distinguish between the *direct* and *indirect* methods of calculating the AMT.

3. **LO.2** Both AMT adjustments and AMT preferences can cause AMTI to increase. Both AMT adjustments and AMT preferences can cause AMTI to decrease. Evaluate these statements.

4. **LO.2, 4** Identify which of the following are tax preferences:
   a. Seven percent of the exclusion associated with gains on the sale of certain small business stock.
   b. Exclusion on the receipt of property by gift or by inheritance.
   c. Exclusion associated with payment of premiums by the employer on group term life insurance for coverage not in excess of $50,000.
   d. Percentage depletion in excess of the property's adjusted basis.
   e. Exclusion of life insurance proceeds received as the result of death.
   f. Exclusion to the employee on the employer's payments of health insurance premiums for employees.

5. **LO.2, 4** Identify which of the following are tax preferences:
   a. Exclusion for qualified employee discount provided by employer.
   b. Exclusion to employee on the employer's contribution to the employee's pension plan.
   c. Excess of deduction for circulation expenditures for regular income tax purposes over the deduction for AMT purposes.
   d. Excess of amortization allowance over depreciation on pre-1987 certified pollution control facilities.
   e. Excess of accelerated over straight-line depreciation on real property placed in service before 1987.

6. **LO.2** Describe the tax formula for the AMT.

7. **LO.2** An AMT results if the tentative AMT exceeds the regular income tax liability. But what happens if the regular income tax liability exceeds the tentative AMT? Does a negative AMT develop to the extent of this excess that can be carried to other years?

8. **LO.2** John and Mabel, unrelated individuals, have the same filing status (single). However, Mabel's AMT exemption amount is $48,450, while John's is $0. Explain.

9. **LO.2** Alfred is single, and his AMTI of $350,000 consists of the following:

Ordinary income	$250,000
Long-term capital gains	70,000
Qualified dividends	30,000

What tax rates are applicable in calculating Alfred's tentative AMT?

10. **LO.2** Can any nonrefundable credits, other than the foreign tax credit, reduce the regular income tax liability below the amount of the tentative AMT?

11. **LO.3** In 1997, Andy placed a warehouse in service in his business. For both regular income tax and AMT purposes, he calculates the cost recovery using the straight-line method. Andy concludes that there will be no AMT adjustment for 2011 because he uses the straight-line method. Evaluate Andy's conclusion.

12. **LO.3** Nell recently purchased a weekly newspaper that has been generating losses. Nell is convinced that she can turn the newspaper around with a new editorial style and increased circulation expenditures. What are the tax benefits and potential tax pitfalls, if any, of increasing the circulation expenses?

13. **LO.3, 8** Rick, who is single, incurs mining exploration and development costs associated with his energy company. He would expense the costs in the current year in order to reduce his regular income tax but is aware that this would create a positive adjustment for AMT purposes. His AGI is large enough to reduce the AMT exemption amount to zero. Therefore, he is considering electing to amortize the mining exploration and development costs over 10 years to avoid having to pay any AMT. Advise Rick.

ISSUE ID

14. **LO.3** Both Janice and April own and operate construction companies. Janice uses the completed contract method, while April uses the percentage of completion method. Why does Janice have to be concerned with the AMT, while April does not?

15. **LO.3** Megan, a corporate executive, plans to exercise an incentive stock option (ISO) granted by her employer to purchase 200 shares of the corporation's stock for an option price of $25 per share. The stock is freely transferable. The stock is currently selling for $60 per share.
   a. Discuss the tax effects if Megan exercises the option.
   b. Can AMT adjustments be avoided if Megan disposes of the stock in the same tax year that she exercises the stock option?

16. **LO.3** Three years ago, Lilly acquired a machine (seven-year property) for $140,000. She depreciated it using an accelerated method under MACRS. When she sells the machine at a gain this year, will her recognized gain for regular income tax and AMT purposes be the same? Explain.

17. **LO.3, 8** Celine is going to be subject to the AMT in 2011. She owns an investment building and is considering disposing of it and investing in other realty. Based on an appraisal of the building's value, the realized gain would be $85,000. Ed has offered to

ISSUE ID

purchase the building from Celine with the closing date being December 29, 2011. Ed wants to close the transaction in 2011 because certain beneficial tax consequences will result only if the transaction is closed prior to the beginning of 2012. Abby has offered to purchase the building with the closing date being January 2, 2012. The building has a $95,000 greater AMT adjusted basis. For regular income tax purposes, Celine expects to be in the 25% tax bracket in 2011 and the 28% tax bracket in 2012. What are the relevant tax issues that Celine faces in making her decision?

18. **LO.3** Passive activity losses are not deductible in computing either taxable income or AMTI. Explain why an adjustment for passive activity losses may be required for AMT purposes.

19. **LO.3, 4** What effect do adjustments and preferences have on the calculation of the ATNOLD?

20. **LO.3** For which of the following itemized deductions is the tax treatment the same for regular income tax and AMT purposes?

- Medical expenses.
- Casualty losses.
- Miscellaneous itemized deductions subject to the 2% floor.
- State income taxes.
- Real estate taxes.
- Charitable contributions.

ISSUE ID

21. **LO.3, 4, 8** Matt, who is single, has always elected to itemize deductions rather than take the standard deduction. In prior years, his itemized deductions always exceeded the standard deduction by a substantial amount. As a result of paying off the mortgage on his residence, he projects that his itemized deductions for 2011 will exceed the standard deduction by only $500. Matt anticipates that the amount of his itemized deductions will remain about the same in the foreseeable future. Matt's AGI is $150,000. He is investing the amount of his former mortgage payment each month in tax-exempt bonds that were issued four years ago. A friend recommends that Matt buy a beach house in order to increase his itemized deductions with the mortgage interest deduction. What are the relevant tax issues for Matt?

22. **LO.3** How does the treatment of medical expenses differ for AMT and regular income tax purposes?

23. **LO.3** In computing the AMT itemized deduction for interest, it is possible that some interest allowed for regular income tax purposes will not be allowed. Explain.

24. **LO.3** When converting taxable income to AMTI, what is the reason for a positive adjustment as to personal and dependency exemptions?

25. **LO.4** Kevin owns a mineral deposit that qualifies for percentage depletion. In 2011, he deducts $90,000 for regular income tax purposes. Cost depletion for the year would have been $55,000.
   a. Does the fact that percentage depletion exceeds cost depletion produce an AMT preference?
   b. Under what circumstances would Kevin have an AMT preference for depletion?

DECISION MAKING

26. **LO.4** During the year, Fran earned $18,000 of interest income on private activity bonds that she had purchased in 2008. She also incurred interest expense of $7,000 in connection with amounts borrowed to purchase the bonds. What is the effect on Fran's taxable income? On her AMT? Could there be a related beneficial effect in calculating AMTI?

27. **LO.6** What is the purpose of the AMT credit? Briefly describe how the credit is computed.

28. **LO.2, 7** Discuss the similarities and differences between the individual and the corporate AMT.

29. **LO.7** Some observers believe that the ACE adjustment causes corporations to change some of the methods they use for financial accounting and tax accounting purposes. Comment.

ISSUE ID

30. **LO.2, 8** Is it ever advisable for a taxpayer to defer deductions from an AMT year into a non-AMT year when the regular income tax applies? Explain and give an example of how such a deferral might be accomplished.

PROBLEMS

31. **L0.2** Use the following data to calculate Reba's AMT base in 2011:

Taxable income	$160,000
Positive AMT adjustments	80,000
Negative AMT adjustments	60,000
AMT preferences	45,000

Reba will file as a single taxpayer.

32. **L0.2** Arthur Wesson, an unmarried individual who is age 68, has taxable income of $160,000 in 2011. He has AMT positive adjustments of $40,000 and tax preferences of $35,000.

COMMUNICATIONS

   a. What is Arthur's AMT?
   b. What is the total amount of Arthur's tax liability?
   c. Draft a letter to Arthur explaining why he must pay more than the regular income tax liability. Arthur's address is 100 Colonel's Way, Conway, SC 29526.

33. **L0.2** Calculate the AMT for the following cases in 2011. The taxpayer has regular taxable income of $450,000 and does not have any credits.

	Tentative AMT	
Filing Status	**Case 1**	**Case 2**
Single	$200,000	$180,000
Married, filing jointly	200,000	180,000

34. **L0.2** Calculate the exemption amount for the following cases in 2011 for a single taxpayer, a married taxpayer filing jointly, and a married taxpayer filing separately.

Case	AMTI
1	$155,000
2	290,000
3	700,000

35. **L0.2** Leona has nonrefundable credits of $70,000 for 2011. None of these nonrefundable credits are personal credits that qualify for special treatment. Her regular income tax liability before credits is $145,000, and her tentative AMT is $98,000.
   a. What is the amount of Leona's AMT?
   b. What is the amount of Leona's regular income tax liability after credits?

36. **L0.2, 3, 8** Angela, who is single, incurs circulation expenditures of $153,000 during 2011. She is in the process of deciding whether to expense the $153,000 or to capitalize it and elect to deduct it over a three-year period. Angela already knows that she will be subject to the AMT for 2011 at both the 26% and the 28% rates. Angela is in the 28% bracket for regular income tax purposes this year (has regular taxable income of $153,000 before considering the circulation expenses) and expects to be in the 28% bracket in 2012 and 2013. Advise Angela on whether she should elect the three-year write-off rather than expensing the $153,000 in 2011.

DECISION MAKING

37. **L0.2, 3** Vito owns and operates a news agency (as a sole proprietorship). During 2011, he incurred expenses of $450,000 to increase circulation of newspapers and magazines that his agency distributes. For regular income tax purposes, he elected to expense the $450,000 in 2011. In addition, he incurred $120,000 in circulation expenditures in 2012 and again elected expense treatment. What AMT adjustments will be required in 2011 and 2012 as a result of the circulation expenditures?

38. **L0.3** Lonzo owns two apartment buildings. He acquired Forsythia Acres on February 21, 1998, for $300,000 ($90,000 allocated to the land) and Square One on November 12, 2011, for $800,000 ($100,000 allocated to the land). Neither apartment complex qualifies

as low-income housing. If Lonzo elects to write off the cost of each building as fast as possible, what is the effect of depreciation (cost recovery) on his AMTI for:

a.   1998?

b.   2011?

DECISION MAKING

COMMUNICATIONS

39. **L0.3, 8** In March 2011, Helen Carlon acquired used equipment for her business at a cost of $300,000. The equipment is five-year class property for regular income tax purposes and for AMT purposes.

a.   If Helen depreciates the equipment using the method that will produce the greatest deduction for 2011 for regular income tax purposes, what is the amount of the AMT adjustment? Helen does not elect § 179 limited expensing. Helen elected not to take additional first-year depreciation.

b.   How can Helen reduce the AMT adjustment to $0? What circumstances would motivate her to do so?

c.   Draft a letter to Helen regarding the choice of depreciation methods. Helen's address is 500 Monticello Avenue, Glendale, AZ 85306.

DECISION MAKING

40. **L0.3, 8** In 2011, Geoff incurred $600,000 of mining and exploration expenditures. He elects to deduct the expenditures as quickly as the tax law allows for regular income tax purposes.

a.   How will Geoff's treatment of mining and exploration expenditures affect his regular income tax and AMT computations for 2011?

b.   How can Geoff avoid having AMT adjustments related to the mining and exploration expenditures?

c.   What factors should Geoff consider in deciding whether to deduct the expenditures in the year incurred?

41. **L0.3** Josepi's construction company uses the completed contract method. During the three-year period 2011–2013, Josepi recognized the following income on his two construction contracts:

Year	Contract 1	Contract 2
2011	$700,000*	$ –0–
2012	–0–	–0–
2013	–0–	800,000**

  *Construction completed in 2011.

**Construction completed in 2013.

If Josepi had used the percentage of completion method, he would have recognized the following income:

Year	Contract 1	Contract 2
2011	$40,000	$275,000
2012	–0–	225,000
2013	–0–	300,000

Calculate the AMT adjustment for 2011, 2012, and 2013.

42. **L0.3** Burt, the CFO of Amber, Inc., is granted stock options in 2011 that qualify as incentive stock options. In 2016, the rights in the stock become freely transferable and not subject to a substantial risk of forfeiture. Burt exercises the stock options in 2015 when the option price is $75,000 and the fair market value of the stock is $90,000. He sells the stock in 2019 for $150,000. What are the regular income tax consequences and the AMT consequences for Burt in:

a.   2011?

b.   2015?

c.   2016?

d.   2019?

43. **LO.3** In 2006, Diego exercised an incentive stock option (ISO), acquiring 1,000 shares of stock at a price of $75 per share. The fair market value of the stock on this date was $98 per share. In 2011, the stock rights became freely transferable (i.e., no longer subject to a substantial risk of forfeiture). Diego sells the 1,000 shares of stock in 2012 for $120 per share. How do these transactions affect Diego's AMTI for 2006, 2011, and 2012?

44. **LO.3** Alicia owns two investment properties that she acquired several years ago. Her adjusted basis for each is as follows:

	Regular Income Tax	AMT
Land	$100,000	$100,000
Apartment building	450,000	490,000

Alicia sells the land for $250,000 and the building for $800,000.
   a. Calculate Alicia's recognized gain or loss on the sale of each asset for regular income tax and AMT purposes.
   b. Determine the AMT adjustment on the sale of each asset.

45. **LO.3** Freda acquired a passive activity in 2011 for $870,000. Gross income from operations of the activity was $160,000. Operating expenses, not including depreciation, were $122,000. Regular income tax depreciation of $49,750 was computed under MACRS. AMT depreciation, computed under ADS, was $41,000. Compute Freda's passive loss deduction and passive loss suspended for regular income tax purposes and for AMT purposes.

46. **LO.3** Wally and Gloria incur and pay medical expenses in excess of insurance reimbursements during the year as follows:

For Wally	$15,000
For Gloria (spouse)	5,000
For Chuck (son)	1,500
For Carter (Gloria's father)	13,000

Wally and Gloria's AGI is $175,000. They file a joint return. Chuck and Carter are Wally and Gloria's dependents.
   a. What is Wally and Gloria's medical expense deduction for regular income tax purposes?
   b. What is Wally and Gloria's medical expense deduction for AMT purposes?
   c. What is the amount of the AMT adjustment for medical expenses?

47. **LO.3** Wolfgang's AGI is $125,000. He has the following itemized deductions for 2011:

Medical expenses [$15,000 − (7.5% × $125,000)]	$ 5,625
State income taxes	4,200
Charitable contributions	4,000
Home mortgage interest on his personal residence	8,000
Casualty loss (after $100 and 10% reductions)	1,800
Miscellaneous itemized deductions [$3,500 − 2%($125,000)]	1,000
	$24,625

   a. Calculate Wolfgang's itemized deductions for AMT purposes.
   b. What is the amount of the AMT adjustment?

48. **LO.3** Walter, who is single, owns a personal residence in the city. He also owns a cabin near a ski resort in the mountains. He uses the cabin as a vacation home. In August 2011, he borrowed $60,000 on a home equity loan and used the proceeds to reduce credit card obligations and other debt. During 2011, he paid the following amounts of interest:

On his personal residence	$16,000
On the cabin	7,000
On the home equity loan	2,500

On credit card obligations	$1,500
On purchase of SUV	1,350

What amount, if any, must Walter recognize as an AMT adjustment in 2011?

49. **LO.3** Gail pays investment interest of $52,000. She has interest income of $21,000 on taxable bonds, $12,000 on tax-exempt private activity bonds (issued in 2007), and $14,000 on regular tax-exempt bonds. Her other investment expenses are $4,000, none of which relates to the tax-exempt bonds.
   a. What is Gail's deduction for investment interest for regular income tax purposes?
   b. What is the amount of her investment interest carryover for regular income tax purposes?
   c. What is the amount of the adjustment for AMT purposes?

50. **LO.3** Bill, who is single with no dependents, had AGI of $100,000 in 2011. His AGI included net investment income of $15,000 and gambling income of $1,100. Bill incurred the following itemized deductions for income tax purposes:

Medical expenses (before 7.5%-of-AGI floor)	$11,000
State income taxes	3,200
Personal property tax	2,000
Real estate tax	8,400
Interest on personal residence	12,200
Interest on home (never rented to others)	3,800
Interest on home equity loan (proceeds were used to buy a new automobile)	2,700
Investment interest expense	3,300
Charitable contribution	5,000
Casualty loss (after $100 floor, before 10%-of-AGI floor)	13,000
Unreimbursed employee expenses (before 2%-of-AGI floor)	2,400
Gambling losses	900

What is the amount of Bill's AMT adjustment for itemized deductions, and is it positive or negative?

51. **LO.2, 3** Paula is single and has no dependents. She has taxable income of $155,000 and tax preferences of $57,000 in 2011. She does not itemize deductions for regular income tax purposes. Compute Paula's AMT exemption and AMTI for 2011.

52. **LO.3, 4** Merle purchased a copper mine several years ago for $750,000. His adjusted basis at the beginning of the year is $425,000. For the year, he deducts depletion of $550,000 (greater of cost depletion of $230,000 or percentage depletion of $550,000) for regular income tax purposes. Calculate Merle's:
   a. AMT adjustment.
   b. Adjusted basis for regular income tax purposes.
   c. Adjusted basis for AMT purposes.

53. **LO.4** Amos incurred and expensed intangible drilling costs (IDC) of $70,000. His net oil and gas income was $60,000. What is the amount of Amos's tax preference item for IDC?

54. **LO.2, 3, 4** Jerry, who is single with no dependents and does not itemize, provides you with the following information for 2011:

Short-term capital loss	$ 7,000
Long-term capital gain	25,000
Municipal bond interest received on private activity bonds acquired in 1997	9,000
Dividends from Procter & Gamble	2,300
Excess of FMV over cost of ISOs (the rights became freely transferable and not subject to a substantial risk of forfeiture in 2011)	35,000

What is the total amount of Jerry's tax preference items and AMT adjustments for 2011?

55. **LO.2, 3, 4** Pat, who is single with no dependents, received a salary of $90,000 in 2011. She had interest income of $1,000, dividend income of $5,000, gambling income of $4,000, and interest income from private activity bonds (issued in 2006) of $40,000. The dividends are not qualified dividends. The following additional information is relevant:

Medical expenses (before 7.5%-of-AGI floor)	$12,000
State income taxes	4,100
Real estate taxes	2,800
Mortgage interest on residence	3,100
Investment interest expense	1,800
Gambling losses	5,100

   Compute Pat's tentative minimum tax for 2011.

56. **LO.2, 5** Renee and Sanjeev, who are married, had taxable income of $273,000 for 2011. They had positive AMT adjustments of $38,000, negative AMT adjustments of $14,000, and tax preference items of $67,500.
    a. Compute their AMTI.
    b. Compute their tentative minimum tax.

57. **LO.2, 3, 4, 5** Farr, who is single, has no dependents and does not itemize. She has the following items relative to her tax return for 2011:

Bargain element from the exercise of an ISO (no restrictions apply to the stock)	$ 45,000
MACRS depreciation on shopping mall building acquired after 1986 and before 1999 (ADS depreciation would have yielded $26,000)	49,000
Percentage depletion in excess of property's adjusted basis	50,000
Taxable income for regular income tax purposes	121,000

    a. Determine Farr's AMT adjustments and preferences for 2011.
    b. Calculate the AMT (if any) for 2011.

58. **LO.2, 3, 4, 5** Larry is single and has the following items for 2011:

Income—	
Salary	$145,000
Interest from bank savings account	12,000
Interest on corporate bonds	7,000
Short-term capital gain	8,000
Expenses—	
Unreimbursed employee business expenses (no meals or entertainment)	4,000
Total medical expenses	24,000
State income taxes	6,500
Real property taxes	6,800
Home mortgage (qualified housing) interest	7,200
Casualty loss on vacation home—	
Decline in value	20,000
Adjusted basis	70,000
Insurance proceeds	12,000
Tax preferences	116,000

   Compute Larry's tax liability for 2011 before credits or prepayments.

59. **LO.5, 6** Bonnie, who is single, has taxable income of $0 in 2011. She has positive timing adjustments of $200,000 and AMT exclusion items of $100,000 for the year. What is the amount of Bonnie's AMT credit for carryover to 2012?

60. **LO.7** Aqua, Inc., a calendar year corporation, has the following gross receipts and taxable income for 2001–2011:

Year	Gross Receipts	Taxable Income
2001	$6,000,000	$1,450,000
2002	6,200,000	1,375,000
2003	6,100,000	1,425,000
2004	8,000,000	1,400,000
2005	7,000,000	1,312,000
2006	7,500,000	985,000
2007	7,200,000	1,002,000
2008	7,100,000	1,010,000
2009	6,500,000	990,000
2010	6,300,000	982,000
2011	7,800,000	850,000

    a.   When is Aqua first exempt from the AMT as a small corporation?
    b.   Is Aqua subject to the AMT for 2011?

61. **LO.7** Gray Corporation (a calendar year corporation) reports the following information for the years listed below:

	2010	2011	2012
Unadjusted AMTI	$3,000	$2,000	$5,000
Adjusted current earnings	4,000	3,000	2,000

Compute the ACE adjustment for each year.

62. **LO.7** In each of the following independent situations, determine the tentative AMT:

	AMTI (Before the Exemption Amount)
Quincy Corporation	$150,000
Redland Corporation	160,000
Tanzen Corporation	320,000

63. **LO.7** Amber, Inc., has taxable income of $200,000. During the year, Amber paid dividends of $30,000. The corporation had $20,000 of positive AMT adjustments and $25,000 of tax preferences.
    a.   Calculate Amber's regular income tax liability.
    b.   Calculate Amber's AMTI and AMT.

CUMULATIVE PROBLEMS

TAX RETURN PROBLEM

64. Robert A. Kliesh, age 41, is single and has no dependents. Robert's Social Security number is 111–11–1111. His address is 201 Front Street, Missoula, MT 59812. He is independently wealthy as a result of having inherited sizable holdings in real estate and corporate stocks and bonds. Robert is a minister at First Presbyterian Church, but he accepts no salary from the church. However, he does reside in the church's parsonage free of charge. The fair rental value of the parsonage is $3,000 a month. The church also provides him a cash grocery allowance of $200 a week. Examination of Robert's financial records provides the following information for 2010:
    a.   On January 16, 2010, Robert sold 1,000 shares of stock for a gain of $10,000. The stock was acquired fourteen months ago.
    b.   He received $30,000 of interest on private activity bonds that he had purchased in 2007. He also received $40,000 of interest on tax-exempt bonds that are not private activity bonds.
    c.   He received gross rent income of $190,000 from an apartment complex he owns. He qualifies as an active participant.

d. Expenses related to the apartment complex, which he acquired in 1987, were $225,000.
e. Robert's interest income (on CDs) totaled $23,000. Since he invests only in growth stocks, he has no dividend income.
f. He won $60,000 on the lottery.
g. On October 9, 2008, Robert exercised his rights under Falcon Corporation's incentive stock option plan. For an option price of $20,000, he acquired stock worth $75,000. The stock became freely transferable in 2010. At the date the stock became freely transferable, the fair market value was $95,000.
h. Robert was the beneficiary of an $800,000 life insurance policy on his Uncle Jake. He received the proceeds in October.
i. Robert had the following potential itemized deductions *from* AGI:

- $5,200 fair market value of stock contributed to Presbyterian Church (basis of stock was $3,000). He had owned the stock for two years.
- $4,200 interest on consumer purchases.
- $3,900 state and local income tax.
- $6,500 medical expenses (before 7.5% floor) for himself. He also paid $15,000 of medical expenses for a parishioner who died.
- $300 for a safe deposit box that is used to store investments and related legal documents.
- $5,000 paid for lottery tickets associated with playing the state lottery. Robert contributed $5,000 of his winnings to the church.
- $5,000 contribution to his traditional IRA.
- Since Robert lived in Montana, he had no sales tax.
- $750 contribution to the campaign of the Democratic candidate for governor.

j. Robert made estimated tax payments of $27,500.

Use Forms 1040 and 6251 and Schedules A, B, D, and E to compute the tax liability (including AMT) for Robert A. Kliesh for 2010. Suggested software: H&R BLOCK At Home.

65. Robert M. and Jane R. Armstrong live at 1802 College Avenue, Carmel, IN 46302. They are married and file a joint return for 2011. The Armstrongs have two dependent children, Ellen J. and Sean M., who are 10-year-old twins. Ellen's Social Security number is 123–45–6788, and Sean's is 123–45–6787. Robert pays child support of $12,000 for Amy, his 17-year-old daughter from his previous marriage. Amy's Social Security number is 123–45–6786. According to the divorce decree, Margaret, Robert's former wife, has legal custody of Amy. Margaret provides the balance of Amy's support (about $6,000).

TAX COMPUTATION PROBLEM

COMMUNICATIONS

Robert (111–11–1111) is a factory foreman, and Jane (123–45–6789) is a computer systems analyst. The Armstrongs' W–2 Forms for 2011 reflect the following information:

	Robert	Jane
Salary (Indiana Foundry, Inc.)	$95,000	
Salary (Carmel Computer Associates)		$110,000
Federal income tax withheld	24,750	27,000
Social Security wages	95,000	106,800
Social Security tax withheld	3,990	4,486
Medicare wages	95,000	110,000
Medicare tax withheld	1,378	1,595
State wages	95,000	110,000
State income tax withheld	4,900	5,500

In addition to their salaries, the Armstrongs had the following income items in 2011:

Interest income (Carmel Sanitation District Bonds)	$23,500
Interest income (Carmel National Bank)	2,900
Qualified dividend income (Able Computer Corporation)	15,000
Gambling income	4,500
Gift from Uncle Raymond to Robert	8,000

Jane inherited $750,000 from her grandfather in January and invested the money in the Carmel Sanitation District Bonds, which are private activity bonds. These bonds were initially issued in April 2008. Jane was selected as the "Citizen of the Year" and received an award of $5,000. She used the $5,000 to pay credit card debt.

The Armstrongs incurred the following expenses during 2011:

Medical expenses (doctor and hospital bills)	$21,000
Real property tax on personal residence	6,900
Mortgage interest on personal residence (reported on Form 1098)	7,400
Investment interest expense	2,300
Contributions	11,500
Gambling losses	5,800
Sales taxes (from sales tax table)	1,851

On March 1, Robert and Jane contributed Ace stock to the Carmel Salvation Army, a public charity. They had acquired the stock on February 9, 1999, for $6,500. The stock was listed on the New York Stock Exchange at a value of $9,000 on the date of the contribution. In addition, Robert and Jane contributed $2,500 during the year to Second Church.

Robert sold five acres of land to a real estate developer on October 12, 2011, for $100,000. He had acquired the land on May 15, 2006, for $81,000.

Compute the tax liability (including AMT) for Robert and Jane Armstrong for 2011. Write a letter to the Armstrongs indicating whether they have a refund or balance due for 2011, and suggest possible tax planning strategies for 2012.

RESEARCH PROBLEMS

THOMSON REUTERS

Checkpoint® Student Edition

Note: Solutions to Research Problems can be prepared by using the Checkpoint® Student Edition online research product, which is available to accompany this text. It is also possible to prepare solutions to the Research Problems by using tax research materials found in a standard tax library.

Research Problem 1. Samuel had worked for Pearl, Inc., for 35 years when he was discharged and his position filled by a much younger person. He filed and pursued a suit for age discrimination and received an award of $1.5 million. Under the contingent fee arrangement with his attorney, one-third of the award was paid directly to the attorney with the balance going to Samuel. Samuel reported the $1 million on his income tax return but did not include the $500,000 paid to the attorney.

The IRS audited Samuel's return and included the $500,000 contingency fee in his gross income. Additionally, Samuel was allowed a miscellaneous itemized deduction (subject to the 2% floor) for the fee paid to the attorney. The IRS adjustment caused a tax deficiency to be assessed for both the regular income tax and the AMT.

Evaluate the result reached.

Research Problem 2. Jolene receives tax-exempt interest of $33,000 on bonds that are classified as private activity bonds. She properly excludes the $33,000 from her gross income for regular income tax purposes [under §§ 103(a) and 103(b)(1)]. Jolene asks your advice on the treatment of the interest for AMT purposes. Locate the Code Section that covers this matter and advise Jolene accordingly.

Research Problem 3. Masha Quigly filed her return for 2009 and reported taxable income of $48,350. This consisted of the following:

AGI (includes $2,000 state income tax refund previously deducted with a tax benefit)	$80,000
Personal exemption	(3,650)
Miscellaneous itemized deductions in excess of 2% of AGI	(28,000)
Taxable income	$48,350

Although Masha had state and local tax expense of $9,000, she chose not to deduct them in calculating taxable income. Masha believed that if she claimed the state and local taxes, she would be subject to the AMT. As a result, she reported a tax liability of $8,281.

Upon audit of the return, the IRS concluded that Masha should have included the $9,000 of state and local taxes in her itemized deductions. Thus, her decision to not deduct the state and local taxes did not relieve her from being subject to the AMT.

Who is right?

Research Problem 4. On his 2010 Federal income tax return, Walter deducted state income taxes of $8,000 for amounts withheld and estimated tax payments made in 2010. When he filed his 2010 state income tax return in April 2011, he discovered that he had overpaid his state income taxes by $1,500. Rather than having the $1,500 refunded to him, he treated it as a 2011 estimated tax payment. The year 2010 was not an AMT year for Walter.

In preparing his 2011 Federal income tax return, Walter is confused about how he should treat the $1,500 in calculating his Federal income tax liability. He knows that under the § 111 tax benefit rule, he should include the $1,500 in gross income in calculating his regular taxable income. However, since he is going to be subject to the AMT, he is uncertain as to how he should treat the $1,500 in calculating AMT. He thinks that the amount could be treated as a negative adjustment in converting taxable income to AMTI if 2010 had been an AMT year. Since it was not, Walter is unsure of the treatment.

Advise Walter on the appropriate treatment of the $1,500 in calculating his 2011 Federal income tax liability.

Use the tax resources of the Internet to address the following questions. Do not restrict your search to the Web, but include a review of newsgroups and general reference materials, practitioner sites and resources, primary sources of the tax law, chat rooms and discussion groups, and other opportunities.

INTERNET
activity

Research Problem 5. Locate a current proposal to modify the structure or scope of the AMT for individuals. Describe the proposal, the entity making the proposal, and potential motivations for submitting the modification to Congress.

Research Problem 6. Go to one of the tax newsgroups and post a short note on one of the following items relative to individuals who are subject to the AMT:
a. Interest deductions on vacation homes.
b. Charitable contributions of appreciated securities.
c. Tax preparation fees.
d. Adequacy of the exemption amount.
e. Indexing of AMT rates.
f. Local property tax.
g. Tax benefit rule.

COMMUNICATIONS

Research Problem 7. Ascertain if your state's income tax has an AMT component. If your state does not levy an income tax, choose a contiguous state that does.

Tax Credits and Payment Procedures

LEARNING OBJECTIVES

After completing Chapter 13, you should be able to:

LO.1

Explain how tax credits are used as a tool of Federal tax policy.

LO.2

Distinguish between refundable and nonrefundable credits and understand the order in which they can be used by taxpayers.

LO.3

Describe various business-related tax credits.

LO.4

Describe various tax credits that are available primarily to individual taxpayers.

LO.5

Understand the tax withholding and payment procedures applicable to employers.

LO.6

Understand the payment procedures applicable to self-employed persons.

LO.7

Identify tax planning opportunities related to tax credits and payment procedures.

OUTLINE

For the latest in changes to tax legislation, visit **www.cengage.com/taxation/swft.**

FRAMEWORK 1040:

Tax Formula for Individuals

This chapter covers the boldfaced portions of the Tax Formula for Individuals that was introduced in Figure 3.1 on p. 3-3. Below those portions are the sections of Form 1040 where the results are reported.

Income (broadly conceived)	$xx,xxx
Less: Exclusions	(x,xxx)
Gross income	$xx,xxx
Less: Deductions for adjusted gross income	(x,xxx)
Adjusted gross income.	$xx,xxx
Less: The greater of total itemized deductions *or* the standard deduction	(x,xxx)
Personal and dependency exemptions	(x,xxx)
Taxable income	$xx,xxx
Tax on taxable income (see Tax Tables or Tax Rate Schedules)	$ x,xxx
Less: Tax credits (including income taxes withheld and prepaid)	(xxx)

FORM 1040 (p. 2)

47	Foreign tax credit. Attach Form 1116 if required	47
48	Credit for child and dependent care expenses. Attach Form 2441	48
49	Education credits from Form 8863, line 23	49
50	Retirement savings contributions credit. Attach Form 8880	50
51	Child tax credit (see instructions)	51
52	Residential energy credits. Attach Form 5695	52
53	Other credits from Form: **a** ☐ 3800 **b** ☐ 8801 **c** ☐ ____	53
54	Add lines 47 through 53. These are your **total credits**	

Tax due (or refund). . . . . $ xxx

THE BIG PICTURE   **Tax Solutions for the Real World**

EDUCATION TAX CREDITS

Tom and Jennifer Snyder have two children in college. Lora is a freshman, and her tuition and required fees in 2011 total $14,000. Lora has a partial scholarship amounting to $6,500, and the Snyders paid the balance of her tuition ($7,500), plus room and board of $8,500. Sam is a junior, and the Snyders paid $8,100 for his tuition plus $7,200 for his room and board. Both students qualify as Tom and Jennifer's dependents.

The Snyders have AGI of $158,000. They would like to know what tax options are available to them related to these educational expenses. They have heard about education tax credits, but they believe that their income is too high for them to get any benefit. Are they correct? **Read the chapter and formulate your response.**

A s explained in Chapter 1, Federal tax law often serves purposes besides merely raising revenue for the government. Evidence of equity, social, and economic considerations, among others, is found throughout the tax law. These considerations also bear heavily in the area of **tax credits**. Consider the following examples:

Paul and Peggy, husband and wife, are both employed outside the home. Their combined salaries are $50,000. However, after paying for child care expenses of $2,000 on behalf of their daughter, Polly, the net economic benefit from both spouses working is $48,000. The child care expenses are, in a sense, business related since they would not have been incurred if both spouses did not work outside the home. If no tax benefits are associated with the child care expenditures, $50,000 is subject to tax.

Another couple, Alicia and Diego, also have a child, John. Diego stays at home to care for John (the value of those services is $2,000) while Alicia earns a $48,000 salary. Because the value of Diego's services rendered is not subject to tax, only Alicia's earnings of $48,000 are subject to tax. ■

The credit for child and dependent care expenses mitigates the inequity felt by working taxpayers who must pay for child care services in order to work outside the home.

Graham, age 66, is a retired taxpayer who receives $17,000 of Social Security benefits as his only source of income in 2011. His Social Security benefits are excluded from gross income. Therefore, Graham's income tax is $0. In 2011, Olga, a single taxpayer 66 years of age, has, as her sole source of income, $17,000 from a pension plan funded by her former employer. Assuming Olga has no itemized deductions or deductions *for* AGI, her income tax for 2011 (before credits) is $605, based on the following computation:

Pension plan benefits	$17,000
Less: Basic standard deduction	(5,800)
Additional standard deduction	(1,450)
Personal exemption	(3,700)
Taxable income	$ 6,050
Income tax (at 10%)	$ 605

■

The tax credit for elderly or disabled taxpayers was enacted to mitigate this inequity.

Jane is a single parent who depends on the government's "safety net" for survival—she receives benefits under the Temporary Assistance to Needy Families program in the amount of $15,000 per year. However, she very much wishes to work. Jane has located a job that will pay $15,500 per year and has found an individual to care for her child at no cost. But, with the $875.75 ($15,500 × 5.65% in 2011) withholding for Social Security and Medicare taxes, the economic benefit from working is less than remaining reliant on the government ($14,624.25 versus $15,000). ■

To help offset the effect of Social Security and Medicare taxes on wages of the working poor and to provide an incentive to work, the earned income credit is used to increase the after-tax earnings of qualified individuals. In addition, the earned income credit helps offset the regressive nature of certain taxes, such as the Social Security and Medicare taxes, which impose a relatively larger burden on low-income taxpayers than on more affluent taxpayers.

These tax credits and many of the other important tax credits available to individuals and other types of taxpayers are a major focus of this chapter. The chapter begins by discussing important tax policy considerations relevant to tax credits. Tax credits are categorized as being either refundable or nonrefundable.

TAX in the NEWS

TAX CREDITS ENABLE MANY TAXPAYERS TO BECOME "NONPAYERS"

One of the key domestic policy initiatives of recent administrations has been to reduce marginal tax rates and then to retain a lower marginal rate structure than under prior law. Many opponents of this policy have argued that the main beneficiaries of the lower tax rates are upper-income taxpayers who are the most affluent individuals in our country. However, Tax Foundation economists have estimated that these policies have also led to more Americans than ever before being relieved of any Federal income tax liability.

Since 2000, the number of "nonpayers" has grown by about 59 percent. In 2008, almost 52 million Americans filed a tax return and did not owe any taxes because of deductions and credits available to them. Thus, more than 36 percent of all filers were "nonpayers."

Source: Adapted from "Record Number of Tax Filers Paid No Federal Income Taxes in 2008," *Tax Foundation,* March 10, 2010.

The distinction between refundable and nonrefundable credits is important because it may affect the taxpayer's ability to enjoy a tax benefit from a particular credit.

Next, an overview of the priority of tax credits is presented. The chapter continues with a discussion of the credits available to businesses and to individual taxpayers and the ways in which credits enter into the calculation of the tax liability.

The Federal tax system has long been based on the pay-as-you-go concept. That is, taxpayers or their employers are required to make regular deposits with the Federal government during the year as payment toward the tax liability that will be determined at the end of the tax year. These deposits are in effect refundable credits. The chapter concludes with a discussion of procedures used in calculating tax deposits, special problems encountered by self-employed persons when estimating their tax payments, and penalties imposed on underpayments.

13.1 TAX POLICY CONSIDERATIONS

LO.1

Explain how tax credits are used as a tool of Federal tax policy.

Congress has generally used tax credits to achieve social or economic objectives or to promote equity among different types of taxpayers. For example, the disabled access credit was enacted to accomplish a social objective: to encourage taxpayers to renovate older buildings so they would be in compliance with the Americans with Disabilities Act. This Act requires businesses and institutions to make their facilities more accessible to persons with various types of disabilities. As another example, the foreign tax credit, which has been a part of the law for decades, has as its purpose the economic and equity objectives of mitigating the burden of multiple taxation on a single stream of income.

A tax credit should not be confused with an income tax deduction. Certain expenditures of individuals (e.g., business expenses) are permitted as deductions from gross income in arriving at adjusted gross income (AGI). Additionally, individuals are allowed to deduct certain nonbusiness and investment-related expenses *from* AGI. While the tax benefit received from a tax deduction depends on the tax rate, a tax credit is not affected by the tax rate of the taxpayer.

EXAMPLE 4

Assume Congress wishes to encourage a certain type of expenditure. One way to accomplish this objective is to allow a tax credit of 25% for such expenditures. Another way is to allow an itemized deduction for the expenditures. Assume that Abby's tax rate is 15%, while Bill's tax rate is 35%, and that each itemizes deductions. In addition, assume that Carmen does not incur enough qualifying expenditures to itemize deductions. The following tax benefits are available to each taxpayer for a $1,000 expenditure:

TAX in the NEWS — FEDERAL TAX LAW IS A KEY COMPONENT OF U.S. ENERGY POLICY

To help stem the increasing dependence of the United States on foreign sources of energy, Congress enacted the Energy Tax Incentives Act of 2005. The legislation provides numerous tax breaks for power producers as well as for consumers, many of which take the form of tax credits. The primary goals of the tax provisions are to improve energy-related infrastructure, provide more incentives for traditional fossil fuel production, and encourage higher levels of energy conservation.

Some of the more widely applicable provisions include credits for:

- Builders who construct energy-efficient homes.
- Individuals who make energy-saving improvements to their residences.
- Manufacturers that make energy-efficient appliances.

- Businesses that buy fuel cell and microturbine power plants.
- Taxpayers who purchase alternative power motor vehicles and refueling property.

Like many other tax credits, the energy credits have been designed to modify taxpayer behavior. More specifically, in this case, Congress's intention is that these credits will lead to greater conservation and more efficient use of energy. At the bill-signing ceremony, President Bush remarked that the legislation is "not a bill for today or necessarily a bill for tomorrow, but it's a bill for the future." Only time will tell whether Congress's intentions and President Bush's prediction of greater energy independence for the United States will prove to be true.

	Abby	Bill	Carmen
Tax benefit if a 25% credit is allowed	$250	$250	$250
Tax benefit if an itemized deduction is allowed	150	350	–0–

As these results indicate, tax credits provide benefits on a more equitable basis than do tax deductions. Equally apparent is that the deduction approach in this case benefits only taxpayers who itemize deductions, while the credit approach benefits all taxpayers who make the specified expenditure. ■

For many years, Congress has used the tax credit provisions of the Code liberally in implementing tax policy. Although budget constraints and economic considerations often have dictated the repeal of some credits, other credits, such as those applicable to expenses incurred for child and dependent care, have been kept to respond to important social policy considerations. Still other credits, such as the one available to low-income workers, have been retained based on economic and equity considerations. Finally, as the myriad of tax proposals so frequently pending before Congress makes clear, the use of tax credits as a tax policy tool continues to evolve as economic and political circumstances change.

13.2 OVERVIEW AND PRIORITY OF CREDITS

REFUNDABLE VERSUS NONREFUNDABLE CREDITS

As illustrated in Exhibit 13.1, certain credits are refundable while others are nonrefundable. **Refundable credits** are paid to the taxpayer even if the amount of the credit (or credits) exceeds the taxpayer's tax liability.

L0.2

Distinguish between refundable and nonrefundable credits and understand the order in which they can be used by taxpayers.

EXAMPLE 5

Ted, who is single, had taxable income of $21,000 in 2011. His income tax from the 2011 Tax Rate Schedule is $2,725. During 2011, Ted's employer withheld income tax of $3,200. Ted is entitled to a refund of $475 because the credit for tax withheld on wages is a refundable credit. ■

EXHIBIT 13.1	Partial Listing of Refundable and Nonrefundable Credits

Refundable Credits

Taxes withheld on wages

Earned income credit

First-time homebuyer credit

Nonrefundable Credits

Credit for child and dependent care expenses

Credit for elderly or disabled

Adoption expenses credit

Child tax credit*

Education tax credits**

Credit for certain retirement plan contributions

Foreign tax credit

General business credit, which includes the following:
- Tax credit for rehabilitation expenditures
- Jobs credit
- Work opportunity tax credit
- Research activities credit
- Low-income housing credit
- Disabled access credit
- Credit for small employer pension plan startup costs
- Credit for employer-provided child care

*The credit is refundable to the extent of 15 percent of the taxpayer's earned income in excess of $3,000 for 2011. Parents with three or more qualifying children may compute the refundable portion using an alternative method.

**Forty percent of the American Opportunity credit is refundable.

Nonrefundable credits are not paid if they exceed the taxpayer's tax liability.

EXAMPLE 6

Tina is single, age 67, and retired. Her taxable income for 2011 is $1,320, and the tax on this amount is $132. Tina's tax credit for the elderly is $225. This credit can be used to reduce her net tax liability to zero, but it will not result in a refund, even though the credit ($225) exceeds Tina's tax liability ($132). This result occurs because the tax credit for the elderly is a nonrefundable credit. ■

Some nonrefundable credits, such as the foreign tax credit, are subject to carry-over provisions if they exceed the amount allowable as a credit in a given year. Other nonrefundable credits, such as the tax credit for the elderly (refer to Example 6), are lost if they exceed the limitations. Because some credits are refundable and others are not and because some credits are subject to carryover provisions while others are not, the order in which credits are offset against the tax liability can be important.[1]

---

[1]With the passage of the Tax Relief Reconciliation Act of 2001, the ordering rules and limitations applied when offsetting tax credits against both the regular income tax liability and the alternative minimum tax liability have become increasingly complex. In addition, different variations of these rules will apply over time as this legislation is fully implemented. Further discussion of the intricacies of these rules is beyond the scope of this chapter.

GENERAL BUSINESS CREDIT

As shown in Exhibit 13.1, the **general business credit** is composed of a number of other credits, each of which is computed separately under its own set of rules. The general business credit combines these credits into one amount to limit the amount of business credits that can be used to offset a taxpayer's income tax liability. The idea behind combining the credits is to prevent a taxpayer from completely avoiding an income tax liability in any one year by offsetting it with business credits that would otherwise be available.

Two special rules apply to the general business credit. First, any unused credit must be carried back 1 year, then forward 20 years. Second, for any tax year, the general business credit is limited to the taxpayer's *net income tax* reduced by the greater of:[2]

- The *tentative minimum tax.*
- 25 percent of *net regular tax liability* that exceeds $25,000.[3]

In order to understand the general business credit limitation, several terms need defining:

- *Net income tax* is the sum of the regular tax liability and the alternative minimum tax reduced by certain nonrefundable tax credits.
- *Tentative minimum tax* for this purpose is reduced by the foreign tax credit allowed.
- *Regular tax liability* is determined from the appropriate tax table or tax rate schedule, based on taxable income. However, the regular tax liability does not include certain taxes (e.g., alternative minimum tax).
- *Net regular tax liability* is the regular tax liability reduced by certain nonrefundable credits (e.g., credit for child and dependent care expenses, foreign tax credit).

EXAMPLE 7

Floyd's general business credit for the current year is $70,000. His net income tax is $150,000, tentative minimum tax is $130,000, and net regular tax liability is $150,000. He has no other tax credits. Floyd's general business credit allowed for the tax year is computed as follows:

Net income tax	$ 150,000
Less: The greater of	
$130,000 (tentative minimum tax)	
$31,250 [25% × ($150,000 − $25,000)]	(130,000)
Amount of general business credit allowed for tax year	$ 20,000

Floyd then has $50,000 ($70,000 − $20,000) of unused general business credits that may be carried back or forward as discussed below. ∎

TREATMENT OF UNUSED GENERAL BUSINESS CREDITS

Unused general business credits are initially carried back one year and are applied to reduce the tax liability during that year. Thus, the taxpayer may receive a tax refund as a result of the carryback. Any remaining unused credits are then carried forward 20 years.[4]

A FIFO method is applied to the carrybacks, carryovers, and utilization of credits earned during a particular year. The oldest credits are used first in determining the amount of the general business credit. The FIFO method minimizes the potential for loss of a general business credit benefit due to the expiration of credit carryovers, since the earliest years are used before the current credit for the taxable year.

---

[2]§ 38(c).

[3]This amount is $12,500 for married taxpayers filing separately unless one of the spouses is not entitled to the general business credit.

[4]§ 39(a)(1).

EXAMPLE 8

This example illustrates the use of general business credit carryovers.

General business credit carryovers		
2008	$ 4,000	
2009	6,000	
2010	2,000	
Total carryovers	$12,000	
2011 general business credit		$ 40,000
Total credit allowed in 2011 (based on tax liability)	$50,000	
Less: Utilization of carryovers		
2008	(4,000)	
2009	(6,000)	
2010	(2,000)	
Remaining credit allowed in 2011	$38,000	
Applied against		
2011 general business credit		(38,000)
2011 unused amount carried forward to 2012		$ 2,000

13.3 SPECIFIC BUSINESS-RELATED TAX CREDIT PROVISIONS

LO.3

Describe various business-related tax credits.

Each component of the general business credit is determined separately under its own set of rules. Some of the more important credits that make up the general business credit are explained here in the order listed in Exhibit 13.1.

TAX CREDIT FOR REHABILITATION EXPENDITURES

Taxpayers are allowed a tax credit for expenditures incurred to rehabilitate industrial and commercial buildings and certified historic structures. The **rehabilitation expenditures credit** is intended to discourage businesses from moving from older, economically distressed areas (e.g., inner cities) to newer locations and to encourage the preservation of historic structures. The current operating features of this credit follow:[5]

Rate of the Credit for Rehabilitation Expenses	Nature of the Property
10%	Nonresidential buildings and residential rental property, other than certified historic structures, originally placed in service before 1936
20%	Nonresidential and residential certified historic structures

When taking the credit, the basis of a rehabilitated building must be reduced by the full rehabilitation credit allowed.[6]

EXAMPLE 9

Juan spent $60,000 to rehabilitate a building (adjusted basis of $40,000) that had originally been placed in service in 1932. He is allowed a $6,000 (10% × $60,000) credit for rehabilitation expenditures. Juan then increases the basis of the building by $54,000 [$60,000 (rehabilitation expenditures) − $6,000 (credit allowed)]. If the building were a historic structure, the credit allowed would be $12,000 (20% × $60,000), and the building's depreciable basis would increase by $48,000 [$60,000 (rehabilitation expenditures) − $12,000 (credit allowed)]. ■

---

[5]§ 47.   [6]§ 50(c).

TABLE 13.1	Recapture Calculation for Rehabilitation Expenditures Credit

If the Property Is Held for	The Recapture Percentage Is
Less than 1 year	100
One year or more but less than 2 years	80
Two years or more but less than 3 years	60
Three years or more but less than 4 years	40
Four years or more but less than 5 years	20
Five years or more	0

To qualify for the credit, buildings must be substantially rehabilitated. A building has been *substantially rehabilitated* if qualified rehabilitation expenditures exceed the greater of:

- The adjusted basis of the property before the rehabilitation expenditures, or
- $5,000.

Qualified rehabilitation expenditures do not include the cost of acquiring a building, the cost of facilities related to a building (such as a parking lot), and the cost of enlarging an existing building.

Recapture of Tax Credit for Rehabilitation Expenditures

The rehabilitation credit taken must be recaptured if the rehabilitated property is disposed of prematurely or if it ceases to be qualifying property. The **rehabilitation expenditures credit recapture** is based on a holding period requirement of five years and is added to the taxpayer's regular tax liability in the recapture year. The recapture amount is also *added* to the adjusted basis of the rehabilitation expenditures for purposes of determining the amount of gain or loss realized on the property's disposition.

The portion of the credit recaptured is a specified percentage of the credit that was taken by the taxpayer. This percentage is based on the period the property was held by the taxpayer, as shown in Table 13.1.

EXAMPLE 10

On March 15, 2008, Rashad placed in service $30,000 of rehabilitation expenditures on a building qualifying for the 10% credit. A credit of $3,000 ($30,000 × 10%) was allowed, and the basis of the building was increased by $27,000 ($30,000 − $3,000). The building was sold on December 15, 2011. Rashad must recapture a portion of the rehabilitation credit based on the schedule in Table 13.1. Because he held the rehabilitated property for more than three years but less than four, 40% of the credit, or $1,200, is added to his 2011 tax liability. Also, the adjusted basis of the rehabilitation expenditures is increased by the $1,200 recapture amount. ∎

JOBS CREDIT

Under the Hiring Incentives to Restore Employment Act of 2010, a $1,000 **jobs credit** is allowed for every unemployed individual who is hired from February 4 through December 31, 2010, and who works for the employer for at least 52 consecutive weeks and whose wages during the last 26 weeks of employment equal at least 80 percent of the wages for the first 26 weeks. The credit applies to any tax year ending after the 2010 date of enactment.

WORK OPPORTUNITY TAX CREDIT

The **work opportunity tax credit** was enacted to encourage employers to hire individuals from one or more of a number of targeted and economically disadvantaged groups.[7]

[7]§ 51. The credit is available only if qualifying employees start work by December 31, 2011.

Examples of such targeted persons include qualified ex-felons, high-risk youths, food stamp recipients, veterans, summer youth employees, and long-term family assistance recipients.

Computation of the Work Opportunity Tax Credit: General

The credit is generally equal to 40 percent of the first $6,000 of wages (per eligible employee) for the first 12 months of employment. Thus, the credit is not available for any wages paid to an employee after the *first year* of employment. If the employee's first year overlaps two of the employer's tax years, however, the employer may take the credit over two tax years. If the credit is taken, the employer's tax deduction for wages is reduced by the amount of the credit.

For an employer to qualify for the 40 percent credit, the employee must (1) be certified by a designated local agency as being a member of one of the targeted groups and (2) have completed at least 400 hours of service to the employer. If an employee meets the first condition but not the second, the credit rate is reduced to 25 percent provided the employee has completed a minimum of 120 hours of service to the employer.

EXAMPLE 11

In January 2011, Green Company hires four individuals who are certified to be members of a qualifying targeted group. Each employee works 800 hours and is paid wages of $8,000 during the year. Green Company's work opportunity credit is $9,600 [($6,000 × 40%) × 4 employees]. If the tax credit is taken, Green must reduce its deduction for wages paid by $9,600. No credit is available for wages paid to these employees after their first year of employment. ∎

EXAMPLE 12

On June 1, 2011, Maria, a calendar year taxpayer, hires Joe, a certified member of a targeted group. During the last seven months of 2011, Joe is paid $3,500 for 500 hours of work. Maria is allowed a credit of $1,400 ($3,500 × 40%) for 2011. Joe continues to work for Maria in 2012 and is paid $7,000 through May 31, 2012. Because up to $6,000 of first-year wages are eligible for the credit, Maria is allowed a 40% credit on $2,500 [$6,000 − $3,500 (wages paid in 2011)] of wages paid in 2012, or $1,000 ($2,500 × 40%). None of Joe's wages paid after May 31, the end of the first year of employment, is eligible for the credit. ∎

Computation of the Work Opportunity Tax Credit: Qualified Summer Youth Employees

The credit for qualified summer youth employees is allowed on wages for services during any 90-day period between May 1 and September 15. The maximum wages eligible for the credit are $3,000 per summer youth employee. The credit rate is the same as the general work opportunity tax credit rate. If the employee continues employment after the 90-day period as a member of another targeted group, the amount of the wages eligible for the general work opportunity tax credit as a member of the new target group is reduced by the wages paid to the employee as a qualified summer youth employee.

A *qualified summer youth employee* must be age 16 or 17 on the hiring date. In addition, the individual's principal place of abode must be within an empowerment zone, enterprise community, or renewal community.

Computation of the Work Opportunity Tax Credit: Long–Term Family Assistance Recipient

The credit[8] is available to employers hiring individuals who have been long-term recipients of family assistance welfare benefits. In general, *long-term recipients* are those individuals who are certified by a designated local agency as being a member of a family receiving assistance under a public aid program for at least an 18-month period ending on the hiring date. Unlike the work opportunity credit for other targeted groups, which applies only to first-year wages paid to qualified individuals, the credit is available for qualified wages paid in the *first two years* of employment if the

[8]Prior to 2007, this component of the work opportunity tax credit was the welfare-to-work credit, which was provided for under § 51A. Under current law, long-term family assistance recipients are a designated targeted group under the work opportunity tax credit [§ 51(d)(1)(I)], and the maximum credit is now slightly more generous than under prior law.

employee is a long-term family assistance recipient. If an employee's first and second work years overlap two or more of the employer's tax years, the employer may take the credit during the applicable tax years.

The credit is equal to 40 percent of the first $10,000 of qualified wages paid to an employee in the first year of employment, plus 50 percent of the first $10,000 of qualified wages paid in the second year of employment, resulting in a maximum credit per qualified employee of $9,000 [$4,000 (year 1) + $5,000 (year 2)]. The credit rate is higher for second-year wages to encourage employers to retain qualified individuals, thereby promoting the overall welfare-to-work goal.

EXAMPLE 13

In April 2011, Blue Company hired three individuals who are certified as long-term family assistance recipients. Each employee is paid $12,000 during 2011. Two of the three individuals continue to work for Blue Company in 2012, earning $9,000 each during the year. Blue Company's work opportunity tax credit is $12,000 [(40% × $10,000) × 3 employees] for 2011 and $9,000 [(50% × $9,000) × 2 employees] for 2012. In each year, Blue must reduce its deduction for wages paid by the amount of the credit for that year. ∎

RESEARCH ACTIVITIES CREDIT

To encourage research and experimentation, usually described as research and development (R&D), a credit is allowed for certain qualifying expenditures paid or incurred by a taxpayer. The **research activities credit** is the *sum* of three components: an incremental research activities credit, a basic research credit, and an energy research credit.[9]

Incremental Research Activities Credit

The incremental research activities credit is equal to 20 percent of the *excess* of qualified research expenses for the taxable year over the base amount.[10]

In general, *research expenditures* qualify if the research relates to discovering technological information that is intended for use in the development of a new or improved business component of the taxpayer. Such expenses qualify fully if the research is performed in-house (by the taxpayer or employees). If the research is conducted by persons outside the taxpayer's business (under contract), only 65 percent of the amount paid qualifies for the credit.[11]

EXAMPLE 14

George incurs the following research expenditures:

In-house wages, supplies, computer time	$50,000
Paid to Cutting Edge Scientific Foundation for research	30,000

George's qualified research expenditures are $69,500 [$50,000 + ($30,000 × 65%)]. ∎

Beyond the general guidelines described above, the Code does not give specific examples of qualifying research. However, the credit is *not* allowed for research that falls into certain categories, including the following:[12]

- Research conducted after the beginning of commercial production of the business component.
- Surveys and studies such as market research, testing, or routine data collection.
- Research conducted *outside* the United States (other than research undertaken in Puerto Rico or possessions of the United States).
- Research in the social sciences, arts, or humanities.

Determining the *base amount* involves a relatively complex series of computations meant to approximate recent historical levels of research activity by the taxpayer.

---

[9]§ 41. Each component of the research credit is available only if qualifying expenditures are paid or incurred by December 31, 2011.

[10]In lieu of determining the incremental research credit as described here, a taxpayer may elect to calculate the credit using an alternative simplified credit procedure. See §§ 41(c)(4) and (5).

[11]In the case of payments to a qualified research consortium, § 41(b)(3)(A) provides that 75% of the amount paid qualifies for the credit. In contrast, for amounts paid to an energy research consortium, § 41(b)(3)(D) allows the full amount to qualify for the credit.

[12]§ 41(d). See also Reg. §§ 1.41–1 through 1.41–7.

Thus, the credit is allowed only for increases in research expenses. A discussion of these computations is beyond the scope of this presentation.

EXAMPLE 15

Jack, a calendar year taxpayer, incurs qualifying research expenditures of $200,000 at the beginning of the year. Assuming the base amount is $100,000, the incremental research activities credit is $20,000 [($200,000 − $100,000) × 20%]. ■

Qualified research and experimentation expenditures are not only eligible for the 20 percent credit, but can also be *deducted* in the year incurred.[13] In this regard, a taxpayer has two choices:[14]

- Use the full credit and reduce the expense deduction for research expenses by 100 percent of the credit.
- Retain the full expense deduction and reduce the credit by the product of 100 percent of the credit times the maximum corporate tax rate (35 percent).

As an alternative to the expense deduction, the taxpayer may *capitalize* the research expenses and *amortize* them over 60 months or more. In this case, the amount capitalized and subject to amortization is reduced by the full amount of the credit *only* if the credit exceeds the amount allowable as a deduction.

EXAMPLE 16

Assume the same facts as in Example 15, which shows that the potential incremental research activities credit is $20,000. In the current year, the expense that the taxpayer can deduct and the credit amount are as follows:

	Credit Amount	Deduction Amount
Full credit and reduced deduction		
$20,000 − $0	$20,000	
$200,000 − $20,000		$180,000
Reduced credit and full deduction		
$20,000 − [(100% × $20,000) × 35%]	13,000	
$200,000 − $0		200,000
Full credit and capitalize and elect to amortize costs over 60 months		
$20,000 − $0	20,000	
($200,000/60) × 12		40,000

■

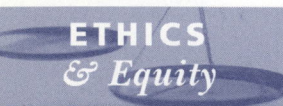

ETHICS & Equity   **WHEN DOES "RESEARCH" QUALIFY AS R&D?**

The research activities credit is designed to encourage taxpayers to engage in research related to the discovery of technological information for use in developing a new or improved business component of the taxpayer.

You are employed as a staff accountant for a privately held corporation that manufactures medical equipment. During the current year, the corporation purchases new communications software and related document-management systems with the goal of enhancing employee efficiency and productivity. To familiarize employees with these new systems, an outside firm is hired to conduct numerous training

seminars during the first six months after the software is installed. Substantial costs are incurred in connection with these training seminars. Not surprisingly, the firm encounters various inefficiencies until the employees have had sufficient training and time to learn the new systems.

The corporation's new president, ever mindful of the company's profitability and tax position, urges you to claim the research activities credit with respect to the software training costs. The president justifies this position on the grounds that the employees were "researching" the new software and its use. How do you respond?

---

[13]§ 174. Also refer to the discussion of rules for deducting research and experimental expenditures in Chapter 7.

[14]§ 280C(c).

Basic Research Credit

Corporations (other than S corporations or personal service corporations) are allowed an additional 20 percent credit for basic research payments made in *excess* of a base amount. This credit is not available to individual taxpayers. *Basic research payments* are defined as amounts paid in cash to a qualified basic research organization, such as a college or university or a tax-exempt organization operated primarily to conduct scientific research.

Basic research is defined generally as any original investigation for the advancement of scientific knowledge not having a specific commercial objective. The definition excludes basic research conducted outside the United States and basic research in the social sciences, arts, or humanities. This reflects the intent of Congress to encourage high-tech research in the United States.

The calculation of this additional credit for basic research expenditures is complex and is based on expenditures in excess of a specially defined base amount. The portion of the basic research expenditures not in excess of the base amount is treated as a part of the qualifying expenditures for purposes of the regular credit for incremental research activities.

EXAMPLE 17

Orange Corporation, a qualifying corporation, pays $75,000 to a university for basic research. Assume that Orange's base amount for the basic research credit is $50,000. The basic research activities credit allowed is $5,000 [($75,000 − $50,000) × 20%]. The $50,000 of basic research expenditures that equal the base amount are treated as research expenses for purposes of the regular incremental research activities credit. ∎

Energy Research Credit

This component of the research credit is intended to stimulate additional energy research. The calculation of the credit is relatively straightforward and is equal to 20 percent of the amounts paid or incurred by a taxpayer to an energy research consortium for energy research.

LOW-INCOME HOUSING CREDIT

To encourage building owners to make affordable housing available for low-income individuals, Congress has made a credit available to owners of qualified low-income housing projects.[15]

More than any other, the **low-income housing credit** is influenced by nontax factors. For example, certification of the property by the appropriate state or local agency authorized to provide low-income housing credits is required. These credits are issued based on a nationwide allocation.

The amount of the credit is based on the qualified basis of the property. The qualified basis depends on the number of units rented to low-income tenants. Tenants are low-income tenants if their income does not exceed a specified percentage of the area median gross income. The amount of the credit is determined by multiplying the qualified basis by a credit rate.[16] The credit is allowed over a 10-year period if the property continues to meet the required conditions.

EXAMPLE 18

Sarah spends $1 million to build a qualified low-income housing project that is completed on January 1 of the current year. The entire project is rented to low-income families. Assume the credit rate for property placed in service during January is 7.67%. Sarah may claim a credit of $76,700 ($1,000,000 × 7.67%) in the current year and in each of the following nine years. Generally, first-year credits are prorated based on the date the project is placed in service. A full year's credit is taken in each of the next nine years, and any remaining first-year credit is claimed in the eleventh year. ∎

---

[15]§ 42.

[16]The rate is subject to adjustment every month by the IRS.

Recapture of a portion of the credit may be required if the number of units set aside for low-income tenants falls below a minimum threshold, if the taxpayer disposes of the property or the interest in it, or if the taxpayer's amount at risk decreases.

A "Win-Win" Situation?

Tom and Sarah Prentice rent an apartment in a complex owned by Steve Heatherton, who has been a close friend since high school. About a week ago, Steve told Tom about the tax savings he has received by claiming the low-income housing credit on all of his apartment complexes—including the one in which the Prentices live. Initially, Tom was pleased that Steve had been able to use this government "subsidy" to reduce his tax burden because, in general, he believes that the government rarely uses its resources wisely. However, during the conversation, Steve inadvertently let slip the fact that the apartment complex in which the Prentices live qualifies for the credit only because he overstates the percentage of low-income tenants living in the facility. Steve admitted that by claiming that the Prentices are low-income tenants (even though they aren't), the percentage of low-income tenants is just enough for Steve to "qualify" for the credit on the complex. Steve said that because Tom and Sarah are his friends, he was passing along some of his tax savings to them in the form of lower rent.

Tom knows that if he were to report Steve to the IRS, Steve would not only lose the economic benefits of the credit, but would also have legal troubles—and could be sentenced to prison. In addition, Tom and Sarah would see an increase in their rent. Tom has come to you for advice. What course of action would you recommend to Tom?

DISABLED ACCESS CREDIT

The **disabled access credit** is designed to encourage small businesses to make their facilities more accessible to disabled individuals. The credit is available for any eligible access expenditures paid or incurred by an eligible small business. The credit is calculated at the rate of 50 percent of the eligible expenditures that exceed $250 but do not exceed $10,250. Thus, the maximum amount for the credit is $5,000 ($10,000 × 50%).[17]

An *eligible small business* is one that during the previous year either had gross receipts of $1 million or less or had no more than 30 full-time employees. An eligible business can include a sole proprietorship, partnership, regular corporation, or S corporation.

Eligible access expenditures are generally any reasonable and necessary amounts that are paid or incurred to make certain changes to facilities. These changes must involve the removal of architectural, communication, physical, or transportation barriers that would otherwise make a business inaccessible to disabled and handicapped individuals. Examples of qualifying projects include installing ramps, widening doorways, and adding raised markings on elevator control buttons. However, eligible expenditures do *not* include amounts that are paid or incurred in connection with any facility that has been placed in service after the enactment of the credit (i.e., November 5, 1990).

To the extent a disabled access credit is available, no deduction or credit is allowed under any other provision of the tax law. The adjusted basis for depreciation is reduced by the amount of the credit.

EXAMPLE 19

This year Red, Inc., an eligible business, makes $11,000 of capital improvements to business realty that had been placed in service in June 1990. The expenditures are intended to make Red's business more accessible to the disabled and are considered eligible expenditures for purposes of the disabled access credit. The amount of the credit is $5,000 [($10,250 − $250) × 50%]. Although $11,000 of eligible expenditures are incurred, only the excess of $10,250 over $250 qualifies for the credit. Further, the depreciable basis of the capital improvement is $6,000 because the basis must be reduced by the amount of the credit [$11,000 (cost) − $5,000 (amount of the credit)]. ∎

---

[17]§ 44.

CREDIT FOR SMALL EMPLOYER PENSION PLAN STARTUP COSTS

Small businesses are entitled to a nonrefundable credit for administrative costs associated with establishing and maintaining certain qualified retirement plans.[18] While such costs (e.g., payroll system changes, consulting fees) generally are deductible as ordinary and necessary business expenses, the credit is intended to lower the after-tax cost of establishing a qualified retirement program and thereby encourage qualifying businesses to offer retirement plans for their employees. The **credit for small employer pension plan startup costs** is available for eligible employers at the rate of 50 percent of qualified startup costs. An eligible employer is one with fewer than 100 employees who have earned at least $5,000 of compensation. Qualified startup costs include ordinary and necessary expenses incurred in connection with establishing or maintaining an employer pension plan and retirement-related education costs.[19] The maximum credit is $500 (based on a maximum $1,000 of qualifying expenses), and the deduction for the startup costs incurred is reduced by the amount of the credit. The credit can be claimed for qualifying costs incurred in each of the three years beginning with the tax year in which the retirement plan becomes effective (maximum total credit over three years of $1,500).

EXAMPLE 20

Maple Company decides to establish a qualified retirement plan for its employees. In the process, it pays consulting fees of $1,200 to a firm that will provide educational seminars to Maple's employees and will assist the payroll department in making necessary changes to the payroll system. Maple may claim a credit for the pension plan startup costs of $500 ($1,200 of qualifying costs, limited to $1,000 × 50%), and its deduction for these expenses is reduced to $700 ($1,200 − $500). ∎

CREDIT FOR EMPLOYER-PROVIDED CHILD CARE

The scope of § 162 trade or business expenses includes an employer's expenditures incurred to provide for the care of children of employees as ordinary and necessary business expenses. Alternatively, employers may claim a credit for qualifying expenditures incurred while providing child care facilities to their employees during normal working hours.[20] The **credit for employer-provided child care**, limited annually to $150,000, is composed of the aggregate of two components: 25 percent of qualified child care expenses and 10 percent of qualified child care resource and referral services. *Qualified child care expenses* include the costs of acquiring, constructing, rehabilitating, expanding, and operating a child care facility. *Child care resource and referral services* include amounts paid or incurred under a contract to provide child care resource and referral services to an employee. Any qualifying expenses otherwise deductible by the taxpayer must be reduced by the amount of the credit. In addition, the taxpayer's basis for any property acquired or constructed and used for qualifying purposes is reduced by the amount of the credit. If within 10 years of being placed in service, a child care facility ceases to be used for a qualified use, the taxpayer will be required to recapture a portion of the credit previously claimed.[21]

EXAMPLE 21

During the year, Tan Company constructed a child care facility for $400,000 to be used by its employees who have preschool-aged children in need of child care services while their parents are at work. In addition, Tan incurred salaries for child care workers and other administrative costs associated with the facility of $100,000. As a result, Tan's credit for employer-provided child care is $125,000 [($400,000 + $100,000) × 25%]. Correspondingly, the basis of the facility is reduced to $300,000 ($400,000 − $100,000), and the deduction for salaries and administrative costs is reduced to $75,000 ($100,000 − $25,000). ∎

---

[18]§ 45E. Currently, this credit is scheduled to expire for years after December 31, 2012.

[19]§§ 45E(c)(1) and (d)(1).

[20]§ 45F. Currently, this credit is scheduled to expire for years after December 31, 2012.

[21]§ 45F(d).

| TABLE 13.2 | Earned Income Credit and Phaseout Percentages | | | | | | |

Tax Year	Number of Qualifying Children	Earned Income Base Amount	Credit Percentage	Maximum Credit	Phaseout Base	Phaseout Percentage	Phaseout Ends at Income of
2011	*Married, Filing Jointly:*						
	No children	$ 6,070	7.65	$ 464	$12,670	7.65	$18,740
	One child	9,100	34.00	3,094	21,770	15.98	41,132
	Two children	12,780	40.00	5,112	21,770	21.06	46,044
	Three or more children	12,780	45.00	5,751	21,770	21.06	49,078
	Other Taxpayers:						
	No children	$ 6,070	7.65	$ 464	$ 7,590	7.65	$13,660
	One child	9,100	34.00	3,094	16,690	15.98	36,052
	Two children	12,780	40.00	5,112	16,690	21.06	40,964
	Three or more children	12,780	45.00	5,751	16,690	21.06	43,998
2010	*Married, Filing Jointly:*						
	No children	$ 5,980	7.65	$ 457	$12,490	7.65	$18,470
	One child	8,970	34.00	3,050	21,460	15.98	40,545
	Two children	12,590	40.00	5,036	21,460	21.06	45,372
	Three or more children	12,590	45.00	5,666	21,460	21.06	48,362
	Other Taxpayers:						
	No children	$ 5,980	7.65	$ 457	$ 7,480	7.65	$13,460
	One child	8,970	34.00	3,050	16,450	15.98	35,535
	Two children	12,590	40.00	5,036	16,450	21.06	40,363
	Three or more children	12,590	45.00	5,666	16,450	21.06	43,352

13.4 OTHER TAX CREDITS

LO.4

Describe various tax credits that are available primarily to individual taxpayers.

EARNED INCOME CREDIT

The **earned income credit**, which has been a part of the law for many years, consistently has been justified as a means of providing tax equity to the working poor. In addition, the credit has been designed to help offset regressive taxes that are a part of our tax system, such as the gasoline tax. Further, the credit is intended to encourage economically disadvantaged individuals to become contributing members of the workforce.[22]

The earned income credit is determined by multiplying a maximum amount of earned income by the appropriate credit percentage (see Table 13.2). Generally, earned income includes employee compensation and net earnings from self-employment but excludes items such as interest, dividends, pension benefits, nontaxable employee compensation, and alimony. If a taxpayer has children, the credit percentage used in the calculation depends on the number of qualifying children. For 2009 through 2012, the American Recovery and Reinvestment Tax Act of 2009 and the Tax Relief Act of 2010 increased the credit percentage for families with three or more children and increased the phaseout threshold amounts for married taxpayers filing joint returns. Thus, in 2011, the maximum earned income credit for a taxpayer with one qualifying child is $3,094 ($9,100 × 34%), $5,112 ($12,780 × 40%) for a taxpayer with two qualifying children, and $5,751 ($12,780 × 45%) for a taxpayer with three or more qualifying children. However, the maximum earned income credit is phased out completely if the taxpayer's earned income or AGI exceeds certain thresholds as shown in Table 13.2.[23] To the extent that the greater of earned income or AGI exceeds

---

[22]§ 32. The earned income credit is not available if the taxpayer's unearned income (e.g., interest, dividends) exceeds $3,150 in 2011 ($3,100 in 2010). See § 32(i).

[23]§ 32(a)(2)(B).

$21,770 in 2011 for married taxpayers filing a joint return ($16,690 for other taxpayers), the difference, multiplied by the appropriate phaseout percentage, is subtracted from the maximum earned income credit.

EXAMPLE 22

In 2011, Grace Brown, who is married, files a joint return and otherwise qualifies for the earned income credit. Grace receives wages of $26,000, and she and her husband have no other income. The Browns have one qualifying child. The current earned income credit is $3,094 ($9,100 × 34%) reduced by $676 [($26,000 − $21,770) × 15.98%]. Thus, the earned income credit is $2,418. If, instead, the Browns have three or more qualifying children, the calculation produces a credit of $5,751 ($12,780 × 45%) reduced by $891 [($26,000 − $21,770) × 21.06%]. Thus, the Browns' earned income credit is $4,860 if they have three or more children. ■

Earned Income Credit Table

It is not necessary to compute the credit as shown in Example 22. To simplify the compliance process, the IRS issues an Earned Income Credit Table for the determination of the appropriate amount of the credit. This table and a worksheet are included in the instructions available to individual taxpayers.

Eligibility Requirements

Eligibility for the credit depends not only on the taxpayer meeting the earned income and AGI thresholds, but also on whether he or she has a qualifying child. The term *qualifying child* generally has the same meaning here as it does for purposes of determining who qualifies as a dependent (see Chapter 3).

In addition to being available for taxpayers with qualifying children, the earned income credit is also available to certain *workers without children*. However, this provision is available only to taxpayers aged 25 through 64 who cannot be claimed as a dependent on another taxpayer's return. As shown in Table 13.2, the credit for 2011 is calculated on a maximum earned income of $6,070 times 7.65 percent and reduced by 7.65 percent of earned income over $12,670 for married taxpayers filing a joint return ($7,590 for other taxpayers).

EXAMPLE 23

Walt, who is single, 28 years of age, and is not claimed as a dependent on anyone else's return, earns $8,000 during 2011. Even though he does not have any qualifying children, he qualifies for the earned income credit. His credit is $464 ($6,070 × 7.65%) reduced by $31 [($8,000 − $7,590) × 7.65%]. Thus, Walt's earned income credit is $433. If, instead, Walt's earned income is $7,000, his earned income credit is $464. In this situation, there is no phaseout of the maximum credit because his earned income is not in excess of $7,590. ■

ETHICS & Equity

HOLDING ON TO THE EARNED INCOME CREDIT WITH THE AID OF A TRANSIENT CHILD

For many years, Loretta Johnson, a single mother of three children, has been struggling to make ends meet by working at two jobs that barely pay the minimum wage and together provide just over $10,000. Fortunately, her housing and food costs have been partially subsidized through various government programs. In addition, she has been able to take advantage of the earned income credit, which has provided almost $3,000 annually to help her with living expenses. The credit truly has made a difference in the lives of Loretta and her family by helping them keep their creditors at bay. Loretta is proud that she has worked hard and provided for her family for many years without having to accept welfare.

Now, however, Loretta faces a problem as her children have grown up and moved out of her home. With no qualifying children in her household, she no longer qualifies for the earned income credit. Although she will continue working her two jobs, such a significant loss to her household budget cuts into her ability to be self-reliant. As a survival strategy and as a way of keeping the earned income credit, Loretta arranges to have one of her grandchildren live with her for just over six months every year. This enables almost 30 percent of her household budget to be secure. How do you react to Loretta's tax strategy?

TAX *in the NEWS*

WHAT ARE THE CHANCES OF AN IRS AUDIT?

Even though most taxpayers try to comply with the rules, most also worry that their return may be audited by the IRS. Are these taxpayers worrying needlessly? What are the chances that a particular return will be selected for audit?

The IRS picks returns for audit on the basis of a "DIF" score. "DIF" stands for "discriminant function"—a statistical technique that assigns a score to each individual return after it has been processed. The higher a return's DIF score, the higher the likelihood that it will be selected for audit. What generates a high DIF score? The biggest factor is the amount of deductions and credits claimed relative to income.

For most taxpayers, the chances of an audit are low. In 2007, only about 1 percent of Federal individual income tax returns were selected for audit. For the self-employed and those with complex returns or high income, however, the

odds increase. For example, the audit rate was about 6 percent for proprietorship returns showing total gross receipts between $100,000 and $200,000. For individual returns reporting total income of $1 million or more, the audit rate was about 9 percent.

But the IRS also devotes a great deal of attention to low-income taxpayers. Because there have been many fraudulent claims of the earned income credit in the past, taxpayers who claim the credit have a good chance of finding themselves under scrutiny. Taxpayers who claimed the earned income credit in 2007 had a better than 36 percent chance of being audited.

Source: Adapted from "Assessing the Risk of IRS Audit for Your Tax Return," *The Dallas Morning News* (online), March 28, 2008.

Advance Payment

The earned income credit is a form of negative income tax (a refundable credit for taxpayers who do not have a tax liability). An eligible individual may elect to receive advance payments of the earned income credit from his or her employer (rather than receiving the credit from the IRS upon filing the tax return). The amount that can be received in advance is limited to 60 percent of the credit that is available to a taxpayer with only one qualifying child. If this election is made, the taxpayer must file a certificate of eligibility (Form W–5) with his or her employer and *must* file a tax return for the year the income is earned.[24] The advance payment provision expired at the end of 2010.

TAX CREDIT FOR ELDERLY OR DISABLED TAXPAYERS

The credit for the elderly was originally enacted to provide tax relief on retirement income for individuals who were not receiving substantial benefits from tax-free Social Security payments.[25] Currently, the **tax credit for the elderly or disabled** applies to the following:

- Taxpayers age 65 or older.
- Taxpayers under age 65 who are retired with a **permanent and total disability** and who have disability income from a public or private employer on account of the disability. A person generally is considered permanently and totally disabled if he or she is unable to engage in any substantial gainful activity due to a physical or mental impairment for a period of at least 12 months (or lesser period if the disability results in death).

The *maximum* allowable credit is $1,125 (15% × $7,500 of qualifying income), but the credit will be less for a taxpayer who receives Social Security benefits or has AGI exceeding specified amounts. Under these circumstances, the qualifying income base amount used in the credit computation is reduced. Many taxpayers receive Social Security benefits or have AGI high enough to reduce the base for the credit to zero. In addition, because the credit is nonrefundable, the allowable credit cannot exceed the taxpayer's tax liablity.

---

[24]§ 3507.   [25]§ 22. This credit is not subject to indexation.

TABLE 13.3	Base and Threshold Amounts for Tax Credit for Elderly or Disabled Taxpayers		
Status		**Base Amount**	**Threshold Amount**
Single, head of household, or surviving spouse		$5,000	$ 7,500
Married, joint return, only one spouse qualifies		5,000	10,000
Married, joint return, both spouses qualify		7,500	10,000
Married, separate returns, spouses live apart the entire year (amount for each spouse)		3,750	5,000

The eligibility requirements and the tax computation are somewhat complicated. Consequently, an individual may elect to have the IRS compute his or her tax and the amount of the tax credit.

The credit generally is based on a qualifying income amount (referred to as the *base amount*) and the filing status of the taxpayer in accordance with Table 13.3. To qualify for the credit, married taxpayers who live together must file a joint return. For taxpayers under age 65 who are retired on permanent and total disability, the base amounts could be less than those shown in Table 13.3 because these amounts are limited to taxable disability income.

This initial base amount is *reduced* by (1) Social Security, Railroad Retirement, and certain excluded pension benefits and (2) one-half of the taxpayer's AGI in excess of a threshold amount (see Table 13.3), which is a function of the taxpayer's filing status.

EXAMPLE 24

Paul and Peggy, husband and wife, are both over age 65 and receive Social Security benefits of $1,000 in the current year. On a joint return, they report AGI of $21,000.

Base amount (from Table 13.3)		$7,500
Less: Social Security benefits	$1,000	
One-half of excess of AGI over threshold amount (from Table 13.3) [($21,000 − $10,000) × ½]	5,500	
Total reductions		(6,500)
Remaining base amount		$1,000
Multiply remaining base amount by 15%—this is the tax credit allowed, subject to tax liability limitation		$ 150 ∎

Schedule R of Form 1040 is used to calculate and report the credit.

FOREIGN TAX CREDIT

Both individual taxpayers and corporations may claim a tax credit for foreign income tax paid on income earned and subject to tax in another country or a U.S. possession.[26] As an alternative, a taxpayer may claim a deduction instead of a credit.[27] In most instances, the **foreign tax credit (FTC)** is advantageous since it provides a direct offset against the tax liability.

The purpose of the FTC is to mitigate double taxation since income earned in a foreign country is subject to both U.S. and foreign taxes. However, the FTC is subject to an overall limitation. This limitation may result in some form of double taxation or taxation at rates in excess of U.S. rates when the foreign tax rates are higher than

---

[26]Section 27 provides for the credit, but the qualifications and calculation procedure for the credit are contained in §§ 901–908.

[27]§ 164.

the U.S. rates. This is a distinct possibility because U.S. tax rates are lower than those of many foreign countries.

Other special tax treatments applicable to taxpayers working outside the United States include the foreign earned income exclusion (see Chapter 5) and limitations on deducting expenses of employees working outside the United States (see Chapter 9). Recall from the earlier discussion that a taxpayer may not take advantage of *both* the FTC and the foreign earned income exclusion.

Computation

Taxpayers are required to compute the FTC based upon an overall limitation.[28] The FTC allowed is the *lesser* of the foreign taxes imposed or the *overall limitation* determined according to the following formula:

$$\frac{\text{Foreign-source taxable income}}{\text{Worldwide taxable income}} \times \text{U.S. tax before FTC}$$

For individual taxpayers, worldwide taxable income in the overall limitation formula is determined *before* personal and dependency exemptions are deducted.

EXAMPLE 25

In 2011, Carlos, a calendar year taxpayer, has $10,000 of income from Country Y, which imposes a 15% tax, and $20,000 from Country Z, which imposes a 50% tax. He has taxable income of $55,200 from within the United States, is married filing a joint return, and claims two dependency exemptions. Thus, although Carlos's taxable income for purposes of determining U.S. tax is $85,200, taxable income amounts used in the limitation formula are not reduced by personal and dependency exemptions. Thus, for this purpose, taxable income is $100,000 [$85,200 + (4 × $3,700)]. Assume that Carlos's U.S. tax before the credit is $13,550. Overall limitation:

$$\frac{\text{Foreign-source taxable income}}{\text{Worldwide taxable income}} = \frac{\$30,000}{\$100,000} \times \$13,550 = \$4,065$$

In this case, $4,065 is allowed as the FTC because this amount is less than the $11,500 of foreign taxes imposed [$1,500 (Country Y) + $10,000 (Country Z)]. ■

Thus, the overall limitation may result in some of the foreign income being subjected to double taxation. Unused FTCs [e.g., the $7,435 ($11,500 − $4,065) from Example 25] can be carried back 1 year and forward 10 years.[29]

Only foreign income taxes, war profits taxes, and excess profits taxes (or taxes paid in lieu of such taxes) qualify for the credit.[30] In determining whether or not a tax is an income tax, U.S. criteria are applied. Thus, value added taxes (VAT), severance taxes, property taxes, and sales taxes do not qualify because they are not regarded as taxes on income. Such taxes may be deductible, however.

ADOPTION EXPENSES CREDIT

Adoption expenses paid or incurred by a taxpayer may give rise to the **adoption expenses credit**.[31] The provision is intended to assist taxpayers who incur nonrecurring costs directly associated with the adoption process, such as adoption fees, attorney fees, court costs, social service review costs, and transportation costs.

In 2011, up to $13,360 of costs incurred to adopt an eligible child qualify for the credit.[32] An eligible child is one who is:

• under 18 years of age at the time of the adoption or
• physically or mentally incapable of taking care of himself or herself.

---

[28]§ 904.

[29]§ 904(c) and Reg. § 1.904–2(g), Example 13–1. This treatment of unused FTCs applies to tax years ending after October 22, 2004. Prior law provided a two-year carryback and a five-year carryforward.

[30]Reg. § 1.901–1(a)(3)(i).

[31]§ 23.

[32]§ 23(b)(1). In 2010, after amendment by the Health Care Act of 2010, the maximum amount of eligible costs was $13,170. This ceiling is adjusted for inflation annually. Special rules are used in calculating the credit when adopting "a child with special needs." See § 23(d)(3).

Sourcing Income in Cyberspace—Getting It Right When Calculating the Foreign Tax Credit

The overall limitation on the foreign tax credit (FTC) plays a critical role in restricting the amount of the credit available to a taxpayer. In the overall limitation formula, the taxpayer must characterize the year's taxable income as either earned (or sourced) inside the United States or earned from sources outside the United States. As a general rule, a relatively greater percentage of foreign-source income in the formula will lead to a larger FTC. Therefore, determining the source of various types of income is critical in the proper calculation of the credit. However, classifying income as either foreign or U.S. source is not always a simple matter.

For example, consumers and businesses are using the Internet to conduct more and more commerce involving both products and services. The problem is that the existing income-sourcing rules were developed long before the existence of the Internet, and taxing authorities are finding it challenging to apply these rules to Internet transactions. Where does a sale take place when the web server is in Scotland, the seller is in India, and the customer is in Illinois? Where is a service performed when all activities take place over the Net? These questions and more will have to be answered by the United States and its trading partners as the Internet economy grows in size and importance.

A taxpayer may claim the credit in the year qualifying expenses were paid or incurred if they were paid or incurred *during or after* the tax year in which the adoption was finalized. For qualifying expenses paid or incurred in a tax year *prior* to the year when the adoption was finalized, the credit must be claimed in the tax year following the tax year during which the expenses are paid or incurred. A married couple must file a joint return.

EXAMPLE 26

In late 2010, Sam and Martha pay $4,000 in legal fees, adoption fees, and other expenses directly related to the adoption of an infant daughter, Susan. In 2011, the year in which the adoption becomes final, they pay an additional $10,000. Sam and Martha are eligible for a $13,360 credit in 2011 (for expenses of $14,000, limited by the $13,360 ceiling, paid in 2010 and 2011). ∎

The amount of the credit that is otherwise available is phased out for taxpayers whose AGI (modified for this purpose) exceeds $185,210 in 2011, and the credit is completely eliminated when AGI reaches $225,210. The resulting credit is calculated by reducing the allowable credit (determined without this reduction) by the allowable credit multiplied by the ratio of the excess of the taxpayer's AGI over $185,210 to $40,000.[33]

EXAMPLE 27

Assume the same facts as in the previous example, except that Sam and Martha's AGI is $210,210 in 2011. As a result, their available credit in 2011 is reduced from $13,360 to $5,010 {$13,360 − [$13,360 × ($25,000/$40,000)]}. ∎

The credit is nonrefundable and is available to taxpayers only in a year in which this credit and the other nonrefundable credits do not exceed the taxpayer's tax liability. However, any unused adoption expenses credit may be carried over for up to five years, being utilized on a first-in, first-out basis.

---

[33]§ 23(b)(2). The AGI threshold amount is indexed for inflation. In 2010, the phaseout of the credit began when AGI exceeded $182,520.

CHILD TAX CREDIT

The **child tax credit** provisions allow individual taxpayers to take a tax credit based solely on the *number* of their qualifying children. This credit is one of several "family-friendly" provisions that currently are part of our tax law. To be eligible for the credit, the child must be under age 17, a U.S. citizen, and claimed as a dependent on the taxpayer's return.

Maximum Credit and Phaseouts

Under current law, the maximum credit available is $1,000 per child.[34] The available credit is phased out for higher-income taxpayers beginning when AGI reaches $110,000 for joint filers ($55,000 for married taxpayers filing separately) and $75,000 for single taxpayers. The credit is phased out by $50 for each $1,000 (or part thereof) of AGI above the threshold amounts.[35] Since the maximum credit amount available to taxpayers depends on the number of qualifying children, the income level at which the credit is phased out completely also depends on the number of children qualifying for the credit.[36]

EXAMPLE 28	Juanita and Alberto are married and file a joint tax return claiming their two children, ages six and eight, as dependents. Their AGI is $122,400. Juanita and Alberto's maximum child tax credit is $2,000 ($1,000 × 2 children). Since Juanita and Alberto's AGI is in excess of the $110,000 threshold, the maximum credit must be reduced by $50 for every $1,000 (or part thereof) above the threshold amount {$50 × [($122,400 − $110,000)/ $1,000]}. Thus, the credit reduction equals $650 [$50 × 13 (rounded from 12.4)]. Therefore, Juanita and Alberto's child tax credit is $1,350. ∎

CREDIT FOR CHILD AND DEPENDENT CARE EXPENSES

A credit is allowed to taxpayers who incur employment-related expenses for child or dependent care.[37] The **credit for child and dependent care expenses** is a specified percentage of expenses incurred to enable the taxpayer to work or to seek employment. Expenses on which the credit for child and dependent care expenses is based are subject to limitations.

Eligibility

To be eligible for the credit, an individual must have either of the following:

- A dependent under age 13.
- A dependent or spouse who is physically or mentally incapacitated and who lives with the taxpayer for more than one-half of the year.

Generally, married taxpayers must file a joint return to obtain the credit.

Eligible Employment–Related Expenses

Eligible expenses include amounts paid for household services and care of a qualifying individual that are incurred to enable the taxpayer to be employed. Child and dependent care expenses include expenses incurred in the home, such as payments for a housekeeper. Out-of-the-home expenses incurred for the care of a dependent under the age of 13 also qualify for the credit. In addition, out-of-the-home expenses incurred for an older dependent or spouse who is physically or mentally incapacitated qualify for the credit if that person regularly spends at least eight hours each day in the taxpayer's household. This makes the credit available to taxpayers who

---

[34]§ 24. The maximum credit per child is scheduled to remain at $1,000 through 2012.

[35]AGI is modified for purposes of this calculation. The threshold amounts are *not* indexed for inflation. See §§ 24(a) and (b).

[36]The child tax credit is generally refundable to the extent of 15% of the taxpayer's earned income in excess of an inflation-adjusted amount.

The American Recovery and Reinvestment Tax Act of 2009 set this amount at $3,000 for 2009 and 2010, and the Tax Relief Act of 2010 extends this provision through 2012. Prior to the ARRTA of 2009, the 2009 threshold was $12,550.

[37]§ 21.

keep handicapped older children and elderly relatives in the home instead of institutionalizing them. Out-of-the-home expenses incurred for services provided by a dependent care center will qualify only if the center complies with all applicable laws and regulations of a state or unit of local government.

Child care payments to a relative are eligible for the credit unless the relative is a child (under age 19) of the taxpayer.

EXAMPLE 29

Wilma is an employed mother of an eight-year-old child. She pays her mother, Rita, $1,500 per year to care for the child after school. Wilma pays her daughter Eleanor, age 17, $900 for the child's care during the summer. Of these amounts, only the $1,500 paid to Rita qualifies as employment-related child care expenses. ∎

Earned Income Ceiling

Qualifying employment-related expenses are limited to an individual's earned income. For married taxpayers, this limitation applies to the spouse with the *lesser* amount of earned income. Special rules are provided for taxpayers with nonworking spouses who are disabled or are full-time students. If a nonworking spouse is physically or mentally disabled or is a full-time student, he or she is *deemed* to have earned income for purposes of this limitation. The deemed amount is $250 per month if there is one qualifying individual in the household or $500 per month if there are two or more qualifying individuals in the household. In the case of a student-spouse, the student's income is *deemed* to be earned only for the months that the student is enrolled on a full-time basis at an educational institution.[38]

Calculation of the Credit

In general, the credit is equal to a percentage of *unreimbursed* employment-related expenses up to $3,000 for one qualifying individual and $6,000 for two or more individuals. The credit rate varies between 20 percent and 35 percent, depending on the taxpayer's AGI. The following chart shows the applicable percentage for taxpayers as AGI increases:

Adjusted Gross Income		Applicable Rate of Credit
Over	But Not Over	
$ 0	$15,000	35%
15,000	17,000	34%
17,000	19,000	33%
19,000	21,000	32%
21,000	23,000	31%
23,000	25,000	30%
25,000	27,000	29%
27,000	29,000	28%
29,000	31,000	27%
31,000	33,000	26%
33,000	35,000	25%
35,000	37,000	24%
37,000	39,000	23%
39,000	41,000	22%
41,000	43,000	21%
43,000	No limit	20%

---

[38]§ 21(d).

EXAMPLE 30	Nancy, who has two children under age 13, worked full-time while her spouse, Ron, was attending college for 10 months during the year. Nancy earned $22,000 and incurred $6,200 of child care expenses. Ron is *deemed* to be fully employed and to have earned $500 for each of the 10 months (or a total of $5,000). Since Nancy and Ron have AGI of $22,000, they are allowed a credit rate of 31%. Nancy and Ron are limited to $5,000 in qualified child care expenses ($6,000 maximum expenses, limited to Ron's deemed earned income of $5,000). Therefore, they are entitled to a tax credit of $1,550 (31% × $5,000) for the year. ∎

Dependent Care Assistance Program

Recall from Chapter 5 that a taxpayer is allowed an exclusion from gross income for a limited amount reimbursed for child or dependent care expenses. However, the taxpayer is not allowed both an exclusion from gross income and a child and dependent care credit on the same amount. The $3,000 and $6,000 ceilings for allowable child and dependent care expenses are reduced dollar for dollar by the amount of reimbursement.[39]

EXAMPLE 31	Assume the same facts as in Example 30, except that of the $6,200 paid for child care, Nancy was reimbursed $2,500 by her employer under a qualified dependent care assistance program. Under the employer's plan, the reimbursement reduces Nancy's taxable wages. Thus, Nancy and Ron have AGI of $19,500 ($22,000 − $2,500). The maximum amount of child care expenses for two or more dependents of $6,000 is reduced by the $2,500 reimbursement, resulting in a tax credit of $1,120 [32% × ($6,000 − $2,500)]. ∎

Reporting Requirements

The credit is claimed by completing and filing Form 2441, Credit for Child and Dependent Care Expenses.

EDUCATION TAX CREDITS

Two credits, the **American Opportunity credit** and the **lifetime learning credit**,[40] are available to help qualifying low- and middle-income individuals defray the cost of higher education. The credits are available for qualifying tuition and related expenses incurred by students pursuing undergraduate or graduate degrees or vocational training. Books and other course materials are eligible for the American Opportunity credit (but not the lifetime learning credit).[41] Room and board are ineligible for both credits.

Maximum Credit

The American Opportunity credit permits a maximum credit of $2,500 per year (100 percent of the first $2,000 of tuition expenses plus 25 percent of the next $2,000 of tuition expenses) for the *first four years* of postsecondary education.[42] The lifetime learning credit permits a credit of 20 percent of qualifying expenses (up to $10,000 per year) incurred in a year in which the American Opportunity credit is not claimed with respect to a given student. Generally, the lifetime learning credit is used for individuals who are beyond the first four years of postsecondary education.

Eligible Individuals

Both education credits are available for qualified expenses incurred by a taxpayer, taxpayer's spouse, or taxpayer's dependent. The American Opportunity credit is

---

[39]§ 21(c).

[40]§ 25A. The HOPE scholarship credit was modified and renamed the American Opportunity tax credit by the American Recovery and Reinvestment Tax Act of 2009 for the 2009 and 2010 tax years. The Tax Relief Act of 2010 extends this credit through 2012. Without congressional intervention, the HOPE scholarship credit will return in 2013.

[41]§ 25A(i)(3).

[42]In years prior to 2009, the qualifying expense base for the HOPE scholarship credit was subject to inflation adjustment. The base was $1,200 in 2008, $1,100 in 2007 and 2006, and $1,000 for years prior to 2006.

available per eligible student, while the lifetime learning credit is calculated per taxpayer. To be eligible for the American Opportunity credit, a student must take at least one-half the full-time course load for at least one academic term at a qualifying educational institution. No comparable requirement exists for the lifetime learning credit. Therefore, taxpayers who are seeking new job skills or maintaining existing skills through graduate training or continuing education are eligible for the lifetime learning credit. Taxpayers who are married must file a joint return in order to claim either education credit.

Income Limitations and Refundability

Both education credits are subject to income limitations, which differ for 2009 through 2012.[43] In addition, the American Opportunity credit is partially refundable and may be used to offset a taxpayer's alternative minimum tax (AMT) liability (the lifetime learning credit is neither refundable nor an AMT liability offset).

The American Opportunity credit amount is phased out, beginning when the taxpayer's AGI (modified for this purpose) reaches $80,000 ($160,000 for married taxpayers filing jointly).[44] The reduction is equal to the extent to which AGI exceeds $80,000 ($160,000 for married taxpayers filing jointly) as a percentage of a $10,000 phaseout range ($20,000 for married taxpayers filing jointly). As a result, the credit is completely eliminated when modified AGI reaches $90,000 ($180,000 for married taxpayers filing jointly). The entire credit allowed may be used to reduce a taxpayer's AMT liability. In addition, 40 percent of the American Opportunity credit is refundable.[45]

The lifetime learning credit amount is phased out, beginning when the taxpayer's AGI (modified for this purpose) reaches $51,000 ($102,000 for married taxpayers filing jointly).[46] The reduction is equal to the extent to which AGI exceeds $51,000 ($102,000 for married filing jointly) as a percentage of a $10,000 ($20,000 for married filing jointly) phaseout range. The credit is completely eliminated when AGI reaches $61,000 ($122,000 for married filing jointly).

EXAMPLE 32 THE BIG PICTURE

Return to the facts of *The Big Picture* on p. 13-2. Recall that Tom and Jennifer Snyder are married, file a joint tax return, have modified AGI of $158,000, and have two children, Lora and Sam. The Snyders paid $7,500 of tuition and $8,500 for room and board for Lora (a freshman) and $8,100 of tuition plus $7,200 for room and board for Sam (a junior). Both Lora and Sam are full-time students and are Tom and Jennifer's dependents. Lora's tuition and Sam's tuition are qualified expenses for the American Opportunity credit. For 2011, Tom and Jennifer may claim a $2,500 American Opportunity credit [(100% × $2,000) + (25% × $2,000)] for both Lora's and Sam's expenses (in total, a $5,000 American Opportunity credit). ■

EXAMPLE 33 THE BIG PICTURE

Return to the facts of *The Big Picture* on p. 13-2. Now assume that Tom and Jennifer's modified AGI for 2011 is $172,000 instead of $158,000. Tom and Jennifer are eligible to claim a $2,000 American Opportunity credit for 2011. Their $5,000 available American Opportunity credit must be reduced because their AGI exceeds the $160,000 limit for married taxpayers. The percentage reduction is computed as the amount by which modified AGI exceeds the limit, expressed as a percentage of the phaseout range, or [($172,000 − $160,000)/$20,000)], resulting in a 60% reduction. Therefore, the maximum available credit for 2011 is $2,000 ($5,000 × 40% allowable portion). ■

---

[43]In 2008 and prior years, the HOPE scholarship and lifetime learning credits were combined and subject to a single modified AGI limitation.
[44]These amounts are not adjusted for inflation.
[45]If the credit is claimed for a taxpayer subject to § 1(g) (the "kiddie tax"), the credit is not refundable.
[46]§ 25A(d). For 2009 and 2010, the AGI bases were $50,000 and $100,000. § 25A(b)(2)(A).

EXAMPLE 34	Return to the facts of *The Big Picture* on p. 13-2. Now assume that Tom and Jennifer's

EXAMPLE 34
THE BIG PICTURE

Return to the facts of *The Big Picture* on p. 13-2. Now assume that Tom and Jennifer's modified AGI is $116,000. In addition, assume that Tom is going to school on a part-time basis to complete a graduate degree and pays qualifying tuition and fees of $4,000 during 2011. As Tom and Jennifer's modified AGI is below $160,000, a $5,000 American Opportunity credit is available to them. In addition, Tom's qualifying expenses are eligible for the lifetime learning credit. The available lifetime learning credit of $800 ($4,000 × 20%) must be reduced because their modified AGI exceeds the $102,000 limit for married taxpayers. As their modified AGI exceeds the $102,000 limit by $14,000 and the phaseout range is $20,000, their lifetime learning credit is reduced by 70%. Therefore, their lifetime learning credit for 2011 is $240 ($800 × 30%), and their total education credits amount to $5,240 ($5,000 American Opportunity credit and $240 lifetime learning credit). ∎

Restrictions on Double Tax Benefit

Taxpayers are prohibited from receiving a double tax benefit associated with qualifying educational expenses. Therefore, taxpayers who claim an education credit may not deduct the expenses, nor may they claim the credit for amounts that are otherwise excluded from gross income (e.g., scholarships, employer-paid educational assistance). However, a taxpayer may claim an education tax credit and exclude from gross income amounts distributed from a Coverdell Education Savings Account as long as the distribution is not used for the same expenses for which the credit is claimed.

FIRST-TIME HOMEBUYER CREDIT

Designed to encourage home ownership and to alleviate the surplus of unsold houses, the **first-time homebuyer credit** provides a tax incentive for home purchases. For home purchases from January 1, 2009 through April 30, 2010,[47] a credit of 10 percent of the purchase price is allowed but not to exceed $8,000 ($4,000 for married individuals filing separately). In this regard, single taxpayers and married persons filing jointly are treated alike, and each is subject to the same $8,000 maximum.[48]

The credit is available only if the purchase price of the home is $800,000 or less.[49] In addition, the credit is phased out for more affluent taxpayers. The phaseout range is based on modified AGI and occurs between $125,000 and $145,000 for single taxpayers and $225,000 and $245,000 for married persons filing jointly.[50]

Eligible Individuals

In general, the credit is available to *first-time buyers*.[51] This means that the taxpayer has not owned a principal residence during the three-year period before the purchase (i.e., when title to the property passes).[52] However, for purchases made after November 6, 2009, the credit is also available to *existing homeowners* who are "*long-term residents.*" A long-term resident is one who has maintained the same principal residence for any five-consecutive-year period during the eight-year period ending on the date of the purchase of a subsequent principal residence.[53] The maximum allowable credit for existing homeowners is limited to $6,500 ($3,250 for married individuals filing separately).[54]

---

[47]§ 36(h). The credit also applies to the purchase of a principal residence with a written binding contract in place by April 30, 2010, that includes a requirement to close on the purchase before July 1, 2010. Congress did not extend this credit.

[48]§§ 36(a) and (h). For homes purchased from April 9, 2008 through December 31, 2008, the maximum credit was $7,500 ($3,750 for married individuals filing separately).

[49]§ 36(b)(3). There is no phaseout mechanism to this limit (i.e., a home purchased with a price in excess of $800,000 will not qualify for the credit). No price limit existed for purchases before November 7, 2009.

[50]§ 36(b)(2)(A). For purchases before November 7, 2009, the phaseout range was between $75,000 and $95,000 for singles and $150,000 to $170,000 for married persons filing jointly.

[51]§ 36(c)(1). The statute also contains a variety of anti-abuse provisions; see §§ 36(b)(4) and 36(d)(3) and (4).

[52]§ 36(c)(3).

[53]§ 36(c)(6).

[54]§ 36(b)(1)(D).

The term *principal residence* carries the same meaning as in the rules for the exclusion of gain on the sale of a residence.[55] For this purpose, the ownership of a vacation home is not a disqualification as it is not a principal residence.

As long as the time limitations for the purchase are met, the credit may be claimed in either the year of purchase or the prior taxable year.[56]

EXAMPLE 35

The Nelsons always file jointly, and their modified AGI varies from $130,000 to $140,000. They decide not to renew the lease on their apartment, and in March 2010, they purchase a new home for $750,000. If the Nelsons already filed their return for 2009, they can file an amended return claiming a credit of $8,000. If not claimed on their 2009 return, the $8,000 credit can be claimed on their 2010 return. Note that if the Nelsons had purchased a house with a value in excess of $800,000, no credit would be allowed. ■

Recapture of Credit

Although the homebuyer credit contains a recapture provision, this provision is waived for homes purchased after December 31, 2008 (even if the taxpayer claimed the credit in 2008).[57] For homes purchased in 2008, the first-time homebuyer credit must be repaid beginning two years after the home was purchased. The credit is repaid in equal installments over 15 years.[58] In effect, a credit claimed on a home purchased in 2008 is merely an interest-free loan to the homebuyer.

EXAMPLE 36

Assume the same facts as in the previous example and that the Nelsons purchased their home on November 20, 2008. Beginning in 2010, the Nelsons must add $500 ($7,500 credit allowed/15 years) to their tax liability for each year through 2024. ■

If a home purchased in 2008 is disposed of before the 15-year period is up, recapture of the unpaid balance occurs.[59] Homes purchased after December 31, 2008, are also subject to an accelerated recapture rule. If such a home is disposed of within 36 months from the date of purchase, the entire homebuyer credit must be recaptured.[60] However, the recapture cannot exceed any gain from the sale of the residence. Recapture also can occur if the property ceases to be the taxpayer's principal residence. But recapture does not occur on the death of the taxpayer, an involuntary conversion, or a transfer between spouses incident to a divorce.[61]

The home purchase credit is classified as a refundable credit. In certain situations, therefore, it could generate a payment from the IRS for the taxpayer in excess of any tax liability.

ENERGY CREDITS

The Internal Revenue Code contains a variety of credits for businesses and individuals to encourage the conservation of natural resources and the development of energy sources other than oil and gas. Exhibit 13.2 provides a summary of several of the more important energy tax credits.

CREDIT FOR CERTAIN RETIREMENT PLAN CONTRIBUTIONS

Taxpayers may claim a nonrefundable **credit for certain retirement plan contributions** based on eligible contributions of up to $2,000 to certain qualified retirement plans, such as traditional and Roth IRAs and § 401(k) plans.[62] This credit, sometimes referred to as the "saver's credit," is intended to encourage lower- and middle-income taxpayers to contribute to qualified retirement plans. The benefit provided by this credit is in addition to any deduction or exclusion that otherwise is available due to the qualifying contribution. In calculating the credit, the qualifying

---

[55]§ 36(c)(2), § 121, and Reg. § 1.121–1(b).

[56]§ 36(g).

[57]§ 36(f)(4)(D), as modified by the American Recovery and Reinvestment Tax Act of 2009.

[58]§§ 36(f)(1) and (7).

[59]§ 36(f)(2).

[60]§ 36(f)(4)(D)(ii), as added by the American Recovery and Reinvestment Tax Act of 2009.

[61]§ 36(f)(4).

[62]§ 25B.

EXHIBIT 13.2	Energy Credits Summary

Home Energy Efficiency Improvement Tax Credits

Consumers who purchase and install specific products, such as energy-efficient windows, insulation, doors, roofs, and heating and cooling equipment, in the home can receive a tax credit of up to $1,500 for property placed in service before January 1, 2011 (§ 25C). In addition, consumers who purchase photovoltaic, fuel cell, and/or solar water heating property can receive a credit equal to 30% of the purchase price. Improvements must be made to the taxpayer's principal residence and must be completed before January 1, 2017 (§ 25D).

Plug-in Electric Drive Motor Vehicles

Consumers who purchase new plug-in electric drive motor vehicles before January 1, 2015, can qualify for a credit of $2,500 plus $417 for each kilowatt-hour of battery capacity in excess of 5 kilowatt-hours. The maximum credit is $7,500 (§ 30D).

Business Energy Tax Credits

Businesses are eligible for tax credits for producing alternative fuels, building energy-efficient buildings, producing energy-efficient products, and producing energy using alternative means.

- *Biodiesel/Alternative Fuels—Small Producer Biodiesel and Renewable Diesel* (§ 40) and *Ethanol Credit* (§ 40A). Small agri-biodiesel producers are provided a tax credit measured in varying cents per gallon for producing these fuels (with varying maximums per year). The credit is available for sales through December 31, 2011.
- *Credit for Business Installation of Qualified Fuel Cells, Stationary Microturbine Power Plants, Solar, and Small Wind Energy Equipment.* A tax credit—based on the purchase price—is provided for installing qualified fuel cell power plants (a 30% credit), qualifying stationary microturbine power plants (a 10% credit), qualifying solar energy equipment (a 30% credit), and small wind energy equipment (a 30% credit). The credit applies to property placed in service before January 1, 2017 (§ 48).
- *Credit for Building Energy-Efficient New Homes.* A $2,000 tax credit is provided to eligible contractors for each qualified new energy-efficient home constructed through December 31, 2011. The credit applies to manufactured homes meeting ENERGY STAR® criteria and other homes (§ 45L).
- *Manufacturing Energy-Efficient Appliances.* A tax credit is provided to the manufacturer of energy-efficient dishwashers, clothes washers, and refrigerators. Credits vary depending on the efficiency of the unit and relate, generally, to production through December 31, 2011 (§ 45M).
- *Energy Credit for Producing Electricity via Wind, Solar, Geothermal, and Other Property.* A tax credit is provided for producing energy via qualified wind, solar, geothermal, and other property. The tax credit—based on the number of kilowatt-hours of electricity produced—applies to production through the end of 2013 (except for wind energy, which applies to production through the end of 2012) (§ 45).

contributions are reduced by taxable distributions from any of the qualifying plans received by the taxpayer and spouse during the tax year and the two previous tax years and during the period prior to the due date of the return.

The credit rate applied to the eligible expenses depends on the taxpayer's AGI[63] and filing status as shown in Table 13.4. However, the maximum credit allowed to an individual is $1,000 ($2,000 × 50%). As the taxpayer's AGI increases, the rate applied to contributions in calculating the credit is reduced, and once AGI exceeds the upper end of the applicable range, no credit is available. To qualify for the credit, the taxpayer must be at least 18 years of age and cannot be a dependent of another taxpayer or a full-time student.

EXAMPLE 37	Earl and Josephine, married taxpayers, each contribute $2,500 to their respective § 401(k) plans offered through their employers. The AGI reported on their joint return is $45,000. The maximum amount of contributions that may be taken into account in calculating the credit is limited to $2,000 for Earl and $2,000 for Josephine. As a result, they may claim a credit for their retirement plan contributions of $400 [($2,000 × 2) × 10%]. They would not qualify for the credit if their AGI had exceeded $56,500. ∎

---

[63]For years beginning after 2006, the AGI thresholds are indexed for inflation. The amounts shown in Table 13–4 are the relevant thresholds for 2011. For purposes of this credit, the AGI thresholds are modified to include certain excluded income items. See § 25B(e).

| TABLE 13.4 | "Saver's" Credit Rate and AGI Thresholds |

Joint Return		Head of Household		All Other Cases		Applicable Percentage
Over	Not Over	Over	Not Over	Over	Not Over	
$ 0	$34,000	$ 0	$25,500	$ 0	$17,000	50%
34,000	36,500	25,500	27,375	17,000	18,250	20%
36,500	56,500	27,375	42,375	18,250	28,250	10%
56,500		42,375		28,250		0%

SMALL EMPLOYER HEALTH INSURANCE CREDIT

Under the Health Care Act of 2010, a tax credit is provided for a qualified small employer for nonelective contributions to purchase health insurance for its employees beginning in 2010.[64] To qualify for the credit, the employer must have no more than 25 full-time equivalent employees whose annual full-time wages average no more than $50,000. The employer must pay at least half the cost of the health insurance premiums.[65] The credit is 35 percent of the health insurance premiums paid in 2010 through 2013 (50 percent in years after 2013). It is subject to a phaseout if the employer has more than 10 full-time equivalent employees and/or has annual full-time wages that average more than $25,000.[66]

13.5 PAYMENT PROCEDURES

The tax law contains elaborate rules that require the prepayment of various Federal taxes. Consistent with the pay-as-you-go approach to the collection of taxes, these rules carry penalties for lack of compliance.[67] Prepayment procedures fall into two major categories: those applicable to employers and those applicable to self-employed persons. For employers, both payroll taxes (FICA and FUTA) and income taxes may be involved. With self-employed taxpayers, the focus is on the income tax and the self-employment tax.

L0.5
Understand the tax withholding and payment procedures applicable to employers.

PROCEDURES APPLICABLE TO EMPLOYERS

Employment taxes include FICA (Federal Insurance Contributions Act) and FUTA (Federal Unemployment Tax Act). The employer usually is responsible for withholding the employee's share of FICA (commonly referred to as Social Security tax) and appropriate amounts for income taxes. In addition, the employer must match the FICA portion withheld and fully absorb the cost of FUTA. The sum of the employment taxes and the income tax withholdings must be paid to the IRS at specified intervals.

The key to employer compliance in this area involves the resolution of the following points:

- Ascertaining which employees and wages are covered by employment taxes and are subject to withholding for income taxes.
- Arriving at the amount to be paid and/or withheld.
- Reporting and paying employment taxes and income taxes withheld to the IRS on a timely basis through the use of proper forms and procedures.

[64]§ 45R.
[65]§§ 45R(d)(1) and (4). The wage amount is indexed for inflation beginning in 2014.
[66]§ 45R(c). The credit percentage for tax-exempt employers is 25% in 2010 through 2013 and 35% in subsequent years.

[67]See, for example, § 3403 (employer liable for any taxes withheld and not paid over to the IRS), § 6656 (penalty on amounts withheld and not paid over), and § 6654 (penalty for failure by an individual to pay estimated income taxes).

CONCEPT SUMMARY 13.1

Tax Credits

Credit	Computation	Comments
Tax withheld on wages (§ 31)	Amount is reported to employee on Form W–2.	Refundable credit.
Earned income (§ 32)	Amount is determined by reference to Earned Income Credit Table published by IRS. Computations of underlying amounts in Earned Income Credit Table are illustrated in Example 22.	Refundable credit. A form of negative income tax to assist low-income taxpayers. Earned income and AGI must be less than certain threshold amounts. Generally, one or more qualifying children must reside with the taxpayer.
Child and dependent care (§ 21)	Rate ranges from 20% to 35% depending on AGI. Maximum base for credit is $3,000 for one qualifying individual, $6,000 for two or more.	Nonrefundable personal credit. No carryback or carryforward. Benefits taxpayers who incur employment-related child or dependent care expenses in order to work or seek employment. Eligible taxpayers must have a dependent under age 13 or a dependent (any age) or spouse who is physically or mentally incapacitated.
Elderly or disabled (§ 22)	15% of sum of base amount minus reductions for (1) Social Security and other nontaxable benefits and (2) excess AGI. Base amount is fixed by law (e.g., $5,000 for a single taxpayer).	Nonrefundable personal credit. No carryback or carryforward. Provides relief for taxpayers not receiving substantial tax-free retirement benefits.
Adoption expenses (§ 23)	Up to $13,360 of costs incurred to adopt an eligible child qualify for the credit. Taxpayer claims the credit in the year qualified expenses were paid or incurred if they were paid or incurred during or after year in which adoption was finalized. For expenses paid or incurred in a year prior to when adoption was finalized, credit must be claimed in tax year following the tax year during which the expenses are paid or incurred.	Nonrefundable credit. Unused credit may be carried forward five years. Purpose is to assist taxpayers who incur nonrecurring costs associated with the adoption process.
Child (§ 24)	Credit is based on *number* of qualifying children under age 17. Maximum credit is $1,000 per child. Credit is phased out for higher-income taxpayers.	Generally a nonrefundable credit. Refundable in certain cases. Purpose is to provide tax relief for low- to moderate-income families with children.
Education (§ 25A)	American Opportunity credit is available for qualifying education expenses of students in first two years of postsecondary education. Maximum credit is $2,500 per year per eligible student. Credit is phased out for higher-income taxpayers.	Credit is partially refundable. Credit is designed to help defray costs of first four years of higher education for low- to middle-income families.
	Lifetime learning credit permits a credit of 20% of qualifying expenses (up to $10,000 per year) provided American Opportunity credit is not claimed with respect to those expenses. Credit is calculated per taxpayer, not per student, and is phased out for higher-income taxpayers.	Nonrefundable credit. Credit is designed to help defray costs of higher education beyond first four years, and for costs incurred in maintaining or improving existing job skills, for low- to middle-income taxpayers.
Credit for certain retirement plan contributions (§ 25B)	Calculation is based on amount of contribution multiplied by a percentage that depends on the taxpayer's filing status and AGI.	Nonrefundable credit. Purpose is to encourage contributions to qualified retirement plans by low- and middle-income taxpayers.
Foreign tax (§ 27)	Foreign taxable income/total worldwide taxable income × U.S. tax = overall limitation. Lesser of foreign taxes imposed or overall limitation.	Nonrefundable credit. Unused credits may be carried back 1 year and forward 10 years. Purpose is to prevent double taxation of foreign income.

Credit	Computation	Comments
First-time homebuyer credit (§ 36)	Credit is limited to 10% of the home's purchase price, but no more than $8,000 ($4,000 for married individuals filing separately). Applies to homes purchased from January 1, 2009 through April 30, 2010 (including those under contract, provided the purchase closes before July 1, 2010). Homes purchased after November 6, 2009, with a price in excess of $800,000 do not qualify for the credit. For homes purchased after November 6, 2009, the credit is phased out for taxpayers with modified AGI between $125,000 and $145,000 (single) and $225,000 and $245,000 (married). Lower phaseout ranges apply to home purchases from January 1, 2009 through November 6, 2009 ($75,000 to $95,000 for singles and $150,000 to $170,000 for married).	Refundable credit. A credit to encourage home ownership and to alleviate the surplus of unsold homes. For homes purchased from April 9, 2008 through December 31, 2008, the maximum credit is $7,500 ($3,750 for married individuals filing separately), and the credit must be repaid in equal installments over 15 years. For homes purchased from January 1, 2009 through April 30, 2010, the maximum credit is $8,000 ($4,000 for married individuals filing separately). For such homes, there is no requirement that the credit be repaid.
General business (§ 38)	May not exceed net income tax minus the greater of tentative minimum tax or 25% of net regular tax liability that exceeds $25,000.	Nonrefundable credit. Components include tax credit for rehabilitation expenditures, work opportunity tax credit, research activities credit, low-income housing credit, disabled access credit, credit for small employer pension plan startup costs, and credit for employer-provided child care. Unused credit may be carried back 1 year and forward 20 years. FIFO method applies to carrybacks, carryovers, and credits earned during current year.
Rehabilitation expenditures (§ 47)	Qualifying investment times rehabilitation percentage, depending on type of property. Regular rehabilitation rate is 10%; rate for certified historic structures is 20%.	Nonrefundable credit. Part of general business credit and therefore subject to same carryback, carryover, and FIFO rules. Purpose is to discourage businesses from moving from economically distressed areas to newer locations.
Research activities (§ 41)	Incremental credit is 20% of excess of computation year expenditures over the base amount. Basic research credit is allowed to certain corporations for 20% of cash payments to qualified organizations that exceed a specially calculated base amount.	Nonrefundable credit. Part of general business credit and therefore subject to same carryback, carryover, and FIFO rules. Purpose is to encourage high-tech and energy research in the United States.
Low-income housing (§ 42)	Appropriate rate times eligible basis (portion of project attributable to low-income units). Credit is available each year for 10 years. Recapture may apply.	Nonrefundable credit. Part of general business credit and therefore subject to same carryback, carryover, and FIFO rules. Purpose is to encourage construction of housing for low-income individuals.
Disabled access (§ 44)	Credit is 50% of eligible access expenditures that exceed $250 but do not exceed $10,250. Maximum credit is $5,000. Available only to eligible small businesses.	Nonrefundable credit. Part of general business credit and therefore subject to same carryback, carryover, and FIFO rules. Purpose is to encourage small businesses to become more accessible to disabled individuals.
Credit for small employer pension plan startup costs (§ 45E)	Credit equals 50% of qualified startup costs incurred by eligible employers. Maximum annual credit is $500. Deduction for related expenses is reduced by the amount of the credit.	Nonrefundable credit. Part of general business credit and therefore subject to same carryback, carryover, and FIFO rules. Purpose is to encourage small employers to establish qualified retirement plans for their employees.
Credit for employer-provided child care (§ 45F)	Credit is equal to 25% of qualified child care expenses plus 10% of qualified expenses for child care resource and referral services. Maximum credit is $150,000. Deduction for related expenses or basis must be reduced by the amount of the credit.	Nonrefundable credit. Part of general business credit and therefore subject to same carryback, carryover, and FIFO rules. Purpose is to encourage employers to provide child care for their employees' children during normal working hours.
Work opportunity (§ 51)	Credit is limited to 40% of the first $6,000 of wages paid to each eligible employee. For long-term family assistance recipients, credit is limited to 40% of first $10,000 of wages paid to each eligible employee in first year of employment, plus 50% of first $10,000 of wages paid to each eligible employee in second year of employment.	Nonrefundable credit. Part of the general business credit and therefore subject to the same carryback, carryover, and FIFO rules. Purpose is to encourage employment of individuals in specified groups.

Coverage Requirements

Circular E, *Employer's Tax Guide* (Publication 15), issued by the IRS, contains a listing of which employees and which wages require withholdings for income taxes and employment taxes. Excerpts from Circular E appear in Exhibit 13.3. In working with Exhibit 13.3, consider the following observations:

- The designation "Exempt" in the income tax withholding column does not mean that the amount paid is nontaxable to the employee. It merely relieves the employer from having to withhold.

EXAMPLE 38

Lee works for Yellow Corporation and has the type of job where tips are not common but do occur. If Lee's total tips amount to less than $20 per month, Yellow Corporation need not withhold Federal income taxes on the tips (see Exhibit 13.3). Nevertheless, Lee must include the tips in his gross income. ■

- In some cases, income tax withholding is not required but is voluntary. This is designated "Exempt (withhold if both employer and employee agree)."

EXAMPLE 39

Pat is employed as a gardener by a wealthy family. In the past, he has encountered difficulty in managing his finances so as to be in a position to pay the income tax due every April 15. To ease the cash-flow problem that develops in April, Pat asks his employer to withhold income taxes from his wages. ■

- The Social Security and Medicare (FICA) column refers to the employer's share. The same is true of the Federal Unemployment (FUTA) column since the employee does not contribute to this tax.

Amount of FICA Taxes

The FICA tax has two components: Social Security tax (old age, survivors, and disability insurance) *and* Medicare tax (hospital insurance). The tax rates and wage base under FICA have increased substantially over the years. The base amount is adjusted each year for inflation. As Table 13.5 shows, the top base amount differs for the Medicare portion (now unlimited) and for the Social Security portion. Table 13.5 represents the employee's share of the tax. The employer must match the employee's portion. The Tax Relief Act of 2010 reduces the employee's (but not the employer's) Social Security tax rate from 6.2 percent to 4.2 percent for 2011. A similar 2 percent reduction applies to self-employed taxpayers (discussed later in this chapter). So, for 2011, the total Social Security tax rate is 10.4 percent (4.2 percent plus 6.2 percent).

Withholdings from employees must continue until the maximum base amount is reached. In 2011, for example, FICA withholding ceases for the Social Security portion (4.2 percent) once the employee has earned wages subject to FICA in the amount of $106,800. For the Medicare portion (1.45 percent), however, the employer is required to withhold on all wages without limit. This contrasts with years prior to 1994 when a maximum base existed for the Medicare portion also.

EXAMPLE 40

In 2011, Keshia earned a salary of $140,000 from her employer. Therefore, FICA taxes withheld from her salary are $4,485.60 ($106,800 × 4.2%) plus $2,030 ($140,000 × 1.45%) for a total of $6,515.60. In addition to paying the amount withheld from Keshia's salary to the government, her employer pays $8,651.60 [($106,800 × 6.2%) + ($140,000 × 1.45%)]. ■

In at least two situations, it is possible for an employee to have paid excess FICA taxes.

EXHIBIT 13.3 | **Withholding Classifications**

Special Classes of Employment and Special Types of Payments	Treatment under Employment Taxes		
	Income Tax Withholding	Social Security and Medicare	Federal Unemployment
Employee business expense reimbursement:			
1. Accountable plan.			
a. Amounts not exceeding specified government rate for per diem or standard mileage.	Exempt	Exempt	Exempt
b. Amounts in excess of specified government rate for per diem or standard mileage.	Withhold	Taxable	Taxable
2. Nonaccountable plan.	Withhold	Taxable	Taxable
Family employees:			
1. Child employed by parent (or partnership in which each partner is a parent of the child).	Withhold	Exempt until age 18; age 21 for domestic service.	Exempt until age 21
2. Parent employed by child.	Withhold	Taxable if in course of the son's or daughter's business.	Exempt
3. Spouse employed by spouse.	Withhold	Taxable if in course of spouse's business.	Exempt
Household employees: Domestic service in private homes. Farmers see Publication 51 (Circular A).	Exempt (withhold if both employer and employee agree).	Taxable if paid $1,700 or more in cash in 2011. Exempt if performed by an individual under age 18 during any portion of the calendar year and is not the principal occupation of the employee.	Taxable if employer paid total cash wages of $1,000 or more in any quarter in the current or preceding calendar year.
Interns working in hospitals.	Withhold	Taxable	Exempt
Newspaper carriers under age 18.	Exempt (withhold if both employer and employee agree).	Exempt	Exempt
Salespersons:			
1. Common law employees.	Withhold	Taxable	Taxable
2. Statutory employees.	Exempt	Taxable	Taxable, except for full-time life insurance sales agents.
Scholarships and fellowship grants: [includible in income under § 117(c)].	Withhold	Taxability depends on the nature of the employment and the status of the organization.	Taxability depends on the nature of the employment and the status of the organization.
Severance or dismissal pay.	Withhold	Taxable	Taxable
Tips, if less than $20 in a month.	Exempt	Exempt	Exempt
Worker's compensation.	Exempt	Exempt	Exempt

TABLE 13.5	FICA Rates and Base

	Social Security Tax			Medicare Tax			
	Percent	×	Base Amount	+	Percent	×	Base Amount	=	Maximum Tax
1991	6.20%	×	$ 53,400	+	1.45%	×	$125,000	=	$5,123.30
1992	6.20%	×	55,500	+	1.45%	×	130,200	=	5,328.90
1993	6.20%	×	57,600	+	1.45%	×	135,000	=	5,528.70
1994	6.20%	×	60,600	+	1.45%	×	Unlimited	=	Unlimited
1995	6.20%	×	61,200	+	1.45%	×	Unlimited	=	Unlimited
1996	6.20%	×	62,700	+	1.45%	×	Unlimited	=	Unlimited
1997	6.20%	×	65,400	+	1.45%	×	Unlimited	=	Unlimited
1998	6.20%	×	68,400	+	1.45%	×	Unlimited	=	Unlimited
1999	6.20%	×	72,600	+	1.45%	×	Unlimited	=	Unlimited
2000	6.20%	×	76,200	+	1.45%	×	Unlimited	=	Unlimited
2001	6.20%	×	80,400	+	1.45%	×	Unlimited	=	Unlimited
2002	6.20%	×	84,900	+	1.45%	×	Unlimited	=	Unlimited
2003	6.20%	×	87,000	+	1.45%	×	Unlimited	=	Unlimited
2004	6.20%	×	87,900	+	1.45%	×	Unlimited	=	Unlimited
2005	6.20%	×	90,000	+	1.45%	×	Unlimited	=	Unlimited
2006	6.20%	×	94,200	+	1.45%	×	Unlimited	=	Unlimited
2007	6.20%	×	97,500	+	1.45%	×	Unlimited	=	Unlimited
2008	6.20%	×	102,000	+	1.45%	×	Unlimited	=	Unlimited
2009	6.20%	×	106,800	+	1.45%	×	Unlimited	=	Unlimited
2010	6.20%	×	106,800	+	1.45%	×	Unlimited	=	Unlimited
2011	4.20% / 6.20%	×	106,800	+	1.45%	×	Unlimited	=	Unlimited
2012 on	6.20%	×	*	+	1.45%	×	Unlimited	=	Unlimited

*Not yet determined.

EXAMPLE 41

During 2011, Kevin changed employers in the middle of the year and earned $60,000 (all of which was subject to FICA) from each job. As a result, each employer withheld $3,390 [(4.2% × $60,000) + (1.45% × $60,000)] for a total of $6,780. Although each employer acted properly, Kevin's total FICA tax liability for the year is only $6,225.60 [(4.2% × $106,800) + (1.45% × $120,000)]. Thus, Kevin has overpaid his share of FICA taxes by $554.40 [$6,780 (amount paid) − $6,225.60 (amount of correct liability)]. He should claim this amount as a tax credit when filing his income tax return for 2011. The tax credit will reduce any income tax Kevin might owe or, possibly, generate a tax refund. ■

EXAMPLE 42

During 2011, Lori earned $94,000 from her regular job and $26,000 from a part-time job (all of which was subject to FICA). As a result, one employer withheld $5,311 [(4.2% × $94,000) + (1.45% × $94,000)] while the other employer withheld $1,469 [(4.2% × $26,000) + (1.45% × $26,000)] for a total of $6,780. Lori's total FICA tax liability for the year is only $6,225.60 [(4.2% × $106,800) + (1.45% × $120,000)]. Thus, Lori has overpaid her share of FICA taxes by $554.40 [$6,780 (amount paid) − $6,225.60 (amount of correct liability)]. She should claim this amount as a tax credit when filing her income tax return for 2011. ■

In Examples 41 and 42, the employee is subject to overwithholding. In both cases, however, the employee was able to obtain a credit for the excess withheld. The same result does not materialize for the portion paid by the employer. Since this amount is not refundable, in some situations employers may pay more FICA taxes than the covered employees. The mere fact that a husband and wife are both employed does not, by itself, result in overwithholding of FICA taxes.

EXAMPLE 43

During 2011, Jim and Betty (husband and wife) are both employed, and each earns wages subject to FICA of $60,000. Accordingly, each has $3,390 FICA withheld [(4.2% × $60,000) + (1.45% × $60,000)] for a total of $6,780. Since neither spouse paid FICA tax on wages in excess of $106,800 (Social Security tax) [see Table 13.5], there is no over-withholding. ■

A spouse employed by another spouse is subject to FICA. However, children under the age of 18 who are employed in a parent's trade or business are exempted.

Amount of Income Tax Withholding

Arriving at the amount to be withheld for income tax purposes is not so simple. It involves three basic steps:[68]

- Have the employee complete Form W–4, Employee's Withholding Allowance Certificate.
- Determine the employee's payroll period.
- Compute the amount to be withheld, usually using either the wage-bracket tables or the percentage method.

Form W–4 reflects the employee's marital status and **withholding allowances**. Generally, it need not be filed with the IRS and is retained by the employer as part of the payroll records.

The employer need not verify the number of exemptions claimed. Any misinformation on the form will be attributed to the employee. However, if the employer has reason to believe that the employee made a false statement, the IRS should be notified. In the meantime, the Form W–4 should be honored. Employees are subject to both civil and criminal penalties for filing false withholding statements.

On the current Form W–4, an employee may claim *withholding allowances* for the following: personal exemptions for self and spouse and dependency exemptions. One *special withholding allowance* may be claimed if the employee is single and has only one job, if the employee is married and has only one job and the spouse is not employed, or if wages from a second job or a spouse's wages (or both) are $1,000 or

[68]The withholding provisions are contained in §§ 3401 and 3402. These Sections will not be referenced specifically in the discussion that follows.

less. An additional allowance is available if the employee expects to file using the head-of-household status or if the employee expects to claim a credit for child and dependent care expenses on qualifying expenditures of at least $1,900. A taxpayer qualifying for the child tax credit may claim one or two additional allowances for each eligible child. An employee who plans to itemize deductions or claim adjustments to income (e.g., alimony, deductible IRA contributions) should use the worksheet provided on Form W–4 to determine the correct number of additional allowances.

To avoid having too little tax withheld, some employees may find it necessary to reduce their withholding allowances. This might be the case for an employee who has more than one job or who has other sources of income that are not subject to adequate withholding. Likewise, a married employee who has a working spouse or more than one job might wish to claim fewer allowances.

If both spouses of a married couple are employed, they may allocate their total allowances between themselves as they see fit. The same allocation procedure is required if a taxpayer has more than one job. In no event should the same allowance be claimed more than once at the same time. It is permissible to declare *fewer* allowances than the taxpayer is entitled to in order to increase the amount of withholding. Doing so, however, does not affect the number of personal and dependency exemptions allowable on the employee's income tax return. An employee is also permitted to have the employer withhold a certain dollar amount in addition to the required amount. This additional dollar amount can be arbitrary or calculated in accordance with a worksheet on Form W–4.

EXAMPLE 44

Carl, who earns $75,000, is married to Carol, who earns $85,000. They have three dependent children and will claim the standard deduction. Assume they do not qualify to claim the child tax credit. Together they should be entitled to five allowances [2 (for personal exemptions) + 3 (for dependency exemptions)]. The special withholding allowance is not available since both spouses earn more than $1,000. If Carl is the spouse first employed and his Form W–4 reflects five allowances, Carol's Form W–4 should report none. They could, however, reallocate their allowances between them as long as the total claimed does not exceed five. ∎

The period of service for which an employee is paid is known as the *payroll period*. Daily, weekly, biweekly, semimonthly, and monthly periods are the most common arrangements. If an employee has no regular payroll period, he or she is considered to be paid on a daily basis.

Once the allowances are known (as reflected on Form W–4) and the payroll period determined, the amount to be withheld for Federal income taxes can be computed. The computation usually is made by using the wage-bracket tables or the percentage method.

Wage-bracket tables are available for daily, weekly, biweekly, semimonthly, and monthly payroll periods for single (including heads of household) and married taxpayers. An extract of the tables dealing with married persons on a monthly payroll period is reproduced in Table 13.6. The data in Table 13.6 are for wages paid in 2011. Example 45 illustrates the use of withholding tables.

EXAMPLE 45

Tom is married and has three dependent children and no additional withholding allowances are available. In his job with Pink Corporation, he earns $4,500 in May 2011. Assuming Tom's wife has a part-time job for which she earns $5,000 for the year and all available allowances are claimed on his Form W–4, Pink should withhold $274 a month from his wages. This amount is taken from the five allowances column in the $4,480–$4,520 wage bracket. The five allowances result from personal exemptions (two) plus dependency exemptions (three). Note that an additional withholding allowance is not available for Tom's wife because she has a job for which she earned more than $1,000. ∎

TABLE 13.6	Wage-Bracket Withholding Table

MARRIED Persons—MONTHLY Payroll Period
(For Wages Paid through December 2011)

And the wages are—		And the number of withholding allowances claimed is—										
At least	But less than	0	1	2	3	4	5	6	7	8	9	10
		The amount of income tax to be withheld is—										
$3,400	$3,440	$343	$297	$251	$205	$158	$122	$91	$60	$30	$0	$0
3,440	3,480	349	303	257	211	164	126	95	64	34	3	0
3,480	3,520	355	309	263	217	170	130	99	68	38	7	0
3,520	3,560	361	315	269	223	176	134	103	72	42	11	0
3,560	3,600	367	321	275	229	182	138	107	76	46	15	0
3,600	3,640	373	327	281	235	188	142	111	80	50	19	0
3,640	3,680	379	333	287	241	194	148	115	84	54	23	0
3,680	3,720	385	339	293	247	200	154	119	88	58	27	0
3,720	3,760	391	345	299	253	206	160	123	92	62	31	0
3,760	3,800	397	351	305	259	212	166	127	96	66	35	4
3,800	3,840	403	357	311	265	218	172	131	100	70	39	8
3,840	3,880	409	363	317	271	224	178	135	104	74	43	12
3,880	3,920	415	369	323	277	230	184	139	108	78	47	16
3,920	3,960	421	375	329	283	236	190	144	112	82	51	20
3,960	4,000	427	381	335	289	242	196	150	116	86	55	24
4,000	4,040	433	387	341	295	248	202	156	120	90	59	28
4,040	4,080	439	393	347	301	254	208	162	124	94	63	32
4,080	4,120	445	399	353	307	260	214	168	128	98	67	36
4,120	4,160	451	405	359	313	266	220	174	132	102	71	40
4,160	4,200	457	411	365	319	272	226	180	136	106	75	44
4,200	4,240	463	417	371	325	278	232	186	140	110	79	48
4,240	4,280	469	423	377	331	284	238	192	146	114	83	52
4,280	4,320	475	429	383	337	290	244	198	152	118	87	56
4,320	4,360	481	435	389	343	296	250	204	158	122	91	60
4,360	4,400	487	441	395	349	302	256	210	164	126	95	64
4,400	4,440	493	447	401	355	308	262	216	170	130	99	68
4,440	4,480	499	453	407	361	314	268	222	176	134	103	72
4,480	4,520	505	459	413	367	320	274	228	182	138	107	76
4,520	4,560	511	465	419	373	326	280	234	188	142	111	80
4,560	4,600	517	471	425	379	332	286	240	194	147	115	84
4,600	4,640	523	477	431	385	338	292	246	200	153	119	88
4,640	4,680	529	483	437	391	344	298	252	206	159	123	92
4,680	4,720	535	489	443	397	350	304	258	212	165	127	96
4,720	4,760	541	495	449	403	356	310	264	218	171	131	100
4,760	4,800	547	501	455	409	362	316	270	224	177	135	104
4,800	4,840	553	507	461	415	368	322	276	230	183	139	108
4,840	4,880	559	513	467	421	374	328	282	236	189	143	112
4,880	4,920	565	519	473	427	380	334	288	242	195	149	116
4,920	4,960	571	525	479	433	386	340	294	248	201	155	120
4,960	5,000	577	531	485	439	392	346	300	254	207	161	124
5,000	5,040	583	537	491	445	398	352	306	260	213	167	128
5,040	5,080	589	543	497	451	404	358	312	266	219	173	132
5,080	5,120	595	549	503	457	410	364	318	272	225	179	136
5,120	5,160	601	555	509	463	416	370	324	278	231	185	140
5,160	5,200	607	561	515	469	422	376	330	284	237	191	145
5,200	5,240	613	567	521	475	428	382	336	290	243	197	151
5,240	5,280	619	573	527	481	434	388	342	296	249	203	157
5,280	5,320	625	579	533	487	440	394	348	302	255	209	163
5,320	5,360	631	585	539	493	446	400	354	308	261	215	169
5,360	5,400	637	591	545	499	452	406	360	314	267	221	175
5,400	5,440	643	597	551	505	458	412	366	320	273	227	181
5,440	5,480	649	603	557	511	464	418	372	326	279	233	187
5,480	5,520	655	609	563	517	470	424	378	332	285	239	193
5,520	5,560	661	615	569	523	476	430	384	338	291	245	199
5,560	5,600	667	621	575	529	482	436	390	344	297	251	205
5,600	5,640	673	627	581	535	488	442	396	350	303	257	211
5,640	5,680	679	633	587	541	494	448	402	356	309	263	217
5,680	5,720	685	639	593	547	500	454	408	362	315	269	223
5,720	5,760	691	645	599	553	506	460	414	368	321	275	229
5,760	5,800	697	651	605	559	512	466	420	374	327	281	235
5,800	5,840	703	657	611	565	518	472	426	380	333	287	241
5,840	5,880	709	663	617	571	524	478	432	386	339	293	247

$5,880 and over   Use Table 4(b) for a **MARRIED person** on page 36. Also see the instructions on page 35.

TABLE 13.7	Conversion Chart for 2011
Payroll Period	**Amount of One Allowance**
Daily	$ 14.23
Weekly	71.15
Biweekly	142.31
Semimonthly	154.17
Monthly	308.33
Quarterly	925.00
Semiannual	1,850.00
Annual	3,700.00

Although the wage-bracket table requires few, if any, calculations, the percentage method is equally acceptable. Its use may be necessary for payroll periods where no wage-bracket tables are available (quarterly, semiannual, and annual payroll periods) and where wages paid exceed the amount allowed for use of the wage-bracket tables. The percentage method is particularly useful when payroll computations are computerized. This method, however, requires the use of a conversion chart based on one withholding allowance. That is, the amount of one allowance is equal to the personal and dependency exemption amount divided by the number of payroll periods in a year. For example, the amount of one allowance for a taxpayer who is paid weekly is $71.15 ($3,700/52 payroll periods)—see Table 13.7.

To use the percentage method, proceed as follows:

Step1. Multiply the amount of one allowance (as specified in the conversion chart in Table 13.7) by the employee's total allowances (taken from Form W–4).

Step2. Subtract the product reached in step 1 from the employee's wages. The remainder is called "amount of wages."

Step3. Using the result derived in step 2, compute the income tax withholding under the proper percentage-method table.

The table used in applying the percentage method for those with monthly payroll periods is reproduced in Table 13.8. An illustration of the percentage method follows.

EXAMPLE 46

Assume the same facts as in Example 45, except that Tom's income tax withholding is determined using the percentage method.

Step1. $308.33 (amount of one allowance for a monthly payroll period) × 5 (total allowances) = $1,541.65.

Step2. $4,500.00 (monthly salary) − $1,541.65 (step 1) = $2,958.35 (amount of wages).

Step3. Referring to Table 13.8: $141.70 + 15%($2,958.35 − $2,075.00) = $274.20. ∎

Note that the wage-bracket tables yield an amount for income tax withholding of $274 (refer to Example 45) while the percentage method results in $274.20 (refer to Example 46). The difference occurs because the wage-bracket table amounts are derived by computing the withholding on the median wage within each bracket and rounded to the nearest dollar.

TABLE 13.8	Table for Percentage Method of Withholding for Wages Paid through 2011

TABLE 4—MONTHLY Payroll Period

(a) SINGLE person (including head of household)—

If the amount of wages (after subtracting withholding allowances) is: The amount of income tax to withhold is:

Not over $175 . . . . $0

Over—	But not over—		of excess over—
$175	—$883	. . . $0.00 plus 10%	—$175
$883	—$3,050	. . . $70.80 plus 15%	—$883
$3,050	—$7,142	. . . $395.85 plus 25%	—$3,050
$7,142	—$14,708	. . . $1,418.85 plus 28%	—$7,142
$14,708	—$31,771	. . . $3,537.33 plus 33%	—$14,708
$31,771	. . . .	. . $9,168.12 plus 35%	—$31,771

(b) MARRIED person—

If the amount of wages (after subtracting withholding allowances) is: The amount of income tax to withhold is:

Not over $658 . . . . $0

Over—	But not over—		of excess over—
$658	—$2,075	. . . $0.00 plus 10%	—$658
$2,075	—$6,408	. . . $141.70 plus 15%	—$2,075
$6,408	—$12,271	. . . $791.65 plus 25%	—$6,408
$12,271	—$18,350	. . . $2,257.40 plus 28%	—$12,271
$18,350	—$32,254	. . . $3,959.52 plus 33%	—$18,350
$32,254	. . . .	. . $8,547.84 plus 35%	—$32,254

Reporting and Payment Procedures

Proper handling of employment taxes and income tax withholdings requires considerable compliance efforts by the employer. Among the Federal forms that have to be filed are the following:

Tax Form	Title
SS–4	Application for Employer Identification Number
W–2	Wage and Tax Statement
W–3	Transmittal of Wage and Tax Statements
940 or 940 EZ	Employer's Annual Federal Unemployment (FUTA) Tax Return
941	Employer's Quarterly Federal Tax Return

Form SS–4 is the starting point since it provides the employer with an identification number that must be used on all of the other forms filed with the IRS and the Social Security Administration. The number issued consists of nine digits and is hyphenated between the second and third digits (e.g., 98–7654321).

Form W–2 furnishes essential information to employees concerning wages paid, FICA, and income tax withholdings. Copies of Form W–2 are distributed to several parties for various purposes: to enable the employee to complete his or her income tax return, to inform the Social Security Administration of the amount of FICA wages earned by the employee, and to serve as a permanent record for the employer and employee of the payroll information contained on the form. Form W–2 (reporting information for the previous calendar year) must be furnished to an employee not later than January 31. If an employee leaves a place of employment before the end of the year, Form W–2 can be given to him or her at any time after employment ends but no later than the following January 31. However, if the terminated employee asks for Form W–2, it must be given to him or her within 30 days after the request or the final wage payment, whichever is later.

Form W–3 must accompany the copies of Forms W–2 filed by the employer with the Social Security Administration. Its basic purpose is to summarize and reconcile the amounts withheld for FICA and income taxes from *all* employees.

Form 940 (or Form 940 EZ) constitutes the employer's annual accounting for FUTA purposes. Generally, it must be filed on or before January 31 of the following year and must be accompanied by the payment of any undeposited FUTA due the Federal government.

THE TAX GAP INCLUDES $58 BILLION IN PAYROLL TAXES

The "tax gap"—the difference between what taxpayers owe to the Federal government in taxes and what they pay—is approaching $400 billion annually. A significant portion of that amount consists of delinquent payroll taxes—the money withheld from employees' salaries by employers for FICA taxes (Social Security and Medicare taxes).

According to a study by the Government Accountability Office (GAO), more than 1.6 million businesses together owe in excess of $58 billion related to delinquent payroll taxes. Of that amount, $26 billion represents actual taxes owed, $18 billion is for interest, and $14 billion is for penalties. In contrast, businesses owe only $24 billion in delinquent corporate income taxes. Businesses in the construction, professional services, and health care industries have the largest payroll tax delinquencies.

Collecting payroll taxes seems to be a perennial problem. The GAO study pointed out that delinquencies today are about the same as they were a decade ago when 1.8 million businesses owed about $49 billion. Today, though, debts are more likely to be longstanding. About

500 employers owe at least 10 years' worth of taxes, and nearly 15,000 owe 5 years' worth. About half of the $58 billion owed is from 2002 or earlier. Since then the IRS has stepped up its enforcement efforts through the use of liens and levies on businesses that fail to pay over the taxes withheld.

In July 2009, the Treasury Department released its own study of the tax gap that generally confirmed the data in the GAO study. Further, beginning in November 2009, the IRS launched a National Research Program that is conducting detailed examinations of employment tax collections. Approximately 5,000 employers will be randomly selected for audit over a three-year period. In addition to potential assessments, these audits will provide the IRS with a better understanding of overall employment tax compliance.

Sources: Adapted from "Businesses Owe IRS $58 Billion," *USA Today* (online), July 28, 2008; U.S. Department of the Treasury, "Update on Reducing the Federal Tax Gap and Improving Voluntary Compliance," July 9, 2009.

Whether or not deposits[69] are required, most employers must settle their employment taxes every quarter. To do this, Form 941 must be filed on or before the last day of the month following the end of each calendar quarter.

Backup Withholding

Some types of payments made to individuals by banks or businesses are subject to backup withholding under certain conditions. Backup withholding is designed to ensure that income tax is collected on interest and other payments reported on a Form 1099. If backup withholding applies in 2011, the payor must withhold 28 percent of the gross amount. Backup withholding applies when the taxpayer does not give the business or bank his or her identification number in the required manner and in certain other situations.[70]

LO.6

Understand the payment procedures applicable to self-employed persons.

PROCEDURES APPLICABLE TO SELF-EMPLOYED PERSONS

Although the following discussion largely centers on self-employed taxpayers, some of the procedures may be applicable to employed persons. In many cases, for example, employed persons may be required to pay estimated tax if they have income other than wages that is not subject to withholding. An employee may conduct a second trade or business in a self-employment capacity. Depending on the circumstances, the second job may require the payment of a self-employment tax. In addition, taxpayers whose income consists primarily of rentals, dividends, or interest (this list is not all-inclusive) may be required to pay estimated tax.

Estimated Tax for Individuals

Estimated tax is the amount of tax (including AMT and self-employment tax) an individual expects to owe for the year after subtracting tax credits and income tax

---

[69]Deposit requirements are specified in each current issue of Circular E, *Employer's Tax Guide*, IRS Publication 15. Under current rules, employers must make deposits on either a monthly or a semiweekly basis.

[70]§ 3406(a). The backup withholding rate is equal to the fourth lowest tax rate for single filers.

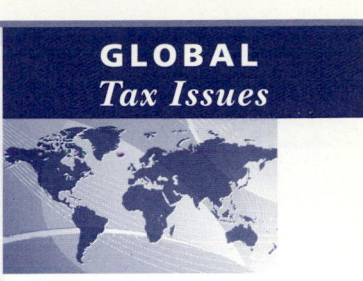

FOREIGN "WITHHOLDING TAX" PERFORMS AN IMPORTANT ROLE

GLOBAL *Tax Issues*

Taxpayers in the United States are accustomed to having their employer withhold a portion of their salary or wages and then forward the amounts to the government in payment of their income tax liabilities. As a rule, other types of income, such as dividends, interest, and annuities, are not subject to withholding because the IRS has adequate mechanisms in place to assure a high level of tax compliance. But for payments of U.S.-source income to foreign taxpayers, the IRS would not be as confident that it is getting its due were it not for the so-called withholding tax.

To ensure the collection of the income tax on amounts paid to nonresident aliens and foreign corporations, the person *paying* the income, rather than the recipient, is required to withhold and forward the appropriate payment to the government. Although the withholding rate is typically 30 percent, the rate can vary in certain situations. In some situations, this withholding mechanism will also prevent the taxpayer from having to file an income tax return with the U.S. government.

withheld. Any individual who has estimated tax for the year of $1,000 or more *and* whose withholding does not equal or exceed the required annual payment (discussed below) must make quarterly payments.[71] Otherwise, a penalty may be assessed. No quarterly payments are required (and no penalty will apply on an underpayment) if the taxpayer's estimated tax is under $1,000. No penalty will apply if the taxpayer had no tax liability for the preceding tax year *and* the preceding tax year was a taxable year of 12 months *and* the taxpayer was a citizen or resident for the entire preceding tax year. In this regard, having no tax liability is not the same as having no additional tax to pay.

The required annual payment must first be computed. This is the *smaller* of the following amounts:

- Ninety percent of the tax shown on the current year's return.
- One hundred percent of the tax shown on the preceding year's return (the return must cover the full 12 months of the preceding year). If the AGI on the preceding year's return exceeds $150,000 ($75,000 if married filing separately), the 100 percent requirement is increased to 110 percent.

In general, one-fourth of this required annual payment is due on April 15, June 15, and September 15 of the tax year and January 15 of the following year.

An equal part of withholding is deemed paid on each due date. Thus, the quarterly installment of the required annual payment reduced by the applicable withholding is the estimated tax to be paid. Payments are to be accompanied by the payment voucher for the appropriate date from Form 1040–ES.

Married taxpayers may make joint estimated tax payments even though a joint income tax return is not subsequently filed. In such event, the estimated tax payments may be applied against the separate return liability of the spouses as they see fit. If a husband and wife cannot agree on a division of the estimated tax payments, the Regulations provide that the payments are to be allocated in proportion to the tax liability on the separate returns.

Penalty on Underpayments

A nondeductible penalty is imposed on the amount of underpayment of estimated tax. The rate for this penalty is adjusted quarterly to reflect changes in the average prime rate.

An *underpayment* occurs when any installment (the sum of estimated tax paid and income tax withheld) is less than 25 percent of the required annual payment. The

---

[71]§§ 6654(c)(1) and 6654(e)(1).

penalty is applied to the amount of the underpayment for the period of the under-payment.[72]

EXAMPLE 47

Marta made the following payments of estimated tax for 2011 and had no income tax withheld:

April 18, 2011	$1,400
June 15, 2011	2,300
September 15, 2011	1,500
January 17, 2012	1,800

Marta's actual tax for 2011 is $8,000, and her tax in 2010 was $10,000. Therefore, each installment should have been at least $1,800 [($8,000 × 90%) × 25%]. Of the payment on June 15, $400 will be credited to the unpaid balance of the first quarterly installment due on April 18,[73] thereby effectively stopping the underpayment penalty for the first quarterly period. Of the remaining $1,900 payment on June 15, $100 is credited to the September 15 payment, resulting in this third quarterly payment being $200 short. Then $200 of the January 17 payment is credited to the September 15 shortfall, ending the period of underpayment for that portion due. The January 17, 2012 installment is now underpaid by $200, and a penalty will apply from January 17, 2012, to April 16, 2012 (unless paid sooner). Marta's underpayments for the periods of underpayment are as follows:

1st installment due:	$400 from April 18 to June 15
2nd installment due:	Paid in full
3rd installment due:	$200 from September 15, 2011 to January 17, 2012
4th installment due:	$200 from January 17 to April 16, 2012 ■

If a possible underpayment of estimated tax is indicated, Form 2210 should be filed to compute the penalty due or to justify that no penalty applies.

Self-Employment Tax

The tax on self-employment income is levied to provide Social Security and Medicare benefits (old age, survivors, and disability insurance and hospital insurance) for self-employed individuals. Individuals with net earnings of $400 or more from self-employment are subject to the **self-employment tax**.[74] For 2011, the self-employment tax is 13.3 percent of self-employment income up to $106,800 and 2.9 percent of self-employment income in excess of $106,800. In other words, for 2011 the self-employment tax is 10.4 percent of self-employment earnings up to $106,800 (for the Social Security portion) *plus* 2.9 percent of the total amount of self-employment earnings (for the Medicare portion)—see Table 13.9.

Currently, self-employed taxpayers are allowed a deduction from net earnings from self-employment, at one-half of the self-employment rate, for purposes of determining self-employment tax[75] *and* an income tax deduction (normally, one-half the amount of self-employment tax paid).[76] For 2011, the 2 percent Social Security rate reduction is not taken into account in determining the appropriate base for the self-employment tax.[77] In other words, the 2011 deduction remains at 7.65 percent. The income tax deduction allowed under § 164(f) for 2011 is computed at the rate of 59.6 percent of the Social Security tax paid plus one-half of the Medicare tax paid.[78]

Determining the amount of self-employment tax to be paid for 2011 involves completing the steps in Figure 13.1. The result of step 3 or 4 is the amount of self-employment tax to be paid. For *income tax purposes*, the amount to be reported is

---

[72]§ 6654(b)(2).

[73]Payments are credited to unpaid installments in the order in which the installments are required to be paid. § 6654(b)(3).

[74]§ 6017.

[75]§ 1402(a)(12).

[76]§ 164(f).

[77]The Tax Relief Act of 2010, § 601(b)(1).

[78]The Tax Relief Act of 2010, § 601(b)(2). This revised percentage replaces the 50% deduction allowed under current law for 2011. This revised percentage allows the taxpayer to deduct the full amount of the employer portion of Social Security taxes. The employer Social Security tax rate remains at 6.2%, while the employee portion falls to 4.2% for 2011. Thus, the employer share of total Social Security taxes is 6.2 divided by 10.4 (or 59.6%).

TABLE 13.9	Self-Employment Tax: Social Security and Medicare Portions		
Year		**Tax Rate**	**Ceiling Amount**
2011	Social Security portion	10.4%	$106,800
	Medicare portion	2.9%	Unlimited
	Aggregate rate	13.3%	
2010	Social Security portion	12.4%	$106,800
	Medicare portion	2.9%	Unlimited
	Aggregate rate	15.3%	

FIGURE 13.1   2011 Self-Employment Tax Worksheet

1.	Net earnings from self-employment.	_____
2.	Multiply line 1 by 92.35%.	_____
3.	If the amount on line 2 is $106,800 or less, multiply the line 2 amount by 13.3%. This is the self-employment tax.	_____
4.	If the amount on line 2 is more than $106,800, multiply the excess of line 2 over $106,800 by 2.9% and add $14,204.40. This is the self-employment tax.	_____

net earnings from self-employment before the deduction for one-half of the self-employment tax. Then the taxpayer is allowed a deduction *for* AGI of 59.6 percent of the self-employment tax.

EXAMPLE 48

Using the format in Figure 13.1, the self-employment tax is determined for two taxpayers with net earnings from self-employment for 2011 as follows: Ned, $55,000 and Terry, $120,000.

Ned's Self-Employment Tax Worksheet

1.	Net earnings from self-employment.	$ 55,000.00
2.	Multiply line 1 by 92.35%.	$ 50,792.50
3.	If the amount on line 2 is $106,800 or less, multiply the line 2 amount by 13.3%. This is the self-employment tax.	$ 6,755.40
4.	If the amount on line 2 is more than $106,800, multiply the excess of line 2 over $106,800 by 2.9% and add $14,204.40. This is the self-employment tax.	_____

Terry's Self-Employment Tax Worksheet

1.	Net earnings from self-employment.	$120,000.00
2.	Multiply line 1 by 92.35%.	$110,820.00
3.	If the amount on line 2 is $106,800 or less, multiply the line 2 amount by 13.3%. This is the self-employment tax.	_____
4.	If the amount on line 2 is more than $106,800, multiply the excess of line 2 over $106,800 by 2.9% and add $14,204.40. This is the self-employment tax.	$ 14,320.98

For income tax purposes, Ned has net earnings from self-employment of $55,000 and a deduction *for* AGI of $3,884.81 [($50,792.50 × .104 × .596) + ($50,792.50 × .029 × .5)]. Terry has net earnings from self-employment of $120,000 and a deduction *for* AGI of $8,226.78 [($106,800.00 × .104 × .596) + ($110,820.00 × .029 × .5)]. Both taxpayers benefit from the deduction for one-half of the self-employment tax paid. ∎

FIGURE 13.2	2010 Self-Employment Tax Worksheet

1. Net earnings from self-employment. _____
2. Multiply line 1 by 92.35%. _____
3. If the amount on line 2 is $106,800 or less, multiply the line 2 amount by 15.3%. This is the self-employment tax. _____
4. If the amount on line 2 is more than $106,800, multiply the excess of line 2 over $106,800 by 2.9% and add $16,340.40. This is the self-employment tax. _____

For 2010, the self-employment tax computations are identical to those for 2011, except for the rate, as the tax base is the same in both years (see Table 13.9 and Figure 13.2).

If an individual also receives wages subject to FICA tax, the ceiling amount of the Social Security portion on which the self-employment tax is computed is reduced. Thus, the self-employment tax may be reduced if a self-employed individual also receives FICA wages in excess of the ceiling amount.

EXAMPLE 49

In 2011, Kelly had $76,000 of net earnings from the conduct of a bookkeeping service (trade or business activity). She also received wages as an employee amounting to $40,000 during the year. The amount of Kelly's self-employment income subject to the Social Security portion (10.4%) is $66,800 ($106,800 − $40,000), producing a tax of $6,947.20 ($66,800 × 10.4%). All of Kelly's net self-employment earnings are subject to the Medicare portion of the self-employment tax of 2.9%. Therefore, the self-employment tax on this portion is $2,035.39 ($70,186 × 2.9%).

	Social Security Portion
Ceiling amount	$106,800
Less: FICA wages	(40,000)
Net ceiling	$ 66,800
Net self-employment income ($76,000 × 92.35%)	$ 70,186
Lesser of net ceiling or net self-employment income	$ 66,800

Net earnings from self-employment include gross income from a trade or business less allowable trade or business deductions, the distributive share of any partnership income or loss derived from a trade or business activity, and net income from rendering personal services as an independent contractor. Gain or loss from the disposition of property (including involuntary conversions) is excluded from the computation of self-employment income unless the property involved is inventory.[79]

TAX PLANNING:

13.6 FOREIGN TAX CREDIT

L0.7

Identify tax planning opportunities related to tax credits and payment procedures.

A U.S. citizen or resident working abroad (commonly referred to as an *expatriate*) may elect to take either a foreign tax credit or the foreign earned income exclusion. In cases where the income tax of a foreign country is higher than the U.S. income

---

[79]For 2010, any self-employed health insurance deduction (see p. 10-7) may be used to reduce net earnings from self-employment.

tax, the credit choice usually is preferable. If the reverse is true, electing the foreign earned income exclusion probably reduces the overall tax burden.

Unfortunately, the choice between the credit and the earned income exclusion is not without some limitations. The election of the foreign earned income exclusion, once made, can be revoked for a later year. However, once revoked, the earned income exclusion will not be available for a period of five years unless the IRS consents to an earlier date. This will create a dilemma for expatriates whose job assignments over several years shift between low- and high-bracket countries.

EXAMPLE 50

In 2010, Ira, a calendar year taxpayer, is sent by his employer to Saudi Arabia (a low-tax country). For 2010, therefore, Ira elects the foreign earned income exclusion. In 2011, Ira's employer transfers him to France (a high-tax country). Accordingly, he revokes the foreign earned income exclusion election for 2011 and chooses instead to use the foreign tax credit. If Ira is transferred back to Saudi Arabia (or any other low-tax country) within five years, he may not utilize the foreign earned income exclusion. ∎

13.7 CREDIT FOR CHILD AND DEPENDENT CARE EXPENSES

A taxpayer may incur employment-related expenses that also qualify as medical expenses (e.g., a nurse is hired to provide in-the-home care for an ill and incapacitated dependent parent). Such expenses may be either deducted as medical expenses (subject to the 7.5 percent limitation) or utilized in determining the credit for child and dependent care expenses. If the credit for child and dependent care expenses is chosen and the employment-related expenses exceed the limitation ($3,000, $6,000, or earned income, as the case may be), the excess may be considered a medical expense. If, however, the taxpayer chooses to deduct qualified employment-related expenses as medical expenses, any portion that is not deductible because of the 7.5 percent limitation may not be used in computing the credit for child and dependent care expenses.

EXAMPLE 51

Alicia has the following tax position for 2011:

Adjusted gross income		$30,000
Potential itemized deductions *from* AGI—		
Other than medical expenses	$3,500	
Medical expenses	6,600	$10,100

All of Alicia's medical expenses were incurred to provide nursing care for her disabled father while she was working. The father lives with Alicia and qualifies as her dependent. ∎

What should Alicia do in this situation? One approach would be to use $3,000 of the nursing care expenses to obtain the maximum credit for child and dependent care expenses allowed of $810 (27% × $3,000). The balance of these expenses should be claimed as medical expenses. After a reduction of 7.5 percent of AGI, this would produce a medical expense deduction of $1,350 [$3,600 (remaining medical expenses) − (7.5% × $30,000)].

Another approach would be to claim the full $6,600 as a medical expense and forgo the credit for child and dependent care expenses. After the 7.5 percent adjustment of $2,250 (7.5% × $30,000), a deduction of $4,350 remains.

The choice, then, is between a credit of $810 plus a deduction of $1,350 or a credit of $0 plus a deduction of $4,350. Which is better, of course, depends on the relative tax savings involved, which in turn are dependent on the taxpayer's marginal tax bracket.

One of the traditional goals of *family tax planning* is to minimize the total tax burden within the family unit. With proper planning and implementation, the credit for child and dependent care expenses can be used to help achieve this goal. For example, payments to certain relatives for the care of qualifying dependents and children qualify for the credit if the care provider is *not* a child (under age 19) of the taxpayer. Thus, if the care provider is in a lower tax bracket than the taxpayer, the following benefits result:

* Income is shifted to a lower-bracket family member.
* The taxpayer qualifies for the credit for child and dependent care expenses.

In addition, the goal of minimizing the family income tax liability can be enhanced in some other situations, but only if the credit's limitations are recognized and avoided. For example, tax savings may still be enjoyed even if the qualifying expenditures incurred by a cash basis taxpayer have already reached the annual ceiling ($3,000 or $6,000). To the extent that any additional payments can be shifted into future tax years, the benefit from the credit may be preserved on these excess expenditures.

EXAMPLE 52	Andre, a calendar year and cash basis taxpayer, has spent $3,000 by December 1 on qualifying child care expenditures for his dependent 11-year-old son. The $250 that is due the care provider for child care services rendered in December does not generate a tax credit benefit if the amount is paid in the current year because the $3,000 ceiling has been reached. However, if the payment can be delayed until the next year, the total credit over the two-year period for which Andre is eligible may be increased. ■

A similar shifting of expenditures to a subsequent year may be wise if the potential credit otherwise generated would exceed the tax liability available to absorb the credit.

13.8 ADJUSTMENTS TO INCREASE WITHHOLDING

The penalty for underpayment of estimated tax by individuals is computed for each quarter of the tax year. A taxpayer can play *catch-up* to a certain extent. Each quarterly payment is credited to the unpaid portion of any previous required installment. Thus, the penalty stops on that portion of the underpayment for the previous quarter. However, since income tax withheld is assumed to have been paid evenly throughout the year and is allocated equally among the four installments in computing any penalty, a taxpayer who would otherwise be subject to a penalty for underpayment should increase withholdings late in the year. This can be done by changing the number of allowances claimed on Form W–4 or by special arrangement with the employer to increase the amount withheld.

A similar way to avoid (or reduce) a penalty for underpayment is to have the employer continue Social Security withholding beyond the base amount.

EXAMPLE 53	Rose, a calendar year taxpayer, earns $125,000 from her job. In late October 2011, she realizes that she will be subject to a penalty for underpayment of estimated tax due to income from outside sources. Consequently, she instructs her employer to continue FICA withholdings for the rest of 2011. If this is done, an extra $18,200 [$125,000 (annual salary) − $106,800 (base amount of the Social Security portion for 2011)] will be subject to the 4.2% Social Security portion of the FICA tax [5.65% (total FICA rate) − 1.45% (Medicare portion of the FICA rate)]. Thus, Rose generates an additional $764.40 (4.2% × $18,200) that will be deemed withheld ratably during 2011. ■

13.9 ADJUSTMENTS TO AVOID OVERWITHHOLDING

Publication 505, *Tax Withholding and Estimated Tax*, contains worksheets that taxpayers may use to take advantage of special provisions for avoiding overwithholding. Extra exemptions for withholding purposes are allowed if the taxpayer has unusually large itemized deductions, deductions *for* AGI, or tax credits. Net losses from Schedules C, D, E, and F may be considered in computing the number of extra withholding exemptions. Net operating loss carryovers may also be considered in the computation. A taxpayer who is entitled to extra withholding exemptions for any of these reasons should file a new Form W–4, Employee's Withholding Allowance Certificate, with his or her employer.

REFOCUS ON THE BIG PICTURE

EDUCATION TAX CREDITS

The American Recovery and Reinvestment Tax Act (ARRTA) of 2009 made a significant change in education credits, and the American Opportunity tax credit provides some relief for Tom and Jennifer Snyder.

Both Lora and Sam qualify for the American Opportunity credit in 2011 as they are both in their first four years of postsecondary education. Lora and Sam both qualify for a $2,500 credit (100 percent of the first $2,000 and 25 percent of the next $2,000 of qualified expenses).

These credits phase out over a range of $20,000 once married taxpayers' AGI exceeds $160,000. As the Snyders' AGI ($158,000) is less than this amount, the total education credits available to them amount to $5,000, and they may claim this amount as a credit on their 2011 income tax return. Further, this credit may be used to offset any AMT liability, and 40 percent ($2,000) is refundable to the Snyders.

What If?

What if the Snyders' AGI is $188,000? In 2011, the Snyders would not qualify for any education credits (their income exceeds the limits for both the American Opportunity and the lifetime learning credits). Although a deduction *for* AGI is allowed for qualified tuition and related expenses involving higher education, their AGI exceeds the $160,000 maximum allowed for a deduction (see Chapter 9 for additional details).

KEY TERMS

Adoption expenses credit, 13–20

American Opportunity credit, 13–24

Child tax credit, 13–22

Credit for certain retirement plan contributions, 13–27

Credit for child and dependent care expenses, 13–22

Credit for employer-provided child care, 13–15

Credit for small employer pension plan startup costs, 13–15

Disabled access credit, 13–14

Earned income credit, 13–16

Employment taxes, 13–29

Estimated tax, 13–40

First-time homebuyer credit, 13-26

Foreign tax credit (FTC), 13–19

General business credit, 13–7

Jobs credit, 13–9

Lifetime learning credit, 13–24

Low-income housing credit, 13–13

Nonrefundable credits, 13–6

Permanent and total disability, 13–18

Refundable credits, 13–5

Rehabilitation expenditures credit, 13–8

Rehabilitation expenditures credit recapture, 13–9

Research activities credit, 13–11

Self-employment tax, 13–42

Tax credit for the elderly or disabled, 13–18

Tax credits, 13–3

Withholding allowances, 13–35

Work opportunity tax credit, 13–9

DISCUSSION QUESTIONS

1. **LO.1** Would an individual taxpayer receive greater benefit from deducting an expenditure or from taking a credit equal to 25% of the expenditure? How would your response change if the item would only be deductible *from* AGI?

2. **LO.2** What is a refundable credit? Give examples. What is a nonrefundable credit? Give examples.

3. **LO.2** Tax credits are offset against the tax liability in a prescribed order. Explain why the order in which credits are utilized is important.

4. **LO.2, 3** Identify the components of the general business credit and discuss the treatment of unused general business credits.

ISSUE ID

5. **LO.2** Clint, a self-employed engineering consultant, is contemplating purchasing an old building for renovation. After the work is completed, Clint plans to rent out two-thirds of the floor space to businesses and to live and work in the remaining portion. Identify the relevant tax issues for Clint.

ISSUE ID

6. **LO.3** Sonja is considering the purchase and renovation of an old building. She has heard about the tax credit for rehabilitation expenditures, but does not know the specific rules applicable to the credit. Explain the most important and relevant provisions for her.

7. **LO.3** Discuss the purpose of the work opportunity tax credit. Who receives the tax benefits from the credit? Give examples of the types of individuals who, if hired, give rise to the credit.

8. **LO.3** Explain the alternatives a taxpayer has in claiming the deduction and credit for research and experimentation expenditures.

9. **LO.3** Explain the purpose of the disabled access credit and identify several examples of the type of structural changes to a building that qualify for the credit.

10. **LO.4** Is the earned income credit a form of negative income tax? Why or why not?

11. **LO.4** Briefly discuss the requirements that must be satisfied for a taxpayer to qualify for the earned income credit.

12. **LO.4** Individuals who receive substantial Social Security benefits are usually not eligible for the tax credit for the elderly or disabled because these benefits effectively eliminate the base upon which the credit is computed. Explain.

13. **LO.4, 7** In general, when would an individual taxpayer find it more beneficial to use the foreign earned income exclusion rather than the foreign tax credit in computing his or her income tax liability?

ISSUE ID

14. **LO.4, 7** Tim was recently called into the partner's office and offered a two-year assignment in his public accounting firm's Shanghai office. Realizing that Tim will face incremental expenses while in Shanghai, such as for foreign income taxes and rent, the firm will try to make him "whole" from a financial perspective by increasing his salary to help offset the expenses he will incur while living overseas. If Tim takes the assignment, he will likely rent his personal residence and sell several major tangible assets such as his personal automobile. Identify the relevant tax issues.

15. **LO.4** Do all payments of foreign taxes qualify for the U.S. foreign tax credit? Explain.

16. **LO.4** Discuss, in general, the calculation of the adoption expenses credit.

17. **LO.4** Distinguish between the child tax credit and the credit for child and dependent care expenses.

18. **LO.4** Discuss the rationale underlying the enactment of the following tax credits:
    a. Rehabilitation expenditures credit.
    b. Research activities credit.
    c. Low-income housing credit.
    d. Earned income credit.
    e. Foreign tax credit.

19. **LO.4, 7** Polly and her spouse, Leo, file a joint return and expect to report AGI of $70,000 in 2011. Polly's employer offers a child and dependent care reimbursement plan that allows up to $3,500 of qualifying expenses to be reimbursed in exchange for a $3,500 reduction in the employee's salary. Because Polly and Leo have one minor child requiring child care that costs $3,500 each year, she is wondering if she should sign up for the program instead of taking advantage of the credit for child and dependent care expenses. Assuming Polly and Leo are in the 25% tax bracket, analyze the effect of the two alternatives. How would your answer differ if Polly and Leo's AGI was $14,000 instead of $70,000? Assume in this case that their marginal tax rate is 10%.

> **DECISION MAKING**

20. **LO.4** Mark and Lisa are approaching an exciting time in their lives as their oldest son, Austin, graduates from high school and moves on to college. What are some of the tax issues Mark and Lisa should consider as they think about paying for Austin's college education?

> **ISSUE ID**

21. **LO.4** Explain the purpose of the first-time homebuyer credit and describe the general characteristics of its computation.

22. **LO.3, 4** Identify two tax credits enacted by Congress that are designed to encourage the establishment of or contributions to qualified retirement plans.

23. **LO.5** Elaborate rules exist that require employers to prepay various types of Federal taxes. Summarize the major issues that an employer must resolve if it is to comply with the requirements.

> **ISSUE ID**

24. **LO.5** If an employer is not required to withhold income taxes on an item of income paid to an employee, does this mean that the item is nontaxable? Explain.

25. **LO.5** Kathy, a sole proprietor, owns and operates a grocery store. Kathy's husband and her 16-year-old daughter work in the business and are paid wages. Will the husband and daughter be subject to FICA? Explain.

26. **LO.5** Under what circumstances will the special withholding allowance be allowed for purposes of determining income tax withholding?

27. **LO.6** Describe the exposure (i.e., wage base and tax rate) that a self-employed individual has to the self-employment tax for 2011.

PROBLEMS

28. **LO.2** Dick has a tentative general business credit of $70,000 for the current year. His net regular tax liability before the general business credit is $88,000, and his tentative minimum tax is $82,000. Compute Dick's allowable general business credit for the year.

29. **LO.2** Pine Corporation has the following general business credit carryovers:

2007	$ 40,000
2008	70,000
2009	60,000
2010	30,000
Total carryovers	$200,000

If the general business credit generated by activities during 2011 equals $185,000 and the total credit allowed during the current year is $300,000 (based on tax liability), what amounts of the current general business credit and carryovers are utilized against the 2011 income tax liability? What is the amount of unused credit carried forward to 2012?

30. **LO.3, 7** In the current year, Paul Chaing (4522 Fargo Street, Geneva, IL 60134) acquires a qualifying historic structure for $350,000 (excluding the cost of the land) and plans to substantially rehabilitate the structure. He is planning to spend either $320,000 or $380,000 on rehabilitation expenditures. Write a letter to Paul and a memo for the tax files explaining, for the two alternative expenditures, (1) the computation that determines the rehabilitation expenditures tax credit available to Paul, (2) the impact of the credit on Paul's adjusted basis in the property, and (3) the cash-flow differences as a result of the tax consequences related to his expenditure choice.

> **DECISION MAKING**
>
> **COMMUNICATIONS**

31. **LO.3** Green Corporation hires six individuals on January 4, 2011, all of whom qualify for the work opportunity credit. Three of these individuals receive wages of $8,500 during 2011, and each individual works more than 400 hours during the year. The other three individuals work 300 hours and receive wages of $5,000 during the year.
    a. Calculate the amount of Green's work opportunity credit for 2011.
    b. If Green pays total wages of $140,000 to its employees during the year, how much of this amount is deductible in 2011 assuming the work opportunity credit is taken?

32. **LO.3** In March 2011, Sparrow Corporation hired three individuals—Austin, Adam, and Angela—all of whom are certified as long-term family assistance recipients. Each of these individuals earned $11,000 during 2011. Only Adam continued to work for Sparrow in 2012, and he earned $13,500. In March 2012, Sparrow hired Sam, who is also certified as a long-term family assistance recipient. During 2012, Sam earned $12,000.
    a. Compute Sparrow Corporation's work opportunity credit for 2011 and 2012.
    b. If Sparrow Corporation pays total wages to its employees of $325,000 in 2011 and $342,000 in 2012, how much may Sparrow claim as a wage deduction in 2011 and 2012?

DECISION MAKING

33. **LO.3, 7** Sarah, a calendar year taxpayer, informs you that during the year she incurs expenditures of $30,000 that qualify for the incremental research activities credit. In addition, it is determined that her base amount for the year is $22,800.
    a. Determine Sarah's incremental research activities credit for the year.
    b. Sarah is in the 25% tax bracket. Determine which approach to the research expenditures and the research activities credit (other than capitalization and subsequent amortization) would provide the greater tax benefit to Sarah.

COMMUNICATIONS

34. **LO.3** Dan DeRose (333 East Shore Drive, Wyckoff, NJ 07481), one of your clients, owns two retail establishments in downtown Wyckoff and has come to you seeking advice concerning the tax consequences of complying with the Americans with Disabilities Act. He understands that he needs to install various features at his stores (e.g., ramps, doorways, and restrooms that are handicapped accessible) to make them more accessible to disabled individuals. He asks whether any tax credits will be available to help offset the cost of the necessary changes. He estimates the cost of the planned changes to his facilities as follows:

Location	Projected Cost
Oak Street	$18,000
Maple Avenue	12,400

He reminds you that the Oak Street store was constructed in 2004 while the Maple Avenue store is in a building that was constructed in 1912. Dan operates his business as a sole proprietorship and has approximately eight employees at each location. Write a letter to Dan in which you summarize your conclusions concerning the tax consequences of his proposed capital improvements.

35. **LO.4** Which of the following individuals qualify for the earned income credit for 2011?
    a. Thomas is single, 21 years of age, and has no qualifying children. His income consists of $9,000 in wages.
    b. Shannon, who is 27 years old, maintains a household for a dependent 11-year-old son and is eligible for head-of-household tax rates. Her income consists of $16,050 of salary and $50 of taxable interest (Shannon's AGI is $16,100).
    c. Keith and Susan, both age 30, are married and file a joint return. Keith and Susan have no dependents. Their combined income consists of $28,500 of salary and $100 of taxable interest (their AGI is $28,600).
    d. Colin is a 26-year-old, self-supporting, single taxpayer. He has no qualifying children and generates earnings of $9,000.

36. **LO.4** Jason, a single parent, lives in an apartment with his three minor children, whom he supports. Jason earned $27,400 during 2011, paid $800 in qualified moving expenses during 2011, and uses the standard deduction. Calculate the amount, if any, of Jason's earned income credit.

DECISION MAKING

37. **LO.4, 7** Joyce, a widow, lives in an apartment with her two minor children (ages 8 and 10) whom she supports. Joyce earns $33,000 during 2011. She uses the standard deduction.

a. Calculate the amount, if any, of Joyce's earned income credit.

b. During the year, Joyce is offered a new job that has greater future potential than her current job. If she accepts the job offer, her earnings for the year would be $39,000; however, she is afraid she will not qualify for the earned income credit. Using after-tax cash-flow calculations, determine whether Joyce should accept the new job offer.

38. **LO.4** Robert, age 68, and Tanya, age 66, are married retirees who receive the following income and retirement benefits during the current year:

Fully taxable pension from Robert's former employer	$ 8,000
Dividends and interest	2,500
Social Security benefits	4,000
Total	$14,500

Assume Robert and Tanya file a joint tax return, have no deductions *for* AGI, and use the standard deduction. Are they eligible for the tax credit for the elderly? If so, calculate the amount of the credit, assuming the credit is not limited by their tax liability.

39. **LO.4, 7** Kim, a U.S. citizen and resident, owns and operates a novelty goods business. During 2011, Kim has taxable income of $100,000, made up as follows: $50,000 from foreign sources and $50,000 from U.S. sources. In calculating taxable income, the standard deduction is used. The income from foreign sources is subject to foreign income taxes of $26,000. For 2011, Kim files a joint return claiming his three children as dependents.

DECISION MAKING

a. Assuming Kim chooses to claim the foreign taxes as an income tax credit, what is his income tax liability for 2011?

b. Recently, Kim has become disenchanted with the location of his business and is considering moving his foreign operation to a different country. Based on his research, if he moves his business to his country of choice, all relevant revenues and costs would remain approximately the same except that the income taxes payable to that country would be only $8,000. Given that all of the foreign income taxes paid are available to offset the U.S. tax liability (whether he operates in a high-tax or a low-tax foreign jurisdiction), what impact will this have on his decision regarding the potential move?

40. **LO.4** Blue Horizons, Inc., a U.S. corporation, is a manufacturing concern that sells most of its products in the United States. It also does some business in the European Union through various branches. During the current year, Blue Horizons has taxable income of $700,000, of which $500,000 is U.S.-sourced and $200,000 is foreign-sourced. Foreign income taxes paid amounted to $45,000. Blue Horizons' U.S. income tax liability is $238,000. What is its U.S. income tax liability net of the allowable foreign tax credit?

41. **LO.4** Ann and Bill were on the list of a local adoption agency for several years seeking to adopt a child. Finally, in 2010, good news comes their way and an adoption seems imminent. They pay qualified adoption expenses of $4,000 in 2010 and $11,000 in 2011. Assume the adoption becomes final in 2011. Ann and Bill always file a joint income tax return.

a. Determine the amount of the adoption expenses credit available to Ann and Bill assuming their combined annual income is $100,000. What year(s) will they benefit from the credit?

b. Assuming Ann and Bill's modified AGI in 2010 and 2011 is $200,000, calculate the amount of the adoption expenses credit.

42. **LO.4** Durell and Earline are married, file a joint return, and claim dependency exemptions for their two children, ages 5 years and 6 months. They also claim Earline's son from a previous marriage, age 18, as a dependent. Durell and Earline's combined AGI is $68,000.

a. Compute Durell and Earline's child tax credit.

b. Assume the same facts, except that Durell and Earline's combined AGI is $122,000. Compute their child tax credit.

43. **LO.4** Paul and Karen are married, and both are employed (Paul earned $44,000 and Karen earned $9,000 during 2011). Paul and Karen have two dependent children, both under the age of 13. In order to work, Paul and Karen pay $3,800 to various unrelated parties to care for their children while they are working. Assuming that Paul and Karen file a joint return, what, if any, is their tax credit for child and dependent care expenses?

44. **L0.4** Jim and Mary Jean are married and have two dependent children under the age of 13. Both parents are gainfully employed and during 2011 earn salaries as follows: $16,000 (Jim) and $5,200 (Mary Jean). To care for their children while they work, they pay Eleanor (Jim's mother) $5,600. Eleanor does not qualify as a dependent of Jim and Mary. Assuming Jim and Mary Jean file a joint tax return, what, if any, is their credit for child and dependent care expenses?

45. **L0.4, 7** Bernadette, a longtime client of yours, is an architect and president of the local Rotary chapter. To keep up-to-date with the latest developments in her profession, she attends continuing education seminars offered by the architecture school at State University. During 2011, Bernadette spends $2,000 on course tuition to attend such seminars. She also spends another $400 on architecture books during the year. Bernadette's son is a senior majoring in engineering at the University of the Midwest. During the 2011 calendar year, Bernadette's son incurs the following expenses: $8,200 for tuition ($4,100 per semester) and $750 for books and course materials. Bernadette's son, whom she claims as a dependent, lives at home while attending school full-time. Bernadette is married, files a joint return, and has a combined AGI with her husband of $103,000.
    a. Calculate Bernadette's education tax credit for 2011.
    b. In her capacity as president of the local Rotary chapter, Bernadette has asked you to make a 30–45 minute speech outlining the different ways the tax law helps defray (1) the cost of higher education and (2) the cost of continuing education once someone is in the workforce. Prepare an outline of possible topics for presentation. A tentative title for your presentation is "How Can the Tax Law Help Pay for College and Continuing Professional Education?"

46. **L0.4** Kathleen and Glenn decide that this is the year to begin getting serious about saving for their retirement by participating in their employers' § 401(k) plans. As a result, they each have $3,000 of their salary set aside in their qualified plans.
    a. Calculate the credit for certain retirement plan contributions available to Kathleen and Glenn if the AGI on their joint return is $35,000.
    b. Kathleen and Glenn persuade their dependent 15-year-old son, Joel, to put $500 of his part-time earnings into a Roth IRA during the year. What is the credit for certain retirement plan contributions available to Joel? His AGI is $7,000.

47. **L0.5** In each of the following independent situations, determine the amount of FICA that should be withheld from the employee's 2011 salary by the employer.
    a. Harry earns a $50,000 salary, files a joint return, and claims four withholding allowances.
    b. Hazel earns a $110,000 salary, files a joint return, and claims four withholding allowances.
    c. Tracy earns a $190,000 salary, files a joint return, and claims four withholding allowances.
    d. Alicia's 17-year-old son, Carlos, earns $10,000 at the family sole proprietorship.

48. **L0.5** During 2011, Greg Cruz (1401 Orangedale Road, Troy, MI 48084) works for Maple Corporation and Gray Company. He earns $70,000 at Maple Corporation where he is a full-time employee. Greg also works part-time for Gray Company for wages of $45,000.
    a. Did Greg experience an overwithholding of FICA taxes? Write a letter to Greg and a memo for the tax files in which you explain your conclusion.
    b. Did Maple Corporation and Gray Company overpay the employer's portion of FICA? Explain.

49. **L0.5** In each of the following independent situations, determine the maximum withholding allowances permitted Eli (an employee) on Form W–4.
    a. Eli is single with no dependents.
    b. Eli is married to a nonemployed spouse, and they have no dependents.
    c. Eli is married to Vera, an employed spouse who earns $25,000, and they have three dependent children. Eli and Vera do not qualify for the child tax credit. On the Form W–4 that she filed with the employer, Vera claimed zero allowances.
    d. Assume the same facts as in (c), except that Eli and Vera fully support Eli's mother, who lives with them. The mother (age 70 and blind) qualifies as their dependent. (Refer to Chapter 3.)
    e. Eli is single with no dependents but works for two employers, one on a full-time basis and the other on a part-time basis. The Form W–4 filed with the first employer (the

full-time job) reflects two withholding exemptions. The wages from each job exceed $1,000.

f. Assume the same facts as in (e), except that Eli is married to a nonemployed spouse.

DECISION MAKING

50. **LO.5** Jane, who is expecting to finish college in May 2011, is fortunate to have already arranged full-time employment after graduation. She will begin work on July 1, 2011, as a staff accountant at a nearby professional services firm with a starting salary of $48,600 per year. Jane is married to Craig, who plans to be a full-time student throughout the year. They anticipate generating no income for the year other than the salary from her new position.

a. How many withholding allowances would you expect Jane to claim on her Form W–4?

b. Assuming Jane receives her salary on a monthly basis, what amount will be withheld if her employer uses the wage-bracket tables to calculate withholdings?

c. Assuming Jane receives her salary on a monthly basis, what amount will be withheld if her employer uses the percentage method to calculate withholdings?

d. Assuming Jane and Craig use the standard deduction, calculate the Federal income tax liability on their projected taxable income for 2011. What changes would you recommend Jane make to her W–4 to correct any over- or under-withholding for the current year?

e. What further changes should she make to her W–4 at the beginning of 2012?

51. **LO.5** Norm is married to a nonemployed spouse and has four dependents. He is employed by Beige Corporation and is paid a monthly salary of $4,245 ($50,940 per year). Using these facts, determine the amount to be withheld by Beige Corporation for Federal income tax purposes under the wage-bracket tables and under the percentage method for 2011.

52. **LO.6** Julie, being self-employed, is required to make estimated payments of her tax liability for the year. Her tax liability for 2010 was $25,000, and her AGI was less than $150,000. For 2011, Julie ultimately determines that her income tax liability is $18,000. During the year, however, she made the following payments, totaling $13,000:

April 18, 2011	$ 4,500
June 15, 2011	2,800
September 15, 2011	4,100
January 17, 2012	1,600
	$13,000

Because she prepaid so little of her ultimate income tax liability, she now realizes that she may be subject to the penalty for underpayment of estimated tax.

a. Determine Julie's exposure to the penalty for underpayment of estimated tax.

b. The same as (a) except that Julie's tax liability for 2010 was $15,960.

53. **LO.6** In 2011, Maria has self-employed earnings of $125,000. Using the format illustrated in the text, compute Maria's self-employment tax liability and the allowable income tax deduction for the self-employment tax paid.

CUMULATIVE PROBLEMS

54. Beth R. Jordan lives at 2322 Skyview Road, Mesa, AZ 85201. She is a tax accountant with Mesa Manufacturing Company, 1203 Western Avenue, Mesa, AZ 85201 (employer identification number 11–1111111). She also writes computer software programs for tax practitioners and has a part-time tax practice. Beth is single and has no dependents. Beth's birthday is July 4, 1971, and her Social Security number is 123–45–6789. She wants to contribute $3 to the Presidential Election Campaign Fund.

TAX RETURN PROBLEM

The following information is shown on Beth's Wage and Tax Statement (Form W–2) for 2010.

Line	Description	Amount
1	Wages, tips, other compensation	$63,000.00
2	Federal income tax withheld	10,500.00
3	Social Security wages	63,000.00
4	Social Security tax withheld	3,906.00
5	Medicare wages and tips	63,000.00
6	Medicare tax withheld	913.50
15	State	Arizona
16	State wages, tips, etc.	63,000.00
17	State income tax withheld	1,650.00

During 2010, Beth received interest of $1,300 from Arizona Federal Savings and Loan and $400 from Arizona State Bank. Each financial institution reported the interest income on a Form 1099–INT. She received qualified dividends of $800 from Blue Corporation, $750 from Green Corporation, and $650 from Orange Corporation. Each corporation reported Beth's dividend payments on a Form 1099–DIV.

Beth received a $1,100 income tax refund from the state of Arizona on April 29, 2010. On her 2009 Federal income tax return, she reported total itemized deductions of $8,200, which included $2,200 of state income tax withheld by her employer.

Fees earned from her part-time tax practice in 2010 totaled $3,800. She paid $600 to have the tax returns processed by a computerized tax return service.

On February 8, 2010, Beth bought 500 shares of Gray Corporation common stock for $17.60 a share. On September 12, Beth sold the stock for $14 a share.

Beth bought a used sport utility vehicle for $6,000 on June 5, 2010. She purchased the vehicle from her brother-in-law, who was unemployed and was in need of cash. On November 2, 2010, she sold the vehicle to a friend for $6,500.

On January 2, 2010, Beth acquired 100 shares of Blue Corporation common stock for $30 a share. She sold the stock on December 19, 2010, for $55 a share.

During 2010, Beth received royalties of $16,000 on a software program she had written. Beth incurred the following expenditures in connection with her software-writing activities:

Cost of personal computer (100% business use)	$7,000
Cost of printer (100% business use)	2,000
Furniture	3,000
Supplies	650
Fee paid to computer consultant	3,500

Beth elected to expense the maximum portion of the cost of the computer, printer, and furniture allowed under the provisions of § 179. This equipment and furniture were placed in service on January 15, 2010.

Although her employer suggested that Beth attend a convention on current developments in corporate taxation, Beth was not reimbursed for the travel expenses of $1,420 she incurred in attending the convention. The $1,420 included $200 for the cost of meals.

During 2010, Beth paid $300 for prescription medicines and $2,875 for doctor bills and hospital bills. Medical insurance premiums were paid for her by her employer. Beth paid real property taxes of $1,766 on her home. Interest on her home mortgage was $3,845, and interest to credit card companies was $320. Beth contributed $30 each week to her church and $10 each week to the United Way. Professional dues and subscriptions totaled $350. Beth maintained her sales tax receipts. The total is $1,954.

Beth paid estimated taxes of $1,000.

Part 1—Tax Computation

Compute the net tax payable or refund due for Beth R. Jordan for 2010. If you use tax forms for your solution, you will need Forms 1040, 2106–EZ, and 4562 and Schedules A, B, C, D, and SE. Suggested software: H&R BLOCK At Home.

Part 2—Tax Planning

Beth is anticipating significant changes in her life in 2011, and she has asked you to estimate her taxable income and tax liability for 2011. She just received word that she has been qualified to adopt a two-year-old daughter. Beth expects the adoption will be finalized in 2011 and that she will incur approximately $2,000 of adoption expenses. In addition, she expects to incur approximately $3,500 of child and dependent care expenses relating to the care of her new daughter, which will enable her to keep her job at Mesa Manufacturing Company. However, with the additional demands on her time because of her daughter, she has decided to discontinue her two part-time jobs (i.e., the part-time tax practice and her software business), and she will cease making estimated income tax payments. In your computations, assume all other income and expenditures will remain at approximately the same levels as in 2010.

55. Tim and Sarah Lawrence are married and file a joint return. Tim's Social Security number is 123–45–6789, and Sarah's Social Security number is 111–11–1111. They reside at 100 Olive Lane, Covington, LA 70400. They have two dependent children, Sean and Debra, ages 12 and 16, respectively. Sean's Social Security number is 123–45–6788, and Debra's Social Security number is 123–45–6787. Tim is a self-employed businessman (sole proprietor of an unincorporated business), and Sarah is a corporate executive. Tim has the following income and expenses from his business:

TAX COMPUTATION PROBLEM

Gross income	$280,000
Business expenses	156,000

Records related to Sarah's employment provide the following information:

Salary	$130,000
Unreimbursed travel expenses (including $400 of meals)	1,800
Unreimbursed entertainment expenses	700

Other pertinent information relating to 2011 follows:

Proceeds from sale of stock acquired on July 15, 2011 (cost of $16,500), and sold on August 1, 2011	$14,300
Proceeds from sale of stock acquired on September 18, 2010 (cost of $7,000), and sold on October 5, 2011	5,800
Wages paid to full-time domestic worker for housekeeping and child supervision	10,000
Interest income received	9,000
Total itemized deductions (not including any potential deductions above)	27,900
Federal income tax withheld	36,000
Estimated payments of Federal income tax	24,000

Compute the net tax payable or refund due for Tim and Sarah Lawrence for 2011.

RESEARCH PROBLEMS

Note: Solutions to Research Problems can be prepared by using the **Checkpoint®** **Student Edition** online research product, which is available to accompany this text. It is also possible to prepare solutions to the Research Problems by using tax research materials found in a standard tax library.

THOMSON REUTERS
Checkpoint® Student Edition

Research Problem 1. Ashby and Curtis, a young professional couple, have a two-year-old son, Jason. Curtis works full-time as an electrical engineer, but Ashby has not worked outside the home since Jason was born. As Jason is getting older, Ashby feels that he would benefit from attending nursery school several times a week, which would give her an opportunity to reinvigorate her love of painting at a nearby art studio. Ashby thinks that if she is lucky, the proceeds from the sale of her paintings will pay for the nursery school tuition. But, in addition, she is planning to claim the credit for child and dependent care expenses because the care provided Jason at the nursery school is required for her to pursue her art. Can Ashby and Curtis claim the credit for child and dependent care expenses for the nursery school expenditure?

Research Problem 2. Your ophthalmologist, Dr. Hunter Francis (55 Wheatland Drive, Hampton, CT 06247), has been very pleased with the growth of his practice in the 15 years he has been in business. This growth has resulted, at least in part, because he has aggressively marketed his services and tried to accommodate clients with various needs. This year Dr. Francis purchased a sophisticated piece of equipment that enables him to diagnose persons with mental handicaps, hearing impairments, and physical disabilities without having to go through a series of questions. In addition, he can treat his patients who are not disabled much more accurately and efficiently by using this equipment. Since purchasing the machine this year for $9,500, Dr. Francis has used it on many occasions. Unfortunately, he has not been able to attract any disabled patients, even though previously he referred such people to other ophthalmologists who owned the necessary equipment. Therefore, the primary purpose for acquiring the equipment (i.e., to attract disabled patients) has not been realized, but he has put it to good use in treating other patients. Write a letter to Dr. Francis explaining whether he may claim the disabled access credit for this acquisition.

Research Problem 3. You recently read an article in your school newspaper about Professor Rodney Taylor, one of your favorite professors in the religious studies department. According to the article, he and the university have been negotiating an early retirement package and have reached a stumbling block. Under the agreement, Professor Taylor is to receive a lump-sum payment equal to one year's salary in exchange for his retirement and the release of any and all rights associated with his tenure status. While recognizing that the payment would be subject to income tax, Taylor contends that the amount is not earned income and thus should not be subject to the FICA tax. The university negotiators say that they are not aware of any authority that supports Taylor's view. In fact, they have learned that other universities in the state system have been withholding amounts for FICA for years in situations involving early retirement buyout packages for high-level administrators. The university's position is that lacking the authority to not withhold for FICA and given the precedent set in similar early retirement packages at other universities, they are obligated to withhold FICA from the payment. You want to come to the aid of Professor Taylor. Obviously, if the payments are considered wages subject to the FICA tax, the value of the offer to Professor Taylor will be significantly reduced. Can you find any authority for his position?

Research Problem 4. During a recent Sunday afternoon excursion, Miriam, an admirer of early twentieth-century architecture, discovers a 1920s-era house in the countryside outside Mobile, Alabama. She desires not only to purchase and renovate this particular house, but also to move the structure into Mobile so her community can enjoy its architectural features. Being aware of the availability of the tax credit for rehabilitation expenditures, she wishes to maximize her use of the provision, if it is available in this case, once the renovation work begins in Mobile. Miriam also informs you that she will pursue the purchase, relocation, and renovation of the house only if the tax credit is available. Comment on Miriam's decision and whether any renovation expenditures incurred will qualify for the tax credit for rehabilitation expenditures.

Partial list of research aids:
George S. Nalle III v. Comm., 93–2 USTC ¶50,468, 72 AFTR 2d 93–5705, 997 F.2d 1134 (CA–5, 1993).

INTERNET *activity*

Use the tax resources of the Internet to address the following questions. Do not restrict your search to the Web, but include a review of newsgroups and general reference materials, practitioner sites and resources, primary sources of the tax law, chat rooms and discussion groups, and other opportunities.

Research Problem 5. The IRS has unveiled a web-based tool to help taxpayers determine whether they or their clients are eligible for the earned income credit. Locate this tool at the IRS website and then apply the facts related to a hypothetical taxpayer and determine if the earned income credit is available.

Research Problem 6. The foreign tax credit is especially valuable when a U.S. individual works in a country whose income tax rates exceed those of the United States. List five countries whose tax rates on individuals exceed those of the United States and five where the corresponding U.S. rates are higher.

Research Problem 7. Download a copy of Form W–4 and complete the accompanying worksheet. File the worksheet with your employer if you discover that you currently are being under- or overwithheld.

Property Transactions

Part 5 presents the tax treatment of sales, exchanges, and other dispositions of property. Included are the determination of the realized gain or loss, recognized gain or loss, and the classification of the recognized gain or loss as capital or ordinary. The topic of basis is evaluated both in terms of its effect on the calculation of the gain or loss and in terms of the determination of the basis of any contemporaneous or related subsequent acquisitions of property.

Property Transactions: Determination of Gain or Loss and Basis Considerations

After completing Chapter 14, you should be able to:

LO.1

Understand the computation of realized gain or loss on property dispositions.

LO.2

Distinguish between realized and recognized gain or loss.

LO.3

Apply the recovery of capital doctrine.

LO.4

Explain how basis is determined for various methods of asset acquisition.

LO.5

Describe various loss disallowance provisions.

LO.6

Identify tax planning opportunities related to selected property transactions.

OUTLINE

Income (broadly conceived).	$ xx,xxx
Less: Exclusions	(x,xxx)
Gross income	**$xx,xxx**
Less: Deductions for adjusted gross income.	**(x,xxx)**

FORM 1040 (p. 1)

12	Business income or (loss). Attach Schedule C or C-EZ	
13	Capital gain or (loss). Attach Schedule D if required. If not required, check here ▶	☐
14	Other gains or (losses). Attach Form 4797	

Adjusted gross income.	$ xx,xxx
Less: The greater of total itemized deductions *or* the standard deduction	(x,xxx)
Personal and dependency exemptions	(x,xxx)
Taxable income	$ xx,xxx
Tax on taxable income (see Tax Tables or Tax Rate Schedules)	$ x,xxx
Less: Tax credits (including income taxes withheld and prepaid)	(xxx)
Tax due (or refund)	$ xxx

THE BIG PICTURE   Tax Solutions for the Real World

PROPOSED SALE OF A HOUSE AND OTHER PROPERTY TRANSACTIONS

Alice owns a house that she received from her mother seven months ago. Her mother's cost for the house was $275,000. Alice is considering selling the house to her favorite nephew, Dan, for $275,000. Alice anticipates she will have no gain or loss on the transaction. She comes to you for advice.

As Alice's tax adviser, you need answers to the following questions:

- You are aware that Alice's mother died around the time Alice indicates she received the house from her mother. Did Alice receive the house by gift prior to her mother's death? If so, what was the mother's adjusted basis? Did Alice instead inherit the house from her mother? If so, what was the fair market value of the house on the date of her mother's death?
- Has the house been Alice's principal residence during the period she has owned it? Was it her principal residence before she received it from her mother?
- How long did Alice's mother own the house?
- What is the fair market value of the house?
- Does Alice intend for the transaction with Dan to be a sale or part sale and part gift?
- What does Alice intend to do with the sale proceeds?

Alice would also like to know the tax consequences of selling her car, which she purchased for $22,000 four months ago and has used exclusively for personal use.

She has been disappointed with its performance. Based on the "Blue Book" value, she anticipates that she can sell it for $20,000 to $23,000.

In addition, earlier this year Alice sold some stock at a realized loss and subsequently repurchased some shares of the same stock. She has also asked you about the tax consequences of these transactions.

Once you have more information, you can advise Alice on the tax consequences of these various transactions. **Read the chapter and formulate your response.**

T his chapter and the following three chapters are concerned with the income tax consequences of property transactions (the sale or other disposition of property). The following questions are considered with respect to the sale or other disposition of property:

- Is there a realized gain or loss?
- If so, is the gain or loss recognized?
- If the gain or loss is recognized, is it ordinary or capital?
- What is the basis of any replacement property that is acquired?

Chapters 14 and 15 discuss the determination of realized and recognized gain or loss and the basis of property. Chapters 16 and 17 cover the classification of the recognized gain or loss as ordinary or capital.

14.1 DETERMINATION OF GAIN OR LOSS

REALIZED GAIN OR LOSS

Realized gain or loss is the difference between the amount realized from the sale or other disposition of property and the property's adjusted basis on the date of disposition. If the amount realized exceeds the property's adjusted basis, the result is a **realized gain**. Conversely, if the property's adjusted basis exceeds the amount realized, the result is a **realized loss**.[1]

> **LO.1**
>
> Understand the computation of realized gain or loss on property dispositions.

> **EXAMPLE 1**
>
> Tab sells Swan Corporation stock with an adjusted basis of $3,000 for $5,000. Tab's realized gain is $2,000. If Tab had sold the stock for $2,000, he would have had a realized loss of $1,000. ∎

Sale or Other Disposition

The term *sale or other disposition* is defined broadly in the tax law and includes virtually any disposition of property. Thus, transactions such as trade-ins, casualties, condemnations, thefts, and bond retirements are treated as dispositions of property. The most common disposition of property is through a sale or exchange. Usually, the key factor in determining whether a disposition has taken place is whether an identifiable event has occurred[2] as opposed to a mere fluctuation in the value of the property.[3]

---

[1]§ 1001(a) and Reg. § 1.1001–1(a).
[2]Reg. § 1.1001–1(c)(1).

[3]*Lynch v. Turrish*, 1 USTC ¶18, 3 AFTR 2986, 38 S.Ct. 537 (USSC, 1918).

EXAMPLE 2

Lori owns Tan Corporation stock that cost $3,000. The stock has appreciated in value by $2,000 since Lori purchased it. Lori has no realized gain since mere fluctuation in value is not a disposition or identifiable event for tax purposes. ■

EXAMPLE 3

Assume the same facts as in Example 2, except that the stock has declined in value by $2,000 since Lori purchased it. Lori has no realized loss since the decline is associated with a mere fluctuation in value. ■

Amount Realized

The **amount realized** from a sale or other disposition of property is the sum of any money received plus the fair market value of other property received. The amount realized also includes any real property taxes treated as imposed on the seller that are actually paid by the buyer.[4] The reason for including these taxes in the amount realized is that by paying the taxes, the purchaser is, in effect, paying an additional amount to the seller of the property.

The amount realized also includes any liability on the property disposed of, such as a mortgage debt, if the buyer assumes the mortgage or the property is sold subject to the mortgage.[5] The amount of the liability is included in the amount realized even if the debt is nonrecourse and the amount of the debt is greater than the fair market value of the mortgaged property.[6]

EXAMPLE 4

Barry sells property on which there is a mortgage of $20,000 to Cole for $50,000 cash. Barry's amount realized from the sale is $70,000 if Cole assumes the mortgage or takes the property subject to the mortgage. ■

The **fair market value** of property received in a sale or other disposition has been defined by the courts as the price at which property will change hands between a willing seller and a willing buyer when neither is compelled to sell or buy.[7] Fair market value is determined by considering the relevant factors in each case.[8] An expert appraiser is often required to evaluate these factors in arriving at fair market value. When the fair market value of the property received cannot be determined, the value of the property given up by the taxpayer may be used.[9]

In calculating the amount realized, selling expenses such as advertising, commissions, and legal fees relating to the disposition are deducted. The amount realized is the net amount that the taxpayer received directly or indirectly, in the form of cash or anything else of value, from the disposition of the property.

Adjusted Basis

The **adjusted basis** of property disposed of is the property's original basis adjusted to the date of disposition.[10] Original basis is the cost or other basis of the property on the date the property is acquired by the taxpayer. Considerations involving original basis are discussed later in this chapter. *Capital additions* increase and *recoveries of capital* decrease

---

[4]§ 1001(b) and Reg. § 1.1001–1(b). Refer to Chapter 10 for a discussion of this subject.

[5]*Crane v. Comm.*, 47–1 USTC ¶9217, 35 AFTR 776, 67 S.Ct. 1047 (USSC, 1947). Although a legal distinction exists between the direct assumption of a mortgage and taking property subject to a mortgage, the tax consequences in calculating the amount realized are the same.

[6]*Comm. v. Tufts*, 83–1 USTC ¶9328, 51 AFTR 2d 83–1132, 103 S.Ct. 1826 (USSC, 1983).

[7]*Comm. v. Marshman*, 60–2 USTC ¶9484, 5 AFTR 2d 1528, 279 F.2d 27 (CA–6, 1960).

[8]*O'Malley v. Ames*, 52–1 USTC ¶9361, 42 AFTR 19, 197 F.2d 256 (CA–8, 1952).

[9]*U.S. v. Davis*, 62–2 USTC ¶9509, 9 AFTR 2d 1625, 82 S.Ct. 1190 (USSC, 1962).

[10]§ 1011(a) and Reg. § 1.1011–1.

the original basis so that on the date of disposition the adjusted basis reflects the unrecovered cost or other basis of the property.[11] Adjusted basis is determined as follows:

Cost (or other adjusted basis) on date of acquisition
+ Capital additions
− Capital recoveries
= Adjusted basis on date of disposition

Capital Additions

Capital additions include the cost of capital improvements and betterments made to the property by the taxpayer. These expenditures are distinguishable from expenditures for the ordinary repair and maintenance of the property, which are neither capitalized nor added to the original basis (refer to Chapter 6). The latter expenditures are deductible in the current taxable year if they are related to business or income-producing property. Amounts representing real property taxes treated as imposed on the seller but paid or assumed by the buyer are part of the cost of the property.[12] Any liability on property that is assumed by the buyer is also included in the buyer's original basis of the property. The same rule applies if property is acquired subject to a liability. Amortization of the discount on bonds increases the adjusted basis of the bonds.[13]

Capital Recoveries

Capital recoveries decrease the adjusted basis of property. The following are examples of capital recoveries:

1. *Depreciation and cost recovery allowances.* The original basis of depreciable property is reduced by the annual depreciation charges (or cost recovery allowances) while the property is held by the taxpayer. The amount of depreciation that is subtracted from the original basis is the greater of the *allowed* or *allowable* depreciation calculated on an annual basis.[14] In most circumstances, the allowed and allowable depreciation amounts are the same (refer to Chapter 8).
2. *Casualties and thefts.* A casualty or theft may result in the reduction of the adjusted basis of property.[15] The adjusted basis is reduced by the amount of the deductible loss. In addition, the adjusted basis is reduced by the amount of insurance proceeds received. However, the receipt of insurance proceeds may result in a recognized gain rather than a deductible loss. The gain increases the adjusted basis of the property.[16]

EXAMPLE 5

An insured truck that Marvin used in his trade or business is destroyed in an accident. The adjusted basis is $8,000, and the fair market value is $6,500. Marvin receives insurance proceeds of $6,500. The amount of the casualty loss is $1,500 ($6,500 insurance proceeds − $8,000 adjusted basis). The adjusted basis is reduced by the $1,500 casualty loss and the $6,500 of insurance proceeds received. ∎

EXAMPLE 6

An insured truck that Marvin used in his trade or business is destroyed in an accident. The adjusted basis is $6,500, and the fair market value is $8,000. Marvin receives insurance proceeds of $8,000. The amount of the casualty gain is $1,500 ($8,000 insurance

---

[11]§ 1016(a) and Reg. § 1.1016–1.
[12]Reg. §§ 1.1001–1(b)(2) and 1.1012–1(b). Refer to Chapter 10 for a discussion of this subject.
[13]See Chapter 16 for a discussion of bond discount and the related amortization.

[14]§ 1016(a)(2) and Reg. § 1.1016–3(a)(1)(i).
[15]Refer to Chapter 7 for the discussion of casualties and thefts.
[16]Reg. § 1.1016–6(a).

proceeds − $6,500 adjusted basis). The adjusted basis is increased by the $1,500 casualty gain and is reduced by the $8,000 of insurance proceeds received ($6,500 basis before casualty + $1,500 casualty gain − $8,000 insurance proceeds = $0 basis). ■

3. *Certain corporate distributions.* A corporate distribution to a shareholder that is not taxable is treated as a return of capital, and it reduces the basis of the shareholder's stock in the corporation.[17] For example, if a corporation makes a cash distribution to its shareholders and has no earnings and profits, the distributions are treated as a return of capital. Once the basis of the stock is reduced to zero, the amount of any subsequent distributions is a capital gain if the stock is a capital asset. These rules are illustrated in Example 25 of Chapter 20.

4. *Amortizable bond premium.* The basis in a bond purchased at a premium is reduced by the amortizable portion of the bond premium.[18] Investors in taxable bonds may *elect* to amortize the bond premium, but the premium on tax-exempt bonds *must be* amortized.[19] The amount of the amortized premium on taxable bonds is permitted as an interest deduction. Therefore, the election enables the taxpayer to take an annual interest deduction to offset ordinary income in exchange for a larger capital gain or smaller capital loss on the disposition of the bond. No such interest deduction is permitted for tax-exempt bonds.

   The amortization deduction is allowed for taxable bonds because the premium is viewed as a cost of earning the taxable interest from the bonds. The reason the basis of taxable bonds is reduced is that the amortization deduction is a recovery of the cost or basis of the bonds. The basis of tax-exempt bonds is reduced even though the amortization is not allowed as a deduction. No amortization deduction is permitted on tax-exempt bonds because the interest income is exempt from tax and the amortization of the bond premium merely represents an adjustment of the effective amount of such income.

EXAMPLE 7

Antonio purchases Eagle Corporation taxable bonds with a face value of $100,000 for $110,000, thus paying a premium of $10,000. The annual interest rate is 7%, and the bonds mature 10 years from the date of purchase. The annual interest income is $7,000 (7% × $100,000). If Antonio elects to amortize the bond premium, the $10,000 premium is deducted over the 10-year period. Antonio's basis for the bonds is reduced each year by the amount of the amortization deduction. Note that if the bonds were tax-exempt, amortization of the bond premium and the basis adjustment would be mandatory. However, no deduction would be allowed for the amortization. ■

5. *Easements.* An easement is the legal right to use another's land for a special purpose. Historically, easements were commonly used to obtain rights-of-way for utility lines and roads. In recent years, grants of conservation easements have become a popular means of obtaining charitable contribution deductions and reducing the value of real estate for transfer tax (i.e., estate and gift) purposes. Likewise, scenic easements are used to reduce the value of land as assessed for ad valorem property tax purposes.

   If the taxpayer does not retain any right to the use of the land, all of the basis is assigned to the easement. However, if the use of the land is only partially restricted, an allocation of some of the basis to the easement is appropriate.

---

[17]§ 1016(a)(4) and Reg. § 1.1016–5(a).

[18]§ 1016(a)(5) and Reg. § 1.1016–5(b). The accounting treatment of bond premium amortization is the same as for tax purposes. The amortization results in a decrease in the bond investment account.

[19]§ 171(c).

CONCEPT SUMMARY 14.1

Recognized Gain or Loss

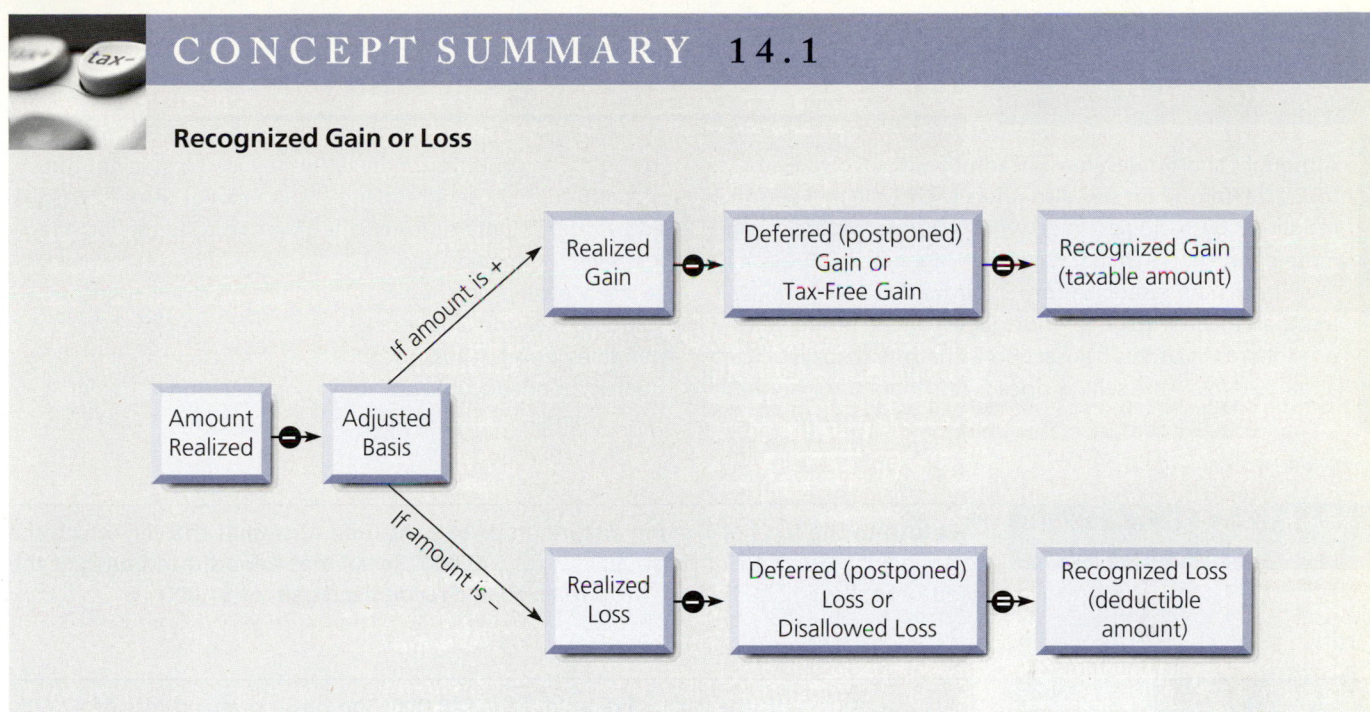

RECOGNIZED GAIN OR LOSS

Recognized gain is the amount of the realized gain that is included in the taxpayer's gross income.[20] A **recognized loss**, on the other hand, is the amount of a realized loss that is deductible for tax purposes.[21] As a general rule, the entire amount of a realized gain or loss is recognized.[22]

Concept Summary 14.1 summarizes the realized gain or loss and recognized gain or loss concepts.

> **LO.2**
> Distinguish between realized and recognized gain or loss.

NONRECOGNITION OF GAIN OR LOSS

In certain cases, a realized gain or loss is not recognized upon the sale or other disposition of property. One such case involves nontaxable exchanges, which are covered in Chapter 15. Others include losses realized upon the sale, exchange, or condemnation of personal use assets (as opposed to business or income-producing property) and gains realized upon the sale of a residence (see Chapter 15). In addition, realized losses from the sale or exchange of business or income-producing property between certain related parties are not recognized.[23]

Sale, Exchange, or Condemnation of Personal Use Assets

A realized loss from the sale, exchange, or condemnation of personal use assets (e.g., a personal residence or an automobile not used at all for business or income-producing purposes) is not recognized for tax purposes. An exception exists for casualty or theft losses from personal use assets (see Chapter 7). In contrast, any gain realized from the sale or other disposition of personal use assets is, generally, fully taxable.

---

[20]§ 61(a)(3) and Reg. § 1.61–6(a).
[21]§ 165(a) and Reg. § 1.165–1(a).

[22]§ 1001(c) and Reg. § 1.1002–1(a).
[23]§ 267(a)(1).

TAX *in* the *NEWS*

TRIPLE THE MISERY!

Although short sales have traditionally involved stocks, today the term *short sale* also refers to the sale of a personal residence by a homeowner who is "underwater," owing more on the home than it is worth. In a short sale, the homeowner sells the residence for its fair market value, which is less than the mortgage (or mortgages) on the property. One possible result of this transaction is that the taxpayer incurs a realized loss—the selling price is less than his or her basis in the property. Unfortunately, the realized loss cannot be recognized because a residence is a personal use asset. To add to the trauma of losing the home in a nondeductible loss sale, the mortgage company may require the taxpayer to keep paying on the portion of the mortgage still outstanding (i.e., the amount of the mortgage in excess of the net sales price). Thus, the taxpayer has triple misery: no home, a nondeductible loss, and an outstanding debt to pay.

EXAMPLE 8
THE BIG PICTURE

Return to the facts of *The Big Picture* on p. 14-2. Assume Alice sells the car, which she has held exclusively for personal use, for $23,000. Recall that her adjusted basis of the automobile is $22,000. Alice has a realized and recognized gain of $1,000. ∎

EXAMPLE 9
THE BIG PICTURE

Assume Alice sells the car in Example 8 for $20,000. She has a realized loss of $2,000, but the loss is not recognized. ∎

LO.3

Apply the recovery of capital doctrine.

RECOVERY OF CAPITAL DOCTRINE

Doctrine Defined

The **recovery of capital doctrine** pervades all the tax rules relating to property transactions. The doctrine derives its roots from the very essence of the income tax—a tax on income. Under the doctrine, as a general rule, a taxpayer is entitled to recover the cost or other original basis of property acquired and is not taxed on that amount.

The cost or other original basis of depreciable property is recovered through annual depreciation deductions. The basis is reduced as the cost is recovered over the period the property is held. Therefore, when property is sold or otherwise disposed of, it is the adjusted basis (unrecovered cost or other basis) that is compared with the amount realized from the disposition to determine realized gain or loss.

Relationship of the Recovery of Capital Doctrine to the Concepts of Realization and Recognition

If a sale or other disposition results in a realized gain, the taxpayer has recovered more than the adjusted basis of the property. Conversely, if a sale or other disposition results in a realized loss, the taxpayer has recovered less than the adjusted basis.

The general rules for the relationship between the recovery of capital doctrine and the realized and recognized gain and loss concepts are summarized as follows:

Rule 1. A realized gain that is *never recognized* results in the *permanent recovery* of more than the taxpayer's cost or other basis for tax purposes. For example, all or a portion of the realized gain on the sale of a personal residence can be excluded from gross income under § 121.

Rule 2. A realized gain on which *recognition is postponed* results in the *temporary recovery* of more than the taxpayer's cost or other basis for tax purposes. For example, an exchange of like-kind property under § 1031 and an involuntary conversion under § 1033 are both eligible for postponement treatment.

Rule 3. A realized loss that is *never recognized* results in the *permanent recovery* of less than the taxpayer's cost or other basis for tax purposes. For example, a loss on the sale of an automobile held for personal use is not deductible.

Rule 4. A realized loss on which *recognition is postponed* results in the *temporary recovery* of less than the taxpayer's cost or other basis for tax purposes. For example, the realized loss on the exchange of like-kind property under § 1031 is postponed.

These rules are illustrated in discussions to follow in this and the next chapter.

14.2 BASIS CONSIDERATIONS

DETERMINATION OF COST BASIS

LO.4

Explain how basis is determined for various methods of asset acquisition.

As noted earlier, the basis of property is generally the property's cost. Cost is the amount paid for the property in cash or other property.[24] This general rule follows logically from the recovery of capital doctrine; that is, the cost or other basis of property is to be recovered tax-free by the taxpayer.

A *bargain purchase* of property is an exception to the general rule for determining basis. A bargain purchase may result when an employer transfers property to an employee at less than the property's fair market value (as compensation for services) or when a corporation transfers property to a shareholder at less than the property's fair market value (a dividend). The amount included in income either as compensation for services or dividend income is the difference between the bargain purchase price and the property's fair market value. The basis of property acquired in a bargain purchase is the property's fair market value.[25] If the basis of the property were not increased by the bargain amount, the taxpayer would be taxed on this amount again at disposition.

EXAMPLE 10

Wade buys land from his employer for $10,000 on December 30. The fair market value of the land is $15,000. Wade must include the $5,000 difference between the cost and the fair market value of the land in gross income for the taxable year. The bargain element represents additional compensation to Wade. His basis for the land is $15,000, the land's fair market value. ∎

Identification Problems

Cost identification problems are frequently encountered in securities transactions. For example, the Regulations require that the taxpayer adequately identify the particular stock that has been sold.[26] A problem arises when the taxpayer has purchased separate lots of stock on different dates or at different prices and cannot adequately identify the lot from which a particular sale takes place. In this case, the stock is presumed to come from the first lot or lots purchased (a FIFO presumption).[27] When securities are left in the custody of a broker, it may be necessary to provide specific instructions and receive written confirmation as to which securities are being sold.

EXAMPLE 11

Polly purchases 100 shares of Olive Corporation stock on July 1, 2009, for $5,000 ($50 a share) and another 100 shares of Olive stock on July 1, 2010, for $6,000 ($60 a share). She sells 50 shares of the stock on January 2, 2011. The cost of the stock sold, assuming Polly cannot adequately identify the shares, is $50 a share, or $2,500. This is the cost Polly will compare with the amount realized in determining the gain or loss from the sale. ∎

Allocation Problems

When a taxpayer acquires *multiple assets in a lump-sum purchase*, the total cost must be allocated among the individual assets.[28] Allocation is necessary for several reasons:

- Some of the assets acquired may be depreciable (e.g., buildings), while others may not be (e.g., land).

---

[24]§ 1012 and Reg. § 1.1012–1(a).

[25]Reg. §§ 1.61–2(d)(2)(i) and 1.301–1(j). See the discussion in Chapter 5 of the circumstances under which what appears to be a taxable bargain purchase is an excludible qualified employee discount.

[26]Reg. § 1.1012–1(c)(1).

[27]*Kluger Associates, Inc.,* 69 T.C. 925 (1978).

[28]Reg. § 1.61–6(a).

- Only a portion of the assets acquired may be sold.
- Some of the assets may be capital or § 1231 assets that receive special tax treatment upon subsequent sale or other disposition.

The lump-sum cost is allocated on the basis of the fair market values of the individual assets acquired.

| EXAMPLE 12 | Harry purchases a building and land for $800,000. Because of the depressed nature of the industry in which the seller was operating, Harry was able to negotiate a very favorable purchase price. Appraisals of the individual assets indicate that the fair market value of the building is $600,000 and that of the land is $400,000. Harry's basis for the building is $480,000 [($600,000/$1,000,000) × $800,000], and his basis for the land is $320,000 [($400,000/$1,000,000) × $800,000]. ∎ |

If a business is purchased and **goodwill** is involved, a special allocation rule applies. Initially, the purchase price is assigned to the assets, excluding goodwill, to the extent of their total fair market value. This assigned amount is allocated among the assets on the basis of the fair market value of the individual assets acquired. Goodwill is then assigned the residual amount of the purchase price. The resultant allocation is applicable to both the buyer and the seller.[29]

| EXAMPLE 13 | Rocky sells his business to Paul. They agree that the values of the individual assets are as follows:

Inventory	$ 50,000
Building	500,000
Land	200,000
Goodwill	150,000

After negotiations, Rocky and Paul agree on a sales price of $1 million. Applying the residual method with respect to goodwill results in the following allocation of the $1 million purchase price:

Inventory	$ 50,000
Building	500,000
Land	200,000
Goodwill	250,000

---

[29]§ 1060.

The residual method requires that all of the excess of the purchase price over the fair market value of the assets ($1,000,000 − $900,000 = $100,000) be allocated to goodwill. Without this requirement, the purchaser could allocate the excess pro rata to all of the assets, including goodwill, based on their respective fair market values. This would have resulted in only $166,667 [$150,000 + ($150,000 ÷ $900,000 × $100,000)] being assigned to goodwill. ∎

In the case of *nontaxable stock dividends*, the allocation depends on whether the dividend is a common stock dividend on common stock or a preferred stock dividend on common stock. If the dividend is common on common, the cost of the original common shares is allocated to the total shares owned after the dividend.[30]

EXAMPLE 14

Susan owns 100 shares of Sparrow Corporation common stock for which she paid $1,100. She receives a 10% common stock dividend, giving her a new total of 110 shares. Before the stock dividend, Susan's basis was $11 per share ($1,100 ÷ 100 shares). The basis of each share after the stock dividend is $10 ($1,100 ÷ 110 shares). ∎

If the nontaxable stock dividend is preferred stock on common, the cost of the original common shares is allocated between the common and preferred shares on the basis of their relative fair market values on the date of distribution.[31]

EXAMPLE 15

Fran owns 100 shares of Cardinal Corporation common stock for which she paid $1,000. She receives a nontaxable stock dividend of 50 shares of preferred stock on her common stock. The fair market values on the date of distribution of the preferred stock dividend are $30 a share for common stock and $40 a share for preferred stock.

Fair market value of common ($30 × 100 shares)	$3,000
Fair market value of preferred ($40 × 50 shares)	2,000
	$5,000
Basis of common: 3/5 × $1,000	$ 600
Basis of preferred: 2/5 × $1,000	$ 400

The basis per share for the common stock is $6 ($600/100 shares). The basis per share for the preferred stock is $8 ($400/50 shares). ∎

The holding period for a nontaxable stock dividend, whether received in the form of common stock or preferred stock, includes the holding period of the original shares.[32] The significance of the holding period for capital assets is discussed in Chapter 16.

In the case of *nontaxable stock rights*, the basis of the rights is zero unless the taxpayer elects or is required to allocate a portion of the cost of the stock already held to the newly received stock rights. If the fair market value of the rights is 15 percent or more of the fair market value of the stock, the taxpayer is required to allocate. If the value of the rights is less than 15 percent of the fair market value of the stock, the taxpayer may elect to allocate.[33] When allocation is required or elected, the cost of the stock on which the rights are received is allocated between the stock and the rights on the basis of their relative fair market values.

EXAMPLE 16

Donald receives nontaxable stock rights with a fair market value of $1,000. The fair market value of the stock on which the rights were received is $8,000 (cost $10,000). Donald does not elect to allocate. The basis of the rights is zero. If he exercises the rights, the basis of the new stock is the exercise (subscription) price. ∎

---

[30]§§ 305(a) and 307(a).
[31]Reg. § 1.307–1(a).

[32]§ 1223(5) and Reg. § 1.1223–1(e).
[33]§ 307(b).

EXAMPLE 17

Assume the same facts as in Example 16, except the fair market value of the rights is $3,000. Donald must allocate because the value of the rights ($3,000) is 15% or more of the value of the stock ($3,000/$8,000 = 37.5%).

- The basis of the stock is $7,273 [($8,000/$11,000) × $10,000].
- The basis of the rights is $2,727 [($3,000/$11,000) × $10,000].

If Donald exercises the rights, the basis of the new stock is the exercise (subscription) price plus the basis of the rights. If he sells the rights, he recognizes gain or loss equal to the difference between the amount realized and the basis of the rights. This allocation rule applies only when the rights are exercised or sold. Therefore, if the rights are allowed to lapse (expire), they have no basis, and the basis of the original stock is the stock's cost, $10,000. ■

The holding period of nontaxable stock rights includes the holding period of the stock on which the rights were distributed. However, if the rights are exercised, the holding period of the newly acquired stock begins with the date the rights are exercised.[34]

GIFT BASIS

When a taxpayer receives property as a gift, there is no cost to the donee (recipient). Thus, under the cost basis provision, the donee's basis would be zero. However, this would violate the statutory intent that gifts not be subject to the income tax.[35] With a zero basis, if the donee sold the property, all of the amount realized would be treated as realized gain. Therefore, a basis is assigned to the property received depending on the following:

- The date of the gift.
- The basis of the property to the donor.
- The amount of the gift tax paid.
- The fair market value of the property.

Gift Basis Rules If No Gift Tax Is Paid

Property received by gift can be referred to as *dual basis* property; that is, the basis for gain and the basis for loss might not be the same amount. The present basis rules for gifts of property are as follows:

- If the donee disposes of gift property in a transaction that results in a gain, the basis to the donee is the same as the donor's adjusted basis.[36] The donee's basis in this case is referred to as the *gain basis*. Therefore, a *realized*

---

[34]§ 1223(5) and Reg. §§ 1.1223–1(e) and (f).

[35]§ 102(a).

[36]§ 1015(a) and Reg. § 1.1015–1(a)(1). See Reg. § 1.1015–1(a)(3) for cases in which the facts necessary to determine the donor's adjusted basis are unknown. Refer to Example 24 for the effect of depreciation deductions by the donee.

gain results if the amount realized from the disposition exceeds the donee's gain basis.

EXAMPLE 18

Melissa purchased stock in 2010 for $10,000. She gave the stock to her son, Joe, in 2011, when the fair market value was $15,000. No gift tax is paid on the transfer, and Joe subsequently sells the property for $15,000. Joe's basis is $10,000, and he has a realized gain of $5,000. ■

- If the donee disposes of gift property in a transaction that results in a loss, the basis to the donee is the *lower* of the donor's adjusted basis or the fair market value on the date of the gift. The donee's basis in this case is referred to as the *loss basis*. Therefore, a *realized loss* results if the amount realized from the disposition is less than the donee's loss basis.

EXAMPLE 19

Burt purchased stock in 2010 for $10,000. He gave the stock to his son, Cliff, in 2011, when the fair market value was $7,000. No gift tax is paid on the transfer. Cliff later sells the stock for $6,000. Cliff's basis is $7,000 (fair market value is less than donor's adjusted basis of $10,000), and the realized loss from the sale is $1,000 ($6,000 amount realized − $7,000 basis). ■

The amount of the loss basis will *differ* from the amount of the gain basis only if, at the date of the gift, the adjusted basis of the property exceeds the property's fair market value. Note that the loss basis rule prevents the donee from receiving a tax benefit from a decline in value that occurred while the donor held the property. Therefore, in Example 19, Cliff has a loss of only $1,000 rather than a loss of $4,000. The $3,000 difference represents the decline in value that occurred while Burt held the property. Ironically, however, the gain basis rule may result in the donee being subject to income tax on the appreciation that occurred while the donor held the property, as illustrated in Example 18.

If the amount realized from a sale or other disposition is *between* the basis for loss and the basis for gain, no gain or loss is realized.

EXAMPLE 20

Assume the same facts as in Example 19, except that Cliff sells the stock for $8,000. Application of the gain basis rule produces a loss of $2,000 ($8,000 − $10,000). Application of the loss basis rule produces a gain of $1,000 ($8,000 − $7,000). Because the amount realized is between the gain basis and the loss basis, Cliff recognizes neither a gain nor a loss. ■

Adjustment for Gift Tax

If gift taxes are paid by the donor, the donee's gain basis may exceed the adjusted basis of the property to the donor. This occurs only if the fair market value of the property at the date of the gift is greater than the donor's adjusted basis (the property has appreciated in value). The portion of the gift tax paid that is related to the appreciation is added to the donor's basis in calculating the donee's gain basis for the property. In this circumstance, the following formula is used for calculating the donee's gain basis:[37]

Donee's gain basis = Donor's adjusted basis + (Unrealized appreciation / Taxable gift*) × Gift tax paid

*The taxable gift is the fair market value of the gift less the per donee annual exclusion.

---

[37]§ 1015(d)(6) and Reg. § 1.1015–5(c)(2).

EXAMPLE 21

In 2011, Bonnie made a gift of stock (adjusted basis of $15,000) to Peggy. The stock had a fair market value of $50,000, and the transfer resulted in a gift tax of $4,000. The unrealized appreciation of the stock is $35,000 ($50,000 fair market value − $15,000 adjusted basis), and the taxable gift is $37,000 ($50,000 fair market value of gift − $13,000 annual exclusion). Peggy's basis in the stock is $18,800, determined as follows:

Donor's adjusted basis	$15,000
Gift tax attributable to appreciation— $35,000/$37,000 = 95% (rounded) × $4,000	3,800
Donee's gain basis	$18,800

EXAMPLE 22

Don made a gift of stock to Matt in 2011, when the fair market value of the stock was $50,000. Don paid gift tax of $4,000. Don had purchased the stock in 1991 for $65,000. Because there is no unrealized appreciation at the date of the gift, none of the gift tax paid is added to Don's basis in calculating Matt's gain basis. Therefore, Matt's gain basis is $65,000. ■

For *gifts made before 1977*, the full amount of the gift tax paid is added to the donor's basis. However, the ceiling on this total is the fair market value of the property at the date of the gift. Thus, in Example 21, if the gift had been made before 1977, the basis of the property would be $19,000 ($15,000 + $4,000). In Example 22, the gain basis would still be $65,000 ($65,000 + $0).

Holding Period

The **holding period** for property acquired by gift begins on the date the donor acquired the property if the gain basis rule applies.[38] The holding period starts on the date of the gift if the loss basis rule applies.[39] The significance of the holding period for capital assets is discussed in Chapter 16.

The following example summarizes the basis and holding period rules for gift property:

EXAMPLE 23

Jill acquired 100 shares of Wren Corporation stock on December 30, 1993, for $40,000. On January 3, 2011, when the stock has a fair market value of $38,000, Jill gives it to Dennis and pays gift tax of $4,000. The basis is not increased by a portion of the gift tax paid because the property has not appreciated in value at the time of the gift. Therefore, Dennis's gain basis is $40,000. Dennis's basis for determining loss is $38,000 (fair market value) because the fair market value on the date of the gift is less than the donor's adjusted basis.

- If Dennis sells the stock for $45,000, he has a recognized gain of $5,000. The holding period for determining whether the capital gain is short term or long term begins on December 30, 1993, the date Jill acquired the property.
- If Dennis sells the stock for $36,000, he has a recognized loss of $2,000. The holding period for determining whether the capital loss is short term or long term begins on January 3, 2011, the date of the gift.
- If Dennis sells the property for $39,000, there is no loss because the amount realized is less than the gain basis of $40,000 and more than the loss basis of $38,000. ■

Basis for Depreciation

The basis for depreciation on depreciable gift property is the donee's gain basis.[40] This rule is applicable even if the donee later sells the property at a loss and uses the loss basis rule in calculating the amount of the realized loss.

---

[38]§ 1223(2) and Reg. § 1.1223–1(b).
[39]Rev.Rul. 59–86, 1959–1 C.B. 209.

[40]§ 1011 and Reg. §§ 1.1011–1 and 1.167(g)–1.

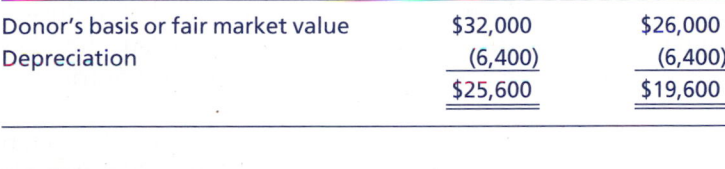

Vito gave a machine to Tina in 2011. At that time, the adjusted basis was $32,000 (cost of $40,000 − accumulated depreciation of $8,000), and the fair market value was $26,000. No gift tax was paid. Tina's gain basis at the date of the gift is $32,000, and her loss basis is $26,000. During 2011, Tina deducts depreciation (cost recovery) of $6,400 ($32,000 × 20%). (Refer to Chapter 8 for the cost recovery tables.) At the end of 2011, Tina's gain basis and loss basis are calculated as follows:

	Gain Basis	Loss Basis
Donor's basis or fair market value	$32,000	$26,000
Depreciation	(6,400)	(6,400)
	$25,600	$19,600

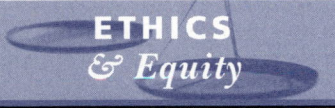

ETHICS & Equity

LOOKING A GIFT HORSE IN THE EYE

Walter rarely sees his Uncle George because George is a devoted world traveler. On January 15, 2011, Walter received an envelope that George had mailed to him from Singapore on December 13, 2010. The envelope contained a Christmas card from George and 1,000 shares of stock of Lavender, Inc.

In October 2011, Walter decides to pay off credit card debt and buy a new car, so he sells the stock for $45,000.

In early April 2012, the accountant who is preparing Walter's tax return tells him that she needs to know his uncle's adjusted basis for the stock and the amount of any gift tax paid. Since Walter is unable to contact his uncle by April 15, 2012, he requests a filing extension on Form 4868. He sends a letter to Uncle George requesting this information and thanking him for the gift. Walter is able to ascertain from a stock service that during the past 10 years, the stock price has ranged from $10 to $50 per share.

On August 10, 2012, Uncle George unexpectedly calls from Florence. He says he has not filed any type of Federal income tax return in years. He thinks he won the stock in a poker game in Monaco about 15 years ago when another player used it to cover a $15,000 bet.

Walter wants to file his tax return by the October 15, 2012 due date. He does not think it is a good idea to tell the return preparer how his uncle acquired the stock or about his uncle not filing income tax returns. Consequently, he tells the accountant that his uncle's basis for the stock is $15,000 and that no gift taxes were paid.

The return is completed and filed with a Schedule D reporting a long-term capital gain of $30,000 from the sale of the Lavender stock. Comment on the propriety of Walter's actions.

PROPERTY ACQUIRED FROM A DECEDENT

General Rules

The basis of property acquired from a decedent is generally the property's fair market value at the date of death (referred to as the *primary valuation amount*).[41] The property's basis is the fair market value six months after the date of death if the executor or administrator of the estate *elects* the alternate valuation date for estate tax purposes. This amount is referred to as the *alternate valuation amount*.

EXAMPLE 25
THE BIG PICTURE

Return to the facts of *The Big Picture* on p. 14-2. Alice and various other family members inherited property from Alice's mother, who died in 2011. At the date of death, the mother's adjusted basis for the property Alice inherited—her mother's house—was $275,000. The house's fair market value at the date of death was $475,000. The alternate valuation date was not elected. Alice's basis for income tax purposes is $475,000. This is commonly referred to as a *stepped-up basis*. ∎

---

[41]§§ 1014(a) and 1022. Congress did re-enact the estate tax and the related fair market value income tax basis rules for decedents dying in 2011 and 2012. The estate tax exemption amount was increased and the maximum estate tax rate was reduced. However, for deaths in 2010 the executor of an estate can elect to avoid any estate tax by choosing a modified carryover basis for the assets of the estate. See the discussion in the Tax in the News on p. 14-17.

EXAMPLE 26	Assume the same facts as in Example 25, except the house's fair market value at the
THE BIG PICTURE	date of the mother's death was $260,000. Alice's basis for income tax purposes is $260,000. This is commonly referred to as a *stepped-down basis*. ∎

No estate tax return must be filed for estates below a threshold amount. In such cases, the alternate valuation date and amount are not available. Even if an estate tax return is filed and the executor elects the alternate valuation date, the six months after death date is available only for property that the executor has not distributed before this date. For any property distributed or otherwise disposed of by the executor during the six-month period preceding the alternate valuation date, the adjusted basis to the beneficiary will equal the fair market value on the date of distribution or other disposition.[42]

The alternate valuation date can be *elected only* if, as a result of the election, both the value of the gross estate and the estate tax liability are lower than they would have been if the primary valuation date had been used. This provision prevents the alternate valuation election from being used to increase the basis of the property to the beneficiary for income tax purposes without simultaneously increasing the estate tax liability (because of estate tax deductions or credits).[43]

EXAMPLE 27	Nancy inherited all the property of her father, who died in 2011. Her father's adjusted basis for the property at the date of death was $650,000. The property's fair market value was $3,750,000 at the date of death and $3,760,000 six months after death. The alternate valuation date cannot be elected because the value of the gross estate has increased during the six-month period. Nancy's basis for income tax purposes is $3,750,000. ∎

EXAMPLE 28	Assume the same facts as in Example 27, except the property's fair market value six months after death was $3,745,000. If the executor elects the alternate valuation date, Nancy's basis for income tax purposes is $3,745,000. ∎

EXAMPLE 29	Assume the same facts as in the previous example, except the property is distributed four months after the date of the decedent's death. At the distribution date, the property's fair market value is $3,747,500. Since the executor elected the alternate valuation date, Nancy's basis for income tax purposes is $3,747,500. ∎

For inherited property, both unrealized appreciation and decline in value are taken into consideration in determining the basis of the property for income tax purposes. Contrast this with the carryover basis rules for property received by gift.

Deathbed Gifts

The Code contains a provision designed to eliminate a tax avoidance technique referred to as *deathbed gifts*. With this technique, a donor makes a gift of appreciated property to a dying person with the understanding that the donor (or the donor's spouse) will inherit the property on the donee's death. If the time period between the date of the gift and the date of the donee's death is not longer than one year, the usual basis rule (stepped-up basis) for inherited property may not apply. The adjusted basis of such property inherited by the donor or his or her spouse from the donee is the same as the decedent's adjusted basis for the property rather than the fair market value at the date of death or the alternate valuation date.[44]

---

[42]§ 2032(a)(1) and Rev.Rul. 56–60, 1956–1 C.B. 443.   [44]§ 1014(e).

[43]§ 2032(c).

TAX *in the NEWS*

SPECIAL RULE FOR THE BASIS OF PROPERTY INHERITED IN 2010

Enacted in 2001 in connection with the scheduled revocation of the estate tax, new § 1022 provides for a modified carryover basis for inherited property. Apparently, Congress had forgotten the disastrous result experienced with its prior attempt to impose the carryover basis approach to property passing by death. Applicable to property acquired after 1979, former Code §1023 caused such complexity and confusion that it was repealed with retroactive effect one year later.

For decedents dying in 2010, the executor of the estate can avoid any estate tax by electing a modified carryover basis rather than a fair market value basis. Section 1022 of the Code provides that the carryover basis amount for the estate can be increased by $1.3 million (plus any NOL carryovers and capital loss carryovers) of the decedent. In addition, a special $3 million step-up amount can be added for the surviving spouse. Such carryover basis as adjusted cannot exceed the fair market value of an asset.

EXAMPLE 30

Ned gives stock to his uncle, Vern, in 2011. Ned's basis for the stock is $100,000, and the fair market value is $900,000. No gift tax is paid. Eight months later, Ned inherits the stock from Vern. At the date of Vern's death, the fair market value of the stock is $980,000. Ned's adjusted basis for the stock is $100,000. ∎

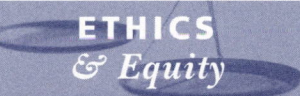

ETHICS *& Equity*

HELPING A FRIEND INCREASE BASIS: TO LIVE OR TO DIE?

Louise owns stock, adjusted basis of $4,500 and fair market value of $12,000, that is expected to continue appreciating. Beverly, Louise's best friend, has a terminal illness. Beverly's life expectancy is predicted to be between 6 and 18 months.

One day at lunch while the two friends were discussing their tax problems, Beverly mentioned that she had read a newspaper article about a tax planning opportunity that might be suitable for Louise. Under the scheme, Louise would make a gift of the appreciated stock to Beverly. In her will, Beverly would bequeath the stock to Louise. Since Beverly is confident that she will live longer than a year, the basis of the stock to Louise would be the fair market value on the date of Beverly's death. Beverly would "feel good" because she had helped Louise "beat the tax system."

You are Louise's tax adviser. How will you respond to Beverly's proposal to Louise?

Survivor's Share of Property

Both the decedent's share and the survivor's share of *community property* have a basis equal to the fair market value on the date of the decedent's death.[45] This result applies to the decedent's share of the community property since the property is included in the estate and assumes a fair market value basis. Because the surviving spouse's share of the community property is treated as if it is acquired from the decedent, it also has a basis equal to the fair market value.

EXAMPLE 31

Floyd and Vera are married and reside in a community property state. They own as community property 200 shares of Crow stock acquired in 1986 for $100,000. Floyd dies in 2011, when the securities are valued at $300,000. One-half of the Crow stock is included in Floyd's estate. If Vera inherits Floyd's share of the community property, the basis for determining gain or loss is $300,000, determined as follows:

Vera's one-half of the community property (stepped up from $50,000 to $150,000 due to Floyd's death)	$150,000
Floyd's one-half of the community property (stepped up from $50,000 to $150,000 due to inclusion in his gross estate)	150,000
Vera's new basis	$300,000

∎

---

[45]§ 1014(b)(6). See the listing of community property states in Chapter 4.

In a *common law* state, only one-half of jointly held property of spouses (tenants by the entirety or joint tenants with rights of survivorship) is included in the estate.[46] In such a case, no adjustment of the basis is permitted for the excluded property interest (the surviving spouse's share).

EXAMPLE 32

Assume the same facts as in the previous example, except that the property is jointly held by Floyd and Vera who reside in a common law state. Floyd purchased the property and made a gift of one-half of the property to Vera when the stock was acquired. No gift tax was paid. Only one-half of the Crow stock is included in Floyd's estate. Vera's basis for determining gain or loss in the excluded half is not adjusted upward for the increase in value to date of death. Therefore, Vera's basis is $200,000, determined as follows:

Vera's one-half of the jointly held property (carryover basis of $50,000)	$ 50,000
Floyd's one-half of the jointly held property (stepped up from $50,000 to $150,000 due to inclusion in his gross estate)	150,000
Vera's new basis	$200,000

Holding Period of Property Acquired from a Decedent

The holding period of property acquired from a decedent is *deemed to be long term* (held for the required long-term holding period). This provision applies regardless of whether the property is disposed of at a gain or at a loss.[47]

DISALLOWED LOSSES

LO.5

Describe various loss disallowance provisions.

Related Taxpayers

Section 267 provides that realized losses from sales or exchanges of property, directly or indirectly, between certain related parties are not recognized. This loss disallowance provision applies to several types of related-party transactions. The most common involve (1) members of a family and (2) an individual and a corporation in which the individual owns, directly or indirectly, more than 50 percent in value of the corporation's outstanding stock. Section 707 provides a similar loss disallowance provision where the related parties are a partner and a partnership in which the partner owns, directly or indirectly, more than 50 percent of the capital interests or profits interests in the partnership. The rules governing the relationships covered by § 267 were discussed in Chapter 6. See Chapter 15 for the discussion of the special rules under § 1041 for property transfers between spouses or incident to divorce.

If income-producing or business property is transferred to a related taxpayer and a loss is disallowed, the basis of the property to the recipient is the property's cost to the transferee. However, if a subsequent sale or other disposition of the property by the original transferee results in a realized gain, the amount of gain is reduced by the loss that was previously disallowed.[48] This *right of offset* is not applicable if the original sale involved the sale of a personal use asset (e.g., the sale of a personal residence between related taxpayers). Furthermore, the right of offset is available only to the original transferee (the related-party buyer).

EXAMPLE 33

Pedro sells business property with an adjusted basis of $50,000 to his daughter, Josefina, for its fair market value of $40,000. Pedro's realized loss of $10,000 is not recognized.

- How much gain does Josefina recognize if she sells the property for $52,000? Josefina recognizes a $2,000 gain. Her realized gain is $12,000 ($52,000 less her basis of $40,000), but she can offset Pedro's $10,000 loss against the gain.
- How much gain does Josefina recognize if she sells the property for $48,000? Josefina recognizes no gain or loss. Her realized gain is $8,000

---

[46]§ 2040(b).
[47]§ 1223(11).

[48]§ 267(d) and Reg. § 1.267(d)–1(a).

($48,000 less her basis of $40,000), but she can offset $8,000 of Pedro's $10,000 loss against the gain. Note that Pedro's loss can only offset Josefina's gain. It cannot create a loss for Josefina.
- How much loss does Josefina recognize if she sells the property for $38,000? Josefina recognizes a $2,000 loss, the same as her realized loss ($38,000 less $40,000 basis). Pedro's loss does not increase Josefina's loss. His loss can be offset only against a gain. Since Josefina has no realized gain, Pedro's loss cannot be used and is never recognized. This part of the example assumes that the property is business or income-producing property to Josefina. If not, her $2,000 loss is personal and is not recognized. ∎

The loss disallowance rules are designed to achieve two objectives. First, the rules prevent a taxpayer from directly transferring an unrealized loss to a related taxpayer in a higher tax bracket who could receive a greater tax benefit from recognition of the loss. Second, the rules eliminate a substantial administrative burden on the Internal Revenue Service as to the appropriateness of the selling price (fair market value or not). The loss disallowance rules are applicable even where the selling price is equal to the fair market value and can be validated (e.g., listed stocks).

The holding period of the buyer for the property is not affected by the holding period of the seller. That is, the buyer's *holding period* includes only the period of time he or she has held the property.[49]

Wash Sales

Section 1091 stipulates that in certain cases, a realized loss on the sale or exchange of stock or securities is not recognized. Specifically, if a taxpayer sells or exchanges stock or securities and within 30 days before *or* after the date of the sale or exchange acquires substantially identical stock or securities, any loss realized from the sale or exchange is not recognized because the transaction is a **wash sale**.[50] The term *acquire* means acquire by purchase or in a taxable exchange and includes an option to purchase substantially identical securities. *Substantially identical* means the same in all important particulars. Corporate bonds and preferred stock normally are not considered substantially identical to the corporation's common stock. However, if the bonds and preferred stock are convertible into common stock, they may be considered substantially identical under certain circumstances.[51] Attempts to avoid the application of the wash sales rules by having a related taxpayer repurchase the securities have been unsuccessful.[52] The wash sales provisions do *not* apply to gains.

Recognition of the loss is disallowed because the taxpayer is considered to be in substantially the same economic position after the sale and repurchase as before the sale and repurchase. This disallowance rule does not apply to taxpayers engaged in the business of buying and selling securities.[53] Investors, however, are not allowed to create losses through wash sales to offset income for tax purposes.

Realized loss that is not recognized is added to the *basis* of the substantially identical stock or securities whose acquisition resulted in the nonrecognition of loss.[54] In other words, the basis of the replacement stock or securities is increased by the amount of the unrecognized loss. If the loss were not added to the basis of the newly acquired stock or securities, the taxpayer would never recover the entire basis of the old stock or securities.

The basis of the new stock or securities includes the unrecovered portion of the basis of the formerly held stock or securities. Therefore, the *holding period* of the new stock or securities begins on the date of acquisition of the old stock or securities.[55]

[49]§§ 267(d) and 1223(2) and Reg. § 1.267(d)–1(c)(3).
[50]§ 1091(a) and Reg. §§ 1.1091–1(a) and (f).
[51]Rev.Rul. 56–406, 1956–2 C.B. 523.
[52]*McWilliams v. Comm.*, 47–1 USTC ¶9289, 35 AFTR 1184, 67 S.Ct. 1477 (USSC, 1947).
[53]Reg. § 1.1091–1(a).
[54]§ 1091(d) and Reg. § 1.1091–2(a).
[55]§ 1223(4) and Reg. § 1.1223–1(d).

EXAMPLE 34
THE BIG PICTURE

Return to the facts of *The Big Picture* on p. 14-2. Alice owned 100 shares of Green Corporation stock (adjusted basis of $20,000). She sold 50 shares for $8,000. Ten days later, she purchased 50 shares of the same stock for $7,000. Alice's realized loss of $2,000 ($8,000 amount realized − $10,000 adjusted basis of 50 shares) is not recognized because it resulted from a wash sale. Alice's basis in the newly acquired stock is $9,000 ($7,000 purchase price + $2,000 unrecognized loss from the wash sale). ■

A taxpayer may acquire fewer shares than the number sold in a wash sale. In this case, the loss from the sale is prorated between recognized and unrecognized loss on the basis of the ratio of the number of shares acquired to the number of shares sold.[56]

CONVERSION OF PROPERTY FROM PERSONAL USE TO BUSINESS OR INCOME-PRODUCING USE

As discussed previously, losses from the sale of personal use assets are not recognized for tax purposes, but losses from the sale of business and income-producing assets are deductible. Can a taxpayer convert a personal use asset that has declined in value to business or income-producing use and then sell the asset to recognize a business or income-producing loss? The tax law prevents this practice by specifying that the *original basis for loss* on personal use assets converted to business or income-producing use is the *lower* of the property's adjusted basis or fair market value on the date of conversion.[57] The *gain basis* for converted property is the property's adjusted basis on the date of conversion. The tax law is not concerned with gains on converted property because gains are recognized regardless of whether property is business, income-producing, or personal use.

EXAMPLE 35

Diane's personal residence has an adjusted basis of $175,000 and a fair market value of $160,000. Diane converts the personal residence to rental property. Her basis for loss is $160,000 (lower of $175,000 adjusted basis and fair market value of $160,000). The $15,000 decline in value is a personal loss and can never be recognized for tax purposes. Diane's basis for gain is $175,000. ■

The basis for loss is also the *basis for depreciating* the converted property.[58] This is an exception to the general rule that the basis for depreciation is the gain basis (e.g., property received by gift). This exception prevents the taxpayer from recovering a personal loss indirectly through depreciation of the higher original basis. After the property is converted, both its basis for loss and its basis for gain are adjusted for depreciation deductions from the date of conversion to the date of disposition. These rules apply only if a conversion from personal to business or income-producing use has actually occurred.

EXAMPLE 36

At a time when his personal residence (adjusted basis of $140,000) is worth $150,000, Keith converts one-half of it to rental use. Assume the property is not MACRS recovery property. At this point, the estimated useful life of the residence is 20 years, and there is no estimated salvage value. After renting the converted portion for five years, Keith sells the property for $144,000. All amounts relate only to the building; the land has been accounted for separately. Keith has a $2,000 realized gain from the sale of the personal use portion of the residence and a $19,500 realized gain from the sale of the rental portion. These gains are computed as follows:

---

[56]§ 1091(b) and Reg. § 1.1091–1(c).   [58]Reg. § 1.167(g)–1.

[57]Reg. § 1.165–9(b)(2).

	Personal Use	Rental
Original basis for gain and loss—adjusted basis on date of conversion (fair market value is greater than the adjusted basis)	$70,000	$70,000
Depreciation—five years	None	17,500
Adjusted basis—date of sale	$70,000	$52,500
Amount realized	72,000	72,000
Realized gain	$ 2,000	$19,500

As discussed in Chapter 15, Keith may be able to exclude the $2,000 realized gain from the sale of the personal use portion of the residence under § 121. If the § 121 exclusion applies, only $17,500 (equal to the depreciation deducted) of the $19,500 realized gain from the rental portion is recognized.

EXAMPLE 37

Assume the same facts as in the previous example, except that the fair market value on the date of conversion is $130,000 and the sales proceeds are $90,000. Keith has a $25,000 realized loss from the sale of the personal use portion of the residence and a $3,750 realized loss from the sale of the rental portion. These losses are computed as follows:

	Personal Use	Rental
Original basis for loss—fair market value on date of conversion (fair market value is less than the adjusted basis)	*	$65,000
Depreciation—five years	None	16,250
Adjusted basis—date of sale	$70,000	$48,750
Amount realized	45,000	45,000
Realized loss	($25,000)	($ 3,750)

*Not applicable.

The $25,000 loss from the sale of the personal use portion of the residence is not recognized. The $3,750 loss from the rental portion is recognized. ■

ADDITIONAL COMPLEXITIES IN DETERMINING REALIZED GAIN OR LOSS

Amount Realized

The calculation of the amount realized may appear to be one of the least complex areas associated with property transactions. However, because numerous positive and negative adjustments may be required, this calculation can be complex and confusing. In addition, determining the fair market value of the items received by the taxpayer can be difficult. The following example provides insight into various items that can affect the amount realized.

EXAMPLE 38

Ridge sells an office building and the associated land on October 1, 2011. Under the terms of the sales contract, Ridge is to receive $600,000 in cash. The purchaser is to assume Ridge's mortgage of $300,000 on the property. To enable the purchaser to obtain adequate financing, Ridge is to pay the $15,000 in points charged by the lender. The broker's commission on the sale is $45,000. The purchaser agrees to pay the $12,000 in property taxes for the entire year. The amount realized by Ridge is calculated as follows:

Selling price		
Cash	$600,000	
Mortgage assumed by purchaser	300,000	
Seller's property taxes paid by purchaser ($12,000 × $^9/_{12}$)	9,000	$909,000
Less		
Broker's commission	$ 45,000	
Points paid by seller	15,000	(60,000)
Amount realized		$849,000

Adjusted Basis

Three types of issues tend to complicate the determination of adjusted basis. First, the applicable tax provisions for calculating the adjusted basis depend on how the property was acquired (e.g., purchase, taxable exchange, nontaxable exchange, gift, inheritance). Second, if the asset is subject to depreciation, cost recovery, amortization, or depletion, adjustments must be made to the basis during the time period the asset is held by the taxpayer. Upon disposition of the asset, the taxpayer's records for both of these items may be deficient. For example, the donee does not know the amount of the donor's basis or the amount of gift tax paid by the donor, or the taxpayer does not know how much depreciation he or she has deducted. Third, the complex positive and negative adjustments encountered in calculating the amount realized are also involved in calculating the adjusted basis.

EXAMPLE 39

Jane purchased a personal residence in 2002. The purchase price and the related closing costs were as follows:

Purchase price	$325,000
Recording costs	140
Title fees and title insurance	815
Survey costs	225
Attorney's fees	750
Appraisal fee	250

Other relevant tax information for the house during the time Jane owned it is as follows:

- Constructed a swimming pool for medical reasons. The cost was $20,000, of which $5,000 was deducted as a medical expense.
- Added a solar heating system. The cost was $18,000.
- Deducted home office expenses of $6,000. Of this amount, $5,200 was for depreciation.

The adjusted basis for the house is calculated as follows:

Purchase price	$325,000
Recording costs	140
Title fees and title insurance	815
Survey costs	225
Attorney's fees	750
Appraisal fee	250
Swimming pool ($20,000 − $5,000)	15,000
Solar heating system	18,000
	$360,180
Less: Depreciation deducted on home office	(5,200)
Adjusted basis	$354,980

SUMMARY OF BASIS ADJUSTMENTS

Some of the more common items that either increase or decrease the basis of an asset appear in Concept Summary 14.2.

CONCEPT SUMMARY 14.2

Adjustments to Basis

Item	Effect	Refer to Chapter	Explanation
Amortization of bond discount.	Increase	16	Amortization is mandatory for certain taxable bonds and elective for tax-exempt bonds.
Amortization of bond premium.	Decrease	14	Amortization is mandatory for tax-exempt bonds and elective for taxable bonds.
Amortization of covenant not to compete.	Decrease	8	Covenant must be for a definite and limited time period. The amortization period is a statutory period of 15 years.
Amortization of intangibles.	Decrease	8	Intangibles are amortized over a 15-year period.
Assessment for local benefits.	Increase	10	To the extent not deductible as taxes (e.g., assessment for streets and sidewalks that increase the value of the property versus one for maintenance or repair or for meeting interest charges).
Bad debts.	Decrease	7	Only the specific charge-off method is permitted.
Capital additions.	Increase	14	Certain items, at the taxpayer's election, can be capitalized or deducted (e.g., selected medical expenses).
Casualty.	Decrease	7	For a casualty loss, the amount of the adjustment is the sum of the deductible loss and the insurance proceeds received. For a casualty gain, the amount of the adjustment is the insurance proceeds received reduced by the recognized gain.
Condemnation.	Decrease	15	See casualty explanation.
Cost recovery.	Decrease	8	§ 168 is applicable to tangible assets placed in service after 1980 whose useful life is expressed in terms of years.
Depletion.	Decrease	8	Use the greater of cost or percentage depletion. Percentage depletion can still be deducted when the basis is zero.
Depreciation.	Decrease	8	§ 167 is applicable to tangible assets placed in service before 1981 and to tangible assets not depreciated in terms of years.
Easement.	Decrease	14	If the taxpayer does not retain any use of the land, all of the basis is allocable to the easement transaction. However, if only part of the land is affected by the easement, only part of the basis is allocable to the easement transaction.
Improvements by lessee to lessor's property.	Increase	5	Adjustment occurs only if the lessor is required to include the fair market value of the improvements in gross income under § 109.
Imputed interest.	Decrease	18	Amount deducted is not part of the cost of the asset.
Inventory: lower of cost or market.	Decrease	18	Not available if the LIFO method is used.
Limited expensing under § 179.	Decrease	8	Occurs only if the taxpayer elects § 179 treatment.
Medical capital expenditure permitted as a medical expense.	Decrease	10	Adjustment is the amount of the deduction (the effect on basis is to increase it by the amount of the capital expenditure net of the deduction).

Adjustments to Basis—continued

Item	Effect	Refer to Chapter	Explanation
Real estate taxes: apportionment between the buyer and seller.	Increase or decrease	10	To the extent the buyer pays the seller's pro rata share, the buyer's basis is increased. To the extent the seller pays the buyer's pro rata share, the buyer's basis is decreased.
Rebate from manufacturer.	Decrease		Since the rebate is treated as an adjustment to the purchase price, it is not included in the buyer's gross income.
Stock dividend.	Decrease	5	Adjustment occurs only if the stock dividend is nontaxable. While the basis per share decreases, the total stock basis does not change.
Stock rights.	Decrease	14	Adjustment to stock basis occurs only for nontaxable stock rights and only if the fair market value of the rights is at least 15% of the fair market value of the stock or, if less than 15%, the taxpayer elects to allocate the basis between the stock and the rights.
Theft.	Decrease	7	See casualty explanation.

In discussing the topic of basis, a number of specific techniques for determining basis have been presented. Although the various techniques are responsive to and mandated by transactions occurring in the marketplace, they do possess enough common characteristics to be categorized as follows:

- The basis of the asset may be determined by reference to the asset's cost.
- The basis of the asset may be determined by reference to the basis of another asset.
- The basis of the asset may be determined by reference to the asset's fair market value.
- The basis of the asset may be determined by reference to the basis of the asset to another taxpayer.

TAX PLANNING:
14.3 COST IDENTIFICATION AND DOCUMENTATION CONSIDERATIONS

LO.6

Identify tax planning opportunities related to selected property transactions.

When multiple assets are acquired in a single transaction, the contract price must be allocated for several reasons. First, some of the assets may be depreciable, while others are not. From the different viewpoints of the buyer and the seller, this may produce a tax conflict that needs to be resolved. That is, the seller prefers a high allocation for nondepreciable assets, whereas the purchaser prefers a high allocation for depreciable assets (see Chapters 16 and 17). Second, the seller needs to know the amount realized on the sale of the capital assets and the ordinary income assets so that the recognized gains and losses can be classified as capital or ordinary. For example, an allocation to goodwill or to a covenant not to compete (see Chapters 8, 16, and 17) produces different tax consequences to the seller. Third, the buyer needs the adjusted basis of each asset to calculate the realized gain or loss on a subsequent sale or other disposition of each asset.

14.4 SELECTION OF PROPERTY FOR MAKING GIFTS

A donor can achieve several tax advantages by making gifts of appreciated property. The donor avoids income tax on the unrealized gain that would have occurred had the donor sold the property. A portion of this amount can be permanently avoided because the donee's adjusted basis is increased by part or all of any gift tax paid by the donor. Even without this increase in basis, the income tax liability on the sale of the property by the donee can be less than the income tax liability that would have resulted from the donor's sale of the property, if the donee is in a lower tax bracket than the donor. In addition, any subsequent appreciation during the time the property is held by the lower tax bracket donee results in a tax savings on the sale or other disposition of the property. Such gifts of appreciated property can be an effective tool in family tax planning.

Taxpayers should generally not make gifts of depreciated property (property that, if sold, would produce a realized loss) because the donor does not receive an income tax deduction for the unrealized loss element. In addition, the donee receives no benefit from this unrealized loss upon the subsequent sale of the property because of the loss basis rule. The loss basis rule provides that the donee's basis is the lower of the donor's basis or the fair market value at the date of the gift. If the donor anticipates that the donee will sell the property upon receiving it, the donor should sell the property and take the loss deduction, assuming the loss is deductible. The donor can then give the proceeds from the sale to the donee.

14.5 SELECTION OF PROPERTY FOR MAKING BEQUESTS

A taxpayer should generally make bequests of appreciated property in his or her will. Doing so enables both the decedent and the heir to avoid income tax on the unrealized gain because the recipient takes the fair market value as his or her basis.

Taxpayers generally should not make bequests of depreciated property (property that, if sold, would produce a realized loss) because the decedent does not receive an income tax deduction for the unrealized loss element. In addition, the heir will receive no benefit from this unrealized loss upon the subsequent sale of the property.

EXAMPLE 40

On the date of her death in 2011, Marta owned land held for investment purposes. The land had an adjusted basis of $130,000 and a fair market value of $100,000. If Marta had sold the property before her death, the recognized loss would have been $30,000. If Roger inherits the property and later sells it for $90,000, the recognized loss is $10,000 (the decline in value since Marta's death). In addition, regardless of the period of time Roger holds the property, the holding period is long term (see Chapter 16). ■

From an income tax perspective, it is preferable to transfer appreciated property as a bequest rather than as a gift. The reason is that inherited property receives a step-up in basis, whereas property received by gift has a carryover basis to the donee. However, in making this decision, the estate tax consequences of the bequest should also be weighed against the gift tax consequences of the gift.

14.6 Disallowed Losses

SECTION 267 DISALLOWED LOSSES

Taxpayers should be aware of the desirability of avoiding transactions that activate the loss disallowance provisions for related parties. This is so even in light of the provision that permits the related-party buyer to offset his or her realized gain by the related-party seller's disallowed loss. Even with this offset, several inequities exist. First, the tax benefit associated with the disallowed loss ultimately is realized by the wrong party (the related-party buyer rather than the related-party seller). Second, the tax benefit of this offset to the related-party buyer does not occur until the buyer disposes of the property. Therefore, the longer the time period between the purchase and disposition of the property by the related-party buyer, the less the economic benefit. Third, if the property does not appreciate to at least its adjusted basis to the related-party seller during the time period the related-party buyer holds it, part or all of the disallowed loss is permanently lost. Fourth, since the right of offset is available only to the original transferee (the related-party buyer), all of the disallowed loss is permanently lost if the original transferee subsequently transfers the property by gift or bequest.

EXAMPLE 41

Tim sells property with an adjusted basis of $35,000 to Wes, his brother, for $25,000, the fair market value of the property. The $10,000 realized loss to Tim is disallowed by § 267. If Wes subsequently sells the property to an unrelated party for $37,000, he has a recognized gain of $2,000 (realized gain of $12,000 reduced by disallowed loss of $10,000). Therefore, from the perspective of the family unit, the original $10,000 realized loss ultimately is recognized. However, if Wes sells the property for $29,000, he has a recognized gain of $0 (realized gain of $4,000 reduced by disallowed loss of $4,000 necessary to offset the realized gain). From the perspective of the family unit, $6,000 of the realized loss of $10,000 is permanently wasted ($10,000 realized loss − $4,000 offset permitted). ■

WASH SALES

The wash sales provisions can be avoided if the security that was sold is replaced within the statutory time period with a similar rather than a substantially identical security. For example, a sale of Dell, Inc. common stock accompanied by a purchase of Hewlett-Packard common stock is not treated as a wash sale. Such a procedure can enable the taxpayer to use an unrealized capital loss to offset a recognized capital gain. The taxpayer can sell the security before the end of the taxable year, offset the recognized capital loss against the capital gain, and invest the sales proceeds in a similar security.

Because the wash sales provisions do not apply to gains, it may be desirable to engage in a wash sale before the end of the taxable year. The recognized capital gain may be used to offset capital losses or capital loss carryovers from prior years. Since the basis of the replacement stock or securities will be the purchase price, the taxpayer in effect has exchanged a capital gain for an increased basis for the stock or securities.

REFOCUS ON THE BIG PICTURE

**PROPOSED
SALE OF A
HOUSE AND
OTHER PROPERTY
TRANSACTIONS**

Alice's tax adviser asked a number of questions in order to advise her on her proposed transaction for the house. Alice provided the following answers (refer to Example 25):

- Alice inherited the house from her mother. The fair market value of the house at the date of her mother's death, based on the estate tax return, was $475,000. Based on an appraisal, the house currently is worth $485,000. Alice's mother lived in the house for 38 years. According to the mother's attorney, her adjusted basis for the house was $275,000.
- As a child, Alice lived in the house for 10 years. She has not lived there during the 25 years she has been married.
- The house has been vacant during the seven months that Alice has owned it. She has been trying to decide whether she should sell it for its fair market value or sell it to her nephew for $275,000. Alice has suggested a $275,000 price for the sale to Dan because she believes this is the amount at which she will have no gain or loss.
- Alice intends to invest the $275,000 in stock.

You advise Alice that her adjusted basis for the house is the $475,000 fair market value on the date of her mother's death. If Alice sells the house for $485,000 (assuming no selling expenses), she would have a recognized gain of $10,000 ($485,000 amount realized − $475,000 adjusted basis). The house is a capital asset, and Alice's holding period is long term since she inherited the house. Thus, the gain would be classified as a long-term capital gain. If, instead, Alice sells the house to her nephew for $275,000, she will have a part sale and part gift. The realized gain on the sale of $5,670 is recognized.

Amount realized	$ 275,000
Less: Adjusted basis	(269,330)*
Realized gain	$ 5,670
Recognized gain	$ 5,670

*[($275,000/$485,000) × $475,000] = $269,330.

The gain is classified as a long-term capital gain. Alice is then deemed to have made a gift to Dan of $210,000 ($485,000 − $275,000). With this information, Alice can make an informed selection between the two options.

See Examples 8 and 9 for the tax consequences associated with Alice's questions regarding selling the car. See Example 34 for the tax consequences associated with Alice's questions regarding the wash sale of the stock.

KEY TERMS

Adjusted basis, 14–4	Holding period, 14–14	Recognized loss, 14–7
Amount realized, 14–4	Realized gain, 14–3	Recovery of capital doctrine, 14–8
Fair market value, 14–4	Realized loss, 14–3	Wash sale, 14–19
Goodwill, 14–10	Recognized gain, 14–7	

DISCUSSION QUESTIONS

1. **L0.1** Upon the sale or other disposition of property, what four questions should be considered for income tax purposes?

2. **L0.1** Define each of the following terms:
   a. Amount realized.
   b. Realized gain.
   c. Realized loss.

3. **L0.1** In addition to sales and exchanges, what are some other transactions that are treated as dispositions of property?

4. **L0.1** Ivan invests in land and Grace invests in taxable bonds. The land appreciates by $8,000 each year, and the bonds earn interest of $8,000 each year. After holding the land and bonds for five years, Ivan and Grace sell them. There is a $40,000 realized gain on the sale of the land and no realized gain or loss on the sale of the bonds. Are the tax consequences to Ivan and Grace the same for each of the five years? Explain.

5. **L0.1** Carol and Dave each purchase 100 shares of stock of Burgundy, Inc., a publicly owned corporation, in July for $10,000 each. Carol sells her stock on December 31 for $8,000. Since Burgundy's stock is listed on a national exchange, Dave is able to ascertain that his shares are worth $8,000 on December 31. Does the tax law treat the decline in value of the stock differently for Carol and Dave? Explain.

6. **L0.1** If a taxpayer sells property for cash, the amount realized consists of the net proceeds from the sale. For each of the following, indicate the effect on the amount realized:
   a. The property is sold on credit.
   b. A mortgage on the property is assumed by the buyer.
   c. A mortgage on the property is assumed by the seller.
   d. The buyer acquires the property subject to a mortgage of the seller.
   e. Stock that has a basis to the purchaser of $6,000 and a fair market value of $10,000 is received by the seller as part of the consideration.

7. **L0.1** Adrian owns real property for which the annual property taxes are $3,650. He sells the property to Shelley on February 28, 2011, for $200,000. Shelley pays the real property taxes for the entire year on August 1.
   a. How much of the property taxes can be deducted by Adrian and how much by Shelley?
   b. What effect does the property tax apportionment have on Shelley's adjusted basis in the property?
   c. What effect does the apportionment have on Adrian's amount realized from the sale?
   d. How would the answers in (b) and (c) differ if the taxes were paid by Adrian?

8. **L0.1** Troy is negotiating to buy some land. Under the first option, Troy will give Ella $150,000 and assume her mortgage on the land for $80,000. Under the second option, Troy will give Ella $230,000, and she will immediately pay off the mortgage. Troy wants his basis for the land to be as high as possible. Given this objective, which option should Troy select?

9. **L0.1** Eve purchases land from Gillen. Eve gives Gillen $100,000 in cash and agrees to pay Gillen an additional $400,000 one year later plus interest at 6%.
   a. What is Eve's adjusted basis for the land at the acquisition date?
   b. What is Eve's adjusted basis for the land one year later?

10. **L0.1** A taxpayer owns land and a building (held for investment) with an adjusted basis of $75,000 and a fair market value of $240,000. The property is subject to a mortgage of $360,000. Since the taxpayer is in arrears on the mortgage payments, the creditor is willing to accept the property in return for canceling the amount of the mortgage.
    a. How can the adjusted basis of the property be less than the amount of the mortgage?
    b. If the creditor's offer is accepted, what are the effects on the amount realized, the adjusted basis, and the realized gain or loss?
    c. Does it matter in (b) if the mortgage is recourse or nonrecourse?

11. **LO.1** Distinguish between the terms *allowed depreciation* and *allowable depreciation*. What effect does the difference have on adjusted basis?

12. **LO.1** Chuck and Teresa became engaged after they graduated from college in May 2011. As a graduation present, Chuck received a new car worth $29,000 from his uncle, which he uses for personal purposes. Since Teresa is employed, she purchases a car just like the one Chuck received from his uncle and uses it 60% for business.
    a. Why can Teresa deduct depreciation on her car, whereas Chuck cannot?
    b. If Chuck and Teresa each later sell their cars for $24,000, why is Teresa's realized gain recognized, while Chuck's realized loss is disallowed?

13. **LO.1** Abby owns stock in Orange Corporation and Blue Corporation. She receives a $1,000 distribution from both corporations. The instructions from Orange state that the $1,000 is a dividend. The instructions from Blue state that the $1,000 is not a dividend. What could cause the instructions to differ as to the tax consequences?

14. **LO.1** On July 1, 2011, Katrina purchased tax-exempt bonds (face value of $75,000) for $82,000. The bonds mature in five years, and the annual interest rate is 6%. The market rate of interest is 2%.
    a. How much interest income and/or interest expense must Katrina report in 2011?
    b. What is Katrina's adjusted basis for the bonds on January 1, 2012?

15. **LO.2** Sandra is considering selling two personal use assets that she owns. One has appreciated in value by $14,000, and the other has declined in value by $18,000. Sandra believes that she should sell both assets in the same tax year so that the loss of $18,000 can offset the gain of $14,000.
    a. Advise Sandra regarding the tax consequences of her plan.
    b. Could Sandra achieve better tax results by selling the assets in different tax years?

DECISION MAKING

16. **LO.2** Ron sold his sailboat for a $5,000 loss in the current year because he was diagnosed as having skin cancer. His spouse wants him to sell his Harley Davidson motorcycle because her brother broke his leg while riding his motorcycle. Since Ron no longer has anyone to ride with, he is seriously considering accepting his wife's advice. Because the motorcycle is a classic, Ron has received two offers. Each offer would result in a $5,000 gain. Joe would like to purchase the motorcycle before Christmas, and Jeff would like to purchase it after New Year's. Identify the relevant tax issues Ron faces in making his decision.

ISSUE ID

17. **LO.3** Monty owns a life insurance policy that will pay $500,000 to Pearlie, his spouse, on his death. At the date of Monty's death, he had paid total premiums of $115,000 on the policy. In accordance with § 101(a)(1), Pearlie excludes the $500,000 of insurance proceeds. Discuss the relationship, if any, between the § 101 exclusion and the recovery of capital doctrine.

18. **LO.4** Melba purchases a one-acre lot from her employer, a real estate developer, for $80,000. Is it possible that Melba's adjusted basis for the lot could be $100,000? $90,000? $75,000? Explain.

19. **LO.4** How is cost allocated when a taxpayer acquires multiple assets in a lump-sum purchase?

20. **LO.4** Distinguish between the procedures for determining the basis of stock received as a nontaxable stock dividend when the stock dividend is:
    a. Common stock on common stock.
    b. Preferred stock on common stock.

21. **LO.1, 2, 4** Marla bought a small sailboat for $20,000 in 2007. In January 2011, when the fair market value of the sailboat is $12,000, Marla makes a gift of it to Janine. No gift tax is due on the transfer. Six months later, Janine sells the boat for $10,500. What is Janine's:
    a. Adjusted basis in the sailboat?
    b. Recognized gain or loss on the sale?
    c. How would the answer to (b) change if the fair market value at the date of the gift was $22,500?

22. **LO.1, 2, 4, 6** In January, Agnes is diagnosed as having a terminal disease. Her nephew, Stan, will graduate from college in May, and she would like to give him $50,000 as a graduation present. She has stock worth $50,000 that she could either give him directly or sell and transfer the cash. Since she may not be alive in May, Agnes is considering

ISSUE ID

making the gift now (four months prior to graduation). If Agnes should die before making the gift, her will stipulates that Stan will receive the stock. Identify the relevant tax issues that Agnes should consider in making her decision.

23. **L0.4** Different rules apply as to the basis for property received by gift and property received by inheritance. Under what circumstances will the basis be the same for property received by gift and by inheritance in 2011?

24. **L0.4** Robin inherits 1,000 shares of Wal-Mart stock from her aunt in 2011. According to the information received from the executor of her aunt's estate, Robin's adjusted basis for the stock is $55,000. Albert, Robin's fiancé, receives 1,000 shares of Wal-Mart stock from his uncle as a gift in 2011. His uncle tells Albert that his adjusted basis for the Wal-Mart stock is $7,000. What could cause the substantial difference in the adjusted basis for Robin's and Albert's respective 1,000 shares of Wal-Mart stock?

25. **L0.4** Gary makes a gift of an appreciated building to Carmen. She dies three months later, and Gary inherits the building from her. During the period that Carmen held the building, she deducted depreciation and made a capital expenditure. What effect might these items have on Gary's basis for the inherited building?

26. **L0.4** Thelma inherited land from Sadie on June 7, 2011. The land appreciated in value by 100% during the six months that it was owned by Sadie. The value has remained stable during the three months that Thelma has owned it, and she expects it to continue to do so in the near future. Although she would like to sell the land now, Thelma has decided to postpone the sale for another three months. The delay is to enable the recognized gain to qualify for long-term capital gain treatment. Evaluate Thelma's understanding of the tax law.

DECISION MAKING

27. **L0.5** Marilyn owns land that she acquired three years ago as an investment for $250,000. Since the land has not appreciated in value as she anticipated, she sells it to her brother, Amos, for its fair market value of $180,000. Amos sells the land two years later for $240,000.
    a. Explain why Marilyn's realized loss of $70,000 ($180,000 amount realized − $250,000 adjusted basis) is disallowed.
    b. Explain why Amos has neither a recognized gain nor a recognized loss on his sale of the land.
    c. Is the family unit treated fairly under the related-party disallowance rule under § 267?
    d. Which party wins and which party loses?
    e. How could Marilyn have avoided the loss disallowance on her sale of the land?

DECISION MAKING

28. **L0.5, 6** On December 18, 2011, Amber sells 500 shares of John Deere stock for a realized loss of $5,000. On January 8, 2012, Amber purchases 500 shares of John Deere stock for $8,000 more than she received on the December sale.
    a. Why is Amber's December realized loss of $5,000 disallowed?
    b. How does Amber calculate the basis of the 500 shares purchased in January 2012?
    c. What could Amber have done differently to enable her to recognize the $5,000 loss in 2011?

PROBLEMS

29. **L0.1** Anne sold her home for $290,000 in 2011. Selling expenses were $17,400. She had purchased it in 2004 for $200,000. During the period of ownership, Anne had done the following:

    • Deducted $50,500 office-in-home expenses, which included $4,500 in depreciation. (Refer to Chapter 9.)
    • Deducted a casualty loss in 2007 for residential trees destroyed by a hurricane. The total loss was $19,000 (after the $100 floor and the 10%-of-AGI floor), and Anne's insurance company reimbursed her for $13,500. (Refer to Chapter 7.)
    • Paid street paving assessment of $7,000 and added sidewalks for $8,000.
    • Installed an elevator for medical reasons. The total cost was $20,000, and Anne deducted $13,000 as medical expenses. (Refer to Chapter 10.)

    What is Anne's realized gain?

30. **LO.1** Kareem bought a rental house in October 2006 for $250,000, of which $50,000 is allocated to the land and $200,000 to the building. Early in 2008, he had a tennis court built in the backyard at a cost of $5,000. Kareem has deducted $30,900 for depreciation on the house and $1,300 for depreciation on the court. In January 2011, he sells the house and tennis court for $400,000 cash.
    a.   What is Kareem's realized gain or loss?
    b.   If an original mortgage of $75,000 is still outstanding and the buyer assumes the mortgage in addition to the cash payment, what is Kareem's realized gain or loss?
    c.   If the buyer takes the property subject to the mortgage, rather than assuming it, what is Kareem's realized gain or loss?

31. **LO.1** Norm is negotiating the sale of a tract of his land to Pat. Use the following classification scheme to classify each of the items contained in the proposed sales contract:

Legend

DARN = Decreases amount realized by Norm
IARN = Increases amount realized by Norm
DABN = Decreases adjusted basis to Norm
IABN = Increases adjusted basis to Norm
DABP = Decreases adjusted basis to Pat
IABP = Increases adjusted basis to Pat

---

    a.   Norm is to receive cash of $50,000.
    b.   Norm is to receive Pat's note payable for $25,000, payable in three years.
    c.   Pat assumes Norm's mortgage of $5,000 on the land.
    d.   Pat agrees to pay the realtor's sales commission of $8,000.
    e.   Pat agrees to pay the property taxes on the land for the entire year. If each party paid his or her respective share, Norm's share would be $1,000, and Pat's share would be $3,000.
    f.   Pat pays legal fees of $500.
    g.   Norm pays legal fees of $750.

32. **LO.1** Gayla owns a building (adjusted basis of $375,000 on January 1, 2011) that she rents to Len who operates a restaurant in the building. The municipal health department closed the restaurant for two months during 2011 because of health code violations. Under MACRS, the cost recovery deduction for 2011 would be $24,000. However, Gayla deducted cost recovery only for the 10 months the restaurant was open since she waived the rent income during the two-month period the restaurant was closed.
    a.   What is the amount of the cost recovery deduction that Gayla should report on her 2011 income tax return?
    b.   Calculate the adjusted basis of the building at the end of 2011.

33. **LO.1, 2** Melanie owns a personal use boat that has a fair market value of $32,500 and an adjusted basis of $45,000. Melanie's AGI is $90,000. Calculate the realized and recognized gain or loss if:
    a.   Melanie sells the boat for $32,500.
    b.   Melanie exchanges the boat for another boat worth $32,500.
    c.   The boat is stolen and Melanie receives insurance proceeds of $32,500.
    d.   Would your answer in (a) change if the fair market value and the selling price of the boat were $48,000?

34. **LO.1** Butch owns stock in Dove Corporation. His adjusted basis for the stock is $70,000. During the year, he receives a distribution from the corporation of $50,000 that is labeled a return of capital (i.e., Dove has no earnings and profits).
    a.   Determine the tax consequences to Butch.
    b.   Assume instead that the amount of the distribution is $140,000. Determine the tax consequences to Butch.
    c.   Assume instead in (a) that the $50,000 distribution is labeled a taxable dividend (i.e., Dove has earnings and profits of at least $50,000).

35. **LO.1, 2** Chee purchases Tan, Inc. bonds for $108,000 on January 2, 2011. The face value of the bonds is $100,000, the maturity date is December 31, 2015, and the annual interest rate is 5%. Chee will amortize the premium only if he is required to do so. Chee sells the bonds on July 1, 2013, for $106,000.

a. Determine the interest income Chee should report for 2011.
b. Calculate Chee's recognized gain or loss on the sale of the bonds in 2013.

36. **LO.1, 2** Which of the following results in a recognized gain or loss?
   a. Kay sells her vacation cabin (adjusted basis of $100,000) for $150,000.
   b. Adam sells his personal residence (adjusted basis of $150,000) for $100,000.
   c. Carl's personal residence (adjusted basis of $65,000) is condemned by the city. He receives condemnation proceeds of $55,000.
   d. Olga's land is worth $40,000 at the end of the year. She had purchased the land six months earlier for $25,000.
   e. Vera's personal vehicle (adjusted basis of $22,000) is stolen. She receives $23,000 from the insurance company and does not plan to replace the automobile.
   f. Jerry sells used clothing (adjusted basis of $500) to a thrift store for $50.

37. **LO.1, 2** Yancy's personal residence is condemned as part of an urban renewal project. His adjusted basis for the residence is $405,000. He receives condemnation proceeds of $390,000 and invests the proceeds in stocks and bonds.
   a. Calculate Yancy's realized and recognized gain or loss.
   b. If the condemnation proceeds are $450,000, what are Yancy's realized and recognized gain or loss?
   c. What are Yancy's realized and recognized gain or loss in (a) if the house was rental property?

38. **LO.4** Buddy Morris is a real estate agent for Presidential Estates, a residential real estate development. Because of his outstanding sales performance, Buddy is permitted to buy a lot that normally would sell for $280,000 for $250,000. Buddy is the only real estate agent for Presidential Estates who is permitted to do so.
   a. Does Buddy have gross income from the transaction?
   b. What is Buddy's adjusted basis for the land?
   c. Write a letter to Buddy informing him of the tax consequences of his acquisition of the lot. His address is 100 Tower Road, San Diego, CA 92182.

39. **LO.1, 2, 4** Karen makes the following purchases and sales of stock:

Transaction	Date	Number of Shares	Company	Price per Share
Purchase	1–1–2009	300	MDG	$ 75
Purchase	6–1–2009	150	GRU	300
Purchase	11–1–2009	60	MDG	70
Sale	12–3–2009	180	MDG	70
Purchase	3–1–2010	120	GRU	375
Sale	8–1–2010	90	GRU	330
Sale	1–1–2011	150	MDG	90
Sale	2–1–2011	75	GRU	500

Assuming that Karen is unable to identify the particular lots that are sold with the original purchase, what is the recognized gain or loss on each type of stock as of the following dates:
   a. 7–1–2009.
   b. 12–31–2009.
   c. 12–31–2010.
   d. 7–1–2011.

40. **LO.1, 2, 4** Kevin purchases 1,000 shares of Bluebird Corporation stock on October 3, 2011, for $300,000. On December 12, 2011, Kevin purchases an additional 750 shares of Bluebird stock for $210,000. According to market quotations, Bluebird stock is selling for $285 per share on December 31, 2011. Kevin sells 500 shares of Bluebird stock on March 1, 2012, for $162,500.
   a. What is the adjusted basis of Kevin's Bluebird stock on December 31, 2011?
   b. What is Kevin's recognized gain or loss from the sale of Bluebird stock on March 1, 2012, assuming the shares sold are from the shares purchased on December 12, 2011?

c. What is Kevin's recognized gain or loss from the sale of Bluebird stock on March 1, 2012, assuming Kevin cannot adequately identify the shares sold?

41. **LO.4** Irene Andrews is purchasing the assets of a sole proprietorship from Seth. The fair market values of the assets as agreed to by Irene and Seth are as follows:

COMMUNICATIONS

Asset	Seth's Adjusted Basis	Fair Market Value
Accounts receivable	$ –0–	$ 10,000
Notes receivable	15,000	20,000
Machinery and equipment	85,000	110,000
Building	100,000	320,000
Land	200,000	350,000

The purchase price is $950,000.
a. Calculate Seth's realized and recognized gain.
b. Determine Irene's basis for each of the assets.
c. Write a letter to Irene informing her of the tax consequences of the purchase. Her address is 300 Riverside Drive, Cincinnati, OH 45207.

42. **LO.4** Donna owns 800 shares of common stock in Macaw Corporation (adjusted basis of $40,000). She receives a 5% stock dividend when the stock is selling for $60 per share.
a. How much gross income must Donna recognize because of the stock dividend?
b. What is Donna's basis for her 840 shares of stock?

43. **LO.4** Paula owns stock in Yellow, Inc., which she purchased for $5,000. The stock has a fair market value of $6,000. Because Yellow is experiencing a cash flow problem, it chooses to distribute nontaxable stock rights instead of cash to its shareholders.
a. What effect does this distribution have on Paula's basis in her Yellow stock if the fair market value of the stock rights is $1,000?
b. What is Paula's basis for the nontaxable stock rights?
c. What is Paula's recognized gain or loss if she sells the stock rights for $1,200?
d. What is Paula's recognized gain or loss if she allows the stock rights to lapse?
e. If the fair market value of the stock rights is $750 (not $1,000), how will this change the answers to parts (a) and (b)?

44. **LO.1, 2, 4** Roberto has received various gifts over the years. He has decided to dispose of the following assets that he received as gifts:
a. In 1951, he received land worth $32,000. The donor's adjusted basis was $35,000. Roberto sells the land for $95,000 in 2011.
b. In 1956, he received stock in Gold Company. The donor's adjusted basis was $19,000. The fair market value on the date of the gift was $34,000. Roberto sells the stock for $40,000 in 2011.
c. In 1962, he received land worth $15,000. The donor's adjusted basis was $20,000. Roberto sells the land for $9,000 in 2011.
d. In 2003, he received stock worth $30,000. The donor's adjusted basis was $42,000. Roberto sells the stock for $38,000 in 2011.

What is the recognized gain or loss from each of the preceding transactions? Assume for each of the gift transactions that no gift tax was paid.

45. **LO.1, 2, 4** Nicky receives a car from Sam as a gift. Sam paid $40,000 for the car. He had used it for business purposes and had deducted $16,000 for depreciation up to the time he gave the car to Nicky. The fair market value of the car is $21,000.
a. Assuming Nicky uses the car for business purposes, what is her basis for depreciation?
b. Assume Nicky deducts depreciation of $5,500 and then sells the car for $20,000. What is her recognized gain or loss?
c. Assume Nicky deducts depreciation of $5,500 and then sells the car for $14,000. What is her recognized gain or loss?

46. **LO.4** Laura receives a gift of real estate with an adjusted basis of $125,000 and a fair market value of $100,000. The donor paid gift tax of $14,000 on the transfer. If Laura later sells the property for $110,000, what is her recognized gain or loss?

47. **LO.4** Natalie receives an original Matisse painting as a gift from her aunt. At the date of the gift, the adjusted basis of the painting is $825,000, and its fair market value is $1,120,000. Her aunt paid gift tax of $392,000.
    a.   What is Natalie's adjusted basis in the painting?
    b.   If the fair market value of the painting at the date of the gift is $824,000 (not $1,120,000), what is Natalie's adjusted basis?

48. **LO.1, 2, 4, 6** Ira Cook is planning to make a charitable contribution of Crystal, Inc. stock worth $20,000 to the Boy Scouts. The stock has an adjusted basis of $15,000. A friend has suggested that Ira sell the stock and contribute the $20,000 in proceeds rather than contribute the stock.
    a.   Should Ira follow the friend's advice? Why?
    b.   Assume the fair market value is only $13,000. In this case, should Ira follow the friend's advice? Why?
    c.   Rather than make a charitable contribution to the Boy Scouts, Ira is going to make a gift to Nancy, his niece. Advise Ira regarding (a) and (b).
    d.   Write a letter to Ira regarding whether in (a) he should sell the stock and contribute the cash or contribute the stock. He has informed you that he purchased the stock six years ago. Ira's address is 500 Ireland Avenue, De Kalb, IL 60115.

49. **LO.4** As sole heir, Dazie receives all of Mary's property (adjusted basis of $1,400,000 and fair market value of $3,820,000). Six months after Mary's death in 2011, the fair market value is $3,835,000.
    a.   Can the executor of Mary's estate elect the alternate valuation date and amount?
    b.   What is Dazie's basis for the property?
    c.   Assume, instead, that the fair market value six months after Mary's death is $3.8 million. Respond to (a) and (b).

50. **LO.4** The portion of Earl's estate distributed to Robert, one of Earl's beneficiaries, is valued as follows:

Asset	Earl's Adjusted Basis	FMV at Date of Death	FMV at Alternate Valuation Date
Cash	$10,000	$ 10,000	$ 10,000
Stock	40,000	125,000	60,000
Apartment building	60,000	300,000	325,000
Land	75,000	100,000	110,000

Although the fair market value of the stock six months after Earl's death in 2011 turned out to be $60,000, the executor of the estate distributed it to Robert one month after Earl's death when it was worth $85,000. Determine Robert's basis for the assets if:
    a.   The primary valuation date applies.
    b.   The executor elects the alternate valuation date.

51. **LO.4** Emily makes a gift of 100 shares of appreciated stock to her uncle, George, on January 5, 2011. The basis of the stock is $3,000, and the fair market value is $6,000. George dies on November 8, 2011. Under the provisions of George's will, Emily inherits 100 shares of the stock. The value of the stock for Federal estate tax purposes is $95 per share.
    a.   What is the basis of the inherited stock to Emily?
    b.   What would have been the basis of the inherited stock to Emily if she had given the stock to George on January 5, 2010?

52. **LO.4** Helene and Pauline are twin sisters who live in Louisiana and Mississippi, respectively. Helene is married to Frank, and Pauline is married to Richard. Frank and Richard are killed in an auto accident in 2011 while returning from a sporting event.
    Helene and Frank jointly owned some farmland in Louisiana (value of $940,000, cost of $450,000). Pauline and Richard jointly owned some farmland in Mississippi (value of $940,000, cost of $450,000). Assume all of Frank's and Richard's property passes to their surviving wives.
    a.   Calculate Helene's basis in the land.
    b.   Calculate Pauline's basis in the land.
    c.   What causes the difference?

53. **LO.4, 5** Joyce owns undeveloped real estate with an adjusted basis of $120,000. She sells the real estate to her sister, Iris, for its fair market value of $115,000.

    a. Calculate Joyce's realized and recognized gain or loss.

    b. If Iris later sells the real estate for $119,000, calculate her realized and recognized gain or loss.

    c. Assume instead that Joyce sold the real estate to Iris for its fair market value of $130,000. Calculate Joyce's realized and recognized gain or loss.

    d. Assume instead that Joyce sold the real estate to Hector, a friend, for its fair market value of $115,000. Calculate Joyce's realized and recognized gain or loss.

    e. Advise Joyce whether she should sell the real estate to Iris or Hector for its fair market value of $115,000.

DECISION MAKING

54. **LO.1, 2, 4, 5** Louis owns three pieces of land with an adjusted basis as follows: parcel A, $75,000; parcel B, $125,000; and parcel C, $175,000. Louis sells parcel A to his uncle for $50,000, parcel B to his partner for $120,000, and parcel C to his mother for $150,000.

    a. What is the recognized gain or loss from the sale of each parcel?

    b. If Louis's uncle eventually sells his land for $90,000, what is his recognized gain or loss?

    c. If Louis's partner eventually sells his land for $130,000, what is his recognized gain or loss?

    d. If Louis's mother eventually sells her land for $165,000, what is her recognized gain or loss?

55. **LO.1, 2, 4, 5** Tyneka inherited 1,000 shares of Aqua, Inc. stock from Joe. Joe's basis was $35,000, and the fair market value on July 1, 2011 (the date of death) was $45,000. The shares were distributed to Tyneka on July 15, 2011. Tyneka sold the stock on July 30, 2012, for $33,000. After giving the matter more thought, she decides that Aqua is a good investment and purchases 1,000 shares for $30,000 on August 20, 2012.

    a. What is Tyneka's basis for the 1,000 shares purchased on August 20, 2012?

    b. What would be Tyneka's basis for the 1,000 Aqua shares inherited from Joe if she had given 1,000 Aqua shares to Joe on March 1, 2011 (assuming no gift tax was paid)? Her basis at the date of the gift was $35,000, and the fair market value was $45,000.

    c. Could Tyneka have obtained different tax consequences in (a) if she had sold the 1,000 shares on December 27, 2011, and purchased the 1,000 shares on January 5, 2012?

DECISION MAKING

56. **LO.1, 2, 5** Sarah owns 100 shares of Drake, Inc. (adjusted basis of $50,000). On October 11, 2011, she sells the 100 shares for their fair market value of $45,000. On November 5, 2011, she purchases 125 shares of Drake stock for $57,500.

    a. What is Sarah's realized and recognized gain or loss on the 100 shares sold on October 11, 2011?

    b. What is Sarah's adjusted basis for the 125 shares purchased on November 5, 2011?

    c. How would your answers in (a) and (b) change if Sarah purchased only 75 shares for $34,500 on November 5, 2011?

    d. How would your answers in (a) and (b) change if Sarah purchased 125 shares on November 15, 2011, instead of November 5, 2011? Which purchase date would you recommend?

DECISION MAKING

57. **LO.1, 2, 5** Abby's home had a basis of $360,000 ($160,000 attributable to the land) and a fair market value of $340,000 ($155,000 attributable to the land) when she converted 70% of it to business use by opening a bed and breakfast. Four years after the conversion, Abby sells the home for $500,000 ($165,000 attributable to the land).

    a. Calculate Abby's basis for gain, loss, and cost recovery for the portion of her personal residence that was converted to business use.

    b. Calculate the cost recovery deducted by Abby during the four-year period of business use, assuming the bed and breakfast is opened on January 1 of year 1 and the house is sold on December 31 of year 4.

    c. What is Abby's recognized gain or loss on the sale of the business use portion?

58. **LO.5, 6** Surendra's personal residence originally cost $340,000 (ignore land). After living in the house for five years, he converts it to rental property. At the date of conversion, the fair market value of the house is $320,000. As to the rental property, calculate Surendra's basis for:

DECISION MAKING

a. Loss.
b. Depreciation.
c. Gain.
d. Could Surendra have obtained better tax results if he had sold his personal residence for $320,000 and then purchased another house for $320,000 to hold as rental property?

59. **LO.4, 6** Hun, age 93, has accumulated substantial assets during his life. Among his many assets are the following, which he is considering giving to Koji, his grandson.

Asset	Adjusted Basis	Fair Market Value
Silver Corporation stock	$900,000	$700,000
Red Corporation stock	70,000	71,000
Emerald Corporation stock	200,000	500,000

Hun has been in ill health for the past five years. His physician has informed him that he probably will not live for more than six months. Advise Hun on which of the stocks should be transferred as gifts and which as bequests.

CUMULATIVE PROBLEMS

60. Alton Newman, age 67, is married and files a joint return with his wife, Clair, age 65. Alton and Clair are both retired, and during 2010, they received Social Security benefits of $10,000. Alton's Social Security number is 111–11–1111, and Clair's is 123–45–6789. They reside at 210 College Drive, Columbia, SC 29201.

Alton, who retired on January 1, 2010, receives benefits from a qualified pension plan of $750 a month for life. His total contributions to the plan (none of which were deductible) were $68,250. In January 2010, he received a bonus of $2,000 from his former employer for service performed in 2009. Although the former employer accrued the bonus in 2009, it was not paid until 2010.

Clair, who retired on December 31, 2009, started receiving benefits of $900 a month on January 1, 2010. Her contributions to the qualified pension plan (none of which were deductible) were $74,100.

Clair had casino winnings for the year of $4,500 and casino losses of $2,100 while Alton won $17,000 on a $1 lottery ticket.

On September 27, 2010, Alton and Clair received a 10% stock dividend on 600 shares of stock they owned. They had bought the stock on March 5, 2003, for $20 a share. On December 16, 2010, they sold the 60 dividend shares for $55 a share.

On October 10, 2010, Clair sold the car she had used in commuting to and from work for $17,000. She had paid $31,000 for the car in 2004.

On July 14, 2002, Alton and Clair received a gift of 1,000 shares of stock from their son, Thomas. Thomas's basis in the stock was $35 a share (fair market value at the date of gift was $25). No gift tax was paid on the transfer. Alton and Clair sold the stock on October 8, 2010, for $24 a share.

On May 1, 2010, Clair's mother died, and Clair inherited her personal residence. In February 2010, her mother had paid the property taxes for 2010 of $2,100. The residence had a fair market value of $235,000 and an adjusted basis to the mother of $160,000. Clair listed the house with a real estate agent who estimated it was worth $240,000 as of December 31, 2010.

Clair received rent income of $6,000 on a beach house she inherited three years ago from her Uncle Chuck. She had rented the property for one week during the July 4th weekend and one week during the Thanksgiving holidays. Uncle Chuck's adjusted basis in the beach house was $150,000, and its fair market value on the date of his death was $240,000. Clair and Alton used the beach house for personal purposes for 56 days during the year. Expenses associated with the house were $3,700 for utilities, maintenance, and repairs; $2,200 for property taxes; and $800 for insurance. There are no mortgages on the property.

Clair and Alton paid estimated Federal income tax of $3,100 and had itemized deductions of $6,800 (excluding any itemized deductions associated with the beach house and gambling). If they have overpaid their Federal income tax, they want the amount refunded. Both Clair and Alton wish to have $3 go to the Presidential Election Campaign Fund.

Compute their net tax payable or refund due for 2010. If you use tax forms for your computations, you will need Form 1040 and Schedule D. Suggested software: H&R BLOCK At Home.

61. John Custer, age 35, is single. His Social Security number is 111–11–1111, and he resides at 150 Highway 51, Tangipahoa, LA 70443.

    John has a five-year-old child, Kendra, who lives with her mother, Katy. John pays alimony of $24,000 per year to Katy and child support of $6,000. The $6,000 of child support covers 70% of Katy's costs of rearing Kendra. Kendra's Social Security number is 123–45–6789, and Katy's is 123–45–6788.

    John's mother, Sally, lived with him until her death in early September 2011. He incurred and paid medical expenses for her of $12,500 and other support payments of $10,000. Sally's only sources of income were $4,500 of interest income on certificates of deposit and $5,600 of Social Security benefits, which she spent on her medical expenses and helping to maintain John's household. Sally's Social Security number was 123–45–6787.

    John is employed by the Highway Department of the State of Louisiana in an executive position. His salary is $95,000. The appropriate amounts of Social Security tax ($5,890) and Medicare tax ($1,378) were withheld. In addition, $13,500 was withheld for Federal income taxes, and $4,500 was withheld for state income taxes.

    In addition to his salary, John's employer provides him with the following fringe benefits:

- Group term life insurance with a maturity value of $95,000. The cost of the premiums for the employer was $425.
- Group health insurance plan. John's employer paid premiums of $5,600 for his coverage. The plan paid $2,800 for John's medical expenses during the year.

    Upon the death of his Aunt Josie in December 2010, John, her only recognized heir, inherited the following assets:

Asset	Josie's Adjusted Basis	FMV at Date of Death
Car	$ 35,000	$ 15,000
Land—300 acres	275,000	500,000
IBM stock	100,000	160,000
Cash	50,000	50,000

Six months prior to her death, Josie gave John a mountain cabin. Her adjusted basis for the mountain cabin was $270,000, and the fair market value was $390,000. She paid gift tax of $20,000.

During the year, John had the following transactions:

- On February 1, 2011, he sold for $45,000 Microsoft stock that he inherited from his father four years ago. His father's adjusted basis was $49,000, and the fair market value at the date of the father's death was $41,000.
- The car John inherited from Josie was destroyed in a wreck on October 1, 2011. He had loaned the car to Katy to use for a two-week period while the engine in her car was being replaced. Fortunately, neither Katy nor Kendra was injured. John received insurance proceeds of $12,500, the fair market value of the car on October 1, 2011.
- On October 30, 2011, John gambled away the $50,000 he inherited at a casino in Biloxi. He had hoped this activity would help with the bouts of depression he had been suffering since Sally's death.
- On December 28, 2011, John sold the 300 acres of land to his brother, James, for its fair market value of $475,000. James planned on using the land for his dairy farm.

Other sources of income for John were as follows:

Dividend income	$18,000
Interest income:	
Guaranty Bank	12,000
City of Kentwood water bonds	24,000
Award from State of Louisiana for outstanding suggestion for highway beautification	7,500

Potential itemized deductions for John, in addition to items already mentioned, were as follows:

Property taxes paid on his residence	$4,500
Property taxes paid on personalty	2,500
Estimated Federal income taxes paid	4,300
Estimated state income taxes paid	2,300
Charitable contributions	5,500
Mortgage interest on his residence	7,100
Orthodontic expenses for Kendra	4,000
Psychiatric expenses for John	3,500
Sales taxes paid	7,500

Part 1—Tax Computation

Compute John's net tax payable or refund due for 2011.

Part 2—Tax Planning

Assume that rather than selling the land to James, John is considering leasing it to him for $30,000 annually with the lease beginning on October 1, 2011. James would prepay the lease payments through December 31, 2011. Thereafter, he would make monthly lease payments at the beginning of each month. What effect would this have on John's 2011 tax liability? What potential problem might John encounter? Write a letter to John in which you advise him of the tax consequences of leasing versus selling. Also, prepare a memo for the tax files.

RESEARCH PROBLEMS

THOMSON REUTERS

Checkpoint® Student Edition

Note: Solutions to Research Problems can be prepared by using the **Checkpoint®** **Student Edition** online research product, which is available to accompany this text. It is also possible to prepare solutions to the Research Problems by using tax research materials found in a standard tax library.

Research Problem 1. Inez Butler is the sole shareholder of Pelican, Inc., which owns car dealerships. Pelican purchases the assets of a Chevrolet dealership. The purchase price of $12 million is allocated to the purchased assets based on the fair market values. This includes $3.5 million that is allocated to goodwill.

In addition to the price of $12 million, Pelican incurred legal fees of $250,000 associated with the purchase. According to an itemized invoice provided by the attorney, 80% of the legal fees relate to the acquisition of inventory. Consequently, Pelican assigned $200,000 of the legal fees to inventory with the balance being capitalized as goodwill. The expectation is that 60% of the $200,000 will become part of cost of goods sold in the current year with the remaining 40% doing so in the following year.

The IRS has concluded that § 1060 limits the amount that may be assigned to the fair market value of the inventory. Therefore, the $200,000 of legal fees cannot be added to the basis of the inventory. Instead, it must be included in goodwill under the residual method. Who is correct?

Research Problem 2. Terry owns real estate with an adjusted basis of $600,000 and a fair market value of $1.1 million. The amount of the nonrecourse mortgage on the property is $2.5 million. Because of substantial past and projected future losses associated with the real estate development (occupancy rate of only 37% after three years), Terry deeds the property to the creditor.

a. What are the tax consequences to Terry?

b. Assume the data are the same, except the fair market value of the property is $2,525,000. Therefore, when Terry deeds the property to the creditor, she also receives $25,000 from the creditor. What are the tax consequences to Terry?

Research Problem 3. As the result of a large inheritance from her grandmother, Marcy has a substantial investment portfolio. The securities are held in street name by her brokerage firm. Marcy's broker, Max, has standing oral instructions from her on sales transactions to sell the shares with the highest cost basis.

In October 2009, Marcy phoned Max and instructed him to sell 6,000 shares of Color, Inc. Her portfolio has 15,000 shares of Color, which were purchased in several transactions over a three-year period. At the end of each month, the brokerage firm provides Marcy with a monthly statement that includes sales transactions. It does not identify the specific certificates transferred.

In filing her 2009 income tax return, Marcy used the specific identification method to calculate the $75,000 recognized gain on the sale. On audit of her 2009 return, the IRS has taken the position that under Reg. § 1.1012–1(c) Marcy should have used the FIFO method to report the sale of the Color shares, resulting in a gain of $140,000. According to this interpretation of the Regulations, Marcy may not use the specific identification method (and must use the FIFO method) because the broker did not provide written confirmation of Marcy's sales instructions.

Marcy has come to you for tax advice with respect to this issue.

Research Problem 4. Ruth Ames died on January 10, 2011. In filing the estate tax return, her executor, Melvin Sims, elects the primary valuation date and amount (fair market value on the date of death). On March 12, 2011, Melvin invests $30,000 of cash that Ruth had in her money market account in acquiring 1,000 shares of Orange, Inc. ($30 per share). On January 10, 2011, Orange was selling for $29 per share. The stock is distributed to a beneficiary, Annette Rust, on June 1, 2011, when it is selling for $33 per share. Melvin wants you to determine the amount at which the Orange shares should appear on the estate tax return and the amount of Annette's adjusted basis for the stock. Write a letter to Melvin in which you respond to his inquiry and prepare a memo for the tax files. His address is 100 Center Lane, Miami, FL 32124.

Research Problem 5. Amanda purchased the following lots of stock of Pearl, Inc. (a pharmaceutical company) during 2008:

Date	Number of Shares	Cost per Share
February 1	100	$150
July 25	100	140
November 3	100	130

On December 20, 2010, Amanda sold the 300 shares for $145 each.

In early January 2011, the Food and Drug Administration granted approval for a new drug developed by Pearl. Expecting the stock to continue to increase in value, Amanda purchased 300 shares on January 5, 2011, for $175 per share.

Amanda calculated her recognized gain as $1,500 ($43,500 amount realized – $42,000 adjusted basis). The IRS contends that the transaction must be treated as the sale of three lots of stock because of the wash sale rules. As a result, the $500 realized gain on the sale of the second lot and the $1,500 realized gain on the sale of the third lot must be recognized, and the $500 realized loss on the sale of the first lot is disallowed under § 1091. Who is correct?

Research Problem 6. Cecelia owned 30% of the stock of Lime, Inc., a family corporation. Her basis for the stock was $280,000. As a result of a dispute with the majority shareholder regarding a projected expansion of the company, the corporation redeemed her stock for $900,000. Cecelia received $300,000 in cash plus a $600,000 interest-bearing promissory note. Cecelia had been the vice president of Lime, but after the redemption, she was no longer employed by the corporation.

The contract describing the stock redemption and the termination of employment included a three-year covenant not to compete by Cecelia in the citrus industry in Florida. The contract did not allocate any of the purchase price to the covenant. Cecelia was well

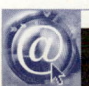

known in the industry, highly respected among her associates, and had many business contacts.

The promissory note was payable in three installments over a three-year period. The note contained a provision that any breach of the covenant not to compete could result in a right of offset. This meant that future payments on the note could be offset against any damages caused by Cecelia's breach of the covenant.

Six months after the stock redemption, Cecelia's CPA informed her that there would have been tax benefits to Lime if part of the payment to her had been allocated to the covenant (i.e., § 197 amortization treatment). Otherwise, no deduction results when a corporation redeems its stock. Therefore, if Cecelia would renegotiate the agreement and accept such an allocation, she would receive additional payments or a reduction in the three-year noncompete period. Although meetings were held, no modification of the original agreement was made.

Cecelia reported all of the $900,000 of payments received as the amount realized from the stock redemption (i.e., eligible for the beneficial capital gains tax rate of 15%). Lime treated $400,000 of the payments as a § 197 intangible for the covenant and amortized it under § 197.

Not wishing to be whipsawed by these inconsistent positions, the IRS levied assessments against *both* Cecelia and Lime. For Cecelia, it disallowed part of her capital gain and treated it as ordinary income (i.e., proceeds from a covenant not to compete). For Lime, it disallowed the § 197 deduction and classified the payments as a nondeductible redemption of stock. Which party should prevail?

INTERNET *activity*

COMMUNICATIONS

Use the tax resources of the Internet to address the following questions. Do not restrict your search to the Web, but include a review of newsgroups and general reference materials, practitioner sites and resources, primary sources of the tax law, chat rooms and discussion groups, and other opportunities.

Research Problem 7. Many see the "step-up in basis at death" rule of § 1014 as an expensive tax loophole enjoyed by the wealthy. Find the latest estimates of the revenue loss to the Treasury that is attributable to this rule.

a. How does Canada's tax law determine the basis of property acquired from a decedent?
b. Send an e-mail message to a member of the House Ways and Means Committee expressing a preference for the preservation of the current § 1014 rule or the modifications made to it by the Tax Relief Reconciliation Act of 2001 and the Tax Relief Act of 2010.

Research Problem 8. The specific identification method is important when one invests in mutual funds. When taxpayers sell part of their holdings, the basis of the surrendered shares can be difficult to compute. Go to the site of an investment adviser or mutual fund to find instructions on how to compute the basis of the shares sold. What options are available to the taxpayer according to this information? Illustrate each of the alternatives.

CHAPTER

15

Property Transactions: Nontaxable Exchanges

LEARNING OBJECTIVES

After completing Chapter 15, you should be able to:

LO.1
Understand the rationale for nonrecognition (postponement) of gain or loss in certain property transactions.

LO.2
Apply the nonrecognition provisions and basis determination rules for like-kind exchanges.

LO.3
Explain the nonrecognition provisions available on the involuntary conversion of property.

LO.4
Describe the provision for the permanent exclusion of gain on the sale of a personal residence.

LO.5
Identify other nonrecognition provisions contained in the Code.

LO.6
Identify tax planning opportunities related to the nonrecognition provisions discussed in the chapter.

OUTLINE

FRAMEWORK 1040:

Tax Formula for Individuals

This chapter covers the boldfaced portions of the Tax Formula for Individuals that was introduced in Figure 3.1 on p. 3-3. Below those portions are the sections of Form 1040 where the results are reported.

Income (broadly conceived)	$ xx,xxx
Less: Exclusions	(x,xxx)
Gross Income	**$xx,xxx**
Less: Deductions for adjusted gross income	**(x,xxx)**

FORM 1040 (p. 1)

12	Business income or (loss). Attach Schedule C or C-EZ	
13	Capital gain or (loss). Attach Schedule D if required. If not required, check here ▶	☐
14	Other gains or (losses). Attach Form 4797	

Adjusted gross income.	$ xx,xxx
Less: The greater of total itemized deductions *or* the standard deduction.	(x,xxx)
Personal and dependency exemptions.	(x,xxx)
Taxable income	$ xx,xxx
Tax on taxable income (see Tax Tables or Tax Rate Schedules)	$ x,xxx
Less: Tax credits (including income taxes withheld and prepaid)	(xxx)
Tax due (or refund).	$ xxx

THE BIG PICTURE   Tax Solutions for the Real World

ALTERNATIVE USES OF PROPERTY

Recall the situation introduced in "The Big Picture" in Chapter 14. After 11 months, Alice has changed her mind about selling the house to her nephew for $275,000. As a result of a recent groundbreaking for an upscale real estate development nearby, the appraised value of the house has increased to $600,000. Alice has decided she needs to do something with the house other than let it remain vacant. She is considering the following options and has come to you for advice.

- Sell the house for approximately $600,000 using the services of a real estate agent (commission rate of 5 percent).
- Convert the house to a vacation home (100 percent personal use by Alice and her family), then sell it in two years.
- Convert the house to a vacation home (projected 40 percent rental use and 60 percent personal use), then sell it in two years.
- Sell her current home and move into the inherited house. She has owned and lived in the current home for 15 years, and her gain on the sale would be about $200,000. Since she is nearing retirement, she would live in the inherited house for only the required two-year minimum period and then sell it.

Alice expects the inherited house to continue to appreciate in value by about 5 percent per year. She plans on retiring from her job in two years and moving to a warmer climate. Until then, she is neutral as to which house she lives in. What advice can you offer Alice? **Read the chapter and formulate your response.**

15.1 GENERAL CONCEPT OF A NONTAXABLE EXCHANGE

A taxpayer who is going to replace a productive asset (e.g., machinery) used in a trade or business may structure the transactions as a sale of the old asset and the purchase of a new asset. When this approach is used, any realized gain or loss on the asset sale is recognized. The basis of the new asset is its cost. Alternatively, the taxpayer may be able to trade the old asset for the new asset. This exchange of assets may produce beneficial tax consequences by qualifying for nontaxable exchange treatment.

The tax law recognizes that nontaxable exchanges result in a change in the *form* but not in the *substance* of the taxpayer's relative economic position. The replacement property received in the exchange is viewed as substantially a continuation of the old investment.[1] Additional justification for nontaxable exchange treatment is that this type of transaction does not provide the taxpayer with the wherewithal to pay the tax on any realized gain.

The nonrecognition provisions for nontaxable exchanges do not apply to realized losses from the sale or exchange of personal use assets. Such losses are not recognized (are disallowed) because they are personal in nature and not because of any nonrecognition provision.

In a **nontaxable exchange**, realized gains or losses are not recognized. However, the nonrecognition is usually temporary. The recognition of gain or loss is *postponed* (deferred) until the property received in the nontaxable exchange is subsequently disposed of in a taxable transaction. This is accomplished by assigning a carryover basis to the replacement property.

> **LO.1**
> Understand the rationale for nonrecognition (postponement) of gain or loss in certain property transactions.

EXAMPLE 1

Debra exchanges property with an adjusted basis of $10,000 and a fair market value of $12,000 for property with a fair market value of $12,000. The transaction qualifies for nontaxable exchange treatment. Debra has a realized gain of $2,000 ($12,000 amount realized − $10,000 adjusted basis). Her recognized gain is $0. Her basis in the replacement property is a carryover basis of $10,000. Assume the replacement property is nondepreciable and Debra subsequently sells it for $12,000. Her realized and recognized gain will be the $2,000 gain that was postponed (deferred) in the nontaxable transaction. If the replacement property is depreciable, the carryover basis of $10,000 is used in calculating depreciation. ∎

In some nontaxable exchanges, only part of the property involved in the transaction qualifies for nonrecognition treatment. If the taxpayer receives cash or other nonqualifying property, part or all of the realized gain from the exchange is recognized. In these instances, gain is recognized because the taxpayer has changed or improved his or her relative economic position and has the wherewithal to pay income tax to the extent of cash or other property received.

It is important to distinguish between a nontaxable disposition, as the term is used in the statute, and a tax-free transaction. First, a direct exchange is not required in all circumstances (e.g., replacement of involuntarily converted property). Second, as previously mentioned, the term *nontaxable* refers to postponement of recognition via a carryover basis. In a *tax-free* transaction, the nonrecognition is permanent (e.g., see the discussion later in the chapter of the § 121 exclusion of realized gain on the sale of a personal residence). Therefore, the basis of any property acquired in a tax-free transaction does not depend on the basis of the property disposed of by the taxpayer.

---

[1]Reg. § 1.1002–1(c).

15.2 LIKE-KIND EXCHANGES—§ 1031

LO.2

Apply the nonrecognition provisions and basis determination rules for like-kind exchanges.

Section 1031 provides for nontaxable exchange treatment if the following requirements are satisfied:[2]

• The form of the transaction is an exchange.
• Both the property transferred and the property received are held either for productive use in a trade or business or for investment.
• The property is like-kind property.

Like-kind exchanges include business for business, business for investment, investment for business, or investment for investment property. Property held for personal use, inventory, and partnership interests (both limited and general) do not qualify under the like-kind exchange provisions. Securities, even though held for investment, do not qualify for like-kind exchange treatment.

The nonrecognition provision for like-kind exchanges is *mandatory* rather than elective. A taxpayer who wants to recognize a realized gain or loss will have to structure the transaction in a form that does not satisfy the statutory requirements for a like-kind exchange. This topic is discussed further under Tax Planning.

LIKE-KIND PROPERTY

"The words 'like-kind' refer to the nature or character of the property and not to its grade or quality. One kind or class of property may not . . . be exchanged for property of a different kind or class."[3]

The term *like-kind* is intended to be interpreted very broadly. However, three categories of exchanges are not included. First, livestock of different sexes do not qualify as like-kind property. Second, real estate can be exchanged only for other real estate, and personalty can be exchanged only for other personalty. For example, the exchange of a machine (personalty) for an office building (realty) is not a like-kind exchange. *Real estate* (or realty) includes principally rental buildings, office and store buildings, manufacturing plants, warehouses, and land. It is immaterial whether real estate is improved or unimproved. Thus, unimproved land can be exchanged for an apartment house. Personalty includes principally machines, equipment, trucks, automobiles, furniture, and fixtures. Third, real property located in the United States exchanged for foreign real property (and vice versa) does not qualify as like-kind property.

---

[2]§ 1031(a) and Reg. § 1.1031(a)–1(a).

[3]Reg. § 1.1031(a)–1(b).

TAX in the NEWS

MORE IRS OVERSIGHT OF § 1031 EXCHANGES

The IRS has announced that it is stepping up its oversight and enforcement of § 1031 like-kind exchanges. The announcement is in response to a report issued by the Treasury Inspector General for Tax Administration. According to the report, clearer IRS guidance on § 1031 exchanges will:

- Help taxpayers understand the qualification requirements for a § 1031 exchange.
- Help deter unscrupulous promoters from trying to abuse the use of § 1031 exchanges.

Common abuses include using properties that are not like kind, failing to comply with the statutory requirements by including related parties in an exchange, and incorrectly determining the basis for the properties involved.

Section 1031 exchanges are reported on Form 8824 when the taxpayer files his or her income tax return. During the period from 1998 to 2004, the number of Forms 8824 filed doubled (from 338,500 to 677,000). During the same period, the deferred income resulting from § 1031 exchanges more than tripled to $73.6 billion. Of the Forms 8824 filed, 65 percent were attached to Forms 1040 with the balance being filed by partnerships and corporations.

EXAMPLE 2

Wade made the following exchanges during the taxable year:

a. Inventory for a machine used in business.
b. Land held for investment for a building used in business.
c. Stock held for investment for equipment used in business.
d. A light-duty business truck for a light-duty business truck.
e. An automobile used for personal transportation for an automobile used in business.
f. Livestock for livestock of a different sex.
g. Land held for investment in New York for land held for investment in London.

Exchanges (b), investment real property for business real property, and (d), business personalty for business personalty, qualify as exchanges of like-kind property. Exchanges (a), inventory; (c), stock; (e), personal use automobile (not held for business or investment purposes); (f), livestock of different sexes; and (g), U.S. and foreign real estate do not qualify. ■

A special provision relates to the location where personal property is used. Personal property used predominantly within the United States and personal property used predominantly outside the United States are not like-kind property. The location of use for the personal property given up is its location during the two-year period ending on the date of disposition of the property. The location of use for the personal property received is its location during the two-year period beginning on the date of the acquisition.

EXAMPLE 3

In October 2010, Walter exchanges a machine used in his factory in Denver for a machine that qualifies as like-kind property. In January 2011, the factory, including the machine, is moved to Berlin, Germany. As of January 2011, the exchange is not an exchange of like-kind property. The predominant use of the original machine was in the United States, whereas the predominant use of the new machine is foreign. ■

Another special provision applies if the taxpayers involved in the exchange are *related parties* under § 267(b). To qualify for like-kind exchange treatment, the taxpayer and the related party must not dispose of the like-kind property received in the exchange within the two-year period following the date of the exchange. If such an early disposition does occur, the postponed gain is recognized as of the date of the early disposition. Dispositions due to death, involuntary conversions, and certain non-tax avoidance transactions are not treated as early dispositions.

Regulations dealing with § 1031 like-kind exchange treatment provide that if the exchange transaction involves multiple assets of a business (e.g., a television station for another television station), the determination of whether the assets qualify as like-kind property will not be made at the business level.[4] Instead, the underlying assets must be evaluated.

The Regulations also provide for greater specificity in determining whether depreciable tangible personal property is of a like kind or class. Such property held for productive use in a business is of a like class only if the exchanged property is within the same *general business asset class* (as specified by the IRS in Revenue Procedure 87–57 or as subsequently modified) or the same *product class* (as specified by the Department of Commerce). Property included in a general business asset class is evaluated under this system rather than under the product class system.

The following are examples of general business asset classes:

- Office furniture, fixtures, and equipment.
- Information systems (computers and peripheral equipment).
- Airplanes.
- Automobiles and taxis.
- Buses.
- Light general-purpose trucks.
- Heavy general-purpose trucks.

These Regulations have made it more difficult for depreciable tangible personal property to qualify for § 1031 like-kind exchange treatment. For example, the exchange of office equipment for a computer does not qualify as an exchange of like-kind property. Even though both assets are depreciable tangible personal property, they are not like-kind property because they are in different general business asset classes.

EXCHANGE REQUIREMENT

The transaction must involve a direct exchange of property to qualify as a like-kind exchange. The sale of old property and the purchase of new property, even though like kind, is generally not an exchange. However, if the two transactions are mutually dependent, the IRS may treat them as a like-kind exchange. For example, if the taxpayer sells an old business machine to a dealer and purchases a new one from the same dealer, like-kind exchange treatment could result.[5]

The taxpayer may want to avoid nontaxable exchange treatment. Recognition of gain gives the taxpayer a higher basis for depreciation (see Example 35). To the extent that such gains would, if recognized, either receive favorable capital gain treatment or be passive activity income that could offset passive activity losses, it might be preferable to avoid the nonrecognition provisions through an indirect exchange transaction. For example, a taxpayer may sell property to one individual, recognize the gain, and subsequently purchase similar property from another individual. The taxpayer may also want to avoid nontaxable exchange treatment so that a realized loss can be recognized.

If the exchange is a delayed (nonsimultaneous) exchange, there are time limits on its completion. In a delayed like-kind exchange, one party fails to take immediate title to the new property because it has not yet been identified. The Code provides that the delayed swap will qualify as a like-kind exchange if the following requirements are satisfied:

- *Identification period.* The new property must be identified within 45 days of the date when the old property was transferred.
- *Exchange period.* The new property must be received by the earlier of the following:
  - *Within 180 days of the date when the old property was transferred.*
  - *The due date (including extensions) for the tax return covering the year of the transfer.*

---

[4]Reg. § 1.1031(j)–1.   [5]Rev.Rul. 61–119, 1961–1 C.B. 395.

TAX in the NEWS

WHAT HAPPENS TO § 1031 DEFERRAL IF THE QUALIFIED INTERMEDIARY DEFAULTS?

Normally, the IRS takes the position that the provisions of § 1031 are to be interpreted narrowly with respect to delayed § 1031 like-kind exchanges. In Revenue Procedure 2010–14, however, the IRS has announced an exception to this strict compliance requirement.

The exception applies if the 180-day time requirement for a delayed § 1031 like-kind exchange is not satisfied because the qualified intermediary defaults due to a bankruptcy or receivership proceeding. In this situation, no gain is recognized by the taxpayer until a payment is received from the qualified intermediary or the bankruptcy trustee. As payments are received, gain is recognized using the gross profit ratio method.

Are these time limits firm, or can they be extended due to unforeseen circumstances? Indications are that the IRS will allow no deviation from either the identification period or the exchange period even when events outside the taxpayer's control preclude strict compliance. See the exception to strict compliance provided for in Revenue Procedure 2010–14 in the Tax in the News above.

BOOT

If the taxpayer in a like-kind exchange gives or receives some property that is not like-kind property, recognition may occur. Property that is not like-kind property, including cash, is referred to as **boot**. Although the term *boot* does not appear in the Code, tax practitioners commonly use it rather than saying "property that is not like-kind property."

The *receipt* of boot will trigger recognition of gain if there is realized gain. The amount of the recognized gain is the *lesser* of the boot received or the realized gain (realized gain serves as the ceiling on recognition).

EXAMPLE 4

Emily and Fran exchange machinery, and the exchange qualifies as like kind under § 1031. Since Emily's machinery (adjusted basis of $20,000) is worth $24,000 and Fran's machine has a fair market value of $19,000, Fran also gives Emily cash of $5,000. Emily's recognized gain is $4,000, the lesser of the realized gain ($24,000 amount realized − $20,000 adjusted basis = $4,000) or the fair market value of the boot received ($5,000). ■

EXAMPLE 5

Assume the same facts as in the previous example, except that Fran's machine is worth $21,000 (not $19,000). Under these circumstances, Fran gives Emily cash of $3,000 to make up the difference. Emily's recognized gain is $3,000, the lesser of the realized gain of $4,000 ($24,000 amount realized − $20,000 adjusted basis) or the fair market value of the boot received of $3,000. ■

The receipt of boot does not result in recognition if there is realized loss.

EXAMPLE 6

Assume the same facts as in Example 4, except that the adjusted basis of Emily's machine is $30,000. Emily's realized loss is $6,000 ($24,000 amount realized − $30,000 adjusted basis). The receipt of the boot of $5,000 does not trigger recognition. Therefore, the recognized loss is $0. ■

The *giving* of boot usually does not trigger recognition. If the boot given is cash, no realized gain or loss is recognized.

EXAMPLE 7

Fred and Gary exchange equipment in a like-kind exchange. Fred receives equipment with a fair market value of $25,000 and transfers equipment worth $21,000 (adjusted basis of $15,000) and cash of $4,000. Fred's realized gain is $6,000 ($25,000 amount realized − $15,000 adjusted basis − $4,000 cash). However, none of the realized gain is recognized. ■

If, however, the boot given is appreciated or depreciated property, gain or loss is recognized to the extent of the difference between the adjusted basis and the fair market value of the boot. For this purpose, *appreciated or depreciated property* is defined as property whose adjusted basis is not equal to the fair market value.

EXAMPLE 8

Assume the same facts as in the previous example, except that Fred transfers equipment worth $10,000 (adjusted basis of $12,000) and boot worth $15,000 (adjusted basis of $9,000). Fred's realized gain appears to be $4,000 ($25,000 amount realized − $21,000 adjusted basis). Since realization previously has served as a ceiling on recognition, it appears that the recognized gain is $4,000 (lower of realized gain of $4,000 or amount of appreciation on boot of $6,000). However, the recognized gain actually is $6,000 (full amount of the appreciation on the boot). In effect, Fred must calculate the like-kind and boot parts of the transaction separately. That is, the realized loss of $2,000 on the like-kind property is not recognized ($10,000 fair market value − $12,000 adjusted basis), and the $6,000 realized gain on the boot is recognized ($15,000 fair market value − $9,000 adjusted basis). ∎

BASIS AND HOLDING PERIOD OF PROPERTY RECEIVED

If an exchange does not qualify as nontaxable under § 1031, gain or loss is recognized, and the basis of property received in the exchange is the property's fair market value. If the exchange qualifies for nonrecognition, the basis of property received must be adjusted to reflect any postponed (deferred) gain or loss. The *basis of like-kind property* received in the exchange is the property's fair market value less postponed gain or plus postponed loss. If the exchange partially qualifies for nonrecognition (if recognition is associated with boot), the basis of like-kind property received in the exchange is the property's fair market value less postponed gain or plus postponed loss. The *basis* of any *boot* received is the boot's fair market value.

If there is a postponed loss, nonrecognition creates a situation in which the taxpayer has recovered *less* than the cost or other basis of the property exchanged in an amount equal to the unrecognized loss. If there is a postponed gain, the taxpayer has recovered *more* than the cost or other basis of the property exchanged in an amount equal to the unrecognized gain.

EXAMPLE 9

Jaime exchanges a building (used in his business) with an adjusted basis of $30,000 and a fair market value of $38,000 for land with a fair market value of $38,000. The land is to be held as an investment. The exchange qualifies as like kind (an exchange of business real property for investment real property). Thus, the basis of the land is $30,000 (the land's fair market value of $38,000 less the $8,000 postponed gain on the building). If the land is later sold for its fair market value of $38,000, the $8,000 postponed gain is recognized. ∎

EXAMPLE 10

Assume the same facts as in the previous example, except that the building has an adjusted basis of $48,000 and a fair market value of only $38,000. The basis in the newly acquired land is $48,000 (fair market value of $38,000 plus the $10,000 postponed loss on the building). If the land is later sold for its fair market value of $38,000, the $10,000 postponed loss is recognized. ∎

The Code provides an alternative approach for determining the basis of like-kind property received:

    Adjusted basis of like-kind property surrendered
    + Adjusted basis of boot given
    + Gain recognized
    − Fair market value of boot received
    − Loss recognized
    = *Basis of like-kind property received*

This approach is logical in terms of the recovery of capital doctrine. That is, the unrecovered cost or other basis is increased by additional cost (boot given) or decreased by cost recovered (boot received). Any gain recognized is included in the basis of the new property. The taxpayer has been taxed on this amount and is now entitled to recover it tax-free. Any loss recognized is deducted from the basis of the new property. The taxpayer has received a tax benefit on that amount.

The holding period of the property surrendered in the exchange carries over and *tacks on* to the holding period of the like-kind property received.[6] The holding period for boot received in a like-kind exchange begins with the date of the exchange. See Chapter 16 for a discussion of the relevance of the holding period.

Depreciation recapture potential carries over to the property received in a like-kind exchange.[7] See Chapter 17 for a discussion of this topic.

The following comprehensive example illustrates the like-kind exchange rules.

EXAMPLE 11

Vicki exchanged the following old machines for new machines in five independent like-kind exchanges:

Exchange	Adjusted Basis of Old Machine	Fair Market Value of Old Machine	Fair Market Value of New Machine	Adjusted Basis of Boot Given	Fair Market Value of Boot Received
1	$4,000	$ 9,000	$9,000	$ –0–	$ –0–
2	4,000	6,000	9,000	3,000	–0–
3	4,000	3,000	9,000	6,000	–0–
4	4,000	12,000	9,000	–0–	3,000
5	4,000	3,800	3,500	–0–	300

Vicki's realized and recognized gains and losses and the basis of each of the like-kind properties received are as follows:

Exchange	Realized Gain (Loss)	Recognized Gain (Loss)	Old Adj. Basis	+	Boot Given	+	Gain Recognized	–	Boot Received	=	New Basis
1	$ 5,000	$ –(0)–	$4,000	+	$ –0–	+	$ –0–	–	$ –0–	=	$ 4,000*
2	2,000	–(0)–	4,000	+	3,000	+	–0–	–	–0–	=	7,000*
3	(1,000)	–(0)–	4,000	+	6,000	+	–0–	–	–0–	=	10,000**
4	8,000	3,000	4,000	+	–0–	+	3,000	–	3,000	=	4,000*
5	(200)	–(0)–	4,000	+	–0–	+	–0–	–	300	=	3,700**

*Basis may be determined in gain situations under the alternative method by subtracting the gain not recognized from the fair market value of the new property:
$9,000 – $5,000 = $4,000 for exchange 1.
$9,000 – $2,000 = $7,000 for exchange 2.
$9,000 – $5,000 = $4,000 for exchange 4.

**In loss situations, basis may be determined by adding the loss not recognized to the fair market value of the new property:
$9,000 + $1,000 = $10,000 for exchange 3.
$3,500 + $200 = $3,700 for exchange 5.
The basis of the boot received is the boot's fair market value. ∎

If the taxpayer either assumes a liability or takes property subject to a liability, the amount of the liability is treated as boot given. For the taxpayer whose liability is assumed or whose property is taken subject to the liability, the amount of the liability is treated as boot received. Example 12 illustrates the effect of such a liability. In

[6]§ 1223(1) and Reg. § 1.1223–1(a). For this carryover holding period rule to apply to like-kind exchanges after March 1, 1954, the like-kind property surrendered must have been either a capital asset or § 1231 property. See Chapters 16 and 17 for the discussion of capital assets and § 1231 property.
[7]Reg. §§ 1.1245–2(a)(4) and 1.1250–2(d)(1).

addition, the example illustrates the tax consequences for both parties involved in the like-kind exchange.

EXAMPLE 12

Jane and Leo exchange real estate investments. Jane gives up property with an adjusted basis of $250,000 (fair market value of $400,000) that is subject to a mortgage of $75,000 (assumed by Leo). In return for this property, Jane receives property with a fair market value of $300,000 (adjusted basis of $200,000) and cash of $25,000.

- Jane's realized gain is $150,000. She gave up property with an adjusted basis of $250,000. Jane received $400,000 from the exchange ($300,000 fair market value of like-kind property plus $100,000 boot received). The boot received consists of the $25,000 cash received from Leo and Jane's mortgage of $75,000, which Leo assumes.
- Jane's recognized gain is $100,000. The realized gain of $150,000 is recognized to the extent of boot received.
- Jane's basis in the real estate received from Leo is $250,000. This basis can be computed by subtracting the postponed gain ($50,000) from the fair market value of the real estate received ($300,000). It can also be computed by adding the recognized gain ($100,000) to the adjusted basis of the real estate given up ($250,000) and subtracting the boot received ($100,000).
- Leo's realized gain is $100,000. Leo gave up property with an adjusted basis of $200,000 plus boot of $100,000 ($75,000 mortgage assumed + $25,000 cash) or a total of $300,000. Leo received $400,000 from the exchange (fair market value of like-kind property received).
- Leo has no recognized gain because he did not receive any boot. The entire realized gain of $100,000 is postponed.
- Leo's basis in the real estate received from Jane is $300,000. This basis can be computed by subtracting the postponed gain ($100,000) from the fair market value of the real estate received ($400,000). It can also be computed by adding the boot given ($75,000 mortgage assumed by Leo + $25,000 cash) to the adjusted basis of the real estate given up ($200,000).[8] ∎

REPORTING CONSIDERATIONS

Section 1031 transactions are reported on Form 8824 (Like-Kind Exchanges). This form should be used even though the like-kind exchange transaction results in no recognized gain or loss. It must be filed with the regular return for the tax year in which the taxpayer transfers property in a like-kind exchange.

If the like-kind exchange is with a related party, additional Forms 8824 must be filed for the following two years.

15.3 INVOLUNTARY CONVERSIONS—§ 1033

LO.3

Explain the nonrecognition provisions available on the involuntary conversion of property.

Section 1033 provides that a taxpayer who suffers an involuntary conversion of property may postpone recognition of *gain* realized from the conversion. The objective of this provision is to provide relief to the taxpayer who has suffered hardship and does not have the wherewithal to pay the tax on any gain realized from the conversion. Postponement of realized gain is permitted to the extent that the taxpayer *reinvests* the amount realized from the conversion in replacement property. The rules for nonrecognition of gain are as follows:

- If the amount reinvested in replacement property *equals or exceeds* the amount realized, realized gain is *not recognized*.
- If the amount reinvested in replacement property is *less than* the amount realized, realized gain *is recognized* to the extent of the deficiency.

---

[8]Example (2) of Reg. § 1.1031(d)–2 illustrates a special situation in which both the buyer and the seller transfer liabilities that are assumed by the other party or both parties acquire property that is subject to a liability.

TAX *in* the NEWS	ECONOMIC DEVELOPMENT GONE WRONG

One of the messages of the U.S. Supreme Court in *Kelo v. City of New London* was that eminent domain proceedings can be justified if the "taking" potentially will lead to future economic development. Now it appears that the message may be a two-way street: a city may attempt to use eminent domain proceedings against a developer if promised development does not occur.

The city of Boston is threatening such a taking if a prominent property is not developed soon. The site was the location of Filene's Basement, a popular retailer that closed in September 2007. A group of investors led by Vornado Realty Trust acquired the property and nearby buildings, planning to erect a $700 million mixed-use development on the site. Most of the buildings were demolished in 2008, but then construction stalled. At present, the site is a vacant lot flanked by two partially demolished structures. The city, led by Mayor Thomas Menino, claims that the property is an eyesore and that the city has the right to seize it if it is not developed soon.

Source: Adapted from Christina S. N. Lewis, "Mayor Battles Vornado in Boston," *Wall Street Journal*, April 14, 2010, p. B1.

If a *loss* occurs on an involuntary conversion, § 1033 does not modify the normal rules for loss recognition. That is, if a realized loss would otherwise be recognized, § 1033 does not change the result.

INVOLUNTARY CONVERSION DEFINED

An **involuntary conversion** results from the destruction (complete or partial), theft, seizure, requisition or condemnation, or sale or exchange under threat or imminence of requisition or condemnation of the taxpayer's property.[9] To prove the existence of a threat or imminence of condemnation, the taxpayer must obtain confirmation that there has been a decision to acquire the property for public use. In addition, the taxpayer must have reasonable grounds to believe the property will be taken.[10] The property does not have to be sold to the authority threatening to condemn it to qualify for § 1033 postponement. If the taxpayer satisfies the confirmation and reasonable grounds requirements, he or she can sell the property to another party.[11] Likewise, the sale of property to a condemning authority by a taxpayer who acquired the property from its former owner with the knowledge that the property was under threat of condemnation also qualifies as an involuntary conversion under § 1033.[12] A voluntary act, such as a taxpayer destroying the property by arson, is not an involuntary conversion.[13]

COMPUTING THE AMOUNT REALIZED

The amount realized from the condemnation of property usually includes only the amount received as compensation for the property.[14] Any amount received that is designated as severance damages by both the government and the taxpayer is not included in the amount realized. *Severance awards* usually occur when only a portion of the property is condemned (e.g., a strip of land is taken to build a highway). Severance damages are awarded because the value of the taxpayer's remaining property has declined as a result of the condemnation. Such damages are a tax-free recovery of capital and reduce the basis of the property. However, if either of the following

[9]§ 1033(a) and Reg. §§ 1.1033(a)−1(a) and −2(a)
[10]Rev.Rul. 63–221, 1963–2 C.B. 332, and *Joseph P. Balistrieri*, 38 TCM 526, T.C.Memo. 1979–115.
[11]Rev.Rul. 81–180, 1981–2 C.B. 161.
[12]Rev.Rul. 81–181, 1981–2 C.B. 162.
[13]Rev.Rul. 82–74, 1982–1 C.B. 110.
[14]*Pioneer Real Estate Co.*, 47 B.T.A. 886 (1942), *acq.* 1943 C.B. 18.

requirements is satisfied, the nonrecognition provision of § 1033 applies to the severance damages:

- The severance damages are used to restore the usability of the remaining property.
- The usefulness of the remaining property is destroyed by the condemnation, and the property is sold and replaced at a cost equal to or exceeding the sum of the condemnation award, severance damages, and sales proceeds.

EXAMPLE 13	The government condemns a portion of Ron's farmland to build part of an interstate highway. Because the highway denies his cattle access to a pond and some grazing land, Ron receives severance damages in addition to the condemnation proceeds for the land taken. Ron must reduce the basis of the property by the amount of the severance damages. If the amount of the severance damages received exceeds the adjusted basis, Ron recognizes gain. ■

EXAMPLE 14	Assume the same facts as in the previous example, except that Ron uses the proceeds from the condemnation and the severance damages to build another pond and to clear woodland for grazing. Therefore, all the proceeds are eligible for § 1033 treatment. There is no possibility of gain recognition as the result of the amount of the severance damages received exceeding the adjusted basis. ■

REPLACEMENT PROPERTY

The requirements for replacement property generally are more restrictive than those for like-kind property under § 1031. The basic requirement is that the replacement property be similar or related in service or use to the involuntarily converted property.[15]

Different interpretations of the phrase *similar or related in service or use* apply depending on whether the involuntarily converted property is held by an *owner-user* or by an *owner-investor* (e.g., lessor). A taxpayer who uses the property in his or her trade or business is subject to a more restrictive test in terms of acquiring replacement property. For an owner-user, the *functional use test* applies, and for an owner-investor, the *taxpayer use test* applies.

Taxpayer Use Test

The taxpayer use test for owner-investors provides the taxpayer with more flexibility in terms of what qualifies as replacement property than does the functional use test for owner-users. Essentially, the properties must be used by the taxpayer (the owner-investor) in similar endeavors. For example, rental property held by an owner-investor qualifies if replaced by other rental property, regardless of the type of rental property involved. The test is met when an investor replaces a manufacturing plant with a wholesale grocery warehouse if both properties are held for the production of rent income.[16] The replacement of a rental residence with a personal residence does not meet the test.[17]

Functional Use Test

The functional use test applies to owner-users (e.g., a manufacturer whose manufacturing plant is destroyed by fire is required to replace the plant with another facility of similar functional use). Under this test, the taxpayer's use of the replacement property and of the involuntarily converted property must be the same. Replacing a manufacturing plant with a wholesale grocery warehouse does not meet this test. Neither does replacing a rental residence with a personal residence.

---

[15]§ 1033(a) and Reg. § 1.1033(a)–1.

[16]*Loco Realty Co. v. Comm.*, 62–2 USTC ¶9657, 10 AFTR 2d 5359, 306 F.2d 207 (CA–8, 1962).

[17]Rev.Rul. 70–466, 1970–2 C.B. 165.

CONCEPT SUMMARY 15.1

Replacement Property Tests

Type of Property and User	Like-Kind Test	Taxpayer Use Test	Functional Use Test
Land used by a manufacturing company is condemned by a local government authority.	X		
Apartment and land held by an investor are sold due to the threat or imminence of condemnation.	X		
An investor's rented shopping mall is destroyed by fire; the mall may be replaced by other rental properties (e.g., an apartment building).		X	
A manufacturing plant is destroyed by fire; replacement property must consist of another manufacturing plant that is functionally the same as the property converted.			X
Personal residence of taxpayer is condemned by a local government authority; replacement property must consist of another personal residence.			X

Special Rules

Under one set of circumstances, the broader replacement rules for like-kind exchanges are substituted for the narrow replacement rules normally used for involuntary conversions. This beneficial provision applies if business real property or investment real property is condemned. This provision gives the taxpayer substantially more flexibility in selecting replacement property. For example, improved real property can be replaced with unimproved real property.

The rules concerning the nature of replacement property are illustrated in Concept Summary 15.1.

TIME LIMITATION ON REPLACEMENT

The taxpayer normally has a two-year period after the close of the taxable year in which gain is realized from an involuntary conversion to replace the property (*the latest date*).[18] This rule affords as much as three years from the date of realization of gain to replace the property if the realization of gain took place on the first day of the taxable year.[19] If the involuntary conversion involved the condemnation of real property used in a trade or business or held for investment, a three-year period is substituted for the normal two-year period. In this case, the taxpayer can actually have as much as four years from the date of realization of gain to replace the property.

EXAMPLE 15

Megan's warehouse is destroyed by fire on December 16, 2010. The adjusted basis is $325,000. Megan receives $400,000 from the insurance company on January 10, 2011. She is a calendar year taxpayer. The latest date for replacement is December 31, 2013 (the end of the taxable year in which realized gain occurred plus two years). The critical date is not the date the involuntary conversion occurred, but rather the date of gain realization. ■

EXAMPLE 16

Assume the same facts as in the previous example, except that Megan's warehouse is condemned. The latest date for replacement is December 31, 2014 (the end of the taxable year in which realized gain occurred plus three years). ■

---

[18]§§ 1033(a)(2)(B) and (g)(4) and Reg. § 1.1033(a)–2(c)(3).

[19]The taxpayer can apply for an extension of this time period anytime before its expiration [Reg. § 1.1033(a)–2(c)(3)]. Also, the period for filing the application for extension can be extended if the taxpayer shows reasonable cause.

The *earliest date* for replacement typically is the date the involuntary conversion occurs. However, if the property is condemned, it is possible to replace the condemned property before this date. In this case, the earliest date is the date of the threat or imminence of requisition or condemnation of the property. The purpose of this provision is to enable the taxpayer to make an orderly replacement of the condemned property.

EXAMPLE 17

Assume the same facts as in Example 16. Megan can replace the warehouse before December 16, 2010 (the condemnation date). The earliest date for replacement is the date of the threat or imminence of requisition or condemnation of the warehouse. ∎

NONRECOGNITION OF GAIN

Nonrecognition of gain can be either mandatory or elective, depending on whether the conversion is direct (into replacement property) or indirect (into money).

Direct Conversion

If the conversion is directly into replacement property rather than into money, non-recognition of realized gain is *mandatory*. In this case, the basis of the replacement property is the same as the adjusted basis of the converted property. Direct conversion is rare in practice and usually involves condemnations.

EXAMPLE 18

Lupe's property, with an adjusted basis of $20,000, is condemned by the state. Lupe receives property with a fair market value of $50,000 as compensation for the property taken. Since the nonrecognition of realized gain is mandatory for direct conversions, Lupe's realized gain of $30,000 is not recognized, and the basis of the replacement property is $20,000 (adjusted basis of the condemned property). ∎

Conversion into Money

If the conversion is into money, at the election of the taxpayer, the realized gain is recognized only to the extent the amount realized from the involuntary conversion exceeds the cost of the qualifying replacement property.[20] This is the usual case, and nonrecognition (postponement) is *elective*. If the election is not made, the realized gain is recognized.

The basis of the replacement property is the property's cost less postponed (deferred) gain.[21] If the election to postpone gain is made, the holding period of the replacement property includes the holding period of the converted property.

Section 1033 applies *only to gains* and *not to losses*. Losses from involuntary conversions are recognized if the property is held for business or income-producing purposes. Personal casualty losses are recognized, but condemnation losses related to personal use assets (e.g., a personal residence) are neither recognized nor postponed.

EXAMPLE 19

Walt's building (used in his trade or business), with an adjusted basis of $50,000, is destroyed by fire on October 5, 2011. Walt is a calendar year taxpayer. On November 17, 2011, he receives an insurance reimbursement of $100,000 for the loss. Walt invests $80,000 in a new building.

- Walt has until December 31, 2013, to make the new investment and qualify for the nonrecognition election.
- Walt's realized gain is $50,000 ($100,000 insurance proceeds received − $50,000 adjusted basis of old building).
- Assuming the replacement property qualifies as similar or related in service or use, Walt's recognized gain is $20,000. He reinvested $20,000 less than the insurance proceeds received ($100,000 proceeds − $80,000 reinvested). Therefore, his realized gain is recognized to that extent.

---

[20]§ 1033(a)(2)(A) and Reg. § 1.1033(a)–2(c)(1).   [21]§ 1033(b).

- Walt's basis in the new building is $50,000. This is the building's cost of $80,000 less the postponed gain of $30,000 (realized gain of $50,000 − recognized gain of $20,000).
- The computation of realization, recognition, and basis would apply even if Walt was a real estate dealer and the building destroyed by fire was part of his inventory. Unlike § 1031, § 1033 generally does not exclude inventory. ∎

Assume the same facts as in the previous example, except that Walt receives only $45,000 of insurance proceeds. He has a realized and recognized loss of $5,000. The basis of the new building is the building's cost of $80,000. If the destroyed building had been held for personal use, the recognized loss would have been subject to the following additional limitations.[22] The loss of $5,000 would have been limited to the decline in fair market value of the property, and the amount of the loss would have been reduced first by $100 and then by 10% of adjusted gross income (refer to Chapter 7). ∎

INVOLUNTARY CONVERSION OF A PERSONAL RESIDENCE

The tax consequences of the involuntary conversion of a personal residence depend on whether the conversion is a casualty or condemnation and whether a realized loss or gain results.

Loss Situations

If the conversion is a condemnation, the realized loss is not recognized. Loss from the condemnation of a personal use asset is never recognized. If the conversion is a casualty (a loss from fire, storm, etc.), the loss is recognized subject to the personal casualty loss limitations (refer to Chapter 7).

Gain Situations

If the conversion is a casualty, theft, or condemnation, the gain may be postponed under § 1033 or excluded under § 121. That is, the taxpayer may treat the involuntary conversion as a sale under the exclusion of gain rules relating to the sale of a personal residence under § 121 (presented subsequently).

Under certain circumstances, the taxpayer may use both the § 121 exclusion of gain and the § 1033 postponement of gain provisions. See the discussion under Involuntary Conversion and Using §§ 121 and 1033 later in this chapter.

REPORTING CONSIDERATIONS

Involuntary conversions from casualty and theft are reported first on Form 4684, Casualties and Thefts. Casualty and theft losses on personal use property for the individual taxpayer are carried from Form 4684 to Schedule A of Form 1040. For other casualty and theft items, the Form 4684 amounts are generally reported on Form 4797, Sales of Business Property, unless Form 4797 is not required. In the latter case, the amounts are reported directly on the tax return involved.

Except for personal use property, recognized gains and losses from involuntary conversions other than by casualty and theft are reported on Form 4797. As stated previously, if the property involved in the involuntary conversion (other than by casualty and theft) is personal use property, any realized loss is not recognized. Any realized gain is treated as gain on a voluntary sale.

What procedure should be followed if the taxpayer intends to acquire qualifying replacement property but has not done so by the time the tax return is filed? The taxpayer should elect § 1033 and report all of the details of the transaction on a statement attached to the return. Though a tax form (Form 8824) is available for § 1031 like-kind exchanges, no special form is provided for § 1033 transactions. When the qualifying replacement property is acquired, the taxpayer

---

[22]§ 165(c)(3) and Reg. § 1.165–7.

should attach a statement to the tax return that contains relevant information on the replacement property.

An amended return must be filed if qualified replacement property is not acquired during the statutory time period allowed. An amended return also is required if the cost of the replacement property is less than the amount realized from the involuntary conversion. In this case, the return would recognize the portion of the realized gain that can no longer be deferred.

15.4 SALE OF A RESIDENCE—§ 121

LO.4

Describe the provision for the permanent exclusion of gain on the sale of a personal residence.

A taxpayer's **personal residence** is a personal use asset. Therefore, a realized loss from the sale of a personal residence is not recognized.[23]

A realized gain from the sale of a personal residence is subject to taxation. However, favorable relief from recognition of gain is provided in the form of the **§ 121 exclusion**. Under this provision, a taxpayer can exclude up to $250,000 of realized gain on the sale.[24]

REQUIREMENTS FOR EXCLUSION TREATMENT

To qualify for exclusion treatment, at the date of the sale, the residence must have been *owned* and *used* by the taxpayer as the principal residence for at least two years during the five-year period ending on the date of the sale.[25]

EXAMPLE 21

Melissa sells her principal residence on September 18, 2011. She had purchased it on July 5, 2009, and lived in it since then. The sale of Melissa's residence qualifies for the § 121 exclusion. ■

The five-year window enables the taxpayer to qualify for the § 121 exclusion even though the property is not his or her principal residence at the date of the sale.

EXAMPLE 22

Benjamin sells his former principal residence on August 16, 2011. He had purchased it on April 1, 2003, and lived in it until July 1, 2010, when he converted it to rental property. Even though the property is rental property on August 16, 2011, rather than Benjamin's principal residence, the sale qualifies for the § 121 exclusion.[26] During the five-year period from August 16, 2006, to August 16, 2011, Benjamin owned and used the property as his principal residence for at least two years. ■

Taxpayers might be tempted to make liberal use of the § 121 exclusion as a means of speculating when the price of residential housing is rising. Without any time restriction on its use, § 121 would permit the exclusion of realized gain on multiple sales of principal residences. The Code curbs this approach by denying the application of the § 121 exclusion to sales occurring within two years of its last use.[27]

EXAMPLE 23

Seth sells his principal residence (the first residence) in June 2010 for $150,000 (realized gain of $60,000). He then buys and sells the following (all of which qualify as principal residences):

	Date of Purchase	Date of Sale	Amount Involved
Second residence	July 2010		$160,000
Second residence		April 2011	180,000
Third residence	May 2011		200,000

---

[23]§ 165(c).

[24]§ 121(b).

[25]§ 121(a). However, § 121(d)(10) provides that exclusion treatment does not apply if the residence was acquired in a like-kind exchange within the prior five years of the sale of the residence.

[26]However, any realized gain on the sale that is attributable to depreciation is not eligible for the § 121 exclusion. See Example 40.

[27]§ 121(b)(3).

Because multiple sales have taken place within a period of two years, § 121 does not apply to the sale of the second residence. Thus, the realized gain of $20,000 [$180,000 (selling price) − $160,000 (purchase price)] must be recognized. ∎

EXCEPTIONS TO THE TWO-YEAR OWNERSHIP RULE

The two-year ownership and use requirement and the "only once every two years" provision could create a hardship for taxpayers in certain situations that are beyond their control. Thus, under the following special circumstances, the requirements are waived:[28]

* Change in place of employment.
* Health.
* To the extent provided in the Regulations, other unforeseen circumstances.

These three exceptions have recently been amplified by the IRS and are discussed in the sections that follow.

Change in Place of Employment

In order for this exception to apply, the distance requirements applicable to the deductibility of moving expenses must be satisfied (see Chapter 9).[29] Consequently, the location of the taxpayer's new employment must be at least 50 miles further from the old residence than the old residence was from the old job. The house must be used as the principal residence of the taxpayer at the time of the change in the place of employment. Employment includes the commencement of employment with a new employer, the continuation of employment with the same employer, and the commencement or continuation of self-employment.

> **EXAMPLE 24**
>
> Assume the same facts as in the previous example, except that in March 2011, Seth's employer transfers him to a job in another state that is 400 miles away. Thus, the sale of the second residence and the purchase of the third residence were due to relocation of employment. Consequently, the § 121 exclusion is partially available on the sale of the second residence. ∎

Keep in mind, however, that the change in place of employment exception, or any of the other exceptions noted below, does not make the full amount of the exclusion available. See the discussion under Relief Provision later in this chapter for determining the amount of the partial exclusion allowed.

Health Considerations

For the health exception to apply, health must be the primary reason for the sale or exchange of the residence.[30] A sale or exchange that is merely beneficial to the general health or well-being of the individual will not qualify. A safe harbor applies if there is a physician's recommendation for a change of residence (1) to obtain, provide, or facilitate the diagnosis, cure, mitigation, or treatment of disease, illness, or injury or (2) to obtain or provide medical or personal care for an individual suffering from a disease, illness, or injury. If the safe harbor is not satisfied, then the determination is made using a facts and circumstances approach. Examples that qualify include the following:

* A taxpayer who is injured in an accident is unable to care for herself. She sells her residence and moves in with her daughter.

---

[28]§ 121(c)(2)(B).
[29]Reg. § 1.121–3T(c).
[30]Reg. § 1.121–3T(d).

| **TAX** *in* **the NEWS** | A TAX BREAK FOR THOSE WHO SERVE |

To qualify for exclusion treatment on the gain from the sale of a principal residence, a two-year ownership and occupancy requirement during the five-year period preceding the sale must be satisfied. As satisfying this provision was difficult for those in the military, Congress enacted the Military Family Tax Relief Act of 2003 to provide some relief. The two-out-of-five-years requirement still must be satisfied, but at the election of the taxpayer, the running of the five-year period can be suspended during any period that the taxpayer or spouse is serving on qualified official extended duty in the military. Since this extension is limited to 10 years, the maximum period allowed is 15 years. This provision is retroactive to home sales after May 6, 1997.

- A taxpayer's father has a chronic disease. The taxpayer sells his house in order to move into the father's house to provide the care the father requires as a result of the disease.
- A taxpayer's son suffers from a chronic disease. The taxpayer sells his house and moves his family so the son can begin a new treatment recommended by the son's physician that is available at a medical facility 100 miles away.
- A taxpayer suffers from chronic asthma. Her physician recommends that she move to a warm, dry climate. She moves from Minnesota to Arizona.

Unforeseen Circumstances

For the unforeseen circumstances exception to apply, the primary reason for the sale or exchange of the residence must be an event that the taxpayer did not anticipate before purchasing and occupying the residence.[31] This requirement is satisfied under a safe-harbor provision by any of the following:

- Involuntary conversion of the residence.
- Natural or human-made disasters or acts of war or terrorism resulting in a casualty to the residence.
- Death of a qualified individual.
- Cessation of employment that results in eligibility for unemployment compensation.
- Change in employment or self-employment that results in the taxpayer being unable to pay housing costs and reasonable basic living expenses for the taxpayer's household.
- Divorce or legal separation.
- Multiple births resulting from the same pregnancy.

If the safe harbor is not satisfied, then the determination is made using a facts and circumstances approach.

EXAMPLE 25

Debra and Roy are engaged and buy a house (sharing the mortgage payments) and live in it as their personal residence. Eighteen months after the purchase, they cancel their wedding plans, and Roy moves out of the house. Because Debra cannot afford to make the payments alone, they sell the house. While the sale does not fit under the safe harbor, the sale does qualify under the unforeseen circumstances exception. ∎

---

[31]Reg. § 1.121–3T(e).

CALCULATION OF THE AMOUNT OF THE EXCLUSION

General Provisions

The amount of the available § 121 exclusion on the sale of a principal residence is $250,000.[32] If the realized gain does not exceed $250,000, there is no recognized gain.

Realized gain is calculated in the normal manner. The *amount realized* is the selling price less the selling expenses, which include items such as the cost of advertising the property for sale, real estate broker commissions, legal fees in connection with the sale, and loan placement fees paid by the taxpayer as a condition of arranging financing for the buyer. Repairs and maintenance performed by the seller to aid in selling the property are treated neither as selling expenses nor as adjustments to the taxpayer's adjusted basis for the residence.

EXAMPLE 26
THE BIG PICTURE

Return to the facts of *The Big Picture* on p. 15-2. Recall that one of Alice's options is to sell her current house and move into the inherited house. Assume that Alice, who is single, sells her current personal residence (adjusted basis of $130,000) for $348,000. She has owned and lived in the house for 15 years. Her selling expenses are $18,000. Three weeks prior to the sale, Alice pays a carpenter and a painter $1,000 to make some repairs and paint the two bathrooms. Her recognized gain would be calculated as follows:

Amount realized ($348,000 − $18,000)	$ 330,000
Adjusted basis	(130,000)
Realized gain	$ 200,000
§ 121 exclusion	(200,000)
Recognized gain	$ –0–

Since the available § 121 exclusion of $250,000 would exceed Alice's realized gain of $200,000, her recognized gain would be $0. ■

EXAMPLE 27
THE BIG PICTURE

Continue with *The Big Picture* and the facts of Example 26, except that the selling price is $490,000.

Amount realized ($490,000 − $18,000)	$ 472,000
Adjusted basis	(130,000)
Realized gain	$ 342,000
§ 121 exclusion	(250,000)
Recognized gain	$ 92,000

Since the realized gain of $342,000 would exceed the § 121 exclusion amount of $250,000, Alice's recognized gain would be $92,000 ($342,000 − $250,000). ■

---

[32]§ 121(b)(1).

Effect on Married Couples

If a married couple files a joint return, the $250,000 amount is increased to $500,000 if the following requirements are satisfied:[33]

- Either spouse meets the at-least-two-years *ownership* requirement.
- Both spouses meet the at-least-two-years *use* requirement.
- Neither spouse is ineligible for the § 121 exclusion on the sale of the current principal residence because of the sale of another principal residence within the prior two years.

EXAMPLE 28

Margaret sells her personal residence (adjusted basis of $150,000) for $650,000. She has owned and lived in the residence for six years. Her selling expenses are $40,000. Margaret is married to Ted, and they file a joint return. Ted has lived in the residence since they were married two and one-half years ago.

Amount realized ($650,000 − $40,000)	$ 610,000
Adjusted basis	(150,000)
Realized gain	$ 460,000
§ 121 exclusion	(460,000)
Recognized gain	$ –0–

Since the realized gain of $460,000 is less than the available § 121 exclusion amount of $500,000, no gain is recognized. ∎

Starting in 2008, a surviving spouse can continue to use the $500,000 exclusion amount on the sale of a personal residence for the next two years following the deceased spouse's death. If the sale occurs in the year of death, however, a joint return must be filed by the surviving spouse.

If each spouse owns a qualified principal residence, each spouse can separately qualify for the $250,000 exclusion on the sale of his or her own residence even if the couple files a joint return.[34]

---

[33]§ 121(b)(2).   [34]§ 121(b)(1).

EXAMPLE 29

Anne and Samuel are married on August 1, 2011. Each owns a residence that is eligible for the § 121 exclusion. Anne sells her residence on September 7, 2011, and Samuel sells his residence on October 9, 2011. Relevant data on the sales are as follows:

	Anne	Samuel
Selling price	$320,000	$425,000
Selling expenses	20,000	25,000
Adjusted basis	190,000	110,000

Anne and Samuel intend to rent a condo in Florida or Arizona and to travel. The recognized gain of each is calculated as follows:

	Anne	Samuel
Amount realized	$ 300,000	$ 400,000
Adjusted basis	(190,000)	(110,000)
Realized gain	$ 110,000	$ 290,000
§ 121 exclusion	(110,000)	(250,000)
Recognized gain	$ –0–	$ 40,000

Anne has no recognized gain because the available $250,000 exclusion amount exceeds her realized gain of $110,000. Samuel's recognized gain is $40,000 as his realized gain of $290,000 exceeds the $250,000 exclusion amount. The recognized gains calculated above result regardless of whether Anne and Samuel file a joint return or separate returns. ∎

Relief Provision

As discussed earlier in Requirements for Exclusion Treatment, partial § 121 exclusion treatment may be available when not all of the statutory requirements are satisfied. Under the relief provision, the § 121 exclusion amount ($250,000 or $500,000) is multiplied by a fraction, the numerator of which is the number of qualifying months and the denominator of which is 24 months. The resulting amount is the excluded gain.[35]

EXAMPLE 30

On October 1, 2010, Rich and Audrey, who file a joint return and live in Chicago, sell their personal residence, which they have owned and lived in for eight years. The realized gain of $325,000 is excluded under § 121. They purchase another personal residence for $525,000 on October 2, 2010. Audrey's employer transfers her to the Denver office in August 2011. Rich and Audrey sell their Chicago residence on August 2, 2011, and purchase a residence in Denver shortly thereafter. The realized gain on the sale is $300,000.

The $325,000 gain on the first Chicago residence is excluded under § 121. The sale of the second Chicago residence is within the two-year window of the prior sale, but because it resulted from a change in employment, Rich and Audrey can qualify for partial § 121 exclusion treatment as follows:

Realized gain	$ 300,000
§ 121 exclusion:	
$\dfrac{10 \text{ months}}{24 \text{ months}} \times \$500,000$	(208,333)
Recognized gain	$ 91,667

∎

Basis of New Residence

Because § 121 is an exclusion provision rather than a postponement of gain provision, the basis of a new residence is its cost.[36]

[35]§ 121(c)(1).

[36]§ 1012.

Reduction in Exclusion for Prior Use as a Vacation Home

A vacation home does not qualify for the § 121 exclusion because it does not satisfy the requirement of being the taxpayer's principal residence. Suppose, however, that the taxpayer converts the vacation home into a principal residence and subsequently satisfies the at least two-out-of-five-years ownership and use requirements. Prior to 2009, the converted vacation home qualified for the § 121 exclusion.

The Housing Assistance Tax Act of 2008 has reduced this opportunity to use the § 121 exclusion for converted vacation homes as to sales and exchanges occurring after December 31, 2008.[37] For periods of nonqualified use, the realized gain that otherwise is eligible for the § 121 exclusion is reduced by the proportion of the periods of nonqualified use compared to the period the property was owned by the taxpayer.

EXAMPLE 31

Monica purchases a house for use as a vacation home (100% personal use) on January 1, 2011, for $600,000. She uses it as a vacation home until January 1, 2013, when she makes it her principal residence. She continues to use it as her principal residence until she sells it on December 31, 2015, for $950,000 (selling expenses of $50,000).

Monica's realized gain is calculated as follows:

Amount realized ($950,000 − $50,000)	$ 900,000
Adjusted basis	(600,000)
Realized gain	$ 300,000

The sale of Monica's principal residence is subject to the proration required under the Act for nonqualified use.

$$\frac{2 \text{ years (periods of nonqualified use)}}{5 \text{ years (period of ownership)}} = 40\%$$

Thus, $120,000 ($300,000 × 40%) of the gain is ineligible for the § 121 exclusion, while the remaining gain of $180,000 ($300,000 − $120,000) is eligible for the § 121 exclusion. As a result, Monica's recognized gain is $120,000. ∎

EXAMPLE 32

Assume the same facts as in Example 31, except that the realized gain is $500,000. Of this amount, $200,000 ($500,000 × 40%) is ineligible for the § 121 exclusion, and of the remaining gain of $300,000 ($500,000 − $200,000), $250,000 is offset by the § 121 exclusion. So Monica's recognized gain is $250,000 ($200,000 + $50,000). ∎

The period the property was owned by the taxpayer includes any period before 2009. The period of nonqualified use includes only the period after 2008.

PRINCIPAL RESIDENCE

To be eligible for the § 121 exclusion, the residence must have been owned and used by the taxpayer as the principal residence for at least two years during the five-year window (subject to partial exclusion treatment under the relief provision). Whether property is the taxpayer's principal residence "depends upon all of the facts and circumstances in each case."[38]

EXAMPLE 33

Mitch graduates from college and moves to Boston, where he is employed. He decides to rent an apartment in Boston because of its proximity to his place of employment. He purchases a beach condo in the Cape Cod area that he occupies most weekends. Mitch does not intend to live at the beach condo except on weekends. The apartment in Boston is his principal residence. ∎

---

[37]§ 121(b)(4).

[38]Regulation § 1.121–1(b)(2) includes factors to be considered in determining a taxpayer's principal residence.

TAX *in* the NEWS

THE BROADENING GRIP OF FORECLOSURES OR FORECLOSURES FOR ALL

Residential home foreclosures are usually associated with lower-income and middle-income taxpayers who obtained subprime mortgages and/or lost their jobs in the recession. Most residential foreclosures have occurred in this segment of the market.

But now the rich and famous (i.e., upper-income taxpayers) including some prominent actors and Wall Street executives are also experiencing foreclosures. The forclosure rate for residential mortgages of $5 million or more is rising sharply.

By some measures, big borrowers are more likely to default on their mortgages than small borrowers. According to American CoreLogic, which tracks more than 80 percent of the overall home mortgage market, 14.8 percent of loans with balances of $4 million or more were 90 days or more past due in early 2010 compared with 8.7 percent of all loans tracked. Sam Khater, a senior economist at First American, thinks big borrowers may be more likely than small borrowers to stop making payments when the house is underwater (i.e., debt exceeds fair market value).

Source: Adapted from Craig Karmin and James R. Hagerty, "Foreclosures Hit Rich and Famous," *Wall Street Journal*, April 9, 2010, p. A1.

A residence does not have to be a house. For example, a houseboat, a house trailer, or a motor home can qualify.[39] Land, under certain circumstances, can qualify for exclusion treatment. The lot on which a house is built obviously qualifies. An adjacent lot can qualify if it is regularly used by the owner as part of the residential property. To qualify, the land must be sold along with the residence or within two years before or after the sale of the residence.

HOW CLOSE TO THE WATER?

Sixteen years ago, Steve and Madeline Wilson purchased from a single seller the following properties located at the confluence of the York River and Chesapeake Bay near West Point, Virginia.

Property	Description	Cost
101 Main Street	½ acre of land with house across the street from the water	$290,000
102 Main Street	½ acre of land on the water	300,000

The house at 101 Main Street is used as their principal residence. It has spectacular river/bay views, but no direct access to the water.

The Wilsons purchased the lot at 102 Main Street because it provides access to the water. Also, owning this lot would prevent someone else from building a house that would impair their river/bay views. In addition, they regarded the lot as a sound investment.

Three months after the purchase, the Wilsons installed a dock and boat lift at a cost of $75,000 at the lot at 102 Main Street. They also added a barbeque pit there at a cost of $2,000 that they use for recreation and entertaining their friends.

Now Madeline, an advertising executive, has been transferred to Raleigh, North Carolina. Steve works out of an office in Washington, D.C., as a political consultant and will rent an apartment there. Consequently, the Wilsons decide to sell the two properties in a single transaction with the sale price allocated as follows:

101 Main Street	$695,000
102 Main Street	500,000

The Wilsons treat the sale of the two properties as the sale of their principal residence under § 121 and calculate the gain as follows:

Amount realized ($695,000 + $500,000)	$1,195,000
Basis ($290,000 + $300,000 + $75,000 + $2,000)	(667,000)
Realized gain	$ 528,000
§121 exclusion	(500,000)
Recognized gain	$ 28,000

Evaluate the validity of the Wilsons' calculation of recognized gain.

---

[39]Reg. § 1.1034–1(c)(3)(i).

INVOLUNTARY CONVERSION AND USING §§ 121 AND 1033

As mentioned earlier (see Involuntary Conversion of a Personal Residence), a taxpayer can use both the § 121 exclusion of gain provision and the § 1033 postponement of gain provision.[40] The taxpayer initially can elect to exclude realized gain under § 121 to the extent of the statutory amount. Then a qualified replacement of the residence under § 1033 can be used to postpone the remainder of the realized gain. In applying § 1033, the amount of the required reinvestment is reduced by the amount of the § 121 exclusion.

EXAMPLE 34	Angel's principal residence is destroyed by a tornado. Her adjusted basis for the residence is $140,000. She receives insurance proceeds of $480,000.

If Angel does not elect to use the § 121 exclusion, her realized gain on the involuntary conversion of her principal residence is $340,000 ($480,000 amount realized − $140,000 adjusted basis). Thus, to postpone the $340,000 realized gain under § 1033, she would need to acquire qualifying property costing at least $480,000.

Using the § 121 exclusion enables Angel to reduce the amount of the required reinvestment for § 1033 purposes from $480,000 to $230,000. That is, by using § 121 in conjunction with § 1033, the amount realized, for § 1033 purposes, is reduced to $230,000 ($480,000 − $250,000 § 121 exclusion).

Note that if Angel does not acquire qualifying replacement property for § 1033 purposes, her recognized gain is $90,000 ($480,000 − $140,000 adjusted basis − $250,000 § 121 exclusion). ∎

If § 1033 is used in conjunction with the § 121 exclusion on an involuntary conversion of a principal residence, the holding period of the replacement residence includes the holding period of the involuntarily converted residence. This can be beneficial in satisfying the § 121 two-out-of-five-years ownership and use requirement on a subsequent sale of the replacement residence.

15.5 OTHER NONRECOGNITION PROVISIONS

LO.5
Identify other nonrecognition provisions contained in the Code.

The typical taxpayer experiences the sale of a personal residence or an involuntary conversion more frequently than the other types of nontaxable exchanges. Several less common nonrecognition provisions are treated briefly in the remainder of this chapter.

EXCHANGE OF STOCK FOR PROPERTY—§ 1032

Under § 1032, a corporation does not recognize gain or loss on the receipt of money or other property in exchange for its stock (including treasury stock). In other words, a corporation does not recognize gain or loss when it deals in its own stock. This provision is consistent with the accounting treatment of such transactions.

CERTAIN EXCHANGES OF INSURANCE POLICIES—§ 1035

Under § 1035, no gain or loss is recognized from the exchange of certain insurance contracts or policies. The rules relating to exchanges not solely in kind and the basis of the property acquired are the same as under § 1031. Exchanges qualifying for nonrecognition include the following:

- The exchange of life insurance contracts.
- The exchange of a life insurance contract for an endowment or annuity contract.
- The exchange of an endowment contract for another endowment contract that provides for regular payments beginning at a date not later than the date payments would have begun under the contract exchanged.
- The exchange of an endowment contract for an annuity contract.
- The exchange of annuity contracts.

---

[40]§ 121(d)(5).

EXCHANGE OF STOCK FOR STOCK OF THE SAME CORPORATION—§ 1036

Section 1036 provides that a shareholder does not recognize gain or loss on the exchange of common stock solely for common stock in the same corporation or from the exchange of preferred stock for preferred stock in the same corporation. Exchanges between individual shareholders as well as between a shareholder and the corporation are included. The rules relating to exchanges not solely in kind and the basis of the property acquired are the same as under § 1031. For example, a nonrecognition exchange occurs when common stock with different rights, such as voting for nonvoting, is exchanged. A shareholder usually recognizes gain or loss from the exchange of common for preferred or preferred for common even though the stock exchanged is in the same corporation.

CERTAIN REACQUISITIONS OF REAL PROPERTY—§ 1038

Under § 1038, no loss is recognized from the repossession of real property sold on an installment basis. Gain is recognized to a limited extent.

TRANSFERS OF PROPERTY BETWEEN SPOUSES OR INCIDENT TO DIVORCE—§ 1041

Section 1041 provides that transfers of property *between spouses or former spouses incident to divorce* are nontaxable transactions. Therefore, the basis to the recipient is a carryover basis. To be treated as incident to the divorce, the transfer must be related to the cessation of marriage or occur within one year after the date on which the marriage ceases.

Section 1041 also provides for nontaxable exchange treatment on property transfers *between spouses during marriage.* The basis to the recipient spouse is a carryover basis.

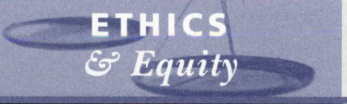

ETHICS & Equity — **INCIDENT TO DIVORCE OR NOT?**

Randy and Judy are divorced on December 28, 2010, after being married for 10 years. Several years ago, they purchased a beach lot for $300,000 and planned to construct a beach house there for vacation purposes.

On December 21, 2011, Randy transfers his interest in the beach lot to Judy for $325,000 (i.e., 50 percent of the fair market value of $650,000). According to both Randy and Judy, the sale was not associated with the divorce but was made to enable Randy to invest the cash in a new business. They treat the transaction as the sale of Randy's one-half interest to Judy. Accordingly, Randy recognizes a capital gain of $175,000 ($325,000 − $150,000), which is eligible for the 15 percent alternative tax rate. Judy considers her adjusted basis to be $475,000 ($150,000 + $325,000).

Evaluate Randy and Judy's treatment of this transaction.

ROLLOVERS INTO SPECIALIZED SMALL BUSINESS INVESTMENT COMPANIES—§ 1044

A postponement opportunity is available for some sellers of publicly traded securities under § 1044. If the amount realized is reinvested in the common stock or partnership interest of a specialized small business investment company (SSBIC), the realized gain is not recognized. Any amount not reinvested will trigger recognition of the realized gain to the extent of the deficiency. The taxpayer must reinvest the proceeds within 60 days of the date of sale in order to qualify. In calculating the basis of the SSBIC stock, the amount of the purchase price is reduced by the amount of the postponed gain.

Statutory ceilings are imposed on the amount of realized gain that can be postponed for any taxable year as follows:

- For an individual taxpayer, the lesser of:
  - *$50,000 ($25,000 for married filing separately).*
  - *$500,000 ($250,000 for married filing separately) reduced by the amount of such non-recognized gain in prior taxable years.*

- For a corporate taxpayer, the lesser of:
  - *$250,000.*
  - *$1 million reduced by the amount of such nonrecognized gain in prior taxable years.*

Investors *ineligible* for this postponement treatment include partnerships, S corporations, estates, and trusts.

ROLLOVER OF GAIN FROM QUALIFIED SMALL BUSINESS STOCK INTO ANOTHER QUALIFIED SMALL BUSINESS STOCK—§ 1045

Under § 1045, realized gain from the sale of qualified small business stock held for more than six months may be postponed if the taxpayer acquires other qualified small business stock within 60 days. Any amount not reinvested will trigger the recognition of the realized gain on the sale to the extent of the deficiency. In calculating the basis of the acquired qualified small business stock, the amount of the purchase price is reduced by the amount of the postponed gain.

Qualified small business stock is stock of a qualified small business that is acquired by the taxpayer at its original issue in exchange for money or other property (excluding stock) or as compensation for services. A qualified small business is a domestic corporation that satisfies the following requirements:

- The aggregate gross assets prior to the issuance of the small business stock do not exceed $50 million.
- The aggregate gross assets immediately after the issuance of the small business stock do not exceed $50 million.

TAX PLANNING:

15.6 LIKE-KIND EXCHANGES

LO.6

Identify tax planning opportunities related to the nonrecognition provisions discussed in the chapter.

Since application of the like-kind exchange provisions is mandatory rather than elective, in certain instances it may be preferable to avoid qualifying for § 1031 nonrecognition. To avoid the application of a deferral under § 1031, the taxpayer should structure the transaction so that at least one of the statutory requirements for a § 1031 like-kind exchange is not satisfied. If the like-kind exchange provisions do not apply, the end result may be the recognition of capital gain in exchange for a higher basis in the newly acquired asset. Also, the immediate recognition of gain may be preferable in certain situations. Examples where immediate recognition is beneficial include the following:

- Taxpayer has unused net operating loss carryovers.
- Taxpayer has unused general business credit carryovers.
- Taxpayer has suspended or current passive activity losses.

EXAMPLE 35

Alicia disposes of a machine (used in her business) with an adjusted basis of $3,000 for $4,000. She also acquires a new business machine for $9,000. If § 1031 applies, the $1,000 realized gain is not recognized, and the basis of the new machine is reduced by $1,000 (from $9,000 to $8,000). If § 1031 does not apply, a $1,000 gain is recognized and may receive favorable capital gain treatment to the extent that the gain is not recognized as ordinary income due to the depreciation recapture provisions (see Chapter 17). In addition, the basis for depreciation on the new machine is $9,000 rather than $8,000 since there is no unrecognized gain. ∎

The application of § 1031 nonrecognition treatment should also be avoided when the adjusted basis of the property being disposed of exceeds the fair market value.

EXAMPLE 36

Assume the same facts as in the previous example, except that the fair market value of the machine is $2,500. If § 1031 applies, the $500 realized loss is not recognized. To recognize the loss, Alicia should sell the old machine and purchase the new one. The purchase and sale transactions should be with different taxpayers. ■

On the other hand, the like-kind exchange procedure can be utilized to control the amount of recognized gain.

EXAMPLE 37

Rex has property with an adjusted basis of $40,000 and a fair market value of $100,000. Sandra wants to buy Rex's property, but Rex wants to limit the amount of recognized gain on the proposed transaction. Sandra acquires other like-kind property (from an outside party) for $80,000. She then exchanges this property and $20,000 cash for Rex's property. Rex has a realized gain of $60,000 ($100,000 amount realized − $40,000 adjusted basis). His recognized gain is only $20,000, the lower of the $20,000 boot received or the $60,000 realized gain. Rex's basis for the like-kind property is $40,000 ($40,000 adjusted basis + $20,000 gain recognized − $20,000 boot received). If Rex had sold the property to Sandra for its fair market value of $100,000, the result would have been a $60,000 recognized gain ($100,000 amount realized − $40,000 adjusted basis) to him. It is permissible for Rex to identify the like-kind property that he wants Sandra to purchase.[41] ■

In the present economic environment, however, there is another consideration. The beneficial result of tax deferral of realized gain could be more than offset by future tax rate increases. Some real estate investors are following this approach, particularly with respect to undeveloped land. They are willing to accept current taxation at 15 percent to avoid the possibility of future taxation at a much higher rate. Many believe that the capital gains tax rate could rise to 20 or 25 percent in the near future. Although turning down a tax deferral may sound like a strange strategy, it fits the notion of "pay a tax today to avoid a higher tax tomorrow."

15.7 INVOLUNTARY CONVERSIONS

In certain cases, a taxpayer may prefer to recognize gain from an involuntary conversion. Keep in mind that § 1033, unlike § 1031 (dealing with like-kind exchanges), generally is an elective provision.

EXAMPLE 38

Ahmad has a $40,000 realized gain from the involuntary conversion of an office building. He reinvests the entire proceeds of $450,000 in a new office building. He does not elect to postpone gain under § 1033, however, because of an expiring net operating loss carryover that is offset against the gain. Therefore, none of the realized gain of $40,000 is postponed. Because Ahmad did not elect § 1033 postponement, his basis in the replacement property is the property's cost of $450,000 rather than $410,000 ($450,000 reduced by the $40,000 realized gain). ■

15.8 SALE OF A PRINCIPAL RESIDENCE

ELECTION TO FORGO

The § 121 exclusion automatically applies if the taxpayer is eligible. That is, the taxpayer does not have to make an election. However, if the taxpayer wishes to avoid § 121 exclusion treatment on an otherwise eligible sale, the taxpayer may elect to do so.[42]

---

[41]*Franklin B. Biggs*, 69 T.C. 905 (1978); Rev.Rul. 73–476, 1973–2 C.B. 300; and *Starker v. U.S.*, 79–2 USTC ¶9541, 44 AFTR 2d 79–5525, 602 F.2d 1341 (CA–9, 1979).

[42]§ 121(f).

EXAMPLE 39

George owns two personal residences that satisfy the two-year ownership and use test with respect to the five-year window. The Elm Street residence has appreciated by $25,000, and the Maple Street residence has appreciated by $230,000. He intends to sell both of them and move into rental property. He sells the Elm Street residence in December 2011 and expects to sell the Maple Street residence early next year.

Unless George elects not to apply the § 121 exclusion to the sale of the Elm Street residence, he will exclude the $25,000 realized gain on that residence in 2011. In 2012, however, he will have a recognized gain of $230,000 on the sale of the Maple Street residence.

If George makes the election to forgo, he will report a recognized gain of $25,000 on the sale of the Elm Street residence in 2011. But by using the § 121 exclusion in 2012, he will eliminate the recognized gain of $230,000 on the sale of the Maple Street residence. ∎

NEGATIVE EFFECT OF RENTING OR USING AS A HOME OFFICE

The residence does not have to be the taxpayer's principal residence at the date of sale to qualify for the § 121 exclusion. During part of the five-year window, it could have been rental property (e.g., either a vacation home or entirely rental property). In addition, the taxpayer can have used part of the principal residence as a qualifying home office. In either of these circumstances, the taxpayer may claim deductions for the expenses attributable to the rental or business use. But what effect, if any, do such deductions have on a later sale of the residence? Will the sales proceeds still qualify for nonrecognition of gain treatment under § 121?

Concern that the § 121 exclusion might be denied may have deterred some taxpayers from claiming legitimate deductions, particularly in the case of an office in the home. As noted below, however, the IRS has clarified its position regarding the effect of any such depreciation.

In either the rental or the home office setting, the taxpayer will have deducted depreciation. Any realized gain on the sale that is attributable to depreciation claimed after May 5, 1997, is not eligible for the § 121 exclusion.[43]

EXAMPLE 40

On December 5, 2011, Amanda sells her principal residence, which qualifies for the § 121 exclusion. Her realized gain is $190,000. From January through November 2010, she was temporarily out of town on a job assignment in another city and rented the residence to a college student. For this period, she deducted MACRS cost recovery of $7,000. Without the depreciation provision, Amanda could exclude the $190,000 realized gain. However, the depreciation taken requires her to recognize $7,000 of the realized gain. ∎

The gain recognized associated with prior depreciation deductions is determined first before calculating the amount of recognized gain associated with periods of nonqualified use.[44]

EXAMPLE 41

Assume the same facts as in Example 31, except that the vacation home was used partially for rental use before being converted to Monica's personal residence and that $25,000 of depreciation was deducted during the periods that the vacation home was rented. Monica's realized gain is calculated as follows:

Amount realized ($950,000 − $50,000)	$ 900,000
Adjusted basis ($600,000 − $25,000)	(575,000)
Realized gain	$ 325,000

Since $25,000 of depreciation was deducted by Monica, $25,000 of the realized gain is recognized. The sale of Monica's principal residence is subject to the proration required for nonqualified use.

---

[43]§ 121(d)(6).   [44]§ 121(b)(4)(D).

$$\frac{2\,\text{years (periods of nonqualified use)}}{5\,\text{years (period of ownership)}} = 40\%$$

Thus, $120,000 ($300,000 × 40%) of the remaining gain is ineligible for the § 121 exclusion, and the remaining gain of $180,000 ($300,000 − $120,000) is eligible for the § 121 exclusion. Consequently, Monica's recognized gain is $145,000 ($25,000 + $120,000). ∎

QUALIFICATION FOR § 121 EXCLUSION

The key requirement for the § 121 exclusion is that the taxpayer must have *owned* and *used* the property as a principal residence for at least two years during the five-year window. As taxpayers advance in age, they quite frequently make decisions such as the following:

- Sell the principal residence and buy a smaller residence or rent the principal residence.
- Sell vacation homes they own.
- Sell homes they are holding as rental property.

These properties may have experienced substantial appreciation during the ownership period. Clearly, the sale of the principal residence is eligible for the § 121 exclusion. Less clear, however, is that proper planning can make it possible for a vacation home or rental property to qualify for the exclusion. Although this strategy may require taxpayers to be flexible about where they live, it can result in substantial tax savings.

EXAMPLE 42

Thelma and David are approaching retirement. They have substantial appreciation on their principal residence and on a house they own at the beach (about two hours away). After retirement, they plan to move to Florida. They have owned and lived in the principal residence for 28 years and have owned the beach house for 9 years. If they sell their principal residence, it qualifies for the § 121 exclusion. At retirement, they could move into their beach house for two years and make it eligible for the exclusion. If the beach house were not so far away, they could sell the principal residence now and move into the beach house to start the running of the two-year use period. Note that any realized gain on the beach house attributable to depreciation is not eligible for the § 121 exclusion. Note also the provision that now requires a reduction in the § 121 exclusion for prior use as a vacation home (see Examples 31 and 41). ∎

RECORD KEEPING

Since the amount of the available exclusion ($250,000 or $500,000) for most taxpayers will exceed the realized gain on the sale of the residence, the IRS has discontinued the form that previously was used to report the sale of a principal residence. If the sale of the residence does result in a gain that is not excluded from gross income, the gain is reported on Schedule D of Form 1040 (Capital Gains and Losses).

However, it is a good idea for all taxpayers who own residences to continue to maintain records on the adjusted basis of the residence including the original cost, any capital improvements, and any deductions that decrease basis (e.g., depreciation on a home office or on rental use) for the following reasons:

- The sale of the residence may not qualify for the § 121 exclusion.
- The realized gain may exceed the § 121 exclusion amount.
- The residence may be converted to rental or business use.
- If part of the residence has been rental or business use property (e.g., a qualifying home office) and depreciation has been deducted, the realized gain is recognized to the extent of the depreciation deducted.

Chapter 15 has covered certain situations in which realized gains or losses are not recognized (nontaxable exchanges). Chapters 16 and 17 are concerned with the *classification* of recognized gains and losses. That is, if a gain or loss is recognized, is it an ordinary or a capital gain or loss? Chapter 16 discusses the tax consequences of capital gains and losses.

REFOCUS ON THE BIG PICTURE

ALTERNATIVE USES OF PROPERTY

Alice needs to be aware of the different tax consequences of her proposals and whether there are any limits to these consequences.

- *Sale of the inherited house.* This is by far the simplest transaction for Alice. Based on the available data, her recognized gain would be:

Amount realized ($600,000 − $30,000)	$ 570,000
Adjusted basis	(475,000)
Recognized gain	$ 95,000

  Because the sale of the house is not eligible for the § 121 exclusion, the tax liability is $14,250 ($95,000 × 15%). So Alice's net cash flow would be $555,750 ($570,000 − $14,250).

- *Conversion into a vacation home with only personal use.* With this alternative, the only tax benefit Alice would receive is the deduction for property taxes as an itemized deduction. She would continue to incur upkeep costs (e.g., repairs, utilities, insurance). At the end of the two-year period, the sales results are similar to those of a current sale. The sale of the house would not be eligible for the § 121 exclusion.

- *Conversion into a vacation home with partial personal use and partial rental use.* In this case, Alice would be able to deduct 40 percent of the costs such as property taxes, agent's management fee, depreciation, maintenance and repairs, utilities, and insurance. However, this amount cannot exceed the rent income generated. The remaining 60 percent of the property taxes can be claimed as an itemized deduction.

  At the end of the two-year period, the sales results would be similar to those of a current sale. In determining recognized gain, adjusted basis must be reduced by the amount of the depreciation claimed. The sale of the house would not be eligible for the § 121 exclusion.

- *Current sale of present home with sale of inherited home in two years.* The present sale of her current principal residence and the future sale of her inherited residence would enable Alice to qualify for the § 121 exclusion as to each sale. She would satisfy the two-year ownership requirement, the two-year use requirement, and the allowance of the § 121 exclusion only once every two years. Alice must be careful to occupy the inherited residence for at least two years. Also, the period between the sales of the first and second houses must be greater than two years. Qualifying for the § 121 exclusion of up to $250,000 would allow Alice to avoid any Federal income tax liability.

With this information, Alice can make an informed choice. In all likelihood, she probably will select the strategy of selling her current house now and the inherited house in the future. A noneconomic benefit of this option is that she will have to sell only one house at the time of her retirement.

KEY TERMS

Boot, 15–7	Like-kind exchanges, 15–4	Personal residence, 15–16
Involuntary conversion, 15–11	Nontaxable exchange, 15–3	§ 121 Exclusion, 15–16

DISCUSSION QUESTIONS

1. **LO.1** In most nontaxable exchanges, is the nonrecognition of the realized gain or loss temporary or permanent? Explain.

2. **LO.1** Distinguish between a loss that is not recognized on a nontaxable exchange and a loss that is not recognized on the sale or exchange of a personal use asset.

3. **LO.2** What are the three requirements that must be satisfied for a transaction to qualify for nontaxable exchange treatment under § 1031?

4. **LO.2** Can the exchange of personal use property for property held for productive use in a trade or business qualify for like-kind exchange treatment? Explain.

5. **LO.2, 6** Can property held for productive use in a trade or business be exchanged for investment property and qualify for like-kind exchange treatment? Explain.

6. **LO.2** Which of the following qualify as like-kind exchanges under § 1031?
   a. Improved for unimproved real estate.
   b. Vending machine (used in business) for inventory.
   c. Rental house for personal residence.
   d. Business equipment for securities.
   e. Warehouse for office building (both used for business).
   f. Truck for computer (both used in business).
   g. Rental house for land (both held for investment).
   h. Ten shares of stock in Blue Corporation for 10 shares of stock in Red Corporation.
   i. Office furniture for office equipment (both used in business).
   j. Unimproved land in Jackson, Mississippi, for unimproved land in Toledo, Spain.
   k. General partnership interest for a general partnership interest.
   l. Limited partnership interest for a limited partnership interest.
   m. Limited partnership interest for a general partnership interest.

7. **LO.2** Address the following issues:
   a. Melissa owns a residential lot in Spring Creek, Louisiana, that has appreciated substantially in value. She holds the lot for investment. She is considering exchanging the lot with her father for a residential lot in McComb, Mississippi, that she also will hold for investment. Identify the relevant tax issues for Melissa.
   b. Assume instead that the lot Melissa receives from her father is located in Paris, France. Identify the relevant tax issues for Melissa.

ISSUE ID

8. **LO.2** Ross would like to dispose of some land that he acquired five years ago because he believes that it will not continue to appreciate. Its value has increased by $50,000 over the five-year period. He also intends to sell stock that has declined in value by $50,000 during the eight-month period he has owned it. Ross has four offers to acquire the stock and land:

ISSUE ID

Buyer number 1:	Exchange land.
Buyer number 2:	Purchase land for cash.
Buyer number 3:	Exchange stock.
Buyer number 4:	Purchase stock for cash.

Identify the tax issues relevant to Ross in disposing of this land and stock.

9. **LO.2** Samuel is a 10% limited partner in the SVI limited partnership. He exchanges his partnership interest in SVI for a 25% limited partnership interest in DRI. Both partnerships are in the oil drilling business. Samuel's adjusted basis for his SVI partnership interest is $80,000, and the fair market value of the partnership interest he receives in DRI is $120,000.
   a. What is Samuel's recognized gain or loss associated with the exchange?
   b. Would the answer in (a) be different if Samuel exchanged a general partnership interest for a general partnership interest?

10. **LO.2** When no boot is given or received in a like-kind exchange, the basis of the property received is the same as the basis of the property transferred. What effect does the receipt of boot have on the basis of the like-kind property received? What if boot is given?

11. **L0.2** In connection with like-kind exchanges, discuss each of the following:
    a. Realized gain.
    b. Realized loss.
    c. Recognized gain.
    d. Recognized loss.
    e. Postponed gain.
    f. Postponed loss.
    g. Basis of like-kind property received.
    h. Basis of boot received.

12. **L0.2** Beverly exchanges undeveloped real estate for developed real estate on March 3, 2011. The fair market value of each property is $260,000. Beverly had purchased the undeveloped real estate on February 25, 2008, for $325,000.
    a. When does Beverly's holding period begin for the developed real estate?
    b. Assume instead that Beverly's cost for the undeveloped real estate was $200,000. When does her holding period begin for the developed real estate?

13. **L0.2** Mortgaged real estate may be received in a like-kind exchange. If the taxpayer's mortgage is assumed, what effect does the mortgage have on the recognition of realized gain? On the basis of the real estate received?

14. **L0.3** Andrea's retail store building (basis of $270,000) is destroyed by a fire. She receives insurance proceeds of $250,000 (the appraised value of the building prior to its destruction).
    a. How much can Andrea reinvest in another retail store building and still recognize a $20,000 loss?
    b. Assume instead that the insurance proceeds are $300,000. How much must Andrea reinvest in another retail store building in order not to have any recognized gain?

15. **L0.3** What constitutes an involuntary conversion?

16. **L0.3** Ed receives severance damages from the state government for a public road built across his property. Under what circumstances can the § 1033 involuntary conversion provision apply to prevent the recognition of gain?

17. **L0.3** Vera owns an office building that she leases to tenants. If the building is destroyed by a tornado, is the functional use test or the taxpayer use test applied as to replacement property? Explain the differences between the two tests.

18. **L0.3** On June 5, 2011, Amber, Inc., a calendar year taxpayer, receives cash of $525,000 from the county upon condemnation of its warehouse building (adjusted basis of $390,000 and fair market value of $525,000).
    a. What must Amber do to qualify for § 1033 postponement of gain treatment?
    b. How would your advice to Amber differ if the adjusted basis was $550,000?

19. **L0.3** Reba, a calendar year taxpayer, owns an office building that she uses in her business. The building is involuntarily converted on November 15, 2011. On January 5, 2012, Reba receives enough proceeds to produce a realized gain. What is the latest date she can replace the building and qualify for § 1033 postponement treatment if the conversion event is:
    a. A flood?
    b. A condemnation?
    c. A tornado?

20. **L0.3** Bob is notified by the city public housing authority on May 3, 2011, that his apartment building is going to be condemned as part of an urban renewal project. On June 1, 2011, Carol offers to buy the building from Bob. Bob sells the building to Carol on June 30, 2011. Condemnation occurs on September 1, 2011, and Carol receives the condemnation proceeds from the city. Assume both Bob and Carol are calendar year taxpayers.
    a. What is the earliest date on which Bob can dispose of the building and qualify for § 1033 postponement treatment?
    b. Does the sale to Carol qualify as a § 1033 involuntary conversion?
    c. What is the latest date on which Carol can acquire qualifying replacement property and qualify for postponement of the realized gain?
    d. What type of property will be qualifying replacement property?

21. **LO.3** A warehouse owned by Martha and used in her business (i.e., to store inventory) is being condemned by the city to provide a right of way for a highway. The warehouse has appreciated by $180,000 based on Martha's estimate of its fair market value. In the negotiations, the city is offering $35,000 less than what Martha believes the property is worth. Alan, a real estate broker, has offered to purchase Martha's property for $20,000 more than the city's offer. Martha plans to invest the proceeds she will receive in an office building that she will lease to various tenants.
    a. Identify the relevant tax issues for Martha.
    b. Would the answer in (a) change if Martha's warehouse was property held for invest-ment rather than being used in her business?

22. **LO.3** When does the holding period begin for replacement property acquired in an involuntary conversion?

23. **LO.4** Samantha wants to retire, sell the house that she has occupied as her residence for 20 years, and travel. She would have a $120,000 realized loss on the sale of the residence. She intends to use the net proceeds to fund her travels.
    a. Can Samantha recognize the loss?
    b. Would the answer in (a) be different if the realized loss was, instead, a $120,000 realized gain?

24. **LO.4** Gary, who is single, sells his principal residence (owned and occupied by him for seven years) in November 2011 for a realized gain of $148,000. He had purchased a more expensive new residence eight months prior to the sale. He anticipates that he will occupy this new house as his principal residence for only about 18 additional months. He expects it to appreciate substantially while he owns it. Gary would like to recognize the realized gain on the 2011 sale to offset a large investment loss from the sale of stock. Can he recognize the realized gain of $148,000 on the sale of his principal residence in 2011?

25. **LO.4** Sandy owns a personal residence in which she has lived since she acquired it. It has appreciated by $90,000 during this period. Now, however, the school board has redrawn the boundaries for the school districts, and her son will have to transfer to a different high school for his senior year. Sandy is considering selling her residence and buying another one that will enable her son to remain in the same high school. Without this reason, she would not sell the house. Identify the relevant tax issues for Sandy.

26. **LO.4** Explain how the following are determined on the sale or exchange of a principal residence:
    a. Realized gain.
    b. Recognized gain.
    c. Postponed gain.
    d. Basis of new residence.

27. **LO.4** What is a principal residence? Can a taxpayer have several principal residences at the same time?

28. **LO.5** On May 5, 2011, Nancy sells her stock (adjusted basis of $13,000) in Lime, Inc., a publicly traded company, for $17,000. On May 31, 2011, she pays $20,000 for stock in Rose, Inc., a specialized small business investment company. Nancy believes that her adjusted basis for the Rose stock is $10,000.
    a. Evaluate Nancy's calculation of the adjusted basis for her Rose stock.
    b. How would your answer change if Nancy purchased the replacement stock on July 15 rather than on May 31?

PROBLEMS

29. **LO.2** Martha owns developed land with an adjusted basis of $300,000. She exchanges it for undeveloped land worth $360,000.
    a. What are Martha's realized and recognized gain or loss?
    b. What is Martha's basis in the undeveloped land she receives?
    c. Would the answers in (a) and (b) change if Martha exchanged the developed land for land and a building?

30. **LO.2** Kareem owns a pickup truck that he uses exclusively in his business. The adjusted basis is $22,000, and the fair market value is $14,000. Kareem exchanges the truck for a truck that he will use exclusively in his business.
    a.   What are Kareem's realized and recognized gain or loss?
    b.   What is his basis in the new truck?
    c.   What are the tax consequences to Kareem in (a) and (b) if he used the old truck and will use the new truck exclusively for personal purposes?

31. **LO.2** Tanya Fletcher owns undeveloped land (adjusted basis of $80,000 and fair market value of $92,000) on the East Coast. On January 4, 2011, she exchanges it with her sister, Lisa, for undeveloped land on the West Coast and $3,000 cash. Lisa has an adjusted basis of $72,000 for her land, and its fair market value is $89,000. As the real estate market on the East Coast is thriving, on September 1, 2012, Lisa sells the land she acquired for $120,000.
    a.   What are Tanya's recognized gain or loss and adjusted basis for the West Coast land on January 4, 2011?
    b.   What are Lisa's recognized gain or loss and adjusted basis for the East Coast land on January 4, 2011?
    c.   What is Lisa's recognized gain or loss from the September 1, 2012 sale?
    d.   What effect does Lisa's 2012 sale have on Tanya?
    e.   Write a letter to Tanya advising her on how she could avoid any recognition of gain associated with the January 4, 2011 exchange prior to her actual sale of the land. Her address is The Corral, El Paso, TX 79968.

32. **LO.2** Sarah exchanges a yellow bus (used in her business) for Tyler's gray bus and some garage equipment (used in his business). The assets have the following characteristics:

	Adjusted Basis	Fair Market Value
Yellow bus	$6,000	$15,000
Gray bus	3,000	11,000
Equipment	2,000	4,000

    a.   What are Sarah's recognized gain or loss and basis for the gray bus and garage equipment?
    b.   What are Tyler's recognized gain or loss and basis for the yellow bus?

33. **LO.2, 6** In two unrelated transactions, Laura exchanges property that qualifies for like-kind exchange treatment. In the first exchange, Laura gives up office equipment purchased in May 2009 (adjusted basis of $20,000; fair market value of $17,000) in exchange for new office equipment (fair market value of $15,000) and $2,000 cash. In the second exchange, Laura receives a parking garage (to be used in her business) with a fair market value of $50,000 in exchange for a plot of land she had held for investment. The land was purchased in April 2003 for $12,000 and has a current fair market value of $48,000. In addition to transferring the land, Laura pays an additional $2,000 to the other party.
    a.   What is Laura's adjusted basis for the new office equipment?
    b.   When does the holding period begin?
    c.   What is Laura's adjusted basis for the parking garage?
    d.   When does the holding period begin?
    e.   How could Laura structure either of the transactions differently to produce better tax consequences?

34. **LO.2** Samantha owns an SUV that she uses exclusively for personal purposes. Its original cost was $48,000, and the fair market value is $24,000. She exchanges the SUV and $27,000 cash with an online dealer for a new SUV.
    a.   Calculate Samantha's realized and recognized gain or loss.
    b.   Calculate Samantha's basis for the new SUV.
    c.   Determine when Samantha's holding period for the new SUV begins.
    d.   Would the answers in (a), (b), and (c) change if Samantha first sold the old SUV to an unrelated party for $24,000 and then purchased the new SUV from the online dealer for $51,000?

35. **LO.2** Tom owns land and a building that he uses in his business (adjusted basis of $125,000 and fair market value of $275,000). Tom exchanges the land and building for land (fair market value of $175,000) that he will use as a parking lot in his business. In addition, he receives stock worth $100,000.
    a. What is Tom's realized gain or loss?
    b. His recognized gain or loss?
    c. The basis of the land and the stock received?
    d. Would the answers in (a), (b), and (c) change if the stock is worth $175,000 (not $100,000) and the land Tom receives has a fair market value of $100,000 (not $175,000)?

36. **LO.2** Ed owns investment land with an adjusted basis of $35,000. Polly has offered to purchase the land from Ed for $175,000 for use in a real estate development. The amount offered by Polly is $10,000 in excess of what Ed perceives as the fair market value of the land. Ed would like to dispose of the land to Polly but does not want to incur the tax liability that would result. He identifies an office building with a fair market value of $175,000 that he would like to acquire. Polly purchases the office building and then exchanges the office building for Ed's land.
    a. Calculate Ed's realized and recognized gain on the exchange and his basis for the office building.
    b. Calculate Polly's realized and recognized gain on the exchange and her basis in the land.

37. **LO.2** What is the basis of the new property in each of the following exchanges?
    a. Apartment building held for investment (adjusted basis of $145,000) for office building to be held for investment (fair market value of $225,000).
    b. Land and building used as a barber shop (adjusted basis of $190,000) for land and building used as a grocery store (fair market value of $350,000).
    c. Office building (adjusted basis of $45,000) for bulldozer (fair market value of $42,000), both held for business use.
    d. IBM common stock (adjusted basis of $20,000) for ExxonMobil common stock (fair market value of $28,000).
    e. Rental house (adjusted basis of $90,000) for mountain cabin to be held for rental use (fair market value of $225,000).
    f. General partnership interest (adjusted basis of $400,000) for a limited partnership interest (fair market value of $580,000).

38. **LO.2** Steve owns Machine A (adjusted basis of $12,000 and fair market value of $15,000), which he uses in his business. Steve sells Machine A for $15,000 to Aubry (a dealer) and then purchases Machine B for $15,000 from Joan (also a dealer). Machine B would normally qualify as like-kind property.
    a. What are Steve's realized and recognized gain on the sale of Machine A?
    b. What is Steve's basis for Machine B?
    c. What factors would motivate Steve to sell Machine A and purchase Machine B rather than exchange one machine for the other?
    d. Assume that the adjusted basis of Machine A is $15,000 and the fair market value of both machines is $12,000. Respond to (a) through (c).

39. **LO.2** Tab exchanges real estate used in his business plus stock for real estate to be held for investment. The stock transferred has an adjusted basis of $42,000 and a fair market value of $50,000. The real estate transferred has an adjusted basis of $59,000 and a fair market value of $200,000. The real estate acquired has a fair market value of $250,000.
    a. What is Tab's realized gain or loss?
    b. His recognized gain or loss?
    c. The basis of the newly acquired real estate?

40. **LO.2, 6** Tom and Frank are brothers. Each owns investment property in the other's hometown. To make their lives easier, they decide to legally exchange the investment properties. Under the terms of the exchange, Frank will transfer realty (adjusted basis of $52,000; fair market value of $80,000), and Tom will exchange realty (adjusted basis of $60,000; fair market value of $92,000). Tom's property is subject to a mortgage of $12,000 that will be assumed by Frank.

DECISION MAKING

a. What are Frank's and Tom's recognized gains?

b. What are their adjusted bases?

c. As an alternative, Frank has proposed that rather than assuming the mortgage, he will transfer cash of $12,000 to Tom. Tom would use the cash to pay off the mortgage. Advise Tom on whether this alternative would be beneficial to him from a tax perspective.

41. **LO.2** Determine the realized, recognized, and postponed gain or loss and the new basis for each of the following like-kind exchanges:

	Adjusted Basis of Old Machine	Boot Given	Fair Market Value of New Asset	Boot Received
a.	$ 7,000	$ –0–	$12,000	$4,000
b.	14,000	2,000	15,000	–0–
c.	3,000	7,000	8,000	500
d.	22,000	–0–	32,000	–0–
e.	10,000	–0–	11,000	1,000
f.	10,000	–0–	8,000	–0–

42. **LO.2** Shontelle owns an apartment house that has an adjusted basis of $760,000 but is subject to a mortgage of $192,000. She transfers the apartment house to Dave and receives from him $120,000 in cash and an office building with a fair market value of $780,000 at the time of the exchange. Dave assumes the $192,000 mortgage on the apartment house.

a. What is Shontelle's realized gain or loss?

b. What is her recognized gain or loss?

c. What is the basis of the newly acquired office building?

43. **LO.3** Monica's roadside vegetable stand (adjusted basis of $305,000) is destroyed by a tractor-trailer accident. She receives insurance proceeds of $288,000 ($360,000 fair market value less $72,000 coinsurance). Monica immediately uses the proceeds plus additional cash of $45,000 to build another roadside vegetable stand at the same location. What are the tax consequences to Monica?

44. **LO.3** Albert owns 100 acres of land on which he grows spruce Christmas trees. His adjusted basis for the land is $100,000. He receives condemnation proceeds of $10,000 when the city's new beltway takes 5 acres along the eastern boundary of his property. He also receives a severance award of $6,000 associated with the possible harmful effects of exhaust fumes on his Christmas trees. Albert invests the $16,000 in a growth mutual fund. Determine the tax consequences to Albert of the:

a. Condemnation proceeds.

b. Severance award.

45. **LO.3** For each of the following involuntary conversions, indicate whether the property acquired qualifies as replacement property, the recognized gain, and the basis for the property acquired:

a. Frank owns a warehouse that is destroyed by a tornado. The space in the warehouse was rented to various tenants. The adjusted basis was $470,000. Frank uses all of the insurance proceeds of $700,000 to build a shopping mall in a neighboring community where no property has been damaged by tornadoes. The shopping mall is rented to various tenants.

b. Ivan owns a warehouse that he uses in his business. The adjusted basis is $300,000. The warehouse is destroyed by fire. Because of economic conditions in the area, Ivan decides not to rebuild the warehouse. Instead, he uses all of the insurance proceeds of $400,000 to build a warehouse to be used in his business in another state.

c. Ridge's personal residence is condemned as part of a local government project to widen the highway from two lanes to four lanes. The adjusted basis is $170,000. Ridge uses all of the condemnation proceeds of $200,000 to purchase another personal residence.

d. Juanita owns a building that she uses in her retail business. The adjusted basis is $250,000. The building is destroyed by a hurricane. Because of an economic downturn in the area caused by the closing of a military base, Juanita decides to rent space for her retail outlet rather than to replace the building. She uses all of the insurance proceeds of $300,000 to buy a four-unit apartment building in another city. A real estate agent in that city will handle the rental of the apartments for her.

e. Susan and Rick's personal residence is destroyed by a tornado. They had owned it for 15 months. The adjusted basis was $170,000. Since they would like to travel, they decide not to acquire a replacement residence. Instead, they invest all of the insurance proceeds of $200,000 in a duplex, which they rent to tenants.

f. Ellen and Harry's personal residence (adjusted basis of $245,000) is destroyed in a flood. They had owned it for 18 months. Of the insurance proceeds of $350,000, they reinvest $342,000 in a replacement residence four months later.

46. **LO.3** Jason, a calendar year taxpayer, is the sole proprietor of a hardware store. His adjusted basis for the building and the related land is $150,000. On March 4, 2011, state authorities notify Jason that his property is going to be condemned so that the highway can be widened. On June 1, Jason's property is officially condemned, and he receives an award of $212,000. Since Jason's business has been successful in the past, he would like to reopen the hardware store in a new location.

a. What is the earliest date Jason can acquire a new hardware store and qualify for § 1033 postponement?

b. On June 30, Jason purchases land and a building for $200,000. Assuming he elects postponement of gain under § 1033, what is his recognized gain?

c. What is Jason's adjusted basis for the new land and building?

d. If he does not elect § 1033, what are Jason's recognized gain and adjusted basis?

e. Suppose he invests the $212,000 condemnation proceeds in the stock market on June 30. What is Jason's recognized gain?

47. **LO.3** Edith's warehouse (adjusted basis of $450,000) is destroyed by a hurricane in October 2011. Edith, a calendar year taxpayer, receives insurance proceeds of $525,000 in January 2012. Calculate Edith's realized gain or loss, recognized gain or loss, and basis for the replacement property if she:

a. Acquires a new warehouse for $550,000 in January 2012.

b. Acquires a new warehouse for $500,000 in January 2012.

c. Does not acquire replacement property.

48. **LO.3** Cabel's warehouse, which has an adjusted basis of $380,000 and a fair market value of $450,000, is condemned by an agency of the Federal government to make way for a highway interchange. The initial condemnation offer is $410,000. After substantial negotiations, the agency agrees to transfer to Cabel a surplus warehouse that he believes is worth $450,000. Cabel is a calendar year taxpayer. The condemnation and related asset transfer occur during September 2011.

DECISION MAKING

a. What are the recognized gain or loss and the basis of the replacement warehouse if Cabel's objective is to recognize as much gain as possible?

b. Advise Cabel regarding what he needs to do by what date in order to achieve his objective.

49. **LO.3** What are the *maximum* postponed gain or loss and the basis for the replacement property for the following involuntary conversions?

	Property	Type of Conversion	Amount Realized	Adjusted Basis	Amount Reinvested
a.	Drugstore (business)	Casualty	$160,000	$130,000	$110,000
b.	Apartments (investment)	Condemned	100,000	125,000	175,000
c.	Grocery store (business)	Casualty	400,000	300,000	450,000
d.	Residence (personal)	Casualty	16,000	18,000	17,000
e.	Vacant lot (investment)	Condemned	240,000	160,000	220,000
f.	Residence (personal)	Casualty	20,000	18,000	19,000
g.	Residence (personal)	Condemned	18,000	20,000	26,000
h.	Apartments (investment)	Condemned	150,000	100,000	200,000

50. **LO.3, 6** Wanda, a calendar year taxpayer, owned a building (adjusted basis of $250,000) in which she operated a bakery that was destroyed by fire in December 2011. She receives

DECISION MAKING

insurance proceeds of $290,000 for the building the following March. Wanda is considering two options regarding the investment of the insurance proceeds. First, she could purchase a local building (suitable for a bakery) that is for sale for $275,000. Second, she could buy a new home for $290,000 and go back to college and finish her degree.

   a.   To minimize her tax liability, which of these alternatives should Wanda choose?

   b.   What is the latest date on which Wanda can replace the involuntarily converted property to qualify for § 1033?

   c.   What is the latest date on which Wanda can replace the involuntarily converted property to qualify for § 1033 if the involuntary conversion is a condemnation?

51. **LO.4, 6** After living in a residence during 2009 as a tenant, Katie exercised an option to purchase the residence for $180,000 on January 2, 2010. On June 1, 2011, Katie sells the residence for $335,000, and on June 13, 2011, she purchases a new residence for $360,000.

   a.   What is Katie's recognized gain? Her basis for the new residence?

   b.   Assume instead that Katie purchased her original residence on January 2, 2009 (rather than on January 2, 2010). What is Katie's recognized gain? Her basis for the new residence?

   c.   In (a), what could Katie do to minimize her recognized gain?

52. **LO.4** Taylor has owned and occupied her personal residence (adjusted basis of $190,000) for four years. In April 2011, she sells the residence for $300,000 (selling expenses are $20,000). On the same day as the sale, Taylor purchases another house for $350,000. Because of noisy neighbors, she sells the new house after just 10 months. The selling price is $483,000 (selling expenses are $18,000).

   a.   What is Taylor's recognized gain on the sale of the first residence?

   b.   What is Taylor's basis for her second residence?

   c.   What is Taylor's recognized gain on the sale of the second residence?

   d.   Assume instead that the sale of the second residence was due to Taylor's job transfer to another state. What is her recognized gain on the sale of the second residence?

53. **LO.4** Milton, who is single, listed his personal residence with a real estate agent on March 3, 2011, at a price of $250,000. He rejected several offers in the $200,000 range during the summer. Finally, on August 16, 2011, he and the purchaser signed a contract to sell for $245,000. The sale (i.e., closing) took place on September 7, 2011. The closing statement showed the following disbursements:

Real estate agent's commission	$ 14,000
Appraisal fee	500
Exterminator's certificate	300
Recording fees	400
Mortgage to First Bank	180,000
Cash to seller	49,800

Milton's adjusted basis for the house is $150,000. He owned and occupied the house for eight years. On October 1, 2011, Milton purchases another residence for $210,000.

   a.   Calculate Milton's recognized gain on the sale.

   b.   What is Milton's adjusted basis for the new residence?

   c.   Assume instead that the selling price is $735,000. What is Milton's recognized gain? His adjusted basis for the new residence?

54. **LO.4** Bruce and Libby are married and file a joint return. On January 1, 2011, they purchased a house for $270,000 to be used by them and family members for vacations. They continued to use it for this purpose through December 31, 2013. On January 1, 2014, they converted it to their principal residence. On December 31, 2015, they sold it for $460,000 (selling expenses of $29,000). What is Bruce and Libby's recognized gain on the sale of their principal residence?

55. **LO.4** Jill bought a house in April 2007 for $190,000. She lived in it until August 2009 when she moved to Mack's new home. Mack and Jill got married and filed a joint return in 2010 and subsequent years. In January 2011, Jill sells her house for $350,000 (selling expenses are $17,500).

   a.   Do Mack and Jill qualify for the § 121 exclusion? What is the maximum amount of exclusion available on the sale of Jill's house? What is her recognized gain?

b. On May 22, 2012, Mack and Jill sell Mack's house for $625,000. Selling expenses are $37,500, and Mack's adjusted basis is $260,000. What is the maximum amount of the § 121 exclusion available on the sale of Mack's home? What is the recognized gain?

c. Would the result in part (b) change if Mack's house is not sold until June 2013?

56. **LO.4** Nell, Nina, and Nora Sanders, who are sisters, sell their principal residence (owned as tenants in common) in which they have lived for the past 25 years. The youngest of the sisters is age 60. The selling price is $960,000, selling expenses and legal fees are $63,000, and the adjusted basis is $120,000 (the fair market value of the residence when inherited from their parents 25 years ago). Since the sisters are going to live in rental housing, they do not plan to acquire another residence. Nell has contacted you on behalf of the three sisters regarding the tax consequences of the sale.

COMMUNICATIONS

a. Write a letter to Nell advising her of the tax consequences and how taxes can be minimized. Nell's address is 100 Oak Avenue, Billings, MT 59101.

b. Prepare a memo for the tax files.

57. **LO.4** Ben owns a beach house (five years) and a cabin in the mountains (four years). His adjusted basis is $280,000 in the beach house and $315,000 in the mountain cabin. Ben also rents a townhouse in the city where he is employed. During the year, he occupies each of the three residences as follows:

DECISION MAKING

Townhouse	120 days
Beach house	170 days
Mountain cabin	75 days

The beach house is close enough to the city so that he can commute to work during the spring and early fall. While this level of occupancy may vary slightly from year to year, it is representative during the time period that Ben has owned the two residences.

As Ben plans on retiring in several years, he sells both residences. The mountain cabin is sold on March 3, 2011, for $540,000 (related selling expenses of $30,000). The beach house is sold on December 10, 2011, for $600,000 (related selling expenses of $36,000).

a. Calculate Ben's lowest recognized gain on the sale of the two residences.

b. Assume instead that both residences satisfy the two-year ownership and use tests as Ben's principal residence. Since the mountain cabin is sold first, is it possible for Ben to apply the § 121 exclusion to the sale of the beach house?

58. **LO.4, 6** Cisco, a calendar year taxpayer who is age 63, owns a residence in which he has lived for 21 years. The residence is destroyed by fire on August 8, 2011. The adjusted basis is $190,000, and the fair market value is $320,000. Cisco receives insurance proceeds of $320,000 for the residence on September 1, 2011. He is trying to decide whether to purchase a comparable house. He anticipates that he will retire in two years and will move to a warmer climate where he will rent in case he decides to live in different places.

DECISION MAKING

a. Advise Cisco of the tax consequences of replacing versus not replacing the residence.

b. Which do you recommend to him?

c. How would your answer in (a) change if the fair market value and insurance proceeds received were $510,000?

59. **LO.4, 6** Tina, age 28, has owned her principal residence (adjusted basis of $175,000) for five years. During the first three years of ownership, she occupied it as her principal residence. During the past two years, she was in graduate school and rented the residence. After graduate school, Tina returned to the same location where she previously worked. At this point, she purchased another residence for $300,000 and listed her old residence for sale at $240,000. Due to a slow real estate market, 11 months later Tina finally receives an offer of $230,000.

DECISION MAKING

a. What is Tina's recognized gain if she immediately accepts the $230,000 offer (i.e., 11 months after the listing date)?

b. What is Tina's recognized gain if she rejects the $230,000 offer and accepts another offer of $240,000 three months later (i.e., 14 months after the listing date)?

c. Advise Tina on which offer she should accept (assume she is in the 28% tax bracket).

60. **LO.5** Roby and Sid have been married for 12 years. Roby sells Peach, Inc. stock that she has owned for four years to Sid for its fair market value of $120,000. Her adjusted basis is $150,000.

DECISION MAKING

a. Calculate Roby's recognized gain or recognized loss.

b. Calculate Sid's adjusted basis for the stock.

c. How would the tax consequences in (a) and (b) differ if Roby had made a gift of the stock to Sid? Which form of the transaction would you recommend?

61. **L0.5** On September 1, 2011, Marsha sells stock in Orange, Inc., for $90,000. The stock is qualified small business stock and was purchased on August 16, 2010, for $60,000. On September 30, 2011, Marsha purchases $85,000 of Blue, Inc., also qualified small business stock.
    a. What is Marsha's realized and recognized gain (or loss) on the sale of the Orange stock?
    b. What is Marsha's basis in the Blue stock?

CUMULATIVE PROBLEMS

62. Devon Bishop, age 40, is single. He lives at 1507 Rose Lane, Albuquerque, NM 87131. His Social Security number is 111–11–1111. Devon does not wish to have $3 go to the Presidential Election Campaign Fund.

Devon was divorced in 2006 after 15 years of marriage. He pays alimony of $18,000 a year to his former spouse, Ariane. Ariane's Social Security number is 123–45–6789. Devon's son, Tom, who is age 16, resides with Ariane. Devon pays child support of $12,000 per year. Ariane has provided Devon with a signed Form 8332 in which she releases the dependency deduction to him for 2010. Tom's Social Security number is 123–45–6788.

Devon owns a sole proprietorship for which he uses the accrual method of accounting. His revenues and expenses for 2010 are as follows:

Sales revenue	$740,000
Cost of goods sold	405,000
Salary expense	88,000
Rent expense	30,000
Utilities	8,000
Telephone	6,500
Advertising	4,000
Bad debts	5,000
Depreciation	21,000
Health insurance*	26,000
Accounting and legal fees	7,000
Supplies	1,000

*$18,000 for employees and $8,000 for Devon.

Other income received by Devon includes the following:

Dividend income:	
Swan, Inc.	$ 10,000
Wren, Inc.	2,000
Interest income:	
First Bank	11,000
Second Bank	2,500
City of Asheville bonds	17,000
Lottery winnings (tickets purchased cost $500)	10,000

During the year, Devon and his sole proprietorship had the following property transactions:
a. Sold Blue, Inc. stock for $45,000 on March 12, 2010. He had purchased the stock on September 5, 2007, for $50,000.
b. Received an inheritance of $300,000 from his Uncle Henry. Devon used $200,000 to purchase Green, Inc. stock on May 15, 2010, and invested $100,000 in Gold, Inc., stock on May 30, 2010.
c. Received Orange, Inc. stock worth $9,500 as a gift from his Aunt Jane on June 17, 2010. Her adjusted basis for the stock was $5,000. No gift taxes were paid on the

transfer. Aunt Jane had purchased the stock on April 1, 2004. Devon sold the stock on July 1, 2010, for $22,000.

d. On July 15, 2010, Devon sold one-half of the Green, Inc. stock for $40,000.

e. Devon was notified on August 1, 2010, that Yellow, Inc. stock he purchased from a colleague on September 1, 2009, for $52,500 had become worthless. While he perceived that the investment was risky, he did not anticipate that the corporation would declare bankruptcy.

f. On August 15, 2010, Devon received a parcel of land in Phoenix worth $220,000 in exchange for a parcel of land he owned in Tucson. Since the Tucson parcel was worth $245,000, he also received $25,000 cash. Devon's adjusted basis for the Tucson parcel was $210,000. He originally purchased it on September 18, 2007.

g. On December 1, 2010, Devon sold the condominium in which he had been living for the past 10 years. The sales price was $480,000, selling expenses were $28,500, and repair expenses related to the sale were $9,400. Devon and Ariane had purchased the condominium as joint owners for $180,000. Devon had received Ariane's ownership interest as part of the divorce proceedings. The fair market value at that time was $240,000.

Devon's potential itemized deductions, exclusive of the aforementioned information, are as follows:

Medical expenses (before the 7.5% floor)	$ 9,500
Property taxes on residence	5,300
State income taxes	4,000
Charitable contributions	10,000
Mortgage interest on residence	9,900
Sales taxes paid	5,000

During the year, Devon makes estimated Federal income tax payments of $40,000.

Compute Devon's lowest net tax payable or refund due for 2010, assuming he makes any available elections that will reduce the tax. If you use tax forms for your computations, you will need Forms 1040, 4562, 8332, and 8824 and Schedules A, B, C, D, and SE. Suggested software: H&R BLOCK At Home.

63. Tammy Walker, age 37, is a self-employed accountant. Tammy's Social Security number is 123–45–6789. Her address is 101 Glass Road, Richmond, VA 23236. Her income and expenses associated with her accounting practice for 2011 are as follows:

TAX COMPUTATION PROBLEM

DECISION MAKING

COMMUNICATIONS

Revenues (cash receipts during 2011)	$ 192,000
Expenses	
Salaries	$ 95,000
Office supplies	2,100
Postage	2,900
Depreciation of equipment	40,000
Telephone	800
	$ 140,800

Since Tammy is a cash method taxpayer, she does not record her receivables as revenue until she receives cash payment. At the beginning of 2011, her accounts receivable were $65,000, and the balance had decreased to $20,000 by the end of the year.

Tammy used one room in her 10-room house as the office for her accounting practice (300 square feet out of a total square footage of 3,000). She paid the following expenses related to the house during 2011:

Utilities	$4,200
Insurance	1,800
Property taxes	4,700
Repairs	3,000

Tammy had purchased the house on September 1, 2010, for $290,000 (exclusive of land cost).

Tammy has one child, Thomas, age 16. Thomas's Social Security number is 123–45–6788. Thomas lives with his father during the summer and with Tammy for the rest of the year. Tammy can document that she spent $16,000 during 2011 for the child's support. The father normally provides about $9,000 per year, but this year he gave Thomas a new car for Christmas. The cost of the car was $20,000. The divorce decree is silent regarding the dependency exemption for Thomas. Tammy does not provide her former spouse with a signed Form 8332 for 2011.

Under the terms of the divorce decree, Tammy is to receive alimony of $10,000 per month. The payments will terminate at Tammy's death or at her remarriage.

Tammy provides part of the support of her mother, age 67. Her mother's Social Security number is 123–45–6787. The total support in 2011 for her mother was as follows:

Social Security benefits	$5,200
From Tammy	2,900
From Bob, Tammy's brother	2,000
From Susan, Tammy's sister	2,200

Bob and Susan have both indicated their willingness to sign a multiple support waiver form if it will benefit Tammy.

Tammy's deductible itemized deductions during 2011, excluding any itemized deductions related to the house, were $19,000. She made estimated tax payments of $38,000.

Part 1—Tax Computation
Compute Tammy's lowest net tax payable or refund due for 2011.

Part 2—Tax Planning
Tammy and her former husband have been discussing the $10,000 alimony he pays her each month. Because his new wife has a health problem, he does not feel that he can afford to continue to pay the $10,000 each month. He is in the 15% tax bracket. If Tammy will agree to decrease the amount by 25%, he will agree that the amount paid is not alimony for tax purposes. Assume that Tammy projects her marginal tax rate in 2012 will be 33% (both with and without the alimony decrease). Write a letter to Tammy that contains your advice on whether she should agree to her former husband's proposal. Also prepare a memo for the tax files.

RESEARCH PROBLEMS

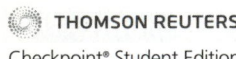

Checkpoint® Student Edition

Note: Solutions to Research Problems can be prepared by using the **Checkpoint**® **Student Edition** online research product, which is available to accompany this text. It is also possible to prepare solutions to the Research Problems by using tax research materials found in a standard tax library.

Research Problem 1. Charlene and Alton Dutro had lived in their home for two and one-half years when they decided to enlarge and remodel the house. However, their architect advised them that more stringent building and permit restrictions had been imposed since the house was built 10 years earlier. So the Dutros decided to demolish the house and to rebuild on the same site. Rather than occupying the new house, however, the Dutros sold it for a realized gain in excess of $500,000.

In calculating the recognized gain on their Federal income tax return, the Dutros reduced the realized gain of more than $500,000 by the $500,000 exclusion of § 121. The IRS has issued an income tax deficiency notice on the grounds that the Dutros did not satisfy the two-out-of-five-years requirement of § 121(a).

Who is correct?

Partial list of research aids:
§ 121(a)(1).
David A. Gates, 135 T.C. ___, No.1 (2010).

Research Problem 2. For three years, Amos, a calendar year taxpayer, has owned stock that is qualified small business stock under § 1045. The stock has an adjusted basis of $10,000. On July 2, 2011, he sells the stock for $100,000. On August 3, 2011, he uses the sales proceeds of $100,000 to purchase other qualified small business stock. If possible, Amos would like to defer any recognized gain on the sale of the stock. Advise Amos on the tax consequences of the sale and the subsequent purchase and the procedure he must follow to achieve his deferral objective.

Research Problem 3. April owned an annuity contract (cash balance of $250,000) issued by Teal Insurance Company. She decides to switch to an annuity contract issued by Brown Insurance Company. To make the change, April instructed Teal to cash out her annuity by issuing a check to Brown. Teal refused to do so and issued a check for $250,000 payable to April.

April intended that the exchange of annuity contracts qualify for tax deferral treatment under § 1035(a)(3). Consequently, rather than depositing or cashing the check from Teal, she endorsed it and sent it to Brown.

On audit, an IRS agent contends that the transaction does not qualify under § 1035(a)(3). For tax deferral to apply, the initial annuity contract must be directly exchanged for the new annuity contract. Evaluate the positions of the parties.

Research Problem 4. Milly and Doug carried out a § 1031 exchange on September 1, 2011. They transferred to Asa a parcel of land (adjusted basis of $375,000; fair market value of $600,000). Once the like-kind property to be received was identified, Asa was to purchase it for them. On October 1, they identified two parcels of land, one located near Austin and the other located near Fort Worth. Either of the parcels was acceptable, although their preference was for the Austin property.

Asa entered into negotiations with the owner of the Austin parcel and expected to close the deal well before the end of the year. The closing was scheduled for December 15, 2011. Shortly before the scheduled closing, the owner of the Austin parcel raised the purchase price, and the deal fell through. Asa began negotiations with the owner of the Fort Worth parcel and purchased it for Milly and Doug on January 1, 2012.

Determine the tax consequences of this exchange for Milly and Doug.

Research Problem 5. Taylor owns a 150-unit motel that was constructed in the late 1960s. It is located on 10 acres on the main highway leading into the city. Taylor renovated the motel three years ago.

Taylor's motel is condemned by the city, which is going to use 2 of the 10 acres for a small park. The other 8 acres are to be sold to a timeshare developer who intends to build 400 units on the property. The developer has already secured approval from the city planning commission.

Taylor's attorney advises him not to contest the condemnation of the 2 acres for the park. Under the eminent domain provision, the city does have the right to take "private property for public use." However, the attorney advises Taylor to contest the condemnation of the remaining property. According to the attorney, the city does not have the right to take "private property for private use."

The city's position is that the condemnation will result in a substantial number of new jobs and additional tax revenue for the city.

Will Taylor be successful if he follows the attorney's advice?

Research Problem 6. Walter Albers, a physician, and his wife Maud owned and occupied a house in Hampton, Virginia, from 2005 through 2008. Dr. Albers's medical practice was located in a rental office building in Hampton.

In January 2009, Walter accepted employment in a medical practice in Richmond (75 miles from Hampton). During the same month, he and Maud purchased a home in Richmond that they occupied in February 2009. They did not sell the Hampton home because they planned to live there after retirement. Walter became dissatisfied with his employment in Richmond, so he quit and became a partner in a three-physician medical practice in West Point, Virginia (75 miles from Hampton and 30 miles from Richmond). Maud moved back into the Hampton residence. Walter commuted daily to his medical practice in West Point from either the residence in Richmond or the residence in Hampton. He normally spent four nights each week with Maud in the Hampton house and three nights each week by himself in the Richmond house. Maud occasionally spent a few nights at the Richmond residence during the periods Walter was there. They did not sell the Richmond house because it was closer to Walter's West Point office.

Even though Maud moved back to the Hampton house and Walter lived there part of the time, they retained the following associated with the Richmond house:

- Address listed on their Federal and state income tax returns.
- Address listed on their driver's licenses, automobile registrations, and voter registration cards.
- Address listed for their bills and correspondence.
- Location of their bank accounts.

They continued to use the Richmond address so that they would have a single address for all their correspondence. Though Maud attended church in Hampton, Walter was not a member.

In October 2011, Walter retired, and the Albers moved to Tucson. They listed both houses for sale. The closing for the Hampton house was on December 15, 2011, and resulted in a realized gain of $650,000. On their 2011 Form 1040, they reported a recognized gain of $150,000 ($650,000 − $500,000 § 121 exclusion).

The IRS has concluded that the sale does not qualify for § 121 treatment because the Hampton house was not the principal residence of Walter and Maud for at least two years during the five-year period ending December 15, 2011. Evaluate the positions of the Albers and the IRS.

INTERNET
activity

Use the tax resources of the Internet to address the following questions. Do not restrict your search to the Web, but include a review of newsgroups and general reference materials, practitioner sites and resources, primary sources of the tax law, chat rooms and discussion groups, and other opportunities.

Research Problem 7. Find two newspaper stories about transactions to which you believe the involuntary conversion rules could apply. Do not limit your search to individual taxpayers.

Research Problem 8. A number of public policy think tanks, taxpayer unions, and other private interest groups have proposed changes to the tax rules that apply to like-kind exchanges of realty. Summarize several of these proposals, including your assessment of the motivations underlying the suggested changes.

Research Problem 9. Find and print a Form 8824, Like-Kind Exchanges. Fill in the form as part of the requirements for Problem 35.

Research Problem 10. The U.S. government has established various programs to help homeowners avoid foreclosure on the mortgage covering their principal residence. Locate a newspaper article that describes one of these programs.

Property Transactions: Capital Gains and Losses

LEARNING OBJECTIVES

After completing Chapter 16, you should be able to:

LO.1
Understand the rationale for separate reporting of capital gains and losses.

LO.2
Distinguish capital assets from ordinary assets.

LO.3
Understand the relevance of a sale or exchange to classification as a capital gain or loss and apply the special rules for the capital gain or loss treatment of the retirement of corporate obligations, options, patents, franchises, and lease cancellation payments.

LO.4
Determine whether the holding period for a capital asset is long term or short term.

LO.5
Describe the beneficial tax treatment for capital gains and the detrimental tax treatment for capital losses for noncorporate taxpayers.

LO.6
Describe the tax treatment for capital gains and the detrimental tax treatment for capital losses for corporate taxpayers.

LO.7
Identify tax planning opportunities arising from the sale or exchange of capital assets.

OUTLINE

FRAME WORK 1040:
Tax Formula for Individuals

This chapter covers the boldfaced portions of the Tax Formula for Individuals that was introduced in Figure 3.1 on p. 3-3. Below those portions are the sections of Form 1040 where the results are reported.

Income (broadly conceived).. $ xx,xxx
Less: Exclusions .... (x,xxx)
Gross income .... **$xx,xxx**
Less: Deductions for adjusted gross income .... **(x,xxx)**

FORM 1040 (p. 1)		
12	Business income or (loss). Attach Schedule C or C-EZ	
13	Capital gain or (loss). Attach Schedule D if required. If not required, check here ▶ ☐	
14	Other gains or (losses). Attach Form 4797	

Adjusted gross income.. $ xx,xxx
Less: The greater of total itemized deductions *or* the standard deduction .... (x,xxx)
    Personal and dependency exemptions .... (x,xxx)
Taxable income .... $ xx,xxx
Tax on taxable income (see Tax Tables or Tax Rate Schedules) .... **$ x,xxx**

FORM 1040 (p. 2)		
44	**Tax** (see instructions). Check if any tax is from: **a** ☐ Form(s) 8814 **b** ☐ Form 4972 .	

Less: Tax credits (including income taxes withheld and prepaid) .... (xxx)
Tax due (or refund) .... $ xxx

THE BIG PICTURE   Tax Solutions for the Real World

MANAGING CAPITAL ASSET TRANSACTIONS

Maurice has come to you for tax advice regarding his investments. He inherited $500,000 from his Uncle Joe. A financial adviser suggested he make the following investments, which he did nine months ago.

- $200,000 in the stock of Purple, a publicly held bank that follows a policy of not paying dividends. At one time, the stock had appreciated to $300,000, but now it is worth only $210,000. Maurice is considering unloading this stock.
- $50,000 for a 50 percent interest in a patent that Kevin, a college roommate who is an unemployed inventor, had obtained for a special battery he had developed to power "green" cars. To date, Kevin has been unable to market the battery to an auto manufacturer or supplier, but he has high hopes of doing so given the current price of gasoline.
- $150,000 in tax-exempt bonds. The interest rate is only 3 percent. Maurice is considering moving this money into taxable bonds that pay 3.5 percent.
- $100,000 for a 10 percent ownership interest as a limited partner in a real estate development. Lots in the development are selling well.

Maurice read an article that talked about the beneficial tax rates for capital assets and dividends. He really liked the part about "costless" capital gains, although he did not understand it.

Maurice has retained his job as a toll booth operator at the municipal airport. His annual compensation is $35,000. He likes the job and has met some really interesting people there.

Respond to Maurice's inquiries. **Read the chapter and formulate your response.**

16.1 General Considerations

RATIONALE FOR SEPARATE REPORTING OF CAPITAL GAINS AND LOSSES

Fourteen years ago, a taxpayer purchased 100 shares of IBM stock for $17 a share. This year the taxpayer sells the shares for $129 a share. Should the $112 per share gain receive any special tax treatment? The $112 gain has built up over 14 years, so it may not be fair to tax it the same as income that was all earned this year.

What if the stock had been purchased for $129 per share and sold for $17 a share? Should the $112 loss be fully deductible? The tax law has an intricate approach to answering these investment activity-related questions.

As you study this chapter, keep in mind that how investment-related gains and losses are taxed can dramatically affect whether taxpayers make investments and which investments are made. Except for a brief discussion in Chapter 3, earlier chapters dwelt on how to determine the amount of gain or loss from a property disposition, but did not discuss the classification of gains and losses. This chapter will focus on that topic.

The tax law requires **capital gains** and **capital losses** to be separated from other types of gains and losses. There are two reasons for this treatment. First, long-term capital gains may be taxed at a lower rate than ordinary gains. An *alternative tax computation* is used to determine the tax when taxable income includes net long-term capital gain. Capital gains and losses must therefore be matched with one another to see if a net long-term capital gain exists. The alternative tax computation is discussed later in the chapter under Tax Treatment of Capital Gains and Losses of Noncorporate Taxpayers.

The second reason the Code requires separate reporting of gains and losses and a determination of their tax character is that a net capital loss is only deductible up to $3,000 per year. Excess loss over the annual limit carries over and may be deductible in a future tax year. Capital gains and losses must be matched with one another to see if a net capital loss exists.

For these reasons, capital gains and losses must be distinguished from other types of gains and losses. Most of this chapter and the next chapter describe the intricate rules for determining what type of gains and losses the taxpayer has.

As a result of the need to distinguish and separately match capital gains and losses, the individual tax forms include very extensive reporting requirements for capital gains and losses. This chapter explains the principles underlying the forms. The forms are illustrated with an example at the end of the chapter.

GENERAL SCHEME OF TAXATION

Recognized gains and losses must be properly classified. Proper classification depends upon three characteristics:

- The tax status of the property.
- The manner of the property's disposition.
- The holding period of the property.

The three possible tax statuses are capital asset, § 1231 asset, or ordinary asset. Property disposition may be by sale, exchange, casualty, theft, or condemnation.

There are two holding periods: short term and long term. The short-term holding period is one year or less. The long-term holding period is more than one year.

The major focus of this chapter is capital gains and losses. Capital gains and losses usually result from the disposition of a capital asset. The most common disposition is a sale of the asset. Capital gains and losses can also result from the disposition of § 1231 assets, which is discussed in Chapter 17.

UNCERTAINTY OVER CAPITAL GAIN RATES

During the fall of 2010, there was a great deal of uncertainty over what the special tax rates on long-term capital gains would be in 2011. Existing legislation would have raised the special tax rates, but proposed legislation would have kept the rates the same as in 2010. Late in the fall, a political compromise yielded the special rates that are discussed later in this chapter.

16.2 CAPITAL ASSETS

LO.2

Distinguish capital assets from ordinary assets.

DEFINITION OF A CAPITAL ASSET

Personal use assets and investment assets are the most common capital assets owned by individual taxpayers. Personal use assets usually include items such as clothing, recreational equipment, a residence, and automobiles. Investment assets usually include investments in mutual funds, corporate stocks and bonds, government bonds, and vacant land. Remember, however, that losses from the sale or exchange of personal use assets are not recognized. Therefore, the classification of such losses as capital losses can be ignored.

Due to the historical preferential treatment of capital gains, taxpayers have preferred that gains be capital gains rather than ordinary gains. As a result, a great many statutes, cases, and rulings have accumulated in the attempt to define what is and what is not a capital asset.

Capital assets are not directly defined in the Code. Instead, § 1221(a) defines what is *not* a capital asset. A **capital asset** is property held by the taxpayer (whether or not it is connected with the taxpayer's business) that is *not* any of the following:

- Inventory or property held primarily for sale to customers in the ordinary course of a business. The Supreme Court, in *Malat v. Riddell*, defined *primarily* as meaning *of first importance* or *principally*.[1]
- Accounts and notes receivable acquired from the sale of inventory or acquired for services rendered in the ordinary course of business.
- Depreciable property or real estate used in a business.
- Certain copyrights; literary, musical, or artistic compositions; or letters, memoranda, or similar property held by (1) a taxpayer whose efforts created the property; (2) in the case of a letter, memorandum, or similar property, a taxpayer for whom it was produced; or (3) a taxpayer in whose hands the basis of the property is determined, for purposes of determining gain from a sale or exchange, in whole or in part by reference to the basis of such property in the hands of a taxpayer described in (1) or (2). When a sale or exchange involves musical compositions or copyrights in musical works either (1) created by the taxpayer's personal efforts or (2) having a basis determined by reference to the basis in the hands of a taxpayer whose personal efforts created the compositions or copyrights, the taxpayer may elect to treat the sale or exchange as the disposition of a capital asset.[2]
- U.S. government publications that are (1) received by a taxpayer from the U.S. government other than by purchase at the price at which they are offered for sale to the public or (2) held by a taxpayer whose basis, for

purposes of determining gain from a sale or exchange, is determined by reference to a taxpayer described in (1).
- Supplies of a type regularly used or consumed in the ordinary course of a business.

The Code defines what is not a capital asset. From the preceding list, it is apparent that inventory, accounts and notes receivable, supplies, and most fixed assets of a business are not capital assets. Often, the only business asset that is a capital asset is goodwill. The following discussion provides further detail on each part of the capital asset definition.

Inventory

What constitutes inventory is determined by the taxpayer's business.

	EXAMPLE 1

Green Company buys and sells used cars. Its cars are inventory. Its gains from the sale of the cars are ordinary income. ■

	EXAMPLE 2

Soong sells her personal use automobile at a $500 gain. The automobile is a personal use asset and, therefore, a capital asset. The gain is a capital gain. ■

Accounts and Notes Receivable

Collection of an accrual basis account receivable usually does not result in a gain or loss because the amount collected equals the receivable's basis. The sale of an account or note receivable may generate a gain or loss, and the gain or loss is ordinary because the receivable is not a capital asset. The sale of an accrual basis receivable may result in a gain or loss because it will probably be sold for more or less than its basis. A cash basis account receivable has no basis. Sale of such a receivable generates a gain. Collection of a cash basis receivable generates ordinary income rather than a gain. A gain usually requires a sale of the receivable. See the discussion of Sale or Exchange later in this chapter.

	EXAMPLE 3

Oriole Company has accounts receivable of $100,000. Because it needs working capital, it sells the receivables for $83,000 to a financial institution. If Oriole is an accrual basis taxpayer, it has a $17,000 ordinary loss. Revenue of $100,000 would have been recorded and a $100,000 basis would have been established when the receivable was created. If Oriole is a cash basis taxpayer, it has $83,000 of ordinary income because it would not have recorded any revenue earlier; thus, the receivable has no tax basis. ■

Business Fixed Assets

Depreciable personal property and real estate (both depreciable and nondepreciable) used by a business are not capital assets. Thus, *business fixed assets* are generally not capital assets.

The Code has a very complex set of rules pertaining to such property. One of these rules is discussed under Real Property Subdivided for Sale in this chapter; the remainder of the rules are discussed in Chapter 17. Although business fixed assets are not capital assets, a long-term capital gain can sometimes result from their sale. Chapter 17 discusses the potential capital gain treatment for business fixed assets under § 1231.

Copyrights and Creative Works

Generally, the person whose efforts led to the copyright or creative work has an ordinary asset, not a capital asset. *Creative works* include the works of authors, composers, and artists. Also, the person for whom a letter, memorandum, or other similar property was created has an ordinary asset. Finally, a person receiving a copyright, creative work, letter, memorandum, or similar property by gift from the creator or the person for whom the work was created has an ordinary asset. Note the exception mentioned earlier that permits the taxpayer to elect to treat the sale or exchange of a musical composition or a copyright of a musical work as the disposition of a capital asset.

EXAMPLE 4

Wanda is a part-time music composer. A music publisher purchases one of her songs for $5,000. Wanda has a $5,000 ordinary gain from the sale of an ordinary asset unless she elects to treat the gain as a capital gain. ■

EXAMPLE 5

Ed received a letter from the President of the United States in 1982. In the current year, Ed sells the letter to a collector for $300. Ed has a $300 ordinary gain from the sale of an ordinary asset (because the letter was created for Ed). ■

EXAMPLE 6

Isabella gives a song she composed to her son. The son sells the song to a music publisher for $5,000. The son has a $5,000 ordinary gain from the sale of an ordinary asset unless he elects to treat the gain as a capital gain. If the son inherits the song from Isabella, his basis for the song is its fair market value at Isabella's death. In this situation, the song is a capital asset because the son's basis is not related to Isabella's basis for the song. ■

(Patents are subject to special statutory rules discussed later in the chapter.)

ETHICS & Equity   WHO OWNS THE SONG?

Jason is the lead singer in a hip-hop band. He also handles all business arrangements for the band, such as bookings, negotiating contracts, and collecting payments for band performances. After each performance, Jason pays all of the band members in cash for their services that night. Jason and the other band members created a song that has gone viral on the Web. A music publisher has offered to purchase the song for $100,000. Jason has not told the other band members about this opportunity. Evaluate some of the issues facing Jason.

U.S. Government Publications

U.S. government publications received from the U.S. government (or its agencies) for a reduced price are not capital assets. This prevents a taxpayer from later donating the publications to charity and claiming a charitable contribution equal to the fair market value of the publications. A charitable contribution of a capital asset generally yields a deduction equal to the fair market value. A charitable contribution of an ordinary asset generally yields a deduction equal to less than the fair market value. If such property is received by gift from the original purchaser, the property is not a capital asset to the donee. (For a more comprehensive explanation of charitable contributions of property, refer to Chapter 10.)

EFFECT OF JUDICIAL ACTION

Court decisions play an important role in the definition of capital assets. Because the Code only lists categories of what are *not* capital assets, judicial interpretation is sometimes required to determine whether a specific item fits into one of those categories. The Supreme Court follows a literal interpretation of the categories. For instance, corporate stock is not mentioned in § 1221. Thus, corporate stock is *usually* a capital asset. However, what if corporate stock is purchased for resale to customers? Then it is *inventory* and not a capital asset because inventory is one of the categories in § 1221. (See the discussion of Dealers in Securities that follows.)

A Supreme Court decision was required to distinguish between capital asset and non-capital asset status when a taxpayer who normally did not acquire stock for resale to customers acquired stock with the intention of resale.[3] The Court decided that since the stock was not acquired primarily for sale to customers (the taxpayer did not sell the stock to its regular customers), the stock was a capital asset.

Often the crux of the capital asset determination hinges on whether the asset is held for investment purposes (capital asset) or business purposes (ordinary asset). The taxpayer's *use* of the property often provides objective evidence.

David's business buys an expensive painting. If the painting is used to decorate David's office and is not of investment quality, the painting is depreciable and, therefore, not a capital asset. If David's business is buying and selling paintings, the painting is inventory and, therefore, an ordinary asset. If the painting is of investment quality and the business purchased it for investment, the painting is a capital asset, even though it serves a decorative purpose in David's office. *Investment quality* generally means that the painting is expected to appreciate in value. If David depreciates the painting, that would be objective evidence that the painting is held for use in his business, is not being held for investment or as inventory, and is not a capital asset. ■

Because of the uncertainty associated with capital asset status, Congress has enacted several Code Sections to clarify the definition. These statutory expansions of the capital asset definition are discussed in the following section.

STATUTORY EXPANSIONS

Congress has often expanded the § 1221 general definition of what is *not* a capital asset.

Dealers in Securities

As a general rule, securities (stocks, bonds, and other financial instruments) held by a dealer are considered to be inventory and are, therefore, not subject to capital gain or loss treatment. A *dealer in securities* is a merchant (e.g., a brokerage firm) that regularly engages in the purchase and resale of securities to customers. The dealer must identify any securities being held for investment. Generally, if a dealer clearly identifies certain securities as held for investment purposes by the close of business on the acquisition date, gain from the securities' sale will be capital gain. However, the gain will not be capital gain if the dealer ceases to hold the securities for investment prior to the sale. Losses are capital losses if at any time the securities have been clearly identified by the dealer as held for investment.[4]

Tracy is a securities dealer. She purchases 100 shares of Swan stock. If Tracy takes no further action, the stock is inventory and an ordinary asset. If she designates in her records that the stock is held for investment, the stock is a capital asset. Tracy must designate the investment purpose by the close of business on the acquisition date. If Tracy maintains her investment purpose and later sells the stock, the gain or loss is capital gain or loss. If Tracy redesignates the stock as held for resale (inventory) and then sells it, any gain is ordinary, but any loss is capital loss. Stock designated as held for investment and then sold at a loss always yields a capital loss. ■

Real Property Subdivided for Sale

Substantial real property development activities may result in the owner being considered a dealer for tax purposes. Income from the sale of real estate property lots is treated as the sale of inventory (ordinary income) if the owner is considered to be a dealer. However, § 1237 allows real estate investors capital gain treatment if they

---

[3] *Arkansas Best v. Comm.*, 88–1 USTC ¶9210, 61 AFTR 2d 88–655, 108 S.Ct. 971 (USSC, 1988).

[4] §§ 1236(a) and (b) and Reg. §§ 1.1236–1(a) and (b).

engage *only* in *limited* development activities. To be eligible for § 1237 treatment, the following requirements must be met:

- The taxpayer may not be a corporation.
- The taxpayer may not be a real estate dealer.
- No substantial improvements may be made to the lots sold. *Substantial* generally means more than a 10 percent increase in the value of a lot. Shopping centers and other commercial or residential buildings are considered substantial, while filling, draining, leveling, and clearing operations are not.
- The taxpayer must have held the lots sold for at least 5 years, except for inherited property. The substantial improvements test is less stringent if the property is held at least 10 years.

If the preceding requirements are met, all gain is capital gain until the tax year in which the *sixth* lot is sold. Sales of contiguous lots to a single buyer in the same transaction count as the sale of one lot. Beginning with the tax year the *sixth* lot is sold, some of the gain may be ordinary income. Five percent of the revenue from lot sales is potential ordinary income. That potential ordinary income is offset by any selling expenses from the lot sales. Practically, sales commissions often are at least 5 percent of the sales price, so none of the gain is treated as ordinary income.

Section 1237 does not apply to losses. A loss from the sale of subdivided real property is an ordinary loss unless the property qualifies as a capital asset under § 1221. The following example illustrates the application of § 1237.

EXAMPLE 9

Jack owns a large tract of land and subdivides it for sale. Assume Jack meets all the requirements of § 1237 and during the tax year sells the first 10 lots to 10 different buyers for $10,000 each. Jack's basis in each lot sold is $3,000, and he incurs total selling expenses of $4,000 on the sales. Jack's gain is computed as follows:

Selling price (10 × $10,000)	$100,000	
Less: Selling expenses (10 × $400)	(4,000)	
Amount realized		$ 96,000
Basis (10 × $3,000)		(30,000)
Realized and recognized gain		$ 66,000
Classification of recognized gain:		
Ordinary income		
Five percent of selling price (5% × $100,000)	$ 5,000	
Less: Selling expenses	(4,000)	
Ordinary gain		1,000
Capital gain		$ 65,000

Nonbusiness Bad Debts

A loan not made in the ordinary course of business is classified as a nonbusiness receivable. In the year the receivable becomes completely worthless, it is a *nonbusiness*

> ### TAX*in* the NEWS — BANKRUPTCY AND WORTHLESS STOCK
>
> During 2009, General Motors went into bankruptcy, was reorganized, and emerged from bankruptcy. However, the common shareholders of the General Motors that went into bankruptcy were not the common shareholders of the General Motors that emerged from bankruptcy. The original common shareholders lost their entire investment because their stock became worthless. The holding period of their stock ended for tax purposes on December 31,
>
> 2009, because of the worthless stock rules. They had a capital loss equal to whatever their basis was for the worthless shares. The debtors of General Motors accepted common shares in the General Motors that emerged from bankruptcy. Generally, the exchange of debt for common shares in a bankruptcy reorganization is not a taxable transaction, and the basis of the debt becomes the basis for the shares.

bad debt, and the bad debt is treated as a short-term capital loss. Even if the receivable was outstanding for more than one year, the loss is still a short-term capital loss. Chapter 7 discusses nonbusiness bad debts more thoroughly.

16.3 SALE OR EXCHANGE

Recognition of capital gain or loss usually requires a sale or exchange of a capital asset. The Code uses the term **sale or exchange**, but does not define it. Generally, a property sale involves the receipt of money by the seller and/or the assumption by the purchaser of the seller's liabilities. An exchange involves the transfer of property for other property. Thus, an involuntary conversion (casualty, theft, or condemnation) is not a sale or exchange. In several situations, the determination of whether a sale or exchange has taken place has been clarified by the enactment of Code Sections that specifically provide for sale or exchange treatment.

Recognized gains or losses from the cancellation, lapse, expiration, or any other termination of a right or obligation with respect to personal property (other than stock) that is or would be a capital asset in the hands of the taxpayer are capital gains or losses.[5] See the discussion under Options later in the chapter for more details.

> **LO.3**
>
> Understand the relevance of a sale or exchange to classification as a capital gain or loss and apply the special rules for the capital gain or loss treatment of the retirement of corporate obligations, options, patents, franchises, and lease cancellation payments.

WORTHLESS SECURITIES AND § 1244 STOCK

Occasionally, securities such as stock and, especially, bonds may become worthless due to the insolvency of their issuer. If such a security is a capital asset, the loss is deemed to have occurred as the result of a sale or exchange on the *last day* of the tax year.[6] This last-day rule may have the effect of converting what otherwise would have been a short-term capital loss into a long-term capital loss. (See Treatment of Capital Losses later in this chapter.) Worthless securities are discussed in Chapter 7 at pp. 7–7 and 7–27.

Section 1244 allows an ordinary deduction on disposition of stock at a loss. The stock must be that of a small business company, and the ordinary deduction is limited to $50,000 ($100,000 for married individuals filing jointly) per year. For a more detailed discussion, refer to Chapter 7, pp. 7–8 and 7–27.

SPECIAL RULE—RETIREMENT OF CORPORATE OBLIGATIONS

A debt obligation (e.g., a bond or note payable) may have a tax basis in excess of or less than its redemption value because it may have been acquired at a premium or

---

[5]§ 1234A.

[6]§ 165(g)(1).

discount. Consequently, the collection of the redemption value may result in a loss or gain. Generally, the collection of a debt obligation is *treated* as a sale or exchange.[7] Therefore, any loss or gain can be a capital loss or capital gain because a sale or exchange has taken place. However, if the debt obligation was issued by a human being prior to June 9, 1997, and/or purchased by the taxpayer prior to June 9, 1997, the collection of the debt obligation is not a sale or exchange.

EXAMPLE 10

Fran acquires $1,000 of Osprey Corporation bonds for $980 in the open market. If the bonds are held to maturity, the $20 difference between Fran's collection of the $1,000 redemption value and her cost of $980 is treated as capital gain. If the obligation had been issued to Fran by an individual prior to June 9, 1997, her $20 gain would be ordinary, since she did not sell or exchange the debt. ■

Original Issue Discount

The benefit of the sale or exchange exception that allows a capital gain from the collection of certain obligations is reduced when the obligation has original issue discount. **Original issue discount (OID)** arises when the issue price of a debt obligation is less than the maturity value of the obligation. OID must generally be amortized over the life of the debt obligation using the effective interest method. The OID amortization increases the basis of the bond. Most new publicly traded bond issues do not carry OID since the stated interest rate is set to make the market price on issue the same as the bond's face amount. In addition, even if the issue price is less than the face amount, the difference is not considered to be OID if the difference is less than one-fourth of 1 percent of the redemption price at maturity multiplied by the number of years to maturity.[8]

In the case where OID does exist, it may or may not have to be amortized, depending upon the date the obligation was issued. When OID is amortized, the amount of gain upon collection, sale, or exchange of the obligation is correspondingly reduced. The obligations covered by the OID amortization rules and the method of amortization are presented in §§ 1272–1275. Similar rules for other obligations can be found in §§ 1276–1288.

EXAMPLE 11

Jerry purchases $10,000 of newly issued White Corporation bonds for $6,000. The bonds have OID of $4,000. Jerry must amortize the discount over the life of the bonds. The OID amortization *increases* his interest income. (The bonds were selling at a discount because the market rate of interest was greater than the bonds' interest rate.) After Jerry has amortized $1,800 of OID, he sells the bonds for $8,000. Jerry has a capital gain of $200 [$8,000 − ($6,000 cost + $1,800 OID amortization)]. The OID amortization rules prevent him from converting ordinary interest income into capital gain. Without the OID amortization, Jerry would have capital gain of $2,000 ($8,000 − $6,000 cost). ■

OPTIONS

Frequently, a potential buyer of property wants some time to make the purchase decision, but wants to control the sale and/or the sale price in the meantime. **Options** are used to achieve these objectives. The potential purchaser (grantee) pays the property owner (grantor) for an option on the property. The grantee then becomes the option holder. The option usually sets a price at which the grantee can buy the property and expires after a specified period of time.

Sale of an Option

A grantee may sell or exchange the option rather than exercising it or letting it expire. Generally, the grantee's sale or exchange of the option results in capital gain or loss if the option property is (or would be) a capital asset to the grantee.[9]

---

[7]§ 1271.
[8]§ 1273(a)(3).

[9]§ 1234(a) and Reg. § 1.1234–1(a)(1). Stock options are discussed in Chapter 19.

EXAMPLE 12

Rosa wants to buy some vacant land for investment purposes. She cannot afford the full purchase price. Instead, she convinces the landowner (grantor) to sell her the right to purchase the land for $100,000 anytime in the next two years. Rosa (grantee) pays $3,000 to obtain this option to buy the land. The option is a capital asset for Rosa because if she actually purchased the land, the land would be a capital asset. Three months after purchasing the option, Rosa sells it for $7,000. She has a $4,000 ($7,000 − $3,000) short-term capital gain on this sale since she held the option for one year or less. ∎

Failure to Exercise Options

If an option holder (grantee) fails to exercise the option, the lapse of the option is considered a sale or exchange on the option expiration date. Thus, the loss is a capital loss if the property subject to the option is (or would be) a capital asset in the hands of the grantee.

The grantor of an option on *stocks, securities, commodities, or commodity futures* receives short-term capital gain treatment upon the expiration of the option. Options on property other than stocks, securities, commodities, or commodity futures result in ordinary income to the grantor when the option expires. For example, an individual investor who owns certain stock (a capital asset) may sell a call option, entitling the buyer of the option to acquire the stock at a specified price higher than the value at the date the option is granted. The writer of the call receives a premium (e.g., 10 percent) for writing the option. If the price of the stock does not increase during the option period, the option will expire unexercised. Upon the expiration of the option, the grantor must recognize short-term capital gain. These provisions do not apply to options held for sale to customers (the inventory of a securities dealer).

Exercise of Options by Grantee

If the option is exercised, the amount paid for the option is added to the optioned property's selling price. This increases the gain (or reduces the loss) to the grantor resulting from the sale of the property. The grantor's gain or loss is capital or ordinary depending on the tax status of the property. The grantee adds the cost of the option to the basis of the property purchased.

EXAMPLE 13

On September 1, 2007, Wes purchases 100 shares of Eagle Company stock for $5,000. On April 1, 2011, he writes a call option on the stock, giving the grantee the right to buy the stock for $6,000 during the following six-month period. Wes (the grantor) receives a call premium of $500 for writing the call.

- If the call is exercised by the grantee on August 1, 2011, Wes has $1,500 ($6,000 + $500 − $5,000) of long-term capital gain from the sale of the stock. The grantee has a $6,500 ($500 option premium + $6,000 purchase price) basis for the stock.
- Assume that Wes decides to sell his stock prior to exercise for $6,000 and enters into a closing transaction by purchasing a call on 100 shares of Eagle Company stock for $5,000. Since the Eagle stock is selling for $6,000, Wes must pay a call premium of $1,000. He recognizes a $500 short-term capital loss [$1,000 (call premium paid) − $500 (call premium received)] on the closing transaction. On the actual sale of the Eagle stock, Wes has a long-term capital gain of $1,000 [$6,000 (selling price) − $5,000 (cost)]. The grantee is not affected by Wes's closing transaction. The original option is still in existence, and the grantee's tax consequences will depend on what action the grantee takes—exercising the option, letting the option expire, or selling the option.
- Assume that the original option expired unexercised. Wes has a $500 short-term capital gain equal to the call premium received for writing the option. This gain is not recognized until the option expires. The grantee has a loss from expiration of the option. The nature of the loss will depend upon whether the option was a capital asset or an ordinary asset. ∎

Concept Summary 16.1 summarizes the rules for options.

CONCEPT SUMMARY 16.1

Options

Event	Effect on	
	Grantor	**Grantee**
Option is granted.	Receives value and has a contract obligation (a liability).	Pays value and has a contract right (an asset).
Option expires.	Has a short-term capital gain if the option property is stocks, securities, commodities, or commodity futures. Otherwise, gain is ordinary income.	Has a loss (capital loss if option property would have been a capital asset for the grantee).
Option is exercised.	Amount received for option increases proceeds from sale of the option property.	Amount paid for option becomes part of the basis of the option property purchased.
Option is sold or exchanged by grantee.	Result depends upon whether option later expires or is exercised (see above).	Could have gain or loss (capital gain or loss if option property would have been a capital asset for the grantee).

PATENTS

Transfer of a **patent** is treated as the sale or exchange of a long-term capital asset when all substantial rights to the patent (or an undivided interest that includes all such rights) are transferred by a holder.[10] The transferor/holder may receive payment in virtually any form. Lump-sum or periodic payments are most common. The amount of the payments may also be contingent on the transferee/purchaser's productivity, use, or disposition of the patent. If the transfer meets these requirements, any gain or loss is *automatically a long-term* capital gain or loss. Whether the asset was a capital asset for the transferor, whether a sale or exchange occurred, and how long the transferor held the patent are not relevant.

This special long-term capital gain or loss treatment for patents is intended to encourage technological progress. Ironically, authors, composers, and artists are not eligible for capital gain treatment when their creations are transferred. Books, songs, and artists' works may be copyrighted, but copyrights and the assets they represent are not capital assets. Thus, the disposition of those assets by their creators usually results in ordinary gain or loss (unless the exception for musical compositions applies, as noted earlier). The following example illustrates the special treatment for patents.

EXAMPLE 14
THE BIG PICTURE

Return to the facts of *The Big Picture* on p. 16-2. Kevin transfers his rights in the battery patent to the Green Battery Company in exchange for $1 million plus $.50 for each battery sold. Assuming Kevin has transferred all substantial rights, the question of whether the transfer is a sale or exchange of a capital asset is not relevant. Kevin automatically has a long-term capital gain from both his share of the lump-sum payment of $2 million and the $1 per battery royalty to the extent that these proceeds exceed his basis for the patent. Kevin also had an automatic long-term capital gain when he sold 50% of his rights in the patent to Maurice, because Kevin transferred an undivided interest that included all substantial rights in the patent. Whether Maurice gets long-term capital gain treatment on the transfer to Green Battery will depend on whether he is a holder (see the discussion below and in Example 15). ∎

Substantial Rights

To receive favorable capital gain treatment, all *substantial rights* to the patent (or an undivided interest in it) must be transferred. All substantial rights to a patent means all rights (whether or not then held by the grantor) that are valuable at the time the

[10]§ 1235.

patent rights (or an undivided interest in the patent) are transferred. All substantial rights have not been transferred when the transfer is limited geographically within the issuing country or when the transfer is for a period less than the remaining life of the patent. The circumstances of the entire transaction, rather than merely the language used in the transfer instrument, are to be considered in deciding whether all substantial rights have been transferred.[11]

Holder Defined

The *holder* of a patent must be an *individual* and is usually the invention's creator. A holder may also be an individual who purchases the patent rights from the creator before the patented invention is reduced to practice. However, the creator's employer and certain parties related to the creator do not qualify as holders. Thus, in the common situation where an employer has all rights to an employee's inventions, the employer is not eligible for long-term capital gain treatment. More than likely, the employer will have an ordinary asset because the patent was developed as part of its business.

> **EXAMPLE 15**
> **THE BIG PICTURE**
>
> Return to the facts of *The Big Picture* on p. 16-2. Continuing with the facts of Example 14, Kevin is clearly a holder of the patent because he is the inventor and was not an employee when he invented the battery. When Maurice purchased a 50% interest in the patent nine months ago, he became a holder if the patent had not yet been reduced to practice. Since the patent apparently was not being manufactured at the time of the purchase, it had not been reduced to practice. Consequently, Maurice is also a holder, and he also has an automatic long-term capital gain or loss when the patent is transferred to Green Battery Company. Maurice's basis for his share of the patent is $50,000, and his share of the proceeds is $1 million plus $.50 for each battery sold. Thus, Maurice has a long-term capital gain even though he has not held his interest in the patent for more than one year. ■

FRANCHISES, TRADEMARKS, AND TRADE NAMES

A mode of operation, a widely recognized brand name (trade name), and a widely known business symbol (trademark) are all valuable assets. These assets may be licensed (commonly known as franchising) by their owner for use by other businesses. Many fast-food restaurants (such as McDonald's and Taco Bell) are franchises. The franchisee usually pays the owner (franchisor) an initial fee plus a contingent fee. The contingent fee is often based upon the franchisee's sales volume.

For Federal income tax purposes, a **franchise** is an agreement that gives the franchisee the right to distribute, sell, or provide goods, services, or facilities within a specified area.[12] A franchise transfer includes the grant of a franchise, a transfer by one franchisee to another person, or the renewal of a franchise.

A franchise transfer is generally not a sale or exchange of a capital asset. Section 1253 provides that a transfer of a franchise, trademark, or trade name is not a transfer of a capital asset when the transferor retains any significant power, right, or continuing interest in the property transferred.

Significant Power, Right, or Continuing Interest

Significant powers, rights, or continuing interests include control over assignment, quality of products and services, and sale or advertising of other products or services, and the right to require that substantially all supplies and equipment be purchased from the transferor. Also included are the right to terminate the franchise at will and the right to substantial contingent payments. Most modern franchising operations involve some or all of these powers, rights, or continuing interests.

In the unusual case where no significant power, right, or continuing interest is retained by the transferor, a sale or exchange may occur, and capital gain or loss treatment may be available. For capital gain or loss treatment to be available, the asset transferred must qualify as a capital asset.

---

[11]Reg. § 1.1235–2(b)(1). [12]§ 1253(b)(1).

| EXAMPLE 16 | Orange, Inc., a franchisee, sells the franchise to a third party. Payments to Orange are not contingent, and all significant powers, rights, and continuing interests are transferred. The gain (payments − adjusted basis) on the sale is a capital gain to Orange. ∎ |

Noncontingent Payments

When the transferor retains a significant power, right, or continuing interest, the transferee's noncontingent payments to the transferor are ordinary income to the transferor. The franchisee capitalizes the payments and amortizes them over 15 years. The amortization is subject to recapture under § 1245.[13]

| EXAMPLE 17 | Grey Company signs a 10-year franchise agreement with DOH Donuts. Grey (the franchisee) makes payments of $3,000 per year for the first 8 years of the franchise agreement—a total of $24,000. Grey cannot deduct $3,000 per year as the payments are made. Instead, Grey may amortize the $24,000 total over 15 years. Thus, Grey may deduct $1,600 per year for each of the 15 years of the amortization period. The same result would occur if Grey made a $24,000 lump-sum payment at the beginning of the franchise period. Assuming DOH Donuts (the franchisor) retains significant powers, rights, or a continuing interest, it will have ordinary income when it receives the payments from Grey. ∎ |

Contingent Payments

Whether or not the transferor retains a significant power, right, or continuing interest, contingent franchise payments are ordinary income for the franchisor and an ordinary deduction for the franchisee. For this purpose, a payment qualifies as a contingent payment only if the following requirements are met:

- The contingent amounts are part of a series of payments that are paid at least annually throughout the term of the transfer agreement.
- The payments are substantially equal in amount or are payable under a fixed formula.

| EXAMPLE 18 | TAK, a spicy chicken franchisor, transfers an eight-year franchise to Otis. TAK retains a significant power, right, or continuing interest. Otis, the franchisee, agrees to pay TAK 15% of sales. This contingent payment is ordinary income to TAK and a business deduction for Otis as the payments are made. ∎ |

Sports Franchises

Professional sports franchises (e.g., the Detroit Tigers) are subject to § 1253.[14] Player contracts are usually one of the major assets acquired with a sports franchise. These contracts last only for the time stated in the contract. By being classified as § 197 intangibles, the player contracts and other intangible assets acquired in the purchase of the sports franchise are amortized over a statutory 15-year period.[15]

Concept Summary 16.2 summarizes the rules for franchises.

LEASE CANCELLATION PAYMENTS

The tax treatment of payments received for canceling a lease depends on whether the recipient is the **lessor** or the **lessee** and whether the lease is a capital asset or not.

Lessee Treatment

Lease cancellation payments received by a lessee are treated as an exchange.[16] Thus, these payments are capital gains if the lease is a capital asset. Generally, a lessee's lease is a capital asset if the property (either personalty or realty) is used for the lessee's

---

[13]See Chapter 17 for a discussion of the recapture provisions.

[14]Section 1253(e) previously exempted sports franchises from § 1253, but was repealed for franchises acquired after October 22, 2004.

[15]§ 197(a).

[16]§ 1241 and Reg. § 1.1241–1(a).

CONCEPT SUMMARY 16.2

Franchises

Event	Effect on Franchisor	Effect on Franchisee
Franchisor Retains Significant Powers and Rights		
Noncontingent payment	Ordinary income.	Capitalized and amortized over 15 years as an ordinary deduction; if franchise is sold, amortization is subject to recapture under § 1245.
Contingent payment	Ordinary income.	Ordinary deduction.
Franchisor Does *Not* Retain Significant Powers and Rights		
Noncontingent payment	Ordinary income if franchise rights are an ordinary asset; capital gain if franchise rights are a capital asset (unlikely).	Capitalized and amortized over 15 years as an ordinary deduction; if the franchise is sold, amortization is subject to recapture under § 1245.
Contingent payment	Ordinary income.	Ordinary deduction.

personal use (e.g., his or her residence). A lessee's lease is an ordinary asset if the property is used in the lessee's trade or business and the lease has existed for one year or less when it is canceled. A lessee's lease is a § 1231 asset if the property is used in the lessee's trade or business and the lease has existed for more than a year when it is canceled.[17]

EXAMPLE 19

Mark owns an apartment building that he is going to convert into an office building. Vicki is one of the apartment tenants and receives $1,000 from Mark to cancel the lease. Vicki has a capital gain of $1,000 (which is long term or short term depending upon how long she has held the lease). Mark has an ordinary deduction of $1,000. ■

Lessor Treatment

Payments received by a lessor for a lease cancellation are always ordinary income because they are considered to be in lieu of rental payments.[18]

EXAMPLE 20

Floyd owns an apartment building near a university campus. Hui-Fen is one of the tenants. Hui-Fen is graduating early and offers Floyd $800 to cancel the apartment lease. Floyd accepts the offer. Floyd has ordinary income of $800. Hui-Fen has a nondeductible payment since the apartment was personal use property. ■

16.4 HOLDING PERIOD

Property must be held more than one year to qualify for long-term capital gain or loss treatment.[19] Property not held for the required long-term period results in short-term capital gain or loss. To compute the **holding period**, start counting on the day after the property was acquired and include the day of disposition.

LO.4
Determine whether the holding period for a capital asset is long term or short term.

EXAMPLE 21 THE BIG PICTURE

Return to the facts of *The Big Picture* on p. 16-2. Assume that Maurice purchased the Purple stock on January 15, 2010. If he sells it on January 16, 2011, Maurice's holding period is more than one year. If instead Maurice sells the stock on January 15, 2011, the holding period is exactly one year, and the gain or loss is short term. ■

[17]Reg. § 1.1221–1(b) and PLR 200045019.
[18]Reg. § 1.61–8(b).
[19]§ 1222(3).

TAX in the NEWS

UNCERTAINTY ABOUT THE HOLDING PERIOD

During the fall of 2010, a tornado struck a small town in Ohio. A local investor had purchased a 20-acre plot with a stand of trees to use for hunting. The tornado destroyed the trees and made the land useless for hunting. Three months after the tornado, the land was sold "as is" to the insurance company that had insured it. The investor had owned the land for 10 months when the tornado struck and 13 months when it was sold to the insurance company. The land was sold at a loss. The loss is long term because the sale date occurred after the land had been held for more than one year.

To be held for more than one year, a capital asset acquired on the last day of any month must not be disposed of until on or after the first day of the thirteenth succeeding month.[20]

EXAMPLE 22

Leo purchases a capital asset on February 28, 2010. If Leo sells the asset on February 28, 2011, the holding period is one year, and Leo will have a short-term capital gain or loss. If Leo sells the asset on March 1, 2011, the holding period is more than one year, and he will have a long-term capital gain or loss. ■

REVIEW OF SPECIAL HOLDING PERIOD RULES

There are several special holding period rules.[21] The application of these rules depends on the type of asset and how it was acquired.

Nontaxable Exchanges

The holding period of property received in a like-kind exchange includes the holding period of the former asset if the property that has been exchanged is a capital asset or a § 1231 asset. In certain nontaxable transactions involving a substituted basis, the holding period of the former property is *tacked on* to the holding period of the newly acquired property.

EXAMPLE 23

Vern exchanges a business truck for another truck in a like-kind exchange. The holding period of the exchanged truck tacks on to the holding period of the new truck. ■

Certain Nontaxable Transactions Involving a Carryover of Another Taxpayer's Basis

A former owner's holding period is tacked on to the present owner's holding period if the transaction is nontaxable and the former owner's basis carries over to the present owner.

EXAMPLE 24

Kareem acquires 100 shares of Robin Corporation stock for $1,000 on December 31, 2007. He transfers the shares by gift to Megan on December 31, 2010, when the stock is worth $2,000. Kareem's basis of $1,000 becomes the basis for determining gain or loss on a subsequent sale by Megan. Megan's holding period begins with the date the stock was acquired by Kareem. ■

EXAMPLE 25

Assume the same facts as in Example 24, except that the fair market value of the shares is only $800 on the date of the gift. The holding period begins on the date of the gift if Megan sells the stock for a loss. The value of the shares at the date of the gift is used in the determination of her basis for loss. If she sells the shares for $500 on April 1, 2011,

---

[20]Rev.Rul. 66–7, 1966–1 C.B. 188. [21]§ 1223.

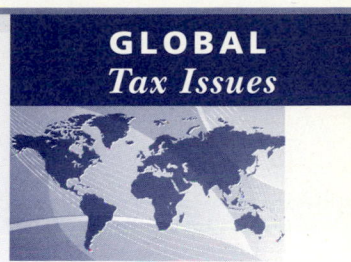

GLOBAL
Tax Issues

TRADING ADRS ON U.S. STOCK EXCHANGES

Many non-U.S. companies now have subsidiaries that were formerly U.S. companies. For instance, Chrysler Corporation is a subsidiary of Fiat. Shares in such foreign companies generally cannot be traded directly on U.S. stock exchanges. Instead, the foreign companies issue instruments called American Depository Receipts (ADRs) that can be traded on U.S. stock exchanges. Purchases and sales of ADRs are treated for tax purposes as though the ADRs were shares in the corporation that issued them.

Megan has a $300 recognized capital loss, and the holding period is from December 31, 2010, to April 1, 2011 (thus, the loss is short term). ∎

Certain Disallowed Loss Transactions

Under several Code provisions, realized losses are disallowed. When a loss is disallowed, there is no carryover of holding period. Losses can be disallowed under § 267 (sale or exchange between related taxpayers) and § 262 (sale or exchange of personal use assets) as well as other Code Sections. Taxpayers who acquire property in a disallowed loss transaction will have a new holding period begin and will have a basis equal to the purchase price.

EXAMPLE 26

Janet sells her personal automobile at a loss. She may not deduct the loss because it arises from the sale of personal use property. Janet purchases a replacement automobile for more than the selling price of her former automobile. Janet has a basis equal to the cost of the replacement automobile, and her holding period begins when she acquires the replacement automobile. ∎

Inherited Property

The holding period for inherited property is treated as long term no matter how long the property is actually held by the heir. The holding period of the decedent or the decedent's estate is not relevant for the heir's holding period.[22]

EXAMPLE 27

Shonda inherits Blue Company stock from her father who died in 2011. She receives the stock on April 1, 2011, and sells it on November 1, 2011. Even though Shonda did not hold the stock more than one year, she receives long-term capital gain or loss treatment on the sale. ∎

SPECIAL RULES FOR SHORT SALES

General

The Code provides special rules for determining the holding period of property sold short.[23] A **short sale** occurs when a taxpayer sells borrowed property and repays the lender with substantially identical property either held on the date of the sale or purchased after the sale. Short sales usually involve corporate stock. The seller's objective is to make a profit in anticipation of a decline in the stock's price. If the price declines, the seller in a short sale recognizes a profit equal to the difference between the sales price of the borrowed stock and the price paid for the replacement stock.

---

[22]The estate tax was repealed for 2010, and not all inherited assets will receive an automatic long-term holding period. However, Congress has enacted legislation that will continue the estate tax for 2011 (and later years) and continue an automatic long-term holding period for all inherited assets.

[23]§ 1233.

A *short sale against the box* occurs when the stock is borrowed from a broker by a seller who already owns the same stock. The box is the safe deposit box where stock owners routinely used to keep stock certificates. Although today stockbrokers generally keep stock for their customers, the terminology "short sale against the box" is still used.

EXAMPLE 28

Chris does not own any shares of Brown Corporation. However, Chris sells 30 shares of Brown. The shares are borrowed from Chris's broker and must be replaced within 45 days. Chris has a short sale because he was short the shares he sold. He will *close* the short sale by purchasing Brown shares and delivering them to his broker. If the original 30 shares were sold for $10,000 and Chris later purchases 30 shares for $8,000, he has a gain of $2,000. Chris's hunch that the price of Brown stock would decline was correct. Chris was able to profit from selling high and buying low. If Chris had to purchase Brown shares for $13,000 to close the short sale, he would have a loss of $3,000. In this case, Chris would have sold low and bought high—not the result he wanted! Chris would be making a short sale against the box if he borrowed shares from his broker to sell and then closed the short sale by delivering other Brown shares he owned at the time he made the short sale. ∎

A short sale gain or loss is a capital gain or loss to the extent that the short sale property constitutes a capital asset of the taxpayer. The gain or loss is not recognized until the short sale is closed. Generally, the holding period of the short sale property is determined by how long the property used to close the short sale was held. However, if *substantially identical property* (e.g., other shares of the same stock) is held by the taxpayer, the short-term or long-term character of the short sale gain or loss may be affected:

- If substantially identical property has *not* been held for the long-term holding period on the short sale date, the short sale *gain or loss* is short term.
- If substantially identical property has *been* held for the long-term holding period on the short sale date, the short sale *gain* is long term if the substantially identical property is used to close the short sale and short term if it is not used to close the short sale.
- If substantially identical property has *been* held for the long-term holding period on the short sale date, the short sale *loss* is long term whether or not the substantially identical property is used to close the short sale.
- If substantially identical property is acquired *after* the short sale date and on or before the closing date, the short sale *gain or loss* is short term.

Concept Summary 16.3 summarizes the short sale rules. These rules are intended to prevent the conversion of short-term capital gains into long-term capital gains and long-term capital losses into short-term capital losses.

Disposition Rules for Short Sales against the Box

In a short sale against the box, the taxpayer either owns securities that are substantially identical to the securities sold short at the short sale date or acquires such securities before the closing date. To remove the taxpayer's flexibility as to when the short sale gain must be reported, a constructive sale approach is used. If the taxpayer has not closed the short sale by delivering the short sale securities to the broker *before* January 31 of the year following the short sale, the short sale is deemed to have been closed on the *earlier* of two events:

- On the short sale date if the taxpayer owned substantially identical securities at that time.
- On the date during the year of the short sale that the taxpayer acquired substantially identical securities.[24]

[23]§ 1233.

CONCEPT SUMMARY 16.3

Short Sales of Securities

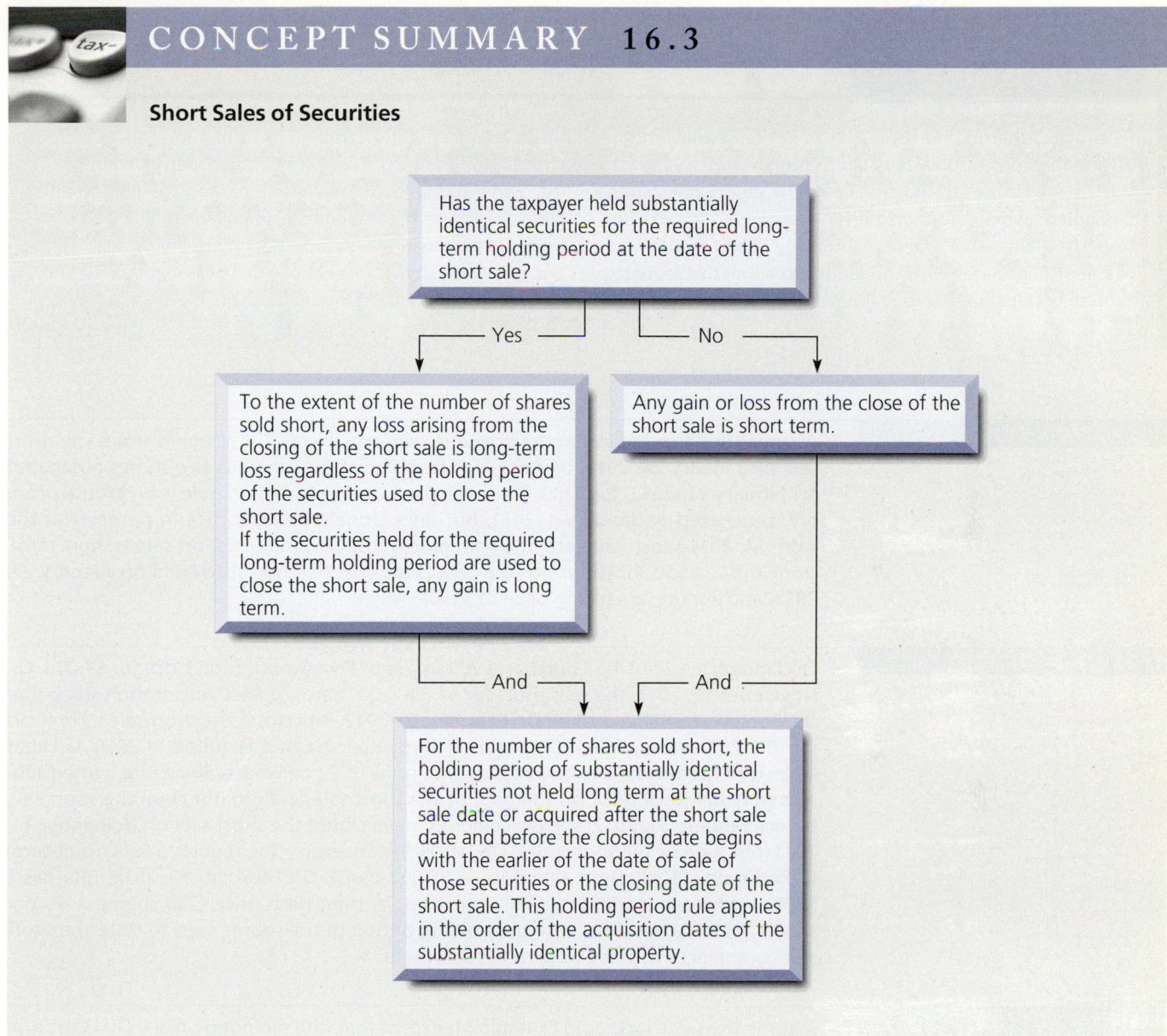

The basis of the shares in the deemed transfer of shares is used to compute the gain or loss on the short sale. Later, when shares are *actually* transferred to the broker to close the short sale, there may be a gain or loss because the shares transferred will have a basis equal to the short sale date price and the value at the *actual* short sale closing date may be different from the short sale date price.

Illustrations

The following examples illustrate the treatment of short sales and short sales against the box.

EXAMPLE 29

On January 4, 2011, Donald purchases five shares of Osprey Corporation common stock for $100. On April 14, 2011, he engages in a short sale of five shares of the same stock for $150. On August 15, Donald closes the short sale by repaying the borrowed stock with the five shares purchased on January 4. Donald has a $50 short-term capital gain from the short sale because he had not held substantially identical shares for the long-term holding period on the short sale date. ∎

SHORT SALES IN REAL ESTATE

Recently, the term "short sale" has taken on a meaning in real estate transactions that is different from its use with regard to securities transactions. A short sale in real estate takes place when the mortgage on property exceeds the property's fair market value. A property owner in this predicament negotiates with the lender to allow the property to be sold at its fair market value with the lender accepting the sales price in full satisfaction of the mortgage. Lenders typically will not negotiate with such property owners until the owner has failed to make required mortgage payments and foreclosure by the lender is imminent. If the negotiations are successful, the property owner avoids foreclosure but may have debt cancellation income for the difference between the mortgage and the sales price.

EXAMPLE 30

Assume the same facts as in the previous example, except that Donald closes the short sale on January 28, 2012, by repaying the borrowed stock with five shares purchased on January 27, 2012, for $200. The stock used to close the short sale was not the property purchased on January 4, 2011, but since Donald held short-term property at the April 14, 2011 short sale date, the gain or loss from closing the short sale is short term. Donald has a $50 short-term capital loss ($200 cost of stock purchased on January 27, 2012, and a short sale selling price of $150). ■

EXAMPLE 31

On January 18, 2010, Rita purchases 200 shares of Owl Corporation stock for $1,000. On November 11, 2011, she sells short for $1,300 200 shares of Owl Corporation stock that she borrows from her broker. On February 10, 2012, Rita closes the short sale by delivering the 200 shares of Owl Corporation stock that she had acquired in 2010. On that date, Owl Corporation stock had a market price of $3 per share. Since Rita owned substantially identical stock on the date of the short sale and did not close the short sale before January 31, 2012, she is *deemed* to have closed the short sale on November 11, 2011 (the date of the short sale). On her 2011 tax return, she reports a $300 long-term capital gain ($1,300 short sale price − $1,000 basis). On February 10, 2012, Rita has a $700 short-term capital loss [$600 short sale closing date price (200 shares × $3 per share) − $1,300 basis] because the holding period of the shares used to close the short sale commences with the date of the short sale. ■

EXAMPLE 32

Assume the same facts as in Example 31, except that Rita did not own any Owl Corporation stock on the short sale date and acquired the 200 shares of Owl Corporation stock for $1,000 on December 12, 2011 (after the November 11, 2011 short sale date). The *deemed* closing of the short sale is December 12, 2011, because Rita held substantially identical shares at the end of 2011 and did not close the short sale before January 31, 2012. Her 2011 short sale gain is a *short-term* gain of $300 ($1,300 short sale price − $1,000 basis), and she still has a short-term capital loss of $700 on February 10, 2012. ■

16.5 TAX TREATMENT OF CAPITAL GAINS AND LOSSES OF NONCORPORATE TAXPAYERS

LO.5

Describe the beneficial tax treatment for capital gains and the detrimental tax treatment for capital losses for noncorporate taxpayers.

All taxpayers net their capital gains and losses. Short-term gains and losses (if any) are netted against one another, and long-term gains and losses (if any) are netted against one another. The results will be net short-term gain or loss and net long-term gain or loss. If these two net positions are of opposite sign (one is a gain and one is a loss), they are netted against one another.

Six possibilities exist for the result after all possible netting has been completed. Three of these final results are gains, and three are losses. One possible result is a net long-term capital gain (NLTCG). Net long-term capital gains of noncorporate taxpayers are subject to beneficial treatment. A second possibility is a net short-term capital gain (NSTCG). Third, the netting may result in both NLTCG and NSTCG.

The NLTCG portion of these results is eligible for an alternative tax calculation. As many as four different tax rates may be used in the calculation—0, 15, 25, and 28 percent. The tax savings from the alternative tax calculation range from a low of 10 percentage points (10 percent regular tax rate − 0 percent alternative tax rate) to a high of 20 percentage points (35 percent regular tax rate − 15 percent alternative tax rate). The alternative tax computation is discussed later in the chapter under Alternative Tax on Net Capital Gain.

The last three results of the capital gain and loss netting process are losses. Thus, a fourth possibility is a net long-term capital loss (NLTCL). A fifth result is a net short-term capital loss (NSTCL). Finally, a sixth possibility includes both an NLTCL and an NSTCL. Neither NLTCLs nor NSTCLs are treated as ordinary losses. Treatment as an ordinary loss generally is preferable to capital loss treatment since ordinary losses are deductible in full while the deductibility of capital losses is subject to certain limitations. An individual taxpayer may deduct a maximum of $3,000 of net capital losses for a taxable year.[25]

CAPITAL GAIN AND LOSS NETTING PROCESS

Holding Periods for Capital Gain and Loss Netting Purposes

As mentioned earlier in this chapter, there are two holding periods for purposes of the capital gain and loss netting process:

- *Short term*—Assets held one year or less.
- *Long term*—Assets held more than one year.

Net short-term capital gain is not eligible for any special tax rate. It is taxed at the same rate as the taxpayer's other taxable income. *Net long-term capital gain* is eligible for one or more of *four* alternative tax rates: 0 percent, 15 percent, 25 percent, and 28 percent. The 25 percent and 28 percent rates are used only in somewhat unusual circumstances, so the discussion below concentrates more heavily on the other two rates. The net long-term capital gain components are referred to as the *0%/15% gain*, the *25% gain*, and the *28% gain*.

The *25% gain* is technically called the **unrecaptured § 1250 gain** and is related to gain from disposition of § 1231 assets. Gains and losses from disposition of § 1231 assets are discussed in Chapter 17. In this chapter, the discussion will focus only on how the *25% gain* is taxed and not how it is determined. The *28% gain* relates to collectibles and § 1202 gain (see Chapter 5). Collectibles gain is discussed later in this chapter.

The *0% gain* portion of the *0%/15% gain* applies when the taxable income before taxing the *0%/15% gain* does not put the taxpayer out of the 15 percent bracket. Once the taxable income (including any portion of the *0%/15% gain* taxed at 0 percent) puts the taxpayer above the 15 percent bracket, the remaining portion of the *0%/15% gain* is taxed at 15 percent rather than at the regular tax rate.

When the long-term capital gain exceeds short-term capital loss, a **net capital gain (NCG)** exists.[26] Net capital gain qualifies for beneficial alternative tax treatment (see the coverage later in the chapter).

---

[25]§ 1211(b).　　　　　　[26]§ 1222(11).

Since there are both short- and long-term capital gains and losses and because the long-term capital gains may be taxed at various rates, an *ordering procedure* is required. The ordering procedure tends to preserve the lowest tax rate long-term capital gain when there is a net long-term capital gain. This ordering procedure is explained in the steps below and then illustrated by several examples.

Step 1. Group all gains and losses into short term and 28%, 25%, and 0%/15% long term.

Step 2. Net the gains and losses within each group.

Step 3. Offset the net 28% and net 25% amounts if they are of opposite sign.

Step 4. Offset the results after step 3 against the 0%/15% amount if they are of opposite sign. If the 0%/15% amount is a loss, offset it against the *highest taxed gain first.* After this step, there is a net long-term capital gain or loss. If there is a net long-term capital gain, it may consist of only 28% gain, only 25% gain, only 0%/15% gain, or some combination of all of these gains. If there is a net long-term capital loss, it is simply a net long-term capital loss.

Step 5. Offset the net short-term amount against the results of step 4 if they are of opposite sign. The netting rules offset net short-term capital loss against the *highest taxed gain first.* Consequently, if there is a net short-term capital loss and a net gain from step 4, the short-term capital loss offsets first the 28% gain, then the 25% gain, and finally the 0%/15% gain.

If the result of step 5 is *only* a short-term capital gain, the taxpayer is not eligible for a reduced tax rate. If the result of step 5 is a loss, the taxpayer may be eligible for a *capital loss deduction* (discussed later in this chapter). If there was no offsetting in step 5 because the short-term and step 4 results were both gains *or* if the result of the offsetting is a long-term gain, a net capital gain exists, and the taxpayer may be eligible for a reduced tax rate. The net capital gain may consist of *28% gain, 25% gain, and/or 0%/15% gain.*

The five steps outlined above can have many unique final results. See Concept Summary 16.5 later in the chapter for a summary of the netting rules and how capital gains and losses are taxed. The following series of examples illustrates the capital gain and loss netting process.

EXAMPLE 33

This example shows how a net short-term capital gain may result from the netting process.

		Long-Term Gains and Losses			
Step	Short Term	28%	25%	0%/15%	Comment
1	$13,000	$ 12,000		$ 3,000	
	(2,000)	(20,000)			
2	$11,000	($ 8,000)		$ 3,000	
3					No 28%/25% netting because no opposite sign.
4		3,000 →		(3,000)	Netted because of opposite sign.
		($ 5,000)		$ –0–	
5	(5,000) ←	5,000			The net short-term capital gain is taxed as ordinary income.
	$ 6,000	$ –0–			
	Net short-term capital gain				

■

EXAMPLE 34

This example shows how a net long-term capital gain may result from the netting process.

Step	Short Term	Long-Term Gains and Losses 28%	25%	0%/15%	Comment
1	$ 3,000 (5,000)	$15,000 (7,000)	$4,000	$ 3,000 (8,000)	
2	($ 2,000)	$ 8,000	$4,000	($ 5,000)	
3					No 28%/25% netting because no opposite sign.
4		(5,000) $ 3,000	←	5,000 $ –0–	Netted because of opposite sign. Net 0%/15% loss is netted against 28% gain first.
5	2,000 → $ –0–	(2,000) $ 1,000 Net 28% gain	$4,000 Net 25% gain		The net short-term capital loss is netted against 28% gain first. The net long-term capital gain is $5,000 ($1,000 + $4,000).

EXAMPLE 35

This example shows how a net long-term capital loss may result from the netting process.

Step	Short Term	Long-Term Gains and Losses 28%	25%	0%/15%	Comment
1	$ 3,000	$ 1,000		$ 3,000 (8,000)	
2	$ 3,000	$ 1,000		($ 5,000)	
3					No 28%/25% netting because no opposite sign.
4		(1,000) $ –0–	→	1,000 ($ 4,000)	Netted because of opposite sign.
5	(3,000) $ –0–	→	→	3,000 ($ 1,000) Net long-term capital loss	The net short-term capital gain is netted against the net long-term capital loss, and the remaining loss is eligible for the capital loss deduction.

Use of Capital Loss Carryovers

A short-term capital loss carryover to the current year retains its character as short term and is combined with the short-term items of the current year. A long-term net capital loss carries over as a long-term capital loss and is combined with the current-year long-term items. The long-term loss carryover is first offset with 28% gain of the current year, then 25% gain, and then 0%/15% gain until it is absorbed.

EXAMPLE 36	In 2011, Abigail has a $4,000 short-term capital gain, a $36,000 28% long-term capital gain, and a $13,000 0%/15% long-term capital gain. She also has a $3,000 short-term capital loss carryover and a $2,000 long-term capital loss carryover from 2010. This produces a $1,000 net short-term capital gain ($4,000 − $3,000), a $34,000 net 28% long-term capital gain ($36,000 − $2,000), and a $13,000 net 0%/15% long-term capital gain for 2011. ∎

Definition of Collectibles

Capital assets that are collectibles, even though they are held long term, are not eligible for the *0%/15%* alternative tax rate. Instead, a 28 percent alternative tax rate applies.

For capital gain or loss purposes, **collectibles** include:[27]

- Any work of art.
- Any rug or antique.
- Any metal or gem.
- Any stamp.
- Any alcoholic beverage.
- Most coins.
- Any historical objects (documents, clothes, etc.).

ETHICS & Equity — DELAYING A MARRIAGE TO GET A TAX ADVANTAGE

Jennifer and Fred are planning to marry on December 10. Jennifer has a very large stock portfolio that includes stocks that have substantially appreciated in value and have been held long term. Jennifer plans to sell the appreciated stocks and use the proceeds to purchase a home for Fred and herself. Jennifer's tax adviser has suggested that she sell these stocks before her wedding and that the wedding be postponed until next year. This tax strategy will result in significantly lower taxes for Jennifer because she will still be single at the end of the tax year in which she sells the stock. Fred feels that postponing the wedding for such "commercial" reasons is not romantic and is unethical besides. What do you think?

QUALIFIED DIVIDEND INCOME

Dividends paid from current or accumulated earnings and profits of domestic and certain foreign corporations are eligible to be taxed at the 0%/15% long-term capital gain rates if they are **qualified dividend income**. The question of which dividends constitute qualified dividend income is discussed more fully in Chapter 4. Here the discussion focuses on how the qualified dividend income is taxed.

After the net capital gain or loss has been determined, the qualified dividend income is added to the net long-term capital gain portion of the net capital gain and is taxed as *0%/15% gain.* If there is a net capital loss, the net capital loss is still deductible *for* AGI up to $3,000 per year with the remainder of the loss (if any) carrying forward. In this case, the qualified dividend income is still eligible to be treated as *0%/15% gain* in the alternative tax calculation (it is *not* offset by the net capital loss).

EXAMPLE 37	Refer to Example 34, but assume there is qualified dividend income of $2,500 in addition to the items shown. The qualified dividend income *is not* netted against the capital gains and losses. Instead, the taxpayer has $1,000 of 28% gain, $4,000 of 25% gain, *and* $2,500 of qualified dividend income taxed at 0%/15%. ∎

EXAMPLE 38	Refer to Example 35, but assume there is qualified dividend income of $2,500 in addition to the items shown. The qualified dividend income *is not* netted against the net

---

[27]§ 408(m)(2) and Reg. § 1.408–10(b).

capital loss. The taxpayer has a $1,000 capital loss deduction *and* $2,500 of qualified dividend income taxed at 0%/15%. ∎

ALTERNATIVE TAX ON NET CAPITAL GAIN

Section 1 contains the statutory provisions that enable the *net capital gain* to be taxed at special rates (0, 15, 25, and 28 percent). This calculation is referred to as the **alternative tax** on net capital gain.[28] The alternative tax applies only if taxable income includes some long-term capital gain (there is net capital gain). Taxable income includes *all* of the net capital gain unless taxable income is less than the net capital gain. In addition, the net capital gain is taxed *last*, after other taxable income (including any short-term capital gain).

Joan, an unmarried taxpayer, has 2011 taxable income of $98,000, including a $12,000 net capital gain. The last $12,000 of her $98,000 taxable income is the layer related to the net capital gain. The first $86,000 ($98,000 − $12,000) of her taxable income is not subject to any special tax rate, so it is taxed using the regular tax rates. ∎	**EXAMPLE 39**

Since the net capital gain may be made up of various *rate layers*, it is important to know in what order those layers will be taxed. For *each* of the layers, the taxpayer compares the regular tax rate on that layer of income and the alternative tax rate on that portion of the net capital gain. The layers are taxed in the following order: *25% gain, 28% gain*, the 0 percent portion of the *0%/15% gain*, and then the 15 percent portion of the *0%/15% gain*. As a result of this layering, the taxpayer will benefit from the 0 percent portion of the net capital gain if the taxpayer is still in the 10 percent or 15 percent regular rate bracket after taxing other taxable income and the 25 percent and 28 percent portions of the net capital gain.

Assume that Joan's $12,000 net capital gain in Example 39 is made up of $10,000 *25% gain* and $2,000 *0%/15% gain*. Examination of the 2011 tax rates reveals that $86,000 of taxable income for a single individual puts Joan at a marginal tax rate of 28%. Consequently, she will use the alternative tax on both the $10,000 gain and the $2,000 gain. Her alternative tax liability for 2011 is $20,497 [$17,697 (tax on $86,000 of taxable income) + $2,500 ($10,000 × .25) + $300 ($2,000 × .15)]. Since the combination of the $86,000 taxable income and her $10,000 *25% gain* puts her above the 15% regular tax bracket, none of the $2,000 *0%/15% gain* is taxed at 0%. Her regular tax liability on $98,000 would be $21,057. Thus, Joan saves $560 ($21,057 − $20,497) by using the alternative tax calculation. ∎	**EXAMPLE 40**

Joan, an unmarried taxpayer, has 2011 taxable income of $25,000. Of this amount, $12,000 is net capital gain, and $13,000 is other taxable income. The net capital gain is made up of $8,300 of *25% gain* and $3,700 of *0%/15% gain* (including $1,000 of qualified dividend income). Her alternative tax liability for 2011 is $2,770 [$1,525 (tax on $13,000 of taxable income) + $1,245 (tax on $8,300 *25% gain* at 15%) + $0 (tax on $3,700 *0%/15% gain* at 0%)]. Since her marginal rate is still 15% after taxing the $13,000 of other taxable income, she uses the 15% regular tax rate rather than the 25% alternative tax rate on the $8,300 *25% gain*. After taxing the $13,000 and the $8,300, a total of $21,300 of the $25,000 taxable income has been taxed. Since her marginal rate is still 15%, she uses the 0% alternative rate for the $3,700 of *0%/15% gain*. The $1,000 qualified dividend income is included in the $3,700 and, thus, is also taxed at 0%. Joan's regular tax liability on $25,000 would be $3,325. Thus, she saves $555 ($3,325 − $2,770) by using the alternative tax calculation. ∎	**EXAMPLE 41**

The alternative tax computation allows the taxpayer to receive the *lower of* the regular tax or the alternative tax on *each layer* of net capital gain or *portion of each layer* of net capital gain.

---

[28]§ 1(h) Note: Examples 40, 41, and 42 use the 2011 Tax Rate Schedules rather than the 2011 Tax Table to calculate the tax on the non-long-term capital gain portion of taxable income. This approach is used to better illustrate the concepts under discussion. The actual tax on the non-long-term portion of taxable income would be calculated using the Tax Tables since that income is less than $100,000.

CONCEPT SUMMARY 16.4

Income Layers for Alternative Tax on Capital Gain Computation

Compute tax on:	Ordinary taxable income (including net short-term capital gain) using the regular tax rates.
Compute tax on:	Each of the layers below using the *lower* of the alternative tax rate or the regular tax rate for that layer (or portion of a layer) of taxable income.

+   25% long-term capital gain (unrecaptured § 1250 gain) portion of taxable income

+   28% long-term capital gain

+   0% long-term capital gain (portion of 0%/15% capital gain that is taxed at 0%; available only if ordinary taxable income plus 25% and 28% capital gain layers do not put the taxpayer above the 15% bracket; 0% rate is no longer available once income including the portion of the gain taxed at 0% puts the taxpayer out of the 15% bracket)*

+   15% long-term capital gain (remaining portion of 0%/15% capital gain)*

=   Alternative tax on taxable income

*May include qualified dividend income.

EXAMPLE 42

Assume the same facts as in Example 41 except that Joan's taxable income is $36,000, consisting of $12,000 of net capital gain and $24,000 of other taxable income. Not all of the $3,700 of *0%/15% gain* is taxed at 0% because Joan's taxable income exceeds $34,500, taking her out of the 15% bracket. Consequently, the last $1,500 ($36,000 − $34,500) of the $3,700 of *0%/15% gain* is taxed at 15% rather than 0%. Her tax liability using the alternative tax computation is $4,645 [$3,175 (tax on $24,000 of taxable income) + $1,245 (tax on $8,300 *25% gain* at 15%) + $0 (tax on $2,200 of *0%/15% gain* at 0%) + $225 (tax on $1,500 of *0%/15% gain* at 15%)]. Joan's regular tax liability on $36,000 would be $5,125. Thus, she saves $480 ($5,125 − $4,645) by using the alternative tax calculation. ∎

Concept Summary 16.4 summarizes the alternative tax computation.

TREATMENT OF CAPITAL LOSSES

Computation of Net Capital Loss

A **net capital loss (NCL)** results if capital losses exceed capital gains for the year. An NCL may be all long term, all short term, or part long and part short term.[29] The characterization of an NCL as long or short term is important in determining the capital loss deduction (discussed later in this chapter).

EXAMPLE 43

Three different individual taxpayers have the following capital gains and losses during the year:

Taxpayer	LTCG	LTCL	STCG	STCL	Result of Netting	Description of Result
Robert	$1,000	($ 2,800)	$1,000	($ 500)	($ 1,300)	NLTCL
Carlos	1,000	(500)	1,000	(2,800)	(1,300)	NSTCL
Troy	400	(1,200)	500	(1,200)	(1,500)	NLTCL ($800)
						NSTCL ($700)

Robert's NCL of $1,300 is all long term. Carlos's NCL of $1,300 is all short term. Troy's NCL is $1,500, $800 of which is long term and $700 of which is short term. ∎

---

[29]Section 1222(10) defines a net capital loss as the net loss after the capital loss deduction. However, that definition confuses the discussion of net capital loss. Therefore, net capital loss is used here to mean the result after netting capital gains and losses and before considering the capital loss deduction. The capital loss deduction is discussed under Treatment of Net Capital Loss in this chapter.

| **TAX** *in* the *NEWS* | A SIMPLE SOLUTION TO AVOIDING THE **$3,000** LIMIT ON DEDUCTING CAPITAL LOSSES AGAINST ORDINARY INCOME |

Tom Herman wrote a weekly tax column in the *Wall Street Journal* for more than 16 years. In his final column, which appeared on April 15, 2009 (a very appropriate day!), he told about a question from a senior citizen on how to get around the $3,000 limit on deducting net capital losses.

It seems that the individual had amassed capital losses in the stock market of $2.1 million, but at $3,000 per year, he would not come close to living long enough to offset that amount of losses. His accountant had advised him to marry a woman with large capital gains. The couple would not even have to live together. In fact, after the $2.1 million loss was used up to offset capital gains, they could get a divorce. Of course, a prenuptial agreement would protect each spouse's separate assets.

The senior citizen liked the accountant's advice. So why was he writing to Tom Herman? First, he wanted Tom's advice on how to "find such a lady." Second, should he offer a reward (and how much) to anyone who would help him find her?

Source: Adapted from Tom Herman, "What I Learned in Over 16 Years on the Tax Beat," *Wall Street Journal*, April 15, 2009, p. Dl.

Treatment of Net Capital Loss

An NCL is deductible from gross income to the extent of $3,000 per tax year.[30] Capital losses exceeding the loss deduction limits carry forward indefinitely. Thus, although there may or may not be beneficial treatment for capital gains, there is *unfavorable* treatment for capital losses in terms of the $3,000 annual limitation on deducting NCL against ordinary income. If the NCL includes both long-term and short-term capital loss, the short-term capital loss is counted first toward the $3,000 annual limitation.

> **EXAMPLE 44**
>
> Burt has an NCL of $5,500, of which $2,000 is STCL and $3,500 is LTCL. Burt has a capital loss deduction of $3,000 ($2,000 of STCL and $1,000 of LTCL). He has an LTCL carryforward of $2,500 ($3,500 − $1,000). ■

Carryovers

Taxpayers are allowed to carry over unused capital losses indefinitely. The short-term capital loss (STCL) retains its character as STCL. Likewise the long-term capital loss retains its character as LTCL.

> **EXAMPLE 45**
>
> In 2011, Mark incurred $1,000 of STCL and $11,000 of LTCL. In 2012, Mark has a $400 LTCG.
>
> - Mark's NCL for 2011 is $12,000. Mark deducts $3,000 ($1,000 STCL and $2,000 LTCL). He has $9,000 of LTCL carried forward to 2012.
> - Mark combines the $9,000 LTCL carryforward with the $400 LTCG for 2012. He has an $8,600 NLTCL for 2012. Mark deducts $3,000 of LTCL in 2012 and carries forward $5,600 of LTCL to 2013. ■

When a taxpayer has both a capital loss deduction and negative taxable income, a special computation of the capital loss carryover is required.[31] Specifically, the capital loss carryover is the NCL minus the lesser of:

- The capital loss deduction claimed on the return.
- The negative taxable income increased by the capital loss deduction claimed on the return and the personal and dependency exemption deduction.

Without this provision, some of the tax benefit of the capital loss deduction would be wasted when the deduction drives taxable income below zero. However, the capital

---

[30]§ 1211(b)(1). Married persons filing separate returns are limited to a $1,500 deduction per tax year.

[31]§ 1212(b).

CONCEPT SUMMARY 16.5

Some Possible Final Results of the Capital Gain and Loss Netting Process and How They Are Taxed

Result	Maximum Tax Rate	Comments
Net short-term capital loss	—	Eligible for capital loss deduction ($3,000 maximum per year).
Net long-term capital loss	—	Eligible for capital loss deduction ($3,000 maximum per year).
Net short-term capital loss *and* net long-term capital loss	—	Eligible for capital loss deduction ($3,000 maximum per year). Short-term capital losses are counted first toward the deduction.
Net short-term capital gain	10–35%	Taxed as ordinary income.
Net long-term capital gain	0–28%	The net long-term capital gain may have as many as four tax rate components: 25%, 28%, and 0%/15%.
• The net long-term capital gain is the *last* portion of taxable income.		The components are taxed in the following order: 25%, 28%, 0%, 15%. They are taxed *after* the non-long-term capital gain portion of taxable income has been taxed. The 0%/15% component may include qualified dividend income.
• Each net long-term capital gain component of taxable income is taxed at the *lower* of the regular tax on that component or the alternative tax.		The alternative tax on net long-term capital gain can never increase the tax on taxable income, but it can reduce the tax on taxable income.
Net short-term capital gain *and* net long-term capital gain	10–35% on net short-term capital gain; 0–28% on net long-term capital gain	The net short-term capital gain is taxed as ordinary income; the net long-term capital gain is taxed as discussed above for just net long-term capital gain.

loss deduction is not reduced if taxable income before the exemption deduction is a positive number or zero. In that situation, it is the exemption deduction, and not the capital loss deduction, that is creating the negative taxable income.

EXAMPLE 46

In 2011, Joanne has a $13,000 NCL (all long term), a $3,700 personal exemption deduction, and $4,000 negative taxable income. The negative taxable income includes a $3,000 capital loss deduction. The capital loss carryover to 2012 is $10,300, computed as follows:

- The $4,000 negative taxable income is treated as a negative number, but the capital loss deduction and personal exemption deduction are treated as positive numbers.
- The normal ceiling on the capital loss deduction is $3,000.
- However, if the $3,000 capital loss deduction and the $3,700 exemption deduction are added back to the $4,000 negative taxable income, only $2,700 of the $3,000 capital loss deduction is needed to make taxable income equal to zero.
- Therefore, this special computation results in only $2,700 of the $13,000 NCL being consumed. The LTCL carryforward is $10,300 ($13,000 − $2,700). ∎

Concept Summary 16.5 summarizes the rules for noncorporate taxpayers' treatment of capital gains and losses.

SCHEDULE D (Form 1040) Department of the Treasury Internal Revenue Service (99)	**Capital Gains and Losses** ► Attach to Form 1040 or Form 1040NR. ► See Instructions for Schedule D (Form 1040). ► Use Schedule D-1 to list additional transactions for lines 1 and 8.	OMB No. 1545-0074 20**10** Attachment Sequence No. **12**

Name(s) shown on return *Joan Rapson*	Your social security number *123 45 6789*

Part I **Short-Term Capital Gains and Losses—Assets Held One Year or Less**

	(a) Description of property (Example: 100 sh. XYZ Co.)	**(b)** Date acquired (Mo., day, yr.)	**(c)** Date sold (Mo., day, yr.)	**(d)** Sales price (see page D-7 of the instructions)	**(e)** Cost or other basis (see page D-7 of the instructions)	**(f)** Gain or (loss) Subtract (e) from (d)
1	*100 shares* *Blue stock*	*01/21/10*	*11/11/10*	*11,000*	*17,000*	*(6,000)*

2	Enter your short-term totals, if any, from Schedule D-1, line 2	**2**	
3	**Total short-term sales price amounts.** Add lines 1 and 2 in column (d)	**3**	*11,000*

4	Short-term gain from Form 6252 and short-term gain or (loss) from Forms 4684, 6781, and 8824 .	**4**	
5	Net short-term gain or (loss) from partnerships, S corporations, estates, and trusts from Schedule(s) K-1	**5**	
6	Short-term capital loss carryover. Enter the amount, if any, from line 10 of your **Capital Loss Carryover Worksheet** on page D-7 of the instructions	**6** ( )	
7	**Net short-term capital gain or (loss).** Combine lines 1 through 6 in column (f)	**7**	*(6,000)*

Part II **Long-Term Capital Gains and Losses—Assets Held More Than One Year**

	(a) Description of property (Example: 100 sh. XYZ Co.)	**(b)** Date acquired (Mo., day, yr.)	**(c)** Date sold (Mo., day, yr.)	**(d)** Sales price (see page D-7 of the instructions)	**(e)** Cost or other basis (see page D-7 of the instructions)	**(f)** Gain or (loss) Subtract (e) from (d)
8	*100 shares* *Yellow stock*	*09/12/05*	*10/12/10*	*36,000*	*20,000*	*16,000*
	100 shares *Purple stock*	*03/14/08*	*10/12/10*	*14,000*	*12,000*	*2,000*

9	Enter your long-term totals, if any, from Schedule D-1, line 9	**9**	
10	**Total long-term sales price amounts.** Add lines 8 and 9 in column (d).	**10**	*50,000*

11	Gain from Form 4797, Part I; long-term gain from Forms 2439 and 6252; and long-term gain or (loss) from Forms 4684, 6781, and 8824	**11**	
12	Net long-term gain or (loss) from partnerships, S corporations, estates, and trusts from Schedule(s) K-1	**12**	
13	Capital gain distributions. See page D-2 of the instructions	**13**	
14	Long-term capital loss carryover. Enter the amount, if any, from line 15 of your **Capital Loss Carryover Worksheet** on page D-7 of the instructions	**14** ( )	
15	**Net long-term capital gain or (loss).** Combine lines 8 through 14 in column (f). Then go to Part III on the back	**15**	*18,000*

For Paperwork Reduction Act Notice, see your tax return instructions.	Cat. No. 11338H	Schedule D (Form 1040) 2010

Schedule D (Form 1040) 2010   Page **2**

Part III	**Summary**

16 Combine lines 7 and 15 and enter the result . . . . | **16** | *12,000* |

- If line 16 is a **gain**, enter the amount from line 16 on Form 1040, line 13, or Form 1040NR, line 14. Then go to line 17 below.
- If line 16 is a **loss**, skip lines 17 through 20 below. Then go to line 21. Also be sure to complete line 22.
- If line 16 is **zero**, skip lines 17 through 21 below and enter -0- on Form 1040, line 13, or Form 1040NR, line 14. Then go to line 22.

17 Are lines 15 and 16 **both** gains?
- ☐ **Yes.** Go to line 18.
- ☐ **No.** Skip lines 18 through 21, and go to line 22.

18 Enter the amount, if any, from line 7 of the **28% Rate Gain Worksheet** on page D-8 of the instructions . . . . ▶ | **18** | *0* |

19 Enter the amount, if any, from line 18 of the **Unrecaptured Section 1250 Gain Worksheet** on page D-9 of the instructions . . . . ▶ | **19** | *0* |

20 Are lines 18 and 19 **both** zero or blank?
- ☐ **Yes.** Complete Form 1040 through line 43, or Form 1040NR through line 41. Then complete the **Qualified Dividends and Capital Gain Tax Worksheet** in the Instructions for Form 1040, line 44 (or in the Instructions for Form 1040NR, line 42). **Do not** complete lines 21 and 22 below.

- ☐ **No.** Complete Form 1040 through line 43, or Form 1040NR through line 41. Then complete the **Schedule D Tax Worksheet** on page D-10 of the instructions. **Do not** complete lines 21 and 22 below.

21 If line 16 is a loss, enter here and on Form 1040, line 13, or Form 1040NR, line 14, the **smaller** of:

- The loss on line 16 or
- ($3,000), or if married filing separately, ($1,500)

. . . . | **21** (|) |

Note. When figuring which amount is smaller, treat both amounts as positive numbers.

22 Do you have qualified dividends on Form 1040, line 9b, or Form 1040NR, line 10b?

- ☐ **Yes.** Complete Form 1040 through line 43, or Form 1040NR through line 41. Then complete the **Qualified Dividends and Capital Gain Tax Worksheet** in the Instructions for Form 1040, line 44 (or in the Instructions for Form 1040NR, line 42).
- ☐ **No.** Complete the rest of Form 1040 or Form 1040NR.

Schedule D (Form 1040) 2010

REPORTING PROCEDURES

The following discusses the 2010 tax forms because the 2011 tax forms were not available at the time of this writing.

Capital gains and losses are reported on Schedule D of the 2010 Form 1040 (reproduced on pp. 16–29 and 16–30 using the data from Example 47). Part I of Schedule D is used to report short-term capital gains and losses. Part II of Schedule D is used to report long-term capital gains and losses. Part III summarizes the results of Parts I and II and indicates whether the taxpayer has a net capital gain or a net capital loss. Part III then helps determine which alternative tax worksheet is used to

Qualified Dividends and Capital Gain Tax Worksheet—Line 44

Keep for Your Records

Before you begin:	✓	See the instructions for line 44 on page 35 to see if you can use this worksheet to figure your tax.
	✓	If you do not have to file Schedule D and you received capital gain distributions, be sure you checked the box on line 13 of Form 1040.

1. Enter the amount from Form 1040, line 43. However, if you are filing Form 2555 or 2555-EZ (relating to foreign earned income), enter the amount from line 3 of the worksheet on page 36 . . . . **1.** 78,000

2. Enter the amount from Form 1040, line 9b* **2.** 300

3. Are you filing Schedule D?*

   ☒ **Yes.** Enter the **smaller** of line 15 or 16 of Schedule D. If either line 15 or line 16 is blank or a loss, enter -0-

   ☐ **No.** Enter the amount from Form 1040, line 13 } **3.** 12,000

4. Add lines 2 and 3 . . . . **4.** 12,300

5. If filing Form 4952 (used to figure investment interest expense deduction), enter any amount from line 4g of that form. Otherwise, enter -0- **5.** 0

6. Subtract line 5 from line 4. If zero or less, enter -0- **6.** 12,300

7. Subtract line 6 from line 1. If zero or less, enter -0- **7.** 65,700

8. Enter:

   $34,000 if single or married filing separately,
   $68,000 if married filing jointly or qualifying widow(er),
   $45,550 if head of household. } **8.** 34,000

9. Enter the smaller of line 1 or line 8 . . . . **9.** 34,000

10. Enter the smaller of line 7 or line 9 . . . . **10.** 34,000

11. Subtract line 10 from line 9. This amount is taxed at 0% **11.** 0

12. Enter the smaller of line 1 or line 6 . . . . **12.** 12,300

13. Enter the amount from line 11 . . . . **13.** 0

14. Subtract line 13 from line 12 . . . . **14.** 12,300

15. Multiply line 14 by 15% (.15) **15.** 1,845

16. Figure the tax on the amount on line 7. If the amount on line 7 is less than $100,000, use the Tax Table to figure this tax. If the amount on line 7 is $100,000 or more, use the Tax Computation Worksheet **16.** 12,613

17. Add lines 15 and 16 . . . . **17.** 14,458

18. Figure the tax on the amount on line 1. If the amount on line 1 is less than $100,000, use the Tax Table to figure this tax. If the amount on line 1 is $100,000 or more, use the Tax Computation Worksheet **18.** 15,688

19. **Tax on all taxable income.** Enter the **smaller** of line 17 or line 18. Also include this amount on Form 1040, line 44. If you are filing Form 2555 or 2555-EZ, do not enter this amount on Form 1040, line 44. Instead, enter it on line 4 of the worksheet on page 36 . . . . **19.** 14,458

If you are filing Form 2555 or 2555-EZ, see the footnote in the worksheet on page 36 before completing this line.

calculate the alternative tax on long-term capital gains and qualified dividends. If the taxpayer has a net long-term capital gain that does not include any 28% or 25% long-term capital gain, then the alternative tax is calculated using the Qualified Dividends and Capital Gain Worksheet from the Form 1040 instructions. If the taxpayer has a net long-term capital gain that does include either 28% or 25% long-term capital gain, then the alternative tax is calculated using the Schedule D Tax Worksheet from the Schedule D instructions. These worksheets do not have to be filed with the tax return, but are kept for the taxpayer's records.

EXAMPLE 47

During 2010, Joan Rapson (Social Security number 123–45–6789) had the following sales of capital assets. In addition, she has other taxable income of $66,000, including $300 of qualified dividend income.

Description	Acquired On	Date Sold	Sales Price	Tax Basis	Gain or Loss	Character
100 shares Blue stock	1/21/10	11/11/10	$11,000	$17,000	($ 6,000)	STCL
100 shares Yellow stock	9/12/05	10/12/10	36,000	20,000	16,000	LTCG
100 shares Purple stock	3/14/08	10/12/10	14,000	12,000	2,000	LTCG

Joan has a net capital gain of $12,000 ($16,000 *0%/15% gain* + $2,000 *0%/15% gain* − $6,000 short-term capital loss). Consequently, all of the net capital gain is composed of *0%/15% gain*. Joan's $78,000 taxable income includes $65,700 ($66,000 − $300) of other taxable income. This example is filled in on the Schedule D on pp. 16–29 through 16–31. Joan's total stock sales were reported to her on Form 1099–B by her stockbroker. ■

16.6 Tax Treatment of Capital Gains and Losses of Corporate Taxpayers

LO.6

Describe the tax treatment for capital gains and the detrimental tax treatment for capital losses for corporate taxpayers.

The treatment of a corporation's net capital gain or loss differs from the rules for individuals. Briefly, the differences are as follows:

- There is an NCG alternative tax rate of 35 percent.[32] However, since the maximum corporate tax rate is 35 percent, the alternative tax is not beneficial.
- Capital losses offset only capital gains. No deduction of capital losses is permitted against ordinary taxable income (whereas a $3,000 deduction is allowed to individuals).[33]
- Corporations may carry back net capital losses (whether long term or short term) as short-term capital losses for three years; if losses still remain after the carryback, the remaining losses may be carried forward five years.[34] Individuals may carry forward unused capital losses indefinitely, but there is no carryback.

EXAMPLE 48

Sparrow Corporation has a $15,000 NLTCL for the current year and $57,000 of ordinary taxable income. Sparrow may not offset the $15,000 NLTCL against its ordinary income by taking a capital loss deduction. The $15,000 NLTCL becomes a $15,000 STCL for carryback and carryover purposes. This amount may be offset by capital gains in the three-year carryback period or, if not absorbed there, offset by capital gains in the five-year carryforward period. ■

The rules applicable to corporations are discussed in greater detail in Chapter 20.

TAX PLANNING:

16.7 Importance of Capital Asset Status

LO.7

Identify tax planning opportunities arising from the sale or exchange of capital assets.

Why is capital asset status important? Capital asset status enables the taxpayer to be eligible for the alternative tax on net capital gain. For a taxpayer in the 25, 28, 33, or 35 percent regular tax bracket, a 15 percent rate is available on assets held longer than one year. For a taxpayer in the 10 or 15 percent regular tax bracket, a 0 percent

---

[32]§ 1201.
[33]§ 1211(a).

[34]§ 1212(a)(1).

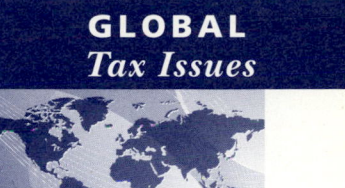

CAPITAL GAIN TREATMENT IN THE UNITED STATES AND OTHER COUNTRIES

The United States currently requires a very complex tax calculation when taxable income includes net long-term capital gain. However, the alternative tax on net long-term capital gain can generate tax savings even when the taxpayer is in the lowest regular tax bracket (10 percent) because there is an alternative tax rate of 0 percent. Many other countries do not have an alternative tax rate on long-term capital gains. Instead, those gains are taxed the same as other income. Consequently, even though the U.S. system is complex, it may be preferable because of the lower tax rates and because the lower rates are available to taxpayers in all tax brackets.

rate is available on assets held longer than one year. Thus, individuals who can receive income in the form of long-term capital gains or qualified dividend income have an advantage over taxpayers who cannot receive income in these forms.

Capital asset status is also important because capital gains must be offset by capital losses. If a net capital loss results, the maximum deduction is $3,000 per year.

Consequently, capital gains and losses must be segregated from other types of gains and losses and must be reported separately on Schedule D of Form 1040.

16.8 PLANNING FOR CAPITAL ASSET STATUS

It is important to keep in mind that capital asset status often is a question of objective evidence. Thus, property that is not a capital asset to one party may qualify as a capital asset to another party.

EXAMPLE 49

Diane, a real estate dealer, transfers by gift a tract of land to Jeff, her son. The land was recorded as part of Diane's inventory (it was held for resale) and was therefore not a capital asset to her. Jeff, however, treats the land as an investment. The land is a capital asset in Jeff's hands, and any later taxable disposition of the property by him will yield a capital gain or loss. ■

If proper planning is carried out, even a dealer may obtain long-term capital gain treatment on the sale of the type of property normally held for resale.

EXAMPLE 50

Jim, a real estate dealer, segregates tract A from the real estate he regularly holds for resale and designates the property as being held for investment purposes. The property is not advertised for sale and is disposed of several years later. The negotiations for the subsequent sale were initiated by the purchaser and not by Jim. Under these circumstances, it would appear that any gain or loss from the sale of tract A should be a capital gain or loss.[35] ■

When a business is being sold, one of the major decisions usually concerns whether a portion of the sales price is for goodwill. For the seller, goodwill generally represents the disposition of a capital asset. Goodwill has no basis and represents a residual portion of the selling price that cannot be allocated reasonably to the known assets. The amount of goodwill thus represents capital gain.

From a legal perspective, the buyer may prefer that the residual portion of the purchase price be allocated to a covenant not to compete (a promise that the seller will not compete against the buyer by conducting a business similar to the one that

---

[35]*Toledo, Peoria & Western Railroad Co.*, 35 TCM 1663, T.C.Memo. 1976–366.

the buyer has purchased). Both purchased goodwill and a covenant not to compete are § 197 intangibles. Thus, both must be capitalized and can be amortized over a 15-year statutory period.

To the seller, a covenant produces ordinary income. Thus, the seller would prefer that the residual portion of the selling price be allocated to goodwill—a capital asset. If the buyer does not need the legal protection provided by a covenant, the buyer is neutral regarding whether the residual amount be allocated to a covenant or to goodwill. Since the seller would receive a tax advantage from labeling the residual amount as goodwill, the buyer should factor this into the negotiation of the purchase price.

EXAMPLE 51

Marcia is buying Jack's dry cleaning proprietorship. An appraisal of the assets indicates that a reasonable purchase price would exceed the value of the known assets by $30,000. If the purchase contract does not specify the nature of the $30,000, the amount will be for goodwill, and Jack will have a long-term capital gain of $30,000. Marcia will have a 15-year amortizable $30,000 asset. If Marcia is paying the extra $30,000 to prevent Jack from conducting another dry cleaning business in the area (a covenant not to compete), Jack will have $30,000 of ordinary income. Marcia will have a $30,000 deduction over the statutory 15-year amortization period rather than over the actual life of the covenant (e.g., 5 years). ■

16.9 EFFECT OF CAPITAL ASSET STATUS IN TRANSACTIONS OTHER THAN SALES

The nature of an asset (capital or ordinary) is important in determining the tax consequences that result when a sale or exchange occurs. It may, however, be just as significant in circumstances other than a taxable sale or exchange. When a capital asset is disposed of, the result is not always a capital gain or loss. Rather, in general, the disposition must be a sale or exchange. Collection of a debt instrument having a basis less than the face value results in a capital gain if the debt instrument is a capital asset. The collection is a sale or exchange. Sale of the debt shortly before the due date for collection will produce a capital gain.[36] If selling the debt in such circumstances could produce a capital gain but collecting could not, the consistency of what constitutes a capital gain or loss would be frustrated. Another illustration of the sale or exchange principle involves a donation of certain appreciated property to a qualified charity. Recall that in certain circumstances, the measure of the charitable contribution is fair market value when the property, if sold, would have yielded a long-term capital gain [refer to Chapter 10 and the discussion of § 170(e)].

EXAMPLE 52

Sharon wants to donate a tract of unimproved land (basis of $40,000 and fair market value of $200,000) held for the required long-term holding period to State University (a qualified charitable organization). However, Sharon currently is under audit by the IRS for capital gains she reported on certain real estate transactions during an earlier tax year. Although Sharon is not a licensed real estate broker, the IRS agent conducting the audit is contending that she has achieved dealer status by virtue of the number and frequency of the real estate transactions she has conducted. Under these circumstances, Sharon would be well-advised to postpone the donation to State University until her status is clarified. If she has achieved dealer status, the unimproved land may be inventory (refer to Example 50 for another possible result), and Sharon's charitable contribution deduction would be limited to $40,000. If not, and if the land is held as an investment, Sharon's deduction is $200,000 (the fair market value of the property). ■

---

[36]§ 1271(b).

16.10 STOCK SALES

The following rules apply in determining the date of a stock sale:

- The date the sale is executed is the date of the sale. The execution date is the date the broker completes the transaction on the stock exchange.
- The settlement date is the date the cash or other property is paid to the seller of the stock. This date is *not* relevant in determining the date of sale.

EXAMPLE 53

Lupe, a cash basis taxpayer, sells stock that results in a gain. The sale was executed on December 29, 2010. The settlement date is January 2, 2011. The date of sale is December 29, 2010 (the execution date). The holding period for the stock sold ends with the execution date. ■

16.11 MAXIMIZING BENEFITS

Ordinary losses generally are preferable to capital losses because of the limitations imposed on the deductibility of net capital losses and the requirement that capital losses be used to offset capital gains. The taxpayer may be able to convert what would otherwise have been capital loss to ordinary loss. For example, business (but not nonbusiness) bad debts, losses from the sale or exchange of small business investment company stock, and losses from the sale or exchange of small business company stock all result in ordinary losses.[37]

Although capital losses can be carried over indefinitely, *indefinite* becomes definite when a taxpayer dies. Any loss carryovers not used by the taxpayer are permanently lost. That is, no tax benefit can be derived from the carryovers subsequent to death.[38] Therefore, the potential benefit of carrying over capital losses diminishes when dealing with older taxpayers.

It is usually beneficial to spread gains over more than one taxable year. In some cases, this can be accomplished through the installment sales method of accounting.

16.12 YEAR-END PLANNING

The following general rules can be applied for timing the recognition of capital gains and losses near the end of a taxable year:

- If the taxpayer already has recognized more than $3,000 of capital loss, sell assets to generate capital gain equal to the excess of the capital loss over $3,000.

EXAMPLE 54

Kevin has already incurred a $7,000 STCL. Kevin should generate $4,000 of capital gain. The gain will offset $4,000 of the loss. The remaining loss of $3,000 can be deducted against ordinary income. ■

- If the taxpayer already has recognized capital gain, sell assets to generate capital loss equal to the capital gain. The gain will not be taxed, and the loss will be fully *deductible* against the gain.
- Generally, if the taxpayer has a choice between recognizing short-term capital gain or long-term capital gain, long-term capital gain should be recognized because it has the lower tax rate.

---

[37]§§ 166(d), 1242, and 1244. Refer to the discussion in Chapter 7. [38]Rev.Rul. 74–175, 1974–1 C.B. 52.

REFOCUS ON THE BIG PICTURE

MANAGING CAPITAL ASSET TRANSACTIONS

You explain to Maurice that your area of expertise is tax, so you are providing tax advice and not investment advice. From an overall perspective, he is correct that certain capital gains and dividends are eligible for either a 0 percent or a 15 percent tax rate rather than the regular tax rates that go as high as 35 percent. You then discuss the potential tax consequences of each of his investments.

- *Purple stock.* To qualify for the beneficial tax rate, the holding period for the stock must be longer than one year. From a tax perspective, Maurice should retain his stock investment for at least an additional three months and a day. To be eligible for the "costless" capital gains, his taxable income should not exceed $34,500 for 2011.
- *Patent.* Since he is a "holder" of the patent, it will qualify for the beneficial capital gain rate regardless of the holding period if the patent should produce income in excess of his $50,000 investment. However, if he loses money on the investment, he will be able to deduct only $3,000 of the loss per year against his ordinary income (assuming there are no offsetting capital gains).
- *Tax-exempt bonds.* The after-tax return on the taxable bonds would be less than the 3 percent on the tax-exempt bonds. In addition, the interest on the taxable bonds would increase his taxable income, possibly moving it out of the desired 15 percent marginal tax rate into the 25 percent marginal tax rate.
- *Partnership interest.* Whether Maurice receives capital or ordinary treatment associated with his partnership interest depends on whether he is reporting his share of profits or losses (ordinary income or ordinary loss) or is reporting recognized gain or loss from the sale of his partnership interest (capital gain or capital loss).

You conclude your tax advice to Maurice by telling him that whatever he does regarding his investments should make economic sense. There are no 100 percent tax rates. For example, disposing of the bank stock in the current market could be the wise thing to do.

KEY TERMS

Alternative tax, 16–25	Holding period, 16–15	Original issue discount (OID), 16–10
Capital asset, 16–4	Lessee, 16–14	Patent, 16–12
Capital gains, 16–3	Lessor, 16–14	Qualified dividend income, 16–24
Capital losses, 16–3	Net capital gain (NCG), 16–21	Sale or exchange, 16–9
Collectibles, 16–24	Net capital loss (NCL), 16–26	Short sale, 16–17
Franchise, 16–13	Options, 16–10	Unrecaptured § 1250 gain, 16–21

DISCUSSION QUESTIONS

ISSUE ID

1. **LO.2, 4, 5** Gynn inherited 400 shares of stock, 200 shares of Orange and 200 shares of Ecru. She has a stockbroker sell the shares for her, uses the proceeds for personal expenses, and thinks nothing further about the transactions. What issues does she face when she prepares her Federal income tax return?

ISSUE ID

2. **LO.2** An individual taxpayer sells some used assets at a rummage sale. Why are none of the proceeds taxable in most situations?

3. **LO.2, 4** Shaneka owns a sculpture that she received as a gift from her uncle two years ago. The uncle created the sculpture. Shaneka has displayed the sculpture in her home and has never attempted to sell it. Recently, a visitor noticed the sculpture and has offered Shaneka $50,000 for it. If Shaneka decides to sell the sculpture, what tax issues does she face? **ISSUE ID**

4. **LO.2** Are the lyrics to a song a capital asset or an ordinary asset? Why or why not?

5. **LO.2** Is an account receivable that arose in the ordinary course of a cash basis dentist's business a capital asset? Why or why not?

6. **LO.2** Why do Internal Revenue Code provisions play an important role in the definition of capital assets?

7. **LO.2** Harmon is a "stock trader" who buys and sells publicly traded stocks regularly for his own account. His cousin, who purports to be a tax expert, but is not a CPA, has told Harmon that since the shares of stock Harmon holds are held for resale, they are ordinary assets and not capital assets. Is this always true?

8. **LO.2** Gabrielle is holding vacant land for investment. She wants to subdivide it into 25 lots, put in utilities (sewer, water, cable, electricity, and natural gas) for each lot, and pave the streets running through the subdivision. Is this transaction eligible for the "real property subdivided for sale" provisions?

9. **LO.3** What is the difference between a "worthless security" and "§ 1244 stock"?

10. **LO.3** Lila purchased an original issue discount bond several years ago. She paid $188,000 for the $200,000 face value bond. She sold the bond this year for $193,000. Is all of Lila's gain long-term capital gain? Why or why not?

11. **LO.3** Carl receives $58,000 from a real estate developer for an option to purchase land Carl is holding for investment. Fourteen months later, the option expires unexercised. How is the $58,000 taxed to Carl?

12. **LO.3** Hubert purchases all the rights in a patent from the inventor who developed the patented product. After holding the patent for two years, Hubert sells all the rights in the patent for a substantial gain. What issues does Hubert face if he wants to treat the gain as a long-term capital gain? **ISSUE ID**

13. **LO.3** Green Corporation and Red Corporation are engaged in a contract dispute over the use of Green's trademarked name, Big Blue Taco. For a one-time payment of $45,000, Green licensed Red to use the name Big Blue Taco, but the license did not require that Red use the same materials in its version of Big Blue Taco that Green uses. Red also did not have to make any contingent payments to Green or buy any supplies from Green. Did Red purchase a franchise right from Green, or did Red purchase the name Big Blue Taco from Green?

14. **LO.4** Siva purchased corporate stock for $20,000 on April 10, 2009. On July 14, 2011, when the stock was worth $12,000, he gave it to his son, Mithra. What has to happen to the value of the property while Mithra holds it if Mithra is to tack Siva's holding period on to his own holding period? **ISSUE ID**

15. **LO.4** At the date of a short sale, Betty had not held substantially identical securities for more than 12 months. What is the nature of any gain or loss from the close of her short sale?

16. **LO.5** After netting all her short-term and long-term capital gains and losses, Minerva has a net short-term capital gain and a net long-term capital gain. Can she net these against each other?

17. **LO.2, 5** Bill sells his graphic comic book collection at a profit. He had acquired all of the comic books for his personal pleasure and sold all of them for more than he paid for them. What is the tax status of the comic books, and is his gain a 28% gain?

18. **LO.2, 5, 7** Near the end of 2011, Byron realizes that he has a net short-term capital loss of $13,000 for the year. Byron has taxable income (not including the loss) of $123,000 and is single. He owns numerous stocks that could be sold for a long-term capital gain. What should he do before the end of 2011? **ISSUE ID**

PROBLEMS

19. **LO.2** During the year, Eric had the four property transactions summarized below. Eric is a collector of antique automobiles and occasionally sells one to get funds to buy another. What are the amount and nature of the gain or loss from each of these transactions?

Property	Date Acquired	Date Sold	Adjusted Basis	Sales Price
Antique truck	06/18/01	05/23/11	$37,000	$32,000
Blue Growth Fund (100 shares)	12/23/02	11/22/11	22,000	38,000
Orange bonds	02/12/03	04/11/11	34,000	42,000*
Green stock (100 shares)	02/14/11	11/23/11	13,000	11,000

*The sales price included $750 of accrued interest.

DECISION MAKING

20. **LO.2, 5** Revez owns an antique shop. He buys property from estates, often at much less than the retail value of the property. Recently, Revez sold for $4,000 an antique clock for which he had paid $1,250. Revez had held the clock in his shop for 36 months before selling it. Revez would like the gain on the sale of the clock to be a long-term capital gain. How can he achieve that objective?

21. **LO.2** Chalmers is the owner of numerous houses. His intention is to hold the houses until they increase in value and then sell them. He rents the houses to tenants while he is holding them. In 2011, he sold one house for $45,000. Chalmers had held the house for six years, and it had a tax basis of $20,000. Was the house a capital asset? Why or why not?

22. **LO.2, 4** Wilma purchased a swing set at a yard sale for $50 in May. She is not in the business of buying and selling anything. She researched the swing set on the Internet and discovered that it was worth $200. She sold it on an Internet auction site for $180 in July. Was the swing set a capital asset, and what were the amount and nature of Wilma's gain or loss from its sale?

23. **LO.2** Cyan is a corporation that buys and sells furniture. It purchases furniture from furniture merchants that need cash immediately and cannot wait to sell in the normal course of their business. Cyan pays about 35% of the wholesale value of the furniture and then sells the furniture to other furniture dealers for about 85% of wholesale value. Does Cyan have a capital gain when it sells the furniture?

COMMUNICATIONS

24. **LO.2** Faith Godwin is a dealer in securities. She has spotted a fast-rising company and would like to buy and hold its stock for investment. The stock is currently selling for $2 per share, and Faith thinks it will climb to $40 a share within two years. Faith's co-workers have told her that there is "no way" she can get long-term capital gain treatment when she purchases stock because she is a securities dealer. Faith has asked you to calculate her potential gain and tell her whether her co-workers are right. Draft a letter to Faith responding to her request. Her address is 200 Catamon Drive, Pelham, IA 59406.

25. **LO.2** Maria meets all the requirements of § 1237 (subdivided realty). In 2011, she begins selling lots and sells four separate lots to four different purchasers. She also sells two contiguous lots to another purchaser. The sales price of each lot is $30,000. Maria's basis for each lot is $15,000. Selling expenses are $500 per lot.
    a. What are the realized and recognized gain?
    b. Explain the nature of the gain (i.e., ordinary income or capital gain).
    c. Would your answers change if, instead, the lots sold to the fifth purchaser were not contiguous? If so, how?

DECISION MAKING

26. **LO.3, 5** Kate has had a bad year with her investments. She lent a friend $5,700; the friend did not repay the loan when it was due and then declared bankruptcy. The loan is totally uncollectible. Kate also was notified by her broker that the Elm corporate bonds she owned became worthless on October 13, 2011. She had purchased the bonds for $22,000 on November 10, 2010. Kate also had a $30,000 loss on the disposition of § 1244 corporate stock that she purchased several years ago. Kate is single.

a.   What are the nature and amount of Kate's losses?
b.   What is Kate's AGI for 2011 assuming she has $65,000 of ordinary gross income from sources other than those discussed above?
c.   What are the nature and amount of Kate's loss carryforwards?

27. **LO.2, 3** Jason purchased $400,000 of Cherry Corporation face value bonds for $320,000 on November 13, 2010. The bonds had been issued with $80,000 of original issue discount because Cherry was in financial difficulty in 2010. On December 3, 2011, Jason sold the bonds for $383,000 after amortizing $1,000 of the original issue discount. What are the nature and amount of Jason's gain or loss?

28. **LO.3** Frank is an investor in vacant land. When he thinks he has identified property that would be a good investment, he approaches the landowner, pays the landowner for a "right of first refusal" to purchase the land, records this right in the property records, and then waits to see if the land increases in value. The right of first refusal is valid for four years. Fourteen months ago, Frank paid a landowner $4,000 for a right of first refusal. The land was selected as the site of a new shopping center, and the landowner was offered $4 million for the land. In its title search on the land, the buyer discovered Frank's right of first refusal and involved him in the purchase negotiations. Ultimately, the landowner paid Frank $120,000 to give up his right of first refusal; the landowner then sold the land to the buyer for $4,120,000. Frank has a marginal tax rate of 35%.
a.   What difference does it make whether or not Frank treats the right of first refusal as an option to purchase the land?
b.   What difference does it make whether or not Frank is a "dealer" in land?

DECISION MAKING

29. **LO.3** Crissie was the owner of vacant land that she was holding for investment. She paid $1 million for the land in 2008. Kazi was an investor in vacant land. He thought Crissie's land might be the site of an exit ramp from a new freeway. Kazi gave Crissie $836,000 for an option on her land in 2009. The option was good for two years and gave Kazi the ability to purchase Crissie's land for $4,765,000. The freeway was not approved by the government, and Kazi's option expired in 2011. Does Crissie have $836,000 of long-term capital gain upon the expiration of the option?

30. **LO.3** Helen purchased all the rights to a patent on a new sewing tool developed by a friend of hers who was an amateur inventor. The inventor had obtained the patent rights, set up a manufacturing company to produce and sell the sewing tool, and produced substantial quantities of the tool, but he then became discouraged when no large sewing company would agree to distribute the tool for him. Helen purchased the patent rights (but not the manufacturing company) for $320,000 on October 24, 2010. Helen had never engaged in such a transaction before, but she is a salesperson in the sewing industry and thought she could succeed where her friend had failed. On June 27, 2011, she sold all the patent rights to Sewing Tool Company for $2,233,000. Sewing Tool will manufacture the tool in its own factory and sell it to its customers. What is the nature of Helen's gain from this transaction?

31. **LO.3, 4, 7** Mac, an inventor, obtained a patent on a chemical process to clean old aluminum siding so that it can be easily repainted. Mac has a $50,000 tax basis in the patent. Mac does not have the capital to begin manufacturing and selling this product, so he has done nothing with the patent since obtaining it two years ago. Now a group of individuals has approached him and offered two alternatives. Under one alternative, they will pay Mac $600,000 (payable evenly over the next 15 years) for the exclusive right to manufacture and sell the product. Under the other, they will form a business and contribute capital to it to begin manufacturing and selling the product; Mac will receive 20% of the company's shares of stock in exchange for all of his patent rights. Discuss which alternative is better for Mac.

DECISION MAKING

32. **LO.3** Freys, Inc., sells a 12-year franchise to Reynaldo. The franchise contains many restrictions on how Reynaldo may operate his store. For instance, Reynaldo cannot use less than Grade 10 Idaho potatoes, must fry the potatoes at a constant 410 degrees, dress store personnel in Freys-approved uniforms, and have a Freys sign that meets detailed specifications on size, color, and construction. When the franchise contract is signed, Reynaldo makes a noncontingent $160,000 payment to Freys. During the same year, Reynaldo pays Freys $300,000—14% of Reynaldo's sales. How does Freys treat each of these payments? How does Reynaldo treat each of the payments?

33. **LO.3** Alice owns numerous office buildings. A major tenant of one of the buildings wished to cancel its lease because it was moving to another city. After lengthy negotiations, the tenant paid Alice $78,000 to cancel its obligations under the lease. If the tenant had fulfilled the lease terms, Alice would have received rent of $322,000. What factors should Alice consider to determine the amount and character of her income from these circumstances?

34. **LO.3** Sally rented an apartment from the same company that employs her. Her lease began on August 1, 2011, and was due to expire on July 31, 2012, but her landlord/employer needed the building to expand its warehouse facilities. Therefore, Sally's landlord/employer paid her $23,000 to cancel the lease. Sally received the $23,000 on November 30, 2011, moved out, and rented another apartment. How should Sally treat the $23,000?

35. **LO.4** Chandra held vacant land that qualified as an investment asset. She had purchased the vacant land on April 10, 2010. She exchanged the vacant land for a rental house in a qualifying like-kind exchange on January 22, 2011. Chandra intended to hold the rental house for several years and then sell it, but she received an "offer she could not refuse" and sold the house on November 22, 2011, for a substantial gain. What was Chandra's holding period for the rental house?

36. **LO.4** Nick inherited 130 shares of Beige stock when his mother, Cherie, died. Cherie had acquired the stock for a total of $300,000 on November 15, 2010. She died on August 10, 2011, and the shares were worth a total of $225,000 at that time. Nick sold the shares for $236,000 on December 22, 2011. How much gain or loss does Nick have, and what is the nature of that gain or loss?

37. **LO.4** Sarah received a gift of farmland from her father. The land was worth $4 million at the date of the gift, had been farmed by her father for 40 years, and had a tax basis for her father of $30,000. Sarah never farmed the land and sold it eight months after receiving it from her father for $4.2 million. What is Sarah's holding period for the farmland, and what is the nature of the gain from its disposition?

38. **LO.5** Dennis sells short 100 shares of ARC stock at $20 per share on January 15, 2011. He buys 200 shares of ARC stock on April 1, 2011, at $25 per share. On May 2, 2011, he closes the short sale by delivering 100 of the shares purchased on April 1.
   a. What are the amount and nature of Dennis's loss upon closing the short sale?
   b. When does the holding period for the remaining 100 shares begin?
   c. If Dennis sells (at $27 per share) the remaining 100 shares on January 20, 2012, what will be the nature of his gain or loss?

39. **LO.5** Elaine Case (single with no dependents) has the following transactions in 2011:

AGI (exclusive of capital gains and losses)	$240,000
Long-term capital gain	22,000
Long-term capital loss	(8,000)
Short-term capital gain	19,000
Short-term capital loss	(23,000)

What is Elaine's net capital gain or loss? Draft a letter to Elaine describing how the net capital gain or loss will be treated on her tax return. Assume Elaine's income from other sources puts her in the 35% bracket. Elaine's address is 300 Ireland Avenue, Shepherdstown, WV 25443.

40. **LO.3, 5** In 2011, Betty (head of household with three dependents) had an $18,000 loss from the sale of a personal residence. She also purchased from an individual inventor for $18,000 (and resold in two months for $7,000) a patent on a rubber bonding process. The patent had not yet been reduced to practice. Betty purchased the patent as an investment. Additionally, she had the following capital gains and losses from stock transactions:

Long-term capital loss	($ 5,000)
Long-term capital loss carryover from 2010	(12,000)
Short-term capital gain	21,000
Short-term capital loss	(6,000)

What is Betty's net capital gain or loss? Draft a letter to Betty explaining the tax treatment of the sale of her personal residence. Assume Betty's income from other sources puts her in the 35% bracket. Betty's address is 1120 West Street, Ashland, OR 97520.

41. **LO.2, 4, 5** Bridgette is known as the "doll lady." She started collecting dolls as a child, always received one or more dolls as gifts on her birthday, never sold any dolls, and eventually owned 600 dolls. She is retiring and moving to a small apartment and has decided to sell her collection. She lists the dolls on an Internet auction site and, to her great surprise, receives an offer from another doll collector of $45,000 for the entire collection. Bridgette sells the entire collection, except for five dolls that she purchased during the last year. She had owned all the dolls sold for more than a year. What tax factors should Bridgette consider in deciding how to report the sale?

ISSUE ID

42. **LO.5** Phil and Susan are married, filing a joint return. The couple have two dependent children. Susan has wages of $34,000 in 2011. Phil does not work due to a disability, but he is a buyer and seller of stocks on the Internet. He generally buys and holds for long-term gain, but occasionally gets in and out of a stock quickly. The couple's 2011 stock transactions are detailed below. In addition, they have $2,300 of qualifying dividends.

Item	Date Acquired	Date Sold	Cost	Sales Price
Blue stock	11/10/10	03/12/11	$ 3,000	$ 6,000
Puce stock	12/13/09	05/23/11	36,000	32,000
Beige stock	12/14/06	07/14/11	13,000	14,500
Red stock	06/29/10	05/18/11	26,000	27,000
Black stock	05/15/10	10/18/11	67,000	67,800
Gray stock	04/23/09	10/18/11	89,000	88,200

What is Phil and Susan's AGI?

43. **LO.5** Phil has the following long-term capital gains and losses for 2011: $35,000 28% gain, $13,000 28% loss, $18,000 25% gain, and $34,000 0%/15% gain. He also has a $23,000 short-term loss and a $5,000 short-term gain. What is Phil's AGI from these transactions, and if he has a net long-term capital gain, what is its makeup in terms of the alternative tax rates?

44. **LO.5** Hiawatha has the following long-term capital gains and losses for 2011: $45,000 28% gain, $33,000 28% loss, $18,000 25% gain, and $34,000 0%/15% loss. He also has a $23,000 short-term loss and a $75,000 short-term gain. What is Hiawatha's AGI from these transactions, and if he has a net long-term capital gain, what is its makeup in terms of the alternative tax rates?

45. **LO.5** For 2011, Ashley has gross income of $8,350 and a $5,000 long-term capital loss. She claims the standard deduction. Ashley is 35 years old and single with two dependent children. How much of Ashley's $5,000 capital loss carries over to 2012?

46. **LO.5** Jane and Blair are married filing jointly and have 2011 taxable income of $97,000. The taxable income includes $5,000 of gain from a capital asset held for five years, $2,100 of gain from a capital asset held seven months, and $13,000 of gain from a capital asset held four years. All the capital assets were stock in publicly traded corporations. Jane and Blair also have qualified dividend income of $3,000. What is the couple's tax on taxable income?

47. **LO.5** For 2011, Wilma has properly determined taxable income of $36,000, including $3,000 of unrecaptured § 1250 gain and $8,200 of 0%/15% gain. Wilma qualifies for head-of-household filing status. Compute Wilma's tax liability and the tax savings from the alternative tax on net capital gain.

48. **LO.5** Asok's AGI for 2011 is $133,050. Included in this AGI is a $45,000 25% long-term capital gain and a $13,000 0%/15% long-term capital gain. Asok is single, uses the standard deduction, and has only his personal exemption. Compute his taxable income, the tax liability, and the tax savings from the alternative tax on net capital gain.

49. **LO.6** Chartreuse, Inc., a C corporation, has taxable income from operations of $1,432,000 for 2011. It also has a net long-term capital loss of $455,000 from the sale of a

subsidiary's stock. The year 2011 is the first year in the last 10 years that Chartreuse has not had at least $500,000 per year of net long-term capital gains. What is Chartreuse's 2011 taxable income, and what, if anything, can it do with any unused capital losses?

DECISION MAKING

50. **LO.2, 3, 7** Hsui, who is single, is the owner of a sole proprietorship. Two years ago, Hsui developed a process for preserving fresh fruit that gives the fruit a much longer shelf life. The process is not patented or copyrighted, but only Hsui knows how it works. Hsui has been approached by a company that would like to buy the process. Hsui insists that she receive a long-term employment contract with the acquiring company as well as be paid for the rights to the process. The acquiring company offers Hsui a choice of two options: (1) $850,000 in cash for the process and a 10-year covenant not to compete at $45,000 per year or (2) $850,000 in cash for a 10-year covenant not to compete and $45,000 per year for 10 years in payment for the process. Which option should Hsui accept? What is the tax effect on the acquiring company of each approach?

CUMULATIVE PROBLEMS

TAX RETURN PROBLEM

51. Susan Panda lives at 1310 Willow Lane, Wayne, OH 23412, and her Social Security number is 123–45–6789. Susan is single and has a 20-year-old son, Karl. His Social Security number is 111–11–1111. Karl lives with Susan, and she fully supports him. Karl spent 2010 traveling in Europe and was not a college student. He had gross income of $4,355 in 2010.

Susan owns the Panda Enterprises, LLC sole proprietorship, a data processing service (98–7654321), which is located at 456 Hill Street, Wayne, OH 23401. The business activity code is 514210. Her 2010 Form 1040, Schedule C for Wayne Enterprises shows revenues of $155,000, office expenses of $66,759, employee salary of $23,000, employee payroll taxes of $1,760, meals and entertainment expenses (before the 50% reduction) of $22,000, and rent expense of $34,000. The rent expense includes payments related to renting an office ($30,000) and payments related to renting various equipment ($4,000). There is no depreciation because all depreciable equipment owned has been fully depreciated in previous years. No fringe benefits are provided to the employee. Susan personally purchases health insurance on herself and Karl. The premiums are $23,000 per year.

Susan has an extensive stock portfolio and has prepared the following analysis:

Stock	Number of Shares	Date Purchased	Date Sold	Per Share Cost	Per Share Selling Price	Total Dividends
Beige	10	10/18/09	10/11/10	$80	$ 74	$30
Garland	30	10/11/03	10/11/10	43	157	70
Puce	15	3/10/10	8/11/10	62	33	45

NOTE: The per-share cost includes commissions, and the per-share selling price is net of commissions. Also, the dividends are the actual dividends received in 2010.

Susan had $800 of interest income from State of Ohio bonds and $600 of interest income on her Wayne Savings Bank account. She received $25,000 of alimony from her former husband. His Social Security number is 123–45–6788.

Susan itemizes her deductions and had the following items, which may be relevant to her return:

Item	Amount	Comment
Unreimbursed medical expenses for Susan (all for visits to doctors)	$1,786	Does not include health insurance premiums.
State income taxes paid	1,830	
Real property taxes on personal residence	3,230	
Interest paid on home mortgage (Form 1098)	8,137	The loan is secured by the residence and was incurred when the home was purchased.
Charitable contributions	940	Cash paid to Susan's church.
Sales taxes	619	Amount per sales tax table.

Susan made a $3,000 estimated Federal income tax payment, does not wish any of her taxes to finance presidential elections, has no foreign bank accounts or trusts, and wishes any refund to be applied against her 2011 taxes.

Compute Susan's net tax payable or refund due for 2010. If you use tax forms for your computations, you will need Form 1040 and Schedules A, C, D, and SE. Suggested software: H&R BLOCK At Home.

52. Paul Barrone is a graduate student at State University. His 10-year-old son, Jamie, lives with him, and Paul is Jamie's sole support. Paul's wife died in 2010, and Paul has not remarried. Paul received $320,000 of life insurance proceeds (related to his wife's death) in early 2011 and immediately invested the entire amount as shown below:

Item	Date Acquired	Cost	Date Sold	Selling Price	Dividends/ Interest
1,000 shares Blue	01/23/11	$ 14,000	12/03/11	$ 3,500	None
400 shares Magenta	01/23/11	23,000			$750
600 shares Orange	01/23/11	230,000			$2,300
100 shares Brown	06/23/05	2,800	01/23/11	14,000	None
Green bonds	01/23/11	23,000			$1,200
Gold money market account	01/23/11	30,000			$600

Paul had $42,000 of taxable graduate assistant earnings from State University and also received a $10,000 scholarship. He used $8,000 of the scholarship to pay his tuition and fees for the year and $2,000 for Jamie's day care. Jamie attended Little Kids Daycare Center, a state certified child care facility. Paul received a statement related to the Green bonds saying that there was $45 of original issue discount amortization during 2011. Paul maintains the receipts for the sales taxes he paid of $735.

Paul lives at 1610 Cherry Lane, State College, MD 34212, and his Social Security number is 111–11–1111. Jamie's Social Security number is 123–45–6789. The university withheld $3,000 of Federal income tax from Paul's salary. Paul is not itemizing his deductions.

Part 1—Tax Computation
Compute Paul's lowest tax liability for 2011.

Part 2—Tax Planning
Paul is concerned because the Green bonds were worth only $18,000 at the end of 2011, $5,000 less than he paid for them. He is an inexperienced investor and wants to know if this $5,000 is deductible. The bonds had original issue discount of $2,000 when he purchased them, and he is also curious about how that affects his investment in the bonds. The bonds had 20 years left to maturity when he purchased them. Draft a brief letter to Paul explaining how to handle these items. Also, prepare a memo for Paul's tax file.

RESEARCH PROBLEMS

Note: Solutions to Research Problems can be prepared by using the **Checkpoint®** **Student Edition** online research product, which is available to accompany this text. It is also possible to prepare solutions to the Research Problems by using tax research materials found in a standard tax library.

Research Problem 1. Ali owns 100 shares of Brown Corporation stock. He purchased the stock at five different times and at five different prices per share as indicated:

Share Block	Number of Shares	Per Share Price	Purchase Date
A	10	$60	10/10/95
B	20	20	8/11/96
C	15	15	10/24/96
D	35	30	4/23/98
E	20	25	7/28/98

THOMSON REUTERS
Checkpoint® Student Edition

On April 28, 2011, Ali will sell 40 shares of Brown stock for $40 per share. All of Ali's shares are held by his stockbroker. The broker's records track when the shares were purchased. May Ali designate the shares he sells, and, if so, which shares should he sell? Assume Ali wants to maximize his gain because he has a capital loss carryforward.

COMMUNICATIONS

Research Problem 2. Clean Corporation runs a chain of dry cleaners. Borax is used heavily in Clean's dry cleaning process and has been in short supply several times in the past. Clean Corporation buys a controlling interest in Dig Corporation—a borax mining concern. Clean's sole reason for purchasing the Dig stock is to assure Clean of a continuous supply of borax if another shortage develops. Although borax must be refined before it is usable for dry cleaning purposes, a well-established commodities market exists for trading unrefined borax for refined borax. After owning the Dig stock for several years, Clean sells the stock at a loss because Dig is in difficult financial straits. Clean no longer needs to own Dig because Clean has obtained an alternative source of borax. What is the nature of Clean's loss on the disposition of the Dig Corporation stock? Write a letter to the controller, Salvio Guitterez, that contains your advice and prepare a memo for the tax files. The mailing address of Clean Corporation is 4455 Whitman Way, San Mateo, CA 44589.

Research Problem 3. Clyde had worked for many years as the chief executive of Red Industries, Inc., and had also been a major shareholder. Clyde and the company had a falling out, and Clyde was terminated. Clyde and Red executed a document under which Clyde's stock in Red would be redeemed and Clyde would agree not to compete against Red in its geographic service area. After extensive negotiations between the parties, Clyde agreed to surrender his Red stock in exchange for $600,000. Clyde's basis in his shares was $143,000, and he had held the shares for 17 years. The agreement made no explicit allocation of any of the $600,000 to Clyde's agreement not to compete against Red. How should Clyde treat the $600,000 payment on his 2010 tax return?

Research Problem 4. Siva Nathaniel owns various plots of land in Fulton County, Georgia. He acquired the land at various times during the last 20 years. About every fourth year, Siva subdivides one of the properties he owns into lots. He then has water, sewer, natural gas, and electricity hookups put in on each lot and paves the new streets. Siva has always treated his sales of such lots as sales of capital assets. His previous tax returns were prepared by an accountant whose practice you recently purchased. Has the proper tax treatment been used on the prior tax returns?

Partial list of research aids:
§§ 1221 and 1237 and *Jesse W. and Betty J. English,* 65 T.C.M. 2160, T.C.Memo, 1993–111.

INTERNET *activity*

Use the tax resources of the Internet to address the following questions. Do not restrict your search to the Web, but include a review of newsgroups and general reference materials, practitioner sites and resources, primary sources of the tax law, chat rooms and discussion groups, and other opportunities.

Research Problem 5. Find a website that discusses the income tax in Australia. Determine whether Australia has an alternative tax on net long-term capital gains similar to that in the United States.

Research Problem 6. Find a website, other than the IRS website, that discusses the taxation of short sales of securities.

Property Transactions: § 1231 and Recapture Provisions

FRAMEWORK 1040:
Tax Formula for Individuals

This chapter covers the boldfaced portions of the Tax Formula for Individuals that was introduced in Figure 3.1 on p. 3-3. Below those portions are the sections of Form 1040 where the results are reported.

Income (broadly conceived)	$ xx,xxx
Less: Exclusions	(x,xxx)
Gross income	**$xx,xxx**
Less: Deductions for adjusted gross income	**(x,xxx)**

FORM 1040 (p. 1)

12	Business income or (loss). Attach Schedule C or C-EZ	
13	Capital gain or (loss). Attach Schedule D if required. If not required, check here ▶ ☐	
14	Other gains or (losses). Attach Form 4797	

Adjusted gross income..	$ xx,xxx
Less: The greater of total itemized deductions *or* the standard deduction.................	(x,xxx)
Personal and dependency exemptions	(x,xxx)
Taxable income	$ xx,xxx
Tax on taxable income (see Tax Tables or Tax Rate Schedules)	**$ x,xxx**

FORM 1040 (p. 2)

44	Tax (see instructions). Check if any tax is from: **a** ☐ Form(s) 8814	**b** ☐ Form 4972 .	

Less: Tax credits (including income taxes withheld and prepaid)	(xxx)
Tax due (or refund)...	$ xxx

THE BIG PICTURE   Tax Solutions for the Real World

DEPRECIATION RECAPTURE

Hazel Brown (a sole proprietor filing a Form 1040 Schedule C) owns and operates a retail arts and crafts store. In 2008, she remodeled the store and replaced the store equipment (counters, display racks, etc.) at a cost of $450,000. All of the equipment was used (she bought it from a competitor that was going out of business). The equipment is seven-year MACRS property, and she took $250,000 of § 179 expense on it and depreciated the balance. As of June 30, 2011, the equipment has an adjusted basis of $74,960 ($450,000 cost − $250,000 § 179 expense − $125,040 of regular MACRS depreciation). Now, Hazel is again planning on replacing the store equipment, and she has determined that she can sell all of the existing equipment for $128,000.

If Hazel completes this transaction, what will be the impact on her 2011 tax return? **Read the chapter and formulate your response.**

Generic Motors Corporation sold machinery, office furniture, and unneeded production plants for $100 million last year. The corporation's disposition of these assets resulted in $60 million of gains and $13 million of losses. How are these gains and losses treated for tax purposes? Do any special tax rules apply? Could any of the gains and losses receive capital gain or loss treatment? This chapter answers these questions by explaining how to *classify* gains and losses from the disposition of assets that are used in the business rather than held for resale. Chapter 8 discussed how to *depreciate* such assets. Chapters 14 and 15 discussed how to determine the *adjusted basis* and the *amount* of gain or loss from their disposition.

A long-term capital gain was defined in Chapter 16 as the recognized gain from the sale or exchange of a capital asset held for the required long-term holding period.[1] Long-term capital assets are capital assets held more than one year.

This chapter is concerned with classification under § 1231, which applies to the sale or exchange of business properties and to certain involuntary conversions. The business properties are not capital assets because they are depreciable and/or real property used in business or for the production of income. Section 1221(a)(2) provides that such assets are not capital assets. Nonetheless, these business properties may be held for long periods of time and may be sold at a gain. Congress decided many years ago that such assets deserved *limited* capital gain-type treatment. Unfortunately, this limited capital gain-type treatment is very complex and difficult to understand.

Because the limited capital gain-type treatment sometimes gives too much tax advantage if assets are eligible for depreciation (or cost recovery), certain recapture rules may prevent the capital gain treatment when depreciation is taken. Thus, this chapter also covers the recapture provisions that tax as ordinary income certain gains that might otherwise qualify for long-term capital gain treatment.

17.1 SECTION 1231 ASSETS

RELATIONSHIP TO CAPITAL ASSETS

Depreciable property and real property used in business are not capital assets.[2] Thus, the recognized gains from the disposition of such property (principally machinery, equipment, buildings, and land) would appear to be ordinary income rather than capital gain. Due to § 1231, however, *net gain* from the disposition of such property is sometimes *treated* as *long-term capital gain*. A long-term holding period requirement must be met; the disposition must generally be from a sale, exchange, or involuntary conversion; and certain recapture provisions must be satisfied for this result to occur. Section 1231 may also apply to involuntary conversions of capital assets. Since an involuntary conversion is not a sale or exchange, such a disposition normally would not result in a capital gain.

If the disposition of depreciable property and real property used in business results in a *net loss*, § 1231 *treats* the *loss* as an *ordinary loss* rather than as a capital loss. Ordinary losses are fully deductible *for* adjusted gross income (AGI). Capital losses are offset by capital gains, and, if any loss remains, the loss is deductible to the extent of $3,000 per year for individuals and currently is not deductible at all by regular corporations. It seems, therefore, that § 1231 provides the *best* of both potential results: net gain may be treated as long-term capital gain, and net loss is treated as ordinary loss.

> **LO.1**
>
> Understand the rationale for and the nature and treatment of gains and losses from the disposition of business assets.

---

[1] § 1222(3). To be eligible for any beneficial tax treatment, the holding period must be more than one year.

[2] § 1221(a)(2).

EXAMPLE 1 THE BIG PICTURE	Return to the facts of *The Big Picture* on p. 17-2. If Hazel sells the store equipment, she will have disposed of a § 1231 asset because it was depreciable property used in a trade or business and held for more than 12 months. Her gain will be $53,040 ($128,000 selling price − $74,960 adjusted basis). Part of the gain may (depending on the recapture rules discussed later in this chapter) be treated as a long-term capital gain under § 1231. ∎

EXAMPLE 2	Samantha sells business equipment at a $10,000 loss and business land at a $2,000 gain. Both properties were held for the long-term holding period. Samantha's net loss is $8,000, and that net loss is an ordinary loss. ∎

The rules regarding § 1231 treatment do *not* apply to *all* business property. Important in this regard are the holding period requirements and the fact that the property must be either depreciable property or real estate used in business. Nor is § 1231 necessarily limited to business property. Transactions involving certain capital assets may fall into the § 1231 category. Thus, § 1231 singles out only some types of business property.

As discussed in Chapter 16, long-term capital gains receive beneficial tax treatment. Section 1231 requires netting of **§ 1231 gains and losses**. If the result is a gain, it may be treated as a long-term capital gain. The net gain is added to the "real" long-term capital gains (if any) and netted with capital losses (if any). Thus, the net § 1231 gain may eventually be eligible for beneficial capital gain treatment or help avoid the unfavorable net capital loss result. The § 1231 gain and loss netting may result in a loss. In this case, the loss is an ordinary loss and is deductible *for* AGI. Finally, § 1231 assets are treated the same as capital assets for purposes of the appreciated property charitable contribution provisions (refer to Chapter 10).

JUSTIFICATION FOR FAVORABLE TAX TREATMENT

The favorable capital gain/ordinary loss treatment sanctioned by § 1231 can be explained by examining several historical developments. Before 1938, business property had been included in the definition of capital assets. Thus, if such property was sold for a loss (not an unlikely possibility during the depression years of the 1930s), a capital loss resulted. If, however, the property was depreciable and could be retained for its estimated useful life, much (if not all) of its costs could be recovered in the form of depreciation. Because the allowance for depreciation was fully deductible whereas capital losses were not, the tax law favored those who did not dispose of an asset. Congress recognized this inequity when it removed business property from the capital asset classification. During the period 1938–1942, therefore, all such gains and losses were ordinary gains and losses.

With the advent of World War II, two developments in particular forced Congress to reexamine the situation regarding business assets. First, the sale of business assets at a gain was discouraged because the gain would be ordinary income. Gains were common because the war effort had inflated prices. Second, taxpayers who did not want to sell their assets often were required to because the government acquired them through condemnation. Often, as a result of the condemnation awards, taxpayers who were forced to part with their property experienced large gains and were deprived of the benefits of future depreciation deductions. Of course, the condemnations constituted involuntary conversions, so taxpayers could defer the gain by timely reinvestment in property that was "similar or related in service or use." But where was such property to be found in view of wartime restrictions and other governmental condemnations? The end result did not seem equitable: a large ordinary gain due to government action and no possibility of deferral due to government restrictions.

In recognition of these conditions, in 1942, Congress eased the tax bite on the disposition of some business property by allowing preferential capital gain treatment. Thus, the present scheme of § 1231 and the dichotomy of capital gain/ordinary loss treatment evolved from a combination of economic considerations existing in 1938 and 1942.

PROPERTY INCLUDED

Section 1231 property generally includes the following assets if they are held for more than one year:

- Depreciable or real property used in business or for the production of income (principally machinery and equipment, buildings, and land).
- Timber, coal, or domestic iron ore to which § 631 applies.
- Livestock held for draft, breeding, dairy, or sporting purposes.
- Unharvested crops on land used in business.
- Certain *purchased* intangible assets (such as patents and goodwill) that are eligible for amortization.

These assets are ordinary assets until they have been held for more than one year. Only then do they become § 1231 assets.

LO.2

Distinguish § 1231 assets from ordinary assets and capital assets and calculate the § 1231 gain or loss.

PROPERTY EXCLUDED

Section 1231 property generally does *not* include the following:

- Property not held for the long-term holding period. Since the benefit of § 1231 is long-term capital gain treatment, the holding period must correspond to the more-than-one-year holding period that applies to capital assets. Livestock must be held at least 12 months (24 months in some cases). Unharvested crops do not have to be held for the required long-term holding period, but the land must be held for the long-term holding period.
- Nonpersonal use property where casualty losses exceed casualty gains for the taxable year. If a taxpayer has a net casualty loss, the individual casualty gains and losses are treated as ordinary gains and losses.
- Inventory and property held primarily for sale to customers.
- Copyrights; literary, musical, or artistic compositions, etc.; and certain U.S. government publications.
- Accounts receivable and notes receivable arising in the ordinary course of the trade or business.

SPECIAL RULES FOR CERTAIN § 1231 ASSETS

A rather diverse group of assets is included under § 1231. The following discussion summarizes the special rules for some of those assets.

Timber

Congress has provided preferential treatment relative to the natural growth value of timber, which takes a relatively long time to mature. Congress believed that this preferential treatment would encourage reforestation of timber lands. A taxpayer disposing of timber held for the long-term holding period has a long-term capital gain or loss if the timber was held for investment, has a § 1231 gain or loss if the timber was used in a trade or business, but, without special statutory treatment, would have ordinary income or loss if the timber was held as inventory. Section 631(a) allows the taxpayer to *elect* to treat the cutting of timber as a sale or exchange and, if the election is made, to treat the sale as the disposition of a § 1231 asset.[3]

The recognized § 1231 gain or loss is determined at the time the timber is cut and is equal to the difference between the timber's fair market value as of the *first day* of the taxable year and the adjusted basis for depletion. If a taxpayer sells the timber for more or less than the fair market value as of the first day of the taxable year in which it is cut, the difference is ordinary income or loss.

---

[3]§ 631(a) and Reg. § 1.631–1. To receive § 631 treatment, the holding period for the timber must be greater than one year.

EXAMPLE 3

Several years ago, Tom, a timber dealer, purchased a tract of land with a substantial stand of trees on it. The land cost $40,000, and the timber cost $100,000. On the first day of 2011, the timber was appraised at $250,000. In August 2011, Tom cut the timber and sold it for $265,000. Tom elects to treat the cutting as a sale or exchange under § 1231. He has a $150,000 § 1231 gain ($250,000 − $100,000) and a $15,000 ordinary gain ($265,000 − $250,000).

What if the timber had been sold for $235,000? Tom would still have a $150,000 § 1231 gain, but he would also have a $15,000 ordinary loss. The price for computing § 1231 gain is the price at the beginning of the tax year. Any difference between that price and the sales price is ordinary gain or loss. Here, since the price declined by $15,000, Tom has an ordinary loss in that amount. ■

Livestock

Cattle and horses must be held 24 months or more and other livestock must be held 12 months or more to qualify under § 1231.[4] The primary reason for enacting this provision was the considerable amount of litigation over the character of livestock [whether livestock was held primarily for sale to customers (ordinary income) or for use in a trade or business (§ 1231 property)]. Poultry is not livestock for purposes of § 1231.

Section 1231 Assets Disposed of by Casualty or Theft

When § 1231 assets are disposed of by casualty or theft, a special netting rule is applied. For simplicity, the term *casualty* is used to mean both casualty and theft dispositions. First, the casualty gains and losses from § 1231 assets *and* the casualty gains and losses from **long-term nonpersonal use capital assets** are determined. A nonpersonal use capital asset might be an investment painting or a baseball card collection held by a nondealer in baseball cards.

Next, the § 1231 asset casualty gains and losses and the nonpersonal use capital asset casualty gains and losses are netted together (see Concept Summary 17.1). If the result is a *net loss*, the § 1231 casualty gains and the nonpersonal use capital asset casualty gains are treated as ordinary gains, the § 1231 casualty losses are deductible *for* AGI, and the nonpersonal use capital asset casualty losses are deductible *from* AGI subject to the 2 percent-of-AGI limitation.

If the result of the netting is a *net gain*, the net gain is treated as a § 1231 gain. Thus, a § 1231 asset disposed of by casualty may or may not get § 1231 treatment, depending on whether the netting process results in a gain or a loss. Also, a nonpersonal use capital asset disposed of by casualty may get § 1231 treatment or ordinary treatment, but will not get capital gain or loss treatment!

Personal use property casualty gains and losses are not subject to the § 1231 rules. If the result of netting these gains and losses is a gain, the net gain is a capital gain. If the netting results in a loss, the net loss is a deduction *from* AGI to the extent it exceeds 10 percent of AGI.

---

[4]Note that the holding period is "12 months or more" and not "more than 12 months."

TAX *in the NEWS*

LOSS FROM CATTLE RUSTLING

A newspaper in "cattle country" reported that rustlers had stolen 20 head of prime milk cows from a local ranch. The rancher never recovered the cows. According to the article, the rancher had no insurance on the cows and was upset because he had no way of recovering his loss. A CPA might advise the rancher that he could be entitled to a special "theft loss" for tax purposes because the theft loss rules apply to § 1231 assets such as cattle held for 24 months or more.

CONCEPT SUMMARY 17.1

Section 1231 Netting Procedure

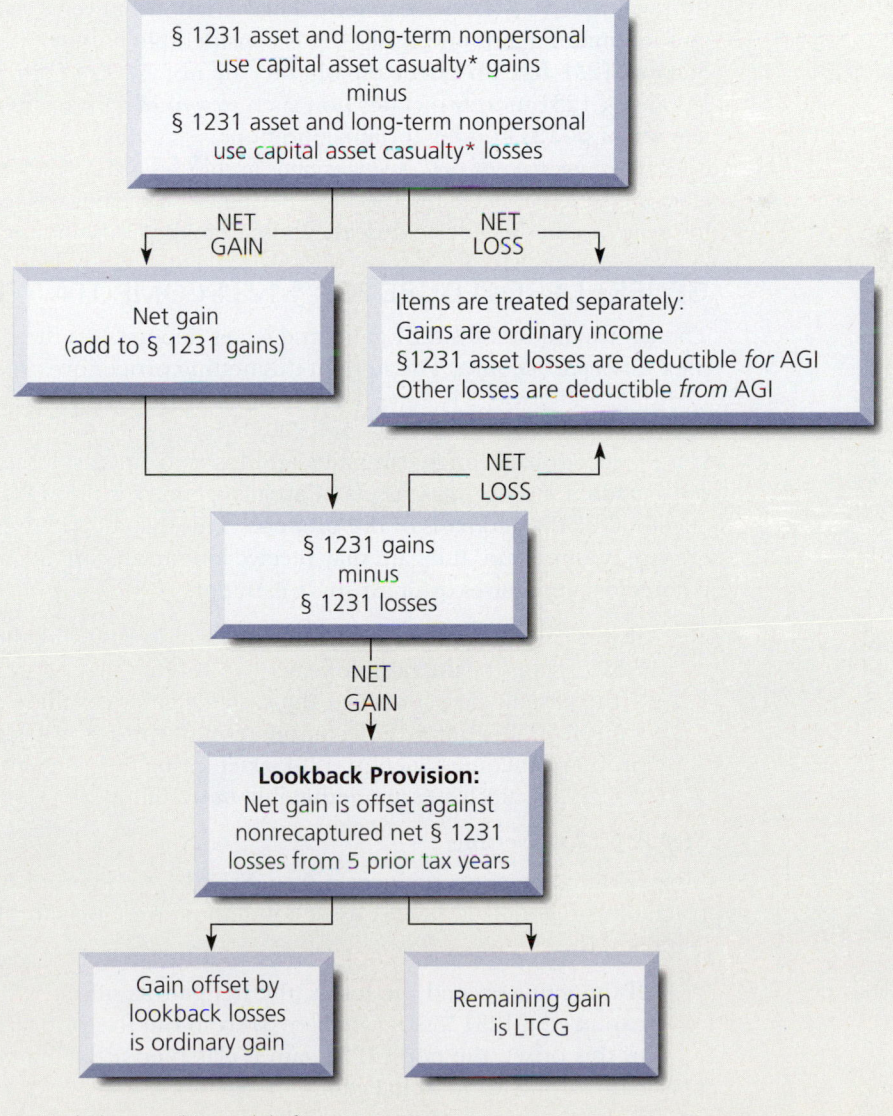

§ 1231 asset and long-term nonpersonal use capital asset casualty* gains
minus
§ 1231 asset and long-term nonpersonal use capital asset casualty* losses

NET GAIN → Net gain (add to § 1231 gains)

NET LOSS → Items are treated separately:
Gains are ordinary income
§1231 asset losses are deductible *for* AGI
Other losses are deductible *from* AGI

§ 1231 gains minus § 1231 losses

NET LOSS

NET GAIN

Lookback Provision:
Net gain is offset against nonrecaptured net § 1231 losses from 5 prior tax years

Gain offset by lookback losses is ordinary gain

Remaining gain is LTCG

*Includes casualties and thefts.

GLOBAL
Tax Issues

CANADIAN SLOW DEPRECIATION

A manufacturer has a division in Canada that manufactures auto components. The components are shipped to Detroit and become part of U.S.-manufactured automobiles. Due to slow auto sales, the manufacturer closes the Canadian plant and moves its machinery to the United States. Later, the manufacturer sells the machinery and has a tax loss because the machinery's adjusted basis is much higher than that of similar equipment that was used exclusively in the United States. The adjusted basis of the formerly Canadian equipment is higher because straight-line tax depreciation was required for the Canadian property (see Chapter 8).

Casualties, thefts, and condemnations are *involuntary conversions*. Involuntary conversion gains may be deferred if conversion proceeds are reinvested; involuntary conversion losses are recognized currently (refer to Chapter 15) regardless of whether the conversion proceeds are reinvested. Thus, the special netting process discussed previously for casualties and thefts would not include gains that are not currently recognizable because the insurance proceeds are reinvested.

The special netting process for casualties and thefts also does not include condemnation gains and losses. Consequently, a § 1231 asset disposed of by condemnation will receive § 1231 treatment. This variation between recognized casualty and condemnation gains and losses sheds considerable light on what § 1231 is all about. Section 1231 has no effect on whether or not *realized* gain or loss is recognized. Instead, § 1231 merely dictates how such *recognized* gain or loss is *classified* (ordinary, capital, or § 1231) under certain conditions.

Personal use property condemnation gains and losses are not subject to the § 1231 rules. The gains are capital gains (because personal use property is a capital asset), and the losses are nondeductible because they arise from the disposition of personal use property.

GENERAL PROCEDURE FOR § 1231 COMPUTATION

The tax treatment of § 1231 gains and losses depends on the results of a rather complex *netting* procedure. The steps in this netting procedure are as follows.

Step 1: Casualty Netting

Net all recognized long-term gains and losses from casualties of § 1231 assets and nonpersonal use capital assets. Casualty gains result when insurance proceeds exceed the adjusted basis of the property. This casualty netting is beneficial because if there is a net gain, the gain may receive long-term capital gain treatment. If there is a net loss, it receives ordinary loss treatment.

a. If the casualty gains exceed the casualty losses, add the excess to the other § 1231 gains for the taxable year.
b. If the casualty losses exceed the casualty gains, exclude all casualty losses and gains from further § 1231 computation. If this is the case, all casualty gains are ordinary income. Section 1231 asset casualty losses are deductible *for* AGI. Other casualty losses are deductible *from* AGI.

Step 2: § 1231 Netting

After adding any net casualty gain from Step 1a to the other § 1231 gains and losses (including recognized § 1231 asset condemnation gains and losses), net all § 1231 gains and losses.

a. If the gains exceed the losses, the net gain is offset by the "lookback" nonrecaptured § 1231 losses (see Step 3) from the five prior tax years. To the extent of this offset, the net § 1231 gain is classified as ordinary gain. Any remaining gain is long-term capital gain.
b. If the losses exceed the gains, all gains are ordinary income. Section 1231 asset losses are deductible *for* AGI. Other casualty losses are deductible *from* AGI.

TAX *in* the *NEWS*

CONDEMNATIONS AND § 1231

A recent newspaper article discussed the condemnation of local properties as part of an expressway project. One taxpayer had both his home and his retail store (which were on adjacent real estate parcels) condemned. He had a loss on the home disposition, but a gain on the business real estate disposition. The loss from the condemnation of the home is nondeductible because, although the home was a capital asset, losses resulting from dispositions by condemnation of personal use activity assets are not deductible. The gain from the disposition of the retail store resulted from the disposition of a § 1231 asset (assuming it had been held more than one year). This gain is not part of the special netting process for nonpersonal use casualty and theft gains and losses.

Step 3: § 1231 Lookback Provision

The net § 1231 gain from Step 2a is offset by the nonrecaptured net § 1231 losses for the five preceding taxable years. For 2011, the lookback years are 2006, 2007, 2008, 2009, and 2010. To the extent of the nonrecaptured net § 1231 loss, the current-year net § 1231 gain is ordinary income. The *nonrecaptured* net § 1231 losses are those that have not already been used to offset net § 1231 gains. Only the net § 1231 gain exceeding this net § 1231 loss carryforward is given long-term capital gain treatment. Concept Summary 17.1 summarizes the § 1231 computational procedure. Examples 6 and 7 illustrate the **§ 1231 lookback** provision.

Examples 4 through 7 illustrate the application of the § 1231 computation procedure.

EXAMPLE 4

During 2011, Ross had $125,000 of AGI before considering the following recognized gains and losses:

Capital Gains and Losses	
Long-term capital gain	$3,000
Long-term capital loss	(400)
Short-term capital gain	1,000
Short-term capital loss	(200)

Casualties	
Theft of diamond ring (owned four months)	($ 800)*
Fire damage to personal residence (owned 10 years)	(400)*
Gain from insurance recovery on fire loss to business building (owned two years)	200

§ 1231 Gains and Losses from Depreciable Business Assets Held Long Term	
Asset A	$ 300
Asset B	1,100
Asset C	(500)

Gains and Losses from Sale of Depreciable Business Assets Held Short Term	
Asset D	$ 200
Asset E	(300)

*As adjusted for the $100 floor on personal casualty losses.

Ross had no net § 1231 losses in tax years before 2011.

Disregarding the recapture of depreciation (discussed later in the chapter), Ross's gains and losses receive the following tax treatment:

- The diamond ring and the residence are personal use assets. Therefore, these casualties are not § 1231 transactions. The $800 (ring) plus $400 (residence) losses are potentially deductible *from* AGI. However, the total loss of $1,200 does not exceed 10% of AGI. Thus, only the business building (a § 1231 asset) casualty gain remains. The netting of the § 1231 asset and nonpersonal use capital asset casualty gains and losses contains only one item—the $200 gain from the business building. Consequently, there is a net gain and that gain is treated as a § 1231 gain (added to the § 1231 gains).

- The gains from § 1231 transactions (Assets A, B, and C and the § 1231 asset casualty gain) exceed the losses by $1,100 ($1,600 − $500). This excess is a long-term capital gain and is added to Ross's other long-term capital gains.

- Ross's net long-term capital gain is $3,700 ($3,000 + $1,100 from § 1231 trans-actions − $400 long-term capital loss). Ross's net short-term capital gain is $800 ($1,000 − $200). The result is capital gain net income of $4,500. The $3,700 net long-term capital gain portion is eligible for beneficial capital gain treatment [assume all the gain is 0%/15% gain (see the discussion in Chapter 16)]. The $800 net short-term capital gain is subject to tax as ordinary income.[5]

- Ross treats the gain and loss from Assets D and E (depreciable business assets held for less than the long-term holding period) as ordinary gain and loss.

Results of the Gains and Losses on Ross's Tax Computation	
NLTCG	$ 3,700
NSTCG	800
Ordinary gain from sale of Asset D	200
Ordinary loss from sale of Asset E	(300)
AGI from other sources	125,000
AGI	$129,400

- Ross will have personal use property casualty losses of $1,200 [$800 (dia-mond ring) + $400 (personal residence)]. A personal use property casualty loss is deductible only to the extent it exceeds 10% of AGI. Thus, none of the $1,200 is deductible ($129,400 × 10% = $12,940). ■

EXAMPLE 5

Assume the same facts as in Example 4, except the loss from Asset C was $1,700 instead of $500.

- The treatment of the casualty losses is the same as in Example 4.
- The losses from § 1231 transactions now exceed the gains by $100 ($1,700 − $1,600). As a result, the gains from Assets A and B and the § 1231 asset casu-alty gain are ordinary income, and the loss from Asset C is a deduction *for* AGI (a business loss). The same result can be achieved by simply treating the $100 net loss as a deduction *for* AGI.
- Capital gain net income is $3,400 ($2,600 long term + $800 short term). The $2,600 net long-term capital gain portion is eligible for beneficial capital gain treatment, and the $800 net short-term capital gain is subject to tax as ordinary income.

Results of the Gains and Losses on Ross's Tax Computation	
NLTCG	$ 2,600
NSTCG	800
Net ordinary loss on Assets A, B, and C and § 1231 casualty gain	(100)
Ordinary gain from sale of Asset D	200
Ordinary loss from sale of Asset E	(300)
AGI from other sources	125,000
AGI	$128,200

- None of the personal use property casualty losses will be deductible since $1,200 does not exceed 10% of $128,200. ■

EXAMPLE 6

Assume the same facts as in Example 4, except that Ross has a $700 nonrecaptured net § 1231 loss from 2010.

---

[5]Ross's taxable income (unless the itemized deductions and the personal exemption and dependency deductions are extremely large) will put him in at least the 28% bracket. Thus, the alternative tax computation will yield a lower tax. See Example 40 in Chapter 16.

- The treatment of the casualty losses is the same as in Example 4.
- The 2011 net § 1231 gain of $1,100 is treated as ordinary income to the extent of the 2010 nonrecaptured § 1231 loss of $700. The remaining $400 net § 1231 gain is a long-term capital gain and is added to Ross's other long-term capital gains.
- Ross's net long-term capital gain is $3,000 ($3,000 + $400 from § 1231 transactions − $400 long-term capital loss). Ross's net short-term capital gain is still $800 ($1,000 − $200). The result is capital gain net income of $3,800. The $3,000 net long-term capital gain portion is eligible for beneficial capital gain treatment, and the $800 net short-term capital gain is subject to tax as ordinary income.

Results of the Gains and Losses on Ross's Tax Computation

NLTCG	$ 3,000
NSTCG	800
Ordinary gain from recapture of § 1231 losses	700
Ordinary gain from sale of Asset D	200
Ordinary loss from sale of Asset E	(300)
AGI from other sources	125,000
AGI	$129,400

- None of the personal use property casualty losses will be deductible since $1,200 does not exceed 10% of $129,400. ■

EXAMPLE 7

Assume the same facts as in Example 4, except that Ross had a net § 1231 loss of $2,700 in 2009 and a net § 1231 gain of $300 in 2010.

- The treatment of the casualty losses is the same as in Example 4.
- The 2009 net § 1231 loss of $2,700 will have carried over to 2010 and been offset against the 2010 net § 1231 gain of $300. Thus, the $300 gain will have been classified as ordinary income, and $2,400 of nonrecaptured 2009 net § 1231 loss will carry over to 2011. The 2011 net § 1231 gain of $1,100 will be offset against this loss, resulting in $1,100 of ordinary income. The nonrecaptured net § 1231 loss of $1,300 ($2,400 − $1,100) carries over to 2012.
- Capital gain net income is $3,400 ($2,600 net long-term capital gain + $800 net short-term capital gain). The $2,600 net long-term capital gain portion is eligible for beneficial capital gain treatment, and the $800 net short-term capital gain is subject to tax as ordinary income.

Results of the Gains and Losses on Ross's Tax Computation

NLTCG	$ 2,600
NSTCG	800
Ordinary gain from recapture of § 1231 losses	1,100
Ordinary gain from sale of Asset D	200
Ordinary loss from sale of Asset E	(300)
AGI from other sources	125,000
AGI	$129,400

- None of the personal use property casualty losses will be deductible since $1,200 does not exceed 10% of $129,400. ■

ETHICS & Equity

PREPARING RETURNS WITHOUT PROPER INFORMATION

A CPA firm is preparing the tax return of a new client who says he has had numerous transactions involving sales of business depreciable property in prior years. The client lost all his tax records in a recent tornado. The client's transactions for the current year result in a net § 1231 gain. Can the CPA firm complete this return without further information?

17.2 SECTION 1245 RECAPTURE

LO.3

Determine when § 1245 recapture applies and how it is computed.

Now that the basic rules of § 1231 have been introduced, it is time to add some complications. The Code contains two major *recapture* provisions—§§ 1245 and 1250. These provisions cause *gain* to be treated *initially* as ordinary gain. Thus, what may appear to be a § 1231 gain is ordinary gain instead. These recapture provisions may also cause a gain in a nonpersonal use casualty to be *initially* ordinary gain rather than casualty gain. Classifying gains (and losses) properly initially is important because improper initial classification may lead to incorrect mixing and matching of gains and losses. This section discusses the § 1245 recapture rules, and the next section discusses the § 1250 recapture rules.

Section 1245 requires taxpayers to treat all gain as ordinary gain unless the property is disposed of for more than was paid for it. This result is accomplished by requiring that all gain be treated as ordinary gain to the extent of the depreciation taken on the property disposed of. Section 1231 gain results only when the property is disposed of for more than its original cost. The excess of the sales price over the original cost is § 1231 gain. Section 1245 applies *primarily* to non-real-estate property such as machinery, trucks, and office furniture. Section 1245 does not apply if property is disposed of at a loss. Generally, the loss will be a § 1231 loss unless the form of the disposition is a casualty.

EXAMPLE 8

Alice purchased a $100,000 business machine and deducted $70,000 depreciation before selling it for $80,000. If it were not for § 1245, the $50,000 gain would be § 1231 gain ($80,000 amount realized − $30,000 adjusted basis). Section 1245 prevents this potentially favorable result by treating as ordinary income (not as § 1231 gain) any gain to the extent of depreciation taken. In this example, the entire $50,000 gain would be ordinary income. If Alice had sold the machine for $120,000, she would have a gain of $90,000 ($120,000 amount realized − $30,000 adjusted basis). The § 1245 gain would be $70,000 (equal to the depreciation taken), and the § 1231 gain would be $20,000 (equal to the excess of the sales price over the original cost). ■

Section 1245 recapture provides, in general, that the portion of recognized gain from the sale or other disposition of § 1245 property that represents depreciation [including § 167 depreciation, § 168 cost recovery, § 179 immediate expensing, § 168(k) additional first-year depreciation, and § 197 amortization] is *recaptured* as ordinary income. Thus, in Example 8, $50,000 of the $70,000 depreciation taken is recaptured as ordinary income when the business machine is sold for $80,000. Only $50,000 is recaptured rather than $70,000 because Alice is only required to recognize § 1245 recapture ordinary gain equal to the lower of the depreciation taken or the gain recognized.

The method of depreciation (e.g., accelerated or straight-line) does not matter. All depreciation taken is potentially subject to recapture. Thus, § 1245 recapture is often referred to as *full recapture*. Any remaining gain after subtracting the amount recaptured as ordinary income will usually be § 1231 gain. If the property is disposed of in a casualty event, however, the remaining gain will be casualty gain. If the business machine in Example 8 had been disposed of by casualty and the $80,000 received had been an insurance recovery, Alice would still have a gain of $50,000, and the gain would still be recaptured by § 1245 as ordinary gain. The § 1245 recapture rules apply before there is any casualty gain. Since all the $50,000 gain is recaptured, no casualty gain arises from the casualty.

The following examples illustrate the general application of § 1245.

EXAMPLE 9

On January 1, 2011, Gary sold for $13,000 a machine acquired several years ago for $12,000. He had taken $10,000 of depreciation on the machine.

- The recognized gain from the sale is $11,000. This is the amount realized of $13,000 less the adjusted basis of $2,000 ($12,000 cost − $10,000 depreciation taken).
- Depreciation taken is $10,000. Therefore, since § 1245 recapture gain is the lower of depreciation taken or gain recognized, $10,000 of the $11,000 recognized gain is ordinary income, and the remaining $1,000 gain is § 1231 gain.
- The § 1231 gain of $1,000 is also equal to the excess of the sales price over the original cost of the property ($13,000 − $12,000 = $1,000 § 1231 gain). ■

EXAMPLE 10

Assume the same facts as in the previous example, except the asset is sold for $9,000 instead of $13,000.

- The recognized gain from the sale is $7,000. This is the amount realized of $9,000 less the adjusted basis of $2,000.
- Depreciation taken is $10,000. Therefore, since the $10,000 depreciation taken exceeds the recognized gain of $7,000, the entire $7,000 recognized gain is ordinary income.
- The § 1231 gain is zero. There is no § 1231 gain because the selling price ($9,000) does not exceed the original purchase price ($12,000). ■

EXAMPLE 11

Assume the same facts as in Example 9, except the asset is sold for $1,500 instead of $13,000.

- The recognized loss from the sale is $500. This is the amount realized of $1,500 less the adjusted basis of $2,000.
- Since there is a loss, there is no depreciation recapture. All of the loss is § 1231 loss. ■

If § 1245 property is disposed of in a transaction other than a sale, exchange, or involuntary conversion, the maximum amount recaptured is the excess of the property's fair market value over its adjusted basis. See the discussion under Considerations Common to §§ 1245 and 1250 later in the chapter.

SECTION 1245 PROPERTY

Generally, **§ 1245 property** includes all depreciable personal property (e.g., machinery and equipment), including livestock. Buildings and their structural components generally are not § 1245 property. The following property is *also* subject to § 1245 treatment:

- Amortizable personal property such as goodwill, patents, copyrights, and leaseholds of § 1245 property. Professional baseball and football player contracts are § 1245 property.
- Amortization of reforestation expenditures.
- Expensing of costs to remove architectural and transportation barriers that restrict the handicapped and/or elderly.
- Section 179 immediate expensing of depreciable tangible personal property costs.
- Elevators and escalators acquired before January 1, 1987.
- Certain depreciable tangible real property (other than buildings and their structural components) employed as an integral part of certain activities such as manufacturing and production. For example, a natural gas storage tank where the gas is used in the manufacturing process is § 1245 property.
- Pollution control facilities, railroad grading and tunnel bores, on-the-job training, and child care facilities on which amortization is taken.
- Single-purpose agricultural and horticultural structures and petroleum storage facilities (e.g., a greenhouse or silo).

- Fifteen-year, 18-year, and 19-year nonresidential real estate for which accelerated cost recovery is used is subject to the § 1245 recapture rules, although it is technically not § 1245 property. Such property would have been placed in service after 1980 and before 1987.

EXAMPLE 12

James acquired nonresidential real property on December 1, 1986, for $100,000. He used the statutory percentage method to compute the ACRS cost recovery. He sells the asset on January 15, 2011, for $120,000. The amount and nature of James's gain are computed as follows:

Amount realized		$120,000
Adjusted basis		
Cost	$ 100,000	
Less cost recovery: 1986–2009	(100,000)	
2010–2011	(–0–)	
January 15, 2011 adjusted basis		(–0–)
Gain realized and recognized		$120,000

The gain of $120,000 is treated as ordinary income to the extent of *all* depreciation taken because the property is 19-year nonresidential real estate for which accelerated depreciation was used. Thus, James reports ordinary income of $100,000 and § 1231 gain of $20,000 ($120,000 − $100,000). ∎

OBSERVATIONS ON § 1245

- In most instances, the total depreciation taken will exceed the recognized gain. Therefore, the disposition of § 1245 property usually results in ordinary income rather than § 1231 gain. Thus, generally, no § 1231 gain will occur unless the § 1245 property is disposed of for more than its original cost. Refer to Examples 9 and 10.
- Recapture applies to the total amount of depreciation allowed or allowable regardless of the depreciation method used.
- Recapture applies regardless of the holding period of the property. Of course, the entire recognized gain would be ordinary income if the property were held for less than the long-term holding period because § 1231 would not apply.
- Section 1245 does not apply to losses, which receive § 1231 treatment.
- Gains from the disposition of § 1245 assets may also be treated as passive activity gains (see Chapter 11).

17.3 SECTION 1250 RECAPTURE

LO.4

Determine when § 1250 recapture applies and how it is computed.

Generally, **§ 1250 property** is depreciable real property (principally buildings and their structural components) that is not subject to § 1245.[6] Intangible real property, such as leaseholds of § 1250 property, is also included.

Section 1250 recapture rarely applies since only the amount of *additional depreciation* is subject to recapture. To have additional depreciation, accelerated depreciation must have been taken on the asset. Straight-line depreciation is not recaptured (except for property held one year or less). Since depreciable real property placed in service after 1986 can generally only be depreciated using the straight-line method, there will usually be *no § 1250 depreciation recapture* on such property. Nor does § 1250 apply if the real property is sold at a loss.

---

[6]As noted above, in one limited circumstance, § 1245 does apply to nonresidential real estate. If the nonresidential real estate was placed in service after 1980 and before 1987 and accelerated depreciation was used, the § 1245 recapture rules rather than the § 1250 recapture rules apply.

If depreciable real property has been held for many years before it is sold, however, the § 1250 recapture rules may apply and are therefore discussed here. **Additional depreciation** is the excess of the accelerated depreciation actually deducted over depreciation that would have been deductible if the straight-line method had been used. Section 1250 recapture may apply when either (1) residential rental real property was acquired after 1975 and before 1987 and accelerated depreciation was taken or (2) nonresidential real property was acquired before 1981 and accelerated depreciation was taken after December 31, 1969. Also, § 168(k) additional first-year depreciation for certain leasehold improvements (nonresidential real property used in business) is depreciation subject to recapture under § 1250.

If § 1250 property with additional depreciation is disposed of in a transaction other than a sale, exchange, or involuntary conversion, the depreciation recapture is limited to the excess of the property's fair market value over the adjusted basis. For instance, if a corporation distributes real property to its shareholders as a dividend and the fair market value of the real property is greater than its adjusted basis, the corporation will recognize a gain. If accelerated depreciation was taken on the property, § 1250 recapture will apply.

It is important to know what assets are defined as § 1250 property because even when there is no additional depreciation, the gain from such property may be subject to a special 25 percent tax rate. See the discussion of Unrecaptured § 1250 Gain later in this chapter.

The discussion below describes the computational steps when § 1250 recapture applies and indicates how that recapture is reflected on Form 4797 (Sales of Business Property).

COMPUTING RECAPTURE ON NONRESIDENTIAL REAL PROPERTY

For § 1250 property other than residential rental property, the potential recapture is equal to the amount of additional depreciation taken since December 31, 1969. This nonresidential real property includes buildings such as offices, warehouses, factories, and stores. (The definition of and rules for residential rental housing are discussed later in the chapter.) The lower of the potential § 1250 recapture amount or the recognized gain is ordinary income. The following general rules apply:

- Additional depreciation is depreciation taken in excess of straight-line after December 31, 1969, on property that was acquired before 1981.
- Additional first-year depreciation [§ 168(k)] exceeding straight-line depreciation taken on leasehold improvements, qualified restaurant property, and qualified retail improvement property is additional depreciation.
- Immediate expense deduction [§ 179(f)] exceeding straight-line depreciation taken on leasehold improvements, qualified restaurant property, and qualified retail improvement property is additional depreciation.
- If the property is held for one year or less (usually not the case), all depreciation taken, even under the straight-line method, is additional depreciation.

The following procedure is used to compute recapture on nonresidential real property that was acquired before 1981 and for which accelerated depreciation was taken after December 31, 1969, under § 1250:

- Determine the recognized gain from the sale or other disposition of the property.
- Determine the additional depreciation (if any).
- The lower of the recognized gain or the additional depreciation is ordinary income.
- If any recognized gain remains (total recognized gain less recapture), it is § 1231 gain. However, it would be casualty gain if the disposition was by casualty.

The following example shows the application of the § 1250 computational procedure.

EXAMPLE 13

On January 3, 1980, Larry acquired a new building at a cost of $200,000 for use in his business. The building had an estimated useful life of 50 years and no estimated salvage value. Depreciation has been taken under the 150% declining-balance method through December 31, 2010. Pertinent information with respect to depreciation taken follows:

Year	Undepreciated Balance (Beginning of the Year)	Current Depreciation Provision	Straight-Line Depreciation	Additional Depreciation
1980–2009	$200,000	$122,230	$120,000	$2,230
2010	77,770	3,070	4,000	(930)
Total 1980–2010		$125,300	$124,000	$1,300

On January 2, 2011, Larry sold the building for $180,000. Compute the amount of his § 1250 ordinary income and § 1231 gain.

- Larry's recognized gain from the sale is $105,300. This is the difference between the $180,000 amount realized and the $74,700 adjusted basis ($200,000 cost − $125,300 depreciation taken).
- Additional depreciation is $1,300.
- The amount of ordinary income is $1,300. Since the additional depreciation of $1,300 is less than the recognized gain of $105,300, the entire gain is not recaptured.
- The remaining $104,000 ($105,300 − $1,300) gain is § 1231 gain. ∎

EXAMPLE 14

Blue Corporation is the lessor of an office building. Blue spent $250,000 on qualified leasehold improvements to the building during 2003. The improvements were placed in service on May 10, 2003, qualified for § 168(k) additional depreciation, and had a 39-year MACRS life.

Year	Undepreciated Balance (Beginning of the Year)	Current Depreciation Provision	Straight-Line Depreciation	Additional Depreciation
2003	$250,000	$127,006	$ 4,013	$122,993
2004–2010	122,994	20,165	40,330	(20,165)
2011	102,829	935	1,870	(935)
Total 2003–2011		$148,106	$46,213	$101,893

On April 20, 2011, the improvements were sold for $220,000. Compute the amount of Blue's § 1250 ordinary gain and § 1231 gain on the improvements.

- Blue's recognized gain from the sale is $118,106. This is the difference between the $220,000 amount realized and the $101,894 adjusted basis ($250,000 cost − $148,106 depreciation taken).
- Additional depreciation is $101,893.

- The amount of ordinary income due to § 1250 recapture is $101,893. Since the additional depreciation of $101,893 is less than the $118,106 recognized gain, the entire gain is not recaptured.
- The remaining $16,213 ($118,106 − $101,893) gain is § 1231 gain.■

COMPUTING RECAPTURE ON RESIDENTIAL RENTAL HOUSING

Section 1250 recapture sometimes applies to the sale or other disposition of residential rental housing. Property qualifies as *residential rental housing* only if at least 80 percent of gross rent income is rent income from dwelling units.[7] The rules are the same as for other § 1250 property, except that only the post-1975 additional depreciation may be recaptured on property acquired before 1987. If any of the recognized gain is not absorbed by the recapture rules pertaining to the post-1975 period, the remaining gain is § 1231 gain.

Assume the same facts as in Example 13, except the building is residential rental housing.	**EXAMPLE 15**

- Post-1975 ordinary income is $1,300 (post-1975 additional depreciation of $1,300).
- The remaining $104,000 ($105,300 − $1,300) gain is § 1231 gain. ■

Under § 1250, when straight-line depreciation is used, there is no § 1250 recapture potential unless the property is disposed of in the first year of use. Generally, however, the § 1250 recapture rules do not apply to depreciable real property unless the property is disposed of in the first year of use.

Sanjay acquires a residential rental building on January 1, 2010, for $300,000. He receives an offer of $450,000 for the building in 2011 and sells it on December 23, 2011.	**EXAMPLE 16**

- Sanjay takes $20,909 {($300,000 × .03485) + [$300,000 × .03636 × (11.5/12)] = $20,909} of total depreciation for 2010 and 2011, and the adjusted basis of the property is $279,091 ($300,000 − $20,909).
- Sanjay's recognized gain is $170,909 ($450,000 − $279,091).
- All of the gain is § 1231 gain. ■

SECTION 1250 RECAPTURE SITUATIONS

The § 1250 recapture rules apply to the following property for which accelerated depreciation was used:

- Additional first-year depreciation [§ 168(k)] exceeding straight-line depreciation taken on leasehold improvements, qualified restaurant property, and qualified retail improvement property.
- Immediate expense deduction [§ 179(f)] exceeding straight-line depreciation taken on leasehold improvements, qualified restaurant property, and qualified retail improvement property.
- Residential rental real estate acquired before 1987.
- Nonresidential real estate acquired before 1981.
- Real property used predominantly outside the United States.
- Certain government-financed or low-income housing.[8]

Concept Summary 17.2 compares and contrasts the § 1245 and § 1250 depreciation recapture rules.

UNRECAPTURED § 1250 GAIN (REAL ESTATE 25% GAIN)

This section will explain what gain is eligible for the 25 percent tax rate on **unrecaptured § 1250 gain**. This gain is used in the alternative tax computation for net capital gain discussed in Chapter 16. Unrecaptured § 1250 gain (*25% gain*) is some or all of the § 1231 gain that is treated as long-term capital gain and relates to a sale of depreciable real estate.

---

[7]§ 168(e)(2)(A). Note that there may be residential, nonrental housing (e.g., a bunkhouse on a cattle ranch). Such property is commonly regarded as "nonresidential real estate." The rules for such property were discussed in the previous section.

[8]Described in § 1250(a)(1)(B).

CONCEPT SUMMARY 17.2

Comparison of § 1245 and § 1250 Depreciation Recapture

	§ 1245	§ 1250
Property affected	All depreciable personal property, but also nonresidential real property acquired after December 31, 1980, and before January 1, 1987, for which accelerated cost recovery was used. Also includes miscellaneous items such as § 179 expense and § 197 amortization of intangibles such as goodwill, patents, and copyrights.	Nonresidential real property acquired after December 31, 1969, and before January 1, 1981, on which accelerated depreciation was taken. Residential rental real property acquired after December 31, 1975, and before January 1, 1987, on which accelerated depreciation was taken. Additional first-year depreciation [§ 168(k)] exceeding straight-line depreciation taken on leasehold improvements, qualified restaurant property, and qualified retail property. Immediate expense deduction [§ 179(f)] exceeding straight-line depreciation taken on leasehold improvements, qualified restaurant property, and qualified retail improvement property.
Depreciation recaptured	Potentially all depreciation taken. If the selling price is greater than or equal to the original cost, all depreciation is recaptured. If the selling price is between the adjusted basis and the original cost, only some depreciation is recaptured.	Additional depreciation (the excess of accelerated cost recovery over straight-line cost recovery or the excess of accelerated depreciation over straight-line depreciation).
Limit on recapture	Lower of depreciation taken or gain recognized.	Lower of additional depreciation or gain recognized.
Treatment of gain exceeding recapture gain	Usually § 1231 gain.	Usually § 1231 gain.
Treatment of loss	No depreciation recapture; loss is usually § 1231 loss.	No depreciation recapture; loss is usually § 1231 loss.

The maximum amount of this *25%* gain is the depreciation taken on real property sold at a recognized gain. That maximum amount is reduced in one or more of the following ways:

- The recognized gain from disposition is less than the depreciation taken. The *25%* gain is reduced to the recognized gain amount. Refer to Example 13. The depreciation taken was $125,300, but the recognized gain was only $105,300. Consequently, *all* of the recognized gain is potential *25%* § 1231 gain.

- There is § 1250 recapture because there is additional first-year depreciation [§ 168(k)] exceeding straight-line depreciation taken on leasehold improvements, qualified restaurant property, and qualified retail property and/or there is § 1250 recapture because there is immediate expense deduction [§ 179(f)] exceeding straight-line depreciation taken on leasehold improvements, qualified restaurant property, and qualified retail improvement property. The § 1250 recapture reduces the *25%* gain. Refer to Example 14. Of the $118,106 gain, $101,893 was recaptured by § 1250 as ordinary gain, leaving $16,213 of potential *25%* § 1231 gain.

- There is § 1250 depreciation recapture because the property is residential real estate acquired before 1987 on which accelerated depreciation was taken. The § 1250 recapture reduces the *25%* gain. Refer to Example 15. Of the $105,300 recognized gain, $1,300 was recaptured by § 1250 as ordinary income, leaving $104,000 of the potential *25%* § 1231 gain.

- There is § 1245 depreciation recapture because the property is nonresidential real estate acquired in 1981–1986 on which accelerated depreciation was taken. No *25%* § 1231 gain will be left because § 1245 will recapture all of the depreciation or the recognized gain, whichever is less. Refer to Example 12. Depreciation of $100,000 was taken, but all of it was recaptured as ordinary income by § 1245. Thus, there is no remaining potential *25% § 1231* gain. The entire $20,000 § 1231 gain in Example 12 is potential *0%/15%* gain.

- Section 1231 loss from disposition of other § 1231 assets held long term reduces the gain from real estate.
- Section 1231 lookback losses convert some or all of the potential *25%* § 1231 gain to ordinary income.

Special 25% Gain Netting Rules

Where there is a § 1231 gain from real estate and that gain includes both potential *25%* gain and potential *0%/15%* gain, any § 1231 loss from disposition of other § 1231 assets *first offsets* the *0%/15%* portion of the § 1231 gain and then offsets the *25%* portion of the § 1231 gain. Also, any § 1231 lookback loss *first recharacterizes* the *25%* portion of the § 1231 gain and then recharacterizes the *0%/15%* portion of the § 1231 gain as ordinary income.

Net § 1231 Gain Limitation

The amount of unrecaptured § 1250 gain may not exceed the net § 1231 gain that is eligible to be treated as long-term capital gain. The unrecaptured § 1250 gain is the *lesser of* the unrecaptured § 1250 gain or the net § 1231 gain that is treated as capital gain. Thus, if there is a net § 1231 gain, but it is all converted to ordinary income by the five-year § 1231 lookback loss provision, there is no surviving § 1231 gain or unrecaptured § 1250 gain.

Refer to Example 6. There was $200 of § 1231 gain from the building fire that would also be potential *25%* gain if at least $200 of depreciation was taken. The net § 1231 gain was $1,100 including the $200 building gain. (The $500 loss from Asset C would offset the potential *0%/15%* § 1231 gain and not the potential *25%* gain, so all of the potential *25%* gain of $200 is in the $1,100 net § 1231 gain.) However, the $700 of § 1231 lookback losses would *first* absorb the $200 building gain, so the $400 of § 1231 gain that is treated as long-term capital gain includes no *25%* gain.

Section 1250 Property for Purposes of the Unrecaptured § 1250 Gain

Section 1250 property includes any real property (other than § 1245 property) that is or has been depreciable. Land is *not* § 1250 property because it is not depreciable.

EXAMPLE 17

Bill is a single taxpayer with 2011 taxable income of $84,000 composed of:

- $64,000 ordinary taxable income,
- $3,000 short-term capital loss,
- $15,000 long-term capital gain from sale of stock, and
- $8,000 § 1231 gain that is all unrecaptured § 1250 gain (the actual unrecaptured gain was $11,000, but net § 1231 gain is only $8,000).

Bill's net capital gain is $20,000 ($15,000 long-term capital gain + $8,000 unrecaptured § 1250 gain/net § 1231 gain − $3,000 short-term capital loss). The $3,000 short-term capital loss is offset against the $8,000 unrecaptured § 1250 gain, reducing that gain to $5,000 (see the discussion in Chapter 16 concerning netting of capital losses). Bill's adjusted net capital gain is $15,000 ($20,000 net capital gain − $5,000 unrecaptured § 1250 gain). Bill's total tax (using the alternative tax calculation discussed in Chapter 16) is $15,625 [$12,125 (tax on ordinary taxable income) + $1,250 ($5,000 unrecaptured § 1250 gain × 25%) + $2,250 ($15,000 adjusted net capital gain × 15%)]. ∎

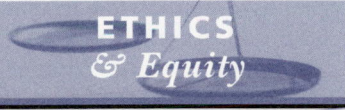

ETHICS & Equity   **FLOW-THROUGH 25% GAIN**

While preparing an individual Form 1040, the tax return preparer examines a Schedule K–1 from a partnership in which the taxpayer has an ownership interest. The Schedule K–1 includes a $23,000 § 1231 gain and $12,300 of unrecaptured § 1250 gain. The tax return preparer has no idea what unrecaptured § 1250 gain means and does nothing with it in preparing the individual return. Could this affect the tax computation on the individual income tax return?

GLOBAL *Tax Issues*

EXCHANGE FOR FOREIGN PROPERTY YIELDS RECOGNIZED RECAPTURE GAIN

Tangible personal property used in a trade or business may be the subject of a § 1031 like-kind exchange, and the postponed gain is most likely postponed § 1245 gain. However, tangible personal property used predominantly within the United States cannot be exchanged for tangible personal property used predominantly outside the United States. Thus, such an exchange would cause recognized gain, and, as long as the fair market value of the property given up does not exceed its original cost, all of the gain is § 1245 depreciation recapture gain.

17.4 CONSIDERATIONS COMMON TO §§ 1245 AND 1250

LO.5

Understand considerations common to §§ 1245 and 1250.

EXCEPTIONS

Recapture under §§ 1245 and 1250 does not apply to the following transactions.

Gifts

The recapture potential carries over to the donee.[9]

> **EXAMPLE 18**
>
> Wade gives his daughter, Helen, § 1245 property with an adjusted basis of $1,000. The amount of recapture potential is $700. Helen uses the property in her business and claims further depreciation of $100 before selling it for $1,900. Helen's recognized gain is $1,000 ($1,900 amount realized − $900 adjusted basis), of which $800 is recaptured as ordinary income ($100 depreciation taken by Helen + $700 recapture potential carried over from Wade). The remaining gain of $200 is § 1231 gain. Even if Helen used the property for personal purposes, the $700 recapture potential would still be carried over. ∎

Death

Although not a very attractive tax planning approach, death eliminates all recapture potential.[10] In other words, any recapture potential does not carry over from a decedent to an estate or heir.

> **EXAMPLE 19**
>
> Assume the same facts as in Example 18, except that Helen receives the property as a result of Wade's death. The $700 recapture potential from Wade is extinguished. Helen has a basis for the property equal to the property's fair market value (assume $1,700) at Wade's death. She will have a $300 gain when the property is sold because the selling price ($1,900) exceeds the property's adjusted basis of $1,600 ($1,700 original basis to Helen − $100 depreciation) by $300. Because of § 1245, $100 is ordinary income. The remaining gain of $200 is § 1231 gain. ∎

Charitable Transfers

The recapture potential reduces the amount of the charitable contribution deduction under § 170.[11]

> **EXAMPLE 20**
> **THE BIG PICTURE**
>
> Return to the facts of *The Big Picture* on p. 17-2. If instead of selling the old equipment Hazel gives it to a charity, her charitable contribution is limited to zero. The potential § 1245 recapture on the equipment is $375,040 (the depreciation taken). When that amount is subtracted from the equipment's $128,000 fair market value, the result is zero since the charitable contribution cannot be less than zero. ∎

---

[9]§§ 1245(b)(1) and 1250(d)(1) and Reg. §§ 1.1245–4a(1) and 1.1250–3(a)(1).

[10]§§ 1245(b)(2) and 1250(d)(2).

[11]§ 170(e)(1)(A) and Reg. § 1.170A–4(b)(1). In certain circumstances, § 1231 gain also reduces the amount of the charitable contribution. See § 170(e)(1)(B).

Certain Nontaxable Transactions

In certain transactions, the transferor's adjusted basis of property carries over to the transferee.[12] The recapture potential also carries over to the transferee.[13] Included in this category are transfers of property pursuant to the following:

- Nontaxable incorporations under § 351.
- Certain liquidations of subsidiary companies under § 332.
- Nontaxable contributions to a partnership under § 721.
- Nontaxable reorganizations.

Gain may be recognized in these transactions if boot is received. If gain is recognized, it is treated as ordinary income to the extent of the recapture potential or recognized gain, whichever is lower.[14]

Like-Kind Exchanges (§ 1031) and Involuntary Conversions (§ 1033)

Realized gain will be recognized to the extent of boot received under § 1031. Realized gain also will be recognized to the extent the proceeds from an involuntary conversion are not reinvested in similar property under § 1033. Such recognized gain is subject to recapture as ordinary income under §§ 1245 and 1250. The remaining recapture potential, if any, carries over to the property received in the exchange. Realized losses are not recognized in like-kind exchanges, but are recognized in involuntary conversions (see Chapter 15).

EXAMPLE 21

Anita exchanges § 1245 property with an adjusted basis of $300 for § 1245 property with a fair market value of $6,000. The exchange qualifies as a like-kind exchange under § 1031. Anita also receives $1,000 cash (boot). Her realized gain is $6,700 ($7,000 amount realized − $300 adjusted basis of property). Assuming the recapture potential is $7,500, Anita recognizes § 1245 gain of $1,000 because she received boot of $1,000. The remaining recapture potential of $6,500 carries over to the like-kind property received. ∎

OTHER APPLICATIONS

Sections 1245 and 1250 apply notwithstanding any other provisions in the Code.[15] That is, the recapture rules under these Sections *override* all other Sections. Special applications include installment sales and property dividends.

Installment Sales

Recapture gain is recognized in the year of the sale regardless of whether gain is otherwise recognized under the installment method.[16] All gain is ordinary income until the recapture potential is fully absorbed. Nonrecapture (§ 1231) gain is recognized under the installment method as cash is received.

Gain is also recognized on installment sales in the year of the sale in an amount equal to the § 179 (immediate expensing) deduction taken with respect to the property sold.

EXAMPLE 22
THE BIG PICTURE

Return to the facts of *The Big Picture* on p. 17-2. Assume Hazel could sell the used equipment for $28,000 down and the balance in five yearly installments of $20,000 plus interest. She would have to recognize her entire $53,040 gain ($128,000 sale price − $74,960 adjusted basis) in 2011. All of the gain is § 1245 depreciation recapture gain because the $375,040 depreciation taken exceeds the $53,040 recognized gain. ∎

---

[12]§§ 1245(b)(3) and 1250(d)(3) and Reg. §§ 1.1245–4(c) and 1.1250–3(c).

[13]Reg. §§ 1.1245–2(a)(4) and −2(c)(2) and 1.1250–2(d)(1) and (3) and −3(c)(3).

[14]§§ 1245(b)(3) and 1250(d)(3) and Reg. §§ 1.1245–4(c) and 1.1250–3(c). Some of these special corporate problems are discussed in Chapter 20. Partnership contributions are also discussed in Chapter 20.

[15]§§ 1245(d) and 1250(i).

[16]§ 453(i). The installment method of reporting gains on the sale of property is discussed in Chapter 18.

Property Dividends

A corporation generally recognizes gain if it distributes appreciated property as a dividend. Recapture under §§ 1245 and 1250 applies to the extent of the lower of the recapture potential or the excess of the property's fair market value over the adjusted basis.[17]

EXAMPLE 23

Emerald Corporation distributes § 1245 property as a dividend to its shareholders. The amount of the recapture potential is $300, and the excess of the property's fair market value over the adjusted basis is $800. Emerald recognizes $300 of ordinary income and $500 of § 1231 gain. ■

Concept Summary 17.3 integrates the depreciation recapture rules with the § 1231 netting process. It is an expanded version of Concept Summary 17.1.

17.5 SPECIAL RECAPTURE PROVISIONS

L0.6

Apply the special recapture provisions for related parties and IDC and be aware of the special recapture provision for corporations.

SPECIAL RECAPTURE FOR CORPORATIONS

Corporations selling depreciable real estate may have ordinary income in addition to that required by § 1250.[18] See the discussion of this topic in Chapter 20.

GAIN FROM SALE OF DEPRECIABLE PROPERTY BETWEEN CERTAIN RELATED PARTIES

When the sale or exchange of property, which in the hands of the *transferee* is depreciable property (principally machinery, equipment, and buildings, but not land), is between certain related parties, any gain recognized is ordinary income.[19] This provision applies to both direct and indirect sales or exchanges. A **related party** is defined as an individual and his or her controlled corporation or partnership or a taxpayer and any trust in which the taxpayer (or the taxpayer's spouse) is a beneficiary.

EXAMPLE 24

Isabella sells a personal use automobile (therefore nondepreciable) to her controlled corporation. The automobile, which was purchased two years ago, originally cost $5,000 and is sold for $7,000. The automobile is to be used in the corporation's business. If the related-party provision did not exist, Isabella would realize a $2,000 long-term capital gain. The income tax consequences would be favorable because Isabella's controlled corporation is entitled to depreciate the automobile based upon the purchase price of $7,000. Under the related-party provision, Isabella's $2,000 gain is ordinary income. ■

INTANGIBLE DRILLING COSTS

Taxpayers may elect to either *expense or capitalize* intangible drilling and development costs for oil, gas, or geothermal properties.[20] **Intangible drilling and development costs (IDC)** include operator (one who holds a working or operating interest in any tract or parcel of land) expenditures for wages, fuel, repairs, hauling, and supplies. These expenditures must be incident to and necessary for the drilling of wells and preparation of wells for production. In most instances, taxpayers elect to expense IDC to maximize tax deductions during drilling.

---

[17]§ 311(b) and Reg. §§ 1.1245–1(c) and –6(b) and 1.1250–1(a)(4), –1(b)(4), and –1(c)(2).

[18]§ 291(a)(1).

[19]§ 1239.

[20]§ 263(c).

CONCEPT SUMMARY 17.3

Depreciation Recapture and § 1231 Netting Procedure

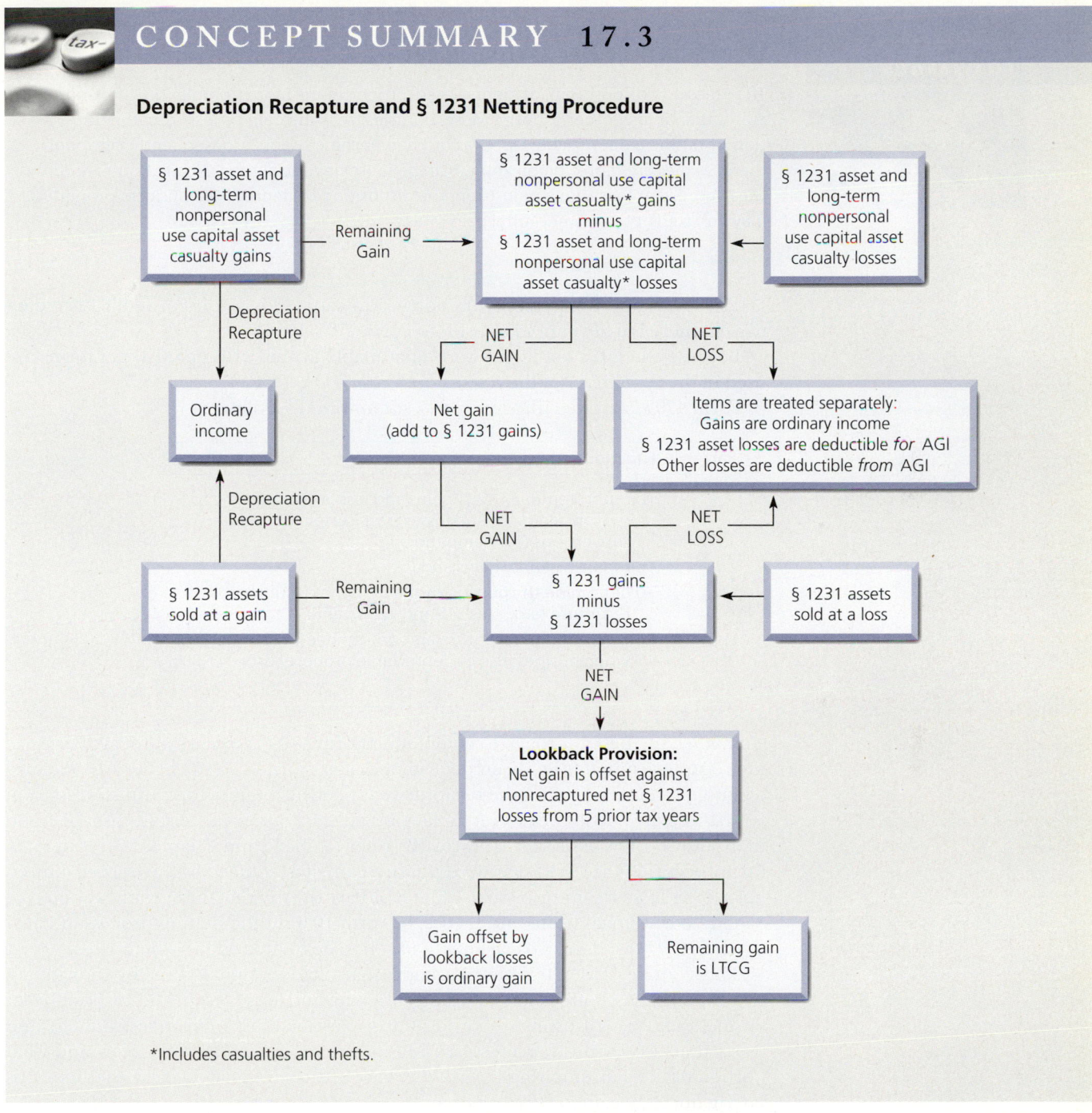

*Includes casualties and thefts.

Intangible drilling and development costs are subject to § 1254 recapture when the property is disposed of. The gain on the disposition of the property is subject to recapture as ordinary income.

17.6 REPORTING PROCEDURES

Noncapital gains and losses are reported on Form 4797, Sales of Business Property. Before filling out Form 4797, however, Form 4684, Casualties and Thefts, Part B, must be completed to determine whether any casualties will enter into the § 1231 computation procedure. Recall that recognized gains from § 1231 asset casualties may be recaptured by § 1245 or § 1250. These gains will not appear on Form 4684. The § 1231 gains and nonpersonal use long-term capital gains are netted against

LO.7

Describe and apply the reporting procedures for §§ 1231, 1245, and 1250.

GLOBAL *Tax Issues*

DEPRECIATION RECAPTURE IN OTHER COUNTRIES

The rules for dispositions of depreciated property are more complex in the United States than in any other country. Most countries treat the gain or loss from the disposition of business depreciable assets as ordinary income or loss. Consequently, although the U.S. rules are more complex, they can be more beneficial than those of other countries because at least some gains from the disposition of depreciable business property may be taxed at the lower capital gain rates.

§ 1231 losses and nonpersonal use long-term capital losses on Form 4684 to determine if there is a net gain to transfer to Form 4797, Part I.

Because the 2011 tax forms were unavailable at this writing, 2010 tax forms are used in the remainder of the discussion.

Form 4797 is divided into four parts, summarized as follows:

Part	Function
I	To report regular § 1231 gains and losses [including recognized gains and losses from certain involuntary conversions (condemnations)].
II	To report ordinary gains and losses.
III	To determine the portion of the gain that is subject to recapture (e.g., §§ 1245 and 1250 gain).
IV	Computation of recapture amounts under §§ 179 and 280F when business use of depreciable property drops to 50% or less.

Generally, the best approach to completing Form 4797 is to start with Part III. Once the recapture amount has been determined, it is transferred to Part II. The balance of any gain remaining after the recapture has been accounted for is transferred from Part III to Part I. Also transferred to Part I is any net gain from certain casualties and thefts as reported on Form 4684, Part B (refer to above and Chapter 15). If the netting process in Form 4797, Part I, results in a gain, it is reduced by the nonrecaptured net § 1231 losses from prior years (line 8 of Part I). Any remaining gain is shifted to Schedule D, Capital Gains and Losses, of Form 1040. If the netting process in Part I of Form 4797 results in a loss, it goes to Part II to be treated as an ordinary loss.

The complex rules for the alternative tax on net capital gain for individuals, estates, and trusts affect the reporting of gains and losses from the disposition of business and rental assets. S corporations, partnerships, individuals, estates, and trusts that use Form 4797 must provide information sufficient to determine what portion of the gain surviving Form 4797, Part I (the gain that goes to Schedule D) is *28%* gain, *25%* gain, or *0%/15%* gain.

The process explained below is based upon an analysis of Form 1040, Schedule D, and Form 4797 and their instructions. One key point to remember is that all the gains and losses that end up being treated as ordinary gains and losses (and, therefore, end up in Part II of Form 4797) are not eligible for any of the special tax rates for net capital gain. Another key point is that the gain that goes from Part I of Form 4797 to Schedule D will go to line 11 of Schedule D (long-term capital gains and losses). The entire gain from Form 4797 goes in column 11(f) of Schedule D.

The *25%* gain (if any) from Form 4797 is part of the Schedule D, line 11(f) gain. *Nothing on the face of Form 4797 or Schedule D identifies this gain.* Only when the alternative tax on net capital gain is computed is the *25%* gain portion of the Form 4797 net gain specifically mentioned on line 19.

Also remember that § 1231 assets are assets held more than one year. Therefore, no gain or loss is reportable on Form 4797, Part I, unless that holding period requirement is satisfied.

For 2010, Troy Williams, a single taxpayer (Social Security number 111–11–1111), has taxable income of $133,000 *including* the following recognized gains and losses (a 2010 example has been used since 2011 forms were unavailable):

Sale of Depreciable Business Assets Held Long Term

Asset A (Note 1)	$36,500
Asset B (Note 2)	20,126
Asset C (Note 3)	(880)

Sale of Depreciable Business Assets Held Short Term

Asset D (Note 4)	($ 600)

Capital Assets

Long-term gain (Note 5)	$ 3,000
Short-term loss (Note 6)	(200)

Note 1. Asset A was acquired on June 23, 2007, for $50,000. It was five-year MACRS property, and four years' cost recovery allowances totaled $38,480. The property was sold for $48,020 on August 31, 2010.

Note 2. Asset B was purchased on May 10, 2000, for $37,000. It was 27.5-year residential rental real estate, and straight-line depreciation totaled $14,126. Asset B was sold for $43,000 on November 10, 2010.

Note 3. Asset C was purchased on December 9, 2007, for $16,000. It was five-year MACRS property, and four years' cost recovery totaled $12,314. The property was sold for $2,806 on December 30, 2010.

Note 4. Asset D was purchased for $7,000 on July 27, 2010. It was five-year MACRS property but proved unsuitable to Troy's business. Troy sold it for $6,400 on November 3, 2010.

Note 5. The LTCG resulted from the sale of 100 shares of Orange Corporation stock purchased for $10,000 on April 5, 2008. The shares were sold on October 21, 2010, for $13,223. Expenses of sale were $223.

Note 6. The STCL resulted from the sale of 50 shares of Blue Corporation stock purchased for $350 on March 14, 2010. The shares were sold for $170 on August 20, 2010. Expenses of sale were $20.

The sale of asset A at a gain results in the recapture of cost recovery deductions. That recapture is shown in Part III of Form 4797. The gain from the sale of asset B is carried from line 32 to Part I, line 6, of Form 4797. On line 2, the loss from asset C appears. Part I is where the § 1231 netting process takes place. Assume Troy Williams has no nonrecaptured net § 1231 losses from prior years. The net gain on line 7 is transferred to Schedule D, line 11. In Part II of Form 4797, the ordinary gains are accumulated. On line 13, the recapture from line 31 (Part III) is shown. On line 10, the loss from asset D is shown. The net gain on line 18 is ordinary income and is transferred to Form 1040, line 14.

Schedule D, Part I, line 1, reports the short-term capital loss from the Blue Corporation stock. Part II of Schedule D has the net § 1231 gain transferred from Form 4797 on line 11 and the Orange Corporation gain on line 8. The net capital gain is determined on line 16, Part III. The capital gain is then carried to line 13 of Form 1040.

On Form 4797, Part III, the $20,126 § 1231 gain from Asset B is made up of $14,126 (equals depreciation taken) of potential *25%* gain and $6,000 of potential *0%/15%* gain. The $880 § 1231 loss from Form 4797, Part I, line 2, offsets the potential *0%/15%* portion of the $20,126 § 1231 gain on Form 4797, Part I, line 6. Consequently, of the $19,246 § 1231 gain that goes from Form 4797, Part I, line 7, to Schedule D, line 11, $14,126 is *25%* gain and $5,120 is *0%/15%* gain. Schedule D, Part III, line 19, shows an unrecaptured § 1250 gain of $13,926. This gain results from the $14,126 *25%* gain being reduced by the $200 short-term capital loss from Schedule D, line 7. Troy's 2010 tax liability is $29,476: $24,776 tax on ordinary taxable income of $110,954 ($133,000 taxable income − $22,046 net long-term capital gain), $3,482 tax on the *25%* gain ($13,926 × .25), and $1,218 tax on the *0%/15%* gain ($8,120 × .15). ∎

The 2010 tax form solution for Example 25 appears on the following pages.

Form **4797**	**Sales of Business Property**	OMB No. 1545-0184
Department of the Treasury Internal Revenue Service (99)	(Also Involuntary Conversions and Recapture Amounts Under Sections 179 and 280F(b)(2)) ► Attach to your tax return. ► See separate instructions.	**2010** Attachment Sequence No. **27**

Name(s) shown on return	Identifying number
Troy Williams	*111 - 11 - 1111*

1 Enter the gross proceeds from sales or exchanges reported to you for 2010 on Form(s) 1099-B or 1099-S (or substitute statement) that you are including on line 2, 10, or 20 (see instructions) . . . . **| 1 |**

Part I   Sales or Exchanges of Property Used in a Trade or Business and Involuntary Conversions From Other Than Casualty or Theft—Most Property Held More Than 1 Year (see instructions)

2	(a) Description of property	(b) Date acquired (mo., day, yr.)	(c) Date sold (mo., day, yr.)	(d) Gross sales price	(e) Depreciation allowed or allowable since acquisition	(f) Cost or other basis, plus improvements and expense of sale	(g) Gain or (loss) Subtract (f) from the sum of (d) and (e)
	Asset C	*12/09/07*	*12/30/10*	*2,806*	*12,314*	*16,000*	*(880)*

3 Gain, if any, from Form 4684, line 42	**3**	
4 Section 1231 gain from installment sales from Form 6252, line 26 or 37	**4**	
5 Section 1231 gain or (loss) from like-kind exchanges from Form 8824	**5**	
6 Gain, if any, from line 32, from other than casualty or theft.	**6**	*20,126*
7 Combine lines 2 through 6. Enter the gain or (loss) here and on the appropriate line as follows:	**7**	*19,246*

Partnerships (except electing large partnerships) and S corporations. Report the gain or (loss) following the instructions for Form 1065, Schedule K, line 10, or Form 1120S, Schedule K, line 9. Skip lines 8, 9, 11, and 12 below.

Individuals, partners, S corporation shareholders, and all others. If line 7 is zero or a loss, enter the amount from line 7 on line 11 below and skip lines 8 and 9. If line 7 is a gain and you did not have any prior year section 1231 losses, or they were recaptured in an earlier year, enter the gain from line 7 as a long-term capital gain on the Schedule D filed with your return and skip lines 8, 9, 11, and 12 below.

8 Nonrecaptured net section 1231 losses from prior years (see instructions)	**8**	
9 Subtract line 8 from line 7. If zero or less, enter -0-. If line 9 is zero, enter the gain from line 7 on line 12 below. If line 9 is more than zero, enter the amount from line 8 on line 12 below and enter the gain from line 9 as a long-term capital gain on the Schedule D filed with your return (see instructions)	**9**	

Part II   Ordinary Gains and Losses (see instructions)

10 Ordinary gains and losses not included on lines 11 through 16 (include property held 1 year or less):

	Asset D	*07/27/10*	*11/03/10*	*6,400*	*·0*	*7,000*	*(600)*

11 Loss, if any, from line 7	**11** ( )
12 Gain, if any, from line 7 or amount from line 8, if applicable	**12**	
13 Gain, if any, from line 31	**13**	*36,500*
14 Net gain or (loss) from Form 4684, lines 34 and 41a	**14**	
15 Ordinary gain from installment sales from Form 6252, line 25 or 36	**15**	
16 Ordinary gain or (loss) from like-kind exchanges from Form 8824.	**16**	
17 Combine lines 10 through 16	**17**	*35,900*

18 For all except individual returns, enter the amount from line 17 on the appropriate line of your return and skip lines a and b below. For individual returns, complete lines a and b below:

a If the loss on line 11 includes a loss from Form 4684, line 38, column (b)(ii), enter that part of the loss here. Enter the part of the loss from income-producing property on Schedule A (Form 1040), line 28, and the part of the loss from property used as an employee on Schedule A (Form 1040), line 23. Identify as from "Form 4797, line 18a." See instructions . .	**18a**	
b Redetermine the gain or (loss) on line 17 excluding the loss, if any, on line 18a. Enter here and on Form 1040, line 14	**18b**	*35,900*

For Paperwork Reduction Act Notice, see separate instructions.   Cat. No. 13086I   Form **4797** (2010)

Form 4797 (2010)   Page **2**

Part III Gain From Disposition of Property Under Sections 1245, 1250, 1252, 1254, and 1255
(see instructions)

19	(a) Description of section 1245, 1250, 1252, 1254, or 1255 property:	**(b)** Date acquired (mo., day, yr.)	**(c)** Date sold (mo., day, yr.)
A	*Asset A*	*06/23/07*	*08/31/10*
B	*Asset B*	*05/10/00*	*11/10/10*
C			
D			

	These columns relate to the properties on lines 19A through 19D. ▶		**Property A**	**Property B**	**Property C**	**Property D**
20	Gross sales price (**Note:** *See line 1 before completing.*) .	20	*48,020*	*43,000*		
21	Cost or other basis plus expense of sale	21	*50,000*	*37,000*		
22	Depreciation (or depletion) allowed or allowable. . .	22	*38,480*	*14,126*		
23	Adjusted basis. Subtract line 22 from line 21	23	*11,520*	*22,874*		
24	Total gain. Subtract line 23 from line 20	24	*36,500*	*20,126*		
25	**If section 1245 property:**					
a	Depreciation allowed or allowable from line 22 . . .	25a	*38,480*			
b	Enter the **smaller** of line 24 or 25a	25b	*36,500*			
26	**If section 1250 property:** If straight line depreciation was used, enter -0- on line 26g, except for a corporation subject to section 291.					
a	Additional depreciation after 1975 (see instructions) .	26a				
b	Applicable percentage multiplied by the **smaller** of line 24 or line 26a (see instructions)	26b				
c	Subtract line 26a from line 24. If residential rental property **or** line 24 is not more than line 26a, skip lines 26d and 26e	26c				
d	Additional depreciation after 1969 and before 1976. .	26d				
e	Enter the **smaller** of line 26c or 26d	26e				
f	Section 291 amount (corporations only)	26f				
g	Add lines 26b, 26e, and 26f.	26g		*0*		
27	**If section 1252 property:** Skip this section if you did not dispose of farmland or if this form is being completed for a partnership (other than an electing large partnership).					
a	Soil, water, and land clearing expenses	27a				
b	Line 27a multiplied by applicable percentage (see instructions)	27b				
c	Enter the **smaller** of line 24 or 27b	27c				
28	**If section 1254 property:**					
a	Intangible drilling and development costs, expenditures for development of mines and other natural deposits, mining exploration costs, and depletion (see instructions)	28a				
b	Enter the **smaller** of line 24 or 28a	28b				
29	**If section 1255 property:**					
a	Applicable percentage of payments excluded from income under section 126 (see instructions)	29a				
b	Enter the **smaller** of line 24 or 29a (see instructions) .	29b				

Summary of Part III Gains. Complete property columns A through D through line 29b before going to line 30.

30	Total gains for all properties. Add property columns A through D, line 24	30	*56,626*
31	Add property columns A through D, lines 25b, 26g, 27c, 28b, and 29b. Enter here and on line 13	31	*36,500*
32	Subtract line 31 from line 30. Enter the portion from casualty or theft on Form 4684, line 36. Enter the portion from other than casualty or theft on Form 4797, line 6	32	*20,126*

Part IV Recapture Amounts Under Sections 179 and 280F(b)(2) When Business Use Drops to 50% or Less
(see instructions)

			(a) Section 179	**(b) Section 280F(b)(2)**
33	Section 179 expense deduction or depreciation allowable in prior years.	33		
34	Recomputed depreciation (see instructions)	34		
35	Recapture amount. Subtract line 34 from line 33. See the instructions for where to report . .	35		

Form **4797** (2010)

| SCHEDULE D
(Form 1040)

Department of the Treasury
Internal Revenue Service (99) | **Capital Gains and Losses**

► **Attach to Form 1040 or Form 1040NR.**   ► **See Instructions for Schedule D (Form 1040).**
► **Use Schedule D-1 to list additional transactions for lines 1 and 8.** | OMB No. 1545-0074

20**10**
Attachment
Sequence No. **12** |

Name(s) shown on return		Your social security number
Troy Williams		*111 11 1111*

Part I   Short-Term Capital Gains and Losses—Assets Held One Year or Less

(a) Description of property (Example: 100 sh. XYZ Co.)	(b) Date acquired (Mo., day, yr.)	(c) Date sold (Mo., day, yr.)	(d) Sales price (see page D-7 of the instructions)	(e) Cost or other basis (see page D-7 of the instructions)	(f) Gain or (loss) Subtract (e) from (d)
1 *Blue Corp. (50 shares)*	*03/14/10*	*08/20/10*	*170*	*370*	*(200)*

2 Enter your short-term totals, if any, from Schedule D-1, line 2	**2**	
3 **Total short-term sales price amounts.** Add lines 1 and 2 in column (d)	**3**	*170*

4 Short-term gain from Form 6252 and short-term gain or (loss) from Forms 4684, 6781, and 8824 . | **4** |

5 Net short-term gain or (loss) from partnerships, S corporations, estates, and trusts from Schedule(s) K-1 . . . . | **5** |

6 Short-term capital loss carryover. Enter the amount, if any, from line 10 of your **Capital Loss Carryover Worksheet** on page D-7 of the instructions . . . . | **6** ( ) |

7 **Net short-term capital gain or (loss).** Combine lines 1 through 6 in column (f) . . . . | **7** | *(200)* |

Part II   Long-Term Capital Gains and Losses—Assets Held More Than One Year

(a) Description of property (Example: 100 sh. XYZ Co.)	(b) Date acquired (Mo., day, yr.)	(c) Date sold (Mo., day, yr.)	(d) Sales price (see page D-7 of the instructions)	(e) Cost or other basis (see page D-7 of the instructions)	(f) Gain or (loss) Subtract (e) from (d)
8 *Orange Corp. (100 shares)*	*04/05/08*	*10/21/10*	*13,223*	*10,223*	*3,000*

9 Enter your long-term totals, if any, from Schedule D-1, line 9	**9**	
10 **Total long-term sales price amounts.** Add lines 8 and 9 in column (d).	**10**	*13,223*

11 Gain from Form 4797, Part I; long-term gain from Forms 2439 and 6252; and long-term gain or (loss) from Forms 4684, 6781, and 8824 . . . . | **11** | *19,246* |

12 Net long-term gain or (loss) from partnerships, S corporations, estates, and trusts from Schedule(s) K-1 . . . . | **12** |

13 Capital gain distributions. See page D-2 of the instructions . . . . | **13** |

14 Long-term capital loss carryover. Enter the amount, if any, from line 15 of your **Capital Loss Carryover Worksheet** on page D-7 of the instructions . . . . | **14** ( ) |

15 **Net long-term capital gain or (loss).** Combine lines 8 through 14 in column (f). Then go to Part III on the back . . . . | **15** | *22,246* |

For Paperwork Reduction Act Notice, see your tax return instructions.   Cat. No. 11338H   **Schedule D (Form 1040) 2010**

Schedule D (Form 1040) 2010   Page **2**

Part III   Summary

16 Combine lines 7 and 15 and enter the result **16**   *22,046*

   - If line 16 is a **gain**, enter the amount from line 16 on Form 1040, line 13, or Form 1040NR, line 14. Then go to line 17 below.
   - If line 16 is a **loss**, skip lines 17 through 20 below. Then go to line 21. Also be sure to complete line 22.
   - If line 16 is **zero**, skip lines 17 through 21 below and enter -0- on Form 1040, line 13, or Form 1040NR, line 14. Then go to line 22.

17 Are lines 15 and 16 **both** gains?
   ☒ **Yes.** Go to line 18.
   ☐ **No.** Skip lines 18 through 21, and go to line 22.

18 Enter the amount, if any, from line 7 of the **28% Rate Gain Worksheet** on page D-8 of the instructions . . . . ▶ **18**   *0*

19 Enter the amount, if any, from line 18 of the **Unrecaptured Section 1250 Gain Worksheet** on page D-9 of the instructions . . . . ▶ **19**   *13,926*

20 Are lines 18 and 19 **both** zero or blank?
   ☐ **Yes.** Complete Form 1040 through line 43, or Form 1040NR through line 41. Then complete the **Qualified Dividends and Capital Gain Tax Worksheet** in the Instructions for Form 1040, line 44 (or in the Instructions for Form 1040NR, line 42). **Do not** complete lines 21 and 22 below.

   ☒ **No.** Complete Form 1040 through line 43, or Form 1040NR through line 41. Then complete the **Schedule D Tax Worksheet** on page D-10 of the instructions. **Do not** complete lines 21 and 22 below.

21 If line 16 is a loss, enter here and on Form 1040, line 13, or Form 1040NR, line 14, the **smaller** of:

   - The loss on line 16 or
   - ($3,000), or if married filing separately, ($1,500)   . . . . **21** (   )

   Note. When figuring which amount is smaller, treat both amounts as positive numbers.

22 Do you have qualified dividends on Form 1040, line 9b, or Form 1040NR, line 10b?

   ☐ **Yes.** Complete Form 1040 through line 43, or Form 1040NR through line 41. Then complete the **Qualified Dividends and Capital Gain Tax Worksheet** in the Instructions for Form 1040, line 44 (or in the Instructions for Form 1040NR, line 42).
   ☐ **No.** Complete the rest of Form 1040 or Form 1040NR.

Schedule D (Form 1040) 2010

ETHICS & Equity

INCORRECT DEPRECIATION AND RECOGNIZED GAIN

A staff accountant for a large international company is calculating the tax gain from disposition of business equipment. The equipment was seven-year MACRS property and has been fully depreciated for tax purposes. The staff accountant notices that the equipment was used in Germany, not the United States, although it is listed as an asset of the U.S. company for which the staff accountant works. Since the property was used outside the United States, it should have been depreciated using straight-line over a nine-year life. Consequently, the tax depreciation has been overstated, and the tax basis should be greater than zero, causing a smaller gain. What should the staff accountant do?

TAX PLANNING:

17.7 TIMING OF § 1231 GAIN

LO.8

Identify tax planning opportunities associated with §§ 1231, 1245, and 1250.

Although §§ 1245 and 1250 recapture much of the gain from the disposition of business property, sometimes § 1231 gain is still substantial. For instance, land held as a business asset will generate either § 1231 gain or § 1231 loss. If the taxpayer already has a capital loss for the year, the sale of land at a gain should be postponed so that the net § 1231 gain is not netted against the capital loss. The capital loss deduction will therefore be maximized for the current tax year, and the capital loss carryforward (if any) may be offset against the gain when the land is sold. If the taxpayer already has a § 1231 loss, § 1231 gains might be postponed to maximize the ordinary loss deduction this year. However, the carryforward of unrecaptured § 1231 losses will make some or all of the § 1231 gain next year an ordinary gain.

In the examples below, the 2011 and 2012 long-term capital gain rates are assumed to be the same.

EXAMPLE 26

Mark has a $2,000 net STCL for 2011. He could sell business land held 27 months for a $3,000 § 1231 gain. He will have no other capital gains and losses or § 1231 gains and losses in 2011 or 2012. He has no nonrecaptured § 1231 losses from prior years. Mark is in the 28% tax bracket in 2011 and will be in the 25% bracket in 2012. If he sells the land in 2011, he will have a $1,000 net LTCG ($3,000 § 1231 gain − $2,000 STCL) and will pay a tax of $150 ($1,000 × 15%). If Mark sells the land in 2012, he will have a 2011 tax savings of $560 ($2,000 capital loss deduction × 28% tax rate on ordinary income). In 2012, he will pay tax of $450 ($3,000 × 15%). By postponing the sale by a year, Mark gets the use of $710 ($560 + $150) of tax savings until he has to pay $450 in 2012, for a net savings of $260 between the two years without considering the time value of money and other factors. ∎

EXAMPLE 27

Beth has a $15,000 § 1231 loss in 2011. She could sell business equipment held 30 months for a $20,000 § 1231 gain and a $12,000 § 1245 gain. Beth is in the 28% tax bracket in 2011 and will be in the 25% bracket in 2012. She has no nonrecaptured § 1231 losses from prior years. If she sells the equipment in 2011, she will have a $5,000 net § 1231 gain and $12,000 of ordinary gain. Her tax would be $4,110 [($5,000 § 1231 gain × 15%) + ($12,000 ordinary gain × 28%)].

If Beth postpones the equipment sale until 2012, she would have a 2011 ordinary loss of $15,000 and tax savings of $4,200 ($15,000 × 28%). In 2012, she would have $5,000 of § 1231 gain (the 2011 § 1231 loss carries over and recaptures $15,000 of the 2012 § 1231 gain as ordinary income) and $27,000 of ordinary gain. Her tax would be $7,500 [($5,000 § 1231 gain × 15%) + ($27,000 ordinary gain × 25%)]. By postponing the sale of the § 1231 property until 2012, Beth gets the use of $8,310 ($4,200 + $4,110) of tax savings until she has to pay $7,500 in 2012, for a net savings of $810 between the two years without considering the time value of money and other factors. ∎

17.8 TIMING OF RECAPTURE

Since recapture is usually not triggered until the property is sold or disposed of, it may be possible to plan for recapture in low-bracket or loss years. If a taxpayer has net operating loss (NOL) carryovers that are about to expire, the recognition of ordinary income from recapture may be advisable to absorb the loss carryovers.

EXAMPLE 28

Ahmad has a $15,000 NOL carryover that will expire this year. He owns a machine that he plans to sell in the early part of next year. The expected gain of $17,000 from the sale of the machine will be recaptured as ordinary income under § 1245. Ahmad sells the machine before the end of this year and offsets $15,000 of the ordinary income against the NOL carryover. ■

17.9 POSTPONING AND SHIFTING RECAPTURE

It is also possible to postpone recapture or to shift the burden of recapture to others. For example, recapture is avoided upon the disposition of a § 1231 asset if the taxpayer replaces the property by entering into a like-kind exchange. In this instance, recapture potential is merely carried over to the newly acquired property (refer to Example 21).

Recapture can be shifted to others through the gratuitous transfer of § 1245 or § 1250 property to family members. A subsequent sale of such property by the donee will trigger recapture to the donee rather than the donor (refer to Example 18). This procedure would be advisable only if the donee is in a lower income tax bracket than the donor.

17.10 AVOIDING RECAPTURE

The immediate expensing election (§ 179) is subject to § 1245 recapture. If the election is not made, the § 1245 recapture potential will accumulate more slowly (refer to Chapter 8). Since using the immediate expense deduction complicates depreciation and book accounting for the affected asset, not taking the deduction may make sense even though the time value of money might indicate it should be taken.

REFOCUS ON THE BIG PICTURE

DEPRECIATION RECAPTURE

Hazel maximized her depreciation deductions when she acquired the store equipment in 2008. When she sells the equipment in 2011, however, she has a gain because of the low adjusted basis resulting from the § 179 immediate expensing and the rapid seven-year MACRS depreciation. Section 1245 "recaptures" this gain as ordinary income. One way Hazel could avoid currently recognizing the $53,040 ($128,000 − $74,960) gain would be to do a like-kind exchange of the equipment acquired in 2008 for the replacement equipment to be acquired in 2011 [see Like-Kind Exchanges (§ 1031) on p. 17-21]. She would likely have to give up the 2008 equipment plus cash to acquire the replacement equipment. Thus, there would be no "boot received" and, therefore, no current gain recognized. However, the depreciation recapture potential on the 2008 equipment would carry over to the replacement equipment.

KEY TERMS

Additional depreciation, 17–15	§ 1231 Gains and losses, 17–4	§ 1250 Property, 17–14
Intangible drilling and development costs (IDC), 17–22	§ 1231 Lookback, 17–9	Section 1250 recapture, 17–14
	Section 1231 property, 17–5	Unrecaptured § 1250 gain, 17–17
Long-term nonpersonal use capital assets, 17–6	§ 1245 Property, 17–13	
Related party, 17–22	Section 1245 recapture, 17–12	

DISCUSSION QUESTIONS

ISSUE ID

1. **LO.1, 2** Harriet, an organic farmer, has owned depreciable farm equipment for several years. Is the equipment a capital asset? Why or why not?

2. **LO.1** If there is a net loss from the sale of depreciable business property held long term, what is the character of the loss, and how is it deducted (*for* or *from* AGI)?

3. **LO.1** If there is a net gain from the sale of land used in a business, is it possible that the gain could be treated as a long-term capital gain? If so, how?

4. **LO.1** Why is a depreciable asset, held 12 months or less when it was sold, not a § 1231 asset?

ISSUE ID

5. **LO.1, 2** Nate, a farmer, is thinking about raising llamas. Llama milk is highly sought after because it is high in protein and low in saturated fat. Nate would like to know what tax issues he would face if he decides to raise llamas in addition to the pigs he is currently raising.

ISSUE ID

6. **LO.1, 2** Bernice, a sole proprietor, sold two business assets during the year. As a result, she has an ordinary loss and a § 1231 gain. The loss asset was office furniture that was held for eight months, and the gain asset is land that was held for five years. Why doesn't the ordinary loss offset the § 1231 gain?

ISSUE ID

7. **LO.1, 2** Hakim's rental building was not insured when it was destroyed by a hurricane. His adjusted basis for the building was substantial, but was less than he had paid for the building in 2007. The building was Hakim's only asset that was damaged by the hurricane. How should Hakim handle this situation?

ISSUE ID

8. **LO.1, 2** Sammy established a sole proprietorship in 2003. He sold § 1231 assets at a loss in 2009 and 2010. He had not sold any § 1231 assets before 2009. In 2011, he could sell a § 1231 asset at a gain and would like to have the gain taxed as a long-term capital gain. What issue is Sammy facing?

9. **LO.2** As a result of a casualty event, Thelma disposed of tangible personal property (a § 1231 asset) at a realized and recognized gain. At the time of the casualty, the property was worth substantially less than Thelma had paid for it and had an adjusted basis of zero. This was her only business casualty, and she has some § 1231 lookback loss. Is the resulting gain a casualty gain taxed as a long-term capital gain, a gain taxed as an ordinary gain, or a casualty gain taxed as a § 1231 gain?

ISSUE ID

10. **LO.2** An individual taxpayer had a net § 1231 loss in 2008 and a net § 1231 gain in 2009, 2010, and 2011. What factors will influence whether any of the 2011 net § 1231 gain will be treated as long-term capital gain?

11. **LO.2** Review Examples 4 and 6 in the text. In both examples, the taxpayer's AGI is $129,400 even though in Example 6 there is $700 of nonrecaptured § 1231 loss from 2010. Explain why the two AGI amounts are the same.

12. **LO.3** A taxpayer owns depreciable business real property held for the long-term holding period. What would have to be true for the real property to generate a § 1231 loss when it is sold?

13. **LO.3** A depreciable business dump truck has been owned for four years and is no longer useful to the taxpayer. What would have to be true for the disposition of the dump truck to generate at least some § 1231 gain?

14. **LO.1, 2, 3** Sissie owns two items of business equipment. They were both purchased in 2007 for $100,000, both have a seven-year recovery period, and both have an adjusted basis of $37,490. Sissie is considering selling these assets in 2011. One of them is worth $50,000, and the other is worth $33,000. Since both items were used in her business, Sissie simply assumes that the loss on one will be offset against the gain from the other and the net gain or loss will increase or reduce her business income. Is she correct?

ISSUE ID

15. **LO.1, 3** If depreciable equipment used in a business is sold at a recognized gain on July 10, 2011, and it was purchased on August 21, 2010, does § 1245 depreciation recapture apply to the asset?

16. **LO.3** A professional football player's contract is sold at a gain after it has been held for two years. What issues should the team consider in determining the nature of this gain?

ISSUE ID

17. **LO.3** A farmer's silo is destroyed by a tornado, but is insured for its replacement cost. Consequently, the farmer has a $40,000 gain after receiving the insurance proceeds. The silo is not replaced because the farmer spends the insurance proceeds on additional cattle. What is the nature of the gain if the silo originally cost $100,000 three years ago and had an adjusted basis of $60,000 at the time of its destruction?

18. **LO.4** Nonresidential real estate leasehold improvements are sold at a loss. In what circumstances would the loss be subject to § 1250 depreciation recapture?

19. **LO.4** An apartment building was acquired in 2004. Depreciation of $123,000 was taken on the building, and the building was sold for a $34,000 gain. What is the maximum amount of 25% gain?

20. **LO.4** In the current year, an individual taxpayer has net long-term capital gain from the disposition of capital assets and also has unrecaptured § 1250 gain. Under what circumstances would the unrecaptured § 1250 gain be taxed at 25%?

21. **LO.4** An individual has $25,000 of § 1231 loss from the disposition of an office building. Straight-line depreciation of $43,000 was deducted on the building. The taxpayer also has a § 1231 gain of $56,000 from the sale of business land. How much of the gain or loss is taxed as unrecaptured § 1250 gain?

22. **LO.3, 5** Mary receives tangible personal property as a gift. The property was depreciated by the donor, and Mary will also depreciate it. At the date of the gift, the property was worth more than the donor's adjusted basis. What is the impact of these facts on Mary when she sells the property at a gain several years after she acquired it?

23. **LO.3, 5** Thomas receives tangible personal property as an inheritance from a decedent who died in 2011. The property was depreciated by the deceased, and Thomas will also depreciate it. At the date of the deceased's death, the property was worth more than the deceased's adjusted basis. What is the impact of these facts on Thomas when he sells the property at a gain several years after he acquired it?

24. **LO.3, 5** Dino contributes to charity some tangible personal property that he had used in his business and depreciated. At the date of the donation, the property has a fair market value greater than its adjusted basis, but less than the original cost. What is the impact of these facts on Dino's charitable contribution?

25. **LO.3, 5** Desiree contributes to her wholly owned corporation some tangible personal property that she had used in her sole proprietorship business and depreciated. At the date of the contribution, the property has a fair market value greater than its adjusted basis. What is the impact of these facts on the corporation?

26. **LO.3, 5** A corporation distributes a truck it has owned for three years to its sole shareholder. The shareholder will use the truck for personal use activity. The truck's fair market value at the time of the distribution is greater than its adjusted basis, but less than its original cost. Does the corporation recognize a gain? If so, what is the character of the gain?

27. **LO.6** A corporation distributes a truck it has owned for three years to its sole shareholder. The shareholder will use the truck for business activity. The truck's fair market value at the time of the distribution is greater than its adjusted basis, but less than its original cost. Does the corporation recognize a gain? If so, what is the character of the gain?

28. **LO.7** Refer to Form 4797 near the end of this chapter. Where would a § 1231 loss be entered on the form?

29. **LO.7** Refer to Form 4797 near the end of this chapter. Where would a § 1231 gain on the disposition of business land be entered on the form?

30. **LO.7** Refer to Form 4797 near the end of this chapter. Where would a § 1231 lookback loss be entered on the form?

PROBLEMS

31. **LO.1, 2** Sally purchased timber on a 100-acre tract of land in Montana in March 2008 for $200,000. On January 1, 2010, the timber had a fair market value of $230,000. Because of careless cutting in November 2010, when the fair market value was $245,000, the wood was sold on January 30, 2011, for $78,000.
    a. What gain (loss) was recognized in 2009, 2010, and 2011 if Sally elects to treat the cutting as a sale?
    b. What was the nature of the gains (losses) in (a)?
    c. Does the answer change if the timber was sold in December 2010? Why?
    d. If the timber was worth only $48,000 on January 1, 2010, was cut in November when it was worth $21,000, and was sold in December for $49,000, how would the answers to (a) and (b) change?

32. **LO.2** Bernie owns a farming sole proprietorship. During the year, Bernie sold a breeding bull that he had owned for 15 months and a workhorse that he had owned for 66 months. The bull had an adjusted basis of $38,000 and was sold for $25,000. The horse had an adjusted basis of $750 and was sold for $4,000. Bernie also has a $200 long-term capital loss from the sale of corporate stock. He has $55,000 of other AGI (not associated with the items above) for the year. He has $4,000 nonrecaptured § 1231 losses from the previous five years. What is the nature of the gains or losses from the disposition of the farm animals, and what is Bernie's AGI for the year?

COMMUNICATIONS

33. **LO.2** A sculpture that Korliss Kane held for investment was destroyed in a flood. The sculpture was insured, and Korliss had a $60,000 gain from this casualty. He also had a $17,000 loss from an uninsured antique vase that was destroyed by the flood. The vase was also held for investment. Korliss had no other property transactions during the year and has no nonrecaptured § 1231 losses from prior years. Both the sculpture and the vase had been held more than one year when the flood occurred. Compute Korliss's net gain or loss and identify how it would be treated. Also, write a letter to Korliss explaining the nature of the gain or loss. Korliss's address is 2367 Meridian Road, Hannibal Point, MO 34901.

34. **LO.2** Keshara has the following net § 1231 results for each of the years shown. What would be the nature of the net gains in 2010 and 2011?

Tax Year	Net § 1231 Loss	Net § 1231 Gain
2006	$16,000	
2007	33,000	
2008	32,000	
2009		$41,000
2010		30,000
2011		41,000

DECISION MAKING

35. **LO.2, 8** Jinjie owns two parcels of business land (§ 1231 assets). One parcel can be sold at a loss of $60,000, and the other parcel can be sold at a gain of $70,000. Jinjie has no nonrecaptured § 1231 losses from prior years. The parcels could be sold at any time because potential purchasers are abundant. Jinjie has a $35,000 short-term capital loss carryover from a prior tax year and no capital assets that could be sold to generate long-term capital gains. Both the land parcels have been held more than one year. What should Jinjie do based upon these facts? (Assume tax rates are constant and ignore the present value of future cash flow.)

36. **LO.1, 2, 3** Siena Industries (a sole proprietorship) sold three § 1231 assets during 2011. Data on these property dispositions are as follows:

Asset	Cost	Acquired	Depreciation	Sold for	Sold on
Rack	$100,000	10/10/07	$65,000	$75,000	10/10/11
Forklift	35,000	10/16/08	23,000	5,000	10/10/11
Bin	87,000	03/12/10	34,000	60,000	10/10/11

a. Determine the amount and the character of the recognized gain or loss from the disposition of each asset.

b. Assuming Siena has no nonrecaptured net § 1231 losses from prior years, how much of the 2011 recognized gains is treated as capital gains?

37. **L0.2, 3** Amber Industries (a sole proprietorship) sold three § 1231 assets during 2011. Data on these property dispositions are as follows:

Asset	Cost	Acquired	Depreciation	Sold for	Sold on
Rack	$100,000	10/10/07	$100,000	$135,000	10/10/11
Forklift	35,000	10/16/08	23,000	3,000	10/10/11
Bin	87,000	03/12/10	34,000	60,000	10/10/11

a. Determine the amount and the character of the recognized gain or loss from the disposition of each asset.

b. Assuming Amber has $5,000 nonrecaptured net § 1231 losses from the five prior years, how much of the 2011 recognized gains is treated as capital gains?

38. **L0.2, 3** Copper Industries (a sole proprietorship) sold three § 1231 assets during 2011. Data on these property dispositions are as follows:

Asset	Cost	Acquired	Depreciation	Sold for	Sold on
Rack	$110,000	10/10/08	$60,000	$55,000	10/10/11
Forklift	45,000	10/16/07	21,000	15,000	10/10/11
Bin	97,000	03/12/10	34,000	60,000	10/10/11

a. Determine the amount and the character of the recognized gain or loss from the disposition of each asset.

b. Assuming Copper has $2,000 nonrecaptured net § 1231 losses from prior years, how much of the 2011 recognized gains is treated as capital gains?

39. **L0.2, 3** On December 1, 2009, Lavender Manufacturing Company (a corporation) purchased another company's assets, including a patent. The patent was used in Lavender's manufacturing operations; $49,500 was allocated to the patent, and it was amortized at the rate of $275 per month. On July 30, 2011, Lavender sold the patent for $70,000. Twenty months of amortization had been taken on the patent. What are the amount and nature of the gain Lavender recognizes on the disposition of the patent? Write a letter to Lavender discussing the treatment of the gain. Lavender's address is 6734 Grover Street, Back Bay Harbor, ME 23890. The letter should be addressed to Bill Cubit, Controller.

COMMUNICATIONS

40. **L0.2, 4** On June 1, 2007, Sparrow Enterprises (not a corporation) acquired a retail store building for $500,000 (with $100,000 being allocated to the land). The store building was 39-year real property, and the straight-line cost recovery method was used. The property was sold on June 21, 2011, for $385,000.

a. Compute the cost recovery and adjusted basis for the building using Table 8.6 from Chapter 8.

b. What are the amount and nature of Sparrow's gain or loss from disposition of the building? What amount, if any, of the gain is unrecaptured § 1250 gain?

41. **L0.2, 3, 4** On May 2, 1986, Hannah acquired residential rental real estate for $450,000. Of the cost, $100,000 was allocated to the land and $350,000 to the building. On January 20, 2011, the building, which then had an adjusted basis of $0, was sold for $445,000 and the land for $500,000.

a. Determine the amount and character of the recognized gain from the sale of the building.

b. Determine the amount and character of the recognized gain from the sale of the land.

42. **LO.2, 3, 4** Larry is the sole proprietor of a trampoline shop. During 2011, the following transactions occurred:

- Unimproved land adjacent to the store was condemned by the city on February 1. The condemnation proceeds were $25,000. The land, acquired in 1984, had an allocable basis of $40,000. Larry has additional parking across the street and plans to use the condemnation proceeds to build his inventory.

- A truck used to deliver trampolines was sold on January 2 for $3,500. The truck was purchased on January 2, 2007, for $6,000. On the date of sale, the adjusted basis was zero.

- Larry sold an antique rowing machine at an auction. Net proceeds were $3,900. The rowing machine was purchased as used equipment 17 years ago for $5,200 and is fully depreciated.

- Larry sold an apartment building for $200,000 on September 1. The rental property was purchased on September 1, 2008, for $150,000 and was being depreciated over a 27.5-year life using the straight-line method. At the date of sale, the adjusted basis was $124,783.

- Larry's personal yacht was stolen on September 5. The yacht had been purchased in August at a cost of $25,000. The fair market value immediately preceding the theft was $19,600. Larry was insured for 50% of the original cost, and he received $12,500 on December 1.

- Larry sold a Buick on May 1 for $9,600. The vehicle had been used exclusively for personal purposes. It was purchased on September 1, 2007, for $20,800.

- Larry's trampoline stretching machine (owned two years) was stolen on May 5, but the business's insurance company will not pay any of the machine's value because Larry failed to pay the insurance premium. The machine had a fair market value of $8,000 and an adjusted basis of $6,000 at the time of theft.

- Larry had AGI of $402,000 from sources other than those described above.

- Larry has no nonrecaptured § 1231 lookback losses.

a. For each transaction, what are the amount and nature of recognized gain or loss?
b. What is Larry's 2010 AGI?

43. **LO.2, 4** On January 1, 2002, Stephanie Bridges acquired depreciable real property for $50,000. She used straight-line depreciation to compute the asset's cost recovery. The asset was sold for $96,000 on January 3, 2011, when its adjusted basis was $38,000.

a. What are the amount and nature of the gain if the real property was residential?
b. Stephanie is curious about how the recapture rules differ for residential rental real estate acquired in 1986 and for residential rental real estate acquired in 1987 and thereafter. Write a letter to Stephanie explaining the differences. Her address is 2345 Westridge Street #23, Homer, MT 67342.

44. **LO.2, 3, 5, 8** Joanne is in the 35% tax bracket and owns depreciable business equipment that she purchased several years ago for $135,000. She has taken $100,000 of depreciation on the equipment, and it is worth $85,000. Joanne's niece, Susan, is starting a new business and is short of cash. Susan has asked Joanne to gift the equipment to her so that Susan can use it in her business. Joanne no longer needs the equipment. Identify the alternatives available to Joanne if she wishes to help Susan and the tax effects of those alternatives. (Assume all alternatives involve the business equipment in one way or another, and ignore the gift tax.)

45. **LO.2, 3, 5** Hazel received tangible personal property with a fair market value of $55,000 as a gift in 2009. The donor had purchased the property for $77,000 and taken $77,000 of depreciation. Hazel used the property in her business. Hazel sells the property for $13,000 in 2011. What are the tax status of the property and the nature of the recognized gain when she sells the property?

46. **LO.2, 3, 5** Evan receives tangible personal property as an inheritance in 2009. The property was depreciated by the deceased (Evan's father), and Evan will also depreciate it. At the date of the deceased's death, the property was worth $432,000. The deceased had purchased it for $900,000 and taken $623,000 of depreciation on the property. Evan takes $123,000 of depreciation on the property before selling it for $482,000 in 2011. What are the tax status of the property and the nature of the recognized gain when Evan sells the property?

47. **LO.5** David contributes to charity some tangible personal property that he had used in his business and depreciated. At the date of the donation, the property has a fair market value of $233,000 and an adjusted basis of zero; it was originally acquired for $400,000. What is the amount of David's charitable contribution?

48. **LO.2, 3, 5** Dedriea contributes to her wholly owned corporation some tangible personal property that she had used in her sole proprietorship business and depreciated. She had acquired the property for $566,000 and taken $431,000 of depreciation on it before contributing it to the corporation. At the date of the contribution, the property had a fair market value of $289,000. The corporation took $100,000 of depreciation on the property and then sold it for $88,000 in 2011. What are the tax status of the property to the corporation and the nature of the recognized gain or loss when the corporation sells the property?

49. **LO.2, 3, 6** Magenta Corporation purchased depreciable tangible personal property for $100,000 in 2008 and immediately expensed the entire cost under § 179. In 2011, when the property was worth $40,000, Magenta distributed it as a dividend to the corporation's sole shareholder. What was the tax status of this property for Magenta, and what is the nature of the recognized gain or loss from the distribution of the property?

50. **LO.4, 7** Jeremiah is the tenant of a shopping center. In 2004, he installed $450,000 of capitalized leasehold improvements in his store at the mall. He took $316,508 of depreciation on the leasehold improvements before selling them for $420,000 to the lessee who took over his lease in 2010. Straight-line depreciation on the leasehold improvements up to the point of sale would have been $67,253. Jeremiah's depreciation was so much larger than straight-line depreciation because he took § 168(k) depreciation in 2004. What is Jeremiah's recognized gain, what is the nature of that gain, and how is the transaction reported on a 2010 Form 4797?

51. **LO.4** Jasmine owned rental real estate that she sold to her tenant in an installment sale. Jasmine had acquired the property in 2000 for $400,000, had taken $178,000 of depreciation on it, and sold it for $210,000, receiving $25,000 immediately and the balance (plus interest at a market rate) in equal payments of $18,500 for 10 years. What is the nature of the recognized gain or loss from this transaction?

52. **LO.4, 7** Sasha and Tara are married, filing jointly. Their correctly determined 2011 taxable income is $127,000. This taxable income includes a $5,000 § 1231 gain from the sale of business land that was included in their $22,000 of net long-term capital gain. None of the net long-term capital gain was from collectibles.
    a. In addition to their Form 1040, what tax forms related to their property transactions would the couple include in their income tax return?
    b. Calculate the couple's tax on taxable income using the alternative tax on net capital gain method.

53. **LO.2, 7** On August 10, 2009, Jasper purchased business equipment for $40,000. On his 2009 tax return, $40,000 of § 179 immediate expense was taken on the equipment. On July 14, 2010, Jasper sold the equipment for $12,000. What is the nature of the gain or loss from the disposition, and where is it reported on the 2010 Form 4797?

54. **LO.7** Adrian has a 2010 Form 4797, line 9 gain of $56,000. He also has one transaction on his 2010 Form 1040 Schedule D Part I—a loss of $58,000. What is Adrian's AGI from these events?

55. **LO.7** Theresa has a 2010 Form 1040 Schedule D, line 16 gain of $45,000. There is also a $45,000 gain on the form's line 19. What is the nature of the gain, and what alternative tax rate applies to it?

56. **L0.3, 8** Jay sold three items of business equipment for a total of $300,000. None of the equipment was appraised to determine its value. Jay's cost and adjusted basis for the assets are as follows:

Asset	Cost	Adjusted Basis
Skidder	$230,000	$ 40,000
Driller	120,000	60,000
Platform	620,000	–0–
Total	$970,000	$100,000

Jay has been unable to establish the fair market values of the three assets. All he can determine is that combined they were worth $300,000 to the buyer in this arm's length transaction. How should Jay allocate the sales price and figure the gain or loss on the sale of the three assets?

CUMULATIVE PROBLEMS

57. Justin Stone was an employee of DataCare Services, Inc. His salary was $45,000 through November 10, 2010, when he was laid off. He received $7,000 of unemployment compensation from November 11, 2010, through December 31, 2010. FICA withholdings were as follows: Social Security of $2,790 ($45,000 × 6.2%) and Medicare of $653 ($45,000 × 1.45%). Justin lives at 112 Green Road, Sandusky, ID 45623. His Social Security number is 111–11–1111. Justin owned an apartment building until November 22, 2010, when he sold it for $200,000. For 2010, he had rent revenue of $33,000. He incurred and paid expenses as follows: $4,568 of repairs, $22,000 of mortgage interest, and $1,000 of miscellaneous expenses. He had purchased the building on January 2, 2004, for $125,000. The building generated an operating profit each year that Justin owned it.

Other information follows:

- On November 22, 2010, Justin sold for $3,500 equipment that had been used for repairing various items in the apartments. The equipment was purchased for $25,000 on July 10, 2003, and was fully depreciated prior to 2010.
- Justin has $3,000 of unrecaptured § 1231 losses from prior years.
- Justin is age 38, single, divorced, and has custody of his nine-year-old son, Flint. Justin provides more than 50% of Flint's support. Flint's Social Security number is 123–45–6789.
- Justin had $1,000 interest income from Blue Corporation bonds.
- Justin had $1,500 interest income from a State Bank certificate of deposit.
- Justin had a $2,000 *0%/15%* long-term capital gain distribution from the Brown Stock Investment Fund.
- Justin had the following itemized deductions: $5,600 real estate taxes on his home; $8,900 mortgage interest on his home; $760 charitable contributions (all in cash, properly documented, and no single contribution exceeded $25); $7,300 state income tax withholding during 2010; $2,000 state estimated income tax payments during 2010; $2,600 sales taxes paid.
- Justin does not wish to donate to the Presidential Election Campaign Fund.
- He had $12,000 of Federal income tax withholding during 2010 and made total Federal estimated income tax payments of $14,000 during 2010.

Compute Justin's 2010 net tax payable or refund due. If you use tax forms for your computations, you will need Form 1040 and Schedules A, B, D, and E. You will also need Form 4797, but ignore Form 6251. Suggested software: H&R BLOCK At Home.

58. Glen and Diane Okumura are married, file a joint return, and live at 39 Kaloa Street, Honolulu, HI 56790. Glen's Social Security number is 111–11–1111 and Diane's is 123–45–6789. The Okumuras have two dependent children, Amy (age 15) and John (age 9). Amy's Social Security number is 123–45–6788, and John's Social Security number

is 123–45–6787. Glen works for the Hawaii Public Works Department, and Diane works in a retail dress shop. The Okumuras had the following transactions during 2011:

a. Glen earned $87,000 in wages and had Federal income tax withholding of $8,000.

b. Diane earned $38,000 in wages from the dress shop and had Federal income tax withholding of $3,000.

c. The Okumuras sold a small apartment building for $199,980 on November 15, 2011. The building was acquired in October 2005 for $300,000; cost recovery was $86,820.

d. The Okumuras received $3,000 in qualified dividends on various domestic corporation stocks that they own.

e. The Okumuras sold stock on November 5 for a $7,000 long-term capital gain and other stock on December 10 at a $2,000 short-term capital loss.

f. The Okumuras had the following itemized deductions: $11,000 unreimbursed medical expenses; $10,500 personal use real property taxes; $7,000 qualified residence interest; $1,500 of Glen's unreimbursed employee business expenses; $535 of investment-related expenses; $2,700 of state income taxes paid; and $1,061 of sales taxes from the sales tax table.

g. The Okumuras spent $3,000 on qualifying child care expenses during the year.

Compute the Okumuras' 2011 net tax payable or refund due. Also write a letter to the Okumuras describing how the sale of the apartment building affects their return.

RESEARCH PROBLEMS

Note: Solutions to Research Problems can be prepared by using the **Checkpoint®** **Student Edition** online research product, which is available to accompany this text. It is also possible to prepare solutions to the Research Problems by using tax research materials found in a standard tax library.

THOMSON REUTERS
Checkpoint® Student Edition

COMMUNICATIONS

Research Problem 1. Sidney owns a professional football franchise. He has received an offer of $80 million for the franchise, all the football equipment, the rights to concession receipts, the rights to a stadium lease, and the rights to all the player contracts he owns. Most of the players have been with the team for quite a long time and have contracts that were signed several years ago. The contracts have been substantially depreciated. Sidney is concerned about potential § 1245 recapture when the contracts are sold. He has heard about "previously unrecaptured depreciation with respect to initial contracts" and would like to know more about it. Find a definition for that phrase and write an explanation of it.

Research Problem 2. Walter is both a real estate developer and the owner and manager of residential rental real estate. Walter is retiring and is going to sell both the land he is holding for future development and the rental properties he owns. Straight-line depreciation was used to depreciate the rental real estate. The rental properties will be sold at a substantial loss, and the development property will be sold at a substantial gain. What is the nature of these gains and losses?

Partial list of research aids:
§§ 1221 and 1231.
Zane R. Tollis, 65 TCM 1951, T.C.Memo. 1993–63.

Research Problem 3. An individual cash basis taxpayer sells rental real estate on the installment basis. The gain from the disposition is $45,000: $30,000 of potential *25%* gain and $15,000 of potential *0%/15%* gain. In what sequence are these gains recognized as gain on the installment sale?

Research Problem 4. In 2007, a taxpayer made leasehold improvements that were eligible for a 15-year MACRS life. Straight-line depreciation was taken on the improvements. Will these improvements be subject to either § 1245 or § 1250 depreciation recapture if they are eventually disposed of at a recognized gain?

INTERNET
activity

Use the tax resources of the Internet to address the following questions. Do not restrict your search to the Web, but include a review of newsgroups and general reference materials, practitioner sites and resources, primary sources of the tax law, chat rooms and discussion groups, and other opportunities.

Research Problem 5. Summarize tax planning strategies related to each of the following topics that are presented on the Internet by tax advisers looking for clients:

a. A strategy for maximizing gains that are eligible for the 0%/15% alternative tax rate rather than the 25% rate.

b. A strategy for maximizing gains that are eligible for the 0%/15% alternative tax rate rather than the 28% rate.

Research Problem 6. Determine whether Australia has an equivalent to § 1231 treatment for gains from the disposition of business depreciable assets.

Research Problem 7. Find a state website that has tax forms and instructions for that state. Let's call that state "X." Find a discussion in those sources that reveals whether state X taxes gains from the sale of real estate that is located in state Y when the taxpayer is an individual and is a full-time resident of state X.

Accounting Periods, Accounting Methods, and Deferred Compensation

Part 6 provides a more comprehensive examination of the accounting periods and accounting methods that were introduced in Part 2. A discussion of special accounting methods is also included. Part 6 concludes with an analysis of the tax consequences of deferred compensation transactions.

Accounting Periods and Methods

After completing Chapter 18, you should be able to:

LO.1

Understand the relevance of the accounting period concept, the different types of accounting periods, and the limitations on their use.

LO.2

Apply the cash method, accrual method, and hybrid method of accounting.

LO.3

Utilize the procedure for changing accounting methods.

LO.4

Determine when the installment method of accounting can be utilized and apply the related calculation techniques.

LO.5

Understand the alternative methods of accounting for long-term contracts (the completed contract method and the percentage of completion method) including the limitations on the use of the completed contract method.

LO.6

Know when accounting for inventories must occur, recognize the types of costs that must be included in inventories, and apply the LIFO method.

LO.7

Identify tax planning opportunities related to accounting periods and accounting methods.

OUTLINE

For the latest in changes to tax legislation, visit **www.cengage.com/taxation/swft.**

FRAMEWORK 1040:
Tax Formula for Individuals

This chapter covers the boldfaced portions of the Tax Formula for Individuals that was introduced in Figure 3.1 on p. 3-3. Below those portions are the sections of Form 1040 where the results are reported.

Income (broadly conceived)	$ xx,xxx
Less: Exclusions	(x,xxx)
Gross income	**$xx,xxx**

FORM 1040 (p. 1)

12	Business income or (loss). Attach Schedule C or C-EZ	

Less: Deductions for adjusted gross income	(x,xxx)
Adjusted gross income.	$ xx,xxx
Less: The greater of total itemized deductions *or* the standard deduction.	(x,xxx)
Personal and dependency exemptions.	(x,xxx)
Taxable income	$ xx,xxx
Tax on taxable income (see Tax Tables or Tax Rate Schedules)	$ x,xxx
Less: Tax credits (including income taxes withheld and prepaid)	(xxx)
Tax due (or refund).	$ xxx

THE BIG PICTURE   Tax Solutions for the Real World

ACCOUNTING PERIOD

Belinda, Pearl, Inc. (a C corporation), and Tweety, Inc. (an S corporation), are going to form a partnership (Silver Partnership). The ownership interests and tax years of the partners are as follows:

Partner	Partnership Interest	Tax Year Ends
Belinda	25%	December 31
Pearl, Inc.	35%	November 30
Tweety, Inc.	40%	June 30

The partnership will begin business on April 1, 2011. The partners have several issues they would like for you to address.

- A potential conflict exists among the partners regarding when the tax year should end for Silver. Belinda and Pearl would like a year-end close to their own year-ends while Tweety would like to have a June 30 year-end. Is this a decision that Tweety can make since it owns more of the partnership than either of the other two partners? Is this a decision that Belinda and Pearl can make since collectively they own more of the partnership than Tweety?
- Since Silver will begin business on April 1, 2011, will the first tax year be a "short" tax year or a "long" tax year? Will annualization of the net income of the partnership be required?
- How will the partners know when their share of Silver's net income or net loss should be reported on their respective income tax returns?

Read the chapter and formulate your response.

Tax practitioners must deal with the issue of *when* particular items of income and expense are recognized as well as the basic issue of *whether* the items are includible in taxable income. Earlier chapters discussed the types of income subject to tax (gross income and exclusions) and allowable deductions (the *whether* issue).[1] This chapter focuses on the related issue of the periods in which income and deductions are reported (the *when* issue). Generally, a taxpayer's income and deductions must be assigned to particular 12-month periods—calendar years or fiscal years.

Income and deductions are placed within particular years through the use of tax accounting methods. The basic accounting methods are the cash method, accrual method, and hybrid method. Other special purpose methods, such as the installment method and the methods used for long-term construction contracts, are available for specific circumstances or types of transactions.

Over the long run, the accounting period used by a taxpayer will not affect the aggregate amount of reported taxable income. However, taxable income for any particular year may vary significantly due to the use of a particular reporting period. Also, through the choice of accounting methods or accounting periods, it is possible to postpone the recognition of taxable income and to enjoy the benefits from deferring the related tax. This chapter discusses the taxpayer's alternatives for accounting periods and accounting methods.

18.1 ACCOUNTING PERIODS

IN GENERAL

A taxpayer who keeps adequate books and records may be permitted to elect a **fiscal year**, a 12-month period ending on the *last day* of a month other than December, for the **accounting period**. Otherwise, a *calendar year* must be used.[2] Frequently, corporations can satisfy the record-keeping requirements and elect to use a fiscal year.[3] Often the fiscal year conforms to a natural business year (e.g., a summer resort's fiscal year may end on September 30, after the close of the season). Individuals seldom use a fiscal year because they do not maintain the necessary books and records and because complications can arise as a result of changes in the tax law (e.g., often the transition rules and effective dates differ for fiscal year taxpayers).

Generally, a taxable year may not exceed 12 calendar months. However, if certain requirements are met, a taxpayer may elect to use an annual period that varies from 52 to 53 weeks.[4] In that case, the year-end must be on the same day of the week (e.g., the Tuesday falling closest to October 31 or the last Tuesday in October). The day of the week selected for ending the year will depend upon business considerations. For example, a retail business that is not open on Sundays may end its tax year on a Sunday so that it can take an inventory without interrupting business operations.

> **L0.1**
>
> Understand the relevance of the accounting period concept, the different types of accounting periods, and the limitations on their use.

EXAMPLE 1

Wade is in the business of selling farm supplies. His natural business year terminates at the end of October with the completion of harvesting. At the end of the fiscal year, Wade must take an inventory, which is most easily accomplished on a Tuesday. Therefore, Wade could adopt a 52–53 week tax year ending on the Tuesday closest to October 31. If Wade selects this method, the year-end date may fall in the following month if that Tuesday is closer to October 31. The tax year ending in 2011 will contain 52 weeks beginning on Wednesday, November 3, 2010, and ending on Tuesday, November 1, 2011. The tax year ending in 2012 will have 52 weeks beginning on Wednesday, November 2, 2011, and ending on Tuesday, October 30, 2012. ■

---

[1]See Chapters 4, 5, and 6.
[2]§ 441(c) and Reg. § 1.441–1(b)(1)(ii).
[3]Reg. § 1.441–1(e)(2).
[4]§ 441(f).

SPECIFIC PROVISIONS FOR PARTNERSHIPS, S CORPORATIONS, AND PERSONAL SERVICE CORPORATIONS

Partnerships and S Corporations

When a partner's tax year and the partnership's tax year differ, the partner will enjoy a deferral of income. This results because the partner reports his or her share of the partnership's income and deductions for the partnership's tax year ending within or with the partner's tax year.[5] For example, if the tax year of the partnership ends on January 31, a calendar year partner will not report partnership profits for the first 11 months of the partnership tax year until the following year. Therefore, partnerships are subject to special tax year requirements.

In general, the partnership tax year must be the same as the tax year of the majority interest partners. The **majority interest partners** are the partners who own a greater-than-50 percent interest in the partnership capital and profits. If there are no majority interest partners, the partnership must adopt the same tax year as its principal partners. A **principal partner** is a partner with a 5 percent or more interest in the partnership capital or profits.[6]

EXAMPLE 2

The RST Partnership is owned equally by Rose Corporation, Silver Corporation, and Tom. The partners have the following tax years.

	Partner's Tax Year Ending
Rose Corporation	June 30
Silver Corporation	June 30
Tom	December 31

The partnership's tax year must end on June 30. If Silver Corporation's as well as Tom's year ended on December 31, the partnership would be required to adopt a calendar year. ■

If the principal partners do not all have the same tax year and no majority of partners have the same tax year, the partnership must use a year that results in the *least aggregate deferral* of income.[7] Under the **least aggregate deferral method**, the different tax years of the principal partners are tested to determine which produces the least aggregate deferral. This is calculated by first multiplying the combined percentages of the principal partners with the same tax year by the months of deferral for the test year. Once this is done for each set of principal partners with the same tax year, the resulting products are summed to produce the aggregate deferral. After calculating the aggregate deferral for each of the test years, the test year with the smallest summation (the least aggregate deferral) is the tax year for the partnership.

EXAMPLE 3
THE BIG PICTURE

Return to the facts of *The Big Picture* on p. 18-2. The Code and Regulations eliminate the need for the Silver partners to bargain among themselves over the tax year-end. The partnership's tax year must end on November 30 because using that year-end results in the least aggregate deferral of partnership income as demonstrated below:

	Test for Tax Year Ending December 31		
	1	2	1 × 2
Partner's Year-End	Profit Percentage	Months Income Deferred	Aggregate Months of Deferral
Belinda 12–31	25%	0	0
Pearl, Inc. 11–30	35%	11	3.85
Tweety, Inc. 6–30	40%	6	2.40
			6.25

---

[5]Reg. § 1.706–1(a).
[6]§§ 706(b)(1)(B) and 706(b)(3).
[7]Reg. § 1.706–1(b)(3).

Test for Tax Year Ending November 30

	Partner's Year-End	Profit Percentage	Months Income Deferred	Aggregate Months of Deferral
Belinda	12–31	25%	1	0.25
Pearl, Inc.	11–30	35%	0	0
Tweety, Inc.	6–30	40%	7	2.80
				3.05

Test for Tax Year Ending June 30

	Partner's Year-End	Profit Percentage	Months Income Deferred	Aggregate Months of Deferral
Belinda	12–31	25%	6	1.50
Pearl, Inc.	11–30	35%	5	1.75
Tweety, Inc.	6–30	40%	0	0
				3.25

Generally, S corporations must adopt a calendar year.[8] However, partnerships and S corporations may *elect* an otherwise *impermissible year* under any of the following conditions:

- A business purpose for the year can be demonstrated.[9]
- The partnership's or S corporation's year results in a deferral of not more than three months' income, and the entity agrees to make required tax payments.[10]
- The entity retains the same year as was used for the fiscal year ending in 1987, provided the entity agrees to make required tax payments.

Business Purpose

The only business purpose for a fiscal year that the IRS has acknowledged is the need to conform the tax year to the natural business year of a business.[11] Generally, only seasonal businesses have a natural business year. For example, the natural business year for a department store may end on January 31, after Christmas returns have been processed and clearance sales have been completed.

Required Tax Payments

Under the required payments system, tax payments are due from a fiscal year partnership or S corporation by April 15 of each tax year.[12] The amount due is computed by applying the highest individual tax rate plus 1 percentage point to an estimate of the deferral period income. The deferral period runs from the close of the fiscal year to the end of the calendar year. Estimated income for this period is based on the average monthly earnings for the previous fiscal year. The amount due is reduced by the amount of required tax payments for the previous year.[13]

---

[8]§§ 1378(a) and (b).

[9]§§ 706(b)(1)(C) and 1378(b)(2).

[10]§ 444.

[11]Rev.Rul. 87–57, 1987–2 C.B. 117.

[12]§§ 444(c) and 7519. No payment is required if the calculated amount is $500 or less.

[13]§ 7519(b).

EXAMPLE 4

Brown, Inc., an S corporation, elected a fiscal year ending September 30. Bob is the only shareholder. For the fiscal year ending September 30, 2011, Brown earned $100,000. The required tax payment for the previous year was $5,000. The corporation must pay $4,000 by April 15, 2012, calculated as follows:

$$(\$100,000 \times {}^3\!/_{12} \times 36\%{}^*) - \$5,000 = \$4,000$$

*Maximum § 1 rate of 35% + 1%. ∎

WHO BENEFITS FROM THE CHANGE IN TAX YEAR?

A public accounting sole practitioner has reached a break-ing point. All of his clients use the calendar year to report income. Many of the clients are S corporations and part-nerships. His workload the first four months of the year is so heavy that it is putting the quality of his work at risk. He is considering asking some of his S corporations and partnerships to switch to a fiscal year ending September 30. The accountant believes that he can convince the shareholders and partners to make the change. Although the shareholders and partners would be subject to the "required tax payments" rules, the accountant will sell the plan by promising better service. Evaluate the plan pro-posed by the accountant.

Personal Service Corporations

A **personal service corporation (PSC)** is a corporation whose shareholder-employees provide personal services (e.g., medical, dental, legal, accounting, engineering, actuarial, consulting, or performing arts). Generally, a PSC must use a calendar year.[14] However, a PSC can *elect* a fiscal year under any of the following conditions:

- A business purpose for the year can be demonstrated.
- The PSC year results in a deferral of not more than three months' income, the corporation pays the shareholder-employee's salary during the portion of the calendar year after the close of the fiscal year, and the salary for that period is at least proportionate to the shareholder-employee's salary received for the preceding fiscal year.[15]
- The PSC retains the same year it used for the fiscal year ending in 1987, provided it satisfies the latter two requirements in the preceding option.

EXAMPLE 5

Nancy's corporation paid Nancy a salary of $120,000 during its fiscal year ending September 30, 2011. The corporation cannot satisfy the business purpose test for a fiscal year. The corporation can continue to use its fiscal year without any negative tax effects, provided Nancy receives at least $30,000 [(3 months/12 months) × $120,000] as salary during the period October 1 through December 31, 2011. ∎

If the salary test is not satisfied, the PSC can retain the fiscal year, but the corpora-tion's deduction for salary for the fiscal year is limited to the following:

---

[14]§ 441(i).   [15]§§ 444 and 280H.

$$A + A(F/N)$$

where A = Amount paid after the close of the fiscal year.
    F = Number of months in the fiscal year minus number of months from the end of the fiscal year to the end of the ongoing calendar year.
    N = Number of months from the end of the fiscal year to the end of the ongoing calendar year.

EXAMPLE 6

Assume the corporation in the previous example paid Nancy $10,000 of salary during the period October 1 through December 31, 2011. The deduction for Nancy's salary for the corporation's fiscal year ending September 30, 2012, is thus limited to $40,000 calculated as follows:

$$\$10,000 + \left[\$10,000\left(\frac{12-3}{3}\right)\right] = \$10,000 + \$30,000 = \$40,000 \quad \blacksquare$$

MAKING THE ELECTION

A taxpayer elects to use a calendar or fiscal year by the timely filing of his or her initial tax return. For all subsequent years, the taxpayer must use this same period unless approval for change is obtained from the IRS.[16]

CHANGES IN THE ACCOUNTING PERIOD

A taxpayer must obtain consent from the IRS before changing the tax year.[17] This power to approve or not to approve a change is significant in that it permits the IRS to issue authoritative administrative guidelines that must be met by taxpayers who wish to change their accounting period. An application for permission to change tax years must be made on Form 1128, Application for Change in Accounting Period. The application must be filed on or before the fifteenth day of the second calendar month following the close of the short period that results from the change in accounting period.[18]

EXAMPLE 7

Beginning in 2011, Gold Corporation, a calendar year taxpayer, would like to switch to a fiscal year ending March 31. The corporation must file Form 1128 by May 15, 2011. ■

IRS Requirements

The IRS will not grant permission for the change unless the taxpayer can establish a substantial business purpose for the request. One substantial business purpose is to change to a tax year that coincides with the *natural business year* (the completion of an annual business cycle). The IRS applies an objective gross receipts test to determine if the entity has a natural business year. At least 25 percent of the entity's gross receipts for the 12-month period must be realized in the final two months of the 12-month period for three consecutive years.[19]

---

[16]Reg. §§ 1.441–1(b)(3) and 1.441–1(b)(4).

[17]§ 442. Under certain conditions, corporations are allowed to change tax years without obtaining IRS approval. See Reg. § 1.442–1(c)(1).

[18]Reg. § 1.442–1(b)(1). In Example 7, the first period after the change in accounting period (January 1, 2011 through March 31, 2011) is less than a 12-month period and is referred to as a *short period*.

[19]Rev.Proc. 87–32, 1987–1 C.B. 131; Rev.Rul. 87–57, 1987–2 C.B. 117; and Rev.Proc. 2002–39, 2002–1 C.B. 1046.

EXAMPLE 8

A Virginia Beach motel had gross receipts as follows:

	2009	2010	2011
July–August receipts	$ 300,000	$250,000	$ 325,000
September 1–August 31 receipts	1,000,000	900,000	1,250,000
Receipts for final 2 months divided by receipts for 12 months	30.0%	27.8%	26.0%

Since it satisfies the natural business year test, the motel will be allowed to use a fiscal year ending August 31. ■

The IRS usually establishes certain conditions that the taxpayer must accept if the approval for change is to be granted. In particular, if the taxpayer has a net operating loss (NOL) for the short period, the IRS requires that the loss be carried forward; the loss cannot be carried back to prior years.[20] As you may recall (refer to Chapter 7), NOLs are ordinarily carried back for 2 years and forward for 20 years.

EXAMPLE 9

Parrot Corporation changed from a calendar year to a fiscal year ending September 30. The short-period return for the nine months ending September 30, 2011, reflected a $60,000 NOL. The corporation had taxable income for 2009 and 2010. As a condition for granting approval, the IRS requires Parrot to carry the loss forward rather than carrying the loss back to the two preceding years (the usual order for applying an NOL). ■

TAXABLE PERIODS OF LESS THAN ONE YEAR

A **short taxable year** (or **short period**) is a period of less than 12 calendar months. A taxpayer may have a short year for (1) the first income tax return, (2) the final income tax return, or (3) a change in the tax year. If the short period results from a change in the taxpayer's annual accounting period, the taxable income for the period must be annualized. Due to the progressive tax rate structure, taxpayers could reap benefits from a short-period return if some adjustments were not required. Thus, the taxpayer is required to do the following:

1. Annualize the short-period income.

$$\text{Annualized income} = \text{Short-period income} \times \frac{12}{\text{Number of months in the short period}}$$

2. Compute the tax on the annualized income.
3. Convert the tax on the annualized income to a short-period tax.

$$\text{Short-period income} = \text{Tax on annualized income} \times \frac{\text{Number of months in the short period}}{12}$$

EXAMPLE 10

Gray Corporation obtained permission to change from a calendar year to a fiscal year ending September 30, beginning in 2011. For the short period January 1 through September 30, 2011, the corporation's taxable income was $48,000. The relevant tax rates and the resultant short-period tax are as follows:

Amount of Taxable Income	Tax Rates
$1–$50,000	15% of taxable income
$50,001–$75,000	$7,500 plus 25% of taxable income in excess of $50,000

---

[20]Rev.Proc. 2002–39, 2002–1 C.B. 1046.

Calculation of Short-Period Tax

Annualized income
$$(\$48,000 \times {}^{12}/_9) = \underline{\$64,000}$$

Tax on annualized income
$$\$7,500 + .25(\$64,000 - \$50,000) =$$
$$\$7,500 + \$3,500 = \underline{\$11,000}$$

Short-period tax = $(\$11,000 \times {}^9/_{12}) = \underline{\$8,250}$

Annualizing the income increased the tax by $1,050:

Tax with annualizing	$ 8,250
Tax without annualizing (.15 × $48,000)	(7,200)
	$ 1,050

Rather than annualize the short-period income, the taxpayer can (1) elect to calculate the tax for a 12-month period beginning on the first day of the short period and (2) convert the tax in (1) to a short-period tax as follows:[21]

$$\frac{\text{Taxable income for short period}}{\text{Taxable income for the 12-month period}} \times \text{Tax on the 12 months of income}$$

> **EXAMPLE 11**
>
> Assume Gray Corporation's taxable income for the calendar year 2011 was $60,000. The tax on the full 12 months of income would have been $10,000 [$7,500 + .25($60,000 − $50,000)]. The short-period tax would be $8,000 [($48,000/$60,000) × $10,000]. Thus, if the corporation utilized this option, the tax for the short period would be $8,000 (rather than $8,250, as calculated in Example 10). ∎

For individuals, annualizing requires some special adjustments:[22]

- Deductions must be itemized for the short period (the standard deduction is not allowed).
- Personal and dependency exemptions must be prorated.

Fortunately, individuals rarely change tax years.

MITIGATION OF THE ANNUAL ACCOUNTING PERIOD CONCEPT

Several provisions in the Code are designed to give the taxpayer relief from the seemingly harsh results that may be produced by the combined effects of an arbitrary accounting period and a progressive rate structure. For example, under the NOL carryback and carryover rules, a loss in one year can be carried back and offset against taxable income for the preceding two years. Unused NOLs are then carried over for 20 years.[23] In addition, the Code provides special relief provisions for casualty losses pursuant to a disaster and for the reporting of insurance proceeds from destruction of crops.[24]

Farm Relief

Farmers and fishermen are often subject to wide fluctuations in income between years, some of which are due to the weather. Congress has provided these taxpayers a special method of computing their tax on income from farming or fishing. In the high-income years, these taxpayers can elect to compute their tax on income from farming or fishing as though it were earned equally in the three previous years.[25] Thus, the tax on the farming or fishing income for the year is the sum of the

---

[21]§§ 443(b)(1) and (2).
[22]§ 443(b)(3), § 443(c), and Reg. § 1.443–1(b).
[23]§ 172. Refer to Chapter 7.
[24]§§ 165(i) and 451(d). Refer to Chapter 7.
[25]§ 1301. The tax is calculated on Schedule J.

TAX *in*
the NEWS

EXECUTIVE COMPENSATION CLAWBACKS

In recent years, there has been a public outcry over the compensation of executives. With many companies receiving taxpayer-funded bailouts, both taxpayers and shareholders have demanded that executives repay the excessive amounts to the corporation. If executives are required to repay a portion of their salaries and bonuses, an executive's marginal tax rate may be greater in the year the income was received than in the year of repayment. This appears to be a situation that § 1341 should address. However, when the original amount received was based on an existing contract, the compensation was received under the executive's actual rights and is not income received under a mere claim of right. Therefore, the amount of the "clawback" is not eligible for § 1341 treatment.

additional tax that would have been due in the three previous years if one-third of the income had been earned in each of those years. This averaging system enables the taxpayer to avoid the higher marginal tax rates associated with a large amount of income received in one year.

The income pattern for farmers can also be disrupted by natural disasters that are covered by insurance. The disaster may occur and the **crop insurance proceeds** may be received in a year before the income from the crop would have been realized. Under these circumstances, § 451(d) permits the farmer to defer reporting the income until the year following the disaster. Section 451(e) provides similar relief when livestock must be sold on account of drought or other weather-related conditions.

Restoration of Amounts Received under a Claim of Right

The court-made **claim of right doctrine** applies when the taxpayer receives property as income and treats it as his or her own but a dispute arises over the taxpayer's rights to the income.[26] According to the doctrine, the taxpayer must include the amount as income in the year of receipt. The rationale for the doctrine is that the Federal government cannot await the resolution of all disputes before exacting a tax. As a corollary to the doctrine, if the taxpayer is later required to repay the funds, generally a deduction is allowed in the year of repayment.[27]

EXAMPLE 12

In 2011, Pedro received a $5,000 bónus computed as a percentage of profits. In 2012, Pedro's employer determined that the 2011 profits had been incorrectly computed, and Pedro had to refund the $5,000 in 2012. Pedro was required to include the $5,000 in his 2011 gross income, but he can claim a $5,000 deduction in 2012. ■

In Example 12 the transactions were a wash; that is, the income and deduction were the same ($5,000). Suppose, however, that Pedro was in the 35 percent tax bracket in 2011 but in the 15 percent bracket in 2012. Without some relief provision, the mistake would be costly to Pedro. He paid $1,750 tax in 2011 (.35 × $5,000), but the deduction reduced his tax liability in 2012 by only $750 (.15 × $5,000). The Code does provide the needed relief in such cases. Under § 1341, when income that has been taxed under the claim of right doctrine must later be repaid, in effect, the taxpayer gets to apply to the deduction the tax rate of the year that will produce the greatest tax benefit. Thus, in Example 12, the repayment in 2012 would reduce Pedro's 2012 tax liability by the higher 2011 rate (.35) applied to the $5,000. However, relief is provided only in cases where the tax is significantly different; that is, when the deduction for the amount previously included in income exceeds $3,000.

---

[26]*North American Consolidated Oil Co. v. Burnet,* 3 USTC ¶943, 11 AFTR 16, 52 S.Ct. 613 (USSC, 1932).

[27]*U.S. v. Lewis,* 51–1 USTC ¶9211, 40 AFTR 258, 71 S.Ct. 522 (USSC, 1951).

SPECIAL TAX RELIEF

A taxpayer who is required to report income in one year, but must repay the income in a subsequent year, is granted special tax relief. If the taxpayer is in a lower marginal tax bracket in the year the income is repaid than in the year it was received, the deduction reduces the tax for the year of repayment by using the higher tax rate that applied to the income when it was received.

In contrast, if a taxpayer takes a deduction in one year and receives a refund of the amount giving rise to the deduction in a subsequent year, the refund is taxed at the marginal tax rate in the year of refund. This is true even though the taxpayer's marginal tax rate in the year of receipt is higher than that in the year of the deduction.

Should both adjustments to income and adjustments to deductions receive the same tax relief? Or should neither situation be granted special relief?

18.2 ACCOUNTING METHODS

L0.2

Apply the cash method, accrual method, and hybrid method of accounting.

PERMISSIBLE METHODS

Section 446 requires the taxpayer to compute taxable income using the method of accounting regularly employed in keeping his or her books, provided the method clearly reflects income. The Code recognizes the following as generally permissible **accounting methods**:

- The cash receipts and disbursements method.
- The accrual method.
- A hybrid method (a combination of cash and accrual).

The Regulations refer to these alternatives as *overall methods* and add that the term *method of accounting* includes not only the taxpayer's overall method of accounting but also the accounting treatment of any item.[28]

Generally, any of the three methods of accounting may be used if the method is consistently employed and clearly reflects income. However, in most cases the taxpayer is required to use the accrual method for sales and cost of goods sold if inventories are an income-producing factor to the business.[29] Other situations in which the accrual method is required are discussed later. Special methods are also permitted for installment sales, long-term construction contracts, and farmers.

A taxpayer who has more than one trade or business may use a different method of accounting for each trade or business activity. Furthermore, a taxpayer may use one method of accounting to determine income from a trade or business and use another method to compute nonbusiness items of income and deductions.[30]

EXAMPLE 13

Linda operates a grocery store and owns stock and bonds. The sales and cost of goods sold from the grocery store must be computed by the accrual method because inventories are material. However, Linda can report her dividends and interest from the stocks and bonds under the cash method. ■

The Code grants the IRS broad powers to determine whether the taxpayer's accounting method *clearly reflects income*. Thus, if the method employed does not clearly reflect income, the IRS has the power to prescribe the method to be used by the taxpayer.[31]

[28]Reg. § 1.446–1(a)(1).
[29]Reg. § 1.446–1(a)(4)(i). As discussed subsequently, as a matter of administrative convenience, the IRS will permit taxpayers to use the cash method even though inventory is a material income-producing factor, if average annual gross receipts are not more than $1 million for the most recent three-year period.
[30]§ 446(d) and Reg. § 1.446–1(c)(1)(iv)(b).
[31]§ 446(b).

TAX in the NEWS

WHO WANTS TO BE A PRODUCER?

For many years, small businesses wanted to be considered service providers rather than producers of products. Service provider classification meant that the cash method could be used. Now, however, classification as a producer can be advantageous. As a result of the American Jobs Creation Act of 2004, producers can deduct 9 percent of their qualifying domestic production activities income in calculating taxable income for 2011. Thus, a company that develops advertising materials might argue that it is a producer rather than a provider of advertising services.

CASH RECEIPTS AND DISBURSEMENTS METHOD—CASH BASIS

Most individuals and many businesses use the cash basis to report income and deductions. The popularity of this method can largely be attributed to its simplicity and flexibility.

Under the **cash method**, income is not recognized until the taxpayer actually receives, or constructively receives, cash or its equivalent (e.g., the receipt of accounts receivable does not trigger income until collected). Cash is constructively received if it is available to the taxpayer.[32] Generally, a cash equivalent is anything with a fair market value, including a note receivable from a customer.

EXAMPLE 14
THE BIG PICTURE

Return to the facts of *The Big Picture* on p. 4-2 in Chapter 4. Recall that Dr. Cliff Payne has opened a dental practice as a sole proprietorship and does not accept credit cards. In the second year of his business, he adopts a new policy of requiring that his patients either pay cash at the time the services are performed or give him a note receivable with interest at the market rate. Generally, the notes can be sold to the local banks for 95% of their face amount. At the end of the second year, Dr. Payne has $60,000 in notes receivable from patients. The notes receivable are a cash equivalent and have a fair market value of $57,000 ($60,000 × 95%). Therefore, Dr. Payne must include the $57,000 in his gross income for this year. ∎

Deductions are generally permitted in the year of payment. Thus, year-end accounts payable and accrued expenses are not deducted in the determination of taxable income.

In many cases, a taxpayer using the cash method can choose the year in which a deduction is claimed simply by postponing or accelerating the payment of expenses. For fixed assets, however, the cash basis taxpayer claims deductions through depreciation or amortization, the same as an accrual basis taxpayer does. In addition, prepaid expenses must be capitalized and amortized if the life of the asset extends substantially beyond the end of the tax year.[33]

The Regulations have established a **one-year rule for prepaid expenses** that permits the taxpayer to deduct expenditures for rights that do not extend beyond the earlier of (1) 12 months after the first date on which the taxpayer realizes the right or (2) the end of the tax year following the year of payment. Both cash basis and accrual basis taxpayers are permitted to use the one-year rule.[34]

Restrictions on Use of the Cash Method

Using the cash method to measure income from a merchandising or manufacturing operation would often yield a distorted picture of the results of operations. Income for the period would largely be a function of when payments were made for goods or materials. Thus, the Regulations prohibit the use of the cash method (and require the accrual method) to measure sales and cost of goods sold if inventories are material to the business.[35]

---

[32]Reg. § 1.451–1(a). Refer to Chapter 4 for a discussion of constructive receipt.

[33]Reg. § 1.461–1(a)(1).

[34]Reg. § 1.263(a)–4(f). Refer to Chapter 6 for further discussion of the one-year rule.

[35]Reg. § 1.446–1(a)(4)(i).

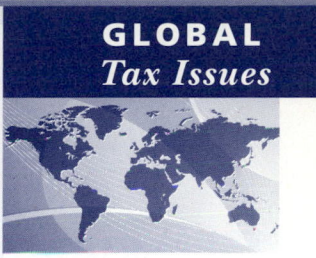

TAX ACCOUNTING METHODS AS AN INCENTIVE TO GO FOREIGN

GLOBAL Tax Issues

Some foreign countries allow a corporation to defer income by using tax accounting methods that are not permitted in the United States. For example, a producer or retailer may be allowed to use the cash method of accounting even though inventory is present. Under the cash method, the cost of goods sold is deducted in the tax year the goods are paid for, and income is not recognized until receivables are collected. Thus, if a U.S. corporation creates a foreign subsidiary in a country that permits the cash method in association with inventory, tax savings occur that would not be available in the United States. The corporation obtains additional deductions in the first year equal to the ending inventory and additional deferrals equal to the ending accounts receivable. The company would continue to benefit until it has no more receivables or inventory.

The prohibition on the use of the cash method if inventories are material and the rules regarding prepaid expenses (discussed previously) are intended to assure that annual income is clearly reflected. However, certain taxpayers may not use the cash method of accounting for Federal income tax purposes regardless of whether inventories are material. The accrual basis must be used to report the income earned by (1) a corporation (other than an S corporation), (2) a partnership with a corporate partner, and (3) a tax shelter. This accrual basis requirement has three exceptions:[36]

- A farming business.
- A qualified personal service corporation (a corporation performing services in health, law, engineering, architecture, accounting, actuarial science, performing arts, or consulting).
- An entity that is not a tax shelter whose average annual gross receipts for the most recent three-year period are $5 million or less.

As a matter of administrative convenience, the IRS will permit any entity with average annual gross receipts of not more than $1 million for the most recent three-year period to use a modified form of the cash method even if the taxpayer is buying and selling inventory. Sales can be reported on the cash method, but the cost of such inventoriable items is deductible only in the year of sale, or in the year the taxpayer actually pays for the inventoriable items, whichever is later.

Also as a matter of administrative convenience, the IRS will permit certain entities whose average annual gross receipts are greater than $1 million but are not more than $10 million for the most recent three-year period to use the cash method. However, under the $10 million exception, inventory on hand at the end of the tax year cannot be deducted until the inventory is sold (i.e., must be capitalized). Not eligible for the cash method under the $10 million exception are entities whose principal business activity (the activity producing the largest percentage of gross receipts) is selling goods, manufacturing, mining, and certain publishing activities. Also not eligible are the C corporations, partnerships, and tax shelters discussed above that must use the accrual method. The major beneficiaries of the $10 million exception are small construction companies and small service businesses that sell some goods in conjunction with the services provided.[37]

Special Rules for Small Farmers

Although inventories are material to farming operations and the accrual method would appear to be required, the IRS long ago created an exception to the general rule that allows small farmers to use the cash method of accounting.[38] The purpose of the exception is to relieve the small farmer from the bookkeeping burden of accrual accounting. Generally, this exception applies to unincorporated farms and closely held farming corporations with gross receipts for the year of less than $25 million.[39]

---

[36]§§ 448(a) and 448(b). For this purpose, the hybrid method of accounting is considered the same as the cash method.

[37]Rev.Proc. 2001–10, 2001–1 C.B. 272, and Rev.Proc. 2002–28, 2002–1 C.B. 815.

[38]Reg. § 1.471–6(a).

[39]See §§ 447(c) and 464.

GLOBAL
Tax Issues

CHANGES IN THE TAX RATES LEAD TO INCOME SHIFTING

In 2006, statistical evidence indicated that the German economy was booming. On further analysis of the data, however, it became clear that businesses were taking steps to shift their income from 2007 to 2006. Generally, businesses do not wish to accelerate their income because their taxes on the income will also be accelerated. In this case, though, German income tax rates were to increase in 2007. For many companies, the tax savings were worth the earlier-than-necessary recognition of the income.

Source: Adapted from Brian Wesbury, "A One-Year Wonder; Germany Is Booming, Pulling the Rest of Europe Along. Or Is It?" *Newsweek*, International Edition, March 12, 2007.

Cash method farmers must nevertheless capitalize their costs of raising trees that have a preproduction period of more than two years.[40] Thus, an apple farmer generally must capitalize the costs of raising the trees until they produce apples in merchantable quantities. However, to simplify the farmer's tax accounting, the cash method farmer is given an option: the preproduction cost of the trees can be expensed if the taxpayer elects to use the alternative depreciation system (refer to Chapter 8) for all the farming assets.

Farmers who produce crops that take more than a year from planting to harvesting (e.g., pineapples) can elect to use the crop method to report the income. Under the **crop method**, the costs of raising the crop are capitalized as those costs are incurred and then deducted in the year the income from the crop is realized.[41] This method is analogous to the completed contract method used by contractors (discussed later in this chapter).

Generally, a cash basis farmer must capitalize the purchase price of an animal, whether it is acquired for sale or for breeding. However, the cost of raising the animal can be expensed.[42]

ACCRUAL METHOD

All Events Test for Income

Under the **accrual method**, an item is generally included in gross income for the year in which it is earned, regardless of when the income is collected. An item of income is earned when (1) all the events have occurred to fix the taxpayer's right to receive the income and (2) the amount of income (the amount the taxpayer has a right to receive) can be determined with reasonable accuracy.[43]

EXAMPLE 15

Andre, a calendar year taxpayer who uses the accrual basis of accounting, was to receive a bonus equal to 6% of Blue Corporation's net income for its fiscal year ending each June 30. For the fiscal year ending June 30, 2011, Blue Corporation had net income of $240,000, and for the six months ending December 31, 2011, the corporation's net income was $150,000. Andre will report $14,400 (.06 × $240,000) for 2011 because his right to the amount became fixed when Blue Corporation's year closed. However, Andre would not accrue income based on the corporation's profits for the last six months of 2011 since his right to the income does not accrue until the close of the corporation's tax year. ∎

An accrual basis taxpayer's amount of income and the tax year the income is recognized are based on his or her right to receive the income. Thus, the fair market value of a receivable is irrelevant.

EXAMPLE 16

Marcey, an accrual basis taxpayer, has provided services to clients and has the right to receive $60,000. The clients have signed notes receivable to Marcey that have a fair market value of $57,000. Marcey must include $60,000, the amount she has the right to receive, in her gross income, rather than the fair market value of the notes of $57,000. ∎

---

[40]§ 263A(d).
[41]Reg. §§ 1.61–4 and 1.162–12(a).

[42]Reg. § 1.162–12(a).
[43]Reg. § 1.451–1(a). Refer to Chapter 4 for further discussion of the accrual basis.

As discussed in Chapter 4, when an accrual basis taxpayer receives prepaid income for services that will not all be earned by the end of the tax year following the tax year of receipt, generally the income that is not earned by the end of the year of receipt must be allocated to the following year.

EXAMPLE 17

Troy sells computers and two-year service contracts on the computers. On November 1, 2011, Troy sold a 24-month service contract and received $240. He recognizes $20 gross income in 2011 ($240 × $^2/_{24}$) and $220 ($240 − $20) in 2012. ∎

However, the deferral of prepaid income is not available for prepaid rent and prepaid interest.

In a situation where the accrual basis taxpayer's right to income is being contested and the income has not yet been collected, generally no income is recognized until the dispute has been settled.[44] Before the settlement, "all of the events have not occurred that fix the right to receive the income."

All Events and Economic Performance Tests for Deductions

An **all events test** applies to accrual basis deductions. A deduction cannot be claimed until (1) all the events have occurred to create the taxpayer's liability and (2) the amount of the liability can be determined with reasonable accuracy.[45] Once these requirements are satisfied, the deduction will be permitted only if economic performance has occurred.[46]

The **economic performance test** addresses situations in which the taxpayer has either of the following obligations:

1. To pay for services or property to be provided in the future.
2. To provide services or property (other than money) in the future.

When services or property are to be provided to the taxpayer in the future (situation 1), economic performance occurs when the property or services are actually provided by the other party.

EXAMPLE 18

An accrual basis calendar year taxpayer, JAB, Inc., promoted a boxing match held in the company's arena on December 31, 2011. CLN, Inc., had contracted to clean the arena for $5,000, but did not actually perform the work until January 1, 2012. JAB, Inc., did not pay the $5,000 until 2013. Although financial accounting rules would require JAB, Inc., to accrue the $5,000 cleaning expense in 2011 to match the revenues from the fight, the economic performance test was not satisfied until 2012, when CLN, Inc., performed the service. Thus, JAB, Inc., must deduct the expense in 2012. ∎

If the taxpayer is obligated to provide property or services (situation 2), economic performance occurs (and thus the deduction is allowed) in the year the taxpayer provides the property or services.

EXAMPLE 19

Copper Corporation, an accrual basis taxpayer, is in the strip mining business. According to the contract with the landowner, the company must reclaim the land. The estimated cost of reclaiming land mined in 2011 was $500,000, but the land was not actually reclaimed until 2013. The all events test was satisfied in 2011. The obligation existed, and the amount of the liability could be determined with reasonable accuracy. However, the economic performance test was not satisfied until 2013. Therefore, the deduction is not allowed until 2013.[47] ∎

The economic performance test is waived, and thus year-end accruals can be deducted, if all the following conditions (*recurring item exception*) are met:

[44]*Burnet v. Sanford & Brooks Co.*, 2 USTC ¶636, 9 AFTR 603, 51 S.Ct. 150 (USSC, 1931).
[45]§ 461(h)(4).
[46]§ 461(h).
[47]See § 468 for an elective method for reporting reclamation costs.

TAX *in*
the NEWS

PAYMENT IS NOT ECONOMIC PERFORMANCE

In recent pronouncements, the IRS has reiterated the point that when an accrual basis taxpayer has contracted to receive future services whose cost is deductible, the time for the deduction is when economic performance is satisfied. Moreover, economic performance can occur before or after the taxpayer pays for the services. Generally, economic per-formance is satisfied when the other party provides the ser-vices. If the taxpayer pays for the services before they are provided, the taxpayer has acquired an asset (prepaid expense). The deduction for the cost of the asset is not allowed until the services are actually received, unless the requirements for the recurring item exception are satisfied.

- The obligation exists and the amount of the liability can be reasonably esti-mated.
- Economic performance occurs within a reasonable period (but not later than 8½ months after the close of the taxable year).
- The item is recurring in nature and is treated consistently by the taxpayer.
- Either the accrued item is not material, or accruing it results in a better matching of revenues and expenses.

EXAMPLE 20

Green Corporation often sells goods that are on hand but cannot be shipped for another week. Thus, the sales account usually includes revenues for some items that have not been shipped at year-end. Green Corporation is obligated to pay shipping costs. Although the company's obligation for shipping costs can be determined with reasonable accuracy, economic performance is not satisfied until Green (or its agent) actually delivers the goods. However, accruing shipping costs on sold items will better match expenses with revenues for the period. Therefore, the company should be allowed to accrue the shipping costs on items sold but not shipped at year-end. ■

The economic performance test as set forth in the Code does not address all possible accrued expenses. That is, in some cases, the taxpayer incurs cost even though no property or services were received. In these instances, according to the Regulations, economic performance generally is not satisfied until the liability is paid. The following liabilities are cases in which payment is generally the only means of satisfying economic performance:[48]

1. Workers' compensation.
2. Torts.
3. Breach of contract.
4. Violation of law.
5. Rebates and refunds.
6. Awards, prizes, and jackpots.
7. Insurance, warranty, and service contracts.[49]
8. Taxes.

EXAMPLE 21

Yellow Corporation sold defective merchandise that injured a customer. Yellow admit-ted liability in 2011, but did not pay the claim until January 2012. The customer's tort claim cannot be deducted until it is paid. ■

However, items (5) through (8) above are eligible for the aforementioned recur-ring item exception.

EXAMPLE 22

Pelican Corporation filed its 2011 state income tax return in March 2012. At the time the return was filed, Pelican was required to pay an additional $5,000. The state taxes are

---

[48]Reg. §§ 1.461–4(g)(2)–(6) and 1.461–5(c).

[49]This item applies to contracts the taxpayer enters into for his or her own protection, rather than the taxpayer's liability as insurer, warrantor, or ser-vice provider.

FINANCIAL DISCLOSURE *Insights* | TAX DEFERRALS FROM RESERVES

The tax law generally applies the economic performance test in determining when an expense is deductible. Accordingly, the use of reserves for financial accounting purposes does not carry over to the tax return. When a business creates a reserve, say, to account for warranty obligations to customers or vacation pay for employees, book expenses are allowed, but the corresponding tax deduction usually is delayed until an expenditure is actually incurred. The temporary book-tax difference typically creates or adds to a deferred tax asset on the entity's balance sheet.

Deferred tax assets and liabilities are classified as *current* or *noncurrent* for balance sheet purposes. This classification is determined by the following:

- The nature of the underlying asset; for example, deferral of a bad debt relates to an account receivable, typically a current asset.

- Any knowledge by the entity as to when the required expenditure will occur; for example, as to the timing and amounts of a legal settlement or award.

For instance, suppose that Best Buy sells a product and a three-year warranty contract to provide maintenance to the customer. In the simplest case, one-third of the costs associated with the contract are deductible in the year that the contract is sold and used by the customer. Of the remaining warranty costs, one-half generates a current deferred tax asset (the costs will actually be incurred within the next tax year), and one-half generates a noncurrent deferred tax asset (for the third contract year).

Current versions of the related IFRS provisions eliminate the classification of deferred tax assets as current or noncurrent. Under IAS 1, all deferred tax assets are deemed to be noncurrent.

---

eligible for the recurring item exception. Thus, the $5,000 of state income taxes can be deducted on the corporation's 2011 Federal tax return. The deduction is allowed because all the events had occurred to fix the liability as of the end of 2011, the payment was made within 8½ months after the end of the tax year, the item is recurring in nature, and allowing the deduction in 2011 produces a good matching of revenues and expenses. ∎

Reserves

Generally, the all events and economic performance tests will prevent the use of reserves (e.g., for product warranty expense) frequently used in financial accounting to match expenses with revenues. However, small banks are allowed to use a bad debt reserve.[50] Furthermore, an accrual basis taxpayer in a service business is permitted to not accrue revenue that appears uncollectible based on experience. In effect, this approach indirectly allows a reserve.[51]

HYBRID METHOD

A **hybrid method** of accounting involves the use of more than one method. For example, a taxpayer who uses the accrual basis to report sales and cost of goods sold but uses the cash basis to report other items of income and expense is employing a hybrid method. The Code permits the use of a hybrid method provided the taxpayer's income is clearly reflected.[52] A taxpayer who uses the accrual method for business expenses must also use the accrual method for business income (the cash method may not be used for income items if the taxpayer's expenses are accounted for under the accrual method).

It may be preferable for a business that is required to report sales and cost of goods sold on the accrual method to report other items of income and expense under the cash method. The cash method permits greater flexibility in the timing of income and expense recognition.

---

[50]§ 585.
[51]§ 448(d)(5).
[52]§ 446(c).

CHANGE OF METHOD

The taxpayer, in effect, makes an election to use a particular accounting method when an initial tax return is filed using that method. If a subsequent change in method is desired, the taxpayer must obtain the permission of the IRS. The request for change is made on Form 3115, Application for Change in Accounting Method. Generally, the form must be filed within the taxable year of the desired change.[53]

As previously mentioned, the term *accounting method* encompasses not only the overall accounting method used by the taxpayer (the cash or accrual method) but also the treatment of any material item of income or deduction.[54] Thus, a change in the method of deducting property taxes from a cash basis to an accrual basis that results in a deduction for taxes in a different year constitutes a change in an accounting method. Another example of an accounting method change is a change involving the method or basis used in the valuation of inventories. However, a change in treatment resulting from a change in the underlying facts does not constitute a change in the taxpayer's method of accounting.[55] For example, a change in employment contracts so that an employee accrues one day of vacation pay for each month of service rather than 12 days of vacation pay for a full year of service is a change in the underlying facts and is therefore not an accounting method change.

Correction of an Error

A change in accounting method should be distinguished from the *correction of an error*. The taxpayer can correct an error (by filing amended returns) without permission, and the IRS can simply adjust the taxpayer's liability if an error is discovered on audit of the return. Some examples of errors are incorrect postings, errors in the calculation of tax liability or tax credits, deductions of business expense items that are actually personal, and omissions of income and deductions.[56] Unless the taxpayer or the IRS corrects the error within the statute of limitations, the taxpayer's total lifetime taxable income will be overstated or understated by the amount of the error.

Change from an Incorrect Method

An *incorrect accounting method* is the consistent (year-after-year) use of an incorrect rule to report an item of income or expense. The incorrect accounting method generally will not affect the taxpayer's total lifetime income (unlike the error). That is, an incorrect method has a self-balancing mechanism. For example, deducting freight on inventory in the year the goods are purchased, rather than when the inventory is sold, is an incorrect accounting method. The total cost of goods sold over the life of the business is not affected, but the year-to-year income is incorrect.[57]

If a taxpayer is employing an incorrect method of accounting, permission must be obtained from the IRS to change to a correct method. An incorrect method is not treated as a mechanical error that can be corrected by merely filing an amended tax return.

The tax return preparer as well as the taxpayer will be subject to penalties if the tax return is prepared using an incorrect method of accounting and permission for a change to a correct method has not been requested.[58]

Net Adjustments Due to Change in Accounting Method

In the year of a change in accounting method, some items of income and expense may have to be adjusted to prevent the change from distorting taxable income.

EXAMPLE 23

In 2011, White Corporation, with consent from the IRS, switched from the cash to the accrual basis for reporting sales and cost of goods sold. The corporation's accrual basis gross profit for the year was computed as follows:

---

[53]Rev.Proc. 2002–9, 2002–1 C.B. 327. See Rev.Proc. 2008–52, I.R.B. No. 36, 587, which permits certain changes in methods requested with a timely filed return.

[54]Reg. § 1.446–1(a)(1).

[55]Reg. § 1.446–1(e)(2)(ii).

[56]Reg. § 1.446–1(e)(2)(ii)(b).

[57]But see *Korn Industries v. U.S.*, 76–1 USTC ¶9354, 37 AFTR 2d 76–1228, 532 F.2d 1352 (Ct.Cls., 1976).

[58]§ 446(f). See *South-Western Federal Taxation: Corporations, Partnerships, Estates, and Trusts*, Chapter 17.

Sales		$100,000
Beginning inventory	$ 15,000	
Purchases	60,000	
Less: Ending inventory	(10,000)	
Cost of goods sold		(65,000)
Gross profit		$ 35,000

At the end of the previous year, White Corporation had accounts receivable of $25,000 and accounts payable for merchandise of $34,000. The accounts receivable from the previous year in the amount of $25,000 were never included in gross income since White was on the cash basis and did not recognize the uncollected receivables. In the current year, the $25,000 was not included in the accrual basis sales since the sales were made in a prior year. Therefore, a $25,000 adjustment to income is required to prevent the receivables from being omitted from income.

The corollary of the failure to recognize a prior year's receivables is the failure to recognize a prior year's accounts payable. The beginning of the year's accounts payable were not included in the current or prior year's purchases. Thus, a deduction for the $34,000 was not taken in either year and is therefore included as an adjustment to income for the period of change.

An adjustment is also required to reflect the $15,000 beginning inventory that White deducted (due to the use of a cash method of accounting) in the previous year. In this instance, the cost of goods sold during the year of change was increased by the beginning inventory and resulted in a double deduction.

The net adjustment due to the change in accounting method is computed as follows:

Beginning inventory (deducted in prior and current year)	$ 15,000
Beginning accounts receivable (omitted from income)	25,000
Beginning accounts payable (omitted from deductions)	(34,000)
Net increase in taxable income	$ 6,000

■

Disposition of the Net Adjustment

Required changes in accounting methods are the result of an IRS examination. The IRS usually will examine all years that are open under the statute of limitations. Generally, this means that the three preceding years are examined. The IRS will not require a change unless the net adjustment is positive. That adjustment generally must be included in gross income for the year of the change. Additional tax and interest on the tax will be due. However, if the adjustment is greater than $3,000, the taxpayer can elect to calculate the tax by spreading the adjustment over one or more previous years.[59] The election is beneficial if the taxpayer's marginal tax rate for the prior years is lower than the marginal tax rate for the year of the change.

To encourage taxpayers to *voluntarily* change from incorrect methods and to facilitate changes from one correct method to another, the IRS generally allows the taxpayer to spread a positive adjustment into future years. One-fourth of the adjustment is applied to the year of the change, and one-fourth of the adjustment is applied to each of the next three taxable years. A negative adjustment can be deducted in the year of the change.[60]

EXAMPLE 24

White Corporation in Example 23 voluntarily changed from an incorrect method (the cash basis was incorrect because inventories were material to the business) to a correct method. The company must add $1,500 (¼ × $6,000 positive adjustment) to its 2011, 2012, 2013, and 2014 income. ■

---

[59]§ 481(b). See also Notice 98–31, 1998–1 C.B. 1165.   [60]Rev.Proc. 2002–9, 2002–1 C.B. 327, and Rev.Proc. 2002–19, 2002–1 C.B. 696.

CHANGE IN ACCOUNTING METHOD

The IRS faces a difficult choice when it deals with taxpayers who use incorrect accounting methods. On the one hand, the taxpayer who has used an incorrect accounting method may be just as culpable as a person who has omitted income or taken an improper deduction. On the other hand, it is often difficult to discover that a taxpayer is using an incorrect accounting method. Therefore, the IRS relies to some extent on self-reporting by taxpayers. The Service encourages voluntary changes in incorrect accounting methods by waiving penalties for underpayment of prior years' taxes and permitting the taxpayer, in effect, to pay the related taxes over a four-year period. Is this equitable treatment?

18.3 SPECIAL ACCOUNTING METHODS

Generally, accrual basis taxpayers recognize income when goods are sold and shipped to the customer. Cash basis taxpayers generally recognize income from a sale on the collection of cash from the customer. The tax law provides special accounting methods for certain installment sales and long-term contracts. These special methods were enacted, in part, to assure that the tax will be due when the taxpayer is best able to pay the tax.

INSTALLMENT METHOD

LO.4

Determine when the installment method of accounting can be utilized and apply the related calculation techniques.

Under the general rule for computing the gain or loss from the sale of property, the taxpayer recognizes the entire amount of gain or loss upon the sale or other disposition of the property.

EXAMPLE 25

Mark sells property to Fran for $10,000 cash plus Fran's note (fair market value and face amount of $90,000). Mark's basis for the property was $15,000. Gain or loss is computed under either the cash or accrual basis as follows:

Selling price	
Cash down payment	$ 10,000
Note receivable	90,000
	$100,000
Basis in the property	(15,000)
Realized gain	$ 85,000

In Example 25, the general rule for recognizing gain or loss requires Mark to pay a substantial amount of tax on the gain in the year of sale even though he received only $10,000 cash. Congress enacted the installment sales provisions to prevent this sort of hardship by allowing the taxpayer to spread the gain from installment sales over the collection period. The installment method is a very important planning tool because of the tax deferral possibilities.

Eligibility and Calculations

The **installment method** applies to *gains* (but not losses) from the sale of property by a taxpayer who will receive at least one payment *after* the year of sale. For many years, practically all gains from the sale of property were eligible for the installment method. However, over the years, the Code has been amended to *deny* the use of the installment method for the following:[61]

---
[61]§§ 453(b), (i), and (l).

| TAX *in* the *NEWS* | SEARCHING FOR THE GOLD IN ACCOUNTING METHOD CHANGES |

A negative amount due to a change in accounting method is like gold to the client because it can result in an immediate refund of taxes paid in prior years. This possibility has led to the development of a specialized service called "cost segregation." Consultants analyze a company's asset classifications to determine whether some costs that were capitalized as part of the cost of a building should have been treated as tangible personal property. The cost recovery period for tangible personal property is much shorter than that for buildings. Therefore, if a client classified costs as part of a building when the costs should have been capitalized as equipment, the cost recovery in those prior years was understated. The correction is achieved by changing the taxpayer's accounting method for such items, increasing accumulated depreciation, and creating a negative adjustment to income due to the change in accounting method. The result is a refund of taxes overpaid in prior years.

- Gains on property held for sale in the ordinary course of business.
- Depreciation recapture under § 1245 or § 1250.
- Gains on stocks or securities traded on an established market.

As an exception to the first item, the installment method may be used to report gains from sales of the following:[62]

- Time-share units (e.g., the right to use real property for two weeks each year).
- Residential lots (if the seller is not to make any improvements).
- Any property used or produced in the trade or business of farming.

The Nonelective Aspect

As a general rule, eligible sales *must* be reported by the installment method.[63] A special election is required to report the gain by any other method of accounting (see the discussion in a subsequent section of this chapter).

Computing the Gain for the Period

The gain reported on each sale is computed by the following formula:

$$\frac{\text{Total gain}}{\text{Contract price}} \times \text{Payments received} = \text{Recognized gain}$$

The taxpayer must compute each variable as follows:

1. *Total gain* is the selling price reduced by selling expenses and the adjusted basis of the property. The selling price is the total consideration received by the seller, including notes receivable from the buyer and the seller's liabilities assumed by the buyer.
2. *Contract price* is the selling price less the seller's liabilities that are assumed by the buyer. Generally, the contract price is the amount, other than interest, the seller will receive from the purchaser.
3. *Payments received* are the collections on the contract price received in the tax year. This generally is equal to the cash received less the interest income collected for the period. If the buyer pays any of the seller's expenses, the seller regards the amount paid as a payment received.

---

[62]§ 453(l)(2).   [63]§ 453(a).

TAX in the NEWS

SELLER FINANCING IS POPULAR IN TROUBLED TIMES

As financial institutions are applying stringent loan requirements and real estate investors are anxious to sell, seller financing is becoming more common. In other words, instead of the financing being done by a financial institution, the seller of the property finances the transaction. The seller receives a down payment and a mortgage for the balance on the contract. If the buyer turns out to be unable to pay, the seller regains ownership of the property. Thus, even under this worst case scenario, the seller is still in a better position than if the original sale had not been made.

EXAMPLE 26

The seller is not a dealer, and the facts are as follows:

Sales price		
Cash down payment	$ 1,000	
Seller's mortgage assumed	3,000	
Notes payable to the seller	13,000	$ 17,000
Selling expenses		(500)
Seller's basis		(10,000)
Total gain		$ 6,500

The contract price is $14,000 ($17,000 − $3,000). Assuming the $1,000 is the only payment in the year of sale, the recognized gain in that year is computed as follows:

$$\frac{\$6,500 \text{ total gain}}{\$14,000 \text{ contract price}} \times \$1,000 = \$464 \text{ (gain recognized in year of sale)} \quad \blacksquare$$

If the sum of the seller's basis and selling expenses is less than the liabilities assumed by the buyer, the difference must be added to the contract price and to the payments (treated as *deemed payments*) received in the year of sale.[64] This adjustment to the contract price is required so that the ratio of total gain to contract price will not be greater than one. The adjustment also accelerates the reporting of income from the deemed payments.

EXAMPLE 27

Assume the same facts as in Example 26, except that the seller's basis in the property is only $2,000. The total gain, therefore, is $14,500 [$17,000 − ($2,000 + $500)]. Payments in the year of sale are $1,500 and are calculated as follows:

Down payment	$1,000
Excess of mortgage assumed over seller's basis and selling expenses ($3,000 − $2,000 − $500)	500
	$1,500

The contract price is $14,500 [$17,000 (selling price) − $3,000 (seller's mortgage assumed) + $500 (excess of mortgage assumed over seller's basis and selling expenses)]. The gain recognized in the year of sale is computed as follows:

$$\frac{\$14,500 \text{ total gain}}{\$14,500 \text{ contract price}} \times \$1,500 = \$1,500$$

In subsequent years, all amounts the seller collects on the note principal ($13,000) will be recognized gain ($13,000 × 100%). ■

As previously discussed, gains attributable to ordinary income recapture under §§ 1245 and 1250 are *ineligible* for installment reporting. Therefore, the § 1245 or

---

[64]Temp.Reg. § 15a.453–1(b)(3)(i).

§ 1250 gain realized must be recognized in the year of sale, and the installment sale gain is the remaining gain.

EXAMPLE 28

Olaf sold an apartment building for $50,000 cash and a $75,000 note due in two years. Olaf's cost of the property was $90,000, and he had deducted depreciation of $65,000, $40,000 of which was in excess of what the straight-line amount would have been. Thus, the basis in the property was $25,000, and he recaptured $40,000 ordinary income under § 1250.

Olaf's realized gain is $100,000 ($125,000 − $25,000), and the $40,000 recapture must be recognized in the year of sale. Of the $60,000 remaining § 1231 gain, $24,000 must be recognized in the year of sale:

$$\frac{\text{§ 1231 gain}}{\text{Contract price}} \times \text{Payments received} = \frac{\$125,000 - \$25,000 - \$40,000}{\$125,000} \times \$50,000$$

$$= \frac{\$60,000}{\$125,000} \times \$50,000 = \$24,000$$

The remaining realized gain of $36,000 ($60,000 − $24,000) will be recognized as the $75,000 note is collected. ∎

Character of the Gain on Depreciable Real Estate

As discussed in Chapter 17, recognized gains from the sale of depreciable real estate may be subject to a 25 percent tax rate. The gain to the extent of straight-line depreciation taken is subject to the special rate and is referred to as "unrecaptured § 1250 gain." The recognized gain in excess of the depreciation is a § 1231 gain eligible for the 15 percent rate. Under the installment sale rules, when the sale results in both 25% gain and 15% gain, the 25% gain is reported first and then the 15% gain.

EXAMPLE 29

Continuing with the facts in Example 28, the realized gain was $100,000, of which $40,000 was § 1250 ordinary income. The straight-line depreciation would have been $25,000 (total depreciation of $65,000 less excess depreciation of $40,000). Therefore, the unrecaptured § 1250 gain is $25,000. The recognized installment gain in the year of sale of $24,000 was less than the unrecaptured § 1250 gain of $25,000. Therefore, the $24,000 recognized gain in the year of sale is subject to the 25% tax rate. ∎

Imputed Interest

If a deferred payment contract for the sale of property with a selling price greater than $3,000 does not contain a reasonable interest rate, a reasonable rate is imputed.[65] The imputing of interest effectively restates the selling price of the property to equal the sum of the payments at the date of the sale and the discounted present value of the future payments. The difference between the present value of a future payment and the payment's face amount is taxed as interest income, as discussed in the following paragraphs. Thus, the **imputed interest** rules prevent sellers of capital assets from increasing the selling price to reflect the equivalent of unstated interest on deferred payments and thereby converting ordinary (interest) income into long-term capital gains. In addition, the imputed interest rules are important because they affect the timing of income recognition.

Generally, if the contract does not charge at least the Federal rate, interest will be imputed at the Federal rate. The Federal rate is the interest rate the Federal government pays on new borrowing and is published monthly by the IRS.[66]

---

[65]§§ 483 and 1274.

[66]§ 1274(d)(1). There are three Federal rates: short term (not over three years), midterm (over three years but not over nine years), and long term (over nine years).

As a general rule, the buyer and seller must account for interest on the accrual basis with semiannual compounding.[67] Requiring the use of the accrual basis assures that the seller's interest income and the buyer's interest expense are reported in the same tax year. Under pre-1984 law, the cash basis seller did not report interest income until it was actually collected, but an accrual basis buyer could deduct the interest as it accrued. The following example illustrates the calculation and amortization of imputed interest.

EXAMPLE 30

Peggy, a cash basis taxpayer, sold land on January 1, 2011, for $200,000 cash and $6 million due on December 31, 2012, with 5% interest payable December 31, 2011, and December 31, 2012. At the time of the sale, the Federal rate was 8% (compounded semiannually). Because Peggy did not charge at least the Federal rate, interest will be imputed at 8% (compounded semiannually).

Date	Payment	Present Value (at 8%) on 1/1/2011	Imputed Interest
12/31/2011	$ 300,000	$ 277,500	$ 22,500
12/31/2012	6,300,000	5,386,500	913,500
	$6,600,000	$5,664,000	$936,000

Thus, the selling price will be restated to $5,864,000 ($200,000 + $5,664,000) rather than $6,200,000 ($200,000 + $6,000,000), and Peggy will recognize interest income in accordance with the following amortization schedule:

	Beginning Balance	Interest Income (at 8%)*	Received	Ending Balance
2011	$5,664,000	$462,182	$ 300,000	$5,826,182
2012	5,826,182	473,818	6,300,000	–0–

*Compounded semiannually.   ■

Congress has created several exceptions regarding the rate at which interest is imputed and the method of accounting for the interest income and expense. The general rules and exceptions are summarized in Concept Summary 18.1.

Related-Party Sales of Nondepreciable Property

If the Code did not contain special rules, a taxpayer could make an installment sale of property to a related party (e.g., a family member) who would obtain a basis in the property equal to the purchase price (the fair market value of the property). Then, the purchasing family member could immediately sell the property to an unrelated party for cash with no recognized gain or loss (the amount realized would equal the basis). The related-party purchaser would not pay the installment note to the selling family member until a later year or years. The net result would be that the family has the cash, but no taxable gain is recognized until the intrafamily transfer of the cash (when the purchasing family member makes payments on the installment note).

Under special rules designed to combat the scheme described above, the proceeds from the subsequent sale (the second sale) by the purchasing family member are treated as though they were used to pay the installment note due the selling

---

[67]§§ 1274(a), 1273(a), and 1272(a).

CONCEPT SUMMARY 18.1

Interest on Installment Sales

	Imputed Interest Rate
General rule	Federal rate
Exceptions:	
• Principal amount not over $2.8 million.[1]	Lesser of Federal rate or 9%
• Sale of land (with a calendar year ceiling of $500,000) between family members (the seller's spouse, brothers, sisters, ancestors, or lineal descendants).[2]	Lesser of Federal rate or 6%

	Method of Accounting for Interest	
	Seller's Interest Income	**Buyer's Interest Expense**
General rule[3]	Accrual	Accrual
Exceptions:		
• Total payments under the contract are $250,000 or less.[4]	Taxpayer's overall method	Taxpayer's overall method
• Sale of a farm (sales price of $1 million or less).[5]	Taxpayer's overall method	Taxpayer's overall method
• Sale of a principal residence.[6]	Taxpayer's overall method	Taxpayer's overall method
• Sale for a note with a principal amount of not over $2 million, the seller is on the cash basis, the property sold is not inventory, and the buyer agrees to report expense by the cash method.[7]	Cash	Cash

[1]§ 1274A(b). This amount is adjusted annually for inflation. For 2011, the amount is $5,201,300.
[2]§§ 1274(c)(3)(F) and 483(e).
[3]§§ 1274(a) and 1272(a)(3).
[4]§§ 1274(c)(3)(C) and 483.
[5]§§ 1274(c)(3)(A) and 483.
[6]§§ 1274(c)(3)(B) and 483.
[7]§ 1274A(c). This amount is adjusted annually for inflation. For 2011, the amount is $3,715,200.

family member (the first sale). As a result, the recognition of gain from the original sale between the related parties is accelerated.[68]

However, even with these special rules, Congress did not eliminate the benefits of all related-party installment sales.

• Related parties include the first seller's brothers, sisters, ancestors, lineal descendants, controlled corporations, and partnerships, trusts, and estates in which the seller has an interest.[69]
• There is no acceleration if the second disposition occurs more than two years after the first sale.[70]

Thus, if the taxpayer can sell the property to an unrelated party (not a related party) or patient family member, the intrafamily installment sale is still a powerful tax planning tool. Other exceptions also can be applied in some circumstances.[71]

---

[68]§ 453(e).
[69]§ 453(f)(1), cross-referencing §§ 267(b) and 318(a). Although spouses are related parties, the exemption of gain between spouses (§ 1041) makes the second-disposition rules inapplicable when the first sale was between spouses.

[70]§ 453(e)(2). But see § 453(e)(2)(B) for extensions of the two-year period.
[71]See §§ 453(e)(6) and (7).

Related-Party Sales of Depreciable Property

The installment method cannot be used to report a gain on the sale of depreciable property to a controlled entity. The purpose of this rule is to prevent the seller from deferring gain (until collections are received) while the related purchaser is enjoying a stepped-up basis for depreciation purposes.[72]

The prohibition on the use of the installment method applies to sales between the taxpayer and a partnership or corporation in which the taxpayer holds a more-than-50 percent interest. Constructive ownership rules are used in applying the ownership test (e.g., the taxpayer is considered to own stock owned by a spouse and certain other family members).[73] However, if the taxpayer can establish that tax avoidance was not a principal purpose of the transaction, the installment method can be used to report the gain.

EXAMPLE 31

Alan purchased an apartment building from his controlled corporation, Emerald Corporation. Alan was short of cash at the time of the purchase (December 2011), but was to collect a large cash payment in January 2012. The agreement required Alan to pay the entire arm's length price in January 2012. Alan had good business reasons for acquiring the building. Emerald Corporation should be able to convince the IRS that tax avoidance was not a principal purpose for the installment sale because the tax benefits are not overwhelming. The corporation will report all of the gain in the year following the year of sale, and the building must be expensed over 27.5 years (the cost recovery period). ■

DISPOSITION OF INSTALLMENT OBLIGATIONS

Generally, a taxpayer must recognize the deferred profit from an installment sale when the obligation is transferred to another party or otherwise relinquished. The rationale for accelerating the gain is that the deferral should continue for no longer than the taxpayer owns the installment obligation.[74]

The gift or cancellation of an installment note is treated as a taxable disposition by the donor. The amount realized from the cancellation is the face amount of the note if the parties (obligor and obligee) are related to each other.[75]

EXAMPLE 32

Liz cancels a note issued by Tina (Liz's daughter) that arose in connection with the sale of property. At the time of the cancellation, the note had a basis to Liz of $10,000, a face amount of $25,000, and a fair market value of $20,000. Presuming the initial sale by Liz qualified as an installment sale, the cancellation results in gain of $15,000 ($25,000 − $10,000) to Liz. ■

Certain exceptions to the recognition of gain provisions are provided for transfers of installment obligations pursuant to tax-free incorporations under § 351, contributions of capital to a partnership, certain corporate liquidations, transfers due to the taxpayer's death, and transfers between spouses or incident to divorce.[76] In such situations, the deferred profit is merely shifted to the transferee, who is responsible for the payment of tax on the subsequent collections of the installment obligations.

---

[72]§ 453(g).
[73]§§ 1239(b) and (c).
[74]§ 453B(a).
[75]§ 453B(f)(2).
[76]§§ 453B(c), (d), and (g). See Chapter 20 for a discussion of some of these subjects.

INTEREST ON DEFERRED TAXES

With the installment method, the seller earns interest on the receivable. The receivable includes the deferred gain. Thus, one could argue that the seller is earning interest on the deferred taxes. Some commentators reason that the government is, in effect, making interest-free loans to taxpayers who report gains by the installment method. Following the argument that the amount of the deferred taxes is a loan, the taxpayer is required to pay interest on the deferred taxes in some situations.[77]

The taxpayer is required to pay interest on the deferred taxes only if *both* of the following requirements are met:

- The installment obligation arises from the sale of property (other than farming property) for more than $150,000.
- Such installment obligations outstanding at the close of the tax year exceed $5 million.

Interest on the deferred taxes is payable only for the portion of the taxes that relates to the installment obligations in *excess* of $5 million. The interest is calculated using the underpayment rate in § 6621.

ELECTING OUT OF THE INSTALLMENT METHOD

A taxpayer can *elect not to use* the installment method. The election is made by reporting on a timely filed return the gain computed by the taxpayer's usual method of accounting (cash or accrual).[78] However, the Regulations provide that the amount realized by a cash basis taxpayer cannot be less than the value of the property sold. This rule differs from the usual cash basis accounting rules (discussed earlier),[79] which measure the amount realized in terms of the fair market value of the property received. The net effect of the Regulations is to allow the cash basis taxpayer to report his or her gain as an accrual basis taxpayer. The election is frequently applied to year-end sales by taxpayers who expect to be in a higher tax bracket in the following year.

EXAMPLE 33

On December 31, 2011, Kurt sold land to Jodie for $20,000 (fair market value). He had owned the land for seven years. The cash was to be paid on January 4, 2012. Kurt is a cash basis taxpayer, and his basis in the land is $8,000. Kurt has a large casualty loss that, when combined with his other income in 2011, puts him at a marginal tax rate of 15% in 2011. He expects his tax rate to increase to 35% in 2012.

The transaction constitutes an installment sale because a payment will be received in a tax year after the tax year of disposition. Jodie's promise to pay Kurt is an installment obligation, and under the Regulations, the value of the installment obligation is equal to the value of the property sold ($20,000). If Kurt elects out of the installment method, he would shift $12,000 of gain ($20,000 − $8,000) from the expected higher rate in 2012 of 15% to the 0% rate for long-term capital gains in 2011. The expected tax savings based on the rate differential may exceed the benefit of the tax deferral available with the installment method. ∎

Revocation of the Election

Permission of the IRS is required to revoke an election not to use the installment method.[80] The stickiness of the election is an added peril.

---

[77]§ 453A.
[78]§ 453(d) and Temp.Reg. § 15a.453–1(d). See also Rev.Rul. 82–227, 1982–2 C.B. 89.
[79]Refer to Chapter 4, Example 6.
[80]§ 453(d)(3) and Temp.Reg. § 15a.453–1(d)(4).

LONG-TERM CONTRACTS

<table>
<tr><td>

LO.5

Understand the alternative methods of accounting for long-term contracts (the completed contract method and the percentage of completion method) including the limitations on the use of the completed contract method.

</td></tr>
</table>

A **long-term contract** is a building, installation, construction, or manufacturing contract that is entered into but not completed within the same tax year. However, a *manufacturing* contract is long term *only* if the contract is to manufacture (1) a unique item not normally carried in finished goods inventory or (2) items that normally require more than 12 calendar months to complete.[81] An item is *unique* if it is designed to meet the customer's particular needs and is not suitable for use by others. A contract to perform services (e.g., auditing or legal services) is not considered a contract for this purpose and thus cannot qualify as a long-term contract.

EXAMPLE 34

Rocky, a calendar year taxpayer, entered into two contracts during the year. One contract was to construct a building foundation. Work was to begin in October 2011 and was to be completed by June 2012. The contract is long term because it will not be entered into and completed in the same tax year. The fact that the contract requires less than 12 calendar months to complete is not relevant because the contract is not for manufacturing. The second contract was for architectural services to be performed over two years. These services will not qualify for long-term contract treatment because the taxpayer will not build, install, construct, or manufacture a product. ∎

Generally, the taxpayer must accumulate all of the direct and indirect costs incurred under a contract. This means the production costs must be accumulated and allocated to individual contracts. Furthermore, mixed services costs, costs that benefit contracts as well as the general administrative operations of the business, must be allocated to production. Exhibit 18.1 lists the types of costs that must be accumulated and allocated to contracts. The taxpayer must develop reasonable bases for cost allocations.[82]

EXAMPLE 35

Falcon, Inc., uses detailed cost accumulation records to assign labor and materials to its contracts in progress. The total cost of fringe benefits is allocated to a contract on the following basis:

$$\frac{\text{Labor on the contract}}{\text{Total salaries and labor}} \times \text{Total cost of fringe benefits}$$

Similarly, storage and handling costs for materials are allocated to contracts on the following basis:

$$\frac{\text{Contract materials}}{\text{Materials purchases}} \times \text{Storage and handling costs}$$

The cost of the personnel operations, a mixed services cost, is allocated between production and general administration based on the number of employees in each function. The personnel cost allocated to production is allocated to individual contracts on the basis of the formula used to allocate fringe benefits. ∎

The accumulated costs are deducted when the revenue from the contract is recognized. Generally, two methods of accounting are used in varying circumstances to determine when the revenue from a contract is recognized:[83]

- The completed contract method.
- The percentage of completion method.

The *completed contract method may be used* for (1) home construction contracts (contracts in which at least 80 percent of the estimated costs are for dwelling units in buildings with four or fewer units) and (2) certain other real estate construction

---

[81]§ 460(f) and Reg. § 1.460–2(a).
[82]Reg. §§ 1.460–5(b) and 1.263A–1(e).

[83]§ 460.

EXHIBIT 18.1   **Contract Costs, Mixed Services Costs, and Current Expense Items for Contracts**

	Contracts Eligible for the Completed Contract Method	Other Contracts
Contract costs:		
Direct materials (a part of the finished product).	Capital	Capital
Indirect materials (consumed in production but not in the finished product, e.g., grease and oil for equipment).	Capital	Capital
Storage, handling, and insurance on materials.	Expense	Capital
Direct labor (worked on the product).	Capital	Capital
Indirect labor (worked in the production process but not directly on the product, e.g., a construction supervisor).	Capital	Capital
Fringe benefits for direct and indirect labor (e.g., vacation, sick pay, unemployment, and other insurance).	Capital	Capital
Pension costs for direct and indirect labor:		
Current cost.	Expense	Capital
Past service costs.	Expense	Capital
Depreciation on production facilities:		
For financial statements.	Capital	Capital
Tax depreciation in excess of financial statements.	Expense	Capital
Depreciation on idle facilities.	Expense	Expense
Property taxes, insurance, rent, and maintenance on production facilities.	Capital	Capital
Bidding expenses—successful.	Expense	Capital
Bidding expenses—unsuccessful.	Expense	Expense
Interest to finance real estate construction.	Capital	Capital
Interest to finance personal property:		
Production period of one year or less.	Expense	Expense
Production period exceeds one year and costs exceed $1 million.	Capital	Capital
Production period exceeds two years.	Capital	Capital
Mixed services costs:		
Personnel operations.	Expense	Allocate
Data processing.	Expense	Allocate
Purchasing.	Expense	Allocate
Selling, general, and administrative expenses (including an allocated share of mixed services).	Expense	Expense
Losses.	Expense	Expense

contracts. Other real estate contracts can qualify for the completed contract method if the following requirements are satisfied:

• The contract is expected to be completed within the two-year period beginning on the commencement date of the contract.
• The contract is performed by a taxpayer whose average annual gross receipts for the three taxable years preceding the taxable year in which the contract is entered into do not exceed $10 million.

All other contractors must use the percentage of completion method.

Completed Contract Method

Under the **completed contract method**, no revenue from the contract is recognized until the contract is completed and accepted. However, a taxpayer may not delay completion of a contract for the principal purpose of deferring tax.[84]

---

[84]Reg. § 1.451–3(b)(2).

In some situations, the original contract price may be disputed, or the buyer may want additional work to be done on a long-term contract. If the disputed amount is substantial (it is not possible to determine whether a profit or loss will ultimately be realized on the contract), the Regulations provide that no amount of income or loss is recognized until the dispute is resolved. In all other cases, the profit or loss (reduced by the amount in dispute) is recognized in the current period on completion of the contract. However, additional work may need to be performed with respect to the disputed contract. In this case, the difference between the amount in dispute and the actual cost of the additional work is recognized in the year the work is completed rather than in the year in which the dispute is resolved.[85]

EXAMPLE 36

Ted, a calendar year taxpayer utilizing the completed contract method of accounting, constructed a building for Brad under a long-term contract. The gross contract price was $500,000. Ted finished construction in 2011 at a cost of $475,000. When Brad examined the building, he insisted that the building be repainted or the contract price be reduced. The estimated cost of repainting is $10,000. Since under the terms of the contract, Ted is assured of a profit of at least $15,000 ($500,000 − $475,000 − $10,000) even if the dispute is ultimately resolved in Brad's favor, Ted must include $490,000 ($500,000 − $10,000) in gross income and is allowed deductions of $475,000 for 2011.

In 2012, Ted and Brad resolve the dispute, and Ted repaints certain portions of the building at a cost of $6,000. Ted must include $10,000 in 2012 gross income and may deduct the $6,000 expense in that year. ∎

EXAMPLE 37

Assume the same facts as in the previous example, except the estimated cost of repainting the building is $50,000. Since the resolution of the dispute completely in Brad's favor would mean a net loss on the contract for Ted ($500,000 − $475,000 − $50,000 = $25,000 loss), Ted does not recognize any income or loss until the year the dispute is resolved. ∎

Frequently, a contractor receives payment at various stages of completion. For example, when the contract is 50 percent complete, the contractor may receive 50 percent of the contract price less a retainage. The taxation of these payments is generally governed by Regulation § 1.451–5, "advance payments for goods and long-term contracts" (discussed in Chapter 4). Generally, contractors are permitted to defer the advance payments until the payments are recognized as income under the taxpayer's method of accounting.

Percentage of Completion Method

The percentage of completion method must be used to account for long-term contracts unless the taxpayer qualifies for one of the two exceptions that permit the completed contract method to be used (home construction contracts and certain other real estate construction contracts).[86] Under the **percentage of completion method**, a portion of the gross contract price is included in income during each period as the work progresses. The revenue accrued each period (except for the final period) is computed as follows:[87]

$$\frac{C}{T} \times P$$

where   C = Contract costs incurred during the period
        T = Estimated total cost of the contract
        P = Contract price

---

[85]Reg. §§ 1.451–3(d)(2)(ii)–(vii), Example (2).
[86]Certain residential construction contracts that do not qualify for the completed contract method may nevertheless use that method to account for 30% of the profit from the contract, with the remaining 70% reported by the percentage of completion method.
[87]§ 460(b)(1)(A).

All of the costs allocated to the contract during the period are deductible from the accrued revenue.[88] The revenue reported in the final period is simply the unreported revenue from the contract. Because T in this formula is an estimate that frequently differs from total actual costs, which are not known until the contract has been completed, the profit on a contract for a particular period may be overstated or understated.

EXAMPLE 38

Tan, Inc., entered into a contract that was to take two years to complete, with an estimated cost of $2,250,000. The contract price was $3,000,000. Costs of the contract for 2010, the first year, totaled $1,350,000. The gross profit reported by the percentage of completion method for 2010 was $450,000 [($1,350,000/$2,250,000 × $3,000,000) − $1,350,000]. The contract was completed at the end of 2011 at a total cost of $2,700,000. In retrospect, 2010 profit should have been $150,000 [($1,350,000/$2,700,000 × $3,000,000) − $1,350,000]. Thus, taxes were overpaid for 2010. ∎

A *de minimis* rule enables the contractor to delay the recognition of income for a particular contract under the percentage of completion method. If less than 10 percent of the estimated contract costs have been incurred by the end of the taxable year, the taxpayer can elect to defer the recognition of income and the related costs until the taxable year in which cumulative contract costs are at least 10 percent of the estimated contract costs.[89]

Lookback Provisions

In the year a contract is completed, a *lookback* provision requires the recalculation of annual profits reported on the contract under the percentage of completion method. Interest is paid to the taxpayer if taxes were overpaid, and interest is payable by the taxpayer if there was an underpayment.[90] For a corporate taxpayer, the lookback interest paid by the taxpayer is deductible, but for an individual taxpayer, it is nondeductible personal interest associated with a tax liability.

EXAMPLE 39

Assume Tan, Inc., in Example 38, was in the 35% tax bracket in both years and the relevant interest rate was 10%. For 2010, the company paid excess taxes of $105,000 [($450,000 − $150,000) × .35]. When the contract is completed at the end of 2011, Tan, Inc., should receive interest of $10,500 for one year on the tax overpayment ($105,000 × .10). ∎

18.4 INVENTORIES

Generally, tax accounting and financial accounting for inventories are much the same:

- The use of inventories is necessary to clearly reflect the income of any business engaged in the production and sale or purchase and sale of goods.[91]
- The inventories should include all finished goods, goods in process, and raw materials and supplies that will become part of the product (including containers).
- Inventory rules must give effect to the *best* accounting practice of a particular trade or business, and the taxpayer's method should be consistently followed from year to year.
- All items included in inventory should be valued at either (1) cost or (2) the lower of cost or market value.

---

[88]Reg. § 1.451–3(c)(3).
[89]§ 460(b)(5).

[90]§§ 460(b)(2) and (6). The taxpayer can elect to not apply the lookback method in situations where the cumulative taxable income as of the close of each prior year is within 10% of the correct income for each prior year.
[91]§ 471(a) and Reg. §§ 1.471–1 and –2.

The following are *not* acceptable methods or practices in valuing inventories:

- A deduction for a reserve for anticipated price changes.
- The use of a constant price or nominal value for a so-called normal quantity of materials or goods in stock (e.g., the base stock method).
- The inclusion in inventory of stock in transit to which title is not vested in the taxpayer.
- The direct costing approach (excluding fixed indirect production costs from inventory).
- The prime costing approach (excluding all indirect production costs from inventory).

The reason for the similarities between tax and financial accounting for inventories is that § 471 sets forth what appears to be a two-prong test. Under this provision "inventories shall be taken . . . on such basis . . . as conforming as nearly as may be to the *best accounting practice* in the trade or business and as most *clearly reflecting the income.*" The best accounting practice is synonymous with generally accepted accounting principles (GAAP). However, the IRS determines whether an inventory method clearly reflects income.

In *Thor Power Tool Co. v. Comm.*, there was a conflict between the two tests.[92] The taxpayer's method of valuing obsolete parts was in conformity with GAAP. The IRS, however, successfully argued that the clear reflection of income test was not satisfied because the taxpayer's procedures for valuing its inventories were contrary to the Regulations. Under the taxpayer's method, inventories for parts in excess of estimated future sales were written off (expensed), although the parts were kept on hand and their asking prices were not reduced. [Under Regulation § 1.471–4(b), inventories cannot be written down unless the selling prices also are reduced.] The taxpayer contended that conformity to GAAP creates a presumption that the method clearly reflects income. The Supreme Court disagreed, concluding that the clear reflection of income test was *paramount*. Moreover, it is the opinion of the IRS that controls in determining whether the method of inventory clearly reflects income. Thus, the best accounting practice test was rendered practically meaningless. It follows that the taxpayer's method of inventory must strictly conform to the Regulations regardless of what GAAP may require.

DETERMINING INVENTORY COST

For merchandise purchased, cost is the invoice price less trade discounts plus freight and other handling charges.[93] Cash discounts approximating a fair interest rate can be deducted or capitalized at the taxpayer's option, providing the method used is consistently applied.

Uniform Capitalization (UNICAP)

Section 263A provides that for inventory and property produced by the taxpayer, "(A) the direct cost of such property, and (B) such property's share of those indirect costs (including taxes) part or all of which are allocable to such property" must be capitalized. The Committee Reports observe that Congress is attempting to achieve a set of capitalization rules that will apply to all types of businesses: contractors, manufacturers, farmers, wholesalers, and retailers.[94] Congress has labeled the system the **uniform capitalization (UNICAP) rules**, and practitioners refer to the rules as a *super-full absorption costing system*.

To value inventory under the UNICAP rules, a *producer* must apply the following steps:

---

[92]79–1 USTC ¶9139, 43 AFTR 2d 79–362, 99 S.Ct. 773 (USSC, 1979).

[93]Reg. § 1.471–3(b).

[94]H. Rep. 99–841, 99th Cong., 2nd Sess., 1986, pp. 302–309. See also Reg. § 1.263A–1(a).

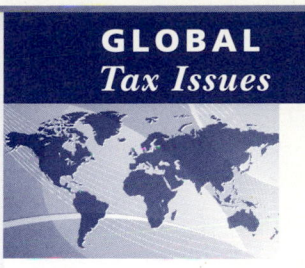

INVENTORY ACQUIRED FROM A FOREIGN SUBSIDIARY

Generally, a parent corporation and its foreign subsidiaries are treated as separate corporations. If a foreign subsidiary is producing goods in a country whose tax rates are lower than the U.S. tax rates, tax savings can accrue to the group if the foreign subsidiary's prices to the U.S. parent are as high as permissible. This will increase the income in the foreign country, but will reduce taxable income subject to the higher U.S. rates. Section 482 is the IRS's weapon against such income shifting. Under § 482, the prices charged on transactions between related parties must be equal to an "arm's length price."

- Classify all costs into three categories: (1) production, (2) general administrative expense, and (3) mixed services.
- Allocate mixed services costs to production and general administrative expenses.[95]
- Allocate the production costs between the cost of goods sold and the ending inventory.

Exhibit 18.1 (see the "Other Contracts" column) lists typical items that are included in the three classes of costs. The mixed services costs should be allocated to production on a rational basis. For example, the costs of operating the personnel department may be allocated between production and general administration based on the number of applications processed or the number of employees. In lieu of allocating each mixed services cost, the taxpayer can elect a *simplified method* whereby the total of all mixed services costs is allocated to production as follows:[96]

$$MSP = \frac{TP}{TC} \times TMS$$

where   MSP = Mixed services costs allocated to production
          TP = Total production costs, other than interest and mixed services
          TC = Total costs, other than interest; state, local, or foreign income taxes; and mixed services costs
        TMS = Total mixed services costs

The usual cost accounting techniques (e.g., average cost per equivalent unit) can be used to allocate the costs between the cost of goods sold and the ending inventory.

Alternatively, the producer can elect to allocate mixed services costs to production on the basis of labor charges only (production labor as a percentage of total labor costs).

The costs included in the inventory of *wholesalers and retailers* are comparable to those of the producer. However, many of these costs are captured in the price these taxpayers pay for the goods. The following additional costs must be capitalized by these taxpayers:

- All storage costs for wholesalers.
- Offsite storage costs for retailers.
- Purchasing costs (e.g., buyers' wages or salaries).
- Handling, processing, assembly, and repackaging.
- The portion of mixed services costs allocable to these functions.

Mixed services costs must be allocated to offsite storage, purchasing, and packaging on the basis of direct labor costs of these departments as a percentage of total

---

[95]Producers with mixed services costs of less than $200,000 for the year are not required to allocate mixed services costs if the simplified method is used to allocate their production costs. Reg. § 1.263A–1(b)(12).

[96]Reg. § 1.263A–1(h)(5).

payroll. Thus, the storage, purchasing, and packaging costs allocated to ending inventory include some mixed services costs.

The UNICAP rules may result in some costs being capitalized for tax purposes but not for financial accounting purposes. For example, a wholesaler's or a manufacturer's storage costs are generally expensed for financial reporting purposes, but are capitalized for tax purposes. Also, the taxpayer may capitalize straight-line depreciation of production equipment for financial accounting purposes, but the total tax depreciation must be capitalized under uniform capitalization.

The Farmer's Exemption

A farmer who is permitted to use the cash method is not required to apply the UNICAP rules to (1) any animals or (2) any plants with a preproduction period of two years or less that the farmer produces. In exchange for this concession, the farmer is required to use the alternative depreciation system (see Chapter 8) for property used in the farming business.[97]

Lower of Cost or Market

Except for those taxpayers who use the LIFO method, inventories may be valued at the **lower of cost or market (replacement cost)**.[98] Taxpayers using LIFO must value inventory at cost. However, the write-down of damaged or shopworn merchandise and goods that are otherwise unsalable at normal prices is not considered to be an application of the lower of cost or market method. Such items should be valued at bona fide selling price less direct cost of disposal.[99]

In the case of excess inventories (as in *Thor Power Tool Co.*, discussed previously), the goods can be written down only to the taxpayer's offering price. If the offering price on the goods is not reduced, the goods must be valued at cost.

EXAMPLE 40

The Cardinal Publishing Company invested $50,000 in printing 10,000 copies of a book. Although only 7,000 copies were sold in the first 3 years and none in the next 5 years, management is convinced that the book will become a classic in 20 years. Cardinal leaves the price the same as it was when the book was first distributed ($15 per copy). The remaining 3,000 books must be valued at cost ($15,000). Note that the tax law provides an incentive for the taxpayer to destroy or abandon its excess inventory and obtain an immediate deduction rather than wait for the event of future sales. ■

In applying the lower of cost or market method, *each* item included in the inventory must be valued at the lower of its cost or market value.[100]

EXAMPLE 41

The taxpayer's ending inventory is valued as follows:

Item	Cost	Market	Lower of Cost or Market
A	$5,000	$ 4,000	$4,000
B	3,000	2,000	2,000
C	1,500	6,000	1,500
	$9,500	$12,000	$7,500

Under the lower of cost or market method, the taxpayer's inventory is valued at $7,500 rather than $9,500. ■

---

[97]§§ 263A(d) and (e)(3).
[98]Reg. § 1.472–4.
[99]Reg. § 1.471–2(c).
[100]Reg. § 1.471–4(c).

Inventory Shrinkage

The difference between the inventory per physical count and according to the company's records is referred to as *inventory shrinkage.* Inventory shrinkage is the result of accidents, theft, and errors in recording. Many companies take physical inventories at times other than the last day of the tax year and adjust their inventory per books to agree with the physical count. The inventory of the last day of the tax year, which is used to compute cost of goods sold, is based on the perpetual records. Such companies often adjust the ending inventory for the estimated shrinkage that has occurred between the date of the physical inventory and the last day of the tax year. The adjustment is often based on the historical relationship between inventory shrinkage and sales.[101]

Determining Cost—Specific Identification, FIFO, and LIFO

In some cases, it is feasible to determine the cost of the particular item sold. For example, an automobile dealer can easily determine the specific cost of each automobile that has been sold. However, in most businesses it is necessary to resort to a flow of goods assumption such as *first in, first out* (*FIFO*), *last in, first out* (*LIFO*), or an *average cost* method. A taxpayer may use any of these methods, provided the method selected is consistently applied from year to year.

During a period of rising prices, LIFO will generally produce a lower ending inventory valuation and will result in a greater cost of goods sold than would be obtained under the FIFO method. The following example illustrates how LIFO and FIFO affect the computation of the cost of goods sold.

EXAMPLE 42

On January 1, 2011, the taxpayer opened a retail store to sell refrigerators. At least 10 refrigerators must be carried in inventory to satisfy customer demands. The initial investment in the 10 refrigerators is $5,000. During the year, 10 refrigerators were sold at $750 each and were replaced at a cost of $6,000 ($600 each). Gross profit under the LIFO and FIFO methods is computed as follows:

		FIFO		LIFO
Sales (10 × $750)		$ 7,500		$ 7,500
Beginning inventory	$ 5,000		$ 5,000	
Purchases	6,000		6,000	
	$11,000		$11,000	
Ending inventory				
10 × $600	(6,000)			
10 × $500			(5,000)	
Cost of goods sold		(5,000)		(6,000)
Gross profit		$ 2,500		$ 1,500

Dollar-Value LIFO

In the previous example, the taxpayer was buying and selling a single product, a particular model of a refrigerator. The taxpayer employed the specific goods LIFO technique. Under the specific goods approach, if the identical items are not on hand at the end of the period, the LIFO inventory is depleted, and all of the deferred profit must be recaptured. Thus, taxpayers who frequently change the items carried in inventory would realize little benefit from LIFO. However, the dollar-value LIFO technique avoids the LIFO depletion problem associated with the specific goods technique.

Under **dollar-value LIFO**, each inventory item is assigned to a pool. A *pool* is a collection of similar items and is treated as a separate inventory. Determining whether items are similar involves considerable judgment. In general, however, the taxpayer would prefer broad pools so that when a particular item is sold out, it can be

---

[101]§ 471(b).

TAX in the NEWS

LIFO COULD STALL ACCEPTANCE OF INTERNATIONAL FINANCIAL REPORTING STANDARDS

The movement for the United States to adopt international accounting standards likely will meet resistance from companies that currently use the LIFO inventory method. The international standards do not permit the use of LIFO, and the Internal Revenue Code requires companies that use LIFO for tax purposes to use LIFO in preparing their financial statements as well. Thus, changing to the international standards would require the taxpayers currently using

LIFO to change their method of accounting for inventory. The House Ways and Means Committee has estimated that the change would increase the total tax liabilities of these companies by more than $100 billion—that is serious money.

Source: Adapted from David M. Katz, "How LIFO Could Stall Global Accounting," CFO.com, December 7, 2008.

replaced by increases in other items in the same pool. Generally, all products manufactured at a particular plant can be treated as a pool.[102] A department store may have a separate pool for each department. An automobile dealer may have separate pools for new cars, lightweight trucks, heavy-duty trucks, and car and truck parts.

At the end of the period, the ending inventory must be valued at the current-year prices and then at the LIFO base period (the year LIFO was adopted). The ratio of the ending inventory at current prices to the ending inventory at base period prices is the *LIFO index*. If the total current inventory at base period prices is greater than the base period inventory at base period prices, a LIFO layer must be added. The LIFO index is applied to the LIFO layer to convert it to current prices.

EXAMPLE 43

Black Company adopted LIFO effective January 1, 2011. The base LIFO inventory (from December 31, 2010) was $1,000,000. On December 31, 2011, the inventory was $1,320,000 at end-of-2011 prices and $1,200,000 at end-of-2010 (the base period) prices. Thus, Black added a 2011 layer of $200,000 ($1,200,000 − $1,000,000) at base period prices. The layer must be converted to 2011 prices as follows:

$$\text{LIFO index} = \$1,320,000 / \$1,200,000 = 1.10$$
$$2011 \text{ layer} \times \text{LIFO index} = \$200,000 \times 1.10 = \$220,000$$

Therefore, the 2011 ending inventory is $1,000,000 + $220,000 = $1,220,000.

The inventory on December 31, 2012, is $1,325,000 using 2012 prices and $1,250,000 using base period prices. Thus, the LIFO index for 2012 is $1,325,000/$1,250,000 = 1.06. The LIFO inventory is $1,273,000, computed as follows:

	BLACK COMPANY **LIFO Inventory** **December 31, 2012**		
	Base Period Cost	**LIFO Index**	**LIFO Layers**
Base inventory	$1,000,000	1.00	$1,000,000
2011 layer	200,000	1.10	220,000
2012 layer	50,000	1.06	53,000
	$1,250,000		$1,273,000

---

[102]See, generally, Reg. § 1.472–8.

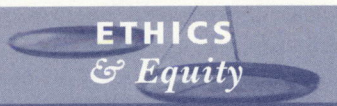

PRESERVING THE LIFO RESERVE

Blanch Corporation has been using the dollar-value LIFO inventory method for 20 years. The company maintains one inventory pool that includes raw materials, goods in process, and finished goods. The LIFO deferral is several million dollars. At the end of the current year, the corporation's inventory of finished goods was almost depleted because the company's major competitor had to recall a substantial portion of its products. Blanch's management is aware that if the inventory is not replenished, the corporation will be required to recognize income that has been deferred for the past 20 years. The controller has suggested that the company buy sufficient raw materials to substitute for the depleted finished goods. This will require having on hand at the end of the year the raw materials required for the next 18 months, when ordinarily the company has only a three-month supply on hand. The controller argues that the cost of carrying the additional inventory is much less than the additional taxes that will be due if the inventories are allowed to decrease.

The operations manager has suggested that the company buy the raw materials before the end of the year and have the supplier store the materials. Furthermore, the supplier would act as Blanch's agent to sell the excess materials. This would minimize the actual investment in inventory. Do you think the corporation should follow either proposal?

THE LIFO ELECTION

A taxpayer may adopt LIFO by merely using the method in the tax return for the year of the change and by attaching Form 970 (Application to Use LIFO Inventory Method) to the tax return. Thus, a taxpayer does not have to request approval for the change. Once the election is made, it cannot be revoked. However, a prospective change from LIFO to any other inventory method can be made only if the consent of the IRS is obtained.[103]

The beginning inventory valuation for the first year LIFO is used is computed by the costing method employed in the preceding year. Thus, the beginning LIFO inventory is generally the same as the closing inventory for the preceding year. However, since lower of cost or market cannot be used in conjunction with LIFO, previous write-downs to market for items included in the beginning inventory must be restored to income. The amount the inventories are written up is an adjustment due to a change in accounting method.[104] However, the usual rules for disposition of the adjustments under Revenue Procedure 2002–9 are not applicable.[105] The taxpayer is allowed to spread the adjustment ratably over the year of the change and the two succeeding years.

> **EXAMPLE 44**
>
> In 2010, Paul used the lower of cost or market FIFO inventory method. The FIFO cost of his ending inventory was $30,000, and the market value of the inventory was $24,000. Therefore, the ending inventory for 2010 was $24,000. Paul switched to LIFO in 2011 and was required to write up the beginning inventory to $30,000. Paul must add $2,000 ($6,000 ÷ 3) to his income for each of the years 2011, 2012, and 2013. ∎

Congress added this provision to the Code to overrule the previous IRS policy of requiring the taxpayer to include the entire adjustment in income for the year preceding the change to LIFO.[106]

Once the LIFO election is made for tax purposes, the taxpayer's financial reports to owners and creditors must also be prepared on the basis of LIFO.[107] The

---

[103]Reg. §§ 1.472–3(a) and 1.472–5 and Rev.Proc. 84–74, 1984–2 C.B. 736 at 742.

[104]Reg. § 1.472–2(c). In Rev.Rul. 76–282, 1976–2 C.B. 137, the IRS required the restoration of write-downs for damaged and shopworn goods when the taxpayer switched to LIFO.

[105]2002–1 C.B. 327.

[106]§ 472(d), overruling the IRS position cited in Footnote 104.

[107]§ 472(c).

conformity of financial reports to tax reporting is specifically required by the Code and is strictly enforced by the IRS. However, the Regulations permit the taxpayer to make a footnote disclosure of the net income computed by another method of inventory valuation (e.g., FIFO).[108]

SPECIAL INVENTORY METHODS RELATING TO FARMING AND RANCHING

Farmers who do not use the cash method and therefore account for inventories may elect to use the **farm price method** or the **unit-livestock-price method** rather than one of the inventory methods discussed above. Under the farm price method, the inventory is valued at its market price less disposition costs (e.g., transportation and selling expenses).[109] If the taxpayer uses the unit-livestock-price method, the animals are valued at a standard cost, which is based on the average cost of raising an animal with the characteristics of the animals included in the ending inventory.[110] The farmer can also elect to use the lower of cost or market inventory method.

TAX PLANNING:

18.5 TAXABLE YEAR

LO.7

Identify tax planning opportunities related to accounting periods and accounting methods.

Under the general rules for tax years, partnerships and S corporations frequently will be required to use a calendar year. However, if the partnership or S corporation can demonstrate a business purpose for a fiscal year, the IRS will allow the entity to use the requested year. The advantage to a fiscal year is that the calendar year partners and S corporation shareholders may be able to defer from tax the income earned from the close of the fiscal year until the end of the calendar year. Tax advisers for these entities should apply the IRS's gross receipts test described in Revenue Procedure 87–32 to determine if permission for the fiscal year will be granted.[111]

18.6 CASH METHOD OF ACCOUNTING

The cash method of accounting gives the taxpayer considerable control over the recognition of expenses and some control over the recognition of income. This method can be used by proprietorships, partnerships, and small corporations (gross receipts of $5 million or less) that provide services (inventories are not material to the service business). Farmers (except certain farming corporations) can also use the cash method.

18.7 INSTALLMENT METHOD

Unlike the cash and accrual methods, the installment method often results in an interest-free loan (of deferred taxes) from the government. The installment method is not available for the sale of inventory. Nevertheless, the installment method is an important tax planning technique and should be considered when a sale of eligible property is being planned. That is, if the taxpayer can benefit from deferring the tax, the terms of sale can be arranged so that the installment method rules apply. If, on the other hand, the taxpayer expects to be in a higher tax bracket when the payments will be received, he or she can elect not to use the installment method.

---

[108]Reg. § 1.472–2(e).
[109]Reg. § 1.471–6(d).

[110]Reg. § 1.471–6(e). See also IRS Pub. 225 (Farmers Tax Guide), p. 7.
[111]See also Rev.Proc. 2002–38, 2002–1 C.B. 1037.

RELATED PARTIES

Intrafamily installment sales can still be a useful family tax planning tool. If the related party holds the property more than two years, a subsequent sale will not accelerate the gain from the first disposition. Patience and forethought are rewarded.

The 6 percent limitation on imputed interest on sales of land between family members (see Concept Summary 18.1) enables the seller to convert ordinary income into capital gain or make what is, in effect, a nontaxable gift. If the selling price is raised to adjust for the low interest rate charges on an installment sale, the seller has more capital gain but less ordinary income than would be realized from a sale to an unrelated party. If the selling price is not raised and the specified interest of 6 percent is charged, the seller enables the relative to have the use of the property without having to pay its full market value. As an additional benefit, the bargain sale is not a taxable gift.

DISPOSITION OF INSTALLMENT OBLIGATIONS

A disposition of an installment obligation is also a serious matter. Gifts of the obligations will accelerate income to the seller. The list of taxable and nontaxable dispositions of installment obligations should not be trusted to memory. In each instance where transfers of installment obligations are contemplated, the practitioner should conduct research to be sure he or she knows the consequences.

18.8 COMPLETED CONTRACT METHOD

Generally, large contractors must use the percentage of completion method of accounting for reporting the income from long-term contracts. Under the percentage of completion method, the taxpayer must recognize profit in each period costs are incurred. Profit is reported in proportion to the cost incurred for the period as a proportion of the total contract cost. However, small contractors (average annual gross receipts do not exceed $10 million) working on contracts that are completed within a two-year period can elect to use the completed contract method and defer profit until the year in which the contract is completed.

18.9 INVENTORIES

LOWER OF COST OR MARKET

Generally, under tax accounting rules, a deduction cannot be taken for a loss before the loss is realized. Inventories with a replacement cost below their original cost are the major exception to this rule. The rationale for the lower of cost or market method is that when the replacement cost of the goods has decreased, the taxpayer's selling price must likewise be reduced. Under the lower of cost or market method, the taxpayer is allowed to anticipate a reduction in the expected selling price of the goods by taking a deduction in the period the replacement cost decreases, rather than waiting until the goods are actually sold. Thus, the lower of cost or market method is a tax deferral technique.

LIFO

While the lower of cost or market method defers tax when replacement costs are declining, LIFO defers tax when prices are rising. However, when some goods are increasing in value while others are decreasing, the taxpayer cannot use the lower of cost or market method for the goods declining in value and LIFO for the goods whose replacement costs are rising. That is, LIFO cannot be used in conjunction with the lower of cost or market method. Assuming that prices generally are rising, the taxpayer generally should elect LIFO. The only major disadvantage to LIFO is the financial-tax conformity requirement. However, even this disadvantage can be overcome through footnote disclosure of earnings as computed under FIFO.

REFOCUS ON THE BIG PICTURE

ACCOUNTING PERIOD

Selection of a Tax Year

An entity's tax form will govern the rules for determining the entity's tax year. Since Silver is a partnership, the Code's provisions for partnerships are applicable.

In this case, Tweety's 40 percent ownership interest in Silver is not sufficient to enable it to control the selection of the partnership's tax year. Likewise, Belinda and Pearl's collective controlling interest will not allow them to control the selection of the tax year for the partnership.

The Code and related Regulations have a very precise set of rules regarding the selection of a tax year for a partnership. The partnership applies these rules in the following sequence:

- *Majority interest tax year.* The tax year of the partners who have a common year-end and collectively own a greater-than-50 percent interest in the partnership capital and profits.
- *Principal partners' tax year.* The tax year if all the principal partners (5 percent or greater interest in capital or profits) have the same tax year.
- *Least aggregate deferral tax year.* The tax year of the principal partners (grouped by a common year-end) that produces the least aggregate deferral of income.

Alternatively, the partnership can select its tax year based on a business purpose for the tax year selected. However, this requires the approval of the IRS, which is unlikely to be granted. The only business purpose the IRS has acknowledged is the need to conform the tax year to the entity's natural business year.

Therefore, from the data provided, it appears that Silver will determine its tax year by using the least aggregate deferral method. Based on this method, Silver's tax year will end on November 30 (see the calculations in Example 3).

Short Tax Year

Silver will have a short tax year that begins on April 1, 2011, and ends on November 30, 2011, as determined by the least aggregate deferral method. Silver will not have to annualize the income reported on its first income tax return. Note, however, that annualization will be required if Silver ever changes its tax year.

Partner's Reporting of Share of Net Income

Each of the partners will receive a Schedule K–1 that reports the partner's share of net income. From a timing perspective, the partner will include the Schedule K–1 items on the partner's income tax return only if a partnership tax year ends within or with the partner's tax year.

KEY TERMS

DISCUSSION QUESTIONS

1. **LO.1** Would a tax year ending December 31 be appropriate for a department store?

2. **LO.1** In the case of a profitable partnership whose partners are all individuals, what would be the advantage of using a tax year ending January 31 if this was permissible?

3. **LO.1** A law practice was incorporated on January 1, 2011, and expects to earn $25,000 per month before deducting the lawyer's salary. The lawyer owns 100% of the stock. The corporation and the lawyer both use the cash method of accounting. The corporation does not need to retain any of the earnings in the business; thus, the salary of the lawyer (a calendar year taxpayer) will equal the corporation's net income before salary expense. If the corporation could choose any tax year it wished and pay the lawyer's salary at the time that would be the most tax efficient (but at least once every 12 months), what tax year should the corporation choose, and when should the salary be paid each year?

DECISION MAKING

4. **LO.1** Pale Hotel, Inc., was a C corporation using a fiscal year ending April 30 for tax purposes for all tax years through April 30, 2011. In May 2011, the corporation made an S election. What are the implications of the election for Pale's tax year?

5. **LO.1** Fred, a cash basis taxpayer, received a $75,000 bonus from his employer in 2011. The bonus was based on the company's profits for the year 2010. In 2012, the company discovered that its 2010 profits were incorrectly computed. As a result, Fred was required to repay his employer $25,000 of the bonus. Fred's marginal tax rate was 35% in 2011 and 15% in 2012. Sue, a cash basis taxpayer, earned a $75,000 bonus in 2011 that her employer failed to pay until 2012. Sue was in the 15% marginal tax bracket in 2011 and the 35% bracket in 2012. What special tax relief is available to Fred that is not available to Sue?

ISSUE ID

6. **LO.1** How are farmers treated differently from other producers in regard to tax accounting?

7. **LO.2** In December 2011, Nell, a cash basis taxpayer, paid insurance premiums of $12,000 on rental property for the period February 1, 2012, through January 31, 2013. How much of the premiums can Nell deduct in 2011?

8. **LO.2** In 2011, the taxpayer became ineligible to use the cash method of accounting. At the beginning of the year, accounts receivable totaled $240,000, accounts payable for merchandise totaled $80,000, and the inventory on hand totaled $320,000. What is the amount of the adjustment due to the change in accounting method?

9. **LO.2** Osprey Corporation, an accrual basis taxpayer, had taxable income for 2011. The company filed its 2011 state income tax return in August 2012 and paid the $8,000 state income tax due for 2011. In December 2011, the company received a notice from the state tax commission that an additional $4,000 of income tax was due for 2010 because of an error on the return. The company acknowledged the error in December 2011 and paid the additional $4,000 in tax in February 2012. Can the $8,000 and $4,000 in state income tax be deducted on Osprey's 2011 Federal income tax return?

10. **LO.2** Compare the cash basis and accrual basis of accounting as applied to the following:
    a. Fixed assets.
    b. Prepaid expenses.
    c. Prepaid income for services.
    d. A note received for services performed if the market value and face amount of the note differ.

11. **LO.2** Edgar uses the cash method to report the income from his software consulting business. A large publicly held corporation has offered to invest in Edgar's business as a limited partner. What tax accounting complications would be created if Edgar and the corporation become partners?

DECISION MAKING

12. **LO.2** Samantha, a cash basis taxpayer, subscribes to a service that updates a database used in her business. In December 2011, Samantha paid the $120,000 subscription for the period December 2011 through November 2012. What is Samantha's deduction for 2011?

13. **LO.2** Emerald Motors is an automobile dealer. The company has made a special offer to its new car customers for 2011. The dealer will not charge for the first four manufacturer's recommended service visits (i.e., at 3,000, 6,000, 9,000, and 12,000 miles). It is a virtual certainty that all customers will exercise their rights to the service. The controller asks you whether the company can accrue as an expense in 2011 the normal charge for service visits on cars sold in 2011 but not to be serviced until 2012.

DECISION MAKING

14. **LO.4, 7** Irene has made Sara an offer on the purchase of a capital asset. Irene will pay (1) $200,000 cash or (2) $50,000 cash and a 6% installment note for $150,000 guaranteed by City Bank of New York. If Sara sells for $200,000 cash, she will invest the after-tax proceeds in certificates of deposit yielding 6% interest. Sara's cost of the asset is $25,000. Why would Sara prefer the installment sale?

15. **LO.4** Arnold gave land to his son, Bruce. Arnold's basis in the land was $70,000, and its fair market value at the date of the gift was $80,000. Bruce borrowed $150,000 that he used to improve the property. He sold the property to Della for $300,000. Della paid Bruce $60,000 in cash, assumed his $150,000 mortgage, and agreed to pay $90,000 in two years. Bruce's selling expenses were $10,000. Della is going to pay adequate interest. What is Bruce's installment sale gain in the year of sale?

16. **LO.4** A seller and buyer agree that the sales/purchase price for land is $150,000 down and five payments of $50,000 each. In addition, the seller would like the contract to read that the total selling price is $372,600 and that the five payments of $50,000 each include interest at 4%, which is the current Federal intermediate-term rate. The buyer counters that the price should be stated as $360,600, with a 6% stated rate on the five payments of $50,000 each. The land is a capital asset to the seller, and the holding period is four years. Because the total amount received by the seller and the amount paid by the buyer are the same [$150,000 + 5($50,000) = $400,000], why does it matter how the price and interest rate are stated in the contract?

DECISION MAKING

17. **LO.4, 7** On June 1, 2009, Father sold land to Son for $300,000. Father reported the gain by the installment method, with the gain to be spread over five years. In May 2011, Son received an offer of $400,000 for the land, to be paid over three years. What would be the tax consequences of Son's sale? How could the tax consequences be improved?

DECISION MAKING

18. **LO.4, 7** In December 2011, Carl Corporation sold land it held as an investment. The corporation received $50,000 in 2011 and a note payable (with adequate interest) for $150,000 to be paid in 2013. Carl Corporation's cost of the land was $80,000. The corporation has a $90,000 net capital loss carryover that will expire in 2011. Should Carl Corporation report the sale in 2011 or use the installment method to report the income as payments are received?

19. **LO.2, 5** What are the similarities between the crop method used for farming and the completed contract method used for long-term construction?

20. **LO.5** Nathan uses the percentage of completion method to report income from his real estate construction contracts. A contract was begun in 2011 and completed in 2012. In 2011, Nathan reported gross income from the partial completion of the contract. In 2012, however, costs had decreased below the original estimate. The contract was completed with the actual profit on the contract being more than the income from the contract reported in 2011. What mechanism should be used to correct for the underpayment of tax in 2011?

21. **LO.5** Neal uses the percentage of completion method to report his gross income from long-term contracts that were to begin in 2011. In 2012, he completes a contract for less than the estimate of total costs that was used in the prior year. What are the tax accounting implications of the incorrect estimate?

22. **LO.5** The Hawk Corporation builds yachts. The vessels it currently produces are practically identical and are completed in approximately 8 months. A customer has approached Hawk about constructing a larger yacht that would take approximately 15 months to complete. What are the tax implications of accepting the contract proposal?

ISSUE ID

23. **LO.6** Largo Company is an engineering consulting business that uses the accrual method of accounting for its services. Mango Company is a manufacturer of nuts and bolts that

also uses the accrual method to account for its sales. Each company has a personnel department. How should the cost of personnel operations be treated by each of the two companies?

24. **LO.6** Amber Auto Parts adopted the dollar-value LIFO inventory method. The company has consistently used a retail price index when it should have used a producer's price index. As a result, its LIFO layers have been consistently undervalued. What should the company do?

ISSUE ID

25. **LO.6** Opal, Inc., is about to make its first attempt to borrow from a local bank. The company uses LIFO for tax purposes, solely to defer taxes, and believes that income computed using the FIFO method would better reflect its income. The company also uses the double-declining balance method of depreciation for tax, although the straight-line method better reflects the actual depreciation. The company would like to present its financial position in the most favorable light. Therefore, Opal's CEO intends to provide the bank with an income statement prepared using the FIFO inventory method and straight-line depreciation. What types of problems will presenting the income statement to the bank in this fashion cause for Opal?

ISSUE ID

26. **LO.6** Blue and Gold are competitors in the automotive supply business. In calculating its ending inventory at the end of the tax year, Blue includes an estimate of inventory shrinkage, but Gold does not. What could account for this difference?

ISSUE ID

PROBLEMS

27. **LO.1** Red, White, and Blue are unrelated corporations engaged in real estate development. The three corporations formed a joint venture (treated as a partnership) to develop a tract of land. Assuming the venture does not have a natural business year, what tax year must the joint venture adopt under the following circumstances?

		Tax Year Ending	Interest in Joint Venture
a.	Red	March 31	60%
	Blue	June 30	20%
	White	October 31	20%
b.	Red	October 31	30%
	White	September 30	40%
	Blue	January 31	30%

28. **LO.1, 7** The Cardinal Wholesale Company is an S corporation that began business on March 1, 2011. Robert, a calendar year taxpayer, owns 100% of the Cardinal stock. He has $400,000 taxable income from other sources each year. Robert will work approximately 30 hours a week for the corporation. Cardinal sells swimming pool supplies, and its natural business year ends in September. Approximately 80% of Cardinal's gross receipts occur in June through September.
    a. What tax year should Cardinal elect, assuming that Robert anticipates the company will produce a net profit for all years?
    b. What tax year should Cardinal elect, assuming it will lose $10,000 a month for the first 12 months and an average of $5,000 a month for the next 12 months? In the third year, the corporation will earn taxable income.

DECISION MAKING

29. **LO.1** Zorn conducted his professional practice through Zorn, Inc. The corporation uses a fiscal year ending September 30 even though the business purpose test for a fiscal year cannot be satisfied. For the year ending September 30, 2011, the corporation paid Zorn a salary of $240,000, and during the period January through September 2011, the corporation paid him a salary of $120,000.
    a. How much salary should Zorn receive during the period October 1 through December 31, 2011?
    b. Assume Zorn received only $30,000 salary during the period October 1 through December 31, 2011. What would be the consequences to Zorn, Inc.?

DECISION MAKING

30. **LO.1** Mauve Corporation began operations as a farm supplies business and used a fiscal year ending September 30. The company gradually went out of the farm supplies business and into the mail-order Christmas gifts business. The company has received permission from the IRS to change to a fiscal year ending January 31, effective for the year ending January 31, 2011. For the short period October 1, 2010, through January 31, 2011, Mauve earned $32,000. Calculate Mauve's tax liability for the short period October 1, 2010, through January 31, 2011.

31. **LO.1** In 2010, Juan entered into a contract to write a book. The publisher advanced Juan $50,000, which was to be repaid out of future royalties. If the book was not completed by the end of 2011, however, Juan would be required to repay the publisher for the advance. Juan did not complete the book in 2011, and in accordance with the agreement, he repaid the $50,000 to the publisher in 2012. Juan is a cash basis taxpayer. His marginal tax rate was 35% in 2010 and 15% in 2012. What are the tax consequences to Juan of the repayment?

COMMUNICATIONS

32. **LO.2** Gold, Inc., is an accrual basis taxpayer. In 2011, an employee accidentally spilled hazardous chemicals on leased property. The chemicals destroyed trees on neighboring property, resulting in $30,000 of damages. In 2011, the owner of the property sued Gold, Inc., for the $30,000. Gold's attorney feels that it is liable and the only issue is whether the neighbor will also seek punitive damages that could be as much as three times the actual damages. In addition, as a result of the spill, Gold was in violation of its lease and was therefore required to pay the landlord $15,000. However, the amount due for the lease violation is not payable until the termination of the lease in 2014. None of these costs were covered by insurance. Jeff Stuart, the president of Gold, Inc., is generally familiar with the accrual basis tax accounting rules and is concerned about when the company will be allowed to deduct the amounts the company is required to pay as a result of this environmental disaster. Write Mr. Stuart a letter explaining these issues. Gold's address is 200 Elm Avenue, San Jose, CA 95192.

33. **LO.2** Compute Mary's income or deductions for 2011 using (1) the cash basis and (2) the accrual basis for each of the following:
    a. In May 2011, Mary paid a license fee of $1,200 for the period June 1, 2011, through May 31, 2012.
    b. In December 2011, Mary collected $10,000 for January 2012 rents. In January 2012, Mary collected $2,000 for December 2011 rents.
    c. In June 2011, Mary paid $7,200 for an office equipment service contract for the period July 1, 2011, through December 31, 2012.
    d. In June 2011, Mary purchased office furniture for $273,000. She paid $131,000 in cash and gave a $142,000 interest-bearing note for the balance. The office furniture has an MACRS cost recovery period of seven years. Mary did not make the § 179 election and elected not to take additional first-year depreciation.

34. **LO.2, 5** What accounting method (cash or accrual) would you recommend for the following businesses?
    a. An incorporated retail hardware store with annual gross receipts of $4.5 million.
    b. An incorporated engineering firm with annual gross receipts of $12 million.
    c. A dry wall subcontractor who works on residences and has annual gross receipts of $3 million.
    d. An incorporated insurance agency with annual gross receipts of $6 million.

DECISION MAKING

35. **LO.2** Blue Company, an architectural firm, has a bookkeeper who maintains a cash receipts and disbursements journal. At the end of the year, the company hires you to convert the cash receipts and disbursements into accrual basis revenues and expenses. The total cash receipts are summarized as follows:

Cash sales	$150,000
Collections on accounts receivable	450,000
Bank loan	90,000
Total cash receipts	$690,000

The accounts receivable from customers at the end of the year are $210,000. You note that the accounts receivable at the beginning of the year were $160,000. The cash sales included $60,000 of prepayments for services to be provided over the next 36 months (i.e., 12 months of such services relate to 2011).

a.   Compute the company's accrual basis gross income for 2011.

b.   Would you recommend that Blue use the cash method or the accrual method?

c.   The company does not maintain an allowance for uncollectible accounts. Would you recommend that such an allowance be established for tax purposes?

36. **LO.2** How do the all events and economic performance requirements apply to the following transactions by an accrual basis taxpayer?

a.   The company guarantees its products for six months. At the end of 2011, customers had made valid claims for $600,000 that were not paid until 2012. Also, the company estimates that another $400,000 in claims from 2011 sales will be filed and paid in 2012.

b.   The accrual basis taxpayer reported $200,000 in corporate taxable income for 2011. The state income tax rate was 6%. The corporation paid $7,000 in estimated state income taxes in 2011 and paid $2,000 on 2010 state income taxes when it filed its 2010 state income tax return in March 2011. The company filed its 2011 state income return in March 2012 and paid the remaining $5,000 of its 2011 state income tax liability.

c.   An employee was involved in an accident while making a sales call. The company paid the injured victim $15,000 in 2011 and agreed to pay the victim $15,000 a year for the next nine years.

37. **LO.3** Ross Company is a computer consulting firm. The company also sells equipment to its clients. The sales of equipment account for approximately 40% of the company's gross receipts. The company has consistently used the cash method to report its income from services and the accrual method to report its income from the sale of inventory. In June of the current year, Ross's accountant discovered that as a small business the company qualifies to use the cash method for all of its activities. The company is a calendar year taxpayer. As of the beginning of the current year, the company had $120,000 of inventory on hand and $90,000 of accounts receivable from the sales of equipment and $30,000 of receivables from the consulting services.

a.   Compute the adjustment due to the change in accounting method.

b.   Is the adjustment positive or negative? Explain.

c.   When can the adjustment be taken into account in computing taxable income?

38. **LO.2, 3** Raven Finance Company experiences bad debts of about 3% of its outstanding loans. At the end of the year, the company had outstanding receivables of $30 million. This balance included $2 million of accrued interest receivable. Raven's loan loss reserve for the year was computed as follows:

DECISION MAKING

Balance, January 1, 2011	$850,000
Accounts written off as uncollectible	
Loans made in 2011	(70,000)
Loans made in prior years	(10,000)
Collections on loans previously written off	25,000
Adjustment to required balance	100,000
Balance, December 31, 2011	$895,000

a.   Determine the effects of the above on Raven's taxable income for 2011.

b.   Assume that Raven has used the reserve method to compute its taxable income for the 10 years the company has been in existence. In 2011, you begin preparing Raven's tax return. What should be done with regard to the reserve?

39. **LO.2, 3, 6** Jeffrey Boyd, the president of Eagle Furniture Company (average annual gross receipts of $4 million), has prepared the company's financial statements and income tax returns for the past 15 years. In July 2012, however, he hired you to prepare the 2011 corporate income tax return because he has not studied taxes for over 20 years and suspects the rules may have changed. Eagle uses the accrual method of accounting. Based on an initial examination of Eagle's trial balance and some account analyses, you have determined that the following items may require adjustments:

COMMUNICATIONS

- The company uses the FIFO inventory method, as valued at cost. However, all freight expenses on incoming merchandise have been expensed for the 15 years the company has been in business.
- The company experiences inventory shrinkage (due to breakage and theft) of about 1% of sales each year. The shrinkage is not taken into account until the company takes a physical inventory each October, but the corporation's fiscal year ends January 31.

- The company has used an allowance for uncollectible accounts, which has a balance of $60,000. In the past, the company has been able to accurately predict its actual bad debt expense.
- The company sells a three-year service contract on its appliances. The company treats $1/36$ of the contract price as earned each month. At the beginning of the year, the company had $120,000 in its account for unearned revenues from the service contracts.
- The company deducts its state income tax in the year paid. Thus, the 2011 state income tax expense includes the estimated taxes paid in 2011 and the additional amount paid in 2011 on 2010 taxes.

Write a letter to Mr. Boyd explaining what adjustments will be required and how they will be implemented. The address of Eagle Furniture Company is 1000 East Maryland Street, Evansville, IL 47722.

DECISION MAKING

40. **LO.4, 7** Floyd, a cash basis taxpayer, has received an offer to purchase his land. The buyer will either pay him $100,000 at closing or pay $50,000 at closing and $52,000 one year after the date of closing. If Floyd recognizes the entire gain in the current year, his marginal tax rate will be 35% (combined Federal and state rates). However, if he spreads the gain over the two years, his marginal tax rate on the gain will be only 25%. Floyd does not consider the buyer a credit risk, but he realizes that the deferred payment will, in effect, earn only 4% interest ($2,000/$50,000 = 4%). Floyd believes he can earn a 10% before-tax rate of return on his after-tax cash. Floyd's adjusted basis for the land is $25,000, the buyer is also a cash basis taxpayer, and the short-term Federal rate is 4%. Floyd has asked you to evaluate the two alternatives on an after-tax basis.

DECISION MAKING

41. **LO.4, 7** Ted purchased equipment and used materials to develop a patent. The development costs were deducted on prior returns. The bases and fair market values of the assets are presented below.

Assets	Fair Market Value		Basis
Equipment	$350,000	Cost	$ 450,000
		Less: Depreciation	(350,000)
Patent	250,000		–0–
	$600,000		$ 100,000

Sarah has made an offer to purchase the assets. Under one plan, she would pay $200,000 now and $400,000 plus interest at 5% (the Federal rate) in one year. Alternatively, Ted would incorporate the assets and then sell the stock to Sarah. Incorporating the assets would not be a taxable event to Ted, and his basis in the stock would equal his basis in the assets of $100,000. The corporation's basis in the assets would also be $100,000, the same as Ted's basis for the stock. Because the corporation would have a basis in the assets of less than the fair market value, and therefore there would be less depreciation and amortization than with an asset sale by Ted, Sarah would pay $200,000 in the current year but only $350,000, plus interest at 5%, in one year. Assume Ted's marginal tax rate is 35%.
a.   What is Ted's gain in the year of sale from the installment sale of his assets?
b.   Assuming that Ted's time value of money is 5%, would he prefer the sale of the assets or the sale of the stock?

42. **LO.4** Kay, who is not a dealer, sold an apartment house to Polly during the current year (2011). The closing statement for the sale is as follows:

Total selling price		$ 160,000
Add: Polly's share of property taxes (6 months) paid by Kay		2,500
Less: Kay's 8% mortgage assumed by Polly	$55,000	
Polly's refundable binder ("earnest money") paid in 2010	1,000	
Polly's 8% installment note given to Kay	90,000	
Kay's real estate commissions and attorney's fees	7,500	(153,500)
Cash paid to Kay at closing		$ 9,000
Cash due from Polly = $9,000 + $7,500 expenses		$ 16,500

During 2011, Kay collected $4,000 in principal on the installment note and $2,000 of interest. Kay's basis in the property was $70,000 [$85,000 − $15,000 (depreciation)]. The Federal rate is 6%.

a. Compute the following:
   1. Total gain.
   2. Contract price.
   3. Payments received in the year of sale.
   4. Recognized gain in the year of sale and the character of such gain.
   (*Hint:* Think carefully about the manner in which the property taxes are handled before you begin your computations.)

b. Same as (a)(2) and (3), except Kay's basis in the property was $45,000.

43. **L0.4** On June 30, 2011, Kelly sold property for $250,000 cash and a $750,000 note due on September 30, 2012. The note will also pay 6% interest, which is slighty higher than the Federal rate. Kelly's cost of the property was $400,000. She is concerned that Congress may increase the tax rate that will apply when the note is collected. Kelly's after-tax rate of return on investments is 7%.

a. What can Kelly do to avoid the expected higher tax rate?

b. Assuming Kelly's marginal combined Federal and state tax rate is 20% in 2011, how much would the tax rates need to increase to make the option identified in (a) advisable?

DECISION MAKING

44. **L0.4** On December 30, 2010, Maud sold land to her son, Charles, for $50,000 cash and a 7% installment note for $350,000, payable over 10 years. Maud's cost of the land was $150,000. In October 2012, after Charles had paid $60,000 on the principal of the note, he received an offer to sell the land for $500,000 cash. What advice can you provide Charles that will minimize the present value of the tax liability for Maud and Charles?

DECISION MAKING

45. **L0.4** George sold land to an unrelated party in 2010. His basis in the land was $45,000, and the selling price was $120,000—$30,000 payable at closing and $30,000 (plus 10% interest) due January 1, 2011, 2012, and 2013. What would be the tax consequences of the following? [Treat each part independently and assume (1) George did not elect out of the installment method and (2) the installment obligations have values equal to their face amounts. Ignore interest in your calculations.]

a. In 2011, George gave to his daughter the right to collect all future payments on the installment obligations.

b. In 2011, after collecting the payment due on January 1, George transferred the installment obligation to his 100%-controlled corporation in exchange for additional shares of stock.

c. On December 31, 2011, George received the payment due on January 1, 2012. On December 15, 2012, George died, and the remaining installment obligation was transferred to his estate. The estate collected the amount due on January 1, 2013.

46. **L0.5** The Wren Construction Company reports its income by the completed contract method. At the end of 2011, the company completed a contract to construct a building at a total cost of $800,000. The contract price was $1.2 million. However, the customer refused to accept the work and would not pay anything on the contract because he claimed the roof did not meet specifications. Wren's engineers estimated it would cost $140,000 to bring the roof up to the customer's standards. In 2012, the dispute was settled in the customer's favor; the roof was improved at a cost of $165,000, and the customer accepted the building and paid the $1.2 million.

a. What would be the effects of the above on Wren's taxable income for 2011 and 2012?

b. Same as (a), except Wren had $1.1 million accumulated cost under the contract at the end of 2011.

47. **L0.5** Rust Company is a real estate construction company with average annual gross receipts of $4 million. Rust uses the completed contract method, and the contracts require 18 months to complete.

a. Which of the following costs would be allocated to construction in progress by Rust?
   1. The payroll taxes on direct labor.
   2. The current services pension costs for employees whose wages are included in direct labor.
   3. Accelerated depreciation on equipment used on contracts.

COMMUNICATIONS

4. Freight charges on materials assigned to contracts.
5. The past service costs for employees whose wages are included in direct labor.
6. Bidding expenses for contracts awarded.

b. Assume that Rust generally builds commercial buildings under contracts with the owners and reports the income by the completed contract method. The company is considering building a series of similar stores for a retail chain. The gross profit margin would be a low percentage, but the company's gross receipts would triple. Write a letter to your client, Rust Company, explaining the tax accounting implications of entering into these contracts. Rust's mailing address is P.O. Box 1000, Harrisonburg, VA 22807.

48. **LO.5** On March 31, 2009, Big Boats Company entered into a contract with Vacations Unlimited to produce a state-of-the-art cruise ship, to be completed within three years. Big Boats estimated the total cost of building the ship at $300 million. The contract price was $400 million. The ship was completed on February 15, 2012.

a. What tax accounting method must Big Boats use for the contract? Why?
b. Using the financial data provided relating to the contract's performance, complete the following schedule:

Date	Total Costs Incurred to Date	Total Percentage of Contract Completed	Current-Year Revenue Accrued	Current-Year Costs Deductible
12/31/09	$ 60 million	———	———	———
12/31/10	180 million	———	———	———
12/31/11	280 million	———	———	———
12/31/12	340 million	N/A	———	———

c. What are the consequences of the total cost of $340 million exceeding the estimated total cost of $300 million?

49. **LO.5** Ostrich Company makes gasoline storage tanks. Everything produced is under contract (that is, the company does not produce until it gets a contract for a product). Ostrich makes three basic models. However, the tanks must be adapted to each individual customer's location and needs (e.g., the location of the valves, the quality of the materials and insulation). Discuss the following issues relative to Ostrich's operations:

a. An examining IRS agent contends that each of the company's contracts is to produce a "unique product." What difference does it make whether the product is unique or a "shelf item"?
b. Producing one of the tanks takes over one year from start to completion, and the total cost is in excess of $1 million. What costs must be capitalized for this contract that are not subject to capitalization for a contract with a shorter duration and lower cost?
c. What must Ostrich do with the costs of bidding on contracts?
d. Ostrich frequently makes several cost estimates for a contract, using various estimates of materials costs. These costs fluctuate almost daily. Assuming Ostrich must use the percentage of completion method to report the income from the contract, what will be the consequence if the company uses the highest estimate of a contract's cost and the actual cost is closer to the lowest estimated cost?

COMMUNICATIONS

50. **LO.5, 7** Swallow Company is a large real estate construction company that has made a Subchapter S election. The company reports its income using the percentage of completion method. In 2012, the company completed a contract at a total cost of $4.8 million. The contract price was $7.2 million. At the end of 2011, the year the contract was begun, Swallow estimated the total cost of the contract would be $5.4 million. Total accumulated cost on the contract at the end of 2011 was $1.8 million. The relevant tax rate is 35%, and the relevant Federal interest rate is 5%. Assume that all income tax returns were filed and taxes were paid on March 15 following the end of the calendar tax year.

a. Compute the gross profit on the contract for 2011 and 2012.
b. Compute the lookback interest due or receivable with the 2012 tax return.
c. Before bidding on a contract, Swallow generally makes three estimates of total contract costs: (1) optimistic, (2) pessimistic, and (3) most likely (based on a blending of

optimistic and pessimistic assumptions). The company has asked you to write a letter explaining which of these estimates should be used for percentage of completion purposes. In writing your letter, you should consider the fact that Swallow is incorporated and has made an S corporation election. Therefore, the income and deductions flow through to the shareholders who are all individuals in the 35% marginal tax bracket. The relevant Federal interest rate is 8%. Swallow's mailing address is 400 Front Avenue, Ashland, OR 97520.

51. **LO.6** Grouse Company is a furniture retailer whose average annual gross receipts for the three preceding years exceeded $10 million. In the current tax year, the company purchased merchandise with an invoice price of $12 million, less a 2% discount for early payment. However, the company had to borrow on a bank line of credit to take advantage of the discount for early payment. Freight on the merchandise totaled $360,000. The company has three stores and operates a warehouse where it stores goods. The cost of operating the warehouse was $300,000. The $300,000 includes labor, depreciation, taxes, and insurance on the building. The cost of the purchasing operations totaled $420,000. The jurisdiction where the company operates imposes a tax on inventories on hand as of January 1. The inventory tax for this year is $24,000. The invoice cost of goods on hand at the end of the year is $3 million. Compute Grouse's ending inventory using the FIFO method.

52. **LO.6, 7** Lavender Manufacturing Company began business in the current year. The company uses the simplified method to allocate mixed services costs to production. The company's costs and expenses for the year were as follows:

DECISION MAKING

Direct labor	$2,950,000
Direct materials	2,500,000
Factory supervision	500,000
Personnel department	300,000
Computer operations	150,000
General administration	400,000
Marketing	310,000
State income tax	90,000
	$7,200,000

a. Determine Lavender's total production costs for the year.
b. Assume that the hourly pay for direct labor is much higher than the hourly pay for employees in general administration and that the employee turnover is much higher for general administration than for production employees. Also, general administration receives much more in services from computer operations than is received by production. How should these facts affect the company's decision to use the simplified mixed services method to allocated mixed services costs to production?

53. **LO.6** Silver Creek Ranch, LLC, is a small, family-owned cattle ranch that began operations in the current year. The ranch will grow hay that will be fed to its purebred cattle. It will take approximately three years to build up the herd and to begin producing a positive cash flow. The owners' other income will equal their deductions, so they will not be able to utilize farm losses for the first three years. The owners have asked you to discuss the tax accounting issues related to their cattle business.

ISSUE ID

54. **LO.3, 6** In 2011, Gail changed from the lower of cost or market FIFO method to the LIFO inventory method. The ending inventory for 2010 was computed as follows:

Item	FIFO Cost	Replacement Cost	Lower of Cost or Market
A	$26,000	$15,000	$15,000
B	52,000	55,000	52,000
C	30,000	7,000	7,000
			$74,000

Item C was damaged goods, and the replacement cost used was actually the estimated selling price of the goods. The actual cost to replace item C was $32,000.

a. What is the correct beginning inventory for 2011 under the LIFO method?

b. What immediate tax consequences (if any) will result from the switch to LIFO?

55. **LO.6** Wren Manufacturing Company's 2011 Federal income tax return was examined by an IRS agent. One of the proposed adjustments was for the $140,000 cost of rebuilding some production equipment. Wren deducted the $140,000 as a repair expense, but the agent thinks the cost should be capitalized and depreciated as seven-year property. What would be the consequences of the agent's adjustment under the following circumstances?

a. The taxpayer uses the FIFO inventory method, and 25% of goods produced during the period were included in the ending inventory.

b. The taxpayer uses the LIFO inventory method, and no new LIFO layer was added during the current year.

56. **LO.6** Amber Company has used the dollar-value LIFO technique for the past three years. The company has only one inventory pool. Its beginning inventory for the current year was computed as follows:

	Base Period Cost	LIFO Index	LIFO Layer
Base period inventory	$1,400,000	1.00	$1,400,000
Year 1 layer	200,000	1.03	206,000
Year 2 layer	400,000	1.05	420,000
	$2,000,000		$2,026,000

The current-year ending inventory at current prices is $2,226,000, and the LIFO index is 1.06. Determine the company's LIFO inventory as of the end of the current year.

DECISION MAKING

COMMUNICATIONS

57. **LO.4, 7** Your client, Bob Young, is negotiating a sale of investment real estate for $12 million. Bob believes that the buyer would pay cash of $8 million and a note for $4 million, or $3 million cash and a note for $9 million. The notes will pay interest at slightly above the market rate. Bob realizes that the second option involves more risks of collection, but he is willing to accept that risk if the tax benefits of the installment sale are substantial. Write a letter to Bob advising him of the tax consequences of choosing the lower down payment and larger note option, assuming he has no other installment receivables. Bob's address is 200 Jerdone, Gettysburg, PA 17325.

RESEARCH PROBLEMS

Note: Solutions to Research Problems can be prepared by using the **Checkpoint®** **Student Edition** online research product, which is available to accompany this text. It is also possible to prepare solutions to the Research Problems by using tax research materials found in a standard tax library.

Research Problem 1. Your client is not permitted to deduct a year-end accrual for vacation pay earned but not paid. This result occurs because the tax law considers this to be deferred compensation that is ineligible for the recurring item exception, unless it is paid by March 15 of the year following the accrual [see §§ 404(a)(5) and (6)]. Your client has asked whether the related accrued Social Security taxes on the vacation pay can be accrued under the general recurring item exception because these taxes will be paid by the fifteenth day of the ninth month after the close of the tax year.

Research Problem 2. Your client manufactures products and must pay royalties to an inventor of the production process. The royalties are calculated as a percentage of sales. The client uses the simplified production method. An IRS agent contends that the royalties paid are part of the cost of production and therefore the simplified method requires that the royalties be allocated between ending inventory and cost of goods sold. You believe that because the royalties do not accrue until the goods are sold, the royalties are a selling expense and therefore are deductible when the sale is made. Can you locate an authority to support your intuition.

Research Problem 3. Your client is an electric utility company. During the year, the company made some improvements to its distribution lines. While the improvements were being made, the company had to temporarily move some lines so that customer service would not be interrupted. The company needs to know whether the temporary relocation costs can be allocated to electric distribution costs or must be capitalized as part of the cost of the improvements. You locate Revenue Ruling 73–203, which permits a current deduction for the cost of temporarily relocating the lines. The client notes that the ruling is old and that the uniform capitalization rules might change the results. Can you locate more current authority on the issue?

Research Problem 4. Your client is a manufacturer. For several years, the company buried empty paint cans on its property. The paint was used in the production process. Recently, a state environmental agency informed the company that it was required to dig up the paint cans and decontaminate the land. The company spent a substantial amount for this environmental cleanup in the current year. An IRS agent contends that the cost must be added to the basis in the land because the cleanup improved the land. The company's CFO has asked you to determine if any authority exists that would support a current deduction for these costs.

Research Problem 5. In 2011, your client, Clear Corporation, changed from the cash to the accrual method of accounting for its radio station. The company had a positive § 481 adjustment of $2.4 million as a result of the change and began amortizing the adjustment in 2011. In 2012, Clear received an offer to purchase the assets of the radio station business (this would be considered a sale of a trade or business under § 1060). If the offer is accepted, Clear plans to purchase a satellite television business. Clear has asked you to explain the consequences of the sale of the radio station on the amortization of the § 481 adjustment.

Use the tax resources of the Internet to address the following questions. Do not restrict your search to the Web, but include a review of newsgroups and general reference materials, practitioner sites and resources, primary sources of the tax law, chat rooms and discussion groups, and other opportunities.

INTERNET *activity*

Research Problem 6. What tax form is used to elect the LIFO inventory method?

Research Problem 7. Has the National Federation of Independent Businesses (NFIB) taken a position on whether the LIFO method should be repealed?

Deferred Compensation

LEARNING OBJECTIVES

After completing Chapter 19, you should be able to:

LO.1
Distinguish between qualified (defined contribution and defined benefit) and nonqualified compensation arrangements.

LO.2
Identify the qualification requirements for qualified plans.

LO.3
Discuss the tax consequences of qualified plans.

LO.4
Calculate the limitations on contributions to and benefits from qualified plans.

LO.5
Understand the qualified plan (Keogh plan) available to a self-employed person.

LO.6
Describe the benefits of the different types of Individual Retirement Accounts (IRAs).

LO.7
Understand the rationale for nonqualified deferred compensation plans and the related tax treatment.

LO.8
Explain the value of restricted property plans.

LO.9
Differentiate the tax treatment of qualified and nonqualified stock options.

LO.10
Identify tax planning opportunities available with deferred compensation.

OUTLINE

For the latest in changes to tax legislation, visit **www.cengage.com/taxation/swft.**

THE BIG PICTURE   Tax Solutions for the Real World

A TAXPAYER WHO SAVES

Joyce is a junior finance major at State University. Recently, Dr. Sanchez, the professor in her finance class, delivered a lecture on retirement savings that emphasized the need for a long-term savings horizon and multiple retirement plans. Near the end of the lecture, Dr. Sanchez mentioned that she has four different retirement plans. Joyce was surprised to hear this because she knows that her father has only a single retirement plan that is provided by his employer (an automobile manufacturer).

Joyce drops in on the professor during office hours. Her goal is to find out more about how a person can have multiple retirement plans. **Read the chapter and formulate your response.**

Compensation is important in any type of organization. If you have not chosen a career, consider becoming a professional golfer, basketball player, race car driver, boxer, or soccer player. *Forbes*'s latest list of the World's Top-Earning Athletes included 15 basketball players, 8 motorsports drivers, and 6 soccer players.[1] In order, the 10 top-earning athletes were as follows:

Rank	Athlete	Age	Earnings
1.	Tiger Woods (golf)	35	$105,000,000
2.	Floyd Mayweather (boxing)	33	65,000,000
3.	Kobe Bryant (basketball)	32	48,000,000
4.	Phil Mickelson (golf)	40	46,000,000
5.	David Beckham (soccer)	35	43,700,000
6.	Roger Federer (tennis)	29	43,000,000
7.	LeBron James (basketball)	26	42,800,000
8.	Manny Pacquiao (boxing)	32	42,000,000
9.	Eli Manning (football)	29	39,900,000
10.	Terrell Suggs (football)	28	38,300,000

The top earner, Tiger Woods, is paid $30 million annually by Nike.

For comparison, a second lieutenant in the U.S. Army receives approximately $47,000 (after factoring in the exclusion benefit for the meal and housing allowance), and an entry-level accountant earns approximately $55,000.

Compensation, however, whether in sports or otherwise does not guarantee commensurate performance. Consider the top 10 PER scores of NBA basketball players for the 2009–2010 season. PER, or player efficiency rating, was created by ESPN.com columnist John Hollinger. It sums up all of a player's accomplishments, subtracts the negative accomplishments, and returns a per-minute rating of a player's performance.

[1]Adapted from slide show: "The World's 50 Top-Earning Athletes," **www.Forbes.com/2010/07/20/most-valuable-athletes**.

CHAPTER 19 *Deferred Compensation*

	PER	Salary	Salary Divided by PER
1. LeBron James (Miami)	31.19	$14,500,000	$464,893
2. Dwyane Wade (Miami)	28.10	14,000,000	498,221
3. Kevin Durant (Oklahoma)	26.23	6,053,662	230,792
4. Chris Bosh (Miami)	25.11	14,500,000	577,459
5. Tim Duncan (San Antonio)	24.79	18,700,000	754,336
6. Dwight Howard (Orlando)	24.07	16,509,000	685,875
7. Chris Paul (New Orleans)	23.74	14,940,152	629,324
8. Greg Oden (Portland)	23.14	6,796,524	293,713
9. Dirk Nowitzki (Dallas)	23.01	17,300,000	751,847
10. Pau Gasol (L.A. Lakers)	22.97	17,822,187	775,890

When a player's PER score is divided into his salary, Kevin Durant of Oklahoma ($230,792) emerges as the most productive player, followed by Greg Oden of Portland ($293,713). Pau Gasol of the Los Angeles Lakers ($775,890) was the least productive of the 10 players using this measure. However, the two highest-paid players, Kobe Bryant (L.A. Lakers), with a PER of 21.95 and salary of $24,806,250, and Rashard Lewis (Orlando), with a PER of 14.0 and salary of $20,514,000, had atrocious "salary divided by PER" scores of $1,130,125 and $1,465,286, respectively.

Before you decide to give up your future career in accounting, education, or the military and jump into major league sports, also consider the tax consequences. A professional athlete's lifetime sports income is compressed into about 10 years. For example, tennis star Pete Sampras, a 14-time Grand Slam winner, retired in 2003 at the age of 32. Andre Agassi, another tennis star, retired in 2006 at age 36. Yet income averaging is not allowed for Federal income tax purposes. As a result, the athlete will lose a larger portion of lifetime earned income in the form of taxes than someone with a comparable amount of earned income over a typical work/life cycle. The athlete does, however, have a method available for reducing the Federal income tax liability in the form of deferred compensation.

This chapter discusses the various types of deferred compensation arrangements available to employees and self-employed individuals. With **deferred compensation**, an employee receives compensation for services in a later period than that in which the services were performed—quite often during retirement years. The tax law encourages employers to offer deferred compensation plans to their employees to supplement the Federal Social Security retirement system.

Qualified deferred compensation plans receive particularly favorable tax treatment. The amounts that may be deferred under these plans are limited, so they might not be perfect for Tiger Woods or Phil Mickelson. For employers and more traditional employees, however, they provide tax advantages that are exceedingly helpful. For example, contributors to qualified pension, profit sharing, or stock bonus plans receive three major tax advantages:

* Contributions are immediately deductible by the employer.
* Employees are not taxed until these funds are distributed to them.
* Income earned by the plan trust, which has received the contributions, is not subject to tax until made available to the employees, and thus grows at a tax-free rate.
* Employer contributions to and benefits payable under qualified plans generally are not subject to FICA and FUTA taxes.

Compared to nonqualified plans, though, qualified plans have some disadvantages including the following:

* The employer must make contributions for most employees on a nondiscriminatory basis.
* There are a number of limits on contributions to defined contribution plans and on benefits that may be paid under defined benefit plans.
* Qualified plans have higher startup and administrative costs.

TAX in the NEWS

FORBES'S EFFICIENT CEOs

Are high pay and efficiency related when it comes to corporate CEOs? According to *Forbes*, the two highest-paid CEOs, H. Lawrence Culp Jr. at Danaher (pay of $141.36 million) and Lawrence J. Ellison at Oracle (pay of $130.23 million), have efficiency ratings of only 90 and 82, respectively. The most efficient CEOs are as follows:

Rank	Name	Company	Pay ($ Millions)	5-Year Pay ($ Millions)	Shares Owned ($ Millions)	Age	Efficiency
135	Jeffery H. Boyd	Priceline.com	7.49	16.99	53.4	53	1
463	Jeffrey P. Bezos	Amazon.com	1.28	6.11	12,990.6	46	2
286	Leonard Bell	Alexion Pharma	4.26	19.10	47.0	51	3
427	Neal L. Patterson	Cerner	1.86	10.01	645.0	60	4
295	Paul H. Stebbins	World Fuel Services	4.05	35.94	27.9	53	5
341	Craig S. Donohue	CME Group	3.08	43.99	8.7	48	6
133	James D. Taiclet Jr.	American Tower	7.58	39.03	4.8	49	7
182	Debra A. Cafaro	Ventas	6.18	48.10	36.0	52	8
312	Keith O. Rattie	Questar	3.90	19.67	12.4	55	9
412	Daniel R. DiMicco	Nucor	1.99	26.68	22.0	59	10
373	Blake W. Nordstrom	Nordstrom	2.58	19.64	88.4	49	11
431	Ronald L. Havner Jr.	Public Storage	1.81	36.23	3.3	52	12
157	Robert Greifeld	Nasdaq OMX Group	6.81	34.28	5.9	52	13
23	David B. Snow Jr.	Medco Health	25.05	67.49	19.3	55	14
130	John P. Wiehoff	CH Robinson Worldwide	7.81	33.74	54.7	48	14

Source: Adapted from "CEO Compensation," **www.forbes.com/lists/2010/12/boss-10_CEO-Compensation_Rank.html**, April 28, 2010.

A variety of deferred compensation arrangements are being offered to employees, including the following:

- Qualified profit sharing plans.
- Qualified pension plans.
- Cash or deferred arrangement plans.
- SIMPLE IRAs and § 401(k) plans.
- Tax-deferred annuities.
- Incentive stock option plans.
- Nonqualified deferred compensation plans.
- Restricted property plans.
- Cafeteria benefit plans.
- Employee stock purchase plans.

In addition to the various types of deferred compensation, employees may receive other valuable fringe benefits, some of which may be tax-free. Examples of such benefits include group term life insurance, medical reimbursement plans, company-supplied automobiles, education expense reimbursement plans, qualified transportation benefits, and group legal services.[2]

---

[2]Refer to the discussions in Chapters 4 and 5.

19.1 QUALIFIED PENSION, PROFIT SHARING, AND STOCK BONUS PLANS

To ensure that retired people will not be dependent solely on government programs, the Federal government encourages private pension and profit sharing plans. Therefore, the Federal tax law provides substantial tax benefits for plans that meet certain requirements (qualified plans). The major requirement for qualification is that a plan not discriminate in favor of highly compensated employees.

LO.1
Distinguish between qualified (defined contribution and defined benefit) and nonqualified compensation arrangements.

TYPES OF PLANS

Qualified plans can be conveniently divided into four groups: pension, profit sharing, stock bonus, and cash balance plans.

Pension Plans

A **pension plan** is a deferred compensation arrangement that provides for systematic payments of definitely determinable retirement benefits to employees who meet the requirements set forth in the plan. Employer contributions under a qualified pension plan must *not* depend on profits. A pension plan normally must pay benefits out as lifetime annuities to provide retirement income to retired employees.

There are basically two types of qualified pension plans: defined benefit plans and defined contribution plans.

A **defined benefit plan** includes a formula that defines the benefits employees are to receive.[3] Benefits are generally measured by and based on such factors as years of service and employee compensation. Under such a plan, an employer must make annual contributions based upon actuarial computations that will be sufficient to fund the retirement benefits. If a plan document permits, employees may make contributions to the pension fund. A separate account is not maintained for each participant. A defined benefit plan provides some sense of security for employees since the benefits may be expressed in fixed dollar amounts. In a defined benefit plan, the employer (not the employee) assumes the market risk because the employer promises to pay fixed benefits. Since an expense is not deductible for tax purposes until paid, there often will be a book-tax difference because the employer accounts for the expense on an accrual basis for accounting purposes.

A **defined contribution pension plan** (or money purchase plan) defines the amount the employer is required to contribute (e.g., a flat dollar amount, an amount based on a special formula, or an amount equal to a certain percentage of compensation). A separate account must be maintained for each participant. Benefits are based solely on (1) the amount contributed and (2) income from the fund that accrues to the participant's account.[4] Consequently, actuarial calculations are not required to determine the employer's annual contribution. Upon retirement, an employee's pension amount depends on the value of his or her account. Although it is not mandatory, a plan may require or permit employee contributions to the pension fund. Since employers record the expense for both tax and accounting purposes when funding an employee's account, book-tax differences do not often occur.

The qualified pension plan of Rose Company calls for both the employer and the employee to contribute annually to the pension trust an amount equal to 5% of the employee's compensation. Since the employer's rate of contribution is fixed, this pension plan is a defined contribution plan. If the plan called for contributions sufficient to provide retirement benefits equal to 30% of the employee's average salary for the last five years of employment, it would be a defined benefit plan. ■

EXAMPLE 1

---

[3]§ 414(j).   [4]§ 414(i).

CONCEPT SUMMARY 19.1

Defined Benefit Plan and Defined Contribution Plan Compared

Defined Benefit Plan	Defined Contribution Plan
Includes a pension plan.	Includes profit sharing, stock bonus, money purchase, target benefit, qualified cash or deferred compensation, employee stock ownership plans, and some pension plans.
Determinable benefits based upon years of service and average compensation. Benefits calculated by a formula.	An account for each participant. Ultimate benefits depend upon contributions and investment performance.
Maximum annual *benefits* payable may not exceed the smaller of (1) $195,000 (in 2011)* or (2) 100% of the participant's average earnings in the three highest years of employment.	Maximum annual *contribution* to an account may not exceed the smaller of (1) $49,000** (in 2011) or (2) 100% of the participant's compensation (25% for a profit sharing plan, money purchase plan, or stock bonus plan).
Employer bears the investment risk and reward.	Employee bears the investment risk and reward.
Forfeitures must reduce subsequent funding costs and cannot increase the benefits any participant can receive under the plan.	Forfeitures may be allocated to the accounts of remaining participants.
Subject to minimum funding requirement in order to avoid penalties.	Exempt from funding requirements.
Greater administrative and actuarial costs and greater reporting requirements.	Costs and reporting requirements less burdensome.
Subject to Pension Benefit Guaranty Corporation (PBGC) plan termination insurance rules.	Not subject to PBGC plan termination insurance rules.
More favorable to employees who are older when plan is adopted since it is possible to fund higher benefits over a shorter period.	More favorable to younger employees since, over a longer period, higher benefits may result.

*This amount is subject to indexing annually in $5,000 increments.
**This amount is subject to indexing annually in $1,000 increments.

Concept Summary 19.1 compares and contrasts a defined benefit plan and a defined contribution plan.

Profit Sharing Plans

A **profit sharing plan** is a deferred compensation arrangement established and maintained by an employer to provide for employee participation in the company's profits. Contributions are paid from the employer to a trustee and are commingled in a single trust fund. Despite the name, an employer does not have to have current or accumulated profits to make a contribution. The contribution formula can be based on compensation, earnings, gross sales, or any other measurement chosen by the employer.

In a profit sharing plan, a separate account is maintained for each participant. The plan must provide a definite, predetermined formula for allocating the contributions made to the trustee among the participants. Likewise, it must include a definite, predetermined formula for distributing the accumulated funds after a fixed number of years, on the attainment of a stated age, or on the occurrence of certain events such as illness, layoff, retirement, or termination of the plan. A company is not required to contribute a definite, predetermined amount to the plan every year, although substantial and recurring contributions must be made to meet the permanency requirement. Forfeitures arising under this plan may be used to increase the individual accounts of the remaining participants as long as these increases do not result in prohibited discrimination.[5] Benefits to employees may normally be distributed through lump-sum payouts in a profit sharing plan. A § 401(k) cash or deferred arrangement plan is the most common type of profit sharing plan.

Stock Bonus Plans

A **stock bonus plan** is another form of deferred compensation. The employer establishes and maintains the plan in order to contribute shares of its stock. The contributions need not be dependent on the employer's profits. A stock bonus plan is subject to the same requirements as a profit sharing plan for purposes of allocating and distributing the stock among the employees.[6] Also, as with profit sharing plans, benefits are paid out of each separate account, and participants bear the investment risks and rewards. Any benefits of the plan normally are distributable in the form of stock of the employer company, except that distributable fractional shares may be paid in cash. Employee stock ownership plans (ESOPs) may be either profit sharing or stock bonus plans.

Cash Balance Plans

A **cash balance plan** is a controversial hybrid form of pension plan that is similar in many aspects to a defined benefit plan. These plans are funded by the employer, and the employer bears the investment risks and rewards. Thus, the employer bears the mortality risk if an employee elects to receive benefits in the form of a lifetime annuity and lives beyond normal life expectancy. But like defined contribution plans, a cash balance plan accrues benefits to individual accounts. The benefits for an employee depend on how much builds up over time in the employee's account and not on a formula based on years of service and preretirement pay. Cash balance plans are better for younger, mobile employees, and the companies save money by reducing pension payouts for older and longer-service employees.

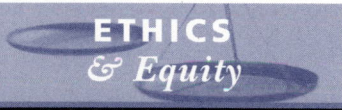

ETHICS & Equity

DO CASH BALANCE PLANS DISCRIMINATE AGAINST OLDER EMPLOYEES?

Older employees often suffer under both state and Federal laws when employers convert traditional pension plans to cash balance plans. Under a traditional pension plan, a company adopts a formula that calculates pension benefits by multiplying years of service by a factor based on average salary, which causes benefits to escalate rapidly in value in later years. Should a company be allowed to reduce a long-term employee's benefits significantly by converting to a cash balance plan?

QUALIFICATION REQUIREMENTS

To be *qualified*, and thereby to receive favorable tax treatment, a plan generally must satisfy the following requirements:

- Exclusive benefit requirement.
- Nondiscrimination requirements.
- Participation and coverage requirements.
- Vesting requirements.
- Distribution requirements.
- Minimum funding requirements.

> **LO.2**
>
> Identify the qualification requirements for qualified plans.

---

[5]Reg. §§ 1.401–1(b) and 1.401–4(a)(1)(iii).   [6]Reg. § 1.401–1(b)(1)(iii).

These qualification rules are highly technical and numerous. As a result, the IRS maintains a staggered determination letter request process that allows plan sponsors to file a plan document with the IRS for approval. A favorable determination letter (similar to a letter ruling) indicates that the form of the plan meets the qualification requirements and that the form of the plan's trust meets the requirements for exemption. However, the ultimate qualification of the plan depends upon its actual administration and operations. Therefore, the operations of the plan should be reviewed periodically. Favorable determination letters have an expiration date with individually designed plans on a five-year schedule and preapproved plans on a six-year schedule.

The IRS has an Employee Plans Compliance Resolution System (EPCRS) that allows sponsors of retirement plans to correct failures to satisfy requirements for a period of time. By using this system to correct failures, plan sponsors can avoid disqualification and continue to provide employees with retirement benefits on a tax-favored basis. The components of EPCRS include the Self-Correction Program (SCP), the Voluntary Correction Program (VCP), and the Audit Closing Agreement Program (Audit CAP).

Nondiscrimination Requirements

The contributions and benefits under a plan must *not discriminate* in favor of highly compensated employees. A plan is not considered discriminatory merely because contributions and benefits are proportional to compensation.[7] For example, a pension plan that provides for the allocation of employer contributions based upon a flat 3 percent of each employee's compensation would not be discriminatory solely because highly paid employees receive greater benefits.

Participation and Coverage Requirements

A qualified plan must provide, at a minimum, that all employees in the covered group who are 21 years of age are eligible to participate after completing one year of service. A year of service is generally defined as the completion of 1,000 hours of service within a measuring period of 12 consecutive months. As an alternative, where the plan provides that 100 percent of an employee's accrued benefits will be vested upon entering the plan, the employee's participation may be postponed until the later of age 21 or two years from the date of employment. Once the age and service requirements are met, an employee must begin participating no later than the *earlier* of the following:

- The first day of the first plan year beginning after the date on which the requirements were satisfied.
- Six months after the date on which the requirements were satisfied.[8]

EXAMPLE 2	Coffee Corporation has a calendar year retirement plan covering its employees. The corporation adopts the most restrictive eligibility rules permitted. Wilma, age 21, is hired on January 31, 2010, and meets the service requirement over the next 12 months (completes at least 1,000 hours by January 31, 2011). Wilma must be included in this plan no later than July 31, 2011, because the six-month limitation would be applicable. If the company had adopted the two-year participation rule, Wilma must be included in the plan no later than July 31, 2012. ∎

Since a qualified plan must be primarily for the benefit of employees and be nondiscriminatory, the plan has to cover a reasonable percentage of the company employees. A plan will be qualified only if it satisfies one of the following tests:[9]

- The plan benefits a percentage of non-highly compensated employees equal to at least 70 percent of the percentage of highly compensated employees benefiting under the plan (the *ratio percentage test*).
- The plan meets the *average benefits test*, which is described below.

---

[7]§§ 401(a)(4) and (5).
[8]§§ 410(a)(1)(A) and (B) and 410(a)(4).

[9]§ 410(b).

If a company has no highly compensated employees, the retirement plan will automatically satisfy the coverage rules.

To satisfy the *average benefits test*, the plan must benefit any employees who qualify under a classification set up by the employer and found by the Secretary of the Treasury not to be discriminatory in favor of highly compensated employees (the classification test). In addition, the average benefit percentage for non-highly compensated employees must be at least 70 percent of the average benefit percentage for highly compensated employees. The *average benefit percentage* means, with respect to any group of employees, the average of the benefit percentages calculated separately for each employee in the group. The term *benefit percentage* means the employer-provided contributions (including forfeitures) or benefits of an employee under all qualified plans of the employer, expressed as a percentage of that employee's compensation.

An employee is a **highly compensated employee** if, at any time during the year or the preceding year, the employee satisfies *either* of the following:[10]

- Was a 5 percent owner of the company.
- Received more than $110,000 (in 2011) in annual compensation from the employer *and* was a member of the top-paid group of the employer.[11] The top-paid group clause is applicable only if the employer elects to have it apply. An employee whose compensation is in the top 20 percent of the employees is a member of the top-paid group.

An additional *minimum participation test* must also be met for some plans. A plan must cover at least 40 percent of all employees or, if fewer, at least 50 employees on one representative day of the plan year. In determining all employees, nonresident aliens, certain union members, and employees not fulfilling the minimum age or years-of-service requirement of the plan may be excluded.[12]

EXAMPLE 3

Assume that Rust Corporation's retirement plan automatically meets the 70% test (the ratio percentage test) because 70% of all non-highly compensated employees benefit. The company has 100 employees, but only 38 of these employees are covered by the plan. Therefore, this retirement plan does not meet the minimum participation requirement. ∎

Vesting Requirements

The purpose of the **vesting requirements** is to protect an employee who has worked a reasonable period of time for an employer from losing employer contributions because of being fired or changing jobs. An employee's right to accrued benefits derived from his or her own contributions to a defined benefit plan must be nonforfeitable from the date of contribution. The accrued benefits derived from employer contributions must be nonforfeitable in accordance with one of *two alternative minimum vesting schedules* or an even more generous vesting schedule.

To satisfy the *first alternative*, a participant must have a nonforfeitable right to 100 percent of his or her accrued benefits derived from employer contributions upon completion of not more than five years of service (five-year or cliff vesting). The *second alternative* is satisfied if a participant has a nonforfeitable right at least equal to a percentage of the accrued benefits derived from employer contributions as depicted in Table 19.1 (graded vesting). Of the two alternatives, cliff vesting minimizes administration expenses for a company and provides more vesting for a long-term employee.

EXAMPLE 4

Mitch has six years of service completed as of February 2, 2011, his employment anniversary date. If his defined benefit plan has a five-year (cliff) vesting schedule, 100% of Mitch's accrued benefits are vested. If the plan uses the graded vesting rule, Mitch's nonforfeitable percentage is 80%. ∎

---

[10] §§ 401(a)(4) and 414(q).
[11] The $110,000 amount is indexed annually in $5,000 increments.
[12] §§ 401(a)(26) and 410(b)(3) and (4).

TABLE 19.1	Three- to Seven-Year Vesting
Years of Service	**Nonforfeitable Percentage**
3	20%
4	40%
5	60%
6	80%
7 or more	100%

TABLE 19.2	Two- to Six-Year Vesting
Years of Service	**Nonforfeitable Percentage**
2	20%
3	40%
4	60%
5	80%
6 or more	100%

After 2006, defined contribution plans also must satisfy one of the following minimum vesting schedules: two- to six-year graded vesting as shown in Table 19.2, three-year cliff vesting, or an even more generous vesting schedule.

EXAMPLE 5

Millie has five years of service completed as of February 2, 2011, her employment anniversary date. If her defined contribution plan uses three-year cliff vesting, Millie must be 100% vested. Under a two- to six-year vesting plan, Millie must be 80% vested. ∎

Distribution Requirements

Uniform *minimum distribution rules* exist for all qualified defined benefit and defined contribution plans, traditional Individual Retirement Accounts (IRAs) and annuities, unfunded deferred compensation plans of state and local governments and tax-exempt employers, and tax-sheltered custodial accounts and annuities. Distributions to a participant must begin by April 1 of the calendar year *following the later* of (1) the calendar year in which the employee attains age 70½ or (2) the calendar year in which the employee retires. Thus, an employee can delay receiving distributions until retirement. However, distributions to a 5 percent owner or a traditional IRA holder must begin no later than April 1 of the calendar year *following* the year in which the 5 percent owner or the IRA holder reaches age 70½.[13] A holder of a Roth IRA does *not* have to take a distribution by April 1 of the calendar year following the calendar year in which the holder attains age 70½. That is, the holder of a Roth IRA is not required to begin receiving distributions at any point in time during his or her life.

Minimum annual distributions must be made over the life of the participant or the lives of the participant and a designated individual beneficiary. The amount of the required minimum distribution for a particular year is determined by dividing the

---

[13]§ 401(a)(9).

TAX in the NEWS

SPIKING YOUR RETIREMENT PLAN

"Spiking" is more than a baseball player injuring an opponent with the spikes on his shoes or a player sharply spiking a volleyball over the net. Spiking also refers to the practice of increasing one's salary just before retirement to boost pension payouts. Spiking has been common in California because of favorable terms in pension contracts negotiated by powerful unions.

For example, Pete Nowicki was receiving a salary of $186,000 shortly before he retired in January 2009 as chief of a Northern California fire department. Three days before he retired, he increased his salary by selling unused vacation days and holidays. This spiking increased his annual pension payment to $241,000. Of course, spiking creates a larger shortfall between what the participant has paid into the plan and what the plan must pay out.

The Virginia state legislature has enacted a law with the primary intent of preventing spiking at the College of William and Mary. Previously, William and Mary had provided its retiring faculty members with 8 and 7 percent raises during their last two years of employment. The effect was to build retirement pay for those faculty members participating in the state's defined benefit plan, since the benefit formula looked at the final three years of employment.

Sources: Adapted from Craig Karmin, "Pension Calculus Draws New Scrutiny," *Wall Street Journal*, July 20, 2009, p. A3; and Susan Robertson, "State Quits Paying Extra Retirement," *Virginia Gazette*, June 26, 2010, p. A1

account balance as of December 31 of the prior year by the applicable life expectancy. The life expectancy of the owner and his or her beneficiary is based upon the expected return multiples in the Regulations, using ages attained within the calendar year the participant reaches age 70½.[14]

EXAMPLE 6

Beth reaches age 70½ in 2011, and she will also be age 71 in 2011. Her retirement account has a balance of $120,000 on December 31, 2010. If Beth is retired, a 5% owner, or the holder of a traditional IRA, she must withdraw $7,843 ($120,000 ÷ 15.3) for the 2011 calendar year, assuming her multiple is 15.3. This distribution need not be made until April 1, 2012, but a second distribution must be made by December 31, 2012. ∎

Failure to make a minimum required distribution to a particular participant results in a *50 percent nondeductible excise tax* on the excess in any taxable year of the amount that should have been distributed over the amount that actually was distributed. The tax is imposed on the individual required to take the distribution (the payee).[15] The Secretary of the Treasury is authorized to waive the tax for a given taxpayer year if the taxpayer is able to establish that the shortfall is due to reasonable error and that reasonable steps are being taken to remedy the shortfall.

If a taxpayer receives an *early distribution* from a qualified retirement plan, a 10 percent additional tax is levied on the full amount of any distribution includible in gross income.[16] For this purpose, the term *qualified retirement plan* includes a qualified defined benefit plan or defined contribution plan, a tax-sheltered annuity or custodial account, or a traditional IRA. The following distributions, however, are *not* treated as early distributions:

- Distributions made on or after the date the employee attains age 59½.
- Distributions made to a beneficiary (or the estate of an employee) on or after the death of the employee.
- Distributions attributable to the employee's being disabled.
- Distributions made as part of a scheduled series of substantially equal periodic payments (made not less frequently than annually) for the life of the participant (or the joint lives of the participant and the participant's beneficiary).

[14]Reg. § 1.72–9. Refer to Chapter 4.
[15]§ 4974(a).
[16]§ 72(t). See Ltr.Rul. 8837071.

- Distributions made to an employee after separation from service because of early retirement under the plan after attaining age 55. This exception to early distribution treatment does not apply to a traditional IRA.
- Distributions used to pay medical expenses to the extent that the expenses are deductible under § 213 (determined regardless of whether or not the taxpayer itemizes deductions).
- IRA distributions that are used to pay qualified higher education expenses of the taxpayer, the spouse, or any child or grandchild of the taxpayer or the taxpayer's spouse.
- IRA distributions up to $10,000 that are used to pay expenses incurred by qualified first-time homebuyers.

Minimum Funding Requirements

Minimum funding requirements apply to defined benefit plans, money purchase plans, and target benefit plans to regulate the amount that an employer must contribute to ensure that the plan is properly funded. The amount of contributions required for a plan year is the amount needed to fund benefits earned during a plan year (e.g., normal costs) plus the portion of other liabilities that are amortized over a period of years (e.g., investment losses). A special account called a funding standard account is required, and contribution amounts are determined under one of several acceptable actuarial cost methods. A tax equal to 10 percent of the aggregate unpaid required contribution is imposed on a single-employer plan (5 percent for a multiemployer plan). If an accumulated funding deficit is not corrected, a 100 percent tax is imposed.[17]

<table>
<tr><td>LO.3</td></tr>
<tr><td>Discuss the tax consequences of qualified plans.</td></tr>
</table>

TAX CONSEQUENCES TO THE EMPLOYEE AND EMPLOYER

In General

Although employer contributions to qualified plans are generally deductible immediately (subject to contribution and deductibility rules), these amounts are not subject to taxation until distributed to employees.[18] If benefits are paid with respect to an employee (to a creditor of the employee, a child of the employee, etc.), the benefits paid are treated as if paid to the employee. When benefits are distributed to employees, or paid with respect to an employee, the employer does not receive another deduction.

The tax benefit to the employee amounts to a substantial tax deferral and may be viewed as an interest-free loan from the government to the trust fund. Another advantage of a qualified plan is that any income earned by the trust is not taxable to the trust.[19] Employees, in effect, are taxed on such earnings when they receive the retirement benefits.

The taxation of amounts received by employees in periodic or installment payments is generally subject to the annuity rules in § 72 (refer to Chapter 4). In any situation where employee contributions have been subject to tax previously, they are included in the employee's *investment in the contract*. Two other alternative options generally are available for benefit distributions. A taxpayer may (1) receive the distribution in a lump-sum payment or (2) roll over the benefits into an IRA or another qualified employer retirement plan.

Lump-Sum Distributions from Qualified Plans

A **lump-sum distribution** occurs when an employee receives his or her entire payout from a qualified plan in a single payment rather than receiving the amount in installments. The annuity rules do not apply to a lump-sum distribution. All such payments are thrown into one year. Since lump-sum payments have been accumulated over a number of years, bunching retirement benefits into one taxable year may impose a

[17]§ 412.
[18]§ 402(a)(1).

[19]§ 501(a).

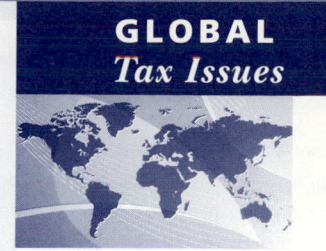

COVERING EXPATRIATE EMPLOYEES

GLOBAL Tax Issues

Can an employer cover individuals employed outside the United States in a qualified retirement plan? This question often arises when an employee is transferred from the United States to a foreign affiliate of the employer.

The hurdle to overcome is the exclusive benefit rule in § 401(a): the qualified plan must be maintained for the exclusive benefit of the employees of the company that sponsors the plan.

If a company conducts its foreign operations through branches that are part of the U.S. entity, the employee can qualify for the plan. Likewise, all employees of all corporations that are members of a controlled group of corporations can be covered. A controlled group would include both a brother-sister group and a parent-subsidiary group.

high tax burden because of progressive rates. To overcome this bunching effect, for many years the tax law has provided favorable treatment for certain lump-sum distributions. Major changes were made in the lump-sum distribution rules by TRA of 1986. Transitional provisions allow a participant who reached age 50 before January 1, 1986 (born before 1936), to elect the pre-1987 rules on a limited basis. These pre-1987 rules permit a 10-year forward averaging technique and a limited capital gain allocation.[20]

Rollover Treatment

A taxpayer who receives a distribution can avoid current taxation by rolling the distribution into another qualified employer retirement plan or into an IRA.[21] The taxation of the distribution is deferred until distributions are made from the recipient's qualified employer retirement plan or IRA. The rollover can be *direct* with the balance in the account going directly from a qualified employer retirement plan to another qualified employer retirement plan or an IRA (sometimes called a conversion). The rollover can be *indirect* with the proceeds going to the taxpayer who has 60 days to transfer the proceeds into another qualified employer retirement plan or an IRA. One can use an indirect rollover to borrow from an IRA, but the "loan" must be fully reinvested in another retirement plan or IRA within the 60-day window. A benefit of the direct rollover is that it is not subject to the 20 percent withholding applicable to indirect rollovers.[22]

LIMITATIONS ON CONTRIBUTIONS TO AND BENEFITS FROM QUALIFIED PLANS

LO.4

Calculate the limitations on contributions to and benefits from qualified plans.

In General

The annual limitations on contributions to and benefits from qualified plans appearing in § 415 must be written into a qualified plan. Section 404 sets the limits on deductibility applicable to the employer. The limit on the amount deductible under § 404 may have an impact on the amount the employer is willing to contribute. In fact, a defined benefit plan or defined contribution plan is not allowed a deduction for the amount that exceeds the § 415 limitations.[23]

Defined Contribution Plans

Under a *defined contribution plan*, the annual addition to an employee's account cannot exceed the smaller of $49,000 (in 2011) or 100 percent of the employee's compensation.[24] However, this individual percentage limitation of 100 percent normally

---

[20]§ 402(e)(1)(C) of the IRC of 1954.
[21]§ 402(c).
[22]§ 3405(c).

[23]§ 404(j).
[24]§§ 415(c) and (d).

TAX *in* the *NEWS*   A TSUNAMI AVERTED?

Now is the time when the baby boomers are supposed to be starting to retire. Could this produce a retirement tsunami? The answer may be "no"—at least for now.

According to a survey of state and local government managers by the Center for State and Local Government Excellence, two-thirds of the managers said that workers are delaying retirement because of the recession.

Should these survey results ease fears that the baby boomers will retire en masse? The answer may be "yes"— but only for the time being. The Center's communications manager believes that the tsunami is merely being postponed for a few years.

Source: Adapted from Sara Murray, "State, Local Employees Delay Retirement," *Wall Street Journal*, May 14, 2009, p. D5.

is not attainable for small plans because the employer's deduction limit cannot exceed 25 percent of eligible compensation for all participants. The $49,000 amount is indexed (in $1,000 increments).[25]

Defined Benefit Plans

Under a *defined benefit plan*, the annual benefit payable to an employee is limited to the smaller of $195,000 (in 2011)[26] or 100 percent of the employee's average compensation for the highest three years of employment. This benefit limit is subject to a $10,000 *de minimis* floor. The $195,000 limitation is reduced actuarially if the benefits begin before the Social Security normal retirement age (currently age 65 and 10 months) and is increased actuarially if the benefits begin after the Social Security normal retirement age. The dollar limit on annual benefits ($195,000) is reduced by one-tenth for each year of *participation* under 10 years by the employee. Furthermore, the 100 percent of compensation limitation and the $10,000 *de minimis* floor are reduced proportionately for a participant who has less than 10 years of *service* with the employer.[27]

EXAMPLE 7
THE BIG PICTURE

Return to the facts of *The Big Picture* on p. 19-2. The university has offered Joyce's professor, Dr. Sanchez, a choice between a defined benefit pension plan and a defined contribution plan. Dr. Sanchez expects to work at a number of universities during her career. A colleague has recommended that Dr. Sanchez choose the defined contribution plan because of its mobility (i.e., she can take the plan with her). So she needs to decide if this mobility factor is significant in making her choice and how much she can contribute annually to a defined contribution plan. ■

EXAMPLE 8

Adam's average compensation for the highest three years of employment is $87,000. The defined benefit plan would not qualify if the plan provides for benefits in excess of the smaller of (1) $87,000 or (2) $195,000 for Adam in 2011 (assuming normal retirement age). ■

EXAMPLE 9

Peggy has participated for four years in a defined benefit plan and has six years of service with her employer. Her average compensation for the three highest years is $60,000. Her four years of participation reduce her dollar limitation to $78,000 ($195,000 × $4/10$). Her six years of service reduce her 100% of compensation limitation to 60%. Therefore, her limit on annual benefits is $36,000 ($60,000 × 60%). ■

The amount of compensation that may be taken into account under any plan is limited to $245,000 (in 2011).[28] Thus, the benefits highly compensated individuals

---

[25]§ 415(d)(4).
[26]This amount is indexed annually in $5,000 increments.

[27]§ 415(b).
[28]§§ 401(a)(17) and 404(l). This amount is indexed in $5,000 increments.

receive may be smaller as a percentage of their pay than those received by non-highly compensated employees.

> **EXAMPLE 10**
>
> Swan Corporation has a defined contribution plan with a 10% contribution formula. An employee earning less than $245,000 in 2011 would not be affected by this includible compensation limitation. However, an employee earning $490,000 in 2011 would have only 5% of compensation allocated to his or her account because of the $245,000 limit on includible compensation. ■

The maximum deduction a corporation is permitted for contributions to pension plans may be determined by either of two methods. First, an aggregate cost method allows an actuarially determined deduction based on a level amount, or a level percentage, of compensation over the remaining future service of covered participants. Second, the employer is permitted to deduct the so-called normal cost plus no more than 10 percent of the past service costs. The *normal cost* represents the estimated contribution required associated with work performed by employees in the current year. *Past service costs* are costs relating to the inception of the plan and costs that result from changes in the retirement plan.

The employer's contribution is deductible in the tax year such amounts are allocated or credited to the pension trust. However, both cash and accrual basis employers may defer the payment of contributions with respect to any tax year until the date fixed for filing the taxpayer's Federal income tax return for that year (including extensions).[29] In effect, the corporation is allowed a deduction to the extent it is compelled to make such contributions to satisfy the funding requirement. If an amount in excess of the allowable amount is contributed in any tax year, the excess may be carried forward and deducted in succeeding tax years (to the extent the carryover plus the succeeding year's contribution does not exceed the deductible limitation for that year).[30]

> **EXAMPLE 11**
>
> During 2011, Green Corporation contributes $17,500 to its qualified pension plan. Normal cost for this year is $7,200, and the amount necessary to pay retirement benefits on behalf of employee services before 2011 is $82,000 (past service costs). The corporation's maximum deduction is $15,400. This amount consists of the $7,200 normal cost plus 10% ($8,200) of the past service costs. The corporation has a $2,100 [$17,500 (contribution) − $15,400 (deduction)] contribution carryover. ■

> **EXAMPLE 12**
>
> Assume in the previous example that Green Corporation has normal cost of $7,200 in 2012 and contributes $10,000 to the pension trust. The corporation's maximum deduction would be $15,400. Green Corporation may deduct $12,100, composed of this year's contribution ($10,000) plus the $2,100 contribution carryover. ■

A 10 percent excise tax is imposed on nondeductible contributions. The tax is levied on the employer making the contribution. The tax applies to nondeductible contributions for the current year and any nondeductible contributions for the preceding year that have not been eliminated by the end of the current year (as a carryover or by being returned to the employer in the current year).[31]

Profit Sharing and Stock Bonus Plan Limitations

The maximum deduction permitted to an employer each year for contributions to profit sharing and stock bonus plans is 25 percent of the compensation paid or accrued with respect to plan participants in the aggregate. The maximum amount of compensation for an employee that may be taken into account under a plan for deduction calculations or any other purposes is $245,000 (in 2011), and the

---

[29]§§ 404(a)(1) and (6).   [31]§ 4972.
[30]§ 404(a)(1)(D).

maximum deduction allowed is $49,000 (in 2011). Any nondeductible excess, a so-called contribution carryover, may be carried forward indefinitely and deducted in subsequent years. The maximum deduction in any succeeding year is 25 percent of all compensation paid or accrued in the aggregate during that taxable year.[32]

SECTION 401(K) Plans

In General

A **§ 401(k) plan** allows participants to elect either to receive up to $16,500 (in 2011)[33] in cash (taxed currently) or to have a contribution made on their behalf to a profit sharing or stock bonus plan. The plan may also be in the form of a salary-reduction agreement between an eligible participant and an employer under which a contribution will be made only if the participant elects to reduce his or her compensation or to forgo an increase in compensation.

Any pretax amount elected by the employee as a plan contribution is not includible in gross income in the year of deferral and is 100 percent vested. Any employer contributions are tax deferred until distributed, as are earnings on contributions in the plan.

EXAMPLE 13

Sam participates in a § 401(k) plan of his employer. The plan permits the participants to choose between a full salary or a reduced salary where the reduction becomes a before-tax contribution to a retirement plan. Sam elects to contribute 10% of his annual compensation of $30,000 to the plan. Income taxes are paid on only $27,000. No income taxes are paid on the $3,000—or on any earnings—until it is distributed from the plan to Sam. The main benefit of a § 401(k) plan is that Sam can shift a portion of his income to a later taxable year. ■

The maximum annual elective contribution to a § 401(k) plan is $16,500 (in 2011), but that amount is reduced dollar-for-dollar by other salary-reduction contributions to tax-sheltered annuities, simplified employee pension plans, and § 401(k) plans. Elective contributions in excess of the maximum limitation are taxable in the year of deferral. These amounts may be refunded from the plan tax-free before April 15 of the following year. Excess amounts not timely distributed will be double-taxed because they will be taxable in the year of distribution, even though they were included in income in the year of deferral. Annual elective contributions are also limited by complicated nondiscrimination requirements designed to encourage

---

[32]§§ 404(a)(3)(A) and (a)(7).

[33]§§ 402(g)(1) and (4). Starting in 2003, this amount was increased in $1,000 increments until it reached $15,000 in 2006. It is indexed in $500 incre-ments in years after 2006. The amount was $12,000 for 2003; $13,000 for 2004; $14,000 for 2005; $15,000 for 2006; $15,500 for 2007; $15,500 for 2008; $16,500 for 2009; and $16,500 for 2010.

GLOBAL REMUNERATION APPROACH

A multinational firm may find it desirable to develop a global remuneration strategy. According to Bowker Consulting International, a nonglobal remuneration approach has several disadvantages:

- U.S. compensation and benefit programs are imposed worldwide, without regard to local laws, employee expectations, and competitive practices.
- U.S. compensation and benefit programs are layered on top of local programs, resulting in a confusing and often overly generous total remuneration package.
- Perceived "U.S." philosophy and principles that might have important global application if properly communicated may be rejected in favor of local programs that do not reflect overall business objectives, performance standards, and corporate values.
- An "us against them" attitude may develop between the corporation and local employees, preventing constructive dialogue in creating and implementing an appropriate rewards structure for a particular country.

Source: Adapted from **www.bowkerconsulting.com/services**.

participation by non-highly compensated employees and by the general defined contribution plan limitations.

	EXAMPLE 14
Return to the facts of *The Big Picture* on p. 19-2. Although Dr. Sanchez is not eligible to participate in a § 401(k) plan, she does participate in a § 403(b) tax-deferred annuity plan for employees of § 501(c)(3) not-for-profit organizations (similar in many respects to a § 401(k) plan). ∎	THE BIG PICTURE

A person who has attained age 50 by the end of the tax year can make catch-up contributions of $1,000 for 2002, $2,000 for 2003, $3,000 for 2004, $4,000 for 2005, and $5,000 for 2006 and thereafter.[34]

	EXAMPLE 15
Return to the facts of *The Big Picture* on p. 19-2. Dr. Sanchez indicates that since she is age 51, she is eligible to make catch-up contributions to her § 403(b) annuity. ∎	THE BIG PICTURE

A 10 percent excise tax is imposed on the employer for excess elective deferral contributions not withdrawn from the plan within 2½ months after the close of the plan year. The plan may lose its qualified status if these excess contributions (and any related income) are not withdrawn by the end of the plan year following the plan year in which the excess contributions were made.[35]

	EXAMPLE 16
Carmen, age 36, is an employee of a manufacturing corporation. She defers $18,500 in a § 401(k) plan in 2011. The $2,000 excess over the $16,500 limit, along with the appropriate earnings, must be returned to Carmen by April 15, 2012. This $2,000 excess amount	

---

[34]The $5,000 amount is indexed in $500 increments in 2007 and thereafter. For 2007 and 2008, the amount remained at $5,000. For 2009, the amount increased to $5,500. For 2010, the amount remained at $5,500. For 2011, the amount remains at $5,500.

[35]§ 4979(a).

MORE OR LESS BENEFICIAL TREATMENT FOR § 403(B) PLANS

Recently issued Regulations are intended to make § 403(b) plans more transparent and understandable for covered employees. Section 403(b) plans are similar to § 401(k) plans, but apply only to employees of certain not-for-profit, educational, governmental, and religious organizations.

These Regulations have substantially lessened the number of investment options for employees and have also reduced participants' access to loans and hardship distributions. They also have increased the burden on the employers who oversee these items. While some see these changes as detrimental, others disagree. John Kevin, the investment officer for the Montgomery County Public Schools in Maryland, which has approximately $1 billion in its § 403(b) plan, believes the new rules will prove advantageous for employees. He thinks that greater employer scrutiny of the plans will result in lower costs and better investment options.

Source: Adapted from Eleanor Laise, "Workers Struggle to Deal with Changes to 403(b) Plans," *Wall Street Journal,* May 3, 2010, p. R1.

plus related income is taxable to her in 2011 and will be taxed again upon distribution (if made after April 15, 2012). There will be a 10% tax on Carmen's employer on any excess contributions not returned within 2½ months after the close of the plan year. ■

For self-employed individuals, matching contributions are not treated as elective contributions under a cash or deferred election.[36] Beginning in 2008, there is a qualified automatic enrollment arrangement (QAEA), whereby companies may automatically enroll employees in a § 401(k) plan with a prescribed percentage (not to exceed 10 percent) of the employee's pay automatically withdrawn from each paycheck (unless the employee elects otherwise). This stated percentage must be applied uniformly to all eligible employees.

If certain requirements are met, the plan administrator may choose the investments for the participants and be protected from liability involving investment choices. A § 401(k) plan consisting solely of contributions made under a QAEA also is exempt from the top-heavy rules.[37] Finally, after 2009, small employers may establish a combined defined benefit/§ 401(k) plan (a DB/K plan); the § 401(k) component of the DB/K plan must have automatic enrollment, with an employee being treated as having elected to make deferrals of 4 percent of pay, and must provide a minimum match of 50 percent of elective deferrals up to 4 percent of pay.[38]

SIMPLE Plans

Employers with 100 or fewer employees who do not maintain another qualified retirement plan may establish a *savings incentive match plan for employees* (SIMPLE plan).[39] The plan can be in the form of a § 401(k) plan or an IRA. A SIMPLE § 401(k) plan is not subject to the nondiscrimination rules that are normally applicable to § 401(k) plans.

All employees who received at least $5,000 in compensation from the employer during any two preceding years and who reasonably expect to receive at least $5,000 in compensation during the current year must be eligible to participate in the plan. The decision to participate is up to the employee. A self-employed individual may also participate in the plan.

---

[36]Prop.Reg. § 1.401(k)–1(a)(6)(ii).

[37]§§ 401(a)(3)(G), 401(k)(8)(E), 401(k)(13), 401(m)(6)(A), 401(m)(12), and 414(w).

[38]§ 414(x) and ERISA § 210(e).

[39]§ 408(p).

The contributions made by the employee (a salary-reduction approach) must be expressed as a percentage of compensation rather than as a fixed dollar amount. The SIMPLE plan must not permit the SIMPLE elective employee contribution for the year to exceed $11,500 (in 2011).[40] The SIMPLE elective deferral limit is increased under the catch-up provision for employees age 50 and over. The amount is $500 for 2002, $1,000 for 2003, $1,500 for 2004, $2,000 for 2005, and $2,500 for 2006 and thereafter. The $2,500 amount is indexed for inflation in $500 increments beginning in 2007 (remains at $2,500 for 2007, 2008, 2009, 2010 and 2011).

Generally, the employer must either match elective employee contributions up to 3 percent of the employee's compensation or provide nonmatching contributions of 2 percent of compensation for each eligible employee. Thus, the maximum amount that may be contributed to the plan for an employee under age 50 for 2011 is $18,850 [$11,500 employee contributions + $7,350 ($245,000 compensation ceiling × 3%) employer match].

No other contributions may be made to the plan other than the employee elective contribution and the required employer matching contribution (or nonmatching contribution under the 2 percent rule). All contributions are fully vested. An employer is required to make the required matching or nonmatching contributions to a SIMPLE § 401(k) plan once it is established, whereas an employer's contributions to a traditional § 401(k) plan generally may be discretionary.

An employer's deduction for contributions to a SIMPLE § 401(k) plan is limited to the greater of 25 percent of the compensation paid or accrued or the amount that the employer is required to contribute to the plan. Thus, an employer may deduct contributions to a SIMPLE § 401(k) plan in excess of 25 percent of the $245,000 salary cap. A traditional § 401(k) plan is limited to 25 percent of the total compensation of plan participants for the year (excluding age 50 catch-ups).

An employer is allowed a deduction for matching contributions only if the contributions are made by the due date (including extensions) for the employer's tax return. Contributions to a SIMPLE plan are excludible from the employee's gross income, and the SIMPLE plan is tax-exempt.

EXAMPLE 17

The Mauve Company has a SIMPLE plan for its employees under which it provides non-matching contributions of 2% of compensation for each eligible employee. The maximum amount that can be added to each participant's account in 2011 is $16,400, composed of the $11,500 employee salary reduction plus an employer contribution of $4,900($245,000 × 2%). ∎

Distributions from a SIMPLE plan are taxed under the IRA rules. Tax-free rollovers can be made from one SIMPLE account to another. A SIMPLE account can be rolled over to an IRA tax-free after the expiration of a two-year period since the individual first participated in the plan. Withdrawals of contributions during the two-year period beginning on the date an employee first participates in the SIMPLE plan are subject to a 25 percent early withdrawal tax rather than the 10 percent early withdrawal tax that otherwise would apply.

Designated Roth Contributions

Starting in 2006, § 401(k) plans and § 403(b) plans may be amended to permit employees to irrevocably designate some or all of their future salary deferral contributions as Roth § 401(k) or Roth § 403(b) contributions.[41] These designated amounts are currently includible in the employee's gross income and are maintained in a separate plan account. The earnings on these elective contributions build up in the plan on a tax-free basis. Future qualified distributions made from

---

[40]For 2004, the limit was $9,000. The $10,000 amount for 2005 is indexed for inflation in $500 increments in 2006 and thereafter. For 2006, the amount remained at $10,000. For 2007 and 2008, it increased to $10,500. For 2009, it increased to $11,500. For 2010, it remained at $11,500. § 408(p)(2)(E)(i).

[41]§ 402A.

IRA LOSSES FROM A PONZI SCHEME

The Bernard Madoff and Mark Stanford Ponzi schemes have affected many taxpayers who had IRA plans with Madoff or Stanford. If a taxpayer had a traditional IRA and all contributions were deductible, the individual has a zero basis, so no loss deduction is available for the losses associated with these Ponzi schemes. If the IRA included some nondeductible contributions, a loss might be deductible if the individual withdraws the entire amount from the IRA. The miscellaneous itemized deduction, subject to the 2 percent floor, would be the difference between the basis and the amount withdrawn. Of course, there may be a 10 percent penalty tax if the withdrawal is an early withdrawal.

A taxpayer with a Roth IRA is more likely to obtain a loss deduction associated with these Ponzi schemes because Roth IRA contributions are nondeductible. The miscellaneous itemized deduction would be the amount contributed (i.e., the basis) less the value of any assets distributed to the Roth IRA owner.

designated contributions are excludible from gross income. The adjusted gross income (AGI) limitation (discussed later in the chapter) does not apply to these designated contributions, so a Roth § 401(k) should be attractive to highly paid officers and employees.

Roth § 401(k)s must comply with the nondiscrimination requirements. The contributions are treated like regular § 401(k) contributions for other purposes and may not exceed the annual limitation ($16,500 in 2011) without regard to any catch-up contributions. A person should be able to roll a designated Roth contributions (DRCs) account into another designated Roth account or into a Roth IRA to preserve the tax-free nature of the account after age 70½ and to avoid the minimum distribution requirements. A "qualified distribution" from a designated Roth account is a distribution that is made after the person has participated for five years and that occurs on or after the date the person attains age 59½, dies, or becomes disabled. If a distribution is not a qualified distribution, such a distribution is taxable to the participant (or a beneficiary) to the extent it consists of earnings (in a pro rata manner).

EXAMPLE 18

A designated Roth account has $18,800 of DRCs and $1,200 of earnings. If a qualified distribution of $10,000 is made to the participant, the entire amount is excluded from gross income. However, if the distribution is not a qualified distribution, $9,400 is a return of capital (excluded from gross income), but a pro rata amount of $600 is included in gross income [($10,000 ÷ $20,000) × $1,200]. ■

19.2 RETIREMENT PLANS FOR SELF-EMPLOYED INDIVIDUALS

LO.5

Understand the qualified plan (Keogh plan) available to a self-employed person.

Self-employed individuals (e.g., partners and sole proprietors) and their employees are eligible to receive qualified retirement benefits under the SIMPLE plans described previously or under what are known as **H.R. 10 (Keogh) plans**. Because of contribution limitations and other restrictions, self-employed plans previously were less attractive than corporate plans. Contributions and benefits of a self-employed person now are subject to the general corporate provisions, putting self-employed persons on a parity with corporate employees. Consequently, Keogh plans can provide a self-employed person with an adequate retirement base.

A variety of funding vehicles can be used for Keogh investments, such as mutual funds, annuities, real estate shares, certificates of deposit, debt instruments, commodities, securities, and personal properties. Investment in most collectibles is not allowed in a self-directed plan. When an individual decides to make all investment decisions, a self-directed retirement plan is established. However, the individual may prefer to invest the funds with a financial institution such as a broker, a bank, or a savings and loan institution.

COVERAGE REQUIREMENTS

Generally, the corporate coverage rules apply to Keogh plans. Thus, the ratio percentage and average benefits tests previously discussed also apply to self-employed plans.[42] An individual covered under a qualified corporate plan as an employee may also establish a Keogh plan for earnings from self-employment.

CONTRIBUTION LIMITATIONS

A self-employed individual may annually contribute the smaller of $49,000 (in 2011) or 100 percent of earned income to a *defined contribution* Keogh plan.[43] However, if the defined contribution plan is a profit sharing plan or stock bonus plan, a 25 percent deduction limit applies. Under a *defined benefit* Keogh plan, the annual benefit payable to an employee is limited to the smaller of $195,000 (in 2011) or 100 percent of the employee's average compensation for the three highest years of employment.[44] An employee includes a self-employed person.

Return to the facts of *The Big Picture* on p. 19-2. Joyce's professor, Dr. Sanchez, has a forensic consulting practice in addition to her position at the university. Also, she receives book royalties from a textbook. Therefore, since she is self-employed (she will report her earnings on a Schedule C), she is able to establish a Keogh plan. ■	**EXAMPLE 19** **THE BIG PICTURE**

Earned income refers to net earnings from self-employment as defined in § 1402(a).[45] Net earnings from self-employment means the gross income derived by an individual from any trade or business carried on by that individual, less appropriate deductions, plus the distributive share of income or loss from a partnership.[46] Earned income is reduced by contributions to a Keogh plan on the individual's behalf and by 50 percent of any self-employment tax.[47]

Pat, a partner, has earned income of $150,000 in 2011 (after the deduction for one-half of self-employment tax). The maximum contribution Pat may make to a defined contribution Keogh plan is $49,000, the lesser of $150,000 or $49,000. ■	**EXAMPLE 20**

For discrimination purposes, the 25 percent limitation on the employee contribution to a profit sharing plan or stock bonus plan is computed on the first $245,000 (in 2011) of earned income. Thus, the maximum contribution in 2011 is $49,000 ($245,000 − .25X = X; X = $196,000). Therefore, $245,000 − $196,000 = $49,000. Alternatively, this can be calculated by multiplying $245,000 by 20 percent.

Terry, a self-employed accountant, has a profit sharing plan with a contribution rate of 15% of compensation. Terry's earned income after the deduction of one-half of self-employment tax, but before the Keogh contribution, is $250,000. Terry's contribution is limited to $31,957 ($245,000 − .15X = X), since X = $213,043 and .15 × $213,043 = $31,957. ■	**EXAMPLE 21**

Although a Keogh plan must be established before the end of the year in question, contributions may be made up to the normal filing date for that year.

---

[42]§ 401(d).

[43]§ 415(c)(1).

[44]§ 415(b)(1). This amount is indexed annually.

[45]§ 401(c)(2).

[46]§ 1402(a).

[47]§§ 401(c)(2)(A)(v) and 164(f).

19.3 INDIVIDUAL RETIREMENT ACCOUNTS (IRAs)

LO.6

Describe the benefits of the different types of Individual Retirement Accounts (IRAs).

GENERAL RULES

Employees not covered by another qualified plan can establish their own tax-deductible **Individual Retirement Accounts (IRAs)**. For years 2005–2007, the contribution ceiling was the smaller of $4,000 (or $8,000 for spousal IRAs) or 100 percent of compensation. For 2008, 2009, 2010, and 2011, the contribution ceiling is the smaller of $5,000 (or $10,000 for spousal IRAs) or 100 percent of compensation.[48] The contribution ceiling applies to all types of IRAs (traditional deductible, traditional nondeductible, and Roth).

An individual who attains the age of 50 by the end of the tax year can make additional catch-up IRA contributions. The maximum contribution limit is increased by $500 for the period 2002 through 2005 and $1,000 for years after 2005.

The amount accumulated in an IRA can be substantial. For example, if a husband and wife each contribute only $4,000 annually to an IRA from age 25 to age 65 (and earn 6 percent annually), their account balances together would be approximately $1.4 million at retirement. If the taxpayer is an *active participant* in a qualified plan, the traditional IRA deduction limitation is phased out *proportionately* between certain AGI ranges, as shown in Table 19.3.[49]

AGI is calculated taking into account any § 469 passive losses and § 86 taxable Social Security benefits and ignoring any § 911 foreign income exclusion, § 135 savings bonds interest exclusion, and the IRA deduction. There is a $200 floor on the IRA deduction limitation for individuals whose AGI is not above the phaseout range.

EXAMPLE 22

Dan, who is single, has compensation income of $62,000 in 2011. He is an active participant in his employer's qualified retirement plan. Dan contributes $5,000 to a traditional IRA. The deductible amount is reduced from $5,000 by $3,000 because of the phaseout mechanism:

$$\frac{\$6,000}{\$10,000} \times \$5,000 = \$3,000 \text{ reduction}$$

Therefore, of the $5,000 contribution, Dan can deduct only $2,000 ($5,000 − $3,000). ∎

EXAMPLE 23

Ben, an unmarried individual, is an active participant in his employer's qualified retirement plan in 2011. With AGI of $65,800, he would normally have an IRA deduction limit of $100 {$5,000 − [($65,800 − $56,000)/$10,000 × $5,000]}. However, because of the special floor provision, Ben is allowed a $200 IRA deduction. ∎

An individual is not considered an active participant in a qualified plan merely because the individual's spouse is an active participant in such a plan for any part of a plan year. Thus, most homemakers may take a full $5,000 deduction regardless of the participation status of their spouse, unless the couple has AGI above $169,000. If their AGI is above $169,000, the phaseout of the deduction begins at $169,000 and ends at $179,000 (phaseout over the $10,000 range) rather than beginning and ending at the phaseout amounts in Table 19.3.[50]

---

[48]§§ 219(b)(1) and (c)(2). The ceiling was $3,000 for 2002–2004. After 2008, the limit is adjusted annually for inflation in $500 increments.

[49]§ 219(g).

[50]§ 219(g)(7). However, a special rule in § 219(g)(4) allows a married person filing a separate return to avoid the phaseout rules even though the spouse is an active participant. The individual must live apart from the spouse at all times during the taxable year and must not be an active participant in another qualified plan.

TABLE 19.3	Phaseout of IRA Deduction of an Active Participant in 2011	
AGI Filing Status	**Phaseout Begins***	**Phaseout Ends**
Single and head of household	$56,000	$ 66,000
Married, filing joint return	90,000	110,000
Married, filing separate return	–0–	10,000

*These amounts are indexed annually for inflation.

Nell is covered by a qualified employer retirement plan at work. Her husband, Nick, is not an active participant in a qualified plan. If Nell and Nick's combined AGI is $135,000, Nell cannot make a deductible IRA contribution because she exceeds the income threshold for an active participant in Table 19.3. However, since Nick is not an active participant, and their combined AGI does not exceed $169,000, he can make a deductible contribution of $5,000 to an IRA. ■

To the extent that an individual is ineligible to make a deductible contribution to an IRA, *nondeductible contributions* can be made to separate accounts.[51] The nondeductible contributions are subject to the same dollar limits as deductible contributions ($5,000 of earned income, $10,000 for a spousal IRA). Income in the account accumulates tax-free until distributed. Only the account earnings are taxed upon distribution because the account basis equals the contributions made by the taxpayer. A taxpayer may elect to treat deductible IRA contributions as nondeductible. If an individual has no taxable income for the year after taking into account other deductions, the election would be beneficial. The election is made on the individual's tax return for the taxable year to which the designation relates.

Starting in 2002, there is a nonrefundable credit for contributions to a traditional IRA or elective deferrals for a § 401(k) plan (see Chapter 13).

For distributions made in tax years 2006, 2007, 2008, 2009, 2010, and 2011, an exclusion from gross income is available for traditional IRA distributions made to charity.[52] The amount of the distribution that is eligible for this beneficial exclusion treatment is limited to $100,000.

Amber has a traditional deductible IRA, so her basis is $0 (see the later discussion under Taxation of Benefits). Therefore, in 2011 she can have an IRA distribution of $100,000 made to a charity and exclude the $100,000 from her gross income. Assume instead that Amber has a traditional nondeductible IRA with a basis of $75,000. If she has a $100,000 IRA distribution made to a charity, she can exclude $25,000 ($100,000 − $75,000) from her gross income. ■

Roth IRAs

Introduced by Congress to encourage individual savings, a **Roth IRA** is a *nondeductible* alternative to the traditional deductible IRA. Earnings inside a Roth IRA are not taxable, and all qualified distributions from a Roth IRA are tax-free.[53] The maximum allowable annual contribution to a Roth IRA for 2011 is the smaller of $5,000 ($10,000 for spousal IRAs) or 100 percent of the individual's compensation for the year. Contributions to a Roth IRA must be made by the due date (excluding extensions) of the taxpayer's tax return. Roth IRAs are not subject to the minimum distribution rules that apply to traditional IRAs. Contributions to a Roth IRA (unlike a

---

[51]§ 408(o).
[52]§ 408(d)(8)(A). This provision may be extended by Congress.

[53]§ 408A.

traditional IRA) may continue beyond age 70½ so long as the person generates compensation income and is not barred by the AGI limits.

A taxpayer can make tax-free withdrawals from a Roth IRA after an initial five-year holding period if any of the following requirements is satisfied:

- The distribution is made on or after the date on which the participant attains age 59½.
- The distribution is made to a beneficiary (or the participant's estate) on or after the participant's death.
- The participant becomes disabled.
- The distribution is used to pay for qualified first-time homebuyer's expenses (statutory ceiling of $10,000).

EXAMPLE 26

Edith establishes a Roth IRA at age 42 and contributes $5,000 per year for 20 years. The account is now worth $149,400, consisting of $100,000 of nondeductible contributions and $49,400 in accumulated earnings that have not been taxed. Edith may withdraw the $149,400 tax-free from the Roth IRA because she is over age 59½ and has met the five-year holding period requirement. ∎

If the taxpayer receives a distribution from a Roth IRA and does not satisfy the aforementioned requirements, the distribution may be taxable. If the distribution represents a return of capital, it is not taxable. Conversely, if the distribution represents a payout of earnings, it is taxable. Under the ordering rules for Roth IRA distributions, distributions are treated as first made from contributions (return of capital).

EXAMPLE 27

Assume the same facts as in the previous example, except that Edith is only age 50 and receives a distribution of $55,000. Since her adjusted basis for the Roth IRA is $100,000 (contributions made), the distribution is tax-free, and her adjusted basis is reduced to $45,000 ($100,000 − $55,000). ∎

Roth IRAs are subject to income limits. In 2011, the maximum annual contribution of $5,000 is phased out beginning at AGI of $107,000 for single taxpayers and $169,000 for married couples who file a joint return. The phaseout range is $10,000 for married filing jointly and $15,000 for single taxpayers. For a married taxpayer filing separately, the phaseout begins with AGI of $0 and is phased out over a $10,000 range.[54]

EXAMPLE 28

Bev, who is single, would like to contribute $5,000 to her Roth IRA. However, her AGI is $117,000, so her contribution is limited to $1,667 ($5,000 − $3,333) calculated as follows:

$$\frac{\$10,000}{\$15,000} \times \$5,000 = \$3,333 \text{ reduction}$$

∎

EXAMPLE 29
THE BIG PICTURE

Return to the facts of *The Big Picture* on p. 19-2. Joyce's professor, Dr. Sanchez, also contributes annually to a traditional IRA. She would prefer a Roth IRA, but her AGI exceeds the phaseout limit. ∎

---

[54]The income limits for Roth IRA contributions are indexed for tax years after 2006.

For distributions made in tax years 2006, 2007, 2008, 2009, 2010, and 2011, an exclusion from gross income is available for Roth IRA distributions made to charity.[55] This exclusion treatment is beneficial for Roth IRA distributions that otherwise are not eligible for Roth IRA exclusion treatment.

Coverdell Education Savings Accounts (CESAs)

Distributions from a **Coverdell Education Savings Account (CESA)** to pay for qualified education expenses receive favorable tax treatment.[56] Qualified education expenses include tuition, fees, books, supplies, and related equipment. Room and board qualify if the student's course load is at least one-half of the full-time course load. If the CESA is used to pay the qualified education expenses of the designated beneficiary, the withdrawals are tax-free. To the extent the distributions during a tax year exceed qualified education expenses, part of the excess is treated as a return of capital (the contributions), and part is treated as a distribution of earnings under the § 72 annuity rules. Thus, the distribution is presumed to be pro rata from each category. The exclusion for the distribution of earnings part is calculated as follows:

$$\frac{\text{Qualified education expenses}}{\text{Total distributions}} \times \text{Earnings} = \text{Exclusion}$$

EXAMPLE 30

Meg receives a $2,500 distribution from her CESA. She uses $2,000 to pay for qualified education expenses. On the date of the distribution, Meg's CESA balance is $10,000, $6,000 of which represents her contributions. Since 60% ($6,000/$10,000) of her account balance represents her contributions, $1,500($2,500 × 60%) of the distribution is a return of capital, and $1,000 ($2,500 × 40%) is a distribution of earnings. The excludible amount of the earnings is calculated as follows:

$$\frac{\$2,000}{\$2,500} \times \$1,000 = \$800$$

Thus, Meg must include $200($1,000 − $800) in her gross income. ∎

The maximum amount that can be contributed annually to a CESA for a beneficiary is $2,000. A beneficiary must be an individual and cannot be a group of children or an unborn child. The contributions are not deductible. A CESA is subject to income limits. The maximum annual contribution is phased out beginning at $95,000 for single taxpayers and $190,000 for married couples who file a joint return. The phaseout range is $30,000 for married filing jointly and $15,000 for single taxpayers. Contributions cannot be made to a CESA after the date on which the designated beneficiary attains age 18. Thus, a total of up to $36,000 can be contributed for each beneficiary—$2,000 in the year of birth and in each of the following 17 years. A 6 percent excise tax is imposed on excess contributions to a CESA. A 10 percent excise tax is imposed on any distributions that are included in gross income.

The balance in a CESA must be distributed within 30 days after the death of the beneficiary or within 30 days after the beneficiary reaches age 30. Any balance at the close of either 30-day period is considered to be distributed at such time, and the earnings portion is included in the beneficiary's gross income. Before a beneficiary reaches age 30, any balance can be rolled over tax-free into another CESA for a member of the beneficiary's family who is under age 30.

The CESA exclusion may be available in a tax year in which the beneficiary claims the American Opportunity credit or the lifetime learning credit (see Chapter 13). However, any excluded amount of the CESA distribution cannot be used for the same educational expenses for which the American Opportunity credit or the lifetime learning credit is claimed.

---

[55]§ 408(d)(8)(A).   [56]§ 530.

CONCEPT SUMMARY 19.2

Keogh Plan and SEP Compared

	Keogh	SEP
Form	Trust.	IRA.
Establishment	By end of year.	By extension due date of employer.
Type of plan	Qualified.	Qualified.
Contributions to plan	By extension due date.	By extension due date of employer.
Vesting rules	Qualified plan rules.	100% immediately.
Participants' rules	Flexible.	Stricter.
Lump-sum distributions and averaging	Yes, favorable 10-year forward averaging.	No, ordinary income.
Deduction limitation	Varies.*	Smaller of $49,000 (in 2011) or 25% of earned income.**
Self as trustee	Yes.	No.

*For a defined contribution pension plan, the limit is the smaller of $49,000 (in 2011) or 100% of self-employment income (after one-half of self-employment tax is deducted). A defined contribution profit sharing plan has a 25% deduction limit. A defined benefit Keogh plan's limit is the smaller of $195,000 (in 2011) or 100% of the employee's average compensation for the highest three years of employment.

**Only $245,000 of income can be taken into consideration.

Contributions cannot be made to a beneficiary's CESA during any year in which contributions are made to a qualified tuition program on behalf of the same beneficiary (see Chapter 5).

Simplified Employee Pension Plans

An employer may contribute to an IRA covering an employee an amount equal to the lesser of $49,000 (in 2011) or 25 percent of the employee's earned income. In such a plan, the employer must make contributions for *each* employee who has reached age 21, has performed service for the employer during the calendar year and at least three of the five preceding calendar years, and has received at least $550 (in 2011) in compensation from the employer for the year.[57] Known as **simplified employee pension (SEP) plans**, these plans are subject to many of the same restrictions applicable to qualified plans (e.g., age and period-of-service requirements, and nondiscrimination limitations). Concept Summary 19.2 compares a SEP with a Keogh plan.

EXAMPLE 31

In 2011, Ryan's compensation before his employer's contribution to a SEP is $30,000. Ryan's employer may contribute and deduct up to $7,500 ($30,000 × 25%) for 2011. ∎

The amounts contributed to a SEP by an employer on behalf of an employee and the elective deferrals of an employee under a SEP are excludible from gross income. Elective deferrals under a SEP are subject to a statutory ceiling of $16,500 (in 2011),[58] which is increased under the catch-up provision for employees at least 50 years of age by the end of the tax year. Only $245,000 (in 2011) in compensation may be taken into account in making the SEP computation. An employer is

[57]§§ 408(j) and (k)(2). This amount is indexed annually. For 2007, 2008, and 2009, the amount was $500. For 2010, the amount was $550.

[58]Elective deferrals by an employee were repealed by the Small Business Job Protection Act of 1996 effective after December 31, 1996. However, if the employer plan was established before January 1, 1997, contributions can continue to be made under the pre-repeal provisions.

permitted to elect to use its taxable year rather than the calendar year for purposes of determining contributions to a SEP.[59]

Simple IRA

A SIMPLE plan can be in the form of an IRA. See the earlier discussion under SIMPLE Plans.

Spousal IRA

If both spouses work, each can individually establish an IRA. Deductible IRA contributions of up to $5,000 may be made by each spouse if the combined compensation of both spouses is at least equal to the contributed amount. Thus, if each spouse has compensation of at least $5,000, they each may contribute a maximum of $5,000. Likewise, if only one spouse is employed, they each may contribute a maximum of $5,000 if the employed spouse has compensation of at least $10,000. Finally, if both spouses are employed, but one has compensation of less than $5,000, they each may contribute a maximum of $5,000 if their combined compensation is at least $10,000.

For the spousal IRA provision to apply, a joint return must be filed.[60] The spousal IRA deduction is also proportionately reduced for active participants whose AGI exceeds the above target ranges.

EXAMPLE 32

Tony, who is married, is eligible to establish an IRA. He received $30,000 in compensation in 2011, and his spouse does not work outside the home. Tony can contribute up to $10,000 to two IRAs, to be divided in any manner between the two spouses, except that no more than $5,000 can be allocated to either spouse. ∎

EXAMPLE 33

Assume the same facts as in the previous example, except that Tony's wife has compensation income of $2,200. Without the spousal IRA provision, Tony could contribute $5,000 to his IRA, and his spouse could contribute only $2,200 to her IRA. With the spousal IRA provision, they both can contribute $5,000 to their IRAs. ∎

Alimony is considered to be earned income for purposes of IRA contributions. Thus, a person whose only income is alimony can contribute to an IRA.

Timing of Contributions

Contributions (both deductible and nondeductible) can be made to an IRA anytime before the due date of the individual's tax return.[61] For example, an individual can establish and contribute to an IRA through April 16, 2012 (the return due date), and deduct this amount on his or her tax return for 2011. IRA contributions that are made during a tax return extension period do not satisfy the requirement of being made by the return due date. An employer can make contributions up until the time of the due date for filing the return (including extensions) and treat those amounts as a deduction for the prior year.[62] As noted earlier, a similar rule applies to Keogh plans. However, the Keogh plan must be established before the end of the tax year. Contributions to the Keogh plan may then be made anytime before the due date of the individual's tax return.

PENALTY TAXES FOR EXCESS CONTRIBUTIONS

A cumulative, nondeductible 6 percent excise penalty tax is imposed on the smaller of (1) any excess contributions or (2) the market value of the plan assets determined as of the close of the tax year. *Excess contributions* are any contributions that exceed

---

[59]§ 404(h)(1)(A). The $16,500 and $245,000 amounts are indexed annually. The elective deferral amount was increased in $1,000 annual increments until it reached $15,000 and then became subject to indexing.
[60]§ 219(c).
[61]§ 219(f)(3).
[62]§ 404(h)(1)(B).

the maximum limitation and contributions that are made to a traditional IRA during or after the tax year in which the individual reaches age 70½.[63] Contributions can be made to a Roth IRA during or after the tax year in which the individual reaches age 70½. A taxpayer is not allowed a deduction for excess contributions. If the excess is corrected by contributing less than the deductible amount for a later year, a deduction then is allowable in the later year as a *makeup* deduction.

An excess contribution is taxable annually until returned to the taxpayer or reduced by the underutilization of the maximum contribution limitation in a subsequent year. The 6 percent penalty tax can be avoided if the excess amounts are returned.[64]

EXAMPLE 34

Nancy, age 45, establishes a traditional IRA in 2011 and contributes $5,300 in cash to the plan. She has earned income of $22,000. Nancy is allowed a $5,000 deduction *for AGI* for 2011. Assuming the market value of the plan assets is at least $300, there is a nondeductible 6% excise penalty tax of $18 ($300 × 6%). The $300 may be subject to an additional penalty tax in future years if it is not returned to Nancy or reduced by underutilization of the $5,000 maximum contribution limitation (ignoring any catch-up contributions). ∎

TAXATION OF BENEFITS

A participant has a zero basis in the *deductible* contributions of a traditional IRA because the contributions were deducted.[65] Therefore, all withdrawals from a deductible IRA are taxed as ordinary income in the year of receipt. They are not eligible for the 10-year averaging allowed for certain lump-sum distributions.

A participant has a basis equal to the contributions made for a *nondeductible* traditional IRA. Therefore, only the earnings component of withdrawals is included in gross income. Such amounts are taxed as ordinary income in the year of receipt and are not eligible for the 10-year averaging allowed for certain lump-sum distributions.

In addition to being included in gross income, payments from IRAs made to a participant before age 59½ are subject to a nondeductible 10 percent penalty tax on such actual, or constructive, payments.[66] However, an individual may make penalty-free withdrawals to pay for medical expenses in excess of 7.5 percent of AGI, to pay for qualified higher education expenses, and to pay for qualified, first-time homebuyer expenses (up to $10,000). Note that a qualified first-time homebuyer is defined as an individual (and spouse) who has not owned a principal residence in the two-year period preceding the date of acquisition of a principal residence. Further, an individual who has received unemployment compensation for at least 12 consecutive weeks may use IRA withdrawals to pay for health insurance for himself or herself, the spouse, and dependents without incurring the 10 percent penalty tax.[67]

All traditional IRAs of an individual are treated as one contract, and all distributions during a taxable year are treated as one distribution. See the earlier discussion of the special rules for distributions from Roth IRAs and traditional IRAs. If an individual who previously has made both deductible and nondeductible IRA contributions makes a withdrawal from a traditional IRA during a taxable year, the excludible amount must be calculated. The amount excludible from gross income for the taxable year is calculated by multiplying the amount withdrawn by a percentage. The percentage is calculated by dividing the individual's aggregate nondeductible IRA contributions by the aggregate balance of all of his or her traditional IRAs (including rollover IRAs and SEPs).[68]

---

[63]§§ 4973(a)(1) and (b).

[64]§§ 408(d)(4) and 4973(b)(2).

[65]§ 408(d)(1).

[66]§ 72(t). There are limited exceptions to the penalty on early distributions.

[67]§§ 72(t)(2)(B), (D), (E), and (F). For purposes of the unemployment provision, a self-employed individual who otherwise would have been eligible for unemployment compensation will qualify.

[68]§ 408(d)(2).

<table>
<tr><td>

Carl, age 59, has a $12,000 deductible traditional IRA and a $2,000 nondeductible traditional IRA (without any earnings). Carl withdraws $1,000 from the nondeductible IRA. The excludible portion is $143 [($2,000/$14,000) × $1,000], and the includible portion is $857 [($12,000/$14,000) × $1,000]. Carl must also pay a 10% penalty tax on the prorated portion considered withdrawn from the deductible IRA and earnings in either type of IRA. Thus, the 10% penalty tax is $85.70 (10% × $857). ∎

</td><td>

EXAMPLE 35

</td></tr>
</table>

Rollovers: General Provisions

As introduced earlier, an IRA may be the recipient of a rollover from another qualified plan, including another IRA. Such a distribution from a qualified plan is not included in gross income if it is transferred within 60 days of receipt to an IRA or another qualified plan. For a series of distributions that constitute a lump-sum distribution, the 60-day period does not begin until the last distribution. Amounts received from IRAs may be rolled over tax-free only once in a 12-month period. If a person has more than one IRA, the one-year waiting period applies separately to each IRA.[69]

<table>
<tr><td>

Nonemployer stock worth $60,000 is distributed to an employee from a qualified retirement plan. Hubert, the employee, sells the stock within 60 days for $60,000 and transfers one-half of the proceeds to a traditional IRA. Hubert has $30,000 of ordinary income, which is not eligible for 10-year forward averaging or for capital gain treatment under the pre-1987 rules. One-half of the distribution, or $30,000, does escape taxation because of the rollover. ∎

</td><td>

EXAMPLE 36

</td></tr>
</table>

A tax-free rollover for distributions from qualified plans is an alternative to the taxable 10-year forward averaging technique. Any rollover amount in a traditional IRA may later be rolled over into another qualified plan if the IRA consists of only the amounts from the original plan and the receiving plan permits it. The amount of nondeductible employee contributions included in a distribution may not be rolled over, but that amount is tax-free because the contributions were made with after-tax dollars. Partial rollovers are allowed, but the maximum amount that may be rolled over may not exceed the portion of the distribution that is otherwise includible in gross income. Rollovers are not available for required distributions under the minimum distribution rules once age 70½ is reached.

<table>
<tr><td>

Return to the facts of *The Big Picture* on p. 19-2. Dr. Sanchez withdraws $15,000 from her traditional IRA on May 2, 2011, but she redeposits it in the same IRA on June 28, 2011. Although the withdrawal and redeposit was a partial rollover and Dr. Sanchez may have used the funds for a limited time, this is a tax-free rollover.[70] ∎

</td><td>

EXAMPLE 37
THE BIG PICTURE

</td></tr>
</table>

A rollover is different from a direct transfer of funds from a qualified plan to an IRA or another qualified plan by a trustee or issuer. A direct transfer is not subject to the one-year waiting period and the withholding rules.[71] Further, in many states, IRA amounts are subject to claims of creditors, which is not the case for some employer plans.

An employer must withhold 20 percent of any lump-sum distributions unless the transfer is a direct transfer to an IRA or another qualified plan.[72]

<table>
<tr><td>

Kay receives a distribution from a qualified retirement plan. The amount of the distribution would have been $20,000, but Kay receives only $16,000 ($20,000 − $4,000) as a result of the 20% withholding provision. After several weeks, Kay decides to contribute $20,000 (the gross amount of the distribution) to her traditional IRA. Since she received only $16,000, she will need to contribute $4,000 from another source in order to make

</td><td>

EXAMPLE 38

</td></tr>
</table>

[69]§ 408(d)(3)(B) and Reg. § 1.408–4(b)(4).
[70]Ltr.Rul. 9010007.
[71]Reg. § 35.3405–1.
[72]§ 3405(c).

CONCEPT SUMMARY 19.3

Comparison of IRAs

	Traditional			Coverdell Education Savings Account (CESA)
	Deductible IRA	**Nondeductible IRA**	**Roth IRA**	
Maximum contribution (per year)	$5,000*	$5,000*	$5,000*	$2,000
Tax-deductible contribution	Yes	No	No	No
Tax-free growth of income	Yes	Yes	Yes	Yes
Beginning of AGI phaseout for active participant (2011)	$56,000 single, $90,000 joint	N/A	$107,000 single, $169,000 joint	$95,000 single, $190,000 joint
Income tax on distributions	Yes, for entire distribution	Yes, for the earnings portion	No, if satisfy 5-year holding period**	No, if used for education expenses
50% excise tax: age 70½ insufficient distributions	Yes	Yes	No	No
10% early withdrawal penalty (before age 59½)	Yes, with exceptions†	Yes, with exceptions†	Yes, with exceptions†	Yes††

*The total of deductible, nondeductible, and Roth IRA contributions may not exceed $5,000 per year.

**In addition, the distribution must satisfy one of the following: after age 59½, for qualified first-time homebuyer expenses, participant is disabled, or made to a beneficiary on or after the participant's death.

†Qualified education and first-time homebuyer costs (up to $10,000) avoid the 10% penalty.

††On early withdrawals not used for education costs. Qualified first-time homebuyer costs (up to $10,000) avoid 10% penalty.

a $20,000 contribution. Kay will be able to claim a refund for the $4,000 that was withheld when she files her tax return for the year. ■

Distributions from a traditional IRA are generally not eligible for 10-year averaging or capital gain treatment. An exception applies in the case of a *conduit IRA*, where the sole assets of a qualified plan are rolled over into an IRA, and the assets are then rolled into a qualified plan. With a conduit IRA, the lump-sum distribution from the original plan is still eligible for the special tax treatments.

Rollovers and Conversions: Roth IRAs

A Roth IRA may be rolled over tax-free into another Roth IRA.

A traditional IRA may be rolled over or converted to a Roth IRA. A conversion occurs when the taxpayer notifies the IRA trustee that the IRA is now a Roth IRA. A rollover or conversion of a traditional IRA to a Roth IRA can occur only if the following requirements are satisfied:[73]

- The participant's AGI does not exceed $100,000 (excluding the amount included in gross income resulting from the rollover or conversion).
- The participant is not married filing a separate return.
- The rollover occurs within 60 days of the IRA distribution.

The $100,000 AGI limitation for conversions and rollovers goes away in 2010 and 2011. Thus, contributions made to a traditional IRA could be converted to a Roth IRA in 2010. Taxes are due on the conversion amount in 2010, but these taxes can be spread over two years.[74] For 2011 conversions, this two-year option goes away (tax is currently due). Further, unlike a traditional IRA, which requires withdrawals at age 70½, there are no required withdrawals from a Roth IRA. Thus, money can be accumulated over the taxpayer's lifetime and then passed to heirs without tax penalties.

[73]§ 408A(c)(3)(B).   [74]§ 408A(d)(3)(A).

When a traditional IRA is rolled over or converted to a Roth IRA, the tax consequences depend on whether the traditional IRA was deductible or nondeductible. If deductible, then the basis for the IRA is zero. Thus, the entire amount of the rollover or conversion is included in gross income. If nondeductible, then the basis for the IRA is equal to the sum of the contributions. Thus, only the IRA earnings included in the rollover or conversion are included in gross income. The 10 percent penalty tax will not apply in either case.[75]

Starting in 2008, distributions from qualified retirement plans, § 403(b) annuities, and governmental § 457 plans can be rolled over into a Roth IRA.[76] However, for this rollover to be permitted, the $100,000 AGI limit must be satisfied. Note that, as mentioned previously, the $100,000 limit was eliminated for 2010 and for future years. Although this rollover is a taxable transaction, it enables subsequent earnings to be excluded from gross income.

19.4 NONQUALIFIED DEFERRED COMPENSATION PLANS

UNDERLYING RATIONALE FOR TAX TREATMENT

Nonqualified deferred compensation (NQDC) plans provide a flexible way for taxpayers, particularly those in the 35 percent tax bracket, to defer income taxes on income payments until a potentially lower tax bracket year. When the deferred compensation is credited with annual earnings until payment, the entire deferred compensation, not just the after-tax amount, is generating investment income. Also, most NQDC plans do not have to meet the discrimination, funding, coverage, and other requirements of qualified plans. In addition to these advantages for the employee, the employer may not have a current cash outflow. The IRS will issue rulings on deferred compensation plans.

> **LO.7**
>
> Understand the rationale for nonqualified deferred compensation plans and the related tax treatment.

TAX TREATMENT TO THE EMPLOYER AND EMPLOYEE

New rules apply after 2004 to nonqualified arrangements that defer the receipt of compensation income to a year later than that in which it is earned. During a taxable year in which an NQDC plan does not meet certain conditions in § 409A or is not operating in accordance with these conditions, all amounts deferred under the arrangement will be included in the participant's gross income to the extent they are not subject to a substantial risk of forfeiture. In addition, a 20 percent penalty tax is imposed on such income along with interest at the underpayment rate plus 1 percent.[77]

A three-pronged analysis determines whether a plan to defer compensation faces these punitive actions. First, does the deferred compensation fall within the NQDC provisions under § 409A? Second, are the benefits subject to a substantial risk of forfeiture (SRF)? SRF is discussed later in this chapter under Restricted Property Plans, but the definition of SRF for NQDCs differs from the normal definition. For example, a covenant not to compete can never be an SRF under § 409A, nor will conditions under the discretionary control of the employee be an SRF under § 409A. Also, an elective extension of a forfeiture period will generally be disregarded as an SRF unless there are substantial additional considerations for such an extension. Third, at the time the arrangement is not covered by an SRF, has the plan suffered a "plan failure"?

Certain compensation arrangements do not fall within § 409A, including a qualified employer plan, any bona fide vacation leave, sick leave, educational benefits, legal settlements, indemnification arrangements, compensatory time, disability pay, and a death benefit plan.[78] Excluded qualified employer plans include tax-qualified

---

[75]§ 408A(d)(3)(A)(ii).
[76]§ 402(c)(8)(B).

[77]§409A(a)(1).
[78]§409A(d)(1).

pension, profit sharing, or § 401(k) plans; a § 403(b) tax-deferred annuity; a simplified employee pension plan; or an eligible § 457(b) plan for state, government, or tax-exempt employees.

In general, a § 409A deferral occurs where an employee has a legally binding right to compensation that has been deferred to the future. The section casts a wide net and may even cover nonqualified stock options and stock appreciation rights (SARs). These rules do not cover restricted property under § 83, as well as nondiscounted stock options, nondiscounted SARs, and statutory stock options. Discounted stock options, discounted SARs, phantom stock, and restricted stock units are covered.

Generally, funded NQDC plans must be forfeitable to keep the compensation payments from being taxable immediately. In most instances, employees prefer to have some assurance that they will ultimately receive benefits from the NQDC (that the plan provides for nonforfeitable benefits). In such instances, the plan will have to be unfunded to prevent immediate taxation to the employee. Note that most funded NQDC plans are subject to many of the provisions that apply to qualified plans, including the nondiscrimination requirements, and are impractical as a result.

To be effective, an unfunded deferred compensation plan must meet and comply with the following requirements under § 409A.[79]

- The NQDC plan may not distribute the deferred compensation to the employee except in these six situations: separation of service, disability, death, specified time or fixed schedule, change in employer control, or unforeseeable emergency.
- The plan must not permit any participant to accelerate the time or scheduled date of distributions (subject to some exceptions).
- A participant must elect to postpone the compensation for the current year no later than the close of the preceding tax year (initial deferral election).
- The employee must decide on the form and time of the benefits (e.g., installment payments or lump sum) when the deferral election is made if the plan permits an election between alternatives, or the NQDC plan must specify the form and time of distribution when the deferral election is made.
- A participant must not change the time or form of benefits unless the employee does so at least 12 months before the scheduled distribution date and also postpones the scheduled distribution date by at least five years.
- The plan should specify the amount payable (or the terms of the formula determining the amount), along with the payment schedule or triggering events that result in payment.
- Publicly held companies must provide for a six-month delay requirement for the top 50 officers with incomes of at least $130,000 (along with certain owner-employees).

EXAMPLE 39

Eagle Corporation and Bill, a cash basis employee, enter into an employment agreement that provides an annual salary of $120,000 to Bill. Of this amount, $100,000 is paid in current monthly installments, and $20,000 is to be paid in 10 annual installments beginning at Bill's retirement or death. Although Eagle Corporation maintains a separate account for Bill, that account is not funded. Bill is merely an unsecured creditor of the corporation. The $20,000 is not considered constructively received and is deferred. Compensation of $100,000 is currently taxable to Bill and deductible to Eagle. The other $20,000 will be taxable and deductible when paid in future years. ∎

---

[79]§409A(a)(2),(3), and (4).

A deferred compensation arrangement occurs when an employee receives compensation after the 2½-month period following the end of an employer's corporate tax year in which such services were performed.[80] An employer's deduction of NQDC must be delayed to match the employee's recognition of income regardless of the employer's method of accounting.[81]

Beige, Inc., a calendar year employer, has an accrued NQDC liability of $300,000 on December 31, 2010. During 2011, the company accrues another $60,000 of NQDC. On February 13, 2012, the company pays the entire $360,000 to the employee. Since the $60,000 was paid within 2½ months after the end of 2011, only $300,000 ever met the requirement for deferred compensation. The entire $360,000 may be deducted by the company only in the year ending December 31, 2012, when the employee receives the cash and recognizes the income. ∎

When to Use an NQDC Arrangement

As a general rule, NQDC plans are more appropriate for executives in a financially secure company. Because of the need for currently disposable income, such plans are usually not appropriate for young employees.

An NQDC plan can reduce an employee's overall tax payments by deferring the taxation of income to later years (possibly when the employee is in a lower tax bracket). In effect, these plans may produce a form of income averaging. Further, unfunded NQDC plans may discriminate in favor of shareholders, officers, specific highly compensated key employees, or a single individual.

Certain disadvantages should be noted, however. As mentioned earlier, nonqualified plans are usually required to be unfunded, which means that an employee is not assured that funds ultimately will be available to pay the benefits. In other words, the deferred amounts are recorded as a liability on the company's books, and the employee will be an unsecured creditor in the event of the firm's bankruptcy.

Golden Parachute Arrangements

Golden parachute arrangements promise monetary benefits to key employees if they lose their jobs as a result of a change in ownership of the corporation. In essence, these are unfunded NQDC plans that do not vest until the change in ownership. These payments may be unreasonable or not really for services rendered. The term **golden parachute payments**, as used in the Code, means *excess severance pay*.

These excessive severance payments to employees are penalized. The Code denies a deduction to an employer who makes a payment of cash or property to an employee or independent contractor that satisfies both of the following conditions:

- The payment is contingent on a change of ownership of a corporation through a stock or asset acquisition.
- The aggregate present value of the payment equals or exceeds three times the employee's (or independent contractor's) average annual compensation.[82]

The disallowed amount is the excess of the payment over a statutory base amount (a five-year average of taxable compensation if the taxpayer was an employee for the entire five-year period). Further, a 20 percent excise tax is imposed on the recipient on the receipt of these parachute payments; the tax is withheld at the time of payment.[83]

Irene, an executive, receives a golden parachute payment of $380,000 from her employer. Her average annual compensation for the most recent five tax years is $120,000. The corporation will be denied a deduction for $260,000 ($380,000 payment − $120,000 base amount). Irene's excise tax is $52,000 ($260,000 × 20%). ∎

---

[80]Temp.Reg. § 1.404(b)–1T.
[81]§ 404(a)(5); Reg. § 1.404(a)–12(b)(1).

[82]§ 280G.
[83]§ 4999.

Golden parachute payments do not include payments to or from qualified pension, profit sharing, stock bonus, annuity, or simplified employee pension plans. Also excluded is the amount of the payment that, in fact, represents reasonable compensation for personal services actually rendered or to be rendered. Such excluded payments are not taken into account when determining whether the threshold (the aggregate present value calculation) is exceeded.

S corporations are not subject to the golden parachute rules. Generally, corporations that do not have stock that is readily tradable on an established securities market or elsewhere are also exempt.

Publicly Held Companies' Compensation Limitation

For purposes of both the regular income tax and the alternative minimum tax, the deductible compensation for the top five executives of publicly traded companies is limited to $1 million for each executive. A company is publicly held if the corporation has common stock listed on a national securities exchange.[84] This $1 million deduction limitation is decreased by any nondeductible golden parachute payments made to the employee during the same year. The $1 million deduction limitation becomes $500,000 during the period in which financial assistance under the Troubled Asset Relief Program (TARP) remains outstanding for a TARP participant company.

This deduction limitation applies when the compensation deduction would otherwise be taken. For example, in the case of a nonqualified stock option (NQSO), which is discussed later in this chapter, the deduction is normally taken in the year the NQSO is exercised, even though the option was granted with respect to services performed in a prior year.

Certain types of compensation are *not* subject to this deduction limit and are not taken into account in determining whether other compensation exceeds $1 million:

- Compensation payable on a commission basis.
- Compensation payable solely on account of the attainment of one or more performance goals when certain requirements involving the approval of outside directors and shareholders are met.
- Payments to a tax-qualified retirement plan (including salary-reduction contributions).

---

[84]§ 162(m).

- Amounts that are excludible from an executive's gross income (such as employer-provided health benefits and miscellaneous fringe benefits).

The most important exception is performance-based compensation. Compensation qualifies for this exception only if the following conditions are satisfied:

- The compensation is paid solely on account of the attainment of one or more performance goals.
- The performance goals are established by a compensation committee consisting solely of two or more outside directors.
- The material terms under which the compensation is to be paid (including the performance goals) are disclosed to and approved by the shareholders in a separate vote prior to payment.
- Prior to payment, the compensation committee certifies that the performance goals and any other material terms were in fact satisfied.

Disallowance of the compensation deduction can occur even where the employee's contract contains performance-based criteria if the employee also can receive compensation for employment that is terminated without cause or for voluntary retirement.

Compensation (other than stock options or other stock appreciation rights) is not treated as paid solely on account of the attainment of one or more performance goals unless the compensation is paid to the particular executive under a preestablished objective performance formula or standard that precludes discretion. In essence, a third party with knowledge of the relevant performance results could calculate the amount to be paid to the particular executive. A performance goal is broadly defined and includes, for example, any objective performance standard that is applied to the individual executive, a business unit (e.g., a division or a line of business), or the corporation as a whole. Performance standards could include increases in stock price, market share, sales, or earnings per share.

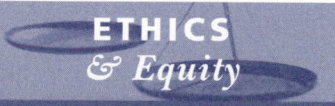

ETHICS & Equity   **ADMINISTRATORS AND COACHES VERSUS PROFESSORS**

As university and college priorities have changed, resources are being shifted from classroom instructors (e.g., professors) to paper pushers (e.g., administrators). The median total compensation in the 2008–2009 academic year for university presidents was $436,111, reflecting a 2.3 percent increase over the 2007–2008 academic year. Last year their pay rose 7.6 percent. E. Gordon Lee at Ohio State University received total annual compensation of $1,346,225.

University football coaches also are doing well. The University of Alabama's Nick Saban earns in excess of $4 million, as do the University of Texas's Mack Brown and the University of Oklahoma's Bob Stoops.

Meanwhile, the average salary for an assistant professor is $45,000 to $65,000; for an associate professor, $60,000 to $80,000; and for a full professor, $70,000 to $85,000. Instructors and adjuncts make much less.

Should administrators and coaches be paid so much more than classroom professors?

Source: Adapted from "Highest-Paid Presidents of Public Universities," **http://images.businessweek/com/ss/09/02/2016_college_pres/1**.

19.5 RESTRICTED PROPERTY PLANS

GENERAL PROVISIONS

A **restricted property plan** is an arrangement whereby an employer transfers property (e.g., stock of the employer-corporation) to an employee or other provider of services at no cost or at a bargain price. The usual purpose of a restricted stock plan is to retain the services of key employees who might otherwise leave. The employer hopes that such compensation arrangements will encourage company growth and

LO.8

Explain the value of restricted property plans.

attainment of performance objectives. Section 83 was enacted in 1969 to provide rules for the taxation of incentive compensation arrangements, which previously were governed by judicial and administrative interpretations. Although the following discussion refers to an employee as the provider of the services, the services may be performed by an independent contractor.

As a general rule, if an employee performs services and receives property (e.g., stock), the fair market value of that property in excess of any amount paid by the employee is includible in his or her gross income. The time for inclusion is the earlier of (1) the time the property is no longer subject to a substantial risk of forfeiture or (2) the time the property is transferable by the employee. The fair market value of the property is determined without regard to any restriction, except a restriction that by its terms will never lapse.[85] Since the amount of the compensation is determined at the date that the restrictions lapse or when the property is transferable, the opportunity to generate capital gain treatment on the property is denied during a period when the ordinary income element is being deferred.

EXAMPLE 42	On October 1, 2007, Blue Corporation sold 100 shares of its stock to Ahmad, an employee, for $10 per share. At the time of the sale, the fair market value of the stock was $100 per share. Under the terms of the sale, each share of stock was nontransferable and subject to a substantial risk of forfeiture (which was not to lapse until October 1, 2011). Evidence of these restrictions was stamped on the face of the stock certificates. On October 1, 2011, the fair market value of the stock was $250 per share. Since the stock was nontransferable and was subject to a substantial risk of forfeiture, Ahmad did not include any compensation in gross income during 2007 (assuming no special election was made). Instead, Ahmad was required to include $24,000 of compensation in gross income [100 shares × ($250 − $10 per share)] during 2011. If for some reason the forfeiture had occurred (e.g., the plan required Ahmad to surrender the stock to the corporation if he voluntarily terminated his employment with the company before October 1, 2011) and Ahmad never received the stock certificates, he would have been allowed a capital loss of $1,000 (the extent of his investment). ∎

SUBSTANTIAL RISK OF FORFEITURE

A **substantial risk of forfeiture (SRF)** exists if a person's rights to full enjoyment of property are conditioned upon the future performance, or the refraining from the performance, of substantial services by that individual.[86] For example, if an employee must return the property (receiving only his or her original cost, if any) should there be a failure to complete a substantial period of service (for any reason), the property is subject to an SRF. Another such situation exists when an employer can compel an employee to return the property due to a breach of a substantial covenant not to compete. Any SRF should be stated on the face of the stock certificates. Assuming that an SRF does not exist, the property received is valued at its fair market value, ignoring any restrictions, except for one instance dealing with closely held stock.

SPECIAL ELECTION AVAILABLE

An employee may elect within 30 days after the receipt of restricted property to recognize immediately as ordinary income the fair market value in excess of the amount paid for the property. Any appreciation in the value of the property after receipt is classified as capital gain instead of ordinary income. No deduction is allowed to the employee for taxes paid on the original amount included in income if the property is subsequently forfeited.[87] The employee is permitted to take a capital

---

[85] § 83(a)(1); *Miriam Sakol*, 67 T.C. 986 (1977); *T. M. Horwith*, 71 T.C. 932 (1979).

[86] § 83(c). Regulation § 1.83–3(c)(2) includes several examples of restricted property arrangements.
[87] § 83(b).

loss for any amounts that were actually paid for the property. Furthermore, in such a case, the employer must repay taxes saved by any compensation deduction taken in the earlier year.[88]

Any increase in value between the time the property is received and the time it becomes either nonforfeitable or transferable is taxed as ordinary income if the employee does not make this special election. However, if the employee elects to be taxed immediately on the difference between the cost and fair market value on the date of issue, any future appreciation is treated as capital gain. In determining whether the gain is long term or short term, the holding period starts when the employee is taxed on the ordinary income.[89]

EXAMPLE 43

On July 1, 2001, Sparrow Company sold 100 shares of its preferred stock, worth $15 per share, to Diane (an employee) for $5 per share. The sale was subject to Diane's agreement to resell the preferred shares to the company for $5 per share if she terminated her employment during the following 10 years. The stock had a value of $25 per share on July 1, 2011, and Diane sold the stock for $30 per share on October 10, 2011. Diane made the special election to include the original spread (between the value of $15 in 2001 and the amount paid of $5) in income for 2001. Diane was required to recognize $1,000 of compensation income in 2001 ($15 − $5 = $10 × 100 shares), at which time her holding period in her stock began. Diane's tax basis in the stock was $1,500 ($1,000 + $500). When the preferred stock was sold in 2011, Diane recognized a $1,500 long-term capital gain ($30 × 100 shares − $1,500). ■

EXAMPLE 44

Assume the same facts as in the previous example, except that Diane sells the stock in 2012 (rather than 2011). She would not recognize any gain in 2011 when the SRF lapses. Instead, Diane would recognize the $1,500 long-term capital gain in 2012. ■

This special provision is usually not elected since it results in an immediate recognition of income and adverse tax consequences result from a subsequent forfeiture. However, the special election may be attractive in the following situations:

- The bargain element is relatively small.
- Substantial appreciation is expected in the future.
- A high probability exists that the restrictions will be met.

EMPLOYER DEDUCTIONS

At the time the employee is required to include the compensation in income, the employer is allowed a tax deduction for the same amount. The employer must withhold on this amount in accordance with § 3402. In the no-election situation, the deduction is limited to the fair market value of the restricted property (without regard to the restrictions) at the time the restrictions lapse, reduced by the amount originally paid for the property by the employee.[90] When the employee elects to be taxed immediately, the corporate deduction also is accelerated and deductible in like amount. In cases of deferred income recognition, the employer can receive a sizable deduction if the property has appreciated.

EXAMPLE 45

On March 14, 2009, Gold Corporation sold to Harry, an employee, 10 shares of Gold common stock for $100 per share. Both the corporation and Harry were calendar year taxpayers. The common stock was subject to an SRF and was nontransferable; both conditions were to lapse on March 14, 2011. At the time of the sale, the fair market value of the common stock (without considering the restrictions) was $1,000 per

---

[88]Reg. §§ 1.83–6(c) and 2(a).
[89]§ 1223(6).

[90]Reg. § 1.83–6(a).

share. On March 14, 2011, when the fair market value of the stock is $2,000 per share, the restrictions lapse. Harry did not make the special election. In 2011, Harry realizes ordinary income of $19,000 (10 shares at $2,000 per share less the $100 per share he had paid). Likewise, Gold Corporation is allowed a $19,000 compensation deduction in 2011. ■

EXAMPLE 46

In the previous example, assume that Harry had made the special election. Since he was taxed on $9,000 in 2009, the corporation was allowed to deduct a like amount in 2009. No deduction would be available in 2011. ■

19.6 STOCK OPTIONS

L0.9

Differentiate the tax treatment of qualified and nonqualified stock options.

IN GENERAL

Various equity types of stock option programs are available for an employee's compensation package. Some authorities believe that some form of *equity kicker* is needed to attract new management, convert key officers into *partners* by giving them a share of the business, and retain the services of executives who might otherwise leave. Encouraging the managers of a business to have a proprietary interest in its successful operation should provide executives with a key motive to expand the company and improve its profits. In addition, under certain conditions, stock options may fall outside the $1 million limitation on the salaries of the top five executives of publicly traded companies. Sometimes an executive's stock option income may far exceed cash salaries and bonuses. For example, in 2006 CEO Barry Diller of InterActiveCorp received a $730,000 salary and exercised stock options valued at approximately $290.2 million.

A **stock option** gives an individual the right to purchase a stated number of shares of stock from a corporation at a certain price within a specified period of time. The optionee must be under no obligation to purchase the stock, and the option may be revocable by the corporation. The option must be in writing, and its terms must be clearly expressed.[91]

INCENTIVE STOCK OPTIONS

An equity type of stock option called an *incentive stock option (ISO)* is available. There are no tax consequences for either the issuing corporation or the recipient when the option is granted. However, the *spread* (the excess of the fair market value of the share at the date of exercise over the option price)[92] is a tax preference item to the recipient for purposes of the alternative minimum tax. The determination of fair market value is made without regard to any lapse restrictions (a restriction that will expire after a period of time). After the option is exercised and when the stock is sold, any gain from the sale is taxed as a long-term capital gain if certain holding period requirements are met. For a gain to qualify as a long-term capital gain, the employee must not dispose of the stock within two years after the option is granted or within one year after acquiring the stock.[93] If the employee meets the holding period requirements, none of these transactions generates any business deduction for the employer.[94] If the employee pays anything for the option and does not exercise the option, any amount paid is recognized as a capital loss.

EXAMPLE 47

Wren Corporation granted an ISO for 100 shares of its stock to Rocky, an employee, on March 18, 2008. The option price was $100, and the fair market value was $100 on the date of the grant. Rocky exercised the option on April 1, 2010, when the fair

---

[91]Reg. §§ 1.421–1(a)(1) and –7(a)(1).
[92]§§ 422(a), 421(a)(1), 57(a)(3), and 1234(a)(1) and (2).

[93]§ 422(a)(1).
[94]§ 421(a)(2).

market value of the stock was $200 per share. He sells the stock on April 6, 2011, for $300 per share. Rocky did not recognize any ordinary income on the date of the grant or the exercise date since the option qualified as an ISO. Wren received no compensation deduction. Rocky has a $10,000 tax preference item on the exercise date. He has a long-term capital gain of $20,000 [($300 − $100) × 100] on the sale of the stock in 2011, because the one-year and two-year holding periods and other requirements have been met. ■

As a further requirement for ISO treatment, the option holder must be an employee of the issuing corporation from the date the option is granted until 3 months (12 months if disabled) before the date of exercise. The holding period and the employee-status rules just described (the one-year, two-year, and three-month requirements) are waived in the case of the death of an employee.[95]

EXAMPLE 48

Assume the same facts as in the previous example, except that Rocky was not employed by Wren Corporation for six months before the date he exercised the options. Rocky must recognize ordinary income to the extent of the spread, assuming there was no SRF. Thus, Rocky recognizes $10,000 [($200 − $100) × 100] of ordinary income on the exercise date, because he was not an employee of Wren Corporation at all times during the period beginning on the grant date and ending three months before the exercise date. Wren is allowed a deduction at the same time that Rocky reports the ordinary income. ■

If the holding period requirements are not satisfied but all other conditions are met, the tax is still deferred to the point of the sale. However, the difference between the option price and the value of the stock at the date the option was exercised is treated as ordinary income. The difference between the amount realized for the stock and the value of the stock at the date of exercise is short-term or long-term capital gain, depending on the holding period of the stock itself. The employer is allowed a deduction equal to the amount recognized by the employee as ordinary income. The employee does not have a tax preference for alternative minimum tax purposes.

EXAMPLE 49

Assume the same facts as in Example 47, except that Rocky sells the stock on March 22, 2011, for $290 per share. Since Rocky did not hold the stock itself for more than one year, $10,000 of the gain is treated as ordinary income in 2011, and Wren Corporation is allowed a $10,000 compensation deduction in 2011. The remaining $9,000 is a short-term capital gain ($29,000 − $20,000). ■

Qualification Requirements for Incentive Stock Option Plans

An **incentive stock option (ISO)** is an option to purchase stock of a corporation granted to an individual for any reason connected with his or her employment that meets specific qualification requirements.[96] The option is granted by the employer-corporation or by a parent or subsidiary corporation of the employer-corporation. An ISO plan may permit an employee to use company stock to pay for the exercise of the option without disqualifying the ISO plan.

For an option to qualify as an ISO, the terms of the option must identify it as an ISO and meet the following conditions:

* The option must be granted under a plan specifying the number of shares of stock to be issued and the employees or class of employees eligible to receive the options. The plan must be approved by the shareholders of the corporation within 12 months before or after the plan is adopted.

---

[95]§§ 422(a)(2) and (c)(3). Exceptions are made for parent and subsidiary situations, corporate reorganizations, and liquidations. Also, in certain situations involving an insolvent employee, the holding period rules are modified.

[96]§ 422(b).

- The option must be granted within 10 years of the date the plan is adopted or of the date the plan is approved by the shareholders, whichever date is earlier.
- The option must by its terms be exercisable only within 10 years of the date it is granted.
- The option price must equal or exceed the fair market value of the stock at the time the option is granted. This requirement is deemed satisfied if there has been a good faith attempt to value the stock accurately, even if the option price is less than the stock value.
- The option by its terms must be nontransferable other than at death and must be exercisable during the employee's lifetime only by the employee.
- The employee must not, immediately before the option is granted, own stock representing more than 10 percent of the voting power or value of all classes of stock in the employer-corporation or its parent or subsidiary. (Here, the attribution rules of § 267 are applied in modified form.) However, the stock ownership limitation will be waived if the option price is at least 110 percent of the fair market value (at the time the option is granted) of the stock subject to the option and the option by its terms is not exercisable more than five years from the date it is granted.[97]

An overall limitation is imposed on the amount of ISOs that can be first exercisable in one year by an employee. This limit is set at $100,000 per year based on the value of the stock determined at the time the option is granted. For example, an ISO plan may permit acquisition of up to $600,000 worth of stock if it provides that the options are exercisable in six installments, each of which becomes exercisable in a different year and does not exceed $100,000.

Because of these regulatory conditions and the fact that a company may never receive a tax deduction, employers may view ISOs less favorably than nonqualified stock options.

NONQUALIFIED STOCK OPTIONS

A **nonqualified stock option (NQSO)** does not satisfy the statutory requirements for ISOs. In addition, a stock option that otherwise would qualify as an ISO will be treated as an NQSO if the terms of the stock option provide that it is not an ISO. If the NQSO has a readily ascertainable fair market value (e.g., the option is traded on an established exchange), the value of the option must be included in the employee's income at the date of grant. Thereafter, capital gain or loss is recognized only upon the disposal of the optioned stock. The employee's basis is the amount paid for the stock plus any amount reported as ordinary income. The employer obtains a corresponding tax deduction at the same time and to the extent that ordinary income is recognized by the employee.[98]

EXAMPLE 50

On February 1, 2010, Janet was granted an NQSO to purchase 100 shares of stock from her employer at $10 per share. On this date, the option was selling for $2 on an established exchange. Janet exercised the option on March 30, 2011, when the stock was worth $20 per share. On November 5, 2011, Janet sold the optioned stock for $22 per share.

- Janet must report ordinary income of $200 ($2 × 100 shares) on the date of grant (February 1, 2010), because the option has a readily ascertainable fair market value.
- Janet's adjusted basis for the stock is $1,200 ($1,000 cost + $200 recognized gain).

---

[97]§ 422(c)(5).   [98]Reg. §§ 1.421–6(c), (d), (e), and (f); Reg. § 1.83–7.

FINANCIAL DISCLOSURE *Insights*

ACCOUNTING FOR EXECUTIVE COMPENSATION

The recent crash of the financial sector of the U.S. economy has shed light on the high levels of bonuses, commissions, health care coverage, and other compensation devices that some firms use to attract and retain managerial talent. Payments to qualified retirement plans are limited in amount and timing, but other "IOUs" are made available to managers, typically as unfunded but enforceable promises to make large payments or stock transfers, say, after the executive retires or works for the firm for a certain number of years. These arrangements embarrassed some of the employers who provided them while receiving bailouts from the Federal government, but the high levels of executive pay and deferred compensation live on today.

Bonus and retirement arrangements like these create a book-tax difference, as they represent compensation expenses for GAAP purposes, but no tax deduction is allowed until the compensation is paid or becomes fully funded and vested, say, through a trust or escrow account. Some firms do fund the deferred payments—no book-tax difference or

deferred tax asset amount would result in that case. Usually, the employer also includes in this book-tax difference the amount by which current compensation paid to employees exceeds the tax law maximum deduction amount of §162(m).

Recent financial statements revealed the following amounts in the deferred tax asset accounts of the employer, using "deferred compensation" or "employee benefits and pay" as the line item in the tax footnote.

Employer	Deferred Tax Asset for Executive Compensation ($000)
Goldman Sachs	11,800
JPMorgan Chase	8,200
Citigroup	5,000
Bank of America	1,300
Cisco	1,200
Eli Lilly	1,150

- Upon the sale of the stock (November 5, 2011), Janet must report a long-term capital gain of $1,000 [($22 − $12) × 100 shares].
- At the date of grant (February 1, 2010), the employer receives a tax deduction of $200, the amount of ordinary income reported by Janet. ∎

If an NQSO does not have a readily ascertainable fair market value, an employee does not recognize income at the grant date. However, as a general rule, ordinary income must then be reported in the year of exercise (the difference between the fair market value of the stock at the exercise date and the option price).[99] The amount paid by the employee for the stock plus the amount reported as ordinary income becomes the basis. Any appreciation above that basis is taxed as a long-term capital gain upon disposition (assuming the stock is held for the required long-term holding period after exercise). The corporation receives a corresponding tax deduction at the same time and to the extent that ordinary income is recognized by the employee.

EXAMPLE 51

On February 3, 2009, Maria was granted an NQSO for 100 shares of common stock at $10 per share. On the date of the grant, there was no readily ascertainable fair market value for the option. Maria exercised the options on January 3, 2010, when the stock was selling for $15 per share. She sold one-half of the shares on April 15, 2010, and the other half on September 17, 2011. The sale price on both dates was $21 per share. Maria would not recognize any income on the grant date (February 3, 2009) but would recognize $500 ($1,500 − $1,000) of ordinary income on the exercise date (January 3, 2010). She would recognize a short-term capital gain of $300 on the sale of the first half in 2010 and a $300 long-term capital gain on the sale of the second batch of stock in 2011 [½($2,100 − $1,500)]. ∎

---

[99]Reg. § 1.83–7(a); Reg. § 1.421–6(d).

The major *advantages* of NQSOs can be summarized as follows:

• A tax deduction is available to the corporation without a cash outlay.
• The employee receives capital gain treatment on any appreciation in the stock starting either at the exercise date if the option does not have a readily ascertainable fair market value or at the date of grant if the option has a readily ascertainable fair market value.
• Options can be issued at more flexible terms than under ISO plans (e.g., longer exercise period and granted to nonemployees).

A major *disadvantage* is that the employee must recognize ordinary income on the exercise of the option or at the date of grant without receiving cash to pay the tax. Another negative factor is that the exercise price for NQSOs must not be lower than the underlying stock's fair market value on the grant date because of § 409A restrictions.

TAX PLANNING:

19.7 DEFERRED COMPENSATION

LO.10

Identify tax planning opportunities available with deferred compensation.

With the individual tax rate being as high as 35 percent in 2011, taxpayers are motivated to try to lower their tax burden by participating in more deferred compensation arrangements. The $1 million annual limit on the compensation deduction for the top five executives of publicly traded companies may cause a shift into § 401(k) plans, qualified retirement plans, and especially nonqualified deferred compensation arrangements. However, only $245,000 of compensation can be taken into consideration for purposes of calculating contributions or benefits under a qualified pension or profit sharing plan. The $5,000 allowed for traditional IRAs and Roth IRAs should encourage more participation in retirement vehicles. The spousal IRA option should expand retirement coverage even further.

19.8 QUALIFIED PLANS

Qualified plans provide maximum tax benefits for employers, because the employer receives an immediate tax deduction for contributions to a plan's trust and the income that is earned on the contributions is not taxable to the employer. The employer's contributions and the trust earnings are not taxed to the employees until those funds are made available to them.

TAX *in* the NEWS

UNDERFUNDED PENSION PLANS POSE PROBLEMS FOR THE STATES

In February 2010, the Pew Center on the States released a study indicating that state pension plans are underfunded by nearly $1 trillion. The states have promised retirement benefits of $3.25 trillion but have only $2.35 trillion on hand. Part of the shortfall is due to investment losses, but many of the states simply fell behind on their payments—and that was before the recent recession. Some states such as Illinois and Kansas have less than 60 percent of the assets needed to meet long-term pension obligations. J. D. Rauh predicts that at the current rate, the Illinois pension system could run out of money by 2018. Nevertheless, public employees' unions in most states are likely to resist any efforts to reduce benefits or to increase the retirement age.

Sources: Adapted from Robert Powell, "Pension Systems on the Brink," *Market Watch*, February 19, 2010, **http://quote.yahoo.com/focus-retirement/article/108868/pension-system**; and Mary Williams Walsh, "In Budget Crisis, States Take Aim at Pension Costs," *New York Times*, January 19, 2010, **www.nytimes.com/2010/06/20/business/20pension.html**.

Qualified plans are most appropriate where it is desirable to provide benefits for a cross section of employees. In some closely held corporations, the primary objective is to provide benefits for the officer-shareholder group and other highly paid personnel. The nondiscrimination requirements that must be met in a qualified plan may prevent such companies from attaining these objectives. Thus, a nonqualified arrangement may be needed as a supplement to, or used in lieu of, the qualified plan.

Cash balance plans are better for younger, mobile employees, and the converting company saves money by reducing pension payouts for older and longer-service employees. If a participant moves or retires, he or she can roll over the lump-sum payment into an IRA or another qualified plan.

Although defined benefit plans are being eliminated by larger companies, many small-business owners with few or no employees (or a young, low-paid, transient staff) are adopting them.

19.9 SELF-EMPLOYED RETIREMENT PLANS

A Keogh or traditional deductible IRA participant may make a deductible contribution for a tax year up to the time prescribed for filing the individual's tax return. A Keogh plan must have been established by the end of the tax year (e.g., December 31) to obtain a current deduction for the contribution made in the subsequent year. An individual can establish an IRA after the end of the tax year and still receive a current deduction for the contribution made in the subsequent year. However, since the deductibility of contributions to IRAs has been restricted for many middle-income and upper-income taxpayers, Keogh plans are likely to become more important.

19.10 INDIVIDUAL RETIREMENT ACCOUNTS

Unlike a traditional IRA, which defers taxes on the entire account, a Roth IRA allows the earnings to accumulate completely tax-free. All ordinary income and capital gains earned inside a Roth IRA are never taxed (assuming the five-year holding period provision is satisfied). Thus, a Roth IRA runs contrary to the general principle that it is usually better for a taxpayer to postpone the payment of any tax. In many situations, a retirement plan participant will earn more wealth with a Roth IRA than with a traditional IRA. This potential for tax-free growth is so advantageous that taxpayers who have substantial traditional IRA balances and are eligible should evaluate converting at least some of their traditional IRA balances into a Roth IRA.

CONCEPT SUMMARY   19.4

Section 401(k) Plan and IRA Compared

	§ 401(k) Plan	IRA
Deduction limitation	Smaller of $16,500 (in 2011) or approximately 100% of total earnings. Limited by antidiscrimination requirements of § 401(k)(3).	$5,000 or 100% of compensation.
Distributions	Early withdrawal possible if for early retirement (55 or over) or to pay medical expenses.	10% penalty for early withdrawals, except for withdrawals to pay for certain medical expenses and health insurance, qualified education expenses, and qualified first-time homebuyer expenses.
Effect on gross earnings	Gross salary reduction, which may reduce profit sharing contributions, Social Security benefits, and group life insurance.	No effect.
Employer involvement	Must keep records; monitor for compliance with antidiscrimination test.	Minimal.
Lump-sum distributions	Favorable 10-year forward averaging under limited circumstances.	Ordinary income.
Timing of contribution	Within 30 days of plan year-end or due date of employer's return.*	Grace period up to due date of tax return (not including extensions).
Loans from plan	Yes.	No.

*Elective contributions must be made to the plan no later than 30 days after the end of the plan year, and nonelective contributions no later than the due date of the tax return (including extensions).

19.11 COMPARISON OF § 401(K) PLAN WITH IRA

Most employees will find a § 401(k) plan more attractive than an IRA. Probably the biggest limitation of an IRA is the $5,000 maximum shelter in 2011 (ignoring the catch-up provision). Under § 401(k), employees are permitted to shelter compensation up to $16,500 (in 2011).[100] The restrictions on deducting contributions to IRAs for many middle-income and upper-income taxpayers may cause many employees to utilize § 401(k) plans more frequently.

Another difference between § 401(k) plans and IRAs is the manner in which the money is treated. Money placed in an IRA may be tax deductible, whereas dollars placed in a § 401(k) plan are considered to be deferred compensation. Thus, a § 401(k) reduction may reduce profit sharing payments, group life insurance, and Social Security benefits. Finally, many employers "match or partially match" employee elective deferrals with employer money. Concept Summary 19.4 compares a § 401(k) plan with an IRA.

---

[100]These amounts are being increased through a phase-in approach. See Footnotes 33 and 48.

19.12 NONQUALIFIED DEFERRED COMPENSATION (NQDC) PLANS

Nonqualified deferred compensation arrangements such as restricted property plans can be useful to attract executive talent or to provide substantial retirement benefits for executives. A restricted property plan may be used to retain a key employee of a closely held company when management continuity problems are anticipated. Without such employees, the untimely death or disability of one of the owners might cause a disruption of the business with an attendant loss in value for his or her heirs. Such plans may discriminate in favor of officers and other highly paid employees. The employer, however, does not receive a tax deduction until the employee is required to include the deferred compensation in income (upon the lapse of the restrictions).

The principal advantage of NQDC plans over current compensation is that the employee can defer the recognition of income to future periods when his or her income tax bracket may be lower (e.g., during retirement years). The time value benefits from the deferral of income should also be considered. If the current tax rates continue, an executive with a deferred compensation arrangement entered into in a prior year might wish to continue to delay the income into future years. However, if future rates are projected to rise, a different decision would be appropriate.

The principal disadvantage of NQDC plans could be the bunching effect that takes place on the expiration of the period of deferral. In some cases, planning can alleviate this result.

During 2011, Kelly, an executive, enters into an agreement to postpone a portion of her payment for current services until retirement. The deferred amount is not segregated from the company's general assets and is subject to normal business risk. The entire payment, not the after-tax amount, is invested in securities and variable annuity contracts. Kelly is not taxed on the payment in 2011, and the company receives no deduction in 2011. If Kelly receives the deferred payment in a lump sum when she retires, the tax rates might be higher and more progressive than in 2011. Thus, Kelly may wish to arrange for a number of payments to be made to her or a designated beneficiary over a number of years. ∎	**EXAMPLE 52**

19.13 STOCK OPTIONS

Rather than paying compensation in the form of corporate stock, a corporation may issue options to purchase stock at a specific price to an employee. Stock option plans are used more frequently by publicly traded companies than by closely held companies. This difference is due to the problems of determining the value of the stock of a company that is not publicly held, which is a practical requirement now in order to avoid negative treatment under § 409A.

Nonqualified stock options (NQSOs) are more flexible and less restrictive than incentive stock options (ISOs). For example, the holding period for an NQSO is not as long as that for an ISO. However, the option price of an NQSO cannot be less than the fair market value of the stock at the time the option is granted because of § 409A. An NQSO creates an employer deduction that lowers the cost of the NQSO to the employer. The employer may pass along this tax savings to the employee in the form of a cash payment. Both the employer and the employee may be better off by combining NQSOs with additional cash payments rather than using ISOs. See Concept Summary 19.5.

For tax purposes, most companies are able to deduct the expense of options and thereby reduce their taxes. Generally, options carry an exercise price (strike price)

CONCEPT SUMMARY 19.5

Incentive Stock Options and Nonqualified Stock Options Compared

	ISO	NQSO
Granted at any price	No	Yes
May have any duration	No	Yes
Governing Code Section	§ 422	§ 83
Spread subject to alternative minimum tax	Yes	No
Deduction to employer for spread	No	Yes
Type of gain/loss on disposal	Capital	Capital
Statutory amount ($100,000) limitation	Yes	No

equal to the fair market value on the date the options are approved by the board of directors. The Financial Accounting Standards Board (FASB) now requires stock options to be expensed, which lowers a company's earnings. Companies must measure the economic value of the options on the grant date and then amortize this cost equally over the vesting period of the options. Also, § 409A effectively forces stock options to be granted with an exercise price equal to the stock's fair market value.

Stock options are an effective compensation device as long as share prices are rising. When stock prices fall, the options become unexercisable and possibly worthless. In an upmarket, options are great. But during a downturn in the market, these underwater options can be ugly.

Stock options are likely to be a less dominant form of executive compensation in the future. The backdating scandals and the required expensing of stock options for financial statement purposes are causing businesses to turn to other forms of compensation. Performance-based bonuses and § 401(k) plans probably will become more popular.

19.14 FLEXIBLE BENEFIT PLANS

Employees may be permitted to choose from a package of employer-provided fringe benefits.[101] In these so-called **cafeteria benefit plans**, some of the benefits chosen by an employee may be taxable, and some may be statutory nontaxable benefits (e.g., health and accident insurance and group term life insurance).

Under general tax rules, providing a choice to employees would result in all benefits (both taxable and nontaxable) under the cafeteria benefit plan to be taxable. However, if the cafeteria plan rules are met, a special provision applies to prevent this tax result from occurring.

Employer contributions made to a flexible plan are included in an employee's gross income only to the extent that the employee actually elects the taxable benefits. Certain nondiscrimination standards with respect to coverage, eligibility for participation, contributions, and benefits must be met. Thus, such a plan must cover a fair cross section of employees. Also, a flexible plan cannot include an election to defer compensation, and a key employee is not exempt from taxation on the taxable benefits made available where more than 25 percent of the statutory nontaxable benefits are provided to key employees.

[101]§ 125.

19.15 Liquidating Retirement Assets

If a person has funds from sources other than retirement assets, which retirement assets should an individual spend first? The most tax-efficient result is to postpone the income tax obligation for as long as possible. Generally, retirement assets should be taken from assets or accounts in the following order so that the tax-deferred growth continues:

- Taxable accounts.
- Section 457 accounts of government employees since no penalties apply once the employee is separated from employment.
- Section 401(k) and nonprofit § 403(b) plans because the age 55 separation rule may apply.
- Traditional IRAs since a taxpayer must be at least age 59½ to obtain penalty-free withdrawals.
- Roth IRAs since no required minimum distribution rules apply.[102]

REFOCUS ON THE BIG PICTURE

A TAXPAYER WHO SAVES

From her discussion with Dr. Sanchez, Joyce learns that her professor has the following retirement plans:

- *Defined contribution plan.* The university offered its faculty members a choice between a defined benefit pension plan and a defined contribution plan. Dr. Sanchez expects to work at a number of universities during her career, so she chose the defined contribution plan because of its mobility (i.e., she can take the plan with her). The maximum annual contribution the university could make to the plan is $49,000 for 2011. Since the university contribution rate is 15 percent, the actual contribution is $22,500 ($150,000 × 15%).
- *§ 403(b) annuity.* Dr. Sanchez makes contributions to a § 403(b) annuity [i.e., the equivalent of a § 401(k) plan, but available to educators]. The maximum annual contribution she can make in 2011 is $16,500, and Dr. Sanchez has the university deduct this amount from her semimonthly salary paychecks. In addition, because she is at least age 50 (i.e., she is age 51), she has the university deduct an additional $5,500 as a catch-up contribution.
- *Keogh (H.R. 10) plan.* In addition to her position at the university, Dr. Sanchez has a forensic consulting practice. Since she is self-employed, she is able to establish a Keogh plan. She contributes 20 percent of her net earnings from the consulting practice, about $8,000 per year ($40,000 × 20%), to the plan.
- *IRA.* Dr. Sanchez also contributes annually to a traditional IRA. She would prefer a Roth IRA, but her AGI exceeds the $122,000 phaseout limit. Likewise, she cannot deduct her contribution of $5,000 (the maximum) because of the amount of her AGI. Since she cannot deduct her contributions, her basis in the IRA is the summation of her contributions. The $15,000 that Dr. Sanchez withdrew from her traditional IRA is not subject to current taxation and does not reduce her basis for the IRA. This result occurs because Dr. Sanchez successfully completed a tax-free rollover (i.e., recontributed the $15,000 to her IRA within 60 days).

Dr. Sanchez explains that she wants to travel after retirement, so her goal is to retire by age 60 while she is still in good health. She anticipates these plans will enable her to do so.

---

[102]David M. Maloney and James E. Smith, "Distribution Options for Defined Contribution Plans, Part II," *The Tax Adviser,* June 2007, pp. 340 and 341.

KEY TERMS

Cafeteria benefit plans, 19–46

Cash balance plan, 19–7

Coverdell Education Savings Account (CESA), 19–25

Deferred compensation, 19–3

Defined benefit plan, 19–5

Defined contribution pension plan, 19–5

Golden parachute payments, 19–33

Highly compensated employee, 19–9

H.R. 10 (Keogh) plans, 19–20

Incentive stock option (ISO), 19–39

Individual Retirement Accounts (IRAs), 19–22

Lump-sum distribution, 19–12

Nonqualified deferred compensation (NQDC), 19–31

Nonqualified stock option (NQSO), 19–40

Pension plan, 19–5

Profit sharing plan, 19–6

Restricted property plan, 19–35

Roth IRA, 19–23

§401(K) plan, 19–16

Simplified employee pension (SEP) plans, 19–26

Stock bonus plan, 19–7

Stock option, 19–38

Substantial risk of forfeiture (SRF), 19–36

Vesting requirements, 19–9

DISCUSSION QUESTIONS

1. **LO.1** Provide a definition of deferred compensation.

2. **LO.1** List some types of deferred compensation arrangements.

3. **LO.1** List some fringe benefits that may be tax-free.

4. **LO.1** Determine whether each of the following independent statements best applies to a defined contribution plan *(DCP)*, a defined benefit plan *(DBP)*, both *(B)*, or neither *(N)*:
   a. The amount to be received at retirement depends on actuarial calculations.
   b. Forfeitures can be allocated to the remaining participants' accounts.
   c. Requires greater reporting requirements and more actuarial and administrative costs.
   d. Forfeitures can revert to the employer.
   e. More favorable to employees who are older at the time the plan is adopted.
   f. Employee forfeitures can be used to reduce future contributions by the employer.
   g. May exclude employees who begin employment within five years of normal retirement age.
   h. Annual addition to each employee's account may not exceed the smaller of $49,000 or 100% of the employee's salary.
   i. The final benefit to a participant depends upon investment performance.
   j. To avoid penalties, the amount of annual contributions must meet minimum funding requirements.

5. **LO.1** Indicate whether the following statements apply to a pension plan *(P)*, a profit sharing plan *(PS)*, both *(B)*, or neither *(N)*:
   a. Forfeited amounts can be used to reduce future contributions by the employer.
   b. Allocation of forfeitures may discriminate in favor of the prohibited group (highly compensated employees).
   c. Forfeitures can revert to the employer.
   d. Forfeitures can be allocated to participants and increase plan benefits.
   e. An annual benefit of $60,000 could be payable on behalf of a participant.
   f. More favorable to employees who are older at the time the qualified plan is adopted.

6. **LO.1** What are the four groups of qualified plans?

7. **LO.1** What are the two types of qualified pension plans?

8. **LO.1** Which type of people favor a cash balance plan?

9. **LO.1** An employee stock ownership plan (ESOP) has to be a profit sharing plan. Discuss this statement.

10. **LO.1, 4** What is the maximum annual benefit payable under a defined benefit plan?

11. **LO.2, 3, 6** Penny plans to retire in 2011 at age 70. Identify any issues facing Penny with respect to distributions from her qualified retirement plan.

    ISSUE ID

12. **LO.3, 6** Harvey Pehrson, who is age 71, is going to receive a lump-sum distribution from a qualified plan in 2011. He has asked you to provide him with a description of the alternatives available to him for taxing the lump-sum distribution. Draft a letter to Harvey in which you respond. He resides at 3000 East Glenn, Tulsa, OK 74104.

    ISSUE ID

    COMMUNICATIONS

13. **LO.3** Which of the following would be considered a tax benefit or advantage of a qualified retirement plan?
    a. Certain lump-sum distributions may be subject to capital gain treatment.
    b. Employer contributions are deductible by the employer in the year of contribution.
    c. Employee contributions are deductible by the employee in the year of contribution.
    d. The qualified trust is tax-exempt as to all income (other than unrelated business income).

14. **LO.3, 6** Donna is retiring and wishes to know her alternatives for receiving payments from her qualified retirement plan.

    DECISION MAKING

15. **LO.5** Explain the contribution limitations for a defined contribution Keogh plan and for a defined benefit Keogh plan.

16. **LO.6, 10** Should a 31-year-old self-employed single woman establish a traditional deductible IRA, a traditional nondeductible IRA, or a Roth IRA? She has two children, ages 11 and 9.

    DECISION MAKING

17. **LO.6** Joey, who is single, is not covered by another qualified plan and earns $109,000 at his job in 2011. How much can he contribute to a traditional IRA or to a Roth IRA in 2011?

18. **LO.6** Jim Hassel calls you and asks about "designated Roth contributions." Prepare a memo for the tax files about your response.

    COMMUNICATIONS

19. **LO.6** What requirements must be met to receive tax-free withdrawals from a Roth IRA?

20. **LO.6** What happens if too much is contributed to an IRA?

21. **LO.7, 10** During his senior year in college, Sandy is drafted by the Los Angeles Dodgers. When he graduates, he expects to sign a five-year contract in the range of $1.7 million per year. Sandy plans to marry his girlfriend before he reports to the Dodger farm team in California. Identify the relevant tax issues facing this left-handed pitcher.

    ISSUE ID

22. **LO.7** How are golden parachute payments treated by the payor and by the recipient?

23. **LO.8** What is a substantial risk of forfeiture, and what effect does it have on a taxpayer's gross income?

24. **LO.10** Aaron is retiring and wants to know the most tax-efficient sequence for liquidating his retirement assets. What do you tell him?

PROBLEMS

25. **LO.2** Blonde Corporation has a total of 1,000 employees, of whom 700 are non-highly compensated. The retirement plan covers 300 non-highly compensated employees and 200 highly compensated employees. Does this plan satisfy the minimum coverage test?

26. **LO.2** Black Corporation's pension plan benefits 620 of its 1,000 highly compensated employees. How many of its 620 non-highly compensated employees must benefit to meet the ratio percentage test for the minimum coverage requirement?

27. **LO.2** A retirement plan covers 72% of the non-highly compensated individuals. The plan benefits 48 of the 131 employees. Determine if the participation requirement is met.

28. **LO.2** Jacob, Inc., uses a two- to six-year graded vesting approach in its defined contribution plan. Calculate the nonforfeitable percentage for each of the following participants based upon the years of service completed:

Participant	Years of Service
Ryan	1
Sloane	3
Donna	5
Caleb	7

29. **LO.1, 4** Wanda participates in a defined benefit plan that uses a fixed formula providing an employee with a benefit of 2% for each year of service, up to a maximum of 30 years. The total percentage accumulated before retirement is applied to the average of her three highest years of salary. Wanda works for 21 years, and the average of her three highest years of salary is $290,000. Calculate the amount of retirement benefits she will receive each year.

DECISION MAKING

30. **LO.2** Marie has worked for Yellow Corporation for four and one-half years, but she has an offer to move to Red Corporation for a moderate increase in salary. Her average salary for Yellow has been $210,000, and she receives a 2% benefit for each year of service in her retirement plan. The company uses a five-year vesting schedule. Advise Marie as to this possible switch in jobs.

31. **LO.4** Heather has been an active participant in a defined benefit plan for 19 years. During her last 6 years of employment, Heather earned $42,000, $48,000, $56,000, $80,000, $89,000, and $108,000, respectively (representing her highest-income years).
    a. Calculate Heather's maximum allowable benefits from her qualified plan (assume there are fewer than 100 participants).
    b. Assume that Heather's average compensation for her three highest years is $199,700. Calculate her maximum allowable benefits.

32. **LO.4** Determine the maximum annual benefits payable to a participant from a defined benefit plan in the following independent situations:
    a. Frank, age 66, has been a participant for 17 years, and his highest average compensation for 3 years is $127,300.
    b. Ellen, age 65, has been a participant for 9 years (11 years of service), and her highest average compensation for 3 years is $102,600.

33. **LO.4** In 2011, Magenta Corporation paid compensation of $45,300 to the participants in a profit sharing plan. During 2011, Magenta Corporation contributed $13,200 to the plan.
    a. Calculate Magenta's deductible amount for 2011.
    b. Calculate the amount of any contribution carryover from 2011.

DECISION MAKING

34. **LO.4, 10** Amber's employer, Lavender, Inc., has a § 401(k) plan that permits salary deferral elections by its employees. Amber's salary is $99,000, and her marginal tax rate is 33%.
    a. What is the maximum amount Amber can elect for salary deferral treatment for 2011?
    b. If Amber elects salary deferral treatment for the amount in (a), how much can she save in taxes?
    c. What amount would you recommend that Amber elect for salary deferral treatment for 2011?

35. **LO.4** Sally, a single individual, participates in her employer's SIMPLE § 401(k) plan. The plan permits participants to contribute a percentage of their salary. Sally elects to contribute 5% of her annual salary of $111,000 to the plan. On what amount of her salary does Sally pay income taxes in 2011?

36. **LO.2, 4, 5** In 2011, Susan's sole proprietorship earns $300,000 of self-employment net income (after the deduction for one-half of self-employment tax).
    a. Calculate the maximum amount that Susan can deduct for contributions to a defined contribution Keogh plan.
    b. Suppose Susan contributes more than the allowable amount to the Keogh plan. What are the consequences to her?
    c. Can Susan retire and begin receiving Keogh payments at age 58 without incurring a penalty?

37. **LO.4, 5** Harvey is a self-employed accountant with earned income from the business of $120,000 (after the deduction for one-half of his self-employment tax). He has a profit sharing plan (e.g., defined contribution Keogh plan). What is the maximum amount Harvey can contribute to his retirement plan in 2011?

38. **LO.4, 6** Janet, age 29, is unmarried and is an active participant in a qualified retirement plan. Her modified AGI is $61,000 in 2011.
    a.   Calculate the amount that Janet can contribute to a traditional IRA and the amount she can deduct.
    b.   Assume instead that Janet is a participant in a SIMPLE IRA and that she elects to contribute 4% of her compensation to the account, while her employer contributes 3%. What amount will be contributed for 2011? What amount will be vested?

39. **LO.4, 6** Answer the following independent questions with respect to a deductible IRA and § 401(k) contributions for 2011:
    a.   Govind, age 31, earns a salary of $26,000 and is not an active participant in any other qualified plan. His wife has $600 of compensation income. What is the maximum total deductible contribution to their IRAs?
    b.   Danos is a participant in a SIMPLE § 401(k) plan. He contributes 6% of his salary of $42,000, and his employer contributes 3%. What amount will be contributed for the year? What amount will be vested?

40. **LO.6** Answer the following independent questions with respect to traditional IRA contributions for 2011:
    a.   Juan, age 41, earns a salary of $28,000 and is not an active participant in any other qualified plan. His wife, Agnes, has no earned income. What is the maximum total deductible contribution to their IRAs? Juan wishes to contribute as much as possible to his own IRA.
    b.   Abby, age 29, has earned income of $25,000, and her husband, Sam, has earned income of $2,600. They are not active participants in any other qualified plan. What is the maximum contribution to their IRAs?
    c.   Leo's employer makes a contribution of $3,500 to Leo's simplified employee pension plan. If Leo is single, has earned income of $32,000, and has AGI of $29,000, what amount, if any, can he contribute to an IRA?

41. **LO.6** Frank established a Roth IRA at age 25 and contributed a total of $131,244 to it over 38 years. The account is now worth $376,000. How much of these funds can Frank withdraw tax-free?

42. **LO.6** Beth, age 51, has a traditional deductible IRA with an account balance of $221,419, of which $160,400 represents contributions and $61,019 represents earnings. In 2011, she converts her traditional IRA into a Roth IRA. What amount, if any, must Beth include in her gross income in 2011?

43. **LO.6** Carri and Dane, ages 31 and 32, have been married for 11 years, and both are active participants in employer qualified retirement plans. Their total AGI in 2011 is $170,500, and they earn salaries of $87,000 and $81,000, respectively. What amount may Carri and Dane:
    a.   Contribute to regular IRAs?
    b.   Deduct for their contributions in (a)?
    c.   Contribute to Roth IRAs?
    d.   Deduct for their contributions in (c)?
    e.   Contribute to Coverdell Education Savings Accounts for their three children?

44. **LO.4, 6** Heather is a participant in a SIMPLE IRA plan of her employer, Yellow, Inc. During 2011, she contributes 9% of her $52,000 salary, and her employer contributes 3%. What is the total amount that will be vested in her account at the end of 2011?

45. **LO.6** In 2014, Joyce receives a $4,000 distribution from her Coverdell Education Savings Account, which has a fair market value of $10,000. Total contributions to her CESA have been $7,000. Joyce's AGI is $25,000.
    a.   Joyce uses the entire $4,000 to pay for qualified education expenses. What amount should she include in her gross income?
    b.   Assume instead that Joyce uses only $2,500 of the $4,000 distribution for qualified education expenses. What amount should she include in her gross income?

46. **LO.6** Gene, age 34, and Beth, age 32, have been married for nine years. Gene, who is a college student, works part-time and earns $1,500. Beth is a high school teacher and earns a salary of $34,000. Their AGI is $37,000.
    a. What is the maximum amount Gene can contribute to an IRA in 2011?
    b. What is the maximum amount Beth can contribute to an IRA in 2011?

DECISION MAKING

47. **LO.6** Samuel, age 32, loses his job in a corporate downsizing. As a result of his termination, he receives a distribution of the balance in his § 401(k) account of $20,000 ($25,000 − $5,000 withholding) on May 1, 2011. Samuel's marginal tax rate is 28%.
    a. What effect will the distribution have on Samuel's gross income and tax liability if he invests the $20,000 received in a mutual fund?
    b. Same as (a) except that Samuel invests the $20,000 received in a traditional IRA within 60 days of the distribution.
    c. Same as (a) except that Samuel invests the $20,000 received in a Roth IRA within 60 days of the distribution.
    d. How could Samuel have received better tax consequences in (b)?

48. **LO.7** Red, Inc., a calendar year employer, has an accrued NQDC liability of $400,000 on December 31, 2009. During 2010, the company accrues another $70,000 of NQDC. On February 12, 2011, the company pays the entire $470,000 to Otis, a cash basis employee.
    a. What amount is considered to be deferred compensation?
    b. What amount, if any, can the corporation deduct? When?

49. **LO.7** Elba is an officer of a local company that merges with a public company, resulting in a change of ownership. She loses her job as a result of the merger, but she receives a cash settlement of $680,000 from her employer under a golden parachute plan. Her average annual compensation for the past five tax years is $230,000.
    a. What are the tax consequences to Elba and to the company as a result of the $680,000 payment?
    b. Assume instead that Elba's five-year average annual compensation was $130,000, and she receives $420,000 in the settlement. What are the tax consequences to Elba and the company?

DECISION MAKING

50. **LO.8** On February 20, 2011, Tim (an executive of Hawk Corporation) purchased 100 shares of Hawk stock (selling at $20 a share) for $10 a share. A condition of the transaction was that Tim must resell the stock to Hawk at cost if he voluntarily leaves the company within five years of receiving the stock (assume this represents a substantial risk of forfeiture).
    a. Assuming that no special election is made under § 83(b), what amount, if any, is taxable to Tim in 2011?
    b. Five years later when the stock is selling for $40 a share, Tim is still employed by Hawk. What amount of ordinary income, if any, is taxable to Tim?
    c. What amount, if any, is deductible by Hawk as compensation expense five years later?
    d. Should Tim make the § 83(b) special election in 2011? What amount would be taxable in 2011 if he makes the special election?
    e. In (d), what amount would be deductible by Hawk five years later?
    f. Under (d), assume Tim sold all the stock six years later for $65 per share. How much capital gain is included in his gross income?
    g. In (d), what loss is available to Tim if he voluntarily resigns in 2014 before the five-year period and does not sell the stock back to the corporation?
    h. In (g), in the year Tim resigns, what amount, if any, would be taxable to Hawk Corporation?

51. **LO.8** On July 2, 2009, Black Corporation sold 1,000 of its common shares (worth $14 per share) to Earl, an employee, for $5 per share. The sale was subject to Earl's agreement to resell the shares to the corporation for $5 per share if his employment is terminated within the following four years. The shares had a value of $24 per share on July 2, 2013. Earl sells the shares for $31 per share on September 16, 2013. No special election under § 83(b) is made.
    a. What amount, if any, is taxed to Earl on July 2, 2009?
    b. On July 2, 2013?
    c. On September 16, 2013?
    d. What deduction, if any, will Black Corporation obtain? When?

e. Assume the same facts, except that Earl makes an election under § 83(b). What amount, if any, will be taxed to Earl on July 2, 2009, July 2, 2013, and September 16, 2013?

f. Will the assumption made in (e) have any effect on any deduction Black Corporation will receive? Explain.

52. **LO.9** Rosa exercises ISOs for 100 shares of Copper Corporation common stock at the option price of $100 per share on May 21, 2010, when the fair market value is $120 per share. She sells the 100 shares of common stock three and one-half years later for $140.

a. Calculate the long-term capital gain and the ordinary income on the sale.

b. Assume Rosa holds the stock only seven months and sells the shares for $140 per share. Calculate the capital gain and ordinary income on the sale.

c. In (b), what amount can Copper Corporation deduct? When?

d. Assume instead that Rosa holds the stock for two years and sells the shares for $115 per share. Calculate any capital gain and ordinary income on this transaction.

e. In (a), assume the options are nonqualified stock options with a nonascertainable fair market value on the date of the grant. Calculate the long-term capital gain and ordinary income on the date of the sale.

f. In (e), assume that each option has an ascertainable fair market value of $10 on the date of the grant and that no substantial risk of forfeiture exists. Calculate the long-term capital gain and the ordinary income on the date of the sale.

53. **LO.9** On November 19, 2009, Rex is granted a nonqualified stock option to purchase 100 shares of Tan Company. On that date, the stock is selling for $8 per share, and the option price is $9 per share. Rex exercises the option on August 21, 2010, when the stock is selling for $10 per share. Five months later, Rex sells the shares for $11.50 per share.

a. What amount is taxable to Rex in 2009?

b. What amount is taxable to Rex in 2010?

c. What amount and type of gain are taxable to Rex in 2011?

d. What amount, if any, is deductible by Tan Company in 2010?

e. What amount, if any, is recognized in 2011 if the stock is sold for $9.50 per share?

54. **LO.4, 5, 6, 10** Sara Loflin, age 35, is the owner of a small business. She is trying to decide whether to have a § 401(k) plan or a simplified employee pension plan. She is not interested in a SIMPLE § 401(k) plan. Her salary will be approximately $54,000, and she will have no employees. She asks you to provide her with information on the advantages and disadvantages of both types of plans and your recommendation. Draft a letter to Sara that contains your response. Her address is 1000 Canal Avenue, New Orleans, LA 70148.

DECISION MAKING

COMMUNICATIONS

55. **LO.10** Cody's employer provides a qualified cafeteria plan under which he can choose cash of $20,000 or health and accident insurance premiums worth approximately $14,000. If Cody is in the 35% tax bracket, advise him of his tax alternatives.

DECISION MAKING

56. **LO.10** Zariat has the retirement assets listed below. She plans to retire and start withdrawing amounts on which to live. Rank the accounts in the order from which she should make withdrawals so that tax deferral is maximized.

Roth IRA	$923,408
Traditional IRA	118,120
§ 401(k) plan	837,010
§ 457 account	334,090

RESEARCH PROBLEMS

Note: Solutions to Research Problems can be prepared by using the **Checkpoint®** **Student Edition** online research product, which is available to accompany this text. It is also possible to prepare solutions to the Research Problems by using tax research materials found in a standard tax library.

THOMSON REUTERS

Checkpoint® Student Edition

Research Problem 1. On August 4, 2010, Alex Rodriguez hit his 600th home run into the security netting at Yankee Stadium. A security guard at Yankee Stadium named Frankie Babilonia retrieved the ball and gave it to Rodriguez. Frankie in return received a signed baseball bat (worth about $600) from Rodriguez. Assume the baseball is worth $125,000 but cost only $8. Are there any compensation tax aspects? Provide authority.

Research Problem 2. A client comes to your office in 2011 and asks if she should convert her traditional IRA with a balance of $225,750 to a Roth IRA. Provide her with some helpful guidelines regarding conversion.

Research Problem 3. Frequently, a football or basketball coach moves to another university and incurs an obligation to make a payment to the old university under a buyout provision in his or her contract. Football coach Richard Rodriguez was required to pay $4 million to West Virginia when he moved from West Virginia University to Michigan. Coach Rodriguez will pay $1.5 million, and Michigan will pay $2.5 million (plus any legal fees incurred). What are the tax consequences of these payments to Coach Rodriguez (who as of January 2011 is the former Michigan coach)?

Research Problem 4. Jim Raby transfers one-half of his compensatory stock options (ISOs and nonqualified stock options) to his ex-wife as part of a divorce settlement. Discuss the tax aspects of this transfer.

Partial list of research aids:
FSA 200005006.
§§ 424(c)(4)(A) and (B).

Research Problem 5. Debra, a WC employee, exercised nonqualified stock options for 90,300 shares of WC stock valued at $42.125 per share on January 28, 2008. The value of the stock was reflected in a Form W–2 issued to her by WC. Debra disposed of the stock during 2008 and 2009. On June 25, 2010, WC announced a major restatement of its financials, admitting that because of fraudulent accounting practices it incurred undisclosed losses from 2008 to 2009. Debra therefore claimed in a refund action in 2011 that the stock she received in January 2008 was worth only $12.52 per share and that the W–2 issued by WC was grossly inflated. Can Debra obtain a tax refund because her employer cheated on her?

Use the tax resources of the Internet to address the following questions. Do not restrict your search to the Web, but include a review of newsgroups and general reference materials, practitioner sites and resources, primary sources of the tax law, chat rooms and discussion groups, and other opportunities.

INTERNET *activity*

Research Problem 6. Locate and download an Internet retirement calculator. Use this program to help you answer the questions in Problems 38 and 39.

Research Problem 7. Search the Internet to determine how to use serial IRAs to stretch the 60-day rule for IRA rollovers. List the five steps to carry out this technique.

Research Problem 8. Using newspapers, magazine articles, and other resources, determine what criteria the IRS uses to determine what is debt and what is equity in a closely held corporation.

Corporations and Partnerships

The primary orientation of this text is toward basic tax concepts and the individual taxpayer. Although many of these tax concepts also apply to corporations and partnerships, numerous tax concepts apply specifically to corporations or partnerships. An overview of these provisions is presented in Part 7. Comprehensive coverage of these topics appears in *South-Western Federal Taxation: Corporations, Partnerships, Estates & Trusts.*

Corporations and Partnerships

LEARNING OBJECTIVES

After completing Chapter 20, you should be able to:

LO.1
Identify those entities that are treated as corporations for Federal income tax purposes.

LO.2
Contrast the income tax treatment of individuals with that applicable to corporations.

LO.3
Recognize and calculate the tax deductions available only to corporations.

LO.4
Calculate the corporate tax liability and comply with various procedural and reporting requirements.

LO.5
Describe the tax rules governing the formation of corporations.

LO.6
Explain the tax rules governing the operation of corporations.

LO.7
Apply the tax rules governing the liquidation of corporations.

LO.8
Assess the utility and effect of the Subchapter S election.

LO.9
Discuss the tax consequences of forming and operating a partnership.

LO.10
Evaluate the advantages and disadvantages of the various forms for conducting a business.

OUTLINE

 For the latest in changes to tax legislation, visit **www.cengage.com/taxation/swft.**

CHOICE OF BUSINESS ENTITY

The Todd sisters have decided to begin a catering business to handle private parties, weddings, anniversaries, and other large social events. As their parents previously owned several restaurants, the sisters are familiar with food service operations. All sisters will participate in the operation of the business and will provide the funds for capital acquisitions (e.g., delivery trucks, kitchen equipment, and food preparation facilities) and working capital needs. Due to the cost of the premiums, the sisters plan on minimal liability insurance coverage.

In the first few years of operation, the sisters anticipate losses. When and if the business becomes profitable, however, they would consider expansion. Any such expansion would require obtaining additional capital from outside sources.

In what type of entity should the Todd sisters conduct the business? **Read the chapter and formulate your response.**

U ntil now this text has concentrated on the Federal income taxation of individual taxpayers. In terms of conducting a business, an individual will often operate as a sole proprietorship. Although simple and straightforward—a mere Schedule C is involved—this may not be the best choice. Other forms of business organization are available and should be considered. Besides the sole proprietorship, the choices are:

- C corporation.
- S corporation.
- Limited liability company.
- Partnership.

To make an informed choice on what type of entity to choose, familiarity with operational rules and the tax consequences of each is necessary. Starting with the corporate form, this chapter provides an overview of these rules and tax consequences. Limited liability companies are not discussed in depth, since they are usually subject to partnership treatment.

20.1 WHAT IS A CORPORATION?

L0.1

Identify those entities that are treated as corporations for Federal income tax purposes.

COMPLIANCE WITH STATE LAW

A company must comply with the specific requirements for corporate status under state law. For example, it is necessary to draft articles of incorporation and file them with the state regulatory agency, be granted a charter, and issue stock to shareholders.

Compliance with state law, although important, is not the only requirement that must be met to qualify for corporate *tax* status. For example, a corporation qualifying under state law may be disregarded as a taxable entity if it is a mere sham lacking in economic substance. The key consideration is the degree of business activity conducted at the corporate level.

EXAMPLE 1

Gene and Mike are joint owners of a tract of unimproved real estate that they wish to protect from future creditors. Gene and Mike form Falcon Corporation and transfer the land to it in return for all of the corporation's stock. The corporation merely holds title to the land and conducts no other activities. In all respects, Falcon Corporation meets the legal requirements of a corporation under applicable state law. Nevertheless, Falcon might not be recognized as a separate entity for corporate tax purposes under these facts.[1] ■

---

[1]See *Paymer v. Comm.*, 45–2 USTC ¶9353, 33 AFTR 1536, 150 F.2d 334 (CA–2, 1945).

EXAMPLE 2

Assume the same facts as in Example 1. In addition to holding title to the land, Falcon Corporation leases the property, collects rents, and pays the property taxes. Falcon probably would be treated as a corporation for Federal income tax purposes because of the scope of its activities. ∎

In some instances, the IRS has attempted to disregard (or collapse) a corporation in order to make the income taxable directly to the shareholders.[2] In other cases, the IRS has asserted that the corporation is a separate taxable entity so as to assess tax at the corporate level and to tax corporate distributions to shareholders as dividend income (double taxation).[3]

ENTITY CLASSIFICATION PRIOR TO 1997

Can an organization not qualifying as a corporation under state law still be treated as such for Federal income tax purposes? Unfortunately, the tax law defines a corporation as including "associations, joint stock companies, and insurance companies."[4] As the Code contains no definition of an "association," the issue became the subject of frequent litigation.[5]

It was finally determined that an entity would be treated as a corporation if it had a majority of the characteristics common to corporations.[6] For this purpose, the relevant characteristics are:

- Continuity of life.
- Centralized management.
- Limited liability.
- Free transferability of interests.

These criteria did not resolve all of the problems that continued to arise over corporate classification. When a new type of business entity, the **limited liability company (LLC)**, was developed, the IRS was deluged with inquiries about its tax status. As the LLC became increasingly popular with professional groups, all states enacted statutes allowing some form of this entity. The statutes invariably permitted the corporate characteristic of limited liability and, often, that of centralized management. Because continuity of life and free transferability of interests were absent, it was hoped that the entity would be classified as a partnership. This treatment would avoid the double taxation result inherent in the corporate form.

ENTITY CLASSIFICATION AFTER 1996

In late 1996, the IRS issued its so-called **check-the-box Regulations**.[7] Effective beginning in 1997, these Regulations enable taxpayers to classify a business entity for tax purposes without regard to its corporate (or noncorporate) characteristics. These rules have simplified tax administration considerably and eliminated the litigation that arose with regard to association (corporation) status.

Under the rules, an entity with more than one owner can elect to be classified as either a partnership or a corporation. An entity with only one owner can elect to be classified as a corporation or a sole proprietorship. In the event of default (no election is made), entities with multiple owners will be classified as partnerships and single-person businesses as sole proprietorships.

The election is not available to entities that are actually incorporated under state law or to entities that are required to be corporations under Federal law (e.g., certain publicly traded partnerships). For purposes of these prohibitions, LLCs not incorporated under state law can elect either corporation or partnership status.

---

[2]*Floyd Patterson*, 25 TCM 1230, T.C.Memo. 1966–239, *aff'd* in 68–2 USTC ¶9471, 22 AFTR 2d 5810 (CA–2, 1968).

[3]*Raffety Farms Inc. v. U.S.*, 75–1 USTC ¶9271, 35 AFTR 2d 75–811, 511 F.2d 1234 (CA–8, 1975).

[4]§ 7701(a)(3).

[5]See, for example, *U.S. v. Kintner*, 54–2 USTC ¶9626, 46 AFTR 995, 216 F.2d 418 (CA–5, 1954).

[6]See Reg. § 301.7701–2(a) prior to repeal.

[7]Reg. §§ 301.7701–1 through –4, and –7.

Eligible entities make the election as to tax status by filing Form 8832 (Entity Classification Election).[8] New elections are permitted, but only after a 60-month waiting period.

20.2 INCOME TAX CONSIDERATIONS

GENERAL TAX CONSEQUENCES OF DIFFERENT FORMS OF BUSINESS ENTITIES

A business operation may be conducted as a sole proprietorship, as a partnership, or in corporate form.

- Sole proprietorships are not separate taxable entities. The owner of the business reports all business transactions on his or her individual income tax return.
- Partnerships are not subject to the income tax. Under the *conduit* concept, the various tax attributes of the partnership's operations flow through to the individual partners to be reported on their personal income tax returns.
- The regular corporate form (known as a **C corporation**) of doing business carries with it the imposition of the corporate income tax. The corporation is recognized as a separate taxpaying entity. Income is taxed to the corporation as earned and taxed again to the shareholders as dividends when distributed.
- A regular corporation (C corporation) may elect to be taxed as an S corporation. This special treatment follows the conduit concept and is similar (although not identical) to the partnership rules. Income tax is generally avoided at the corporate level, and shareholders are taxed currently on the taxable income of the S corporation.

A desirable characteristic of a business entity is that of limited liability. This means that the owners of the entity are not personally liable for its debts and obligations. Also beneficial is the existence of the conduit concept, which allows the entity to pass through to the owners certain favorable tax attributes (e.g., operating losses).

EXAMPLE 3
THE BIG PICTURE

Return to the facts of *The Big Picture* on p. 20-2. It appears that the Todd sisters should consider a C or an S corporation to obtain limited liability for their catering business. (An LLC will also provide this result.) On the other hand, the conduit effect of an S corporation or a partnership is needed to enable the sisters to take advantage of the initial losses anticipated for the business. Under the conduit concept, such losses could be deducted on their individual income tax returns. ■

LO.2

Contrast the income tax treatment of individuals with that applicable to corporations.

INDIVIDUALS AND CORPORATIONS COMPARED—AN OVERVIEW

Similarities between Corporate and Individual Tax Rules

The gross income of a corporation is determined in much the same manner as for individuals. Both individuals and corporations are entitled to exclusions from gross income, such as interest on municipal bonds. Gains and losses from property transactions are also treated similarly. For example, whether a gain or loss is capital or ordinary depends on the nature and use of the asset rather than the type of taxpayer. Upon the sale or other taxable disposition of depreciable personalty, the recapture rules of § 1245 make no distinction between corporate and noncorporate taxpayers. In the case of the recapture of depreciation on real property (§ 1250), however, corporate taxpayers experience more severe tax consequences. As illustrated later, corporations must recognize as additional ordinary income 20 percent of the excess of the amount that would be recaptured under § 1245 over the amount recaptured under § 1250.

In cases involving nontaxable exchanges and certain transactions allowing the deferral of gain recognition, many of the rules are the same. Thus, both individuals

---

[8]Reg. § 301.7701–3(c).

and corporations can utilize the like-kind exchange provisions of § 1031 and the deferral allowed by § 1033 for involuntary conversions. In contrast, the § 121 exclusion for gain from the sale of a principal residence is a relief measure available only to individual taxpayers.

The business deductions of corporations parallel those available to individuals. Corporate deductions are allowed for all ordinary and necessary expenses paid or incurred in carrying on a trade or business. Corporations may also deduct interest, certain taxes, losses, bad debts, depreciation, cost recovery, charitable contributions subject to corporate limitation rules, net operating losses, research and experimental expenditures, and other less common deductions.

Many of the tax credits available to individuals, such as the foreign tax credit, can be claimed by corporations. Not available to corporations are certain credits that are personal in nature. Examples of credits not available to corporations include the credit for child and dependent care expenses, the credit for the elderly or disabled, and the earned income credit.

Corporations usually have the same choices of accounting periods as do individuals. Like an individual, a corporation may choose a calendar year or a fiscal year for reporting purposes. Corporations do enjoy greater flexibility in the election of a tax year. For example, corporations usually can have different tax years from those of their shareholders. Also, a newly formed corporation generally has a free choice of any approved accounting period without having to obtain the consent of the IRS. As noted in Chapter 18, however, personal service corporations are subject to severe restrictions on the use of a fiscal year.

In terms of methods of accounting, both individuals and corporations must use the *accrual* method in determining cost of goods sold if they maintain inventory for sale to customers. The *accrual* method must also be used by *large* corporations (annual gross receipts in excess of $5 million). The *cash method* of accounting, however, is available to *small* corporations and in the following additional situations:

- An S election is in effect.
- The trade or business is farming or timber.
- A qualified personal service corporation is involved.
- A qualified service provider (e.g., plumbing business) is involved, and annual gross receipts (for the past three years) do not exceed $10 million. This exception applies even if the service provider is buying and selling inventory.

Dissimilarities

Both noncorporate and corporate taxpayers are subject to progressive income tax rates. For individuals, the rates for 2011 are 10, 15, 25, 28, 33, and 35 percent. For corporations, the rates are 15, 25, 34, and 35 percent. Corporate taxpayers lose the benefits of the lower brackets (using a phaseout approach) once taxable income reaches a certain level. Noncorporate taxpayers, however, continue to enjoy the benefits of the lower brackets even though they have reached the higher taxable income levels.

Commencing in 2003, qualified dividends received by individual shareholders are subject to preferential tax rates. For those shareholders in the top four tax brackets (25, 28, 33, and 35 percent), the maximum rate is 15 percent; for those in the bottom two brackets (10 and 15 percent), the rate is 0 percent. As discussed later, corporate shareholders enjoy the alternative of the dividends received deduction.

Many corporate and all noncorporate taxpayers are subject to the alternative minimum tax (AMT). For AMT purposes, many adjustments and tax preference items are the same for both, but other adjustments and tax preferences apply only to corporations or only to individuals. Also, certain small business corporations are effectively exempt from the corporate AMT. Corporate tax rates are discussed later in the chapter. The AMT is discussed at length in Chapter 12. See also the coverage in *South-Western Federal Taxation: Corporations, Partnerships, Estates, and Trusts.*

All allowable corporate deductions are treated as business expenses. The determination of adjusted gross income, so essential for individuals, has no relevance to corporations. Corporations need not be concerned with classifying deductions into *deduction for* and *deduction from* categories.

GLOBAL
Tax Issues

ARE CORPORATE TAXES TOO HIGH?

A recent Treasury report shows that the average statutory corporate tax rate in the United States is 39 percent when both Federal and state income taxes are considered. In contrast, average rates for the European Union and the Asia-Pacific region are 26 percent and 30 percent, respectively. Currently, the United States is second only to Japan in top rates, and that country is considering a rate reduction. The recent downward trend in corporate income tax rates has been particularly prevalent in European countries (e.g., from 34 to 28 percent in France, from 35 to 30 percent in Spain, and from 39 to just under 30 percent in Germany). Meanwhile, in the United States the Federal tax rates on corporations have remained unchanged since they were substantially lowered in 1986!

SPECIFIC PROVISIONS COMPARED

Corporate and individual tax rules also differ in the following areas:

- Capital gains and losses.
- Recapture of depreciation.
- Charitable contributions.
- Domestic production activities deduction.
- Net operating losses.
- Special deductions for corporations.

Capital Gains and Losses

Both corporate and noncorporate taxpayers are required to aggregate gains and losses from the taxable sale or exchange of capital assets. (Refer to Chapter 16 for a description of the netting process that takes place after the aggregation has been completed.) For long-term capital gains (including gains from collectibles and unrecaptured § 1250 gain), individuals enjoy an advantage. Called the alternative tax, the maximum applicable tax rate is 28 percent for collectibles, 25 percent for unrecaptured § 1250 gain, and 15 percent for other capital gains. For the last category, the tax rate is reduced to 0 percent if the taxpayer is in the 15 percent (or lower) tax bracket. In the case of corporations, all capital gains are taxed using the rates for ordinary income. Therefore, the net long-term capital gain of a corporation could be taxed at a rate of 35 percent (the highest rate applicable to corporations).

EXAMPLE 4

In 2011, Rose has taxable income of $80,000, not including a long-term capital gain of $10,000. If Rose is an individual, the alternative tax yields a tax on the capital gain of $1,500 ($10,000 × 15%). If, however, Rose is a C corporation, the tax becomes $3,400 ($10,000 × 34%). ∎

Significant differences exist in the treatment of capital losses for income tax purposes. Individuals, for example, can annually deduct up to $3,000 of net capital losses against ordinary income. If an individual has both net short-term and net long-term capital losses, the short-term capital losses are used first in arriving at the $3,000 ordinary loss deduction. Corporations are not permitted to use net capital losses to offset ordinary income. Net capital losses can be used only to offset past or future capital gains.[9] Unlike individuals, corporations are not allowed an unlimited carryover period for capital losses. Instead, they may carry back excess capital losses to the three preceding years, applying the losses initially to the earliest year. If not

---

[9]§§ 1211(a) and (b).

exhausted by the carryback, remaining unused capital losses may be carried forward for a period of five years from the year of the loss.[10]

When carried back or forward, *both* short-term capital losses and long-term capital losses are treated as short-term capital losses by corporate taxpayers. For noncorporate taxpayers, carryovers of capital losses retain their identity as short or long term.

EXAMPLE 5

Hawk Corporation, a calendar year taxpayer, incurs a long-term net capital loss of $5,000 for 2011. None of the capital loss may be deducted in 2011. Hawk may, however, carry the loss back to years 2008, 2009, and 2010 (in this order) and offset any capital gains recognized in these years. If the carryback does not exhaust the loss, the loss may be carried forward to 2012, 2013, 2014, 2015, and 2016 (in this order). Such capital loss carrybacks or carryovers are treated as short-term capital losses. ■

Recapture of Depreciation

Corporations selling depreciable real estate may have ordinary income in addition to that required by § 1250. Under § 291, the additional ordinary income element is 20 percent of the excess of the § 1245 recapture potential over the § 1250 recapture. As a result, the § 1231 gain is correspondingly decreased by the additional recapture.

Under § 1250, the excess of accelerated depreciation over straight-line depreciation is recaptured as ordinary income as to residential real property. Since all real property purchased since 1986 is depreciated using only the straight-line method, after 2005 the § 1250 amount is zero because the depreciation period (19 years in 1986) has expired and such buildings are fully depreciated.

EXAMPLE 6

Condor Corporation purchases residential real property on November 3, 1997, for $300,000. Straight-line cost recovery is taken in the amount of $143,624 (see Table 8.6 in Chapter 8) before the property is sold on January 5, 2011, for $250,000. (Neither the purchase nor the selling price includes any amount attributable to the land.)

First, determine the recognized gain:

Sales price		$ 250,000
Less adjusted basis:		
Cost of property	$ 300,000	
Less cost recovery	(143,624)	(156,376)
Recognized gain		$ 93,624

Second, determine the § 1245 recapture potential. This is the lesser of $93,624 (recognized gain) or $143,624 (cost recovery claimed).

Third, determine the § 1250 recapture amount:

Cost recovery taken	$ 143,624
Less straight-line cost recovery	(143,624)
§ 1250 ordinary income	$ –0–

Fourth, because the taxpayer is a corporation, determine the additional § 291 amount:

§ 1245 recapture potential	$93,624
Less § 1250 recapture amount	(–0–)
Excess § 1245 recapture potential	$93,624
Apply § 291 percentage	× 20%
Additional ordinary income under § 291	$18,725

---

[10]§ 1212(a).

Condor Corporation's recognized gain of $93,624 is accounted for as follows:

Ordinary income under § 1250	$ –0–
Ordinary income under § 291	18,725
§ 1231 gain	74,899
Total recognized gain	$93,624

Charitable Contributions

Generally, a charitable contribution deduction is allowed only for the tax year in which the payment is made. However, an important exception is made for accrual basis corporations. The deduction may be claimed in the tax year *preceding* payment if the following conditions are satisfied:

- The contribution is authorized by the board of directors by the end of that tax year *and*
- The contribution is paid on or before the fifteenth day of the third month of the next tax year.[11]

EXAMPLE 7

On December 29, 2011, the board of directors of Dove Corporation, a calendar year, accrual basis taxpayer, authorizes a $20,000 donation to a qualified charity. The donation is paid on March 12, 2012. Dove Corporation may claim the $20,000 donation as a deduction for 2011. As an alternative, Dove may claim the deduction in 2012 (the year of payment). ■

Like individuals, corporations are not permitted an unlimited charitable contribution deduction. In any one year, a corporate taxpayer is limited to 10 percent of taxable income. For this purpose, taxable income is computed without regard to the charitable contribution deduction, any net operating loss carryback or capital loss carryback, or the dividends received deduction.[12] Any contributions in excess of the 10 percent limitation are carried forward to the five succeeding tax years. Any carryover must be added to subsequent contributions and is subject to the 10 percent limitation. In applying the limitation, the most recent contributions must be deducted first.[13]

EXAMPLE 8

During 2011, Eagle Corporation (a calendar year taxpayer) had the following income and expenses:

Income from operations	$140,000
Expenses from operations	110,000
Dividends received	10,000
Charitable contributions made in 2011	5,000

For purposes of the 10% limitation only, Eagle's taxable income is $40,000 ($140,000 − $110,000 + $10,000). Consequently, the allowable charitable contribution deduction for 2011 is $4,000 (10% × $40,000). The $1,000 unused portion of the contribution is carried forward to 2012, 2013, 2014, 2015, and 2016 (in that order) until exhausted. ■

EXAMPLE 9

Assume the same facts as in Example 8. In 2012, Eagle Corporation has taxable income (after adjustments) of $50,000 and makes a charitable contribution of $4,800. The maximum deduction allowed for 2012 is $5,000 (10% × $50,000). The first $4,800 of the allowed deduction must be allocated to the 2012 contribution, and the $200 excess is allocated to the carryover from 2011. The remaining $800 of the 2011 contribution is carried over to 2013, etc. ■

---

[11]§ 170(a)(2).
[12]§ 170(b)(2).

[13]§ 170(d)(2).

As noted in Chapter 10, the deduction for charitable contributions of ordinary income property is limited to the lesser of the fair market value or the adjusted basis of the property. A special rule provides an exception that permits a corporation to contribute inventory (ordinary income property) to certain charitable organizations and receive a deduction equal to the adjusted basis plus one-half of the difference between the fair market value and the adjusted basis of the property. In no event, however, may the deduction exceed twice the adjusted basis of the property. To qualify for this exception, the inventory must be used by the charity in its exempt purpose for the care of *children*, the *ill*, or the *needy*.

EXAMPLE 10

In the current year, Robin Company (a retail clothier) donates sweaters and overcoats to Sheltering Arms (a qualified charity caring for the homeless). The clothing is inventory and has a basis of $10,000 and a fair market value of $14,000. If Robin is a corporation, the charitable contribution that results is $12,000 [$10,000 (basis) + $2,000 (50% of the appreciation of $4,000)]. In contrast, if Robin is not a corporation, the charitable contribution is limited to $10,000 (basis). ∎

The special rule allowing the inventory exception also provides further exceptions for gifts of scientific property and computer technology and equipment to be used for educational purposes. If certain conditions are met, 50 percent of the appreciation on such property is allowed as an additional charitable deduction.[14]

Domestic Production Activities Deduction

As noted in Chapter 7, § 199 was designed to replace various export tax benefits that our world trading partners deemed discriminatory. Known as the domestic production activities deduction (DPAD), the provision is equally applicable to C corporations. In the case of C corporations, however, the limitation is based on taxable income, rather than AGI (both computed without considering the deduction). Thus, the DPAD is 9 percent of the *lesser* of qualified production activities income (QPAI) or taxable income. (The DPAD was 6 percent prior to 2010.) As with individual taxpayers, the DPAD cannot exceed 50 percent of the W–2 wages involved (those subject to withholding plus certain elective deferrals). Domestic gross receipts from manufacturing activities are a major source of QPAI. These gross receipts are adjusted by cost of goods sold and other assignable expenses to arrive at QPAI.

For corporations that are members of an affiliated group (based on 50 percent common control), the deduction is determined by treating the group as a single taxpayer. In effect, therefore, each member of the group is treated as being engaged in the activities of every other member. The deduction is then allocated among the members in proportion to each member's respective amount of QPAI.[15]

EXAMPLE 11

Mallard and Pintail Corporations are members of an affiliated group but do not file a consolidated return. Mallard manufactures a machine at a cost of $300 and sells it to Pintail for $500. Pintail incurs additional cost of $100 for marketing and then sells the machine to an unrelated customer for $700. The QPAI deduction is based on $300 ($700 − $300 − $100) even though the seller (Pintail) did not perform any manufacturing.[16] Note that this is the same result that would have been reached if Pintail had not been involved and Mallard had conducted its own marketing function. ∎

EXAMPLE 12

Assume the same facts as in Example 11 except that the parties are not related. Under these circumstances, Mallard has QPAI of $200 ($500 − $300) and Pintail has none. Pintail's activities, when considered alone, are not QPAI because they involve marketing and not manufacturing. ∎

---

[14]These conditions are set forth in §§ 170(e)(4) and (6). The inventory exception is prescribed by § 170(e)(3).
[15]§ 199(d)(4).
[16]Reg. § 1.199–7(c).

In the case of pass-through entities (e.g., partnerships, S corporations, trusts, and estates), special rules apply for handling the DPAD.[17] Because the deduction is determined at the owner level, each partner or shareholder must make the computation separately. Thus, the entity allocates to each owner his or her share of QPAI. The QPAI that is passed through is then combined with any qualifying activities that the owner has from other sources (e.g., a partner also conducts a manufacturing activity on his or her own).

The DPAD can be claimed in computing the alternative minimum tax (including adjusted current earnings). The deduction allowed is the lesser of QPAI or alternative minimum taxable income (AMTI). In the case of an individual taxpayer, AGI is substituted for AMTI in determining the limitation on the amount allowed as a deduction.[18]

Net Operating Losses

The computation of a net operating loss (NOL) for individuals was discussed in Chapter 7. Corporations are not subject to the complex adjustments required for individuals (e.g., a corporation has no adjustments for nonbusiness deductions or capital gains and losses). Corporations are subject to fewer adjustments than individuals are because a corporation's loss more clearly approximates a true economic loss. Artificial deductions (e.g., personal and dependency exemptions) that merely generate paper losses are not permitted for corporations.

In computing the NOL of a corporation, the dividends received deduction (discussed below) can be claimed in determining the amount of the loss. Generally, NOLs may be carried back 2 years and forward 20 years (or taxpayers may elect to forgo the carryback period) to offset taxable income for those years.[19]

EXAMPLE 13

In 2011, Wren Corporation has gross income of $200,000 and deductions of $300,000, excluding the dividends received deduction. Wren received taxable dividends of $100,000 from ExxonMobil stock. Wren has an NOL of $170,000, computed as follows:

Gross income (including ExxonMobil dividends)		$ 200,000
Less: Business deductions	$300,000	
Dividends received deduction (70% × $100,000)	70,000	(370,000)
Taxable income (loss)		($ 170,000) ∎

EXAMPLE 14

Assume the same facts as in Example 13 and that Wren Corporation had taxable income of $40,000 in 2009. The NOL of $170,000 is carried back to 2009 (unless Wren elects not to carry back the loss to that year). The carryover to 2010 is $130,000, computed as follows:

Taxable income for 2009	$ 40,000
Less: NOL carryback from 2011	(170,000)
Carryover of unabsorbed 2011 loss	($ 130,000) ∎

In Example 14, the carryback to 2009 might have been ill-advised if Wren Corporation had little, if any, taxable income in 2009 and 2010 and if it anticipated large amounts of taxable income in the immediate future. In that case, the *election to forgo* the carryback might generate greater tax savings. In this regard, three points should be considered. First, the time value of the tax refund that is lost by not using the carryback procedure must be considered. Second, the election to forgo an NOL carryback is irrevocable. Thus, it cannot be changed later if the future high profits do not materialize. Third, future increases or decreases in corporate income tax rates that can reasonably be anticipated should be considered.

---

[17]§ 199(d)(1).
[18]§ 199(d)(6).

[19]§ 172(b).

> **TAX in the NEWS**
>
> **VARIATIONS IN MITIGATING THE EFFECT OF MULTIPLE TAXATION**
>
> When a corporation receives a dividend from another corporation, multiple taxation of the same income is eased (or avoided) by allowing the corporate shareholder a dividends received deduction. But what happens when these funds are later passed through to the individual shareholders? In the past, such distributions were fully taxed as ordinary income.
>
> This problem of double taxation of corporate distributions at the individual shareholder level was addressed by Congress in 2003. The solution arrived at, however, is different from that used for corporate shareholders. Instead of allowing a deduction for some (or all) of the dividends received, relief is provided through the application of a lower tax rate. Thus, qualified dividends are taxed at the same preferential tax rate available to net capital gains.
>
> In summary, the possible triple taxation of corporate-source income is mitigated by the combination of a deduction (available to corporate shareholders) and a lower tax rate (available to individual shareholders).

DEDUCTIONS AVAILABLE ONLY TO CORPORATIONS

> **LO.3**
>
> Recognize and calculate the tax deductions available only to corporations.

Dividends Received Deduction

The purpose of the **dividends received deduction** is to prevent triple taxation. Without the deduction, income paid to a corporation in the form of a dividend would be subject to taxation for a second time (after being taxed first to the distributing corporation) with no corresponding deduction to the distributing corporation. A third level of tax would be assessed on the shareholders when the recipient corporation distributed the income to its shareholders. Since the dividends received deduction may be less than 100 percent, the law provides only partial relief.

The amount of the dividends received deduction depends upon the percentage of ownership the recipient corporate shareholder holds in the corporation making the dividend distribution.[20] For dividends received or accrued, the *deduction percentage* is summarized as follows:

Percentage of Ownership by Corporate Shareholder	Deduction Percentage
Less than 20%	70%
20% or more (but less than 80%)	80%
80% or more	100%

The dividends received deduction may be limited to a percentage of the taxable income of a corporation computed without regard to the NOL deduction, the dividends received deduction, the DPAD, or any capital loss carryback to the current tax year. The percentage of taxable income limitation corresponds to the deduction percentage. Thus, if a corporate shareholder owns less than 20 percent of the stock in the distributing corporation, the dividends received deduction is limited to 70 percent of taxable income (as previously defined). However, this limitation does not apply if the corporation has an NOL for the current taxable year.[21]

In working with these myriad rules, the following steps need to be taken:

1. Multiply the dividends received by the deduction percentage.
2. Multiply the taxable income (as previously defined) by the deduction percentage.
3. The deduction is limited to the lesser of step 1 or step 2, unless subtracting the amount derived from step 1 from taxable income (as previously defined) generates a negative number. If so, the amount derived in step 1 should be used.

---

[20]§ 243(a). [21]§ 246(b).

EXAMPLE 15

Crane, Osprey, and Gull Corporations, three unrelated calendar year corporations, have the following transactions for 2011:

	Crane Corporation	Osprey Corporation	Gull Corporation
Gross income from operations	$ 400,000	$ 320,000	$ 260,000
Expenses from operations	(340,000)	(340,000)	(340,000)
Dividends received from domestic corporations (less than 20% ownership)	200,000	200,000	200,000
Taxable income before the dividends received deduction	$ 260,000	$ 180,000	$ 120,000

In determining the dividends received deduction, use the step procedure just described:

	Crane Corporation	Osprey Corporation	Gull Corporation
Step 1: (70% × $200,000)	$140,000	$140,000	$140,000
Step 2:			
70% × $260,000 (taxable income)	$182,000		
70% × $180,000 (taxable income)		$126,000	
70% × $120,000 (taxable income)			$ 84,000
Step 3:			
Lesser of step 1 or step 2	$140,000	$126,000	
Generates an NOL			$140,000

Osprey Corporation is subject to the 70 percent of taxable income limitation. It does not qualify for the loss rule treatment, since subtracting $140,000 (step 1) from $180,000 does not yield a loss. Gull Corporation qualifies for the loss rule treatment because subtracting $140,000 (step 1) from $120,000 does yield a loss. In summary, each corporation has the following dividends received deduction for 2011: $140,000 for Crane, $126,000 for Osprey, and $140,000 for Gull. If a corporation already has an NOL before any dividends received deduction is claimed, the full dividends received deduction (as calculated in step 1) is allowed.

Deduction of Organizational Expenditures

A corporation may elect to amortize organizational expenses over a period of 15 years or more. A special exception allows the corporation to immediately expense the first $5,000 of these costs.[22] The exception, however, is phased out on a dollar-for-dollar basis when these expenses exceed $50,000.

EXAMPLE 16

Kingbird Corporation, a calendar year taxpayer, is formed on June 1, 2011. In connection with its formation, it incurs organizational expenditures of $52,000. If Kingbird wants to claim as much of these expenses as soon as possible, its deduction for 2011 is—

$$\text{Expense: } \$5,000 - (\$52,000 - \$50,000) = \$3,000$$

$$\text{Amortization: } \frac{\$52,000 - \$3,000}{180 \text{ months}} \times 7 \text{ (months)} = \$1,906$$

Kingbird deducts a total of $4,906 ($3,000 + $1,906) for 2011. ■

If the election is not made on a timely basis, the expenditures cannot be deducted until the corporation ceases to conduct business and liquidates. The election is made in a statement attached to the corporation's return for its first taxable year. The election

---

[22]§ 248.

GLOBAL Tax Issues

TAXING THE INCOME OF FOREIGN CORPORATIONS

Are foreign corporations subject to the U.S. corporate income tax? If the income is from U.S. sources, the answer is *yes*! This presumes that the income is not insulated from U.S. taxation by a provision in a tax treaty between the United States and the country of incorporation.

The manner of taxation depends upon the nature of the income involved. If the income is fixed, determinable, annual, or periodic (known as FDAP income), it is taxed at 30 percent on the *gross* amount. The tax is collected by virtue of required withholding imposed on the payor. FDAP income generally includes passive income (e.g., dividends, interest, rents, royalties, annuities) that is not effectively connected with a U.S. trade or business.

If, however, the income comes from the conduct of a U.S. trade or business, it is taxed at *net* in much the same manner as the income of domestic corporations. Any FDAP income effectively connected with the trade or business is taxed in the same manner as the business *net* income.

covers all qualifying expenses *incurred* in the corporation's first tax year. Thus, a cash basis taxpayer need not have paid the expenses as long as they were incurred.

Organizational expenditures include the following:

- Legal services incident to organization (e.g., drafting the corporate charter, bylaws, minutes of organizational meetings, terms of original stock certificates).
- Necessary accounting services.
- Expenses of temporary directors and of organizational meetings of directors and shareholders.
- Fees paid to the state of incorporation.

Expenditures connected with issuing or selling shares of stock or other securities (e.g., commissions, professional fees, and printing costs) or with the transfer of assets to a corporation do not qualify. These expenditures are generally added to the capital account and are not subject to amortization.

DETERMINATION OF CORPORATE TAX LIABILITY

Income Tax Rates

The income tax rates for corporations are reproduced in Table 20.1.[23]

> **LO.4**
> Calculate the corporate tax liability and comply with various procedural and reporting requirements.

TABLE 20.1	**Income Tax Rates—Corporations**
Taxable Income	**Tax Rate**
Not over $50,000	15%
Over $50,000 but not over $75,000	25%
Over $75,000 but not over $100,000	34%
Over $100,000 but not over $335,000	39%*
Over $335,000 but not over $10,000,000	34%
Over $10,000,000 but not over $15,000,000	35%
Over $15,000,000 but not over $18,333,333	38%**
Over $18,333,333	35%

*Five percent of this rate represents a phaseout of the benefits of the lower tax rates on the first $75,000 of taxable income.

**Three percent of this rate represents a phaseout of the benefits of the lower tax rate (34% rather than 35%) on the first $10 million of taxable income.

---

[23]§ 11(b).

| EXAMPLE 17 | A calendar year corporation has taxable income of $90,000 for the current year. The income tax liability is $18,850, determined as follows: $7,500 (15% × $50,000) + $6,250 (25% × $25,000) + $5,100 (34% × $15,000). ∎ |

In reviewing Table 20.1, note that the income tax rates begin by being progressive—compare the marginal tax rate applicable to the first $50,000 (taxed at 15 percent) with that on taxable income over $50,000 (taxed at 25 percent). But the phaseout of these lower rates starts with the $100,001 to $335,000 bracket (taxed at 39 percent) and continues with the $15,000,001 to $18,333,333 bracket (taxed at 38 percent). Once taxable income reaches $18,333,334, the progression disappears (i.e., the lower brackets have been phased out), and the marginal rate on every dollar becomes 35 percent. Thus, the tax on $20 million is $7 million (35% × $20,000,000).

Qualified personal service corporations are taxed at a flat 35 percent rate on all taxable income. They do not enjoy the tax savings of the lower brackets. For this purpose, a *qualified* **personal service corporation** is one that is substantially employee owned and engages in one of the following activities: health, law, engineering, architecture, accounting, actuarial science, performing arts, or consulting.

Alternative Minimum Tax

Corporations are subject to an alternative minimum tax (AMT) that is structured in the same manner as that applicable to individuals. The AMT for corporations, as for individuals, defines a more expansive tax base than for the regular tax. Like individuals, corporations are required to apply a minimum tax rate to the expanded base and pay the difference between the tentative AMT liability and the regular tax. Many of the adjustments and tax preference items necessary to arrive at alternative minimum taxable income (AMTI) are the same for individuals and corporations. Although the objective of the AMT is the same for individuals and for corporations, the rate and exemptions are different. As noted in Chapter 12, certain small business corporations are effectively exempt from the corporate AMT.

CORPORATE FILING REQUIREMENTS

A corporation must file a return whether it has taxable income or not.[24] A corporation that was not in existence throughout an entire annual accounting period is required to file a return for the fraction of the year during which it was in existence. In addition, the corporation must file a return even though it has ceased to do business if it has valuable claims for which it will bring suit. It is relieved of filing returns once it ceases business and dissolves.

The corporate return is filed on Form 1120. Corporations making the S corporation election (discussed later in the chapter) file on Form 1120S.

Corporations with less than $250,000 of gross receipts and less than $250,000 in assets do not have to complete Schedule L (balance sheet) and Schedules M–1 and M–2 (see below) of Form 1120. Similar omissions are allowed for Form 1120S. These rules are intended to ease the compliance burden on small business.

The return must be filed on or before the fifteenth day of the third month following the close of the corporation's tax year. Corporations can receive an automatic extension of six months for filing the corporate return by filing Form 7004 by the due date of the return. However, the IRS may terminate an extension by mailing a 10-day notice to the taxpayer corporation.[25]

A corporation must make payments of estimated tax unless its tax liability can reasonably be expected to be less than $500.[26] The payments must equal the lesser of 100 percent of the corporation's final tax or 100 percent of the last year's tax. These payments may be made in four installments due on or before the fifteenth day of the fourth, sixth, ninth, and twelfth months of the corporate taxable year. The full amount of the unpaid tax is due on the date of the return. Failure to make the required estimated tax prepayments will result in a nondeductible penalty being imposed on the corporation. The penalty can be avoided, however, if any of various exceptions apply.[27]

---

[24]§ 6012(a)(2).
[25]§ 6081.

[26]§ 6655(f).
[27]See § 6655 for the penalty involved and the various exceptions.

FINANCIAL DISCLOSURE *Insights*

DEFERRED TAXES ON THE BALANCE SHEET

A business entity that follows GAAP, whether it is incorporated or not, typically records deferred tax assets and liabilities on its Statement of Financial Position (the "balance sheet"). The differences between the entity's total tax expense and its current tax expense can represent sizable amounts on the balance sheet. Because certain transactions result in deferred tax assets, and others in deferred tax liabilities, many balance sheets include dollar amounts for both accounts. For example, some recent financial reports included the following estimates:

	Deferred Tax Liabilities ($000)	Deferred Tax Assets ($000)
General Electric	$34,200	$22,000
ExxonMobil	30,200	11,200
Berkshire Hathaway	22,500	4,300
Ford Motor	14,500	15,000

As deferred tax amounts "reverse" themselves into the Statement of Earnings and Comprehensive Income (the "income statement"), shareholders and investment analysts must determine whether and how the tax deferrals indicate the current and future profitability of the entity. This can be difficult in situations such as the following:

- The taxpayer wins or loses an audit or other appeal with a taxing jurisdiction, creating an unusual amount due or refund.
- Tax rates change, and the amounts of the tax deferrals change accordingly.
- A multinational entity deals with countries outside the United States that apply a different mix of taxes and rates.

Much of the public information regarding tax deferrals is found in the footnotes to the entity's financial statements, but these data can be difficult to interpret for large businesses with complex legal structures.

RECONCILIATION OF CORPORATE TAXABLE INCOME AND ACCOUNTING INCOME

Taxable income and accounting net income are seldom the same amount. For example, a difference may arise if the corporation uses accelerated depreciation for tax purposes and straight-line depreciation for accounting purposes.

Many items of income for accounting purposes, such as proceeds from a life insurance policy on the death of a corporate officer and interest on municipal bonds, may not be includible in calculating taxable income. Some expense items for accounting purposes, such as expenses to produce tax-exempt income, estimated warranty reserves, a net capital loss, and Federal income taxes, are not deductible for tax purposes.

Schedule M–1 on the last page of Form 1120 is used to reconcile accounting net income (net income after Federal income taxes) with taxable income (as computed on the corporate tax return before the deduction for an NOL and the dividends received deduction). In the left-hand column of Schedule M–1, net income per books is added to the following: the Federal income tax liability for the year, the excess of capital losses over capital gains (which cannot be deducted in the current year), income for tax purposes that is not income in the current year for accounting purposes, and expenses recorded on the books that are not deductible on the tax return. In the right-hand column, income recorded on the books that is not currently taxable or is tax-exempt and deductions for tax purposes that are not expenses for accounting purposes are totaled and subtracted from the left-hand column total to arrive at taxable income (before the NOL or dividends received deductions).

EXAMPLE 18

During the current year, Crow Corporation had the following transactions:

Net income per books (after tax)	$92,400
Taxable income	50,000
Federal income tax liability (15% × $50,000)	7,500
Interest income from tax-exempt bonds	5,000

Interest paid on loan, the proceeds of which were used to purchase the tax-exempt bonds	$ 500
Life insurance proceeds received as a result of the death of a key employee	50,000
Premiums paid on key employee life insurance policy	2,600
Excess of capital losses over capital gains	2,000

For book and tax purposes, Crow determines depreciation under the straight-line method. Crow's Schedule M–1 for the current year follows.

Schedule M-1 **Reconciliation of Income (Loss) per Books With Income per Return**
Note: Schedule M-3 required instead of Schedule M-1 if total assets are $10 million or more—see instructions

1	Net income (loss) per books	92,400	7	Income recorded on books this year not included on this return (itemize):	
2	Federal income tax per books	7,500		Tax-exempt interest $ *5,000*	
3	Excess of capital losses over capital gains .	2,000		*Life insurance proceeds on key employee $50,000*	55,000
4	Income subject to tax not recorded on books this year (itemize):		8	Deductions on this return not charged against book income this year (itemize):	
5	Expenses recorded on books this year not deducted on this return (itemize):		a	Depreciation . . . . $	
			b	Charitable contributions $	
a	Depreciation . . . . $				
b	Charitable contributions $				
c	Travel and entertainment $				
	Prem.–life ins. $2,600; Int.–exempt bonds $500	3,100	9	Add lines 7 and 8	55,000
6	Add lines 1 through 5	105,000	10	Income (page 1, line 28)—line 6 less line 9	50,000

Schedule M–2 reconciles unappropriated retained earnings at the beginning of the year with unappropriated retained earnings at year-end. Beginning balance plus net income per books, as entered on line 1 of Schedule M–1, less dividend distributions during the year equals ending retained earnings. Other sources of increases or decreases in retained earnings are also listed on Schedule M–2.

EXAMPLE 19

Assume the same facts as in Example 18. Crow Corporation's beginning balance in unappropriated retained earnings is $125,000, and Crow distributed a cash dividend of $30,000 to its shareholders during the year. Based on these further assumptions, Crow has the following Schedule M–2 for the current year.

Schedule M-2 **Analysis of Unappropriated Retained Earnings per Books (Line 25, Schedule L)**

1	Balance at beginning of year	125,000	5	Distributions:	a Cash	30,000
2	Net income (loss) per books	92,400			b Stock	
3	Other increases (itemize):				c Property . . .	
			6	Other decreases (itemize):		
			7	Add lines 5 and 6		30,000
4	Add lines 1, 2, and 3	217,400	8	Balance at end of year (line 4 less line 7)		187,400

Certain corporations have to file **Schedule M–3**.[28] This schedule, designated "Net Income (Loss) Reconciliation for Corporations With Total Assets of $10 Million or More," is in lieu of Schedule M–1. It has to be filed when the assets reported on Schedule L of Form 1120 total or exceed $10 million. Because it reveals significant differences between book and taxable income, Schedule M–3 will enable the IRS to more quickly identify possible abusive transactions (e.g., use of tax shelter schemes).

[28]Rev.Proc. 2004–45, 2004–2 C.B. 140. Schedule M–3 satisfies some of the disclosure requirements set forth in Reg. § 1.6011–4 when significant book-tax differences occur.

20.3 FORMING THE CORPORATION

CAPITAL CONTRIBUTIONS

LO.5
Describe the tax rules governing the formation of corporations.

The receipt of money or property in exchange for capital stock produces neither recognized gain nor loss to the recipient corporation.[29] Gross income of a corporation does not include shareholders' contributions of money or property to the capital of the corporation.[30] Contributions by nonshareholders are also excluded from the gross income of a corporation.[31] The basis of the property (capital transfers by nonshareholders) to the corporation is zero.

EXAMPLE 20

A city donates land worth $900,000 to Cardinal Corporation as an inducement for it to locate in the city. The receipt of the land does not represent gross income. The land's basis to the corporation is zero. ■

Thin Capitalization

The advantages of capitalizing a corporation with debt may be substantial. Interest on debt is deductible by the corporation, while dividend payments are not. Further, the shareholders are not taxed on loan repayments unless the payments exceed basis.

In certain instances, the IRS will claim **thin capitalization** by holding that debt is really an equity interest and will deny the shareholders the tax advantages of debt financing. If the debt instrument has too many features of stock, it may be treated as a form of stock, and principal and interest payments are treated as dividends.[32]

The form of the instrument will not assure debt treatment, but failure to observe certain formalities in creating the debt may lead to an assumption that the purported debt is a form of stock. The debt should be in proper legal form, bear a legitimate rate of interest, have a definite maturity date, and be repaid on a timely basis. Payments should not be contingent upon earnings. Further, the debt should not be subordinated to other liabilities, and proportionate holdings of stock and debt should be avoided or minimized.

The preferential treatment allowed for qualified dividend income has added another dimension to the thin capitalization issue. Although a corporation would prefer to pay out profits in the form of interest (deductible as an expense) rather

---

[29]§ 1032.
[30]§ 118.
[31]*Edwards v. Cuba Railroad Co.*, 1 USTC ¶139, 5 AFTR 5398, 45 S.Ct. 614 (USSC, 1925).

[32]Section 385 lists several factors that might be used to determine whether a debtor-creditor relationship or a shareholder-corporation relationship exists.

TAX*in*
the NEWS

COMPETING FOR NEW INDUSTRY

The procedure described in Example 20 of the text has become increasingly common during the current economic downturn. In fact, in some cases state and local governments are looking for more than the location of a new plant and are trying to persuade corporations to move their entire business to the area. Also, the inducements offered go beyond the promise of free land and money to include such incentives as tax holidays,

job training, employee relocation services, and even airfare and car rental discounts. Recently, a Fortune 500 corporation accepted a $100 million package to move to the Atlanta area from a midwestern city where it had been based for 125 years.

Source: Adapted from Ansley Haman, "Southern States Poach Businesses Amid Downturn," *Wall Street Journal,* June 13–14, 2009, p. A4.

than as dividends (nondeductible), the shareholders have the opposite tax position. Interest income is ordinary income, while qualified dividends are subject to beneficial net capital gain rates. Nevertheless, the repayment of the debt is not taxed at all as it is a return of capital. Hence, the thin capitalization incentive will continue to exist.

Minimum Capitalization

With many small corporations, particularly nonmanufacturing personal service corporations, the capitalization is minimal. The corporation is formed with whatever investment in stock is required under applicable state law.

EXAMPLE 21
THE BIG PICTURE

Return to the facts of *The Big Picture* on p. 20-2. Suppose that the Todd sisters decide to conduct their catering business in the corporate form—either a C or an S corporation. In forming the corporation, they should probably limit their capital investment to whatever state law requires. The sisters should consider acquiring the capital assets needed to operate the business (e.g., delivery trucks, kitchen equipment, location for food preparation) on their own and leasing them to the corporation. This would allow the sisters to claim the appropriate depreciation and would provide the corporation with a deduction for the rent paid. Although this strategy would force the sisters to recognize rent income rather than preferentially taxed dividends, no dividends will be forthcoming in the early loss years of the business. ■

TRANSFERS TO CONTROLLED CORPORATIONS

Without special provisions in the Code, a transfer of property to a corporation in exchange for its stock would be a sale or exchange of property and would constitute a taxable transaction to the transferor shareholder. Section 351 provides for the nonrecognition of gain or loss upon such transfers of property if the transferors are in control of the corporation immediately after the transfer. Gain or loss is merely postponed in a manner similar to a like-kind exchange (see Chapter15). The following requirements must be met to qualify under § 351:

- The transferors must be in control of the corporation immediately after the exchange. *Control* is defined as ownership of at least 80 percent of the total combined voting power of all classes of stock entitled to vote and at least 80 percent of the total number of shares of all other classes of stock.[33]
- Realized gain (but not loss) is recognized to the extent that the transferors receive property other than stock. Such nonqualifying property is commonly referred to as *boot.*

[33]§ 368(c).

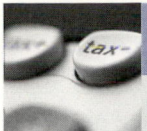

CONCEPT SUMMARY 20.1

Summary of Income Tax Consequences

	Individuals	Corporations
Computation of gross income	§ 61.	§ 61.
Computation of taxable income	§§ 62, 63(b) through (h).	§ 63(a). Concept of AGI has no relevance.
Deductions	Trade or business (§ 162); nonbusiness (§ 212); some personal and employee expenses (generally deductible as itemized deductions).	Trade or business (§ 162).
Charitable contributions	Limited in any tax year to 50% of AGI; 30% for long-term capital gain property unless election is made to reduce fair market value of gift; 20% for long-term capital gain property contributed to private nonoperating foundations.	Limited in any tax year to 10% of taxable income computed without regard to the charitable contribution deduction, net operating loss or capital loss carryback, and dividends received deduction.
	Time of deduction—year in which payment is made.	Time of deduction—year in which payment is made unless accrual basis taxpayer. Accrual basis corporation may take deduction in year preceding payment if contribution was authorized by board of directors by end of that year and contribution is paid by fifteenth day of third month of following year.
	Contribution of ordinary income property is limited to the lesser of adjusted basis or fair market value.	Contribution of certain ordinary income property can include one-half of any appreciation on the property.
	Excess charitable contributions can be carried over for a period of up to five years.	Excess charitable contributions can be carried over for a period of up to five years.
Casualty losses	$100 floor on nonbusiness casualty and theft losses; nonbusiness casualty and theft losses deductible only to extent losses exceed 10% of AGI.	Deductible in full.
Depreciation recapture for § 1250 property	Recaptured to extent accelerated depreciation exceeds straight-line.	20% of excess of amount that would be recaptured under § 1245 over amount recaptured under § 1250 is additional ordinary income under § 291.
Domestic production activities deduction	9% of the lesser of QPAI or AGI.	9% of the lesser of QPAI or taxable income.
Net operating loss	Adjusted for nonbusiness deductions over nonbusiness income and for personal and dependency exemptions.	Generally no adjustments.
Dividends received	Qualified dividends are taxed at the same rate applicable to net long-term capital gains.	Deduction allowed (70%, 80%, or 100%) as to dividends received.
Long-term capital gains	Generally taxed at a rate no higher than 15% (0% if taxpayer is in the 15% or lower tax bracket).	Taxed using regular corporate rates.
Capital losses	Only $3,000 of capital loss can offset ordinary income; loss is carried forward indefinitely to offset capital gains or ordinary income up to $3,000; carryovers of short-term losses remain short term; long-term losses carry over as long term.	Can offset only capital gains; carried back three years and forward five years; carrybacks and carryovers are treated as short-term losses.

	Individuals	Corporations
Passive activity losses	Generally deductible only against income from passive activities.	For regular corporations, no limitation on deductibility. Personal service corporations and certain closely held corporations, however, are subject to same limitations as imposed on individuals. A closely held corporation is one where five or fewer individuals own more than 50% of the stock either directly or indirectly.
Alternative minimum tax	Applied at a graduated rate schedule of 26% and 28% to AMT base (taxable income as modified by certain adjustments plus preference items minus exemption amount); exemption allowed depending on filing status; exemption phaseout begins when AMTI reaches a certain amount (e.g., $150,000 for married filing jointly).	Applied at a 20% rate to AMT base (taxable income as modified by certain adjustments plus preference items minus exemption amount); $40,000 exemption allowed but phaseout begins once AMTI reaches $150,000; adjustments and tax preference items similar to those applicable to individuals but also include 75% of adjusted current earnings (ACE) over AMTI. Certain small business corporations are exempt from the AMT.
Tax rates	Progressive with six rates in 2011 (10%, 15%, 25%, 28%, 33%, and 35%).	Progressive with four rates (15%, 25%, 34%, and 35%); lower brackets phased out at higher levels.

If the requirements of § 351 are satisfied and no boot is involved, nonrecognition of gain or loss is *mandatory*.

Basis Considerations and Computation of Gain

The nonrecognition of gain or loss is accompanied by a carryover of basis. The basis of stock received in a § 351 transfer is determined as follows:

- Start with the adjusted basis of the property transferred by the shareholder.
- Add any gain recognized by the shareholder as a result of the transfer.
- Subtract the fair market value of any boot received by the shareholder from the corporation.[34]

Shareholders who receive noncash boot have a basis in the property equal to the fair market value.

The basis of properties received by the corporation is the basis in the hands of the transferor increased by the amount of any gain recognized to the transferor shareholder.[35]

EXAMPLE 22

Ann and Lori form Bluejay Corporation. Ann transfers property with an adjusted basis of $30,000 and a fair market value of $60,000 for 50% of the stock. Lori transfers property with an adjusted basis of $40,000 and a fair market value of $60,000 for the remaining 50% of the stock. The realized gain ($30,000 for Ann and $20,000 for Lori) is not recognized on the transfer because the transfer qualifies under § 351. The basis of the stock to Ann is $30,000, and the basis of the stock to Lori is $40,000. Bluejay Corporation has a basis of $30,000 in the property transferred by Ann and a basis of $40,000 in the property transferred by Lori. ∎

EXAMPLE 23

Mike and John form Condor Corporation with the following investments: Mike transfers property (adjusted basis of $30,000 and fair market value of $70,000), and John transfers cash of $60,000. Each receives 50 shares of the Condor stock, but Mike also

---

[34]§ 358(a).   [35]§ 362(a).

receives $10,000 in cash. Assume each share of the Condor stock is worth $1,200. Mike's realized gain is $40,000, determined as follows:

Value of the Condor stock received [50 (shares) × $1,200 (value per share)]	$ 60,000
Cash received	10,000
Amount realized	$ 70,000
Less basis of property transferred	(30,000)
Realized gain	$ 40,000

Mike's recognized gain is $10,000, the lesser of the realized gain ($40,000) or the fair market value of the boot received ($10,000). Mike's basis in the Condor stock is $30,000, computed as follows:

Basis in the property transferred	$ 30,000
Plus recognized gain	10,000
	$ 40,000
Less boot received	(10,000)
Basis to Mike of the Condor stock	$ 30,000

Condor Corporation's basis in the property transferred by Mike is $40,000 [$30,000 (basis of the property to Mike) + $10,000 (gain recognized by Mike)]. John neither realizes nor recognizes gain or loss and will have a basis of $60,000 in the Condor stock. ■

ETHICS & Equity — SELECTIVE INCORPORATION

Miguel, a cash basis taxpayer, owns and operates a home renovation business that he decides to incorporate. In forming the corporation, he transfers *most* of the business, which includes unrealized receivables and inventory items. However, he retains the land and building and the trade accounts payable.

For tax purposes, what is Miguel trying to accomplish by being selective in terms of what he transfers to the corporation? Will it work?

The receipt of stock for the performance of *services* always results in ordinary income to the transferor shareholder. An example might be an attorney who does not charge a fee for incorporating a business but instead receives the value equivalent in stock of the newly formed corporation. The basis of stock received for the performance of services is equal to the fair market value of the services.

20.4 OPERATING THE CORPORATION

DIVIDEND DISTRIBUTIONS

Corporate distributions of cash or property to shareholders are treated as dividend income to the extent the corporation has accumulated *or* current earnings and profits (E & P).[36] In determining the source of the distribution, a dividend is deemed to have been made initially from current E & P.

> **L0.6**
> Explain the tax rules governing the operation of corporations.

EXAMPLE 24

As of January 1, 2011, Teal Corporation has a deficit in accumulated E & P of $300,000. For tax year 2011, it has current E & P of $100,000. In 2011, the corporation distributes $50,000 to its shareholders. The $50,000 distribution is treated as a dividend, since it is deemed to have been made from current E & P. This is the case even though Teal still has a deficit in its accumulated E & P at the end of 2011. ■

---
[36]§ 316.

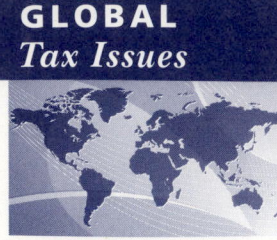

GLOBAL
Tax Issues

TRANSFERRING ASSETS TO FOREIGN CORPORATIONS— FORGET § 351?

Tax-deferred transfers to controlled corporations under § 351 may generate current taxation when those transfers cross national borders. When a U.S. person transfers appreciated assets to a foreign corporation, the United States may lose its ability to tax the deferred gain on those assets (as well as the future income generated by the assets). To protect the U.S. taxing jurisdiction, § 367 provides that transfers of assets outside the U.S. tax net are generally taxable, in spite of the provisions of § 351.

Qualified dividend income is taxed like net long-term capital gain.[37] Consequently, the tax rate on such income cannot exceed 15 percent (0 percent in 2008, 2009, 2010, and 2011 for individual shareholders in the 15 percent or lower tax bracket).[38]

If a corporate distribution is not covered by E & P (either current or past), it is treated as a return of capital (refer to the discussion of the recovery of capital doctrine in Chapter 4). Because this treatment allows the shareholder to apply the amount of the distribution against the basis of the stock investment, the distribution represents a nontaxable return of capital. Any amount received in excess of the stock basis is classified as a capital gain (if the stock is a capital asset in the hands of the shareholder).

EXAMPLE 25

When Mallard Corporation has no E & P (either current or accumulated), it distributes cash of $300,000 to its sole shareholder, Helen. The basis of Helen's stock investment is $200,000. Based on these facts, the $300,000 distribution Helen receives is accounted for as follows:

Return of capital (nontaxable)	$200,000
Capital gain	100,000
Total amount of distribution	$300,000

After the distribution, Helen has a basis of zero in her stock investment. ∎

Concept of Earnings and Profits

The term **earnings and profits** is not defined in the Code, but § 312 does include certain transactions that affect E & P. Although E & P and the accounting concept of retained earnings have certain similarities, they differ in numerous respects. For example, a nontaxable stock dividend is treated as a capitalization of retained earnings for accounting purposes, yet it does not decrease E & P for tax purposes. Taxable dividends do reduce E & P but cannot yield a deficit. Referring to Example 25, after the distribution Mallard Corporation's E & P remains zero rather than being a negative amount.

E & P is an account that reflects a corporation's economic ability to pay dividends to its shareholders. Thus, in converting a corporation's taxable income for any one year to *current E & P*, certain adjustments need to be made. For example, one adjustment is to add back any tax-exempt interest received. Although such interest is not included in taxable income, it is available for distribution as dividends. Some of the other adjustments to taxable income to arrive at current E & P include the following:

---

[37]Qualified dividend income is defined in § 1(h)(11)(B) and is discussed in Chapter 4.

[38]§ 1(h)(1). See the discussion in Chapter 3.

As additions—

- Dividends received deduction.
- Domestic production activities deduction.
- Proceeds of life insurance policies on key employees.

As subtractions—

- Federal income taxes paid.
- Charitable contributions in excess of the 10 percent limitation.
- Excess capital losses (no carryback available).
- Nondeductible items (e.g., fines, penalties, losses between related parties).

Accumulated E & P is the sum of the corporation's past current E & P that has not been distributed as dividends. A more detailed discussion of the concept of E & P is beyond the scope of this chapter.

Property Dividends

A distribution of property to a shareholder is measured by the fair market value of the property on the date of distribution. The shareholder's basis in the property received is also the fair market value.[39]

EXAMPLE 26

Drake Corporation has E & P of $60,000. It distributes land with a fair market value of $50,000 (adjusted basis of $30,000) to its sole shareholder, Art. Art has a taxable dividend of $50,000 and a basis in the land of $50,000. ∎

A corporation that distributes appreciated property to its shareholders as a dividend must recognize the amount of the appreciation as gain.[40]

EXAMPLE 27

Assume the same facts as in Example 26. Drake Corporation must recognize a gain of $20,000 on the distribution it made to Art. ∎

However, if the property distributed has a basis in excess of its fair market value, the distributing corporation cannot recognize any loss.

Constructive Dividends

Many taxpayers mistakenly assume that dividend consequences do not take place unless the distribution carries the formalities of a dividend (declaration date, record date, payment date). They further assume that dividends must be paid out to all shareholders on a pro rata basis. This may not be the case when closely held corporations are involved. Here, the key to dividend treatment depends upon whether the shareholders derive a benefit from the corporation that cannot be otherwise classified (e.g., as reasonable salary). The following are examples of **constructive dividends**:

- Salaries paid to shareholder-employees that are not reasonable (refer to Example 6 in Chapter 6).
- Interest on debt owed by the corporation to shareholders that is reclassified as equity because the corporation is thinly capitalized (refer to the earlier discussion in this chapter).
- Excessive rent paid by a corporation for the use of shareholder property. The arm's length standard is used to test whether the rent is excessive (refer to Example 28 in Chapter 1).
- Advances to shareholders that are not bona fide loans.

---

[39]§ 301.

[40]The tax consequences to a corporation of nonliquidating distributions to shareholders are covered in § 311.

- Interest-free (or below-market) loans to shareholders. In this situation, the dividend component is the difference between the interest provided for, if any, and that calculated using the market rate.
- Shareholder use of corporate property for less than an arm's length rate.
- Absorption by the corporation of a shareholder's personal expenses.
- Bargain purchase of corporate property by shareholders.

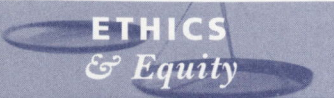

KEEPING IT IN THE FAMILY

Thrasher Company is a very profitable closely held C corporation owned and operated by the Fleming family. When its treasurer, Matilda Fleming, died, Michael Fleming was appointed as a temporary replacement. Although Matilda was 80 years old at death, she was a licensed CPA and had developed a competent accounting staff. Michael is the son of the CEO and major shareholder of Thrasher, but individually he owns no stock in the corporation. He just graduated from high school and plans to attend college full-time with a major in sports management. Thrasher Company will pay Michael the same salary Matilda was receiving. What are the parties trying to accomplish? Will they succeed?

Like regular dividends, constructive dividends must be covered by E & P to carry dividend income consequences to the shareholders. As noted previously, however, constructive dividends need not be available to all shareholders on a pro rata basis.

EXAMPLE 28
THE BIG PICTURE

Return to the facts of *The Big Picture* on p. 20-2. Recall also the suggestions made in Example 21. If they choose the corporate form, the Todd sisters need to take the following into account:

- Any salaries that the sisters pay themselves should satisfy the reasonableness test.
- Rent charged the corporation for the use of capital assets owned by the sisters should meet the arm's length standard.
- Loans made to the corporation for working capital purposes should provide for a market rate of interest to be charged.

Although the constructive dividend issue will not arise until the corporation becomes profitable (and has E & P), these procedures should be structured at the outset so that the parties will be prepared for a possible future challenge by the IRS. ■

Although dividends reduce the E & P of a corporation, they are not deductible for income tax purposes. In this regard, certain constructive dividends could have subtle tax consequences for all parties concerned.

EXAMPLE 29

Grouse Corporation makes a loan to one of its shareholders, Hal. No interest is provided for, but application of the market rate would produce $20,000 of interest for the term of the loan. Presuming the loan is bona fide, the following results occur:

- Hal has dividend income of $20,000.
- Grouse Corporation has interest income of $20,000.
- Hal might obtain an interest deduction of $20,000.

Not only does Grouse Corporation have to recognize income of $20,000, but it also obtains no income tax deduction for the $20,000 constructive dividend. ■

EXAMPLE 30

Assume the same facts as in Example 29, except that the loan to Hal was not bona fide. In this event, the full amount of the loan is regarded as a dividend to Hal. Therefore, the interest element is not a factor since no bona fide loan ever existed. ■

STOCK REDEMPTIONS

If a corporation redeems a shareholder's stock (a **stock redemption**), one of two possible outcomes occurs:

- The redemption may qualify as a sale or exchange under § 302 or § 303. In that case, capital gain or loss treatment usually applies to the qualifying shareholders.
- The redemption will be treated as a dividend under § 301, provided the distributing corporation has E & P.

EXAMPLE 31

Reba owns 300 shares of Snipe Corporation stock as an investment. The shares have a basis to Reba of $100 each, for a total of $30,000. When the fair market value of a share is $300, Snipe redeems 200 of Reba's shares. If the redemption qualifies for sale or exchange treatment, the result is a capital gain to Reba of $40,000 [$60,000 (redemption price) − $20,000 (basis in 200 shares)]. Reba's basis in the remaining 100 shares is $10,000 [$30,000 (basis in the original shares) − $20,000 (basis in the shares redeemed)]. ■

EXAMPLE 32

Assume the same facts as in Example 31, except that the redemption does not qualify for sale or exchange treatment. Presuming adequate E & P, the redemption results in $60,000 dividend income. Reba's basis in the remaining 100 shares now becomes $30,000, or $300 per share. ■

Because dividend income is taxed at the rate applicable to net long-term capital gain, the difference between Examples 31 and 32 is in the amount of recognized gain that is eligible for the beneficial capital gain rate. In Example 32, an extra $20,000 of such gain occurs, since the redeemed stock's basis of $20,000 is not part of the recognized gain calculation.

A stock redemption qualifies as a sale or exchange if it meets any of the safe harbors of § 302 or § 303.

20.5 LIQUIDATING THE CORPORATION

Unlike dividend distributions or stock redemptions, where the distributing corporation continues its operations, **liquidating distributions** occur during the termination of the business. All debts are paid, and any remaining corporate assets are distributed pro rata to the shareholders in exchange for their stock. Once these distributions are completed, the corporation undergoing liquidation will cease to be a separate tax entity.

LO.7

Apply the tax rules governing the liquidation of corporations.

GENERAL RULE OF § 331

Under the general rule, the shareholders recognize gain or loss in a corporate liquidation. The amount of recognized gain or loss is measured by the difference between the fair market value of the assets received from the corporation and the adjusted basis of the stock surrendered. The shareholders recognize capital gain or loss if the stock is a capital asset.[41]

EXAMPLE 33

Pursuant to a complete liquidation, Starling Corporation distributes $100,000 in cash to Edna, one of its shareholders. If Edna's basis in the stock surrendered is $40,000, she must recognize a gain of $60,000. If Edna held the stock as an investment, the $60,000 gain is capital gain—either short term or long term (depending on the holding period). ■

---

[41]If the stock is held as an investment, which is usually the case, gain or loss will be capital. Stock owned by a broker probably will be inventory and therefore will not constitute a capital asset. Thus, the gain or loss on this type of stock is ordinary and not capital.

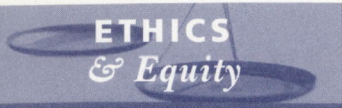

ETHICS & Equity

ELIMINATING BURDENSOME PAPERWORK

For many years, Sophie has owned and operated several apartment buildings. In 1995 and upon the advice of her attorney, Sophie transferred the apartment buildings to a newly created corporation. Her main reason for incorporating the business was to achieve limited liability.

Every year since 1995, Sophie has prepared and filed a Form 1120 for the corporation. No corporate income tax has been paid because, after the deduction of various expenses (including Sophie's "management fee"), the corporation has zero taxable income.

In 2011, Sophie decides that filing Form 1120 is a waste of time and serves no useful purpose. Instead, she plans to report all of the financial activities of the apartment business on her own individual Form 1040.

Comment on the propriety of what Sophie plans to do.

EXCEPTION TO THE GENERAL RULE

Section 332 is an exception to the general rule that the shareholder recognizes gain or loss on a corporate liquidation. If a parent corporation liquidates a subsidiary corporation in which it owns at least 80 percent of the voting power and value of the stock, no gain or loss is recognized by the parent company. The subsidiary must distribute all of its property in complete liquidation of all of its stock within the taxable year or within three years from the close of the tax year in which the first distribution occurred.

BASIS DETERMINATION—§§ 334 AND 338

General Rule

Where gain or loss is recognized upon the complete liquidation of a corporation, the basis of the property received by the shareholders is the property's fair market value.[42]

Subsidiary Liquidation Basis Rules

The general rule is that the property received by the parent corporation in a complete liquidation of its subsidiary under § 332 has the same basis it had in the hands of the subsidiary (a carryover basis).[43] The parent's basis in the stock of the liquidated subsidiary disappears.

EXAMPLE 34

Swallow, the parent corporation, has a basis of $200,000 in the stock of Shrike Corporation, a subsidiary in which it owns 85% of all classes of stock. Swallow purchased the stock of Shrike Corporation 10 years ago. In the current year, Swallow liquidates Shrike Corporation and receives assets worth $500,000 with a tax basis to Shrike of $400,000. Swallow Corporation will have a basis of $400,000 in the assets, with a potential gain upon sale of $100,000. Swallow's original $200,000 basis in the Shrike stock disappears. ■

An exception to the carryover of basis rule is provided in § 338. Under this exception, the parent company may elect to receive a basis for the assets equal to the adjusted basis of the stock of the subsidiary. In effect, the initial acquisition of the subsidiary is treated as if the parent company had acquired the assets (rather than the stock) of the subsidiary.

EFFECT OF THE LIQUIDATION ON THE CORPORATION

At the corporate level, § 336 applies to dictate the tax consequences to the corporation being liquidated. Under § 336, the distributing corporation recognizes gain or loss upon complete liquidation. In this regard, it does not matter whether the corporation distributes the property in kind (*as is*) to the shareholders or first sells the property and then distributes the proceeds.

---

[42]§ 334(a).   [43]§ 334(b)(1).

EXAMPLE 35

Pursuant to a complete liquidation, Grackle Corporation distributes the following assets to its shareholders: undeveloped land held as an investment (basis of $150,000 and fair market value of $400,000) and marketable securities (basis of $260,000 and fair market value of $200,000). Since Grackle is treated as if it had sold the property, a gain of $250,000 results from the land, and a loss of $60,000 results from the securities. ∎

The deductibility of losses may be restricted by the related-party rules (refer to Chapter 6) if certain conditions exist (e.g., the distributions are not pro rata).[44]

A wholly owned subsidiary corporation does not recognize gain or loss when the parent corporation uses the carryover basis option of § 334(b)(1). The reason for the special treatment is that the subsidiary's basis (and all other tax attributes) in the assets carries over to the parent corporation.

20.6 THE S ELECTION

Numerous nontax reasons exist for operating a business in the corporate form (e.g., limited liability). Consequently, the existence of income tax disadvantages (e.g., double taxation of corporate income and shareholder dividends) should not deter businesspeople from using the corporate form. To prevent tax considerations from interfering with the exercise of sound business judgment, Congress enacted Subchapter S of the Code. The Subchapter S election enables taxpayers to use the corporate form for conducting a business without being taxed as a corporation.

LO.8

Assess the utility and effect of the Subchapter S election.

QUALIFICATION FOR S STATUS

To achieve S corporation status, the corporation must meet certain requirements and make an effective election.

Qualifying for the Election

To qualify for **S corporation** status, the corporation must be a **small business corporation**. This includes any corporation that has the following characteristics:

- Is a domestic corporation.
- Has no more than 100 shareholders.
- Has as its shareholders only individuals, estates, and certain trusts.
- Does not have a nonresident alien as a shareholder.
- Has only one class of stock outstanding.

The members of a family who own stock are treated as a single shareholder. Members of a family include all lineal descendants of a shareholder and spouse (or ex-spouse) and the spouses (or ex-spouses) of such lineal descendants.[45]

EXAMPLE 36

Harry, a shareholder in an S corporation dies, and under his will, his stock is distributed among three children and eight grandchildren. The 11 new shareholders are treated as one shareholder for purposes of the 100-shareholder limitation. ∎

These characteristics must continue to exist if an electing S corporation is to maintain S status.

Making the Election

The election is made by filing Form 2553, and *all* shareholders must consent. For this purpose, husbands and wives are counted as a single shareholder.

---

[44]§ 336(d).　　　　　　　　　　　[45]§ 1361(c)(1).

To be effective for the current year, the election must be filed anytime during the preceding taxable year or on or before the fifteenth day of the third month of the current year.[46]

EXAMPLE 37

Heron, a calendar year taxpayer, is a regular corporation that wishes to elect S status for 2011. If the election is filed anytime from January 1, 2010, through March 15, 2011, it will be effective for 2011. ■

The IRS has the authority to waive invalid S elections (e.g., inadvertent failure to obtain all the necessary shareholder consents to the original election) and to treat late elections as timely.

Loss of the Election

The S election may be terminated *voluntarily* (a majority of the shareholders file to revoke the election) or *involuntarily*. An involuntary termination may occur in *any* of the following ways:

- The corporation ceases to qualify as a small business corporation (e.g., the number of shareholders exceeds 100, or a partnership becomes a shareholder).
- The corporation has passive investment income (e.g., interest, dividends) in excess of 25 percent of gross receipts for a period of three consecutive years. This possibility applies only if the corporation was previously a regular corporation and has E & P from that period.

If the holders of a *majority* of the shares consent to a voluntary revocation of S status, the election to revoke must be made on or before the fifteenth day of the third month of the tax year to be effective for that year.

EXAMPLE 38

The shareholders of Stork Corporation, a calendar year S corporation, elect to revoke the election on January 4, 2011. Assuming the election is duly executed and timely filed, Stork will become a regular corporation for calendar year 2011. If the election to revoke is not made until June 2011, Stork will not become a regular corporation until calendar year 2012. ■

Suppose the shareholders in Example 38 file the election to revoke on January 4, 2011, but do not want the revocation to take place until 2012. If the election so specifies, Stork Corporation will cease to have S status as of January 1, 2012.

In the case where S status is lost because of a disqualifying act (involuntarily), the loss of the election takes effect as of the date on which the event occurs.

EXAMPLE 39

Crow Corporation has been a calendar year S corporation for several years. On August 13, 2011, one of its shareholders sells her stock to Kite Corporation. Since Crow Corporation no longer satisfies the definition of a small business corporation (it has another corporation as a shareholder), the election has been involuntarily terminated. For calendar year 2011, therefore, Crow will be an S corporation through August 12 and a regular corporation from August 13 through December 31, 2011. ■

In the event the election is lost through a violation of the passive investment income limitation, the loss of S status starts at the beginning of the next tax year.

Barring certain exceptions, the loss of the election places the corporation in a five-year holding period before S status can be reelected.

---

[46]§ 1362.

TAX in the NEWS

S CORPORATIONS AND SALARIES: A CONTINUING DILEMMA

Devising the most beneficial salary structure has always presented a supreme challenge for many S corporations. The owner-shareholders may want to receive enough salary to be covered under Social Security and private retirement plans. Too much, however, will aggravate the employment tax cost (particularly the Medicare portion, which does not have a cap). (Note that nonsalary distributions to a shareholder are not subject to self-employment tax.) Not infrequently, common sense disappears, and shareholders work for free just to avoid payroll taxes.

The IRS is expected to place increased emphasis on investigating abuses in the area of payroll taxes. Although the major efforts will be directed toward the misclassification of workers (i.e., employees wrongfully treated as independent contractors), the level of compensation will be subject to scrutiny as well. In the case of S corporations, therefore, the IRS is likely to ask, "Are shareholder-employees deliberately underpaying themselves to avoid payroll taxes?" S corporations should anticipate the problem by making certain that they are able to justify the salaries they pay their shareholder-employees.

OPERATIONAL RULES

The S corporation is primarily a tax-reporting rather than a taxpaying entity. In this respect, the entity is taxed much like a partnership.[47] Under the conduit concept, the taxable income and losses of an S corporation flow through to the shareholders who report them on their personal income tax returns.

To ascertain the annual tax consequences to each shareholder, it is necessary to carry out two steps at the S corporation level. First, all corporate transactions that will flow through to the shareholders on an *as is* basis under the conduit approach must be set aside. Second, what remains is aggregated as the taxable income of the S corporation and is allocated to each shareholder on a per-share and per-day of stock ownership basis.[48]

Separately Stated Items

The following are some of the items that do not lose their identity as they pass through the S corporation and are therefore picked up by each shareholder on an *as is* basis:

- Tax-exempt income.
- Long-term and short-term capital gains and losses.
- Section 1231 gains and losses.
- Charitable contributions.
- Domestic production activities deduction (DPAD).
- Qualified dividend income.
- Foreign tax credits.
- Depletion.
- Nonbusiness income or loss under § 212.
- Intangible drilling costs.
- Investment interest, income, and expenses covered under § 163(d).
- Certain portfolio income.
- Passive activity gains, losses, and credits under § 469.
- AMT adjustments and tax preference items.

In the case of the DPAD, the individual components needed to determine the deduction at the shareholder level must be broken out. These components include each shareholder's pro rata portion of QPAI and the W–2 wages paid by the

---

[47]This is not to imply that an S corporation is always free from the income tax. For example, a tax may be imposed on certain built-in gains or certain excessive passive investment income.

[48]§ 1366.

corporation. This information is listed on Schedule K–1 (Form 1120S) and is picked up by the shareholder on lines 7 and 17 of his or her Form 8903 (Domestic Production Activities Deduction).

The items listed above are separately stated because each may lead to a different tax result when combined with a particular shareholder's other transactions.

EXAMPLE 40

Arnold and Jean are equal shareholders in Lark Corporation (an S corporation). For calendar year 2011, each must account for one-half of a corporate short-term capital gain of $6,000. Arnold has no other capital asset transactions, and Jean has a short-term capital loss of $3,000 from the sale of stock in IBM Corporation. In terms of overall effect, the difference between the two taxpayers is significant. Although both must report the short-term capital gain pass-through, Jean will neutralize its inclusion in gross income by offsetting it with the $3,000 short-term capital loss from the sale of the IBM stock. For Arnold, the short-term capital gain pass-through results in a $3,000 increase in his taxable income. ∎

Taxable Income

After the separately stated items have been removed, the balance represents the taxable income of the S corporation. In arriving at taxable income, the dividends received deduction, the DPAD, and the NOL deduction are not allowed. An S corporation does come under the regular corporate rules, however, for purposes of amortization of organizational expenditures.

Once taxable income has been determined, it passes through to each shareholder as of the last day of the S corporation's tax year.

EXAMPLE 41

Harrier Corporation, a calendar year S corporation, had the following transactions during the current year:

Sales		$ 400,000
Cost of goods sold		(230,000)
Other income		
*Tax-exempt interest	$ 3,000	
*Long-term capital gain	5,000	8,000
Other expenses		
*Charitable contributions	$ 4,000	
Advertising expense	15,000	
Other operating expenses	20,000	
*Short-term capital loss	1,500	(40,500)
Net income per books		$ 137,500

When the items that are to be separately stated (those preceded by an asterisk [*]) and shown *as is* by each shareholder are withdrawn, Harrier has the following taxable income:

Sales		$ 400,000
Cost of goods sold		(230,000)
Other expenses		
Advertising expense	$15,000	
Other operating expenses	20,000	(35,000)
Taxable income		$ 135,000

∎

EXAMPLE 42

If Oscar owned 10% of the stock in Harrier Corporation (refer to Example 41) during all of the current year, he must account for the following:

Separately stated items	
Tax-exempt interest	$ 300
Long-term capital gain	500
Charitable contributions	400
Short-term capital loss	150
Taxable income (10% of $135,000)	13,500

Some of the separately stated items (e.g., the tax-exempt interest) must be reported on Oscar's individual income tax return but may not lead to tax consequences. Oscar picks up his share of Harrier's taxable income ($13,500) as ordinary income. ∎

Treatment of Losses

As previously noted, separately stated loss items (e.g., capital losses, § 1231 losses) flow through to the shareholders on an *as is* basis. Their treatment by a shareholder depends on the shareholder's individual income tax position. If the S corporation's taxable income determination results in an operating loss, it also passes through to the shareholders. As is the case with separately stated items, the amount of the loss each shareholder receives depends on the stock ownership during the year.

EXAMPLE 43

In 2011, Oriole Corporation (a calendar year S corporation) incurred an operating loss of $365,000. During 2011, Jason's ownership in Oriole was 20% for 200 days and 30% for 165 days. Jason's share of the loss is determined as follows:

[$365,000 × (200/365)] × 20% =	$40,000
[$365,000 × (165/365)] × 30% =	49,500
Total loss for Jason	$89,500

Presuming the basis limitation does not come into play (see the following discussion), Jason deducts $89,500 in arriving at adjusted gross income. ∎

EXAMPLE 44
THE BIG PICTURE

Return to the facts of *The Big Picture* on p. 20-2. Recall that the Todd sisters anticipate losses in the early years of their catering business. If they form a C corporation, such losses will be of no benefit to the new corporation—no carryback will be available, and there will be only a potential for a delayed carryover. With an S election, however, losses pass through currently. Thus, the sisters will secure limited liability for their business and the immediate tax benefit of any losses. ∎

ETHICS
& Equity   ## INCOME TAX BASIS THAT DOES NOT CHANGE?

In 2000, Howard purchased stock in Green, a C corporation, for $100,000. In 2006, Green made a valid election under Subchapter S. In 2011, Howard sells his stock in Green for $120,000. Since he paid $100,000 for the stock, Howard plans to recognize a long-term capital gain of $20,000 as a result of the sale. Do you agree with Howard's proposed reporting?

Basis Determination

A shareholder's *basis* in the stock of an S corporation, like that of a regular corporation, is the original investment plus additional capital contributions less return of capital distributions. At this point, however, the symmetry disappears. Generally, basis is increased by the pass-through of income items (including those separately stated) and decreased by the loss items (including those separately stated).[49]

---

[49]§ 1367.

EXAMPLE 45

In 2011, Warbler Corporation is formed with an investment of $500,000, of which Janice contributed $100,000 for a 20% stock interest. A timely S election is made, and for 2011, Warbler earns taxable income of $50,000. Janice's basis in her stock investment now becomes $110,000 [$100,000 (original capital contribution) + $10,000 (the 20% share of the corporation's taxable income assigned to Janice)]. ■

Distributions by an S corporation reduce the basis of a shareholder's stock investment. However, if the amount of the distribution exceeds basis, the excess normally receives capital gain treatment.

As previously noted, operating losses of an S corporation pass through to the shareholders and reduce the basis in their stock investment. Because the basis of the stock cannot fall below zero, an excess loss is then applied against the basis of any loans the shareholder may have made to the corporation.

EXAMPLE 46

Flamingo Corporation, a calendar year S corporation, has an operating loss of $60,000 for 2011. Norman, a 50% shareholder, has an adjusted basis of $25,000 in his stock investment and has made loans to the corporation of $5,000. Based on these facts, Norman may take full advantage of the $30,000 loss (50% of $60,000) on his 2011 individual income tax return. Norman's basis in the stock and the loans must be reduced accordingly, and both will be zero after the pass-through. ■

In the event the basis limitation precludes an operating loss from being absorbed, the loss can be carried forward and deducted when and if it is covered by basis.

EXAMPLE 47

Assume the same facts as in Example 46, except that Norman had not made any loans to Flamingo Corporation. Further assume that Flamingo has taxable income of $15,000 in the following year (2012). Norman's tax situation for 2011 and 2012 is summarized as follows:

Ordinary loss for 2011	$25,000
Income to be reported in 2012 (50% of $15,000)	7,500
Restoration of stock basis in 2012 (50% of $15,000)	7,500
Loss allowed for 2012 ($30,000 − $25,000)	5,000
Basis in stock account after 2012 ($7,500 − $5,000)	2,500

Thus, Norman's unabsorbed loss of $5,000 from 2011 carries over to 2012 and is applied against the $7,500 of ordinary income for that year. ■

20.7 PARTNERSHIPS

L0.9

Discuss the tax consequences of forming and operating a partnership.

NATURE OF PARTNERSHIP TAXATION

Unlike corporations, partnerships are not considered separate taxable entities. Each member of a partnership is subject to income tax on the partner's distributive share of the partnership's income, even if an actual distribution is not made. The tax return (Form 1065) required of a partnership serves only to provide information necessary in determining the character and amount of each partner's distributive share of the partnership's income and expense. Because a partnership acts as a conduit, items that pass through to the partners do not lose their identity. For example, tax-exempt income earned by a partnership is picked up by the partners as tax-exempt income. In this regard, partnerships function in much the same fashion as S corporations, which also serve as conduits.

A partnership is considered a separate taxable entity for purposes of making various elections and selecting its taxable year, method of depreciation, and accounting method. A partnership is also treated as a separate legal entity under civil law with the right to own property in its own name and to transact business free from the personal debts of its partners.

PARTNERSHIP FORMATION

Recognition of Gain or Loss

The general rule is that no gain or loss is recognized by a partnership or any of its partners on the contribution of property in exchange for a capital interest in the partnership.[50] The general rule also applies to all subsequent contributions of property.

There are certain exceptions to the nonrecognition of gain or loss rule including the following:

- If a partner transfers property to the partnership and receives money or other consideration (boot) as a result, the transaction will be treated as a sale or exchange rather than as a contribution of capital. Realized gain is recognized to the extent of the fair market value of the boot received.
- If a partnership interest is received in exchange for services rendered or to be rendered by the partner to the partnership, the fair market value of the transferred capital interest is regarded as compensation for services rendered. In such cases, the recipient of the capital interest must recognize the amount as ordinary income in the year actually or constructively received.
- If property that is subject to a liability in excess of its basis is contributed to a partnership, the contributing partner may recognize gain.

Basis of a Partnership Interest

The contributing *partner's basis* in the partnership interest received is the sum of money contributed plus the adjusted basis of any other property transferred to the partnership.[51]

EXAMPLE 48

In return for the contribution of property (with a basis of $50,000 and a fair market value of $80,000) and cash of $10,000 to the Brown Partnership, Marcia receives a 10% capital interest worth $90,000. Although Marcia has a realized gain of $30,000 ($90,000 − $60,000) on the transfer, none of the gain is recognized. The basis of her interest in the Brown Partnership is $60,000 [$50,000 (basis of property contributed) + $10,000 (cash contribution)]. ■

A partner's basis in the partnership interest is determined without regard to any amount reflected on the partnership's books as capital, equity, or a similar account.

EXAMPLE 49

Marge and Clyde form the equal Blue Partnership with a cash contribution of $300,000 from Marge and a property contribution (adjusted basis of $180,000 and fair market value of $300,000) from Clyde. Although the books of the Blue Partnership may reflect a credit of $300,000 to each partner's capital account, only Marge has a tax basis of $300,000 in her partnership interest. Clyde's tax basis in his partnership interest is $180,000, the amount of his tax basis in the property contributed to the partnership. ■

After its initial determination, the basis of a partnership interest is subject to continuous fluctuations. A partner's basis is increased by additional contributions and the sum of his or her current and prior years' distributive share of the following:

- Taxable income of the partnership, including capital gains.
- Tax-exempt income of the partnership.

---

[50]§ 721.   [51]§ 722.

- The excess of the deductions for depletion over the basis of the partnership's property subject to depletion.[52]

Similarly, the basis of a partner's interest is decreased, but not below zero, by distributions of partnership property (including cash) and by the sum of the current and prior years' distributive share of the following:

- Partnership losses, including capital losses.
- Partnership expenditures that are not deductible in computing taxable income or loss and that are not capital expenditures.

Changes in the liabilities (including trade accounts payable, bank loans, etc.) of a partnership also affect the basis of a partnership interest. A partner's basis is increased by his or her assumption of partnership liabilities and by his or her pro rata share of liabilities incurred by the partnership. Likewise, the partner's basis is decreased by the amount of any personal liabilities assumed by the partnership and by the pro rata share of any decreases in the liabilities of the partnership.

EXAMPLE 50

Tony, Martha, and Carolyn form the Orange Partnership with the following contributions: cash of $100,000 from Tony for a 50% interest in capital and profits, cash of $50,000 from Martha for a 25% interest, and property valued at $66,000 from Carolyn for a 25% interest. The property contributed by Carolyn has an adjusted basis of $30,000 and is subject to a mortgage of $16,000, which is assumed by the partnership. Carolyn's basis in her interest in the Orange Partnership is $18,000, determined as follows:

Adjusted basis of Carolyn's contributed property	$ 30,000
Less portion of mortgage assumed by Tony and Martha and treated as a distribution of money to Carolyn (75% of $16,000)	(12,000)
Basis of Carolyn's interest in Orange Partnership	$ 18,000 ∎

EXAMPLE 51

Assuming the same facts as in Example 50, Tony and Martha have a basis in their partnership interests of $108,000 and $54,000, respectively.

	Tony	Martha
Cash contribution	$100,000	$50,000
Plus portion of mortgage assumed and treated as an additional cash contribution:		
(50% of $16,000)	8,000	
(25% of $16,000)		4,000
Basis of interest in Orange Partnership	$108,000	$54,000 ∎

Partnership's Basis in Contributed Property

The *basis of property* contributed to a partnership by a partner is the adjusted basis of the property to the contributing partner at the time of the contribution.[53] Additionally, the holding period of the property for the partnership includes the period during which the property was held by the contributing partner. This is logical, since the partnership's basis in the property is the same basis the property had in the hands of the partner.[54]

EXAMPLE 52

In 2011, Roger contributed equipment with an adjusted basis of $100,000 and fair market value of $300,000 to the Red Partnership in exchange for a one-third interest in the

---

[52]§ 705(a).
[53]§ 723.
[54]§ 1223(2).

partnership. No gain or loss is recognized by Roger. The Red Partnership's basis in the equipment is $100,000. If Roger had acquired the equipment in 2005, the partnership's holding period would include the period from 2005 through 2011. ∎

PARTNERSHIP OPERATION

Measuring and Reporting Partnership Income

Although a partnership is not subject to Federal income taxation, it is required to determine its taxable income and file an income tax return for information purposes.[55] The tax return, Form 1065, is due on the fifteenth day of the fourth month following the close of the taxable year of the partnership.

In measuring and reporting partnership income, certain transactions must be segregated and reported separately on the partnership return. Items such as charitable contributions, the domestic production activities deduction, capital gains and losses, qualified dividend income, and foreign taxes are excluded from partnership taxable income and are allocated separately to the partners.[56] These items must be segregated and allocated separately because they affect the computation of various exclusions, deductions, and credits at the individual partner level. For example, one of the partners may have made personal charitable contributions in excess of the ceiling limitations on his or her individual tax return. Therefore, partnership charitable contributions are excluded from partnership taxable income and are reported separately on the partnership return.

Similar to the procedure for an S corporation, the individual components needed to determine the DPAD at the partner level must be separated. These components include each partner's pro rata portion of QPAI and the W–2 wages paid by the partnership. This information is listed on Schedule K–1 (Form 1065) and is picked up by the partner on lines 7 and 17 of his or her Form 8903 (Domestic Production Activities Deduction).

The separate stating of certain attributes of the partnership is essential as they may result in differing tax consequences when passed through to the various partners.

EXAMPLE 53

Alyssa, Madison, and Brad are equal partners in the Yellow Partnership. All parties use the calendar year for tax purposes. Among other transactions, Yellow had the following separately stated items for 2011: $30,000 in QPAI, $15,000 in long-term capital gains, and $6,000 in charitable contributions. The pass-through of these items generates the following results: Alyssa cannot use all of her $10,000 share of QPAI because of the AGI limitation; Madison's $5,000 long-term capital gain is not subject to tax (i.e., she is in a 15% or lower tax bracket); and Brad cannot benefit from his $2,000 share of the charitable contribution as he chooses not to itemize (i.e., claims the standard deduction). Thus, the pass-through of these separately stated items caused different tax consequences to the partners. ∎

A second step in the measurement and reporting process is the computation of the partnership's ordinary income or loss. The taxable income of a partnership is computed in the same manner as the taxable income of an individual taxpayer. However, a partnership is not allowed the following deductions:[57]

* The deduction for personal and dependency exemptions.
* The deduction for taxes paid to foreign countries or possessions of the United States.
* The deduction for charitable contributions.
* The deduction for net operating losses.
* The additional itemized deductions allowed individuals in §§ 211 through 219.

---

[55]§ 6031.
[56]§ 702(a).

[57]§ 703(a).

The partnership's ordinary income or loss and each of the items requiring separate treatment are reported in the partnership's information return and allocated to the partners in accordance with their distributive shares.

Limitation on Partner's Share of Losses

A partner's deduction of the distributive share of partnership losses (including capital losses) could be limited. The limitation is the adjusted basis of the partnership interest at the end of the partnership year in which the losses were incurred.

The limitation for partnership loss deductions is similar to that applicable to losses of S corporations. Like S corporation losses, partnership losses may be carried forward by the partner and utilized against future increases in the basis of the partnership interest. Such increases might result from additional capital contributions to the partnership, from additional partnership liabilities, or from future partnership income. Unlike S corporations, however, loans to the entity cannot be utilized by a partner to absorb the pass-through of losses.

EXAMPLE 54

Florence and Donald do business as the Green Partnership, sharing profits and losses equally. All parties use the calendar year for tax purposes. As of January 1, 2011, Florence's basis in her partnership interest is $25,000. The partnership sustained an operating loss of $80,000 in 2011 and earned a profit of $70,000 in 2012. For the calendar year 2011, Florence may claim only $25,000 of her $40,000 distributive share of the partnership loss (one-half of the $80,000 loss). As a result, the basis in her partnership interest is reduced to zero as of January 1, 2012, and she must carry forward the remaining $15,000 of partnership losses. ■

EXAMPLE 55

Assuming the same facts as in Example 54, what are the income tax consequences for Florence in 2012? Since the partnership earned a profit of $70,000 for the calendar year 2012, Florence reports income from the partnership of $20,000 ($35,000 distributive share of income for 2012 less the $15,000 loss not allowed for 2011). The adjusted basis of her partnership interest now becomes $20,000. ■

Transactions between Partner and Partnership

A partner engaging in a transaction with the partnership is generally regarded as a nonpartner or outsider. However, the Code includes certain exceptions to prevent unwarranted tax avoidance in related-party situations. For instance, losses from the sale or exchange of property are disallowed if they arise in either of the following cases:

• Between a partnership and a person whose direct or indirect interest in the capital or profits of the partnership is more than 50 percent.
• Between two partnerships in which the same persons own more than a 50 percent interest in the capital or profits.[58]

An indirect interest includes those owned by family members (e.g., parents, children, brothers, and sisters).

EXAMPLE 56

Michael, Samantha, and Sarah (brother and sisters) are equal partners in the Beige Partnership. For purposes of the 50% related-party rules described above, each partner indirectly owns the interests of the others. Thus, Michael has a 100% interest (i.e., his one-third *direct* interest plus the two-thirds *indirect* interests of his sisters) in the Beige Partnership. ■

---

[58]§ 707(b)(1).

In a related-party situation, if one of the purchasers later sells the property, any gain realized will be recognized only to the extent that it exceeds the loss previously disallowed.

EXAMPLE 57

Pat owns a 60% interest in the capital and profits of the Rose Partnership. In the current year, Pat sells property with an adjusted basis of $50,000 to the partnership for its fair market value of $35,000. The $15,000 loss is not deductible since Pat's ownership interest is more than 50%. If the Rose Partnership later sells the property for $40,000, none of the $5,000 gain (sale price of $40,000 less adjusted basis to partnership of $35,000) will be recognized since it is offset by $5,000 of the previously disallowed loss of $15,000. The unused loss of $10,000, however, is of no tax benefit either to the partnership or to Pat. ∎

Payments made by a partnership to one of its partners for services rendered or for the use of capital, to the extent they are determined without regard to the income of the partnership, are treated by the partnership in the same manner as payments made to a person who is not a partner. Referred to as **guaranteed payments**, these are generally deductible by the partnership as a business expense.[59] The payments must be reported as ordinary income by the receiving partner and do not affect the partner's basis in the partnership interest. Their deductibility distinguishes guaranteed payments from a partner's distributive share of income that is not deductible by the partnership.

EXAMPLE 58

Under the terms of the Silver Partnership agreement, Kim is entitled to a fixed annual salary of $60,000 without regard to the income of the partnership. He is also to share in the profits and losses of the partnership as a one-third partner. After deducting the guaranteed payment, the partnership has $300,000 of ordinary income. Kim must include $160,000 as ordinary income on his income tax return for his tax year with or within which the partnership tax year ends ($60,000 guaranteed payment + $100,000 one-third distributive share of partnership income). ∎

Other Partnership Considerations

Complex tax provisions involving liquidating and nonliquidating distributions and the sale of a partnership interest are beyond the scope of this text and are discussed in depth in *South-Western Federal Taxation: Corporations, Partnerships, Estates, and Trusts.*

TAX PLANNING:

20.8 CORPORATE VERSUS NONCORPORATE FORMS OF BUSINESS ORGANIZATION

NONTAX CONSIDERATIONS

> **LO.10**
> Evaluate the advantages and disadvantages of the various forms for conducting a business.

The decision of which entity to use in conducting a trade or business must be weighed carefully. Of prime importance are nontax considerations, including the legal attributes of the business entity chosen. For the corporate form, those commonly include limited liability, continuity of life, free transferability of interests, and centralized management. Many, if not all, of these attributes can also be

---

[59]§ 707(c).

obtained through the use of a limited liability company. When evaluating nontax considerations, close attention must be paid to applicable state law. Many states, for example, place severe restrictions on the use of corporations to practice certain professions (e.g., medicine, law). Likewise, the legal attributes of an LLC may vary from one state to another and may not be identical to those of corporations.

TAX CONSIDERATIONS

The applicable income tax rates will affect the choice of the form of doing business. Because of the wide range of possibilities (10 to 35 percent for individuals in 2011 and 15 to 35 percent for corporations), this factor must be evaluated on a case-by-case basis. For example, the corporate form is very appealing if the anticipated taxable income falls within the 25 percent corporate bracket and the shareholder's individual bracket is 35 percent. Here, the time value of the taxes saved could make operating a business as a corporation advantageous. Do not, moreover, overlook the potential impact of state and local income taxes applicable to individuals and corporations. Also, in those states that do not have an income tax, a franchise tax can pose an added tax burden on corporations (see Chapter 1).

Unless an election is made under Subchapter S, operating as a corporation yields a potential double tax result. Corporate-source income will be taxed twice—once as earned by the corporation and again when distributed to the shareholders. The payment of a dividend does not result in a deduction to the corporation, and the receipt of a dividend generally results in income to a shareholder. In the case of closely held corporations, therefore, a strong incentive exists to avoid the payment of dividends. Instead, a premium is put on bailing out profits in some manner that is deductible by the corporation. This can be accomplished by categorizing the distributions as salaries, interest, or rent—all of which are deductible by the corporation. If not properly structured, however, these devices can generate a multitude of problems. Excessive debt, for example, can lead to its reclassification as equity (under the thin capitalization approach) with a resulting disallowance of any interest deduction. Large salaries could fail the reasonableness test, and rent payments must meet an arm's length standard.

Changes in the tax treatment of qualified dividends have interjected an additional variable that must be taken into account when structuring corporation-shareholder dealings. Prior to 2003, it made little tax difference to an individual shareholder whether a corporate distribution was classified as a dividend, interest, salary, or rent—all were fully taxed as ordinary income. After 2002, however, qualified dividends are taxed in the same manner as net long-term capital gain.[60] Thus, the maximum rate cannot exceed 15 percent (0 percent in some cases). In light of this preferential treatment of qualified dividends, effective planning becomes a matter of deciding who most needs the tax benefit. If it is the corporation, try to pay out profits in a deductible form (i.e., interest, salaries, rents). If it is the shareholder, distribute the profits as dividends. These rules apply only to *qualified* dividends and are subject to a sunset provision.[61]

Other tax considerations having a bearing on the choice of the corporate form to operate a business are summarized below:

- Corporate-source income loses its identity as it passes through the corporation to the shareholders. Thus, items possessing preferential tax treatment (e.g., interest on municipal bonds) are not taxed as such to the shareholders.
- As noted earlier, it may be difficult for shareholders to recover some or all of their investment in the corporation without a dividend income result. Recall that most corporate distributions are treated as dividends to the extent of the corporation's E & P. Structuring the capital of the corporation

---

[60]§ 1(h)(3)(B).

[61]After December 31, 2012, dividend income is scheduled to be taxed at ordinary income rates (i.e., pre-2003 tax treatment is reinstated).

to include debt is a partial solution to this problem. Thus, the shareholder-creditor could recoup part of his or her investment through the tax-free payment of principal. Too much debt, however, may lead to the debt being reclassified as equity.

- Corporate losses cannot be passed through to the shareholders.
- The domestic production activities deduction generated by the corporation is not available to its shareholders. The deduction has become even more attractive as the applicable rate has progressed from 6 percent to 9 percent.
- The liquidation of a corporation may generate tax consequences to both the corporation and its shareholders.
- The corporate form provides the shareholders with the opportunity to be treated as employees for tax purposes if they render services to the corporation. This status makes a number of attractive tax-sheltered fringe benefits available (e.g., group term life insurance). These benefits are not available to partners and sole proprietors.

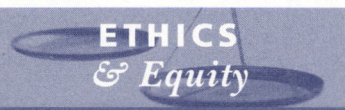

ETHICS & Equity — A YEAR-END CHANGE IN CORPORATE POLICY

Allison and Derek are the key employees and the sole shareholders of Garnet Company, a calendar year C corporation. In early 2011, they have Garnet adopt a policy that travel and entertainment expenses on behalf of the company shall be absorbed by the employee incurring the expense. Allison and Derek believe this policy will shift the deductibility of these expenses to themselves where it will provide a greater tax benefit.

In late December of 2011, Allison and Derek confer with their accountant and are appalled to learn that the employee expenses they were planning to deduct are subject to severe restrictions. First, they must be claimed as itemized deductions. Second, they are reduced by the 2 percent-of-AGI floor. Third, they are subject to a partial phaseout. As a result, it is decided to have Garnet claim these expenses. The corporate policy adopted in January is rescinded, and Garnet reimburses Allison and Derek for the expenses they paid. Garnet deducts the expenses on its Form 1120, and Allison and Derek do not report any of the reimbursement on their individual returns.

Comment on the propriety of what has occurred.

20.9 REGULAR CORPORATION VERSUS S STATUS

Due to the pass-through concept, the use of S status generally avoids the income tax at the corporate level, bringing the individual income tax into play. As noted in the previous section, the differential between the rates applicable to noncorporate and corporate taxpayers makes this a factor to be considered. The S election enables a business to operate in the corporate form, avoid the corporate income tax, and, depending on taxable income, possibly take advantage of the lower rates usually applicable to individuals. Also, losses incurred at the corporate level pass through to the shareholders, who will utilize them on their individual returns.

Electing S status can present several problems, however. First, the election is available only to small business corporations. Consequently, many corporations will not qualify for the election. Second, S corporations are subject to the rules governing regular corporations unless otherwise specified in the Code. For example, § 351 applies on the formation of an S corporation. Likewise, if the S corporation later carries out a stock redemption or is liquidated, the rules governing regular corporations apply. Third, a few states do not recognize S status for purposes of state and local taxation. Therefore, an S corporation might be subject to a state franchise tax or a state or local income tax.

20.10 USE OF AN ENTITY TO REDUCE THE FAMILY INCOME TAX BURDEN

One objective of tax planning is to keep the income from a business within the family unit but to disperse the income in such a manner as to minimize the overall tax burden. To the extent feasible, therefore, income should be shifted from higher-bracket to lower-bracket family members.

A recent legislative change, however, has raised major obstacles to shifting income to children. Beginning in 2008, the kiddie tax applies to all children under age 19 *and* to those who are full-time students under age 24.[62] As a result, shifting investment income (or capital gains) to a child provides no benefit to the extent that the income is taxed at the parents' tax rate.

Unfortunately, the income from property (a business) cannot be shifted to another without also transferring an interest in the property. If, for example, a father wants to assign income from his sole proprietorship to his children, he must form a partnership or incorporate the business. In either case, the transfer of the interest may be subject to the Federal gift tax. But any potential gift tax can be eliminated or controlled through judicious use of the annual exclusion, the election to split gifts (for married donors), and the unified tax credit (refer to the discussion of the Federal gift tax in Chapter 1).

Consequently, the first problem to be resolved becomes which form of business organization will best fit the objective of income shifting. For the partnership form, one major obstacle arises. Family partnership rules preclude the assignment of income to a family member unless capital is a material income-producing factor.[63] If not, the family member must contribute substantial or vital services. Ordinarily, capital is not a material income-producing factor if the income of the business consists principally of compensation for personal services performed by members or employees of the partnership. Conversely, capital is a material income-producing factor if the operation of the business entails a substantial investment in physical assets (e.g., inventory, plant, machinery, or equipment).

Income shifting through the use of a partnership, therefore, may be ineffectual if a personal service business is involved. In fact, it could be hopeless if the assignees are minors. The use of the corporate form usually involves no such impediment. Regardless of the nature of the business, a gift of stock carries with it the attributes of ownership. Thus, dividends paid on stock are taxed to the owner of the stock.

But what if the corporate form is utilized and the S election is made? A new hurdle arises. The Code authorizes the IRS to make adjustments in situations where shareholders are not being adequately compensated for the value of their services or capital provided to an S corporation in a family setting.[64] Thus, an S corporation suffers from the same vulnerability that exists with family partnerships.

A further factor that favors the corporate form (either a regular or an S corporation) as a device for income splitting is the ease with which it can be carried out. Presuming the entity already exists, the transfer of stock merely requires an entry in the corporation's stock ledger account. In contrast, a gift of a partnership interest probably requires an amendment to the articles of copartnership.

Regardless of the form of organization used for the business, income shifting will not take place unless the transfer is complete.[65] If the donor continues to exercise control over the interest transferred and does not recognize and protect the ownership rights of the donee, the IRS may argue that the transfer is ineffective for tax purposes. In that case, the income from the transferred interest continues to be taxed to the donor.

---

[62]The kiddie tax is restricted to *unearned* income (e.g., interest, dividends) and does not apply to *earned* income (e.g., wages, salaries). See the discussion of § 1(g) in Chapter 3.

[63]§ 704(e).

[64]§ 1366(e).

[65]*Ginsberg v. Comm.*, 74–2 USTC ¶9660, 34 AFTR 2d 74–5760, 502 F.2d 965 (CA–6, 1974), and *Michael F. Beirne*, 61 T.C. 268 (1973).

REFOCUS ON THE BIG PICTURE

CHOICE OF BUSINESS ENTITY

A principal concern of the Todd sisters is limited liability. A food preparation business involves a high risk in terms of potential liability (e.g., litigation resulting from food poisoning). This hazard is further magnified by the sisters' intention to carry minimal liability insurance coverage. To obtain limited liability, therefore, the choice of entity cannot be a regular partnership—it must be a C or S corporation or a limited liability company (LLC). (Example 1)

The next concern is the pass-through of losses to the sisters in the early years of the business. This cannot be achieved with a C corporation and is only available with an S corporation or an LLC. (Examples 1 and 44)

In making the choice between a corporation and an LLC, the future must be considered. If the business is successful, the sisters could expand. This is more easily accomplished with a corporation than an LLC. A corporation can raise additional capital for expansion by issuing more stock—even going public if necessary. Issuing additional stock may cause the S corporation election to be lost, but by then S status will have served its purpose (i.e., pass-through of losses).

When forming the corporation, the sisters should take the following into account:

- Key assets (e.g., food preparation facilities) might better be purchased by the sisters and leased to the corporation. This approach leads to a rent deduction for the corporation. (Example 21)
- A viable salary structure should be established for the services the sisters perform. This generates a salary deduction for the corporation. (Example 28)
- Interest should be charged for the funds the sisters loan to the corporation. This yields an interest deduction for the corporation. (Example 28)

If the S corporation becomes a C corporation, these rent, salary, and interest deductions will reduce the taxable income of the corporation and thereby lower any corporate income tax imposed.

KEY TERMS

C corporation, 20–4	Limited liability company (LLC), 20–3	Schedule M–3, 20–16
Check-the-box Regulations, 20–3	Liquidating distributions, 20–25	Small business corporation, 20–27
Constructive dividends, 20–23	Organizational expenditures, 20–13	Stock redemption, 20–25
Dividends received deduction, 20–11	Personal service corporation, 20–14	Thin capitalization, 20–17
Earnings and profits, 20–22	S corporation, 20–27	
Guaranteed payments, 20–37	Schedule M–1, 20–15	

DISCUSSION QUESTIONS

1. **LO.1** What is the role of state law in determining whether an entity will be classified as a corporation for Federal income tax purposes?

2. **LO.1** Under certain circumstances, an entity that qualifies under state law as a corporation may have its corporate status disregarded for tax purposes by the IRS.
   a. Why might the IRS try to disregard a corporate entity?
   b. When might such a challenge by the IRS not be successful?

3. **LO.1, 10** Why are limited liability companies advantageous?

4. **LO.1** What purpose is served by the check-the-box Regulations?

5. **LO.1** Presuming no election is made under the check-the-box Regulations, how will the following businesses be treated for Federal income tax purposes?
   a. A one-person entity not incorporated under state law.
   b. A one-person entity incorporated under state law.
   c. A multi-owner entity not incorporated under state law and possessing all of the characteristics common to corporations (i.e., continuity of life, centralized management, limited liability, and free transferability of interests).

6. **LO.1** For calendar year 2008, Mario filed a Form 8332 and elected to treat his sole proprietorship as a C corporation. For 2011, he wants to revert back to a sole proprietorship for tax purposes.
   a. Why might Mario want to make the change?
   b. Is this change permitted under the check-the-box Regulations?

7. **LO.2** Various tax attributes of the entity's operations flow through to the individual owners to be reported on their personal income tax returns.
   a. What does this statement describe?
   b. To what types of entities does it apply?

8. **LO.2, 3** Contrast the income taxation of individuals and C corporations as to each of the following:
   a. Alternative minimum tax.
   b. Dividend income.
   c. Use of the cash method of accounting.
   d. Accounting period used for tax purposes.
   e. Applicable tax rates.
   f. Due date of the tax return.
   g. Treatment of long-term capital gain.

9. **LO.2, 3** Some tax attributes (e.g., income, deductions, credits) are available to individuals only, corporations only, or both. In this connection, comment on the following:
   a. Foreign tax credit.
   b. Earned income credit.
   c. Nontaxability of certain involuntary conversions.
   d. Domestic production activities deduction.
   e. Recapture of depreciation on disposition of certain business property.
   f. Amortization of organizational expenditures.
   g. Carryback of excess capital losses.

ISSUE ID

10. **LO.2** A C corporation invests and trades in real estate. During the year, it sells a tract of land for a substantial loss. Since the land was held both for resale and as an investment, the loss could arguably be classified as ordinary or capital.
    a. In most cases, which classification will be preferable?
    b. Under what circumstances might the classification of the loss not make any immediate difference?

11. **LO.2, 8, 9** The taxpayer has excess capital losses (both short-term and long-term) for the current year. Discuss the income tax ramifications of the losses if the taxpayer is:
    a. An individual.
    b. A C corporation.
    c. An S corporation.
    d. A partnership.

ISSUE ID

12. **LO.2** In late December 2011, Gray Corporation (a calendar year C corporation) pledges a $50,000 donation to a local relief agency formed to fight AIDS in Africa. Although Gray's board of directors authorized the donation in 2011, the payment is not made until March 2012. What are the issues involved?

13. **LO.2** Colorado Corporation, a calendar year C corporation, has made charitable contributions during 2011, and it also has a charitable contribution carryover from 2010. After applying the 10% of taxable income limitation, which contribution is deducted first for 2011—the carryover from 2010 or the contributions made in 2011? What difference could it make?

14. **LO.2** If a C corporation donates ordinary income property to a qualified charity, the measure of the amount of the deduction is the adjusted basis of the property. Do you agree with this statement? Explain.

15. **LO.2** In connection with the domestic production activities deduction, comment on the following:
    a.   In applying the limitation on the deduction, the difference between individual and C corporation taxpayers.
    b.   How the deduction is determined in the case of an affiliated group of corporations.
    c.   What pass-through situations are, why they are necessary, and how they work.
    d.   Relevance to the imposition of the AMT.

16. **LO.2** What factors should be considered before making the election to forgo the carryback of a net operating loss?

17. **LO.3** One of the purposes of the dividends received deduction is to mitigate *triple taxation* of the same income. Explain.

18. **LO.3** Two small C corporations have invested in the stock of IBM Corporation. Although they own the same number and type of shares, one corporation is able to claim a larger dividends received deduction than the other. Explain why this could be possible.

ISSUE ID

19. **LO.4** Mallard Corporation was formed in December 2010 and plans to use the cash basis of accounting. Mallard incurred one-half of its organizational expenses in December 2010 and one-half in January 2011. The payment of these expenses also occurred in these two months. Do you recognize any income tax problem?

ISSUE ID

20. **LO.4** Citron Corporation has lower taxable income than Drab Corporation. Yet Citron's marginal income tax rate is 39%, while Drab's marginal rate is 35%. Explain how this variance can occur.

ISSUE ID

21. **LO.5** Cynthia and some associates want to form a corporation to develop and operate an industrial park. Cynthia is to contribute the land, which has significantly appreciated in value. She would like to recognize *some* of this gain to offset losses from other sources. In view of the rules governing the application of § 351, what do you suggest?

DECISION MAKING

22. **LO.6** A C corporation makes a cash distribution to its shareholders. Describe the tax effect on the shareholders if the distribution is:
    a.   A qualified dividend.
    b.   A return of capital that does not exceed the basis in the stock investment.
    c.   A return of capital that exceeds the basis in the stock investment.
    d.   What causes the "return of capital" result described in parts (b) and (c) above?

23. **LO.6** When a corporation distributes property as a dividend, what are the tax effects on the corporation and its shareholders under the following assumptions?
    a.   The property has declined in value.
    b.   The property has appreciated in value.

24. **LO.6** The stock of Grouse Corporation (a C corporation) is owned equally by a sister and two brothers: Mary, Rex, and Orson. During the year, the following transactions occur:
    a.   Mary sells property to Grouse Corporation.
    b.   Orson buys property from Grouse Corporation.
    c.   Rex leases property to Grouse Corporation.
    d.   Grouse Corporation pays for Orson's medical bills.
    e.   All shareholders use an airplane owned by Grouse Corporation.
    f.   Orson borrows money from Grouse Corporation.
    g.   Same as (f) with the further stipulation that no interest was provided for.
    h.   All shareholders are paid salaries by Grouse Corporation.

    Discuss any potential tax problems that these transactions might present.

ISSUE ID

25. **LO.7** Angie is the sole shareholder of Rust Corporation (a C corporation). If the corporation is liquidated, what are the tax effects on:
    a.   Rust Corporation?
    b.   Angie?

26. **LO.8** A calendar year corporation has an election under Subchapter S. What will be the effect, if any, of the following events on its S status?
    a.   The board of directors of the corporation revokes its S election in March of the current year.
    b.   A shareholder, who is a citizen of Nigeria and works in Miami, retires and moves back to Nigeria.

c.   The corporation acquires an interest in an LLC.

d.   Because of the death of a shareholder, the total number of shareholders increases from 98 to 101.

e.   A shareholder transfers her stock to a newly formed LLC.

ISSUE ID

27. **LO.8** Alexis, Brayden, Brooke, and Charles are equal shareholders in Azul Corporation (a calendar year S corporation). During the year, Azul has a short-term capital loss, qualified dividend income, charitable contributions, and qualified production activities income (with related W–2 wages). Regarding these transactions, explain the following results:

a.   The short-term capital loss results in no additional tax benefit to Alexis.

b.   Brayden pays no tax on the qualified dividends.

c.   Brooke cannot claim a deduction for the charitable contributions.

d.   Charles cannot claim *all* of the domestic production activities deduction.

ISSUE ID

28. **LO.8** Tracy and Marvin are equal shareholders in Rojo Company, a calendar year S corporation. Each paid the same amount when they originally acquired the stock several years ago. In the current year, Rojo has an operating loss. Tracy can deduct *all* of her share of the loss, but Marvin cannot. Explain the difference in the result.

29. **LO.9** How do changes in the liabilities of a partnership affect the basis of a partnership interest?

30. **LO.9** Indicate whether each of the following will increase (+), decrease (−), or have no effect (*NE*) on a partner's basis in a partnership interest:

a.   Operating loss of the partnership.

b.   Capital gains of the partnership.

c.   Tax-exempt income of the partnership.

d.   Partnership expenditures that are not deductible in computing taxable income.

e.   Withdrawals by a partner that *are not* guaranteed payments.

f.   Withdrawals by a partner that *are* guaranteed payments.

ISSUE ID

31. **LO.9** Blaine, Cassie, and Kirstin are equal partners in the Maize Partnership. During the year, Maize has qualified dividends, charitable contributions, and a domestic production activities deduction. Explain the following results:

a.   Blaine pays less tax than Cassie and Kirstin on his share of the qualified dividends.

b.   Cassie cannot deduct any of her share of the charitable contributions.

c.   Kirstin has a larger domestic production activities deduction than either Blaine or Cassie.

32. **LO.9** To what extent can partners deduct their shares of partnership operating losses?

a.   Can the capital losses of a partnership be included?

b.   Can losses be applied against any loans partners may have made to the partnership?

ISSUE ID

33. **LO.9** Carlos and his parents are equal partners in the Puce Partnership. Carlos sells property to Puce for a realized loss. Puce later sells the property to a third party (i.e., an outsider) for a realized gain. Identify the issues involved.

34. **LO.9** What are guaranteed payments? When might such payments be used?

PROBLEMS

35. **LO.2** Siskin has the following capital asset transactions during 2011:

Long-term capital gain	$6,000
Short-term capital gain	2,000

Further, Siskin has an excess capital loss carryforward of $4,000 from 2010.

a.   What are the tax consequences of these transactions if the $4,000 loss is long term and Siskin is an individual? Siskin is a C corporation?

b.   What are the tax consequences of these transactions if the $4,000 loss is short term and Siskin is an individual? Siskin is a C corporation?

36. **LO.2, 8** Taupe, a calendar year taxpayer, began business in January 2010. It had a short-term capital gain of $6,000 in 2010 and a long-term capital loss of $11,000 in 2011. For

both years, Taupe had an operating profit in excess of $100,000. How are these capital gain and loss transactions handled for income tax purposes if Taupe is:
   a. An individual?
   b. A C corporation?
   c. An S corporation?

37. **LO.2** On December 7, 2011, Kestrel Company (a calendar year taxpayer) authorizes a cash donation of $40,000 to the Memphis Public Library. The pledge is carried out as follows: $10,000 on December 14, 2011; $25,000 on February 14, 2012; and $5,000 on April 14, 2012. What are the alternatives for the year of the charitable contribution deduction if Kestrel is:
   a. An accrual basis partnership?
   b. An accrual basis C corporation?
   c. What is the result under parts (a) and (b) if Kestrel is a cash basis taxpayer?

38. **LO.2** During 2011, Rail Corporation (a C corporation) had the following transactions:

Income from operations	$400,000
Expenses from operations	325,000
Dividends from domestic corporations (less than 20% ownership)	20,000
Dividends received deduction (70% × $20,000)	14,000
Unused short-term capital loss from 2009 (there are no capital gains in 2010 and 2011)	2,500
NOL carryover from 2010	30,000

In June 2011, Rail made a contribution to a qualified charitable organization of $11,500 in cash (not included in any of the items listed above).
   a. How much, if any, of the contribution can be claimed as a deduction for 2011?
   b. What happens to any portion not deductible for 2011?

39. **LO.2** Auburn Company manufactures and sells furnishings for hospitals (e.g., special needs bathroom fixtures). In the current year, it donates some of its inventory to a newly constructed hospice. The hospice is adjacent to a cancer treatment center and is intended to care for indigent and terminal patients. The property donated has an adjusted basis of $40,000 and a fair market value of $90,000. What is the amount of the charitable contribution deduction if Auburn is a:
   a. Sole proprietorship?
   b. C corporation?
   c. Would your answer to part (b) change if the fair market value of the property is $121,000 (not $90,000)?

40. **LO.2** For each of the following *independent* situations, determine the domestic production activities deduction (DPAD) for 2011.

Corporation	Qualified Production Activities Income	Taxable Income (without any DPAD)	Relevant W–2 Wages
Tern	$400,000	$500,000	$200,000
Sparrow	500,000	550,000	100,000
Warbler	600,000	700,000	70,000

41. **LO.3** Determine the dividends received deduction for each of the following *independent* situations. Assume the percentage of stock owned in the corporation paying the dividend is 30% for Green Corporation and less than 20% for Red Corporation and Blue Corporation.

	Red Corporation	Blue Corporation	Green Corporation
Income from operations	$3,000,000	$4,500,000	$8,000,000
Expenses of operations	2,700,000	4,800,000	8,400,000
Qualified dividends received	600,000	150,000	2,000,000

42. **LO.3** Scaup Corporation was formed on June 1, 2011, and incurred qualifying organizational expenditures. It uses a calendar year and wants to accelerate any deductions that are available. Based on this assumption, what is Scaup Corporation's deduction for 2011 if its organizational expenditures are:
    a. $4,000?
    b. $45,000?
    c. $53,000?
    d. $67,000?

43. **LO.4** In each of the following *independent* situations, determine the C corporation's Federal income tax liability for calendar year 2011.

Corporation	Taxable Income
Penguin	$ 45,000
Anhinga	58,000*
Nuthatch	75,000**
Bobwhite	115,000
Puffin	370,000
Skimmer (a personal service corporation)	120,000

   *Does not include a net short-term capital loss of $4,000.

   **Does not include a net long-term capital gain of $3,000.

44. **LO.2, 3, 4** Using the legend provided below, classify each statement.

Legend
I = Applies *only* to the income taxation of individuals
C = Applies *only* to the income taxation of C corporations
B = Applies to the income taxation of *both* individuals and C corporations
N = Applies to the income taxation of *neither* individuals nor C corporations

    a. A foreign tax credit may be available.
    b. The deduction of charitable contributions is subject to percentage limitation(s).
    c. Excess charitable contributions can be carried forward indefinitely.
    d. On the contribution of inventory to charity, the full amount of any appreciation can be claimed as a deduction.
    e. Excess capital losses can be carried forward for five years.
    f. Excess capital losses cannot be carried back.
    g. A net short-term capital gain is subject to the same tax rate as ordinary income.
    h. A domestic production activities deduction may be available.
    i. A dividends received deduction is available.
    j. The like-kind provisions of § 1031 are available.
    k. A taxpayer with a fiscal year of May 1–April 30 has a due date for filing a Federal income tax return of July 15.
    l. Estimated Federal income tax payments may be required.
    m. The determination of the alternative minimum tax may have to take into account an ACE adjustment.

45. **LO.5** Elton, Neil, Courtney, and Zelma form Ecru Corporation with the following investments:

	Basis to Transferor	Fair Market Value	Number of Shares Issued
From Elton—cash	$ 200,000	$ 200,000	200
From Neil—inventory	230,000	270,000	260
From Courtney—machinery and equipment	400,000	370,000	350
From Zelma—land and building	1,270,000	1,300,000	1,200

In addition to its stock, Ecru distributes cash as follows: $10,000 to Neil, $20,000 to Court-ney, and $100,000 to Zelma. Assume that each share of Ecru stock is worth $1,000. Regarding these transactions, provide the following information:

a. Neil's realized and recognized gain (or loss).
b. Neil's basis in the Ecru stock.
c. Ecru's basis in the inventory.
d. Courtney's realized and recognized gain (or loss).
e. Courtney's basis in the Ecru stock.
f. Ecru's basis in the machinery and equipment.
g. Zelma's realized and recognized gain (or loss).
h. Zelma's basis in the Ecru stock.
i. Ecru's basis in the land and building.

46. **LO.6** Ava is the sole shareholder of Garnet Corporation (a C corporation). At a time when Garnet has a deficit in accumulated E & P of $90,000 and current E & P of $50,000, it distributes a cash dividend of $80,000. If Ava's basis in her stock is $20,000, what are the tax consequences of the distribution to:

a. Ava?
b. Garnet Corporation?

47. **LO.6** Verde Corporation, a calendar year taxpayer, has accumulated E & P of $900,000 as of January 1, 2011. For 2011, Verde had taxable income of $360,000 and the following additional transactions:

Distributed a cash dividend to shareholders	$100,000
Received interest on State of Delaware bonds	20,000
Excess capital loss (no carryback available)	30,000
Charitable contributions (in excess of 10% limitation)	10,000
Federal income tax liability	122,400

Determine Verde's current E & P for 2011.

48. **LO.6, 10** The stock of Emerald Corporation is held equally by Barney and Faye. The shareholders would like to receive, as a dividend, value of $800,000 each. The corporation has the following assets it can spare:

DECISION MAKING

COMMUNICATIONS

Asset	Adjusted Basis to Emerald Corporation	Fair Market Value
Unimproved land	$1,040,000	$800,000
Chevron stock	480,000	800,000

Both assets are held as investments. Emerald Corporation has a capital loss carryover from the previous year of $80,000 and has accumulated E & P in excess of $2 million.

Barney and Faye have come to you for advice. Suggest an attractive tax plan to carry out what the parties want. Write a letter (addressed to Emerald Corporation at P.O. Box 940, Rochester, NY 14692) describing your plan and its tax consequences.

49. **LO.6** Justin is one of the shareholders in Flicker, a closely held family C corporation. When his basis in the stock is $120,000, Justin receives a distribution of $150,000 from Flicker. Assume that Flicker Corporation has more than $1 million in E & P. What are Justin's income tax consequences if the distribution from Flicker is treated as

a. A dividend?
b. A stock redemption (i.e., sale or exchange treatment)?

50. **LO.7** In the current year, Carmine Corporation is liquidated under the general rules of § 331 and § 336. It has cash of $200,000 and undeveloped land (basis of $100,000 and fair market value of $400,000). After taxes, Carmine distributes all remaining assets to Amy, its sole shareholder. Amy's basis in the Carmine stock is $50,000.

a. What are Carmine Corporation's income tax consequences?
b. What are Amy's income tax consequences?
c. What basis will Amy have in the land?

51. **LO.7** Ten years ago, Green Corporation purchased all of the stock of Amber Corporation for $800,000. In the current year, Amber has a basis in its assets of $900,000 and a fair market value of $800,000. Green liquidates Amber Corporation and receives all of its assets. The exception to the carryover basis rule does not apply.
    a. Does Green Corporation recognize any gain as a result of the liquidation?
    b. What is Green Corporation's basis for the assets it receives from Amber Corporation?

COMMUNICATIONS

52. **LO.8** During 2011, Junco (a calendar year, accrual basis S corporation) has the following transactions:

Sales	$1,000,000
Cost of goods sold	550,000
Long-term capital gain	5,000
Short-term capital gain	2,000
Salaries	140,000
Qualified dividends from stock investments	20,000
Rent expense	150,000
Advertising expense	70,000
Interest on City of Lancaster bonds	12,000
§ 1231 gain	22,000
Organizational expenditures	2,000
Charitable contributions	4,000
Bad debt (trade account receivable deemed to be uncollectible)	8,000
Cash dividend distributed to shareholders	110,000

    a. Determine Junco Corporation's separately stated items for 2011.
    b. Determine Junco's taxable income for 2011.
    c. Mary Allen is a 30% shareholder in the corporation. She is aware of the tax consequences of the various items listed on the Schedule K–1 (Form 1120S) she received, but does not know of their effect on basis. Since she is considering selling her stock and wants to estimate the gain or loss, she requests your help. Write a letter to Mary (470 Bay Avenue, Bedford, MA 01730) summarizing the changes to stock basis that the 2011 transactions cause.

DECISION MAKING

COMMUNICATIONS

53. **LO.8, 10** Jim Olsen owns all of the stock in Vireo, a calendar year S corporation. For calendar year 2011, Vireo anticipates an operating loss of $160,000 and could, if deemed worthwhile, sell a stock investment that would generate a $10,000 long-term capital loss. Jim has an adjusted basis of $100,000 in the Vireo stock. For the year, he has already realized a short-term capital gain of $8,000. He anticipates no other capital asset transactions and expects to be in the 33% tax bracket in 2011.

    Write a letter to Jim (112 Garden Street, Trenton, NJ 08650) suggesting a course of action that could save him some income taxes.

54. **LO.8** Ida owns 30% of the stock in Mockingbird, a calendar year S corporation. Her basis in the stock as of January 1, 2011, is $120,000. Mockingbird has an operating loss of $500,000 in 2011 and an operating profit of $600,000 in 2012. Ida withdraws $70,000 in cash from the corporation in 2012.
    a. What are Ida's tax consequences in 2011?
    b. 2012?
    c. What is Ida's basis in her Mockingbird stock as of January 1, 2012?
    d. January 1, 2013?

55. **LO.9** Guy, Alma, and Kara form the Ivory Partnership. In exchange for a 30% capital interest, Guy transfers property (basis of $200,000; fair market value of $400,000) subject to a liability of $100,000. The liability is assumed by the partnership. Alma transfers property (basis of $350,000; fair market value of $300,000) for a 30% capital interest. Kara invests cash of $400,000 for the remaining 40% capital interest. Concerning these transactions, provide the following information:
    a. Guy's recognized gain.
    b. Guy's basis in the partnership interest.
    c. Alma's recognized loss.

   d. Alma's basis in the partnership interest.
   e. Kara's basis in the partnership interest.
   f. Ivory Partnership's basis in the property transferred by Guy and Alma.

56. **LO.9** Sam has a 20% capital interest in the Gold Partnership and is entitled to a yearly guaranteed payment of $30,000. As of January 1, 2011, Sam's basis in the partnership interest is $90,000. During tax year 2011, Gold had the following transactions:

Operating profit (after consideration of guaranteed payment)	$300,000
Interest income on City of St. Louis bonds	10,000
Short-term capital loss	4,000
Long-term capital gain	6,000
Funds borrowed from bank to provide working capital	20,000

   During 2011, Sam withdrew cash of $40,000 from Gold to help cover his living expenses. What is Sam's basis in his partnership interest as of January 1, 2012?

57. **LO.9, 10** As of January 1, 2010, Norman has a basis of $90,000 in his 30% capital interest in the Plata Partnership. He and the partnership use the calendar year for tax purposes. The partnership incurs an operating loss of $450,000 for 2010 and a profit of $270,000 for 2011.
   a. How much, if any, loss may Norman recognize for 2010?
   b. How much income must Norman recognize for 2011?
   c. What basis will Norman have in his partnership interest as of January 1, 2011?
   d. What basis will Norman have in his partnership interest as of January 1, 2012?
   e. What year-end tax planning would you suggest to ensure that a partner could deduct all of his or her share of any partnership losses?

> **DECISION MAKING**

58. **LO.9** Rose owns a 65% interest in the capital and profits of the Silver Partnership. In 2011, Rose sells property (adjusted basis of $200,000) to Silver for its fair market value of $90,000. In 2012, Silver Partnership sells the same property to an outside party for $105,000.
   a. What are Rose's tax consequences on the 2011 sale?
   b. What are Silver Partnership's tax consequences on the 2012 sale?
   c. Would the answers to parts (a) and (b) change if Rose owns only a 35% interest and the other 65% interest is owned by her father? Explain.

RESEARCH PROBLEMS

Note: Solutions to Research Problems can be prepared by using the **Checkpoint**® **Student Edition** online research product, which is available to accompany this text. It is also possible to prepare solutions to the Research Problems by using tax research materials found in a standard tax library.

> **THOMSON REUTERS**
> Checkpoint® Student Edition

Research Problem 1. Aaron and Leona (father and daughter) started Pottery Heaven in the late 1990s. Shortly after beginning business, Pottery Heaven was incorporated with stock issued as follows: 700 shares to Aaron and 300 shares to Leona. The business has prospered and by 2011 is in dire need of additional space for customer parking. Fortunately, Aaron owns land adjacent to the business, which he purchased many years ago (cost basis of $40,000 and current value of $200,000). To be suitable for parking, however, the property must be cleared, graded, and paved at a cost of $100,000. To carry out this objective, the parties are considering the three following alternatives:
   a. Aaron makes a capital contribution of the property to Pottery Heaven. To make the needed improvements, Pottery Heaven borrows $100,000 from a bank.
   b. Aaron transfers the property to Pottery Heaven in exchange for 200 shares of its stock. To make the improvements, Pottery Heaven borrows $100,000 from a bank.
   c. Aaron transfers the property to Pottery Heaven in exchange for 200 shares of its stock, while Leona invests cash of $100,000 for 100 shares.

   Evaluate the tax ramifications of each of these alternatives.

Partial list of research aids:
§§ 118, 351, and 1032.
Reg. §§ 1.351–1(a)(1)(ii) and (b)(1).

Research Problem 2. In anticipation that a dividend will be declared, Garnet Corporation purchases $300,000 worth of common stock of Magenta Corporation. Of the $300,000 purchase price, $200,000 is borrowed from a bank. After the dividend is declared and paid, Garnet sells the Magenta stock for a loss. Earlier in the year, Garnet realized a capital gain from the sale of a different investment.

a. What are the hoped-for tax advantages of these transactions?

b. What can go wrong?

COMMUNICATIONS

Research Problem 3. In 2000, Claude received a distribution of $50,000 from Swallow Corporation that purported to be a return of capital. Since Claude's basis in the stock was $80,000, he reduced the basis to $30,000 and recognized no income as to the distribution. In 2005, it was determined that Swallow Corporation had been miscalculating its E & P for a number of years. As a result, the 2000 distribution it made should have been taxed to the shareholders as a dividend. Due to the expiration of the three-year statute of limitations, Claude made no adjustment to his income tax return for 2000.

In 2011, Claude sells his stock in Swallow for $300,000. He feels that he should recognize a gain of only $220,000 from the sale. Since the 2000 distribution was a dividend and not a return of capital, his stock basis should not have been reduced and should remain at the original $80,000. Claude seeks your advice on this matter.

Write a letter to Claude Romano, Box 1340, Clinton, MS 39058, explaining his position. Use layperson terminology, as your client is not well versed in tax matters.

Research Problem 4. Scott and Brooke are the sole shareholders of Tanager Company, a calendar year Subchapter S corporation. After several loss years, in December 2010 Tanager is forced to borrow $300,000 for working capital purposes. Robin State Bank makes the loan to Tanager but only after Scott and Brooke personally guarantee the debt.

Scott and Brooke deduct Tanager's $200,000 operating loss for 2010 on their individual income tax returns. Although they have a zero basis in their stock investment, they consider the guarantee of the bank loan to be debt within the meaning of § 1366(d)(1)(B).

Are Scott and Brooke correct in their reasoning? Explain.

Partial list of research aids:
Milton T. Raynor, 50 T.C. 762 (1968).
William H. Maloof, 89 TCM 1022, T.C.Memo. 2004–75.

INTERNET *activity*

Use the tax resources of the Internet to address the following questions. Do not restrict your search to the Web, but include a review of newsgroups and general reference materials, practitioner sites and resources, primary sources of the tax law, chat rooms and discussion groups, and other opportunities.

Research Problem 5. Does your state permit CPAs to practice public accounting in the corporate form? If not, can they form LLCs? What, if any, special restrictions are imposed?

Research Problem 6. Some C corporations are exempt from the application of the AMT. Review the Instructions to Form 4626 (Alternative Minimum Tax—Corporations) and be prepared to explain and illustrate the small corporation exemption.

Research Problem 7. Does your state recognize a Subchapter S election for state tax purposes? If so, does it treat out-of-state shareholders in the same way as resident shareholders?

Research Problem 8. To report its transactions for the year, a partnership must file a Form 1065 with the IRS.

a. When is this return due?

b. As is the case with individuals and corporations, can a partnership obtain an automatic six-month extension for filing the Form 1065?

c. Does a partnership need to include a Schedule M–3 with its Form 1065? Explain.

Research Problem 9. The Treasury Department's *General Explanation of the Administration's Fiscal Year 2010 Revenue Proposals* (also known as the "Green Book") lists and explains the current administration's tax agenda. Determine the recommendations regarding the following:

a. Income tax rates applicable to individuals.

b. Tax rates applicable to qualified dividends.

c. Tax treatment of long-term capital gains.

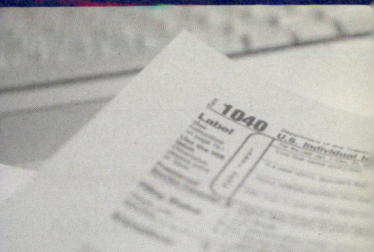

Appendix A

TAX RATE SCHEDULES AND TABLES

(The 2011 Tax Tables and 2011 Sales Tax Tables can be accessed at the IRS website: [http://www.irs.gov] when released.)

2010 Tax Rate Schedules

Single—Schedule X

If taxable income is: Over—	But not over—	The tax is:	of the amount over—
$ 0	$ 8,375	........10%	$ 0
8,375	34,000	$ 837.50 + 15%	8,375
34,000	82,400	4,681.25 + 25%	34,000
82,400	171,850	16,781.25 + 28%	82,400
171,850	373,650	41,827.25 + 33%	171,850
373,650	....	108,421.25 + 35%	373,650

Head of household—Schedule Z

If taxable income is: Over—	But not over—	The tax is:	of the amount over—
$ 0	$ 11,950	........10%	$ 0
11,950	45,550	$ 1,195.00 + 15%	11,950
45,550	117,650	6,235.00 + 25%	45,550
117,650	190,550	24,260.00 + 28%	117,650
190,550	373,650	44,672.00 + 33%	190,550
373,650	....	105,095.00 + 35%	373,650

Married filing jointly or Qualifying widow(er)—Schedule Y–1

If taxable income is: Over—	But not over—	The tax is:	of the amount over—
$ 0	$ 16,750	........10%	$ 0
16,750	68,000	$ 1,675.00 + 15%	16,750
68,000	137,300	9,362.50 + 25%	68,000
137,300	209,250	26,687.50 + 28%	137,300
209,250	373,650	46,833.50 + 33%	209,250
373,650	....	101,085.50 + 35%	373,650

Married filing separately—Schedule Y–2

If taxable income is: Over—	But not over—	The tax is:	of the amount over—
$ 0	$ 8,375	........10%	$ 0
8,375	34,000	$ 837.50 + 15%	8,375
34,000	68,650	4,681.25 + 25%	34,000
68,650	104,625	13,343.75 + 28%	68,650
104,625	186,825	23,416.75 + 33%	104,625
186,825	....	50,542.75 + 35%	186,825

2011 Tax Rate Schedules

Single—Schedule X

If taxable income is: Over—	But not over—	The tax is:	of the amount over—
$ 0	$ 8,500	........10%	$ 0
8,500	34,500	$ 850.00 + 15%	8,500
34,500	83,600	4,750.00 + 25%	34,500
83,600	174,400	17,025.00 + 28%	83,600
174,400	379,150	42,449.00 + 33%	174,400
379,150	....	110,016.50 + 35%	379,150

Head of household—Schedule Z

If taxable income is: Over—	But not over—	The tax is:	of the amount over—
$ 0	$ 12,150	........10%	$ 0
12,150	46,250	$ 1,215.00 + 15%	12,150
46,250	119,400	6,330.00 + 25%	46,250
119,400	193,350	24,617.50 + 28%	119,400
193,350	379,150	45,323.50 + 33%	193,350
379,150	....	106,637.50 + 35%	379,150

Married filing jointly or Qualifying widow(er)—Schedule Y–1

If taxable income is: Over—	But not over—	The tax is:	of the amount over—
$ 0	$ 17,000	........10%	$ 0
17,000	69,000	$ 1,700.00 + 15%	17,000
69,000	139,350	9,500.00 + 25%	69,000
139,350	212,300	27,087.50 + 28%	139,350
212,300	379,150	47,513.50 + 33%	212,300
379,150	....	102,574.00 + 35%	379,150

Married filing separately—Schedule Y–2

If taxable income is: Over—	But not over—	The tax is:	of the amount over—
$ 0	$ 8,500	........10%	$ 0
8,500	34,500	$ 850.00 + 15%	8,500
34,500	69,675	4,750.00 + 25%	34,500
69,675	106,150	13,543.75 + 28%	69,675
106,150	189,575	23,756.75 + 33%	106,150
189,575	....	51,287.00 + 35%	189,575

2010 Tax Table

See the instructions for line 44 on page 35 to see if you must use the Tax Table below to figure your tax.

Example. Mr. and Mrs. Brown are filing a joint return. Their taxable income on Form 1040, line 43, is $25,300. First, they find the $25,300–25,350 taxable income line. Next, they find the column for married filing jointly and read down the column. The amount shown where the taxable income line and filing status column meet is $2,961. This is the tax amount they should enter on Form 1040, line 44.

Sample Table

At least	But less than	Single	Married filing jointly *	Married filing separately	Head of a household
			Your tax is—		
25,200	25,250	3,365	2,946	3,365	3,186
25,250	25,300	3,373	2,954	3,373	3,194
25,300	25,350	3,380	(2,961)	3,380	3,201
25,350	25,400	3,388	2,969	3,388	3,209

If line 43 (taxable income) is—		And you are—			
At least	But less than	Single	Married filing jointly *	Married filing separately	Head of a household
			Your tax is—		
0	5	0	0	0	0
5	15	1	1	1	1
15	25	2	2	2	2
25	50	4	4	4	4
50	75	6	6	6	6
75	100	9	9	9	9
100	125	11	11	11	11
125	150	14	14	14	14
150	175	16	16	16	16
175	200	19	19	19	19
200	225	21	21	21	21
225	250	24	24	24	24
250	275	26	26	26	26
275	300	29	29	29	29
300	325	31	31	31	31
325	350	34	34	34	34
350	375	36	36	36	36
375	400	39	39	39	39
400	425	41	41	41	41
425	450	44	44	44	44
450	475	46	46	46	46
475	500	49	49	49	49
500	525	51	51	51	51
525	550	54	54	54	54
550	575	56	56	56	56
575	600	59	59	59	59
600	625	61	61	61	61
625	650	64	64	64	64
650	675	66	66	66	66
675	700	69	69	69	69
700	725	71	71	71	71
725	750	74	74	74	74
750	775	76	76	76	76
775	800	79	79	79	79
800	825	81	81	81	81
825	850	84	84	84	84
850	875	86	86	86	86
875	900	89	89	89	89
900	925	91	91	91	91
925	950	94	94	94	94
950	975	96	96	96	96
975	1,000	99	99	99	99

1,000

At least	But less than	Single	Married filing jointly *	Married filing separately	Head of a household
1,000	1,025	101	101	101	101
1,025	1,050	104	104	104	104
1,050	1,075	106	106	106	106
1,075	1,100	109	109	109	109
1,100	1,125	111	111	111	111
1,125	1,150	114	114	114	114
1,150	1,175	116	116	116	116
1,175	1,200	119	119	119	119
1,200	1,225	121	121	121	121
1,225	1,250	124	124	124	124
1,250	1,275	126	126	126	126
1,275	1,300	129	129	129	129

If line 43 (taxable income) is—		And you are—			
At least	But less than	Single	Married filing jointly *	Married filing separately	Head of a household
			Your tax is—		
1,300	1,325	131	131	131	131
1,325	1,350	134	134	134	134
1,350	1,375	136	136	136	136
1,375	1,400	139	139	139	139
1,400	1,425	141	141	141	141
1,425	1,450	144	144	144	144
1,450	1,475	146	146	146	146
1,475	1,500	149	149	149	149
1,500	1,525	151	151	151	151
1,525	1,550	154	154	154	154
1,550	1,575	156	156	156	156
1,575	1,600	159	159	159	159
1,600	1,625	161	161	161	161
1,625	1,650	164	164	164	164
1,650	1,675	166	166	166	166
1,675	1,700	169	169	169	169
1,700	1,725	171	171	171	171
1,725	1,750	174	174	174	174
1,750	1,775	176	176	176	176
1,775	1,800	179	179	179	179
1,800	1,825	181	181	181	181
1,825	1,850	184	184	184	184
1,850	1,875	186	186	186	186
1,875	1,900	189	189	189	189
1,900	1,925	191	191	191	191
1,925	1,950	194	194	194	194
1,950	1,975	196	196	196	196
1,975	2,000	199	199	199	199

2,000

At least	But less than	Single	Married filing jointly *	Married filing separately	Head of a household
2,000	2,025	201	201	201	201
2,025	2,050	204	204	204	204
2,050	2,075	206	206	206	206
2,075	2,100	209	209	209	209
2,100	2,125	211	211	211	211
2,125	2,150	214	214	214	214
2,150	2,175	216	216	216	216
2,175	2,200	219	219	219	219
2,200	2,225	221	221	221	221
2,225	2,250	224	224	224	224
2,250	2,275	226	226	226	226
2,275	2,300	229	229	229	229
2,300	2,325	231	231	231	231
2,325	2,350	234	234	234	234
2,350	2,375	236	236	236	236
2,375	2,400	239	239	239	239
2,400	2,425	241	241	241	241
2,425	2,450	244	244	244	244
2,450	2,475	246	246	246	246
2,475	2,500	249	249	249	249
2,500	2,525	251	251	251	251
2,525	2,550	254	254	254	254
2,550	2,575	256	256	256	256
2,575	2,600	259	259	259	259
2,600	2,625	261	261	261	261
2,625	2,650	264	264	264	264
2,650	2,675	266	266	266	266
2,675	2,700	269	269	269	269

If line 43 (taxable income) is—		And you are—			
At least	But less than	Single	Married filing jointly *	Married filing separately	Head of a household
			Your tax is—		
2,700	2,725	271	271	271	271
2,725	2,750	274	274	274	274
2,750	2,775	276	276	276	276
2,775	2,800	279	279	279	279
2,800	2,825	281	281	281	281
2,825	2,850	284	284	284	284
2,850	2,875	286	286	286	286
2,875	2,900	289	289	289	289
2,900	2,925	291	291	291	291
2,925	2,950	294	294	294	294
2,950	2,975	296	296	296	296
2,975	3,000	299	299	299	299

3,000

At least	But less than	Single	Married filing jointly *	Married filing separately	Head of a household
3,000	3,050	303	303	303	303
3,050	3,100	308	308	308	308
3,100	3,150	313	313	313	313
3,150	3,200	318	318	318	318
3,200	3,250	323	323	323	323
3,250	3,300	328	328	328	328
3,300	3,350	333	333	333	333
3,350	3,400	338	338	338	338
3,400	3,450	343	343	343	343
3,450	3,500	348	348	348	348
3,500	3,550	353	353	353	353
3,550	3,600	358	358	358	358
3,600	3,650	363	363	363	363
3,650	3,700	368	368	368	368
3,700	3,750	373	373	373	373
3,750	3,800	378	378	378	378
3,800	3,850	383	383	383	383
3,850	3,900	388	388	388	388
3,900	3,950	393	393	393	393
3,950	4,000	398	398	398	398

4,000

At least	But less than	Single	Married filing jointly *	Married filing separately	Head of a household
4,000	4,050	403	403	403	403
4,050	4,100	408	408	408	408
4,100	4,150	413	413	413	413
4,150	4,200	418	418	418	418
4,200	4,250	423	423	423	423
4,250	4,300	428	428	428	428
4,300	4,350	433	433	433	433
4,350	4,400	438	438	438	438
4,400	4,450	443	443	443	443
4,450	4,500	448	448	448	448
4,500	4,550	453	453	453	453
4,550	4,600	458	458	458	458
4,600	4,650	463	463	463	463
4,650	4,700	468	468	468	468
4,700	4,750	473	473	473	473
4,750	4,800	478	478	478	478
4,800	4,850	483	483	483	483
4,850	4,900	488	488	488	488
4,900	4,950	493	493	493	493
4,950	5,000	498	498	498	498

* This column must also be used by a qualifying widow(er).

(Continued on next page)

2010 Tax Table–*Continued*

If line 43 (taxable income) is— At least	But less than	And you are— Single	Married filing jointly *	Married filing separately	Head of a household
5,000					
5,000	5,050	503	503	503	503
5,050	5,100	508	508	508	508
5,100	5,150	513	513	513	513
5,150	5,200	518	518	518	518
5,200	5,250	523	523	523	523
5,250	5,300	528	528	528	528
5,300	5,350	533	533	533	533
5,350	5,400	538	538	538	538
5,400	5,450	543	543	543	543
5,450	5,500	548	548	548	548
5,500	5,550	553	553	553	553
5,550	5,600	558	558	558	558
5,600	5,650	563	563	563	563
5,650	5,700	568	568	568	568
5,700	5,750	573	573	573	573
5,750	5,800	578	578	578	578
5,800	5,850	583	583	583	583
5,850	5,900	588	588	588	588
5,900	5,950	593	593	593	593
5,950	6,000	598	598	598	598
6,000					
6,000	6,050	603	603	603	603
6,050	6,100	608	608	608	608
6,100	6,150	613	613	613	613
6,150	6,200	618	618	618	618
6,200	6,250	623	623	623	623
6,250	6,300	628	628	628	628
6,300	6,350	633	633	633	633
6,350	6,400	638	638	638	638
6,400	6,450	643	643	643	643
6,450	6,500	648	648	648	648
6,500	6,550	653	653	653	653
6,550	6,600	658	658	658	658
6,600	6,650	663	663	663	663
6,650	6,700	668	668	668	668
6,700	6,750	673	673	673	673
6,750	6,800	678	678	678	678
6,800	6,850	683	683	683	683
6,850	6,900	688	688	688	688
6,900	6,950	693	693	693	693
6,950	7,000	698	698	698	698
7,000					
7,000	7,050	703	703	703	703
7,050	7,100	708	708	708	708
7,100	7,150	713	713	713	713
7,150	7,200	718	718	718	718
7,200	7,250	723	723	723	723
7,250	7,300	728	728	728	728
7,300	7,350	733	733	733	733
7,350	7,400	738	738	738	738
7,400	7,450	743	743	743	743
7,450	7,500	748	748	748	748
7,500	7,550	753	753	753	753
7,550	7,600	758	758	758	758
7,600	7,650	763	763	763	763
7,650	7,700	768	768	768	768
7,700	7,750	773	773	773	773
7,750	7,800	778	778	778	778
7,800	7,850	783	783	783	783
7,850	7,900	788	788	788	788
7,900	7,950	793	793	793	793
7,950	8,000	798	798	798	798

If line 43 (taxable income) is— At least	But less than	And you are— Single	Married filing jointly *	Married filing separately	Head of a household
8,000					
8,000	8,050	803	803	803	803
8,050	8,100	808	808	808	808
8,100	8,150	813	813	813	813
8,150	8,200	818	818	818	818
8,200	8,250	823	823	823	823
8,250	8,300	828	828	828	828
8,300	8,350	833	833	833	833
8,350	8,400	838	838	838	838
8,400	8,450	845	843	845	843
8,450	8,500	853	848	853	848
8,500	8,550	860	853	860	853
8,550	8,600	868	858	868	858
8,600	8,650	875	863	875	863
8,650	8,700	883	868	883	868
8,700	8,750	890	873	890	873
8,750	8,800	898	878	898	878
8,800	8,850	905	883	905	883
8,850	8,900	913	888	913	888
8,900	8,950	920	893	920	893
8,950	9,000	928	898	928	898
9,000					
9,000	9,050	935	903	935	903
9,050	9,100	943	908	943	908
9,100	9,150	950	913	950	913
9,150	9,200	958	918	958	918
9,200	9,250	965	923	965	923
9,250	9,300	973	928	973	928
9,300	9,350	980	933	980	933
9,350	9,400	988	938	988	938
9,400	9,450	995	943	995	943
9,450	9,500	1,003	948	1,003	948
9,500	9,550	1,010	953	1,010	953
9,550	9,600	1,018	958	1,018	958
9,600	9,650	1,025	963	1,025	963
9,650	9,700	1,033	968	1,033	968
9,700	9,750	1,040	973	1,040	973
9,750	9,800	1,048	978	1,048	978
9,800	9,850	1,055	983	1,055	983
9,850	9,900	1,063	988	1,063	988
9,900	9,950	1,070	993	1,070	993
9,950	10,000	1,078	998	1,078	998
10,000					
10,000	10,050	1,085	1,003	1,085	1,003
10,050	10,100	1,093	1,008	1,093	1,008
10,100	10,150	1,100	1,013	1,100	1,013
10,150	10,200	1,108	1,018	1,108	1,018
10,200	10,250	1,115	1,023	1,115	1,023
10,250	10,300	1,123	1,028	1,123	1,028
10,300	10,350	1,130	1,033	1,130	1,033
10,350	10,400	1,138	1,038	1,138	1,038
10,400	10,450	1,145	1,043	1,145	1,043
10,450	10,500	1,153	1,048	1,153	1,048
10,500	10,550	1,160	1,053	1,160	1,053
10,550	10,600	1,168	1,058	1,168	1,058
10,600	10,650	1,175	1,063	1,175	1,063
10,650	10,700	1,183	1,068	1,183	1,068
10,700	10,750	1,190	1,073	1,190	1,073
10,750	10,800	1,198	1,078	1,198	1,078
10,800	10,850	1,205	1,083	1,205	1,083
10,850	10,900	1,213	1,088	1,213	1,088
10,900	10,950	1,220	1,093	1,220	1,093
10,950	11,000	1,228	1,098	1,228	1,098

If line 43 (taxable income) is— At least	But less than	And you are— Single	Married filing jointly *	Married filing separately	Head of a household
11,000					
11,000	11,050	1,235	1,103	1,235	1,103
11,050	11,100	1,243	1,108	1,243	1,108
11,100	11,150	1,250	1,113	1,250	1,113
11,150	11,200	1,258	1,118	1,258	1,118
11,200	11,250	1,265	1,123	1,265	1,123
11,250	11,300	1,273	1,128	1,273	1,128
11,300	11,350	1,280	1,133	1,280	1,133
11,350	11,400	1,288	1,138	1,288	1,138
11,400	11,450	1,295	1,143	1,295	1,143
11,450	11,500	1,303	1,148	1,303	1,148
11,500	11,550	1,310	1,153	1,310	1,153
11,550	11,600	1,318	1,158	1,318	1,158
11,600	11,650	1,325	1,163	1,325	1,163
11,650	11,700	1,333	1,168	1,333	1,168
11,700	11,750	1,340	1,173	1,340	1,173
11,750	11,800	1,348	1,178	1,348	1,178
11,800	11,850	1,355	1,183	1,355	1,183
11,850	11,900	1,363	1,188	1,363	1,188
11,900	11,950	1,370	1,193	1,370	1,193
11,950	12,000	1,378	1,198	1,378	1,199
12,000					
12,000	12,050	1,385	1,203	1,385	1,206
12,050	12,100	1,393	1,208	1,393	1,214
12,100	12,150	1,400	1,213	1,400	1,221
12,150	12,200	1,408	1,218	1,408	1,229
12,200	12,250	1,415	1,223	1,415	1,236
12,250	12,300	1,423	1,228	1,423	1,244
12,300	12,350	1,430	1,233	1,430	1,251
12,350	12,400	1,438	1,238	1,438	1,259
12,400	12,450	1,445	1,243	1,445	1,266
12,450	12,500	1,453	1,248	1,453	1,274
12,500	12,550	1,460	1,253	1,460	1,281
12,550	12,600	1,468	1,258	1,468	1,289
12,600	12,650	1,475	1,263	1,475	1,296
12,650	12,700	1,483	1,268	1,483	1,304
12,700	12,750	1,490	1,273	1,490	1,311
12,750	12,800	1,498	1,278	1,498	1,319
12,800	12,850	1,505	1,283	1,505	1,326
12,850	12,900	1,513	1,288	1,513	1,334
12,900	12,950	1,520	1,293	1,520	1,341
12,950	13,000	1,528	1,298	1,528	1,349
13,000					
13,000	13,050	1,535	1,303	1,535	1,356
13,050	13,100	1,543	1,308	1,543	1,364
13,100	13,150	1,550	1,313	1,550	1,371
13,150	13,200	1,558	1,318	1,558	1,379
13,200	13,250	1,565	1,323	1,565	1,386
13,250	13,300	1,573	1,328	1,573	1,394
13,300	13,350	1,580	1,333	1,580	1,401
13,350	13,400	1,588	1,338	1,588	1,409
13,400	13,450	1,595	1,343	1,595	1,416
13,450	13,500	1,603	1,348	1,603	1,424
13,500	13,550	1,610	1,353	1,610	1,431
13,550	13,600	1,618	1,358	1,618	1,439
13,600	13,650	1,625	1,363	1,625	1,446
13,650	13,700	1,633	1,368	1,633	1,454
13,700	13,750	1,640	1,373	1,640	1,461
13,750	13,800	1,648	1,378	1,648	1,469
13,800	13,850	1,655	1,383	1,655	1,476
13,850	13,900	1,663	1,388	1,663	1,484
13,900	13,950	1,670	1,393	1,670	1,491
13,950	14,000	1,678	1,398	1,678	1,499

* This column must also be used by a qualifying widow(er).

(Continued on next page)

2010 Tax Table–*Continued*

If line 43 (taxable income) is— At least	But less than	Single	Married filing jointly *	Married filing separately	Head of a household
			Your tax is—		
14,000					
14,000	14,050	1,685	1,403	1,685	1,506
14,050	14,100	1,693	1,408	1,693	1,514
14,100	14,150	1,700	1,413	1,700	1,521
14,150	14,200	1,708	1,418	1,708	1,529
14,200	14,250	1,715	1,423	1,715	1,536
14,250	14,300	1,723	1,428	1,723	1,544
14,300	14,350	1,730	1,433	1,730	1,551
14,350	14,400	1,738	1,438	1,738	1,559
14,400	14,450	1,745	1,443	1,745	1,566
14,450	14,500	1,753	1,448	1,753	1,574
14,500	14,550	1,760	1,453	1,760	1,581
14,550	14,600	1,768	1,458	1,768	1,589
14,600	14,650	1,775	1,463	1,775	1,596
14,650	14,700	1,783	1,468	1,783	1,604
14,700	14,750	1,790	1,473	1,790	1,611
14,750	14,800	1,798	1,478	1,798	1,619
14,800	14,850	1,805	1,483	1,805	1,626
14,850	14,900	1,813	1,488	1,813	1,634
14,900	14,950	1,820	1,493	1,820	1,641
14,950	15,000	1,828	1,498	1,828	1,649
15,000					
15,000	15,050	1,835	1,503	1,835	1,656
15,050	15,100	1,843	1,508	1,843	1,664
15,100	15,150	1,850	1,513	1,850	1,671
15,150	15,200	1,858	1,518	1,858	1,679
15,200	15,250	1,865	1,523	1,865	1,686
15,250	15,300	1,873	1,528	1,873	1,694
15,300	15,350	1,880	1,533	1,880	1,701
15,350	15,400	1,888	1,538	1,888	1,709
15,400	15,450	1,895	1,543	1,895	1,716
15,450	15,500	1,903	1,548	1,903	1,724
15,500	15,550	1,910	1,553	1,910	1,731
15,550	15,600	1,918	1,558	1,918	1,739
15,600	15,650	1,925	1,563	1,925	1,746
15,650	15,700	1,933	1,568	1,933	1,754
15,700	15,750	1,940	1,573	1,940	1,761
15,750	15,800	1,948	1,578	1,948	1,769
15,800	15,850	1,955	1,583	1,955	1,776
15,850	15,900	1,963	1,588	1,963	1,784
15,900	15,950	1,970	1,593	1,970	1,791
15,950	16,000	1,978	1,598	1,978	1,799
16,000					
16,000	16,050	1,985	1,603	1,985	1,806
16,050	16,100	1,993	1,608	1,993	1,814
16,100	16,150	2,000	1,613	2,000	1,821
16,150	16,200	2,008	1,618	2,008	1,829
16,200	16,250	2,015	1,623	2,015	1,836
16,250	16,300	2,023	1,628	2,023	1,844
16,300	16,350	2,030	1,633	2,030	1,851
16,350	16,400	2,038	1,638	2,038	1,859
16,400	16,450	2,045	1,643	2,045	1,866
16,450	16,500	2,053	1,648	2,053	1,874
16,500	16,550	2,060	1,653	2,060	1,881
16,550	16,600	2,068	1,658	2,068	1,889
16,600	16,650	2,075	1,663	2,075	1,896
16,650	16,700	2,083	1,668	2,083	1,904
16,700	16,750	2,090	1,673	2,090	1,911
16,750	16,800	2,098	1,679	2,098	1,919
16,800	16,850	2,105	1,686	2,105	1,926
16,850	16,900	2,113	1,694	2,113	1,934
16,900	16,950	2,120	1,701	2,120	1,941
16,950	17,000	2,128	1,709	2,128	1,949

If line 43 (taxable income) is— At least	But less than	Single	Married filing jointly *	Married filing separately	Head of a household
			Your tax is—		
17,000					
17,000	17,050	2,135	1,716	2,135	1,956
17,050	17,100	2,143	1,724	2,143	1,964
17,100	17,150	2,150	1,731	2,150	1,971
17,150	17,200	2,158	1,739	2,158	1,979
17,200	17,250	2,165	1,746	2,165	1,986
17,250	17,300	2,173	1,754	2,173	1,994
17,300	17,350	2,180	1,761	2,180	2,001
17,350	17,400	2,188	1,769	2,188	2,009
17,400	17,450	2,195	1,776	2,195	2,016
17,450	17,500	2,203	1,784	2,203	2,024
17,500	17,550	2,210	1,791	2,210	2,031
17,550	17,600	2,218	1,799	2,218	2,039
17,600	17,650	2,225	1,806	2,225	2,046
17,650	17,700	2,233	1,814	2,233	2,054
17,700	17,750	2,240	1,821	2,240	2,061
17,750	17,800	2,248	1,829	2,248	2,069
17,800	17,850	2,255	1,836	2,255	2,076
17,850	17,900	2,263	1,844	2,263	2,084
17,900	17,950	2,270	1,851	2,270	2,091
17,950	18,000	2,278	1,859	2,278	2,099
18,000					
18,000	18,050	2,285	1,866	2,285	2,106
18,050	18,100	2,293	1,874	2,293	2,114
18,100	18,150	2,300	1,881	2,300	2,121
18,150	18,200	2,308	1,889	2,308	2,129
18,200	18,250	2,315	1,896	2,315	2,136
18,250	18,300	2,323	1,904	2,323	2,144
18,300	18,350	2,330	1,911	2,330	2,151
18,350	18,400	2,338	1,919	2,338	2,159
18,400	18,450	2,345	1,926	2,345	2,166
18,450	18,500	2,353	1,934	2,353	2,174
18,500	18,550	2,360	1,941	2,360	2,181
18,550	18,600	2,368	1,949	2,368	2,189
18,600	18,650	2,375	1,956	2,375	2,196
18,650	18,700	2,383	1,964	2,383	2,204
18,700	18,750	2,390	1,971	2,390	2,211
18,750	18,800	2,398	1,979	2,398	2,219
18,800	18,850	2,405	1,986	2,405	2,226
18,850	18,900	2,413	1,994	2,413	2,234
18,900	18,950	2,420	2,001	2,420	2,241
18,950	19,000	2,428	2,009	2,428	2,249
19,000					
19,000	19,050	2,435	2,016	2,435	2,256
19,050	19,100	2,443	2,024	2,443	2,264
19,100	19,150	2,450	2,031	2,450	2,271
19,150	19,200	2,458	2,039	2,458	2,279
19,200	19,250	2,465	2,046	2,465	2,286
19,250	19,300	2,473	2,054	2,473	2,294
19,300	19,350	2,480	2,061	2,480	2,301
19,350	19,400	2,488	2,069	2,488	2,309
19,400	19,450	2,495	2,076	2,495	2,316
19,450	19,500	2,503	2,084	2,503	2,324
19,500	19,550	2,510	2,091	2,510	2,331
19,550	19,600	2,518	2,099	2,518	2,339
19,600	19,650	2,525	2,106	2,525	2,346
19,650	19,700	2,533	2,114	2,533	2,354
19,700	19,750	2,540	2,121	2,540	2,361
19,750	19,800	2,548	2,129	2,548	2,369
19,800	19,850	2,555	2,136	2,555	2,376
19,850	19,900	2,563	2,144	2,563	2,384
19,900	19,950	2,570	2,151	2,570	2,391
19,950	20,000	2,578	2,159	2,578	2,399

If line 43 (taxable income) is— At least	But less than	Single	Married filing jointly *	Married filing separately	Head of a household
			Your tax is—		
20,000					
20,000	20,050	2,585	2,166	2,585	2,406
20,050	20,100	2,593	2,174	2,593	2,414
20,100	20,150	2,600	2,181	2,600	2,421
20,150	20,200	2,608	2,189	2,608	2,429
20,200	20,250	2,615	2,196	2,615	2,436
20,250	20,300	2,623	2,204	2,623	2,444
20,300	20,350	2,630	2,211	2,630	2,451
20,350	20,400	2,638	2,219	2,638	2,459
20,400	20,450	2,645	2,226	2,645	2,466
20,450	20,500	2,653	2,234	2,653	2,474
20,500	20,550	2,660	2,241	2,660	2,481
20,550	20,600	2,668	2,249	2,668	2,489
20,600	20,650	2,675	2,256	2,675	2,496
20,650	20,700	2,683	2,264	2,683	2,504
20,700	20,750	2,690	2,271	2,690	2,511
20,750	20,800	2,698	2,279	2,698	2,519
20,800	20,850	2,705	2,286	2,705	2,526
20,850	20,900	2,713	2,294	2,713	2,534
20,900	20,950	2,720	2,301	2,720	2,541
20,950	21,000	2,728	2,309	2,728	2,549
21,000					
21,000	21,050	2,735	2,316	2,735	2,556
21,050	21,100	2,743	2,324	2,743	2,564
21,100	21,150	2,750	2,331	2,750	2,571
21,150	21,200	2,758	2,339	2,758	2,579
21,200	21,250	2,765	2,346	2,765	2,586
21,250	21,300	2,773	2,354	2,773	2,594
21,300	21,350	2,780	2,361	2,780	2,601
21,350	21,400	2,788	2,369	2,788	2,609
21,400	21,450	2,795	2,376	2,795	2,616
21,450	21,500	2,803	2,384	2,803	2,624
21,500	21,550	2,810	2,391	2,810	2,631
21,550	21,600	2,818	2,399	2,818	2,639
21,600	21,650	2,825	2,406	2,825	2,646
21,650	21,700	2,833	2,414	2,833	2,654
21,700	21,750	2,840	2,421	2,840	2,661
21,750	21,800	2,848	2,429	2,848	2,669
21,800	21,850	2,855	2,436	2,855	2,676
21,850	21,900	2,863	2,444	2,863	2,684
21,900	21,950	2,870	2,451	2,870	2,691
21,950	22,000	2,878	2,459	2,878	2,699
22,000					
22,000	22,050	2,885	2,466	2,885	2,706
22,050	22,100	2,893	2,474	2,893	2,714
22,100	22,150	2,900	2,481	2,900	2,721
22,150	22,200	2,908	2,489	2,908	2,729
22,200	22,250	2,915	2,496	2,915	2,736
22,250	22,300	2,923	2,504	2,923	2,744
22,300	22,350	2,930	2,511	2,930	2,751
22,350	22,400	2,938	2,519	2,938	2,759
22,400	22,450	2,945	2,526	2,945	2,766
22,450	22,500	2,953	2,534	2,953	2,774
22,500	22,550	2,960	2,541	2,960	2,781
22,550	22,600	2,968	2,549	2,968	2,789
22,600	22,650	2,975	2,556	2,975	2,796
22,650	22,700	2,983	2,564	2,983	2,804
22,700	22,750	2,990	2,571	2,990	2,811
22,750	22,800	2,998	2,579	2,998	2,819
22,800	22,850	3,005	2,586	3,005	2,826
22,850	22,900	3,013	2,594	3,013	2,834
22,900	22,950	3,020	2,601	3,020	2,841
22,950	23,000	3,028	2,609	3,028	2,849

* This column must also be used by a qualifying widow(er).

(Continued on next page)

2010 Tax Table–Continued

23,000

If line 43 (taxable income) is— At least	But less than	Single	Married filing jointly*	Married filing separately	Head of a household
23,000	23,050	3,035	2,616	3,035	2,856
23,050	23,100	3,043	2,624	3,043	2,864
23,100	23,150	3,050	2,631	3,050	2,871
23,150	23,200	3,058	2,639	3,058	2,879
23,200	23,250	3,065	2,646	3,065	2,886
23,250	23,300	3,073	2,654	3,073	2,894
23,300	23,350	3,080	2,661	3,080	2,901
23,350	23,400	3,088	2,669	3,088	2,909
23,400	23,450	3,095	2,676	3,095	2,916
23,450	23,500	3,103	2,684	3,103	2,924
23,500	23,550	3,110	2,691	3,110	2,931
23,550	23,600	3,118	2,699	3,118	2,939
23,600	23,650	3,125	2,706	3,125	2,946
23,650	23,700	3,133	2,714	3,133	2,954
23,700	23,750	3,140	2,721	3,140	2,961
23,750	23,800	3,148	2,729	3,148	2,969
23,800	23,850	3,155	2,736	3,155	2,976
23,850	23,900	3,163	2,744	3,163	2,984
23,900	23,950	3,170	2,751	3,170	2,991
23,950	24,000	3,178	2,759	3,178	2,999

24,000

At least	But less than	Single	Married filing jointly*	Married filing separately	Head of a household
24,000	24,050	3,185	2,766	3,185	3,006
24,050	24,100	3,193	2,774	3,193	3,014
24,100	24,150	3,200	2,781	3,200	3,021
24,150	24,200	3,208	2,789	3,208	3,029
24,200	24,250	3,215	2,796	3,215	3,036
24,250	24,300	3,223	2,804	3,223	3,044
24,300	24,350	3,230	2,811	3,230	3,051
24,350	24,400	3,238	2,819	3,238	3,059
24,400	24,450	3,245	2,826	3,245	3,066
24,450	24,500	3,253	2,834	3,253	3,074
24,500	24,550	3,260	2,841	3,260	3,081
24,550	24,600	3,268	2,849	3,268	3,089
24,600	24,650	3,275	2,856	3,275	3,096
24,650	24,700	3,283	2,864	3,283	3,104
24,700	24,750	3,290	2,871	3,290	3,111
24,750	24,800	3,298	2,879	3,298	3,119
24,800	24,850	3,305	2,886	3,305	3,126
24,850	24,900	3,313	2,894	3,313	3,134
24,900	24,950	3,320	2,901	3,320	3,141
24,950	25,000	3,328	2,909	3,328	3,149

25,000

At least	But less than	Single	Married filing jointly*	Married filing separately	Head of a household
25,000	25,050	3,335	2,916	3,335	3,156
25,050	25,100	3,343	2,924	3,343	3,164
25,100	25,150	3,350	2,931	3,350	3,171
25,150	25,200	3,358	2,939	3,358	3,179
25,200	25,250	3,365	2,946	3,365	3,186
25,250	25,300	3,373	2,954	3,373	3,194
25,300	25,350	3,380	2,961	3,380	3,201
25,350	25,400	3,388	2,969	3,388	3,209
25,400	25,450	3,395	2,976	3,395	3,216
25,450	25,500	3,403	2,984	3,403	3,224
25,500	25,550	3,410	2,991	3,410	3,231
25,550	25,600	3,418	2,999	3,418	3,239
25,600	25,650	3,425	3,006	3,425	3,246
25,650	25,700	3,433	3,014	3,433	3,254
25,700	25,750	3,440	3,021	3,440	3,261
25,750	25,800	3,448	3,029	3,448	3,269
25,800	25,850	3,455	3,036	3,455	3,276
25,850	25,900	3,463	3,044	3,463	3,284
25,900	25,950	3,470	3,051	3,470	3,291
25,950	26,000	3,478	3,059	3,478	3,299

26,000

At least	But less than	Single	Married filing jointly*	Married filing separately	Head of a household
26,000	26,050	3,485	3,066	3,485	3,306
26,050	26,100	3,493	3,074	3,493	3,314
26,100	26,150	3,500	3,081	3,500	3,321
26,150	26,200	3,508	3,089	3,508	3,329
26,200	26,250	3,515	3,096	3,515	3,336
26,250	26,300	3,523	3,104	3,523	3,344
26,300	26,350	3,530	3,111	3,530	3,351
26,350	26,400	3,538	3,119	3,538	3,359
26,400	26,450	3,545	3,126	3,545	3,366
26,450	26,500	3,553	3,134	3,553	3,374
26,500	26,550	3,560	3,141	3,560	3,381
26,550	26,600	3,568	3,149	3,568	3,389
26,600	26,650	3,575	3,156	3,575	3,396
26,650	26,700	3,583	3,164	3,583	3,404
26,700	26,750	3,590	3,171	3,590	3,411
26,750	26,800	3,598	3,179	3,598	3,419
26,800	26,850	3,605	3,186	3,605	3,426
26,850	26,900	3,613	3,194	3,613	3,434
26,900	26,950	3,620	3,201	3,620	3,441
26,950	27,000	3,628	3,209	3,628	3,449

27,000

At least	But less than	Single	Married filing jointly*	Married filing separately	Head of a household
27,000	27,050	3,635	3,216	3,635	3,456
27,050	27,100	3,643	3,224	3,643	3,464
27,100	27,150	3,650	3,231	3,650	3,471
27,150	27,200	3,658	3,239	3,658	3,479
27,200	27,250	3,665	3,246	3,665	3,486
27,250	27,300	3,673	3,254	3,673	3,494
27,300	27,350	3,680	3,261	3,680	3,501
27,350	27,400	3,688	3,269	3,688	3,509
27,400	27,450	3,695	3,276	3,695	3,516
27,450	27,500	3,703	3,284	3,703	3,524
27,500	27,550	3,710	3,291	3,710	3,531
27,550	27,600	3,718	3,299	3,718	3,539
27,600	27,650	3,725	3,306	3,725	3,546
27,650	27,700	3,733	3,314	3,733	3,554
27,700	27,750	3,740	3,321	3,740	3,561
27,750	27,800	3,748	3,329	3,748	3,569
27,800	27,850	3,755	3,336	3,755	3,576
27,850	27,900	3,763	3,344	3,763	3,584
27,900	27,950	3,770	3,351	3,770	3,591
27,950	28,000	3,778	3,359	3,778	3,599

28,000

At least	But less than	Single	Married filing jointly*	Married filing separately	Head of a household
28,000	28,050	3,785	3,366	3,785	3,606
28,050	28,100	3,793	3,374	3,793	3,614
28,100	28,150	3,800	3,381	3,800	3,621
28,150	28,200	3,808	3,389	3,808	3,629
28,200	28,250	3,815	3,396	3,815	3,636
28,250	28,300	3,823	3,404	3,823	3,644
28,300	28,350	3,830	3,411	3,830	3,651
28,350	28,400	3,838	3,419	3,838	3,659
28,400	28,450	3,845	3,426	3,845	3,666
28,450	28,500	3,853	3,434	3,853	3,674
28,500	28,550	3,860	3,441	3,860	3,681
28,550	28,600	3,868	3,449	3,868	3,689
28,600	28,650	3,875	3,456	3,875	3,696
28,650	28,700	3,883	3,464	3,883	3,704
28,700	28,750	3,890	3,471	3,890	3,711
28,750	28,800	3,898	3,479	3,898	3,719
28,800	28,850	3,905	3,486	3,905	3,726
28,850	28,900	3,913	3,494	3,913	3,734
28,900	28,950	3,920	3,501	3,920	3,741
28,950	29,000	3,928	3,509	3,928	3,749

29,000

At least	But less than	Single	Married filing jointly*	Married filing separately	Head of a household
29,000	29,050	3,935	3,516	3,935	3,756
29,050	29,100	3,943	3,524	3,943	3,764
29,100	29,150	3,950	3,531	3,950	3,771
29,150	29,200	3,958	3,539	3,958	3,779
29,200	29,250	3,965	3,546	3,965	3,786
29,250	29,300	3,973	3,554	3,973	3,794
29,300	29,350	3,980	3,561	3,980	3,801
29,350	29,400	3,988	3,569	3,988	3,809
29,400	29,450	3,995	3,576	3,995	3,816
29,450	29,500	4,003	3,584	4,003	3,824
29,500	29,550	4,010	3,591	4,010	3,831
29,550	29,600	4,018	3,599	4,018	3,839
29,600	29,650	4,025	3,606	4,025	3,846
29,650	29,700	4,033	3,614	4,033	3,854
29,700	29,750	4,040	3,621	4,040	3,861
29,750	29,800	4,048	3,629	4,048	3,869
29,800	29,850	4,055	3,636	4,055	3,876
29,850	29,900	4,063	3,644	4,063	3,884
29,900	29,950	4,070	3,651	4,070	3,891
29,950	30,000	4,078	3,659	4,078	3,899

30,000

At least	But less than	Single	Married filing jointly*	Married filing separately	Head of a household
30,000	30,050	4,085	3,666	4,085	3,906
30,050	30,100	4,093	3,674	4,093	3,914
30,100	30,150	4,100	3,681	4,100	3,921
30,150	30,200	4,108	3,689	4,108	3,929
30,200	30,250	4,115	3,696	4,115	3,936
30,250	30,300	4,123	3,704	4,123	3,944
30,300	30,350	4,130	3,711	4,130	3,951
30,350	30,400	4,138	3,719	4,138	3,959
30,400	30,450	4,145	3,726	4,145	3,966
30,450	30,500	4,153	3,734	4,153	3,974
30,500	30,550	4,160	3,741	4,160	3,981
30,550	30,600	4,168	3,749	4,168	3,989
30,600	30,650	4,175	3,756	4,175	3,996
30,650	30,700	4,183	3,764	4,183	4,004
30,700	30,750	4,190	3,771	4,190	4,011
30,750	30,800	4,198	3,779	4,198	4,019
30,800	30,850	4,205	3,786	4,205	4,026
30,850	30,900	4,213	3,794	4,213	4,034
30,900	30,950	4,220	3,801	4,220	4,041
30,950	31,000	4,228	3,809	4,228	4,049

31,000

At least	But less than	Single	Married filing jointly*	Married filing separately	Head of a household
31,000	31,050	4,235	3,816	4,235	4,056
31,050	31,100	4,243	3,824	4,243	4,064
31,100	31,150	4,250	3,831	4,250	4,071
31,150	31,200	4,258	3,839	4,258	4,079
31,200	31,250	4,265	3,846	4,265	4,086
31,250	31,300	4,273	3,854	4,273	4,094
31,300	31,350	4,280	3,861	4,280	4,101
31,350	31,400	4,288	3,869	4,288	4,109
31,400	31,450	4,295	3,876	4,295	4,116
31,450	31,500	4,303	3,884	4,303	4,124
31,500	31,550	4,310	3,891	4,310	4,131
31,550	31,600	4,318	3,899	4,318	4,139
31,600	31,650	4,325	3,906	4,325	4,146
31,650	31,700	4,333	3,914	4,333	4,154
31,700	31,750	4,340	3,921	4,340	4,161
31,750	31,800	4,348	3,929	4,348	4,169
31,800	31,850	4,355	3,936	4,355	4,176
31,850	31,900	4,363	3,944	4,363	4,184
31,900	31,950	4,370	3,951	4,370	4,191
31,950	32,000	4,378	3,959	4,378	4,199

* This column must also be used by a qualifying widow(er).

(Continued on next page)

2010 Tax Table–Continued

If line 43 (taxable income) is— At least	But less than	Single	Married filing jointly *	Married filing separately	Head of a household *
32,000					
32,000	32,050	4,385	3,966	4,385	4,206
32,050	32,100	4,393	3,974	4,393	4,214
32,100	32,150	4,400	3,981	4,400	4,221
32,150	32,200	4,408	3,989	4,408	4,229
32,200	32,250	4,415	3,996	4,415	4,236
32,250	32,300	4,423	4,004	4,423	4,244
32,300	32,350	4,430	4,011	4,430	4,251
32,350	32,400	4,438	4,019	4,438	4,259
32,400	32,450	4,445	4,026	4,445	4,266
32,450	32,500	4,453	4,034	4,453	4,274
32,500	32,550	4,460	4,041	4,460	4,281
32,550	32,600	4,468	4,049	4,468	4,289
32,600	32,650	4,475	4,056	4,475	4,296
32,650	32,700	4,483	4,064	4,483	4,304
32,700	32,750	4,490	4,071	4,490	4,311
32,750	32,800	4,498	4,079	4,498	4,319
32,800	32,850	4,505	4,086	4,505	4,326
32,850	32,900	4,513	4,094	4,513	4,334
32,900	32,950	4,520	4,101	4,520	4,341
32,950	33,000	4,528	4,109	4,528	4,349
33,000					
33,000	33,050	4,535	4,116	4,535	4,356
33,050	33,100	4,543	4,124	4,543	4,364
33,100	33,150	4,550	4,131	4,550	4,371
33,150	33,200	4,558	4,139	4,558	4,379
33,200	33,250	4,565	4,146	4,565	4,386
33,250	33,300	4,573	4,154	4,573	4,394
33,300	33,350	4,580	4,161	4,580	4,401
33,350	33,400	4,588	4,169	4,588	4,409
33,400	33,450	4,595	4,176	4,595	4,416
33,450	33,500	4,603	4,184	4,603	4,424
33,500	33,550	4,610	4,191	4,610	4,431
33,550	33,600	4,618	4,199	4,618	4,439
33,600	33,650	4,625	4,206	4,625	4,446
33,650	33,700	4,633	4,214	4,633	4,454
33,700	33,750	4,640	4,221	4,640	4,461
33,750	33,800	4,648	4,229	4,648	4,469
33,800	33,850	4,655	4,236	4,655	4,476
33,850	33,900	4,663	4,244	4,663	4,484
33,900	33,950	4,670	4,251	4,670	4,491
33,950	34,000	4,678	4,259	4,678	4,499
34,000					
34,000	34,050	4,688	4,266	4,688	4,506
34,050	34,100	4,700	4,274	4,700	4,514
34,100	34,150	4,713	4,281	4,713	4,521
34,150	34,200	4,725	4,289	4,725	4,529
34,200	34,250	4,738	4,296	4,738	4,536
34,250	34,300	4,750	4,304	4,750	4,544
34,300	34,350	4,763	4,311	4,763	4,551
34,350	34,400	4,775	4,319	4,775	4,559
34,400	34,450	4,788	4,326	4,788	4,566
34,450	34,500	4,800	4,334	4,800	4,574
34,500	34,550	4,813	4,341	4,813	4,581
34,550	34,600	4,825	4,349	4,825	4,589
34,600	34,650	4,838	4,356	4,838	4,596
34,650	34,700	4,850	4,364	4,850	4,604
34,700	34,750	4,863	4,371	4,863	4,611
34,750	34,800	4,875	4,379	4,875	4,619
34,800	34,850	4,888	4,386	4,888	4,626
34,850	34,900	4,900	4,394	4,900	4,634
34,900	34,950	4,913	4,401	4,913	4,641
34,950	35,000	4,925	4,409	4,925	4,649

If line 43 (taxable income) is— At least	But less than	Single	Married filing jointly *	Married filing separately	Head of a household *
35,000					
35,000	35,050	4,938	4,416	4,938	4,656
35,050	35,100	4,950	4,424	4,950	4,664
35,100	35,150	4,963	4,431	4,963	4,671
35,150	35,200	4,975	4,439	4,975	4,679
35,200	35,250	4,988	4,446	4,988	4,686
35,250	35,300	5,000	4,454	5,000	4,694
35,300	35,350	5,013	4,461	5,013	4,701
35,350	35,400	5,025	4,469	5,025	4,709
35,400	35,450	5,038	4,476	5,038	4,716
35,450	35,500	5,050	4,484	5,050	4,724
35,500	35,550	5,063	4,491	5,063	4,731
35,550	35,600	5,075	4,499	5,075	4,739
35,600	35,650	5,088	4,506	5,088	4,746
35,650	35,700	5,100	4,514	5,100	4,754
35,700	35,750	5,113	4,521	5,113	4,761
35,750	35,800	5,125	4,529	5,125	4,769
35,800	35,850	5,138	4,536	5,138	4,776
35,850	35,900	5,150	4,544	5,150	4,784
35,900	35,950	5,163	4,551	5,163	4,791
35,950	36,000	5,175	4,559	5,175	4,799
36,000					
36,000	36,050	5,188	4,566	5,188	4,806
36,050	36,100	5,200	4,574	5,200	4,814
36,100	36,150	5,213	4,581	5,213	4,821
36,150	36,200	5,225	4,589	5,225	4,829
36,200	36,250	5,238	4,596	5,238	4,836
36,250	36,300	5,250	4,604	5,250	4,844
36,300	36,350	5,263	4,611	5,263	4,851
36,350	36,400	5,275	4,619	5,275	4,859
36,400	36,450	5,288	4,626	5,288	4,866
36,450	36,500	5,300	4,634	5,300	4,874
36,500	36,550	5,313	4,641	5,313	4,881
36,550	36,600	5,325	4,649	5,325	4,889
36,600	36,650	5,338	4,656	5,338	4,896
36,650	36,700	5,350	4,664	5,350	4,904
36,700	36,750	5,363	4,671	5,363	4,911
36,750	36,800	5,375	4,679	5,375	4,919
36,800	36,850	5,388	4,686	5,388	4,926
36,850	36,900	5,400	4,694	5,400	4,934
36,900	36,950	5,413	4,701	5,413	4,941
36,950	37,000	5,425	4,709	5,425	4,949
37,000					
37,000	37,050	5,438	4,716	5,438	4,956
37,050	37,100	5,450	4,724	5,450	4,964
37,100	37,150	5,463	4,731	5,463	4,971
37,150	37,200	5,475	4,739	5,475	4,979
37,200	37,250	5,488	4,746	5,488	4,986
37,250	37,300	5,500	4,754	5,500	4,994
37,300	37,350	5,513	4,761	5,513	5,001
37,350	37,400	5,525	4,769	5,525	5,009
37,400	37,450	5,538	4,776	5,538	5,016
37,450	37,500	5,550	4,784	5,550	5,024
37,500	37,550	5,563	4,791	5,563	5,031
37,550	37,600	5,575	4,799	5,575	5,039
37,600	37,650	5,588	4,806	5,588	5,046
37,650	37,700	5,600	4,814	5,600	5,054
37,700	37,750	5,613	4,821	5,613	5,061
37,750	37,800	5,625	4,829	5,625	5,069
37,800	37,850	5,638	4,836	5,638	5,076
37,850	37,900	5,650	4,844	5,650	5,084
37,900	37,950	5,663	4,851	5,663	5,091
37,950	38,000	5,675	4,859	5,675	5,099

If line 43 (taxable income) is— At least	But less than	Single	Married filing jointly *	Married filing separately	Head of a household *
38,000					
38,000	38,050	5,688	4,866	5,688	5,106
38,050	38,100	5,700	4,874	5,700	5,114
38,100	38,150	5,713	4,881	5,713	5,121
38,150	38,200	5,725	4,889	5,725	5,129
38,200	38,250	5,738	4,896	5,738	5,136
38,250	38,300	5,750	4,904	5,750	5,144
38,300	38,350	5,763	4,911	5,763	5,151
38,350	38,400	5,775	4,919	5,775	5,159
38,400	38,450	5,788	4,926	5,788	5,166
38,450	38,500	5,800	4,934	5,800	5,174
38,500	38,550	5,813	4,941	5,813	5,181
38,550	38,600	5,825	4,949	5,825	5,189
38,600	38,650	5,838	4,956	5,838	5,196
38,650	38,700	5,850	4,964	5,850	5,204
38,700	38,750	5,863	4,971	5,863	5,211
38,750	38,800	5,875	4,979	5,875	5,219
38,800	38,850	5,888	4,986	5,888	5,226
38,850	38,900	5,900	4,994	5,900	5,234
38,900	38,950	5,913	5,001	5,913	5,241
38,950	39,000	5,925	5,009	5,925	5,249
39,000					
39,000	39,050	5,938	5,016	5,938	5,256
39,050	39,100	5,950	5,024	5,950	5,264
39,100	39,150	5,963	5,031	5,963	5,271
39,150	39,200	5,975	5,039	5,975	5,279
39,200	39,250	5,988	5,046	5,988	5,286
39,250	39,300	6,000	5,054	6,000	5,294
39,300	39,350	6,013	5,061	6,013	5,301
39,350	39,400	6,025	5,069	6,025	5,309
39,400	39,450	6,038	5,076	6,038	5,316
39,450	39,500	6,050	5,084	6,050	5,324
39,500	39,550	6,063	5,091	6,063	5,331
39,550	39,600	6,075	5,099	6,075	5,339
39,600	39,650	6,088	5,106	6,088	5,346
39,650	39,700	6,100	5,114	6,100	5,354
39,700	39,750	6,113	5,121	6,113	5,361
39,750	39,800	6,125	5,129	6,125	5,369
39,800	39,850	6,138	5,136	6,138	5,376
39,850	39,900	6,150	5,144	6,150	5,384
39,900	39,950	6,163	5,151	6,163	5,391
39,950	40,000	6,175	5,159	6,175	5,399
40,000					
40,000	40,050	6,188	5,166	6,188	5,406
40,050	40,100	6,200	5,174	6,200	5,414
40,100	40,150	6,213	5,181	6,213	5,421
40,150	40,200	6,225	5,189	6,225	5,429
40,200	40,250	6,238	5,196	6,238	5,436
40,250	40,300	6,250	5,204	6,250	5,444
40,300	40,350	6,263	5,211	6,263	5,451
40,350	40,400	6,275	5,219	6,275	5,459
40,400	40,450	6,288	5,226	6,288	5,466
40,450	40,500	6,300	5,234	6,300	5,474
40,500	40,550	6,313	5,241	6,313	5,481
40,550	40,600	6,325	5,249	6,325	5,489
40,600	40,650	6,338	5,256	6,338	5,496
40,650	40,700	6,350	5,264	6,350	5,504
40,700	40,750	6,363	5,271	6,363	5,511
40,750	40,800	6,375	5,279	6,375	5,519
40,800	40,850	6,388	5,286	6,388	5,526
40,850	40,900	6,400	5,294	6,400	5,534
40,900	40,950	6,413	5,301	6,413	5,541
40,950	41,000	6,425	5,309	6,425	5,549

* This column must also be used by a qualifying widow(er).

(Continued on next page)

2010 Tax Table–*Continued*

If line 43 (taxable income) is— At least	But less than	Single	Married filing jointly *	Married filing separately	Head of a household

41,000

At least	But less than	Single	MFJ *	MFS	HoH
41,000	41,050	6,438	5,316	6,438	5,556
41,050	41,100	6,450	5,324	6,450	5,564
41,100	41,150	6,463	5,331	6,463	5,571
41,150	41,200	6,475	5,339	6,475	5,579
41,200	41,250	6,488	5,346	6,488	5,586
41,250	41,300	6,500	5,354	6,500	5,594
41,300	41,350	6,513	5,361	6,513	5,601
41,350	41,400	6,525	5,369	6,525	5,609
41,400	41,450	6,538	5,376	6,538	5,616
41,450	41,500	6,550	5,384	6,550	5,624
41,500	41,550	6,563	5,391	6,563	5,631
41,550	41,600	6,575	5,399	6,575	5,639
41,600	41,650	6,588	5,406	6,588	5,646
41,650	41,700	6,600	5,414	6,600	5,654
41,700	41,750	6,613	5,421	6,613	5,661
41,750	41,800	6,625	5,429	6,625	5,669
41,800	41,850	6,638	5,436	6,638	5,676
41,850	41,900	6,650	5,444	6,650	5,684
41,900	41,950	6,663	5,451	6,663	5,691
41,950	42,000	6,675	5,459	6,675	5,699

42,000

At least	But less than	Single	MFJ *	MFS	HoH
42,000	42,050	6,688	5,466	6,688	5,706
42,050	42,100	6,700	5,474	6,700	5,714
42,100	42,150	6,713	5,481	6,713	5,721
42,150	42,200	6,725	5,489	6,725	5,729
42,200	42,250	6,738	5,496	6,738	5,736
42,250	42,300	6,750	5,504	6,750	5,744
42,300	42,350	6,763	5,511	6,763	5,751
42,350	42,400	6,775	5,519	6,775	5,759
42,400	42,450	6,788	5,526	6,788	5,766
42,450	42,500	6,800	5,534	6,800	5,774
42,500	42,550	6,813	5,541	6,813	5,781
42,550	42,600	6,825	5,549	6,825	5,789
42,600	42,650	6,838	5,556	6,838	5,796
42,650	42,700	6,850	5,564	6,850	5,804
42,700	42,750	6,863	5,571	6,863	5,811
42,750	42,800	6,875	5,579	6,875	5,819
42,800	42,850	6,888	5,586	6,888	5,826
42,850	42,900	6,900	5,594	6,900	5,834
42,900	42,950	6,913	5,601	6,913	5,841
42,950	43,000	6,925	5,609	6,925	5,849

43,000

At least	But less than	Single	MFJ *	MFS	HoH
43,000	43,050	6,938	5,616	6,938	5,856
43,050	43,100	6,950	5,624	6,950	5,864
43,100	43,150	6,963	5,631	6,963	5,871
43,150	43,200	6,975	5,639	6,975	5,879
43,200	43,250	6,988	5,646	6,988	5,886
43,250	43,300	7,000	5,654	7,000	5,894
43,300	43,350	7,013	5,661	7,013	5,901
43,350	43,400	7,025	5,669	7,025	5,909
43,400	43,450	7,038	5,676	7,038	5,916
43,450	43,500	7,050	5,684	7,050	5,924
43,500	43,550	7,063	5,691	7,063	5,931
43,550	43,600	7,075	5,699	7,075	5,939
43,600	43,650	7,088	5,706	7,088	5,946
43,650	43,700	7,100	5,714	7,100	5,954
43,700	43,750	7,113	5,721	7,113	5,961
43,750	43,800	7,125	5,729	7,125	5,969
43,800	43,850	7,138	5,736	7,138	5,976
43,850	43,900	7,150	5,744	7,150	5,984
43,900	43,950	7,163	5,751	7,163	5,991
43,950	44,000	7,175	5,759	7,175	5,999

44,000

At least	But less than	Single	MFJ *	MFS	HoH
44,000	44,050	7,188	5,766	7,188	6,006
44,050	44,100	7,200	5,774	7,200	6,014
44,100	44,150	7,213	5,781	7,213	6,021
44,150	44,200	7,225	5,789	7,225	6,029
44,200	44,250	7,238	5,796	7,238	6,036
44,250	44,300	7,250	5,804	7,250	6,044
44,300	44,350	7,263	5,811	7,263	6,051
44,350	44,400	7,275	5,819	7,275	6,059
44,400	44,450	7,288	5,826	7,288	6,066
44,450	44,500	7,300	5,834	7,300	6,074
44,500	44,550	7,313	5,841	7,313	6,081
44,550	44,600	7,325	5,849	7,325	6,089
44,600	44,650	7,338	5,856	7,338	6,096
44,650	44,700	7,350	5,864	7,350	6,104
44,700	44,750	7,363	5,871	7,363	6,111
44,750	44,800	7,375	5,879	7,375	6,119
44,800	44,850	7,388	5,886	7,388	6,126
44,850	44,900	7,400	5,894	7,400	6,134
44,900	44,950	7,413	5,901	7,413	6,141
44,950	45,000	7,425	5,909	7,425	6,149

45,000

At least	But less than	Single	MFJ *	MFS	HoH
45,000	45,050	7,438	5,916	7,438	6,156
45,050	45,100	7,450	5,924	7,450	6,164
45,100	45,150	7,463	5,931	7,463	6,171
45,150	45,200	7,475	5,939	7,475	6,179
45,200	45,250	7,488	5,946	7,488	6,186
45,250	45,300	7,500	5,954	7,500	6,194
45,300	45,350	7,513	5,961	7,513	6,201
45,350	45,400	7,525	5,969	7,525	6,209
45,400	45,450	7,538	5,976	7,538	6,216
45,450	45,500	7,550	5,984	7,550	6,224
45,500	45,550	7,563	5,991	7,563	6,231
45,550	45,600	7,575	5,999	7,575	6,241
45,600	45,650	7,588	6,006	7,588	6,254
45,650	45,700	7,600	6,014	7,600	6,266
45,700	45,750	7,613	6,021	7,613	6,279
45,750	45,800	7,625	6,029	7,625	6,291
45,800	45,850	7,638	6,036	7,638	6,304
45,850	45,900	7,650	6,044	7,650	6,316
45,900	45,950	7,663	6,051	7,663	6,329
45,950	46,000	7,675	6,059	7,675	6,341

46,000

At least	But less than	Single	MFJ *	MFS	HoH
46,000	46,050	7,688	6,066	7,688	6,354
46,050	46,100	7,700	6,074	7,700	6,366
46,100	46,150	7,713	6,081	7,713	6,379
46,150	46,200	7,725	6,089	7,725	6,391
46,200	46,250	7,738	6,096	7,738	6,404
46,250	46,300	7,750	6,104	7,750	6,416
46,300	46,350	7,763	6,111	7,763	6,429
46,350	46,400	7,775	6,119	7,775	6,441
46,400	46,450	7,788	6,126	7,788	6,454
46,450	46,500	7,800	6,134	7,800	6,466
46,500	46,550	7,813	6,141	7,813	6,479
46,550	46,600	7,825	6,149	7,825	6,491
46,600	46,650	7,838	6,156	7,838	6,504
46,650	46,700	7,850	6,164	7,850	6,516
46,700	46,750	7,863	6,171	7,863	6,529
46,750	46,800	7,875	6,179	7,875	6,541
46,800	46,850	7,888	6,186	7,888	6,554
46,850	46,900	7,900	6,194	7,900	6,566
46,900	46,950	7,913	6,201	7,913	6,579
46,950	47,000	7,925	6,209	7,925	6,591

47,000

At least	But less than	Single	MFJ *	MFS	HoH
47,000	47,050	7,938	6,216	7,938	6,604
47,050	47,100	7,950	6,224	7,950	6,616
47,100	47,150	7,963	6,231	7,963	6,629
47,150	47,200	7,975	6,239	7,975	6,641
47,200	47,250	7,988	6,246	7,988	6,654
47,250	47,300	8,000	6,254	8,000	6,666
47,300	47,350	8,013	6,261	8,013	6,679
47,350	47,400	8,025	6,269	8,025	6,691
47,400	47,450	8,038	6,276	8,038	6,704
47,450	47,500	8,050	6,284	8,050	6,716
47,500	47,550	8,063	6,291	8,063	6,729
47,550	47,600	8,075	6,299	8,075	6,741
47,600	47,650	8,088	6,306	8,088	6,754
47,650	47,700	8,100	6,314	8,100	6,766
47,700	47,750	8,113	6,321	8,113	6,779
47,750	47,800	8,125	6,329	8,125	6,791
47,800	47,850	8,138	6,336	8,138	6,804
47,850	47,900	8,150	6,344	8,150	6,816
47,900	47,950	8,163	6,351	8,163	6,829
47,950	48,000	8,175	6,359	8,175	6,841

48,000

At least	But less than	Single	MFJ *	MFS	HoH
48,000	48,050	8,188	6,366	8,188	6,854
48,050	48,100	8,200	6,374	8,200	6,866
48,100	48,150	8,213	6,381	8,213	6,879
48,150	48,200	8,225	6,389	8,225	6,891
48,200	48,250	8,238	6,396	8,238	6,904
48,250	48,300	8,250	6,404	8,250	6,916
48,300	48,350	8,263	6,411	8,263	6,929
48,350	48,400	8,275	6,419	8,275	6,941
48,400	48,450	8,288	6,426	8,288	6,954
48,450	48,500	8,300	6,434	8,300	6,966
48,500	48,550	8,313	6,441	8,313	6,979
48,550	48,600	8,325	6,449	8,325	6,991
48,600	48,650	8,338	6,456	8,338	7,004
48,650	48,700	8,350	6,464	8,350	7,016
48,700	48,750	8,363	6,471	8,363	7,029
48,750	48,800	8,375	6,479	8,375	7,041
48,800	48,850	8,388	6,486	8,388	7,054
48,850	48,900	8,400	6,494	8,400	7,066
48,900	48,950	8,413	6,501	8,413	7,079
48,950	49,000	8,425	6,509	8,425	7,091

49,000

At least	But less than	Single	MFJ *	MFS	HoH
49,000	49,050	8,438	6,516	8,438	7,104
49,050	49,100	8,450	6,524	8,450	7,116
49,100	49,150	8,463	6,531	8,463	7,129
49,150	49,200	8,475	6,539	8,475	7,141
49,200	49,250	8,488	6,546	8,488	7,154
49,250	49,300	8,500	6,554	8,500	7,166
49,300	49,350	8,513	6,561	8,513	7,179
49,350	49,400	8,525	6,569	8,525	7,191
49,400	49,450	8,538	6,576	8,538	7,204
49,450	49,500	8,550	6,584	8,550	7,216
49,500	49,550	8,563	6,591	8,563	7,229
49,550	49,600	8,575	6,599	8,575	7,241
49,600	49,650	8,588	6,606	8,588	7,254
49,650	49,700	8,600	6,614	8,600	7,266
49,700	49,750	8,613	6,621	8,613	7,279
49,750	49,800	8,625	6,629	8,625	7,291
49,800	49,850	8,638	6,636	8,638	7,304
49,850	49,900	8,650	6,644	8,650	7,316
49,900	49,950	8,663	6,651	8,663	7,329
49,950	50,000	8,675	6,659	8,675	7,341

* This column must also be used by a qualifying widow(er).

(Continued on next page)

2010 Tax Table–*Continued*

50,000

If line 43 (taxable income) is— At least	But less than	Single	Married filing jointly *	Married filing separately	Head of a household
			Your tax is—		
50,000	50,050	8,688	6,666	8,688	7,354
50,050	50,100	8,700	6,674	8,700	7,366
50,100	50,150	8,713	6,681	8,713	7,379
50,150	50,200	8,725	6,689	8,725	7,391
50,200	50,250	8,738	6,696	8,738	7,404
50,250	50,300	8,750	6,704	8,750	7,416
50,300	50,350	8,763	6,711	8,763	7,429
50,350	50,400	8,775	6,719	8,775	7,441
50,400	50,450	8,788	6,726	8,788	7,454
50,450	50,500	8,800	6,734	8,800	7,466
50,500	50,550	8,813	6,741	8,813	7,479
50,550	50,600	8,825	6,749	8,825	7,491
50,600	50,650	8,838	6,756	8,838	7,504
50,650	50,700	8,850	6,764	8,850	7,516
50,700	50,750	8,863	6,771	8,863	7,529
50,750	50,800	8,875	6,779	8,875	7,541
50,800	50,850	8,888	6,786	8,888	7,554
50,850	50,900	8,900	6,794	8,900	7,566
50,900	50,950	8,913	6,801	8,913	7,579
50,950	51,000	8,925	6,809	8,925	7,591

51,000

At least	But less than	Single	Married filing jointly *	Married filing separately	Head of a household
51,000	51,050	8,938	6,816	8,938	7,604
51,050	51,100	8,950	6,824	8,950	7,616
51,100	51,150	8,963	6,831	8,963	7,629
51,150	51,200	8,975	6,839	8,975	7,641
51,200	51,250	8,988	6,846	8,988	7,654
51,250	51,300	9,000	6,854	9,000	7,666
51,300	51,350	9,013	6,861	9,013	7,679
51,350	51,400	9,025	6,869	9,025	7,691
51,400	51,450	9,038	6,876	9,038	7,704
51,450	51,500	9,050	6,884	9,050	7,716
51,500	51,550	9,063	6,891	9,063	7,729
51,550	51,600	9,075	6,899	9,075	7,741
51,600	51,650	9,088	6,906	9,088	7,754
51,650	51,700	9,100	6,914	9,100	7,766
51,700	51,750	9,113	6,921	9,113	7,779
51,750	51,800	9,125	6,929	9,125	7,791
51,800	51,850	9,138	6,936	9,138	7,804
51,850	51,900	9,150	6,944	9,150	7,816
51,900	51,950	9,163	6,951	9,163	7,829
51,950	52,000	9,175	6,959	9,175	7,841

52,000

At least	But less than	Single	Married filing jointly *	Married filing separately	Head of a household
52,000	52,050	9,188	6,966	9,188	7,854
52,050	52,100	9,200	6,974	9,200	7,866
52,100	52,150	9,213	6,981	9,213	7,879
52,150	52,200	9,225	6,989	9,225	7,891
52,200	52,250	9,238	6,996	9,238	7,904
52,250	52,300	9,250	7,004	9,250	7,916
52,300	52,350	9,263	7,011	9,263	7,929
52,350	52,400	9,275	7,019	9,275	7,941
52,400	52,450	9,288	7,026	9,288	7,954
52,450	52,500	9,300	7,034	9,300	7,966
52,500	52,550	9,313	7,041	9,313	7,979
52,550	52,600	9,325	7,049	9,325	7,991
52,600	52,650	9,338	7,056	9,338	8,004
52,650	52,700	9,350	7,064	9,350	8,016
52,700	52,750	9,363	7,071	9,363	8,029
52,750	52,800	9,375	7,079	9,375	8,041
52,800	52,850	9,388	7,086	9,388	8,054
52,850	52,900	9,400	7,094	9,400	8,066
52,900	52,950	9,413	7,101	9,413	8,079
52,950	53,000	9,425	7,109	9,425	8,091

53,000

At least	But less than	Single	Married filing jointly *	Married filing separately	Head of a household
53,000	53,050	9,438	7,116	9,438	8,104
53,050	53,100	9,450	7,124	9,450	8,116
53,100	53,150	9,463	7,131	9,463	8,129
53,150	53,200	9,475	7,139	9,475	8,141
53,200	53,250	9,488	7,146	9,488	8,154
53,250	53,300	9,500	7,154	9,500	8,166
53,300	53,350	9,513	7,161	9,513	8,179
53,350	53,400	9,525	7,169	9,525	8,191
53,400	53,450	9,538	7,176	9,538	8,204
53,450	53,500	9,550	7,184	9,550	8,216
53,500	53,550	9,563	7,191	9,563	8,229
53,550	53,600	9,575	7,199	9,575	8,241
53,600	53,650	9,588	7,206	9,588	8,254
53,650	53,700	9,600	7,214	9,600	8,266
53,700	53,750	9,613	7,221	9,613	8,279
53,750	53,800	9,625	7,229	9,625	8,291
53,800	53,850	9,638	7,236	9,638	8,304
53,850	53,900	9,650	7,244	9,650	8,316
53,900	53,950	9,663	7,251	9,663	8,329
53,950	54,000	9,675	7,259	9,675	8,341

54,000

At least	But less than	Single	Married filing jointly *	Married filing separately	Head of a household
54,000	54,050	9,688	7,266	9,688	8,354
54,050	54,100	9,700	7,274	9,700	8,366
54,100	54,150	9,713	7,281	9,713	8,379
54,150	54,200	9,725	7,289	9,725	8,391
54,200	54,250	9,738	7,296	9,738	8,404
54,250	54,300	9,750	7,304	9,750	8,416
54,300	54,350	9,763	7,311	9,763	8,429
54,350	54,400	9,775	7,319	9,775	8,441
54,400	54,450	9,788	7,326	9,788	8,454
54,450	54,500	9,800	7,334	9,800	8,466
54,500	54,550	9,813	7,341	9,813	8,479
54,550	54,600	9,825	7,349	9,825	8,491
54,600	54,650	9,838	7,356	9,838	8,504
54,650	54,700	9,850	7,364	9,850	8,516
54,700	54,750	9,863	7,371	9,863	8,529
54,750	54,800	9,875	7,379	9,875	8,541
54,800	54,850	9,888	7,386	9,888	8,554
54,850	54,900	9,900	7,394	9,900	8,566
54,900	54,950	9,913	7,401	9,913	8,579
54,950	55,000	9,925	7,409	9,925	8,591

55,000

At least	But less than	Single	Married filing jointly *	Married filing separately	Head of a household
55,000	55,050	9,938	7,416	9,938	8,604
55,050	55,100	9,950	7,424	9,950	8,616
55,100	55,150	9,963	7,431	9,963	8,629
55,150	55,200	9,975	7,439	9,975	8,641
55,200	55,250	9,988	7,446	9,988	8,654
55,250	55,300	10,000	7,454	10,000	8,666
55,300	55,350	10,013	7,461	10,013	8,679
55,350	55,400	10,025	7,469	10,025	8,691
55,400	55,450	10,038	7,476	10,038	8,704
55,450	55,500	10,050	7,484	10,050	8,716
55,500	55,550	10,063	7,491	10,063	8,729
55,550	55,600	10,075	7,499	10,075	8,741
55,600	55,650	10,088	7,506	10,088	8,754
55,650	55,700	10,100	7,514	10,100	8,766
55,700	55,750	10,113	7,521	10,113	8,779
55,750	55,800	10,125	7,529	10,125	8,791
55,800	55,850	10,138	7,536	10,138	8,804
55,850	55,900	10,150	7,544	10,150	8,816
55,900	55,950	10,163	7,551	10,163	8,829
55,950	56,000	10,175	7,559	10,175	8,841

56,000

At least	But less than	Single	Married filing jointly *	Married filing separately	Head of a household
56,000	56,050	10,188	7,566	10,188	8,854
56,050	56,100	10,200	7,574	10,200	8,866
56,100	56,150	10,213	7,581	10,213	8,879
56,150	56,200	10,225	7,589	10,225	8,891
56,200	56,250	10,238	7,596	10,238	8,904
56,250	56,300	10,250	7,604	10,250	8,916
56,300	56,350	10,263	7,611	10,263	8,929
56,350	56,400	10,275	7,619	10,275	8,941
56,400	56,450	10,288	7,626	10,288	8,954
56,450	56,500	10,300	7,634	10,300	8,966
56,500	56,550	10,313	7,641	10,313	8,979
56,550	56,600	10,325	7,649	10,325	8,991
56,600	56,650	10,338	7,656	10,338	9,004
56,650	56,700	10,350	7,664	10,350	9,016
56,700	56,750	10,363	7,671	10,363	9,029
56,750	56,800	10,375	7,679	10,375	9,041
56,800	56,850	10,388	7,686	10,388	9,054
56,850	56,900	10,400	7,694	10,400	9,066
56,900	56,950	10,413	7,701	10,413	9,079
56,950	57,000	10,425	7,709	10,425	9,091

57,000

At least	But less than	Single	Married filing jointly *	Married filing separately	Head of a household
57,000	57,050	10,438	7,716	10,438	9,104
57,050	57,100	10,450	7,724	10,450	9,116
57,100	57,150	10,463	7,731	10,463	9,129
57,150	57,200	10,475	7,739	10,475	9,141
57,200	57,250	10,488	7,746	10,488	9,154
57,250	57,300	10,500	7,754	10,500	9,166
57,300	57,350	10,513	7,761	10,513	9,179
57,350	57,400	10,525	7,769	10,525	9,191
57,400	57,450	10,538	7,776	10,538	9,204
57,450	57,500	10,550	7,784	10,550	9,216
57,500	57,550	10,563	7,791	10,563	9,229
57,550	57,600	10,575	7,799	10,575	9,241
57,600	57,650	10,588	7,806	10,588	9,254
57,650	57,700	10,600	7,814	10,600	9,266
57,700	57,750	10,613	7,821	10,613	9,279
57,750	57,800	10,625	7,829	10,625	9,291
57,800	57,850	10,638	7,836	10,638	9,304
57,850	57,900	10,650	7,844	10,650	9,316
57,900	57,950	10,663	7,851	10,663	9,329
57,950	58,000	10,675	7,859	10,675	9,341

58,000

At least	But less than	Single	Married filing jointly *	Married filing separately	Head of a household
58,000	58,050	10,688	7,866	10,688	9,354
58,050	58,100	10,700	7,874	10,700	9,366
58,100	58,150	10,713	7,881	10,713	9,379
58,150	58,200	10,725	7,889	10,725	9,391
58,200	58,250	10,738	7,896	10,738	9,404
58,250	58,300	10,750	7,904	10,750	9,416
58,300	58,350	10,763	7,911	10,763	9,429
58,350	58,400	10,775	7,919	10,775	9,441
58,400	58,450	10,788	7,926	10,788	9,454
58,450	58,500	10,800	7,934	10,800	9,466
58,500	58,550	10,813	7,941	10,813	9,479
58,550	58,600	10,825	7,949	10,825	9,491
58,600	58,650	10,838	7,956	10,838	9,504
58,650	58,700	10,850	7,964	10,850	9,516
58,700	58,750	10,863	7,971	10,863	9,529
58,750	58,800	10,875	7,979	10,875	9,541
58,800	58,850	10,888	7,986	10,888	9,554
58,850	58,900	10,900	7,994	10,900	9,566
58,900	58,950	10,913	8,001	10,913	9,579
58,950	59,000	10,925	8,009	10,925	9,591

* This column must also be used by a qualifying widow(er).

(Continued on next page)

2010 Tax Table–*Continued*

If line 43 (taxable income) is— At least	But less than	And you are— Single	Married filing jointly *	Married filing separately	Head of a household
59,000					
59,000	59,050	10,938	8,016	10,938	9,604
59,050	59,100	10,950	8,024	10,950	9,616
59,100	59,150	10,963	8,031	10,963	9,629
59,150	59,200	10,975	8,039	10,975	9,641
59,200	59,250	10,988	8,046	10,988	9,654
59,250	59,300	11,000	8,054	11,000	9,666
59,300	59,350	11,013	8,061	11,013	9,679
59,350	59,400	11,025	8,069	11,025	9,691
59,400	59,450	11,038	8,076	11,038	9,704
59,450	59,500	11,050	8,084	11,050	9,716
59,500	59,550	11,063	8,091	11,063	9,729
59,550	59,600	11,075	8,099	11,075	9,741
59,600	59,650	11,088	8,106	11,088	9,754
59,650	59,700	11,100	8,114	11,100	9,766
59,700	59,750	11,113	8,121	11,113	9,779
59,750	59,800	11,125	8,129	11,125	9,791
59,800	59,850	11,138	8,136	11,138	9,804
59,850	59,900	11,150	8,144	11,150	9,816
59,900	59,950	11,163	8,151	11,163	9,829
59,950	60,000	11,175	8,159	11,175	9,841
60,000					
60,000	60,050	11,188	8,166	11,188	9,854
60,050	60,100	11,200	8,174	11,200	9,866
60,100	60,150	11,213	8,181	11,213	9,879
60,150	60,200	11,225	8,189	11,225	9,891
60,200	60,250	11,238	8,196	11,238	9,904
60,250	60,300	11,250	8,204	11,250	9,916
60,300	60,350	11,263	8,211	11,263	9,929
60,350	60,400	11,275	8,219	11,275	9,941
60,400	60,450	11,288	8,226	11,288	9,954
60,450	60,500	11,300	8,234	11,300	9,966
60,500	60,550	11,313	8,241	11,313	9,979
60,550	60,600	11,325	8,249	11,325	9,991
60,600	60,650	11,338	8,256	11,338	10,004
60,650	60,700	11,350	8,264	11,350	10,016
60,700	60,750	11,363	8,271	11,363	10,029
60,750	60,800	11,375	8,279	11,375	10,041
60,800	60,850	11,388	8,286	11,388	10,054
60,850	60,900	11,400	8,294	11,400	10,066
60,900	60,950	11,413	8,301	11,413	10,079
60,950	61,000	11,425	8,309	11,425	10,091
61,000					
61,000	61,050	11,438	8,316	11,438	10,104
61,050	61,100	11,450	8,324	11,450	10,116
61,100	61,150	11,463	8,331	11,463	10,129
61,150	61,200	11,475	8,339	11,475	10,141
61,200	61,250	11,488	8,346	11,488	10,154
61,250	61,300	11,500	8,354	11,500	10,166
61,300	61,350	11,513	8,361	11,513	10,179
61,350	61,400	11,525	8,369	11,525	10,191
61,400	61,450	11,538	8,376	11,538	10,204
61,450	61,500	11,550	8,384	11,550	10,216
61,500	61,550	11,563	8,391	11,563	10,229
61,550	61,600	11,575	8,399	11,575	10,241
61,600	61,650	11,588	8,406	11,588	10,254
61,650	61,700	11,600	8,414	11,600	10,266
61,700	61,750	11,613	8,421	11,613	10,279
61,750	61,800	11,625	8,429	11,625	10,291
61,800	61,850	11,638	8,436	11,638	10,304
61,850	61,900	11,650	8,444	11,650	10,316
61,900	61,950	11,663	8,451	11,663	10,329
61,950	62,000	11,675	8,459	11,675	10,341
62,000					
62,000	62,050	11,688	8,466	11,688	10,354
62,050	62,100	11,700	8,474	11,700	10,366
62,100	62,150	11,713	8,481	11,713	10,379
62,150	62,200	11,725	8,489	11,725	10,391
62,200	62,250	11,738	8,496	11,738	10,404
62,250	62,300	11,750	8,504	11,750	10,416
62,300	62,350	11,763	8,511	11,763	10,429
62,350	62,400	11,775	8,519	11,775	10,441
62,400	62,450	11,788	8,526	11,788	10,454
62,450	62,500	11,800	8,534	11,800	10,466
62,500	62,550	11,813	8,541	11,813	10,479
62,550	62,600	11,825	8,549	11,825	10,491
62,600	62,650	11,838	8,556	11,838	10,504
62,650	62,700	11,850	8,564	11,850	10,516
62,700	62,750	11,863	8,571	11,863	10,529
62,750	62,800	11,875	8,579	11,875	10,541
62,800	62,850	11,888	8,586	11,888	10,554
62,850	62,900	11,900	8,594	11,900	10,566
62,900	62,950	11,913	8,601	11,913	10,579
62,950	63,000	11,925	8,609	11,925	10,591
63,000					
63,000	63,050	11,938	8,616	11,938	10,604
63,050	63,100	11,950	8,624	11,950	10,616
63,100	63,150	11,963	8,631	11,963	10,629
63,150	63,200	11,975	8,639	11,975	10,641
63,200	63,250	11,988	8,646	11,988	10,654
63,250	63,300	12,000	8,654	12,000	10,666
63,300	63,350	12,013	8,661	12,013	10,679
63,350	63,400	12,025	8,669	12,025	10,691
63,400	63,450	12,038	8,676	12,038	10,704
63,450	63,500	12,050	8,684	12,050	10,716
63,500	63,550	12,063	8,691	12,063	10,729
63,550	63,600	12,075	8,699	12,075	10,741
63,600	63,650	12,088	8,706	12,088	10,754
63,650	63,700	12,100	8,714	12,100	10,766
63,700	63,750	12,113	8,721	12,113	10,779
63,750	63,800	12,125	8,729	12,125	10,791
63,800	63,850	12,138	8,736	12,138	10,804
63,850	63,900	12,150	8,744	12,150	10,816
63,900	63,950	12,163	8,751	12,163	10,829
63,950	64,000	12,175	8,759	12,175	10,841
64,000					
64,000	64,050	12,188	8,766	12,188	10,854
64,050	64,100	12,200	8,774	12,200	10,866
64,100	64,150	12,213	8,781	12,213	10,879
64,150	64,200	12,225	8,789	12,225	10,891
64,200	64,250	12,238	8,796	12,238	10,904
64,250	64,300	12,250	8,804	12,250	10,916
64,300	64,350	12,263	8,811	12,263	10,929
64,350	64,400	12,275	8,819	12,275	10,941
64,400	64,450	12,288	8,826	12,288	10,954
64,450	64,500	12,300	8,834	12,300	10,966
64,500	64,550	12,313	8,841	12,313	10,979
64,550	64,600	12,325	8,849	12,325	10,991
64,600	64,650	12,338	8,856	12,338	11,004
64,650	64,700	12,350	8,864	12,350	11,016
64,700	64,750	12,363	8,871	12,363	11,029
64,750	64,800	12,375	8,879	12,375	11,041
64,800	64,850	12,388	8,886	12,388	11,054
64,850	64,900	12,400	8,894	12,400	11,066
64,900	64,950	12,413	8,901	12,413	11,079
64,950	65,000	12,425	8,909	12,425	11,091
65,000					
65,000	65,050	12,438	8,916	12,438	11,104
65,050	65,100	12,450	8,924	12,450	11,116
65,100	65,150	12,463	8,931	12,463	11,129
65,150	65,200	12,475	8,939	12,475	11,141
65,200	65,250	12,488	8,946	12,488	11,154
65,250	65,300	12,500	8,954	12,500	11,166
65,300	65,350	12,513	8,961	12,513	11,179
65,350	65,400	12,525	8,969	12,525	11,191
65,400	65,450	12,538	8,976	12,538	11,204
65,450	65,500	12,550	8,984	12,550	11,216
65,500	65,550	12,563	8,991	12,563	11,229
65,550	65,600	12,575	8,999	12,575	11,241
65,600	65,650	12,588	9,006	12,588	11,254
65,650	65,700	12,600	9,014	12,600	11,266
65,700	65,750	12,613	9,021	12,613	11,279
65,750	65,800	12,625	9,029	12,625	11,291
65,800	65,850	12,638	9,036	12,638	11,304
65,850	65,900	12,650	9,044	12,650	11,316
65,900	65,950	12,663	9,051	12,663	11,329
65,950	66,000	12,675	9,059	12,675	11,341
66,000					
66,000	66,050	12,688	9,066	12,688	11,354
66,050	66,100	12,700	9,074	12,700	11,366
66,100	66,150	12,713	9,081	12,713	11,379
66,150	66,200	12,725	9,089	12,725	11,391
66,200	66,250	12,738	9,096	12,738	11,404
66,250	66,300	12,750	9,104	12,750	11,416
66,300	66,350	12,763	9,111	12,763	11,429
66,350	66,400	12,775	9,119	12,775	11,441
66,400	66,450	12,788	9,126	12,788	11,454
66,450	66,500	12,800	9,134	12,800	11,466
66,500	66,550	12,813	9,141	12,813	11,479
66,550	66,600	12,825	9,149	12,825	11,491
66,600	66,650	12,838	9,156	12,838	11,504
66,650	66,700	12,850	9,164	12,850	11,516
66,700	66,750	12,863	9,171	12,863	11,529
66,750	66,800	12,875	9,179	12,875	11,541
66,800	66,850	12,888	9,186	12,888	11,554
66,850	66,900	12,900	9,194	12,900	11,566
66,900	66,950	12,913	9,201	12,913	11,579
66,950	67,000	12,925	9,209	12,925	11,591
67,000					
67,000	67,050	12,938	9,216	12,938	11,604
67,050	67,100	12,950	9,224	12,950	11,616
67,100	67,150	12,963	9,231	12,963	11,629
67,150	67,200	12,975	9,239	12,975	11,641
67,200	67,250	12,988	9,246	12,988	11,654
67,250	67,300	13,000	9,254	13,000	11,666
67,300	67,350	13,013	9,261	13,013	11,679
67,350	67,400	13,025	9,269	13,025	11,691
67,400	67,450	13,038	9,276	13,038	11,704
67,450	67,500	13,050	9,284	13,050	11,716
67,500	67,550	13,063	9,291	13,063	11,729
67,550	67,600	13,075	9,299	13,075	11,741
67,600	67,650	13,088	9,306	13,088	11,754
67,650	67,700	13,100	9,314	13,100	11,766
67,700	67,750	13,113	9,321	13,113	11,779
67,750	67,800	13,125	9,329	13,125	11,791
67,800	67,850	13,138	9,336	13,138	11,804
67,850	67,900	13,150	9,344	13,150	11,816
67,900	67,950	13,163	9,351	13,163	11,829
67,950	68,000	13,175	9,359	13,175	11,841

* This column must also be used by a qualifying widow(er).

(Continued on next page)

2010 Tax Table–*Continued*

If line 43 (taxable income) is—		And you are—			
At least	But less than	Single	Married filing jointly *	Married filing separately	Head of a household
		Your tax is—			

68,000

At least	But less than	Single	Married filing jointly *	Married filing separately	Head of a household
68,000	68,050	13,188	9,369	13,188	11,854
68,050	68,100	13,200	9,381	13,200	11,866
68,100	68,150	13,213	9,394	13,213	11,879
68,150	68,200	13,225	9,406	13,225	11,891
68,200	68,250	13,238	9,419	13,238	11,904
68,250	68,300	13,250	9,431	13,250	11,916
68,300	68,350	13,263	9,444	13,263	11,929
68,350	68,400	13,275	9,456	13,275	11,941
68,400	68,450	13,288	9,469	13,288	11,954
68,450	68,500	13,300	9,481	13,300	11,966
68,500	68,550	13,313	9,494	13,313	11,979
68,550	68,600	13,325	9,506	13,325	11,991
68,600	68,650	13,338	9,519	13,338	12,004
68,650	68,700	13,350	9,531	13,351	12,016
68,700	68,750	13,363	9,544	13,365	12,029
68,750	68,800	13,375	9,556	13,379	12,041
68,800	68,850	13,388	9,569	13,393	12,054
68,850	68,900	13,400	9,581	13,407	12,066
68,900	68,950	13,413	9,594	13,421	12,079
68,950	69,000	13,425	9,606	13,435	12,091

69,000

At least	But less than	Single	Married filing jointly *	Married filing separately	Head of a household
69,000	69,050	13,438	9,619	13,449	12,104
69,050	69,100	13,450	9,631	13,463	12,116
69,100	69,150	13,463	9,644	13,477	12,129
69,150	69,200	13,475	9,656	13,491	12,141
69,200	69,250	13,488	9,669	13,505	12,154
69,250	69,300	13,500	9,681	13,519	12,166
69,300	69,350	13,513	9,694	13,533	12,179
69,350	69,400	13,525	9,706	13,547	12,191
69,400	69,450	13,538	9,719	13,561	12,204
69,450	69,500	13,550	9,731	13,575	12,216
69,500	69,550	13,563	9,744	13,589	12,229
69,550	69,600	13,575	9,756	13,603	12,241
69,600	69,650	13,588	9,769	13,617	12,254
69,650	69,700	13,600	9,781	13,631	12,266
69,700	69,750	13,613	9,794	13,645	12,279
69,750	69,800	13,625	9,806	13,659	12,291
69,800	69,850	13,638	9,819	13,673	12,304
69,850	69,900	13,650	9,831	13,687	12,316
69,900	69,950	13,663	9,844	13,701	12,329
69,950	70,000	13,675	9,856	13,715	12,341

70,000

At least	But less than	Single	Married filing jointly *	Married filing separately	Head of a household
70,000	70,050	13,688	9,869	13,729	12,354
70,050	70,100	13,700	9,881	13,743	12,366
70,100	70,150	13,713	9,894	13,757	12,379
70,150	70,200	13,725	9,906	13,771	12,391
70,200	70,250	13,738	9,919	13,785	12,404
70,250	70,300	13,750	9,931	13,799	12,416
70,300	70,350	13,763	9,944	13,813	12,429
70,350	70,400	13,775	9,956	13,827	12,441
70,400	70,450	13,788	9,969	13,841	12,454
70,450	70,500	13,800	9,981	13,855	12,466
70,500	70,550	13,813	9,994	13,869	12,479
70,550	70,600	13,825	10,006	13,883	12,491
70,600	70,650	13,838	10,019	13,897	12,504
70,650	70,700	13,850	10,031	13,911	12,516
70,700	70,750	13,863	10,044	13,925	12,529
70,750	70,800	13,875	10,056	13,939	12,541
70,800	70,850	13,888	10,069	13,953	12,554
70,850	70,900	13,900	10,081	13,967	12,566
70,900	70,950	13,913	10,094	13,981	12,579
70,950	71,000	13,925	10,106	13,995	12,591

71,000

At least	But less than	Single	Married filing jointly *	Married filing separately	Head of a household
71,000	71,050	13,938	10,119	14,009	12,604
71,050	71,100	13,950	10,131	14,023	12,616
71,100	71,150	13,963	10,144	14,037	12,629
71,150	71,200	13,975	10,156	14,051	12,641
71,200	71,250	13,988	10,169	14,065	12,654
71,250	71,300	14,000	10,181	14,079	12,666
71,300	71,350	14,013	10,194	14,093	12,679
71,350	71,400	14,025	10,206	14,107	12,691
71,400	71,450	14,038	10,219	14,121	12,704
71,450	71,500	14,050	10,231	14,135	12,716
71,500	71,550	14,063	10,244	14,149	12,729
71,550	71,600	14,075	10,256	14,163	12,741
71,600	71,650	14,088	10,269	14,177	12,754
71,650	71,700	14,100	10,281	14,191	12,766
71,700	71,750	14,113	10,294	14,205	12,779
71,750	71,800	14,125	10,306	14,219	12,791
71,800	71,850	14,138	10,319	14,233	12,804
71,850	71,900	14,150	10,331	14,247	12,816
71,900	71,950	14,163	10,344	14,261	12,829
71,950	72,000	14,175	10,356	14,275	12,841

72,000

At least	But less than	Single	Married filing jointly *	Married filing separately	Head of a household
72,000	72,050	14,188	10,369	14,289	12,854
72,050	72,100	14,200	10,381	14,303	12,866
72,100	72,150	14,213	10,394	14,317	12,879
72,150	72,200	14,225	10,406	14,331	12,891
72,200	72,250	14,238	10,419	14,345	12,904
72,250	72,300	14,250	10,431	14,359	12,916
72,300	72,350	14,263	10,444	14,373	12,929
72,350	72,400	14,275	10,456	14,387	12,941
72,400	72,450	14,288	10,469	14,401	12,954
72,450	72,500	14,300	10,481	14,415	12,966
72,500	72,550	14,313	10,494	14,429	12,979
72,550	72,600	14,325	10,506	14,443	12,991
72,600	72,650	14,338	10,519	14,457	13,004
72,650	72,700	14,350	10,531	14,471	13,016
72,700	72,750	14,363	10,544	14,485	13,029
72,750	72,800	14,375	10,556	14,499	13,041
72,800	72,850	14,388	10,569	14,513	13,054
72,850	72,900	14,400	10,581	14,527	13,066
72,900	72,950	14,413	10,594	14,541	13,079
72,950	73,000	14,425	10,606	14,555	13,091

73,000

At least	But less than	Single	Married filing jointly *	Married filing separately	Head of a household
73,000	73,050	14,438	10,619	14,569	13,104
73,050	73,100	14,450	10,631	14,583	13,116
73,100	73,150	14,463	10,644	14,597	13,129
73,150	73,200	14,475	10,656	14,611	13,141
73,200	73,250	14,488	10,669	14,625	13,154
73,250	73,300	14,500	10,681	14,639	13,166
73,300	73,350	14,513	10,694	14,653	13,179
73,350	73,400	14,525	10,706	14,667	13,191
73,400	73,450	14,538	10,719	14,681	13,204
73,450	73,500	14,550	10,731	14,695	13,216
73,500	73,550	14,563	10,744	14,709	13,229
73,550	73,600	14,575	10,756	14,723	13,241
73,600	73,650	14,588	10,769	14,737	13,254
73,650	73,700	14,600	10,781	14,751	13,266
73,700	73,750	14,613	10,794	14,765	13,279
73,750	73,800	14,625	10,806	14,779	13,291
73,800	73,850	14,638	10,819	14,793	13,304
73,850	73,900	14,650	10,831	14,807	13,316
73,900	73,950	14,663	10,844	14,821	13,329
73,950	74,000	14,675	10,856	14,835	13,341

74,000

At least	But less than	Single	Married filing jointly *	Married filing separately	Head of a household
74,000	74,050	14,688	10,869	14,849	13,354
74,050	74,100	14,700	10,881	14,863	13,366
74,100	74,150	14,713	10,894	14,877	13,379
74,150	74,200	14,725	10,906	14,891	13,391
74,200	74,250	14,738	10,919	14,905	13,404
74,250	74,300	14,750	10,931	14,919	13,416
74,300	74,350	14,763	10,944	14,933	13,429
74,350	74,400	14,775	10,956	14,947	13,441
74,400	74,450	14,788	10,969	14,961	13,454
74,450	74,500	14,800	10,981	14,975	13,466
74,500	74,550	14,813	10,994	14,989	13,479
74,550	74,600	14,825	11,006	15,003	13,491
74,600	74,650	14,838	11,019	15,017	13,504
74,650	74,700	14,850	11,031	15,031	13,516
74,700	74,750	14,863	11,044	15,045	13,529
74,750	74,800	14,875	11,056	15,059	13,541
74,800	74,850	14,888	11,069	15,073	13,554
74,850	74,900	14,900	11,081	15,087	13,566
74,900	74,950	14,913	11,094	15,101	13,579
74,950	75,000	14,925	11,106	15,115	13,591

75,000

At least	But less than	Single	Married filing jointly *	Married filing separately	Head of a household
75,000	75,050	14,938	11,119	15,129	13,604
75,050	75,100	14,950	11,131	15,143	13,616
75,100	75,150	14,963	11,144	15,157	13,629
75,150	75,200	14,975	11,156	15,171	13,641
75,200	75,250	14,988	11,169	15,185	13,654
75,250	75,300	15,000	11,181	15,199	13,666
75,300	75,350	15,013	11,194	15,213	13,679
75,350	75,400	15,025	11,206	15,227	13,691
75,400	75,450	15,038	11,219	15,241	13,704
75,450	75,500	15,050	11,231	15,255	13,716
75,500	75,550	15,063	11,244	15,269	13,729
75,550	75,600	15,075	11,256	15,283	13,741
75,600	75,650	15,088	11,269	15,297	13,754
75,650	75,700	15,100	11,281	15,311	13,766
75,700	75,750	15,113	11,294	15,325	13,779
75,750	75,800	15,125	11,306	15,339	13,791
75,800	75,850	15,138	11,319	15,353	13,804
75,850	75,900	15,150	11,331	15,367	13,816
75,900	75,950	15,163	11,344	15,381	13,829
75,950	76,000	15,175	11,356	15,395	13,841

76,000

At least	But less than	Single	Married filing jointly *	Married filing separately	Head of a household
76,000	76,050	15,188	11,369	15,409	13,854
76,050	76,100	15,200	11,381	15,423	13,866
76,100	76,150	15,213	11,394	15,437	13,879
76,150	76,200	15,225	11,406	15,451	13,891
76,200	76,250	15,238	11,419	15,465	13,904
76,250	76,300	15,250	11,431	15,479	13,916
76,300	76,350	15,263	11,444	15,493	13,929
76,350	76,400	15,275	11,456	15,507	13,941
76,400	76,450	15,288	11,469	15,521	13,954
76,450	76,500	15,300	11,481	15,535	13,966
76,500	76,550	15,313	11,494	15,549	13,979
76,550	76,600	15,325	11,506	15,563	13,991
76,600	76,650	15,338	11,519	15,577	14,004
76,650	76,700	15,350	11,531	15,591	14,016
76,700	76,750	15,363	11,544	15,605	14,029
76,750	76,800	15,375	11,556	15,619	14,041
76,800	76,850	15,388	11,569	15,633	14,054
76,850	76,900	15,400	11,581	15,647	14,066
76,900	76,950	15,413	11,594	15,661	14,079
76,950	77,000	15,425	11,606	15,675	14,091

* This column must also be used by a qualifying widow(er).

(Continued on next page)

2010 Tax Table–*Continued*

77,000

At least	But less than	Single	Married filing jointly*	Married filing separately	Head of a household
77,000	77,050	15,438	11,619	15,689	14,104
77,050	77,100	15,450	11,631	15,703	14,116
77,100	77,150	15,463	11,644	15,717	14,129
77,150	77,200	15,475	11,656	15,731	14,141
77,200	77,250	15,488	11,669	15,745	14,154
77,250	77,300	15,500	11,681	15,759	14,166
77,300	77,350	15,513	11,694	15,773	14,179
77,350	77,400	15,525	11,706	15,787	14,191
77,400	77,450	15,538	11,719	15,801	14,204
77,450	77,500	15,550	11,731	15,815	14,216
77,500	77,550	15,563	11,744	15,829	14,229
77,550	77,600	15,575	11,756	15,843	14,241
77,600	77,650	15,588	11,769	15,857	14,254
77,650	77,700	15,600	11,781	15,871	14,266
77,700	77,750	15,613	11,794	15,885	14,279
77,750	77,800	15,625	11,806	15,899	14,291
77,800	77,850	15,638	11,819	15,913	14,304
77,850	77,900	15,650	11,831	15,927	14,316
77,900	77,950	15,663	11,844	15,941	14,329
77,950	78,000	15,675	11,856	15,955	14,341

78,000

At least	But less than	Single	Married filing jointly*	Married filing separately	Head of a household
78,000	78,050	15,688	11,869	15,969	14,354
78,050	78,100	15,700	11,881	15,983	14,366
78,100	78,150	15,713	11,894	15,997	14,379
78,150	78,200	15,725	11,906	16,011	14,391
78,200	78,250	15,738	11,919	16,025	14,404
78,250	78,300	15,750	11,931	16,039	14,416
78,300	78,350	15,763	11,944	16,053	14,429
78,350	78,400	15,775	11,956	16,067	14,441
78,400	78,450	15,788	11,969	16,081	14,454
78,450	78,500	15,800	11,981	16,095	14,466
78,500	78,550	15,813	11,994	16,109	14,479
78,550	78,600	15,825	12,006	16,123	14,491
78,600	78,650	15,838	12,019	16,137	14,504
78,650	78,700	15,850	12,031	16,151	14,516
78,700	78,750	15,863	12,044	16,165	14,529
78,750	78,800	15,875	12,056	16,179	14,541
78,800	78,850	15,888	12,069	16,193	14,554
78,850	78,900	15,900	12,081	16,207	14,566
78,900	78,950	15,913	12,094	16,221	14,579
78,950	79,000	15,925	12,106	16,235	14,591

79,000

At least	But less than	Single	Married filing jointly*	Married filing separately	Head of a household
79,000	79,050	15,938	12,119	16,249	14,604
79,050	79,100	15,950	12,131	16,263	14,616
79,100	79,150	15,963	12,144	16,277	14,629
79,150	79,200	15,975	12,156	16,291	14,641
79,200	79,250	15,988	12,169	16,305	14,654
79,250	79,300	16,000	12,181	16,319	14,666
79,300	79,350	16,013	12,194	16,333	14,679
79,350	79,400	16,025	12,206	16,347	14,691
79,400	79,450	16,038	12,219	16,361	14,704
79,450	79,500	16,050	12,231	16,375	14,716
79,500	79,550	16,063	12,244	16,389	14,729
79,550	79,600	16,075	12,256	16,403	14,741
79,600	79,650	16,088	12,269	16,417	14,754
79,650	79,700	16,100	12,281	16,431	14,766
79,700	79,750	16,113	12,294	16,445	14,779
79,750	79,800	16,125	12,306	16,459	14,791
79,800	79,850	16,138	12,319	16,473	14,804
79,850	79,900	16,150	12,331	16,487	14,816
79,900	79,950	16,163	12,344	16,501	14,829
79,950	80,000	16,175	12,356	16,515	14,841

80,000

At least	But less than	Single	Married filing jointly*	Married filing separately	Head of a household
80,000	80,050	16,188	12,369	16,529	14,854
80,050	80,100	16,200	12,381	16,543	14,866
80,100	80,150	16,213	12,394	16,557	14,879
80,150	80,200	16,225	12,406	16,571	14,891
80,200	80,250	16,238	12,419	16,585	14,904
80,250	80,300	16,250	12,431	16,599	14,916
80,300	80,350	16,263	12,444	16,613	14,929
80,350	80,400	16,275	12,456	16,627	14,941
80,400	80,450	16,288	12,469	16,641	14,954
80,450	80,500	16,300	12,481	16,655	14,966
80,500	80,550	16,313	12,494	16,669	14,979
80,550	80,600	16,325	12,506	16,683	14,991
80,600	80,650	16,338	12,519	16,697	15,004
80,650	80,700	16,350	12,531	16,711	15,016
80,700	80,750	16,363	12,544	16,725	15,029
80,750	80,800	16,375	12,556	16,739	15,041
80,800	80,850	16,388	12,569	16,753	15,054
80,850	80,900	16,400	12,581	16,767	15,066
80,900	80,950	16,413	12,594	16,781	15,079
80,950	81,000	16,425	12,606	16,795	15,091

81,000

At least	But less than	Single	Married filing jointly*	Married filing separately	Head of a household
81,000	81,050	16,438	12,619	16,809	15,104
81,050	81,100	16,450	12,631	16,823	15,116
81,100	81,150	16,463	12,644	16,837	15,129
81,150	81,200	16,475	12,656	16,851	15,141
81,200	81,250	16,488	12,669	16,865	15,154
81,250	81,300	16,500	12,681	16,879	15,166
81,300	81,350	16,513	12,694	16,893	15,179
81,350	81,400	16,525	12,706	16,907	15,191
81,400	81,450	16,538	12,719	16,921	15,204
81,450	81,500	16,550	12,731	16,935	15,216
81,500	81,550	16,563	12,744	16,949	15,229
81,550	81,600	16,575	12,756	16,963	15,241
81,600	81,650	16,588	12,769	16,977	15,254
81,650	81,700	16,600	12,781	16,991	15,266
81,700	81,750	16,613	12,794	17,005	15,279
81,750	81,800	16,625	12,806	17,019	15,291
81,800	81,850	16,638	12,819	17,033	15,304
81,850	81,900	16,650	12,831	17,047	15,316
81,900	81,950	16,663	12,844	17,061	15,329
81,950	82,000	16,675	12,856	17,075	15,341

82,000

At least	But less than	Single	Married filing jointly*	Married filing separately	Head of a household
82,000	82,050	16,688	12,869	17,089	15,354
82,050	82,100	16,700	12,881	17,103	15,366
82,100	82,150	16,713	12,894	17,117	15,379
82,150	82,200	16,725	12,906	17,131	15,391
82,200	82,250	16,738	12,919	17,145	15,404
82,250	82,300	16,750	12,931	17,159	15,416
82,300	82,350	16,763	12,944	17,173	15,429
82,350	82,400	16,775	12,956	17,187	15,441
82,400	82,450	16,788	12,969	17,201	15,454
82,450	82,500	16,802	12,981	17,215	15,466
82,500	82,550	16,816	12,994	17,229	15,479
82,550	82,600	16,830	13,006	17,243	15,491
82,600	82,650	16,844	13,019	17,257	15,504
82,650	82,700	16,858	13,031	17,271	15,516
82,700	82,750	16,872	13,044	17,285	15,529
82,750	82,800	16,886	13,056	17,299	15,541
82,800	82,850	16,900	13,069	17,313	15,554
82,850	82,900	16,914	13,081	17,327	15,566
82,900	82,950	16,928	13,094	17,341	15,579
82,950	83,000	16,942	13,106	17,355	15,591

83,000

At least	But less than	Single	Married filing jointly*	Married filing separately	Head of a household
83,000	83,050	16,956	13,119	17,369	15,604
83,050	83,100	16,970	13,131	17,383	15,616
83,100	83,150	16,984	13,144	17,397	15,629
83,150	83,200	16,998	13,156	17,411	15,641
83,200	83,250	17,012	13,169	17,425	15,654
83,250	83,300	17,026	13,181	17,439	15,666
83,300	83,350	17,040	13,194	17,453	15,679
83,350	83,400	17,054	13,206	17,467	15,691
83,400	83,450	17,068	13,219	17,481	15,704
83,450	83,500	17,082	13,231	17,495	15,716
83,500	83,550	17,096	13,244	17,509	15,729
83,550	83,600	17,110	13,256	17,523	15,741
83,600	83,650	17,124	13,269	17,537	15,754
83,650	83,700	17,138	13,281	17,551	15,766
83,700	83,750	17,152	13,294	17,565	15,779
83,750	83,800	17,166	13,306	17,579	15,791
83,800	83,850	17,180	13,319	17,593	15,804
83,850	83,900	17,194	13,331	17,607	15,816
83,900	83,950	17,208	13,344	17,621	15,829
83,950	84,000	17,222	13,356	17,635	15,841

84,000

At least	But less than	Single	Married filing jointly*	Married filing separately	Head of a household
84,000	84,050	17,236	13,369	17,649	15,854
84,050	84,100	17,250	13,381	17,663	15,866
84,100	84,150	17,264	13,394	17,677	15,879
84,150	84,200	17,278	13,406	17,691	15,891
84,200	84,250	17,292	13,419	17,705	15,904
84,250	84,300	17,306	13,431	17,719	15,916
84,300	84,350	17,320	13,444	17,733	15,929
84,350	84,400	17,334	13,456	17,747	15,941
84,400	84,450	17,348	13,469	17,761	15,954
84,450	84,500	17,362	13,481	17,775	15,966
84,500	84,550	17,376	13,494	17,789	15,979
84,550	84,600	17,390	13,506	17,803	15,991
84,600	84,650	17,404	13,519	17,817	16,004
84,650	84,700	17,418	13,531	17,831	16,016
84,700	84,750	17,432	13,544	17,845	16,029
84,750	84,800	17,446	13,556	17,859	16,041
84,800	84,850	17,460	13,569	17,873	16,054
84,850	84,900	17,474	13,581	17,887	16,066
84,900	84,950	17,488	13,594	17,901	16,079
84,950	85,000	17,502	13,606	17,915	16,091

85,000

At least	But less than	Single	Married filing jointly*	Married filing separately	Head of a household
85,000	85,050	17,516	13,619	17,929	16,104
85,050	85,100	17,530	13,631	17,943	16,116
85,100	85,150	17,544	13,644	17,957	16,129
85,150	85,200	17,558	13,656	17,971	16,141
85,200	85,250	17,572	13,669	17,985	16,154
85,250	85,300	17,586	13,681	17,999	16,166
85,300	85,350	17,600	13,694	18,013	16,179
85,350	85,400	17,614	13,706	18,027	16,191
85,400	85,450	17,628	13,719	18,041	16,204
85,450	85,500	17,642	13,731	18,055	16,216
85,500	85,550	17,656	13,744	18,069	16,229
85,550	85,600	17,670	13,756	18,083	16,241
85,600	85,650	17,684	13,769	18,097	16,254
85,650	85,700	17,698	13,781	18,111	16,266
85,700	85,750	17,712	13,794	18,125	16,279
85,750	85,800	17,726	13,806	18,139	16,291
85,800	85,850	17,740	13,819	18,153	16,304
85,850	85,900	17,754	13,831	18,167	16,316
85,900	85,950	17,768	13,844	18,181	16,329
85,950	86,000	17,782	13,856	18,195	16,341

* This column must also be used by a qualifying widow(er).

(Continued on next page)

2010 Tax Table–*Continued*

If line 43 (taxable income) is—		And you are—			
At least	But less than	Single	Married filing jointly *	Married filing separately	Head of a house-hold
		Your tax is—			

86,000

At least	But less than	Single	Married filing jointly *	Married filing separately	Head of a household
86,000	86,050	17,796	13,869	18,209	16,354
86,050	86,100	17,810	13,881	18,223	16,366
86,100	86,150	17,824	13,894	18,237	16,379
86,150	86,200	17,838	13,906	18,251	16,391
86,200	86,250	17,852	13,919	18,265	16,404
86,250	86,300	17,866	13,931	18,279	16,416
86,300	86,350	17,880	13,944	18,293	16,429
86,350	86,400	17,894	13,956	18,307	16,441
86,400	86,450	17,908	13,969	18,321	16,454
86,450	86,500	17,922	13,981	18,335	16,466
86,500	86,550	17,936	13,994	18,349	16,479
86,550	86,600	17,950	14,006	18,363	16,491
86,600	86,650	17,964	14,019	18,377	16,504
86,650	86,700	17,978	14,031	18,391	16,516
86,700	86,750	17,992	14,044	18,405	16,529
86,750	86,800	18,006	14,056	18,419	16,541
86,800	86,850	18,020	14,069	18,433	16,554
86,850	86,900	18,034	14,081	18,447	16,566
86,900	86,950	18,048	14,094	18,461	16,579
86,950	87,000	18,062	14,106	18,475	16,591

87,000

At least	But less than	Single	Married filing jointly *	Married filing separately	Head of a household
87,000	87,050	18,076	14,119	18,489	16,604
87,050	87,100	18,090	14,131	18,503	16,616
87,100	87,150	18,104	14,144	18,517	16,629
87,150	87,200	18,118	14,156	18,531	16,641
87,200	87,250	18,132	14,169	18,545	16,654
87,250	87,300	18,146	14,181	18,559	16,666
87,300	87,350	18,160	14,194	18,573	16,679
87,350	87,400	18,174	14,206	18,587	16,691
87,400	87,450	18,188	14,219	18,601	16,704
87,450	87,500	18,202	14,231	18,615	16,716
87,500	87,550	18,216	14,244	18,629	16,729
87,550	87,600	18,230	14,256	18,643	16,741
87,600	87,650	18,244	14,269	18,657	16,754
87,650	87,700	18,258	14,281	18,671	16,766
87,700	87,750	18,272	14,294	18,685	16,779
87,750	87,800	18,286	14,306	18,699	16,791
87,800	87,850	18,300	14,319	18,713	16,804
87,850	87,900	18,314	14,331	18,727	16,816
87,900	87,950	18,328	14,344	18,741	16,829
87,950	88,000	18,342	14,356	18,755	16,841

88,000

At least	But less than	Single	Married filing jointly *	Married filing separately	Head of a household
88,000	88,050	18,356	14,369	18,769	16,854
88,050	88,100	18,370	14,381	18,783	16,866
88,100	88,150	18,384	14,394	18,797	16,879
88,150	88,200	18,398	14,406	18,811	16,891
88,200	88,250	18,412	14,419	18,825	16,904
88,250	88,300	18,426	14,431	18,839	16,916
88,300	88,350	18,440	14,444	18,853	16,929
88,350	88,400	18,454	14,456	18,867	16,941
88,400	88,450	18,468	14,469	18,881	16,954
88,450	88,500	18,482	14,481	18,895	16,966
88,500	88,550	18,496	14,494	18,909	16,979
88,550	88,600	18,510	14,506	18,923	16,991
88,600	88,650	18,524	14,519	18,937	17,004
88,650	88,700	18,538	14,531	18,951	17,016
88,700	88,750	18,552	14,544	18,965	17,029
88,750	88,800	18,566	14,556	18,979	17,041
88,800	88,850	18,580	14,569	18,993	17,054
88,850	88,900	18,594	14,581	19,007	17,066
88,900	88,950	18,608	14,594	19,021	17,079
88,950	89,000	18,622	14,606	19,035	17,091

89,000

At least	But less than	Single	Married filing jointly *	Married filing separately	Head of a household
89,000	89,050	18,636	14,619	19,049	17,104
89,050	89,100	18,650	14,631	19,063	17,116
89,100	89,150	18,664	14,644	19,077	17,129
89,150	89,200	18,678	14,656	19,091	17,141
89,200	89,250	18,692	14,669	19,105	17,154
89,250	89,300	18,706	14,681	19,119	17,166
89,300	89,350	18,720	14,694	19,133	17,179
89,350	89,400	18,734	14,706	19,147	17,191
89,400	89,450	18,748	14,719	19,161	17,204
89,450	89,500	18,762	14,731	19,175	17,216
89,500	89,550	18,776	14,744	19,189	17,229
89,550	89,600	18,790	14,756	19,203	17,241
89,600	89,650	18,804	14,769	19,217	17,254
89,650	89,700	18,818	14,781	19,231	17,266
89,700	89,750	18,832	14,794	19,245	17,279
89,750	89,800	18,846	14,806	19,259	17,291
89,800	89,850	18,860	14,819	19,273	17,304
89,850	89,900	18,874	14,831	19,287	17,316
89,900	89,950	18,888	14,844	19,301	17,329
89,950	90,000	18,902	14,856	19,315	17,341

90,000

At least	But less than	Single	Married filing jointly *	Married filing separately	Head of a household
90,000	90,050	18,916	14,869	19,329	17,354
90,050	90,100	18,930	14,881	19,343	17,366
90,100	90,150	18,944	14,894	19,357	17,379
90,150	90,200	18,958	14,906	19,371	17,391
90,200	90,250	18,972	14,919	19,385	17,404
90,250	90,300	18,986	14,931	19,399	17,416
90,300	90,350	19,000	14,944	19,413	17,429
90,350	90,400	19,014	14,956	19,427	17,441
90,400	90,450	19,028	14,969	19,441	17,454
90,450	90,500	19,042	14,981	19,455	17,466
90,500	90,550	19,056	14,994	19,469	17,479
90,550	90,600	19,070	15,006	19,483	17,491
90,600	90,650	19,084	15,019	19,497	17,504
90,650	90,700	19,098	15,031	19,511	17,516
90,700	90,750	19,112	15,044	19,525	17,529
90,750	90,800	19,126	15,056	19,539	17,541
90,800	90,850	19,140	15,069	19,553	17,554
90,850	90,900	19,154	15,081	19,567	17,566
90,900	90,950	19,168	15,094	19,581	17,579
90,950	91,000	19,182	15,106	19,595	17,591

91,000

At least	But less than	Single	Married filing jointly *	Married filing separately	Head of a household
91,000	91,050	19,196	15,119	19,609	17,604
91,050	91,100	19,210	15,131	19,623	17,616
91,100	91,150	19,224	15,144	19,637	17,629
91,150	91,200	19,238	15,156	19,651	17,641
91,200	91,250	19,252	15,169	19,665	17,654
91,250	91,300	19,266	15,181	19,679	17,666
91,300	91,350	19,280	15,194	19,693	17,679
91,350	91,400	19,294	15,206	19,707	17,691
91,400	91,450	19,308	15,219	19,721	17,704
91,450	91,500	19,322	15,231	19,735	17,716
91,500	91,550	19,336	15,244	19,749	17,729
91,550	91,600	19,350	15,256	19,763	17,741
91,600	91,650	19,364	15,269	19,777	17,754
91,650	91,700	19,378	15,281	19,791	17,766
91,700	91,750	19,392	15,294	19,805	17,779
91,750	91,800	19,406	15,306	19,819	17,791
91,800	91,850	19,420	15,319	19,833	17,804
91,850	91,900	19,434	15,331	19,847	17,816
91,900	91,950	19,448	15,344	19,861	17,829
91,950	92,000	19,462	15,356	19,875	17,841

92,000

At least	But less than	Single	Married filing jointly *	Married filing separately	Head of a household
92,000	92,050	19,476	15,369	19,889	17,854
92,050	92,100	19,490	15,381	19,903	17,866
92,100	92,150	19,504	15,394	19,917	17,879
92,150	92,200	19,518	15,406	19,931	17,891
92,200	92,250	19,532	15,419	19,945	17,904
92,250	92,300	19,546	15,431	19,959	17,916
92,300	92,350	19,560	15,444	19,973	17,929
92,350	92,400	19,574	15,456	19,987	17,941
92,400	92,450	19,588	15,469	20,001	17,954
92,450	92,500	19,602	15,481	20,015	17,966
92,500	92,550	19,616	15,494	20,029	17,979
92,550	92,600	19,630	15,506	20,043	17,991
92,600	92,650	19,644	15,519	20,057	18,004
92,650	92,700	19,658	15,531	20,071	18,016
92,700	92,750	19,672	15,544	20,085	18,029
92,750	92,800	19,686	15,556	20,099	18,041
92,800	92,850	19,700	15,569	20,113	18,054
92,850	92,900	19,714	15,581	20,127	18,066
92,900	92,950	19,728	15,594	20,141	18,079
92,950	93,000	19,742	15,606	20,155	18,091

93,000

At least	But less than	Single	Married filing jointly *	Married filing separately	Head of a household
93,000	93,050	19,756	15,619	20,169	18,104
93,050	93,100	19,770	15,631	20,183	18,116
93,100	93,150	19,784	15,644	20,197	18,129
93,150	93,200	19,798	15,656	20,211	18,141
93,200	93,250	19,812	15,669	20,225	18,154
93,250	93,300	19,826	15,681	20,239	18,166
93,300	93,350	19,840	15,694	20,253	18,179
93,350	93,400	19,854	15,706	20,267	18,191
93,400	93,450	19,868	15,719	20,281	18,204
93,450	93,500	19,882	15,731	20,295	18,216
93,500	93,550	19,896	15,744	20,309	18,229
93,550	93,600	19,910	15,756	20,323	18,241
93,600	93,650	19,924	15,769	20,337	18,254
93,650	93,700	19,938	15,781	20,351	18,266
93,700	93,750	19,952	15,794	20,365	18,279
93,750	93,800	19,966	15,806	20,379	18,291
93,800	93,850	19,980	15,819	20,393	18,304
93,850	93,900	19,994	15,831	20,407	18,316
93,900	93,950	20,008	15,844	20,421	18,329
93,950	94,000	20,022	15,856	20,435	18,341

94,000

At least	But less than	Single	Married filing jointly *	Married filing separately	Head of a household
94,000	94,050	20,036	15,869	20,449	18,354
94,050	94,100	20,050	15,881	20,463	18,366
94,100	94,150	20,064	15,894	20,477	18,379
94,150	94,200	20,078	15,906	20,491	18,391
94,200	94,250	20,092	15,919	20,505	18,404
94,250	94,300	20,106	15,931	20,519	18,416
94,300	94,350	20,120	15,944	20,533	18,429
94,350	94,400	20,134	15,956	20,547	18,441
94,400	94,450	20,148	15,969	20,561	18,454
94,450	94,500	20,162	15,981	20,575	18,466
94,500	94,550	20,176	15,994	20,589	18,479
94,550	94,600	20,190	16,006	20,603	18,491
94,600	94,650	20,204	16,019	20,617	18,504
94,650	94,700	20,218	16,031	20,631	18,516
94,700	94,750	20,232	16,044	20,645	18,529
94,750	94,800	20,246	16,056	20,659	18,541
94,800	94,850	20,260	16,069	20,673	18,554
94,850	94,900	20,274	16,081	20,687	18,566
94,900	94,950	20,288	16,094	20,701	18,579
94,950	95,000	20,302	16,106	20,715	18,591

* This column must also be used by a qualifying widow(er).

(Continued on next page)

2010 Tax Table–*Continued*

If line 43 (taxable income) is—		And you are—				If line 43 (taxable income) is—		And you are—				If line 43 (taxable income) is—		And you are—			
At least	But less than	Single	Married filing jointly *	Married filing separately	Head of a household	At least	But less than	Single	Married filing jointly *	Married filing separately	Head of a household	At least	But less than	Single	Married filing jointly *	Married filing separately	Head of a household
		Your tax is—						Your tax is—						Your tax is—			
95,000						**97,000**						**99,000**					
95,000	95,050	20,316	16,119	20,729	18,604	97,000	97,050	20,876	16,619	21,289	19,104	99,000	99,050	21,436	17,119	21,849	19,604
95,050	95,100	20,330	16,131	20,743	18,616	97,050	97,100	20,890	16,631	21,303	19,116	99,050	99,100	21,450	17,131	21,863	19,616
95,100	95,150	20,344	16,144	20,757	18,629	97,100	97,150	20,904	16,644	21,317	19,129	99,100	99,150	21,464	17,144	21,877	19,629
95,150	95,200	20,358	16,156	20,771	18,641	97,150	97,200	20,918	16,656	21,331	19,141	99,150	99,200	21,478	17,156	21,891	19,641
95,200	95,250	20,372	16,169	20,785	18,654	97,200	97,250	20,932	16,669	21,345	19,154	99,200	99,250	21,492	17,169	21,905	19,654
95,250	95,300	20,386	16,181	20,799	18,666	97,250	97,300	20,946	16,681	21,359	19,166	99,250	99,300	21,506	17,181	21,919	19,666
95,300	95,350	20,400	16,194	20,813	18,679	97,300	97,350	20,960	16,694	21,373	19,179	99,300	99,350	21,520	17,194	21,933	19,679
95,350	95,400	20,414	16,206	20,827	18,691	97,350	97,400	20,974	16,706	21,387	19,191	99,350	99,400	21,534	17,206	21,947	19,691
95,400	95,450	20,428	16,219	20,841	18,704	97,400	97,450	20,988	16,719	21,401	19,204	99,400	99,450	21,548	17,219	21,961	19,704
95,450	95,500	20,442	16,231	20,855	18,716	97,450	97,500	21,002	16,731	21,415	19,216	99,450	99,500	21,562	17,231	21,975	19,716
95,500	95,550	20,456	16,244	20,869	18,729	97,500	97,550	21,016	16,744	21,429	19,229	99,500	99,550	21,576	17,244	21,989	19,729
95,550	95,600	20,470	16,256	20,883	18,741	97,550	97,600	21,030	16,756	21,443	19,241	99,550	99,600	21,590	17,256	22,003	19,741
95,600	95,650	20,484	16,269	20,897	18,754	97,600	97,650	21,044	16,769	21,457	19,254	99,600	99,650	21,604	17,269	22,017	19,754
95,650	95,700	20,498	16,281	20,911	18,766	97,650	97,700	21,058	16,781	21,471	19,266	99,650	99,700	21,618	17,281	22,031	19,766
95,700	95,750	20,512	16,294	20,925	18,779	97,700	97,750	21,072	16,794	21,485	19,279	99,700	99,750	21,632	17,294	22,045	19,779
95,750	95,800	20,526	16,306	20,939	18,791	97,750	97,800	21,086	16,806	21,499	19,291	99,750	99,800	21,646	17,306	22,059	19,791
95,800	95,850	20,540	16,319	20,953	18,804	97,800	97,850	21,100	16,819	21,513	19,304	99,800	99,850	21,660	17,319	22,073	19,804
95,850	95,900	20,554	16,331	20,967	18,816	97,850	97,900	21,114	16,831	21,527	19,316	99,850	99,900	21,674	17,331	22,087	19,816
95,900	95,950	20,568	16,344	20,981	18,829	97,900	97,950	21,128	16,844	21,541	19,329	99,900	99,950	21,688	17,344	22,101	19,829
95,950	96,000	20,582	16,356	20,995	18,841	97,950	98,000	21,142	16,856	21,555	19,341	99,950	100,000	21,702	17,356	22,115	19,841
96,000						**98,000**											
96,000	96,050	20,596	16,369	21,009	18,854	98,000	98,050	21,156	16,869	21,569	19,354						
96,050	96,100	20,610	16,381	21,023	18,866	98,050	98,100	21,170	16,881	21,583	19,366						
96,100	96,150	20,624	16,394	21,037	18,879	98,100	98,150	21,184	16,894	21,597	19,379						
96,150	96,200	20,638	16,406	21,051	18,891	98,150	98,200	21,198	16,906	21,611	19,391						
96,200	96,250	20,652	16,419	21,065	18,904	98,200	98,250	21,212	16,919	21,625	19,404						
96,250	96,300	20,666	16,431	21,079	18,916	98,250	98,300	21,226	16,931	21,639	19,416						
96,300	96,350	20,680	16,444	21,093	18,929	98,300	98,350	21,240	16,944	21,653	19,429						
96,350	96,400	20,694	16,456	21,107	18,941	98,350	98,400	21,254	16,956	21,667	19,441						
96,400	96,450	20,708	16,469	21,121	18,954	98,400	98,450	21,268	16,969	21,681	19,454						
96,450	96,500	20,722	16,481	21,135	18,966	98,450	98,500	21,282	16,981	21,695	19,466						
96,500	96,550	20,736	16,494	21,149	18,979	98,500	98,550	21,296	16,994	21,709	19,479						
96,550	96,600	20,750	16,506	21,163	18,991	98,550	98,600	21,310	17,006	21,723	19,491						
96,600	96,650	20,764	16,519	21,177	19,004	98,600	98,650	21,324	17,019	21,737	19,504						
96,650	96,700	20,778	16,531	21,191	19,016	98,650	98,700	21,338	17,031	21,751	19,516						
96,700	96,750	20,792	16,544	21,205	19,029	98,700	98,750	21,352	17,044	21,765	19,529						
96,750	96,800	20,806	16,556	21,219	19,041	98,750	98,800	21,366	17,056	21,779	19,541						
96,800	96,850	20,820	16,569	21,233	19,054	98,800	98,850	21,380	17,069	21,793	19,554						
96,850	96,900	20,834	16,581	21,247	19,066	98,850	98,900	21,394	17,081	21,807	19,566						
96,900	96,950	20,848	16,594	21,261	19,079	98,900	98,950	21,408	17,094	21,821	19,579						
96,950	97,000	20,862	16,606	21,275	19,091	98,950	99,000	21,422	17,106	21,835	19,591						

$100,000 or over — use the Tax Rate Schedules on page A-2

* This column must also be used by a qualifying widow(er)

2010 OPTIONAL SALES TAX TABLES

When Used

The election to deduct state and local general sales taxes requires that the taxpayer forgo any deduction for state and local income taxes. Whether this is advisable or not depends on a comparison of the amounts involved. In making the choice, however, the outcome could be influenced by the additional sales tax incurred due to certain "big ticket" purchases that were made. For example, a taxpayer who chose to deduct state and local income taxes for 2009 might well prefer the sales tax deduction in 2010 if a new boat was purchased or home improvements were made during the year. To make the sales tax election, the taxpayer must enter the amount on Schedule A, line 5, and check box b.

If the sales tax election is made, the amount of the deduction can be determined by use of the *actual expense method* or the *optional sales tax tables* issued by the IRS. The actual expense method can be used only when the taxpayer has actual receipts to support the deduction claimed. In the absence of receipts, the usual case with most taxpayers, resorting to the optional sales tax tables is necessary. Under neither method, however, is the purchase of items used in a taxpayer's trade or business to be considered.

Adjustments Necessary

The optional sales tax tables are based on a number of assumptions that require adjustments to be made. As the starting point for the use of the tables is AGI, nontaxable receipts have not been included. Examples of receipts that should be added include: tax-exempt interest, veterans' benefits, nontaxable combat pay, public assistance payments, workers' compensation, nontaxable Social Security and other retirement benefits. But do not include any large nontaxable items that are not likely to be spent. For example, a $100,000 inheritance should not be added if it was invested in a certificate of deposit.

The tables represent the sales tax on the average (and recurring) expenditures based on level of income by family size and do not include exceptional purchases. Therefore, add to the table amount any sales taxes on major purchases (such as motor vehicles, aircraft, boats, and home building materials, etc.).

When the optional sales tax tables are utilized, special adjustments may be needed when a taxpayer has lived in more than one taxing jurisdiction (e.g., state, county, city) during the year. The adjustments involve apportionment of taxes based on days involved and are illustrated in Instructions for Schedule A (Form 1040), pages A-3 to A-5.

Local Sales Taxes

Local sales taxes (i.e., those imposed by counties, cities, transit authorities) may or may not require a separate determination. In those states where they are not imposed, no further computations are necessary. This is also the case where the local taxes are uniform and are incorporated into the state sales tax table. In other situations, another step is necessary to arrive at the optional sales tax table deduction. Depending on where the taxpayer lives, one of two procedures needs to be used. In one procedure, the local sales tax is arrived at by using the **state table** amount—see the Example 1 worksheet. In the other procedure, special **local tables** issued by the IRS for enumerated state and local jurisdictions are modified (if necessary) and used—see the Example 2 worksheet.

Use Illustrated

EXAMPLE 1 The Archers file a joint return for 2010 reflecting AGI of $88,000 and claiming three exemptions. They have tax-exempt interest of $3,000, and during the year they incurred sales tax of $1,650 on the purchase of an automobile for their dependent teenage son. They live in Bellaire, Texas, where the general sales tax rates are 6.25% for state and 2% for local. Since the IRS *has not issued* optional local sales tax tables for Texas, use the Worksheet below to arrive at the Archers' general sales tax deduction of $3,127.

Sales Tax Deduction Worksheet
(To be used when *no* IRS Optional Local Sales Tax Table Available)

Adjusted Gross Income (AGI) as listed on line 38 of Form 1040	$88,000
Add nontaxable items	3,000
Table income to be used for purposes of line 1 below	$91,000

1. Use table income to determine table amount—go to state of residence and find applicable range of table income and exemption column* for *state* sales tax		$ 1,119
2a. Enter local general sales tax rate	2.0	
2b. Enter state general sales tax rate	6.25	
2c. Divide 2a by 2b	0.32	
2d. Multiply line 1 by line 2c for the local sales tax		358
3. Enter general sales tax on large purchases		1,650
4. Deduction for general sales tax (add lines 1 + 2d + 3) and report on line 5 of Schedule A of Form 1040		$ 3,127

*Use total of personal and dependency exemptions as reported in item 6d of Form 1040.

EXAMPLE 2 The Hardys file a joint return for 2010, reporting AGI of $40,000 and claiming four exemptions (two personal and two dependency). They received $30,000 in nontaxable pension benefits. Although the Hardys do not keep sales tax receipts, they can prove that they paid $4,800 in sales tax on the purchase of a new boat in 2010. The Hardys are residents of Georgia and live in a jurisdiction that imposes a 2% local sales tax. Since the IRS *has issued* optional local sales tax tables for Georgia, use the Worksheet below to arrive at the Hardys' general sales tax deduction of $5,722.

Sales Tax Deduction Worksheet
[To be used for Alaska, Arizona, Arkansas, California (Los Angeles County), Colorado, Georgia, Illinois, Louisiana, Missouri, New York, North Carolina, South Carolina, Tennessee, Utah, and Virginia]

Adjusted Gross Income (AGI) as listed on line 38 of Form 1040	$40,000
Add nontaxable income	30,000
Table income to be used for purpose of line 1 below	$70,000

1. Use the table income to determine *state* sales tax amount—go to table for state of residence and find applicable income range and exemption column*		$ 562
2a. Enter local general sales tax rate	2.0	
2b. Enter IRS *local* sales tax table amount (based on 1%)	$180	
2c. Multiply line 2b by 2a for the local sales tax		360
3. Enter general sales tax on large purchases		4,800
4. Deduction for general sales tax (add lines 1 + 2c + 3) and report on line 5 of Schedule A of Form 1040		$ 5,722

*Use total of personal and dependency exemptions as reported in item 6d of Form 1040.

2010 Optional State and Certain Local Sales Tax Tables

Exemptions columns for each state: 1, 2, 3, 4, 5, Over 5

Alabama 4.0000% / Arizona¹ 6.1863% / Arkansas 6.0000% / California² 8.2500% / Colorado 2.9000%

Income (At least – But less than)	Alabama 1	2	3	4	5	Over 5	Arizona 1	2	3	4	5	Over 5	Arkansas 1	2	3	4	5	Over 5	California 1	2	3	4	5	Over 5	Colorado 1	2	3	4	5	Over 5
$0 – $20,000	235	287	324	353	378	413	253	297	326	349	368	395	302	359	397	427	452	487	326	379	414	441	464	495	122	141	154	164	172	184
20,000 – 30,000	336	409	460	501	535	583	408	476	522	558	588	630	472	559	618	664	702	756	523	605	660	702	737	786	185	213	232	247	259	276
30,000 – 40,000	385	468	525	570	609	663	487	567	622	664	700	749	558	659	728	782	827	890	624	721	785	835	876	934	216	249	271	288	302	321
40,000 – 50,000	426	516	579	629	670	730	555	646	708	756	795	851	630	745	822	883	933	1004	710	820	892	949	995	1061	243	279	304	322	338	360
50,000 – 60,000	463	559	626	680	724	788	616	717	785	837	881	943	695	821	906	972	1027	1105	788	908	989	1051	1102	1174	267	306	333	353	370	393
60,000 – 70,000	495	597	669	725	773	840	671	781	855	912	960	1026	754	890	982	1053	1113	1197	859	989	1076	1144	1199	1277	288	331	359	381	399	424
70,000 – 80,000	525	633	708	767	817	889	724	842	921	982	1033	1105	809	954	1053	1129	1193	1283	926	1066	1159	1231	1291	1374	309	354	384	407	426	453
80,000 – 90,000	553	666	744	806	858	933	773	898	982	1048	1102	1178	860	1014	1118	1199	1267	1362	988	1136	1236	1312	1376	1464	327	375	406	431	451	479
90,000 – 100,000	579	696	778	842	897	974	819	951	1040	1109	1167	1247	908	1070	1180	1266	1337	1437	1047	1204	1308	1389	1456	1549	345	395	428	453	474	504
100,000 – 120,000	613	736	821	889	946	1028	881	1022	1117	1191	1252	1338	971	1144	1261	1353	1428	1535	1125	1292	1404	1490	1562	1662	368	421	456	483	505	536
120,000 – 140,000	659	790	881	953	1014	1100	965	1118	1222	1302	1369	1462	1058	1245	1372	1471	1553	1669	1231	1413	1535	1629	1706	1815	400	456	494	523	547	581
140,000 – 160,000	699	836	932	1008	1071	1162	1038	1202	1313	1399	1471	1571	1133	1333	1468	1574	1661	1785	1324	1519	1649	1750	1833	1949	427	487	527	558	583	619
160,000 – 180,000	739	882	982	1062	1128	1223	1111	1287	1405	1496	1572	1679	1207	1420	1564	1676	1769	1900	1417	1625	1763	1870	1959	2082	454	518	560	593	619	657
180,000 – 200,000	774	923	1027	1110	1179	1278	1178	1362	1487	1584	1664	1777	1274	1498	1649	1767	1865	2003	1501	1720	1866	1979	2072	2203	479	545	590	624	652	691
200,000 or more	947	1123	1246	1344	1425	1542	1508	1741	1898	2020	2121	2262	1605	1883	2072	2219	2341	2512	1921	2195	2378	2520	2637	2800	601	682	735	777	811	858

Connecticut 6.0000% / District of Columbia 6.0000% / Florida 6.0000% / Georgia 4.0000% / Hawaii⁵ 4.0000%

Income (At least – But less than)	CT 1	2	3	4	5	Over 5	DC 1	2	3	4	5	Over 5	FL 1	2	3	4	5	Over 5	GA 1	2	3	4	5	Over 5	HI 1	2	3	4	5	Over 5
$0 – $20,000	235	270	293	310	325	345	186	216	236	252	265	283	262	306	336	359	378	404	169	195	213	226	237	253	262	318	356	386	411	447
20,000 – 30,000	377	431	468	495	518	550	305	353	385	410	431	461	420	488	535	570	600	642	257	295	321	341	357	380	395	477	533	577	614	667
30,000 – 40,000	449	513	556	589	617	654	366	423	462	492	517	552	500	581	635	678	713	762	301	345	375	397	416	442	460	554	619	670	713	774
40,000 – 50,000	510	584	632	670	701	743	419	484	528	563	591	631	568	660	722	769	809	864	338	387	420	445	466	495	515	620	692	749	796	864
50,000 – 60,000	566	647	701	742	776	823	467	539	588	626	657	702	630	731	799	851	895	956	371	425	460	488	511	542	563	678	756	818	870	943
60,000 – 70,000	616	704	763	807	844	896	511	590	643	684	718	766	686	795	869	926	973	1040	401	458	497	526	551	584	607	730	814	880	936	1014
70,000 – 80,000	664	758	821	869	909	964	553	637	694	739	776	827	739	856	935	997	1047	1118	429	490	531	562	588	624	648	778	868	938	997	1081
80,000 – 90,000	708	808	875	926	968	1027	592	682	742	790	829	884	788	913	997	1062	1116	1191	455	519	562	595	623	660	685	823	917	992	1054	1142
90,000 – 100,000	749	856	926	980	1025	1087	628	724	788	838	880	938	834	966	1055	1123	1180	1260	480	547	592	627	655	695	721	865	964	1042	1107	1199
100,000 – 120,000	804	918	993	1051	1099	1165	677	779	848	902	946	1009	895	1036	1131	1204	1265	1350	512	583	631	668	698	740	767	920	1025	1107	1176	1274
120,000 – 140,000	879	1003	1085	1149	1200	1273	744	855	931	989	1038	1106	979	1133	1236	1315	1381	1474	556	633	684	723	756	801	829	994	1107	1196	1270	1375
140,000 – 160,000	944	1077	1166	1233	1289	1366	802	922	1003	1066	1118	1192	1052	1217	1327	1412	1483	1582	594	676	730	772	806	854	883	1058	1178	1272	1351	1463
160,000 – 180,000	1009	1151	1245	1318	1377	1459	861	989	1076	1143	1199	1277	1125	1300	1418	1508	1584	1689	632	718	776	820	856	907	937	1121	1248	1348	1431	1549
180,000 – 200,000	1068	1218	1317	1393	1456	1543	913	1049	1141	1212	1271	1354	1191	1375	1499	1595	1675	1786	666	757	817	863	901	954	985	1178	1311	1415	1503	1626
200,000 or more	1359	1549	1674	1770	1849	1959	1179	1351	1468	1558	1633	1738	1518	1750	1906	2026	2126	2265	836	946	1019	1075	1121	1186	1219	1456	1618	1745	1851	2002

Idaho 6.0000% / Illinois 6.2500% / Indiana 7.0000% / Iowa 6.0000% / Kansas¹ 5.8041%

Income (At least – But less than)	ID 1	2	3	4	5	Over 5	IL 1	2	3	4	5	Over 5	IN 1	2	3	4	5	Over 5	IA 1	2	3	4	5	Over 5	KS 1	2	3	4	5	Over 5
$0 – $20,000	270	320	353	379	401	431	365	447	505	550	589	644	302	354	389	417	439	472	268	312	342	365	383	410	338	417	473	517	554	608
20,000 – 30,000	432	509	562	602	636	684	529	645	725	789	844	921	456	531	581	621	654	700	404	469	512	546	574	613	510	627	709	774	829	908
30,000 – 40,000	513	605	667	715	756	812	608	740	831	904	965	1052	532	618	676	721	759	812	471	546	596	635	667	711	595	730	824	900	963	1054
40,000 – 50,000	583	687	757	812	857	921	675	819	919	999	1066	1162	597	692	756	806	848	906	527	611	667	710	745	795	666	816	921	1005	1076	1177
50,000 – 60,000	646	760	838	898	948	1019	734	889	997	1083	1155	1258	655	757	827	881	926	990	578	669	729	776	815	868	730	893	1007	1098	1175	1285
60,000 – 70,000	703	827	911	977	1031	1108	787	952	1067	1158	1234	1344	707	816	891	949	997	1065	623	721	786	836	877	935	787	962	1085	1182	1265	1383
70,000 – 80,000	757	890	980	1050	1109	1191	836	1010	1131	1227	1308	1424	757	872	951	1012	1063	1135	665	769	838	891	935	997	840	1026	1157	1260	1348	1474
80,000 – 90,000	807	948	1044	1119	1181	1268	882	1064	1190	1291	1376	1497	802	923	1006	1070	1124	1199	705	814	887	943	989	1054	889	1085	1223	1332	1425	1557
90,000 – 100,000	854	1003	1105	1183	1249	1341	924	1114	1246	1351	1439	1565	845	972	1058	1125	1181	1260	741	856	932	991	1040	1107	935	1141	1285	1400	1497	1635
100,000 – 120,000	916	1076	1184	1268	1338	1437	980	1179	1318	1429	1521	1654	901	1035	1126	1197	1256	1339	790	911	992	1054	1105	1177	995	1214	1366	1488	1591	1737
120,000 – 140,000	1000	1175	1293	1384	1461	1568	1056	1268	1416	1534	1633	1774	978	1121	1219	1295	1358	1447	855	986	1073	1140	1195	1272	1077	1312	1477	1608	1718	1876
140,000 – 160,000	1074	1261	1387	1486	1567	1682	1121	1345	1501	1625	1729	1877	1045	1196	1299	1380	1446	1541	912	1051	1143	1214	1273	1354	1148	1398	1572	1711	1828	1995
160,000 – 180,000	1148	1347	1481	1586	1673	1796	1186	1421	1584	1714	1823	1979	1111	1271	1379	1464	1534	1633	968	1115	1212	1287	1349	1435	1219	1482	1666	1813	1937	2113
180,000 – 200,000	1214	1424	1566	1677	1769	1898	1244	1488	1659	1794	1907	2070	1171	1337	1451	1539	1612	1716	1019	1172	1274	1353	1418	1508	1281	1557	1751	1904	2034	2219
200,000 or more	1543	1807	1986	2125	2241	2403	1528	1819	2021	2182	2317	2510	1468	1668	1804	1910	1998	2123	1267	1455	1579	1675	1754	1864	1590	1927	2162	2350	2508	2733

Kentucky 6.0000% / Louisiana 4.0000% / Maine 5.0000% / Maryland 6.0000% / Massachusetts 6.2500%

Income (At least – But less than)	KY 1	2	3	4	5	Over 5	LA 1	2	3	4	5	Over 5	ME 1	2	3	4	5	Over 5	MD 1	2	3	4	5	Over 5	MA 1	2	3	4	5	Over 5
$0 – $20,000	258	301	330	352	370	396	176	205	224	239	251	268	160	186	203	217	228	244	246	286	312	333	350	373	230	260	279	293	305	322
20,000 – 30,000	394	457	499	532	558	596	282	327	357	380	399	426	261	301	329	350	367	392	377	434	473	503	527	562	351	393	421	443	460	484
30,000 – 40,000	462	534	583	620	651	695	336	389	424	452	475	506	312	360	393	418	439	468	442	508	552	587	615	655	410	460	492	516	536	564
40,000 – 50,000	519	600	654	695	730	778	382	442	482	513	539	575	357	411	448	476	500	533	497	570	620	658	689	734	461	516	552	579	601	631
50,000 – 60,000	570	658	716	762	799	852	423	490	534	568	596	636	397	457	498	529	555	592	546	626	679	721	755	804	507	566	605	634	658	691
60,000 – 70,000	616	710	773	822	862	919	461	533	581	618	649	692	434	499	543	577	605	645	591	676	734	778	815	867	548	611	652	684	710	745
70,000 – 80,000	660	760	827	879	921	981	497	574	625	665	698	744	469	539	586	623	653	695	633	724	785	832	871	925	586	653	697	731	758	796
80,000 – 90,000	700	805	876	931	976	1039	530	612	666	709	744	792	501	576	626	665	697	742	672	767	831	881	922	980	622	692	739	774	803	843
90,000 – 100,000	738	848	922	980	1027	1093	561	647	705	750	787	838	532	611	664	705	739	787	709	809	876	928	971	1031	655	729	778	815	845	887
100,000 – 120,000	788	905	983	1044	1094	1164	602	694	756	804	844	899	573	657	714	758	794	845	757	863	934	989	1034	1098	699	778	829	868	900	944
120,000 – 140,000	856	982	1066	1131	1185	1260	658	759	826	878	921	981	629	721	782	830	870	925	824	937	1013	1072	1121	1189	759	844	899	941	975	1022
140,000 – 160,000	915	1049	1138	1207	1264	1344	708	815	887	943	989	1053	678	776	842	894	936	996	881	1001	1082	1144	1196	1268	811	901	959	1004	1040	1090
160,000 – 180,000	974	1115	1209	1282	1343	1427	757	871	948	1007	1056	1125	727	832	902	957	1002	1066	939	1065	1150	1216	1270	1347	863	958	1019	1066	1105	1158
180,000 – 200,000	1027	1174	1273	1350	1413	1501	801	922	1003	1065	1117	1189	771	882	956	1014	1062	1129	990	1122	1211	1280	1337	1417	910	1009	1073	1122	1163	1218
200,000 or more	1288	1469	1590	1683	1760	1867	1021	1173	1275	1354	1419	1509	994	1133	1227	1300	1360	1444	1247	1407	1514	1598	1667	1764	1141	1261	1340	1399	1448	1515

Michigan 6.0000% / Minnesota 6.8750% / Mississippi 7.0000% / Missouri 4.2250% / Nebraska 5.5000%

Income (At least – But less than)	MI 1	2	3	4	5	Over 5	MN 1	2	3	4	5	Over 5	MS 1	2	3	4	5	Over 5	MO 1	2	3	4	5	Over 5	NE 1	2	3	4	5	Over 5
$0 – $20,000	248	287	313	333	349	372	256	296	322	343	360	384	426	520	585	637	680	742	187	223	247	267	283	305	247	289	317	339	357	382
20,000 – 30,000	379	436	474	504	528	561	413	476	518	551	578	616	644	783	879	956	1020	1111	285	338	374	402	426	459	395	461	505	540	569	609
30,000 – 40,000	444	510	554	588	616	655	493	568	618	657	689	734	752	912	1023	1112	1186	1291	334	395	436	469	496	535	470	548	601	642	676	723
40,000 – 50,000	500	573	622	659	690	733	561	646	703	748	784	835	841	1020	1144	1243	1325	1443	375	443	489	525	556	599	534	623	683	729	767	821
50,000 – 60,000	549	629	682	723	756	803	623	717	780	829	869	925	921	1116	1251	1358	1448	1576	412	486	536	576	609	655	592	690	756	807	849	908
60,000 – 70,000	594	679	736	780	816	866	679	782	850	903	947	1008	993	1203	1348	1462	1559	1696	446	524	578	621	656	706	644	751	823	878	924	988
70,000 – 80,000	636	727	787	834	872	925	732	842	916	973	1020	1086	1061	1284	1438	1560	1662	1808	477	561	618	663	701	754	694	808	885	945	994	1063
80,000 – 90,000	675	770	834	883	923	980	781	899	977	1037	1088	1157	1123	1358	1520	1649	1757	1911	506	594	655	702	742	798	740	862	943	1007	1059	1132
90,000 – 100,000	711	812	878	930	972	1031	828	952	1035	1099	1152	1226	1181	1427	1598	1733	1846	2008	533	626	689	739	780	839	783	912	998	1065	1120	1198
100,000 – 120,000	760	866	937	991	1036	1098	889	1022	1111	1179	1236	1315	1257	1518	1700	1843	1963	2134	569	667	735	787	831	893	840	978	1070	1142	1201	1284
120,000 – 140,000	825	940	1016	1074	1123	1190	973	1118	1215	1290	1351	1438	1361	1642	1837	1991	2121	2305	618	724	796	853	900	967	918	1068	1169	1247	1312	1402
140,000 – 160,000	883	1004	1085	1147	1198	1269	1047	1202	1306	1386	1452	1545	1451	1749	1956	2120	2257	2452	661	773	850	910	960	1030	986	1147	1255	1339	1408	1505
160,000 – 180,000	940	1068	1153	1218	1272	1348	1120	1286	1396	1482	1553	1651	1539	1855	2074	2247	2392	2598	703	822	903	966	1019	1093	1054	1226	1341	1430	1504	1607
180,000 – 200,000	991	1125	1214	1283	1339	1418	1186	1361	1478	1568	1643	1747	1619	1950	2179	2360	2512	2728	741	865	950	1017	1072	1150	1115	1297	1418	1512	1590	1699
200,000 or more	1245	1408	1517	1601	1670	1766	1514	1735	1883	1998	2092	2224	2008	2413	2693	2915	3100	3364	930	1081	1185	1266	1333	1428	1419	1648	1801	1920	2018	2155

(Continued on next page)

2010 Optional State and Certain Local Sales Tax Tables *(Continued)*

Nevada[3] 6.8500%

Income (At least / But less than)	1	2	3	4	5	Over 5
$0 – $20,000	288	332	361	384	402	428
20,000 – 30,000	435	499	542	574	602	639
30,000 – 40,000	508	581	630	668	699	743
40,000 – 50,000	569	651	706	747	782	830
50,000 – 60,000	624	713	772	818	855	907
60,000 – 70,000	674	769	832	881	921	977
70,000 – 80,000	721	822	889	940	983	1042
80,000 – 90,000	764	870	941	995	1040	1102
90,000 – 100,000	805	916	990	1047	1093	1158
100,000 – 120,000	858	976	1054	1114	1163	1232
120,000 – 140,000	931	1058	1141	1206	1259	1333
140,000 – 160,000	995	1129	1217	1286	1342	1420
160,000 – 180,000	1058	1199	1293	1364	1424	1506
180,000 – 200,000	1115	1262	1360	1435	1497	1583
200,000 or more	1395	1575	1693	1784	1859	1964

New Jersey[4] 7.0000%

Income (At least / But less than)	1	2	3	4	5	Over 5
$0 – $20,000	274	315	343	364	381	406
20,000 – 30,000	440	504	547	580	607	645
30,000 – 40,000	524	600	651	690	722	767
40,000 – 50,000	596	682	739	784	820	871
50,000 – 60,000	661	756	819	868	908	964
60,000 – 70,000	720	823	891	944	988	1048
70,000 – 80,000	776	886	959	1016	1063	1128
80,000 – 90,000	827	944	1023	1083	1133	1202
90,000 – 100,000	876	1000	1082	1146	1198	1272
100,000 – 120,000	940	1073	1161	1229	1285	1363
120,000 – 140,000	1029	1173	1269	1343	1404	1489
140,000 – 160,000	1106	1260	1362	1442	1507	1598
160,000 – 180,000	1182	1346	1456	1540	1610	1707
180,000 – 200,000	1251	1425	1540	1629	1702	1805
200,000 or more	1595	1813	1958	2070	2162	2291

New Mexico[1] 5.0630%

Income (At least / But less than)	1	2	3	4	5	Over 5
$0 – $20,000	211	248	273	292	308	331
20,000 – 30,000	337	395	434	464	489	525
30,000 – 40,000	400	469	515	551	581	622
40,000 – 50,000	455	533	585	626	659	706
50,000 – 60,000	504	590	647	692	729	781
60,000 – 70,000	548	641	704	752	793	849
70,000 – 80,000	590	690	757	809	852	913
80,000 – 90,000	629	735	807	862	908	972
90,000 – 100,000	665	778	853	912	960	1028
100,000 – 120,000	713	834	915	977	1029	1101
120,000 – 140,000	779	911	999	1067	1123	1202
140,000 – 160,000	837	978	1072	1145	1205	1289
160,000 – 180,000	894	1044	1145	1222	1287	1376
180,000 – 200,000	946	1104	1210	1292	1360	1455
200,000 or more	1203	1402	1535	1638	1724	1843

New York 4.0000%

Income (At least / But less than)	1	2	3	4	5	Over 5
$0 – $20,000	161	187	204	217	228	243
20,000 – 30,000	258	298	324	345	362	386
30,000 – 40,000	307	354	385	410	430	458
40,000 – 50,000	350	402	438	465	488	520
50,000 – 60,000	387	446	485	515	540	575
60,000 – 70,000	422	485	527	560	587	625
70,000 – 80,000	455	522	567	603	632	672
80,000 – 90,000	485	557	605	642	673	716
90,000 – 100,000	513	589	640	679	712	757
100,000 – 120,000	551	632	686	728	763	812
120,000 – 140,000	603	691	750	795	833	886
140,000 – 160,000	648	742	805	854	894	951
160,000 – 180,000	693	793	860	912	955	1015
180,000 – 200,000	733	839	910	965	1010	1073
200,000 or more	935	1067	1156	1225	1282	1361

North Carolina 5.7500%

Income (At least / But less than)	1	2	3	4	5	Over 5
$0 – $20,000	281	336	374	404	428	463
20,000 – 30,000	436	519	576	621	658	711
30,000 – 40,000	513	610	677	729	773	834
40,000 – 50,000	578	687	762	821	870	938
50,000 – 60,000	636	756	838	902	956	1031
60,000 – 70,000	689	818	907	976	1033	1115
70,000 – 80,000	739	877	971	1045	1106	1193
80,000 – 90,000	784	930	1030	1108	1173	1265
90,000 – 100,000	827	981	1086	1168	1237	1333
100,000 – 120,000	884	1048	1159	1247	1319	1422
120,000 – 140,000	961	1138	1259	1353	1432	1543
140,000 – 160,000	1028	1217	1346	1446	1530	1649
160,000 – 180,000	1095	1295	1431	1538	1627	1753
180,000 – 200,000	1154	1365	1508	1620	1714	1846
200,000 or more	1449	1710	1887	2026	2142	2305

North Dakota 5.0000%

Income (At least / But less than)	1	2	3	4	5	Over 5
$0 – $20,000	200	236	261	280	296	319
20,000 – 30,000	305	358	394	423	446	480
30,000 – 40,000	358	419	460	493	520	559
40,000 – 50,000	403	470	516	553	583	626
50,000 – 60,000	443	516	566	606	638	685
60,000 – 70,000	480	558	611	653	688	738
70,000 – 80,000	514	597	654	698	735	788
80,000 – 90,000	545	633	693	739	779	834
90,000 – 100,000	575	667	729	778	819	877
100,000 – 120,000	615	711	778	829	873	934
120,000 – 140,000	668	772	843	899	946	1011
140,000 – 160,000	715	825	900	959	1009	1078
160,000 – 180,000	762	878	957	1019	1071	1145
180,000 – 200,000	804	925	1008	1073	1127	1204
200,000 or more	1013	1159	1260	1339	1404	1498

Ohio 5.5000%

Income (At least / But less than)	1	2	3	4	5	Over 5
$0 – $20,000	242	281	307	327	343	366
20,000 – 30,000	385	445	485	517	542	578
30,000 – 40,000	457	528	576	613	643	685
40,000 – 50,000	520	600	653	695	729	776
50,000 – 60,000	575	664	723	768	806	858
60,000 – 70,000	626	722	785	835	875	932
70,000 – 80,000	674	776	845	897	941	1002
80,000 – 90,000	718	827	900	956	1002	1066
90,000 – 100,000	760	875	951	1011	1059	1127
100,000 – 120,000	815	938	1020	1083	1135	1208
120,000 – 140,000	891	1024	1113	1182	1238	1317
140,000 – 160,000	957	1099	1194	1268	1328	1413
160,000 – 180,000	1022	1174	1275	1353	1418	1508
180,000 – 200,000	1081	1241	1348	1430	1498	1593
200,000 or more	1376	1576	1710	1813	1898	2017

Oklahoma 4.5000%

Income (At least / But less than)	1	2	3	4	5	Over 5
$0 – $20,000	249	304	343	374	400	438
20,000 – 30,000	380	462	519	565	604	659
30,000 – 40,000	445	540	606	659	704	768
40,000 – 50,000	500	606	680	739	788	859
50,000 – 60,000	549	664	745	809	863	940
60,000 – 70,000	594	717	803	872	930	1013
70,000 – 80,000	635	767	859	932	993	1082
80,000 – 90,000	674	812	909	986	1051	1144
90,000 – 100,000	710	855	957	1038	1106	1204
100,000 – 120,000	758	912	1019	1105	1177	1281
120,000 – 140,000	823	988	1104	1197	1274	1386
140,000 – 160,000	879	1055	1178	1276	1358	1477
160,000 – 180,000	936	1121	1251	1354	1442	1566
180,000 – 200,000	986	1180	1316	1425	1516	1647
200,000 or more	1236	1472	1638	1770	1882	2041

Pennsylvania 6.0000%

Income (At least / But less than)	1	2	3	4	5	Over 5
$0 – $20,000	223	256	279	296	310	329
20,000 – 30,000	355	407	441	468	490	520
30,000 – 40,000	422	483	524	555	581	617
40,000 – 50,000	480	548	594	629	658	699
50,000 – 60,000	531	607	657	696	728	773
60,000 – 70,000	578	660	714	756	791	839
70,000 – 80,000	622	710	768	813	850	902
80,000 – 90,000	663	756	818	866	905	960
90,000 – 100,000	702	800	865	916	957	1015
100,000 – 120,000	753	858	927	981	1026	1087
120,000 – 140,000	823	937	1012	1071	1119	1186
140,000 – 160,000	884	1005	1086	1149	1200	1272
160,000 – 180,000	944	1074	1160	1226	1281	1357
180,000 – 200,000	999	1135	1226	1296	1354	1434
200,000 or more	1270	1441	1555	1642	1714	1815

Rhode Island 7.0000%

Income (At least / But less than)	1	2	3	4	5	Over 5
$0 – $20,000	271	311	337	357	373	396
20,000 – 30,000	408	465	503	532	556	589
30,000 – 40,000	476	541	585	618	645	683
40,000 – 50,000	533	605	653	690	720	763
50,000 – 60,000	583	662	714	754	787	833
60,000 – 70,000	629	713	769	812	847	896
70,000 – 80,000	671	761	820	865	903	954
80,000 – 90,000	711	805	867	915	954	1008
90,000 – 100,000	747	846	911	961	1002	1059
100,000 – 120,000	796	900	969	1022	1065	1125
120,000 – 140,000	861	973	1047	1104	1151	1215
140,000 – 160,000	918	1037	1115	1175	1225	1293
160,000 – 180,000	975	1100	1182	1246	1298	1370
180,000 – 200,000	1025	1156	1243	1309	1363	1439
200,000 or more	1273	1432	1537	1617	1683	1774

South Carolina 6.0000%

Income (At least / But less than)	1	2	3	4	5	Over 5
$0 – $20,000	259	301	329	351	369	394
20,000 – 30,000	411	477	521	555	583	622
30,000 – 40,000	487	565	617	658	691	737
40,000 – 50,000	553	641	700	745	783	835
50,000 – 60,000	612	709	774	824	865	922
60,000 – 70,000	665	771	841	895	939	1002
70,000 – 80,000	716	829	904	962	1010	1076
80,000 – 90,000	762	882	962	1024	1074	1145
90,000 – 100,000	807	933	1017	1082	1136	1211
100,000 – 120,000	865	1000	1090	1159	1216	1296
120,000 – 140,000	944	1091	1189	1264	1327	1413
140,000 – 160,000	1013	1170	1275	1356	1422	1515
160,000 – 180,000	1082	1249	1361	1447	1518	1617
180,000 – 200,000	1144	1320	1438	1529	1603	1708
200,000 or more	1451	1673	1821	1934	2028	2159

South Dakota 4.0000%

Income (At least / But less than)	1	2	3	4	5	Over 5
$0 – $20,000	242	297	335	366	391	428
20,000 – 30,000	368	449	506	551	589	644
30,000 – 40,000	429	524	590	642	686	749
40,000 – 50,000	482	587	661	719	768	838
50,000 – 60,000	543	643	723	786	840	916
60,000 – 70,000	570	693	779	847	905	987
70,000 – 80,000	609	740	832	904	965	1053
80,000 – 90,000	645	783	880	957	1021	1113
90,000 – 100,000	678	824	925	1006	1073	1170
100,000 – 120,000	723	877	985	1070	1142	1244
120,000 – 140,000	783	949	1065	1157	1235	1345
140,000 – 160,000	835	1012	1135	1233	1315	1432
160,000 – 180,000	887	1074	1204	1307	1394	1518
180,000 – 200,000	933	1129	1266	1374	1465	1595
200,000 or more	1159	1400	1567	1700	1811	1970

Tennessee 7.0000%

Income (At least / But less than)	1	2	3	4	5	Over 5
$0 – $20,000	398	483	541	587	626	681
20,000 – 30,000	583	703	785	850	905	983
30,000 – 40,000	673	809	903	977	1039	1127
40,000 – 50,000	748	898	1001	1082	1151	1248
50,000 – 60,000	815	976	1087	1175	1249	1354
60,000 – 70,000	875	1046	1165	1259	1337	1449
70,000 – 80,000	930	1112	1237	1336	1419	1537
80,000 – 90,000	982	1172	1303	1407	1494	1617
90,000 – 100,000	1030	1228	1366	1474	1564	1693
100,000 – 120,000	1093	1302	1447	1560	1656	1791
120,000 – 140,000	1178	1402	1556	1678	1780	1925
140,000 – 160,000	1252	1488	1651	1779	1887	2039
160,000 – 180,000	1325	1573	1744	1879	1992	2152
180,000 – 200,000	1391	1649	1827	1968	2085	2253
200,000 or more	1711	2020	2234	2401	2542	2742

Texas 6.2500%

Income (At least / But less than)	1	2	3	4	5	Over 5
$0 – $20,000	276	326	359	386	408	438
20,000 – 30,000	439	517	570	611	646	694
30,000 – 40,000	522	614	677	726	766	823
40,000 – 50,000	593	697	768	823	869	933
50,000 – 60,000	656	772	849	910	960	1031
60,000 – 70,000	714	839	924	989	1044	1121
70,000 – 80,000	769	903	993	1064	1122	1205
80,000 – 90,000	819	961	1058	1133	1195	1283
90,000 – 100,000	867	1017	1119	1198	1264	1356
100,000 – 120,000	929	1090	1199	1283	1354	1453
120,000 – 140,000	1015	1190	1308	1401	1477	1585
140,000 – 160,000	1090	1277	1404	1503	1584	1699
160,000 – 180,000	1164	1364	1499	1604	1691	1814
180,000 – 200,000	1231	1442	1584	1695	1787	1916
200,000 or more	1564	1829	2008	2147	2263	2425

Utah 4.7000%

Income (At least / But less than)	1	2	3	4	5	Over 5
$0 – $20,000	249	300	335	363	386	419
20,000 – 30,000	384	461	514	556	591	640
30,000 – 40,000	451	541	603	651	692	750
40,000 – 50,000	509	609	678	732	778	842
50,000 – 60,000	560	668	745	804	854	925
60,000 – 70,000	606	724	805	869	923	999
70,000 – 80,000	649	775	862	930	987	1068
80,000 – 90,000	690	822	914	986	1047	1132
90,000 – 100,000	727	867	963	1039	1103	1193
100,000 – 120,000	777	926	1028	1108	1176	1272
120,000 – 140,000	845	1005	1116	1203	1276	1379
140,000 – 160,000	904	1074	1192	1285	1362	1472
160,000 – 180,000	962	1143	1268	1366	1448	1564
180,000 – 200,000	1014	1205	1335	1438	1525	1647
200,000 or more	1274	1508	1669	1796	1903	2053

Vermont 6.0000%

Income (At least / But less than)	1	2	3	4	5	Over 5
$0 – $20,000	182	202	216	226	234	245
20,000 – 30,000	273	302	321	336	347	363
30,000 – 40,000	318	352	373	390	403	421
40,000 – 50,000	356	393	417	435	450	470
50,000 – 60,000	390	430	456	475	491	513
60,000 – 70,000	420	463	491	512	529	552
70,000 – 80,000	449	494	524	546	564	588
80,000 – 90,000	475	523	554	577	596	622
90,000 – 100,000	500	550	582	606	626	653
100,000 – 120,000	533	585	619	645	666	694
120,000 – 140,000	577	634	670	697	720	750
140,000 – 160,000	616	675	714	743	766	799
160,000 – 180,000	654	717	757	788	813	847
180,000 – 200,000	688	754	796	828	854	889
200,000 or more	857	936	988	1026	1057	1100

Virginia 4.0000%

Income (At least / But less than)	1	2	3	4	5	Over 5
$0 – $20,000	185	220	244	263	279	301
20,000 – 30,000	276	327	361	389	411	443
30,000 – 40,000	321	379	419	450	476	512
40,000 – 50,000	359	423	467	501	530	570
50,000 – 60,000	393	462	510	547	578	621
60,000 – 70,000	423	498	548	588	621	667
70,000 – 80,000	452	531	584	626	661	710
80,000 – 90,000	478	561	617	661	698	750
90,000 – 100,000	503	590	648	694	733	787
100,000 – 120,000	536	627	689	738	778	835
120,000 – 140,000	580	678	744	797	840	901
140,000 – 160,000	619	722	792	847	893	958
160,000 – 180,000	657	766	840	898	946	1014
180,000 – 200,000	691	805	882	943	993	1065
200,000 or more	861	998	1091	1164	1225	1311

Washington 6.5000%

Income (At least / But less than)	1	2	3	4	5	Over 5
$0 – $20,000	280	330	364	391	414	445
20,000 – 30,000	449	529	583	625	660	709
30,000 – 40,000	536	630	694	744	785	844
40,000 – 50,000	610	717	789	845	892	958
50,000 – 60,000	677	795	874	936	988	1061
60,000 – 70,000	738	865	952	1019	1076	1155
70,000 – 80,000	796	932	1025	1098	1158	1243
80,000 – 90,000	849	994	1093	1170	1234	1325
90,000 – 100,000	899	1053	1157	1239	1306	1402
100,000 – 120,000	966	1130	1242	1329	1401	1503
120,000 – 140,000	1057	1236	1358	1453	1531	1643
140,000 – 160,000	1137	1329	1459	1560	1645	1764
160,000 – 180,000	1216	1421	1560	1668	1758	1885
180,000 – 200,000	1288	1504	1650	1765	1860	1993
200,000 or more	1645	1917	2102	2246	2365	2534

West Virginia 6.0000%

Income (At least / But less than)	1	2	3	4	5	Over 5
$0 – $20,000	306	368	411	445	474	514
20,000 – 30,000	478	573	638	690	733	795
30,000 – 40,000	564	675	752	812	863	934
40,000 – 50,000	637	762	848	916	972	1053
50,000 – 60,000	703	839	934	1008	1070	1158
60,000 – 70,000	762	910	1011	1091	1159	1254
70,000 – 80,000	818	976	1084	1170	1242	1343
80,000 – 90,000	870	1037	1152	1242	1318	1426
90,000 – 100,000	918	1094	1215	1310	1390	1503
100,000 – 120,000	982	1170	1298	1400	1485	1605
120,000 – 140,000	1070	1273	1412	1522	1614	1744
140,000 – 160,000	1146	1362	1511	1628	1726	1865
160,000 – 180,000	1222	1451	1609	1733	1837	1985
180,000 – 200,000	1290	1531	1697	1828	1937	2092
200,000 or more	1626	1926	2131	2293	2429	2621

Wisconsin 5.0000%

Income (At least / But less than)	1	2	3	4	5	Over 5
$0 – $20,000	228	267	294	314	331	355
20,000 – 30,000	362	424	465	497	524	561
30,000 – 40,000	430	503	552	590	621	665
40,000 – 50,000	488	570	626	668	704	754
50,000 – 60,000	540	631	692	739	778	833
60,000 – 70,000	588	686	752	803	845	905
70,000 – 80,000	632	737	808	863	909	972
80,000 – 90,000	678	785	861	919	967	1035
90,000 – 100,000	712	830	910	971	1022	1094
100,000 – 120,000	763	890	975	1041	1095	1171
120,000 – 140,000	834	971	1063	1135	1194	1277
140,000 – 160,000	895	1042	1141	1217	1281	1369
160,000 – 180,000	955	1112	1218	1299	1367	1461
180,000 – 200,000	1010	1176	1287	1373	1444	1543
200,000 or more	1281	1489	1629	1737	1826	1951

Wyoming 4.0000%

Income (At least / But less than)	1	2	3	4	5	Over 5
$0 – $20,000	171	200	219	234	246	264
20,000 – 30,000	274	319	349	373	392	419
30,000 – 40,000	327	380	415	443	466	498
40,000 – 50,000	372	432	472	503	529	565
50,000 – 60,000	412	478	523	557	586	626
60,000 – 70,000	449	521	569	606	637	681
70,000 – 80,000	484	561	613	653	686	732
80,000 – 90,000	516	598	653	696	731	780
90,000 – 100,000	547	633	691	736	773	826
100,000 – 120,000	587	679	741	790	829	885
120,000 – 140,000	642	743	810	863	906	967
140,000 – 160,000	690	798	870	926	973	1038
160,000 – 180,000	738	853	930	990	1039	1109
180,000 – 200,000	781	903	984	1047	1099	1172
200,000 or more	997	1150	1252	1331	1397	1489

Note. Alaska does not have a state sales tax. Alaska residents should follow the instructions on the next page to determine their local sales tax amount.

1 The rates for Arizona, Kansas, and New Mexico increased during 2010, so the rates given are averaged over the year.

2 The California table includes the 1% uniform local sales tax rate in addition to the 7.2500% state sales tax rate.

3 The Nevada table includes the 2.25% uniform local sales tax rate in addition to the 4.6000% state sales tax rate.

4 Residents of Salem County should deduct only half of the amount in the state table.

5 The 4.0% rate for Hawaii is actually an excise tax but is treated as a sales tax for purpose of this deduction.

Which Optional Local Sales Tax Table Should I Use?

IF you live in the state of...	AND you live in...	THEN use Local Table...
Alaska	Any locality	C
Arizona	Mesa or Tucson	A
	Chandler, Gilbert, Glendale, Peoria, Phoenix, Scottsdale, Tempe, Yuma, or any other locality	B
Arkansas	Any locality	C
California	Los Angeles County	A
Colorado	Adams County, Arapahoe County, Boulder County, Centennial, Colorado Springs, Denver City/Denver County, El Paso County, Greeley, Jefferson County, Larimer County, Pueblo County, or any other locality	A
	Arvada, Aurora, City of Boulder, Fort Collins, Lakewood, Longmont, City of Pueblo, Thornton, or Westminster	B
Georgia	Any locality	B
Illinois	Any locality	A
Louisiana	East Baton Rouge Parish	B
	Any other locality	C
Missouri	Any locality	B
New York	New York City	A
	One of the following counties: Albany, Allegany, Cattaraugus, Cayuga, Chemung, Clinton, Cortland, Dutchess, Erie, Essex, Franklin, Fulton, Genesee, Herkimer, Jefferson, Lewis, Livingston, Monroe, Montgomery, Nassau, Niagara, Oneida, Onondaga, Ontario, Orange, Orleans, Oswego, Otsego, Putnam, Rensselaer, Rockland, St. Lawrence, Saratoga, Schenectady, Schoharie, Seneca, Steuben, Suffolk, Sullivan, Tompkins, Ulster, Warren, Washington, Westchester, Wyoming, or Yates Or the City of Oneida	B
	Any other locality	D
North Carolina	Any locality	B
South Carolina	Cherokee County, Chesterfield County, Darlington County, Dillon County, Horry County, Jasper County, Lee County, Lexington County, or Myrtle Beach	B
	Any other locality	C
Tennessee	Any locality	B
Utah	Any locality	B
Virginia	Any locality	B

2010 Optional Local Sales Tax Tables for Certain Local Jurisdictions

(Based on a local sales tax rate of 1 percent)*

Income At least	Income But less than	Local Table A 1	2	3	4	5	Over 5	Local Table B 1	2	3	4	5	Over 5	Local Table C 1	2	3	4	5	Over 5	Local Table D 1	2	3	4	5	Over 5
$0	$20,000	43	50	55	59	62	66	50	60	66	72	76	83	61	75	84	91	97	106	40	47	51	54	57	61
20,000	30,000	65	76	83	89	93	100	76	91	101	109	115	125	93	112	125	136	145	158	65	75	81	86	91	97
30,000	40,000	76	89	97	103	109	116	89	106	118	127	135	146	108	130	146	158	168	183	77	89	96	103	108	115
40,000	50,000	86	99	109	116	122	130	100	119	132	142	151	163	121	146	163	177	188	204	88	101	110	116	122	130
50,000	60,000	94	109	119	127	133	142	110	130	145	156	165	179	132	159	178	193	205	223	97	112	121	129	135	144
60,000	70,000	102	118	128	137	143	153	119	141	156	168	178	193	143	172	192	208	221	240	106	121	132	140	147	156
70,000	80,000	109	126	137	146	153	163	127	151	167	180	190	206	152	183	205	222	236	256	114	131	142	151	158	168
80,000	90,000	116	133	145	154	162	173	135	160	177	190	202	218	161	194	216	234	249	270	121	139	151	161	168	179
90,000	100,000	122	140	153	163	171	182	142	168	186	200	212	229	170	204	227	246	262	284	128	147	160	170	178	189
100,000	120,000	130	150	163	173	182	194	151	179	198	213	226	244	181	217	242	262	278	302	138	158	172	182	191	203
120,000	140,000	141	162	176	187	197	209	164	194	215	231	245	264	195	234	261	283	300	326	151	173	188	199	208	222
140,000	160,000	151	173	188	200	210	223	175	207	229	247	261	281	208	250	278	301	320	346	162	186	201	214	224	238
160,000	180,000	161	184	200	212	223	237	187	220	244	262	277	299	221	265	295	319	339	367	173	198	215	228	239	254
180,000	200,000	169	194	211	223	234	249	197	232	257	276	292	314	233	278	310	335	356	385	183	210	228	241	253	268
200,000 or more		213	242	263	278	291	309	246	290	319	343	362	390	289	344	383	413	439	475	234	267	289	306	321	340

*If your local rate is more than 1 percent, the local portion of your deduction for sales tax will be increased.
See the instructions for line 3 of the *State and Local General Sales Tax Deduction Worksheet.*

Appendix B

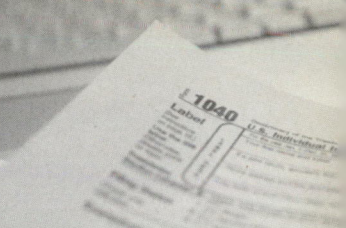

TAX FORMS

*(Tax forms can be obtained from the IRS website: **http://www.irs.gov**)*

Form 1040

Department of the Treasury—Internal Revenue Service

U.S. Individual Income Tax Return 2010

(99)   IRS Use Only—Do not write or staple in this space.

PRINT CLEARLY

Name, Address, and SSN	For the year Jan. 1–Dec. 31, 2010, or other tax year beginning , 2010, ending , 20 OMB No. 1545-0074
	Your first name and initial Last name **Your social security number**
See separate instructions.	If a joint return, spouse's first name and initial Last name **Spouse's social security number**
	Home address (number and street). If you have a P.O. box, see instructions. Apt. no. ▲ Make sure the SSN(s) above and on line 6c are correct.
	City, town or post office, state, and ZIP code. If you have a foreign address, see instructions. Checking a box below will not change your tax or refund.

Presidential Election Campaign   Check here if you, or your spouse if filing jointly, want $3 to go to this fund . . . . . . ▶ ☐ You ☐ Spouse

Filing Status

Check only one box.

1 ☐ Single
2 ☐ Married filing jointly (even if only one had income)
3 ☐ Married filing separately. Enter spouse's SSN above and full name here. ▶
4 ☐ Head of household (with qualifying person). (See instructions.) If the qualifying person is a child but not your dependent, enter this child's name here. ▶
5 ☐ Qualifying widow(er) with dependent child

Exemptions

6a ☐ **Yourself.** If someone can claim you as a dependent, **do not** check box 6a . . . . . .
b ☐ **Spouse** . . . .

c Dependents:			
(1) First name Last name	**(2)** Dependent's social security number	**(3)** Dependent's relationship to you	**(4)** ✓ if child under age 17 qualifying for child tax credit (see page 15)
			☐
			☐
			☐
			☐

If more than four dependents, see instructions and check here ▶ ☐

Boxes checked on 6a and 6b ____
No. of children on 6c who:
• lived with you ____
• did not live with you due to divorce or separation (see instructions) ____
Dependents on 6c not entered above ____
Add numbers on lines above ▶ ☐

d Total number of exemptions claimed . . . .

Income

Attach Form(s) W-2 here. Also attach Forms W-2G and 1099-R if tax was withheld.

If you did not get a W-2, see page 20.

Enclose, but do not attach, any payment. Also, please use Form 1040-V.

7	Wages, salaries, tips, etc. Attach Form(s) W-2	7
8a	**Taxable** interest. Attach Schedule B if required	8a
b	**Tax-exempt** interest. **Do not** include on line 8a . . . 8b	
9a	Ordinary dividends. Attach Schedule B if required	9a
b	Qualified dividends 9b	
10	Taxable refunds, credits, or offsets of state and local income taxes	10
11	Alimony received	11
12	Business income or (loss). Attach Schedule C or C-EZ	12
13	Capital gain or (loss). Attach Schedule D if required. If not required, check here ▶ ☐	13
14	Other gains or (losses). Attach Form 4797	14
15a	IRA distributions . 15a b Taxable amount . . .	15b
16a	Pensions and annuities 16a b Taxable amount . . .	16b
17	Rental real estate, royalties, partnerships, S corporations, trusts, etc. Attach Schedule E	17
18	Farm income or (loss). Attach Schedule F	18
19	Unemployment compensation	19
20a	Social security benefits 20a b Taxable amount . . .	20b
21	Other income. List type and amount _____	21
22	Combine the amounts in the far right column for lines 7 through 21. This is your **total income** ▶	22

Adjusted Gross Income

23	Educator expenses 23	
24	Certain business expenses of reservists, performing artists, and fee-basis government officials. Attach Form 2106 or 2106-EZ 24	
25	Health savings account deduction. Attach Form 8889 . 25	
26	Moving expenses. Attach Form 3903 26	
27	One-half of self-employment tax. Attach Schedule SE . 27	
28	Self-employed SEP, SIMPLE, and qualified plans . 28	
29	Self-employed health insurance deduction 29	
30	Penalty on early withdrawal of savings 30	
31a	Alimony paid b Recipient's SSN ▶ _____ 31a	
32	IRA deduction 32	
33	Student loan interest deduction 33	
34	Tuition and fees. Attach Form 8917 34	
35	Domestic production activities deduction. Attach Form 8903 35	
36	Add lines 23 through 31a and 32 through 35	36
37	Subtract line 36 from line 22. This is your **adjusted gross income** . . . . . ▶	37

For Disclosure, Privacy Act, and Paperwork Reduction Act Notice, see separate instructions.   Cat. No. 11320B   Form **1040** (2010)

Form 1040 (2010)   Page **2**

Tax and Credits

38	Amount from line 37 (adjusted gross income) . . . .
39a	Check if: ☐ **You** were born before January 2, 1946, ☐ Blind. ☐ **Spouse** was born before January 2, 1946, ☐ Blind. } Total boxes checked ▶ 39a
b	If your spouse itemizes on a separate return or you were a dual-status alien, check here ▶ 39b ☐
40	**Itemized deductions** (from Schedule A) **or** your **standard deduction** (see instructions) . .
41	Subtract line 40 from line 38 . . . .
42	**Exemptions.** Multiply $3,650 by the number on line 6d . . . .
43	**Taxable income.** Subtract line 42 from line 41. If line 42 is more than line 41, enter -0- . .
44	**Tax** (see instructions). Check if any tax is from: a ☐ Form(s) 8814 b ☐ Form 4972 .
45	**Alternative minimum tax** (see instructions). Attach Form 6251 . . . .
46	Add lines 44 and 45 . . . . ▶
47	Foreign tax credit. Attach Form 1116 if required	47
48	Credit for child and dependent care expenses. Attach Form 2441	48
49	Education credits from Form 8863, line 23	49
50	Retirement savings contributions credit. Attach Form 8880	50
51	Child tax credit (see instructions)	51
52	Residential energy credits. Attach Form 5695 . . .	52
53	Other credits from Form: a ☐ 3800 b ☐ 8801 c ☐ ____	53
54	Add lines 47 through 53. These are your **total credits** . . . .
55	Subtract line 54 from line 46. If line 54 is more than line 46, enter -0- . . . . . ▶

Other Taxes

56	Self-employment tax. Attach Schedule SE . . . .
57	Unreported social security and Medicare tax from Form: a ☐ 4137 b ☐ 8919 . .
58	Additional tax on IRAs, other qualified retirement plans, etc. Attach Form 5329 if required . .
59	a ☐ Form(s) W-2, box 9 b ☐ Schedule H c ☐ Form 5405, line 16 . . . .
60	Add lines 55 through 59. This is your **total tax** . . . . ▶

Payments

If you have a qualifying child, attach Schedule EIC.

61	Federal income tax withheld from Forms W-2 and 1099 . .	61
62	2010 estimated tax payments and amount applied from 2009 return	62
63	Making work pay credit. Attach Schedule M	63
64a	**Earned income credit (EIC)**	64a
b	Nontaxable combat pay election	64b	
65	Additional child tax credit. Attach Form 8812	65
66	American opportunity credit from Form 8863, line 14 . . .	66
67	First-time homebuyer credit from Form 5405, line 10 . . .	67
68	Amount paid with request for extension to file	68
69	Excess social security and tier 1 RRTA tax withheld . . .	69
70	Credit for federal tax on fuels. Attach Form 4136 . . .	70
71	Credits from Form: a ☐ 2439 b ☐ 8839 c ☐ 8801 d ☐ 8885	71
72	Add lines 61, 62, 63, 64a, and 65 through 71. These are your **total payments** . . . . ▶

Refund

Direct deposit? See instructions.

73	If line 72 is more than line 60, subtract line 60 from line 72. This is the amount you **overpaid**
74a	Amount of line 73 you want **refunded to you.** If Form 8888 is attached, check here . ▶ ☐
▶ b	Routing number ____ ▶ c Type: ☐ Checking ☐ Savings
▶ d	Account number ____
75	Amount of line 73 you want **applied to your 2011 estimated tax** ▶	75

Amount You Owe

76	**Amount you owe.** Subtract line 72 from line 60. For details on how to pay, see instructions ▶
77	Estimated tax penalty (see instructions)	77

Third Party Designee

Do you want to allow another person to discuss this return with the IRS (see instructions)? ☐ **Yes.** Complete below. ☐ **No**

Designee's name ▶   Phone no. ▶   Personal identification number (PIN) ▶

Sign Here

Joint return? See page 12. Keep a copy for your records.

Under penalties of perjury, I declare that I have examined this return and accompanying schedules and statements, and to the best of my knowledge and belief, they are true, correct, and complete. Declaration of preparer (other than taxpayer) is based on all information of which preparer has any knowledge.

Your signature	Date	Your occupation	Daytime phone number
Spouse's signature. If a joint return, **both** must sign.	Date	Spouse's occupation	

Paid Preparer Use Only

Print/Type preparer's name	Preparer's signature	Date	Check ☐ if self-employed	PTIN

Firm's name ▶   Firm's EIN ▶

Firm's address ▶   Phone no.

SCHEDULE A (Form 1040) Department of the Treasury Internal Revenue Service (99)	**Itemized Deductions** ▶ **Attach to Form 1040.** ▶ **See Instructions for Schedule A (Form 1040).**	OMB No. 1545-0074 20**10** Attachment Sequence No. **07**

Name(s) shown on Form 1040		Your social security number

Medical and Dental Expenses	**Caution.** Do not include expenses reimbursed or paid by others.		
	1 Medical and dental expenses (see instructions)	**1**	
	2 Enter amount from Form 1040, line 38 **2**		
	3 Multiply line 2 by 7.5% (.075)	**3**	
	4 Subtract line 3 from line 1. If line 3 is more than line 1, enter -0-		**4**

**Taxes You
Paid**
	5 State and local **(check only one box):**
	  a ☐ Income taxes, **or**
	  b ☐ General sales taxes
		5	

	6 Real estate taxes (see instructions)	**6**	
	7 New motor vehicle taxes from line 11 of the worksheet on back (for certain vehicles purchased in 2009). Skip this line if you checked box 5b	**7**	
	8 Other taxes. List type and amount ▶ _____	**8**	
	9 Add lines 5 through 8		**9**
Interest You Paid **Note.** Your mortgage interest deduction may be limited (see instructions).	10 Home mortgage interest and points reported to you on Form 1098	**10**	
	11 Home mortgage interest not reported to you on Form 1098. If paid to the person from whom you bought the home, see instructions and show that person's name, identifying no., and address ▶ _____ _____	**11**	
	12 Points not reported to you on Form 1098. See instructions for special rules	**12**	
	13 Mortgage insurance premiums (see instructions)	**13**	
	14 Investment interest. Attach Form 4952 if required. (See instructions.)	**14**	
	15 Add lines 10 through 14		**15**
Gifts to Charity If you made a gift and got a benefit for it, see instructions.	16 Gifts by cash or check. If you made any gift of $250 or more, see instructions	**16**	
	17 Other than by cash or check. If any gift of $250 or more, see instructions. You **must** attach Form 8283 if over $500 . . .	**17**	
	18 Carryover from prior year	**18**	
	19 Add lines 16 through 18		**19**
Casualty and Theft Losses	20 Casualty or theft loss(es). Attach Form 4684. (See instructions.)		**20**
Job Expenses and Certain Miscellaneous Deductions	21 Unreimbursed employee expenses—job travel, union dues, job education, etc. Attach Form 2106 or 2106-EZ if required. (See instructions.) ▶ _____	**21**	
	22 Tax preparation fees	**22**	
	23 Other expenses—investment, safe deposit box, etc. List type and amount ▶ _____ _____	**23**	
	24 Add lines 21 through 23	**24**	
	25 Enter amount from Form 1040, line 38 **25**		
	26 Multiply line 25 by 2% (.02)	**26**	
	27 Subtract line 26 from line 24. If line 26 is more than line 24, enter -0-		**27**
Other Miscellaneous Deductions	28 Other—from list in instructions. List type and amount ▶ _____ _____		**28**
Total Itemized Deductions	29 Add the amounts in the far right column for lines 4 through 28. Also, enter this amount on Form 1040, line 40		**29**
	30 If you elect to itemize deductions even though they are less than your standard deduction, check here . . . . ▶ ☐		

For Paperwork Reduction Act Notice, see Form 1040 instructions.	Cat. No. 17145C	Schedule A (Form 1040) 2010

SCHEDULE B	Interest and Ordinary Dividends	OMB No. 1545-0074

SCHEDULE B
(Form 1040A or 1040)

Department of the Treasury
Internal Revenue Service (99)

Interest and Ordinary Dividends

▶ **Attach to Form 1040A or 1040.**   ▶ **See instructions on back.**

OMB No. 1545-0074

2010

Attachment
Sequence No. **08**

Name(s) shown on return

Your social security number

Part I

Interest

(See instructions on the back and the instructions for Form 1040A, or Form 1040, line 8a.)

Note. If you received a Form 1099-INT, Form 1099-OID, or substitute statement from a brokerage firm, list the firm's name as the payer and enter the total interest shown on that form.

1 List name of payer. If any interest is from a seller-financed mortgage and the buyer used the property as a personal residence, see instructions on back and list this interest first. Also, show that buyer's social security number and address ▶

Amount

	1	

2 Add the amounts on line 1 . . . .   **2**

3 Excludable interest on series EE and I U.S. savings bonds issued after 1989. Attach Form 8815 . . . .   **3**

4 Subtract line 3 from line 2. Enter the result here and on Form 1040A, or Form 1040, line 8a . . . . ▶   **4**

Note. If line 4 is over $1,500, you must complete Part III.

Part II

Ordinary Dividends

(See instructions on back and the instructions for Form 1040A, or Form 1040, line 9a.)

Note. If you received a Form 1099-DIV or substitute statement from a brokerage firm, list the firm's name as the payer and enter the ordinary dividends shown on that form.

5 List name of payer ▶

Amount

	5	

6 Add the amounts on line 5. Enter the total here and on Form 1040A, or Form 1040, line 9a . . . . ▶   **6**

Note. If line 6 is over $1,500, you must complete Part III.

Part III

Foreign Accounts and Trusts

(See instructions on back.)

You must complete this part if you **(a)** had over $1,500 of taxable interest or ordinary dividends; **(b)** had a foreign account; or **(c)** received a distribution from, or were a grantor of, or a transferor to, a foreign trust.

	Yes	No
7a At any time during 2010, did you have an interest in or a signature or other authority over a financial account in a foreign country, such as a bank account, securities account, or other financial account? See instructions on back for exceptions and filing requirements for Form TD F 90-22.1		
b If "Yes," enter the name of the foreign country ▶		
8 During 2010, did you receive a distribution from, or were you the grantor of, or transferor to, a foreign trust? If "Yes," you may have to file Form 3520. See instructions on back		

For Paperwork Reduction Act Notice, see your tax return instructions.   Cat. No. 17146N   **Schedule B (Form 1040A or 1040) 2010**

SCHEDULE C (Form 1040) Department of the Treasury Internal Revenue Service (99)	**Profit or Loss From Business** (Sole Proprietorship) ▶ **Partnerships, joint ventures, etc., generally must file Form 1065 or 1065-B.** ▶ **Attach to Form 1040, 1040NR, or 1041.** ▶ **See Instructions for Schedule C (Form 1040).**	OMB No. 1545-0074 20**10** Attachment Sequence No. **09**

Name of proprietor	Social security number (SSN)

A	Principal business or profession, including product or service (see instructions)	**B** Enter code from pages C-9, 10, & 11 ▶		

C Business name. If no separate business name, leave blank.   **D** Employer ID number (EIN), if any

E Business address (including suite or room no.) ▶ --

City, town or post office, state, and ZIP code

F Accounting method: **(1)** ☐ Cash   **(2)** ☐ Accrual   **(3)** ☐ Other (specify) ▶ ----------------------------

G Did you "materially participate" in the operation of this business during 2010? If "No," see instructions for limit on losses   ☐ Yes ☐ No

H If you started or acquired this business during 2010, check here . . . . ▶ ☐

Part I Income

1	Gross receipts or sales. **Caution.** See instructions and check the box if: • This income was reported to you on Form W-2 and the "Statutory employee" box on that form was checked, or • You are a member of a qualified joint venture reporting only rental real estate income not subject to self-employment tax. Also see instructions for limit on losses.	. . ▶ ☐	**1**	
2	Returns and allowances		**2**	
3	Subtract line 2 from line 1		**3**	
4	Cost of goods sold (from line 42 on page 2)		**4**	
5	**Gross profit.** Subtract line 4 from line 3		**5**	
6	Other income, including federal and state gasoline or fuel tax credit or refund (see instructions) . . .		**6**	
7	**Gross income.** Add lines 5 and 6 . . . . ▶		**7**	

Part II Expenses. Enter expenses for business use of your home **only** on line 30.

8	Advertising	**8**		18	Office expense . . .	**18**	
9	Car and truck expenses (see instructions).	**9**		19	Pension and profit-sharing plans .	**19**	
10	Commissions and fees .	**10**		20	Rent or lease (see instructions):		
11	Contract labor (see instructions)	**11**		a	Vehicles, machinery, and equipment	**20a**	
12	Depletion	**12**		b	Other business property . . .	**20b**	
13	Depreciation and section 179 expense deduction (not included in Part III) (see instructions).	**13**		21	Repairs and maintenance . . .	**21**	
				22	Supplies (not included in Part III) .	**22**	
				23	Taxes and licenses	**23**	
				24	Travel, meals, and entertainment:		
				a	Travel	**24a**	
14	Employee benefit programs (other than on line 19) . .	**14**		b	Deductible meals and entertainment (see instructions) .	**24b**	
15	Insurance (other than health)	**15**		25	Utilities	**25**	
16	Interest:			26	Wages (less employment credits) .	**26**	
a	Mortgage (paid to banks, etc.)	**16a**		27	Other expenses (from line 48 on page 2)	**27**	
b	Other	**16b**					
17	Legal and professional services	**17**					

28	**Total expenses** before expenses for business use of home. Add lines 8 through 27 . . . . ▶	**28**	
29	Tentative profit or (loss). Subtract line 28 from line 7	**29**	
30	Expenses for business use of your home. Attach **Form 8829**	**30**	
31	**Net profit or (loss).** Subtract line 30 from line 29. • If a profit, enter on both **Form 1040, line 12,** and **Schedule SE, line 2,** or on **Form 1040NR, line 13** (if you checked the box on line 1, see instructions). Estates and trusts, enter on **Form 1041, line 3.** • If a loss, you **must** go to line 32.	**31**	
32	If you have a loss, check the box that describes your investment in this activity (see instructions). • If you checked 32a, enter the loss on both **Form 1040, line 12,** and **Schedule SE, line 2,** or on **Form 1040NR, line 13** (if you checked the box on line 1, see the line 31 instructions). Estates and trusts, enter on **Form 1041, line 3.** • If you checked 32b, you **must** attach **Form 6198.** Your loss may be limited.	**32a** ☐ All investment is at risk. **32b** ☐ Some investment is not at risk.	

For Paperwork Reduction Act Notice, see your tax return instructions.   Cat. No. 11334P   Schedule C (Form 1040) 2010

Schedule C (Form 1040) 2010   Page **2**

Part III	**Cost of Goods Sold** (see instructions)

33 Method(s) used to
value closing inventory: **a** ☐ Cost   **b** ☐ Lower of cost or market   **c** ☐ Other (attach explanation)

34 Was there any change in determining quantities, costs, or valuations between opening and closing inventory?
If "Yes," attach explanation . . . . ☐ Yes   ☐ No

35	Inventory at beginning of year. If different from last year's closing inventory, attach explanation . . .	35	
36	Purchases less cost of items withdrawn for personal use	36	
37	Cost of labor. Do not include any amounts paid to yourself	37	
38	Materials and supplies	38	
39	Other costs	39	
40	Add lines 35 through 39	40	
41	Inventory at end of year	41	
42	**Cost of goods sold.** Subtract line 41 from line 40. Enter the result here and on page 1, line 4 . . .	42	

Part IV	**Information on Your Vehicle.** Complete this part **only** if you are claiming car or truck expenses on line 9 and are not required to file Form 4562 for this business. See the instructions for line 13 to find out if you must file Form 4562.

43 When did you place your vehicle in service for business purposes? (month, day, year) ▶ _____ / _____ / _____

44 Of the total number of miles you drove your vehicle during 2010, enter the number of miles you used your vehicle for:

a Business _____   **b** Commuting (see instructions) _____   **c** Other _____

45 Was your vehicle available for personal use during off-duty hours? . . . . ☐ Yes   ☐ No

46 Do you (or your spouse) have another vehicle available for personal use? . . . . ☐ Yes   ☐ No

47a Do you have evidence to support your deduction? . . . . ☐ Yes   ☐ No

  b If "Yes," is the evidence written? . . . . ☐ Yes   ☐ No

Part V	**Other Expenses.** List below business expenses not included on lines 8–26 or line 30.

_____	
_____	
_____	
_____	
_____	
_____	
_____	
_____	

48	**Total other expenses.** Enter here and on page 1, line 27	48	

Schedule C (Form 1040) 2010

| SCHEDULE D
(Form 1040)

Department of the Treasury
Internal Revenue Service (99) | **Capital Gains and Losses**

▶ **Attach to Form 1040 or Form 1040NR.** ▶ **See Instructions for Schedule D (Form 1040).**
▶ **Use Schedule D-1 to list additional transactions for lines 1 and 8.** | OMB No. 1545-0074

20**10**
Attachment
Sequence No. **12** |

Name(s) shown on return	Your social security number

Part I   Short-Term Capital Gains and Losses—Assets Held One Year or Less

(a) Description of property (Example: 100 sh. XYZ Co.)	(b) Date acquired (Mo., day, yr.)	(c) Date sold (Mo., day, yr.)	(d) Sales price (see page D-7 of the instructions)	(e) Cost or other basis (see page D-7 of the instructions)	(f) Gain or (loss) Subtract (e) from (d)
1					

2 Enter your short-term totals, if any, from Schedule D-1, line 2	**2**				
3 **Total short-term sales price amounts.** Add lines 1 and 2 in column (d)	**3**				
4 Short-term gain from Form 6252 and short-term gain or (loss) from Forms 4684, 6781, and 8824 .	**4**				
5 Net short-term gain or (loss) from partnerships, S corporations, estates, and trusts from Schedule(s) K-1	**5**				
6 Short-term capital loss carryover. Enter the amount, if any, from line 10 of your **Capital Loss Carryover Worksheet** on page D-7 of the instructions	**6** (				)
7 **Net short-term capital gain or (loss).** Combine lines 1 through 6 in column (f)	**7**				

Part II   Long-Term Capital Gains and Losses—Assets Held More Than One Year

(a) Description of property (Example: 100 sh. XYZ Co.)	(b) Date acquired (Mo., day, yr.)	(c) Date sold (Mo., day, yr.)	(d) Sales price (see page D-7 of the instructions)	(e) Cost or other basis (see page D-7 of the instructions)	(f) Gain or (loss) Subtract (e) from (d)
8					

9 Enter your long-term totals, if any, from Schedule D-1, line 9	**9**				
10 **Total long-term sales price amounts.** Add lines 8 and 9 in column (d).	**10**				
11 Gain from Form 4797, Part I; long-term gain from Forms 2439 and 6252; and long-term gain or (loss) from Forms 4684, 6781, and 8824	**11**				
12 Net long-term gain or (loss) from partnerships, S corporations, estates, and trusts from Schedule(s) K-1	**12**				
13 Capital gain distributions. See page D-2 of the instructions	**13**				
14 Long-term capital loss carryover. Enter the amount, if any, from line 15 of your **Capital Loss Carryover Worksheet** on page D-7 of the instructions	**14** (				)
15 **Net long-term capital gain or (loss).** Combine lines 8 through 14 in column (f). Then go to Part III on the back	**15**				

For Paperwork Reduction Act Notice, see your tax return instructions.   Cat. No. 11338H   **Schedule D (Form 1040) 2010**

Part III	Summary

16 Combine lines 7 and 15 and enter the result **16**

   • If line 16 is a **gain**, enter the amount from line 16 on Form 1040, line 13, or Form 1040NR, line 14. Then go to line 17 below.
   • If line 16 is a **loss**, skip lines 17 through 20 below. Then go to line 21. Also be sure to complete line 22.
   • If line 16 is **zero**, skip lines 17 through 21 below and enter -0- on Form 1040, line 13, or Form 1040NR, line 14. Then go to line 22.

17 Are lines 15 and 16 **both** gains?
   ☐ **Yes.** Go to line 18.
   ☐ **No.** Skip lines 18 through 21, and go to line 22.

18 Enter the amount, if any, from line 7 of the **28% Rate Gain Worksheet** on page D-8 of the instructions . . . . ▶ **18**

19 Enter the amount, if any, from line 18 of the **Unrecaptured Section 1250 Gain Worksheet** on page D-9 of the instructions . . . . ▶ **19**

20 Are lines 18 and 19 **both** zero or blank?
   ☐ **Yes.** Complete Form 1040 through line 43, or Form 1040NR through line 41. Then complete the **Qualified Dividends and Capital Gain Tax Worksheet** in the Instructions for Form 1040, line 44 (or in the Instructions for Form 1040NR, line 42). **Do not** complete lines 21 and 22 below.

   ☐ **No.** Complete Form 1040 through line 43, or Form 1040NR through line 41. Then complete the **Schedule D Tax Worksheet** on page D-10 of the instructions. **Do not** complete lines 21 and 22 below.

21 If line 16 is a loss, enter here and on Form 1040, line 13, or Form 1040NR, line 14, the **smaller** of:

   • The loss on line 16 or
   • ($3,000), or if married filing separately, ($1,500) } . . . . **21** (   )

   Note. When figuring which amount is smaller, treat both amounts as positive numbers.

22 Do you have qualified dividends on Form 1040, line 9b, or Form 1040NR, line 10b?

   ☐ **Yes.** Complete Form 1040 through line 43, or Form 1040NR through line 41. Then complete the **Qualified Dividends and Capital Gain Tax Worksheet** in the Instructions for Form 1040, line 44 (or in the Instructions for Form 1040NR, line 42).
   ☐ **No.** Complete the rest of Form 1040 or Form 1040NR.

SCHEDULE E	Supplemental Income and Loss	OMB No. 1545-0074
(Form 1040)	(From rental real estate, royalties, partnerships, S corporations, estates, trusts, REMICs, etc.)	20**10**
Department of the Treasury Internal Revenue Service (99)	▶ Attach to Form 1040, 1040NR, or Form 1041. ▶ See Instructions for Schedule E (Form 1040).	Attachment Sequence No. **13**

Name(s) shown on return	Your social security number

Part I Income or Loss From Rental Real Estate and Royalties **Note.** If you are in the business of renting personal property, use **Schedule C** or **C-EZ** (see page E-3). If you are an individual, report farm rental income or loss from **Form 4835** on page 2, line 40.

1 List the type and address of each **rental real estate property:**

A ....

B ....

C ....

2 For each rental real estate property listed on line 1, did you or your family use it during the tax year for personal purposes for more than the greater of:
- 14 days **or**
- 10% of the total days rented at fair rental value?

(See page E-3)

	Yes	No
A		
B		
C		

Income:			Properties			Totals (Add columns A, B, and C.)
			A	B	C	
3 Rents received	**3**					**3**
4 Royalties received	**4**					**4**
Expenses:						
5 Advertising	**5**					
6 Auto and travel (see page E-4)	**6**					
7 Cleaning and maintenance	**7**					
8 Commissions	**8**					
9 Insurance	**9**					
10 Legal and other professional fees	**10**					
11 Management fees	**11**					
12 Mortgage interest paid to banks, etc. (see page E-5)	**12**					**12**
13 Other interest	**13**					
14 Repairs	**14**					
15 Supplies	**15**					
16 Taxes	**16**					
17 Utilities	**17**					
18 Other (list) ▶	**18**					
19 Add lines 5 through 18.	**19**					**19**
20 Depreciation expense or depletion (see page E-5)	**20**					**20**
21 Total expenses. Add lines 19 and 20	**21**					
22 Income or (loss) from rental real estate or royalty properties. Subtract line 21 from line 3 (rents) or line 4 (royalties). If the result is a (loss), see page E-5 to find out if you must file **Form 6198**	**22**					
23 Deductible rental real estate loss. **Caution.** Your rental real estate loss on line 22 may be limited. See page E-5 to find out if you must file **Form 8582.** Real estate professionals **must** complete line 43 on page 2	**23** (	)(	)(	)		
24 **Income.** Add positive amounts shown on line 22. **Do not** include any losses						**24**
25 **Losses.** Add royalty losses from line 22 and rental real estate losses from line 23. Enter total losses here						**25** ( )
26 **Total rental real estate and royalty income or (loss).** Combine lines 24 and 25. Enter the result here. If Parts II, III, IV, and line 40 on page 2 do not apply to you, also enter this amount on Form 1040, line 17, or Form 1040NR, line 18. Otherwise, include this amount in the total on line 41 on page 2						**26**

For Paperwork Reduction Act Notice, see your tax return instructions.   Cat. No. 11344L   Schedule E (Form 1040) 2010

Schedule E (Form 1040) 2010   Attachment Sequence No. **13**   Page **2**

Name(s) shown on return. Do not enter name and social security number if shown on other side.	Your social security number

Caution. The IRS compares amounts reported on your tax return with amounts shown on Schedule(s) K-1.

Part II **Income or Loss From Partnerships and S Corporations** **Note.** If you report a loss from an at-risk activity for which **any** amount is **not** at risk, you **must** check the box in column **(e)** on line 28 and attach **Form 6198**. See page E-1.

27   Are you reporting any loss not allowed in a prior year due to the at-risk or basis limitations, a prior year unallowed loss from a passive activity (if that loss was not reported on Form 8582), or unreimbursed partnership expenses? If you answered "Yes," see page E-7 before completing this section.   ☐ **Yes**   ☐ **No**

28

	(a) Name	(b) Enter **P** for partnership; **S** for S corporation	(c) Check if foreign partnership	(d) Employer identification number	(e) Check if any amount is not at risk
A			☐		☐
B			☐		☐
C			☐		☐
D			☐		☐

	Passive Income and Loss		Nonpassive Income and Loss		
	(f) Passive loss allowed (attach **Form 8582** if required)	(g) Passive income from **Schedule K–1**	(h) Nonpassive loss from **Schedule K–1**	(i) Section 179 expense deduction from **Form 4562**	(j) Nonpassive income from **Schedule K–1**
A					
B					
C					
D					
29a Totals					
b Totals					

30	Add columns (g) and (j) of line 29a	30	
31	Add columns (f), (h), and (i) of line 29b	31 (	)
32	**Total partnership and S corporation income or (loss).** Combine lines 30 and 31. Enter the result here and include in the total on line 41 below	32	

Part III **Income or Loss From Estates and Trusts**

33

	(a) Name	(b) Employer identification number
A		
B		

	Passive Income and Loss		Nonpassive Income and Loss	
	(c) Passive deduction or loss allowed (attach **Form 8582** if required)	(d) Passive income from **Schedule K–1**	(e) Deduction or loss from **Schedule K–1**	(f) Other income from **Schedule K–1**
A				
B				
34a Totals				
b Totals				

35	Add columns (d) and (f) of line 34a	35	
36	Add columns (c) and (e) of line 34b	36 (	)
37	**Total estate and trust income or (loss).** Combine lines 35 and 36. Enter the result here and include in the total on line 41 below	37	

Part IV **Income or Loss From Real Estate Mortgage Investment Conduits (REMICs)—Residual Holder**

38

	(a) Name	(b) Employer identification number	(c) Excess inclusion from **Schedules Q,** line 2c (see page E-8)	(d) Taxable income (net loss) from **Schedules Q,** line 1b	(e) Income from **Schedules Q,** line 3b

39	Combine columns (d) and (e) only. Enter the result here and include in the total on line 41 below	39	

Part V **Summary**

40	Net farm rental income or (loss) from **Form 4835.** Also, complete line 42 below	40	
41	**Total income or (loss).** Combine lines 26, 32, 37, 39, and 40. Enter the result here and on Form 1040, line 17, or Form 1040NR, line 18 ▶	41	
42	**Reconciliation of farming and fishing income.** Enter your **gross** farming and fishing income reported on Form 4835, line 7; Schedule K-1 (Form 1065), box 14, code B; Schedule K-1 (Form 1120S), box 17, code U; and Schedule K-1 (Form 1041), line 14, code F (see page E-8)	42	
43	**Reconciliation for real estate professionals.** If you were a real estate professional (see page E-2), enter the net income or (loss) you reported anywhere on Form 1040 or Form 1040NR from all rental real estate activities in which you materially participated under the passive activity loss rules . .	43	

Schedule E (Form 1040) 2010

SCHEDULE F (Form 1040) Department of the Treasury Internal Revenue Service (99)	**Profit or Loss From Farming** ▶ Attach to Form 1040, Form 1040NR, Form 1041, Form 1065, or Form 1065-B. ▶ See Instructions for Schedule F (Form 1040).	OMB No. 1545-0074 20**10** Attachment Sequence No. **14**

Name of proprietor	Social security number (SSN)

A Principal product. Describe in one or two words your principal crop or activity for the current tax year.

B Enter code from Part IV
▶ | | | | | |

D Employer ID number (EIN), if any

C Accounting method: **(1)** ☐ Cash   **(2)** ☐ Accrual

E Did you "materially participate" in the operation of this business during 2010? If "No," see instructions for limit on passive losses.   ☐ Yes   ☐ No

Part I	Farm Income—Cash Method. Complete Parts I and II (Accrual method. Complete Parts II and III, and Part I, line 11.) Do not include sales of livestock held for draft, breeding, sport, or dairy purposes. Report these sales on Form 4797.

1	Sales of livestock and other items you bought for resale	**1**		
2	Cost or other basis of livestock and other items reported on line 1 . . .	**2**		
3	Subtract line 2 from line 1			**3**
4	Sales of livestock, produce, grains, and other products you raised			**4**
5a	Cooperative distributions (Form(s) 1099-PATR) . .	**5a**		**5b** Taxable amount	**5b**
6a	Agricultural program payments (see instructions) . .	**6a**		**6b** Taxable amount	**6b**
7	Commodity Credit Corporation (CCC) loans (see instructions):				
a	CCC loans reported under election			**7a**
b	CCC loans forfeited	**7b**		**7c** Taxable amount	**7c**
8	Crop insurance proceeds and federal crop disaster payments (see instructions):				
a	Amount received in 2010	**8a**		**8b** Taxable amount	**8b**
c	If election to defer to 2011 is attached, check here ▶ ☐ **8d** Amount deferred from 2009			**8d**
9	Custom hire (machine work) income			**9**
10	Other income, including federal and state gasoline or fuel tax credit or refund (see instructions)			**10**
11	**Gross income.** Add amounts in the right column for lines 3 through 10. If you use the accrual method to figure your income, enter the amount from Part III, line 51 . . . . ▶			**11**

Part II	Farm Expenses—Cash and Accrual Method. Do not include personal or living expenses such as taxes, insurance, or repairs on your home.

12	Car and truck expenses (see instructions). Also attach **Form 4562**	**12**		25	Pension and profit-sharing plans	**25**	
13	Chemicals	**13**		26	Rent or lease (see instructions):		
14	Conservation expenses (see instructions)	**14**		a	Vehicles, machinery, and equipment	**26a**	
15	Custom hire (machine work) .	**15**		b	Other (land, animals, etc.) . .	**26b**	
16	Depreciation and section 179 expense deduction not claimed elsewhere (see instructions) . .	**16**		27	Repairs and maintenance . .	**27**	
				28	Seeds and plants	**28**	
				29	Storage and warehousing . .	**29**	
17	Employee benefit programs other than on line 25	**17**		30	Supplies	**30**	
18	Feed	**18**		31	Taxes	**31**	
19	Fertilizers and lime . . .	**19**		32	Utilities	**32**	
20	Freight and trucking . . .	**20**		33	Veterinary, breeding, and medicine	**33**	
21	Gasoline, fuel, and oil . . .	**21**		34	Other expenses (specify):		
22	Insurance (other than health) .	**22**		a	_____	**34a**	
23	Interest:			b	_____	**34b**	
a	Mortgage (paid to banks, etc.)	**23a**		c	_____	**34c**	
b	Other	**23b**		d	_____	**34d**	
24	Labor hired (less employment credits)	**24**		e	_____	**34e**	
				f		**34f**	

35	**Total expenses.** Add lines 12 through 34f. If line 34f is negative, see instructions . . . . ▶	**35**	

36	**Net farm profit or (loss).** Subtract line 35 from line 11. Partnerships, see instructions. • If a profit, enter the profit on both **Form 1040, line 18,** and **Schedule SE, line 1a;** on **Form 1040NR, line 19;** or on **Form 1041, line 6.** • If a loss, you **must** go to line 37.	**36**	

37	If you have a loss, you **must** check the box that describes your investment in this activity and whether you received any applicable subsidy (see instructions). • If you checked 37a, enter the loss on both **Form 1040, line 18,** and **Schedule SE, line 1a;** on **Form 1040NR, line 19;** or on **Form 1041, line 6.** • If you checked 37b, your loss may be limited. See instructions.	**37a** ☐ All investment is at risk and you did not receive a subsidy. **37b** ☐ Some investment is not at risk or you received a subsidy.

For Paperwork Reduction Act Notice, see your tax return instructions.   Cat. No. 11346H   Schedule F (Form 1040) 2010

Schedule F (Form 1040) 2010   Page **2**

Part III **Farm Income—Accrual Method** (see instructions).

Do not include sales of livestock held for draft, breeding, sport, or dairy purposes. Report these sales on Form 4797 and do not include this livestock on line 46 below.

38	Sales of livestock, produce, grains, and other products		**38**	
39a	Cooperative distributions (Form(s) 1099-PATR) . .	**39a**	**39b** Taxable amount	**39b**	
40a	Agricultural program payments	**40a**	**40b** Taxable amount	**40b**	
41	Commodity Credit Corporation (CCC) loans:			
a	CCC loans reported under election		**41a**	
b	CCC loans forfeited	**41b**	**41c** Taxable amount	**41c**	
42	Crop insurance proceeds		**42**	
43	Custom hire (machine work) income		**43**	
44	Other income, including federal and state gasoline or fuel tax credit or refund		**44**	
45	Add amounts in the right column for lines 38 through 44		**45**	
46	Inventory of livestock, produce, grains, and other products at beginning of the year	**46**			
47	Cost of livestock, produce, grains, and other products purchased during the year	**47**			
48	Add lines 46 and 47	**48**			
49	Inventory of livestock, produce, grains, and other products at end of year .	**49**			
50	Cost of livestock, produce, grains, and other products sold. Subtract line 49 from line 48*		**50**	
51	**Gross income.** Subtract line 50 from line 45. Enter the result here and on Part I, line 11 . . . . . ▶		**51**	

*If you use the unit-livestock-price method or the farm-price method of valuing inventory and the amount on line 49 is larger than the amount on line 48, subtract line 48 from line 49. Enter the result on line 50. Add lines 45 and 50. Enter the total on line 51 and on Part I, line 11.

Part IV **Principal Agricultural Activity Codes**

File Schedule C (Form 1040) or Schedule C-EZ (Form 1040) instead of Schedule F if (a) your principal source of income is from providing agricultural services such as soil preparation, veterinary, farm labor, horticultural, or management for a fee or on a contract basis, or (b) you are engaged in the business of breeding, raising, and caring for dogs, cats, or other pet animals.

These codes for the Principal Agricultural Activity classify farms by their primary activity to facilitate the administration of the Internal Revenue Code. These six-digit codes are based on the North American Industry Classification System (NAICS).

Select the code that best identifies your primary farming activity and enter the six digit number on page 1, line B.

Crop Production

111100   Oilseed and grain farming
111210   Vegetable and melon farming
111300   Fruit and tree nut farming
111400   Greenhouse, nursery, and floriculture production
111900   Other crop farming

Animal Production

112111   Beef cattle ranching and farming
112112   Cattle feedlots
112120   Dairy cattle and milk production
112210   Hog and pig farming
112300   Poultry and egg production
112400   Sheep and goat farming
112510   Aquaculture
112900   Other animal production

Forestry and Logging

113000   Forestry and logging (including forest nurseries and timber tracts)

SCHEDULE L
(Form 1040A or 1040)

Department of the Treasury
Internal Revenue Service   (99)

Standard Deduction for Certain Filers

▶ **Attach to Form 1040A or 1040.**   ▶ **See instructions on back.**

OMB No. 1545-0074

20**10**

Attachment
Sequence No. **57**

Name(s) shown on return

Your social security number

> ⚠ **CAUTION**
>
> File this form **only** if you are increasing your standard deduction by certain net disaster losses or new motor vehicle taxes paid in 2010 for certain vehicles purchased in 2009.
>
> **Form 1040 Filers Only:** It may be better for you to itemize your deductions instead. See the Instructions for Schedule A (Form 1040).

1 Enter the amount shown below for your filing status.
- Single or married filing separately—$5,700
- Married filing jointly or Qualifying widow(er)—$11,400 } . . **1**
- Head of household—$8,400

2 Can you (or your spouse if filing jointly) be claimed as a dependent on someone else's return?

☐ **No.** Enter the amount from line 1 on line 4, skip line 3, and go to line 5.

☐ **Yes.** Go to line 3.

3 Is your earned income more than $650 (see instructions)?

☐ **Yes.** Add $300 to your earned income. Enter the total } . . **3**
☐ **No.** Enter $950

4 Enter the **smaller** of line 1 or line 3 . . . . **4**

5 Multiply the number on Form 1040, line 39a, or Form 1040A, line 23a, by $1,100 ($1,400 if single or head of household). If blank, enter -0- **5**

6 Form 1040 filers only, enter from your 2010 Form 4684, line 17, any loss from a disaster declared a federal disaster after 2007 that occurred before 2010 (see instructions) **6**

7 Did you (or your spouse if filing jointly) pay any state or local sales or excise taxes in 2010 for the purchase of any new motor vehicle(s) **after** February 16, 2009, and **before** January 1, 2010 (see instructions)?

☐ **No.** Skip lines 7 through 16, enter -0- on line 17, and go to line 18.

☐ **Yes.** If Form 1040, line 38, or Form 1040A, line 22, is less than $135,000 ($260,000 if married filing jointly), enter the amount of these taxes paid. Otherwise, skip lines 7 through 16, enter -0- on line 17, and go to line 18 **7**

8 Enter the purchase price (**before taxes**) of the new motor vehicle(s) (see instructions) **8**

9 Is the amount on line 8 more than $49,500?

☐ **No.** Enter the amount from line 7.

☐ **Yes.** Figure the **portion** of the tax from line 7 that is attributable to the first $49,500 of the purchase price of each new motor vehicle and enter it here (see instructions) . . **9**

10 Enter the amount from Form 1040, line 38, or Form 1040A, line 22 **10**

11 Form 1040 filers only, enter the total of any—
- Amounts from Form 2555, lines 45 and 50; Form 2555-EZ, line 18; and Form 4563, line 15, and
- Exclusion of income from Puerto Rico **11**

12 Add lines 10 and 11 . . . . **12**

13 Enter $125,000 ($250,000 if married filing jointly) **13**

14 Is the amount on line 12 more than the amount on line 13?

☐ **No.** Skip lines 14 through 16, enter the amount from line 9 on line 17, and go to line 18.

☐ **Yes.** Subtract line 13 from line 12 . . . . **14**

15 Divide the amount on line 14 by $10,000. Enter the result as a decimal (rounded to at least three places). If the result is 1.000 or more, enter 1.000 . . . . **15**

16 Multiply line 9 by line 15 . . . . **16**

17 Subtract line 16 from line 9 . . . . **17**

18 Add lines 4, 5, 6, and 17. Enter the total here and on Form 1040, line 40, or Form 1040A, line 24. **18**

For Paperwork Reduction Act Notice, see your tax return instructions.   Cat. No. 49875F   **Schedule L (Form 1040A or 1040) 2010**

SCHEDULE M
(Form 1040A or 1040)

Department of the Treasury
Internal Revenue Service   (99)

Making Work Pay Credit

▶ Attach to Form 1040A or 1040.   ▶ See separate instructions.

OMB No. 1545-0074

20**10**

Attachment
Sequence No. **166**

Name(s) shown on return

Your social security number

⚠ **CAUTION** *To take the making work pay credit, you must include your social security number (if filing a joint return, the number of either you or your spouse) on your tax return. A social security number does not include an identification number issued by the IRS. Only the Social Security Administration issues social security numbers.*

⚠ **CAUTION** *You cannot take the making work pay credit if you can be claimed as someone else's dependent or if you are a nonresident alien.*

Important: Check the "**No**" box on line 1a and see the instructions if:

(a) You have a net loss from a business,

(b) You received a taxable scholarship or fellowship grant not reported on a Form W-2,

(c) Your wages include pay for work performed while an inmate in a penal institution,

(d) You received a pension or annuity from a nonqualified deferred compensation plan or a nongovernmental section 457 plan, or

(e) You are filing Form 2555 or 2555-EZ.

1a   Do you (and your spouse if filing jointly) have 2010 wages of more than $6,451 ($12,903 if married filing jointly)?

☐ **Yes.** Skip lines 1a through 3. Enter $400 ($800 if married filing jointly) on line 4 and go to line 5.

☐ **No.** Enter your earned income (see instructions) **1a**

b   Nontaxable combat pay included on line 1a
(see instructions) **1b**

2   Multiply line 1a by 6.2% (.062) **2**

3   Enter $400 ($800 if married filing jointly) **3**

4   Enter the **smaller** of line 2 or line 3 (unless you checked "Yes" on line 1a) **4**

5   Enter the amount from Form 1040, line 38*, or Form 1040A, line 22 . . **5**

6   Enter $75,000 ($150,000 if married filing jointly) **6**

7   Is the amount on line 5 more than the amount on line 6?

☐ **No.** Skip line 8. Enter the amount from line 4 on line 9 below.

☐ **Yes.** Subtract line 6 from line 5 . . . . **7**

8   Multiply line 7 by 2% (.02) **8**

9   Subtract line 8 from line 4. If zero or less, enter -0- **9**

10   Did you (or your spouse, if filing jointly) receive an economic recovery payment in **2010**? You may have received this payment in 2010 if you did not receive an economic recovery payment in 2009 but you received social security benefits, supplemental security income, railroad retirement benefits, or veterans disability compensation or pension benefits in November 2008, December 2008, or January 2009 (see instructions).

☐ **No.** Enter -0- on line 10 and go to line 11.

☐ **Yes.** Enter the total of the payments you (and your spouse, if filing jointly) received in **2010**. Do not enter more than $250 ($500 if married filing jointly) **10**

11   **Making work pay credit.** Subtract line 10 from line 9. If zero or less, enter -0-. Enter the result here and on Form 1040, line 63; or Form 1040A, line 40 . . . . **11**

*If you are filing Form 2555, 2555-EZ, or 4563 or you are excluding income from Puerto Rico, see instructions.

For Paperwork Reduction Act Notice, see your tax return instructions.   Cat. No. 52903Q   **Schedule M (Form 1040A or 1040) 2010**

SCHEDULE SE (Form 1040) Department of the Treasury Internal Revenue Service (99)	**Self-Employment Tax** ▶ **Attach to Form 1040 or Form 1040NR.** ▶ **See Instructions for Schedule SE (Form 1040).**	OMB No. 1545-0074 20**10** Attachment Sequence No. **17**

Name of person with **self-employment** income (as shown on Form 1040)	Social security number of person with **self-employment** income ▶

Before you begin: To determine if you must file Schedule SE, see the instructions on page SE-1.

May I Use Short Schedule SE or Must I Use Long Schedule SE?

Note. Use this flowchart **only if** you must file Schedule SE. If unsure, see *Who Must File Schedule SE* on page SE-1.

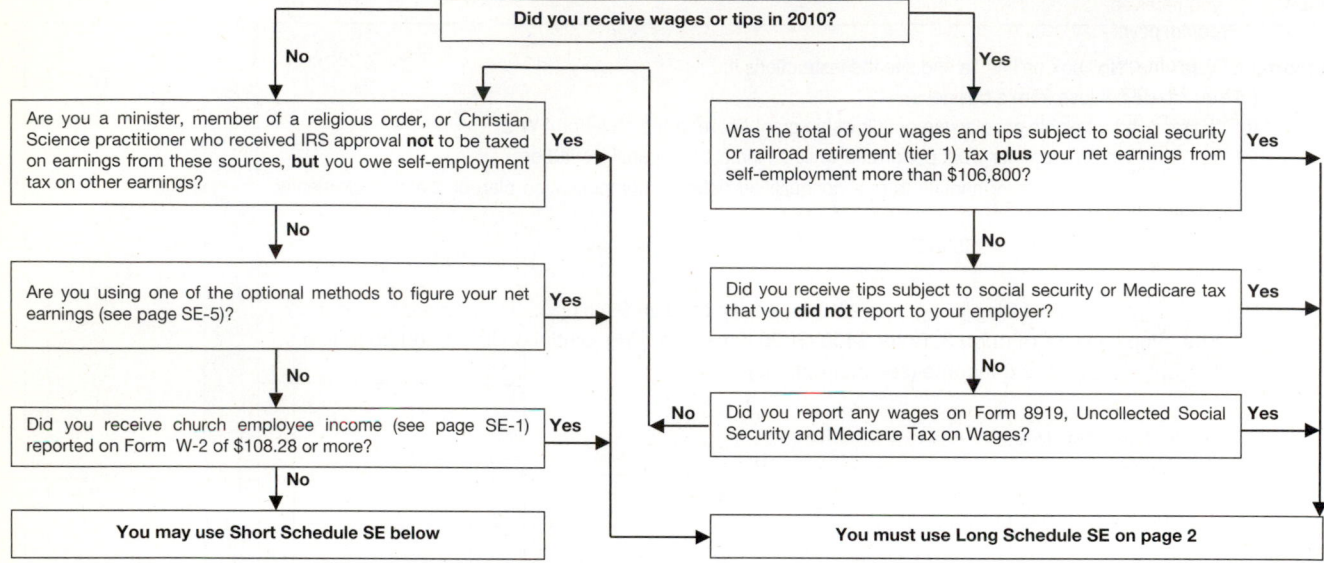

Section A—Short Schedule SE.   Caution. Read above to see if you can use Short Schedule SE.

1a	Net farm profit or (loss) from Schedule F, line 36, and farm partnerships, Schedule K-1 (Form 1065), box 14, code A	**1a**
b	If you received social security retirement or disability benefits, enter the amount of Conservation Reserve Program payments included on Schedule F, line 6b, or listed on Schedule K-1 (Form 1065), box 20, code Y	**1b** ( )
2	Net profit or (loss) from Schedule C, line 31; Schedule C-EZ, line 3; Schedule K-1 (Form 1065), box 14, code A (other than farming); and Schedule K-1 (Form 1065-B), box 9, code J1. Ministers and members of religious orders, see page SE-1 for types of income to report on this line. See page SE-3 for other income to report	**2**
3	Combine lines 1a, 1b, and 2. Subtract from that total the amount on Form 1040, line 29, or Form 1040NR, line 29, and enter the result (see page SE-3)	**3**
4	Multiply line 3 by 92.35% (.9235). If less than $400, you do not owe self-employment tax; **do not** file this schedule unless you have an amount on line 1b . . . . ▶	**4**
	Note. If line 4 is less than $400 due to Conservation Reserve Program payments on line 1b, see page SE-3.	
5	**Self-employment tax.** If the amount on line 4 is: • $106,800 or less, multiply line 4 by 15.3% (.153). Enter the result here and on **Form 1040, line 56,** or **Form 1040NR, line 54** • More than $106,800, multiply line 4 by 2.9% (.029). Then, add $13,243.20 to the result. Enter the total here and on **Form 1040, line 56,** or **Form 1040NR, line 54**	**5**
6	**Deduction for one-half of self-employment tax.** Multiply line 5 by 50% (.50). Enter the result here and on **Form 1040, line 27,** or **Form 1040NR, line 27**	**6**

For Paperwork Reduction Act Notice, see your tax return instructions.   Cat. No. 11358Z   Schedule SE (Form 1040) 2010

Schedule SE (Form 1040) 2010 | Attachment Sequence No. **17** | Page **2**

Name of person with **self-employment** income (as shown on Form 1040)	Social security number of person with **self-employment** income ▶

Section B—Long Schedule SE

Part I Self-Employment Tax

Note. If your only income subject to self-employment tax is **church employee income,** see page SE-3 for specific instructions. Also see page SE-1 for the definition of church employee income.

A If you are a minister, member of a religious order, or Christian Science practitioner **and** you filed Form 4361, but you had $400 or more of **other** net earnings from self-employment, check here and continue with Part I . . . . ▶ ☐

1a	Net farm profit or (loss) from Schedule F, line 36, and farm partnerships, Schedule K-1 (Form 1065), box 14, code A. **Note.** Skip lines 1a and 1b if you use the farm optional method (see page SE-5)	**1a**	
b	If you received social security retirement or disability benefits, enter the amount of Conservation Reserve Program payments included on Schedule F, line 6b, or listed on Schedule K-1 (Form 1065), box 20, code Y	**1b** (	)
2	Net profit or (loss) from Schedule C, line 31; Schedule C-EZ, line 3; Schedule K-1 (Form 1065), box 14, code A (other than farming); and Schedule K-1 (Form 1065-B), box 9, code J1. Ministers and members of religious orders, see page SE-1 for types of income to report on this line. See page SE-4 for other income to report. **Note.** Skip this line if you use the nonfarm optional method (see page SE-5)	**2**	
3	Combine lines 1a, 1b, and 2. Subtract from that total the amount on Form 1040, line 29, or Form 1040NR, line 29, and enter the result (see page SE-3)	**3**	
4a	If line 3 is more than zero, multiply line 3 by 92.35% (.9235). Otherwise, enter amount from line 3 **Note.** If line 4a is less than $400 due to Conservation Reserve Program payments on line 1b, see page SE-3.	**4a**	
b	If you elect one or both of the optional methods, enter the total of lines 15 and 17 here . .	**4b**	
c	Combine lines 4a and 4b. If less than $400, **stop**; you do not owe self-employment tax. **Exception.** If less than $400 and you had **church employee income,** enter -0- and continue ▶	**4c**	
5a	Enter your **church employee income** from Form W-2. See page SE-1 for definition of church employee income **5a**	**5b**	
b	Multiply line 5a by 92.35% (.9235). If less than $100, enter -0-		
6	Add lines 4c and 5b	**6**	
7	Maximum amount of combined wages and self-employment earnings subject to social security tax or the 6.2% portion of the 7.65% railroad retirement (tier 1) tax for 2010	**7**	106,800 00
8a	Total social security wages and tips (total of boxes 3 and 7 on Form(s) W-2) and railroad retirement (tier 1) compensation. If $106,800 or more, skip lines 8b through 10, and go to line 11 **8a**		
b	Unreported tips subject to social security tax (from Form 4137, line 10) **8b**		
c	Wages subject to social security tax (from Form 8919, line 10) **8c**		
d	Add lines 8a, 8b, and 8c	**8d**	
9	Subtract line 8d from line 7. If zero or less, enter -0- here and on line 10 and go to line 11 ▶	**9**	
10	Multiply the **smaller** of line 6 or line 9 by 12.4% (.124)	**10**	
11	Multiply line 6 by 2.9% (.029)	**11**	
12	**Self-employment tax.** Add lines 10 and 11. Enter here and on **Form 1040, line 56,** or **Form 1040NR, line 54**	**12**	
13	**Deduction for one-half of self-employment tax.** Multiply line 12 by 50% (.50). Enter the result here and on **Form 1040, line 27,** or **Form 1040NR, line 27** . **13**		

Part II Optional Methods To Figure Net Earnings (see page SE-4)

Farm Optional Method. You may use this method **only** if **(a)** your gross farm income[1] was not more than $6,720, **or (b)** your net farm profits[2] were less than $4,851.

14	Maximum income for optional methods	**14**	4,480 00
15	Enter the **smaller** of: two-thirds (2/3) of gross farm income[1] (not less than zero) **or** $4,480. Also include this amount on line 4b above	**15**	

Nonfarm Optional Method. You may use this method **only** if **(a)** your net nonfarm profits[3] were less than $4,851 and also less than 72.189% of your gross nonfarm income,[4] **and (b)** you had net earnings from self-employment of at least $400 in 2 of the prior 3 years. **Caution.** You may use this method no more than five times.

16	Subtract line 15 from line 14	**16**	
17	Enter the **smaller** of: two-thirds (2/3) of gross nonfarm income[4] (not less than zero) **or** the amount on line 16. Also include this amount on line 4b above	**17**	

[1] From Sch. F, line 11, and Sch. K-1 (Form 1065), box 14, code B.
[2] From Sch. F, line 36, and Sch. K-1 (Form 1065), box 14, code A—minus the amount you would have entered on line 1b had you not used the optional method.
[3] From Sch. C, line 31; Sch. C-EZ, line 3; Sch. K-1 (Form 1065), box 14, code A; and Sch. K-1 (Form 1065-B), box 9, code J1.
[4] From Sch. C, line 7; Sch. C-EZ, line 1; Sch. K-1 (Form 1065), box 14, code C; and Sch. K-1 (Form 1065-B), box 9, code J2.

Schedule SE (Form 1040) 2010

Appendix C

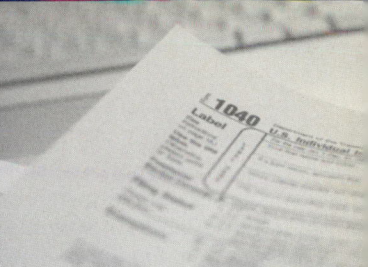

GLOSSARY

The words and phrases in this glossary have been defined to reflect their conventional use in the field of taxation. The definitions may therefore be incomplete for other purposes.

A

Abandoned spouse. The abandoned spouse provision enables a married taxpayer with a dependent child whose spouse did not live in the taxpayer's home during the last six months of the tax year to file as a head of household rather than as married filing separately.

Accelerated cost recovery system (ACRS). A method in which the cost of tangible property is recovered over a prescribed period of time. Enacted by the Economic Recovery Tax Act (ERTA) of 1981 and substantially modified by the Tax Reform Act (TRA) of 1986 (the modified system is referred to as MACRS), the approach disregards salvage value, imposes a period of cost recovery that depends upon the classification of the asset into one of various recovery periods, and prescribes the applicable percentage of cost that can be deducted each year. § 168.

Accelerated death benefits. The amount received from a life insurance policy by the insured who is terminally ill or chronically ill. Any realized gain may be excluded from the gross income of the insured if the policy is surrendered to the insurer or is sold to a licensed viatical settlement provider. § 101(g).

Accelerated depreciation. Various methods of depreciation that yield larger deductions in the earlier years of the life of an asset than the straight-line method. Examples include the double declining-balance and the sum-of-the-years' digits methods of depreciation. § 167.

Accident and health benefits. Employee fringe benefits provided by employers through the payment of health and accident insurance premiums or the establishment of employer-funded medical reimbursement plans. Employers generally are entitled to a deduction for such payments, whereas employees generally exclude the fringe benefits from gross income. §§ 105 and 106.

Accountable plan. An accountable plan is a type of expense reimbursement plan that requires an employee to render an adequate accounting to the employer and return any excess reimbursement or allowance. If the expense qualifies, it will be treated as a deduction *for* AGI.

Accounting income. The accountant's concept of income is generally based upon the realization principle. Financial accounting income may differ from taxable income (e.g., accelerated depreciation might be used for Federal income tax and straight-line depreciation for financial accounting purposes). Differences are included in a reconciliation of taxable and accounting income on Schedule M–1 or Schedule M–3 of Form 1120 for corporations. Seventy-five percent of the excess of adjusted current earnings over alternative minimum taxable income is an adjustment for alternative minimum tax purposes for a corporation. See also *alternative minimum tax* and *economic income*.

Accounting method. The method under which income and expenses are determined for tax purposes. Major accounting methods are the cash basis and the accrual basis. Special methods are available for the reporting of gain on installment sales, recognition of income on construction projects (the completed contract and percentage of completion methods), and the valuation of inventories (last-in, first-out and first-in, first-out). §§ 446–474. See also *accrual method, cash receipts method, completed contract method, percentage of completion method*, etc.

Accounting period. The period of time, usually a year, used by a taxpayer for the determination of tax liability. Unless a fiscal year is chosen, taxpayers must determine and pay their income tax liability by using the calendar year (January 1 through December 31) as the period of measurement. An example of a fiscal year is July 1 through June 30. A change in accounting period (e.g., from a calendar year to a fiscal year) generally requires the consent of the IRS. A new taxpayer, such as a newly formed corporation or an estate created upon the death of an individual taxpayer, is free to select either a calendar or a fiscal year without the consent of the IRS. Limitations exist on the accounting period that may be selected by a partnership, an S corporation, and a personal service corporation. §§ 441–444.

Accrual basis. See *accrual method*.

Accrual method. A method of accounting that reflects expenses incurred and income earned for any one tax year. In contrast to the cash basis of accounting, expenses do not have to be paid to be deductible nor does income have to be received to be taxable. Unearned income (e.g., prepaid interest and rent) generally is taxed in the year of receipt regardless of the method of accounting used by the taxpayer. § 446(c)(2). See also *accounting method, cash receipts method,* and *unearned income.*

Accumulated earnings tax. A special tax imposed on corporations that accumulate (rather than distribute) their earnings beyond the reasonable needs of the business. The tax is imposed on accumulated taxable income and is imposed in addition to the corporate income tax. §§ 531–537.

ACE adjustment. See *adjusted current earnings (ACE) adjustment.*

Acquiescence. In agreement with the result reached. The IRS follows a policy of either acquiescing (*A, Acq.*) or nonacquiescing (*NA, Nonacq.*) in the results reached in certain judicial decisions.

Acquisition indebtedness. Debt incurred in acquiring, constructing, or substantially improving a qualified residence of the taxpayer. The interest on such loans is deductible as *qualified residence interest.* However, interest on such debt is deductible only on the portion of the indebtedness that does not exceed $1,000,000 ($500,000 for married persons filing separate returns). § 163(h)(3). See also *home equity loans.*

ACRS. See *accelerated cost recovery system.*

Active income. Active income includes wages, salary, commissions, bonuses, profits from a trade or business in which the taxpayer is a material participant, gain on the sale or other disposition of assets used in an active trade or business, and income from intangible property if the taxpayer's personal efforts significantly contributed to the creation of the property. The passive activity loss rules require classification of income and losses into three categories with active income being one of them.

Active participation. A term that is relevant for both the at-risk rules and the passive activity loss rules associated with rental real estate activities. For the at-risk rules, the following factors indicate active participation: (1) making decisions involving the operation or management of the activity, (2) performing services for the activity, and (3) hiring and discharging employees. For the passive activity loss rules, the taxpayer must participate in the making of management decisions in a significant and bona fide sense.

Ad valorem tax. A tax imposed on the value of property. The most familiar ad valorem tax is that imposed by states, counties, and cities on real estate. Ad valorem taxes can, however, be imposed upon personal property (e.g., a motor vehicle tax based on the value of an automobile). §§ 164(a)(1) and (2).

Additional depreciation. The excess of the amount of depreciation actually deducted over the amount that would have been deducted had the straight-line method been used. § 1250(b). See also *Section 1250 recapture.*

Additional first-year depreciation. See *Fifty percent additional first-year depreciation* and *one hundred percent additional first-year depreciation.*

Adjusted basis. The cost or other basis of property reduced by depreciation (cost recovery) allowed or allowable and increased by capital improvements. See also *basis* and *realized gain or loss.*

Adjusted current earnings (ACE) adjustment. An adjustment in computing corporate alternative minimum taxable income (AMTI), computed at 75 percent of the excess of adjusted current earnings and profits computations over unadjusted AMTI. ACE computations reflect longer and slower cost recovery deductions and other restrictions on the timing of certain recognition events. Exempt interest, life insurance proceeds, and other receipts that are included in earnings and profits but not in taxable income also increase the ACE adjustment. If unadjusted AMTI exceeds adjusted current earnings and profits, the ACE adjustment is negative. The negative adjustment is limited to the aggregate of the positive adjustments under ACE for prior years, reduced by any previously claimed negative adjustments. See also *alternative minimum tax* and *earnings and profits.*

Adjusted gross income (AGI). A determination peculiar to individual taxpayers. Generally, it represents gross income less business expenses, expenses attributable to the production of rent or royalty income, the allowed capital loss deduction, and certain personal expenses (deductions *for* AGI). § 62. See also *gross income.*

Adoption expenses credit. A provision intended to assist taxpayers who incur nonrecurring costs directly associated with the adoption process such as legal costs, social service review costs, and transportation costs. Up to $13,360 ($13,360 for a child with special needs regardless of the actual adoption expenses) of costs incurred to adopt an eligible child qualify for the credit. A taxpayer may claim the credit in the year qualifying expenses are paid or incurred if the expenses are paid during or after the year in which the adoption is finalized. For qualifying expenses paid or incurred in a tax year prior to the year the adoption is finalized, the credit must be claimed in the tax year following the tax year during which the expenses are paid or incurred. § 23.

Advance payments. In general, prepayments for services or goods are includible in gross income upon receipt of the advance payments (for both accrual and cash basis taxpayers). However, Revenue Procedure 2004–34, 2004–1 C.B. 991, provides guidelines for the deferral of tax on certain advance payments providing specific conditions are met.

AFTR. Published by Research Institute of America (formerly by Prentice-Hall), *American Federal Tax Reports* contains all of the Federal tax decisions issued by the U.S. District Courts, U.S. Court of Federal Claims, U.S. Courts of Appeals, and U.S. Supreme Court.

AFTR 2d. The second series of the *American Federal Tax Reports.*

AFTR 3d. The third series of the *American Federal Tax Reports.*

Alimony and separate maintenance payments. Alimony and separate maintenance payments are includible in the gross income of the recipient and are deductible by the payor. The payments must be made in discharge of a legal obligation arising from a marital or family relationship. Child support and voluntary payments are not treated as alimony. Alimony is deductible *for* AGI. §§ 62(10), 71, and 215. See also *child support payments.*

Alimony recapture. The amount of alimony that previously has been included in the gross income of the recipient and deducted by the payor that now is deducted by the recipient and included in the gross income of the payor as the result of front-loading. § 71(f).

All events test. For accrual method taxpayers, income is earned when (1) all the events have occurred that fix the right to receive the income and (2) the amount can be determined with reasonable accuracy. Accrual of income cannot be postponed simply because a portion of the income may have to be returned in a subsequent period. The all events test also is utilized to determine when expenses can be deducted by an accrual basis taxpayer. The application of the test could cause a variation between the treatment of an item for accounting and for tax purposes. For example, a reserve for warranty expense may be properly accruable under generally accepted accounting principles but not be deductible under the Federal income tax law. Because of the application of the all events test, the deduction becomes available in the year the warranty obligation becomes fixed and the amount is determinable with reasonable certainty. See also *economic performance test.* Reg. §§ 1.446–1(c)(1)(ii) and 1.461–1(a)(2).

Alternate valuation date. Property passing from a person by reason of death may be valued for estate tax purposes as of the date of death or the alternate valuation date. The alternate valuation date is six months from the date of death or the date the property is disposed of by the estate, whichever comes first. To use the alternate valuation date, the executor or administrator of the estate must make an affirmative election. The election of the alternate valuation date is not available unless it decreases both the amount of the gross estate *and* the estate tax liability. §§ 1014(a) and 2032.

Alternative depreciation system (ADS). A cost recovery system that produces a smaller deduction than would be calculated under ACRS or MACRS. The alternative system must be used in certain instances and can be elected in other instances. § 168(g). See also *cost recovery allowance.*

Alternative minimum tax (AMT). The alternative minimum tax is imposed only to the extent it exceeds the regular income tax (in effect, the tax liability is the greater of the tax liability calculated using the AMT rules and that calculated using the regular income tax rules). The AMT rates (26 and 28 percent for the individual taxpayer and 20 percent for the corporate taxpayer) are applied to the AMT base. The AMT base is calculated by modifying taxable income as follows: (1) add tax preferences, (2) add certain adjustments, (3) deduct certain adjustments, and (4) deduct the exemption amount. §§ 55–59. See also *adjusted current earnings (ACE) adjustment.*

Alternative minimum tax credit. The AMT can result from timing differences that give rise to positive adjustments in calculating the AMT base. To provide equity for the taxpayer when these timing differences reverse, the regular tax liability may be reduced by a tax credit for prior year's minimum tax liability attributable to timing differences. § 53.

Alternative tax. An option that is allowed in computing the tax on net capital gain. For the corporate taxpayer, the rate is 35 percent (the same as the highest regular corporate tax rate). Thus, for corporate taxpayers, the alternative tax does not produce a beneficial result. For noncorporate taxpayers, the rate is usually 15 percent (but it is 25 percent for unrecaptured § 1250 gain and is 28 percent for collectibles and § 1202 gain). However, if the noncorporate taxpayer is in either the 10 percent or the 15 percent tax bracket, the alternative tax rate is 0 percent in 2008, 2009, 2010, and 2011 and 5 percent in 2007 and prior years (rather than 15 percent). §§ 1(h) and 1201. See also *collectibles, net capital gain* and *unrecaptured § 1250 gain (25 percent gain).*

Alternative tax NOL deduction (ATNOLD). In calculating the AMT, the taxpayer is allowed to deduct NOL carryovers and carrybacks. A special calculation, referred to as the ATNOLD, is required for this purpose. The regular income tax is modified for AMT adjustments and preferences to produce the ATNOLD. § 56(d).

American Opportunity credit. This credit replaces the HOPE scholarship credit for 2009, 2010, 2011, and 2012 and applies for qualifying expenses for the first four years of postsecondary education. Qualified expenses include tuition and related expenses and books and other course materials. Room and board are ineligible for the credit. The maximum credit available per student is $2,500 (100 percent of the first $2,000 of qualifying expenses and 25 percent of the next $2,000 of qualifying expenses). Eligible students include the taxpayer, taxpayer's spouse, and taxpayer's dependents. To qualify for the credit, a student must take at least one-half the full-time course load for at least one academic term at a qualifying educational institution. The credit is phased out for higher-income taxpayers. See also *HOPE scholarship credit* and *lifetime learning credit.* § 25A.

Amortization. The allocation (and charge to expense) of the cost or other basis of an intangible asset over a statutory period of 15 years. Examples of amortizable intangibles include patents, copyrights, covenants not to compete, acquired goodwill, and leasehold interests. See also *estimated useful life* and *goodwill.* § 197.

Amount realized. The amount received by a taxpayer on the sale or other disposition of property. The amount realized is the sum of the cash and the fair market value of any property or services received, plus any related debt assumed by the buyer. Determining the amount realized is the starting point for arriving at realized gain or loss. The amount realized is defined in § 1001(b) and the related Regulations. See also *realized gain or loss* and *recognized gain or loss.*

AMT adjustments. In calculating AMTI, certain adjustments are added to or deducted from taxable income. These adjustments generally reflect timing differences. § 56.

AMT exclusions. A credit that can be used to reduce the regular tax liability in future tax years is available in connection with the AMT (*AMT credit*). The credit is applicable only with respect to the AMT that results from timing differences. It is not available in connection with AMT exclusions, which include the standard deduction, personal exemptions, medical expenses deductible in calculating the regular income tax that are not deductible in computing the AMT, other itemized deductions that are not allowable for AMT purposes, excess percentage depletion, and tax-exempt interest on specified private activity bonds.

Annuity. A fixed sum payable to a person at specified intervals for a specific period of time or for life. Payments represent a partial return of capital and a return (interest) on the capital investment. Therefore, an exclusion ratio must be used to compute the amount of nontaxable income. The exclusion ratio is used until the annuitant has recovered his or her investment in the annuity contract. Thereafter, all of the annuity payments received are included in gross income. If the annuitant dies before his or her investment is recovered, a deduction is allowed. § 72. See also *qualified pension or profit sharing plan.*

Appellate court. For Federal tax purposes, appellate courts include the Courts of Appeals and the Supreme Court. If the party losing in the trial (or lower) court is dissatisfied with the result, the dispute may be carried to the appropriate appellate court. See also *Court of Appeals* and *trial court.*

Archer medical savings account. See *medical savings account.*

Arm's length transaction. The standard under which unrelated parties would determine an exchange price for a transaction. Suppose, for example, Cardinal Corporation sells property to its sole shareholder for $10,000. In testing whether the $10,000 is an "arm's length" price, one would ascertain the price that would have been negotiated between the corporation and an unrelated party in a bargained exchange.

Asset Depreciation Range (ADR) system. A system of estimated useful lives for categories of tangible assets prescribed by the IRS. The system provides a range for each category that extends from 20 percent above to 20 percent below the guideline class lives prescribed by the IRS.

Assignment of income. A procedure whereby a taxpayer attempts to avoid the recognition of income by assigning the property that generates the income to another. Such a procedure will not avoid the recognition of income by the taxpayer making the assignment if it can be said that the income was earned at the point of the transfer. In this case, usually referred to as an anticipatory assignment of income, the income will be taxed to the person who earns it.

Association. An organization treated as a corporation for Federal tax purposes even though it may not qualify as such under applicable state law. An entity designated as a trust or a partnership, for example, may be classified as an association if it clearly possesses corporate attributes. Corporate attributes include centralized management, continuity of life, free transferability of interests, and limited liability. When the check-the-box Regulations were finalized, the association Regulations were withdrawn. Thus, for most entities, reclassification as an association is unlikely. § 7701(a)(3). See also *check-the-box Regulations*.

At-risk limitation. Under the at-risk rules, a taxpayer's deductible losses from an activity for any taxable year are limited to the amount the taxpayer has at risk at the end of the taxable year. The initial amount considered at risk is generally the sum of the amount of cash and the adjusted basis of property contributed to the activity and amounts borrowed for use in the activity for which the taxpayer is personally liable or has pledged as security property not used in the activity. § 465.

Attribution. Under certain circumstances, the tax law applies attribution (construction ownership) rules to assign to one taxpayer the ownership interest of another taxpayer. If, for example, the stock of Gold Corporation is held 60 percent by Marsha and 40 percent by Sid, Marsha may be deemed to own 100 percent of Gold Corporation if she and Sid are mother and son. In that case, the stock owned by Sid is attributed to Marsha. See, for example, §§ 267 and 318.

Audit. Inspection and verification of a taxpayer's return or other transactions possessing tax consequences. See also *correspondence audit*, *field audit*, and *office audit*.

Automatic mileage method. See *automobile expenses*.

Automobile expenses. Automobile expenses are generally deductible only to the extent the automobile is used in business or for the production of income. Personal commuting expenses are not deductible. The taxpayer may deduct actual expenses (including depreciation and insurance), or the standard (automatic) mileage rate may be used (51 cents for 2011 and 50 cents for 2010). Automobile expenses incurred for medical purposes or in connection with job-related moving expenses are deductible to the extent of actual out-of-pocket expenses or at the rate of 19 cents per mile in 2011 (16.5 cents per mile for 2010). For charitable activities, the rate is 14 cents per mile. See also *transportation expenses*.

B

Bad debts. A deduction is permitted if a business account receivable subsequently becomes partially or completely worthless, providing the income arising from the debt previously was included in income. Available methods are the specific charge-off method and the reserve method. However, except for certain financial institutions, TRA of 1986 repealed the use of the reserve method for 1987 and thereafter. If the reserve method is used, partially or totally worthless accounts are charged to the reserve. A nonbusiness bad debt deduction is allowed as a short-term capital loss if the loan did not arise in connection with the creditor's trade or business activities. Loans between related parties (family members) generally are classified as nonbusiness. § 166. See also *nonbusiness bad debts*.

Basis. The acquisition cost assigned to an asset for income tax purposes. For assets acquired by purchase, the basis is the cost (§ 1012). Special rules govern the basis of property received by virtue of another's death (§ 1014) or by gift (§ 1015), the basis of stock received on a transfer of property to a controlled corporation (§ 358), the basis of the property transferred to the corporation (§ 362), and the basis of property received upon the liquidation of a corporation (§§ 334 and 338). See also *adjusted basis*.

Book value. The net amount of an asset after reduction by a related reserve. The book value of accounts receivable, for example, is the face amount of the receivables less the reserve for bad debts. The book value of a building is the cost less the accumulated depreciation.

Boot. Cash or property of a type not included in the definition of a nontaxable exchange. The receipt of boot will cause an otherwise nontaxable transfer to become taxable to the extent of the lesser of the fair market value of such boot or the realized gain on the transfer. Examples of nontaxable exchanges that could be partially or completely taxable due to the receipt of boot include transfers to controlled corporations [§ 351(b)] and like-kind exchanges [§ 1031(b)]. See also *realized gain or loss* and *recognized gain or loss*.

Bribes and illegal payments. Section 162 denies a deduction for bribes or kickbacks, fines, and penalties paid to a government official or employee for violation of law, and two-thirds of the treble damage payments made to claimants for violation of the antitrust law. Denial of a deduction for bribes and illegal payments is based upon the judicially established principle that allowing such payments would be contrary to public policy.

B.T.A. The Board of Tax Appeals was a trial court that considered Federal tax matters. This court is now the U.S. Tax Court.

Burden of proof. The requirement in a lawsuit to show the weight of evidence and thereby gain a favorable decision. Except in cases of tax fraud, the burden of proof in a tax case generally is on the taxpayer.

Business bad debt. A debt created or acquired in connection with a trade or business of the taxpayer, or a debt the loss from the worthlessness of which is incurred in the taxpayer's trade or business. A business bad debt is deducted as an ordinary deduction. § 166.

Business expenses. See *trade or business expenses.*

Business gifts. Business gifts are deductible only to the extent that each gift does not exceed $25 per person per year. Exceptions are made for gifts costing $4 or less and for certain employee awards. § 274(b).

C

C corporation. A corporation that has not elected conduit treatment under § 1361. See also *S corporation status.*

Cafeteria benefit plan. An employee benefit plan under which an employee is allowed to select from among a variety of employer-provided fringe benefits. Some of the benefits may be taxable and some may be statutory nontaxable benefits (e.g., health and accident insurance and group term life insurance). The employee is taxed only on the taxable benefits selected. A cafeteria benefit plan is also referred to as a flexible benefit plan. § 125.

Cafeteria plan. See *cafeteria benefit plan.*

Canons of taxation. Criteria used in the selection of a tax base that were originally discussed by Adam Smith in *The Wealth of Nations.* Canons of taxation include equality, convenience, certainty, and economy.

Capital asset. Broadly speaking, all assets are capital except those specifically excluded by the Code. Major categories of noncapital assets include property held for resale in the normal course of business (inventory), trade accounts and notes receivable, and depreciable property and real estate used in a trade or business (§ 1231 assets). § 1221. See also *capital gain* and *capital loss.*

Capital contributions. Various means by which a shareholder makes additional funds available to the corporation (placed at the risk of the business) without the receipt of additional stock. Such contributions are added to the basis of the shareholder's existing stock investment and do not generate income to the corporation. § 118.

Capital expenditure. An expenditure that should be added to the basis of the property improved. For income tax purposes, this generally precludes a full deduction for the expenditure in the year paid or incurred. Any capital recovery in the form of a tax deduction must come in the form of depreciation. § 263.

Capital gain. The gain from the sale or exchange of a capital asset. See also *capital asset* and *net capital gain.*

Capital gain net income. If the total capital gains for the tax year exceed the total capital losses, the result is capital gain net income. Note that the term does not distinguish between the long-term and short-term gains. § 1222(9). See also *net capital gain.*

Capital gain or loss holding period. The period of time that a capital asset is held by the taxpayer. To qualify for long-term treatment, the asset must be held for more than one year. If held for one year or less, the holding period is short term. See also *holding period.*

Capital gain property. Property contributed to a charitable organization that, if sold rather than contributed, would have resulted in long-term capital gain to the donor. See also *ordinary income property.*

Capital loss. The loss from the sale or exchange of a capital asset. See also *capital asset.*

Cash balance plan. A hybrid form of pension plan similar in some aspects to a defined benefit plan. Such a plan is funded by the employer, and the employer bears the investment risks and rewards. But like defined contribution plans, a cash balance plan establishes allocations to individual employee accounts, and the payout for an employee depends on investment performance.

Cash basis. See *accounting method* and *cash receipts method.*

Cash equivalent doctrine. Generally, a cash basis taxpayer does not report income until cash is constructively or actually received. Under the cash equivalent doctrine, cash basis taxpayers are required to report income if they receive the equivalent of cash (e.g., property is received) in a taxable transaction.

Cash method. See *cash receipts method.*

Cash receipts method. A method of accounting under which the taxpayer generally reports income when cash is collected and reports expenses when cash payments are made. However, for fixed assets, the cash basis taxpayer claims deductions through depreciation or amortization in the same manner as an accrual basis taxpayer. Prepaid expenses must be capitalized and amortized if the life of the asset extends "substantially beyond" the end of the tax year. See also *constructive receipt.*

Casualty loss. A casualty is defined as "the complete or partial destruction of property resulting from an identifiable event of a sudden, unexpected or unusual nature" (e.g., floods, storms, fires, auto accidents). Individuals may deduct a casualty loss only if the loss is incurred in a trade or business or in a transaction entered into for profit or arises from fire, storm, shipwreck, or other casualty or from theft. Individuals usually deduct personal casualty losses as itemized deductions subject to a $100 ($500 for 2009) nondeductible amount and to an annual floor equal to 10 percent of adjusted gross income that applies after the $100 ($500 for 2009) per casualty floor has been applied. Special rules are provided for the netting of certain casualty gains and losses. § 165. See also *disaster area loss* and *Section 1231 gains and losses.*

Cert. den. By denying the Writ of Certiorari, the U.S. Supreme Court refuses to accept an appeal from a U.S. Court of Appeals. The denial of certiorari does not, however, mean that the U.S. Supreme Court agrees with the result reached by the lower court.

Certiorari. Appeal from a U.S. Court of Appeals to the U.S. Supreme Court is by Writ of Certiorari. The Supreme Court does not have to accept the appeal and usually does not (*cert. den.*) unless there is a conflict among the lower courts that needs to be resolved or a constitutional issue is involved.

Change in accounting method. A change in the taxpayer's method of accounting (e.g., from FIFO to LIFO) generally requires prior approval from the IRS. Generally, a request must be filed within the taxable year of the desired change. In some instances, the permission for change will not be granted unless the taxpayer agrees to certain adjustments prescribed by the IRS.

Change in accounting period. A taxpayer must obtain the consent of the IRS before changing his or her tax year. Income for the short period created by the change must be annualized.

Charitable contributions. Contributions are deductible (subject to various restrictions and ceiling limitations) if made to qualified nonprofit charitable organizations. A cash basis taxpayer is entitled to a deduction solely in the year of payment. Accrual basis corporations may accrue contributions at year-end if payment is properly authorized before the end of the year and payment is made within two and one-half months after the end of the year. § 170.

Check-the-box Regulations. These Regulations enable taxpayers to classify the tax status of a business entity without regard to its corporate or noncorporate characteristics. An entity with more than one owner can elect to be classified either as a partnership or as a corporation. An entity with only one owner can elect to be classified as a sole proprietorship or as a corporation. These Regulations should simplify tax administration and taxpayer compliance and reduce tax litigation.

Child and dependent care expenses credit. A tax credit ranging from 20 percent to 35 percent of employment-related expenses (child and dependent care expenses) for amounts of up to $6,000 is available to individuals who are employed (or deemed to be employed) and maintain a household for a dependent child under age 13, disabled spouse, or disabled dependent. § 21.

Child support payments. Payments for child support do not constitute alimony and are therefore not includible in gross income by the recipient or deductible as alimony by the payor. Generally, none of the amounts paid are regarded as child support unless the divorce decree or separation agreement specifically calls for child support payments, However, if the amount of the payment to the former spouse would be reduced upon the happening of a contingency related to a child (e.g., the child attains age 21 or dies), the amount of the future reduction in the payment will be deemed child support for post-1984 agreements and decrees. § 71(c). See also *alimony and separate maintenance payments.*

Child tax credit. A tax credit based solely on the number of qualifying children under age 17. The maximum credit available is $1,000 per child through 2011. A qualifying child must be claimed as a dependent on a parent's tax return in order to qualify for the credit. Taxpayers who qualify for the child tax credit may also qualify for a supplemental credit. The supplemental credit is treated as a component of the earned income credit and is therefore refundable. The credit is phased out for higher-income taxpayers. § 24.

Circuit Court of Appeals. See *Court of Appeals.*

Circulation expenditures. Expenditures of establishing or increasing the circulation of a periodical that may be either expensed or capitalized. If such expenses are expensed, an adjustment will occur for AMT purposes, since the expenses are deducted over a three-year period for AMT purposes. Over the three-year period, both positive and negative AMT adjustments will be produced. § 173. See also *AMT adjustments.*

Citator. A tax research resource that presents the judicial history of a court case and traces the subsequent references to the case. When these references include the citing case's evaluations of the cited case's precedents, the research can obtain some measure of the efficacy and reliability of the original holding.

Claim of right doctrine. A judicially imposed doctrine applicable to both cash and accrual basis taxpayers that holds that an amount is includible in income upon actual or constructive receipt if the taxpayer has an unrestricted claim to the payment. For the tax treatment of amounts repaid when previously included in income under the claim of right doctrine, see § 1341.

Claims Court. One of three Federal trial courts that consider Federal tax controversies. Now known as the U.S. Court of Federal Claims, appeal from this court (formerly to the U.S. Supreme Court) now goes to the Court of Appeals for the Federal Circuit. See also *trial court.*

Clear reflection of income. The IRS has the authority to redetermine a taxpayer's income using a method that clearly reflects income if the taxpayer's method does not do so. § 446(b). In addition, the IRS may apportion or allocate income among various related businesses if income is not "clearly reflected." § 482.

Closely held corporation. A corporation where the stock ownership is not widely dispersed. Instead, a few shareholders are in control of corporate policy and are in a position to benefit personally from that policy.

Collectibles. A special type of capital asset, the gain from which is taxed at a maximum rate of 28 percent if the holding period is more than one year. Examples include art, rugs, antiques, gems, metals, stamps, some coins and bullion, and alcoholic beverages held for investment.

Community property. Louisiana, Texas, New Mexico, Arizona, California, Washington, Idaho, Nevada, and Wisconsin have community property systems. In Alaska, spouses can choose to have the community property rules apply. The rest of the states are classified as common law jurisdictions. The difference between common law and community property systems centers around the property rights possessed by married persons. In a common law system, each spouse owns whatever he or she earns. Under a community property system, one-half of the earnings of each spouse is considered owned by the other spouse. Assume, for example, Alice and Jeff are husband and wife and their only income is the $50,000 annual salary Jeff receives. If they live in New York (a common law state), the $50,000 salary belongs to Jeff. If, however, they live in Texas (a community property state), the $50,000 salary is divided equally, in terms of ownership, between Jeff and Alice. See also *separate property.*

Compensatory damages. Damages received or paid by the taxpayer can be classified as compensatory damages or as punitive damages. Compensatory damages are those paid to compensate one for harm caused by another. Compensatory damages are excludible from the recipient's gross income. See also *punitive damages.*

Completed contract method. A method of reporting gain or loss on certain long-term contracts. Under this method of accounting, gross income and expenses are recognized in the tax year in which the contract is completed. Reg. § 1.451–3. Limitations exist on a taxpayer's ability to use the completed contract method. § 460. See also *long-term contract* and *percentage of completion method.*

Component depreciation. The process of dividing an asset (e.g., a building) into separate components or parts for the purpose of calculating depreciation. The advantage of dividing an asset into components is to use shorter depreciation lives for selected components under § 167. Generally, the same cost recovery period must be used for all the components of an asset under § 168.

Condemnation. The taking of property by a public authority. The property is condemned as the result of legal action, and the owner is compensated by the public authority. The power to condemn property is known as the right of eminent domain.

Conduit concept. An approach assumed by the tax law in the treatment of certain entities and their owners. Specific tax characteristics pass through the entity without losing their identity. For example, items of income and expense, capital gains and losses, tax credits, etc., realized by a partnership pass through the partnership (a conduit) and are subject to taxation at the partner level. Also, in an S corporation, certain items pass through and are reported on the returns of the shareholders.

Constructive dividends. In addition to dividends formally declared by the board of directors of a corporation (i.e., declaration date, record date, and payment date), a shareholder may receive a distribution that does not have the formalities of a dividend but is treated as a dividend. Examples include salaries paid to shareholder-employees that are not reasonable and the shareholder use of corporate property for less than an arm's length rate.

Constructive ownership. See *attribution*.

Constructive receipt. If income is unqualifiedly available, it will be subject to the income tax even though it is not physically in the taxpayer's possession. An example is accrued interest on a savings account. Under the constructive receipt of income concept, the interest will be taxed to a depositor in the year it is available rather than the year actually withdrawn. The fact that the depositor uses the cash basis of accounting for tax purposes is irrelevant. See Reg. § 1.451–2.

Consumer interest. Interest expense of the taxpayer of a personal nature (not trade or business interest, investment interest, qualified residence interest, or passive activity interest) is not deductible. § 163(h). See also *interest on student loans* and *qualified residence interest*.

Contributions to the capital of a corporation. See *capital contributions*.

Convention expenses. Travel expenses incurred in attending a convention are deductible if the meetings are related to a taxpayer's trade or business or job-related activities. If, however, the convention trip is primarily for pleasure, no deduction is permitted for transportation expenses. Likewise, if the expenses are for attending a convention related to the production of income (§ 212), no deduction is permitted. Specific limitations are provided for foreign convention expenses. See § 274(n) for the limitations on the deductions for meals. § 274(h).

Correspondence audit. An audit conducted by the IRS by mail. Typically, the IRS writes to the taxpayer requesting the verification of a particular deduction, exemption, or credit. The completion of a special form or the remittance of copies of records or other support is all that is requested of the taxpayer. To be distinguished from a *field audit* or an *office audit*.

Cost depletion. Depletion that is calculated based on the adjusted basis of the asset. The adjusted basis is divided by the expected recoverable units to determine the depletion per unit. The depletion per unit is multiplied by the units sold during the tax year to calculate cost depletion. See also *percentage depletion*.

Cost recovery allowance. The portion of the cost of an asset written off under ACRS (or MACRS), which replaced the depreciation system as a method for writing off the cost of an asset for most assets placed in service after 1980 (after 1986 for MACRS). § 168. See also *alternative depreciation system, fifty percent additional first-year depreciation*, and *one hundred percent additional first-year depreciation*.

Cost recovery period. A period specified in the Code for writing off the cost of an asset under ACRS or MACRS.

Court of Appeals. Any of 13 Federal courts that consider tax matters appealed from the U.S. Tax Court, U.S. Court of Federal Claims, or a U.S. District Court. Appeal from a U.S. Court of Appeals is to the U.S. Supreme Court by Writ of Certiorari. See also *appellate court*.

Court of Federal Claims. See *Claims Court*.

Court of original jurisdiction. The Federal courts are divided into courts of original jurisdiction and appellate courts. A dispute between a taxpayer and the IRS is first considered by a court of original jurisdiction (i.e., a trial court). The four Federal courts of original jurisdiction are the U.S. Tax Court, U.S. District Court, the Court of Federal Claims, and the Small Cases Division of the U.S. Tax Court. See also *Court of Appeals*.

Coverdell Education Savings Account (CESA). A savings account established to pay for qualified education expenses (i.e., tuition, fees, books, supplies, related equipment, room and board if the student's course load is at least one-half of the full-time course load). The maximum annual contribution to the savings account of a beneficiary is $2,000. The maximum annual contribution is subject to phaseout beginning at $95,000 for single taxpayers and $150,000 for married couples who file a joint return. Contributions are not deductible and cannot be made to a savings account once the beneficiary attains age 18. Distributions used to pay for qualified education expenses for a designated beneficiary are tax free. § 530.

Credit for certain retirement plan contributions. A nonrefundable credit is available based on eligible contributions of up to $2,000 to certain qualified retirement plans, such as traditional and Roth IRAs and § 401(k) plans, for taxable years beginning after 2001. The benefit provided by this credit is in addition to any deduction or exclusion that otherwise is available resulting from the qualifying contribution. The amount of the credit depends on the taxpayer's AGI and filing status. § 25B.

Credit for child and dependent care expenses. See *child and dependent care expenses credit*.

Credit for employer-provided child care. A nonrefundable credit is available to employers who provide child care facilities to their employees during normal working hours. The credit, limited to $150,000, is comprised of two components. The portion of the credit for qualified child care expenses is equal to 25 percent of these expenses while the portion of the credit for qualified child care resource and referral services is equal to 10 percent of these expenses. Any qualifying expenses otherwise deductible by the taxpayer must be reduced by the amount of the credit. In addition, the taxpayer's basis for any property used for qualifying purposes is reduced by the amount of the credit. § 45F.

Credit for small employer pension plan startup costs. A nonrefundable credit available to small businesses based on administrative costs associated with establishing and maintaining certain qualified plans. While such qualifying costs generally are deductible as ordinary and necessary business expenses, the availability of the credit is intended to lower the costs of starting a qualified retirement program, and therefore encourage qualifying businesses to establish retirement plans for their employees. The credit is available for eligible employers at the rate of 50 percent of qualified startup costs. The maximum credit is $500 (based on a maximum $1,000 of qualifying expenses). § 45E.

Crop insurance proceeds. The proceeds received when an insured crop is destroyed. Section 451(d) permits the farmer to defer reporting the income from the insurance proceeds until the tax year following the taxable year of the destruction.

Crop method. A method of accounting for agricultural crops that are planted in one year but harvested in a subsequent year. Under this method, the costs of raising the crop are accumulated as inventory and are deducted when the income from the crop is realized.

D

Death benefit. A payment made by an employer to the beneficiary or beneficiaries of a deceased employee on account of the death of the employee.

Death tax. See *estate tax.*

Declaration of estimated tax. A procedure whereby individuals and corporations are required to make quarterly installment payments of estimated tax. Individuals are required to make the declaration and file quarterly payments of the estimated tax if certain requirements are met. In 2011, a declaration is not required for an individual whose estimated tax is reasonably expected to be less than $1,000.

Deduction for qualified tuition and related expenses. Taxpayers are allowed a deduction of up to $4,000 for higher education expenses. Certain taxpayers are not eligible for the deduction: those whose AGI exceeds a specified amount and those who can be claimed as a dependent by another taxpayer. These expenses are classified as a deduction *for* AGI and they need not be employment related. § 222.

Deductions for adjusted gross income. See *adjusted gross income.*

Deductions from adjusted gross income. See *itemized deductions.*

Deferred compensation. Compensation that will be taxed when received or upon the removal of certain restrictions on receipt and not when earned. Contributions by an employer to a qualified pension or profit sharing plan on behalf of an employee are an example. The contributions will not be taxed to the employee until the funds are made available or distributed to the employee (e.g., upon retirement). See also *qualified pension or profit sharing plan.*

Deficiency. Additional tax liability owed by a taxpayer and assessed by the IRS. See also *statutory notice of deficiency.*

Defined benefit plan. Qualified plans can be dichotomized into defined benefit plans and defined contribution plans. Under a defined benefit plan, a formula defines the benefits employees are to receive. The formula usually includes years of service, employee compensation, and some stated percentage. The employer must make annual contributions based on actuarial computations that will be sufficient to pay the vested retirement benefits. See also *defined contribution plan* and *pension plan.*

Defined contribution plan. Qualified plans can be dichotomized into defined benefit plans and defined contribution plans. Under a defined contribution plan, a separate account is maintained for each covered employee. The employee's benefits under the plan are based solely on (1) the amount contributed and (2) income from the fund that accrues to the employee's account. The plan defines the amount the employer is required to contribute (e.g., a flat dollar amount, an amount based on a special formula, or an amount equal to a certain percentage of compensation). See also *defined benefit plan* and *pension plan.*

Defined contribution pension plan. See *defined contribution plan.*

De minimis fringe. Benefits provided to employees that are too insignificant to warrant the time and effort required to account for the benefits received by each employee and the value of those benefits. Such amounts are excludible from the employee's gross income. § 132.

Dependency exemption. See *personal and dependency exemptions.*

Depletion. The process by which the cost or other basis of a natural resource (e.g., an oil or gas interest) is recovered upon extraction and sale of the resource. The two ways to determine the depletion allowance are the cost and percentage (or statutory) methods. Under the cost method, each unit of production sold is assigned a portion of the cost or other basis of the interest. This is determined by dividing the cost or other basis by the total units expected to be recovered. Under the percentage (or statutory) method, the tax law provides a special percentage factor for different types of minerals and other natural resources. This percentage is multiplied by the gross income from the interest to arrive at the depletion allowance. §§ 613 and 613A.

Depreciation. The deduction of the cost or other basis of a tangible asset over the asset's estimated useful life. § 167. For intangible assets, see *amortization.* For natural resources, see *depletion.* Also see *estimated useful life.* The depreciation system was replaced by ACRS for most assets placed in service after 1980 (by MACRS for most assets placed in service after 1986) but still applies for assets placed in service before 1981. See also *recapture of depreciation.*

Determination letter. Upon the request of a taxpayer, a District Director will comment on the tax status of a completed transaction. Determination letters are most frequently used to clarify employee versus self-employed status, to determine whether a pension or profit sharing plan qualifies under the Code, and to determine the tax-exempt status of certain nonprofit organizations.

Direct charge-off method. See *specific charge-off method.*

Disabled access credit. A tax credit designed to encourage small businesses to make their facilities more accessible to disabled individuals. The credit is equal to 50 percent of the eligible expenditures that exceed $250 but do not exceed $10,250. Thus, the maximum amount for the credit is $5,000. The adjusted basis for depreciation is reduced by the amount of the credit. To qualify, the facility must have been placed in service before November 6, 1990. § 44. See also *general business credit.*

Disaster area loss. A casualty sustained in an area designated as a disaster area by the President of the United States. In such an event, the disaster loss may be treated as having occurred in the taxable year immediately preceding the year in which the disaster actually occurred. Thus, immediate tax benefits are provided to victims of a disaster. § 165(i). See also *casualty loss.*

Dissent. To disagree with the majority. If, for example, Judge Brown disagrees with the result reached by Judges Charles and Davis (all of whom are members of the same court), Judge Brown could issue a dissenting opinion.

District Court. A Federal District Court is a trial court for purposes of litigating (among others) Federal tax matters. It is the only trial court where a jury trial can be obtained. See also *trial court.*

Dividends received deduction. A deduction allowed a shareholder that is a corporation for dividends received from a domestic corporation. The percentage applied in calculating the dividends received deduction varies according to the percentage of stock ownership. If the stock ownership percentage is less than 20 percent, the percentage is 70 percent of the dividends received. If the stock ownership percentage is at least 20 percent but less than 80 percent, the percentage is 80 percent. If the stock ownership percentage is at least 80 percent, the percentage is 100 percent. §§ 243–246A.

Dollar value LIFO. An inventory technique that focuses on the dollars invested in the inventory rather than the particular items on hand each period. Each inventory item is assigned to a pool. A pool is a collection of similar items and is treated as a separate inventory. At the end of the period, each pool is valued in terms of prices at the time LIFO was adopted (base period prices), whether or not the particular items were actually on hand in the year LIFO was adopted, to compare with current prices to determine if there has been an increase or decrease in inventories.

Domestic production activities deduction (DPAD). See *production activities deduction (PAD)*.

Domestic production gross receipts (DPGR). A key component in computing the domestic production activities deduction (DPAD). Includes receipts from the sale and other disposition of qualified production property produced in significant part within the United States. DPGR is defined in § 199(c)(4). See also *production activities deduction (PAD)*.

E

Earned income. Income from personal services as distinguished from income generated by property. See §§ 32 and 911 and the related Regulations.

Earned income credit. A refundable tax credit designed to provide assistance to certain low-income individuals. To receive the most beneficial treatment, the taxpayer must have qualifying children. However, it is possible to qualify for the credit without having a child. To calculate the credit for a taxpayer with one or more children for 2011, a statutory rate of 34 percent for one child (40 percent for two children and 45 percent for three or more children) is multiplied by the earned income (subject to a statutory maximum of $9,100 with one qualifying child, $12,780 with two qualifying children, and $12,780 for three or more qualifying children). Once the earned income exceeds certain thresholds, the credit is phased out using a 15.98 percent rate for one qualifying child, a 21.06 percent rate for two qualifying children, and a 21.06 rate for three or more qualifying children. For the qualifying taxpayer without children, the credit is calculated on a maximum earned income of $6,070 applying a 7.65 percent rate with the phaseout beginning later applying the same rate. § 32.

Earnings and profits. A tax concept peculiar to corporate taxpayers that measures economic capacity to make a distribution to shareholders that is not a return of capital. Such a distribution will result in dividend income to the shareholders to the extent of the corporation's current and accumulated earnings and profits.

Economic income. The change in the taxpayer's net worth, as measured in terms of market values, plus the value of the assets the taxpayer consumed during the year. Because of the impracticality of this income model, it is not used for tax purposes. See also *accounting income*.

Economic performance test. One of the requirements that must be satisfied in order for an accrual basis taxpayer to deduct an expense. The accrual basis taxpayer first must satisfy the all events test. That test is not deemed satisfied until economic performance occurs. This occurs when property or services are provided to the taxpayer or, in the case in which the taxpayer is required to provide property or services, whenever the property or services are actually provided by the taxpayer. See also *all events test*.

Education expenses. Employees may deduct education expenses that are incurred either (1) to maintain or improve existing job-related skills or (2) to meet the express requirements of the employer or the requirements imposed by law to retain employment status. The expenses are not deductible if the education is required to meet the minimum educational standards for the taxpayer's job or if the education qualifies the individual for a new trade or business. Reg. § 1.162–5. See also *American Opportunity credit*, *HOPE scholarship credit*, and *lifetime learning credit*.

Educational savings bonds. U.S. Series EE bonds whose proceeds are used for qualified higher educational expenses for the taxpayer, the taxpayer's spouse, or a dependent. The interest may be excluded from gross income, provided the taxpayer's adjusted gross income does not exceed certain amounts. § 135.

E-file. The electronic filing of a tax return. The filing is either direct or indirect. As to direct, the taxpayer goes online using a computer and tax return preparation software. Indirect filing occurs when a taxpayer utilizes an authorized IRS e-file provider. The provider often is the tax return preparer.

Employee expenses. The deductions *for* adjusted gross income include reimbursed expenses and certain expenses of performing artists. All other employee expenses are deductible *from* AGI. § 62. See also *trade or business expenses*.

Employment taxes. Employment taxes are those taxes that an employer must pay on account of its employees. Employment taxes include FICA (Federal Insurance Contributions Act) and FUTA (Federal Unemployment Tax Act) taxes. Employment taxes are paid to the IRS in addition to income tax withholdings at specified intervals. Such taxes can be levied on the employees, the employer, or both. See also *FICA tax* and *FUTA tax*.

Entertainment expenses. These expenses are deductible only if they are directly related to or associated with a trade or business. Various restrictions and documentation requirements have been imposed upon the deductibility of entertainment expenses to prevent abuses by taxpayers. See, for example, the provision contained in § 274(n) that disallows 50 percent of entertainment expenses. § 274.

Estate tax. A tax imposed on the right to transfer property by reason of death. Thus, an estate tax is levied on the decedent's estate and not on the heir receiving the property. §§ 2001 and 2002. See also *inheritance tax*.

Estimated tax. The amount of tax (including alternative minimum tax and self-employment tax) an individual expects to owe for the year after subtracting tax credits and income tax withheld. The estimated tax must be paid in installments at designated intervals (e.g. for the individual taxpayer, by

April 15, June 15, September 15, and January 15 of the following year).

Estimated useful life. The period over which an asset will be used by a particular taxpayer. Although the period cannot be longer than the estimated physical life of an asset, it could be shorter if the taxpayer does not intend to keep the asset until it wears out. Assets such as goodwill do not have an estimated useful life. The estimated useful life of an asset is essential to measuring the annual tax deduction for depreciation and amortization. An asset subject to ACRS or MACRS is written off over a specified cost recovery period rather than over its estimated useful life. In addition, most intangibles are now amortized over a 15-year statutory period.

Excise tax. A tax on the manufacture, sale, or use of goods or on the carrying on of an occupation or activity. Also, a tax on the transfer of property. Thus, the Federal estate and gift taxes are, theoretically, excise taxes.

Extraordinary personal services. These are services provided by individuals where the customers' use of the property is incidental to their receipt of the services. For example, a patient's use of a hospital bed is incidental to his or her receipt of medical services. This is one of the six exceptions to determine whether an activity is a passive rental activity. § 469.

F

Fair market value. The amount at which property would change hands between a willing buyer and a willing seller, neither being under any compulsion to buy or sell and both having reasonable knowledge of the relevant facts. Reg. §§ 1.1001–1(a) and 20.2031–1(b).

Farm price method. A method of accounting for agricultural crops. The inventory of crops is valued at its market price less the estimated cost of disposition (e.g., freight and selling expense.)

Federal district court. See *district court*.

FICA tax. An abbreviation for Federal Insurance Contributions Act, commonly referred to as the Social Security tax. The FICA tax is comprised of the Social Security tax (old age, survivors, and disability insurance) and the Medicare tax (hospital insurance) and is imposed on both employers and employees. The employer is responsible for withholding from the employee's wages the Social Security tax at a rate of 6.2 percent on a maximum wage base of $106,800 (for 2010) and the Medicare tax at a rate of 1.45 percent (no maximum wage base). The employer is required to match the employee's contribution. For 2011 the employee's rate is reduced to 4.2 percent for the Social Security tax. The employer's contribution still is at the 6.2 percent rate for 2011. See also *employment taxes*.

Field audit. An audit by the IRS conducted on the business premises of the taxpayer or in the office of the tax practitioner representing the taxpayer. To be distinguished from a *correspondence audit* or an *office audit*.

Fifty percent additional first-year depreciation. This provision, which was effective for property acquired after December 31, 2007 and placed in service before January 1, 2009, provided for an additional cost recovery deduction of 50 percent in the tax year the qualified property is placed in service. Qualified property included most types of new property other than buildings. The American Recovery and Reinvestment Tax Act of 2009 extended the additional first-year depreciation for an additional year. The Small Business Jobs Creation Act of 2010 extended the additional first-year depreciation for an additional year. The taxpayer could elect to forgo this bonus depreciation. See also *cost recovery allowance* and *one hundred percent additional first-year depreciation*.

Finalized Regulation. See *regulations*.

First-in, first-out (FIFO). An accounting method for determining the cost of inventories. Under this method, the inventory on hand is deemed to be the sum of the cost of the most recently acquired units. See also *last-in, first-out (LIFO)*.

Fiscal year. A fiscal year is a 12-month period ending on the last day of a month other than December. In certain circumstances, a taxpayer is permitted to elect a fiscal year instead of being required to use a calendar year. See also *accounting period* and *taxable year*.

Flat tax. In its pure form, it would replace the graduated income tax rates with a single rate (e.g., 17 percent). All deductions are eliminated, and a large personal exemption is allowed to remove low-income and many middle-income taxpayers from the application of the tax.

Flexible spending plan. An employee benefit plan that allows the employee to take a reduction in salary in exchange for the employer paying benefits that can be provided by the employer without the employee being required to recognize income (e.g., medical and child care benefits).

Foreign earned income exclusion. The foreign earned income exclusion is a relief provision that applies to U.S. citizens working in a foreign country. To qualify for the exclusion, the taxpayer must be either a bona fide resident of the foreign country or present in the country for 330 days during any 12 consecutive months. The exclusion is limited to $92,900 per year for 2011 ($91,500 in 2010). § 911.

Foreign tax credit or deduction. Both individual taxpayers and corporations may claim a foreign tax credit on income earned and subject to tax in a foreign country or U.S. possession. As an alternative to the credit, a deduction may be taken for the foreign taxes paid. §§ 27, 164, and 901–905.

Franchise. An agreement that gives the transferee the right to distribute, sell, or provide goods, services, or facilities within a specified area. The cost of obtaining a franchise may be amortized over a statutory period of 15 years. In general, the franchisor's gain on the sale of franchise rights is an ordinary gain because the franchisor retains a significant power, right, or continuing interest in the subject of the franchise. §§ 197 and 1253.

Franchise tax. A tax levied on the right to do business in a state as a corporation. Although income considerations may come into play, the tax usually is based on the capitalization of the corporation.

Fringe benefits. Compensation or other benefits received by an employee that are not in the form of cash. Some fringe benefits (e.g., accident and health plans, group term life insurance) may be excluded from the employee's gross income and therefore are not subject to the Federal income tax.

Fruit and tree metaphor. The courts have held that an individual who earns income from property or services cannot assign that income to another. For example, a father cannot assign his earnings from commissions to his child and escape income tax on those amounts.

F.3d. An abbreviation for the Third Series of the *Federal Reporter*, the official series where decisions of the U.S. Claims Court (before October 1982) and the U.S. Courts of Appeals are published.

F.Supp. The abbreviation for the *Federal Supplement*, the official series where the reported decisions of the U.S. District Courts are published.

FUTA tax. An employment tax levied on employers. Jointly administered by the Federal and state governments, the tax provides funding for unemployment benefits. FUTA applies at a rate of 6.2 percent on the first $7,000 of covered wages paid during the year for each employee. The Federal government allows a credit for FUTA paid (or allowed under a merit rating system) to the state. The credit cannot exceed 5.4 percent of the covered wages. See also *employment taxes*.

G

General business credit. The summation of various non-refundable business credits, including the tax credit for rehabilitation expenditures, business energy credit, work opportunity credit, research activities credit, low-income housing credit, and disabled access credit. The amount of general business credit that can be used to reduce the tax liability is limited to the taxpayer's net income tax reduced by the greater of (1) the tentative minimum tax or (2) 25 percent of the net regular tax liability that exceeds $25,000. Unused general business credits can be carried back 1 year and forward 20 years.

Gift. A transfer of property for less than adequate consideration. Gifts usually occur in a personal setting (such as between members of the same family). Gifts are excluded from the income tax but may be subject to the *gift tax*.

Gift tax. A tax imposed on the transfer of property by gift. The tax is imposed upon the donor of a gift and is based upon the fair market value of the property on the date of the gift. §§ 2501–2524.

Golden parachute payment. A severance payment to employees that meets the following requirements: (1) the payment is contingent on a change of ownership of a corporation through a stock or asset acquisition and (2) the aggregate present value of the payment equals or exceeds three times the employee's average annual compensation. To the extent the severance payment meets these conditions, a deduction is disallowed to the employer for the excess of the payment over a statutory base amount (a five-year average of compensation if the taxpayer was an employee for the entire five-year period). In addition, a 20 percent excise tax is imposed on the employee who receives the excess severance pay. §§ 280G and 4999.

Goodwill. The ability of a business to generate income in excess of a normal rate on assets due to superior managerial skills, market position, new product technology, etc. In the purchase of a business, goodwill represents the difference between the purchase price and the fair market value of the net assets acquired. Goodwill is an intangible asset that possesses an indefinite life. However, since acquired goodwill is a § 197 intangible asset, it is amortized over a 15-year statutory period. Self-created goodwill cannot be amortized. Reg. § 1.167(a)–3. See also *amortization*.

Government bonds issued at a discount. Certain U.S. government bonds (Series EE) are issued at a discount and do not pay interest during the life of the bonds. Instead, the bonds are redeemable at increasing fixed amounts. Thus, the difference between the purchase price and the amount received upon redemption represents interest income to the holder. A cash basis taxpayer may defer recognition of gross income until the bonds are redeemed. For Series EE savings bonds issued after 1989, the interest otherwise taxable at redemption can be excluded if the bonds are qualified educational savings bonds. As an alternative to deferring recognition of gross income until the bonds are redeemed, the taxpayer may elect to include in gross income on an annual basis the annual increase in the value of the bonds. § 454.

Gross income. Income subject to the Federal income tax. Gross income does not include income for which the Code permits exclusion treatment (e.g., interest on municipal bonds). For a manufacturing or merchandising business, gross income means gross profit (gross sales or gross receipts less cost of goods sold). § 61 and Reg. § 1.61–3(a).

Group term life insurance. Life insurance coverage permitted by an employer for a group of employees. Such insurance is renewable on a year-to-year basis and does not accumulate in value (i.e., no cash surrender value is built up). The premiums paid by the employer on the insurance are not taxed to an employee on coverage of up to $50,000 per person. § 79 and Reg. § 1.79–1(a).

Guaranteed payments. Payments made by a partnership to one of its partners for services rendered or for the use of capital, to the extent the payments are determined without regard to the income of the partnership. Such payments generally are deductible by the partnership as a business expense and are reported as ordinary income by the recipient partner. § 707(c).

H

Half-year convention. The half-year convention is a cost recovery convention that assumes all property is placed in service at mid-year and thus provides for a half-year's cost recovery for that year.

Head of household. An unmarried individual who maintains a household for another and satisfies certain conditions set forth in § 2(b). Such status enables the taxpayer to use a set of income tax rates [see § 1(b)] that are lower than those applicable to other unmarried individuals [§ 1(c)] but higher than those applicable to surviving spouses and married persons filing a joint return [§ 1(a)]. See also *tax rate schedules*.

Health savings account. A medical savings account created in legislation enacted in December 2003 that is designed to replace and expand Archer Medical Savings Accounts. See also *medical savings account*.

Highly compensated employee. The employee group is generally divided into two categories for fringe benefit (including pension and profit sharing plans) purposes. These are (1) highly compensated employees and (2) non-highly compensated employees. For most fringe benefits, if the fringe benefit plan discriminates in favor of highly compensated employees, it will not be a qualified plan with respect, at a minimum, to the highly compensated employees.

Hobby loss. A nondeductible loss arising from a personal hobby as contrasted with an activity engaged in for profit. Generally, the law provides a rebuttable presumption that an activity is engaged in for profit if profits are earned during any three or more years during a five-year period. § 183. See also *vacation home*.

Holding period. The period of time property has been held for income tax purposes. The holding period is crucial in determining whether gain or loss from the sale or exchange of a capital asset is long term or short term. § 1223. See also *capital gain or loss holding period.*

Home equity loans. Loans that utilize the personal residence of the taxpayer as security. The interest on such loans is deductible as *qualified residence interest.* However, interest is deductible only on the portion of the loan that does not exceed the lesser of (1) the fair market value of the residence, reduced by the *acquisition indebtedness,* or (2) $100,000 ($50,000 for married persons filing separate returns). A major benefit of a home equity loan is that there are no tracing rules regarding the use of the loan proceeds. § 163(h)(3).

Home office expenses. See *office-in-the-home expenses.*

HOPE scholarship credit. A tax credit for qualifying expenses paid for the first two years of postsecondary education. Room, board, and book costs are ineligible for the credit. The maximum credit available is $1,800 per year per student, computed as 100 percent of the first $1,200 of qualifying expenses, plus 50 percent of the second $1,200 of qualifying expenses. Eligible students include the taxpayer, taxpayer's spouse, and taxpayer's dependents. To qualify for the credit, a student must take at least one-half the full-time course load for at least one academic term at a qualifying educational institution. The credit is phased out for higher-income taxpayers. For 2009, 2010, 2011, and 2012, the HOPE scholarship credit is replaced with the American Opportunity credit. § 25A.

H.R 10 (Keogh) plan. See *self-employment retirement plan.*

Hybrid method. A combination of the accrual and cash methods of accounting. That is, the taxpayer may account for some items of income on the accrual method (e.g., sales and cost of goods sold) and other items (e.g., interest income) on the cash method.

I

Imputed interest. For certain long-term sales of property, the IRS can convert some of the gain from the sale into interest income if the contract does not provide for a minimum rate of interest to be paid by the purchaser. The application of this procedure has the effect of forcing the seller to recognize less long-term capital gain and more ordinary income (interest income). §§ 483 and 1274 and the Regulations thereunder. In addition, interest income and interest expense are imputed (deemed to exist) on interest-free or below-market rate loans between certain related parties. § 7872. See also *interest-free loans.*

Incentive stock option (ISO). A type of stock option that receives favorable tax treatment. If various qualification requirements can be satisfied, there are no recognition tax consequences when the stock option is granted. However, the spread (the excess of the fair market value at the date of exercise over the option price) is a tax preference item for purposes of the alternative minimum tax. The gain on disposition of the stock resulting from the exercise of the stock option will be classified as long-term capital gain if certain holding period requirements are met (the employee must not dispose of the stock within two years after the option is granted or within one year after acquiring the stock). § 422. See also *nonqualified stock option (NQSO).*

Income. For tax purposes, an increase in wealth that has been realized.

Independent contractor. A self-employed person as distinguished from one who is employed as an employee.

Individual retirement account (IRA). A type of retirement plan to which an individual with earned income can contribute a statutory maximum. The maximum amount is $5,000 in 2009, 2010, and 2011. IRAs can be classified as traditional IRAs or Roth IRAs. With a traditional IRA, an individual can contribute and deduct a maximum of $5,000 per tax year in 2011. The deduction is a deduction *for* AGI. However, if the individual is an active participant in another qualified retirement plan, the deduction is phased out proportionally between certain AGI ranges (note that the phaseout limits the amount of the deduction and not the amount of the contribution). With a Roth IRA, an individual can contribute a maximum of $5,000 per tax year in 2011. No deduction is permitted. However, if a five-year holding period requirement is satisfied and if the distribution is a qualified distribution, the taxpayer can make tax-free withdrawals from a Roth IRA. The maximum annual contribution is phased out proportionally between certain AGI ranges. §§ 219 and 408A. See also *simplified employee pension plan.*

Inheritance tax. An excise tax levied on the heir based on the value of property received from a decedent. See also *estate tax.*

Installment method. A method of accounting enabling a taxpayer to spread the recognition of gain on the sale of property over the payout period. Under this procedure, the seller computes the gross profit percentage from the sale (the gain divided by the contract price) and applies it to each payment received to arrive at the gain to be recognized. §§ 453 and 453A.

Intangible drilling and development costs (IDC). Taxpayers may elect to expense or capitalize (subject to amortization) intangible drilling and development costs. However, ordinary income recapture provisions apply to oil and gas properties on a sale or other disposition if the expense method is elected. §§ 263(c) and 1254(a).

Interest-free loans. Bona fide loans that carry no interest (or a below-market rate). If made in a nonbusiness setting, the imputed interest element is treated as a gift from the lender to the borrower. If made by a corporation to a shareholder, a constructive dividend could result. In either event, the lender may recognize interest income, and the borrower may be able to deduct interest expense. § 7872.

Interest on student loans. A limited ability exists to deduct interest on student loans used to pay qualified higher education expenses (i.e., tuition, fees, books, supplies, room and board). The ceiling on the deduction is $2,500. The deduction is a deduction *for* AGI. § 221. See also *consumer interest.*

Interpretive Regulation. A Regulation issued by the Treasury Department that purports to explain the meaning of a particular Code Section. An interpretive Regulation is given less deference than a legislative Regulation. See also *legislative regulation* and *procedural regulation.* § 7805.

Investigation of a new business. Expenditures incurred in the evaluation of prospective business activities by taxpayers who are not engaged in a trade or business (to acquire an existing business or enter into a new trade or business). If the expenditures are general, it is the position of the IRS that no deduction is permitted even if the investigation is abandoned because the taxpayer is not engaged in a trade or business. The courts, however, have permitted a loss deduction providing the expenditures were specific.

Investment income. Gross income from interest, dividends, annuities, and royalties not derived in the ordinary course of a trade or business. Net capital gain attributable to the disposition of property producing these types of income and qualified dividend income normally are not included in investment income. However, a taxpayer may elect to include the capital gains as investment income if the net capital gain qualifying for the *alternative tax* is reduced by an equivalent amount. A similar election can be made for qualified dividends. See also *investment interest.*

Investment indebtedness. If funds are borrowed by noncorporate taxpayers for the purpose of purchasing or continuing to hold investment property, some portion of the interest expense deduction may be disallowed. The interest deduction is generally limited to net investment income. Amounts that are disallowed may be carried forward and treated as investment interest of the succeeding year. § 163(d).

Investment interest. Payment for the use of funds used to acquire assets that produce investment income. The deduction for investment interest is limited to *net investment income* for the tax year. See also *investment income.*

Investment tax credit (ITC). A tax credit that usually was equal to 10 percent (unless a reduced credit was elected) of the qualified investment in tangible personalty used in a trade or business. If the tangible personalty had a recovery period of five years or more, the full cost of the property qualified for the credit. Only 60 percent of cost qualified for property with a recovery period of three years. However, the regular investment tax credit was repealed by TRA of 1986 for property placed in service after December 31, 1985. §§ 46–48. See also *general business credit* and *recapture of investment tax credit.*

Involuntary conversion. The loss or destruction of property through theft, casualty, or condemnation. Any gain realized on an involuntary conversion can, at the taxpayer's election, be postponed (deferred) for Federal income tax purposes if the owner reinvests the proceeds within a prescribed period of time in property that is similar or related in service or use. § 1033. See also *nontaxable exchange.*

IRA. See *individual retirement account.*

Itemized deductions. Certain personal expenditures allowed by the Code as deductions *from* adjusted gross income. Examples include certain medical expenses, interest on home mortgages, state income taxes, and charitable contributions. Itemized deductions are reported on Schedule A of Form 1040. Certain miscellaneous itemized deductions are reduced by 2 percent of the taxpayer's adjusted gross income. In addition, a taxpayer whose adjusted gross income exceeds $100,000 ($50,000 for married filing separately) must reduce the itemized deductions by 3 percent of the excess of adjusted gross income over $100,000. For 2009, the indexed amount for the $100,000 is $166,800, and the indexed amount for the $50,000 is $83,400. Medical, casualty and theft, and investment interest deductions are not subject to the 3 percent reduction. The 3 percent reduction may not reduce itemized deductions that are subject to the reduction to below 20 percent of their initial amount. Beginning in 2006, this reduction is subject to partial phaseout. For 2009, two-thirds of the reduction is phased out, and for 2010 all of the reduction is phased out. Under the sunset provision, the phaseout of itemized deductions was scheduled to be reinstated beginning in 2011. The Tax Relief Act (TRA) of 2010 put off the reinstatement for two years (i.e., 2011 and 2012). §§ 63(d), 67, and 68.

K

Keogh plan. See *self-employment retirement plan.*

Kiddie tax. To reduce the tax savings that result from shifting income from parents to children, the net unearned income of a child under age 19 (or under age 24 if a full-time student) is taxed at the marginal tax rate of the parent(s). For the provision to apply, the child must have at least one living parent and unearned income of more than $1,900 for the tax year. § 1(g). See also *unearned income.*

L

Last-in, first-out (LIFO). An accounting method for valuing inventories for tax purposes. Under this method, it is assumed that the inventory on hand is valued at the cost of the earliest acquired units. § 472 and the related Regulations. See also *first-in, first-out (FIFO).*

Least aggregate deferral method. An algorithm set forth in the Regulations to determine the tax year for a partnership with partners whose tax years differ. The tax year that produces the least aggregate deferral of income for the partners is selected.

Legislative Regulation. Some Code Sections give the Secretary of the Treasury or his delegate the authority to prescribe Regulations to carry out the details of administration or to otherwise complete the operating rules. Regulations issued pursuant to this type of authority truly possess the force and effect of law. In effect, Congress is almost delegating its legislative powers to the Treasury Department. See also *interpretive regulation* and *procedural regulation.*

Lessee. One who rents property from another. In the case of real estate, the lessee is also known as the tenant.

Lessor. One who rents property to another. In the case of real estate, the lessor is also known as the landlord.

Letter rulings. Issued upon a taxpayer's request, by the National Office of the IRS, they describe how the IRS will treat a proposed transaction for tax purposes. They apply only to the taxpayer who asks for and obtains the ruling, but post-1984 rulings may be substantial authority for purposes of avoiding the accuracy-related penalties. The IRS limits the issuance of letter rulings to restricted, preannounced areas of taxation.

Life insurance proceeds. Generally, life insurance proceeds paid to a beneficiary upon the death of the insured are exempt from Federal income tax. An exception is provided when a life insurance contract has been transferred for valuable consideration to another individual who assumes ownership rights. In that case, the proceeds are income to the assignee to the extent that the proceeds exceed the amount paid for the policy plus any subsequent premiums paid. Insurance proceeds may be subject to the Federal estate tax if the decedent retained any incidents of ownership in the policy before death or if the proceeds are payable to the decedent's estate. §§ 101 and 2042.

Lifetime learning credit. A tax credit for qualifying expenses for taxpayers pursuing education beyond the first two years of postsecondary education. Individuals who are completing their last two years of undergraduate studies, pursuing graduate or professional degrees, or otherwise seeking new job skills or maintaining existing job skills are all eligible for the credit. Eligible individuals include the taxpayer, taxpayer's spouse, and taxpayer's dependents. The maximum credit is 20 percent of the first $10,000 of qualifying expenses and is computed per taxpayer. The credit is phased out for higher-income taxpayers. § 25A.

Like-kind exchange. An exchange of property held for productive use in a trade or business or for investment (except inventory, stocks and bonds, and partnership interests) for other investment or trade or business property. Unless non-like-kind property is received (boot), the exchange will be nontaxable. § 1031. See also *boot* and *nontaxable exchange.*

Limited expensing. See *Section 179 expensing.*

Limited liability company. An organization that combines the corporate characteristic of limited liability with treatment as a partnership for Federal income tax purposes.

Liquidating distribution. A distribution of assets by a corporation associated with the termination of the business. See also *liquidation of a corporation.*

Liquidation of a corporation. In a complete or partial liquidation of a corporation, amounts received by the shareholders in exchange for their stock are usually treated as a sale or exchange of the stock resulting in capital gain or loss treatment. § 331. Special rules apply to the liquidation of a subsidiary under § 332. Generally, a liquidation is a taxable event to the corporation. § 336. Special rules apply to a parent corporation that is liquidating a subsidiary. § 337.

Listed property. The term listed property includes (1) any passenger automobile, (2) any other property used as a means of transportation, (3) any property of a type generally used for purposes of entertainment, recreation, or amusement, (4) any computer or peripheral equipment (with an exception for exclusive business use), (5) any cellular telephone (or other similar telecommunications equipment), and (6) any other property of a type specified in the Regulations. If listed property is predominantly used for business, the taxpayer is allowed to use the statutory percentage method of cost recovery. Otherwise, the straight-line cost recovery method must be used. § 280F.

Long-term care insurance. Insurance that helps pay the cost of care when the insured is unable to care for himself or herself. Such insurance is generally thought of as insurance against the cost of an aged person entering a nursing home. The employer can provide the insurance, and the premiums may be excluded from the employee's gross income. § 7702B.

Long-term contract. A building, installation, construction, or manufacturing contract that is entered into but not completed within the same tax year. A manufacturing contract is a long-term contract only if the contract is to manufacture (1) a unique item not normally carried in finished goods inventory or (2) items that normally require more than 12 calendar months to complete. The two available methods to account for long-term contracts are the percentage of completion method and the completed contract method. The completed contract method can be used only in limited circumstances. § 460. See also *completed contract method* and *percentage of completion method.*

Long-term nonpersonal use capital assets. Includes investment property with a long-term holding period. Such property disposed of by casualty or theft may receive § 1231 treatment. See also *Section 1231 gains and losses.*

Lower of cost or market. An elective inventory method, whereby the taxpayer may value inventories at the lower of the taxpayer's actual cost or the current replacement cost of the goods. This method cannot be used in conjunction with the LIFO inventory method.

Low-income housing. Low-income housing is rental housing that is a dwelling unit for low- or moderate-income individuals or families. Beneficial tax treatment is in the form of the *low-income housing credit.* § 42. See also *accelerated cost recovery system (ACRS).*

Low-income housing credit. Beneficial treatment to owners of low-income housing is provided in the form of a tax credit. The calculated credit is claimed in the year the building is placed in service and in the following nine years. § 42. See also *general business credit.*

Lump-sum distribution. Payment of the entire amount due at one time rather than in installments. Such distributions often occur from qualified pension or profit sharing plans upon the retirement or death of a covered employee. The recipient of a lump-sum distribution may recognize both long-term capital gain and ordinary income upon the receipt of the distribution. The ordinary income portion may be subject to a special 10-year income averaging provision. § 402(e).

M

MACRS. See *accelerated cost recovery system (ACRS).*

Majority interest partners. Partners who have more than a 50 percent interest in partnership profits and capital, counting only those partners who have the same taxable year, are referred to as majority interest partners. The term is of significance in determining the appropriate taxable year of a partnership. § 706(b). See also *accounting period* and *principal partner.*

Marital deduction. A deduction allowed upon the transfer of property from one spouse to another. The deduction is allowed under the Federal gift tax for lifetime (inter vivos) transfers or under the Federal estate tax for death (testamentary) transfers. §§ 2056 and 2523.

Marriage penalty. The additional tax liability that results for a married couple compared with what their tax liability would be if they were not married and filed separate returns.

Material participation. If an individual taxpayer materially participates in a nonrental trade or business activity, any loss from that activity is treated as an active loss that can be offset against active income. Material participation is achieved by meeting any one of seven tests provided in the Regulations. § 469(h).

Medical expenses. Medical expenses of an individual, spouse, and dependents are allowed as an itemized deduction to the extent that such amounts (less insurance reimbursements) exceed 7.5 percent of adjusted gross income. § 213.

Medical savings account. A plan available to employees of small firms (50 or fewer employees) with high-deductible health insurance. The employee can place money in the fund and then deduct the contributions (within limits) from gross income. If the employer contributes to the fund, the employee can exclude the contribution from gross income. Income earned from the fund and withdrawals for medical care are not subject to tax. §§ 106(b) and 220.

Mid-month convention. A cost recovery convention that assumes property is placed in service in the middle of the month that it is actually placed in service.

Mid-quarter convention. A cost recovery convention that assumes property placed in service during the year is placed in service at the middle of the quarter in which it is actually placed in service. The mid-quarter convention applies if more than 40 percent of the value of property (other than eligible real estate) is placed in service during the last quarter of the year.

Miscellaneous itemized deductions. A special category of itemized deductions that includes such expenses as professional dues, tax return preparation fees, job-hunting costs, unreimbursed employee business expenses, and certain investment expenses. Such expenses are deductible only to the extent they exceed 2 percent of adjusted gross income. § 67. See also *itemized deductions*.

Mitigation of the annual accounting period concept. Various tax provisions that provide relief from the effect of the finality of the annual accounting period concept. For example, the *net operating loss* provisions provide relief to a taxpayer whose business profits and losses for different taxable years fluctuate. See also *accounting period*.

Modified accelerated cost recovery system (MACRS). See *accelerated cost recovery system (ACRS)*.

Modified adjusted gross income. A key determinant in computing the domestic production activities deduction (DPAD). The deduction is limited to a percentage of the *lesser of* qualified production activities income (QPAI) or modified adjusted gross income. Aside from limited changes required by § 199(d)(2)(A), modified adjusted gross income is AGI as usually determined but without any domestic production activities deduction. See also *production activities deduction (PAD)*.

Moving expenses. A deduction *for* AGI is permitted to employees and self-employed individuals provided certain tests are met. The taxpayer's new job must be at least 50 miles farther from the old residence than the old residence was from the former place of work. In addition, an employee must be employed on a full-time basis at the new location for 39 weeks in the 12-month period following the move. Deductible moving expenses include the cost of moving the household and personal effects, transportation, and lodging expenses during the move. The cost of meals during the move are not deductible. Qualified moving expenses that are paid (or reimbursed) by the employer can be excluded from the employee's gross income. In this case, the related deduction by the employee is not permitted. §§ 62(a)(15), 132(a)(6), and 217.

Multiple support agreement. To qualify for a dependency exemption, the support test must be satisfied. This requires that over 50 percent of the support of the potential dependent be provided by the taxpayer. Where no one person provides more than 50 percent of the support, a multiple support agreement enables a taxpayer to still qualify for the dependency exemption. Any person who contributed more than 10 percent of the support is entitled to claim the exemption if each person in the group who contributed more than 10 percent files a written consent (Form 2120). Each person who is a party to the multiple support agreement must meet all the other requirements for claiming the dependency exemption. § 152(c). See also *personal and dependency exemptions*.

N

National sales tax. Intended as a replacement for the current Federal income tax. Unlike a value added tax (VAT), which is levied on the manufacturer, it would be imposed on the consumer upon the final sale of goods and services. To keep the tax from being regressive, low-income taxpayers would be granted some kind of credit or exemption.

Necessary. Appropriate and helpful in furthering the taxpayer's business or income-producing activity. §§ 162(a) and 212. See also *ordinary*.

Net capital gain. The excess of the net long-term capital gain for the tax year over the net short-term capital loss. The net capital gain of an individual taxpayer is eligible for the alternative tax. § 1222(11). See also *alternative tax*.

Net capital loss. The excess of the losses from sales or exchanges of capital assets over the gains from sales or exchanges of such assets. Up to $3,000 per year of the net capital loss may be deductible by noncorporate taxpayers against ordinary income. The excess net capital loss carries over to future tax years. For corporate taxpayers, the net capital loss cannot be offset against ordinary income, but it can be carried back three years and forward five years to offset net capital gains. §§ 1211, 1212, and 1221(10).

Net investment income. The excess of *investment income* over investment expenses. Investment expenses are those deductible expenses directly connected with the production of investment income. Investment expenses do not include investment interest. The deduction for *investment interest* for the tax year is limited to net investment income. § 163(d).

Net operating loss. To mitigate the effect of the annual accounting period concept, § 172 allows taxpayers to use an excess loss of one year as a deduction for certain past or future years. In this regard, a carryback period of 2 years and a carryforward period of 20 years are allowed. See also *mitigation of the annual accounting period concept*.

Net worth method. An approach used by the IRS to reconstruct the income of a taxpayer who fails to maintain adequate records. Under this approach, the gross income for the year is the increase in net worth of the taxpayer (assets in excess of liabilities) with appropriate adjustment for nontaxable receipts and nondeductible expenditures. The net worth method often is used when tax fraud is suspected.

Ninety-day letter. See *statutory notice of deficiency*.

No-additional-cost services. Services that the employer may provide the employee at no additional cost to the employer. Generally, the benefit is the ability to utilize the employer's excess capacity (vacant seats on an airliner). Such amounts are excludible from the recipient's gross income. § 132.

Nonaccountable plan. An expense reimbursement plan that does not have an accountability feature. The result is that employee expenses must be claimed as deductions *from*

AGI. An exception is moving expenses, which are deductions *for* AGI. See also *accountable plan*.

Nonacquiescence. Announcement of disagreement by the IRS on the result reached in certain judicial decisions. Sometimes abbreviated *Nonacq.* or *NA.* See also *acquiescence*.

Nonbusiness bad debts. A bad debt loss not incurred in connection with a creditor's trade or business. The loss is deductible as a short-term capital loss and is allowed only in the year the debt becomes entirely worthless. In addition to family loans, many investor losses fall into the classification of nonbusiness bad debts. § 166(d). See also *bad debts*.

Nonqualified deferred compensation (NQDC) plans. Compensation arrangements that are frequently offered to executives. Such plans may include stock options, restricted stock, etc. Often, an executive may defer the recognition of taxable income. The employer, however, does not receive a tax deduction until the employee is required to include the compensation in income. See also *restricted property plan*.

Nonqualified stock option (NQSO). A type of stock option that does not satisfy the statutory requirements of an incentive stock option. If the NQSO has a readily ascertainable fair market value (e.g., the option is traded on an established exchange), the value of the option must be included in the employee's gross income at the date of the grant. Otherwise, the employee does not recognize income at the grant date. Instead, ordinary income is recognized in the year of exercise of the option. See also *incentive stock option (ISO)*.

Nonrecourse debt. An obligation on which the endorser is not personally liable. An example of a nonrecourse debt is a mortgage on real estate acquired by a partnership without the assumption of any liability on the mortgage by the partnership or any of the partners. The acquired property generally is pledged as collateral for the loan.

Nonrefundable credit. A nonrefundable credit is a credit that is not paid if it exceeds the taxpayer's tax liability. Some nonrefundable credits qualify for carryback and carryover treatment. See also *refundable credit*.

Nontaxable exchange. A transaction in which realized gains or losses are not recognized. The recognition of gain or loss is postponed (deferred) until the property received in the nontaxable exchange is subsequently disposed of in a taxable transaction. Examples are § 1031 like-kind exchanges and § 1033 involuntary conversions. See also *involuntary conversion* and *like-kind exchange*.

O

Occupational tax. A tax imposed on various trades or businesses. A license fee that enables a taxpayer to engage in a particular occupation.

Office audit. An audit by the IRS of a taxpayer's return that is conducted in the agent's office. To be distinguished from a *correspondence audit* or a *field audit*.

Office-in-the-home expenses. Employment and business-related expenses attributable to the use of a residence (e.g., den or office) are allowed only if the portion of the residence is exclusively used on a regular basis as a principal place of business of the taxpayer or as a place of business that is used by patients, clients, or customers. If the expenses are incurred by an employee, the use must be for the con-

venience of the employer as opposed to being merely appropriate and helpful. § 280A.

One hundred percent additional first-year depreciation. The Tax Relief Act of 2010 provides for a cost recovery deduction of 100 percent in the tax year qualified property is placed in service. Qualified property includes most types of new property other than buildings. This provision is effective for property acquired after December 31, 2010 and placed in service before January 1, 2012. See also *cost recovery allowance* and *fifty percent additional first-year depreciation*.

One-year rule for prepaid expenses. Taxpayers who use the cash method are required to use the accrual method for deducting certain prepaid expenses (i.e., must capitalize the item and can deduct only when used). If a prepayment will not be consumed or expire by the end of the tax year following the year of payment, the prepayment must be capitalized and prorated over the benefit period. Conversely, if the prepayment will be consumed by the end of the tax year following the year of payment, it can be expensed when paid. To obtain the current deduction under the one-year rule, the payment must be a required payment rather than a voluntary payment.

Open transaction. A judicially imposed doctrine that allows the taxpayer to defer all gain until he or she has collected an amount equal to the adjusted basis of assets transferred pursuant to an exchange transaction. This doctrine has been applied where the property received in an exchange has no ascertainable fair market value due to the existence of contingencies. The method is permitted only in very limited circumstances. See also *recovery of capital doctrine*.

Options. The sale or exchange of an option to buy or sell property results in capital gain or loss if the property is a capital asset. Generally, the closing of an option transaction results in short-term capital gain or loss to the writer of the call and the purchaser of the call option. § 1234.

Ordinary. Common and accepted in the general industry or type of activity in which the taxpayer is engaged. It comprises one of the tests for the deductibility of expenses incurred or paid in connection with a trade or business; for the production or collection of income; for the management, conservation, or maintenance of property held for the production of income; or in connection with the determination, collection, or refund of any tax. §§ 162(a) and 212. See also *necessary*.

Ordinary and necessary. See *necessary* and *ordinary*.

Ordinary income property. Property contributed to a charitable organization that, if sold rather than contributed, would have resulted in other than long-term capital gain to the donor (i.e., ordinary income property and short-term capital gain property). Examples are inventory and capital assets held for less than the long-term holding period.

Organizational expenditures. A corporation may elect to immediately expense the first $5,000 (subject to phaseout) of organizational expenses and generally amortize the balance over a period of 180 months. Certain expenses of organizing a company do not qualify for amortization (e.g., expenditures connected with issuing or selling stock or other securities). § 248.

Original issue discount (OID). The difference between the issue price of a debt obligation (e.g., a corporate bond) and the maturity value of the obligation when the issue price is *less than* the maturity value. OID represents interest and must be amortized over the life of the debt obligation using the effective interest method. The difference is not considered to be original issue discount for tax purposes when it is less than one-fourth of 1 percent of the redemption price at maturity multiplied by the number of years to maturity. §§ 1272 and 1273(a)(3).

Outside salesperson. An outside salesperson solicits business away from the employer's place of business on a full-time basis. The employment-related expenses of an outside salesperson are itemized deductions unless reimbursed by the employer. If reimbursed, such expenses are deductible *for* AGI.

P

Partnerships. A partnership is treated as a conduit and is not subject to taxation. Various items of partnership income, expenses, gains, and losses flow through to the individual partners and are reported on the partners' personal income tax returns. §§ 701 and 702.

Passive activity. A trade or business activity in which the taxpayer does not materially participate is subject to limitations on the deduction of losses and credits. Rental activities (subject to exceptions) and limited partnership interests are inherently passive. Relief from passive activity limitation treatment is provided in certain situations, such as for certain rental real estate, if the taxpayer actively participates in the activity. The annual ceiling on this rental real estate relief is $25,000. Relief also is provided for material participation in a real estate trade or business. § 469. See also *passive loss* and *portfolio income.*

Passive investment income. As defined in § 1362(d)(3)(D), passive investment income means gross receipts from royalties, certain rents, dividends, interest, annuities, and gains from the sale or exchange of stock and securities. Revocation of the S corporation election may occur in certain cases when the S corporation has passive investment income in excess of 25 percent of gross receipts for a period of three consecutive years.

Passive loss. Any loss from (1) activities in which the taxpayer does not materially participate or (2) rental activities (subject to certain exceptions). Net passive losses cannot be used to offset income from nonpassive sources. Rather, they are suspended until the taxpayer either generates net passive income (and a deduction of the losses is allowed) or disposes of the underlying property (at which time the loss deductions are allowed in full). One relief provision allows landlords who actively participate in the rental activities to deduct up to $25,000 of passive losses annually. However, a phaseout of the $25,000 amount commences when the landlord's AGI exceeds $100,000. Another relief provision applies for material participation in a real estate trade or business. See also *passive activity* and *portfolio income.*

Patent. A patent is an intangible asset that may be amortized over a statutory 15-year period as a § 197 intangible. The sale of a patent usually results in favorable long-term capital gain treatment. §§ 197 and 1235.

Pension plan. A type of deferred compensation arrangement that provides for systematic payments of definitely determinable retirement benefits to employees who meet the requirements set forth in the plan. See also *defined benefit plan* and *defined contribution plan.*

Percentage depletion. Percentage depletion is depletion based on a statutory percentage applied to the gross income from the property. The taxpayer deducts the greater of cost depletion or percentage depletion. § 613. See also *cost depletion.*

Percentage of completion method. A method of reporting gain or loss on certain long-term contracts. Under this method of accounting, the gross contract price is included in income as the contract is being completed. § 460 and Reg. § 1.451–3. See also *completed contract method* and *long-term contract.*

Permanent and total disability. A person is considered permanently and totally disabled if he or she is unable to engage in any substantial gainful activity due to a physical or mental impairment. In addition, this impairment must be one that can be expected to result in death or that has lasted or can be expected to last for a continuous period of not less than 12 months. The taxpayer generally must provide the IRS a physician's statement documenting this condition.

Personal and dependency exemptions. The tax law provides an exemption for each individual taxpayer and an additional exemption for the taxpayer's spouse if a joint return is filed. An individual may also claim a dependency exemption for each dependent, provided certain tests are met. The amount of the personal and dependency exemptions is $3,650 in 2010 and $3,700 in 2011. The amount is indexed for inflation. The exemption is subject to phaseout once adjusted gross income exceeds certain statutory threshold amounts. This phaseout provision is subject to partial phaseout beginning in 2006. For 2009, two-thirds of the reduction in the exemption amount is phased out, and for 2010 all of the reduction is phased out. Under the sunset provision, the phaseout of personal and dependency exemptions was scheduled to be reinstated in 2011. The Tax Relief Act (TRA) of 2010 put off the reinstatement for two years (i.e., 2011 and 2012). §§ 151 and 152. See also *qualifying child* and *qualifying relative.*

Personal casualty gain. The recognized gain from any involuntary conversion of personal use property arising from fire, storm, shipwreck, or other casualty, or from theft. See also *personal casualty loss.*

Personal casualty loss. The recognized loss from any involuntary conversion of personal use property arising from fire, storm, shipwreck, or other casualty, or from theft. See also *personal casualty gain.*

Personal exemption. See *personal and dependency exemptions.*

Personal expenses. Expenses of an individual for personal reasons that are not deductible unless specifically provided for under the tax law. § 262.

Personal property. Generally, all property other than real estate. It is sometimes referred to as personalty when real estate is termed realty. Personal property also can refer to property that is not used in a taxpayer's trade or business or held for the production or collection of income. When used in this sense, personal property can include both realty (e.g., a personal residence) and personalty (e.g., personal effects such as clothing and furniture).

Personal residence. See *sale of principal residence.*

Personal service corporation (PSC). A corporation the principal activity of which is the performance of personal services (e.g., health, law, engineering, architecture, accounting, actuarial science, performing arts, or consulting), with such services being substantially performed by the employee-owners. The 35 percent statutory rate applies to PSCs.

Personalty. All property other than realty (real estate). Personalty usually is categorized as tangible or intangible property. Tangible personalty includes such assets as machinery and equipment, automobiles and trucks, and office equipment. Intangible personalty includes stocks and bonds, goodwill, patents, trademarks, and copyrights. See also *personal property.*

Points. Loan origination fees that may be deductible as interest by a buyer of property. A seller of property who pays points reduces the selling price by the amount of the points paid for the buyer. While the seller is not permitted to deduct this amount as interest, the buyer may do so. See *prepaid interest* for the timing of the interest deduction.

Pollution control facilities. A certified pollution control facility, the cost of which may be amortized over a 60-month period if the taxpayer elects. § 169.

Portfolio income. The term is relevant in applying the limitation on passive activity losses and credits. Although normally considered passive in nature, for this purpose portfolio income is treated as nonpassive. Therefore, net passive losses and credits cannot be offset against portfolio income. Examples of portfolio income are interest, dividends, annuities, and certain royalties. § 469. See also *passive activity.*

Precedent. A previously decided court decision that is recognized as authority for the disposition of future decisions.

Prepaid expenses. Cash basis as well as accrual basis taxpayers usually are required to capitalize prepayments for rent, insurance, etc., that cover more than one year. Deductions are taken during the period the benefits are received.

Prepaid interest. In effect, the Code places cash basis taxpayers on an accrual basis for purposes of recognizing a deduction for prepaid interest. Thus, interest paid in advance is deductible as an interest expense only as it accrues. The one exception to this rule involves the interest element when a cash basis taxpayer pays points to obtain financing for the purchase of a principal residence (or to make improvements thereto) if the payment of points is an established business practice in the area in which the indebtedness is incurred and the amount involved is not excessive. § 461(g). See also *points.*

Principal partner. A partner with a 5 percent or greater interest in partnership capital or profits. § 706(b)(3). See also *majority interest partners.*

Private activity bond. Interest on state and local bonds is excludible from gross income. § 103. Certain such bonds are labeled private activity bonds. Although the interest on such bonds is excludible for regular income tax purposes, it is treated as a tax preference in calculating the AMT. See also *alternative minimum tax (AMT).*

Prizes and awards. The fair market value of a prize or award generally is includible in gross income. However, exclusion is permitted if the prize or award is made in recognition of religious, charitable, scientific, educational, artistic, literary, or civic achievement, and the recipient transfers the award to a qualified governmental unit or a nonprofit organization. In that case, the recipient must be selected without any action on his or her part to enter a contest or proceeding, and the recipient must not be required to render substantial future services as a condition of receiving the prize or award. § 74.

Procedural Regulation. A Regulation issued by the Treasury Department that is a housekeeping-type instruction indicating information that taxpayers should provide the IRS as well as information about the internal management and conduct of the IRS itself. See also *interpretive regulation* and *legislative regulation.*

Production activities deduction (PAD). A deduction based on 3 percent of the lesser of qualified production activities income (QPAI) or modified adjusted gross income but not to exceed 50 percent of the W–2 production wages paid. In the case of a corporate taxpayer, taxable income is substituted for modified AGI. The deduction rate increases to 6 percent for 2007 to 2009 and to 9 percent for 2010 and thereafter. § 199. See also *qualified production activities income (QPAI).*

Profit sharing plan. A deferred compensation plan established and maintained by an employer to provide for employee participation in the company's profits. Contributions are paid from the employer's current or accumulated profits to a trustee. Separate accounts are maintained for each participant employee. The plan must provide a definite, predetermined formula for allocating the contributions among the participants. It also must include a definite, predetermined formula for distributing the accumulated funds after a fixed number of years, on the attainment of a stated age, or on the occurrence of certain events such as illness, layoff, or retirement.

Proposed Regulation. A Regulation issued by the Treasury Department in proposed, rather than final, form. The interval between the proposal of a Regulation and its finalization permits taxpayers and other interested parties to comment on the propriety of the proposal. See also *regulations* and *temporary regulation.*

Public policy limitation. See *bribes and illegal payments.*

Punitive damages. Damages received or paid by the taxpayer can be classified as compensatory damages or as punitive damages. Punitive damages are those awarded to punish the defendant for gross negligence or the intentional infliction of harm. Such damages are includible in gross income. § 104. See also *compensatory damages.*

Qualified dividend income. Dividends that are eligible for the beneficial 0 percent (5% prior to 2008) or 15 percent tax rate. Excluded are certain dividends from foreign corporations, dividends from tax-exempt entities, and dividends that do not satisfy the holding period requirement. A dividend from a foreign corporation is eligible for qualified dividend status only if one of the following requirements are met: (1) the foreign corporation's stock is traded on an established U.S. securities market, or (2) the foreign corporation is eligible for the benefits of a comprehensive income tax treaty between its country of incorporation and the United States. To satisfy the holding period requirement, the stock on which the dividend is paid must have been held for more than 60 days during the 120-day period beginning 60 days before the ex-dividend date.

Qualified employee discounts. Discounts offered employees on merchandise or services that the employer ordinarily sells or provides to customers. The discounts must be generally available to all employees. In the case of property, the discount cannot exceed the employer's gross profit (the sales price cannot be less than the employer's cost). In the case of services, the discounts cannot exceed 20 percent of the normal sales price. § 132.

Qualified pension or profit sharing plan. An employer-sponsored plan that meets the requirements of § 401. If these requirements are met, none of the employer's contributions to the plan will be taxed to the employee until distributed to him or her (§ 402). The employer will be allowed a deduction in the year the contributions are made (§ 404). See also *annuity* and *deferred compensation.*

Qualified production activities income (QPAI). A key determinant in computing the domestic production activities deduction (DPAD). It consists of domestic production gross receipts (DPGR) reduced by cost of goods sold and other assignable expenses. Thus, QPAI represents the profit derived from production activities. § 199. See also *production activities deduction (PAD)* and *domestic production gross receipts (DPGR).*

Qualified real property business indebtedness. Indebtedness that was incurred or assumed by the taxpayer in connection with real property used in a trade or business and is secured by such real property. The taxpayer must not be a C corporation. For qualified real property business indebtedness, the taxpayer may elect to exclude some or all of the income realized from cancellation of debt on qualified real property. If the election is made, the basis of the property must be reduced by the amount excluded. The amount excluded cannot be greater than the excess of the principal amount of the outstanding debt over the fair market value (net of any other debt outstanding on the property) of the property securing the debt. § 108(c).

Qualified residence interest. A term relevant in determining the amount of interest expense the individual taxpayer may deduct as an itemized deduction for what otherwise would be disallowed as a component of personal interest (consumer interest). Qualified residence interest consists of interest paid on qualified residences (principal residence and one other residence) of the taxpayer. Debt that qualifies as qualified residence interest is limited to $1 million of debt to acquire, construct, or substantially improve qualified residences (acquisition indebtedness) plus $100,000 of other debt secured by qualified residences (home equity indebtedness). The home equity indebtedness may not exceed the fair market value of a qualified residence reduced by the acquisition indebtedness for that residence. § 163(h)(3). See also *consumer interest* and *home equity loans.*

Qualified transportation fringes. Transportation benefits provided by the employer to the employee. Such benefits include (1) transportation in a commuter highway vehicle between the employee's residence and the place of employment, (2) a transit pass, and (3) qualified parking. Qualified transportation fringes are excludible from the employee's gross income to the extent categories (1) and (2) above do not exceed $230 per month in 2011 ($230 in 2010) and category (3) does not exceed $230 per month in 2011 ($230 in 2010). These amounts are indexed annually for inflation. § 132.

Qualified tuition program. A program that allows college tuition to be prepaid for a beneficiary. When amounts in the plan are used, nothing is included in gross income provided they are used for qualified higher education expenses. § 529.

Qualified tuition reduction plan. A type of fringe benefit plan that is available to employees of nonprofit educational institutions. Such employees (and the spouse and dependent children) are allowed to exclude from gross income a tuition waiver pursuant to a qualified tuition reduction plan. The exclusion applies to undergraduate tuition. In limited circumstances, the exclusion also applies to the graduate tuition of teaching and research assistants. § 117(d).

Qualifying child. An individual who, as to the taxpayer, satisfies the relationship, abode, and age tests. To be claimed as a dependent, such an individual must also meet the citizenship and joint return tests and not be self-supporting. §§ 152(a)(1) and (c). See also *personal and dependency exemptions.*

Qualifying relative. An individual who, as to the taxpayer, satisfies the relationship, gross income, support, citizenship, and joint return tests. Such an individual can be claimed as a dependent of the taxpayer. §§ 152(a)(2) and (d). See also *personal and dependency exemptions.*

R

RAR. A Revenue Agent's Report, which reflects any adjustments made by the agent as a result of an audit of the taxpayer. The RAR is mailed to the taxpayer along with the 30-day letter, which outlines the appellate procedures available to the taxpayer.

Realized gain or loss. The difference between the amount realized upon the sale or other disposition of property and the adjusted basis of the property. § 1001. See also *adjusted basis* and *recognized gain or loss.*

Realty. All real estate, including land and buildings. Permanent improvements to a building (fixtures) become realty if their removal would cause significant damage to the property. An example of a fixture is the installation of a central air conditioning or heating system to a building. Thus, personalty can become realty through the fixture reclassification.

Reasonable needs of the business. See *accumulated earnings tax.*

Reasonableness. The Code includes a reasonableness requirement with respect to the deduction of salaries and other compensation for services. What constitutes reasonableness is a question of fact. If an expense is unreasonable, the amount that is classified as unreasonable is not allowed as a deduction. The question of reasonableness generally arises with respect to closely held corporations where there is no separation of ownership and management. § 162(a)(1).

Recapture. To recover the tax benefit of a deduction or a credit previously taken.

Recapture of depreciation. Upon the disposition of depreciable property used in a trade or business, gain or loss is measured by the difference between the consideration received (the amount realized) and the adjusted basis of the property. Before the enactment of the recapture of depreciation provisions of the Code, any such gain recognized could be § 1231 gain and usually qualified for long-term capital gain treatment. The recapture provisions of the Code (e.g., §§ 1245 and 1250) may operate to convert some or all of the previous § 1231 gain into ordinary income. The justification for recapture of depreciation is that it prevents a taxpayer from deducting depreciation at ordinary income rates and having the related gain on disposition taxed at capital gain rates. The recapture of depreciation rules do not apply when the property is disposed of at a loss. See also *residential rental property, Section 1231 gains and losses, Section 1245 recapture*, and *Section 1250 recapture.*

Recapture of investment tax credit. When investment tax credit property is disposed of or ceases to be used in the trade or business of the taxpayer, some or all of the investment tax credit claimed on the property may be recaptured as additional tax liability. The amount of the recapture is the difference between the amount of the credit originally claimed and what should have been claimed in light of the length of time the property was actually held or used for qualifying purposes. § 50. See also *investment tax credit.*

Recapture potential. Reference is to property that, if disposed of in a taxable transaction, would result in the recapture of depreciation (§§ 1245 or 1250) and/or of the investment tax credit (§ 50).

Recognized gain or loss. The portion of realized gain or loss that is considered in computing taxable income. See also *realized gain or loss.*

Recovery of capital doctrine. When a taxable sale or exchange occurs, the seller may be permitted to recover his or her investment (or other adjusted basis) in the property before gain or loss is recognized. See also *open transaction.*

Refundable credit. A refundable credit is a credit that is paid to the taxpayer even if the amount of the credit (or credits) exceeds the taxpayer's tax liability. See also *nonrefundable credit.*

Regulations. Treasury Department Regulations represent the position of the IRS as to how the Internal Revenue Code is to be interpreted. Their purpose is to provide taxpayers and IRS personnel with rules of general and specific application to the various provisions of the tax law. Regulations are published in the *Federal Register* and in all tax services. See also *interpretive regulation, legislative regulation, procedural regulation,* and *proposed regulation.*

Rehabilitation expenditures credit. A credit that is based on expenditures incurred to rehabilitate industrial and commercial buildings and certified historic structures. The credit is intended to discourage businesses from moving from older, economically distressed areas to newer locations and to encourage the preservation of historic structures. § 47. See also *rehabilitation expenditures credit recapture.*

Rehabilitation expenditures credit recapture. When property that qualifies for the rehabilitation expenditures credit is disposed of or ceases to be used in the trade or business of the taxpayer, some or all of the tax credit claimed on the property may be recaptured as additional tax liability. The amount of the recapture is the difference between the amount of the credit claimed originally and what should have been claimed in light of the length of time the property was actually held or used for qualifying purposes. § 50. See also *rehabilitation expenditures credit.*

Related party. Includes certain family members and controlled entities (i.e., partnerships and corporations). §§ 267, 707(b), and 1239. See also *related-party transactions.*

Related-party transactions. The tax law places restrictions upon the recognition of gains and losses between related parties because of the potential for abuse. For example, restrictions are placed on the deduction of losses from the sale or exchange of property between related parties. In addition, under certain circumstances, related-party gains that would otherwise be classified as capital gain are classified as ordinary income. §§ 267, 707(b), and 1239. See also *related party.*

Rental activity. Any activity where payments are received principally for the use of tangible property is a rental activity. Temporary Regulations provide that in certain circumstances activities involving rentals of real and personal property are not to be *treated* as rental activities. The Temporary Regulations list six exceptions.

Research activities credit. A tax credit whose purpose is to encourage research and development. It consists of three components: the incremental research activities credit, the basic research credit, and the energy credit. The incremental research activities credit is equal to 20 percent of the excess of qualified research expenditures over the base amount. The basic research credit is equal to 20 percent of the excess of basic research payments over the base amount. § 41. See also *general business credit.*

Research and experimental expenditures. The Code provides three alternatives for the tax treatment of research and experimentation expenditures. They may be expensed in the year paid or incurred, deferred subject to amortization, or capitalized. If the taxpayer does not elect to expense such costs or to defer them subject to amortization (over 60 months), the expenditures must be capitalized. § 174. Three types of research activities credits are available: the basic research credit, the incremental research activities credit and the energy credit. The rate for each type is 20 percent. § 41. See also *research activities credit.*

Reserve for bad debts. A method of accounting whereby an allowance is permitted for estimated uncollectible accounts. Actual write-offs are charged to the reserve, and recoveries of amounts previously written off are credited to the reserve. The Code permits only certain financial institutions to use the reserve method. § 166. See also *specific charge-off method.*

Reserve method. See *reserve for bad debts.*

Reserves for estimated expenses. Except in the limited case for bad debts, reserves for estimated expenses (e.g., warranty service costs) are not permitted for tax purposes even though such reserves are appropriate for financial accounting purposes. See also *all events test.*

Residential rental property. Buildings for which at least 80 percent of the gross rents are from dwelling units (e.g., an apartment building). This type of building is distinguished from nonresidential (commercial or industrial) buildings in applying the recapture of depreciation provisions. The term also is relevant in distinguishing between buildings that are eligible for a 27.5-year life versus a 39-year (or 31.5-year) life for MACRS purposes. Generally, residential buildings receive preferential treatment. §§ 168(e)(2) and 1250. See also *recapture of depreciation.*

Residential rental real estate. See *residential rental property.*

Restricted property plan. An arrangement whereby an employer transfers property (usually stock) to an employee at a bargain price (for less than the fair market value). If the transfer is accompanied by a substantial risk of forfeiture and the property is not transferable, no compensation results to the employee until the restrictions disappear. An example of a substantial risk of forfeiture would be a requirement that the employee return the property if his or her employment is terminated within a specified period of time. § 83. See also *nonqualified deferred compensation (NQDC) plans* and *substantial risk of forfeiture.*

Retirement of corporate obligations. The retirement of corporate and certain government obligations is considered to be a sale or exchange. Gain or loss, upon the retirement of a corporate obligation, therefore, is treated as capital gain or loss rather than as ordinary income or loss. §§ 1271–1275.

Return of capital doctrine. See *recovery of capital doctrine.*

Revenue neutrality. A description that characterizes tax legislation when it neither increases nor decreases the revenue result. Thus, any tax revenue losses are offset by tax revenue gains.

Revenue Procedure. A matter of procedural importance to both taxpayers and the IRS concerning the administration of the tax law is issued by the National Office of the IRS as a Revenue Procedure (abbreviated Rev.Proc.). A Revenue Procedure is first published in an *Internal Revenue Bulletin* (I.R.B.) and later transferred to the appropriate *Cumulative Bulletin* (C.B.). Both the *Internal Revenue Bulletin* and the *Cumulative Bulletin* are published by the U.S. Government Printing Office.

Revenue Ruling. A Revenue Ruling (abbreviated Rev.Rul.) is issued by the National Office of the IRS to express an official interpretation of the tax law as applied to specific transactions. It is more limited in application than a Regulation. A Revenue Ruling is first published in an *Internal Revenue Bulletin* (I.R.B.) and later transferred to the appropriate *Cumulative Bulletin* (C.B.). Both the *Internal Revenue Bulletin* and the *Cumulative Bulletin* are published by the U.S. Government Printing Office.

S

S corporation. See *S corporation status.*

S corporation status. An elective provision permitting certain small business corporations (§ 1361) and their shareholders to elect (§ 1362) to be treated for income tax purposes in accordance with the operating rules of §§ 1363–1379. Of major significance are the facts that S status avoids the corporate income tax and corporate losses can be claimed by the shareholders. See also *C corporation.*

Sale of principal residence. If a residence has been owned and used by the taxpayer as the principal residence for at least two years during the five-year period ending on the date of sale, up to $250,000 of realized gain is excluded from gross income. For a married couple filing a joint return, the $250,000 is increased to $500,000 if either spouse satisfies the ownership requirement and both spouses satisfy the use requirement. § 121.

Sale or exchange. A requirement for the recognition of capital gain or loss. Generally, the seller of property must receive money or relief from debt in order to have sold the property. An exchange involves the transfer of property for other property. Thus, collection of a debt is neither a sale nor an exchange. The term *sale or exchange* is not defined by the Code.

Sales tax. A transaction tax imposed upon the sale of goods. It usually is based on a specified percentage of the value of the property sold. A sales tax differs from an excise tax, in that a sales tax applies to a broad variety of commodities.

Salvage value. The estimated amount a taxpayer will receive upon the disposition of an asset used in the taxpayer's trade or business. Salvage value is relevant in calculating depreciation under § 167, but is not relevant in calculating cost recovery under § 168.

Schedule M-1. On the Form 1120, a reconciliation of book net income with Federal taxable income. Accounts for timing and permanent differences in the two computations, such as depreciation differences, exempt income, and nondeductible items. On Forms 1120S and 1065, the Schedule M-1 reconciles book income with the owners' aggregate ordinary taxable income.

Schedule M-3. An *expanded* reconciliation of book net income with Federal taxable income (refer to *Schedule M-1* above). Applies to corporations with total assets of $10 million or more.

Scholarships. Scholarships are generally excluded from the gross income of the recipient unless the payments are a disguised form of compensation for services rendered. However, the Code imposes restrictions on the exclusion. The recipient must be a degree candidate. The excluded amount is limited to amounts used for tuition, fees, books, supplies, and equipment required for courses of instruction. Amounts received for room and board are not eligible for the exclusion. § 117.

Section 121 exclusion. See *sale of principal residence.*

Section 179 expensing. The ability to deduct a capital expenditure in the year an asset is placed in service rather than over the asset's useful life or cost recovery period. The annual ceiling on the deduction is $500,000 for 2011 ($250,000 for 2010). However, the deduction is reduced dollar for dollar when § 179 property placed in service during the taxable year exceeds $2 million in 2011 ($800,000 in 2010). In addition, the amount expensed under § 179 cannot exceed the aggregate amount of taxable income derived from the conduct of any trade or business by the taxpayer.

Section 401(k) plan. A cash or deferred arrangement plan that allows participants to elect to receive up to $16,500 in 2011 ($16,500 in 2010) in cash (taxed currently) or to have a contribution made on their behalf to a profit sharing or stock bonus plan (excludible from gross income). The plan may also be in the form of a salary reduction agreement between the participant and the employer.

Section 1231 assets. Depreciable assets and real estate used in a trade or business and held for the required long-term holding period. Under certain circumstances, the classification also includes timber, coal, domestic iron ore, livestock (held for draft, breeding, dairy, or sporting purposes), and unharvested crops. § 1231(b).

Section 1231 gains and losses. If the net result of the combined gains and losses from the taxable dispositions of § 1231 assets plus the net gain from the involuntary conversion of nonpersonal use assets is a gain, the gains and losses from § 1231 assets are treated as long-term capital gains and losses. In arriving at § 1231 gains, however, the depreciation recapture provisions (e.g., §§ 1245 and 1250) are first applied to produce ordinary income. If the net result of the combination is a loss, the gains and losses from § 1231 assets are treated as ordinary gains and losses. § 1231(a). See also *recapture of depreciation.*

Section 1231 lookback. In order for gain to be classified as § 1231 gain, the gain must survive the § 1231 lookback. To the extent of nonrecaptured § 1231 losses for the five prior tax years, the gain is classified as ordinary income. § 1231(c).

Section 1231 property. See *Section 1231 assets.*

Section 1244 stock. Stock issued under § 1244 by qualifying small business corporations. If § 1244 stock is disposed of at a loss or becomes worthless, the shareholders may claim an ordinary loss rather than the usual capital loss. The annual ceiling on the ordinary loss treatment is $50,000 ($100,000 for married individuals filing jointly). See also *worthless securities.*

Section 1245 property. Property that is subject to the recapture of depreciation under § 1245. For a definition of § 1245 property, see § 1245(a)(3). See also *Section 1245 recapture.*

Section 1245 recapture. Upon a taxable disposition of § 1245 property, all depreciation claimed on the property is recaptured as ordinary income (but not to exceed the recognized gain from the disposition). See also *recapture of depreciation.*

Section 1250 property. Real estate that is subject to the recapture of depreciation under § 1250. For a definition of § 1250 property, see § 1250(c). See also *Section 1250 recapture.*

Section 1250 recapture. Upon a taxable disposition of § 1250 property, some or all of the additional depreciation claimed on the property may be recaptured as ordinary income. Various recapture rules apply depending upon the type of property (residential or nonresidential real estate) and the date acquired. Generally, the additional depreciation is recaptured in full to the extent of the gain recognized. See also *additional depreciation* and *recapture of depreciation.*

Self-employment retirement plan. A designation for retirement plans available to self-employed taxpayers. Also referred to as H.R. 10 and Keogh plans. Under such plans, in 2011, a taxpayer may deduct each year up to either 100 percent of net earnings from self-employment or $49,000, whichever is less. If the plan is a profit sharing plan, the percentage is 25 percent.

Self-employment tax. In 2011, a tax of 10.4 percent is levied on individuals with net earnings from self-employment (up to $106,800) to provide Social Security benefits (i.e., the old age, survivors, and disability insurance portion) for such individuals. For 2010, the rate is 12.4 percent. In addition, in 2011, (and 2010) a tax of 2.9 percent is levied on individuals with net earnings from self-employment (with no statutory ceiling) to provide Medicare benefits (i.e., the hospital insurance portion) for such individuals. If a self-employed individual also receives wages from an employer that are subject to FICA, the self-employment tax will be reduced if total income subject to Social Security is more than $106,800 in 2011. A partial deduction is allowed in calculating the self-employment tax. Individuals with net earnings of $400 or more from self-employment are subject to this tax. §§ 1401 and 1402.

Separate property. In a community property jurisdiction, separate property is the property that belongs entirely to one of the spouses. Generally, it is property acquired before marriage or acquired after marriage by gift or inheritance. See also *community property.*

Severance tax. A tax imposed upon the extraction of natural resources.

Short sale. A short sale occurs when a taxpayer sells borrowed property (usually stock) and repays the lender with substantially identical property either held on the date of the short sale or purchased after the sale. No gain or loss is recognized until the short sale is closed, and such gain or loss is generally short term. § 1233.

Short taxable year (short period). A tax year that is less than 12 months. A short taxable year may occur in the initial reporting period, in the final tax year, or when the taxpayer changes tax years.

Significant participation activity. There are seven tests to determine whether an individual has achieved material participation in an activity, one of which is based on more than 500 hours of participation in significant participation activities. A significant participation activity is one in which the individual's participation exceeds 100 hours during the year. Temp.Reg. § 1.469–5T.

Simplified employee pension (SEP) plan. An employer may make contributions to an employee's IRA in amounts not exceeding the lesser of 15 percent of compensation or $49,000 per individual in 2011. These employer-sponsored simplified employee pensions are permitted only if the contributions are nondiscriminatory and are made on behalf of all employees who have attained age 21 and have worked for the employer during at least three of the five preceding calendar years. § 219(b). See also *individual retirement account (IRA).*

Small business corporation. A corporation that satisfies the definition of § 1361(b), § 1244(c)(3), or both. Satisfaction of § 1361(b) permits an S corporation election, and satisfaction of § 1244 enables the shareholders of the corporation to claim an ordinary loss. See also *S corporation status* and *Section 1244 stock.*

Small business stock. See *small business corporation.*

Small cases division. A subsidiary division of the U.S. Tax Court. The jurisdiction of the Small Cases division is limited to small claims (i.e., claims of $50,000 or less). The proceedings of the Small Cases Division are informal, and the findings cannot be appealed.

Specific charge-off method. A method of accounting for bad debts in which a deduction is permitted only when an account becomes partially or completely worthless. See also *reserve for bad debts.*

Standard deduction. The individual taxpayer can either itemize deductions or take the standard deduction. The amount of the standard deduction depends on the taxpayer's filing status (single, head of household, married filing jointly, surviving spouse, or married filing separately). For 2011, the amount of the standard deduction ranges from $5,800 to $11,600. Additional standard deductions of either $1,150 (for married taxpayers) or $1,450 (for single taxpayers) are available if the taxpayer is either blind or age 65 or over. For 2008 and 2009, a real property tax standard deduction is available in the amount of $500 ($1,000 on a joint return). For 2009, there also is a limited auto sales taxes standard deduction. Limitations exist on the amount of the standard deduction of a taxpayer who is another taxpayer's dependent. The standard deduction amounts are adjusted for inflation each year. § 63(c).

Startup expenditures. Expenditures paid or incurred associated with the creation of a business prior to the beginning of business. Examples of such expenditures include advertising, salaries and wages, travel and other expenses incurred in lining up prospective distributors, suppliers, or customers, and salaries and fees to executives, consultants, and professional service providers. A taxpayer may elect to immediately expense the first $5,000 (subject to phaseout) of startup expenditures and generally amortize the balance over a period of 180 months. For 2010, the $5,000 amount was increased to $10,000.

Statute of limitations. Provisions of the law that specify the maximum period of time in which action may be taken on a past event. Code §§ 6501–6504 contain the limitation periods applicable to the IRS for additional assessments, and §§ 6511–6515 relate to refund claims by taxpayers.

Statutory employee. Statutory employees are considered self-employed independent contractors for purposes of reporting income and expenses on their tax returns. Generally, a statutory employee must meet three tests:

- It is understood from a service contract that the services will be performed by the person.
- The person does not have a substantial investment in facilities (other than transportation used to perform the services).
- The services involve a continuing relationship with the person for whom they are performed.

For further information on statutory employees, see Circular E, *Employer's Tax Guide*, IRS Publication 15.

Statutory notice of deficiency. Commonly referred to as the 90-day letter, this notice is sent to a taxpayer upon request, upon the expiration of the 30-day letter, or upon exhaustion by the taxpayer of his or her administrative remedies before the IRS. The notice gives the taxpayer 90 days in which to file a petition with the U.S. Tax Court. If a petition is not filed, the IRS will issue a demand for payment of the assessed deficiency. §§ 6211–6216. See also *thirty-day letter*.

Stock bonus plan. A type of deferred compensation plan in which the employer establishes and maintains the plan and contributes employer stock to the plan for the benefit of employees. The contributions need not be dependent on the employer's profits. Any benefits of the plan are distributable in the form of employer stock, except that distributable fractional shares may be paid in cash.

Stock option. The right to purchase a stated number of shares of stock from a corporation at a certain price within a specified period of time. §§ 421 and 422. See also *incentive stock option (ISO)* and *nonqualified stock option (NQSO)*.

Stock redemption. The redemption of the stock of a shareholder by the issuing corporation is treated as a sale or exchange of the stock if the redemption is not a dividend. §§ 301 and 302.

Substantial risk of forfeiture. A term that is associated with a restricted property plan. Generally, an employee who receives property (e.g., stock of the employer-corporation) from the employer at a bargain price or at no cost must include the bargain element in gross income. However, the employee currently does not have to do so if there is a substantial risk of forfeiture. A substantial risk of forfeiture exists if a person's rights to full enjoyment of property are conditioned upon the future performance, or the refraining from the performance, of substantial services by the individual. § 83. See also *restricted property plan*.

Sunset provision. A provision attached to new tax legislation that will cause such legislation to expire at a specified date. Sunset provisions are attached to tax cut bills for long-term budgetary reasons in order to make their effect temporary. Once the sunset provision comes into play, the tax cut is rescinded and former law is reinstated. An example of a sunset provision is the one contained in the Tax Relief Reconciliation Act of 2001, which relates to the estate tax. After the estate tax is phased out by 2010, a sunset provision reinstates the estate tax as on January 1, 2011.

Super-full absorption costing rules. See *uniform capitalization rules*.

Surviving spouse. The joint return tax rates apply for a surviving spouse. Such rates apply for the two tax years after the tax year of the death of the spouse. To qualify as a surviving spouse, the taxpayer must maintain a household for a dependent child. § 2.

T

Targeted jobs tax credit. See *work opportunity tax credit*.

Taxable year. The annual period over which income is measured for income tax purposes. Most individuals use a calendar year, but many businesses use a fiscal year based on the natural business year. See also *accounting period* and *fiscal year*.

Tax avoidance. The minimization of one's tax liability by taking advantage of legally available tax planning opportunities. Tax avoidance can be contrasted with tax evasion, which entails the reduction of tax liability by illegal means.

Tax benefit rule. A provision that limits the recognition of income from the recovery of an expense or loss properly deducted in a prior tax year to the amount of the deduction that generated a tax benefit. § 111.

Tax Court. The U.S. Tax Court is one of three trial courts of original jurisdiction that decides litigation involving Federal income, estate, or gift taxes. It is the only trial court where the taxpayer need not first pay the deficiency assessed by the IRS. The Tax Court will not have jurisdiction over a case unless the statutory notice of deficiency (90-day letter) has been issued by the IRS and the taxpayer files the petition for hearing within the time prescribed.

Tax credits. Tax credits are amounts that directly reduce a taxpayer's tax liability. The tax benefit received from a tax credit is not dependent on the taxpayer's marginal tax rate, whereas the benefit of a tax deduction or exclusion is dependent on the taxpayer's tax bracket.

Tax credit for the elderly or disabled. An elderly (age 65 and over) or disabled taxpayer may receive a tax credit amounting to 15 percent of $5,000 ($7,500 for qualified married individuals filing jointly). This amount is reduced by Social Security benefits, excluded pension benefits, and one-half of the taxpayer's adjusted gross income in excess of $7,500 ($10,000 for married taxpayers filing jointly). § 22.

Tax-free exchange. Transfers of property specifically exempted from Federal income tax consequences. Examples are a transfer of property to a controlled corporation under §351(a) and a like-kind exchange under § 1031(a). The recognition of gain or loss is postponed, rather than being permanently excluded, through the assignment of a carryover basis to the replacement property. See also *nontaxable exchange*.

Tax home. Since travel expenses of an employee are deductible only if the taxpayer is away from home, the deductibility of such expenses rests upon the definition of tax home. The IRS position is that the tax home is the business location, post, or station of the taxpayer. If an employee is temporarily reassigned to a new post for a period of one year or less, the taxpayer's home should be his or her personal residence, and the travel expenses should be deductible. If the assignment is for more than two years, the IRS position is that it is indefinite or permanent and the taxpayer is therefore not in travel status. If the assignment is for between one and two years, the IRS position is that the location of the tax home will be determined on the basis of the facts and circumstances. The courts are in conflict regarding what constitutes a person's home for tax purposes. The taxpayer will not be treated as temporarily away from home if the employment period exceeds one year. Thus, in this situation, the tax home will be the place of employment. See also *travel expenses.*

Tax preferences. Those items set forth in § 57 that may result in the imposition of the alternative minimum tax. See also *alternative minimum tax (AMT).*

Tax rate schedules. Rate schedules appearing in Appendix A that are used by upper-income taxpayers and those not permitted to use the tax table. Separate rate schedules are provided for married individuals filing jointly, head of household, single taxpayers, estates and trusts, and married individuals filing separate returns. § 1.

Tax research. The method used to determine the best available solution to a situation that possesses tax consequences. Both tax and nontax factors are considered.

Tax shelters. The typical tax shelter generated large losses in the early years of the activity. Investors would offset these losses against other types of income and, therefore, avoid paying income taxes on this income. These tax shelter investments could then be sold after a few years and produce capital gain income, which is taxed at a lower rate than ordinary income. The passive activity loss rules and the at-risk rules now limit tax shelter deductions.

Tax table. A tax table appearing in Appendix A that is provided for taxpayers with less than $100,000 of taxable income. Separate columns are provided for single taxpayers, married taxpayers filing jointly, head of household, and married taxpayers filing separately. § 3.

Technical advice memoranda (TAMs). TAMs are issued by the National Office of the IRS in response to questions raised by IRS field personnel during audits. They deal with completed rather than proposed transactions and are often requested for questions related to exempt organizations and employee plans.

Temporary Regulation. A Regulation issued by the Treasury Department in temporary form. When speed is critical, the Treasury Department issues Temporary Regulations, which take effect immediately. These Regulations have the same authoritative value as final Regulations and may be cited as precedent for three years. Temporary Regulations are also issued as Proposed Regulations. See also *proposed regulation* and *regulations.*

Theft loss. A loss from larceny, embezzlement, and robbery. It does not include misplacement of items. See also *casualty loss.*

Thin capitalization. When debt owed by a corporation to its shareholders is large relative to its capital structure (stock and shareholder equity), the IRS may contend that the corporation is thinly capitalized. In effect, this means that some or all of the debt will be reclassified as equity. The immediate result is to disallow any interest deduction to the corporation on the reclassified debt. To the extent of the corporation's earnings and profits, interest payments and loan repayments on the reclassified debt are treated as dividends to the shareholders. § 385.

Thirty-day letter. A letter that accompanies a Revenue Agent's Report (RAR) issued as a result of an IRS audit of a taxpayer (or the rejection of a taxpayer's claim for refund). The letter outlines the taxpayer's appeal procedure before the IRS. If the taxpayer does not request any such procedures within the 30-day period, the IRS will issue a *statutory notice of deficiency* (the 90-day letter).

Timber. Special rules apply to the recognition of gain from the sale of timber. A taxpayer may elect to treat the cutting of timber that is held for sale or use in a trade or business as a sale or exchange. If the holding period requirements are met, the gain is recognized as § 1231 gain and may therefore receive long-term capital gain treatment. § 631.

Trade or business expenses. Deductions *for* AGI that are attributable to a taxpayer's business or profession. Some employee expenses may also be treated as trade or business expenses. See also *employee expenses.*

Transportation expenses. Transportation expenses for an employee include only the cost of transportation (taxi fares, automobile expenses, etc.) in the course of employment when the employee is not away from home in travel status. Commuting expenses are not deductible. See also *automobile expenses.*

Travel expenses. Travel expenses include meals (generally subject to a 50 percent disallowance) and lodging and transportation expenses while away from home in the pursuit of a trade or business (including that of an employee). See also *tax home.*

Trial court. The court of original jurisdiction; the first court to consider litigation. In Federal tax controversies, trial courts include U.S. District Courts, the U.S. Tax Court, and the U.S. Court of Federal Claims. See also *appellate court.*

U

Unearned income. Also referred to as investment income, it includes such income as interest, dividends, capital gains, rents, royalties, and pension and annuity income. See also *kiddie tax.*

Unearned (prepaid) income. For tax purposes, prepaid income (e.g., rent) is taxable in the year of receipt. In certain cases involving advance payments for goods and services, income may be deferred. See Revenue Procedure 2004–34 (2004–22 I.R.B. 13, 991) and Reg. § 1.451–5. See also *accrual method.*

Uniform capitalization (UNICAP) rules. Under § 263A, the Regulations provide a set of rules that all taxpayers (regardless of the particular industry) can use to determine the items of cost (and means of allocating those costs) that must be capitalized with respect to the production of tangible property.

Unit-livestock-price method. A method of accounting for the cost of livestock. The livestock are valued using a standard cost of raising an animal with the characteristics of that animal to the same age as the animals on hand.

Unreasonable compensation. Under § 162(a)(1), a deduction is allowed for "reasonable" salaries or other compensation for personal services actually rendered. To the extent compensation is excessive ("unreasonable"), no deduction will be allowed. The problem of unreasonable compensation usually is limited to closely held corporations where the motivation is to pay out profits in some form deductible to the corporation. Deductible compensation, therefore, becomes an attractive substitute for nondeductible dividends when the shareholders are also employees of the corporation.

Unrecaptured § 1250 gain (25 percent gain). Gain from the sale of depreciable real estate held more than one year. The gain is equal to or less than the depreciation taken on such property and is reduced by § 1245 gain and § 1250 gain. See also *alternative tax*.

U.S. Court of Federal Claims. See *Claims Court*.

U.S. Supreme Court. The highest appellate court or the court of last resort in the Federal court system and in most states. Only a small number of tax decisions of the U.S. Courts of Appeal are reviewed by the U.S. Supreme Court under its certiorari procedure. The Supreme Court usually grants certiorari to resolve a conflict among the Courts of Appeal (e.g., two or more appellate courts have assumed opposing positions on a particular issue) or when the tax issue is extremely important (e.g., size of the revenue loss to the Federal government).

U.S. Tax Court. See *Tax Court*.

Use tax. A use tax is an ad valorem tax, usually at the same rate as the sales tax, on the use or consumption of tangible personalty. The purpose of a use tax is to prevent the avoidance of a sales tax.

USTC. Published by Commerce Clearing House, *U.S. Tax Cases* contain all of the Federal tax decisions issued by the U.S. District Courts, U.S. Court of Federal Claims, U.S. Courts of Appeals, and the U.S. Supreme Court.

V

Vacation home. The Code places restrictions upon taxpayers who rent their residences or vacation homes for part of the tax year. The restrictions may result in a scaling down of expense deductions for the taxpayers. § 280A. See also *hobby loss*.

Value added tax (VAT). A national sales tax that taxes the increment in value as goods move through the production process. A VAT is much used in other countries, but has not yet been incorporated as part of the U.S. Federal tax structure.

Vesting requirements. A qualified deferred compensation arrangement must satisfy a vesting requirement. Under this provision, an employee's right to accrued plan benefits derived from employer contributions must be nonforfeitable in accordance with one of two vesting time period schedules (or two required alternate vesting schedules for certain employer matching contributions).

W

W–2 wages. The domestic production activities deduction (DPAD) cannot exceed 50 percent of the W–2 wages paid for any particular year. Prop.Reg. § 199–2(f)(2) provides several methods for calculating the W–2 wages, but the payments must involve common law employees. To qualify, the employees need to be involved in the production process. § 199. See also *production activities deduction (PAD)*.

Wash sale. A loss from the sale of stock or securities that is disallowed because the taxpayer within 30 days before or after the sale has acquired stock or securities that are substantially identical to those sold. § 1091.

Welfare-to-work credit. A tax credit available to employers hiring individuals who have been long-term recipients of family assistance welfare benefits. In general, long-term recipients are those individuals who are certified by a designated local agency as being members of a family receiving assistance under a public aid program for at least an 18-month period ending on the hiring date. The welfare-to-work credit is available for qualified wages paid in the first two years of employment. The maximum credit is equal to $9,000 per qualified employee, computed as 40 percent of the first $10,000 of qualified wages paid in the first year of employment, plus 50 percent of the first $10,000 of qualified wages paid in the second year of employment. Starting in 2007, the welfare-to-work credit becomes part of the work opportunity tax credit. § 51(e). See also *general business credit* and *work opportunity tax credit*.

Wherewithal to pay. This concept recognizes the inequity of taxing a transaction when the taxpayer lacks the means with which to pay the tax. Under it, there is a correlation between the imposition of the tax and the ability to pay the tax. It is particularly suited to situations in which the taxpayer's economic position has not changed significantly as a result of the transaction.

Withholding allowances. The number of withholding allowances serves as the basis for determining the amount of income taxes withheld from an employee's salary or wages. The more withholding allowances claimed, the less income tax withheld by an employer. An employee may claim withholding allowances for personal exemptions for self and spouse (unless claimed as a dependent of another person), dependency exemptions, and special withholding allowances.

Working condition fringe. A type of fringe benefit received by the employee that is excludible from the employee's gross income. It consists of property or services provided (paid or reimbursed) by the employer for which the employee could take a tax deduction if the employee had paid for them. § 132.

Work opportunity tax credit. Employers are allowed a tax credit equal to 40 percent of the first $6,000 of wages (per eligible employee) for the first year of employment. Eligible employees include certain hard-to-employ individuals (e.g., qualified ex-felons, high-risk youth, food stamp recipients, and veterans). For an employer to qualify for the 40 percent credit, the employees must (1) be certified by a designated local agency as being members of one of the targeted groups and (2) have completed at least 400 hours of service to the employer. For employees who meet the first condition but not the second, the credit rate is reduced to 25 percent provided the employees meet a minimum employment level of 120 hours of service to the employer. The employer's deduction for wages is reduced by the amount of the credit taken. For qualified summer youth employees, the 40 percent rate is applied to the first $3,000 of qualified wages. See the *welfare-to-work credit* for the calculation for long-term recipients of family assistance welfare benefits. §§ 51 and 52.

Worthless securities. A loss (usually capital) is allowed for a security that becomes worthless during the year. The loss is deemed to have occurred on the last day of the year. Special rules apply to securities of affiliated companies and small business stock. § 165. See also *Section 1244 stock*.

Writ of certiorari. See *certiorari*.

Appendix D-1

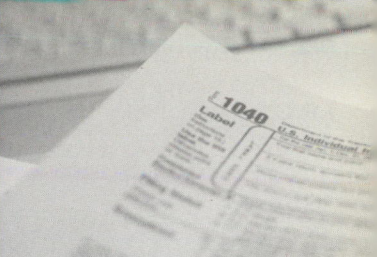

TABLE OF CODE SECTIONS CITED

[See Title 26 U.S.C.A.]

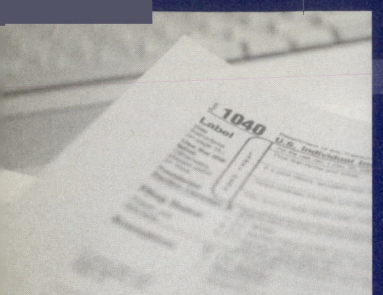

Appendix D-2

TABLE OF REGULATIONS CITED

Appendix D-3

TABLE OF REVENUE PROCEDURES
AND REVENUE RULINGS CITED

Appendix E

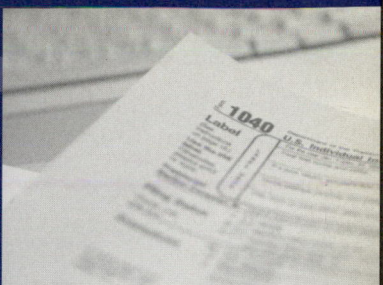

COMPREHENSIVE TAX RETURN PROBLEMS

PROBLEM 1

Paul S. and Ruth N. Hood (ages 42 and 41) are married and live at 4326 Orange Blossom Trail, Tampa, FL 33601. Paul is the regional manager for a budget motel chain (Rest Inn), while Ruth is a self-employed architect. They file a joint return and use the cash basis for tax purposes.

1. Paul receives a yearly salary of $82,000, plus an annual bonus, from Rest Inn. The annual bonus is determined in December of each year but not paid until January of the following year. Paul's bonus is $6,000 for 2009 (received in 2010) and $7,000 for 2010 (received in 2011). Paul also is paid a flat travel allowance of $16,000 per year. The allowance is to cover his expenses in visiting motels in his region to conduct inspections, consult with the local managers, and recruit potential hires. Although Paul maintains substantiation of his travel, he is not required to account for these expenses to Rest Inn. Paul participates in his employer's group health insurance plan to which he contributed $3,600 in 2010 for medical coverage. Rest Inn does not provide any retirement benefits, but it has established a § 401(k) plan to enable its employees to make voluntary contributions. Paul did not contribute to the plan in 2010. The company provides an office for Paul's use that is located at Suite 419, 110 Palm Boulevard, Tampa.

2. Besides the business use of the Impala (see item 3 below), Paul's employment-related expenses for 2010 are as follows:

Airfare	$2,600
Lodging	3,200
Meals	3,400
Entertainment	800
Car rentals, limos, taxis	600
Parking and tolls (during travel)	300
Subscriptions to trade journals	120
Dues to trade association	80
Business gifts	550

   While on business trips in his Impala, Paul was caught in several small-town speed traps and paid fines of $620. The business gifts were made at Christmas and consisted of gift cards ($50 each) to a national chain restaurant. They were sent to 11 key managers of motels in Paul's region.

3. On March 5, 2009, Paul purchased a new Chevrolet Impala for use in his job. The car, a five-passenger sedan, cost $24,000 (including sales tax), with no trade-in involved. The car was driven 14,000 miles in 2009 and 18,000 in 2010 with usage as follows: 20% for

commuting to the office and 80% for business trips. The mileage for 2010 was evenly distributed throughout the year. Paul uses the actual operating cost method and for depreciation purposes uses 200% declining-balance with a half-year convention. No § 179 expensing or additional first-year depreciation has been claimed. (See Table 3 of the Instructions to Form 4562.) Paul's expenses relating to the operation of the Impala for 2010 are as follows:

Gasoline	$2,500
Oil change and lubrication	110
Auto insurance	1,800
Repairs	400
Auto club dues	160
License and registration	120
Interest on car loan	900

4. Ruth is a licensed architect who works part-time on a consulting basis. Her major clients are real estate developers (both residential and commercial) for which she prepares structural designs and construction plans. She also advises on building code requirements regarding the renovation and remodeling of existing structures. Because she limits her engagements, she does not have a separate office but does her work at the client's premises or in her office at home (see item 5 below). Her business expenses for 2010 are summarized below:

Drafting supplies	$4,800
Reproduction materials (e.g., molds, models, photos, blueprints, copies)	3,200
On-site work clothing (e.g., hip boots, safety glasses, safety helmet)	800
Occupation fee	400
Subscriptions to professional journals	250
Dues to professional organizations	240

In addition, she drove the family Acura (purchased on June 7, 2009) 940 miles on her job assignments. Regarding the Acura, Ruth uses the automatic mileage method for tax deduction purposes. She drove the car for 10,000 miles during the year.

5. When the Hoods purchased their home on February 2, 2009, they set aside 300 square feet (out of a total of 2,400 square feet) of living space for Ruth's office. As of January 1, 2010, the home had an adjusted basis of $440,000 for purposes of line 36 of Form 8829 (of which $40,000 is attributable to the land)—the fair market value of the property is in excess of this amount. Relevant information concerning the residence for 2010 appears below:

Homeowner's insurance	$3,200
Repairs and maintenance	1,800
Utilities	6,200
Painting (office area only)	2,500

All of Ruth's office furniture and equipment was previously expensed (under § 179) when acquired. On June 29, 2010, however, she purchased a fireproof file cabinet for $800. The purpose of the acquisition is to further safeguard some of her current and more valuable past architectural drafts and finalized plans. If possible, Ruth prefers to avoid depreciating capital expenditures.

6. One of Ruth's clients was interested in building a shopping center on a tract of land she owned in Levy County. Ruth inherited the property from her aunt when she died on June 6, 1990. At that time, the land was worth $40,000. It has since been rezoned for commercial use and has a current value of $200,000. On February 10, 2010, the following exchange took place in the office of an attorney: Ruth exchanged the Levy parcel for a similar tract in Dixie County (worth $190,000) and cash of $10,000.

7. On September 2, 2010, Ruth sold a tract of land in Citrus County to a farmer who owned the adjoining property. The land was inherited from the same aunt and had a value of $30,000 on June 6, 1990. Under the terms of the sale, Ruth received cash of $20,000 and four notes of $25,000 each payable at one-year intervals with simple interest of 8% provided for. To the extent allowed, Ruth wants to defer recognition of gain as long as possible.

8. During early 2009, Judy Knowles, one of Paul's more competent motel managers, was being subjected to domestic abuse. When the situation became intolerable, she left for parts unknown. Before she left on May 6, 2009, Paul loaned her $5,000 to help her relocate. Paul had her sign an interest-free note due in one year. In late 2010, Paul heard that she had committed suicide after moving to Costa Rica. Paul has no expectation that the loan will ever be repaid.

9. On August 5, 2008, Paul purchased 1,000 shares of NFM common stock for $20 a share as part of its initial public offering. The corporation was formed to establish and operate farmers' markets in mid-size cities throughout the United States. Although some market locations were profitable, as a whole the venture proved to be a failure. By December 2010, NFM was taken over by creditors, and its stock became worthless.

10. Besides the items previously noted, the Hoods had the following receipts for 2010:

Ruth's consulting income		$52,000
Interest income—		
City of Clearwater bonds	$1,400	
Ford Motor Company bonds	900	
CD issued by Wells Fargo Bank	1,100	
Interest on money market account at Tampa State Bank	210	3,610
Refund from SAVALOT (received 1/13/10)		430
Loan repayment by Sarah Duval		4,000
Cash gifts from Ruth's parents		28,000
Federal income tax refund (2009 return)		290

Ruth's consulting income includes a $3,000 payment for work she did in 2009 but does not include $5,000 she billed in November for work performed in 2010. One client who has owed her $6,000 for work done in 2008 was convicted of arson in 2010 and is serving time in state prison. Ruth feels certain that she will never collect the $6,000.

In December 2009, the Hoods made major purchases of household items (e.g., appliances, furniture) at SAVALOT (a discount big box store). They called the manager when they realized they did not receive the advertised sale price. Consequently, the store corrected the mistake and sent a $430 refund.

Four years ago when his sister married, Paul lent her $4,000 to help pay for her honeymoon. Paul was surprised when Sarah paid him back on December 20, 2010.

On March 20 of each year, Ruth's parents always sent her cash as a birthday present. Lately, Ruth has immediately placed the funds in a § 529 plan for her children.

11. In addition to the items already mentioned, the Hoods had the following expenditures for 2010:

Ruth's contribution to her traditional IRA		$5,000
Net gambling loss		1,000
Life insurance premiums		4,200
Medical and dental expense not covered by insurance		6,200
Taxes—		
Ad valorem taxes on personal residence	$4,800	
State and local sales taxes	3,200	8,000
Interest on home mortgage		4,000
Contributions—		
Salvation Army (Tampa branch)	1,200	
Florida governor's election campaign fund	300	1,500

During 2010, the Hoods had gambling winnings of $1,200 and losses of $2,200—all supported by records. The $1,000 listed is the net loss result for the year.

The Hoods maintain whole life insurance policies on each other. The policies were issued by Hawk Assurance Corporation, and the named beneficiaries are their children.

Of the medical expenses listed, $1,200 were incurred in 2009 but not paid until early January 2010.

The Hoods maintain receipts of their purchases and can substantiate the $3,200 in sales taxes paid.

Ruth contributed to the election campaign fund because she thinks the governor's influence was instrumental in getting the Levy County land rezoned for commercial use (see item 6 above).

12. The Hoods maintain a household that includes two children, Anna Marie (age 19) and Roland (age 16). Anna Marie graduated from high school on May 18, 2010, and is undecided about college. Roland is a junior in high school. Anna Marie is an accomplished vocalist and during 2010 was able to earn $7,200 performing at various functions (e.g., weddings, funerals). She placed most of her earnings in a savings account and kept only a small amount to spend on herself.

13. Paul's Form W–2 from Rest Inn shows $15,000 withheld for Federal income tax. The Hoods have made total quarterly income tax payments of $4,000. Ruth's professional activity code is 541310. Relevant Social Security numbers are noted below:

Name	Social Security Number	Birth Date
Paul S. Hood	111–11–1111	07/01/1968
Ruth N. Hood	123–45–6781	03/20/1969
Anna Marie Hood	123–45–6784	05/02/1991
Roland Hood	123–45–6788	06/30/1994

REQUIREMENTS

Prepare an income tax return (with appropriate schedules) for the Hoods for 2010. Make necessary assumptions for facts not stated in the problem. If a refund results, the taxpayers want it sent to them. The Hoods do not wish to contribute to the Presidential Election Campaign Fund. In the past several years, the Hoods have itemized their deductions *from* AGI (have not claimed the standard deduction option).

PROBLEM 2

Alan B. and Paula R. Turner (ages 43 and 39) are married and live at 4603 Dogwood Lane, Raleigh, NC 27611. Alan is a chemist, employed by Old North Chemical Corporation, and Paula is a self-employed doctor of veterinary medicine. They use the cash basis for tax purposes.

1. Old North Chemical Corporation renders chemicals out of forest products and has several plants in the Carolinas and Georgia. Alan is the manager of the Raleigh facility at an annual salary of $90,000. Old North maintains a qualified defined contribution pension plan for its full-time employees, but Alan did not contribute to it in 2010. The company also has a health insurance plan—Alan's contribution for 2010 is $4,000. (The plan covers the employee, spouse, and their dependent children.) Because of the increased risk associated with the type of business involved (i.e., processing of chemicals), Old North provides all of its employees with $200,000 of group term life insurance coverage. (See Table 4.3 in Chapter 4 of the text.) None of these items are included in Alan's Form W-2.

2. After an explosion occurred at Old North's Union (SC) plant killing two employees and injuring several others, Alan began to look for a safer job in the chemical industry. In this connection, he incurred the following expenses during 2010:

Employment agency fee	$3,200
Vita consultation, preparation, and distribution	1,800
Expenses in connection with job interviews	4,100

Alan received several attractive offers but ultimately decided against changing jobs. Influential in his choice was a promotion to regional manager and a $20,000 pay raise (effective in 2011). Apparently, Old North became aware of Alan's job search and reacted accordingly.

3. Old North generally reimburses Alan for all of his employment-related expenses (item 2 above excepted), but not those noted below:

Monthly dinner sessions of the Southern Chemists Association	
(11 meetings in 2010)	$825
Dues to professional organizations	240
Subscriptions to professional journals	180
MIA correspondence study course	230

Each dinner involved the following costs: $40 (fee for speaker), $25 (price of meal), $10 (parking at the Raleigh City Club). Alan goes to the meeting from work and returns home the same night.

The MIA (Management Institute of America) charge was for an online home study course on ways to improve safety measures and avoid accidents in the industrial workplace.

4. Paula Turner is a licensed doctor of veterinary medicine with a specialty in exotic animals (e.g., reptiles, birds). Although she is considering starting her own practice (or buying an existing one), she is not sure the time is right in view of the depressed economy. For the time being, she enjoys working for other veterinarians on a contract basis. By doing this, she is making valuable contacts and benefiting from the experiences of fellow practitioners. For one of her major clients, the Raleigh SPCA, she bills her services at a discount rate. Paula uses her home as her business address. She keeps her records there and otherwise conducts business (e.g., accepts engagements and referrals and renders professional advice) on the premises. Since she does not maintain a specific area for exclusive business use, however, she does not claim an office in the home for tax purposes.

Paula's receipts from her practice during 2010 were $41,000, $6,000 of which was for services performed in 2009. Not included in these amounts is $7,500 she received in January 2011 for services rendered in December 2010.

5. Paula had the following business expenses in 2010:

Medical supplies (e.g., bandages, drugs, instruments)	$1,500
Medical clothing (e.g., lab coats, surgical scrubs)—laundry	
service of $800 *not* included	1,400
Medical malpractice insurance	8,000
State license fee	450
Dues to professional organizations	350
Subscriptions to professional journals	340

In addition she drove the family Suburban (purchased on March 2, 2009) 2,900 miles in connection with her work. She uses the automatic (standard) mileage method. Total mileage for the Suburban is 9,000 miles for the year.

6. In October, Paula saw an ad for the sale of a veterinary practice in Durham (NC). Apparently, the veterinarian had just died, and the executor of his estate was anxious to sell the practice while it still had value. After contacting the executor, Paula went to Durham and spent two days investigating the business. Her expenses for the trip were:

Transportation (rental automobile)	$300
Motel	240
Meals	610

The cost of the meals included a dinner attended by both the executor and the attorney for the estate. Paula turned down the offer as she thought the price was too high. Also, the practice involved mainly large animals (horses, cattle), which are not her specialty.

7. Alan's widowed mother, Loretta, died on January 3, 2010. As her sole heir, Alan inherited her property, which included her home and its furnishings (located at 1320 Cardinal Lane, Raleigh, NC 27611). The costs and values involved are as follows:

	Cost (Includes Some Estimates)	Value on 1/3/10
Lot	$ 10,000	$ 30,000
House	110,000	250,000
Furnishings	55,000	25,000

Because the real estate market was depressed and the home was located in an attractive rental area, Alan decided not to sell. Instead, he rented the property furnished on May 1, 2010. The terms of the lease (executed on April 30) provided for the following: one-year lease at $2,500 per month (payable on the first of each month), last month's rent payable in advance, and damage deposit of $3,000. During 2010, Alan received $25,500 regarding the property. Besides depreciation, his expenses were:

Property taxes	$4,800
Insurance	3,900
Repairs	2,100
Real estate renter's location service	400

Alan plans to use MACRS straight-line depreciation (mid-month convention) for the realty. Regarding the personalty, see Exhibit 8.1 in Chapter 8 of the text.

8. While walking the family dogs in late July, Paula was struck by a delivery van and seriously injured. After being hospitalized for a week, she was released—very bruised but with no permanent impairment. The driver of the van was arrested and ticketed by the police for reckless operation of a vehicle and later was prosecuted for drug use. To forestall the adverse publicity of a lawsuit, the owner of the delivery service paid for Paula's medical expenses and sent her a check on August 16, 2010. The award stated that "$90,000 is a settlement for physical injury sustained." In the negotiations, Paula was represented by her brother who is a practicing attorney. In the interest of family harmony, the brother did not charge for the services he rendered.

9. The Turners had the following property transactions during 2010:

    • On October 5, the City of Raleigh condemned unimproved land owned by Alan for the construction of a fire station. The land consisted of two vacant lots at 3400 and 3402 Cardinal Lane and had been acquired by Alan as an investment on May 25, 2004, for $14,000. In exchange for the lots, the city gave Alan a large lot at 440 Pine Street (worth $20,000). Alan was satisfied with the exchange because the Pine Street property is in a better neighborhood and has a greater potential for appreciation.

    • On November 22, they sold a gun collection for $32,500. The collection was given to Alan by his father on December 25, 2007, when it was worth $22,000. His father's basis in the collection (dating back to 1997) was $14,000.

    • On November 9, they sold 3,000 shares of Dove Pharmaceuticals for $5,000. The stock was purchased by the Turners on December 4, 2009, for $25,000. The investment was motivated by the rumor that Dove was developing a new drug for infertility. After the FDA failed to approve the drug, the Turners decided to cut their losses.

    The Turners have a long-term capital loss carryover of $1,500 from 2009.

10. In March 2010, the Turners were audited by the North Carolina Department of Revenue for tax years 2007 and 2008. As a result of the audit, no change was made for 2007, but they were assessed $250 additional income tax for 2008 (no interest or penalties were included). The Turners paid the $250 immediately.

11. Alan's mother, Loretta, suffered a stroke on December 30, 2009, and died in the hospital on January 3, 2010. Part of Loretta's medical expenses was covered by Medicare, but Alan absorbed the balance. On January 18, 2010, he paid the balance of $9,800, of which half was attributable to expenses incurred in 2009 and the rest in 2010. At the same time, Alan also paid the funeral expenses of $6,000. Although Loretta lived in her own house (see item 7 above), she has been properly claimed as a dependent of the Turners for the past few years.

12. During 2010, Alan was called to serve on a jury. As a result of the service, he was paid $700 and incurred nonreimbursed expenses (e.g., parking) of $60. In conformance with company policy, Alan remitted the $700 of fees to Old North.

13. Besides the items already noted, the Turners had the following receipts in 2010:

Life insurance proceeds		$50,000
State of North Carolina income tax refund (for tax year 2009)		450
Proceeds from garage sale		2,600
Interest income—		
City of Durham general purpose bonds	$480	
CD at Wells Fargo Bank	600	1,080

    The insurance proceeds relate to a policy on Loretta's life in which Alan was the designated beneficiary. The garage sale mainly involved personal items (e.g., camper, furniture, hunting and fishing equipment) belonging to Alan's father and mother (i.e., Loretta). The items sold, based on receipts and some estimates, cost $7,100.

14. In addition to the items already mentioned, the Turners' expenditures for 2010 are summarized below:

Dentist bills not covered by insurance	$3,100
Ad valorem property taxes on personal residence	4,100
Interest on home mortgage	2,600
Charitable contributions of cash	3,600

    As part of a program sponsored by their church, the Turners used the family Suburban to transport senior citizens to religious services for a total of 900 miles. The Suburban also was used for medical purposes (e.g., visits to an orthodontist) for 480 miles.

15. The Turners' household includes two dependent children: Ethan (age 14) and Ava (age 15), both of whom are full-time students. Relevant Social Security numbers appear below:

Name	Social Security Number	Birth Date
Alan B. Turner	123–45–6785	07/14/1967
Paula R. Turner	123–45–6786	02/20/1971
Loretta Turner	123–45–6784	04/09/1938
Ethan Turner	123–45–6787	12/06/1996
Ava Turner	123–45–6788	07/29/1995

    Paula's professional activity code is 541940.

16. Alan's Form W–2 from Old North Chemical Corporation reflects income tax withholding of $6,500 (Federal) and $4,000 (state). The Turners made quarterly income tax payments of $750 (Federal) and $450 (state) for total payments of $3,000 (Federal) and $1,800 (state). They had their Federal income tax refund of $305 (for 2009) applied toward their 2010 income tax.

REQUIREMENTS

Prepare an income tax return (with appropriate schedules) for the Turners for 2010. Make any necessary assumptions for facts not stated in the problem. If a refund results, the taxpayers want it applied toward their 2011 tax liability. The Turners do not wish to contribute to the Presidential Election Campaign Fund. In the past several years, the Turners have itemized their deductions *from* AGI (have not claimed the standard deduction option).

Appendix F

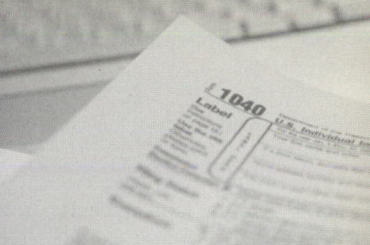

TABLE OF CASES CITED

Appendix G

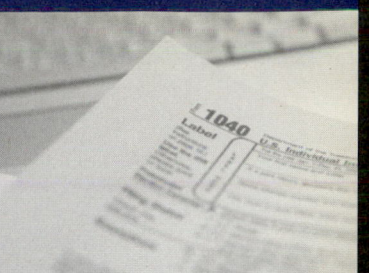

DEPRECIATION

INTRODUCTION

Cost recovery, amortization, and depletion are presented in Chapter 8. For most fixed assets (e.g., machinery, equipment, furniture, fixtures, buildings) placed in service after December 31, 1980, the Economic Recovery Tax Act of 1981 (ERTA) has replaced the depreciation system with the cost recovery system.[1] The general relationship between the depreciation system and the cost recovery system is summarized in Exhibit G.1.

Despite ERTA, a discussion of § 167 depreciation is still relevant for two reasons. First, assets that were placed in service prior to 1981 are still in use. Second, certain assets placed in service after 1980 are not eligible to use the cost recovery system (ACRS and MACRS) and therefore must be depreciated. They include property placed in service after 1980 whose life is not based on years (e.g., units-of-production method).

DEPRECIATION

Section 167 permits a depreciation deduction in the form of a reasonable allowance for the exhaustion, wear and tear, and obsolescence of business property and property held for the production of income (e.g., rental property held by an investor).[2] Obsolescence refers to normal technological change due to reasonably foreseeable

EXHIBIT G.1	Depreciation and Cost Recovery: Relevant Time Periods
System	**Date Property Is Placed in Service**
§ 167 depreciation	Before January 1, 1981, and *certain* property placed in service after December 31, 1980.
Original accelerated cost recovery system (ACRS)	After December 31, 1980, and before January 1, 1987.
Modified accelerated cost recovery system (MACRS)	After December 31, 1986.

---

[1]Depreciation is covered in § 167, and cost recovery (ACRS and MACRS) is covered in § 168.

[2]§ 167(a) and Reg. § 1.167(a)–1.

economic conditions. If rapid or abnormal obsolescence occurs, a taxpayer may change to a shorter estimated useful life if there is a "clear and convincing basis for the redetermination." Depreciation deductions are *not* permitted for personal use property.

The taxpayer must adopt a reasonable and consistent plan for depreciating the cost or other basis of assets over the estimated useful life of the property (e.g., the taxpayer cannot arbitrarily defer or accelerate the amount of depreciation from one year to another). The basis of the depreciable property must be reduced by the depreciation allowed and by not less than the allowable amount.[3] The *allowed* depreciation is the depreciation actually taken, whereas the *allowable* depreciation is the amount that could have been taken under the applicable depreciation method. If the taxpayer does not claim any depreciation on property during a particular year, the basis of the property still must be reduced by the amount of depreciation that should have been deducted (the allowable depreciation).

EXAMPLE 1

On January 1, Ted paid $7,500 for a truck to be used in his business. He chose a five-year estimated useful life, no salvage value, and straight-line depreciation. Thus, the allowable depreciation deduction was $1,500 per year. However, depreciation actually taken (allowed) was as follows:

Year 1	$1,500
Year 2	–0–
Year 3	–0–
Year 4	1,500
Year 5	1,500

The adjusted basis of the truck must be reduced by the amount of allowable depreciation of $7,500 ($1,500 × 5 years) even though Ted claimed only $4,500 depreciation during the five-year period. Therefore, if Ted sold the truck at the end of Year 5 for $1,000, he would recognize a $1,000 gain, since the adjusted basis of the truck is zero. ■

QUALIFYING PROPERTY AND BASIS FOR DEPRECIATION

The use rather than the character of property determines whether a depreciation deduction is permitted. Property must be used in a trade or business or held for the production of income to qualify as depreciable.

EXAMPLE 2

Carol is a self-employed CPA who maintains her office in a room in her home. The room, which is used exclusively for her business, comprises 20% of the square footage of her house. Carol is permitted a depreciation deduction only for the business use part of the house. No depreciation deduction is permitted for the 80% of the square footage of her house that is used as her residence. ■

The basis for depreciation generally is the adjusted cost basis used to determine gain if the property is sold or otherwise disposed of.[4] However, if personal use assets are converted to business or income-producing use, the basis for depreciation *and* for loss is the *lower* of the adjusted basis or fair market value at the time of the conversion of the property.[5] As a result of this lower of basis rule, losses that occurred while the property was personal use property will not be recognized for tax purposes through the depreciation of the property.

[3]§ 1016(a)(2) and Reg. § 1.167(a)–10(a).
[4]§ 167(c).
[5]Reg. § 1.167(g)–1.

EXAMPLE 3

Hans acquires a personal residence for $130,000. Four years later, when the fair market value is only $125,000, he converts the property to rental use. The basis for depreciation is $125,000, since the fair market value is less than the adjusted basis. The $5,000 decline in value is deemed to be personal (since it occurred while the property was held for personal use) and therefore nondeductible. ∎

The Regulations provide that tangible property is depreciable only to the extent that the property is subject to wear and tear, decay or decline from natural causes, exhaustion, and obsolescence.[6] Thus, land and inventory are not depreciable, but land improvements are depreciable (e.g., paved surfaces, fences, landscaping).

OTHER DEPRECIATION CONSIDERATIONS

In determining the amount of the depreciation deduction, the following additional considerations need to be addressed:

- The salvage value of the asset.
- The choice of depreciation methods.
- The useful life of the asset.

For property subject to depreciation under § 167, taxpayers generally must take into account the **salvage value** (assuming there is a salvage value) of an asset in calculating depreciation. An asset cannot be depreciated below its salvage value. However, the Code permits a taxpayer to disregard salvage value for amounts up to 10 percent of the basis in the property. This provision applies to tangible personal property (other than livestock) with an estimated useful life of three years or more.[7]

EXAMPLE 4

Green Company acquired a machine for $10,000 in 1980 with an estimated salvage value of $3,000 after 19 years. The company may disregard salvage value to the extent of $1,000 and compute the machine's depreciation based upon a cost of $10,000 less $2,000 salvage value. The adjusted basis may be reduced to $2,000 (depreciation of $8,000 may be taken) even though the actual salvage value is $3,000. ∎

This provision was incorporated into the law to reduce the number of IRS-taxpayer disputes over the amount of the salvage value that should be used.

Another consideration is the *choice of depreciation methods* from among the several allowed. The following alternative depreciation methods are permitted for property placed into service before January 1, 1981, and for the aforementioned property placed in service after December 31, 1980, for which cost recovery is not permitted:

- The straight-line (SL) method (cost basis less salvage value ÷ estimated useful life).
- The declining-balance method (DB) using a rate not to exceed twice the straight-line rate. Common methods include 200 percent DB (double-declining balance), 150 percent DB, and 125 percent DB. Salvage value is not taken into account under any of the declining-balance methods. However, no further depreciation can be claimed once net book value (cost minus depreciation) and salvage value are the same.
- The sum-of-the-years' digits method (SYD).
- Any other consistent method that does not result in greater total depreciation being claimed during the first two-thirds of the useful life than would have been allowable under the double-declining balance method. Permissible methods include machine hours and the units-of-production method.

---

[6]Reg. § 1.167(a)–2.   [7]Reg. §§ 1.167(a)–1(c) and (f)–1.

EXAMPLE 5

On January 1, 1980, Diego acquired a new machine to be used in his business. The asset cost $10,000 with an estimated salvage value of $2,000 and a four-year estimated useful life.[8] The following amounts of depreciation could be deducted, depending on the method of depreciation used:

	1980	1981	1982	1983
1. Straight-line:				
$10,000 cost less ($2,000 salvage value reduced by 10% of cost) ÷ 4 years	$2,250	$2,250	$2,250	$2,250
2. Double-declining balance:				
a. $10,000 × 50% (twice the straight-line rate)	5,000			
b. ($10,000 − $5,000) × 50%		2,500		
c. ($10,000 − $5,000 − $2,500) × 50%			1,250	
d. ($10,000 − $5,000 − $2,500 − $1,250) × 50%				250[9]
3. Sum-of-the-years' digits:*				
$10,000 cost less ($2,000 salvage value reduced by 10% of cost) or $9,000				
a. $9,000 × 4/10	3,600			
b. $9,000 × 3/10		2,700		
c. $9,000 × 2/10			1,800	
d. $9,000 × 1/10				900

*The formula for the sum-of-the-years' digits (SYD) method is

$$\text{Cost} - \text{Salvage value} \times \frac{\text{Remaining life at the beginning of the year}}{\text{Sum-of-the-years' digits of the estimated life}}$$

In this example, the denominator for SYD is 1 + 2 + 3 + 4, or 10. The numerator is 4 for Year 1 (the number of years left at the beginning of Year 1), 3 for Year 2, etc. The denominator can be calculated by the following formula:

$$S = \frac{Y(Y+1)}{2} \text{ where } Y = \text{estimated useful life}$$

$$S = \frac{4(4+1)}{2} = 10$$

∎

EXAMPLE 6

Using the depreciation calculations in Example 5, the depreciation reserve (accumulated depreciation) and net book value at the end of 1983 are as follows:

	Cost −	Depreciation =	Net Book Value*
Straight-line	$10,000	$9,000	$1,000
Double-declining balance	10,000	9,000	1,000
Sum-of-the-years' digits	10,000	9,000	1,000

*Note that an asset may not be depreciated below its salvage value even when a declining-balance method is used.

∎

In 1969, Congress placed certain restrictions on the use of accelerated methods for new and used realty that are subject to the depreciation rules under § 167. These restrictions were imposed to reduce the opportunities for using real estate investments as tax shelters. The use of accelerated depreciation frequently resulted in the recognition of ordinary tax losses on economically profitable real estate ventures.

---

[8]A four-year life is used to illustrate the different depreciation methods. Note that an asset placed in service in 1980 must have a useful life of at least 32 years in order for depreciation to be deducted in 2011.

[9]Total depreciation taken cannot exceed cost minus estimated salvage value ($1,000 in this example).

The following methods were permitted for residential and nonresidential real property:

	Nonresidential Real Property (Commercial and Industrial Buildings, Etc.)	Residential Real Property (Apartment Buildings, Etc.)
New property acquired after July 24, 1969, and generally before January 1, 1981	150% DB, SL	200% DB, SYD, 150% DB, or SL
Used property acquired after July 24, 1969, and generally before January 1, 1981	SL	125% DB (if estimated useful life is 20 years or greater) or SL

Congress chose to permit accelerated methods (200 percent declining-balance and sum-of-the-years' digits) for new residential rental property. Presumably, the desire to stimulate construction of new housing units justified the need for such accelerated methods.

Restrictions on the use of accelerated methods were not imposed on new tangible personalty (e.g., machinery, equipment, and automobiles). However, the 200 percent declining-balance and sum-of-the-years' digits methods were not permitted for used tangible personal property. The depreciation methods permitted for *used* tangible personal property were as follows:

	Useful Life of Three Years or More	Useful Life of Less Than Three Years
Used tangible personal property acquired after July 24, 1969, and generally before January 1, 1981	150% DB, SL	SL

Since the acquisition of used property does not result in any net addition to gross private investment in our economy, Congress chose not to provide as rapid accelerated depreciation for used property.

The determination of a *useful life* for a depreciable asset often led to disagreement between taxpayers and the IRS. One source of information was the company's previous experience and policy with respect to asset maintenance and utilization. Another source was the guideline lives issued by the IRS.[10] In 1971, the IRS guideline life system was modified and liberalized by the enactment of the **Asset Depreciation Range (ADR) system.**[11]

KEY TERMS

Asset Depreciation Range (ADR) system, G-5

Salvage value, G-3

[10]Rev.Proc. 72–10, 1972–1 C.B. 721, superseded by Rev.Proc. 83–35, 1983–1 C.B. 745.   [11]Reg. § 1.167(a)–11.

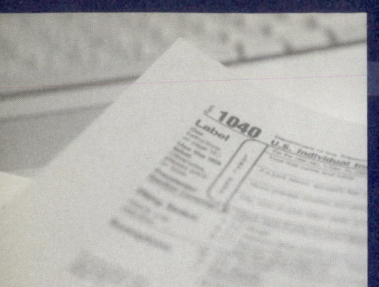

Index

AMT Formula for Individuals

Regular Taxable Income

Plus or minus:	Adjustments
Plus:	Tax preferences
Equals:	Alternative minimum taxable income
Minus:	Exemption
Equals:	Alternative minimum tax base
Times:	26% and 28% graduated rates
Equals:	Tentative minimum tax before foreign tax credit
Minus:	Alternative minimum tax foreign tax credit
Equals:	Tentative minimum tax
Minus:	Regular income tax liability
Equals:	Alternative minimum tax (if amount is positive)

AMT Exemption Phaseout for Individuals for 2011

		Phaseout	
Filing Status	**Exemption**	**Begins at**	**Ends at**
Married, filing jointly	$74,450	$150,000	$447,800
Single or head of household	48,450	112,500	306,300
Married, filing separately	37,225	75,000	223,900

AMT Formula for Corporations

Regular Taxable Income before NOL Deduction

Plus or minus:	Adjustments (except ACE adjustment)
Plus:	Tax preferences
Equals:	AMTI before ATNOL deduction and ACE adjustment
Plus or minus:	ACE adjustment
Equals:	Alternative minimum taxable income (AMTI) before ATNOL deduction
Minus:	ATNOL deduction (limited to 90% of AMTI before ATNOL deduction)
Equals:	Alternative minimum taxable income (AMTI)
Minus:	Exemption
Equals:	Alternative minimum tax base
Times:	20% rate
Equals:	Tentative AMT before AMT foreign tax credit
Minus:	AMT foreign tax credit
Equals:	Tentative minimum tax
Minus:	Regular income tax liability before credits minus regular foreign tax credit
Equals:	Alternative minimum tax (AMT) if positive